2016

Medical Coding Training: CPC®

AAPC
Advancing the Business of Healthcare

Disclaimer

This course was current when it was published. Every reasonable effort has been made to assure the accuracy of the information within these pages. The ultimate responsibility lies with readers to ensure they are using the codes, and following applicable guidelines, correctly. AAPC employees, agents, and staff make no representation, warranty, or guarantee that this compilation of information is error-free, and will bear no responsibility or liability for the results or consequences of the use of this course. This guide is a general summary that explains guidelines and principles in profitable, efficient healthcare organizations.

US Government Rights

This product includes CPT®, which is commercial technical data and/or computer data bases and/or commercial computer software and/or commercial computer software documentation, as applicable, which was developed exclusively at private expense by the American Medical Association, 515 North State Street, Chicago, Illinois, 60610. U.S. Government rights to use, modify, reproduce, release, perform, display, or disclose these technical data and/or computer data bases and/or computer software and/or computer software documentation are subject to the limited rights restrictions of DFARS 252.227-7015(b)(2) (November 1995), as applicable, for U.S. Department of Defense procurements and the limited rights restrictions of FAR 52.227-14 (June 1987) and/or subject to the restricted rights provision of FAR 52.227-14 (June 1987) and FAR 52.227-19 (June 1987), as applicable, and any applicable agency FAR Supplements, for non-Department of Defense Federal procurements.

AMA Disclaimer

CPT® copyright 2015 American Medical Association. All rights reserved.

Fee schedules, relative value units, conversion factors and/or related components are not assigned by the AMA, are not part of CPT®, and the AMA is not recommendation their use. The AMA does not directly or indirectly practice medicine or dispense medical services. The AMA assumes no liability for data contained or not contained herein.

CPT® is a registered trademark of the American Medical Association.

Regarding HCPCS Level II

HCPCS Level II codes and guidelines discussed in this book are current as of press time. The 2016 code set for HCPCS Level II were unavailable when published.

Clinical Examples Used in this Book

AAPC believes it is important in training and testing to reflect as accurate a coding setting as possible to students and examinees. All examples and case studies used in our study guides, exams, and workbooks are *actual, redacted* office visit and procedure notes donated by AAPC members.

To preserve the *real world* quality of these notes for educational purposes, we have not re-written or edited the notes to the stringent grammatical or stylistic standards found in the text of our products. Some minor changes have been made for clarity or to correct spelling errors originally in the notes, but essentially they are as one would find them in a coding setting.

© 2016 AAPC

2233 South Presidents Dr. Suites F-C, Salt Lake City, UT 84120
800-626-2633, Fax 801-236-2258, www.aapc.com
Revised 161115. All rights reserved.
ISBN 978-1-626882-065

Reviewers: Katherine Abel, CPC, CPB, CPMA, CPPM, CPC-I, CMRS
Nicole Benjamin, CPC, CPC-I, CEDC
Brad Ericson, MPC, CPC, COSC
Lindsay-Anne McDonald Jenkins, RN, CPC, COC, CIRCC, CPC-I, CANPC, CPMA, CRNA (Retired)
Kathleen Skolnick, CPC, CPC, CPCO, CPB, CPMA, CPPM, CPC-I, CEMC
Peggy Stilley, CPC, CPB, CPMA, CPC-I, COBGC
Jacqueline J Stack, BSHA, CPC, CPC-I, CPB, CEMC, CFPC, CIMC, CPEDC

Contents

Chapter 6
Introduction to CPT®, Surgery Guidelines, HCPCS, and Modifiers 161

Chapter 7
Integumentary System 199

Chapter 8
Musculoskeletal System 235

Chapter 21
What Lies Ahead

Coding as a Profession

Each time you receive healthcare, a record is maintained of the resulting observations, medical or surgical interventions, and treatment outcomes. This medical record includes information concerning your symptoms and medical history, the results of examinations, reports of X-rays and laboratory tests, diagnoses, and treatment plans.

At its most basic, coding is the process of translating this written or dictated medical record into a series of numeric or alpha-numeric codes. There are separate code sets to describe diagnoses, medical and surgical services/procedures, and supplies. These code sets serve as a common shorthand language to ease data collection (for example, to track disease), to evaluate the quality of care, and to determine costs and reimbursement.

Coders may use several coding systems, such as those required for ambulatory settings, physician offices, or long-term care. Most coders specialize in coding patients' medical information for insurance purposes. Physician-based coders review charts and assign CPT®, HCPCS Level II, and ICD-10-CM codes (about which you will learn more later) for insurance billing. Because coding is tied directly to reimbursement, codes must be assigned correctly to ensure physician livelihood.

Proper code assignment is determined both by the content of the medical record and by the unique rules that govern each code set. Coding rules also may vary depending on who pays for the patient care. For instance, government programs such as Medicare may follow different guidelines than commercial insurers.

Medical care is complex and variable, as are coding requirements. Exceptional precision is required to select appropriate codes. Coders must master anatomy and medical terminology, and must be detail-oriented. Seemingly subtle differences in language, a patient's condition, or the care provided can change code selection completely.

Technicians who specialize in coding are medical coders or coding specialists. Medical coders assign a code to each diagnosis, service/procedure, and (when applicable) supply, using classification systems. The classification system determines the amount healthcare providers will be reimbursed if the patient is covered by Medicare, Medicaid, or other insurance programs using the system.

If the medical record is inaccurate or incomplete, it will not translate properly to the language of codes and reimbursement for services may be lost. The coder must evaluate the medical record for completeness and accuracy and communicate regularly with physicians and other healthcare professionals to clarify diagnoses or to obtain additional patient information. Coders may use computer programs to tabulate and analyze data to improve patient care, for better control of cost, to provide documentation for use in legal actions, or use in research studies.

Technicians who specialize in coding inpatient hospital services are referred to as health information coders, medical record coders, coder/abstractors, or coding specialists. These technicians assign a code to each diagnosis and procedure, relying on their knowledge of disease processes. Coders then use classification system software to assign the patient to one of several hundred Medicare Severity-Diagnosis Related Groups, or MS-DRGs. The MS-DRG determines the amount the hospital will be reimbursed if the patient is covered by Medicare or other insurance programs using the MS-DRG system.

Medical records and health information technicians also may specialize in cancer registry. Cancer (or tumor) registrars maintain facility, regional, and national databases of cancer patients. Registrars review patient records and pathology reports, and assign codes for the diagnosis and treatment of different cancers and selected benign tumors. Registrars conduct annual follow-ups on all patients in the registry to track their treatment, survival, and recovery. Physicians and public health organizations then use this information to calculate survivor rates and success rates of various treatments, locate geographic areas with high incidences of certain cancers, and identify potential participants for clinical drug trials. Public health officials also use cancer registry data to target areas for the allocation of resources to provide intervention and screening.

Regardless of the setting in which they work, continuing education is essential for coders. Code updates and policies are changed as often as quarterly, and it is important to stay abreast of these changes to insure proper coding and reimbursement.

Widespread adoption of electronic health records (EHR)—as opposed to paper-based patient records—will continue to broaden and alter coders' job responsibilities. For example, coders must be familiar with EHR computer software, maintaining EHR security, and analyzing electronic data to improve healthcare information. Coders also may assist with improving EHR software and may contribute to the development and maintenance of health information networks. Finally, coders will take on an auditing role in reviewing EHR code suggestions, based on documentation.

Medical coding is a technical and rapidly-changing field that offers practitioners a variety of career opportunities. For instance, skilled coders may become consultants, educators, or medical auditors. Coding as a profession has evolved over the past several decades, and will continue to do so as the business of medicine embraces new technologies, code sets, and payment methodologies.

The Difference Between Hospital and Physician Services

Outpatient coding focuses on physician services. Outpatient coders will focus on learning CPT®, HCPCS Level II, and ICD-10-CM codes. They work in physician offices, outpatient clinics, and facility outpatient departments. Outpatient facility coders also work with Ambulatory Payment Classifications (APCs).

Inpatient hospital coding focuses on a different subset of skills. Inpatient coders work with ICD-10-CM and ICD-10-PCS. These coders also assign MS-DRGs for reimbursement. Outpatient coders usually have more interaction throughout the day, and must communicate well with physicians; inpatient coders tend to have less interaction throughout the day.

How a Physician Office Works and How the Coder Fits into It

Physician offices vary in size from a single-provider practice to multiple providers and multiple specialties. When you visit a physician, typically, a front desk person obtains your insurance and demographic information, or this information is entered electronically before your visit. After your information has been entered into the practice management system, you are seen by the provider. The provider documents the visit in your medical record and completes an encounter form, or a form to relay the services rendered, to the front desk. Upon completion of your exam, you check out and pay your co-pay. This process may vary from office to office, but each of these steps must be completed.

After you leave the provider's office, someone takes the documentation the provider reported and translates it into codes (CPT®, ICD-10-CM, and HCPCS Level II). This is submitted to the payer to obtain reimbursement. This translation of the documented information from your visit is referred to as coding. Coding can be performed by the physician or the

coder. When the physician performs the coding, the coder takes on the role of auditor to verify the documentation supports the codes the physician selected. In some practices, the physician leaves the responsibility of assigning codes to a trained coding staff.

In this type of setting, the coder reviews the physician's documentation and codes the services based on what is documented in the patient record.

When the documentation has been translated into codes, the codes are attached to a fee and billed to the patient or insurance carrier, also called payer. The charges are billed to the insurance carrier using a CMS-1500 claim form. The claim form can be sent to an insurance carrier on paper or electronically. Many insurance carriers now accept only electronic claims. Electronic claims benefit the provider office by allowing timely submissions to the insurance carrier and proof of transmission of the claim. Once the insurance carrier receives the claim, the insurance carrier uses the codes to identify the services performed, and to determine payment or denial. If a service is denied, there is additional work to validate or appeal the denial. The determination of the payer is then sent to the provider in the form of a remittance advice. The remittance advice explains the detail of outcome of the insurance adjudication on the claim, including the payment amount, denial, and/or reason for denial. The coder's role is extremely important to proper reimbursement and the livelihood of a physician's office.

Understanding the Hierarchy of Providers

Physician offices and hospitals are staffed by a variety of medical providers. Each provider has differing levels of education. As such, each state has guidelines for each level of provider. This is referred to as the state's scope of practice.

Practical Coding Note

Some states provide state-specific guidelines for scope of practice for varying levels of providers. Check your state's health board's website for the scope of practice information.

Physicians undergo four years of college and four years of medical school, plus three to five years or more of residency. Residency is training in a specialty of practice. A physician can continue training in a subspecialty, referred to as a fellowship.

Physicians often have mid-level providers working in the same office. Mid-level providers include physician assistants (PA) and nurse practitioners (NP). Mid-level providers are known also as physician extenders because they extend the work of a physician. PAs are licensed to practice medicine with physician supervision. A PA program takes approximately 26½ months to complete. Nurse Practitioners have a Master's Degree in Nursing.

Mid-level providers often are reimbursed at a lower rate than physicians. Although the scope of practice varies by state, mid-level providers require oversight by a physician.

The Different Types of Payers

Although some patients pay in full for their own medical expenses, most patients have some type of insurance coverage. This is significant because individual payers may specify coding requirements in addition—or even contradictory—to those guidelines found in the CPT® and other codebooks.

Considered most simply, there are only two types of payers: private insurance plans and government insurance plans. Within each of these categories are finer distinctions.

Commercial carriers are private payers that offer both group and individual plans. The contracts they provide vary, but may include hospitalization, basic, and major medical coverage. Blue Cross/Blue Shield organizations also are private payers, and usually operate in the state in which they are based. Blue Cross originally covered hospital benefits and Blue Shield originally covered medical and surgical benefits. They both have since expanded their coverage.

The most significant government insurer is Medicare. Medicare is a federal health insurance program—administered by the Centers for Medicare & Medicaid Services (CMS)—that provides coverage for people over the age of 65, blind, or disabled individuals, and people with permanent kidney failure or end-stage renal disease (ESRD). CMS regulations often serve as the last word in coding requirements for Medicare and non-Medicare payers alike. The Medicare program is made up of several parts:

- Medicare Part A helps to cover inpatient hospital care, as well as care provided in skilled nursing facilities, hospice care, and home healthcare.
- Medicare Part B helps to cover medically necessary doctors' services, outpatient care, and other medical services (including some preventive services) not covered under Medicare Part A. Medicare Part B is an optional benefit for which the patient must pay a premium, and which generally requires a yearly co-insurance. Coders working in physician offices will mainly deal with Medicare Part B.
- Medicare Part C, also called Medicare Advantage, combines the benefits of Medicare Part A, Part B, and—sometimes—Part D. The plans are managed by private insurers approved by Medicare, and may include Preferred Provider Organizations (PPOs), Health Maintenance

Organizations (HMOs), and others. The plans may charge different copayments, coinsurance, or deductibles for services. Accurate and thorough diagnosis coding is important for Medicare Advantage claims because reimbursement is impacted by the patient's health status. The CMS-hierarchical condition category (CMS-HCC) risk adjustment model provides adjusted payments based on a patient's diseases and demographic factors. If a coder does not include all pertinent diagnoses and co-morbidities, the provider may lose out on additional reimbursement for which the provider is entitled.

- Medicare Part D is a prescription drug coverage program available to all Medicare beneficiaries. Private companies approved by Medicare provide the coverage.

Medicaid is a health insurance assistance program for some low-income people (especially children and pregnant women) sponsored by federal and state governments. It is administered on a state-by-state basis, and coverage varies—although each of the state programs adheres to certain federal guidelines.

State-funded insurance programs that provide coverage for children up to 21 years of age may include Crippled Children's Services, Children's Medical Services, Children's Indigent Disability Services, and Children with Special Health Care Needs, among others. Typically, these programs are designed for beneficiaries with specific chronic medical conditions.

Each provider determines whether to contract with an insurance carrier, private or governmental. When contracted with the insurance carrier, the provider is considered a participating provider (par provider). Participating providers are required to accept the allowed payment amount determined by the insurance carrier as the fee for payment and follow all other guidelines stipulated by the contract. The difference between the physician's fee and the insurance carrier's allowed amount is adjusted by the participating provider. The non-participating provider (provider not contracted with the insurance carrier) is not required to make this adjustment. For Medicare services, even if a provider is non-participating, there are limits set on what can be charged for each CPT® code, referred to as a limiting charge.

The Medical Record

Documentation is the recording of pertinent facts and observations about an individual's health history, including past and present illnesses, tests, treatments, and outcomes. The medical record chronologically documents patient care to assist in continuity of care between providers, facilitate claims review and payment, and can serve as a legal document. It is imperative all services provided to a patient be supported and documented in the medical record.

A coder is required to read and understand the documentation in a medical record in order to code accurately the services rendered. Different types of services are documented in the medical record, such as evaluation and management services, operative reports, X-rays, etc.

Evaluation and Management Documentation

Evaluation and management services are often provided in a standard format such as SOAP:

S—Subjective—The patient's statement about his or her health, including symptoms.

O—Objective—The provider assesses and documents the patient's illness using observation, palpation, auscultation, and percussion. Tests and other services performed may be documented here as well.

A—Assessment—Evaluation and conclusion made by the provider. This is usually where the diagnosis(es) for the services are found.

P—Plan—Course of action. Here, the provider will list the next steps for the patient, whether it is ordering additional tests, or taking over the counter medications, etc.

Not all evaluation and management documentation will be documented in a clear SOAP format, but each chart should contain the components of the visit.

Operative Report Documentation

Operative reports are used to document the detail of a procedure performed on a patient. Most operative notes will have a header and a body in the report.

The header might include:

- Date and time of the procedure
- Names of the surgeon, co-surgeon, assistant surgeon
- Type of anesthesia and anesthesia provider name
- Pre-operative and post-operative diagnoses
- Procedure performed
- Complications

The body might include:

- Indication for surgery
- Details of the procedure(s)
- Findings

Typically, approximately 20 percent of an operative report contains words less important to a coder. A coder is tasked with breaking down the information and applying the correct

code. Throughout this textbook, examples of operative reports are dissected to help you locate pertinent information to coding.

Operative Report Coding Tips

1. Diagnosis code reporting—Use the post-operative diagnosis for coding unless there are further defined diagnoses or additional diagnoses found in the body of the operative report. If a pathology report is available, use the findings from the pathology report for the diagnosis.

2. Start with the procedures listed—For the coder who is new to coding a procedure, one way of quickly starting the research process is by focusing on the procedures listed in the header. Read the note in its entirety to verify the procedures performed. Procedures listed in the header may not be listed correctly and procedures documented within the body of the report may not be listed in the header at all; however, it will give a coder a place to start.

3. Look for key words—Key words may include locations and anatomical structures involved, surgical approach, procedure method (debridement, drainage, incision, repair, etc.), procedure type (open, closed, simple, intermediate, etc.), size and number, and the surgical instruments used during the procedure.

4. Highlight unfamiliar words—Research for understanding.

5. Read the body—All procedures reported should be documented within the body of the report. The body may indicate a procedure was abandoned or complicated, possibly indicating the need for a different procedure code or the reporting of a modifier.

Medical Necessity

The term medical necessity relates to whether a procedure or service is considered appropriate in a given circumstance. To cite an extreme example, partial amputation of a limb may be medically necessary to eradicate a tumor or severe infection, but it's certainly not medically necessary to treat a splinter. Generally, a medically necessary service or procedure is the least radical service/procedure that allows for effective treatment of the patient's complaint or condition.

CMS has developed policies regarding medical necessity based on regulations found in title XVIII, §1862(a)(1) of the Social Security Act. The *National Coverage Determinations Manual* describes whether specific medical items, services, treatment procedures, or technologies can be paid for under Medicare. Services and procedures are covered only when linked to designated, approved diagnoses. Non-covered items are deemed not reasonable and necessary.

Medicare (and many insurance plans) may deny payment for a service that is not reasonable and necessary according to the Medicare reimbursement rules. When a physician provides services to a Medicare beneficiary, he or she should bill only those services that meet the Medicare standard of reasonable and necessary for the diagnosis and treatment of a patient.

National Coverage Determinations (NCDs) explain when Medicare will pay for items or services. Each Medicare Administrative Contractor (MAC) is responsible for interpreting national policies into regional policies. These are called Local Coverage Determinations (LCD). The LCDs further define what codes are needed and when an item or service will be covered. LCDs have jurisdiction only within their regional area.

If a NCD doesn't exist for a particular item, it's up to the MAC to determine coverage. According to CMS guidelines (www.cms.gov/transmittals/downloads/R2NCD1.pdf), "Where coverage of an item or service is provided for specified indications or circumstances but is not explicitly excluded for others, or where the item or service is not mentioned at all in the CMS Manual System, the Medicare contractor is to make the coverage decision, in consultation with its medical staff, and with CMS when appropriate, based on the law, regulations, rulings and general program instructions."

Practices should check policies quarterly to maintain compliance.

Below is an example of excerpts of an LCD from Novitas Solutions, a CMS contractor. LCD L30273 is regarding Vitamin D Assay testing.

This snapshot shows the contractor name and numbers and the type of MAC contractor.

Contractor Information

Contractor Name	Contract Number	Contract Type	Jurisdiction
Novitas Solutions, Inc.	12502	A and B MAC	J - L

Back to Top

The LCD includes information on the National Coverage Policy the LCD is attached to:

CMS National Coverage Policy

Title XVIII of the Social Security Act, Section 1862(a)(1)(A) states that no Medicare payment shall be made for items or services which are not reasonable and necessary for the diagnosis or treatment of illness or injury.

Title XVIII of the Social Security Act, Section 1862(a)(7). This section excludes routine physical examinations.

Title XVIII of the Social Security Act, Section 1833(e) states that no payment shall be made to any provider for any claim that lacks the necessary information to process the claim.

The LCD explains when the service is indicated or necessary:

Coverage Guidance

Coverage Indications, Limitations, and/or Medical Necessity

Compliance with the provisions in this policy may be monitored and addressed through post payment data analysis and subsequent medical review audits.

Vitamin D is called a "vitamin" because of its exogenous source, predominately from oily fish in the form of vitamin D2 and vitamin D3. It is more accurate to consider fat-soluble Vitamin D as a steroid hormone, synthesized by the skin and metabolized by the kidney to an active hormone, calcitriol. Clinical disorders related to vitamin D may arise because of altered availability of the parent vitamin D, altered conversion of vitamin D to its predominant metabolites, altered organ responsiveness to dihydroxylated metabolites and disturbances in the interactions of the vitamin D metabolites with PTH and calcitonin. This LCD identifies the indications and limitations of Medicare coverage and reimbursement for these services.

Indications:

Measurement of vitamin D levels is indicated for patients with:

- chronic kidney disease stage III or greater
- cirrhosis
- fibromyalgia
- granuloma forming diseases
- hypocalcemia
- hypercalcemia
- hypovitaminosis D
- hypervitaminosis D
- long term use of anticonvulsants or glucocorticoids and other medications known to lower vitamin D levels
- malabsorption states
- obstructive jaundice
- osteomalacia
- osteoporosis
- osteogenesis imperfecta
- osteosclerosis
- psoriasis
- rickets
- vitamin D deficiency on replacement therapy; to monitor the efficacy of treatment

Limitations:

For Medicare, testing may not be used for routine screening.

All assays of vitamin D and its metabolites need not be performed for each of the above conditions. Often, one type is more appropriate for a certain disease state than another. The most common type of vitamin D deficiency is that of 25 OH vitamin D. A much smaller percentage of 1, 25 dihydroxy vitamin D deficiency exists; mostly in those with renal disease. It is expected that the medical record will justify the tests chosen for a particular disease entity, that all available components of 25 OH vitamin D and other metabolite levels will not be performed routinely on every patient and that supportive documentation for test choices will be available to the Contractor upon request.

This Contractor does not expect to receive billing for the various component sources of 25 OH vitamin D separately (such as stored D or diet derived D). Only one 25 OH vitamin D assay will be considered for reimbursement on any particular day, if medically necessary, for the patient's condition.

Once a beneficiary has been shown to be vitamin D deficient, further testing may be medically necessary only to ensure adequate replacement has been accomplished for this vitamin deficiency, although, generally, other parameters are measured.

Back to Top

The LCD also gives guidance on coverage limitations:

Limitations:

For Medicare, testing may not be used for routine screening.

All assays of vitamin D and its metabolites need not be performed for each of the above conditions. Often, one type is more appropriate for a certain disease state than another. The most common type of vitamin D deficiency is that of 25 OH vitamin D. A much smaller percentage of 1, 25 dihydroxy vitamin D deficiency exists; mostly in those with renal disease. It is expected that the medical record will justify the tests chosen for a particular disease entity, that all available components of 25 OH vitamin D and other metabolite levels will not be performed routinely on every patient and that supportive documentation for test choices will be available to the Contractor upon request.

This Contractor does not expect to receive billing for the various component sources of 25 OH vitamin D separately (such as stored D or diet derived D). Only one 25 OH vitamin D assay will be considered for reimbursement on any particular day, if medically necessary, for the patient's condition.

Once a beneficiary has been shown to be vitamin D deficient, further testing may be medically necessary only to ensure adequate replacement has been accomplished for this vitamin deficiency, although, generally, other parameters are measured.

Back to Top

The LCD describes the specific CPT® codes to which the policy applies:

CPT/HCPCS Codes

Group 1 Paragraph: Italicized and/or quoted material is excerpted from the American Medical Association, *Current Procedural Terminology (CPT) codes.*

Group 1 Codes:

82306	VITAMIN D; 25 HYDROXY, INCLUDES FRACTION(S), IF PERFORMED
82652	VITAMIN D; 1, 25 DIHYDROXY, INCLUDES FRACTION(S), IF PERFORMED

Finally, the LCD will list ICD-10-CM codes that support Medical Necessity for the given service or procedure (below is an example and is not a complete list):

ICD-10 Codes that Support Medical Necessity

Group 1 Paragraph: It is the provider's responsibility to select codes carried out to the highest level of specificity and selected from the ICD-10-CM code book appropriate to the year in which the service is rendered for the claim(s) submitted.

The following ICD-10-CM codes support the medical necessity of CPT code *82306.*

Group 1 Codes:

Show entries: [100 ⬍]

Search: [   ]   Search By: ● Description ○ Code   [SEARCH GROUP]   [CLEAR SEARCH]

ICD-10 CODE	DESCRIPTION
A15.0	Tuberculosis of lung
A15.4	Tuberculosis of intrathoracic lymph nodes
A15.5	Tuberculosis of larynx, trachea and bronchus
A15.6	Tuberculous pleurisy
A15.7	Primary respiratory tuberculosis
A15.8	Other respiratory tuberculosis
A15.9	Respiratory tuberculosis unspecified
A17.0	Tuberculous meningitis
A17.1	Meningeal tuberculoma
A17.81	Tuberculoma of brain and spinal cord
A17.82	Tuberculous meningoencephalitis
A17.83	Tuberculous neuritis
A17.89	Other tuberculosis of nervous system
A17.9	Tuberculosis of nervous system, unspecified
A18.01	Tuberculosis of spine
A18.02	Tuberculous arthritis of other joints
A18.03	Tuberculosis of other bones
A18.09	Other musculoskeletal tuberculosis
A18.10	Tuberculosis of genitourinary system, unspecified
A18.11	Tuberculosis of kidney and ureter
A18.12	Tuberculosis of bladder
A18.13	Tuberculosis of other urinary organs
A18.14	Tuberculosis of prostate
A18.15	Tuberculosis of other male genital organs
A18.16	Tuberculosis of cervix
A18.17	Tuberculous female pelvic inflammatory disease

Source: Novitas Solutions https://www.cms.gov/medicare-coverage-database/details/lcd-details.aspx?LCDId=348 88&ContrId=323&ver=2&ContrVer=1&DocID=L34888&bc=gAAAAgAAAAAA%3d%3d&

If you are providing a service and the Medicare patient's diagnosis does not support the medical necessity requirements per the LCD, the service may not be covered. In such a case, the practice would be responsible for obtaining an Advance Beneficiary Notice of Noncoverage (Advance Beneficiary Notice, or ABN), as explained below.

Commercial (non-Medicare) payers may develop their own medical policies. These policies will not necessarily follow Medicare guidelines, and are specified in private contracts between the payer and the practice or provider. Coders will need to be aware of the contract requirements of the individual commercial payers to which they submit claims.

The Advance Beneficiary Notice

Both Medicare beneficiaries and providers have certain rights and protections related to financial liability. These financial liability and appeal rights and protections are communicated to beneficiaries through notices given by providers.

Providers should use an Advance Beneficiary Notice (ABN) when a Medicare beneficiary requests or agrees to receive a procedure or service that Medicare may not cover. The ABN is a standardized form that explains to the patient why Medicare may deny the particular service or procedure. Additionally, an ABN protects the provider's financial interest by creating a paper trail that CMS requires before a provider can bill the patient for payment if Medicare denies coverage for the stated service or procedure.

The ABN form, entitled Revised ABN CMS-R-131, along with a full set of instructions, is available as a free download on the CMS website: www.cms.gov/Medicare/Medicare-General-Information/BNI/ABN.html. CMS will accept the ABN CMS-R-131 for either a potentially non-covered service or for a statutorily excluded service.

Providers must complete the one-page form in full, giving the patient an explanation as to why Medicare is likely to refuse coverage for the proposed procedure or service. Common reasons Medicare may deny a procedure or service include:

- Medicare does not pay for the procedure/service for the patient's condition
- Medicare does not pay for the procedure/service as frequently as proposed
- Medicare does not pay for experimental procedures/services

The explanation of why Medicare may deny the service or procedure should be as specific as possible. A simple statement of Medicare may not cover this procedure is not sufficient.

The provider must present the patient with a cost estimate for the proposed procedure or service. CMS instructions stipulate, "Notifiers must make a good faith effort to insert a reasonable estimate…the estimate should be within $100 or 25 percent of the actual costs, whichever is greater." Medicare allows an estimate that substantially exceeds the actual costs "would generally still be acceptable" because the beneficiary "would not be harmed if the actual costs were less than predicted."

CMS rules require the provider to present the ABN "far enough in advance that the beneficiary or representative has time to consider the options and make an informed choice." The ABN "must be verbally reviewed with the beneficiary or his/her representative and any questions raised during that review must be answered" *before* the patient signs the ABN.

After the ABN has been completed and reviewed in full, the Medicare beneficiary may choose to proceed with the procedure/service and assume financial responsibility, or may elect to forego the procedure or service. If the patient chooses to proceed, he or she may request the charge be submitted to Medicare for consideration (with the understanding that it will probably be denied). A copy of the completed, signed form must be given to the beneficiary or representative, and the provider must retain the original notice on file.

The patient's signature is not required for assigned claims (that is, claims submitted by and paid to a physician on behalf of the beneficiary). If the beneficiary refuses to sign a properly presented ABN, but still requests the procedure or service, the provider should document the patient's refusal. The provider and a witness should then sign the form.

In the case of unassigned claims (claims are submitted by the provider but the payment is sent to the patient who then reimburses the physician), a signature is required on the ABN to hold the patient financially liable. If the patient refuses to sign, the only options are not to provide the service or procedure (which might raise potential negligence issues), or to provide the service with the understanding the provider may not be able to recoup payment from either Medicare or the beneficiary.

An ABN should not be used to bill the beneficiary for additional fees beyond what Medicare reimburses for a given procedure or service. In particular, an ABN does not allow the provider to shift liability to the beneficiary when Medicare payment for a particular procedure or service is bundled into payment for other, covered procedures or services.

Providers should list on the ABN every recommended procedure or service that might not be covered. Although liability for non-covered services normally rests with the beneficiary, Medicare relieves beneficiaries from financial liability where they did not know and did not have reason to know a service would not be covered. Without a valid ABN, the Medicare beneficiary cannot be held responsible for denied charges.

Note: ABNs are never required in emergency or urgent care situations. In fact, CMS policy prohibits giving an ABN to a patient who is "under duress," including patients who need Emergency Department (ED) services before stabilization. When screening and stabilizing care is denied by Medicare as medically unnecessary, physicians cannot seek payment from beneficiaries.

A. Notifier:

B. Patient Name: **C. Identification Number:**

Advance Beneficiary Notice of Noncoverage (ABN)

<u>NOTE:</u> If Medicare doesn't pay for **D.** _____ below, you may have to pay.
Medicare does not pay for everything, even some care that you or your health care provider have good reason to think you need. We expect Medicare may not pay for the **D.** _____ below.

D.	E. Reason Medicare May Not Pay:	F. Estimated Cost

WHAT YOU NEED TO DO NOW:
- Read this notice, so you can make an informed decision about your care.
- Ask us any questions that you may have after you finish reading.
- Choose an option below about whether to receive the **D.** _____ listed above.
  Note: If you choose Option 1 or 2, we may help you to use any other insurance that you might have, but Medicare cannot require us to do this.

G. OPTIONS: Check only one box. We cannot choose a box for you.
☐ **OPTION 1.** I want the **D.** _____ listed above. You may ask to be paid now, but I also want Medicare billed for an official decision on payment, which is sent to me on a Medicare Summary Notice (MSN). I understand that if Medicare doesn't pay, I am responsible for payment, but **I can appeal to Medicare** by following the directions on the MSN. If Medicare does pay, you will refund any payments I made to you, less co-pays or deductibles.
☐ **OPTION 2.** I want the **D.** _____ listed above, but do not bill Medicare. You may ask to be paid now as I am responsible for payment. **I cannot appeal if Medicare is not billed.**
☐ **OPTION 3.** I don't want the **D.** _____ listed above. I understand with this choice I am **not** responsible for payment, and **I cannot appeal to see if Medicare would pay.**

H. Additional Information:

This notice gives our opinion, not an official Medicare decision. If you have other questions on this notice or Medicare billing, call **1-800-MEDICARE** (1-800-633-4227/**TTY:** 1-877-486-2048).
Signing below means that you have received and understand this notice. You also receive a copy.

I. Signature:	**J. Date:**

According to the Paperwork Reduction Act of 1995, no persons are required to respond to a collection of information unless it displays a valid OMB control number. The valid OMB control number for this information collection is 0938-0566. The time required to complete this information collection is estimated to average 7 minutes per response, including the time to review instructions, search existing data resources, gather the data needed, and complete and review the information collection. If you have comments concerning the accuracy of the time estimate or suggestions for improving this form, please write to: CMS, 7500 Security Boulevard, Attn: PRA Reports Clearance Officer, Baltimore, Maryland 21244-1850.

Form CMS-R-131 (03/11)   Form Approved OMB No. 0938-0566

Source:: CMS www.cms.gov/BNI/02_ABN.asp#TopOfPage

    AAPC   *www.aapc.com*   *9*

Non-Medicare payers may not recognize an ABN. Careful research is needed to determine use of an ABN outside of Medicare. In some instances, health plan contracts may have a "hold harmless" clause found within the language that prohibits billing the patient for anything other than co-pays or deductibles.

Section Review 1.1

1. Which statement below describes a medically necessary service?

   A. Performing a procedure/service based on cost to eliminate wasteful services.

   B. Using the least radical service/procedure that allows for effective treatment of the patient's complaint or condition.

   C. Using the closest facility to perform a service or procedure.

   D. Using the appropriate course of treatment to fit within the patient's lifestyle.

2. According to the example LCD from Novitas Solutions, measurement of vitamin D levels is indicated for patients with which condition?

   A. fatigue

   B. fibromyalgia

   C. hypertension

   D. muscle weakness

3. What form is provided to a patient to indicate a service may not be covered by Medicare and the patient may be responsible for the charges?

   A. LCD

   B. CMS-1500

   C. UB-04

   D. ABN

4. Select the true statement regarding ABNs.

   A. ABNs may not be recognized by non-Medicare payers.

   B. ABNs must be signed for emergency or urgent care.

   C. ABNs are not required to include an estimate cost for the service.

   D. ABNs should be routinely signed by Medicare Beneficiaries in case Medicare does not cover a service.

5. When presenting a cost estimate on an ABN for a potentially noncovered service, the cost estimate should be within what range of the actual cost?

   A. $25 or 10%

   B. $100 or 10%

   C. $100 or 25%

   D. An exact amount

HIPAA was originally sponsored by Sen. Edward Kennedy and Sen. Nancy Kassebaum. This act is sometimes referred to as the "Kennedy-Kassebaum Law" or "Kennedy-Kassebaum Act."

www.hhs.gov/ocr/privacy/hipaa/understanding/coveredentities/index.html

The Health Insurance Portability and Accountability Act of 1996 (HIPAA)

The Health Insurance Portability and Accountability Act of 1996, or HIPAA, is a five-part Act.

Title II—Preventing Healthcare Fraud and Abuse; Administrative Simplification; Medical Liability Reform is the most important Title concerning the position of a medical coder.

Title II of HIPAA is known as Administration Simplification. Administration Simplification speaks to the increasing use of technology in the healthcare industry and addresses the need for:

- National standards for electronic healthcare transactions and code sets;
- National unique identifiers for providers, health plans, and employers;
- Privacy and Security of health data.

Under federal guidelines (www. hhs.gov/ocr/privacy/hipaa/understanding/coveredentities/index.html), a covered entity is any of the following:

- A healthcare provider, such as:
  - Doctors
  - Clinics
  - Psychologists
  - Dentists
  - Chiropractors
  - Nursing Homes
  - Pharmacies

- A health plan, to include:
  - Health Insurance Companies
  - HMOs
  - Company Health Plans
  - Government programs that pay for healthcare, such as Medicare, Medicaid, and the military and veterans healthcare programs

The definition of "health plan" in the HIPAA regulations exclude any policy, plan, or program that provides or pays for the cost of excepted benefits. Excepted benefits include:

- Coverage only for accident, or disability income insurance, or any combination thereof;
- Coverage issued as a supplement to liability insurance;
- Liability insurance, including general liability insurance and automobile liability insurance;
- Workers' compensation or similar insurance;
- Automobile medical payment insurance;
- Credit-only insurance;
- Coverage for on-site medical clinics;
- Other similar insurance coverage, specified in regulations, under which benefits for medical care are secondary or incidental to other insurance benefits.

- A healthcare clearinghouse: This includes entities that process nonstandard health information they receive from another entity into a standard format (such as a standard electronic format or data content), or vice versa.

The Need for National Standards for Electronic Healthcare Transactions and Code Sets

According to CMS, "transactions are electronic exchanges involving transfer of information between two parties for a specific purpose." National standards for electronic healthcare transactions are designed to improve the efficiency and effectiveness of the healthcare system by standardizing the formats used for electronic transactions. The transactions include:

1. Health claims and equivalent encounter information

2. Enrollment and disenrollment in a health plan

3. Eligibility for a health plan

4. Healthcare payment and remittance advice

5. Health plan premium payments

6. Health claim status

7. Referral certification and authorization

8. Coordination of benefits

Any covered entity performing one of these transactions electronically is required to follow the standards set for that transaction. Within the transactions, code sets have been designated for standard use. The code sets include:

- HCPCS (Healthcare Common Procedure Coding System)
- CPT® (Current Procedural Terminology)
- CDT® (Common Dental Terminology)
- ICD-10-CM (Prior to October 1, 2015, this was ICD-9-CM)
- NDC (National Drug Codes)

An additional standard required in all transactions is unique identifiers for providers, health plans, and employers. The identifier for providers has been set as the National Provider Identifier (NPI). The identifier for employers is the Employer Identification Number (EIN) issued to employers by the Internal Revenue Service (IRS).

The Need for Privacy and Security

The Health Insurance Portability and Accountability Act of 1996, or HIPAA, provides federal protections for personal health information when held by *covered entities*.

If an entity is *not* a covered entity as described above, it does not have to comply with the Privacy Rule or the Security Rule.

The Office for Civil Rights (OCR) enforces the HIPAA Privacy Rule, which protects the privacy of individually identifiable health information; the HIPAA Security Rule, which sets national standards for the security of electronic protected health information; and the confidentiality provisions of the Patient Safety Rule, which protect identifiable information being used to analyze patient safety events and improve patient safety.

The OCR released a document called HIPAA Administrative Simplification. The excerpt below discusses the healthcare provider's responsibilities surrounding Protected Health Information (PHI) for Treatment, Payment and Health Care Operations (TPO). Healthcare providers are responsible for developing Notices of Privacy Practices and policies and procedures regarding privacy in their practices.

§ 164.506 uses and disclosures to carry out treatment, payment, or healthcare operations.

(a) *Standard: Permitted uses and disclosures*. Except with respect to uses or disclosures that require an authorization under §164.508(a)(2) and (3), a covered entity may use or disclose protected health information for treatment, payment, or healthcare operations as set forth in paragraph (c) of this section, provided that such use or disclosure is consistent with other applicable requirements of this subpart.

(b) *Standard: Consent for uses and disclosures permitted.*

(1) A covered entity may obtain consent of the individual to use or disclose protected health information to carry out treatment, payment, or healthcare operations.

(2) Consent, under paragraph (b) of this section, shall not be effective to permit a use or disclosure of protected health information when an authorization, under §164.508, is required or when another condition must be met for such use or disclosure to be permissible under this subpart.

(c) *Implementation specifications: Treatment, payment, or healthcare operations.*

(1) A covered entity may use or disclose protected health information for its own treatment, payment, or healthcare operations.

(2) A covered entity may disclose protected health information for treatment activities of a healthcare provider.

(3) A covered entity may disclose protected health information to another covered entity or a healthcare provider for the payment activities of the entity that receives the information.

(4) A covered entity may disclose protected health information to another covered entity for healthcare operations activities of the entity that receives the information, if each entity either has or had a relationship with the individual who is the subject of the protected health information being requested, the protected health information pertains to such relationship, and the disclosure is:

(i) For a purpose listed in paragraph (1) or (2) of the definition of healthcare operations; or

(ii) For the purpose of healthcare fraud and abuse detection or compliance.

(5) A covered entity that participates in an organized healthcare arrangement may disclose protected health information about an individual to another covered entity that participates in the organized healthcare arrangement for any healthcare operations activities of the organized healthcare arrangement.

[67 FR 53268, Aug. 14, 2002]

At the time of publication, since the compliance date in April 2003, HHS has received over 106,522 HIPAA complaints. OCR has resolved ninety-five percent of complaints. OCR has investigated and resolved over 23,314. See www.hhs.gov/ocr/privacy/hipaa/enforcement/highlights/index.html.

How HIPAA Works

A key provision of HIPAA is the "Minimum Necessary" requirement. That is, *only the minimum necessary protected health information* should be shared to satisfy a particular purpose. If information is not required to satisfy a particular purpose, it must be withheld.

Under the Privacy Rule, the minimum necessary standard does not apply to the following:

- Disclosures to or requests by a healthcare provider for treatment purposes.
- Disclosures to the individual who is the subject of the information.
- Uses or disclosures made pursuant to an individual's authorization.
- Uses or disclosures required for compliance with the HIPAA Administrative Simplification Rules.
- Disclosures to the U. S. Department of Health & Human Services (HHS) when disclosure of information is required under the Privacy Rule for enforcement purposes.
- Uses or disclosures that are required by other law.

It is the responsibility of a covered entity to develop and implement policies, best suited to its particular circumstances, to meet HIPAA requirements. As a policy requirement, only those individuals whose job requires it may have access to protected health information. Only the minimum protected information required to do the job should be shared. If the entire medical record is necessary, the covered entity's policies and procedures must state so explicitly and include a justification.

More information on handling requests and disclosures for protected health information may be found at: www.hhs.gov/ocr/privacy/hipaa/understanding/coveredentities/minimum-necessary.pdf

HITECH and Its Impact on HIPAA

The Health Information Technology for Economic and Clinical Health Act, or HITECH, was enacted as part of the American Recovery and Reinvestment Act of 2009 (ARRA) "to promote the adoption and meaningful use of health information technology." Portions of HITECH strengthen HIPAA rules by addressing privacy and security concerns associated with the electronic transmission of health information. HITECH establishes four categories of violations—depending on the covered entity's level of culpability for releasing protected information—and minimum and maximum penalties. HITECH also "lowers the bar" for what constitutes a violation, but provides a 30-day window during which any violation not due to willful neglect may be corrected without penalty.

HITECH allows patients to request an audit trail showing all disclosures of their health information made through an electronic record. HITECH also requires an individual be notified if there is an unauthorized disclosure or use of his or her health information. Some samples of what may constitute breaches under HITECH can be found at www.hhs.gov/ocr/privacy/hipaa/enforcement/examples/allcases.html.

As the use of electronic medical records and transactions become more widespread, so too will concern over the protection and privacy of medical records. All individuals working within healthcare have a role in safeguarding patients' private medical information.

The Need for Compliance Rules and Audits

All physician offices and healthcare facilities should have, and actively use, a *compliance plan*. At its most basic, the compliance plan is a written set of instructions outlining the process for coding and submitting accurate claims, and what to do if mistakes are found. A compliance plan may offer several benefits, among them:

- faster, more accurate payment of claims
- fewer billing mistakes
- diminished chances of a payer audit
- less chance of running afoul of self-referral and anti-kickback statutes

Additionally, the increased accuracy of physician documentation that may result from a compliance program actually may assist in enhancing patient care. Finally, compliance programs show the physician practice is making a good faith effort to submit claims appropriately, and sends a signal to employees that compliance is a priority while providing a means to report erroneous or fraudulent conduct, so that it may be corrected. The Patient Protection and Affordable Care Act (PPACA) makes compliance plans mandatory as a condition of participation in federal healthcare programs; however, there is not yet an implementation date for the mandatory compliance.

The Office of Inspector General (OIG), a government agency tasked "to protect the integrity of Department of Health & Human Services (HHS) programs, as well as the health and welfare of the beneficiaries of those programs," has offered compliance program guidance to form the basis of a voluntary compliance program for a physician practice. The OIG Compliance Program Guidance for Individual and Small Group Physician Practices was published in the *Federal Register* on October 5, 2000. This document still is considered appropriate guidance for compliance in physician offices today.

Key actions of the program include:

- Conduct internal monitoring and auditing through the performance of periodic audits: This ongoing evaluation includes not only whether the physician practice's standards and procedures are in fact current and accurate, but also whether the compliance program is working; eg, whether individuals are properly carrying out their responsibilities and claims are submitted appropriately.

- Implement compliance and practice standards through the development of written standards and procedures: After the internal audit identifies the practice's risk areas, the next step is to develop a method for dealing with those risk areas through the practice's standards and procedures. Written standards and procedures are a central component of any compliance program. Those standards and procedures help to reduce the prospect of erroneous claims and fraudulent activity by identifying risk areas for the practice and establishing tighter internal controls to counter those risks, while also helping to identify any aberrant billing practices.

- Designate a compliance officer or contact(s) to monitor compliance efforts and enforce practice standards: Ideally one member of the staff needs to accept the responsibility of developing a corrective action plan, if necessary, and oversee adherence to that plan. This person can either be in charge of all compliance activities for the practice or play a limited role merely to resolve the current issue.

- Conduct appropriate training and education on practice standards and procedures: Education is important to any compliance program. Ideally, education programs will be tailored to the physician practice's needs, specialty, and size and will include both compliance and specific training.

- Respond appropriately to detected violations through the investigation of allegations and the disclosure of incidents to appropriate government entities: It is important that the compliance contact or other practice employee look into possible violations and, if so, take decisive steps to correct the problem. As appropriate, such steps may involve a corrective action plan, the return of any overpayments, a report to the government, and/or a referral to law enforcement authorities.

- Develop open lines of communication, such as (1) discussions at staff meetings regarding how to avoid erroneous or fraudulent conduct and (2) community bulletin boards, to keep practice employees updated regarding compliance activities: The OIG believes that all practice employees, when seeking answers to questions or reporting potential instances of erroneous or fraudulent conduct, should know to whom to turn for assistance in these matters and should be able to do so without fear of retribution.

- Enforce disciplinary standards through well-publicized guidelines: The OIG recommends that a physician practice's enforcement and disciplinary mechanisms ensure that violations of the practice's compliance policies will result in consistent and appropriate sanctions, including the possibility of termination, against the offending individual.

The above is a highly-condensed summary of the OIG's recommendations. For a complete explanation of the components of an ideal compliance plan, visit the OIG website: oig.hhs.gov/authorities/docs/physician.pdf.

The scope of a compliance program will depend on the size and resources of the physician practice. As a means to implement a compliance program, the OIG encourages physician practices to participate in other provider's compliance programs, such as the compliance programs of the hospitals or other settings in which the physicians practice. Physician practice management companies also may serve as a source of compliance program guidance.

The OIG Work Plan

Each year, in October, the OIG releases a work plan outlining its priorities for the fiscal year ahead. Some of the projects described in the work plan are statutorily required, such as the audit of the department's financial statements, which is mandated by the Government Management Reform Act. Of special interest to healthcare, the work plan announces potential problem areas with claims submissions that it will target for special scrutiny.

For example, an excerpt from the 2015 OIG Work Plan:

Diagnostic Radiology—
Medical Necessity of High-Cost Tests
We will review Medicare payments for high-cost diagnostic radiology tests to determine whether they were medically necessary and the extent to which utilization has increased for these tests. Medicare will not pay for items or services that are not "reasonable and necessary."

(Social Security Act,§1862 (a)(1)(A).) (OAS;W-00-13-35454; W-00-14-35454; various reviews;expected issue date: FY2015)

Source: http://oig.hhs.gov/reports-and-publications/archives/workplan/2015/WP15-2%20Medicare%20AB.pdf

This information guides providers in their delivery of diagnostic radiology services and cautions against the use of over-utilization.

The next example demonstrates the OIG's focus on sleep studies. Because payments totaled approximately $415 million for polysomnography services, and analysis showed high utilization associated with these services, the OIG will investigate to determine why there was such a large increase in providing of services.

Sleep disorder clinics—high utilization of sleep-testing procedures

We will examine Medicare payments to physicians, hospital outpatient departments, and independent di-agnostic testing facilities for sleep-testing procedures to assess the appropriateness of Medicare payments for high utilization sleep-testing procedures and determine whether they were in accordance with Medicare requirements. An OIG analysis of CY2010 Medicare payments for Current Procedural Terminology (CPT) codes 95810 and 95811, which totaled approximately $415 million, showed high utilization associated with these sleep-testing procedures. Medicare will not pay for items or services that are not "reasonable and necessary." (Social Security Act, §1862(a)(1)(A).) To the extent that repeated diagnostic testing is performed on the same beneficiary and the prior test results are still pertinent, repeated tests may not be reasonable and necessary.   Requirements for coverage of sleep tests under Part B are in CMS's Medicare Benefit Policy Manual, Pub.No.100-02, ch.15, §70.

(OAS;W-00-10-35521; W-00-12-35521; W-00-13-35521; W-00-14-35521; various reviews; expected issue date: FY2015)

Source: http://oig.hhs.gov/reports-and-publications/archives/workplan/2015/WP15-2%20Medicare%20AB.pdf

For more information, you can find the most recent OIG Work Plan at oig.hhs.gov

---

Section Review 1.2

1. Who would NOT be considered a covered entity under HIPAA?

    A. Doctors

    B. HMOs

    C. Clearinghouse

    D. Patient

2. Under HIPAA, what would be a policy requirement for "Minimum Necessary?"

    A. Only individuals whose job requires it may have access to protected health information.

    B. Only the patient has access to protected health information.

    C. Only the treating physician has access to protected health information.

    D. Anyone within the provider's office can have access to protected health information.

---

3. Which Act was enacted as part of the American Recovery and Reinvestment Act of 2009 (ARRA) and affected privacy and security?

    A. HIPAA

    B. HITECH

    C. SSA

    D. FECA

4. What document has been created to assist physician offices with the development of compliance manuals?

    A. OIG Compliance Plan Guidance

    B. OIG Work Plan

    C. OIG Suggested Rules and Regulations

    D. OIG Internal Compliance Plan

5. What document should be referred to when looking for potential problem areas identified by the government indicating scrutiny of the services within the coming year?

    A. OIG Compliance Plan Guidance

    B. OIG Security Summary

    C. OIG Work Plan

    D. OIG Document Planner

What AAPC Will Do for You

AAPC was founded in 1988 to provide education and professional certification to physician-based medical coders, and to elevate the standards of medical coding by providing student training, certification, and ongoing education, networking, and job opportunities. AAPC has expanded beyond outpatient coding to include training and credentials in documentation and coding audits, inpatient hospital/facility coding, regulatory compliance, and physician practice management. At press time, AAPC has a membership base of over 150,000 worldwide, of which more than 103,000 are certified.

AAPC credentialed coders have proven mastery of all code sets, evaluation and management principles, and documentation guidelines. Certified Professional Coders (CPCs®) and other AAPC credentialed coders represent the best in the medical coding career field.

AAPC offers more than 400 local chapters. Through local chapters AAPC members can obtain continuing education, gain leadership skills, and network.

AAPC specifies a Code of Ethics to promote and maintain the highest standard of professional service and conduct among its members. As a member of AAPC, a coder is bound by the AAPC Code of Ethics.

AAPC Code of Ethics

Commitment to ethical professional conduct is expected of every AAPC member. The specification of a Code of Ethics enables AAPC to clarify to current and future members, and to those served by members, the nature of the ethical responsibilities held in common by its members. This document establishes principles that define the ethical behavior of AAPC members.

It shall be the responsibility of every AAPC member, as a condition of continued membership, to conduct themselves in all professional activities in a manner consistent with ALL of the following ethical principles of professional conduct:

- Integrity
- Respect
- Commitment
- Competence
- Fairness
- Responsibility

Adherence to these ethical standards assists in assuring public confidence in the integrity and professionalism of AAPC members. Failure to conform professional conduct to these ethical standards, as determined by AAPC's Ethics Committee, may result in the loss of membership with AAPC.

The quality of the AAPC certifications, along with the strength in its membership numbers, offers certified AAPC members credibility in the workforce—as well as higher wages. According to the 2014 AAPC Salary Survey, salaries for credentialed professional coders (CPC) average $50, 030 per year.

Glossary

ABN—Advance Beneficiary Notice.

AMA—American Medical Association.

APC—Ambulatory Payment Classification.

ARRA—American Recovery and Reinvestment Act of 2009.

ASC—Ambulatory Surgical Centers.

CDT—Current Dental Terminology.

CMS—Centers for Medicare & Medicaid Services.

CMS-HCC—Centers for Medicare & Medicaid Services—Hierarchical Condition Category.

CPC®—Certified Professional Coder.

CPT®—Current Procedural Terminology.

EHR—Electronic Health Record.

EIN—Employer Identification Number.

E/M or E&M—Evaluation and Management.

HCPCS—Healthcare Common Procedure Coding System.

HHS—Department of Health & Human Services.

HIPAA—Health Insurance Portability and Accountability Act of 1996.

HITECH—Health Information Technology for Economic and Clinical Health Act.

HMO—Health Maintenance Organization.

ICD-9-CM—International Classification of Disease, 9th Clinical Modification.

ICD-10-CM—International Classification of Disease, Tenth Edition, Clinical Modification

LCD—Local Coverage Determination.

MAC—Medicare Administrative Contractor.

MS-DRG—Medicare Severity Diagnostic Related Group.

NCD—National Coverage Determination.

NP—Nurse Practitioner.

NPI—National Provider Identifier.

OCR—Office for Civil Rights.

OIG—Office of Inspector General.

PA—Physician Assistant.

PHI—Protected Health Information.

PPACA—Patient Protection and Affordable Care Act

SOAP—Standard format for E/M Services—Subjective, Objective, Assessment, Plan.

TPO—Treatment, payment, and healthcare operations.

Medical Terminology and Anatomy Review

Introduction

A thorough knowledge of human anatomy is essential to successful coding, as is the ability to understand medical terminology used to describe and document medical procedures and services. This chapter introduces the basic elements of human anatomy and reviews medical vocabulary and terminology.

Objectives

- Understand the language of medicine
- Review word elements such as combining forms, prefixes, and suffixes
- Acquire an understanding of procedural and diagnostic terms
- Understand anatomy as it relates to coding

Medical Terminology

Every profession has its own language, and medicine is no exception. The language of medicine is more than 2,000 years old. Many medical terms used today derive from the ancient Greeks and Romans. For example, the Latin phrase *pro re nata*, which means when necessary, is the origin of the medical abbreviation PRN. To code medical procedures and diagnoses accurately, you first must learn the language of medicine.

The best way to learn medical terminology is by understanding word parts and elements of medical language — root words, prefixes, and suffixes — which serve as the foundation of our medical vocabulary. When you understand the meanings of each word part, interpretation of tens of thousands of complex medical terms becomes easier.

Word Elements

The base of the word is considered the "root." Root words are terms standing alone as the main portion of a medical term. A prefix, suffix, and/or combining vowel may accompany it. The root word is the word part holding the fundamental meaning of the medical term, and each medical term contains at least one root or base word. A word can have more than one root.

Common root words consistently associated with the major body systems include:

Integumentary System

Term	Definition
Derm/o	skin
Dermat/o	skin
Hidr/o	sweat, perspiration
Kerat/o	keratin, horny layer of skin
Melan/o	dark, black, melanin
Onych/o	nail
Seb/o	sebum, sebaceous gland
Trich/o	hair

CPT® Example: 15780 Dermabrasion; total face

ICD-9-CM Example: 110.1 Onychomycosis

ICD-10-CM Example: L30.1 Dyshidrosis [pompholyx]

Musculoskeletal System

Term	Definition
Arthr/o	joint
Burs/o	bursa, sac of fluid near joint
Chondr/o	cartilage
Erg/o	work
Fasci/o	fascia
Kin/o, kinesi/o	movement
Muscul/o	muscle
My/o	muscle
Myel/o	bone marrow, spinal cord
Oste/o	bone
Synov/i	synovial fluid, joint, or membrane
Ten/o, tendin/o	tendon
Ton/o	tone; pressure

CPT® Example: 23800 Arthrodesis, glenohumeral joint (-desis means binding or fusion; arthrodesis is binding or fusion of the joint)

ICD-9-CM Example: 729.4 Fasciitis, unspecified

ICD-10-CM Example: M46.27 Osteomyelitis of vertebra, lumbosacral region

Respiratory System

Term	Definition
Bronch/o	bronchus
Laryng/o	larynx
Pharyng/o	pharynx
Phren/o	diaphragm
Phrenic/o	phrenic nerve
Pleur/o	pleura
Pneumon/o	lung
Pneum/o, pneumat/o	air, gas; respiration, lung
Pulm/o, pulmon/o	lungs
Rhin/o	nose
Spir/o	breathing
Trache/o	trachea

CPT® Example: 94010 Spirometry, including graphic record, total and timed vital capacity, expiratory flow rate measurement(s), with or without maximal voluntary ventilation.

ICD-9-CM Example: 486 Pneumonia, organism unspecified

ICD-10-CM Example: J00 Acute nasopharyngitis [common cold]

Cardiovascular System

Term	Definition
Angi/o	vessel
Aort/o	aorta
Arter/o, arteri/o	artery
Arteriol/o	arteriole
Atri/o	atrium
Cardi/o	heart
Phleb/o	vein
Valv/o, valvul/o	valve
Vas/o, vascul/o	vessel, duct
Ven/o, ven/i	vein
Ventricul/o	cavity, ventricle

CPT® Example: 33010 Pericardiocentesis; initial

ICD-9-CM Example: 451.84 Phlebitis and thrombophlebitis of upper extremities, unspecified

ICD-10-CM Example: I44.0 Atrioventricular block, first degree

Hemic and Lymphatic Systems

Term	Definition
Erythr/o, erythrocyt/o	red blood cell
Hem/o, hemat/o	blood
Immun/o	immunity, immune system
Leuk/o, leukocyt/o	white blood cell
Lymph/o	lymph, lymphatic system
Lymphaden/o	lymph node
Lymphangi/o	lymphatic vessel
Splen/o	spleen
Thromb/o	blood clot
Thrombocyt/o	platelet, thrombocyte
Thym/o	thymus gland
Tonsil/o	tonsil

CPT® Example: 38308 Lymphangiotomy or other operations on lymphatic channels

ICD-9-CM Example: 453.81 Acute venous embolism and thrombosis of superficial veins of upper extremity

ICD-10-CM: D69.3 Immune thrombocytopenic purpura

Digestive System

Term	Definition
Bucc/o	cheek
Chol/e, chol/o	bile, gall
Cholangi/o	bile duct
Cholecyst/o	gallbladder
Choledoch/o	common bile duct
Enter/o	intestine
Gastr/o	stomach
Gloss/o	tongue
Hepat/o	liver
Labi/o	lip
Lingu/o	tongue
Or/o	mouth
Sial/o	saliva, salivary gland, salivary duct
Stoma, stomat/o	mouth
Proct/o	rectum
Uvul/o	uvula

CPT® Example: 47715 Excision of choledochal cyst

ICD-9-CM Example: 527.2 Sialoadenitis

ICD-10-CM: K14.0 Glossitis

Urinary System

Term	Definition
Cali/o, calic/o	calyx
Cyst/o	urinary bladder
Glomerul/o	glomerulus
Nephr/o	kidney
Pyel/o	renal pelvis
Ren/o	kidney
Ur/o	urine, urinary tract
Ureter/o	ureter
Urethr/o	urethra
Urin/o	urine
Vesic/o	urinary bladder

CPT® Example: 50120 Pyelotomy; with exploration

ICD-9-CM Example: 583.9 Nephritis and nephropathy not specified as acute or chronic with unspecified pathological lesion in kidney

ICD-10-CM Example: N13.71 Vesicoureteral-reflux without reflux nephropathy

Male Reproductive System

Term	Definition
Epididym/o	epididymis
Orchi/o, orchid/o	testis
Osche/o	scrotum
Prostat/o	prostate
Semin/o	semen
Sperm/o, spermat/o	semen, spermatozoa
Test/o	testis, testicle
Vas/o	vas deferens, ductus deferens; also vessel; duct
Vesicul/o	seminal vesicle

CPT® Example: 54522 Orchiectomy, partial

ICD-9-CM Example: 601.0 Acute prostatitis

ICD-10-CM Example: N43.42 Spermatocele of epididymis, multiple

Female Reproductive System

Term	Definition
Colp/o	vagina
Episi/o	vulva
Gyn/o, gynec/o	woman
Hyster/o	uterus
Mast/o	breast, mammary gland
Men/o, mens	menstruation
Metr/o, metr/i	uterus
O/o	ovum, egg cell
Oophor/o	ovary
Ov/o, ovul/o	ovum, egg cell
Salping/o	oviduct, tube

CPT® Example: 58940 Oophorectomy, partial or total, unilateral or bilateral

ICD-9-CM Example: 611.0 Inflammatory disease of breast (Mastitis)

ICD-10-CM Example: O23.521 Salpingo-oophoritis in pregnancy, first trimester

Endocrine System

Term	Definition
Adren/o, adrenal/o	adrenal gland, epinephrine
Adrenocortic/o	adrenal cortex
Endocrin/o	endocrine glands or system
Hypophys/o	pituitary gland, hypophysis
Insul/o	pancreatic islets
Parathyr/o, parathyroid/o	parathyroid gland
Pituitar/o	pituitary gland, hypophysis
Thyr/o, thyroid/o	thyroid gland

CPT® Example: 60240 Thyroidectomy, total or complete

ICD-9-CM Example: 253.6 Other disorders of neurohypophysis

ICD-10-CM Example: E27.1 Primary adrenocortical insufficiency

Nervous System

Term	Definition
Cerebr/o	cerebrum
Cortic/o	cerebral cortex, outer portion
Encephal/o	brain

Term	Definition
Gangli/o, ganglion/o	ganglion
Gli/o	neuroglia cells
Medull/o	medulla oblongata, medulla (inner section), middle, soft, marrow
Mening/o, meninge/o	meninges
Myel/o	spinal cord
Narc/o	stupor, numbness, sleep
Neur/o, neur/i	nervous system, nervous tissue, nerve
Psych/o	mind
Radicul/o	spinal nerve root
Somn/o, somn/i	sleep

CPT® Example: 72240 Myelography, cervical, radiological supervision and interpretation

ICD-9-CM Example: 348.30 Encephalopathy, unspecified

ICD-10-CM Example: G13.0 Paraneoplastic neuromyopathy and neuropathy

Special Senses

Term	Definition
Blephar/o	eyelid
Cochle/o	cochlea of inner ear
Corne/o	cornea
Dacryocyst/o	lacrimal sac
Myring/o	tympanic membrane
Ot/o	ear
Phak/o, phac/o	lens
Retin/o	retina
Salping/o	tube, Eustachian tube
Scler/o	sclera
Tympan/o	tympanic cavity (middle ear), tympanic membrane

CPT® Example: 15820 Blepharoplasty, lower eyelid

ICD-9-CM Example: 381.50 Eustachian salpingitis, unspecified

ICD-10-CM Example: H73.011 Bullous myringitis, right ear

A prefix typically is attached to the beginning of a word to modify or alter its meaning. Not all medical terms will contain

a prefix. Prefixes often (not always) indicate location, time, or number.

Some common prefixes include:

Location

Prefix	Definition
Ec-, ecto-	out; outside
End/o-	in; within
Mes/o	middle
Dextr/o	right
Ab-	away from
Ad-	toward; near
Dia-	through; complete
Per-	through
Trans-	through; across

Time

Prefix	Definition
Ante-	before; forward
Pre-	before, in front of
Pro-	before, in front of
Post-	after, behind

Number

Prefix	Definition
Mon/o	one; single
Bi-	two, twice
Tri-	three
Quadri-	four
Poly-	many, much

The term "suffix" comes from the Latin word subfigure, meaning "to fasten underneath." A suffix traditionally is attached to the end of a word to modify its meaning. Not all medical terms have a suffix. In medical terms, suffixes frequently indicate the procedure, condition, disorder, or disease. Some common suffixes meaning "condition of" include -ia, -ism, -sis, and -y. Suffixes used to show medical specialties include -ian, -iatrics, -iatry, -ics, -ist, and -logy. Some common suffixes for diseases include -itis (inflammation), -oma (tumor), and -pathy (disease of).

Throughout procedural coding, you will see common suffixes used for diagnostic procedures and surgical procedures. To code appropriately, you need to memorize these suffixes:

Suffixes for Diagnostic Procedures

Suffix	Definition
-gram	a record of data
-graph	instrument for recording data
-graphy	act of recording data
-meter	instrument for measuring
-scope	instrument for viewing or examining
-scopy	examination of

CPT® Example: 93000 Electrocardiogram, routine ECG with at least 12 leads; with interpretation and report.

Suffixes for Surgery

Suffix	Definition
-centesis	puncture, tap
-desis	binding, fusion
-ectomy	excision, surgical removal
-pexy	surgical fixation
-plasty	plastic repair, plastic surgery, reconstruction
-rraphy	surgical repair, suture
-stomy	surgical creation of an opening
-tome	instrument for incising (cutting)
-tomy	incision, cutting
-tripsy	crushing

CPT® Example: 58275 Vaginal hysterectomy, with total or partial vaginectomy

Three commonly confused suffixes are -ectomy, -otomy, and -ostomy. Understanding the differences between these will help locate codes within the CPT® codebook.

In most sections of the CPT® codebook, there are subsections for incision and excision. Incision is a cut. This subsection is where you will find -otomy (incision, cutting) and -ostomy (surgical creation of an opening) suffixes. Excision is to cut something out. This subsection is where you will find -ectomy

suffixes. Likewise, the suffix -rraphy (surgical repair, suture) is found in the repair subsections.

Due to Greek and Latin origins of medical terms, the conventions for changing from singular to plural endings are dictated by a specific set of guidelines as in the table below.

Plural Endings

Word Ending	Plural Ending	Singular Example	Plural Example
a	ae	vertebra	vertebrae
en	ina	lumen	lumina
ex, ix, yx	ices	index	indices
is	es	prognosis	prognoses
ma	mata	stigma	stigmata
nx (anx, inx, ynx)	nges	phalanx	phalanges
on	a	phenomenon	phenomena
um	a	serum	sera
us	i	thrombus	thrombi

Using the word parts for translation, you will find the approximate meaning of the complete medical term. For example, the word "cardiomyopathy" tells a provider the patient has a diseased heart muscle. When one sees the combining form "cardio," it is apparent this word element pertains to the heart. It can be used in a variety of combinations with different word elements to relate a plethora of descriptions, illnesses, and conditions to the heart. As such, the word "cardiomyopathy" paints a detailed clinical picture using a single word.

Section Review 2.1

1. Which part is considered the foundation of a word?

    A. Prefix

    B. Combining vowel

    C. Root word

    D. Suffix

2. Blepharoplasty is performed on which part of the body?

    A. Lip

    B. Eyelid

    C. Stomach

    D. Leg

3. Based on word parts, what is the definition of a salpingo-oophorectomy?

    A. Creating a hole in the ovary.

    B. Surgical removal of the ovary.

    C. Surgical repair of the ovary and tube.

    D. Surgical removal of an ovary and tube.

4. Based on word parts, what structure does paronychia refer to?

    A. Hair

    B. Nail

    C. Sweat glands

    D. Parathyroid gland

5. The prefix sub- means beneath. Based on word parts, what is the definition of subfascial?

    A. Beneath the face

    B. Beneath the fascia

    C. Beneath the skin

    D. Beneath the nail

6. Based on word parts, what is the definition of a tracheostomy?

    A. Surgical removal of a portion of the trachea

    B. Creation of a hole in the trachea

    C. Surgical repair of the trachea

    D. Revision of the trachea

7. Leukocytosis refers to an increase in:

    A. White blood cells

    B. Red blood cells

    C. Blood platelets

    D. Blood flow

8. Based on word parts, what is the definition of a glossectomy?

    A. Creating a hole in the glossy part of the eye

    B. Surgical removal of the tongue

    C. Surgical repair of the tongue

    D. Surgical removal of the tear duct in the eye

9. A choledochal cyst is a cyst originating from which structure?

    A. Gallbladder

    B. Liver

    C. Common bile duct

    D. Intestine

10. A cystourethroscopy is examination of what structures?

    A. Bladder and urethra

    B. Gallbladder and urethra

    C. Bladder and ureters

    D. Kidneys and urethra

Introduction to Anatomy

The human body contains multiple organ systems. An organ system is a collection of body parts depending on one another to achieve a mutual objective. The following organ systems will be addressed briefly here, and in greater depth in subsequent coding chapters as relevant:

Integumentary

Musculoskeletal

Cardiovascular

Lymphatic

Respiratory

Digestive

Urinary

Reproductive

Nervous

Organs of sense
- Eye
- Ear

Endocrine

Hematologic

Immune

Anatomical Positions and Planes

For physicians, nurses, and other healthcare personnel to communicate accurately, they must use a standard form for body directions and orientations. This is done by the use of anatomical directions and planes. The standard body position is considered the anatomical position. The anatomical position is an upright, face-forward position with the arms by the side and palms facing forward. The feet are parallel and slightly apart.

Based on the anatomical position, the following directional terms are pertinent to understanding medical documentation:

Anterior (ventral)—toward the front of the body.

Posterior (dorsal)—toward the back of the body.

Medial—toward the midline of the body.

Lateral—toward the side of the body.

Proximal—nearer to the point of attachment or to a given reference point.

Distal—farther from the point of attachment or from a given reference point.

Superior (cranial)—above; toward the head.

Inferior (caudal)—below; toward the lower end of the spine.

Superficial (external)—closer to the surface of the body.

Deep (internal)—closer to the center of the body.

Body Directions

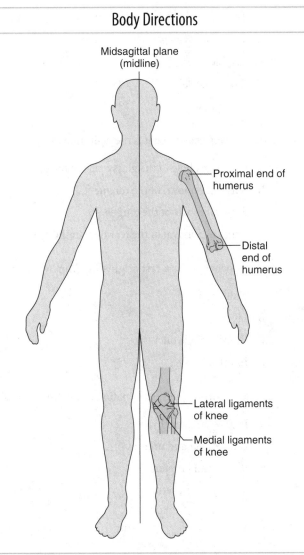

Source: Ehrlich, Medical Terminology for Health Professionals, 6e, ISBN #978-1-4180-7252-0

For radiological studies on the body, the body is often virtually cut along a flat surface called a plane. The most frequently used planes include:

Sagittal—cuts through the midline of the body from front to back and divides the body into right and left sections.

Frontal (coronal)—cuts at a right angle to the midline cut, from side to side, and divides the body into front (anterior) and back (posterior) sections.

Transverse (horizontal) (axial)—cuts horizontally through the body and separates the body into upper (superior) and lower (inferior) sections.

Body Planes

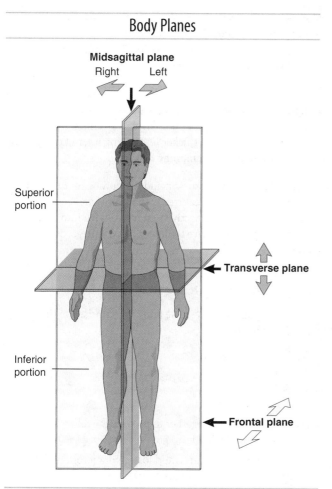

Source: Ehrlich, Medical Terminology for Health Professionals, 6e, ISBN #978-1-4180-7252-0

Application to Documentation

INDICATION: Left vocal cord paralysis

CT NECK WITH CONTRAST

TECHNIQUE: Axial CT cuts were obtained from the top of the orbits down to the thoracic inlet using 100 cc of Isovue 300. 13 mm axial CT cuts were also obtained through the larynx. Sagittal and coronal computer reconstruction images were also obtained.

Use of anatomical planes — axial, sagittal and coronal — explain what types of images were obtained.

Structure of the Human Body

The structure of the human body falls into four categories:

- Cells
- Tissues
- Organs
- Systems

Each structure is a highly organized unit of smaller structures.

The cell is the basic unit of all living things. Human anatomy is composed of cells varying in size and shape according to function:

- Cell membrane forms the boundary of the cell
- Cytoplasm makes up the body of the cell
- Nucleus is the small, round structure in the center of the cell
- Chromosomes are located in the nucleus of the cell; they contain genes determining hereditary characteristics

Tissue is a group of similar cells performing a specific task:

- Muscle tissue produces movement
- Nerve tissue conducts impulses to and from the brain
- Connective tissue connects and supports various body structures: adipose (fat) and osseous (bone)
- Epithelial tissue is found in the skin, lining of the blood vessels, respiratory, intestinal, urinary tracts, and other body systems

Organs are two or more kinds of tissue together performing special body functions. As an example, skin is an organ composed of epithelial, connective, and nerve tissue.

Systems are groups of organs working together to perform complex body functions. For example, the nervous system is made up of the brain, spinal cord, and nerves. Its function is to coordinate and control other body parts.

Medical Terms Related to Cells and Tissues

Cell Membrane—Surrounds and protects the individual cell.

Nucleus—Small, round structure within the cell containing chromosomes and nucleoplasm (DNA [deoxyribonucleic acid] and RNA [ribonucleic acid]).

Chromosome—Linear strand made of DNA carrying genetic information.

Cytology—Study of cells including the formation, structure, and function of cells.

RNA (Ribonucleic acid)—Contained within the nucleus, is transcribed from DNA by enzymes and plays a crucial role in protein synthesis.

Gene—Specific segment of base pairs in chromosomes; functional unit of heredity.

Mitosis—Cells divide and multiply to form two cells.

Body Cavities

The body is not a solid structure as it appears on the outside. It has five cavities, each of which contains an orderly arrangement of internal organs.

1. Cranial Cavity - The space inside the skull, or cranium, containing the brain.

2. Spinal (Vertebral Canal) Cavity - The space inside the spinal column containing the spinal cord. The combined cranial cavity and spinal cavity is known as the dorsal cavity.

3. Thoracic, or Chest, Cavity - The space containing the heart, lungs, esophagus, trachea, bronchi, and thymus.

4. Abdominal Cavity - The space containing the lower portion of the esophagus, the stomach, intestines (excluding the sigmoid colon and rectum), kidneys, liver, gallbladder, pancreas, spleen, and ureters.

5. Pelvic Cavity - The space containing the urinary bladder, certain reproductive organs, part of the large intestine, and the rectum.

Membranes

Membranes line the internal spaces of organs and tubes opening to the outside and line body cavities. There are five types of membranes: mucous membranes, serous membranes, synovial membranes, meninges, and the cutaneous membrane.

Mucous Membranes—Line the interior walls of the organs and tubes opening to the outside of the body, such as those of the digestive, respiratory, urinary, and reproductive systems. These membranes are lined with epithelium, and are involved in absorption and secretion. The mucous membrane is composed of epithelium overlaying a layer of connective tissue called lamina propria. In some instances, the lamina propria rests on a third layer of smooth muscle cells. Not every mucous membrane secretes mucous.

Serous Membranes—Line cavities, including the thoracic cavity and internal organs (eg, heart). They consist of a layer of simple squamous epithelium overlaying a layer of loose connective tissue. Serous membranes support internal organs and compartmentalize the large cavities to hinder spread of infection. The serous membranes are named according to their organ associations. The lungs are covered by pleura and the heart is covered by pericardium. The serous layer also lines the abdominal cavity and is called the peritoneum.

Synovial Membranes—Line joint cavities and are composed of connective tissue. They secrete synovial fluid into the joint cavity; this lubricates the ends of bones so they can move freely.

Meninges—Composed of three connective tissue membranes found within the dorsal cavity and serve as a protective covering of the brain and spinal cord. The meninges from outer layer to inside layer are dura mater, arachnoid, and pia mater.

Cutaneous Membrane—Forms the outer covering of the body and consists of a thin outer layer of stratified squamous epithelium attached to a thicker underlying layer of connective tissue. The cutaneous membrane is skin.

The term "connective tissue" includes a number of different tissues with a common feature. They support and connect tissues of the body. Connective tissue is divided into four general groups: connective tissue proper, cartilage, bone, and blood.

Integumentary System

The largest organ system in the body is comprised of the following structures:

- Skin
- Hair
- Nails

These structures work together to provide the following functions within the body:

- Protection from injury, fluid loss, and microorganisms (eg, bacteria, virus, fungus, yeast)
- Temperature regulation
- Fluid balance—excretion
- Sensation

Skin

Two layers make up human skin: dermis and epidermis. Each layer and its components are listed below. The coder should be familiar with the various layers and be able to apply this knowledge when choosing the appropriate CPT® code.

Epidermis

The epidermis is composed of four to five layers called stratum. The number of stratum varies based on where the epidermis is located. The stratum lucidum layer is normally found only on the palms of the hands and the soles of the feet. The various strata are:

Stratum Corneum—Also called the horny layer; outermost layer.

Stratum Lucidum (Palms and Soles)—Clear layer.

Stratum Granulosum—Granular layer of cells. They accumulate two types of granules; keratohyaline granules and lamellated granules.

Stratum Spinosum—Composed of prickle cells.

Stratum Basale (Stratum Germinativum)—Deepest of the five layers, made of basal cells.

Dermis

The dermis is located just under the epidermis. It has two layers of strata:

Stratum Papillare—Thin superficial layer interlocked with the epidermis.

Stratum Reticulare—Thick layer of dense, irregular connective tissue.

The dermis contains many important structures nourishing and innervating the skin:

- Vessels carrying blood and lymph
- Nerves and nerve endings
- Glands
- Hair follicles

The dermis lies on the subcutaneous (beneath the skin) tissue. The subcutaneous tissue is known as the hypodermis, but is not considered a layer of the skin. The subcutaneous tissues are mostly composed of fatty or adipose tissue, plus some areolar tissue (loose connective tissue consisting of a meshwork of collagen, elastic tissue, and reticular fibers). The hypodermis serves to protect the underlying structures, prevent loss of body heat, and anchor the skin to the underlying musculature. The fibrous connective tissue, referred to as superficial fascia, is included in this layer.

It is imperative to understand the stratification of the tissue layers and the structures lying within when coding for surgical procedures throughout the body—and most particularly those procedures performed on the integument. When applying CPT® codes found in the 10000 section, the coder needs to know in which layer the provider worked.

Application to Documentation

NARRATIVE: After prone positioning and IV sedation, the left upper back was prepped and draped in a sterile manner. Local anesthesia 1% lidocaine and bicarbonate was used. A vertical incision was made over the mass and extended. Deep in the subcutaneous tissue over muscle fascia was an 8 cm lipoma with a lot of lobulations between skin ligaments, and these were all progressively divided to excise the entire mass including a

portion of the muscle fascia. An oblique drain was positioned through an inferior stab wound and secured with Ethilon. All bleeding was controlled with cautery. The subcutaneous tissue was approximated with Vicryl, and the skin was approximated with intracuticular 4-0 Vicryl suture. Steri-Strips and dressings were applied. The patient was awakened and moved to the recovery room in satisfactory condition. There were no complications. Blood loss was minimal.

In the above documentation, understanding the depth of the procedure (eg, which skin tissue layer is involved) is necessary to select the appropriate procedure code.

Medical Terms Relating to Skin

Cutaneous—Pertaining to the skin.

Dermatology—The study of skin.

Dermatologist—Physician specializing in diseases of the skin and subcutaneous tissue.

Decubitus—Pressure ulcer/bedsore.

Ecchymosis—Condition in which blood seeps into the skin causing discoloration.

Hypodermic—Pertaining to under the skin.

Intradermal—Pertaining to within the skin.

Jaundice—Yellowness of skin.

Melanin—Pigment giving color to the skin.

Melanoma—Pigmented tumor of the skin.

Pediculosis—Infestation with lice.

Subcutaneous—Pertaining to below the skin.

Tinea—Ringworm (a fungal infection of the skin).

Hair

By 22 weeks, a developing fetus has its lifetime supply of hair follicles. On average, the body has five million follicles, with the greatest concentration (approximately one million) on the head. Follicles are never added during life, and as the size of the body increases, density of hair follicles on the skin decreases. Hair on the scalp grows approximately .3 to .4 mm/day or about six inches per year.

Hair has two separate structures: follicle and shaft. The follicle contains several layers. At the base is a bulb-like projection, called a papilla. There are capillaries nourishing the bulb. Cells in the bulb divide every 23 to 72 hours. Inner and outer sheaths protect and mold the growing hair shaft surrounding the follicle. The inner sheath ends at the opening of the sebaceous gland, which secretes sebum; it may pocket, causing benign lesions on the scalp (removal of these benign cysts are reported using CPT® codes 11400-11471 range). A muscle called the erector pili, attaches to the outer sheath and causes hair to stand up when it contracts. The shaft is composed of keratin in three layers: the medulla, cortex, and cuticle. Pigment cells in the cortex and medulla give hair its characteristic color.

Nails

The fingernail is made of keratin acting as a protective plate and as a counterforce to the fingertip to increase sensory input of touch. Nails grow all the time, but their rate of growth slows down with age and poor circulation. Fingernails grow at an approximate rate of 3 mm per month; toenails grow more slowly, at approximately 1 mm per month.

The nail is divided into six specific parts: the root, nail bed, nail plate, eponychium (cuticle), perionychium, and hyponychium. The root, also known as the germinal matrix, lies beneath the skin behind the fingernail and extends several millimeters into the finger. The root produces most of the volume of the nail and the nail bed and its edge is the white, crescent-shaped structure called the lunula. The nail bed, called the sterile matrix, extends from the edge of the lunula to the hyponychium. The nail bed contains the blood vessels, nerves, and melanocytes (melanin-producing cells). The nail plate is the actual fingernail, made of translucent keratin. Blood vessels underneath give the nail its pink appearance; the grooves along the inner length of the nail plate anchor the nail to the nail bed. The cuticle, also called the eponychium, is between the skin of the finger and the nail plate fusing the skin of the finger to the nail plate. The perionychium, also known as the paronychial edge, is the skin overlying the nail plate on its sides and is the site of hangnails, ingrown nails, and an infection of the skin called paronychia. The hyponychium is the junction between the free edge of the nail and the skin.

Medical Terms Related to Hair and Nails

Alopecia—Loss of hair.

Follicles—Specialized structures required for hair growth.

Hair Follicles—Sacs holding the root of hair fibers.

Hair Papilla—Knoblike indentation at bottom of hair follicle containing the blood supply to hair root.

Lunula—Little moon area of nail.

Nail Body—Visible part of nail.

Nail Bed—Skin below the nail—epidermis and dermis (sterile matrix).

Onychitis—Inflammation of nail matrix.

CPT® codes in the 10000 range address procedures and services relative to the integumentary system.

Section Review 2.2

1. Squamous cell carcinoma and basal cell carcinoma are both cancers of cell tissue of the skin, lining of the blood vessels, respiratory, intestinal, urinary tracts, and other body systems. What type of tissue are these carcinomas found in?

    A. Muscle tissue

    B. Nerve tissue

    C. Connective tissue

    D. Epithelial tissue

2. The bronchi are found in what body cavity?

    A. Cranial cavity

    B. Spinal cavity

    C. Thoracic cavity

    D. Abdominal cavity

3. Which type of membrane is found lining the interior walls of the digestive system?

    A. Mucous membrane

    B. Serous membrane

    C. Synovial membrane

    D. Cutaneous membrane

4. Which layer of the epidermis is normally found on the palms of the hands and the soles of the feet?

    A. Stratum Corneum

    B. Stratum Lucidum

    C. Stratum Papillare

    D. Stratum Reticulare

5. A procedure requiring the physician to cut down to the superficial fascia is documented as cutting down into the:

    A. Epidermis

    B. Dermis

    C. Hypodermis

    D. Cutaneous tissue

Musculoskeletal System

The musculoskeletal system is a system of muscles, joints, tendons, and ligaments providing movement, form, strength, and protection. Various muscle and bone types work together in this body system.

Bones

Bones are composed of rigid connective tissue and provide the following functions:

- Form the skeleton
- Provide the chief means of support for the body
- Provide the mechanism for motion
- Protect vital organs
- Serve as a production factory for blood cells (eg, marrow)
- Store calcium, phosphorus, and magnesium salts

Bones, classified according to shape are:

Long—Bones longer than they are wide and found in the limbs (eg, femur and humerus). These bones are named for their elongated shape, not their size.

Tubular—Also referred to as long bones.

Short—Roughly cube-shaped bones such as carpal bones of the wrist and tarsal bones of the ankle.

Sesamoid ("shaped like a sesame seed")—A short bone formed within tendons; cartilaginous in early life and osseous (bony) in the adult. The patella is the largest sesamoid bone in the body.

Cuboidal—Also referred to as short bones.

Flat—Consist of a layer of spongy bone between two thin layers of compact bone; cross-section is flat, not rounded. Flat bones have marrow, but lack a bone marrow cavity. Skull and ribs are examples.

Irregular—Bones in the body not fitting into the above categories mentioned; several are found in the face, such as the zygoma. Vertebrae are also considered irregular bones.

Cartilage and Joints

Cartilage is a type of flexible connective tissue, it is nonvascular (has no blood vessels). Cartilage is a matrix made of chondrocytes, collagen, and glycosylated protein called proteoglycans, depending on the type of cartilage.

Joints and articulating surfaces are synonymous and provide a connection between two or more parts of the skeleton. Joints are classified according to the type of connective tissue at the articulating surfaces. There are three types: fibrous, cartilaginous, and synovial. Most joints are synovial and have the following characteristics:

- Articular cartilage that covers the bone ends
- Joint cavity lined with a synovial membrane, which secretes a thick, viscid, slippery mucous that cushions the joint and allow smooth motion
- Joint capsule of fibrous connective tissue that surrounds and provides stability of the joint
- Accessory ligaments that give reinforcement

Human Skeleton

The human skeleton is divided into two parts — the axial and appendicular skeleton:

Axial Skeleton

- Skull
- Hyoid and cervical spine (neck)
- Ribs
- Sternum
- Vertebrae
- Sacrum

Appendicular Skeleton

- Shoulder girdle
- Pelvic girdle
- Extremities

Common Bone Fractures

Closed Fracture—Does not involve a break in the skin.

Compound Fracture—Projects through the skin with a possibility of infection.

Comminuted Fracture—More than two separate bone components—Segmental fracture, bony fragments.

Transverse Fracture—Breaks shaft of a bone across the longitudinal axis.

Greenstick Fracture—Only one side of shaft is broken, and other is bent; common in children.

Spiral Fracture—Spread along length of bone and produced by twisting stress.

Colles' Fracture—Occurs in wrist and affects the distal radius bone.

Compression Fracture—Vertebrae collapse due to trauma, tumor, or osteoporosis.

Epiphyseal Fracture—Occurs when matrix is calcifying and chondrocytes are dying; usually seen in children.

Understanding the type of fracture is essential to proper diagnosis coding. An example of this can be seen when coding a compound fracture. A compound fracture is coded as an open fracture.

Muscles

Muscles have the property of contractility. They also provide form and produce heat for the body. There are three types of muscles found in the body:

Skeletal Muscle—Also called striated muscle, is attached to the skeleton by tendons; contraction of skeletal muscle is under voluntary control.

Cardiac Muscle—Also called heart muscle, contains interlocking involuntary striated muscle as well as smooth muscle, which allow the electrical impulses to pass quickly across the muscle fibers.

Smooth Muscle—Found in the walls of all the hollow organs of the body (except the heart). Its contraction reduces the size of these structures; movement generally is considered involuntary (not under voluntary control).

Medical Terms Related to Musculoskeletal System

Ankylosis—Condition of stiffening of a joint.

Arthralgia—Pain in joint.

Arthritis—Inflammation of a joint.

Arthrodesis—Surgical fixation of a joint.

Arthropathy—Joint disease.

Bursitis—Inflammation of a bursa.

Carpal—Pertaining to the wrist bones.

Chondral—Pertaining to cartilage.

Chondralgia—Pain around and in the cartilage.

Coccygeal—Pertaining to the coccyx.

Connective—Tissue connecting or binding together.

Dactylic—Pertaining to finger or toe.

Femoral—Pertaining to femur and thigh bone.

Iliac—Pertaining to the ilium.

Kyphosis—Abnormal curvature of thoracic spine (humpback).

Lordosis—Abnormal anterior curvature of spine, usually lumbar.

Metacarpal—Long bones of the hand that form the skeletal structure of the palm.

Osteoblast—Bone-forming cell.

Osteocarcinoma—Cancerous tumor of bone.

Osteochondritis—Inflammation of bone and cartilage.

Osteopenia—Lower than average bone density, can be a precursor to osteoporosis.

Osteoporosis—Condition resulting in reduction of bone mass.

Osteorrhaphy—Suture of bone.

Patellar—Pertaining to patella.

Phalangeal—Bones of the fingers and toes.

Scoliosis—Lateral curvature of spine.

Sternotomy—Surgical incision of sternum.

Tendonitis—Inflammation of tendon.

In CPT®, the section containing the 20000 code series pertains primarily to the musculoskeletal system, and is arranged by anatomical regions and structures.

Section Review 2.3

1. What type of fracture is an incomplete fracture commonly found in children?

    A. Compound fracture

    B. Colles' fracture

    C. Spiral fracture

    D. Greenstick fracture

2. Which of the following belongs to the appendicular skeleton as opposed to the axial skeleton?

    A. Ribs

    B. Pelvic Girdle

    C. Sacrum

    D. Hyoid

3. What is an example of a long bone?

    A. Metacarpals

    B. Ribs

    C. Carpals

    D. Patella

4. What type of joint is most common in the human body?

    A. Fibrous

    B. Cartilaginous

    C. Synovial

    D. Stiff

---

5. What is the root word meaning joint?

    A. Arthr/o

    B. Chondr/o

    C. Synov/i

    D. Oste/o

Cardiovascular System

This system is comprised of the heart and the blood vessels working together to move blood throughout the body. Blood provides nutrients and oxygen to all organs within the body.

Blood Vessels

The human body contains three types of blood vessels: arteries, veins, and capillaries.

Arteries carry blood away from the heart. They often are colored red in anatomical drawings to depict the red color of oxygenated blood. All arteries leaving the heart carry oxygenated blood except the pulmonary arteries. The pulmonary arteries carry deoxygenated blood from the right side of the heart to the lungs. These vessels get smaller as the arteries go out into the extremities, turning into arterioles, and eventually they comprise the arterial side of the capillary bed.

The venous side of the circulation begins in the venous side of the capillary bed, enlarging to form venules and eventually forming veins. Most veins bring deoxygenated blood, which is dark reddish brown in color, back to the heart. Veins often are depicted in illustrations as blue (not a true physiological depiction). Veins take deoxygenated blood to the heart except for pulmonary veins which carry oxygenated blood from the pulmonary veins to the left side of the heart.

Capillaries are tiny vessels, usually a single-cell-layer thick. They are semi permeable and facilitate the exchange of fluids, oxygen, nutrients, and waste between local tissues and the blood stream.

Heart

The adult heart is compared to the size of the human fist, and usually weighs less than one pound. The heart pumps blood to two distinct systems for circulation. The first system is the pulmonary circulation, receiving deoxygenated blood into the right atrium from the superior and inferior vena cava. The blood then flows into the right ventricle and is pushed into pulmonary circulation via the pulmonary trunk, which divides into the right and left pulmonary arteries. Blood is circulated through the pulmonary vascular tree in the lungs and sent into the left atrium of the heart through the right and left pulmonary veins. Oxygenated blood is pumped from the left side of the heart to the systemic circulation via the left ventricle to the aorta. Because the left side of the heart is responsible for pumping blood throughout the entire body, the muscle surrounding the left ventricle is stronger and larger than the right ventricle.

The heart is composed of three layers (epicardium, myocardium, and endocardium) and is enclosed in a double-wall lining called the pericardial sac. The pericardial sac prevents the heart from rubbing against other organs or body structures as it beats. The epicardium is the outer layer of the heart. The main muscle of the heart is the myocardium (myo=muscle, cardi=heart). Myocardial tissues allow electrical impulses to pass quickly across muscle fibers as part of the heart's unique electrical conduction system. The inner lining of the heart is the endocardium.

Interior of the Heart

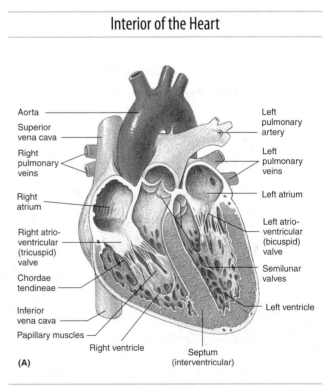

Source: Rizzo, Fundamentals of Anatomy and Physiology, 3e, ISBN #978-1-4354-3871-2

Medical Terms Related to the Cardiovascular System

Anginal—Relating to spasmodic attacks of suffocating pain as related to an inflammatory condition of the throat or mouth or angina pectoris marked by chest pain due to deficient oxygenation of the heart muscle.

Angiocarditis—Inflammation of heart and vessels.

Angioplasty—Surgical repair of vessels.

Arteriosclerosis—Hardening of an artery.

Arteriotomy—Incision into an artery.

Atherosclerosis—A type of arteriosclerosis characterized by lipid deposits causing fibrosis and calcification.

Bradycardia—Slow heartbeat.

Cardiocentesis—Surgical puncture of the heart.

Cardiologist—A physician specializing in diseases of the heart.

Cardiomegaly—Enlargement of the heart.

Cardiopulmonary—Pertaining to heart and lungs.

Carditis—Inflammation of the heart.

Cyanosis—Bluing of skin and mucous membranes caused by oxygen deficiency.

Electrocardiogram—Electrical tracing of the heart and heart muscle activity.

Embolism—Blood clot traveling through a blood vessel to another part of the body.

Hemangioma—Benign tumor of a blood vessel.

Hypertension—Persistent excessive pressure in the arteries.

Pericarditis—Inflammation of the pericardium.

Thrombus—Blood clot formed within a blood vessel.

You need to understand standard medical abbreviations used in medical records documentation. In the cardiovascular section, physicians often dictate using medical abbreviations to indicate the artery or vein involved.

Application to Documentation

The LAD was then dissected out. Arteriotomy was performed and the IMA was anastomosed in an end-to-side fashion to the LAD using running 7-0 Prolene around the heel of the anastomosis. The toe of the anastomosis was closed using interrupted 7-0 Prolene. Rewarming was begun during this anastomosis. The IMA pedicle clamp was released. Rapid resuscitation of the heart was seen as well as rapid distal filling of the LAD. The IMA pedicle was affixed to the epicardium using 5-0 silk suture. The aortic cross-clamp was removed. A partial occlusion clamp was placed on the aorta and three punch arteriotomies were made on the aorta. The vein grafts were measured to length, cut, and spatulated and anastomosed in an end-to-side fashion to the aorta using running 6-0 Prolene. All three proximal vein graft anastomoses were marked with titanium clips. The most distal graft on the aorta is to the posterolateral branch of the circumflex, more proximal is to the ramus, and the vein graft to the PDA was brought to the right side of the aorta. Partial occlusion clamp was removed.

In the documentation above, "IMA" indicates the internal mammary artery, "LAD" indicates the left anterior descending artery, and "PDA" indicates the posterior descending artery.

CPT® codes 33010–37799 address surgical procedures to the cardiovascular system. CPT® codes 92950–93998 address therapeutic and diagnostic procedures and services to the cardiovascular system.

Section Review 2.4

1. The heart receives de-oxygenated blood in the right atrium via which vessel?

    A. Right pulmonary artery

    B. Left pulmonary veins

    C. Inferior and Superior Vena Cava

    D. Aorta

---

2. The heart circulates blood through the lungs and is sent back into the left atrium of the heart via which vessel?

    A. Left pulmonary artery

    B. Left and right pulmonary veins

    C. Vena cava

    D. Aorta

3. What is the term for inflammation of the heart and vessels?

    A. Carditis

    B. Pericarditis

    C. Angiocarditis

    D. Angina

4. What is the inner layer of the heart?

    A. Pericardium

    B. Epicardium

    C. Myocardium

    D. Endocardium

5. What is cyanosis caused by?

    A. Oxygen overload

    B. Oxygen deficiency

    C. Liver excretion

    D. Drinking blue liquids

Lymphatic System

The lymphatic system is comprised of lymph vessels and lymph nodes. This system collects excess fluid from the interstitial spaces (potential spaces between tissues) and returns it to the heart. The venous end of the capillaries reabsorbs fluid pushed from arterial capillaries into the interstitial space; the lymph picks up excess fluid. The lymphatic system operates without a pump using a series of valves to ensure fluid travels in one direction, back to the heart. Lymphoid organs scattered throughout the body house phagocytic cells and lymphocytes essential to the body's defense system and its resistance to disease. Lymphoid organs include the spleen, thymus, tonsils, and Peyer's patches of the intestine.

Lymphatic Vessels

Lymphatic vessels are similar in structure to blood vessels. Lymphatic capillaries are closed off at one end. After lymph fluid is picked up, it is circulated to increasingly larger lymph vessels called lymphatics. Lymphatics empty their contents into either the right lymphatic duct or the thoracic duct. Both of these ducts are situated in the thoracic cavity.

The right lymphatic duct collects lymph fluid from the right arm, right side of the head, and right side of the thorax. The thoracic duct collects lymph from the rest of the body. For the body to maintain an appropriate volume of circulating blood, it is necessary to put fluid back into the main system of circulation. Both lymphatic ducts empty their contents into the subclavian veins. The right lymphatic duct empties into the right subclavian vein and the thoracic duct empties into the left subclavian vein.

Spleen

The spleen is an organ of the lymphatic system in the left upper abdomen filtering and destroying red blood cells that are no longer efficient. It serves as a blood-forming organ early in life, and later as a storage unit for extra red blood cells (RBCs) and platelets.

Thymus

The thymus is an organ consisting of two lobes. It is located in the thoracic region in front of the heart and behind the sternum. The thymus is prominent in newborns, and continues to increase in size during the first year of life. After puberty, the thymus starts to atrophy gradually. The thymus is responsible for the T lymphocyte maturation, enabling these cells to function against specific pathogens in the immune response.

Tonsils

The tonsils are partially encapsulated lymphoid tissue located in the throat. They are the simplest lymphoid organs. Tonsils are named according to their location: palatine tonsils, lingual tonsils, and pharyngeal tonsils (referred to as adenoids if enlarged).

Peyer's Patches & Appendix

Peyer's patches are found in the lining of the intestine and help to protect against invading microorganisms. The appendix is a "finger-like" projection of tissue attached to the cecum, the first part of the large intestine.

Medical Terms Related to the Lymphatic System

Lymphadenitis—Inflammation and enlargement of lymph nodes, usually as a result of infection.

Lymphangitis—Inflammation of lymphatic vessels as a result of bacterial infection.

Lymphedema—Swelling of tissues with lymph caused by obstruction or excision of lymphatic vessels.

Lymphoma—Any neoplastic disease of lymphoid tissue.

Thymitis—Thymus gland inflammation.

Section Review 2.5

1. How does the lymphatic system work to ensure lymph fluid travels one way to the heart?

    A. Travels through blood

    B. Using a pumping system

    C. With a system of one-way valves

    D. Gravity

2. What type of cell is housed by the lymphatic system to help the body's defense system?

    A. Erythrocytes

    B. Phagocytes

    C. Endothelial

    D. Epithelial

3. What procedure is performed when the spleen is removed?

    A. Splenoplasty

    B. Splenorrhaphy

    C. Splenoportography

    D. Splenectomy

---

4. The lymphatic ducts empty their contents into what structure?

    A. Aorta

    B. Subclavian veins

    C. Pulmonary veins

    D. Femoral artery

5. What is the medical term for inflammation of lymphatic vessels due to bacterial infection?

    A. Lymphadenitis

    B. Lymphangitis

    C. Lymphedema

    D. Lymphoma

Respiratory System (Pulmonary System)

The respiratory system includes the nose, nasal cavity, pharynx, larynx, trachea, bronchi, and their smaller branches, lungs, and alveoli. It functions to exchange carbon dioxide for oxygen. Air inspired through the nose and mouth passes to the lungs through a series of branching airways known as the bronchial tree. This series of structures connects the lungs to outside air containing oxygen.

The nose is responsible for providing an airway to breathe (moistening, warming, and filtering inspired air), serving as a resonating chamber for speech, and housing smell receptors.

The pharynx is divided into three regions; nasopharynx (air passageway), oropharynx (air and food passageway), and laryngopharynx (air and food passageway).

The larynx is the voice box. In addition to voice production, it helps provide an open (patent) airway and acts as a switching mechanism to route air and food into proper channels.

The trachea is in the mediastinal region and splits into two bronchi (at the carina) that enter the lungs. There are three lobes in the right lung and two lobes in the left lung.

At the smallest branch of the bronchial tree, airways are called bronchioles. Each of these bronchioles narrow further until they end in a tiny pouch called an alveolar sac. Gases are exchanged across the single-cell layer of tissue comprising the alveolar sac into the pulmonary circulation. Capillaries from the pulmonary circulation are also a single-cell-layer thick. They form a bed around each alveoli; gas is exchanged between the alveoli and the capillaries via the principles of diffusion (molecules flow from levels of higher concentration to lower concentration).

Medical Terms Related to the Respiratory System

Bronchiolitis—Inflammation of the bronchioles.

Bronchoscope—Instrument used to examine the bronchi.

Carina—A projection of the lowest tracheal cartilage where the trachea separates into two bronchi. Used as a landmark for endoscopy (bronchoscopy). The carina is the most sensitive area of the trachea and larynx for triggering a cough reflex.

COPD (Chronic obstructive pulmonary disease)—Any group of chronic, progressive, and debilitative respiratory diseases (emphysema, asthma, bronchitis, etc).

Dyspnea—Difficulty breathing.

Hemothorax—Presence of blood in the pleural space.

Hyperpnea—Rapid or excessive breathing.

Lobectomy—Surgical excision of a lobe of the lung.

Orthopnea—Difficulty breathing unless upright or in a straight position.

Pneumothorax—Collection of air in the chest or pleural cavity.

Rales (crackles)—Abnormal chest sounds heard when air enters small airways or alveoli containing fluid typically during inspiration.

Rhinorrhea—Discharge from the nose.

Rhonchus—Rale or rattling sound in throat or bronchial tube caused by obstructed or inflamed bronchi.

Tachypnea—Fast or rapid breathing.

Thoracotomy—Incision into the chest wall.

Thoracentesis—Removal of fluid from the pleural cavity via surgical puncture; pleural tap.

Wheeze—Whistling sound usually caused by air passageway obstruction, common in asthmatics.

Application to Documentation

TECHNIQUE: After induction of satisfactory general anesthesia, flexible fiberoptic bronchoscopy was performed. Airways were essentially normal with minimal secretions. No endobronchial lesions. The patient was kept supine and his neck was prepared with DuraPrep and draped in sterile fashion. A transverse incision was used and deepened with cautery. The pretracheal fascial plane was entered and the mediastinoscope easily passed. Samples of lymph nodes were taken from the subcarinal area, the right tracheobronchial angle area, and the low pretracheal area. All were negative for neoplasm. The wound was irrigated, checked for hemostasis, and closed with absorbable sutures and a dry sterile dressing was placed. A double-lumen tube was placed and its proper position confirmed bronchoscopically.

In the sample documentation above, it is important to understand anatomy to determine where the biopsies were taken.

The CPT® 30000–32999 code series addresses surgical procedures of the respiratory system.

Section Review 2.6

1. Subcarinal means beneath the carina. Where is the carina located?

    A. At the connection of the larynx and trachea

    B. At the entrance of the bronchi into the lungs

    C. Where the bronchi split into bronchioles

    D. At the bifurcation of the trachea into two bronchi

2. Which structure is responsible for moistening, warming, and filtering inspired air?

    A. Esophagus

    B. Nose

    C. Lungs

    D. Alveoli

3. What is a thoracotomy?

    A. Removal of a lobe of the lung

    B. Incision into the chest wall

    C. Inserting a tube into the chest

    D. Removing the chest wall

4. Where is gas exchanged and moved from the respiratory system into the circulatory system?

    A. Veins and arteries

    B. Lungs and bronchi

    C. Alveoli and capillaries

    D. Pharynx and larynx

5. Which suffix means breathing?

   A. -capnia

   B. -pnea

   C. -oxea

   D. -phonia

Digestive System

The feeding tube begins in the mouth and ends at the anus. This continuous structure winds through several body cavities and encompasses a multitude of structures and organs. The system mechanically and chemically breaks down food into minuscule or molecular size for absorption into the blood stream and use at the cellular level.

Food enters the digestive system via the mouth. The teeth and tongue mechanically break food into small particles to provide greater exposure/surface area for the chemical processes that follow. Chewing is called mastication. Salivary glands surround the mouth and secrete saliva, which is comprised primarily of water, mucus, electrolytes, and salivary amylase. Saliva aids in early phases of chemical digestion and liquefaction of food. Food is swallowed and peristalsis in the esophagus moves food through the upper thoracic cavity into the stomach.

Stomach and Small Intestine

The opening to the stomach is referred to as the cardiac orifice. The fundus of the stomach is the rounded upper portion, above the body of the stomach. The body of the stomach is the main portion, and the lower portion is referred to as the pyloric antrum. The pyloric sphincter leads to the duodenum. Food moves through the stomach into the small intestine, which is divided into three sections. The first section of the small intestine is the duodenum, the second is the jejunum, and the distal portion is the ileum (not to be confused with the ilium, a bone in the pelvis).

Structures of the Stomach

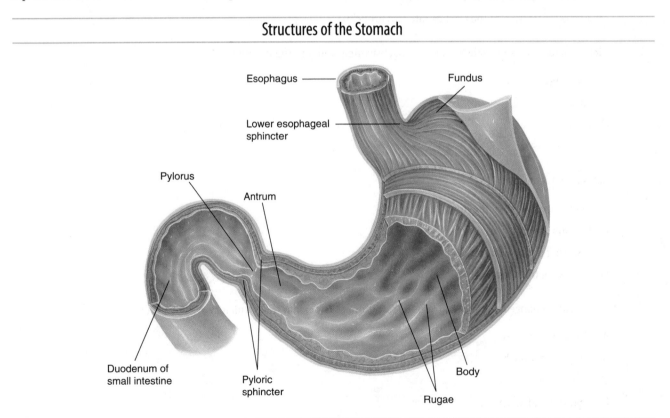

Source: Ehrlich, Medical Terminology for Health Professionals, 6e, ISBN #978-1-4180-7252-0

Large Intestine

The large intestine begins just after the ileocecal valve at the cecum, with the appendix attached at the bottom. There are four portions to the colon: ascending, transverse, descending, and sigmoid or pelvic colon. The ascending colon proceeds from the ileocecal valve upward to the hepatic flexure on the right side of the abdomen. It becomes the transverse colon, and turns downward to become the descending colon at the splenic flexure on the left side of the abdomen. The descending colon gives way to the sigmoid colon and ends at the rectum. The internal and external anal sphincters at the terminus of the rectum control the flow of fecal material leaving the body.

Ancillary Organs

Ancillary organs such as the pancreas, liver, and gallbladder also are considered part of the digestive system because the chemicals they produce are necessary for chemical breakdown of food. The digestive (or exocrine) pancreas is responsible for making digestive enzymes that are secreted into the intestines to help digest food. The gallbladder stores bile produced in the liver. Bile secreted into the intestines from the gallbladder helps digest fats.

Medical Terms Related to the Digestive System

Aphagia—Inability to swallow.

Biliary—Pertaining to bile.

Buccal—Pertaining to the cheek.

Cholecystectomy—Surgical excision of the gallbladder.

Cholecystitis—Inflammation of the gallbladder.

Colectomy—Excision of part of the colon.

Colonoscopy—Examination of the colon and the distal small bowel with an endoscope.

Diverticula of Colon—Herniations of mucosa and submucosa of the colon, which can cause episodes of bleeding and inflammation.

Diverticulitis—Inflammation of the diverticula in the colon.

Diverticulosis—Presence of a number of diverticula of the intestine.

Dysphagia—Difficulty in swallowing.

Epigastric—Region above the stomach.

Esophageal—Pertaining to the esophagus.

Gastralgia—Pain in the stomach.

Gastroenterologist—Physician specializing in the gastrointestinal system.

Hematemesis—Vomiting blood.

Herniotomy—Incision into a hernia.

Ileostomy—Creating an opening through the abdominal wall into the ileum.

Laparotomy—Surgical incision into the abdomen.

Pancreatitis—Inflammation of the pancreas.

Pharyngeal—Pertaining to the pharynx.

Rectocele—Herniation of the rectum into the vagina.

Sigmoidoscope—Instrument used to view the sigmoid.

Splenomegaly—Enlarged spleen.

Stomatitis—Inflammation of the mucous membrane of the mouth.

Sublingual—Below or beneath the tongue. Synonym—subglossal.

The CPT® 40490–49999 codes series address surgical procedures of the digestive system.

Application to Documentation

The patient first was placed into occlusion using Karlis bolts of 8 mm in length. The jaws were put in proper occlusion using 24-gauge stainless steel wires. A buccal incision was made just above the sulcus, carried down through the subcutaneous tissues with the electrocautery. Xylocaine 0.5 % with epinephrine had been injected for hemostasis. The periosteum was elevated, and the patient was noted to have a comminuted fracture of the maxilla creating a Le Fort I fracture. Placement into occlusion had placed the patient in good reduction.

In the documentation above, understanding "buccal" refers to the cheek provides an understanding of where the incision was made.

Section Review 2.7

1. What is the term for the first portion of the small intestine?

    A. Duodenum

    B. Jejunum

    C. Ileum

    D. Cecum

2. Where is bile produced?

    A. Gallbladder

    B. Kidney

    C. Liver

    D. Urinary bladder

3. Which part of the large intestine is between the hepatic flexure and the splenic flexure?

    A. Ascending colon

    B. Transverse colon

    C. Descending colon

    D. Sigmoid colon

4. Which medical term refers to the cheek?

    A. Buccal

    B. Sublingual

    C. Uvula

    D. Palate

5. Food moves through the digestive tract by what means?

    A. Mastication

    B. Gravity

    C. Uvuloptosis

    D. Peristalsis

Urinary System

Production of urine for excretion of metabolic wastes, along with fluid and electrolyte balance, is the main function of the urinary system. This system also provides transportation and temporary storage of urine prior to the intermittent process of urination. Key structures of this system include kidneys, ureters, urinary bladder, and urethra. The kidney also secretes hormones, giving it endocrine function, as well.

Male and female urethras are quite different anatomically in position and length; however, they perform similar functions and are treated similarly for many surgical procedures.

Medical Terms Related to the Urinary System

Albuminuria—Presence of serum protein in the urine.

Bacteriuria—Bacteria in the urine.

Cystectomy—Excision of the bladder or part of the bladder; removal of a cyst.

Cystitis—Inflammation of bladder.

Cystocele—Hernia of the bladder protruding into the vagina.

Cystolithectomy—Excision of a stone from the bladder.

Cystopexy—Surgical fixation of the bladder to the abdominal wall.

Cystoplasty—Surgical repair of the bladder.

Cystorrhagia—Blood bursting forth from the bladder.

Dialysis—Separation of waste material from blood to maintain fluid, electrolyte, and acid-base balance in impaired kidney function or in the absence of a kidney.

Dysuria—Difficult or painful urination.

Hematuria—Blood in urine.

Hydronephrosis—Condition in which urine collects in the renal pelvis due to obstructed outflow, results in dilation of the renal pelvis and calices.

Incontinence—Inability to hold urine.

Nephrectomy—Excision of a kidney.

Nephritis—Inflammation of a kidney.

Nephrologist—A physician treating diseases of the kidney.

Nephropathy—Disease of the kidney.

Nephrosclerosis—Hardening or sclerosis of the kidney.

Polyuria—Excessive urination, profuse micturition

Pyelocystitis—Inflammation of the bladder and renal pelvis.

Pyelonephritis—Inflammation of the kidney and renal pelvis.

Pyuria—Pus in urine.

Uremia—Excess urea and other nitrogenous waste in blood.

Ureteroplasty—Surgical repair of the ureter.

Urethalgia—Pain in the urethra. Syn. - urethrodynia.

Urinalysis—Examination of the urine to detect abnormalities by various diagnostic methods.

Urologist—A physician treating diseases of the urinary system.

CPT® codes dealing with the urinary system are found primarily in the 50010-53899 range.

Reproductive Systems

The organs of the reproductive system differ greatly between male and female; however, functions are similar. Reproduction is achieved through male production of a 23-chromosome gamete called a sperm, and a 23-chromosome gamete called an ovum, or egg, produced by the female. The female also houses, feeds, and protects the growing fetus through the gestational period.

Male and female reproductive organs include external and internal genitalia.

Male Genitalia

External male genitalia include the testes, epididymis, scrotum, and penis. Internal organs of the male genital system include the prostate gland, seminal vesicles, and Cowper's glands. There is also a system of tubes and ducts sperm travel through to leave the body. It is comprised of the vas deferens, ejaculatory duct, and urethra.

Female Genitalia

External female genitalia include the vulva, labia majora and minora, clitoris, external opening of the vagina (also called the introitus), opening of the urethra or urinary meatus, Skene's glands (found on either side of the urinary meatus), and Bartholin's glands (found on either side of the introitus). Internal female genital system organs include the vagina, uterus, two fallopian tubes, and two ovaries.

Medical Terms Related to the Male/Female Reproductive System

Amenorrhea—Absence of menstruation.

Amniocentesis—Surgical puncture of the amniotic sac to obtain a sample of amniotic fluid.

Antepartum—Time period during pregnancy before onset of labor.

Colporrhaphy—Suture or repair of the vaginal wall.

Dysmenorrhea—Painful or difficult menstruation.

Endometriosis—Condition in which the endometrial tissue is found outside of the uterus such as in the abdominal or pelvic cavity.

Epispadias—Congenital defect in which the urethra opens on the upper aspect (dorsum) of the penis.

Fibroma—Fibrous tumor, also called a myoma, fibroid, or leiomyoma.

Genitalia—Male or female reproductive organs, internal and external.

Gynecologist—A physician specializing in the study of the female reproductive system.

Hysterotomy—Surgical incision into the uterus.

Hypospadias—Congenital defect in which the urethra opens on the underside of the penis or on the perineum.

Mammography—A graphic recording of the breast using X-ray technology.

Mastectomy—Surgical excision of the breast.

Menorrhagia—Excessive blood flow during menstruation.

Menorrhea—Normal menstruation.

Myometritis—Inflammation of the muscular wall (myometrium) of the uterus.

Orchiectomy—Surgical excision of a testicle.

Postpartum—Period after childbirth.

Salpingectomy—Surgical excision of fallopian tube(s).

Prostatalgia—Pain in the prostate.

Trimester—Period of three months; in pregnancy—first, second, and third trimesters.

Vaginitis—Inflammation of the vagina.

Vasectomy—Excision of the vas deferens surgically.

CPT® codes for the male and female genitourinary systems can be found in the 54000–58999 range. Maternity care and delivery is found in the 59000–59899 range.

Section Review 2.8

1. Which anatomical structure in the urinary system differs in position and length between male and female, but serves the same function with regards to urine, and is often treated the same?

   A. Ureter

   B. Urethra

   C. Bladder

   D. Kidneys

2. What is the primary function of the urinary system?

   A. Excretion of metabolic wastes, and fluid and electrolyte balance

   B. Produce bile to aid in digestion of fats

   C. Produce bile via emulsification of lipids

   D. Excretion of enzymes and hormones

3. Which structure is an internal organ of the male genital system?

   A. Epididymis

   B. Testes

   C. Cowper's glands

   D. Skene's glands

4. What is the medical term for a congenital defect in which the urethra opens on the dorsum of the penis?

   A. Orchitis

   B. Epispadias

   C. Cryptorchidism

   D. Hypospadias

5. Where are the Bartholin's glands found?

   A. In the pubic symphysis

   B. Below the prostate

   C. In the peritoneal cavity

   D. Either side of the introitus in the female

Nervous System

The nervous system is an enormous network of nerve fibers traversing the human body. The nervous system is composed of central and peripheral portions. The brain and spinal cord are the components of the central nervous system (CNS). The peripheral nervous system (PNS) includes the cranial and spinal nerves. The CNS is the command center and the PNS serves as the communication lines linking all parts of the body to the CNS.

The nervous system functions as both the central operator and central intelligence for the body. It regulates body functions and provides an internal method of communication between the brain and other organs, and between the organism and the environment (for instance, it sends signals from the finger to the brain when a hot, cold, or sharp object is encountered). The brain regulates subconscious body functions such as respiratory rate, body temperature, and peristalsis of the intestines.

Medical Terms Related to the Nervous System

Amnesia—Loss of memory.

Ataxia—Loss of muscular coordination.

Bradykinesia—Abnormal or slowness of motion.

Cephalgia/Cephalagia—Headache.

Cerebrospinal—Pertaining to the brain and spinal cord.

Craniotomy—Surgical incision into the skull.

Discectomy—Surgical excision of an intervertebral disc.

Dysphasia—Impairment of speech. (Syn.- aphasia.)

Encephalomalacia—Softening of the brain often due to ischemia or infarction.

Epidural—Pertaining to above or outside the dura mater.

Hemiparesis—Paralysis on one side of the body.

Intracranial—Within the skull.

Laminectomy—Excision of the vertebral posterior arch or spinal process.

Meningitis—Inflammation of the meninges or the membranes covering the spinal cord or brain.

Myelitis—Inflammation of spinal cord.

Neuralgia—Severe or stabbing pain in the course or distribution of a nerve.

Neuritis—Inflammation of a nerve.

Neurologist—Physician who specializes in diagnosis and treatment of disorders of the nervous system.

Neurolysis—Destruction of nerve tissue or lysis (breaking up) perineural adhesions.

Neurorrhaphy—Repair of severed nerve by suture, graft or with synthetic conduit.

Neurosis—Emotional condition or disorder; anxiety is a primary characteristic.

Paranoia—A mental disorder, often includes delusions involving persecution.

Poliomyelitis—Inflammation of gray matter of the spinal cord.

Psychosis—An Abnormal condition of the mind, gross disorganization, or distortion of mental capacity.

Quadriplegia—Paralysis of all four extremities.

Radiculitis—Inflammation of the spinal nerve roots.

Subdural—Below the dura mater.

Vagotomy—Surgical incision of the vagus nerve.

Procedures of the nervous system are found primarily in the 60000 range of CPT® codes (61000–64999).

Application to Documentation

With a marker, a line was drawn on the skin in the midsagittal plane from the external occipital protuberance to the level of C2. The skin was infiltrated with Marcaine and opened with a scalpel. The midline fascia between the suboccipital muscles was used as a plane of dissection. The dorsal arch of C1 was exposed, and the muscle was dissected off the suboccipital bone bilaterally.

The term "suboccipital" assists in selecting the correct CPT® code for this craniectomy. Another location for this craniectomy could have been "subtemporal."

Organs of Sense — Eye

Organs of sense are classified as a subsection in the nervous system because they ultimately coalesce in nerve endings called sensory receptors. Sensory organs receive and filter sensory input interpreted in the central nervous system.

The eye, the sense organ of sight, is a complex structure situated in the bony orbit or socket formed by seven bones: frontal, maxillary, sphenoid, lacrimal, malar, ethmoid, and palatine bones. The eyeball has three layers: the retina (innermost), choroid (middle), and sclera (outermost). It is separated into an anterior segment filled with aqueous humor and a posterior segment filled with vitreous humor. The crystalline lens separates the two segments.

The anterior segment has two chambers, referred to as an anterior chamber and a posterior chamber. The aqueous humor is a watery substance filling the anterior and posterior chambers of the anterior segment of the eye. It is responsible for intraocular pressure.

A clear gel-like substance filling the posterior segment of the eye is called vitreous, which also is responsible for intraocular pressure and prevents the eyeball from collapsing. The retina is the portion of the posterior segment serving as a light receptor.

The optic nerve (sensory receptor for the eye) emerges in the posterior segment in the posterior-most regions and is known as the optic disk or blind spot.

There are many adnexal or accessory structures to the eye, such as the eyelids, eyelashes, and the lacrimal system. There are six ocular muscles working in opposition to move the eye in multiple directions to facilitate a wide field of vision.

Common Medical Terms for the Eye

Amblyopia—Lazy eye causing dullness of vision.

Ametropia—Defect in the refractive power of the eye.

Aphakia—Absence of lens of the eye.

Astigmatism—Due to an abnormal curve of the cornea, rays of light do not focus on the retina, but are spread over area causing out-of-focus vision.

Blepharitis—An inflammation of the edges of the eyelids.

Corneal—Pertaining to the cornea.

Cycloplegia—Ciliary muscle paralysis.

Diplopia—Double vision.

Ectropion—Turning outward (eyelid).

Entropion—Turning inward (eyelid).

Glaucoma—Disease of the eye characterized by increased intraocular pressure.

Intraocular—Within the eye.

Keratitis—Inflammation of the cornea.

Lacrimal—Tears.

Ocular—Pertaining to the eye.

Ophthalmologist—A physician specializing in diagnosis and treatment of diseases of the eye.

Ophthalmoscope—An instrument used to examine the interior portion of the eye.

Presbyopia—Farsightedness associated with aging and progressive disease.

Retinopathy—Non-inflammatory degenerative disease of the retina.

Tonometer—Instrument to measure intraocular pressure.

Trichiasis—Ingrown eyelashes, can rub against the cornea irritating the eye.

Ophthalmology has its own vocabulary and is a very specialized field of medicine and coding. There are two types of services pertaining to the eye: vision services and surgical services. Vision services can be found in the 92002–92499 range of CPT® codes. Surgical services on the eye can be found in the 65091–68899 range of CPT® codes.

Organs of Sense — Ear

The ear works in tandem with the auditory nerves sending auditory impulses to the temporal lobes of the cerebrum. These structures, working together, form the auditory apparatus. The ear has three distinct and separate anatomical divisions: the outer ear (external ear), middle ear (tympanic cavity), and inner ear (labyrinth). The auditory apparatus uses the ear to capture sound waves and transmits or conducts them into the tiny hair cells in the organ of Corti. Dendrites (nerve endings) of the sensory neurons for hearing are found in the bottom of those tiny hair cells.

Otology (study of the ear) is a very specialized field of medicine and coding. There are two types of services pertaining to the ear: audiometry services (hearing testing) and surgical services.

Surgical services on the ear are found in the 69000-69979 range of CPT® codes. Special otorhinolaryngologic services are found in the 92502-92700 range. The range 92601-92604 is used to report diagnostic analysis of cochlear implants.

Medical Terms for the Ear

Audiology—Study of hearing disorders.

Auricle—External ear.

Labyrinthitis—Inflammation of the labyrinth.

Myringoplasty—Repair of the tympanic membrane.

Otolaryngologist—Physician specializing in diagnosis and treatment of diseases of the ear and larynx.

Otologist—Physician specializing in diagnosis and treatment of diseases of the ear.

Otopyorrhea—Pus draining from the ear.

Otoscope—Instrument used to examine the ear and ear drum.

Tinnitus—Ringing in the ear.

Vertigo—Feeling you or your environment is moving or spinning, caused by a disturbance of equilibrium in the labyrinth.

Section Review 2.9

1. The brain and spinal cord are part of which system?

    A. Somatic Nervous System

    B. Autonomic Nervous System

    C. Central Nervous System

    D. Peripheral Nervous System

2. Which layer is the middle layer of the eyeball?

    A. Iris

    B. Choroid

    C. Retina

    D. Sclera

3. What prevents the eyeball from collapsing?

    A. Crystalline lens

    B. Aqueous humor

    C. Optic nerve

    D. Vitreous humor

---

4. Which structure of the ear is considered the inner ear?

    A. Tympanic cavity

    B. Labyrinth

    C. Dendrites

    D. Cerebrum

5. What term is used for pus draining from the ear?

    A. Labyrinthitis

    B. Otopyorrhea

    C. Tiniitus

    D. Vertigo

Endocrine System

The endocrine system is comprised of glands. A gland is a group of cells secreting or excreting chemicals called hormones. Endocrine glands are ductless glands secreting their hormones directly into the blood stream. Exocrine glands have ducts. Glands secrete hormones eliciting an effect on tissues other than themselves. Glands are found throughout the body. Each gland and its associated hormone have a unique cause and effect.

Exocrine and Endocrine Glands

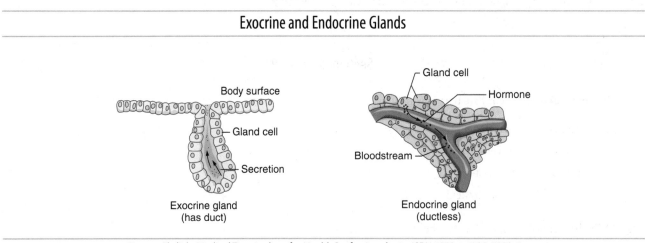

Source: Ehrlich, Medical Terminology for Health Professionals, 6e, ISBN #978-1-4180-7252-0

The following glands are found in the human endocrine system:

Adrenal Glands—Ductless, pyramid-shaped glands are situated on the top of the superior end of each kidney. There are two structural parts of each adrenal gland. The inner portion is called the medulla and the outer portion is the cortex. Each structure performs a separate function. The medulla secretes epinephrine and norepinephrine. The cortex secretes several steroids (eg, glucocorticoids, mineral corticoids, and adrenal estrogens and androgens).

Carotid Body—A structure made of epithelial-like cells located on each side of the body at the bifurcation (division) of the common carotid artery. This has a vascular/sinusoidal bed and a large network of nerve fibers from the glossopharyngeal nerve. This configuration works together to measure concentration of oxygen, carbon dioxide, and free hydrogen atoms in blood. This chemoreceptor organ regulates respiration and pH balance. Although not a true endocrine structure, it is made of both glandular and nonglandular cells. Procedures on this structure are included in the endocrine family of CPT® codes.

Parathyroid Gland—Small round bodies located on the posterior side of the thyroid gland and imbedded in the connective tissue surrounding it. The number of these bodies varies, but usually there are four. These glands regulate calcium and phosphorus metabolism.

Pituitary Gland—Also called the hypophysis cerebri, this single (unpaired) gland has two separate parts located in an area of the brain just under the hypothalamus. One portion is called the posterior pituitary or neurohypophysis. The posterior pituitary secretes oxytocin, a hormone responsible for uterine contractions and "let down" reflex of milk in response to a baby's suckling; and Vasopressin, an antidiuretic. The anterior pituitary manufactures adrenocorticotrophic hormone (ACTH), thyroid stimulating hormone (TSH), follicle stimulating hormone (FSH), luteinizing hormone (LH), growth hormone (somatotrophin or GH), melanocyte stimulating hormone (MSH), and prolactin (PRL).

Thymus Gland—Composed of lymphoid tissue and located in the mediastinum of the chest. The precise functions of this gland are not known entirely. This gland helps regulate humoral (circulating defenses versus cellular defenses) immune functions. The gland does much of its work in early childhood, and is largest shortly after birth. By puberty, it is small and may be replaced by fat.

Thyroid Gland—Regulates metabolism and serum calcium levels through the secretion of thyroid hormone and calcitonin, respectively. This bilobed, ductless gland is located in the neck just below the thyroid cartilage of the trachea. The two lobes sit on either side of the trachea and are joined by a small band of tissue called the isthmus.

When the endocrine system and the nervous system work together, they form a system of internal communication for the human body.

Common Terms in the Endocrine System

Endocrinologist—Physician specializing in diagnosis and treatment of diseases of the endocrine system.

Euthyroid—Normal thyroid gland activity.

Glandular—Pertaining to a gland.

Hyperkalemia—Excessive amounts of potassium in the blood.

Hyperthyroidism—Excessive secretion of thyroid hormone.

Hypothyroidism—Deficient secretion of the thyroid hormone.

Insulin—Hormone secreted by the beta cells in the islets of Langerhans of the pancreas which regulates energy and glucose metabolism. Also used in management of diabetes.

Parathyroid—Glands located behind the thyroid gland.

Thymitis—Inflammation of the thymus gland.

Thyroiditis—Inflammation of the thyroid gland

Thyrotoxicosis—Condition caused by excess thyroid hormone, often due to hyperactivity of the thyroid gland.

The CPT® 60000–60699 codes address surgical procedures of the endocrine system.

Section Review 2.10

1. Which gland secretes thyroid hormone and calcitonin?

    A. Adrenal glands

    B. Parathyroid gland

    C. Pituitary gland

    D. Thyroid gland

2. Which structure is not a true endocrine structure?

    A. Adrenal glands

    B. Carotid body

    C. Pituitary gland

    D. Thyroid gland

---

3. Which gland is larger in early life than in puberty?

    A. Adrenal glands

    B. Parathyroid glands

    C. Thymus gland

    D. Thyroid gland

4. Which gland is also known as the hypophysis cerebri?

    A. Adrenal glands

    B. Pituitary gland

    C. Parathyroid glands

    D. Thymus gland

5. Which gland has two separate structures called the medulla and the cortex?

    A. Adrenal glands

    B. Pituitary gland

    C. Carotid body

    D. Parotid gland

Hematologic (Hemic) System

The hemic system involves the blood. Red cells, white cells, and platelets are produced in the marrow of bones, especially the vertebrae, ribs, hips, skull, and sternum. These essential blood cells fight infection, carry oxygen, and help control bleeding. Plasma is a pale yellow mixture of water, protein, and salt, and acts as a carrier for blood cells, nutrients, enzymes, and hormones.

Red Blood Cells (RBCs or erythrocytes)—Disk-shaped cells containing hemoglobin enabling cells to pick up and deliver oxygen to all parts of the body. Erythropoietin (EPO) is a glycoprotein hormone providing a direct stimulus for erythrocyte formation. Some erythrocyte disorders include anemia and polycythemia.

Hemoglobin transports oxygen and carbon dioxide in the blood. It is composed of globin, a group of amino acids forming a protein, and heme, which contains iron atoms and imparts the red color to hemoglobin. Hemoglobin is an important determinant of anemia (decreased), dehydration (increased), polycythemia (increased), poor diet/nutrition, or a malabsorption problem. Most tests of the hematologic system are performed in the clinical laboratory.

White Blood Cells (WBCs or leukocytes)—The body's primary defense against infection and only account for less than 1

percent of total blood volume. Types of leukocytes include neutrophils, lymphocytes, monocytes, eosinophils, and basophils, each having their own function in defense. Leukocyte disorders include leukopenia, leukemias, and infectious mononucleosis.

Platelets (thrombocytes)—Form clusters to plug small holes in blood vessels and assist in the clotting process.

Some bleeding disorders include thrombocytopenia, impaired liver function, and hemophilia.

Procedures on blood and its components are covered in the 80000 range of CPT® codes.

Immune System

The immune system is classified as a separate system from the hematologic system; however, most immune cells originate in the hematologic system. In medicine, the study of the immune system (immunology) and the study of allergies often go hand in hand because an allergic response is, in fact, an immune response. The human immune system is the body's final line of defense against invading microorganisms, harmful chemicals, and foreign bodies.

There are two kinds of immune cells: B-cells and T-cells. Several types of cells protect the body from infection (eg, neutrophils, lymphocytes, monocytes, eosinophils, and basophils). Neutrophils are the body's main defense against infection and antigens. High levels of neutrophils may indicate an active infection; a low count may indicate a compromised immune system or depressed bone marrow (low neutrophil production).

Lymphocytes are involved in protection of the body from viral infections such as measles, rubella, chicken pox, or infectious mononucleosis. Elevated levels may indicate an active viral infection and a depressed level may indicate an exhausted immune system.

Monocytes fight severe infections and are considered the body's second line of defense against infection. Elevated levels are seen in tissue breakdown, chronic infections, carcinomas, leukemia (monocytic), or lymphomas. Low levels of monocytes indicate a good state of health.

The body uses eosinophils to protect against allergic reactions and parasites; elevated levels may indicate an allergic response. A low count of eosinophils is normal. Basophilic activity is not understood fully, but it is known to carry histamine, heparin, and serotonin. High levels are found in allergic reactions; low levels are normal.

Antigens elicit an immune response in the body. Antigens entering the body from the environment can include:

- Inhaled macromolecules (eg, proteins on cat hairs triggering an asthma attack)
- Ingested macromolecules (eg, shellfish proteins triggering an allergic response)
- Molecules introduced beneath the skin (eg, on a splinter or in an injected vaccine)

Antibodies are immune system related proteins called immunoglobulins. Some antibodies destroy antigens directly; others indirectly by making it easier for white blood cells to destroy the antigen.

Clinical lab tests performed on the function and health of the immune system are found in the 86000–86849 range of CPT® codes and performed in the clinical laboratory.

Medical Terms Related to the Hematologic System and Immune System

Erythropathy—Disease of red blood cells.

Hematocrit—Blood test that measures the red blood cell volume by centrifuge, a technique which separates the plasma and the blood cells.

Hematologist—Physician specializing in the study of blood disorders.

Hemoglobin—The red respiratory protein of RBCs, transports oxygen to the tissues.

Hemolysis—Destruction of red blood cells.

Hemostasis—Control of bleeding.

Hypercalcemia—Excessive amounts of calcium in the blood.

Hyperglycemia—Excessive amounts of sugar in the blood.

Hyperlipemia—Excessive amount of fat in the blood.

Hypoglycemia—Deficient amount of sugar in the blood.

Leukemia—Overproduction of leukocytes resulting in a malignant, acute, or chronic disease.

Mononucleosis—Disease of excessive mononuclear leukocytes in the blood due to infection with the Epstein-Barr virus.

Polycythemia—Abnormal increase in red blood cells.

Septicemia—Pathogenic bacteria present in the blood.

Section Review 2.11

1. Anemia and polycythemia are disorders related to which blood cell?

    A. Erythrocytes

    B. Leukocytes

    C. Lymphocytes

    D. Monocytes

---

2. Which leukocyte protects the body from viral infections?

    A. Neutrophils

    B. Lymphocytes

    C. Monocytes

    D. Eosinophils

3. Which leukocyte is the body's second line of defense against infection?

    A. Neutrophils

    B. Lymphocytes

    C. Monocytes

    D. Eosinophils

4. Which leukocyte does the body use to protect against allergic reactions and parasites?

    A. Neutrophils

    B. Lymphocytes

    C. Monocytes

    D. Eosinophils

5. What is the disease of excessive mononuclear leukocytes in the blood?

    A. Leukopoiesis

    B. Leukopenia

    C. Mononucleosis

    D. Myelocytic leukemia

Introduction

ICD-10 was endorsed by the 43rd World Health Assembly in May 1990 and came into use in World Health Organization (WHO) Member States in 1994. The United States is a member of WHO. The classification is the latest in a series, which has its origins in the 1850s. The first edition, known as the International List of Causes of Death, was adopted by the International Statistical Institute in 1893. WHO took over the responsibility for the ICD at its creation in 1948 when the Sixth Revision, which included causes of morbidity for the first time, was published. The World Health Assembly adopted in 1967 the WHO Nomenclature Regulations that stipulate use of ICD in its most current revision for mortality and morbidity statistics by all Member States.

The ICD is the international standard diagnostic classification for all general epidemiological, many health management purposes and clinical use. These include the analysis of the general health situation of population groups and monitoring of the incidence and prevalence of diseases and other health problems in relation to other variables such as the characteristics and circumstances of the individuals affected, reimbursement, resource allocation, quality, and guidelines.

It is used to classify diseases and other health problems recorded on many types of health and vital records including death certificates and health records. In addition to enabling the storage and retrieval of diagnostic information for clinical, epidemiological and quality purposes, these records also provide the basis for the compilation of national mortality and morbidity statistics by WHO Member States.

The National Center for Health Statistics (NCHS) developed ICD-10-CM (International Classification of Diseases, Tenth Revision, Clinical Modification) in consultation with a technical advisory panel, physician groups, and clinical coders to assure clinical accuracy and utility. There are no codes for procedures in the ICD-10-CM and procedures are coded using the procedure classification appropriate for the encounter setting (eg, Current Procedural Terminology, or CPT®, and ICD-10-PCS).

ICD-10 includes 22 chapters for use; however, in the United States our clinical modification (CM) does not include the letter U. The letter U is not used for international data comparison and the codes are not being used in the United States.

During this chapter, we will discuss:

- Overview of the ICD-10-CM layout
- ICD-10-CM conventions
- How to look up an ICD-10-CM code
- Official ICD-10-CM coding guidelines

Overview of ICD-10-CM Layout

ICD-10-CM is published in two sections:

1. Alphabetic Index or Index to Diseases and Injuries: Diagnostic terms organized in alphabetic order for the disease descriptions in the Tabular List. In this curriculum, the terms Alphabetic Index and Index to Diseases and Injuries are used interchangeably.

2. Tabular List: Diagnosis codes organized in numerical order and divided into chapters based on body system or condition.

ICD-9-CM Application

ICD-9-CM is published in three volumes:

Volume 1—Tabular List of Diseases and Injuries: Diagnosis codes organized in numerical order.

Volume 2—Alphabetic Index or Index to Diseases: Diagnostic terms organized in an alphabetic order for the disease descriptions for Volume 1.

Volume 3 - Alphabetic Index and Tabular List of Procedures: Procedures performed in the inpatient setting.

ICD-9-CM Volume 3 includes procedure codes, and typically is used by facilities only. Hospitals use Volume 3 in the outpatient facility for tracking purposes only; they do not submit outpatient claims using Volume 3. Historically, the ICD-9-CM Volume 3 for procedures had annual updates published each October. The ICD-10-PCS (Procedural Coding System) replaced ICD-9-CM Volume 3 concurrent to ICD-10-CM diagnostic codes in October of 2015.

This guide will focus on the proper use of ICD-10-CM only. Coders use ICD-10-CM to assign diagnosis codes for services rendered, and to establish medical necessity to support those services.

Medical Necessity

One of the most important requirements to receive payment for services is to establish medical necessity. You must justify care provided by presenting the appropriate facts. Payers require the following information to determine the need for care:

1. Knowledge of the emergent nature or severity of the patient's complaint or condition.

2. All signs, symptoms, complaints, or background facts describing the reason for care.

3. The facts must be substantiated by the patient's medical record, and that record must be available to payers on request.

For example, a patient complains of pain in her right knee and the provider performs a knee X-ray. When the claim is submitted, the payer needs to know why the service was performed; that is your diagnosis code. In this example, we select a code to report the X-ray with a diagnosis code for knee pain to support the reason the service was performed. We will discuss the proper selection of diagnosis (ICD-10-CM) codes later in this chapter.

Index to Diseases and Injuries

The Index to Diseases and Injuries (Alphabetic Index) is divided into sections and is organized by main terms:

- Index to Diseases and Injuries
- Neoplasm Table
- Table of Drugs and Chemicals
- Index to External Causes of Injuries

Main terms in the Index to Diseases and Injuries usually reference the disease, condition, or symptom. Subterms modify the main term to describe differences in site, etiology, or clinical type. Main terms are **bold** in the Index to Diseases and Injuries. Subterms add specificity to the main term. The code listed next to the main term is considered the default code. The default code represents the condition most commonly associated with the main term. As with all code assignment, always verify the default code in the Tabular List to assure proper reporting.

Example

Look for the term "Mass" in the Index to Diseases and Injuries in your ICD-10-CM codebook.

Mass
  abdominal R19.00
    epigastric R19.00
    generalized R19.07

  left lower quadrant R19.04
  left upper quadrant R19.02
  periumbilic R19.05
  right lower quadrant R19.03
  right upper quadrant R19.01
  specified site NEC R19.09
  breast N63
  chest R22.2

In this example, the subterms further define the location of the mass.

ICD-9-CM Application

The Index to Diseases in ICD-9-CM utilizes the same main term/subterm indexing systems.

Look for the term "Mass" in the Index to Diseases in your ICD-9-CM codebook.

Mass
  abdominal 789.3
    anus 787.99
    bone 733.90
    breast 611.72
    cheek 784.2

In this example, the subterms further define the location of the mass.

Tabular List

The Tabular List contains 21 chapters and contains categories, subcategories, and codes. Each character for all categories, subcategories, and codes may be either a letter or a number. Codes can be three, four, five, six, or seven characters. The first character of a category is a letter. The second and third characters may be either numbers or alpha characters. Subcategories are either four or five characters and may be either letters or numbers. Codes are three, four, five, or six characters and the final character in a code may be either a letter or number. Certain categories have a seventh character extension (discussed later in this chapter).

There are symbols throughout the Tabular List to identify when a code requires an additional character.

Examples:

- ④ E28 Ovarian dysfunction
- ⑤ G47.5 Parasomnia
- ⑥ H16.33 Sclerosing keratitis
- ⑦ S36.260 Major laceration of head of pancreas
- ⑦ S36.92 Contusion of unspecified intra-abdominal organ

At the beginning of each chapter, there may be "excludes" and "includes" notes that apply to the entire chapter listed here.

Example

Chapter 3—Diseases of the Blood and Blood-Forming Organs and Certain Disorders Involving the Immune Mechanism (D50–D89).

Excludes 2: autoimmune disease (systemic) NOS (M35.9)

certain conditions originating in the perinatal period (P00-P96)

complications of pregnancy, childbirth and the puerperium (O00-O9A)

congenital malformations, deformations and chromosomal abnormalities (Q00-Q99)

endocrine, nutritional and metabolic diseases (E00-E88)

human immunodeficiency virus [HIV] disease (B20)

injury, poisoning and ceratin other consequences of external causes (S00-T88)

neoplasms (C0-D49)

symptoms, signs, and abnormal clinical and laboratory findings, not elsewhere classified (R00-R94)

The fourth character in an ICD-10-CM code further defines the site, etiology, and manifestation or state of the disease or condition. The four character subcategory includes the three character category plus a decimal with an additional character to further identify the condition to the highest level of specificity.

Example

- ④ D56 Thalassemia

  D56.0 Alpha thalassemia

  D56.1 Beta thalassemia

  D56.2 Delta-beta thalassemia

  D56.3 Thalassemia minor

  D56.4 Hereditary persistence of fetal hemoglobin [HPFH]

  D56.5 Hemoglobin E-beta thalassemia

  D56.8 Other thalassemia

  D56.9 Thalassemia, unspecified

The fifth or sixth character subclassifications represent the most accurate level of specificity regarding the patient's condition or diagnosis.

Example

- ⑤ D57.4 Sickle-cell thalassemia

  D57.40 Sickle-cell thalassemia without crisis

- ⑥ D57.41 Sickle-cell thalassemia with crisis

  D57.411 Sickle-cell thalassemia with acute chest syndrome

  D57.412 Sickle-cell thalassemia with splenic sequestration

  D57.419 Sickle-cell thalassemia with crisis, unspecified

Certain ICD-10-CM categories have applicable seven characters. The applicable seventh character is required for all codes within the category, or as the notes in the Tabular List instruct. The seventh character must always be in the seventh position. If a code is three, four, or five characters, but requires a seventh character extension, a placeholder X must be used to fill the empty characters.

 AAPC
www.aapc.com   55

Example

5️⃣   M48.4 Fatigue fracture of vertebra

The appropriate 7th character is to be added to each code from subcategory M48.4:

A   initial encounter for fracture

D   subsequent encounter for fracture with routine healing

G   subsequent encounter for fracture with delayed healing

S   sequela of fracture

7️⃣   M48.40 Fatigue fracture of vertebra, site unspecified

7️⃣   M48.41 Fatigue fracture of vertebra, occipita-atlanto-axial region

In this example, to report codes M48.40 or M48.41 accurately, a seventh character extender is required. Because the codes themselves are only five characters long, the placeholder X must be used for the sixth character so the seventh character stays in the seventh character position:

M48.40XA Fatigue fracture of vertebra, site unspecified, initial encounter for fracture

M48.41XD Fatigue fracture of vertebra, occipita-atlanto-axial region, subsequent encounter for fracture with routine healing.

Note: The application of seventh character extenders will be discussed in later sections.

ICD-9-CM Application

In ICD-9-CM, the Tabular List is an alpha-numerical listing of diseases and injury and is considered Volume 1. Publishers often print Volume 1 after Volume 2 because the code search begins in Volume 2 - Index to Diseases (Alphabetic Index).

There are 17 chapters for the classification of diseases and injury, grouped by etiology (cause) or anatomical (body) site. The Tabular List is organized into three-digit codes and their titles, called category codes. Some three-digit codes are very specific and are not subdivided. These three-digit codes can stand alone to describe the condition being coded.

Most three digit categories (rubrics) have been subdivided with the addition of a decimal point, followed by either one or two additional digits. The fourth digit provides specificity or more information regarding etiology, site, or manifestation. Fourth digit subcategory codes take precedence over three digit category codes. Fourth and fifth digits are required where indicated; they are not optional. A valid diagnosis code can have three, four, or five digits, depending on the disease.

There are symbols throughout the Tabular list to identify when a code requires a fourth or fifth digit.

4️⃣   This symbol alerts the coder a fourth digit is required to accurately report the diagnosis in the category

5️⃣   This symbol alerts the coder a fifth digit is required to accurately report the diagnosis in the category

When fourth and fifth digits are required, the additional digit options may be presented as subterms, or at the beginning of the three-digit category.

Examples:

5️⃣   427.6 Premature beats

      427.60 Premature beats, unspecified

      427.61 Supraventricular premature beats

      427.69 Other

5️⃣   789.0 Abdominal pain

      [0-7, 9]

The digits included in the brackets instruct the coder that the only valid fifth-digit codes will end in a 0-7 or 9. To select the correct fifth digit, refer to the beginning of category 789 for the subclassification designation:

The following fifth-digit subclassification is to be used for codes 789.0, 789.3, 789.4, 789.6.

    0 unspecified site

    1 right upper quadrant

    2 left upper quadrant

    3 right lower quadrant

    4 left lower quadrant

    5 periumbilic

    6 epigastric

    7 generalized

    9 other specified site

Supplementary Classification in Volume 1

1.   Classification of Factors Influencing Health Status and Contact with Health Services, V01–V91

Codes from category V01–V91 are known as V codes. V codes are used when the patient presents for treatment with no complaints. Common reasons to report V codes are for screening tests (eg, mammogram to screen for breast cancer), routine physicals (eg, well child check up), and when a patient has a personal history or family history of a disease or disorder (eg, family history of colon cancer).

2.   Classification of External Causes of Injury, E00.0–E99.9

Codes from category E00.0–E99.9 are known as E codes. E codes are used to report how an injury occurred (eg, motor vehicle accident) and where the injury occurred (eg, injury occurred in the workplace).

Conventions

To apply the diagnosis coding system correctly, coders need to understand and apply the various conventions and terms.

Section I of the Official ICD-10-CM Guidelines for Coding and Reporting includes conventions, general coding guidelines, and chapter specific guidelines. This chapter focuses on the conventions used in the ICD-10-CM codebook and general guidelines. Chapter-specific guidelines are discussed in chapters 4 and 5 of this curriculum.

NEC Not elsewhere classifiable

This abbreviation is used when the ICD-10-CM system does not provide a code specific for the patient's condition. Selecting a code with the NEC classification means that the provider documented more specific information regarding the patient's condition, but there is not a code in ICD-10-CM to report the condition accurately.

Example

The provider documents the patient has a retroperitoneal mass. Look in your ICD-10-CM Index to Diseases and Injuries under the main term Mass, then look for the subterms abdominal/retroperitoneal. There is not a subterm for retroperitoneal under abdominal. There is a subterm in the index under Mass/abdominal for "specified site NEC R19.09" In this example, R19.09 is reported because there is not a specific code for retroperitoneal mass.

NOS Not otherwise specified

This abbreviation is the equivalent of "unspecified" and is used only when the coder lacks the information necessary to code to a more specific diagnosis.

Example

The provider documents the patient has sinusitis. Look in the ICD-10-CM Index to Diseases and Injuries under the main term Sinusitis. There is no further description or detail given on the type of the sinusitis to report a more specific code. The default code listed in the index is J32.9. In the Tabular List, Sinusitis (chronic) NOS is listed as an inclusion term.

J32.9 Chronic sinusitis, unspecified
  Sinusitis (chronic) NOS

[ ] Brackets are used in the Tabular List to enclose synonyms, alternate wording, or explanatory phrases. Brackets are used in the Index to Diseases and Injuries to identify manifestation codes in which multiple coding and sequencing rules will apply.

Example

Look in your ICD-10-CM Tabular List for A30.0

  A30.0 Leprosy [Hansen's Disease]

In this example, if the patient is diagnosed with Hansen's Disease, code A30.0 is reported because it is also known as Leprosy.

Look for encephalitis in your ICD-10-CM Index to Diseases and Injuries.

Encephalitis G04.90
  due to
    human immunodeficiency virus (HIV) disease B20 [G05.3]

In this example, two codes are reported when the encephalitis is due to HIV. The first code reports the cause and the second code reports the manifestation. B20 reports the HIV and G05.3 reports the encephalitis. The code in the brackets is always sequenced after the code that appears before the brackets.

( ) Parentheses are used to enclose supplementary words that may be present or absent in the statement of a disease or procedure, without affecting the code number to which it is assigned. The terms in the parentheses are referred to as nonessential modifiers.

Example

Look for rickets in your ICD-10-CM Index to Diseases and Injuries.

Rickets (active) (acute) (adolescent)(chest wall) (congenital) (current) (infantile) (intestinal) E55.0

If the provider documented "Rickets," the code reported is E55.0. Likewise, if the provider documented "Congenital rickets," the same code, E55.0, is reported.

: The colon is used in the Tabular List after an incomplete term that needs one or more of the modifiers that follow to make it assignable to a given category. Look up the following example in the Tabular List of your ICD-10-CM codebook:

Example

C22   Malignant neoplasm of liver and intrahepatic bile ducts

   EXCLUDES1   malignant neoplasm of biliary tract NOS (C24.9)

   secondary malignant neoplasm of liver and intrahepatic bile duct (C78.7)

   Use additional code to identify:

   alcohol abuse and dependence (F10.-)

   hepatitis B (B16.-, B18.0-B18.1)

   hepatitis C (B17.1-, B18.2)

In this example there are terms and codes listed after the colon. This indicates they can be reported with codes under category code C22 to further support code assignment.

Other Conventions

Other

"Other" or "other unspecified" codes (usually with an 8 or a 9 as the last character) are used when the information in the medical record provides detail for which a specific code does not exist. Index entries with NEC in the line designate "other" codes in the Tabular List. These index entries represent specific diseases for which no specific code exists; therefore, the term is included within the "other" code.

Unspecified

"Unspecified" codes (usually with a 9 or a 0 as the last character) are used when the information in the medical record is not available for coding more specifically. Unspecified codes should be selected only when there is no other option. For example, if the provider documents sinusitis without additional information about the specific location or type of sinusitis, the only option is an unspecified code (J32.9 *Chronic sinusitis, unspecified*).

INCLUDES

The "Includes" note appears immediately under a three-character code title to define further, or to give an example of the contents of the category. Look up the following example in the Tabular List of your ICD-10-CM codebook:

Example

D25 Leiomyoma of uterus

INCLUDES   uterine fibroid

   uterine fibromyoma

   uterine myoma

In ICD-10-CM, there are two types of excludes notes: Excludes1 and Excludes2.

EXCLUDES1 A type 1 excludes note represents "Not coded here." This note indicates that the code excluded should not be used at the same time as the code above the Excludes1 note when the two diagnoses are related. An Excludes1 note includes when two conditions cannot occur together, such as a congenital form versus an acquired form of the same condition.

EXCLUDES2 A type 2 excludes note represents "Not included here." A type 2 excludes note indicates that the condition excluded is not part of the condition represented by the code, but a patient may have both conditions at the same time. When a type 2 excludes note appears under a code, it is acceptable to use both the code and the excluded code together.

Example

N40 Enlarged Prostate

EXCLUDES1   benign neoplasms of prostate (adenoma, benign) (fibroadenoma) (fibroma) (myoma) (D29.1)

EXCLUDES2   malignant neoplasm of prostate (C61)

In this example, we see that if the patient has prostatic adenoma, the correct code is D29.1. The use of "Excludes1" in the Tabular List alerts the coder there is a more appropriate code listed elsewhere for that specific condition than is listed in the current category.

However, if the patient has malignant neoplasm of the prostate (C61) and an enlarged prostate (N40.0-N40.3), both codes may be reported because both conditions exist at the same time.

Practical Coding Note

Pay close attention to the conditions listed under the Excludes1 or Excludes2 notation. This is a clue that you may be looking in the wrong category. Refer to the codes listed next to the Excludes1 or Excludes2 notation to find the appropriate code.

The Includes notation is also important to read because there is often more than one medical term that describes the same condition or multiple conditions that are reported with the same code. If the condition you are coding is listed under the Includes notation, you know you are in the correct category.

ICD-9-CM Application

There is only one type of Excludes note in ICD-9-CM. When a code is listed in the Excludes note, it may only be reported when both conditions exist; however, there are times when the codes may not be reported together. An example of this is when there are codes for both the acquired and congenital conditions, the two codes would not be reported together.

Example

⊕ 461 Acute sinusitis

Excludes chronic or unspecified sinusitis (473.0-473.9)

In this example, sinusitis NOS should not be coded in addition to codes from category 461 Acute sinusitis according to the Excludes note. However, chronic sinusitis can be coded along with acute sinusitis if both conditions exist.

Use additional code

An additional code should be used after a primary code, if the information is available, to provide a more complete picture of the diagnosis. Look up the following example in the Tabular List of your ICD-10-CM codebook.

Example

5⊕ R65.2 Severe sepsis

> Infection with associated acute organ dysfunction
>
> Sepsis with acute organ dysfunction
>
> Sepsis with multiple organ dysfunction
>
> Systemic inflammatory response syndrome due to infectious process with acute organ dysfunction

Code first underlying infection, such as:

> infection following a procedure (T81.4)
>
> infections following infusion, transfusion and therapeutic injections (T80.2-)
>
> puerperal sepsis (O85)
>
> sepsis following complete or unspecified spontaneous abortion (O03.87)
>
> sepsis following ectopic and molar pregnancy (O08.82)
>
> sepsis following incomplete spontaneous abortion (O03.37)
>
> sepsis following (induced) termination of pregnancy (O04.87)

sepsis NOS (A41.9)

Use additional code to specify acute organ dysfunction, such as:

> acute kidney failure (N17.-))
>
> acute respiratory failure (J96.0-)
>
> critical illness myopathy (G72.81)
>
> critical illness polyneuropathy (G62.81)
>
> disseminated intravascular coagulopathy [DIC] (D65)
>
> encephalopathy (metabolic) (septic) (G93.41)
>
> hepatic failure (K72.0-)

In this example, three codes are required. The code for the underlying condition is sequenced first, followed by the code for severe sepsis, which is followed by the code to report the type of acute organ dysfunction. When instructions state "Use additional" this indicates proper sequencing of codes. "Use additional code" indicates that the additional codes are sequenced after the primary code. If a patient had severe sepsis with acute respiratory failure, and the underlying condition was not known, the proper codes in the correct sequence are:

A41.9   Unspecified septicemia

R65.20   Severe sepsis

J96.00   Acute respiratory failure

Code first

This instruction note, used in the Tabular List, is not intended to indicate that a code is to be the principal diagnosis. Instead, the note indicates that two codes are needed to report a condition and requires that the underlying disease (etiology) be recorded first, and the particular manifestation be recorded second. The "Code first" note will only appear in the Tabular List. This is why it is important to always verify codes in the Tabular List to assure proper code sequencing. Look up the following example in the Tabular List of your ICD-10-CM codebook.

Example

I39 Endocarditis and heart valve disorders in diseases classified elsewhere

Code first the underlying disease, such as:

> Q fever (A78)

The "code first" indicates the code(s) listed should be sequenced first. If a patient developed endocarditis due to Q fever, the proper codes and sequencing are A78, I39.

Use additional code, if applicable

The causal condition note indicates that this code may be assigned as a diagnosis when the causal condition is unknown or not applicable. Look up the following example in the Tabular List of your ICD-10-CM codebook.

Example

I27.82 Chronic pulmonary embolism

Use additional code, if applicable, for associated long-term (current) use of anticoagulants (Z79.01)

In this example, report code Z79.01 in addition to I27.82 only if it is documented that the patient is currently taking, or has been taking anticoagulants for an extended period of time.

"Code first" and "Use additional code" notes are also used as sequencing rules in the classification for certain codes that are not a part of an etiology/manifestation combination.

Eponym

An eponym is a disease or syndrome named after a person. An example is Lou Gehrig's disease, which also is known as amyotrophic lateral sclerosis (ALS). It was named after a famous baseball player who was diagnosed with the disease.

Modifiers

Essential modifiers are subterms indented two spaces and listed in alphabetical order below the main term. Nonessential modifiers are subterms that follow the main term and are enclosed in parentheses; they can clarify the diagnosis but are not required. Look up the following example in the Index to Diseases and Injuries of your ICD-10-CM codebook.

Example

Psilosis (sprue) (tropical) K90.1

    nontropical K90.0

In this example, sprue and tropical are nonessential modifiers. Nontropical is an essential modifier and will alter the code assignment.

Notes

Used to define terms, clarify information, or list choices for additional characters in the Tabular List.

Example

Congenital malformation, deformations and chromosomal abnormalities (Q00-Q99)

NOTES Codes from this chapter are not for use on maternal or fetal records.

And

The word "and" in a code description can mean either "and" or "or." Look up the following example in the Tabular List of your ICD-10-CM codebook.

Example

⑤ S49.8- Other specified injuries of shoulder and upper arm

In this case, if the patient has a specified injury of the shoulder, this code would be reported. The patient would not be required to have a specified injury of the upper arm as well for this code to be reported.

With

The word "with" in a code title in the Index to Diseases and Injuries or an instructional note in the Tabular List can mean "associated with" or "due to." Look up the following example in the Tabular List of your ICD-10-CM codebook.

Example

A01.02 Typhoid fever with heart involvement

In the Index to Diseases and Injuries the word "with" is listed immediately under the main term, not in alphabetical order. Look up the following example in the Index to Diseases and Injuries of your ICD-10-CM codebook.

Example

Actinomycosis, actinomycotic A42.9

    with pneumonia A42.0
    abdominal A42.1
    cervicofacial A42.2
    cutaneous A42.89

See

Directs you to a more specific term under which the correct code can be found. Look up the following example in the Index to Diseases and Injuries of your ICD-10-CM codebook.

Example

Atheromatosis—*see* Arteriosclerosis

See also

Indicates additional information is available that may provide an additional diagnostic code. Look up the following example in the Index to Diseases and Injuries of your ICD-10-CM codebook.

Example

Atherosclerosis (*see also* Arteriosclerosis)

Default Code

A code listed next to a main term in the ICD-10-CM Index to Diseases and Injuries is referred to as a default code. The default code represents that condition is the most commonly associated with the main term, or is the unspecified code for the condition. If a condition is documented in a medical record (for example,

appendicitis) without any additional information, such as acute or chronic, the default code (K37) should be assigned.

Example

Diabetes, diabetic (mellitus) (sugar) E11.9

In this example, the default code for Diabetes is E11.9 Type 2 diabetes mellitus without complications if the condition is not given any additional information to report a more specific diabetic code.

.- Point Dash

In the Tabular List you will see a point dash symbol (.-) after certain codes. This indicates that the code is incomplete and go to that category or subcategory of codes to complete that code.

Example

Ⓜ I70.63 Atherosclerosis of nonbiological bypass graft(s) of the right leg with ulceration

INCLUDES any condition classifiable to I70.611 and I70.621

Use additional code to identify severity of ulcer (L97.-)

In this example, you need to turn to category code L97 and report a complete code that has six characters as an additional code.

Section Review 3.1

1. Which coding convention is used in the description of an ICD-10-CM code when the information in the medical record provides detail, but no specific code exists? Refer to ICD-10-CM guidelines, section I.A.6.

    A. Code first

    B. In diseases classified elsewhere

    C. NEC

    D. NOS

2. Cyclic neutropenia is coded with D70.4 *Cyclic neutropenia*. There are additional coding instructions for this code listed under the category D70 *Neutropenia*. Using those instructions, how would you report a patient with cyclic neutropenia with an associated fever?

    A. D70.4

    B. D70.4, R50.81

    C. R50.81, D70.4

    D. R50.81

---

3. Supplementary words enclosed in parentheses in the ICD-10-CM codebook have what affect on the coding? Refer to ICD-10-CM guidelines, section I.A.7.

    A. They indicate to look under another word to locate the ICD-10-CM code.

    B. At least one word in parenthesis is required to be in the documentation to use that code.

    C. They identify manifestation codes that should be coded in addition to the primary code.

    D. They do not affect code assignment.

4. What is a default code? Refer to ICD-10-CM guidelines, section I.A.18.

    A. The first code listed when reporting a condition.

    B. The first code listed in the category of codes.

    C. The code that represents the condition most commonly associated with the main term.

    D. The most specific code that represents the most severe condition most commonly associated with the main term.

5. Three-character ICD-10-CM codes represent what level of code in the ICD-10-CM?

    A. Section

    B. Category

    C. Subcategory

    D. Subclassification

Steps to Look Up a Diagnosis Code

Determine the main term of the diagnosis documented in the medical record. This information usually is found in the assessment and plan for the patient's care, or operative reports, progress notes, or procedure notes. A coder must have a solid foundation in medical terminology and anatomy to effectively review the medical record and determine the documented diseases/conditions that should be reported.

Practical Coding Note

Have medical terminology and anatomy tools available when coding. Use these sources to help you understand what you are coding. Knowing the condition will help you select the proper code.

Look up the main term in the Index to Diseases and Injuries. The main term is the disease, illness, or condition of the patient. Look up the following example in your ICD-10-CM codebook.

Example

Diagnosis: Acute tonsilitis	Main term: Tonsilitis
Diagnosis: Right hip pain	Main term: Pain(s)
Diagnosis: Chronic sinusitis	Main term: Sinusitis

There may be additional descriptive terms that affect code selection, essential modifiers, such as chronic or acute. Review all subterms to determine the most specific code. Review all *see* and *see also* notes. When looking for a code in the Index to Diseases and Injuries, you may not be able to find the exact words the provider has used in his documentation. Let's use the diagnosis of right hip pain shown in the example above. To find this in the Index to Diseases and Injuries, look under the main term Pain(s). Under pain, there is not an entry for hip. To locate this diagnosis, the connection has to be made that the hip is a joint. Look for the subterm joint as a subcategory under the main term Pain(s). Pain(s)/joint/hip directs you to the code selection to verify in the Tabular List.

Refer to the code referenced in the Index to Diseases and Injuries in the Tabular List. Review all the "includes," "excludes," and "use additional code" notations to verify accuracy of the code. The notations and conventions in the ICD-10-CM codebook provide hints to the coder when a more appropriate code should be reported. Information also is provided when more than one code is required to report a diagnosis accurately. Throughout the chapter, we will discuss the coding guidelines that include rules for proper ICD-10-CM code selection and sequencing.

ICD-9-CM Application

In the ICD-10-CM Index to Diseases and Injuries, a code requiring additional characters is indicated by using a dash (-). In the ICD-9-CM Index to Diseases, the requirement for additional digits is indicated by a 4th or 5th icon.

Example

A patient is diagnosed with idiopathic chronic gout in the right ankle without tophus. In this example, the main term is Gout. Look for Gout in the Index to Diseases and Injuries. Next, look for the subterm idiopathic. Next, look for the location ankle. The code referenced in the index is M1A.07 √. There is a dash and a symbol alerting the coder that additional characters are required. Look for M1A.07 in the Tabular List.

⑥ᵗʰ M1A.07 Idiopathic chronic gout, ankle and foot

   ⑦ᵗʰ M1A.071 Idiopathic chronic gout, right ankle and foot

   ⑦ᵗʰ M1A.072 Idiopathic chronic gout, left ankle and foot

   ⑦ᵗʰ M1A.079 Idiopathic chronic gout, unspecified ankle and foot

In this example, the Index to Diseases and Injuries refers to M1A.07 √. Code M1A.07- indicates a sixth character is required.

Code M1A.071 is selected to indicate the right ankle. Code M1A.071 has a symbol to indicate a 7th character is required. To locate the 7th character options, look at the category code M1A Chronic gout. Here, you see:

The appropriate 7th character is to be added to each code from category M1A
0 = without tophus (tophi)
1 = with tophus (tophi)

In this case, the diagnosis is noted without tophus so the seventh character extender 0 is reported. For this example, the correct code is M1A.0710 Idiopathic chronic gout, right ankle and foot, without tophus (tophi).

Following all of the steps to look up diagnosis codes is extremely important to verify accuracy.

ICD-9-CM Application

The steps to look up a diagnosis code in ICD-9-CM are identical to the steps used to locate a code in ICD-10-CM.

Practical Coding Note

Always verify the code referenced in the Index to Diseases and Injuries in the Tabular List before selecting the code. There are important notations and guidance found in the Tabular List that are not found in the Index to Diseases and Injuries. Selecting a code solely from the Index to Diseases and Injuries will lead to coding errors.

Section Review 3.2

1. Applying the coding concept from ICD-10-CM guidelines, section I.B.1., which of the following is the recommended method for using your ICD-10-CM codebook?

    A. Either the Tabular List or Alphabetic Index will take you to the right code.

    B. Locate the main term in the Tabular List, and then verify it in the Alphabetic Index.

    C. Instructional notations in the Alphabetic Index take precedence over those in the Tabular List.

    D. Always consult the Alphabetic Index first. Refer to the Tabular List to locate the selected code.

2. What is the ICD-10-CM code for a bruised left knee?

    A. S81.031A

    B. S80.02XA

    C. S90.912A

    D. S89.92XA

 AAPC

www.aapc.com

63

3. What is the ICD-10-CM code for prostate hyperplasia with urinary retention?

    A. N40.0

    B. N40.0, R33.8

    C. N40.1

    D. N40.1, R33.8

4. What is the ICD-10-CM code for essential hypertension?

    A. I11

    B. I11.9

    C. I12.9

    D. I10

5. What is/are the ICD-10-CM code(s) for bilateral hip pain?

    A. M25.851, M25.852

    B. M25.859

    C. M25.559

    D. M25.551, M25.552

ICD-10-CM Official Guidelines for Coding and Reporting

CMS and NCHS provide the ICD-10-CM Official Guidelines for Coding and Reporting. These guidelines, found in the front of the ICD-10-CM codebook, provide instructions for proper code selection and code sequencing rules. Section I of the official guidelines includes conventions, general coding guidelines, and chapter specific guidelines. Subsection A includes the conventions and punctuation discussed in the beginning of this chapter. Subsection B includes general coding guidelines. Section C includes chapter specific coding guidelines that will be discussed in chapters 4 and 5.

Referencing the Guidelines

Documenting the guidelines is done by referencing the section (Roman numeral), chapter (letter), and sub section (number) of the guidelines being referred to. To understand the reference to the guidelines, start by looking through the Table of Contents for the guidelines. A documented reference appears as Section I.C.4.a.2.

This indicates the guideline is found in:

Section I. Conventions, General Coding Guidelines and Chapter Specific Guidelines

Section I.C. Chapter-Specific Coding Guidelines

Section I.C.4. Chapter 4: Endocrine, Nutritional, and Metabolic Diseases (E00-E89)

Section I.C.4.a. Diabetes mellitus

Section I.C.4.a.2. Type of diabetes mellitus not documented

Look up the following example in your ICD-10-CM codebook.

Example

In your ICD-10-CM Guidelines, you will see (we have emphasized the guideline reference by using a red font below).

Section I. Conventions, General Coding Guidelines and Chapter Specific Guidelines

C. Chapter-Specific Coding Guidelines

4. Chapter 4: Endocrine, Nutritional, and Metabolic Diseases (E00-E89)

a. Diabetes mellitus

The diabetes mellitus codes are combination codes that include the type of diabetes mellitus, the body system affected, and the complications affecting that body system. As many codes within a particular category as are necessary to describe all of the complications of the disease may be used. They should be sequenced based on the reason for a particular encounter. Assign as many codes from categories E08 - E13 as needed to identify all of the associated conditions with which the patient is diagnosed.

1) Type of diabetes

The age of a patient is not the sole determining factor, though most type 1diabetics develop the condition before reaching puberty. For this reason type 1 diabetes mellitus is also referred to as juvenile diabetes.

2) Type of diabetes mellitus not documented

| Guideline referenced Section I.C.4.a.2. |

If the type of diabetes mellitus is not documented in the medical record the default is E11.-, Type 2 diabetes mellitus.

3) Diabetes mellitus and the use of insulin

Section I.B General Coding Guidelines

Use Both Alphabetic Index and Tabular List

Always use both Tabular List and Index to Diseases and Injuries (Alphabetic Index). Verify the code number in the Tabular List. Never code directly from the Index to Diseases and Injuries because important instructions often appear in the Tabular List. Selection of the full code, including laterality and any applicable 7th character can only be done in the Tabular List. A dash (-) at the end of an Alphabetic Index entry indicates that additional characters are required. Even if a dash is not included at the Alphabetic Index entry, it is necessary to refer to the Tabular List to verify that no 7th character is required or additional notes. To locate an ICD-10-CM code, take the following steps:

1. Locate each term in the Alphabetic Index:

- Locate the main term in the Index to Diseases and Injuries (Alphabetic Index).
- Refer to any notes under the main term.
- Read any terms enclosed in parentheses following the main term.
- Refer to any modifiers of the main term.
- Do not skip subterms indented under the main term.
- Follow any cross-reference instructions, such as *see also*.
- Use of a medical dictionary can help you to identify main terms and understand the disease process to assist with accurate coding.

Example

COPD: This acronym is not found in the ICD-10-CM Index to Diseases and Injuries. A medical dictionary can tell you that COPD is an abbreviation for chronic obstructive pulmonary disease (a condition of the lungs). With this information, the coder will be able to identify properly the main term in the Index to Diseases

and Injuries. In the index, COPD can be found under Obstruction, obstructed, obstructive/lung/disease, chronic. The correct code is J44.9 *Chronic obstructive pulmonary disease, unspecified.*

Obstruction, obstructed, obstructive

    lung J98.4
        disease, chronic J44.9

There can be more than one way to find the correct code. For example, to find the code for COPD you could also locate it under Disease, diseased/pulmonary/chronic obstructive.

In searching the Index to Diseases and Injuries, if you start with the wrong main term, you may be directed to the correct term. For example, if you looked under the main term "Pulmonary," there is a note informing you to "*see* condition." This notation instructs you to look under the condition, not the anatomic site.

Practical Coding Note

When trying to determine the main term, it is sometimes helpful to read the diagnosis right to left. For example, Chronic Obstructive Pulmonary Disease (COPD) can be found by looking in the Index to Diseases and Injuries under Disease/pulmonary/chronic obstructive.

2. Verify the code in the Tabular List:

- Find the code in the Tabular List.
- Review any category notes (located under the three character category)
- Review notes for the code including Includes notes, Excludes1 and Excludes2 notes, code first notes, code additional notes, etc.

Level of Detail in Coding

Code to the highest degree of specificity. A three-character code may be used only when the category is not subdivided further. When a three-character code has subdivisions, the appropriate subdivision must be coded. The three-character category may be further subdivided by the use of fourth and/or fifth characters and/or sixth characters, which provide greater detail. Codes may also require a seventh character extender. A code is invalid if it has not been coded to the full number of characters required for that code, including the 7th character, if applicable.

Example

A patient is being seen for follow-up of age-related osteoporosis with current pathological fracture of the left shoulder. The fracture is healing as expected.

M80 Osteoporosis with current pathological fracture

INCLUDES   osteoporosis with current fragility fracture

Use additional code to identify major osseous defect, if applicable (M89.7-)

EXCLUDES1   collapsed vertebra NOS (M48.5)
pathological fracture NOS (M84.4)
wedging of vertebra NOS (M48.5)

EXCLUDES2   personal history of (healed) osteoporosis fracture (Z87.310)

The appropriate 7th character is to be added to each code from category M80

A = initial encounter for fracture

D = subsequent encounter for fracture with routine healing

G = subsequent encounter for fracture with delayed healing

K = subsequent encounter for fracture with nonunion

P = subsequent encounter for fracture with malunion

S = sequela

M80.0 Age-related osteoporosis with current pathological fracture

M80.00 Age-related osteoporosis with current pathological fracture, unspecified site

M80.01 Age-related osteoporosis with current pathological fracture, shoulder

M80.012 Age-related osteoporosis with current pathological fracture, left shoulder

In this example, it is not appropriate to report M80 as a diagnosis because there is further division. Likewise, it is not appropriate to report M80.012 as a diagnosis because a 7th character is required. M80.012D is the correct code to report for this scenario.

Signs and Symptoms

In the outpatient setting, do not code a diagnosis unless it is certain. Examples of language seen in the medical record that identify uncertain diagnoses include:

- Probable
- Suspected
- Questionable
- Rule out
- Differential
- Working

When a definitive diagnosis has not been determined, code the signs, symptoms, and abnormal test result(s) or other reasons for the visit.

Example

Diagnosis: Fatigue, suspect iron deficiency anemia

In this instance, fatigue is reported as the diagnosis because the physician has not confirmed the diagnosis for iron deficiency anemia. To locate the code, look for Fatigue in the Index to Diseases and Injuries. No other subterms apply in this example. The code referred to in the index is R53.83. The Tabular List confirms Fatigue NOS (not otherwise specified) is reported with R53.83.

In the inpatient setting for facility diagnosis coding, it is appropriate to report suspected or rule out diagnoses as if the condition does exist. This is **only** true for facility reporting for inpatient services, for all diagnoses except HIV. HIV is the only condition that must be confirmed if it is to be reported in the inpatient setting.

Conditions that are an Integral Part of a Disease Process

Codes for symptoms, signs, and ill-defined conditions are not to be reported as diagnoses when a related definitive diagnosis has been established, unless otherwise instructed by the classification. If you are unsure if a symptom is part of a disease process, the physician should be queried.

Example

A patient presents with severe abdominal pain, nausea, and vomiting. The provider diagnoses the patient with acute appendicitis. In this case, only a code for the appendicitis is reported because the abdominal pain, nausea, and vomiting are symptoms of appendicitis. To locate the code, look for Appendicitis in the Index to Diseases and Injuries. Then, look for the subterm acute. No additional subterms apply in this example. The code referred to in the index is K35.80, which must be confirmed by reviewing the code in the Tabular List.

Conditions That Are Not an Integral Part of the Disease Process

Codes for signs and symptoms that are not routinely associated with other definite diagnoses should be reported.

Example

A patient presents with runny nose and cough. The provider diagnoses the patient with a URI (Upper Respiratory Infection). The patient also complains of right shoulder pain. In this example, a code is selected for the URI and the right shoulder pain. The runny nose and cough are symptoms of the URI (J06.9) and should not be reported. Right shoulder pain (M25.511) is not related to the URI, and should be coded separately.

URI is found in the Index to Diseases and Injuries under Infection/respiratory (tract)/upper (acute) NOS. Right shoulder pain is found in the Index to Diseases and Injuries under Pain(s)/joint/shoulder. Verification in the Tabular List identifies the 6th character to indicate laterality.

Multiple Coding for a Single Condition

Multiple coding of diagnoses is required for certain conditions not subject to the rules for combination codes.

a. Index to Diseases and Injuries: Codes for both etiology and manifestation of a disease appear following the subentry term, with the second code in brackets. Assign both codes in the same sequence in which they appear in the Index to Diseases and Injuries.

b. Tabular List: Instructional notes that indicate when to use more than one code:

    — Code first
    — Code, if applicable, any causal condition first
    — Code also
    — Use additional code

Example

A patient is diagnosed with amyloid heart disease. In the Index to Diseases and Injuries, look for Disease, diseased/heart (organic)/amyloid. Two codes are listed on the same line — E85.4 [I43]. This indicates both codes are required to describe this diagnosis In the Tabular List, verify the codes. Notice under the code I43 the instructional note "Code first underlying disease, such as: amyloidosis (E85.-)." This statement indicates that E85.4 Organ-limited amyloidosis should be listed first, followed by I43.

The correct diagnosis codes and sequencing are:

E85.4   Organ-limited amyloidosis

I43   Cardiomyopathy in diseases classified elsewhere

Acute and Chronic

When both an acute and a chronic condition are documented, and there is a separate code for each, report both codes. The acute code is sequenced first. For example, the patient is diagnosed with acute and chronic cystitis. From the Index to Diseases and Injuries, look for Cystitis. There is a subterm for acute (N30.00) and a subterm for chronic (N30.20). The acute code is sequenced first:

N30.00   Acute cystitis without hematuria

N30.20   Other chronic cystitis without hematuria

Chronic conditions treated on an ongoing basis may be coded as many times as required for treatment and care of the patient, or when applicable to the patient's care plan. Do not code conditions previously treated, or those that no longer exist. A history of previous conditions should be coded using a Z code if the history affects patient care, or provides the need for a patient to seek medical attention.

Example

Personal history of colon cancer: In this instance, the main term to look for in the Index to Diseases and Injuries is History of/personal, not Cancer. Look under the main term History only if relevant to the current episode of care (for instance, the patient is in for a colonoscopy, or tests are being run to evaluate a cancer suspected in another organ). It would not be appropriate to report the code for a history of colon cancer if the patient is being seen for a condition unrelated to the colon cancer, such as sinus infection.

Combination Code

A combination code is used to fully identify an instance in which two diagnoses, or a diagnosis with an associated secondary process (manifestation) or complication, are included in the description of a single code number. Assign a combination code only when that code fully identifies the diagnostic conditions involved, or when instructed in the Index to Diseases and Injuries.

Example

A patient has type 2 diabetes mellitus and diabetic dermatitis. Instead of reporting the diabetes and dermatitis with two separate codes, it is coded with the combination code E11.620 Type 2 diabetes mellitus with diabetic dermatitis.

Sequelae (Late Effects)

Sequela is "residual effect (condition produced) after the acute portion of an illness or injury has terminated." Key phrases such as "due to an old injury" or "due to previous illness" are indicators that the problem or condition may be a late effect. If these indicators are not present in the diagnostic statement, the injury or condition may be considered a sequela if sufficient time has elapsed between the original condition and the sequela. The residual effect may be apparent early after an acute phase of an illness, as in a cerebrovascular accident, or it may occur much later (one year or more), as with a previous injury or illness (eg, following an auto accident).

When a patient is being treated for a condition that is a sequela of an earlier injury or disease, reference Sequelae in the Index to Diseases and Injuries.

Sequela should be coded according to the nature of the residual condition of the sequela. Two codes usually are required when coding sequela. The residual condition is coded first, and the code(s) for the cause of the sequela are reported as secondary. It may be necessary for the coder to go to the External Cause of Injuries Index to identify and reference the appropriate sequela of an external cause. The documentation in the medical record should support the manifestation or residual effect, as well as the cause.

The code for the cause of the sequela may be used as a principal diagnosis when no residual diagnosis is identified. The following terminology may be used to document sequelae:

- Due to an old injury
- Due to a previous illness
- Due to an illness or injury that occurred one year or more before the current encounter

The code for the acute phase of an illness or injury that leads to the sequela is never used with a code for the cause of the sequela.

The following examples are causes of sequelae:

- Malunion due to old fracture of the left ankle
- Traumatic arthritis following fracture of the left wrist
- Hemiplegia one year following cerebrovascular thrombosis
- Scarring of the left leg due to third degree burns
- Contracture of the left heel tendons due to poliomyelitis

Example

Intellectual disability due to previous poliomyelitis: Here, intellectual disability is the first listed diagnosis code. The sequela (or late effect) of poliomyelitis is the secondary diagnosis. Be sure not to use the code for current poliomyelitis; do not code A80.9 Acute poliomyelitis, unspecified. Instead look in the Index to Diseases and Injuries for the main term Sequela (of), and then the subterm (essential modifier) poliomyelitis (acute). The correct codes are F79 Unspecified intellectual disabilities and B91 Sequelae poliomyelitis.

There are some instances in ICD-10-CM where the code includes both the sequela and the manifestation in one code. In this case, only one code is reported.

Example

I69.120 Aphasia following nontraumatic intracerebral hemorrhage

In this example, aphasia is the late effect of the nontraumatic intracerebral hemorrhage, which is all identified with one code.

ICD-9-CM Application

In ICD-9-CM, sequelae are referred to as late effects. In the ICD-9-CM Index to Diseases, a late effect (or sequela) is located by looking for Late/effect(s) (of).

Impending or Threatened Condition

When a patient is discharged with a condition described as impending or threatened, review the Index to Diseases and Injuries for the sub term impending or threatened under the main term of the condition. If a subterm does not exist, reference Impending or Threatened as the main term, with the condition as a subterm. If a suitable code does not exist, report the signs and symptoms that led the provider to suspect an impending or threatened condition.

Example

A patient is discharged with an impending myocardial infarction. From the Index to Diseases and Injuries, look for Impending/myocardial infarction. You are referred to I20.0. Code I20.0 reports unstable angina or preinfarction angina.

Reporting Same Diagnosis Code More than Once

Do not report the same diagnosis code more than once. There will be instances when a provider will document a bilateral condition, or two different conditions reported with the same diagnosis code. When either situation occurs, report the unique ICD-10-CM code just once.

Laterality

ICD-10-CM allows for the reporting of laterality (right, left, bilateral). For bilateral sites, the final character of the code indicates laterality. An unspecified side code is also provided should the side not be identified in the medical record. If no bilateral code is provided and the condition is bilateral, assign separate codes for both the left and right side.

Example

The specificity of ICD-10-CM codes will modify the reporting of a diagnosis that exists bilaterally, as the laterality of the diagnosis is built into the codes. When a patient complains of pain in his right and left legs, the ICD-10-CM codes reported are:

M79.604 Pain in right leg

M79.605 Pain in left leg

Documentation for BMI and Pressure Ulcer Stages

Codes for body mass index (BMI) and pressure ulcer stage codes can be reported based on documentation from any clinician involved in the patient's case. For example, a nurse caring for the patient's pressure ulcer will provide documentation needed to determine the proper stage of a pressure ulcer. However, the patient's provider must document the underlying condition, such as diabetes or obesity. The BMI codes should only be reported as secondary diagnoses.

Example

ICD-10-CM has codes that report both the ulcer and the stage in one code. Let's look at the diagnosis of pressure ulcer, stage 1, right hip.

Look in the Index to Diseases and Injuries for Ulcer/pressure (pressure area)/stage 1/hip L89.2-.

L89.211 Pressure ulcer of right hip, stage 1

ICD-9-CM Application

Reporting of pressure ulcers in ICD-9-CM requires two codes. Look in the Index to Diseases for Ulcer/pressure/hip 707.04. In the Tabular List, there is an instruction note listed under 707.0 stating to use additional code to identify pressure ulcer stage (707.20-707.25).

707.04 Pressure ulcer, hip

707.21 Pressure ulcer stage 1

Syndromes

When coding syndromes, if the syndrome is not located in the Index to Diseases and Injuries, code the patient's signs and symptoms. For example, a patient is diagnosed with Alstrom syndrome (a rare genetic disease). In the Index to Diseases and Injuries, Syndrome/Alstrom also is not listed; nor is there a listing for Alstrom as a main term in the index. Therefore, review the documentation to report the patient's signs and symptoms.

Documentation of Complications of Care

Not all conditions that occur during or following surgery or other medical care are classified as complications of care. To code a complication of care, there must be a cause-and-effect relationship between the care provided and the condition that the patient has contracted due to the surgery or medical care. The provider must also specifically document that the condition is a complication.

Borderline Diagnosis

Borderline diagnoses are not the same as uncertain diagnoses. Borderline diagnoses are coded as confirmed diagnoses unless there is an index entry of borderline for that classification.

Use of Sign/Symptom/Unspecified Codes

Signs and symptoms are reported unless a definitive diagnosis has been established. Once the definitive diagnosis has been established, the definitive diagnosis is reported. When sufficient clinical information isn't known or available about a particular health condition to assign a more specific code, it is acceptable to report the appropriate "unspecified" code.

Section Review 3.3

1. A patient visits the primary care physician for complaints of nausea and vomiting. Which option is appropriate to report a diagnosis of nausea and vomiting? Apply the coding concept from ICD-10-CM guidelines, section I.B.9.

    A. R11

    B. R11.2

    C. R11.0, R11.10

    D. R11.14

2. Referencing ICD-10-CM guidelines, section I.B.10, what is the time limit when assigning codes as "sequela?"

    A. At least six months beyond the injury or illness causing the sequela.

    B. At least two years beyond the injury or illness causing the sequela.

    C. There is no time limit on sequelae.

    D. There is a sliding scale of time limits on sequelae in the ICD-10-CM appendix.

3. Referencing ICD-10-CM guidelines, section I.B.8, when a patient presents with an acute exacerbation of a chronic condition, and no single code captures both the chronic and acute nature of the illness, how are the codes sequenced?

    A. Code the chronic condition first, followed by the acute condition.

    B. Code the acute condition first, followed by the chronic condition.

    C. Check with the physician to determine whether the acute or chronic condition takes precedence.

    D. Code only the acute condition.

4. Referencing ICD-10-CM guidelines, section I.B.11, what is the appropriate action when a physician documents an impending condition that had not occurred by the time of discharge?

    A. Check the ICD-10-CM Index to Diseases and Injuries to see if there are listings under "threatened" or "impending;" and if not, code the existing underlying condition(s) rather than the condition described as impending.

    B. Code the condition that is impending.

    C. Use a Z code to describe the patient encounter.

    D. Use the appropriate 7th character to indicate the condition is impending or threatened.

5. A patient is brought to the ED with right and left ankle fractures. Applying the coding concepts from ICD-10-CM guidelines, section I.B.12 and I.B.13, which ICD-10-CM code selection should you report?

    A. S82.841D

    B. S82.843A, S82.843S

    C. S82.891A, S82.892A

    D. S82.899A

Selection of the Principal Diagnosis

In Section II of the guidelines, rules for selecting the principal diagnosis in the inpatient setting are discussed. When selecting the proper principal diagnosis, the coding conventions in the Tabular List and Index to Diseases and Injuries take priority over the official coding guidelines. The guidelines used to determine the principal diagnosis are specific to inpatient coding. The rules for selecting the first listed (principal) diagnosis in the outpatient setting, which is the focus of this chapter, will be discussed in the outpatient guidelines found in section IV of the official coding guidelines.

Reporting Additional Diagnoses

When reporting additional diagnoses, only report what is pertinent for the encounter. Conditions that do not have an impact on the presenting problem or treatment of the patient should not be coded.

The guidelines discussed in Section III are specific to inpatient services. The rules for reporting additional diagnosis as they pertain to outpatient coding will be discussed in the next section of this chapter.

The most significant difference in the official coding guidelines between inpatient and outpatient diagnosis coding is the coding of uncertain diagnosis. In the inpatient setting, a condition reported as "probable," "suspected," "likely," "questionable," "possible," "still to be ruled out," or other similar terms indicating uncertainty, is coded as if it existed or was established (with the exception of HIV).

In the outpatient setting, unless the diagnosis is confirmed, it is not reported. For outpatient coding, if the condition is reported as "probable," "suspected," "likely," "questionable," "possible," or "still to be ruled out," report the patient's signs and symptoms. It is extremely important for providers to document conditions they suspect, and the patient's symptoms that prompt the suspicion.

Diagnosis Coding Guidelines for Outpatient Reporting

Diagnostic Coding and Reporting Guidelines for Outpatient Services is described in Section IV of the ICD-10-CM guidelines. These coding guidelines for outpatient diagnoses have been approved for use by hospitals/physicians in coding and reporting hospital-based outpatient services and physician office visits. Review the following guideline sections for coding and reporting outpatient services. Locate Section IV in your ICD-10-CM codebook to visualize where these guidelines are located.

Selection of First Listed Condition

- In the outpatient setting, the first listed diagnosis is used in lieu of principal diagnosis.
- In determining the first listed diagnosis, the coding conventions of ICD-10-CM, as well as the general and disease specific guidelines, take precedence over the outpatient guidelines.

Diagnoses often are not established at the time of the initial encounter/visit. It may take two or more visits before the diagnosis is confirmed.

The most critical rule involves beginning the search for the correct code assignment through the Index to Diseases and Injuries. Never begin searching initially in the Tabular List because this will lead to coding errors.

Example

A middle-aged male presents with a complaint of constant facial pain. The physician ordered diagnostic tests to determine the source of the pain. The initial patient visit is completed with the diagnosis of facial pain (R51) because a definitive diagnosis had not yet been determined.

When a patient presents for outpatient surgery, the reason for the surgery is the first-listed diagnosis even if the surgery is not performed due to complications. When the patient presents for outpatient surgery and develops complications requiring admission to observation, the reason for the surgery is the first-listed diagnosis followed by the codes for the complication(s).

Codes from A00.00 through T88.9, Z00-Z99

The appropriate code or codes from A00.00 through T88.9 and Z00-Z99 must be used to identify diagnoses, signs, symptoms, conditions, problems, complaints, or other reason(s) for the encounter/visit.

Accurate Reporting of ICD-10-CM Diagnosis Codes

For accurate reporting of ICD-10-CM diagnosis codes, the documentation should describe the patient's condition using terminology that includes specific diagnoses, as well as symptoms, problems, or reasons for the encounter. There are ICD-10-CM codes to describe all of these situations.

Example

The physician's documentation indicates that the patient has stable, benign hypertension (I10), with a new onset of nausea (R11.0) and blurred vision (H53.8).

Codes that Describe Symptoms and Signs

Codes that describe symptoms and signs, as opposed to diagnoses, are acceptable for reporting purposes when a physician has not established (confirmed) the diagnosis. Chapter 18 of ICD-10-CM, Symptoms, Signs, and Ill-defined Conditions (codes R00-R99) contains many, but not all, codes for symptoms.

Example

Patient presents to the outpatient clinic complaining of abdominal cramps. The physician performed a complete history and physical examination and could not determine the cause of the cramps. The diagnosis code reported for this encounter is based on the symptom, which is the abdominal cramps (R10.9).

Encounters for Circumstances Other than a Disease or Injury

The Classification of Factors Influencing Health Status and Contact with Health Services (Z00-Z99) are provided to record healthcare encounters for circumstances other than a disease or injury.

Example

Patient presents for follow-up visit after a healed fracture. To locate the diagnosis code, look in the Index to Diseases and Injuries for Examination/follow-up (routine) (following)/fracture to locate Z09.

Level of Detail in Coding

ICD-10-CM is composed of codes with three, four, five, six, or seven characters. Codes with three characters are included in ICD-10-CM as the heading of a category of codes that may be subdivided further with use of additional characters, which provide greater specificity. A three-character code is to be used only if it is not further subdivided.

Where further specificity is provided, additional characters must be assigned. A code is invalid if it has not been coded to the full number of characters (highest level of specificity) required for that code. See also Official ICD-10-CM Guidelines for Coding and Reporting, section I. B.2.

ICD-10-CM Code for the Diagnosis, Condition, Problem or Other Reason for the Encounter

List first the ICD-10-CM code for the diagnosis, condition, problem, or other reason for encounter/visit shown in the medical record to be responsible primarily for the services

provided. List additional codes that describe any co-existing conditions.

Example

The patient presents for evaluation and generalized osteoarthrosis, multiple sites. During the patient encounter, the physician also evaluates the patient's constipation and recommends a change in diet. Diagnosis codes for this encounter are M15.9 *Polyosteosteoarthritis, unspecified* and K59.00 *Constipation, unspecified*.

Uncertain Diagnosis

Do not code diagnoses documented as "probable," "suspected," "questionable," "rule out," or "working diagnosis." Rather, code the condition(s) to the highest degree of certainty for that encounter/visit, such as symptoms, signs, abnormal test results, or other reason for the visit.

Example

The patient presents to the emergency department with low back pain and hematuria. The physician dictates, "rule out kidney stone." Diagnosis codes for this encounter are M54.5 *Low back pain* and R31.9 *Hematuria, unspecified*. The "rule out" condition cannot be assigned a diagnosis code for outpatient services.

Chronic Diseases

Chronic diseases treated on an ongoing basis may be coded and reported as many times as the patient receives treatment and care for the condition(s).

Example

A patient receives treatment every three months for chronic pancreatitis. A diagnosis code K86.1 Other *chronic pancreatitis* is assigned for each medical encounter.

Code All Documented Conditions that Coexist

Code all documented conditions that co-exist at the time of the encounter/visit, and require or affect patient care treatment or management. Do not code conditions that were treated previously and no longer exist. History codes (Z80-Z87) may be used as secondary codes if the historical condition or family history has an impact on current care or influences treatment.

Example

The patient presents with chest pain. The patient's father has a prior diagnosis of ischemic heart disease. Diagnosis codes for this encounter include R07.9 *Chest pain,* unspecified and Z82.49 *Family history of ischemic heart disease and other diseases of the circulatory system.*

Patients Receiving Diagnostic Services Only

For patients receiving diagnostic services only during an encounter/visit, sequence first the diagnosis, condition, problem, or other reason for encounter/visit shown in the medical record to be chiefly responsible for the outpatient services provided during the encounter/visit. Codes for other diagnoses (eg, chronic conditions) may be sequenced as additional diagnoses.

For encounters for routine laboratory/radiology testing in the absence of any signs, symptoms, or associated diagnosis, assign Z01.89 *Encounter for other specified special examinations.*

For outpatient encounters for diagnostic tests that have been interpreted by a physician, and the final report is available at the time of coding, code any confirmed or definitive diagnosis(es). See also ICD-10-CM Official Guidelines for Coding and Reporting, section IV.K). This differs from coding practice in the hospital inpatient setting regarding abnormal findings on test results.

Example

A patient presents for an MRI of the brain with the complaint of dizziness. This patient has been diagnosed with a malignant neoplasm of the bladder and is currently receiving chemotherapy treatment. The diagnosis code R42 *Dizziness and giddiness* is sequenced first because it is the primary reason for the outpatient diagnostic service. Diagnosis code C67.9 *Malignant neoplasm of bladder, unspecified* may be sequenced as the secondary diagnosis code.

Patients Receiving Therapeutic Services Only

For patients receiving therapeutic services only during an encounter/visit, sequence first the diagnosis, condition, problem, or other reason for encounter/visit shown in the medical record to be chiefly responsible for the outpatient services provided during the encounter/visit. Codes for other diagnoses (eg, chronic conditions) may be sequenced as additional diagnoses.

The only exception to this rule is when the primary reason for the admission/encounter is chemotherapy, radiation, or reha-

bilitation. The appropriate Z code for the service is listed first, and the diagnosis or problem for which the service is being performed is listed second.

Example

A patient presents to the outpatient department for chemotherapy to treat cancer of the rectosigmoid junction. Diagnosis codes are sequenced as Z51.11 *Encounter for antineoplastic chemotherapy* and C19 *Malignant neoplasm of rectosigmoid junction.*

Patients Receiving Preoperative Evaluations Only

For patients receiving pre-operative evaluations only, sequence a code from subcategory Z01.81 *Encounter for pre-procedural examinations* to describe the pre-operative consultations. Assign a code for the condition to describe the reason for the surgery as an additional diagnosis. Code also any findings related to the pre-operative evaluation.

Example

A patient presents for a pre-operative screening chest X-ray prior to surgery for a unilateral inguinal hernia. The X-ray detects an undefined abnormality in the right lower lobe, and the radiologist recommends additional imaging studies. Diagnosis sequencing for this encounter includes:

- Z01.818   Encounter for other preprocedural examination
- K40.90   Unilateral inguinal hernia, without obstruction or gangrene, not specified as recurrent
- R91.8   Other nonspecific abnormal finding of lung field

Practical Coding Note

Pre-operative screening exams are found in the Index to Diseases and Injuries by looking for Examination/pre-procedural (pre-operative).

Ambulatory Surgery

For ambulatory surgery, code the diagnosis for which the surgery was performed. If the postoperative diagnosis is known to be different from the preoperative diagnosis at the time the diagnosis is confirmed, select the postoperative diagnosis for coding because it is the most definitive.

Routine Outpatient Prenatal Visits

For routine outpatient prenatal visits when no complications are present, a code from category Z34 *Encounters for supervision of normal pregnancy* should be used as a principal diagnosis. These codes should not be used with chapter 15 codes. It would be inappropriate to code Z34.80 *Encounter supervision*

of other normal pregnancy, unspecified trimester if the patient is diagnosed with a condition that complicates the pregnancy.

For example, if a patient has gestational diabetes, the proper code is O24.419 Gestational diabetes mellitus in pregnancy, unspecified control. The sixth character is selected based on how the diabetes is controlled (diet, insulin, etc.).

Section Review 3.4

1. A patient is admitted for an outpatient cholecystectomy for gallstones. During recovery, the patient developed severe postoperative pain. The patient was admitted to observation to monitor the pain. Applying the coding concept from ICD-10-CM guidelines, section IV.A.2, what is the appropriate ICD-10-CM code selection for the observation?

    A. K80.20, G89.18

    B. G89.18

    C. G89.18, K80.20

    D. K80.20

2. A patient is in outpatient surgery for a laparoscopic oophorectomy for an ovarian cyst. After admission, the anesthesiologist discovered the patient had an upper respiratory infection and the surgery was cancelled. Applying the coding concept from ICD-10-CM guidelines, section IV.A.1, what is the appropriate ICD-10-CM code selection?

    A. J06.9, Z53.09, N83.20

    B. Z53.09

    C. N83.20

    D. N83.20, J06.9, Z53.09

3. A patient sees the physician for chest pain, fever, and cough. The physician orders an X-ray to rule out pneumonia. Applying the coding concept from ICD-10-CM Guideline Section IV.H., which ICD-10-CM code(s) are reported?

    A. J18.9

    B. J10.1

    C. R07.9, R50.9, R05

    D. R07.9, R50.9, R05, J18.9

4. A patient visits her family provider for her annual wellness exam. The provider notices a suspicious skin lesion on her arm and refers her to a dermatologist. Applying the coding concept from ICD-10-CM guideline, section IV.P, which ICD-10-CM code(s) is/are reported?

    A. Z00.00

    B. Z00.01

    C. Z00.00, L98.9

    D. Z00.01, L98.9

5. Mr. Smith is scheduled for a splenectomy for hypersplenism. Before his splenectomy, he is required to have clearance from his pulmonologist. The pulmonologist performs a pre-operative screening. Applying the coding concept from ICD-10-CM guidelines, section IV.M, which ICD-10-CM codes would be reported for the pre-operative clearance?

   A. Z01.811, R09.89

   B. Z01.811, D73.1, R09.89

   C. D73.1, Z01.811

   D. Z01.811, D73.1

Glossary

Acute—A condition with a rapid and short course.

Anatomical—Body site.

And—Can mean either "and" or "or" when it is in the code description.

BMI—Body mass index.

Brackets [ ]—Symbol to enclose synonyms, alternate wording, or explanatory phrases in the Tabular List. Brackets are used in the Index to Diseases and Injuries (Alphabetic Index) to identify manifestation codes in which multiple coding and sequencing rules will apply.

Chronic—A condition that develops slowly and lasts a long time.

Code First—Note in the Tabular List written in italics requiring the underlying disease if reported first.

**Colon: **—Used in the Tabular List after an incomplete term that needs one or more of the modifiers that follow to make it assignable to a given category.

Combination Code—Single code used to classify two diagnoses.

COPD—Chronic Obstructive Pulmonary Disease.

Default Code—The code listed next to the main term and represents the condition most commonly associated with the main term.

Etiology—Cause of the disease.

Eponym—Disease or syndrome named after a person.

Essential Modifiers—Subterms that are listed below the main term in the alphabetical order, and are indented.

Excludes1—Note in the Tabular List to indicate the terms listed are to be reported with a code from another category and are not to be reported with the current selected code.

Excludes2—Note in the Tabular List to indicate the terms listed are to be reported from another category and may be reported with the current selected code if both conditions exist.

Includes—Note in the Tabular List under a three-character code title to define further, or to give an example of the contents of the category.

Index to Diseases and Injuries—Diagnosis codes organized in an Index to Diseases and Injuries (Alphabetic Index).

Main Term—The key word to reference the disease, condition, or symptom in the Index to Diseases and Injuries (Alphabetic Index). Main terms are bolded in the Index to Diseases and Injuries (Alphabetic Index).

NEC—Not elsewhere classified.

Nonessential Modifiers—Subterms that follow the main term and are enclosed in parentheses used to clarify the diagnosis, but are not required.

NOS—Not otherwise specified.

Parentheses ()—Symbol to enclose supplementary words that may be present or absent in the statement of a disease or procedure, without affecting the code number to which it is assigned.

Point Dash (.-)—This symbol is found in the Tabular List after certain codes. It indicates that the code is incomplete and go to that category or subcategory of codes to complete that code.

Rubrics—Three-character categories.

See also—Note in the Index to Diseases and Injuries (Alphabetic Index) that indicates additional information is available that may provide an additional diagnostic code.

See—Note in the Index to Diseases and Injuries (Alphabetic Index) that directs you to a more specific term under which the correct code can be found.

Septicemia—A systemic disease associated with microorganisms or toxins in the blood. These toxins are caused by bacteria, viruses, fungi, or other organisms.

Sepsis—Whole body inflammatory state. It generally refers to SIRS that is due to an infection.

Sequela (late effect)—An inactive, residual effect or condition produced after the acute portion of an injury or illness has passed.

Severe Sepsis—Sepsis with associated acute organ dysfunction.

Subterms—These terms are indented under the main term to describe differences in site, etiology, or clinical type. Subterms add specificity to the main term.

Tabular List—Diagnosis codes organized in numerical order.

Unspecified—Codes are used when the information in the medical record is not available for coding more specificity.

Use Additional Code—Note in the Tabular List instructing you report a second code, if the information is available, to provide a more complete picture of the diagnosis.

Z Codes—Codes used to describe circumstances or conditions that could influence patient care.

With—Means "associated with" or "due to" in a code title in the Index to Diseases and Injuries (Alphabetic Index) or an instructional note in the Tabular List.

Introduction

Proper ICD-10-CM code selection can be accomplished when you follow ICD-10-CM conventions and chapter-specific coding guidelines. The Tabular List is organized into 21 chapters categorized by etiology or anatomic site. Section I.C. of the Official ICD-10-CM Guidelines for Coding and Reporting includes instructions for correct code selection and sequencing specific to each chapter. There are not official guidelines for each three-character category within each chapter of the ICD-10-CM codebook. Coders must know all official coding guidelines, in addition to the conventions discussed in the previous chapter, to select diagnosis codes accurately.

In this chapter, we will discuss the chapter-specific coding guidelines for chapters 1 through 11 of the ICD-10-CM codebook, as well as common diagnoses in each chapter. These chapters include infectious and parasitic diseases, neoplasms, diseases of blood and blood forming organs and disorders involving the immune mechanism, endocrine, nutritional, and metabolic diseases, mental, behavioral and neurodevelopmental disorders, diseases of nervous system, diseases of the eye and adnexa, diseases of the ear and mastoid process, diseases of circulatory system, diseases of respiratory system, and diseases of digestive system. It is important to turn to the official coding guidelines in the front of the ICD-10-CM codebook to take notes for each of the chapter-specific coding guidelines.

The information contained in this chapter is meant as a supplement, and is not intended to replace the official coding guidelines found in the ICD-10-CM codebook. It is important to read and understand every guideline and convention found in ICD-10-CM.

Objectives

- Understand the chapter-specific official coding guidelines for ICD-10-CM chapters 1-11.
- Recognize common diagnoses coded in each ICD-10-CM chapter.
- Recognize main terms to start the code search.
- Follow proper look-up sequences to select diagnosis codes.

Chapter 1: Certain Infectious and Parasitic Diseases (Codes A00–B99)

This chapter includes infectious and parasitic diseases that can be easily transmitted. Infectious and parasitic diseases include communicable diseases, as well as those of unknown origin but possibly due to infectious organisms. Infective organisms in this chapter include bacteria, chlamydia, fungi, helminthes, mycoplasmas, protozoans, rickettsias, and viruses.

When selecting codes from this category, two codes may be required. There are a few different ways codes from this category may be reported:

- Two codes: one for the organism and one for the condition
- A combination code for the organism and condition
- A single code

Example

A patient is diagnosed with cryptococcal meningitis. Refer to meningitis in the Index to Diseases and Injuries. Next, look for the sub term cryptococcal, which directs you to B45.1. In the Tabular List, B45.1 is for cerebral crypotococcosis. The inclusion terms underneath this code verify this code is reported for cryptococcal meningitis.

Next, look at an AIDS patient diagnosed with meningitis caused by histoplasmosis. Look in the Index to Diseases and Injuries for histoplasmosis, which directs you to B39.9. Look for B39.9 in the Tabular List. The category B39 has two notes associated with the category. The "Code First: associated AIDS (B20)" indicates B20 should be the first listed code. The second instructional note states to "Use Additional: code for any associated manifestations." Meningitis (G02) is one of the manifestations listed.

The codes and sequencing reported for this patient are:
B20   Human immunodeficiency virus [HIV] disease
B39.9   Histoplasmosis, unspecified
G02   Meningitis in other infectious and parasitic diseases classi-fied elsewhere

AAPC
www.aapc.com   77

Practical Coding Note

In the Index to Diseases and Injuries, brackets indicate the code within the brackets is sequenced after the code preceding the brackets. It is important to pay close attention to the conventions for proper diagnosis code selection and sequencing.

The chapter-specific coding guidelines for this chapter include: Human Immunodeficiency Virus (HIV) Infections; Infectious Agents as the Cause of Diseases Classified in Other Chapters; Infections Resistant to Antibiotics; Sepsis, Severe Sepsis, and Septic Shock; and Methicillin Resistant Staphylococcus Aureus (MRSA) conditions. Many infectious and parasitic diagnoses are found in the Index to Diseases and Injuries under the type of infection or parasitic disease; such as MRSA indexed under MRSA (Methicillin/resistant Staphylococcus aureus)/infection directing you to code A49.02. Then there are some infectious or parasitic diagnoses that are only found under the word Infection; such as Helicobacter pylori [H. pylori], indexed under Infection/Helicobacter pylori, directing you to code A04.8.

Sepsis and HIV contain some of the most difficult rules in the ICD-10-CM guidelines. This chapter might require more research time if you don't have a good understanding of these conditions. If you are having difficulty grasping these guidelines, move on to the next section and return to these guidelines after you become more familiar with coding in ICD-10-CM.

Human Immunodeficiency Virus (HIV)

HIV causes a broad spectrum of clinical problems that may mimic other diseases. Immediately after infection and for a prolonged period (more than several months in a small number of persons), the exposed individual remains antibody negative, or in a carrier state. During this time, the virus reproduces rapidly until the immune system begins to react and/or targets are exhausted. Some conditions attributable to HIV or complicated by HIV Type 2 [HIV-2] include bacillary angiomatosis, candidiasis, oropharyngeal thrush, vulvovaginitis, cervical dysplasia, and constitutional symptoms such as fever or diarrhea lasting more than one month. Other conditions include hairy leukoplakia, oral herpes zoster (shingles), idiopathic thrombocytopenic purpura (ITP), listeriosis, pelvic inflammatory disease (PID), and peripheral neuropathy.

There are a few things to consider when selecting the proper code for HIV. Is the patient asymptomatic, or known to have had an HIV-related condition in the past? What is the purpose of the admission or encounter? There are sequencing rules to follow when the patient is being treated for an HIV-related condition versus a non-HIV related condition (eg, injury from a car accident).

HIV infection/illness is coded only for confirmed cases. Confirmation does not require documentation of a positive blood test or culture for HIV; the physician's diagnostic statement that the patient is HIV positive or has an HIV-related illness is sufficient. In the inpatient setting, HIV is the only condition that must be confirmed to select the code. All other conditions documented as "probable," suspected," likely," "questionable," "probable," or "still to rule out" are coded as if they exist in the inpatient setting (Section II.H.).

The proper sequencing for HIV depends on the reason for the admission or encounter. When a patient is admitted for an HIV-related condition, B20 is sequenced first, followed by additional diagnosis codes for all reported HIV-related conditions. Conditions always considered HIV-related include Kaposi's sarcoma, lymphoma, Pneumocystis carinii pneumonia (PCP), cryptococcal meningitis, and cytomegaloviral disease. These conditions are considered opportunistic infections. A complete list can be found at AIDS.gov.

Pathologies Associated with AIDS

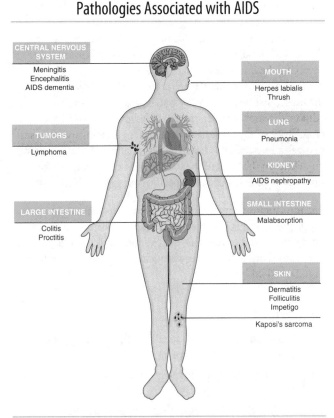

Source: Ehrlich, Medical Terminology for Health Professionals, 6e, ISBN #978-1-4180-7252-0

Example

A patient is admitted for Kaposi's sarcoma in the right lung. The correct codes and sequence are:

- B20 Human immunodeficiency virus [HIV] disease
- C46.51 Kaposi's sarcoma, right lung

In this example, the patient is admitted for an HIV-related condition (Kaposi's sarcoma), so ICD-10-CM code B20 is sequenced first, followed by C46.51. In the Tabular List, you will also note there is a Code First note under category code C46 indicating code B20 is reported as a primary code.

If a patient with HIV disease is admitted for an unrelated condition (eg, fracture), the code for the unrelated condition is sequenced first. Code B20 is reported as an additional diagnosis, as are any HIV-related conditions.

Z21 *Asymptomatic human immunodeficiency virus [HIV] infection status* is applied when the patient is HIV positive and does not have any documented symptoms of an HIV-related illness. Do not use this code if the term AIDS is used. If the patient is treated for any HIV-related illness, or is described as having any condition resulting from HIV positive status, use B20.

Patients with inconclusive HIV serology, and no definitive diagnosis or manifestations of the illness, may be assigned code R75 *Inconclusive laboratory evidence of human immunodeficiency virus [HIV].*

Known prior diagnosis of an HIV-related illness should be coded to B20. After a patient has developed an HIV-related illness, the patient's condition should be assigned code B20 on every subsequent admission/encounter. Never assign R75 or Z21 to a patient with an earlier diagnosis of AIDS or symptomatic HIV (B20).

Practical Coding Note

HIV-related conditions are also known as opportunistic infections. The Centers for Disease Control and Prevention (CDC) developed a list of opportunistic infections that will define the diagnosis of AIDS. This list includes Kaposi's sarcoma, tuberculosis, pneumocystitis carinii pneumonia, among others. A complete list of conditions that move a patient from HIV status to AIDS can be found at aids.gov.

HIV infection status during pregnancy, childbirth, or the puerperium should be reported using the codes from subcategory O98.7- *Human immunodeficiency [HIV] disease complicating pregnancy, childbirth, and the puerperium* and Z21 when the patient is asymptomatic with no history of an HIV-related illness. When the encounter is to treat an HIV-related illness, or the patient has had an HIV-related illness in the past, the proper sequence is O98.7-, B20, and the code for the HIV-related illness if treated during the current encounter. Codes

from ICD-10-CM chapter 15 always take sequencing priority and should be listed first.

Example

A patient who is four weeks pregnant is diagnosed with HIV. She has not experienced any HIV-related conditions. The proper code selection is O98.711, Z21, Z3A.01.

In this example, the patient is in the first trimester of pregnancy. The code from ICD-10-CM chapter 15 (O98.711) is sequenced first. Because the patient neither has any symptoms of HIV nor is there documentation of any past HIV-related illnesses, code Z21 is reported and sequenced second. To find O98.7-, look in the Index to Diseases and Injuries for Pregnancy/complicated by (care of) (management affected by)/HIV O98.71-☑. Sixth character 1 is reported to indicate the patient is in the first trimester. The final code to report for this scenario is to report the weeks of gestation (discussed in Chapter 5 of this curriculum). Look in the Index to Diseases and Injuries for Pregnancy/weeks of gestation/less than 8 weeks Z3A.01.

If a patient is being seen to determine HIV status, use code Z11.4 *Encounter for screening for human immunodeficiency virus [HIV]*. Should a patient with signs, symptoms or illness, or a confirmed HIV-related diagnosis be tested for HIV, code the signs and symptoms or the diagnosis. If the results are positive and the patient is symptomatic, report code B20 with codes for the HIV-related symptoms or diagnosis. The HIV counseling code (Z71.7) may be used if counseling is provided for patients with positive test results. When a patient believes that he/she has been exposed to or has come into contact with the HIV virus code, Z20.6 is reported.

Example

1. A patient with AIDS developed encephalitis as a manifestation of AIDS and is seen in the office for the encephalitis. The appropriate ICD-10-CM codes and sequencing are:

    - B20 Human immunodeficiency virus [HIV] disease; and
    - G05.3 Encephalitis and encephalomyelitis in diseases classified elsewhere

    In the Index to Diseases and Injuries, look for Encephalitis/due to/human immunodeficiency virus [HIV] disease B20 [G05.3]. In this example, encephalitis is the reason for the office visit. The encephalitis is stated as related to AIDS, so B20 is reported first, with G05.3 as a secondary diagnosis.

2. A symptomatic HIV patient is at the initial visit for a sprained left ankle. The appropriate ICD-10-CM codes and sequencing are:

- S93.402A Sprains of unspecified ligament of left ankle, initial encounter;

and

- B20 Human immunodeficiency virus [HIV] disease (followed by additional diagnosis codes for all reported HIV-related conditions).

In this example, the patient is seen for a sprained ankle, which is unrelated to HIV, so it is sequenced first. Because HIV affects treatment for any condition, B20 is reported second. Any additional diagnosis codes for all reported HIV-related conditions would also be reported. Provider documentation should support reporting of HIV under these circumstances.

In the Index to Diseases and Injuries, look for Sprain/ankle S93.40- ☑. In the Tabular List, the sixth character 2 indicates the left ankle. The seventh character A indicates the initial encounter. Then, look in the Index to Diseases and Injuries for HIV B20. Verify code selection in the Tabular List.

Infectious Agents as the Cause of Diseases Classified to Other Chapters

Certain infections are classified in chapters other than chapter 1 and no organism is identified as part of the infection code. In these instances, it is necessary to use an additional code from chapter 1 to identify the organism. A code from category B95 *Streptococcus, Staphylococcus, and Enterococcus as the cause of diseases classified elsewhere*, B96 *Other bacterial agents as the cause of diseases classified elsewhere*, or B97 *Viral agents as the cause of diseases classified elsewhere*, is to be used as an additional code to identify the organism. An instructional note will be found at the infection code advising that an additional organism code is required.

Example

A patient has toxic shock syndrome caused by Staphylococcus aureus. The appropriate ICD-10-CM codes and sequencing are:

- A48.3 Toxic Shock Syndrome
- B95.61 Methicillin susceptible Staphylococcus aureus infection as the cause of diseases classified elsewhere

In the Index to Diseases and Injuries, look for Toxic/shock syndrome A48.3. In the Tabular List, there is a note under A48.3, to use an additional code to identify the organism (B95, B96). Look in the Index to Diseases and Injuries for Staphylococcus, staphylococcal/as cause of disease classified elsewhere/aureus (methicillin susceptible) (MSSA) B95.61. Note that there is an inclusion term under B95.61 for *Staphylococcus aureus infection NOS as the cause of diseases classified elsewhere*, verifying B95.61 is the correct code.

Infections Resistant to Antibiotics

Many bacterial infections are resistant to antimicrobial drugs. It is necessary to identify all infections documented as antibiotic resistant. In the Tabular List, in the beginning of chapter 1, there is a note to assign a code from category Z16, *Resistance to antimicrobial drugs*. A code from category Z16 follows the infection code only if the infection code does not identify drug resistance.

Example

A patient has penicillin-resistant pneumonia.

J18.9　Pneumonia, unspecified organism

Z16.11　Resistance to penicillins

Look in the Index to Diseases and Injuries for Pneumonia J18.9. Then, look for Resistance, resistant (to)/organism(s)/to/drug/penicillins Z16.11. Verify code selection in the Tabular List.

Sepsis, Severe Sepsis, and Septic Shock

Sepsis refers to an infection due to any organism that triggers a systemic inflammatory response, or system inflammatory response syndrome (SIRS). All codes with sepsis in the title include the concept of SIRS. For cases of sepsis that do not result in any associated organ dysfunction, a single code for the type of sepsis is used.

For a diagnosis of sepsis, assign the appropriate code for the underlying systemic infection. If the type of infection or causal organism is not further specified, assign code A41.9 *Sepsis, unspecified organism*. A code from subcategory R65.2 Severe sepsis should not be assigned unless severe sepsis or an associated acute organ dysfunction is documented.

Negative or inconclusive blood cultures do not preclude a diagnosis of sepsis in patients with clinical evidence of the condition, however, the provider should be queried.

Urosepsis is considered a nonspecific term. It is not to be considered synonymous with sepsis. When a provider documents urosepsis, the provider must be queried for further clarification.

Sepsis with an acute organ dysfunction (eg, renal failure) is considered severe sepsis. If a patient has sepsis and associated acute organ dysfunction or multiple organ dysfunction (MOD), follow the instructions for coding severe sepsis.

If a patient has sepsis and an acute organ dysfunction, but the medical record indicates that the acute organ dysfunction is related to a medical condition other than the sepsis, do not assign a code from subcategory R65.2 Severe sepsis. An acute organ dysfunction must be associated with the sepsis in order to assign the severe sepsis code. If the documentation is not clear as to whether an acute organ dysfunction is related to the sepsis or another medical condition, query the provider.

Practical Coding Note

Codes R65.20-R65.21 cannot be sequenced first. A code from this code range is always sequenced following the underlying cause.

Severe sepsis requires a minimum of two codes: First a code for the underlying systemic infection followed by a code from subcategory R65.2 *Severe sepsis*. If the causal organism is not documented, assign code A41.9 *Sepsis, unspecified organism* for the additional infection. Select an additional code to report each appropriate organ dysfunction. If the patient has sepsis with MOD, list a code to identify each organ dysfunction. Do not code severe sepsis if the documentation indicates the acute organ dysfunction is caused by another condition. If the documentation is not clear, query the physician of the cause of the acute organ dysfunction.

Example

The patient's diagnoses include sepsis, acute kidney failure, and bladder cancer. The documentation needs to be reviewed to determine if the acute kidney failure is caused by sepsis or the bladder cancer. If the cause of the acute kidney failure is sepsis, and it is the reason for the admission, the correct coding sequence is:

- A41.9 Sepsis, unspecified organism
- R65.20 Severe sepsis, without septic shock
- N17.9 Acute kidney failure, unspecified
- C67.9 Malignant neoplasm of bladder, part unspecified

Severe sepsis without septic shock (E65.20) is reported because the organ failure is a result of the sepsis, making it severe sepsis. In the Index to Diseases and Injuries, look for Sepsis/with/organ dysfunction (acute) (multiple) and you are directed to code R65.20 which is Severe Sepsis. In addition, there is an inclusion term under code R65.2 for Sepsis with acute organ dysfunction, verifying this is the correct code subcategory.

If the cause of the acute kidney failure is bladder cancer, the correct codes and sequence depend on the condition chiefly responsible for the admission. If the reason for the admission is bladder cancer, the correct codes and sequence are C67.9, N17.9, and A41.9. If the reason for the admission is acute kidney failure, the correct codes and sequence are N17.9, C67.9, and A41.9. This is coded as sepsis (A41.9) and not severe sepsis (A41.9, R65.20) because the acute organ dysfunction is not caused by sepsis.

In the Index to Diseases and Injuries, look for Sepsis/with/organ dysfunction (acute) (multiple) and you are directed to code R65.20. Subcategory R65.2 has a code first note to code

the underlying infection first and then any associated acute organ dysfunction second. The underlying infection is Sepsis, NOS which directs you to A41.9. Acute kidney failure is found by looking for Failure/renal/acute N17.9. Remember renal pertains to the kidneys. For bladder cancer, look for Cancer. This refers you to *see also* Neoplasm, by site, malignant. Go to the Neoplasm Table and look for bladder (urinary) and use the code from the Malignant Primary column C67.9.

Septic shock is circulatory failure associated with severe sepsis. When coding septic shock, always code first the underlying systemic infection followed by R65.21 *Severe sepsis with septic shock*, or code T81.12 *Postprocedural septic shock* and an additional code for the acute organ dysfunction.

If the reason for admission is both sepsis or severe sepsis and a localized infection, such as pneumonia or cellulitis, a code(s) for the underlying systemic infection should be assigned first and the code for the localized infection should be assigned as a secondary diagnosis. If the patient is admitted with a localized infection, such as pneumonia, and sepsis/severe sepsis doesn't develop until after admission, the localized infection should be assigned first, followed by the appropriate sepsis/severe sepsis code.

Following a procedure, a patient may develop sepsis. If the provider documents a causal relationship between the sepsis and the procedure, it is considered a post-procedural complication. The first listed diagnosis indentifies the complication (for example, a code from subcategory T81.4 *Infection following a procedure*) followed by the code for the specific infection. If the patient has severe sepsis, the appropriate code from subcategory R65.2 should also be assigned. An additional diagnosis is reported if any acute organ dysfunctions are documented.

In cases where a postprocedural infection has occurred and has resulted in severe sepsis and postprocedural septic shock, the code for the precipitating complication, such as a code from subcategory T81.4 *Infection following a procedure*, is coded first, followed by code R65.21 *Severe sepsis with septic shock* and a code for the systemic infection.

In some cases, a noninfectious process (condition), such as trauma, may lead to an infection resulting in sepsis or severe sepsis. If sepsis or severe sepsis is documented as associated with a noninfectious condition, such as a burn or serious injury, and this condition meets the definition for principal diagnosis, the code for the noninfectious condition should be sequenced first, followed by the code for the resulting infection. If severe sepsis is present, a code from subcategory R65.2 should also be assigned with any associated organ dysfunction(s) codes. It is not necessary to assign a code from subcategory R65.1 *Systemic inflammatory response syndrome (SIRS) of non-infectious origin* for these cases.

If the infection meets the definition of principal diagnosis, it should be sequenced before the noninfectious condition. When both the associated non-infectious condition and the infection meet the definition of principal diagnosis, either may be assigned as principal diagnosis.

Only one code from category R65 *Symptoms and signs specifically associated with systemic inflammation and infection* should be assigned. Therefore, when a non-infectious condition leads to an infection resulting in severe sepsis, assign the appropriate code from subcategory R65.2 *Severe sepsis*. Do not additionally assign a code from subcategory R65.1. See Section I.C.18.g. SIRS due to non-infectious process. Also refer to ICD-10-CM Official Guidelines I.C.1.d for reporting sepsis, severe sepsis, and septic shock.

Practical Coding Note

To code severe sepsis, it is helpful to go to the Tabular List and highlight the code first note and the use additional code note under R65.2-. Write a brief note to show how the codes are reported and sequenced. Such as:

Underlying infection

R65.2- Severe sepsis

Associated organ dysfunction

To code sepsis and severe sepsis associated with a noninfectious condition, report:

The non-infectious condition

Resulting infection (sepsis or severe sepsis)

There are combination codes in chapter 1 that identify the infection and specific type of causal organism(s) within the code description. For example, sepsis due to Streptococcus Group A is reported with one code A40.0. An additional code for Streptococcus Group A (B95.0) is not reported as an additional code because the code description for A40 includes the type of infection (sepsis) and the causal organism (Streptococcus Group A).

Methicillin Resistant Staphylococcus Aureus (MRSA) Conditions

MRSA is any strain of staphylococcus aureus that has developed a resistance to antibiotics. It is a difficult infection to treat. There are combination codes that report the infection and the causal agent. For example, a patient with methicillin resistant pneumonia due to Staphylococcus aureus is reported with combination code J15.212. If there is not a combination code, report a code for the condition and B95.62 *Methicillin resistant Staphylococcus aureus infection as the cause of diseases classified elsewhere.* Do not assign a code from subcategory X16.11 *Resistance to penicillins* as an additional diagnosis.

If the patient is a carrier of MRSA and does not have an active infection, report code Z22.322 *Carrier or suspected carrier of Methicillin resistant Staphylococcus aureus.* A personal history of MRSA, with no mention of colonization, should be reported with Z86.14.

Example

A patient with a history of MRSA is scheduled for a right hip replacement to treat osteoarthritis of her hip. The correct codes and sequence are:

M16.11 Unilateral primary osteoarthritis, right hip

Z86.14 Personal history of Methicillin resistant Staphylococcus aureus infection

Osteoarthritis is found in the Index to Diseases and Injuries by looking for Osteoarthritis/hip M16.1-☑. In the Tabular List, M16.11 is reported for the osteoarthritis of the right hip. Personal history of MRSA is found in the Index to Diseases and Injuries by looking for History/personal (of)/Methicillin resistant Staphylococcus aureus (MRSA) Z86.14. Verify all codes in the Tabular List.

Key Suffixes and Prefixes

bacteri/o	Bacteria
-coccus (-cocci, pl)	Berry-shaped bacterium
pyr/o	Fever
pyret/o	Fever
pyrex/o	Fever
seps/o	Infection
staphyl/o	Clusters

Acronyms

AIDS	Acquired immune deficiency syndrome
HIV	Human immunodeficiency virus
ICD-10-CM	International Classification of Diseases, 10th Revision, Clinical Modification
MRSA	Methicillin-resistant Staphylococcus aureus
MSSA	Methicillin-susceptible Staphylococcus aureus
OI	Opportunistic infection
SA	Staphylococcus aureus
SIRS	Systemic inflammatory response syndrome

Section Review 4.1

1. A patient is admitted to the hospital for repair of an open fracture, type 1, of the head of the left femur. The patient has been previously diagnosed with symptomatic HIV. Applying the coding concept from ICD-10-CM Guideline Section I.C.1.a.2.b., what ICD-10-CM code(s) is/are reported for the admission?

    A. B20

    B. S72.052B

    C. B20, S72.052B

    D. S72.052B, B20

2. A 22-year-old female is admitted to ICU for acute renal (kidney) failure due to sepsis (causal organism unknown). Applying the coding concept from ICD-10-CM Guideline Section I.C.1.d.1.b., what ICD-10-CM codes are reported (in the correct sequencing)?

    A. A41.9, R65.20, N17.9

    B. N17.9, R65.20, A41.9

    C. R65.21, A41.9, N17.9

    D. N17.9, R65.21, A41.01

3. A patient is admitted to the hospital with pneumonia. Testing indicates the patient's pneumonia is due to Staphylacoccus aureus and is methicillin resistant (MRSA). Applying the coding concept from ICD-10-CM Guideline Section I.C.1.e.1.a., what ICD-10-CM code(s) are reported?

    A. J18.9

    B. J15.212

    C. J15.212, A49.02

    D. J18.9, A49.02

Chapter 2: Neoplasms (Codes C00–D49)

A neoplasm is an abnormal growth of new tissue. There are two ways to begin the search for neoplasm codes. If the histology is documented, look up the term in the Index to Diseases and Injuries. For example, if the patient is diagnosed with basal-squamous cell carcinoma on the forehead, look for Carcinoma/basal-squamous cell, mixed. You are referred to *see* Neoplasm, skin, malignant. This statement is referring you to the Table of Neoplasms, which is found at the end of the Index to Diseases and Injuries. The second way to search for a neoplasm code is to begin in the Table of Neoplasm.

Table of Neoplasms

Information in the Table of Neoplasms is organized alphabetically by site. Using the table, each site is broken into six categories: malignant primary, malignant secondary, Ca in situ, benign, uncertain behavior, and unspecified.

ICD-9-CM Application

In the ICD-9-CM codebook, the Table of Neoplasms is located under Neoplasm in the Alphabetic Index instead of at the end of the index.

	Malignant Primary	Malignant Secondary	Ca in situ	Benign	Uncertain Behavior	Unspecified
Neoplasm, neoplastic	C80.1	C79.9	D09.9	D36.9	D48.9	D49.9
abdomen, abdominal	C76.2	C79.8-	D09.8	D36.7	D48.7	D49.89
Cavity	C76.2	C79.8-	D09.8	D36.7	D48.7	D49.89
Organ	C76.2	C79.8-	D09.8	D36.7	D48.7	D49.89
Viscera	C76.2	C79.8-	D09.8	D36.7	D48.7	D49.89
wall (see also Neoplasm, abdomen, wall, skin)	C44.509	C79.2-	D04.5	D23.5	D48.5	D49.2
connective tissue	C49.4	C79.8-	-	D21.4	D48.1	D49.2
Skin	C44.509					
basal cell carcinoma	C44.519	-	-	-	-	-
specified type NEC	C44.599	-	-	-	-	-
squamous cell carcinoma	C44.529	-	-	-	-	-
abdominopelvic	C76.8	C79.8-	-	D36.7	D48.7	D49.89
accessory sinus—see Neoplasm, sinus						
acoustic nerve	C72.4-	C79.49	-	D33.3	D43.3	D49.7

A primary malignancy is where the cancer originates. A secondary malignancy results from metastasis and forms a new focus of malignancy elsewhere (such as the lymph nodes, liver, lungs, or brain), or develops when the primary cancer has invaded adjacent structures. For example, a patient has brain cancer that metastasizes to the spinal cord. In this case, the primary location is the brain, and the secondary location is the spinal cord.

In situ describes a malignancy confined to the origin site, without invading neighboring tissues. That is, the neoplasm is encapsulated (think of the yolk within the shell of an egg). It may also be called non-infiltrating carcinoma, non-invasive carcinoma, or pre-invasive carcinoma. This type of neoplasm may grow large enough to cause major problems. The pathologist, rather than the physician, designates a diagnosis of Ca *in situ*.

The fourth column of the Table of Neoplasms identifies benign neoplasms, which do not contain precancerous or cancerous cells.

If the pathology report returns with indications of atypia or dysplasia, the neoplasm is in transition from benign to malignant (precancerous). This is a neoplasm of uncertain behavior: It is not benign because benign has no precancerous cells, and it is not malignant because it has not become cancer yet. If the process continues and the mass is left untreated, the neoplasm eventually could become malignant. A diagnosis of "uncertain behavior" is based on the pathologist's report. For example, if the physician documents a mass "of uncertain behavior," you should not select an uncertain behavior code from the Table of Neoplasms. Instead, you would code for the mass.

Unspecified indicates the provider cannot, or has not, determined the neoplasm's nature. If the provider excises a lipoma but does not wait for the pathology report, an unspecified code is reported. It is recommended to wait for the pathology report to report the most specific code.

Practical Coding Note

It is recommended to hold claims for surgical procedures until the pathology report is returned. The pathology report will confirm the morphology of the specimen and allow the most accurate code selection. Until the pathology report is received, the only code option is from the unspecified column in the Table of Neoplasms.

Many kinds of neoplasms are excluded from the Table of Neoplasms. For example, lipomas, melanomas, and Merkel cell carcinomas are not included in the Table of Neoplasms, but are addressed in the Index to Diseases and Injuries. Some polyps and other conditions are indexed to benign neoplasms, but you would know this only by starting in the Index to Diseases and Injuries. The Index to Diseases and Injuries and the Table of Neoplasms each have instructions very useful to coders. Do not skip these steps.

For most neoplasms, coders will start with the Index to Diseases and Injuries, then consult the Table of Neoplasms, then move to the Tabular List. For Merkel cell carcinoma, lipoma, and melanoma, you will flip from the Index to Diseases and Injuries, directly to the Tabular List.

For malignant neoplasms, determine the primary and secondary sites and then code first the site requiring patient care. If the initial or primary cancer is still active and represents the reason for the service, list the code for the primary site first. If a secondary growth is the primary reason for the patient care, choose a code from the secondary column of the table, which is listed first.

One person may have multiple malignant neoplasms in the same site. For example, a woman may have tumors in different quadrants of the same breast. When these sites are next to each other (contiguous), the subcategory for "overlapping lesion" should be assigned. When they are at the same site, but are not contiguous, a code is assigned for each site.

Example

A female patient with a neoplasm in the upper outer quadrant and another contiguous neoplasm in the lower outer quadrant of the right breast. Because the sites are contiguous, one code is reported:

C50.811 Malignant neoplasm of overlapping sites of right female breast.

Example

A female patient with a neoplasm in the upper outer quadrant and another neoplasm in the lower inner quadrant of the right breast. Because these are not contiguous sites, two codes are reported:

C50.411 Malignant neoplasm of upper-outer quadrant of right female breast.

C50.311 Malignant neoplasm of lower-inner quadrant of right female breast.

ICD-9-CM does not provide a code for overlapping sites.

ICD-9-CM does provide a code for overlapping sites, which are listed as other specified codes.

174.8 Other specified site of female breast

Malignant neoplasm of contiguous or overlapping sites of breast whose point of origin cannot be determined

164.8 Other malignant neoplasm of thymus, heart, and mediastinum

Malignant neoplasm of contiguous or overlapping sites of thymus, heart, and mediastinum whose point of origin cannot be determined

153.8 Other specified sites of large intestine

Malignant neoplasm of contiguous or overlapping sites of colon whose point of origin cannot be determined

Malignant neoplasms of ectopic tissue are to be coded to the site of origin mentioned. For example, ectopic malignancy of the thyroid is coded to C73 *Malignant neoplasm of thyroid gland*.

If information regarding the primary site is not available when the encounter is directed at the secondary (metastatic) site, select a code for the secondary site first followed by C80.1.

Example

Metastatic cancer to the right lung; primary unknown. The correct codes are:

C78.01 Secondary malignant neoplasm of right lung; and

C80.1 Malignant (primary) neoplasm, unspecified.

The term "metastatic" indicates a secondary malignancy. In this example, right lung cancer is secondary to another cancer. To find the code for right lung cancer, look in the Table of Neoplasms for lung and select the code from the Secondary Malignancy column. In the Tabular List, C78.01 is selected to indicate the right lung. The origin, or primary site, of cancer is unknown so ICD-10-CM code C78.01 is reported as a secondary diagnosis. To find the unspecified site malignancy, go to the Table of Neoplasms and look for the first listed term at the beginning of the table, Neoplasm, neoplastic and select the code from the Primary Malignancy column. Verify all codes in the Tabular List.

It is not uncommon for a patient with cancer to develop anemia as a result of cancer, or as a result of the cancer treatment (chemotherapy). When the patient develops anemia because of the neoplasm and presents for treatment of the anemia, the code for the malignancy is listed first, followed by the code for the anemia (D63.0). If the anemia is caused by the chemotherapy or radiotherapy, the anemia code is reported first, followed by the appropriate codes for the neoplasm and the adverse effect (T45.1X5 or Y84.2).

ICD-9-CM Application

In ICD-9-CM, the sequencing for anemia associated with a malignancy is reversed. When the patient is being seen for management of the anemia associated with malignancy, the code for anemia is reported first.

When a patient becomes dehydrated because of the malignancy, and only the dehydration is being treated, first sequence the code for dehydration followed by the code to report the malignancy. When an encounter is directed at a surgical complication, the surgical complication is the first listed diagnosis.

After a neoplasm has been treated successfully, it is inappropriate to use the neoplasm codes for follow-up care. Offices should use a code from category Z85 *Personal history of malignant neoplasm* for the following situations:

- The primary malignancy has been removed, and is no longer being treated.
- The patient is not receiving chemotherapy or radiotherapy associated with an active neoplasm.
- There is no evidence of any remaining malignancy.

Example

Colon cancer removed three years ago with no recurrence and no current treatment for colon cancer. The correct code is Z85.038 because there is no active treatment for colon cancer and colon cancer has been removed. To find the code in the Index to Diseases and Injuries, look for History/personal (of)/malignant neoplasm (of)/colon NEC Z85.038. Verify codes in the Tabular List.

When an episode of care involves the surgical removal of a neoplasm followed by chemotherapy or radiation treatment during the same visit, the neoplasm code should be assigned as principal or first listed diagnosis, followed by the code for the therapy.

To report an encounter when the main reason is for administration of chemotherapy (Z51.11), immunotherapy (Z51.12) and radiotherapy (Z51.0), report the Z code first, followed by the active code for the malignant neoplasm (even if that neoplasm

has already been removed). As long as the neoplasm is being treated as adjunctive therapy following a surgical removal of the cancer, it is coded as if the neoplasm still exists. You would not assign a "history of" code because the neoplasm is the reason for the treatment. Instead, the neoplasm is coded as a current or active disease. When treatment for the eradicated neoplasm is completed, a history code can be assigned. If complications develop during an encounter for chemotherapy, immunotherapy or radiotherapy, the code for the chemotherapy, immunotherapy, or radiotherapy is listed first followed by the code for the complication.

Example

A female patient is seen for chemotherapy for right breast cancer previously removed by mastectomy. The correct codes are:

- Z51.11 Encounter for antineoplastic chemotherapy; and
- C50.911 Malignant neoplasm of unspecified site of right female breast.

Even though the patient's cancer has been removed by mastectomy, breast cancer is still being treated with chemotherapy; breast cancer is coded as an active condition instead of a history of code. Find the code for Chemotherapy by looking in the Index to Diseases and Injuries for Chemotherapy (session) (for)/cancer or neoplasm. For breast cancer, look in the Table of Neoplasms for breast and select the code from the Primary Malignancy column. In the Tabular List, C50.911 is selected to indicate the right breast for a female.

When the reason for admission/encounter is to determine the extent of the malignancy, or for a procedure such as paracentesis or thoracentesis, the primary malignancy or appropriate metastatic site is designated as the principal or first listed diagnosis, despite the administration of chemotherapy or radiotherapy.

Symptoms, signs, and ill-defined conditions listed in chapter 18 characteristic of, or associated with, and existing primary or secondary site malignancy cannot be used to replace the malignancy as principal or first-listed diagnosis, regardless of the number of admissions or encounters for treatment and care of the neoplasm. Reference "Factors influencing health status and contact with health services," encounter for prophylactic organ removal (Section I.C.21.c.14).

A patient may have more than one malignant tumor in the same organ. These tumors may represent different primaries or metastatic disease, depending on the site. Should the documentation be unclear, the provider should be queried as to the status of each tumor so that the correct codes can be assigned.

Code C80.0 *Disseminated malignant neoplasm, unspecified* is for use only in those cases where the patient has advanced metastatic disease and no known primary or secondary sites are specified. It should not be used in place of assigning codes for the primary site and all known secondary sites.

Code C80.1 *Malignant (primary) neoplasm, unspecified* equates to cancer, unspecified. This code should only be used when no determination can be made as to the primary site of a malignancy. This code should rarely be used in the inpatient setting.

Sequencing of Neoplasms

Reason for Treatment	Sequencing
Primary malignancy	Primary malignancy is listed first, followed by any metastatic site(s)
Secondary malignancy	Secondary malignancy is listed first, followed by primary malignancy
Pregnant patient with malignant neoplasm	A code from subcategory O9A.1- *Malignant neoplasm complicating pregnancy, childbirth, and the puerperium* is sequenced first followed by a code for the neoplasm
Complication associated with a neoplasm	Complication is listed first, followed by the neoplasm code. An exception to this is anemia
Complication from a surgical procedure for treatment of a neoplasm	The complication is the listed first, followed by a code for the neoplasm or history of neoplasm
Pathologic fracture due to a neoplasm	When the pathologic fracture is the focus of the treatment, a code from subcategory M84.5 *Pathologic fracture in neoplastic disease* is sequenced first, followed by a code for the neoplasm. When the neoplasm is the focus of the treatment, the code for the neoplasm is first, followed by a code for the pathologic fracture.

The categories for leukemia, and category C90, *Multiple myeloma and malignant plasma cell neoplasms*, have codes for when this type of malignancy is in remission. There are also codes Z85.6 *Personal history of leukemia* and Z85.79 *Personal history of other malignant neoplasms of lymphoid, hematopoietic and related tissues*. If the documentation is unclear as to whether the patient is in remission, the provider should be queried.

A malignant neoplasm of a transplanted organ requires three codes. First, report the transplant complication from subcategory T86.- *Complication of transplanted organs and tissue*. Next, report C80.2, followed by the code to specify the malig-

nancy (third code). Notice the note under C80.2, which states, "Code first complication of transplanted organ (T86.-)" and "Use additional code to identify the specific malignancy."

Example

A patient who received a kidney transplant one year ago is diagnosed with right renal (kidney) cancer. From the Index to Diseases and Injuries, look for Complication/transplant/kidney (T86.10). To find the code for the transplanted organ, look in the Table of Neoplasms for Associated with transplanted organ and use the code from the Malignant Primary column. Code C80.2 is listed next. Go to the Table of Neoplasms and look for kidney, and refer to the Malignant Primary column (C64.-). In the Tabular List, C64.1 is selected to indicate the right kidney. The correct coding is:

- T86.10 Unspecified complications of kidney transplant
- C80.2 Malignant neoplasm associated with transplanted organ
- C64.1 Malignant neoplasm of right kidney, except renal pelvis

Merkel Cell Carcinoma

Merkel cell carcinoma is a rare and aggressive form of a skin tumor. Merkel cells release hormones into the blood stream and play a role in skin sensitivity. This type of carcinoma, which has a higher mortality rate than melanoma, is seen most commonly in older people.

Codes for Merkel cell carcinoma are found in the Index to Diseases and Injuries by looking for Carcinoma/Merkel cell. Codes are found in category C4A and are selected based on anatomic site.

Example

Merkel cell carcinoma of the neck is coded with C4A.4. The code is found by looking in the Index to Diseases and Injuries for Carcinoma/Merkel cell/neck.

Melanoma

Melanoma is skin cancer that originates in cells called melanocytes, which produce pigment in the skin. Melanoma often starts as a mole. This is not to say that all moles are melanoma. Many moles are benign, but should be watched closely for changes that are characteristic of melanoma. These characteristics include asymmetry (uneven growth), border irregularity (irregular or ill-defined), color (varying shades of color), and size (progressively increase in size.)

ABCD Signs of Melanoma

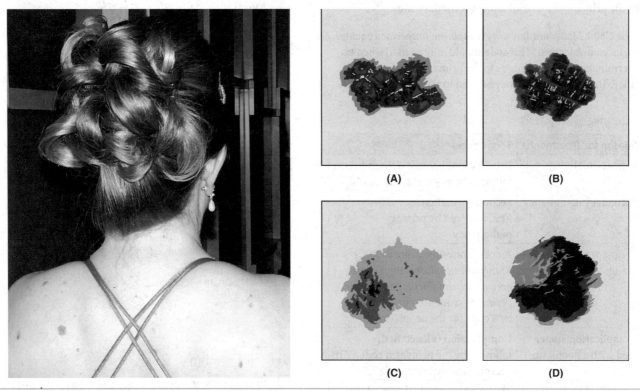

Source: Ehrlich, Medical Terminology for Health Professionals, 6e, ISBN #978-1-4180-7252-0

To locate the correct code, start with the main term Melanoma in the Index to Diseases and Injuries. The sub terms found under melanoma identify the site. Melanoma can develop anywhere but is more common on areas that have sun exposure.

Example

A life guard notices a mole on her left elbow has doubled in size in the last two months. She goes to the dermatologist to have it examined. The dermatologist performs a complete exam of her skin and finds two additional questionable moles on her back. Biopsies are performed on all sites and pathology confirms it is melanoma. She is diagnosed with melanoma on her elbow and her back.

Because there are two separate sites, two codes are required. From the Index to Diseases and Injuries, look up Melanoma/skin/elbow C43.6-. In the Tabular List, C43.62 is selected to indicate the left upper limb. The second code is found by looking for Melanoma/skin/back C43.59. Both codes must be reviewed in the Tabular List to verify the codes are accurate.

Lymphoma

Lymphoma is cancer of the lymphatic system. The lymphatic system is part of the immune system. There are two main types of lymphoma, Hodgkin's and non-Hodgkin's. There are cells found in Hodgkin's lymphoma (Reed Steinberg cells) not found in other types of lymphoma. The codes for lymphoma are selected by type and anatomic site.

Follicular lymphoma is a slow-growing lymphoma that arises from B-cells. It is coded based by grade and are often graded on a scale from 1 to 3, which designates how many large cells (centroblasts - a general term encompassing both large and small noncleaved follicular center cells) are found in a high power field. Large follicular cells are generally more aggressive and therefore while a true Grade 3 follicular lymphoma is not common, they do have a shorter natural history and more aggressive behavior.

The grades are defined as:

Grade 1: 0-5 centroblasts per high power field

Grade 2: 6-15 centroblasts per high power field

Grade 3: > 15 centroblasts per high power field

Grade 3 is further subdivided into:

Grade 3A: centrocytes (smaller cells) are still present

Grade 3B: the follicles consist almost entirely of centroblasts

In order to code follicular lymphomas, a coder must understand not only the grades but also what lymph nodes are affected.

When a patient has a primary cancer that has metastasized to lymph nodes, the code is not reported with category C81-C96. The Tabular List refers you to code category C77.-.

Example

A female patient with left breast cancer has metastatic cancer to the axillary lymph nodes. She is coming in for chemotherapy for the breast cancer and lymph node cancer. The correct codes and sequence are:

- Z51.11 Encounter for antineoplastic chemotherapy;
- C50.912 Malignant neoplasm of unspecified site of left female breast; and
- C77.3 Secondary and unspecified malignant neoplasm of axilla and upper limb lymph nodes

The reason for the visit is chemotherapy, and is listed as the primary diagnosis. It is found in the Index to Diseases and Injuries by looking for Chemotherapy (session) (for)/neoplasm. Next, are the primary and secondary neoplasms. Look in the Table of Neoplasms for breast and use the code from the Malignant Primary column C50.9-. C50.912 is selected for the left breast of a female patient. The lymph node cancer is metastatic indicating it is secondary. In the Table of Neoplasms, find Lymph, lymphatic channel NEC/gland (secondary)/axilla, axillary and select the code from the Malignant Secondary column C77.3.

Neoplasm Related Pain

Code G89.3 is reported when pain is documented as being related, associated with or due to primary or secondary cancer, or tumor. The documentation does not have to state that the pain is acute or chronic to assign this code. Code G89.3 is reported as a primary code when documentation indicates that the reason for the patient's visit is for pain control/pain management that is due to the neoplasm or tumor. The neoplasm code is reported as the additional code. There is no need to report an additional code for the anatomic site of the pain. When documentation indicates the reason for the patient's visit is for management of the neoplasm and the pain associated with the neoplasm, code G89.3 is reported as an additional diagnosis.

Example

A patient is seen for the management of right lung cancer and complains of pain in the rib area due to the cancer. To locate the codes, look in the Table of Neoplasms for lung and select the code from the Malignant Primary column (C34.9-). In the Tabular

List, C34.91 is selected for the right lung. Next, look for Pain/due to malignancy (primary) (secondary) G89.3. Because the patient is seen for the management of lung cancer, the proper codes and sequence for this encounter are:

- C34.91 Malignant neoplasm of unspecified part of right bronchus and lung
- G89.3 Neoplasm related pain (acute) (chronic)

Key Roots, Suffixes, and Prefixes for Neoplasm

ana-	backward
cac/o	bad
carcin/o	cancer, cancerous
chem/o	chemotherapy
cyst/o	sac of fluid
-genesis	formation
neo-	new
-oma	mass, tumor
-plasm	formation, growth
sarc/o	flesh, connective tissue
-therapy	treatment

Acronyms/Abbreviations

Bx	Biopsy
CA	Cancer
Chemo	Chemotherapy
Mets	Metastases/metastatic

Section Review 4.2

1. A 32-year-old female had a mastectomy for breast cancer. The mastectomy completely removed the breast cancer with no further treatment. On a follow-up visit to her oncologist, it is determined the cancer has metastasized to the right lung. The patient is now undergoing a lung resection for the lung cancer. Applying the coding concept from ICD-10-CM guidelines, sections I.C.2.b. and I.C.2.d., what ICD-10-CM codes are reported for the lung resection?

    A. C50.911, C78.01

    B. Z85.3, C78.01

    C. C78.01, C50.911

    D. C78.01, Z85.3

2. A 45-year-old female with ovarian cancer visits her oncologist to receive an injection of Procrit. The Procrit has been prescribed to her for treatment of her anemia resulting from antineoplastic chemotherapy treatment. Applying the coding concept from ICD-10-CM guidelines, section I.C.2.c.2., what ICD-10-CM codes should be reported?

    A. D64.81, T45.1X5A

    B. D64.81, C56.9

    C. C56.9, D64.81

    D. T45.1X5A, D64.81

3. A patient with a Pancoast tumor in the left lung arrives at the oncologist office for chemotherapy. Applying the coding concept from ICD-10-CM guidelines, section I.C.2.e.2., what ICD-10-CM code(s) should be reported? Note: Use the Alphabetic Index instead of the Table of Neoplasms to locate the code for a Pancoast tumor.

    A. C34.12

    B. Z51.11

    C. C34.12, Z51.11

    D. Z51.11, C34.12

Chapter 3: Diseases of Blood and Blood Forming Organs and Certain Disorders Involving the Immune Mechanism (D50-D89)

Blood is pumped throughout the body by the heart. The blood carries nutrients and oxygen needed by tissues and organs and carries wastes away from tissue and organs. Blood is made up of plasma, erythrocytes (red blood cells), leukocytes (white blood cells), and platelets.

Anemia

Anemia occurs when the patient does not have enough red blood cells or does not have enough hemoglobin. Hemoglobin is what oxygen binds to in the red blood cells. There are many different types of anemia. The most common are iron defi-

ciency anemia, vitamin B_{12} deficiency, and folic acid deficiency. When searching for the proper code, start with the main term anemia. Then look for the subterm that identifies the type or cause of the anemia.

Example

A patient with vitamin B_{12} anemia comes in for a routine injection of vitamin B_{12}. From the Index to Diseases and Injuries look for the main term Anemia and the sub terms deficiency/vitamin B12 NOS D51.9. Verify code selection in the Tabular List.

Practical Coding Note

When selecting the code for anemia, review the documentation to see if the provider documented the cause. When the cause is not documented, the code for unspecified anemia (D64.9) is the only option.

Anemia can be caused by other diseases. There are official coding guidelines for the proper code selection and sequencing when a patient develops anemia as a result of neoplastic disease, chemotherapy, or radiotherapy. Management of anemia in neoplastic disease is coded with the appropriate primary code to identify the neoplasm and D63.0 as an additional code for the anemia.

If the anemia is caused by chemotherapy and the treatment is focused on the anemia, the anemia is coded first, followed by a code for the neoplasm and then for adverse effect of antineoplastic chemotherapy (T45.1X5).

If the anemia is caused by the radiotherapy and the treatment is focused on the anemia, the anemia is coded first, followed by a code for the neoplasm and then code Y84.2 *Radiological procedure and radiotherapy as the cause of abnormal reaction of the patient, or of later complication, without mention of misadventure at the time of the procedure.*

You may need to check with the provider to clarify if anemia is related to the neoplasm itself, or if it is related to the treatment of the chemotherapy or radiotherapy for the neoplasm.

When anemia is associated with chronic kidney disease, the code for the chronic kidney diseases is reported first, followed by the code for the anemia.

Example

A patient is treated for anemia caused by stage IV CKD. The proper codes and sequence are:

- N18.4 Chronic kidney disease, stage 4 (severe)
- D63.1 Anemia in chronic kidney disease

Look in the Index to Diseases and Injuries for Anemia/ due to (in) (with)/chronic kidney disease D63.1. In the Tabular List, D63.1 has a code first note indicating to code the underlying chronic kidney disease first. Look in the Index to Diseases and Injuries for Disease/kidney (functional) (pelvis)/chronic/stage 4 (severe) N18.4. Verify all codes in the Tabular List.

ICD-9-CM Application

In ICD-9-CM, there are chapter specific guidelines for Chapter 4: Disease of the Blood and Blood-Forming Organs and Certain Disorders Involving the Immune Mechanism (280-289) for reporting anemia with chronic kidney disease and neoplastic disease.

Key Roots, Suffixes, and Prefixes

coagul/o	clotting
cyt/o	cell
-emia	blood condition
-globulin	protein
ranul/o	granules
hem/o	blood
hemat/o	blood
leuk/o	white

Acronyms

CBC	complete blood count
ESR	erythrocyte sedimentation rate
RBC	red blood count
WBC	white blood count

Section Review 4.3

1. Referencing ICD-10-CM Guideline Section I.A.13, when using a code from category D63 it is also necessary to code first:

    A. The hematocrit level of the patient

    B. A primary (first-listed) diagnosis

    C. The chronic condition causing the anemia

    D. The acute condition presented in the patient encounter

2. Mr. McFarland visits his oncologist for prostate cancer. He is reporting more fatigue than usual. Lab tests determine the patient has anemia due to the cancer. Applying the coding concept from ICD-10-CM guidelines, section I.C.2.c.1, what ICD-10-CM codes should be reported for the visit?

    A. C61, D63.0

    B. C61, D64.81

    C. D63.0, C61

    D. D64.81, C61

3. Mrs. Fryer visits her nephrologists for an erythropoietin (EPO) injection for her anemia. She has Stage III chronic kidney disease, which is the cause of the anemia. Applying the coding concept from ICD-10-CM guidelines, section I.A.13, what ICD-10-CM code(s) should be reported for the EPO injection?

    A. D63.1

    B. N18.3, D63.1

    C. D63.1, N18.3

    D. N18.3

Chapter 4: Endocrine, Nutritional and Metabolic Diseases (E00-E89)

The endocrine system is made up of glands that produce and secrete hormones. Hormones travel through the blood and help with body functions that include metabolism, growth, mood, sexual function, and reproduction. The major glands of the endocrine system are the hypothalamus, pituitary, thyroid, parathyroids, adrenals, pineal body, ovaries, testes, and pancreas.

The categories in this chapter of ICD-10-CM include disorders of the thyroid gland, diabetes mellitus, disorders of the parathyroid gland, diseases of the thymus gland, disorders of adrenal glands, and disorders of the ovaries and testes.

Disorders of the Thyroid Gland

The most common diagnoses that involve the thyroid gland are goiters, hypothyroidism, and hyperthyroidism. A goiter is an enlargement of the thyroid gland. Hypothyroidism,

commonly referred to as an underactive thyroid, is the result of the thyroid gland not producing enough hormones. Common symptoms of hypothyroidism include weight gain, fatigue, hair loss, muscle cramps, and depression. Hyperthyroidism, commonly referred to as an overactive thyroid, is the result of the thyroid gland producing too much hormones. Common symptoms include weight loss, tachycardia (rapid heart rate), sweating, changes in menstrual cycle, and nervousness.

Category E05 *Thyrotoxicosis [hyperthyroidism]* has options for with and without crisis or storm, which means there is an exacerbation of hyperthyroidism that can lead to the dysfunction of one or more organ systems.

Example

A patient complains of weight loss and excessive sweating. The provider performs blood tests and diagnoses the patient with hyperthyroidism.

To locate the diagnosis code, look for the main term Hyperthyroidism in the Index to Diseases and Injuries. Sub terms in this subcategory indicate if the patient has a goiter or thyroid nodule, and if it is a complication in pregnancy or a neonatal condition. The default code is E05.90. Turn to E05.90 in the Tabular List. With the information provided in this case, the correct code is E05.90 because there is no mention of a thyroid crisis or storm (a rare and potentially fatal complication of hyperthyroidism). You do not code the signs and symptoms (weight loss and sweating) because a definitive diagnosis is determined.

Diabetes Mellitus

Diabetes mellitus is one of the most frequently-used category codes in ICD-10-CM, chapter 4 - Endocrine, Nutritional, and Metabolic Diseases. Diabetes mellitus (DM) is a complicated disease to code because of the different types of diabetes and the variety of diseases that manifest because of diabetes mellitus. ICD-10-CM provides combination codes to report diabetes with manifestations.

ICD-9-CM Application

ICD-9-CM requires multiple codes to report diabetes mellitus with manifestations. As an example, let's look at type I diabetes mellitus with gangrene.

ICD-9-CM

Look in the Index to Diseases for Diabetes, diabetic/gangrene 250.7√ [785.4].

250.71 Diabetes with peripheral circulatory disorders, type 1, not stated as uncontrolled

785.4 Gangrene

ICD-10-CM

Look in the Index to Diseases and Injuries for Diabetes, diabetic/type 1/with/gangrene E10.52.

E10.52 Type I diabetes mellitus with diabetic peripheral angiopathy with gangrene

ICD-10-CM codes for diabetes does not differentiate between controlled and uncontrolled like it did in ICD-9-CM.

There are two types of diabetes: Type 1 and Type 2. Type 1 diabetes is an autoimmune disease that results in the destruction of insulin-producing cells in the pancreas. A type I diabetic requires insulin to survive. This type of diabetes usually occurs early in life, typically in childhood or before the patient reaches age 30. Type 2 diabetics still produce insulin, but because of obesity, age, or genetic weakness, the insulin

produced is not enough to keep their blood sugar levels within normal limits.

Diabetes mellitus codes in ICD-10-CM are combination codes that include:

- Type of diabetes mellitus;
- Body system affected; and
- The complications affecting that body system.

There are five diabetes mellitus categories in ICD-10-CM:

- E08 Diabetes mellitus due to an underlying condition
- E09 Drug or chemical induced diabetes mellitus
- E10 Type 1 diabetes mellitus
- E11 Type 2 diabetes mellitus
- E13 Other specified diabetes mellitus

All the categories above with the exception of E10 include a note directing users to use an additional code to identify any insulin use, which is Z79.4. The concept of requiring insulin and non-insulin are not a component of the diabetes mellitus (DM) categories in ICD-10-CM. Code Z79.4 *Long-term (current) use of insulin* is added to identify the use of insulin for diabetic management even if the patient is not insulin dependent in code categories E08–E09 and E11–E13.

The fourth character under these categories refers to underlying conditions with specified complications, whereas, the fifth character defines the specific manifestation such as neuropathy, angiopathy, etc.

Definitions for the types of diabetes mellitus are in the "Includes" notes under each DM categories E10 - E13. Sequencing of diabetes codes from categories E08–E09 have a "Code First" note indicating that diabetes is to be sequenced after the underlying condition, drug or chemical that is responsible for the diabetes. Codes from categories E10–E13 (diabetes mellitus) are sequenced first, followed by codes for any additional complications outside of these categories if applicable.

As many codes within a particular category as are necessary to describe all of the complications of the disease may be used. They should be sequenced based on the reason for a particular encounter. Assign as many codes from categories E08–E13 as needed to identify all of the associated conditions that the patient has.

Example

A patient is diagnosed with stage 3 chronic kidney disease and neuropathic arthropathy as a result of type 2 diabetes. In this case, multiple manifestation codes are required to fully report the patient condition.

> E11.22   Type 2 diabetes mellitus with diabetic chronic kidney disease
>
> N18.3   Chronic kidney disease, stage 3 (moderate)
>
> E11.610 Type 2 diabetes mellitus with diabetic neuropathic arthropathy

Look in the Index to Diseases and Injuries for Diabetes/type 2/with/chronic kidney disease E11.22. In the Tabular List, E11.22 has a note to use an additional code to identify the stage of chronic kidney disease from code range N18.1-N18.6. N18.3 identifies stage 3 chronic kidney disease. Then, look in the Index to Diseases and Injuries for Diabetes/type 2/with/neuropathic arthropathy E11.610.

ICD-9-CM Application

In ICD-9-CM, a code for diabetes is assigned from category 249 *Secondary diabetes mellitus* or 250 *Diabetes mellitus*. For category 250, the type of diabetes in ICD-9-CM is assigned based on the fifth digit assignment:

0 - type 2 or unspecified type, not stated as uncontrolled

1 - type 1 [juvenile type], not stated as uncontrolled

2 - type 2 or unspecified type, uncontrolled

3 - type 1 [juvenile type], uncontrolled

In ICD-10-CM, the concept of controlled or uncontrolled does not apply.

All Type 1 diabetics must use insulin to replace what their bodies do not produce. The use of insulin does not mean a patient is a Type 1 diabetic. Some patients with Type 2 diabetes mellitus are unable to control their blood sugar through diet/exercise and oral medication alone, and do require insulin. If the documentation in a medical record does not indicate the type of diabetes but does indicate the patient uses insulin, a code from category E11 *Type 2 diabetes mellitus* is reported.

For Type 2 patients who routinely use insulin, code Z79.4 *Long-term (current) use of insulin* also should be assigned to indicate the patient uses insulin. Code Z79.4 should not be assigned if insulin is given temporarily to bring a Type 2 patient's blood sugar under control during an encounter.

Example

A patient returns to the physician's office. The patient has been on insulin for nine months since the diabetes was not well-controlled with diet and exercise. The physician determines the patient's type 2 diabetes is well maintained on insulin and has the patient continue insulin use.

> E11.9 Type 2 diabetes mellitus without complications
>
> Z79.4 Long-term (current) use of insulin

Look in the Index to Diseases and Injuries for Diabetes/type 2 E11.9. In the Tabular List, there is a note under category E11 to use an additional code to identify insulin use with Z79.4.

Diabetes Mellitus in a Pregnant Patient

Codes for pregnancy, childbirth, and the puerperium, which are located in chapter 15 of ICD-10-CM, are always sequenced first on the medical record. A patient who has a pre-existing DM who becomes pregnant should be assigned a code from category O24 *Diabetes Mellitus in pregnancy, childbirth, and the puerperium* followed by the diabetes code from chapter 4 of ICD-10-CM. The fourth character subcategory codes identify the type of diabetes as pre-existing Type 1 or Type 2, unspecified, or gestational.

The fifth character indicates whether the diabetes is treated during pregnancy, childbirth, or the puerperium. The sixth character indicates the trimester during which treatment is sought. With gestational diabetes the sixth character identifies whether the gestational diabetes is diet-controlled, insulin controlled, or unspecified control.

Example

A 25-year-old patient with diabetes mellitus type 1 in her second trimester at 18 weeks visited her OB/GYN for her routine follow-up visit. The patient's blood sugar was well controlled and the patient indicated she was doing well with her diet and exercise regimen. The physician scheduled the patient for follow up for one month.

O24.012 Pre-existing diabetes mellitus, type 1, in pregnancy, second trimester

Z3A.18 18 weeks gestation of pregnancy

Example

A 27-year-old patient developed gestational diabetes in her third trimester at 32 weeks 3/7 days. The patient's condition is controlled with diet and exercise.

O24.410 Gestational diabetes mellitus in pregnancy

Z3A.32 32 weeks gestation of pregnancy

Note: See Section I.C.15.g Diabetes mellitus in pregnancy, and section I.C.15.i Gestational (pregnancy induced) diabetes.

Insulin Pump Failure

An under dose of insulin due to an insulin pump failure is assigned using a code from subcategory T85.6 *Mechanical complication of other specified internal and external prosthetic devices, implants and grafts* as the principal or first listed code, followed by code T38.3x6- *Underdosing of insulin and oral hypoglycemic [antidiabetic] drugs*. Additional codes for the type of diabetes mellitus and any associated complications associated with the underdosing are also reported.

The principal or first listed code for an encounter due to an insulin pump malfunction resulting in an overdose of insulin is also a code from subcategory T85.6 *Mechanical complication of other specified internal and external prosthetic devices, implants and grafts*, followed by T38.3x1- *Poisoning by insulin and oral hypoglycemic [antidiabetic] drugs, accidental (unintentional)*.

Secondary Diabetes

Codes under categories E08 *Diabetes mellitus due to underlying condition* and E09 *Drug or chemical induced diabetes mellitus* identify complications/manifestations associated with secondary diabetes mellitus.

Secondary diabetes mellitus is a type of diabetes caused by something other than genetics or environmental factors. It is characterized by elevated blood sugar levels that develop as the result of another medical condition. It also may develop when the pancreatic tissue responsible for the production of insulin is absent because it is destroyed by a disease. Secondary diabetes always is caused by another condition or event.

For patients who routinely use insulin, code Z79.4 *Long-term (current) use of insulin* is also assigned. If insulin is only given temporarily to bring a patient's blood sugar under control during an encounter, Z79.4 is not reported.

For post-pancreatectomy diabetes mellitus, assign code E89.1 *Postprocedural hypoinsulinemia*. Assign a code from category E13 and a code from subcategory Z90.41- *Acquired absence of pancreas* as additional codes. Subcategory code Z90.41- has a use additional note to also code any additional insulin use (Z79.4) and diabetes mellitus, postpancreatectomy (E13.-).

Overweight, Obesity and other Hyperalimentation (E65-E68)

Understanding body mass index (BMI) will help you determine the parameters of the difference between overweight and obesity. BMI is calculated using weight and height and is used because is most often correlates with the amount of body fat the person has.

BMI	Considered
Below 18.5	Underweight
18.5 to 24.9	Healthy weight
25.0 to 29.9	Overweight
30 or higher	Obese

Source: http://www.cdc.gov/obesity/adult/defining.html

In ICD-10-CM, overweight and obesity are separated by coding. The coding for obesity includes the cause of the obesity such as obesity due to excess calories, drug induced and with alveolar hypoventilation. Correct coding of obesity include the cause and if the obesity is considered morbid. A secondary code for the BMI from category Z68 should also be used when the codes for overweight or obesity are used.

Example

A 28-year-old patient presents for consultation for bariatric surgery. Physician has documented that the patient was counseled on controlling her calories. The patient will be seeing a dietician to provide a meal plan for her to lose some weight. Patient states she eats in excess of 3,000 calories a day and does not exercise. Her weight is 290 pounds and BMI is documented at 37. The physician documents morbid obesity.

E66.01 Morbid obesity due to excess calories

Z68.37 Body mass index (BMI) 37.0-37.9, adult

Key Roots, Suffixes, and Prefixes for Endocrine

crin/o	secrete
dips/o	thirst
gluc/o, glyc/o	sugar
hormon/o	hormone
pancreat/o	pancreas
thyr/o, thyroid/o	thyroid
toxic/o	poison
tropin-	act upon
-in	a substance

Section Review 4.4

---

1. Name an example of when a problem caused by diabetes is not sequenced after the code for diabetes. Refer to ICD-10-CM guidelines, section I.C.4.a.5.a.

    A. When a patient's insulin pump malfunctions

    B. When the patient has type 2 diabetes

    C. When the patient has type 1 diabetes

    D. When the patient has end stage renal disease caused by diabetes

2. A 12-year-old's diabetes mellitus is well controlled with oral medications. The patient has no complications. Applying the coding concept from ICD-10-CM guidelines, sections I.C.4.a.1 and I.C.4.a.2, what ICD-10-CM code is reported?

    A. E11.9

    B. E10.9

    C. E13.9

    D. E08.9

3. A type 2 diabetic patient with diabetic retinopathy visits his ophthalmologist for blurred vision. After performing a visual acuity test and a dilated eye exam, the provider states the patient has macular edema. Applying the coding concept from ICD-10-CM guidelines, section I.C. 4.a, what ICD-10-CM code is reported?

    A. E11.311

    B. E11.321

    C. E08.311

    D. E10.311

Chapter 5: Mental, Behavioral and Neurodevelopmental Disorders (F01-F99)

Coding mental disorders is complicated by the availability of another set of widely-used codes in the *Diagnostic and Statistical Manual, fifth Edition* (DSM-5), published by the American Psychiatric Association. If you code for psychiatric services, the DSM-5 should be used as a reference to assist in the determination of a diagnosis. For this course, you will only be required to use the ICD-10-CM for diagnosis coding.

DSM-5 lists the specific DSM-5 code along with a description of the problem, and any diagnostic or associated features. The codes in this manual are similar to those in the ICD-10-CM section of mental disorders and conditions. A part of the mental disorder section of ICD-10-CM was developed with the assistance of the American Psychiatric Association to assist in the selection of appropriate diagnostic codes.

The DSM-5 manual uses a multiaxial coding system. The terms and definitions used for this coding system are listed below. The conditions listed in Axis I-III are used by the coder to assign an ICD-10-CM code. In most cases, the DSM terminology may be more detailed than code descriptions in ICD-10-CM.

Axis I—Clinical disorders and other conditions

Axis II—Personality disorders; intellectual disability

Axis III—General medical condition

Axis IV—Psychosocial problems

Axis V—Global assessment of functioning

Mental disorders usually are self-identifying, but sometimes require explanation.

Guidelines in this chapter cover pain disorders related to psychological factors and the use, abuse, and dependence of psychoactive substances. Another common diagnosis reported from this section is dementia.

Pain Disorders Related to Psychological Factors

Assign code F45.41 for pain that is exclusively psychological. When pain is documented with psychological factors report F45.42. Code F45.42 *Pain disorder with related psychological factors* with an additional code for acute or chronic pain from category G89 *Pain, not elsewhere classified*. See section I.C.6.b.1 - Pain Category G89.

Example

A patient is treated by her psychiatrist for chronic pain syndrome that is causing her depression.

> F45.42 Pain disorder with related psychological factors
> G89.4 Chronic pain syndrome

Look in the Index to Diseases and Injuries for Disorder/pain/with related psychological factors F45.42. In the Tabular List, F45.42 has a note to also code associated acute or chronic pain. In this example, the patient has chronic pain syndrome. Look in the Index to Diseases and Injuries for Pain/chronic/associated with significant psychosocial dysfunction G89.4. The Tabular List confirms this is the code for chronic pain syndrome.

Mental and Behavioral Disorders Due to Psychoactive Substance Use

Selection of codes for *In remission* (categories F10–F19) requires the provider's clinical judgment. The appropriate codes for *In remission* are assigned only on the basis of provider documentation. Working with providers will be essential to correctly assign codes in these categories.

When the provider documentation refers to use, abuse and dependence of the same substance (eg, alcohol, opioid, cannabis, etc.), only one code should be assigned to identify the pattern based on hierarchy:

- If both use and abuse are documented, assign only the code for abuse
- If both abuse and dependence are documented, assign only the code for dependence
- If both use and dependence are documented, assign only the code for dependence
- If use, abuse and dependence are all documented, assign only the code for dependence

Practical Coding Note

Pay attention to the EXCLUDES1 note to remind you that an abuse, use and dependence codes cannot be reported together. For example, under subcategory code F12.22 *Cannabis depen-dence* there is an EXCLUDES1 note that indicates not to report code F12.1- Cannabis abuse or F12.9- *Cannabis use, unspecified* with this code.

As with all other diagnoses, the codes for psychoactive substance use (F10.9-, F11.9-, F12.9-, F13.9-, F14.9-, F15.9-, F16.9-) should only be assigned based on provider documentation and when they meet the definition of a reportable diagnosis. These codes are only to be used when the psychoactive substance use is associated with a mental or behavioral disorder, and such a relationship is documented by the provider.

When severe, acute alcohol intoxication may be accompanied by hypotension, hyperthermia and depression of the gag reflux.

Example

A patient presents to the ED with obvious disinhibition and aggression after showing impaired judgement in a bar. Friends brought him into the ED because he kept repeating the same questions. He was diagnosed with acute alcohol intoxication with delirium.

> F10.121 Alcohol abuse with intoxication delirium

Look in the ICD-10-CM Index to Diseases and Injuries for Abuse/alcohol (non-dependent)/with/intoxication/with delirium F10.121. Verify code selection in the Tabular List.

The categories in block F10-F19 *Mental and behavioral disorders due to psychoactive substance use* indicate the type of substance use with the third character. The fourth characters indicate abuse, dependence, or use. The fifth characters indicates the state of the condition, such as intoxication, alcohol-induced psychotic disorder, mood disorder, and in remission. The codes that require a sixth character indicate further specific complication such as, perceptual disturbance, delirium, delusions, hallucinations, sleep disorder, sexual disorder, and anxiety disorder. This allows the reporting of all disorders related to a substance even when only three character categories are used.

Depression

Depression is a mental illness that can be costly and debilitating to sufferers. Depression can adversely affect the course and outcome of common chronic conditions, such as arthritis, asthma, cardiovascular disease, cancer, diabetes, and obesity. Depression also can result in increased work absenteeism, short-term disability, and decreased productivity.

Understanding the condition is necessary in ICD-10-CM to assign the most appropriate codes. In ICD-10-CM depression is classified by episodes in addition to types such as mild, moderate, severe, and with or without psychotic features.

The ICD-10 classification of Mental and Behavioral Disorders developed in part by the American Psychiatric Association classifies depression by code. In typical, mild, moderate, or severe depressive episodes the patient suffers from lowering of mood, reduction of energy and decrease in activities. The individual's capacity for enjoyment, interest, and concentration is reduced and is marked by tiredness after even a minimum of effort is common. Sleep patterns are usually disturbed and appetite diminished along with reduced self-confidence and self-esteem. Depending on the number and severity of the symptoms, a depressive episode may be specified as mild, moderate, or severe.

Behavioral Syndromes Associated with Physiological Disturbances and Physical Factors

ICD-10-CM contains coding for eating disorders, sleep disorders that are not due to a substance or known physiological conditions and sexual dysfunction that is not due to a substance or known physiological condition. The type of the disorder is needed for coding.

Examples

F50.02	Anorexia nervosa, binge eating/purging type
F51.12	Insufficient sleep syndrome
F52.0	Hypoactive sexual desire disorder

Intellectual Disabilities

An intellectual disability is a term that is used when there are limits to the ability to learn at an expected level and function in daily life. Levels of intellectual disability vary greatly in children. Children with intellectual disability might have a hard time letting others know their wants and needs, and taking care of themselves.

An intellectual disability could cause a child to learn and develop more slowly than other children of the same age and it could take longer for a child to learn to speak, walk, dress, or eat without help, and they could have trouble learning in school. An intellectual disability can be caused by a problem that starts any time before a child turns 18 years-old or even before birth. Some of the most common known causes of an intellectual disability —like Down syndrome, fetal alcohol syndrome, fragile X syndrome, genetic conditions, birth defects, and infections—happen before birth. Others happen while a baby is being born or soon after birth. Still other causes

of intellectual disability do not occur until a child is older; these might include serious head injury, stroke, or certain infections.

To code for these types of intellectual disorders you would first code any associated physical or developmental disorders and then follow with the code for the intellectual disorder. Intellectual disabilities is coded by stage, such as mild, moderate, severe, and profound. Staging is determined by IQ levels.

Example

A 13-year-old has Down syndrome with and IQ level of 25.

Q90.3 Down syndrome, unspecified

F72 Severe intellectual disability

    IQ level 20-25 to 35-40

- Severe mental subnormality

There are other pervasive developmental disorders as well that include autistic disorders, Asperger's syndrome and such.

For patients suffering from behavioral and emotional disorders with the onset usually occurring in childhood and adolescence the conditions are captured in F90-F98.

Attention-deficit hyperactivity disorder (ADHD) is a problem with inattentiveness, over-activity, impulsivity, or a combination. For these problems to be diagnosed as ADHD, they must be out of the normal range for a child's age and development. Coding for ADHD is broken down as to if the condition is predominately hyperactive or inattentive or the combined type.

Example

F90.2 Attention-deficit hyperactivity disorder, combined type

Dementia

Dementia is a group of symptoms affecting memory and cognitive functions such as judgment and communication. Dementia associated with other conditions is coded with category F02. There is a note to "Code first underlying physiological condition, such as:" This note instructs the coder that two codes are required and the code for dementia is sequenced second. To find dementia and associated conditions in the Index to Diseases and Injuries, look for Dementia/with or Dementia/in (due to) and then looking at the indented entries for code selection. Dementia is commonly associated with Parkinson's disease and Alzheimer's disease (these conditions will be discussed in the next chapter).

Key Roots, Suffixes, and Prefixes		Acronyms	
anxi/o	uneasy, anxious, distressed	ADD	attention-deficit disorder
hallucin/o	hallucination	ADHD	attention-deficit hyperactivity disorder
hypo-	deficient	DT	delirium tremens
-mania	obsessive	MDD	major depressive disorder; manic-depressive disorder
ment/o	mind		
para-	abnormal	OCD	obsessive-compulsive disorder
phobia	fear	PTSD	post-traumatic stress disorder
psych/o	mind	SAD	seasonal affective disorder; schizoaffective disorder
schiz/o	split		

Section Review 4.5

1. A patient with a four-year history of eating disorders is seen in the physician's office due to a significant weight loss over the past three months. She went from 82 pounds down to 53 pounds due to restricting her food intake. She is diagnosed with anorexia nervosa. Select the diagnosis code(s).

   A. F50.02

   B. F50.02, R63.4

   C. F50.01, R63.4

   D. R50.01

2. A patient presents to her physician and tells him she drinks each night when she gets home from work. She asks her physician to recommend an alcohol treatment center because her life has become unmanageable and she wishes to quit drinking. The patient is diagnosed with alcohol dependence. Select the diagnosis code.

   A. F10.221

   B. F10.20

   C. F10.239

   D. F10.288

3. A mother brings her son into the doctor because he has been getting in trouble in school for his behavior. He is not paying attention or following the instructions. He is constantly losing his pencil and forgetting to bring in his homework. After evaluating the child, the provider diagnoses him with attention deficit disorder, predominately inattentive type, and sends the patient for a consultation with a psychiatrist to see if medication can help. Select the diagnosis code.

   A. F90.0

   B. F90.9

   C. F90.8

   D. F90.2

Chapter 6: Diseases of Nervous System (G00-G99)

This chapter classifies diseases of the nervous system. The diseases and disorders of the nervous system include the meninges, central nervous system (CNS), and peripheral nervous system (PNS). The CNS includes the brain and spinal cord.

Common diagnoses in this chapter include Parkinson's diseases, Alzheimer's disease, epilepsy, migraines, headaches and pain. The guidelines for this chapter include dominant versus nondominant side for hemiplegia and monoplegia, and pain.

Parkinson's Disease

Parkinson's disease is a disorder of the nervous system that develops gradually. The symptoms include tremors, slowed motions (walking), impaired posture, changes in speech, and dementia. There are very few codes to select from when coding for Parkinson's disease. Refer to the main term Parkinson's diseases, syndrome or tremor in the Index to Diseases and Injuries, which refers you to "*see* Parkinsonism." Review the sub terms to select the most specific code. If you look under the main term disease, then the subterm Parkinson's, you will only be directed to G20. In this case, you will need to pay close attention to the notes in the Tabular List to make sure you have the correct code selection.

Example

A patient diagnosed with Parkinson's disease due to the use of antipsychotic medication, initial encounter.

This type of Parkinson's disease is considered secondary because it is caused by something else, in this case, medication. Look in the Index to Diseases and Injuries for Parkinsonism/secondary/due to/drugs NEC G21.19. Refer to G21.19 in the Tabular List. There is a note to use an additional code for adverse effect to identify the drug. In the Table of Drugs and Chemicals, look for antipsychotic drug and select the code in the Adverse effect column (T43.505). A seventh character extender is selected based on the episode (A for initial encounter, D for subsequent encounter, or S for sequela). The seventh character extender is only appended to the T43.505 code, not the G21.19 code. The codes reported are:

G21.19   Other drug induced secondary parkinsonism

T43.505A   Adverse effect of unspecified antipsychotics and neuroleptics, initial encounter

Alzheimer's Disease

Alzheimer's disease is reported with a code from category G30. It is characterized by degeneration of the brain tissue. The patient's intellectual and social abilities are impaired. The symptoms start as memory loss and confusion and progress to not being able to remember, learn, or reason. Code selection is based on the onset of Alzheimer's disease (eg, early onset, late onset).

Alzheimer's disease is the most common cause of dementia. If the provider documents dementia with Alzheimer's, two codes are required — a code from category G30, selected based on the onset of Alzheimer's disease and code F02.80 or F02.81 for dementia, depending on whether the patient has behavioral disturbances. These codes can be found in the Index to Diseases and Injuries by looking for Disease/Alzheimer's then looking at the indented entries for code selection. In the Tabular List, category code F02 has a note to code first the underlying physiological condition.

Epilepsy

Epilepsy is a seizure disorder. There are different types of epileptic seizures. Code selection is based on the type of seizure. Seizures are divided into two major categories: focal (partial) seizures and generalized seizures. Focal seizures only occur in one part of the brain, while generalized seizures occur in both sides of the brain.

Focal seizures include:

- Simple – the patient remains conscious, but experiences sensations and feelings that are abnormal
- Complex – the patient has a change in or loss of consciousness

Generalized seizures include:

- Absence seizures (petit mal) – the patient may appear to stare into space and/or have twitching muscles
- Tonic seizures – the patient has stiffening of muscles of the body (usually back, legs, and arms)
- Clonic seizures – the patient has repeated jerking movements of muscles on both sides of the body
- Tonic-clonic seizures (grand mal) – the patient has a mixture of symptoms
- Myoclonic seizures – the patient has jerks and twitches of the upper body, arms, or legs
- Atonic seizures – the patient has a loss of normal muscle tone

In the Index to Diseases and Injuries, look for the main term Epilepsy then identify the type of seizures. For example, for an epileptic with grand mal seizures, look in the Index to Diseases and Injuries for Epilepsy/tonic (clonic) which directs you to see Epilepsy, generalized, specified NEC. This is reported with

G40.409. Note that the code selection changes based on whether it is stated as with status epilepticus or whether it is intractable.

Status epilepticus is diagnosed when a seizure lasts an abnormally long time. There is no time limit definition, but it is generally defined when the seizure lasts longer than 5 minutes, according to the National Institute of Neurologic Disorders and Stroke. Intractable means hard to control. According to ICD-10-CM, the terms pharmacoresistant, treatment resistant, refractory, and poorly controlled are equivalent to intractable.

Practical Coding Note

When a patient has a seizure and there is no documentation to support the patient is having an epileptic seizure, a seizure disorder, or there is no history of the patient having recurrent seizures, a code from category R56, *Convulsions, not elsewhere classified* is reported, not a code from categories G40-G47.

For example, the patient is diagnosed with febrile seizures. Code R56.00 is reported. This code is found by looking in the Index to Diseases and Injuries for Convulsions/febrile.

Migraines

Migraines are more intense pulsating and throbbing headaches that are located on one side of the head. Symptoms that accompany a migraine are usually nausea, vomiting, and sensitivity to light and sound. Migraine attacks can last up to hours or several days. Migraines with an aura are when one has warning signs that occur to indicate a migraine is coming. These warning signs can be a type of visual disturbance such as blurred vision, flashes of light, zigzag lines, temporary visual loss or other visual hallucinations. Code selection is based on the type of migraine headaches.

For example, a menstrual migraine is reported with a code from subcategory G43.82 or G43.83. The fifth character identifies whether it is intractable or not intractable. Intractable meaning the migraine cannot be controlled with medication. The sixth character identifies with or without status migrainosus. Migrainosus means that the migraine has been ongoing for more than 72 hours.

Practical Coding Note

A migraine with aura is also known as a classic migraine. A migraine without aura is also known as a common migraine. Aura can be visual (bright flashing dots or lights, wavy or jagged lines, etc.), or affect other senses, such as ringing in the ears, changes in smell, taste, or touch.

Headaches

When specific information regarding the type of headache is documented, a code from ICD-10-CM chapter 6 is assigned. If specific information is not provided, code R51 *Headache*.

Example

A patient is diagnosed with a cluster headache. From the Index to Diseases and Injuries, the main term is headache and the sub term is cluster. Without any further information, code G44.009 is assigned. Review the documentation to determine if the cluster headache is chronic or episodic, which may result in a different code selection.

Dominant/Nondominant Side

Paraplegia is paralysis of both lower limbs. Quadriplegia is paralysis of all four limbs. Hemiplegia is paralysis on one vertical half of the body. Monoplegia is paralysis of one limb. Categories G81 *Hemiplegia and hemiparesis*, G82 *Paraplegia (paraparesis) and quadriplegia (quadriparesis)*, and G83 *Other paralytic syndromes* are only used when there is no further specification.

Codes from category G81 *Hemiplegia and hemiparesis, and subcategories* G83.1 *Monoplegia of lower limb*, G83.2 *Monoplegia of upper limb*, and G83.3 *Monoplegia, unspecified* identify whether the dominant or nondominant side is affected. Should the affected side be documented, but is not specified as dominant or nondominant and the classification does not indicate a default, use the following rules for code selection:

- For ambidextrous patients, the default is dominant
- If the left side is affected, the default is non-dominant
- If the right side is affected, the default is dominant

Pain

The official coding guidelines for this chapter include the proper code selection and sequencing for pain. This chapter includes acute and chronic pain, postoperative pain, pain associated with neoplasms, and chronic pain syndrome.

When selecting a pain code, you need to know if the pain is acute or chronic. Unless the patient presents for pain management, including insertion of a neurostimulator for pain control, code the underlying condition causing the pain instead of a code from category G89. If the encounter is for pain management, select a code from category G89 followed by the code that identifies the underlying condition. An additional code can also be reported to identify the site of the pain.

Example

A patient with chronic lower back pain presents to the office for an epidural for pain management. To locate the codes in the Index to Diseases and Injuries, look up Pain/chronic (G89.29). Next, look for Pain/low back (M54.5). Because the treatment is for pain management for the chronic lower back pain, the proper codes and sequence for this encounter are:

G89.29 Other chronic pain

M54.5   Low back pain

When the encounter is to treat the underlying disease, even if a neurostimulator is inserted, two codes are required. First, select the code for the underlying condition, followed by the pain code.

Coding postoperative pain is based on the provider's documentation. Routine or expected postoperative pain immediately after a surgery is not coded. Postoperative pain not specified as acute or chronic is coded as acute. Sometimes postoperative pain is associated with a specific complication. When the pain is associated with a specific complication, the code for the complication is primary with a code from category G89 reported secondarily. When the pain is not associated with a specific complication, a code from category G89 is reported.

Chronic pain is reported with a code from subcategory G89.2 and is based on the provider's documentation that the pain is chronic. There are no specified clinical parameters to indicate when pain is acute or chronic. Central pain syndrome (G89.0) and chronic pain syndrome (G89.4) are different than chronic pain. These conditions should only be coded when the documentation specifically identifies these conditions.

Key Roots, Suffixes, and Prefixes

-algia	pain
cerebell/o	cerebellum
cerebr/o	cerebrum
dur/o	dura mater
encephal/o	brain
kines/o	movement
-lepsy	seizure
meningi/o	meninges
neur/o	nerve
-paresis	slight paralysis (weakness)
-phasia	speech
-plegia	paralysis
pont/o	pons
thalam/o	thalamus

Acronyms/Abbreviations

CNS	Central nervous system
CSF	Cerebrospinal fluid

Section Review 4.6

1. Referencing ICD-10-CM guidelines, section I.C.6.b.1.a, when should a code from category G89 be reported as a first listed code?

   A. Whenever it is documented

   B. When the pain control or pain management is the purpose of the encounter

   C. Only within the first 72 hours of continuous pain

   D. When the pain is chronic

2. Mr. Elliot visits the surgeon for evaluation for a wedge resection of left lung cancer. During the admission, the patient reports pain in the chest due to the malignancy. Applying the coding concept from ICD-10-CM guidelines, section I.C.6.b.5, what ICD-10-CM code(s) should be reported?

   A. C34.92

   B. C34.92, G89.3

   C. G89.3, C34.92

   D. G89.3

3. Mr. Timmins fell off of a roof and suffered a spinal injury. As a result of the injury he has been suffering from chronic pain in his lower back for several years. Today, he presents for insertion of a neurostimulator for pain control. Applying the coding concept from ICD-10-CM guidelines, sections I.C.6.b.1.a and I.C.6.b.1.b.ii, what ICD-10-CM codes should be reported for the pain? (Do not code the external cause.)

   A. M54.9, G89.21

   B. M54.5, G89.11

   C. G89.21, M54.5

   D. G89.29, M54.9

Chapter 7: Diseases of the Eye and Andexa (H00-H59)

The only guidelines found for chapter 7 pertain to glaucoma. Common diagnoses found in this section include blepharitis, conjunctivitis, cataracts, and strabismus.

Glaucoma

Glaucoma is a condition where the optic nerve is damaged, causing vision loss. Glaucoma codes from category H40 Glaucoma indicate the type and stage of the glaucoma and the affected eye. The fourth character indicates the type of glaucoma. Many of the codes in category H40 require a seventh character extender to indicate the stage of the glaucoma.

Glaucoma can often affect both eyes. Each eye can be affected by a different type of glaucoma, and/or in different stages of glaucoma. When both eyes are affected by the same type of glaucoma, and the same stage, and there is a bilateral code option, only one code is reported.

Example

Bilateral low-tension glaucoma, mild stage is reported with one code:

   H40.1231   Low-tension glaucoma, bilateral, mild stage

Look in the Index to Diseases and Injuries for Glaucoma/low tension, which directs you to see Glaucoma/open-angle/primary/low-tension. This path directs you to H40.12-. In the Tabular List, the sixth character 3 indicates it is bilateral. The seventh character 1 indicates mild stage.

If each eye is affected by a different type and/or stage, a code is reported for each eye to indicate the appropriate type and stage for that eye. When the documentation indicates progression of the stage during an admission, the highest stage documented is coded.

Seventh character 4, indeterminate stage, is reported when the stage cannot be clinically determined. This selection is only reported when it is documented the stage cannot be determined. If the stage is unspecified, seventh character 0 is reported.

ICD-9-CM Application

To code glaucoma in ICD-9-CM, a minimum of two codes is required. In ICD-10-CM, combination codes provide for proper reporting using only one code. Let's look at the coding for primary open angle glaucoma of the right eye, mild stage.

ICD-9-CM

Look in the Index to Diseases for Glaucoma/open angle/primary 365.11. In the Tabular List, subclassification code 365.11 indicates to use an additional code to identify the stage of glaucoma (365.70-365.74). A mild stage is reported with code 365.71.

   365.11 Primary open angle glaucoma

   365.71 Mild stage glaucoma

ICD-10-CM

Look in the Index to Diseases and Injuries for Glaucoma/open angle/primary H40.11-. In the Tabular List, select the 7th character 1 to indicate the mild stage. To make sure the 7th character stays in the seventh position, the placeholder X is appended to H40.11 before the 7th character.

   H40.11x1 Primary open-angle glaucoma, mild stage

Inflammations and Infections

Blepharitis is inflammation of the eyelid that can be caused by seborrheic dermatitis, bacterial infection, clogged or malfunctioning oil glands in your eyelids, allergies, or other conditions. Codes are reported from subcategory H01.0 *Blepharitis* and are selected based on the type of blepharitis and the eyelid affected.

Conjunctivitis is an infection in the eye also known as pink eye. When the eye is exposed to bacteria and other allergic irritants, it may lead to inflammation and infection. The eyes appear red or pink due to inflamed blood vessels in the conjunctiva. Conjunctivitis is reported with a code from category H10 *Conjunctivitis* and is based on the type of conjunctivitis and the eye affected.

Cataracts

A cataract is a clouding of the lens of the eye. The lens is a portion of the eye that is normally clear that assists in focusing rays of light entering the eye onto the retina. In an eye without a cataract, light passes through the transparent lens to the retina. If the lens is cloudy from a cataract, the image striking the retina will be blurry and the vision will be blurry. It is like looking through a fogged up window.

Cataract types include:

- Nuclear—affect the center of the lens
- Cortical—affect the edges of the lens
- Posterior/Anterior subcapsular—occurs behind the lens capsule
- Congenital—present at birth
- Morganian—hypermature cataract
- Traumatic—due to blunt trauma, penetrating trauma, or perforating eye injury

Code selection for cataracts is separated by laterality and type.

Strabismus

Strabismus is a condition of the eye in which there is non-alignment between both eyes. Variations in strabismus are called tropias. In esotropia, the eye deviates inward; in exotropia, outward. In hypertropia, the eye deviates upward; and in hypotropia, downward. Usually, these disorders are corrected in childhood, but sometimes, illness or injury can cause strabismus in adults.

Intraoperative and Postprocedural Complications

Codes from category code H59 *Intraoperative and postprocedural complications and disorders of eye, and andexa, not elsewhere classified* are reported when there is a complication(s) to the eye and adnexa during or after a surgical procedure. Provider's documentation should indicate the condition (e.g. hemorrhage) and the procedure (eg, cataract surgery) for proper code assignment.

Example

Aphakic bullous keratopathy (ABK) development in the left eye as a complication of cataract surgery:

H59.012   Keratopathy (boullous aphakic) following cataract surgery, left eye

Look in the Index to Diseases and Injuries for Complications/postprocedural/following cataract surgery/vitreous (touch) syndrome, which directs you to H59.01-. In the Tabular List, the sixth character 2 indicates left eye.

Key Roots, Suffixes, and Prefixes

blephar/o	eyelid
canth/o	canthus
conjunctiv/o	conjunctiva
cor/o	pupil
corne/o	cornea
dacry/o	tears
glauc/o	gray
lacrim/o	tears
ocul/o	eye
-opia	vision
opt/o	vision
phak/o	lens
retin/o	retina

Acronyms/Abbreviations

ARMD	Age-related macular degeneration
IOLs	Intraocular lenses
MY	Myopia
PDR	Proliferative diabetic retinopathy

Section Review 4.7

1. A patient presents with pigmentary glaucoma bilaterally, moderate stage on the right, mild stage on the left. Reference ICD-10-CM Guideline I.C.7.a.3. What ICD-10-CM code(s) is/are reported?

    A. H40.1332

    B. H40.1312, H40.1322

    C. H40.1332, H40.1331

    D. H40.1312, H40.1321

2. A mother takes her child to the pediatrician because her right eye is red, itchy, with a mucus discharge coming from the eye. The provider documents the child has pink eye. What ICD-10-CM code is reported?

    A. H10.011

    B. H10.021

    C. H10.013

    D. H10.023

3. A patient is having phacoemulsification of an age-related nuclear cataract of the left eye. What ICD-10-CM code is reported?

    A. H25.12

    B. H26.032

    C. H26.9

    D. Q12.0

Chapter 8: Diseases of the Ear and Mastoid Process (H60-H95)

There are no chapter specific coding guidelines for Diseases of the Ear and Mastoid Process (H60–H95). There is a note at the beginning of the chapter that indicates to use an external cause code following the code for the ear condition, if applicable, to identify the cause of the ear condition.

Category H60–H62 contains codes for *Diseases of the external ear*. The external ear consists of the auricula or pinna, and the external acoustic meatus. Conditions covered include otitis externa, disorders of the pinna and other conditions. Laterality as well as designation for both acute and chronic are components of these codes.

Example

Kaleigh was seen today by her pediatrician because of ear pain. She has been swimming and feels like her right ear is not draining. The provider diagnoses her with swimmer's ear and prescribes an antibiotic.

ICD-10-CM H60.331 Swimmer's ear, right ear

Look in the ICD-10-CM Index to Diseases and Injuries for Swimmer's/ear H60.33-. In the Tabular List, sixth character 1 indicates the right ear.

Otitis media (OM) is any inflammation of the middle ear without reference to etiology or pathogenesis. OM can be classified into many variants on the basis of etiology, duration, symptomatology, and physical findings. Acute OM (AOM) implies rapid onset of disease associated with one or more of the following symptoms:

- Otalgia
- Fever
- Otorrhea
- Recent onset of anorexia
- Irritability
- Vomiting
- Diarrhea

These symptoms are accompanied by abnormal otoscopic findings of the tympanic membrane (TM), which may include the following:

- Opacity
- Bulging
- Erythema
- Middle ear effusion (MEE)
- Decreased mobility with pneumatic otoscopy

AOM is a recurrent disease.

OM with effusion (OME), is MEE of any duration that lacks the associated signs and symptoms of infection (eg, fever, otalgia, irritability). OME usually follows an episode of AOM. OME is more common than AOM, and may be caused by viral upper respiratory infections, allergies, or exposure to irritants (such as cigarette smoke).

Chronic suppurative OM is a chronic inflammation of the middle ear that persists at least 6 weeks and is associated with otorrhea through a perforated TM, an indwelling tympanostomy tube, or a surgical myringotomy.

Codes from H65–H75 are codes for *Diseases of the middle ear and mastoid*. Conditions covered in this category include various types of otitis media, perforations of the tympanic membrane and polyps of the middle ear among others.

Category H80–H83 contains codes for *Diseases of the inner ear* and includes such conditions as otosclerosis, labyrinthitis and vertigo.

Category H90-H94 contains codes for *Other disorders of the ear* and includes such conditions as different types of hearing loss, tinnitus, and auditory perception disorders.

Category H95 contains codes for *Intraoperative and postprocedural complications and disorders of ear and mostoid process, note elsewhere classified* and reported for complication(s) for the ear and mastoid process that happen during or after a surgery specific procedure. Provider's documentation should indicate the condition (e.g. inflammation) and the procedure (e.g. postmastoidectomy) for proper code assignment.

ICD-9-CM Application

In coding certain types of ear infections, such as abscess of the left external ear, ICD-9-CM has such a condition under code 380.10 *Infective otitis externa, unspecified.*

ICD-9-CM

Look in the Index to Diseases for Abscess/ear/external 380.10. In the Tabular List, 380.10 lists other conditions that would fall under this code.

380.10 Infective otitis externa, unspecified

Otitis externa (acute):

NOS

circumscribed

diffuse

hemmorrhagica

infective

ICD-10-CM

Look in the Index to Diseases and Injuries for Abscess/ear/external H60.0-. In the Tabular List, select the sixth character for the laterality.

H60.02 Abscess of the left external ear

ICD-10-CM has a specific code for this condition specifying the site and laterality.

There are ICD-10-CM codes for otitis media that indicates if the infection is recurrent.

H65.04 Acute serous otitis media, recurrent, right ear

H65.196 Other acute nonsuppurative otits media, recurrent, bilateral

Key Roots, Suffixes, and Prefixes

myring/o	eardrum
ot/o	ear
-otia	ear condition
salping/o	eustachian tube
tympan/o	eardrum

Acronyms/Abbreviations

AOM	Acute otitis media
COM	Chronic otitis media
MEE	Middle ear effusion
OM	Otitis media
OME	Otits media with effusion
TM	Tympanic membrane

Section Review 4.8

1. A patient presents with right ear pain and fever. The provider diagnoses acute otitis media. What ICD-10-CM code(s) is/are reported?

    A. H92.01, R50.9

    B. H66.90

    C. H92.01

    D. H66.91

2. A patient sees her provider for spontaneous episodes of vertigo lasting for 30 minutes each, fluctuating hearing loss, and tinnitus. The provider performs a hearing test and confirms hearing loss in the right ear. The provider documents the patient has Meniere's disease in the right ear. What ICD-10-CM code(s) is/are reported?

    A. R42, H91.91, H93.11

    B. H81.01

    C. H93.8X1

    D. H81.01, H81.41, H91.21, H93.11

3. A patient sees his family practitioner for a muted feeling in his ears. The provider determines there is impacted cerumen in both ears. What ICD-10-CM code(s) is/are reported?

    A. H61.23

    B. H61.21, H61.22

    C. H61.23, H90.5

    D. H61.21, H61.22, H90.5

Chapter 9: Diseases of Circulatory System (I00-I99)

This chapter classifies diseases of the heart and circulatory system, which includes arteries and veins. Your heart works as a pump that circulates blood to the organs, tissues, and cells of your body. Common diagnoses in this chapter include hypertension, coronary artery disease, myocardial infarction, and cerebrovascular disease.

Hypertension

Hypertension is high blood pressure. Hypertension is reported with ICD-10-CM code I10.

I10   Essential (primary) hypertension

   INCLUDES high blood pressure

            hypertension (arterial)(benign)(essential)(malignant)(primary)(systemic)

EXCLUDES1 hypertensive disease complicating pregnancy, childbirth and the puerperium (O10–O11, O13–O16)

EXCLUDES2 essential (primary) hypertension involving vessels of the brain (I60–I69)

            essential (primary) hypertension involving vessels of eye (H35.0-)

There is also a note added to the hypertensive diseases category to use an additional code to identify exposure to tobacco smoke, history of tobacco use, and current use/abuse of tobacco products. There are also guidelines for reporting hypertension.

    AAPC   www.aapc.com   *107*

ICD-9-CM Application

In ICD-9-CM, hypertension codes are located in the Hypertension Table in the Index to Diseases. The table contains a complete listing of all conditions due to, or associated with, hypertension.

Hypertension, hypertensive	Malignant	Benign	Unspecified
Hypertension, hypertensive (arterial) (arteriolar) (crisis) (degeneration) (disease) (essential) (fluctuating) (idiopathic) (intermittent) (labile) (low renin) (orthostatic) (paroxysmal) (primary) (systemic) (uncontrolled) (vascular)	401.0	401.1	401.9
with			
chronic kidney disease			
stage I through stage IV, or unspecified	403.00	403.10	403.90
stage V or end state renal disease	403.01	403.11	403.91
heart involvement (conditions classifiable to 429.0-429.3, 429.8, 429.9 due to hypertension) (see also Hypertension, Heart)	402.00	402.10	402.90

Each column is labeled. The labels are:

Malignant—an accelerated, severe form of hypertension, manifested by headaches, blurred vision, dyspnea, and uremia; this type of hypertension usually causes permanent organ damage

Benign—a continuous, mild blood pressure elevation

Unspecified—not been specified as either benign or malignant

Some descriptions in the Hypertension Table have a code listed under each category, while other descriptions have only one code listed under just one column. Not every type of hypertension applies in every case. The information is found only in the Hypertension Table; the table replaces the index entries for hypertension. By initially looking for a code in the table located in the Alphabetic Index (Volume 2) the coder will be able to choose the correct code. It is still necessary to verify the code located within the table in the Tabular List (Volume 1).

Hypertension with Heart Disease

High blood pressure can lead to heart disease and heart failure. Heart conditions (I50.-, or I51.4-I51.9) are assigned a code from category I11 *Hypertensive heart disease* when a causal relationship is stated as due to hypertension or is implied as hypertensive. Use an additional code from category I50 to identify the type of heart failure. If the causal relationship between the hypertension and the heart disease is not documented, each condition is coded separately.

Hypertensive Disease with Chronic Kidney Disease

Chronic kidney conditions and hypertension go hand in hand. Assign codes from category I12 *Hypertensive chronic kidney disease* when conditions classified to categories N18 *Chronic kidney disease (CKD)* are present. Unlike hypertension with heart disease, ICD-10-CM presumes a cause-and-effect relationship and classifies renal failure with hypertension as hypertensive renal disease.

The appropriate code from category N18 Chronic kidney disease (CKD) should be reported to identify the stage of the CKD as a secondary diagnosis with a code from category I12.

If the patient has hypertensive chronic kidney disease and acute renal failure, an additional code for the acute renal failure is required.

Hypertensive Heart and Chronic Kidney Disease

Assign codes from combination category I13 *Hypertensive heart and chronic kidney disease* when both hypertensive kidney disease and hypertensive heart disease are stated in the diagnosis. Assume a relationship between the hypertension and the chronic kidney disease, regardless of whether the condition is so designated. Assign an additional code from category I50 to identify the type of heart failure.

The appropriate code from category N18 should be used as a secondary code with a code from category I13 to identify the stage of the chronic kidney disease.

If the patient has hypertensive chronic kidney disease and acute renal failure, an additional code for the acute renal failure is required.

Hypertensive Cerebrovascular Disease

Assign codes from I60-I69 Cerebrovascular Disease followed by the appropriate hypertension code.

Hypertensive Retinopathy

Hypertension in the small vessel of the eyes can cause serious damage and even lead to blindness. In retinopathy, the increased pressure leads to the growth of unstable vessels in the eye. These vessels can fracture and bleed, causing complications to vision and to eye circulation. Two codes are necessary to identify the condition. First assign code from subcategory H35.0 *Background retinopathy and retinal vascular changes*, then an appropriate code from the circulatory categories I10-I15, to indicate the type of hypertension. Hypertensive retinopathy can be found in the Index to Diseases and Injuries by looking for Retinopathy/hypertensive.

Hypertension, Secondary

Just as hypertension can cause other disorders, other disorders can cause hypertension. Endocrine disorders, disorders of the central nervous system, vascular problems, or even certain medications can cause secondary hypertension. Two codes are required to report secondary hypertension: one to identify the underlying etiology and one from category I15 to identify the secondary hypertension. The reason for the encounter determines code sequencing.

Hypertension, Transient

Sometimes, a fleeting bout of high blood pressure readings can occur. One example of this is called "white coat syndrome"—the stress of being in the doctor's office causes a temporary increase in blood pressure. One elevated reading does not constitute a diagnosis of hypertension. Assign code R03.0 *Elevated blood pressure reading without diagnosis of hypertension* as long as the patient does not have an established diagnosis of hypertension.

Assign a code from category O13.- or category O14.- for transient hypertension of pregnancy.

For a statement of elevated blood pressure without further specificity, assign R03.0. This is found in the Index to Diseases and Injuries by looking for Elevated, elevation/blood pressure/reading, no diagnosis of hypertension.

Coronary Artery Disease

Coronary arteries supply the heart muscle with blood. Coronary artery disease (CAD) is a blockage of the coronary arteries. If the arteries become completely occluded, the result is myocardial infarction. The most common type of CAD is atherosclerosis, which is a narrowing of the arteries caused by a buildup of fats. To report CAD, a code is selected from category I25 *Chronic ischemic heart disease.* An additional code should be used to report exposure to or use of tobacco. In addition, a code should be used to report the areas of the atherosclerosis.

If the patient has had a CABG in the past, the code is selected based on the type of graft. An autologous biological bypass graft is a graft that is taken from the patient. The most common vessel used for an autologous graft is the saphenous vein in the leg. A non-autologous biological bypass graft is a graft that is not taken from the patient.

ICD-9-CM Application

In the ICD-9-CM Index to Diseases, the main term "atherosclerosis" in the Index to Diseases refers you to "see arteriosclerosis." The codes are selected based on the type of vessel that is involved. Code 414.01 Coronary atherosclerosis of native coronary artery is selected when it is the patient's artery — meaning the patient has not had a coronary artery bypass graft (CABG). When the provider does not document that the patient has had a previous CABG, select code 414.01.

There are combination codes for atherosclerotic heart disease with angina pectoris. A causal relationship can be assumed in a patient with both atherosclerosis and angina pectoris, unless the documentation indicates the angina is due to something other than the atherosclerosis. When using one of the combination codes, it is not necessary to assign another code for the angina pectoris.

Cerebrovascular Accident

A cerebrovascular accident (CVA) commonly is referred to as a stroke or cerebral infarction. This condition is a result of the lack of blood flow to the brain. The common signs are weakness or paralysis (usually on one side), trouble speaking, change in vision, confusion, severe headache, and problems walking. When the provider documents a stroke or CVA with no additional information, the default code is I63.9 *Cerebral infarction, unspecified*. This can be found by looking in the Index to Diseases and Injuries for Accident/cerebrovascular.

There are sequelae (late effects) that can develop as a result of a CVA. Category I69 is used to indicate conditions classifiable to categories I60-I67 as the causes of sequela. The sequela includes neurological deficits that persist after initial onset of the CVA. The neurologic deficits caused by cerebrovascular disease may be present from the onset or may arise at any time after the onset of the condition. Sequela codes that specify hemiplegia, hemiparesis and monoplegia identify whether the dominant or nondominant side is affected. If not documented, the default is:

- For ambidextrious patients - dominant
- If the left side is affected - nondominant
- If the right side is affected - dominant

Codes for I60-I67 can be reported with sequela codes from category I69 when a patient has a current cerebrovascular disease and residual deficits from an old cerebrovascular disease coexist.

Example

A 45-year-old was admitted today for CVA. He has left-sided hemiplegia as a result of a previous CVA 1 year ago.

I63.9   Cerebral infarction, unspecified

I69.354 Hemiplegia and hemiparesis following cerebral infarction affecting left non-dominant side.

Two codes are reported for this example, the first code to indicate the current CVA. Look in the Index to Diseases and Injuries for Accident/cerebrovascular I63.9. The second code is reported to indicate residual deficits from an old CVA. Look in the Index to Diseases and Injuries for Hemiplegia/following/cerebral infarction I69.35-. Your sixth digit is 4 because it is the left side, and because there is no indication that the left side is dominant or nondominant you default in reporting the nondominant code.

Z86.73 *Personal history of transient ischemic attack (TIA), and cerebral infarction without residual deficits* is reported for patients with a history of CVA with no neurological deficits present. A TIA is often referred to as a mini stroke. It has the same signs as a CVA, but is not long lasting and does not result in permanent damage.

Pay attention to the instructional note *Use additional code*, found throughout category I69 indicating to report the condition, syndrome, or sequelae as a secondary code.

Myocardial Infarction (MI)

Myocardial infarction (heart attack) occurs when blood flow to the heart is blocked. MIs are classified as acute if the duration is four weeks or less. Acute MIs are coded based on location, which is reported with the fourth and fifth characters. If the specific location is not documented, the proper code is I21.3 *ST elevation (STEMI) myocardial infarction unspecified site*.

ICD-9-CM Application

Codes under category 410 *Acute Myocardial Infarction* were coded based on location with the fourth digit. Then a fifth digit is required to identify the episode of care. The fifth digit subclassifications for category 410 include:

- 0-episode of care unspecified
- 1-initial episode of care
- 2-subsequent episode of care

The meaning of each episode of care is defined in the Tabular List under category code 410 where the fifth digits are listed.

Example:

A patient is evaluated by a cardiologist and admitted with an inferolateral wall acute MI. The patient's symptoms started three days prior to his presenting to the emergency department.

From the Index to Diseases, look up Infarct, infarction/myocardium, myocardial/inferolateral. The code referenced in the index is 410.2, which requires a fifth digit. The correct fifth digit is "1" because this is the initial episode of care.

In ICD-9-CM, myocardial infarctions are classified as acute if the duration is eight weeks or less.

Myocardial infarctions also can be classified by whether there is a ST-segment elevation. STEMI (ST elevation myocardial infarction) is coded with subcategories I21.0-I21.3, I22.0, I22.1, and I22.8. In this case, the coronary artery is completely blocked, and nearly all the heart muscle being supplied by the affected artery starts to die. The "ST" refers to the S-T Segment on an ECG.

Electrical Impulses of the Heartbeat

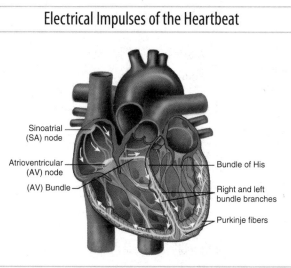

Sinoatrial (SA) node

Atrioventricular (AV) node

(AV) Bundle

Bundle of His

Right and left bundle branches

Purkinje fibers

Source: Ehrlich, Medical Terminology for Health Professionals, 6e, ISBN #978-1-4180-7252-0

NSTEMI (non ST elevation myocardial infarction) describes when the blood clot only partly occludes the artery, and only a portion of the heart muscle being supplied by the affected artery dies. This is coded with subcategory I21.4. A subsequent NSTEMI is reported with I22.2.

If during the encounter STEMI is converted to NSTEMI, select a code for STEMI. If NSTEMI evolves to STEMI, select a code for STEMI.

Code selection also identifies the episode of care. The episode options include:

- episode of care unspecified
- initial episode of care
- subsequent episode of care

Example

A patient is evaluated by a cardiologist and admitted with an inferolateral wall acute STEMI. The patient's symptoms started three days prior to his presenting to the emergency department. From the Index to Diseases and Injuries, look for Infarct, infarction/myocardium, myocardial/ST elevation/inferior I21.19.

A code from category I22 *Subsequent ST elevation (STEMI) and non-ST elevation (NSTEMI) myocardial infarction* is reported when a patient has suffered an AMI and then has a new AMI within four weeks from the initial AMI. A code from category I22 is to be used with a code from category I21. The sequencing of these codes depends on the circumstances of the encounter.

Example

A patient is admitted from the ER for a STEMI acute MI of the anterior wall. Patient had an inferior wall MI involving the right coronary artery three weeks ago.

I22.0 Subsequent ST elevation (STEMI) myocardial infarction of anterior wall

I21.11 ST elevation (STEMI) myocardial infarction of inferior wall involving right coronary artery.

In the Index to Diseases and Injuries look for Infarct, infarction/myocardium, myocardial (acute) (with stated duration of 4 weeks or less)/subsequent (recurrent) (reninfarction)/anterior referring you to I22.0. Next look for Infarct, infarction/myocardium, myocardial (acute) (with stated duration of 4 weeks or less)/ST elevation/involving/right coronary artery referring you to I21.11. Verify codes in the Tabular List.

There is instructional note under categories I21 and I22 in the Tabular List to Use additional code, if documented, to identify use or exposure or dependence to tobacco, or status post administration of tPA (rtPA).

Intraoperative and Postprocedural Complications

Codes from category code I97 *Intraoperative and postprocedural complications and disorders of circulatory system, not elsewhere classified* are reported when there is a complication(s) of the circulatory system during or after a surgery specific procedure. These codes identify a complication that is diagnosis specific (eg, I97.81 *Intraoperative cerebrovascular infarction*). The fourth and fifth characters in this code category (with the exception of codes that end with .8, .88, or .89) indicates the type of complication. A sixth character indicates if the complication followed a cardiac surgery/procedure or other type of surgery/procedure. Provider's documentation should indicate the condition (eg, hematoma) and the procedure (eg, cardiac catheterization) for proper code assignment.

Anticoagulant Therapy

Anticoagulant therapy is when a certain type of medication (eg, Coumadin) is used to prevent clot formations within a blood vessel. This type of therapy is used for different types of vascular disorders such as, atrial fibrillation, pulmonary embolism or venous thrombosis.

When the medical record documents a vascular disorder as a final diagnosis and it is also documents that the patient is currently taking or has a long-term use of an anticoagulant medication, report code Z79.01 as an additional diagnosis. This Z code is indexed under Long-term (current) (prophylactic) drug therapy (use of)/anticoagulants.

Key Roots, Suffixes, and Prefixes

angi/o	vessel
aort/o	aorta
arteri/o	arteries
arteriol/o	arterioles
atri/o	atrium
capillar/o	capillary
coron/o	heart
cardi/o	heart
hem/o	blood
hemat/o	blood
lymph/o	lymph
lymphat/o	lymphatics
lymphan/o	lymph vessels
phleb/o	vein
pleur/o	pleura
sphygm/o	pulse
splen/o	spleen
thromb/o	blood clot
valv/o	valve
valvul/o	valve
vas/o	vessel
vascul/o	vessel
ventricul/o	ventricle

Acronyms/Abbreviations

ASHD	Arteriosclerotic heart disease
AR	Aortic regurgitation
AV	Arteriovenous
BP	Blood pressure
CAD	Coronary artery disease
CHF	Congestive heart failure
HF	Heart failure
HTN	Hypertension
MR	Mitral regurgitation
PAD	Peripheral arterial disease
PDA	Patent ductus arteriosus
PR	Pulmonic regurgitation
TR	Tricuspid regurgitation

Section Review 4.9

1. Applying the coding concept from ICD-10-CM guidelines, section I.C.9.a.5, how do you code hypertensive retinopathy?

    A. First code the hypertension, then the retinopathy.

    B. First code the retinopathy, then the heart disease.

    C. First code the heart disease, then the retinopathy.

    D. Sequencing is based on the reason for the encounter.

2. If an ST elevation myocardial infarction coverts to a non-ST elevation myocardial infarction in the course of thrombolytic therapy, how is it coded? (Reference ICD-10-CM guidelines, section I.C.9.e.1.)

    A. Sequence STEMI first, then NSTEMI

    B. Sequence NSTEMI first, then STEMI

    C. Code only STEMI

    D. Code only NSTEMI

3. Which of the following does NOT require documentation for a cause-and-effect relationship to be coded? (Reference guidelines, sections I.C.9.a.2. and I.C.9.a.3.)

   A. Cerebrovascular hemorrhage due to an operation

   B. Hypertension and chronic kidney disease

   C. Hypertension and heart disease

   D. All require cause and effect to be documented

Chapter 10: Diseases of Respiratory System (J00-J99)

The primary function of the respiratory system is the exchange of gases, which occur as a result of breathing. We take in oxygen and eliminate carbon dioxide. The most common diagnoses in this chapter are chronic obstructive pulmonary disease (COPD), asthma, respiratory failure, influenza, pneumonia, and pleural effusion.

Chronic Obstructive Pulmonary Disease

COPD is chronic bronchitis and emphysema that causes the respiratory passages to narrow. It is not uncommon for COPD to be diagnosed with asthma or with bronchitis. Refer to the appropriate subterm under COPD when diagnosed with another condition to determine if more than one code is needed. COPD is found in the Index to Diseases and Injuries by looking for Disease/pulmonary/chronic obstructive.

Example

A patient who smokes cigarettes is diagnosed with COPD with acute bronchitis and stage II chronic kidney disease. The proper codes and sequence are:

- J44.0   Chronic obstructive pulmonary disease with acute lower respiratory infection
- J20.9   Acute bronchitis, unspecified
- N18.2   Chronic kidney disease, Stage 2 (mild)
- Z72.0   Tobacco use

In the Index to Diseases and Injuries, look up Disease/pulmonary/chronic obstructive/with acute bronchitis J44.0. In the Tabular List, there is a note to use an additional code to identify the infection. For this example, the infection is reported with a code from category code J20 *Acute Bronchitis*. Because there is no indication of the infectious agent for the acute bronchitis, an unspecified code is used. Look for Bronchitis/acute or subacute (with bronchospasm or obstruction) J20.9. There is also a note under category J44 to use an additional code to identify tobacco use. There is not a sub term for CKD under COPD, so an additional code is required to report all of the patient's conditions.

CKD is found in the Index to Diseases and Injuries by looking for Disease/kidney/chronic/stage 2 (mild) N18.2.

Asthma

Asthma is a chronic inflammatory disease of the airway. It can be due to allergies. When coding for asthma, the severity of the asthma should be documented as intermittent, mild persistent, moderate persistent and severe persistent. Acute exacerbation of asthma is an increased severity of asthma. Status asthmaticus indicates the patient is not responding to treatment.

Practical Coding Note

When coding for asthma, review the documentation to determine if the asthma is exacerbated. If asthma is documented without any additional information, the only code choice is J45.909 *Unspecified asthma, uncomplicated*.

The codes in categories J44 *Other chronic obstructive pulmonary disease* and J45 *Asthma* distinguish between uncomplicated cases and those in acute exacerbation. An acute exacerbation is a worsening or a decompensation of a chronic condition.

Respiratory Failure

The codes for respiratory failure are selected by acute, chronic and unspecified and if there is the presence of hypoxia or hypercapnia. The sequencing of acute respiratory failure (ARF) is determined by the reason for the encounter. If a patient is admitted for acute respiratory failure, a code from subcategory J96.0 *Acute respiratory failure* or J96.2 *Acute and chronic respiratory failure* is sequenced first. If the patient is admitted for multiple reasons, select the condition that required the most care. Acute respiratory failure is found in the Index to Diseases and Injuries by looking for Failure, failed/respiration, respiratory/acute.

Influenza

Influenza is caused by a viral infection and attacks the respiratory system. When the virus that caused the influenza is identified, the code is selected based on the type of virus. For example, the avian flu is coded with J09.X2 (found in the Index to Diseases and Injuries by looking for Influenza/avian). This code is reported only when the provider documents the patient has the avian flu. Do not select this code if the provider documents he suspects or wants to rule out the avian flu. In those cases, report a code from category J11.

Pneumonia

Pneumonia is an inflammation of the lungs usually caused by infection. The codes for pneumonia are selected based on the infection that caused the pneumonia. If the infection is not documented, the only choice is J18.9 *Pneumonia, unspecified organism*.

Example

A patient is diagnosed with pneumonia caused by Candida. In the Index to Diseases and Injuries, look for Pneumonia/Candida. You are referred to B37.1. A review of the code in the Tabular List confirms the code is accurate.

Types of pneumonia are named based on the causative agent (for example, bacterial pneumonia or aspiration pneumonia), or based on the location of the pneumonia (for example, lobar pneumonia or bronchopneumonia). Lobar pneumonia affects a lobe of the lung, while bronchopneumonia affects the bronchioles and surrounding alveoli.

Types of Pneumonia

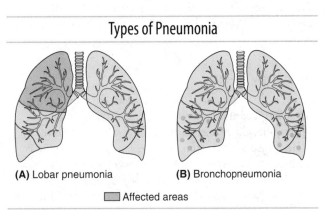

(A) Lobar pneumonia   **(B)** Bronchopneumonia

☐ Affected areas

Source: Ehrlich, Medical Terminology for Health Professionals, 6e, ISBN #978-1-4180-7252-0

Only when pneumonia is documented ventilator associated pneumonia (VAP) should it be coded. When a patient is on a ventilator and develops pneumonia, the provider must document they are associated to code VAP. When VAP is assigned, an additional code from subcategories J12-J18 to identify the type of pneumonia is not coded in addition to VAP.

Pleural Effusion

Pleural effusion results from abnormal fluid accumulation in the pleural spaces. Pleural effusion usually develops as a result of another condition such as congestive heart failure (CHF) or COPD. If pleural effusion is a symptom of an underlying disease, only code for the underlying disease. If the treatment is directed to the pleural effusion or there is no documentation of an underlying disease, a code for pleural effusion is reported. Malignant pleural effusion may be found with cancers such as lung cancers, breast cancers, and lymphomas. If cancer cells are present in the fluid found in the pleura, this would be malignant pleural effusion (J91.0). Documentation needs to indicate the presence of cancers cells in the fluid. Pleural effusion is found in the Index to Diseases and Injuries by looking for Effusion/ pleura, pleurisy, pleuritic, pleuropericardial.

Example

A patient is diagnosed with CHF (congestive heart failure), pleural effusion, and shortness of breath. In this example, select a code for the congestive heart failure (I50.9) only. The pleural effusion and shortness of breath are both symptoms of CHF. CHF is found in the Index to Diseases and Injuries by looking for Failure/heart/ congestive.

Intraoperative and Postprocedural Complications

Codes from category J95 *Intraoperative and postprocedural complications and disorders of respiratory system, not elsewhere classified* are reported when there is a complication(s) of the respiratory system during or after a surgery specific procedure and specific device (eg, ventilator). The subcategories indicated by a diagnosis complication (eg, acute pulmonary insufficiency) or procedure specific complication (eg, tracheostomy stoma).

Key Roots, Suffixes, and Prefixes

alveol/o	alveolus, air sac
bronch/o	bronchial tube
bronchi/o	bronchus
bronchiol/o	bronchiole
cyan/o	blue
laryng/o	larynx, voice box
lob/o	lobe of the lung
nas/o	nose

Key Roots, Suffixes, and Prefixes (continued)		Acronyms/Abbreviations	
pharyng/o	pharynx, throat	ARDS	Acute respiratory distress syndrome
pleur/o	pleura	COPD	Chronic obstructive pulmonary disease
pneum/o	air, lung	OSA	Obstructive sleep apnea
pulmon/o	lung	RDS	Respiratory distress syndrome
sinus/o	sinus, cavity	SOB	Shortness of breath
trache/o	trachea, windpipe	URI	Upper respiratory infection
		RSV	Respiratory syncytial virus

Section Review 4.10

1. What is an acute exacerbation of asthma or COPD? (Reference ICD-10-CM guidelines, section I.C.10.a.1.)

    A. Uncomplicated asthma or COPD

    B. Worsening or decompensation of asthma or COPD

    C. An infection superimposed on asthma or COPD

    D. When a condition is severe enough to be admitted to a hospital

2. A 12-year-old child presents to the ED with an acute exacerbation of asthma. The patient is wheezing and is having difficulty breathing. She is not responding to the therapy. The physician documents as the final diagnosis asthma with status asthmaticus. What ICD-10-CM code(s) is/are reported?

    A. J45.52

    B. J45.901

    C. J45.902

    D. R06.2, J45.901

3. A patient with COPD visits the physician with acute bronchitis. What ICD-10-CM code(s) should be reported?

    A. J20.9

    B. J44.9

    C. J44.0, J20.9

    D. J20.9, J44.0

Chapter 11: Diseases of Digestive System (K00–K95)

The digestive system breaks down food into smaller molecules that can be absorbed and converted to energy, and also eliminates wastes. The organs that make up the digestive system include the mouth, esophagus, stomach, small intestines, large intestines, liver, gallbladder, and pancreas.

There are no chapter-specific coding guidelines for this chapter. Common diagnoses in this chapter include gastroesophageal reflux disease (GERD), cholelithiasis, cholecystitis, and hernias.

Gastroesophageal Reflux Disease

GERD is a result of acid from the stomach flowing back into the esophagus. This condition is commonly called heartburn from the burning sensation the patient feels in their esophagus, which is close to the heart. The codes for reflux are determined based on the location of reflux. Note that GERD (K21.9) is not the same as reflux esophagitis (K21.0), although it may lead to reflux esophagitis. Reflux esophagitis is inflammation of the esophagus causing reflux. GERD can be found in the Index to Diseases and Injuries by looking for GERD (gastroesophageal reflux disease) or Disease/gastroesophageal reflux (GERD).

Cholelithiasis and Cholecystitis

Cholelithiasis is the presence of stones in the bile ducts or gallbladder. Cholecystitis is the inflammation of the gall-bladder. The codes describe a calculus of the gallbladder with different types of cholecystitis, eg, acute, chronic, or both, or without cholecystitis and with or without an obstruction. The obstruction is usually a calculus that has lodged in the neck of the gallbladder or the cystic duct. Code selection identifies the presence or absence of obstruction.

Hernias

A hernia is a protrusion of an internal organ through a weak-ened muscle. There are many types of hernias.

Incisional or ventral hernias may occur either spontaneously or in the area of a prior abdominal incision. The latter develops as the result of a thinning, separation, or tear in the fascial closure from prior surgery, or other causes of separation and weakness unrelated to prior surgery. An umbilical hernia is a protrusion of intestine and/or omentum through a hernia in the abdominal wall near the navel. This type of hernia normally corrects itself after birth. When the hernia doesn't correct itself, surgical repair may be necessary. Epigastric hernias occur through the linea alba above the umbilicus.

The diagnosis for a hernia is selected based on anatomic site and whether an obstruction or gangrene is present. Codes for inguinal hernias also indicate whether it is unilateral or bilat-eral, and if it is recurrent. If it is recurrent, it means the patient has had a hernia in the past.

Example

A 10-year-old with a history of inguinal hernias presents with a new inguinal hernia on the left side. The hernia is on the left side only, and the patient has a history of inguinal hernias. From the Index to Diseases and Injuries, look for Hernia/inguinal/unilateral/recurrent K40.91. The correct code is K40.91 *Unilateral inguinal hernia without obstruction or gangrene, recurrent.*

Practical Coding Note

When selecting a code for inguinal hernias, review the documen-tation for the laterality of the hernia and whether it is recurrent. If the provider does not include this information, the coder's only option is to report K40.90 *Unilateral inguinal hernia, without obstruction or gangrene, unspecified.*

Intraoperative and Postprocedural Complications

Codes from category K91 *Intraoperative and postprocedural complications and disorders of digestive system, not elsewhere classified* are reported when there is a complication(s) of the digestive system during or after a surgery specific procedure. Codes in category K94 are reported for complication(s) of an artificial opening of the digestive system during or after a surgery specific procedure. Codes in category K95 are for complications that deal with bariatric surgery.

Key Roots, Suffixes, and Prefixes

abdomin/o	abdomen
an/o	anus
appendic/o	appendix
bil/i	bile
bilirubin/o	bile pigment
bucc/o	cheek
cec/o	cecum
celi/o	abdomen
cheil/o	lip
chole/o	gall/bile
choleangio/o	bile duct
cholecyst/o	gallbladder
choledoch/o	common bile duct
col/o	colon
diverticul/o	diverticulum
enter/o	small intestine
esophag/o	esophagus
gastr/o	stomach
gloss/o	tongue
hepat/o	liver
herni/o	hernia

Key Roots, Suffixes, and Prefixes (continued)		Acronyms/Abbreviations	
ile/o	ileum	GERD	Gastroesophageal reflux disease
jejun/o	jejunum	GI	Gastrointestinal
lith/o	stone	HJR	Hepatojugular reflux
or/o	mouth		
pancreat/o	pancreas		
polyp/o	polyp		
pylor/o	pylorus		
rect/o	rectum		
sigmoid/o	sigmoid colon		

Section Review 4.11

1. A 39-year-old patient underwent a left femoral hernia repair. The postoperative diagnosis was recurrent left femoral hernia. What is the diagnosis code for this encounter?

    A. K41.41

    B. K41.91

    C. K41.21

    D. K40.91

2. A patient presents for a liver transplant. The provider documents the patient has Laennec's cirrhosis associated with long term alcohol dependent use. What are the diagnosis codes for this encounter?

    A. K74.60, F10.99

    B. K70.30, F10.20

    C. K76.89, F10.20

    D. K70.0, F10.99

3. A patient presents with abdominal pain. The physician performs an abdominal ultrasound and discovers the patient has gallstones and inflammation of the gallbladder. Select the diagnosis code(s).

    A. R10.9, K80.10

    B. K80.10, K80.20

    C. K80.10

    D. K80.70

Documentation Dissection

Case 1

Established patient here today for <u>head congestion, cough, low grade fever, chills, and sweats,</u> [1] which have become worse over the last five days. Felt better after two days but then got worse again. She was exposed to a dog on Tuesday and symptoms started two days later. She has a <u>history of recurrent/chronic sinusitis.</u> [2]

PMH/FamHx/SocHx reviewed. All other ROS negative beyond the above.

Vital signs as listed above. Pleasant female NAD. Voice is nasal. Nares are completely occluded despite using Nasonex. Oropharynx reveals a moderate amount of yellow mucus drainage, mildly hyperemic mucosa. TMs and EACs normal. Neck is supple with bilateral anterior cervical lymphadenopathy, minimally tender, no rigidity. She has tenderness over the nasal bridge and left side of the forehead.

Assessment & Plan

<u>Acute, recurrent sinusitis</u> [3] —Bactrim DS 1 p.o. b.i.d. times 10 days. Referral to Dr. Milligan. I have asked her to increase her Nasonex to twice per day. Medications and side effects reviewed with patient and patient voices understanding.

----

[1] The provider documents the signs and symptoms the patient describes.

[2] The physician documents a past history of recurrent/chronic sinusitis. There is no "history of" code for sinusitis. This is not reported separately.

[3] The provider's final diagnosis is acute sinusitis.

What ICD-10-CM code is reported?

Code(s): J01.91

Rationale: The patient is diagnosed with acute recurrent sinusitis, but the sinus affected is not documented. From the Index to Diseases and Injuries, look up Sinusitis/acute/recurrent J01.91. It is not necessary to code the history of sinusitis because the patient is being treated for acute recurrent sinusitis. ICD-10-CM guidelines, section I.B.8 states when the same condition is described as both acute and chronic with separate subentries in the Alphabetic Index, at the same indentation level, both should be coded with acute listed first; however, acute and chronic are not at the same indentation level making acute more specific.

ICD-9-CM Application

What is the ICD-9-CM code reported?

Code: 461.9

Rationale: The patient is diagnosed with acute recurrent sinusitis, but the sinus affected is not documented. From the Index to Diseases, look up Sinusitis/acute. There is no subentry for recurrent. The proper diagnosis is 461.9. It is not necessary to code the history of sinusitis because the patient is being treated for acute recurrent sinusitis. In addition, ICD-9-CM guidelines, section I.B.10 states when the same condition is described as both acute and chronic with separate subentries in the Alphabetic Index, at the same indentation level, both should be coded with acute listed first; however, acute and chronic are not at the same indentation level making acute more specific.

Case 2

Chief Complaints/Concerns: Patient is here to follow up on chronic illnesses.

1. Diabetes [1] Sugars are: avg 170 Readings: 139, 192, 143,149, 237, 151, 183, 210, 215. Was given Novolin samples and was taking same dose as when taking Novolog. Ran out of insurance, so ran out of all meds. Sugar drop seen, but unable to get to machine to check reading. Had to get sugar in system right away.

Review of Systems

Constitutional: No fever, fatigue, night sweats. No significant weight loss or gain.

HEENT: No vision changes, no chronic nasal congestion, no hearing loss.

Respiratory: No wheezes or cough, respirations are 20/minute.

Neuro/Psychiatric: Negative for headache, psychiatric/emotional problems, Lightheadedness/dizziness.

Dermatologic: No unusual rashes.

Vital Signs: BP: 130/78; Weight: 150 lbs

Assessment/Plan

1. Diabetes, type 2 [2] Fair Control with the long term use of insulin. [3] Will not make drastic changes due to the fact pt was out of meds.

_____

[1] The type of diabetes is not documented. The provider does document the patient is taking Novalin®, which is insulin.

[2] The physician documents the type of diabetes and that it is controlled.

[3] The provider documents the patient takes insulin.

_____

What ICD-10-CM codes are reported?

Code(s): E11.9, Z79.4

Rationale: To select the correct code for diabetes, you need to know the type and any associated manifestations. From the Index to Diseases and Injuries, look for Diabetes, diabetic/type 2 E11.9. The correct code is E11.9. The Official Coding Guidelines, Section I.C.4.a.3., state that Z79.4 is reported for type II diabetics who are routinely taking insulin. This code is indexed under Long-term (current) (prophylactic) drug therapy (use of)/insulin.

ICD-9-CM Application

What ICD-9-CM codes are reported?

Codes: 250.00, V58.67

Rationale: To select the correct code for diabetes, you need to know the type and whether it is controlled or uncontrolled. There is no indication of a diabetic manifestation. From the Index to Diseases, look up Diabetes, diabetic (250.0x). The fifth digit for this case is "0" to indicate the patient has type II diabetes that is controlled. The correct code is 250.00. The Official Coding Guidelines, section I.C.3.a.3 state that V58.67 is reported for type II diabetics who are routinely taking insulin. This V code is indexed under Long-term (current) (prophylactic) drug use/insulin.

Glossary

Acute Exacerbation—Worsening or a decompensation of a chronic condition.

AIDS (Acquired Immune Deficiency Syndrome)—A chronic, potentially life—threatening disease that is caused by HIV. The patient's immune system is compromised, which makes him or her highly susceptible to diseases and infections.

Anemia—Decrease in the number of red blood cells.

Atherosclerosis—Hardening of the arteries caused by fats in the blood.

Benign Hypertension—Continuous, mild blood pressure elevation.

Benign Neoplasm—A non-malignant neoplasm.

Carcinoma *In Situ*—A localized cancer that has not spread to adjacent structures.

Cataracts—Flaws or clouds that develop in the crystalline lens.

Cerebrovascular Accident—The sudden death of some brain cells due to lack of oxygen, when the blood flow to the brain is impaired by blockage or rupture of an artery to the brain.

Cholelithiasis—Gallstones.

Cholecystitis—Inflammation of the gallbladder.

Congestive Heart Failure—The heart is unable to pump away the blood returning to it fast enough, which causes congestion in the veins.

Conjunctivitis—Inflammation or infection of the conjunctiva, which is the transparent layer that lines the part of the eye and eyelid.

Coronary Artery Diseases (CAD)—Blockage of the coronary arteries.

Dementia—A group of symptoms that effect memory and cognitive functions such as judgment and communication.

Epigastric Hernia—A protrusion of internal organ through the epigastrium above the umbilicus.

Epilepsy—Causes disturbances in the electrical activity of the brain.

Glaucoma—A hypertensive condition of the eye caused by too much pressure from fluid.

Goiter—Enlargement of the thyroid gland.

Hernia—Organ or tissue protruding through the wall or cavity that usually contains it.

HIV (Human Immunodeficiency Virus)—A virus that attacks the immune system.

Incisional Hernia—Protrusion of internal organs near an incompletely closed surgical incision site.

Inguinal Hernia—Protrusion of internal organs in the groin.

Intractable (as in migraine)—Severe migraine that does not respond to therapeutic treatment.

Leukemia—Cancer of blood and bone marrow.

Lipoma—Benign tumor made up of fat cells.

Lymphoma—Cancer of the lymphatic system.

Malignant Hypertension—Accelerated, severe form of hypertension that usually causes permanent organ damage.

Malignant Neoplasm—Cancerous tumor that tends to grow, invade, and metastasize.

Manifestation—Condition or symptom that develops as a result of an underlying condition or cause.

Melanoma—Skin cancer that originates in cells called melanocytes, which produce pigment in the skin.

Meningitis—Infection or inflammation of the membranes that surround the head and spinal cord.

Metastases—Spread of cancer from one body area/organ to another.

Myocardial Infarction—Death of tissue in the myocardium.

Neoplastic Disease—Condition related to a tumor or growth.

Neuropathy—Abnormal condition characterized by inflammation or degeneration of peripheral nerves.

NSTEMI—Not ST elevation myocardial infarction; blood clot partly occludes the artery, and only a portion of the heart muscle being supplied by the affected artery dies.

Otitis Media—Middle ear infection.

Parkinson's Disease—Slowly progressive, degenerative neurologic disease.

Pleural Effusion—Abnormal fluid accumulation in the pleural spaces.

Sepsis—A whole body inflammatory state.

Status Asthmaticus—Asthma that is not responding to treatment.

STEMI—ST elevation myocardial infarction; coronary artery completely blocked, and nearly all the heart muscle being supplied by the affected artery starts to die.

Thyrotoxicosis—Morbid condition due to over activity of the thyroid gland.

Umbilical Hernia—Protrusion of internal organs through the abdominal wall around the umbilicus.

Urosepsis—Bacteremia resulting from urinary tract infection.

Ventral Hernia (Incisional Hernia)—Protrusion of internal organs near an incompletely closed surgical incision site.

Chapter
5

ICD-10-CM Coding Chapters 12–21

Introduction

In this chapter, we will discuss coding guidelines specific to Chapters 12–21 in the ICD-10-CM codebook. These chapters include:

- Diseases of the Skin and Subcutaneous Tissue
- Diseases of the Musculoskeletal and Connective Tissue
- Genitourinary System
- Pregnancy, Childbirth, and the Puerperium
- Certain Conditions Originating in the Perinatal Period
- Congenital Malformations, Deformations and Chromosomal Abnormalities
- Symptoms, Signs, and Abnormal Clinical and Laboratory Findings
- Injury, Poisoning and Certain Other Consequences of External Causes
- External Causes of Morbidity
- Factors Influencing Health Status and Contact with Health Services

Objectives

The objectives of this chapter are:

- Understand the chapter specific official coding guidelines for ICD-10-CM Chapters 12–21
- Recognize common diagnoses coded in each ICD-10-CM chapter
- Recognize main terms to start the code search
- Follow proper look up sequences to select diagnosis codes

Chapter 12: Diseases Skin & Subcutaneous Tissue (L00-L99)

Chapter 12 classifies diseases and disorders of the nails, hair, hair follicles, sweat glands, sebaceous glands, epidermis, dermis, and subcutaneous tissue. Common diagnoses in this chapter include cellulitis, dermatitis, and pressure ulcers.

Cellulitis and Acute Lymphangitis

Cellulitis and acute lymphangitis are reported with the same subcategory of codes in ICD-10-CM. Cellulitis is a bacterial infection of the skin and subcutaneous tissue. Common

signs and symptoms include redness, swelling, and pain. A fever may occur, as may regional lymph node enlargement. Lymphangitis is an infection of the lymph vessels which can result from an acute streptococcal infection of the skin caused by staphylococcal infection. Lymphangitis can be a sign that a skin infection is getting worse. Codes are selected based on the anatomic site and type inflammation or infection, can also include if the condition is acute and laterality.

Example

A patient presents to the emergency room complaining of swelling and painful inflammation of his right thigh. The provider performs an exam and diagnoses the patient with cellulitis of his thigh. The correct code is:

- L03.115 Cellulitis of right lower limb

In the Index to Diseases and Injuries, look for Cellulitis/thigh and you are referred to see Cellulitis, lower limb. Look for Cellulitis/lower limb L03.11-. Turn to L03.11 in the Tabular List. 6th character 5 is reported to indicate cellulitis of the right lower limb.

Dermatitis

Dermatitis is inflammation of the skin. It is characterized by itching, swelling, and blistering. There are different types of dermatitis such as seborrheic, atopic, and contact dermatitis. Eczema refers to various skin inflammations with common features such as itching, red patches, and small blisters that burst, causing the skin to become moist and crusty. Atopic eczema (atopic dermatitis) is the most common type, and is associated with an allergic reaction. The block of codes for dermatitis and eczema (L20-L30) uses the terms dermatitis and eczema synonymously. Codes for dermatitis and eczema are selected based on the type or the substance that caused the dermatitis. For example, dermatitis that develops as a result of exposure to an acetone paint solvent is coded L24.2 Irritant contact dermatitis due to solvents. This is found in the Index to Diseases and Injuries by looking for Dermatitis/due to/acetone or Dermatitis/due to/solvents.

Pressure Ulcers

Pressure ulcers also are known as bed sores and decubitus ulcers. Pressure ulcers are areas of damaged skin and tissue developing as a result of compromised circulation. When a patient stays in one position without movement, the weight of the bones against the skin inhibits circulation and causes an ulceration of the tissue. Pressure ulcers usually form near the heaviest bones (buttocks, hips, and heels).

There are stages of pressure ulcers that identify the extent of the tissue damage.

- Stage 1—Persistent focal erythema
- Stage 2—Partial thickness skin loss involving epidermis, dermis, or both
- Stage 3—Full thickness skin loss extending through subcutaneous tissue
- Stage 4—Necrosis of soft tissue extending to muscle and bone

Code selection is based on the location of the ulcer, laterality (if applicable), and the stage of the ulcer. For each location, there is an option to identify an unstageable ulcer. An unstageable ulcer is when the base of the ulcer is covered in eschar or slough so much that it cannot be determined how deep the ulcer is. This diagnosis is determined based on the clinical documentation. This code should not be used if the stage is not documented. In that instance, report the unspecified code for that location.

The category of codes for pressure ulcers (L89) has a note to code first any associated gangrene from category I96.

Practical Coding Note

Because there are several pages of ICD-10-CM codes for pressure ulcers, make a note at the top of each page to remind you to code associated gangrene first, if applicable.

When multiple sites are documented, select a code for each anatomic site and stage. The sequence depends on the pressure ulcer being treated. If all the pressure ulcers are being treated, sequence the code for the most severe pressure ulcer first.

Example

A patient with a stage 3 pressure ulcer on her left heel and a stage 2 pressure ulcer of her left hip is scheduled for debridement. The correct codes and sequence are:

- L89.623 Pressure ulcer of left heel, stage 3
- L89.222 Pressure ulcer of left hip, stage 2

Look in the Index to Diseases and Injuries for Ulcer/pressure then locate the site. In the Tabular List, determine the correct code selection to identify the laterality, and stage.

If the pressure ulcer is healed completely, a code is not reported for the pressure ulcer. There are some cases where the pressure ulcer will get worse during the course of the admission. For example, the patient is admitted for treatment of a stage 2 ulcer that progresses to stage 3. You report the code for the highest stage.

ICD-9-CM Application

The ICD-9-CM and ICD-10-CM Official Guidelines for Coding and Reporting both contain guidelines for coding of pressure ulcers. In ICD-9-CM, two codes are required to identify the site of the pressure ulcer and the stage of the pressure ulcer. In ICD-10-CM, only one code is required to report both the location and the stage. In addition, ICD-9-CM has guidelines for reporting of bilateral pressure ulcers. In ICD-10-CM, the right and left hips have separate codes.

ICD-9-CM:

707.04 Pressure ulcer, hip

707.21 Pressure ulcer, stage I

ICD-10-CM:

L89.201 Pressure ulcer of unspecified hip, stage 1

L89.211 Pressure ulcer of right hip, stage 1

L89.221 Pressure ulcer of left hip, stage 1

Key Roots, Suffixes, and Prefixes

aden/o	gland	kerat/o	hard
adip/o	fat	melan/o	black
albin/o	white	necr/o	death
auto/o	self	pil/o	hair
cutane/o	skin	seb/o	sebum/oil
cyan/o	blue	staphyl/o	cluster
derm/o	skin	trich/o	hair
erythem/o	red	ungu/o	nail
hidr/o	sweat	xanth/o	yellow
ichthy/o	dry/scaly		

Acronyms/Abbreviations

Derm	Dermatology
PPD	Purified protein derivative; skin test for tuberculosis
SLE	Systemic lupus erythematosus
SubQ	Subcutaneous

Section Review 5.1

1. A patient is diagnosed with pressure ulcers on each heel. Select the diagnosis code(s).

    A. L97.409

    B. L89.619

    C. L89.610, L89.620

    D. L89.619, L89.629

2. A patient complains of a rash that is extremely itchy. It began when she started using a new laundry detergent. She is examined and the provider diagnoses her with dermatitis, due to exposure to the laundry detergent. What is the diagnosis code?

    A. L23.9

    B. L20.89

    C. L23.5

    D. L24.0

3. A provider performs an incision and drainage on a large abscess on the patient's left leg. What is the diagnosis code?

    A. L02.416

    B. L02.91

    C. L72.9

    D. L23.9

Chapter 13: Diseases of Musculoskeletal and Connective Tissue (M00–M99)

Chapter 13 covers diseases and disorders of bones, muscles, cartilage, fascia, ligaments, tendons, and bursa. Common diagnoses from this chapter include pathologic fractures, stress fractures, and osteoporosis. In ICD-10-CM, most of the codes within Chapter 13 have site and laterality designation. This means the bone, joint or muscle involved is reported along with the side of the body affected. For certain conditions, the bone may be affected at the upper or lower end of the bone. Although the portion of the bone affected may be part of the joint, the bone will be the site, not the joint.

Example

M87.261 Osteonecrosis due to previous trauma, right tibia

ICD-9-CM Application

In ICD-9-CM, most of the codes in chapter 13 of ICD-9-CM require a fifth digit to identify the site. The fifth digit sub classification used with categories 711–712, 715–716, 718–719, and 730 are defined in the beginning of chapter 13. In each subcategory, there are fifth digit codes in brackets. This informs the coder which fifth digit codes are valid for the subcategory.

Example

718.0x Articular cartilage disorder

[0-5, 7-9]

In this example, the only valid fifth digits are 0-5 or 7-9.

Many musculoskeletal conditions are the result of a previous injury. Codes for these conditions are found in ICD-10-CM Chapter 13. Any current, acute injuries are coded with the appropriate injury code from ICD-10-CM Chapter 19.

Arthritis

Arthritis is an inflammation of joint(s), and also may involve the muscles and connective tissues. Common signs and symptoms include pain, stiffness, inflammation, and movement limitations. The most common types of arthritis are osteoarthritis and rheumatoid arthritis.

Osteoarthritis also is known as degenerative joint disease, which is a condition that develops over time. This is a chronic condition that is a result of the cartilage in the joints wearing down. Cartilage is soft and flexible, and allows easy movement at the joints. If the cartilage wears down, movement at the joints becomes painful because there is bone moving against bone. Codes for osteoarthritis are determined by site and laterality. Also includes the type of arthritis such as primary, secondary or post-traumatic. Primary does not have a known cause. Secondary develops as a result of an injury or disease.

Example

A patient has been complaining of chronic right hip pain. Physician examines the patient and he is diagnosed with primary osteoarthritis of the right hip. Patient is given a prescription for antiflammatory drug to relieve the pain.

M16.11 Unilateral primary osteoarthritis, right hip

Rheumatoid arthritis is an autoimmune disease that affects the whole body. Common symptoms are joint pain and swelling, stiffness in the joints in the morning, red and puffy hands, and fatigue. Codes for rheumatoid arthritis are determined by site, laterality, complication, and with or without rheumatoid factor. Rheumatoid factor is an antibody that is present in the blood of most people with rheumatoid arthritis.

Example

A 65-year-old patient has been complaining of stiffness and pain in her fingers in both hands first thing in the morning. Physician examines the patient, performs an X-ray of the hands and rheumatoid factor blood test. The X-ray reveals the characteristics of early joint damage and the rheumatoid factor is positive. She is diagnosed with rheumatoid arthritis.

M05.841 Other rheumatoid arthritis with rhematoid factor of right hand

M05.842 Other rheumatoid arthritis with rhematoid factor of left hand

---

Pathologic Fractures and Stress Fractures

A pathologic fracture is a broken bone that occurs in an area of weakened bone. The cause is typically due to another disease such as a neoplasm or osteoporosis (see below). A stress fracture is a result of repeated force or overuse. These fractures are considered non-traumatic. These codes are not reported for traumatic fractures (which will be discussed later in this chapter). A code from Category M84 is reported for pathologic or stress fractures. In the Index to Diseases and Injuries look for Fracture, pathological.

A malunion fracture is when the fracture has healed in an undesirable position resulting in a deformity or crooked limb. Different types of deformities are when the fractured bones are healed twisted, bent, or one bone is shorter than normal.

A nonunion fracture is when the fracture is not healing. New bone tissue is not growing to bridge the gap between the broken bones.

In ICD-10-CM, a 7th character extension is used to report the phase of treatment for a pathologic fracture. An example of 7th character extensions is found in category M80 Osteoporosis with current pathological fracture:

A - Initial encounter for fracture

D - Subsequent encounter for fracture with routine healing

G - Subsequent encounter for fracture with delayed healing

K - Subsequent encounter for fracture with nonunion

P - Subsequent encounter for fracture with malunion

S - Sequela

Example

M80.021D Age-related osteoporosis with current pathological fracture, right humerus, subsequent encounter for fracture with routine healing

Seventh character A is for use as long as the patient is receiving active treatment for the fracture. Examples of active treatment are: surgical treatment, emergency department encounter, evaluation and treatment by a new physician. Seventh character D is to be used for encounters after the patient has completed active treatment. The other seventh characters, listed under each subcategory in the Tabular List, are to be used for subsequent encounters for treatment of problems associated with the healing, such as malunions and nonunions, and sequelae. Care for complications of surgical treatment for fracture repairs during the healing or recovery phase should be coded with the appropriate complication codes.

ICD-9-CM Application

In ICD-9-CM, 7th character extenders are not used. Once the patient has completed the active phase of treatment, report the appropriate aftercare code (V code). Aftercare codes can be found in the Index to Diseases under the main term Aftercare. Pathologic fractures can be found in the Index to Diseases by looking for Fracture/pathologic then locating the site.

Malunion and nonunion fractures are identified with their own code in ICD-9-CM. Malunion fractures are reported with code 733.81. Nonunion fractures are reported with code 733.82.

The codes for stress fractures are selected based on site. There is a notation under codes 733.93 - 733.98 which states to report an E code to identify the external cause of the stress fracture. Codes for stress fractures can be found in the Index to Diseases by looking for Fracture/stress and then locating the site.

Osteoporosis

Osteoporosis is a bone disease that decreases bone density. The loss of bone mass can cause pathologic fractures. Osteoporosis is coded based on the type, such as age-related or other, and with or without current pathologic fracture. The site is not required to code osteoporosis when there is not a current pathological fracture. However, when a current pathological fracture occurs with osteoporosis, the site must be known to determine the correct code. One combination code is reported for the pathological fracture and osteoporosis.

For category M80 Osteoporosis with current pathological fracture, you are instructed to use an additional code to identify major osseous defect, if applicable (M89.7). A code from category M80, not a traumatic fracture code, should be used for any patient with known osteoporosis who suffers a fracture, even if the patient had a minor fall or trauma, if that fall or trauma would not usually break a normal, healthy bone.

For category M81 Osteoporosis without current pathological fracture, a history code should also be reported if the patient has had a fracture in the past.

Example

A patient is treated with medication for postmenopausal osteoporosis. The patient had a pathologic fracture one year ago and the physician is following her condition every three months.

M81.0 Age-related osteoporosis without current pathological fracture

Z87.310 Personal history of (healed) osteoporosis fracture

Key Roots, Suffixes, and Prefixes		Acronyms/Abbreviations	
arthr/o	joint	ACL	Anterior cruciate ligament
chondr/o	cartilage	AKA	Above the knee amputation
cost/o	rib	BKA	Below the knee amputation
fasci/o	fibrous tissue	C1–C7	Cervical vertebrae
lamin/o	lamina	CTS	Carpal tunnel syndrome
-malacia	softening	Fx	Fracture
my/o	muscle	L1–L5	Lumbar vertebrae
myel/o	bone marrow/spinal cord	OA	Osteoarthritis
oste/o	bone	RA	Rheumatoid arthritis
spondly/o	vertebra	T1–T12	Thoracic vertebrae
		TMJ	Temporomandibular joint

Section Review 5.2

1. An MRI confirmed the patient has sciatica caused by a herniated disc between L5 and S1. She is scheduled for an injection in this office, after which she will be referred to a physical therapist in an effort to avoid surgery. Select the diagnosis code(s).

    A. M51.17

    B. M51.17, M54.40

    C. M51.15

    D. M51.86

2. A provider performs an arthroscopic procedure to repair an incomplete right degenerative rotator cuff tear on a patient with primary, degenerative arthritis in the same shoulder. Select the diagnosis codes.

    A. M75.111, M19.211

    B. M75.111, M19.011

    C. M66.211, M19.011

    D. S43.421A, M19.011

3. A patient with age-related osteoporosis suffers a pathologic fracture to her right hip. She is being seen for this new fracture today. Select the diagnosis codes.

    A. M81.0, Z87.311

    B. S72.091A, M80.851A

    C. M80.051A

    D. M80.851A

Chapter 14: Diseases of Genitourinary System (N00–N99)

This ICD-10-CM chapter includes diagnoses of the urinary system and male and female genital organs. The urinary system includes the kidneys, bladder, ureters, and urethra. The male genital organs include the prostate, penis, testis, scrotum, and epididymis. The female genital organs include the breast, uterus, fallopian tubes, ovaries, vagina, and external genitalia.

Common diagnoses found in this chapter of ICD-10-CM include chronic kidney disease, acute kidney failure, urinary incontinence, urinary tract infection, kidney stones, benign prostatic hypertrophy, endometriosis, uterine fibroids, dysplasia, and pelvic inflammatory disease.

Chronic Kidney Disease

Chronic kidney disease (CKD) is the only disease in this ICD-10-CM chapter that has official coding guidelines. When reporting chronic kidney disease, select the code with the proper fourth character to identify the stage of CKD. Staging the CKD helps quantify the severity of the disease. Glomerular filtration rate (GFR) is used to determine the stage of CKD. The patient's age, weight, gender, and serum creatinine (waste product in the blood from muscle activity) are used to calculate the GFR. There are five stages of CKD:

- N18.1 Stage I—GFR > 90 ml/min/1.73 m2
- N18.2 Stage II—GFR 60–89 ml/min/1.73 m2
- N18.3 Stage III—GFR 30–59 ml/min/1.73 m2
- N18.4 Stage IV—GFR 15–29 ml/min/1.73 m2
- N18.5 Stage V—GFR < 15 ml/min/1.73 m2
- N18.6 End Stage Renal Disease (ESRD)—GFR < 15 ml/min/1.73 m2, and the patient is on dialysis or undergoing kidney transplant.

Sometimes providers will document CKD and ESRD for the same patient. In such a case, report N18.6 End stage renal disease only. When reporting N18.6, an additional code should also be reported to identify dialysis status.

Example

The patient presents with decreased urine output, nausea, vomiting, and drowsiness. The patient is diagnosed with CKD and ESRD. The decreased urine output, nausea, vomiting, and drowsiness are not reported because all are signs/symptoms of ESRD. According to the Official Coding Guidelines, the only diagnosis code reported for the CKD and ESRD is N18.6. To locate ESRD in the Index to Diseases and Injuries, look for Disease/renal/end-stage (failure). An additional code is reported for the dialysis status (Z99.2) if applicable.

Patients who undergo a kidney transplant may continue to have CKD because the kidneys are not restored to full function. Do not assume a patient who has had a kidney transplant and CKD developed the CKD because of the transplant. Select the code to report the stage of CKD and Z94.0 to report kidney transplant status. Kidney transplant status is found in the Index to Diseases and Injuries under Transplant/kidney Z94.0.

ICD-9-CM Application

Kidney transplant status is found in the ICD-9-CM Index to Diseases by looking for Status/transplant/kidney V42.0.

Patients with CKD can suffer from other conditions, such as hypertension, diabetes mellitus, anemia, and transplant complications. The guidelines for proper code selection and sequencing for CKD and these other conditions are found in the following ICD-10-CM guidelines:

- See I.C.9.a.2.and 3.for hypertensive chronic kidney disease
- See I.C.19.g.3.b. Kidney transplant complications, for instructions on coding documented transplant rejection or failure

Example

A Type II diabetic with stage 3 diabetic CKD presents to his physician's office for a six month follow-up visit. The proper diagnosis codes and sequencing are:

- E11.22 Type 2 diabetes mellitus with diabetic chronic kidney disease
- N18.3 Chronic Kidney Disease, Stage 3 (moderate)

In the Index to Diseases and Injuries, look for Diabetes/type 2/with/chronic kidney disease E11.22. Turn to the Tabular List to verify E11.22. Under E11.22 is a note to use an additional code to identify the stage of chronic kidney disease. Stage 3 CKD is reported with N18.3.

Acute Renal Failure

Acute renal failure (ARF) is the rapid decrease in the kidney's ability to function. Common symptoms include anorexia, nausea, and vomiting. If the condition is left untreated, the patient may have seizures or become comatose. Do not confuse chronic kidney disease and acute renal failure; they are different conditions. CKD develops over time. ARF has a rapid onset. Select the code for the condition documented by the provider.

The code for ARF is found in the Index to Diseases and Injuries by looking for Failure/renal/acute. The fourth character identifies the location of a lesion of necrosis. If a part of the kidney is denied oxygen, the tissue becomes damaged or destroyed. Necrosis in kidney tissues will cause acute renal failure. The most common term you will see documented is ARF or acute kidney failure. Without additional information, the only code option is N17.9 Acute kidney failure, unspecified.

Urinary Incontinence

Urinary incontinence is involuntary loss of urine. This condition can occur in both men and women, but is most common in women. The two most common documented types of urinary incontinence are urge incontinence and stress incontinence. Urge incontinence is a sudden need to urinate followed by the involuntary release of urine. There is not much time from feeling the need to urinate and the loss of the urine. Stress incontinence occurs with an activity such as coughing, sneezing, or exercise. To locate a code for urinary incontinence, you need to know the type of incontinence. If the underlying cause of the incontinence is known, it should be sequenced first.

Example

A patient with uterine prolapse presents to her physician complaining of "wetting herself" every time she sneezes. The provider orders a urinalysis. The patient is diagnosed with uterine prolapse and stress incontinence. The correct codes and sequence are:

- N81.4 Uterovaginal prolapse, unspecified
- N39.3 Stress incontinence (female) (male)

Look in the Index to Diseases and Injuries for Prolapse, proplapsed/uterus (with prolapse of vagina). For stress incontinence, look for Incontinence/urine (urinary)/stress (female) (male). Turn to the Tabular List to verify both codes.

ICD-9-CM Application

In ICD-9-CM, stress incontinence has separate codes depending on whether the patient is male or female. In ICD-10-CM, the same code is used for both male and female.

ICD-9-CM

For females, look in the ICD-9-CM Index to Diseases for Incontinence/urine/stress (female) 625.6. For males, look in the ICD-9-CM Index to Diseases for Incontinence/urine/stress (female)/male NEC 788.32.

625.6 Stress incontinence, female

788.32 Stress incontinence, male

ICD-10-CM

Look in the ICD-10-CM Index to Diseases and Injuries for Incontinence/urine (urinary)/stress (female) (male) N39.3.

N39.3 Stress incontinence (female) (male).

Urinary Tract Infection

Urinary Tract Infection (UTI) is an infection of any of the organs in the urinary tract (kidneys, bladder, or urethra). If the provider documents the specific organ, select a code for the specific organ rather than the code for the UTI. If the specific organ is not documented, the only option is N39.0 Urinary tract infection, site not specified. There is an instruction to "Use additional code to identify infectious agent" found under this code. Depending on the organism, you will report two codes or one combination code.

Example

A patient is diagnosed with a candida UTI. In the Index to Diseases and Injuries, look for Candidiasis, candidal/urogenital site NEC. You are required to know the specific site (urethra, etc.) to report this infection. Turn to the Tabular List to verify B37.49 *Candidiasis of other urogenital sites*. In this example, only one code is needed because the description includes the organism and the site.

Kidney Stones

Kidney stones also are called calculus or nephrolithiasis (Nephr/o = kidney, lith = calculus or stone, iasis = condition of). They are hard deposits made up of minerals forming in the kidneys. Symptoms include pain (lower back, abdomen), the frequent urge to urinate, change in the color of urine, nausea, vomiting, fever, and chills. The diagnosis can be found under several different key terms in the Index to Diseases and Injuries: Stone(s)/kidney; Calculus/kidney; or Nephrolithiasis.

Benign Prostatic Hyperplasia

Benign Prostatic Hyperplasia (Hypertrophy)(BPH) is an enlargement of the prostate gland. The prostate gland surrounds the urethra. When it becomes enlarged, it can cause urinary symptoms such as a weak stream, urgency, and incomplete emptying of the bladder. It can be found in the Index to Diseases and Injuries by looking for Enlargement/prostate or Hyperplasia/prostate. When selecting the diagnosis for BPH, the fourth character identifies whether the patient has urinary obstruction and other urinary tract infections. For example:

N40.0 Enlarged prostate without lower urinary tract symptoms

N40.1 Enlarged prostate with lower urinary tract symptoms

There is the note "use additional code to identify symptoms" under N40.1. Usually you do not code for symptoms when a definitive disease is identified. In this case, the instructional note provides guidance that a code for the symptoms is required.

Example

A patient with BPH develops urinary retention. The proper codes and sequence are:

- N40.1 Enlarged prostate with lower urinary tract symptoms
- R33.8 Urinary retention

Look in the Index to Diseases and Injuries for Enlargement/prostate /with lower urinary tract symptoms (LUTS). Turn to the Tabular List to verify N40.1. Under N40.1, read the note indicating to use an additional code to identify the symptoms; urinary retention (R33.8). Urinary retention can also be found in the Index to Diseases and Injuries by looking under Retention/urine/due to hyperplasia (hypertrophy) of prostate which directs you to see Hyperplasia, prostate. Verify all codes in the Tabular List.

Endometriosis

Endometriosis is a disorder of the female reproductive system where the inner lining (endometrium) of the uterus grows outside of the uterus (fallopian tubes, ovaries, organs in the abdominal, or pelvic organs). Symptoms include pelvic pain, excessive bleeding, painful periods, and infertility. The fourth character identifies where the abnormal growth of tissue is found.

Common Sites of Endometrial Implants

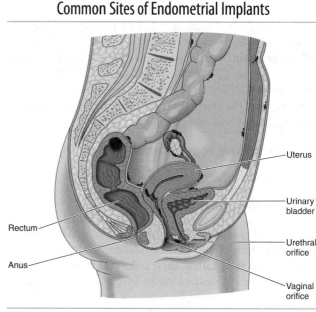

Source: Lindh, Pooler, Tamparo, and Dahl, Delmar's Comprehensive Medical Assisting (Administrative and Clinical Competencies), 4e, ISBN#978-1-4354-1914-8

Example

A patient with very painful periods and excessive menstrual bleeding is diagnosed with endometriosis. The provider performs a laparoscopy to identify the extent of the condition. He documents the endometrial tissue is surrounding the fallopian tubes. He performs a fulguration to remove the abnormal tissue growth. From the Index to Diseases and Injuries, look up Endometriosis/fallopian tube N80.2. Turn to the Tabular List to verify the correct code is N80.2 *Endometriosis of the fallopian tube*. Do not report codes for the symptoms (excessive menstrual bleeding and painful periods) because a definitive diagnosis has been determined.

Uterine Fibroids

Uterine fibroids (leiomyoma) are benign uterine tumors. Symptoms include heavy menstrual bleeding, prolonged periods, pelvic pain, and frequent urination. The fourth character identifies where the fibroid is located. A submucous leiomyoma lies beneath the endometrium. An intramural leiomyoma lies within the uterine wall. A subserous leiomyoma lies under the serous surface of the uterus. In the Index to Diseases and Injuries, look for Leiomyoma/uterus. If you look for Fibroid/uterus you are directed to D25.9; you must look under leiomyoma for the specific locations.

Cervical Dysplasia

Cervical dysplasia, also documented as CIN (Cervical Intraepithelial Neoplasia), is an abnormal growth or premalignant cells of the cervix. There are different grades of CIN diagnosed with a Pap smear. CIN I is mild dysplasia. CIN II is moderate dysplasia. CIN III is severe dysplasia that is considered carcinoma in situ of the cervix. The fourth character identifies the grade of the dysplasia. For example:

N87.9 Dysplasia of cervix uteri, unspecified

N87.0 Mild cervical dysplasia

N87.1 Moderate cervical dysplasia

CIN III is categorized in the Neoplasm section and coded as D06.- Carcinoma in situ of the cervix uteri. The fourth character indicates the location. These codes are found in the Index to Diseases and Injuries looking for Dysplasia/cervix (uteri).

Intraoperative and Postprocedural Complications

Codes from category code N99 *Intraoperative and postprocedural complications and disorders of genitourinary system, not elsewhere classified* are reported when there is a complication(s) to the urinary system, male and female genital organs during or after a surgical procedure. Provider's documentation should indicate the condition (e.g. infection) and the procedure (e.g. cystostomy) for proper code assignment.

Key Roots, Suffixes, and Prefixes

andr/o	male
colp/o	vagina
cyst/o	cyst
dips/o	thirst
glomerul/o	glomerulus
gyn/o	female
hydro/o	water
hyster/o	uterus
ket/o	ketone bodies/ketoacidosis
lith/o	stones
mamm/o	breast
mast/o	breast
meat/o	meatus
men/o	menstruation, month
metro/o	uterus, measure
nephro/o	kidney
obstetr/o	pregnancy/childbirth
olig/o	scant, few
oophor/o	ovary
orch/i	testicle
ov/o	egg
perine/o	perineum
peritone/o	peritoneum
prostat./o	prostate
pyel/o	renal pelvis
ren/o	kidney
salping/o	uterine tube, fallopian tube
test/o	testicle
tryg/o	trigone region/kidney
ur/o	urine
ureter/o	ureter
urethr/o	urethra
uria	urination/urinary condition
urin/o	urine
uter/o	uterus
vagin/o	vagina
vulvu/o	vulva

Acronyms/Abbreviations

ARF	Acute renal failure
BV	Bacterial vaginosis
CPP	Chronic pelvic pain
CKD	Chronic kidney disease
CRF	Chronic renal failure
Cx	Cervix
DUB	Dysfunctional uterine bleeding
ESRD	End stage renal disease
LMP	Last menstrual period
PMS	Premenstrual syndrome
PSA	Prostate specific antigen
SUI	Stress urinary incontinence
UA	Urinalysis
UTI	Urinary tract infection

Section Review 5.3

1. A 55-year-old female with right hydronephrosis presents for a cystourethroscopy with a retrograde pyelogram. What is the correct diagnosis code?

    A. Q62.11

    B. Q62.0

    C. N13.30

    D. N13.6

2. A patient returns to her gynecologist's office to review the results of her ultrasound. She has been experiencing heavy bleeding and painful menstruation. The results of the ultrasound reveal the patient has a uterine fibroid measuring 4.0 cm. Select the diagnosis code(s).

    A. N94.6, N92.0, D25.9

    B. N94.6, N92.1, D25.1

    C. D25.1

    D. D25.9

3. A patient diagnosed with BPH presents with urinary urgency. Select the diagnosis code(s).

    A. N40.0, R39.15

    B. R39.15, N40.1

    C. N40.1, R39.15

    D. N40.1

Chapter 15: Pregnancy, Childbirth, and the Puerperium (O00–O9A)

In this ICD-10-CM chapter, diseases and disorders that occur during pregnancy, childbirth, and puerperium are classified. These codes are reported only on the maternal record. They would not be reported on the newborn's record. Codes from chapter 15 have sequencing priority over codes from all other chapters in ICD-10-CM. Codes from other chapters in ICD-10-CM may be required to document the patient's condition thoroughly, but are sequenced following the code from chapter 15.

Example

A patient with gestational diabetes, controlled with diet, is five months pregnant. If a pregnant patient does not have a previous history of diabetes, a separate ICD-10-CM code to identify the diabetic condition is not required. Look in the ICD-10-CM Index to

Diseases and Injuries for Diabetes/gestational (in pregnancy)/diet controlled O24.410. Turn to the Tabular List to verify the code.

In this example, report O24.410 *Gestational diabetes mellitus in pregnancy, diet controlled.*

Complications related to pregnancy can occur early, during delivery, or during the follow-up period. The puerperium, or follow-up period, is the period from the termination of labor to complete involution of the uterus, which usually is defined as 42 days in length.

The majority of codes for pregnancy require a final character to indicate the trimester of pregnancy. Trimesters are counted from the first day of the last menstrual period:

1st trimester - less than 14 weeks 0 days

2nd trimester - 14 weeks 0 days to less than 28 weeks 0 days

3rd trimester - 28 weeks 0 days until delivery

Example

O46.8X1	Other antepartum hemorrhage, first trimester
O46.8X2	Other antepartum hemorrhage, second trimester
O46.8X3	Other antepartum hemorrhage, third trimester
046.8X9	Other antepartum hemorrhage, unspecified trimester

Practical Coding Note

The trimesters are defined at the beginning of Chapter 15 codes in the Tabular List. Highlight this information and use a tab for easier access to reference back to when needed.

The selection of the trimester is based on the provider's documentation for that encounter. Occasionally, a patient is admitted to the hospital during one trimester and remains in the hospital into a subsequent trimester. In this instance, trimester for the date of admission is used, or for the trimester the complication developed is used, if during that admission. When a delivery occurs during the current admission, and there is a code option for "in childbirth" for the complication, this selection is used for coding. The code for "unspecified trimester" should only be used when documentation in the record is insufficient to determine the trimester and it is not possible to obtain clarification.

Example

O24.1 Pre-existing diabetes mellitus, type 2, in pregnancy, childbirth and the puerperium

Insulin-resistant diabetes mellitus in pregnancy, childbirth and the puerperium
Use additional code (for):
from category E11 to further identify any manifestations
long-term (current) use of insulin (Z79.4)

O24.11 Pre-existing diabetes mellitus, type 2, in pregnancy

O24.111 Pre-existing diabetes mellitus, type 2, in pregnancy, first trimester

O24.112 Pre-existing diabetes mellitus, type 2, in pregnancy, second trimester

O24.113 Pre-existing diabetes mellitus, type 2, in pregnancy, third trimester

O24.119 Pre-existing diabetes mellitus, type 2, in pregnancy, unspecified trimester

O24.12 Pre-existing diabetes mellitus, type 2, in childbirth

O24.13 Pre-existing diabetes mellitus, type 2, in the puerperium

ICD-9-CM Application

A fifth digit sub classification is required for categories 640-649 to denote the current episode of care. Valid fifth digits are in [brackets] under each code.

0 unspecified as to episode of care or not applicable

1 delivered, with or without mention of antepartum condition

2 delivered, with mention of postpartum complications

3 antepartum condition or complication

4 postpartum condition or complication

Example

⑨ 641.8 Other antepartum hemorrhage

[0,1,3] Antepartum or intrapartum hemorrhage associated with:

trauma

uterine leiomyoma

The [0,1,3] in brackets below 641.8 indicates the condition can only be assigned to these fifth digits. That is, the condition can only be assigned during an unspecified episode of care, during the delivery, or as an antepartum condition or complication.

When reporting a code from Chapter 15, a code from category Z3A Weeks of gestation is also reported.

Example

A woman at 16 weeks 2/7 days of her pregnancy presents to her OB/GYN for hemorrhoids.

O22.42 Hemorrhoids in pregnancy, second trimester

Z3A.16 16 weeks gestation of pregnancy

Where applicable, a seventh character is to be assigned for certain categories (O31, O32, O33.3–O33.6, O35, O36, O40, O41, O60.1, O60.2, O64 and O69) to identify the fetus for which the complication code applies. Assign seventh character "0":

- For single gestations
- When the documentation in the record is insufficient to determine the fetus affected and it is not possible to obtain clarification.
- When it is not possible to clinically determine which fetus is affected.

Example

Maternal care for disproportion due to unusually large fetus

O33.5 Maternal care for disproportion due to unusually large fetus

Maternal care for disproportions due to disproportion of fetal origin with normally formed fetus

Maternal care for disproportion due to fetal disproportion NOS

One of the following 7th characters is to be assigned to code O33.5. 7th character 0 is for single gestations and multiple gestations where the fetus is unspecified. 7th characters 1 through 9 are for cases of multiple gestations to identify the fetus for which the code applies. The appropriate code from category O30, Multiple gestation, must also be assigned when assigning code O33.5 with a 7th character of 1 through 9.

0 - not applicable or unspecified

1 - fetus 1

2 - fetus 2

3 - fetus 3

4 - fetus 4

5 - fetus 5

9 - other fetus

O33.5XX0 is reported when the patient has a single gestation that is unusually large.

For routine care, a code from category Z34 *Encounter for supervision of normal pregnancy* is coded. If the patient is seen for an unrelated condition (such as a fracture), Z33.1 *Pregnant state, incidental* may be used as an additional diagnosis. The physician must indicate that the condition being treated is not affecting the pregnancy.

Prenatal complications may range from pregnancy related conditions, such as preeclampsia or hyperemesis gravidarum, to other conditions that can be coded elsewhere but are complicating the pregnancy. It is particularly important to document these encounters because they may be useful in justifying additional prenatal visits. If the patient is considered high risk because of a current condition, the current condition should be noted specifically rather than merely by writing "high risk."

If the patient's current pregnancy appears normal but the patient is considered high risk because of a history of complications, a code from category O09 for Supervision of high risk pregnancy may be used.

There are specific high risk pregnancy codes reported for a patient that is pregnant and will be over the age of 35 at expected date of delivery or younger than 16 years of age at expected date of delivery. If the patient's age is 35-years-old or older at expected date of delivery and has pregnancy complications, there are two subcategories to select a code from. Subcategory O09.5 Supervision of elderly primigravida and multigravida. Primigravida indicates it is the patient's first pregnancy and multigravida indicates she has been pregnant more than once. If the patient is younger than 16 years of age at expected date of delivery, report a code from subcategory O09.6 Supervision of young primigravida and multigravida.

Example

Example 1:

A 42-year-old woman G1P0, at 25 weeks with her first pregnancy comes in to see her obstetrician for follow-up on an ultrasound. The obstetrician reviews the ultrasound and notes the fetus is small and has poor growth.

O36.5920 Maternal care for other known or suspected poor fetal growth, second trimester, not applicable or unspecified fetus

O09.512 Supervision of elderly primigravida, second trimester

Z3A.25 25 weeks gestation of pregnancy

The patient is at 25 weeks which is in the second trimester. In the Index to Diseases and Injuries, look for Pregnancy/complicated by (care of) (management affected by)/fetal (maternal care for)/poor growth guiding you to subcategory code O36.59-. In the Tabular List, sixth character 2 is assigned to indicate the second trimester. Seventh character 0 is assigned to indicate single gestation. The patient is 42 years of age, considered a high risk pregnancy due to her age and has a pregnancy complication. In the Index to Diseases and Injuries look for Pregnancy/complicated by/elderly/primigravida guiding you to subcategory code O09.51-. In the Tabular List, sixth character 2 is assigned to indicate the second trimester. Then look for Pregnancy/weeks of gestation/25 weeks Z3A.25.

Example 2:

A 14-year-old G1P0, at 12 weeks with her first pregnancy is coming in to see the obstetrician for prenatal care. There are no complications and the fetus is doing well.

O09.611 Supervision of young primigravida, first trimester

Z3A.12 12 weeks gestation of pregnancy

The patient is in her 12th week which is the first trimester. Look in the Index to Disease and Injuries under Pregnancy/complicated by/young mother/primgravida guiding you to code O09.61-. From the Tabular List, sixth character 1 is assigned to indicate the first trimester. Then look for Pregnancy/weeks of gestation/12 weeks Z3A.12.

                    AAPC   www.aapc.com   133

Some of the categories in ICD-10-CM Chapter 15 distinguish between conditions of the mother that are pre-existing (existed prior to the pregnancy) and those that are a direct result of the pregnancy. For example, diabetes may occur as a result of the pregnancy (gestational diabetes) or the patient may have had diabetes before becoming pregnant. This distinction must be known to make the correct code choice if the distinction is available within the codes.

Example

A type 2 diabetic patient becomes pregnant and is seen for care in the 10th week of pregnancy. The codes reported are:

O24.111 Pre-existing diabetes mellitus, type 2, in pregnancy, first trimester

Z3A.10 10 weeks gestation of pregnancy

Look in the Alphabetic Index for Pregnancy/complicated by/diabetes (mellitus)/pre-existing/type 2 O24.11-. 10 weeks gestation is in the first trimester. In the Tabular List, sixth character 1 is selected for the first trimester. Then, look in the Alphabetic Index for Pregnancy/weeks of gestation/10 weeks Z3A.10. Verify in the Tabular List.

Another pre-existing condition that affects pregnancy is hypertension. When hypertension exists prior to the pregnancy, and the patient becomes pregnant, a code from category O10 *Pre-existing hypertension* complicating pregnancy, is reported. When the patient has pre-existing hypertensive heart disease or hypertensive chronic kidney disease, it is necessary to add a secondary code from the appropriate hypertension category to specify the type of heart failure or chronic kidney disease.

When a provider documents a fetal condition that is affecting the management of the pregnant patient, a code from categories O35 or O36 is required. The provider must indicate the fetal condition is affecting the management of the pregnant patient. The pregnant patient may require additional diagnostic testing, special care, or termination of the pregnancy. If the provider does not indicate the fetal condition affects the pregnant patient, do not assign a code from categories O35 or O36. If in utero surgery is performed on the fetus, a code from category O35 is reported.

Example

If the provider orders an additional ultrasound at 24 weeks gestation to check the size of the fetus because he is small for dates, the appropriate codes are:

O36.5920 Maternal care for other known or suspected poor fetal growth, second trimester, not applicable or unspecified fetus

Z3A.24 24 weeks gestation of pregnancy

Look in the Alphabetic Index for Pregnancy/complicated by/fetal (maternal care for)/poor growth O36.59-. The patient is at 24 weeks gestation. Turn to the Tabular List for sixth character selection of 2 for the second trimester. Seventh character 0 is reported for single gestation. Then, look in the Alphabetic Index for Pregnancy/weeks of gestation/24 weeks Z3A.24. Verify in the Tabular List.

HIV Infection in Pregnancy, Childbirth and Puerperium

When a pregnant patient is treated for an HIV-related illness, the first listed diagnosis is selected from subcategory O98.7- Human immunodeficiency virus [HIV] disease complicating pregnancy, childbirth and the puerperium, followed by the code(s) for the HIV-related illness(es). If the patient is HIV positive and there is no history of an HIV-related illness, the correct codes are O98.7- and Z21.

Example

A patient in her 11th week of gestation visits her physician for an HIV viral load and CD4 count. She is HIV positive, but has not shown any illness or symptoms.

The diagnosis would be reported as:

- O98.711 Human immunodeficiency virus [HIV] disease complicating pregnancy, first trimester
- Z21 Asymptomatic HIV infection status
- Z3A.11 11 weeks gestation of pregnancy

Look in the Alphabetic Index for Pregnancy/complicated by/human immunodeficiency virus (HIV) disease O98.71-. Turn to the Tabular List for sixth character selection. The patient is at 11 weeks gestation which is the first trimester. Sixth character 1 is selected to indicate the first trimester. For the second code, look in the Alphabetic Index for Human/immunodeficiency virus (HIV) disease (infection)/asymptomatic status Z21. For the weeks of gestation, look in the Alphabetic Index for Pregnancy/weeks of gestation/11 weeks Z3A.11. Verify all codes in the Tabular List.

Diabetes Mellitus and Pregnancy

A patient can be diabetic prior to pregnancy, or develop diabetes during the second or third trimester (gestational diabetes). Diabetes and gestational diabetes complicate the patient's pregnancy. Patients who develop gestational diabetes are at a higher risk of becoming diabetic. Some patients with gestational diabetes only become diabetic during pregnancy, and never develop diabetes mellitus.

Two codes are required when a diabetic patient is pregnant. The first listed code is selected from category O24 *Diabetes mellitus in pregnancy, childbirth, and the puerperium*, followed by a code to report the diabetes mellitus. The secondary code reports the type of diabetes, and must be reported with a code from categories E08-E13. If the patient is a type 2 diabetic being treated with insulin, also report Z79.4 Long-term (current) use of insulin.

Gestational diabetes is reported with a code from subcategory O24.4 Gestational diabetes mellitus. A code from categories E08-E13 are not appropriate when the patient develops gestational diabetes because the diabetic condition was not present prior to the pregnancy.

Practical Coding Note

Next to category code O24 write a small note to report a code from categories E08-E13 as an additional diagnosis. Next to subcategory O24.4 write a small note NOT to report a code from categories E08-E13 with gestational diabetes.

When a patient has sepsis and septic shock complicating abortion, pregnancy, childbirth and the puerperium, a code from subcategory for O98.8 *Other maternal infectious and parasitic diseases complicating pregnancy, childbirth and the puerperium* is reported. The specific type of infection should be assigned as an additional diagnosis. If severe sepsis is present, a code from subcategory R65.2 and code(s) for associated organ dysfunction(s) are also reported.

Puerperal sepsis is an infection in the genital tract that develops during the postpartum period. This condition is not reported with a code from category A40 Streptococcal sepsis or category A41 Other sepsis. Rather, there is a code specific to this condition: Report a code from subcategory O85 Puerperal sepsis with a secondary code that describes the causal organism. If severe sepsis is documented, or if the patient develops acute organ dysfunction, report R65.2- with an additional code to identify the acute organ dysfunction.

Example

A patient is admitted to treat puerperal sepsis caused by Enterococcus fecalis two weeks following her delivery. During the admission, she develops severe sepsis with acute kidney failure. The correct codes and sequence are:

- O85 Puerperal sepsis

- B95.2 Enterococcus as the cause of diseases classified elsewhere
- R65.20 Severe sepsis without septic shock
- N17.9 Acute kidney failure, unspecified

Look in the Alphabetic Index for Sepsis/puerperal, postpartum, childbirth (pelvic) O85. We know the causal organism is Streptococcus fecalis, which is also reported. Look in the Alphabetic Index for Infection/bacterial NOS/as cause of diseases classified elsewhere/Enterococcus B95.2. The patient also has severe sepsis and organ failure; additional codes are reported as indicated by the notes under O85. Look in the Alphabetic Index for Sepsis/severe (R65.20) and for Failure/renal/acute (N17.9). Verify all codes in the Tabular List.

When a mother uses alcohol or any type of tobacco product during pregnancy, it is reported with the appropriate complication of pregnancy, childbirth, and the puerperium code from subcateogry O99.31 or O99.33 along with the code for the alcohol related disorder (F10-) or nicotine dependence (F17-).

Example

Alcohol use

O99.31- Alcohol use complicating pregnancy, childbirth, and the puerperium

F10- Alcohol related disorders

Tobacco use

O99.33- Smoking (tobacco) complicating pregnancy, childbirth, and the puerperium

F17- Nicotine dependence.

When a pregnancy patient has poisoning, toxic effects, adverse effects or underdosing in a pregnant patient, a code from subcategory O9A.2 *Injury, poisoning and certain other consequences of external causes complicating pregnancy, childbirth, and the puerperium*, should be sequenced first, followed by the appropriate injury, poisoning, toxic effect, adverse effect or underdosing code. Additional codes are assigned that specify the condition caused by the poisoning, toxic effect, adverse effect or underdosing are also assigned.

When a patient has a normal delivery, code O80 *Encounter for full-term uncomplicated delivery* or code O82 *Encounter for cesarean delivery* without indication is reported. If a complication occurs during delivery, the code for the complication is reported, do not report an uncomplicated delivery code with a complication pregnancy code. If more than one complication occurs, a code is reported to identify each complication.

Whether the delivery is normal or complicated, a code for the outcome of delivery is required (Z37). The fourth character in this subcategory reports the number of births and status (liveborn or stillborn). The outcome of delivery codes are reported on the maternal record only.

Example

A 30-year-old requires a caesarean section because the baby is breech. She delivers a healthy female newborn. The correct codes and sequence are:

- O32.1XX0 Maternal care for breech presentation, not applicable or unspecified fetus
- Z37.0 Single live birth

Look in the Alphabetic Index for Delivery/cesarean (for)/breech presentation O32.1. Turn to the Tabular List for seventh character selection. Seventh character is 0 is selected because this is a single fetus delivery. The guidelines state to report a code for the outcome of delivery on all deliveries. Look in the Alphabetic Index for Outcome of delivery/single NEC/liveborn Z37.0.

The Peripartum and Postpartum Periods

The peripartum period is defined as the last month of pregnancy to five months postpartum. The postpartum period is six weeks following delivery. A code from ICD-10-CM chapter 15 may be reported when a provider indicates the peripartum or postpartum complication is related to the pregnancy.

When a patient delivers outside of the hospital (eg, at home or in route to the hospital), and no complication is noted, do not report a delivery code. If the patient is admitted for postpartum care, report Z39.0 *Encounter for care and examination of mother immediately after delivery.*

Pregnancy associated cardiomyopathy is unique in that it may be diagnosed in the third trimester of pregnancy but may continue to progress months after delivery. Code O90.3 *Peripartum cardiomyopathy* is only reported when it develops as a result of pregnancy in a woman who did not have pre-existing heart disease.

Code O94 *Sequelae of complication of pregnancy, childbirth and the puerperium* is reported when the initial complication of a pregnancy develops as sequelae (a condition that is the result of a previous disease or injury) requiring care or treatment at a future date. This code may be used any time after the initial postpartum period and is sequenced following the code describing the sequelae of the complication.

Termination of Pregnancy and Spontaneous Abortions

Codes in this category are selected based on the type of abortion. Spontaneous abortion (miscarriage) occurs without any intervention of drugs or instrumentation. Subsequent encounters for retained products of conception (POC) following a spontaneous abortion or elective termination of pregnancy are assigned the following codes, even when the patient was discharged previously with a discharge diagnosis of complete abortion:

1. A code from category O03 Spontaneous abortion;
2. Code O74.4 *Failed attempted termination of pregnancy without complication*; and
3. Z33.2 Encounter for elective termination of pregnancy.

Legally induced abortion (elective abortion) is induced by a medical professional for therapeutic or elective reasons. When an attempted termination of pregnancy results in a liveborn fetus, code Z33.2 *Encounter for elective termination of pregnancy* and a code from category Z37 *Outcome of Delivery* are reported.

Illegally induced abortion is not performed by a qualified individual or in accordance with the law. A failed abortion is when an elective abortion is not successful and the patient is still pregnant.

A missed abortion, code O02.1, is a fetal death before completion of 20 weeks gestation. The retention of a dead fetus remains in the uterus. Missed abortion is not reported if the products of conception are spontaneously expelled or if the patient gets an induced abortion. Missed abortion is when tests show that the fetus no longer has a heartbeat and the pregnancy is no longer developing with the fetus still in the uterus. In the case of a missed abortion, there are no symptoms of miscarriage, no bleeding, cramping or passage of tissue.

Abortions that are a result of a complication in pregnancy require an additional code from categories O07 and O08.

For suspected or confirmed cases of abuse on a pregnant patient, a code from one of the subcategories below is reported as the primary code:

O9A.3- Physical abuse complicating pregnancy, childbirth, and the puerperium

O9A.4- Sexual abuse complicating pregnancy, childbirth, and the puerperium

O9A.5- Psychological abuse complicating pregnancy, childbirth, and the puerperium

Additional codes are reported to specify associated current injuries due to the abuse and to identify the perpetrator of abuse.

Key Roots, Suffixes, and Prefixes		Acronyms/Abbreviations	
amni/o	amnion	AGA	Appropriate for gestational age
ante-	before	ARM	Artificial rupture of membrane
arche/o	first	BV	Bacterial Vaginosis
crypt/o	hidden	CP	Cephalopelvic disproportion
culd/o	cul-de-sac	CS	Cesarean section
endo-	in	EDD	Estimated date of delivery
episi/o	vulva	EFW	Estimated fetal weight
fet/o	fetus	FAS	Fetal alcohol syndrome
galact/o	milk	G	Gravid (pregnant)
gynec/o	female	HSV	Herpes simplex virus
hymen/o	hymen	LGA	Large for gestational age
lact/o	milk	OB	Obstetrics
mamm/o	breast	PROM	Premature rupture of membranes
men/o	menstruation, month	SROM	Spontaneous rupture of membrane
qmulti-	many		
nat/a, nat/i	birth		
neo-	new		
obstetr/o	pregnancy/childbirth		
olig/o	few		
perine/o	perineum		
peritone/o	peritoneum		
post-	after		
prime-	first		
pseudo-	false		
retro-	backwards		

Section Review 5.4

1. A pregnant female, at 21 weeks, is diagnosed with iron-deficiency anemia and is sent to the clinic for a transfusion. Select the diagnosis code(s).

    A. O99.012

    B. D50.9, Z34.92

    C. O99.012, Z3A.21

    D. D50.9, O99.012

2. A woman is readmitted one week after delivery with a diagnosis of delayed hemorrhage due to retained placental fragments. Which ICD-10-CM code(s) should be reported?

    A. O72.2

    B. O72.0

    C. O72.2, O71.9

    D. O72.1

3. A patient presented to the emergency department with second degree burns to both forearms, which makes up 9 percent TBSA (Total Body Surface Area). She is three months pregnant, 12 weeks. The burns are not affecting the pregnancy. Select the diagnosis codes.

    A. T22.212A, T22.211A, T31.0, O09.90

    B. T22.212A, T22.211A, T31.0, Z34.90

    C. T22.212A, T22.211A, T31.0, Z34.80

    D. T22.212A, T22.211A, T31.0, Z33.1

Chapter 16: Certain Conditions Originating in the Perinatal Period (P00-P96)

For coding and reporting, the perinatal period is defined as birth through day 28 following birth. The Official Guidelines for Coding and Reporting for this chapter include:

- General Perinatal Rule: All clinically significant conditions noted on routine newborn exam should be coded. A condition is clinically significant if it requires clinical evaluation, therapeutic treatment, diagnostic procedures, extended length of hospital stay, increased nursing care and monitoring, or has implications for future healthcare needs. Should a condition originate in the perinatal period, and continue throughout the life of the patient, the perinatal code should continue to be used regardless of the patient's age.

- When coding the birth of an infant, assign a code from category Z38 according to the type of birth. A code from this series is assigned as a principal diagnosis and assigned only once to a newborn at the time of birth. If the newborn is transferred to another facility, a code from category Z38 is not used by the receiving hospital.

- Prematurity and Fetal Growth Retardation: Codes from categories P05 *Disorders of newborn related to slow fetal growth and fetal malnutrition* and P07 *Disorders of newborn related to short gestation and low birth weight, NEC* should not be assigned based solely on recorded birth weight or estimated gestational age, but on the attending physician's clinical assessment of maturity of the infant. Because physicians may utilize different criteria in determining prematurity, do not code the diagnosis of prematurity unless the physician documents this condition. When both birth weight and gestational age are available, the code for the birth weight is sequenced before the code for gestational age.

Example

An infant develops a cold and later develops convulsions, originating during the perinatal period. This condition would be coded with ICD-10-CM code P90 *Convulsions of newborn.*

Look in the Alphabetic Index for Convulsions/newborn. Verify the code in the Tabular List. The codes in Chapter 16 are never used on the maternal record.

The codes in the "included" and "excluded" notes throughout this section describe the infant's condition, not the mother's.

Key Roots, Suffixes, and Prefixes

arche/o	first
cephal/o	head
fet/o	fetus
nat/a, nat/l	birth
primi-	first
retro-	backwards
-version	turning

Acronyms/Abbreviations

AGA	Appropriate for gestational age
ARM	Artificial rupture of membrane
CPD	Cephalopelvic disproportion
CMV	Congenital cytomegalovirus
EFW	Estimated fetal weight
FAS	Fetal alcohol syndrome
LBW	Low birth weight
LGA	Large for gestational age
RDS	Respiratory distress syndrome
IUGR	Intrauterine growth retardation

Section Review 5.5

1. Which statement is true regarding the perinatal period?

    A. It begins at six weeks

    B. It ends at 28 days

    C. It ends at 90 days

    D. It begins at 29 days

2. A male newborn, delivered vaginally in the hospital, is born with jaundice. Select the diagnosis code(s) for the newborn's record.

    A. P59.9, Z38.30

    B. R17, O80, Z37.00

    C. P59.9

    D. Z38.00, P59.9

3. Assign the code for feeding problems in newborn.

    A. R63.3

    B. P92.9

    C. P92.01

    D. P76.0

Chapter 17: Congenital Malformations, Deformations and Chromosomal Abnormalities (Q00–Q99)

Congenital anomalies (birth defects) are abnormalities present at birth. Examples of congenital anomalies are spina bifida and cleft palates and lips. Spina bifida is the incomplete closure of the spinal neural tube. Because the neural tube does not close, the meninges sometimes can protrude through the opening. In the most severe cases, the spinal cord itself may protrude. Cleft palate is the result of the palate not closing completely, thereby leaving an opening (fissure). A cleft lip forms when the tissues of the lip fail to join together during the fourth and seventh weeks of pregnancy. It looks like a split lip.

Assign an appropriate code(s) from categories Q00-Q99 Congenital Malformations, Deformations, and Chromosomal Abnormalities when an anomaly is documented. A congenital anomaly may be the first listed diagnosis on a record, or a secondary diagnosis. Use additional secondary codes from other chapters to specify conditions associated with the anomaly, if applicable.

Codes from chapter 17 may be used throughout the life of the patient. If a congenital anomaly has been corrected, a personal history code should be used to identify the history of the anomaly.

For the congenital anomalies reported at the time of birth, the appropriate code from category Z38 Liveborn infants should be sequenced as the principal diagnosis, followed by any congenital anomaly codes from categories Q00-Q99.

Key Roots, Suffixes, and Prefixes

Spin/o	spine
-stenosis	narrowing

Acronyms/Abbreviations		PDA	Patent ductus arteriosus
		PTA	Persistent truncus arteriosus
AVS	Aortic valve stenosis	TAPVR	Total anomalous pulmonary venous return
ASD	Atrial septal defect	TOF	Tetralogy of fallot
CoA	Coarctation of the aorta	VSD	Ventricular septal defect

Section Review 5.6

1. A code from categories Q00-Q99 can be used until the patient reaches what age? Refer to ICD-10-CM Guideline I.C.17.

   A. They can be used throughout the life of the patient unless it has been corrected.

   B. They can be used throughout the life of the patient.

   C. From birth to the 28th day of life

   D. From birth until age 18

2. The hospital documentation states "normal vaginal delivery, live birth, female, with Down Syndrome." Select the correct code(s) for the infant's record.

   A. Q97.1

   B. Q90.9

   C. Z38.00, Q90.9

   D. Q90.9, Z38.00

3. A 4-year-old male is brought to the hospital by his mother. Today he is going to have surgery to repair his Cheiloschisis. Assign the correct code for his condition.

   A. Q38.0

   B. Q38.5

   C. Q36.9

   D. Q37.9

Chapter 18: Symptoms, Signs and Abnormal Clinical and Laboratory Findings (R00–R99)

Signs, Symptoms, and Ill-Defined Conditions in the Tabular List also include abnormal results of investigations and other ill-defined conditions. Use codes from this section when:

- No more-specific diagnoses can be made after investigation.
- Signs and symptoms existing at the time of the initial encounter proved to be transient, or the cause could not be determined.
- A patient fails to return and a provisional diagnosis is the only condition recorded.

- A case is referred elsewhere before a definitive diagnosis could be made.
- A more precise diagnosis was not available for any other reason.
- Certain symptoms, which represent important problems in medical care, exist and might be classified in addition to a known cause.

Do not use the codes from Signs, Symptoms, and Ill-defined Conditions when:

- A definitive diagnosis is available.

Example

The diagnostic statement is "right lower quadrant abdominal pain due to acute appendicitis." Because the reason for the pain is acute appendicitis, the symptom of abdominal pain would not be coded. The only code assigned would be the code for the acute appendicitis. Look in the Alphabetic Index for Appendicitis/acute (K35.80). Verify in the Tabular List.

- The symptom is considered an integral part of the disease process.

Example

The diagnostic statement reads, "cough and fever with pneumonia." Both fever and cough are symptoms of the pneumonia; therefore, codes would not be assigned for either symptom. The only code assigned is the code for the pneumonia. Looking in the Alphabetic Index for Pneumonia and select the default code (J18.9). Verify in the Tabular List.

Combination codes exist that identify both the definitive diagnosis and common symptoms of that diagnosis. When reporting one of these codes, an additional code is not assigned for the symptom because the one code reports both the diagnosis and the symptom.

Example

I70.221 Atherosclerosis of native arteries of extremities with rest pain, right leg

Chapter 18 includes the following guidelines for specific symptoms:

- Assign R03.0 *Elevated blood-pressure reading, without diagnosis of hypertension* is when the patient does not have a formal diagnosis of hypertension. If the patient has an elevated blood-pressure reading that does not mean that the patient has hypertension. Hypertension needs to be documented by the provider to report it.

- Repeated falls - R29.6 is for use when a patient has recently fallen and the reason for the fall is being investigated. When the patient has fallen in the past and is at risk for future falls, code Z91.81 is reported. If the circumstances exist, both codes may be reported on the same encounter.

- Coma scale - The coma scale codes (R40.2-) are primarily for use by trauma registries, but may be used in any setting where the information is collected. The coma scale codes include one code from each of the three subcategories (eyes open, best verbal response, and best

motor response). The total score, subcategory R40.24-*Glascow coma scale, total score*, is only reported when documented in the medical record with the specific individual scores.

- Functional Quadriplegia - R53.2 Functional quadriplegia is the lack of ability to use one's limbs or to ambulate due to extreme debility. This differs from neurologic quadriplegia (G82.5-) and is only reported when the documentation specifically states functional quadriplegia.

- SIRS due to Non-Infectious Process - In some cases a noninfectious process (condition), such as trauma, may lead to an infection which can result in systemic inflammatory response syndrome (SIRS). When SIRS is documented with a noninfectious condition, and no subsequent infection is documented, the code for the underlying condition, such as an injury, is assigned first, followed by code from subcategory R65.1-. If acute organ dysfunction is documented as associated with SIRS, the organ dysfunction is assigned as an additional code. If it is not documented as associated with SIRS, or due to another condition, query the provider.

- Death NOS - When a patient, who has already died, is brought into the facility and is pronounced dead upon arrival, and the cause of mortality is unknown, code R99 is reported. This code is reported only in rare circumstances.

Section Review 5.7

1. Mrs. Bixby, 83, is being admitted for dehydration and anorexia. The probable cause is dementia. She was brought in by her daughter who is visiting from out of town. Her daughter will take her from our office to St. Mary's. The gerontology unit will evaluate her mental condition tomorrow after she is stabilized. How would you code the diagnoses?

    A. F50.00, E86.0

    B. R63.0, E86.0

    C. F50.00, E86.0, F02.80

    D. R63.0, E86.0, F02.80

2. What is the diagnosis code for an elevated blood pressure reading?

    A. I10

    B. R03.0

    C. I15.8

    D. I95.9

3. When should a code for signs and symptoms be reported? Refer to ICD-10-CM Guidelines I.C.18.a. and I.C.18.b.

    A. When it is integral to the definitive diagnosis.

    B. When a probable diagnosis is confirmed.

    C. When it is not integral to the definitive diagnosis.

    D. When it is a confirmed symptom of the diagnosis.

Chapter 19: Injury, Poisoning and Certain Other Consequences of External Causes (S00–T88)

This chapter includes the diagnosis codes for injuries, fractures, burns, adverse effects, poisonings, toxic effects, and complications of care. Most categories in ICD-10-CM chapter 19 require the use of seventh character extenders. The three main seventh character extenders include:

A - Initial encounter which is used while the patient is receiving active treatment for the condition. Active treatment means the provider is actively treating the injury by evaluation from a new provider or surgical treatment. For example, if a patient arrives at the Emergency Department for an injury, it is a new provider and considered active treatment.

D - Subsequent encounter which is used for when the patient is receiving routine care for the condition during the healing or recovery phase. Subsequent care includes cast change or removal, removal of fixation devices (internal or external), medication adjustment, or other follow up visits after an injury. Visits during this time are on the healing side of an injury.

S - Sequela which is used for complications or conditions that arise as a direct result of a condition. For example, a person may have developed a keloid scar after having a bunionectomy. In this case, the keloid scar is the sequela.

There are additional 7th character extensions that apply to categories for traumatic fractures which will be discussed later in this chapter.

Injuries

Injuries are classified according to the type (eg, fracture, burn), site of the injury (eg.blood vessel, thoracic spinal cord), laterality (eg.left, right), and severity (major, superficial). nd site of the injury (eg, fracture, burn). Look in the Index to Diseases and Injuries for the main term describing the injury and then for a subterm identifying the site. When coding multiple injuries, assign separate codes for each injury unless a specific combination code is provided. Traumatic injury codes (S00-

T14.9) are not to be used for normal, healing surgical wounds or to identify complications of surgical wounds.

- List first the code for the most serious injury, as determined by the provider and the focus of care.
- Superficial injuries such as abrasions or contusions are not coded when associated with more severe injuries of the same site (for example, a contusion at the site of a closed fracture, only the fracture would be coded).
- When a primary injury results in minor damage to peripheral nerves or blood vessels, the primary injury is sequenced first with additional code(s) for injuries to nerves and spinal cord (for example, S04), and/or injury to blood vessels (for example S15) reported in addition to the primary code. When the primary injury is to the blood vessels or nerves, that injury is sequenced first.

Traumatic Fractures

Traumatic fractures are coded by the site of the fracture and can be further broken down to the type of fracture (eg.comminuted, Type I, open, closed), pathological or traumatic, and displaced or nondisplaced. When coding multiple traumatic fractures, fractures of specified sites are coded individually by site, in order of severity. An open fracture describes a fracture site exposed to the outside elements; an open fracture should not be coded unless it is documented in the medical record. When a fracture is not specified as open or closed, the fracture is coded as a closed fracture. Many times this injury may be represented as a small puncture wound, but if the fracture site is exposed to air, it is considered an open fracture. A provider may choose to treat a closed fracture with an "open" or incisional treatment, but the approach for treatment should not be confused with an open fracture. The seventh character extender is applied to identify whether the fracture is open or closed.

A displaced fracture is when the bone breaks into two or more parts and the bone moves so that it is no longer aligned in its normal position. When a fracture is not indicated as displaced or non-displaced, it is coded as displaced.

Fractures are coded using seventh character extenders to indicate the episode of care. The seventh character application only applies to specific codes as indicated throughout this section. For example, seventh character C applies to category S52, but not to category S51.

Initial encounter codes for fractures include:

A - Initial encounter for closed fracture

B - Initial encounter for open fracture type I or II

C - Initial encounter for open fracture type IIIA, IIIB, IIIC (see category S52 for an example)

Subsequent care for fractures is reported during the routine healing and follow-up phase. For example, if a patient comes in for a cast change, it is considered subsequent care. Seventh character extenders indicate when the visit is during this phase.

Complication codes (eg, delayed healting) are reported if a complication occurs during healing or recovery phase using the appropriate seventh character extender for complications.

Malunion of a fracture is reported with one of the following seventh character extenders:

P - Subsequent encounter for closed fracture with malunion

Q - Subsequent encounter for open fracture type I or II with malunion

R - Subsequent encounter for open fracture type IIIA, IIIB, or IIIC with malunion

Nonunion of a fracture is reported with one of the following seventh character extenders:

K - Subsequent encounter for closed fracture with nonunion

M - Subsequent encounter for open fracture type I or II with nonunion

N - Subsequent encounter for open fracture type IIIA, IIIB, IIIC with nonunion

Classification of open fractures (type I, II, IIIA, IIIB, IIIC) is based on the Gustillo open fracture classification (discussed further in Chapter) 8. Multiple fractures are sequenced according to the severity of the fracture.

When superficial injuries such as abrasions or contusions are at the same site of a fracture, code only the fracture.

To locate codes for traumatic fractures, look for the main term fracture, traumatic. Remember, that when a patient with known osteoporosis has a fracture that would not have normally occurred due to a fall or other trauma, it is coded as a pathologic fracture instead of a traumatic fracture.

ICD-9-CM Application

ICD-9-CM has separate code for open and closed fractures instead of applying a seventh character extender.

826.0 Fracture of one or more phalanges of foot, closed

826.1 Fracture of one or more phalanges of foot, open

Example

Initial encounter for fractured right hip with dislocation: Because the fracture is not defined as open or closed, it is classified as closed. Also, because the diagnosis includes both fracture and dislocation, code the fracture only. Look in the Index to Diseases and Injuries for Fracture, traumatic/hip and you are directed to see Fracture, femur, neck. Look for Fracture, traumatic/femur, femoral/upper end/neck S72.00-. Look in the Tabular List for the additional characters. Sixth character 1 indicates the right hip. Seventh character A indicates the initial encounter for a closed fracture.

- S72.001A Fracture of unspecified part of neck of right femur, initial encounter for closed fracture.

ICD-9-CM Application

In the Tabular List, the beginning of Category 800–829 has a list of terms describing closed and open fractures. A fracture that is infected, compound, or with foreign body is considered an open fracture.

Burns and Corrosions

To properly code for burns, the burn must be classified as a burn or a corrosion. A burn is for thermal burns, except sunburns (L55.-), come from a heat source such as a fire, a hot appliance, electricity, or radiation. Corrosions are burns due to chemicals.

Categories T20-T25 for current burns are classified by:

- Depth
- Extent
- Agent (X code)

First degree burns are superficial burns through only the epidermis. The area of the burn is usually red, very painful, and blanches to touch. The skin appears intact and no blistering (vesiculation) occurs. In general, the skin involved in a first degree burn does not lose its ability to function. In categories T20-T25, a first degree burn is indicated by using fourth character 1 for burns and 5 for corrosions.

Second degree burns often are referred to as a partial-thickness burn involving the epidermis and the dermis. These burns usually blister immediately and fill with a fluid/serous exudate. The blisters can be superficial or involve deep dermal damage. They are red, extremely painful, and the areas around the blisters will blanch to touch. The nerve endings are exposed

in this level of burn making the extreme pain a characteristic hallmark of their presentation. Those second degree burns with deep dermal involvement often clinically are identical to third degree burns. Second degree burns may leave a scar, depending on the individual's genetic predisposition to scarring. In categories T20-T25, a second degree burn is indicated by using fourth character 2 for burns and fourth character 6 for corrosions.

Third degree burns are full-thickness burns involving the epidermis, dermis, and varying levels of the subcutaneous and underlying structures. Some systems actually classify burns involving the muscles, tendons, and bones as fourth degree. In categories T20-T25, a third degree burn is indicated by using fourth character 3 for burns and 7 for corrosions.

Non-healing burns are coded as acute burns. Necrosis of burned skin is coded as a non-healed burn. A deep third degree burn is when there is deep necrosis of underlying tissues.

Burns to the eye and internal organs (T26-T28) are classified by site, but not by degree.

When a patient is seen for multiple external burns, sequence first the code for the highest degree of burn. When a patient has both external and internal burns, the reason for admission governs the first-listed diagnosis.

Always code to the greatest depth of the burn in a given category/anatomical area. Sequence first the diagnosis that reflects the highest degree of burn when multiple burns are present. Classify burns of the same local site (T20-T25) but of different degrees to the subcategory identifying the highest degree of burn.

Example

A patient is seen in the emergency department for both second and third degree burns on the back. Look in the Index to Diseases and Injuries for Burn/back/third degree (T21.34-) and second degree (T21.24-). Because both burns are coded to the same three digit category (T21), only the highest degree of burn is coded. It would not be appropriate to code both codes from the same category because the deepest level of burn in a given anatomical area or category is sufficient. A seventh character is required to identify the episode. Because there are only five characters in the code, an X is placed in the sixth character to keep the seventh character in the seventh position. Seventh character A is selected for the initial encounter. The correct diagnosis code is:

- T21.34XA |Burn of third degree of lower back, initial encounter

Always list the code for the deepest level of burn first when there are burns to multiple areas. When coding burns, assign separate codes for each burn site. Codes from category *T30 Burn and corrosion, body region unspecified* are extremely vague and should be used only if the locations of the burns are not documented.

ICD-9-CM Application

ICD-9-CM does not distinguish between coding for burns and corrosions; both are coded as burns. Coding for a burn is a situation when a single code cannot describe adequately an entire condition. A burn is coded from categories 940–949 and is selected by site, severity or degree of burn, and total body surface area (TBSA). The category defines the general location, the fourth digit defines the degree of burn, and the fifth digit further defines the location of the burn.

Assign codes from category 948, which classifies burns according to extent of body surface involved, when the site of the burn is not specified or when there is need for additional data. Use category 948 as an additional code for reporting purposes when there is a third degree burn involving 20 percent or more of the body surface. In assigning codes from category 948:

- Fourth digit codes are used to identify the percentage of total body surface area involved in a burn (all degrees).
- Fifth digits are assigned to identify the percentage of body surface involved in a third degree burn.
- Fifth digit zero (0) is assigned when less than 10 percent or when the body surface is involved in a third degree burn.

Category 948 signifies the extent of the body surface involved. The fourth digit in this category describes the percentage of TBSA burned, while the fifth digit classification indicates the TBSA with third degree burns only. The fourth digit assignment represents the percentage of total body surface involved in the burn injury regardless of degree and the fifth digit represents the percentage of body surface with third degree burn. To determine the TBSA, the Rule of Nines is used.

Example

Three-year-old is being treated for second degree burns and third degree burns that cover 15 percent of his body. The third degree burns cover 10 percent of his legs.

948.1x - 10–19 percent of body surface

The fourth digit "1" indicates the total of all degrees of the burns that covers 15 percent of the body.

948.11 - The fifth digit "1" indicates only the third degree burn that covers 10 percent of his legs.

Assign codes from category T31 or T32, which classifies burns according to extent of body surface involved, when the site of the burn is not specified or when there is need for additional data. Use categories T31 and T32 as an additional code for reporting purposes when there is a third degree burn involving 20 percent or more of the body surface. In assigning codes from categories T31 and T32:

- Fourth characters identify the percentage of total body surface area involved in a burn or corrosion (all degrees).
- Fifth characters identify the percentage of body surface involved in a third degree burn or corrosion.
- Fifth character zero (0) is assigned when less than 10 percent of the body surface is involved in a third degree burn or corrosion.

To determine the TBSA, the Rule of Nines is used.

Example

Three-year-old is being treated (initial encounter) for second degree burns and third degree burns from hot liquid that cover 15 percent of his body. The third degree burns cover 10 percent of his legs.

T31.11 - Burns involving 10–19 % of body surface with 10-19% third degree burns

---

Complications such as infections, associated injuries, and co-morbid conditions should be coded in addition to the burn code(s). Examples of co-morbid conditions are diabetes mellitus, cardiovascular disorders, alcoholism, peptic ulcers, and asthma. These co-morbid conditions may influence the healing process.

Encounters for sequela (late effects) of burns or corrosions is reported by appending seventh character S Sequela to the burn or corrosion code. When a patient is seen for both a current burn and sequela of an old burn, it is appropriate to have a code with seventh character A or D and another code with seventh character S.

Coders should sequence the burn code for the highest degree of burn first when coding multiple burns. If a patient has a third degree burn of the palm of the left hand and a second degree burn on the right forearm, the recommended codes for this patient's multiple burns are T23.352- and T22.211-. A seventh character extender is applied to indicate the episode of care.

External cause codes (discussed later in this chapter) are reported with burns and corrosions to identify the source and intent of the burn, as well as the place it occurred. Pay close attention to the code also notes for burn and corrosion codes.

Lund-Browder Classification of Burns

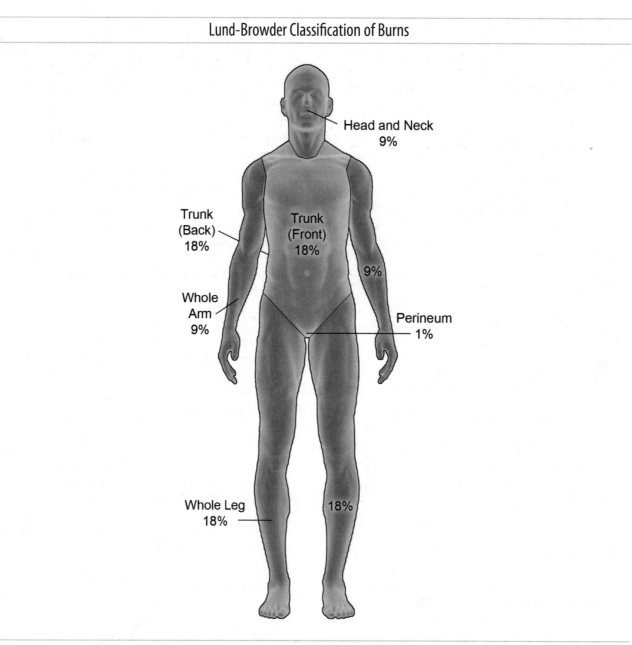

Source: AAPC

Adverse Effects, Poisoning, Underdosing and Toxic Effects

The Table of Drugs and Chemicals (found after the Table of Neoplasms) is used to identify the substances and causes for adverse effects and poisonings. The Table of Drugs and Chemicals organizes codes associated with specific substances. Within the table is an alphabetic list of generic and brand name agents that may cause a reaction or poisoning if taken in the wrong dosage, or if taken in error. It is also for intoxication or poisoning by a drug or other chemical substance. The table contains an extensive list of drugs set in a six column format including industrial solvents, corrosive gases, noxious plants, pesticides, and other toxic agents. The first column provides the codes for the substance involved. The next five columns identify the circumstances of poisoning.

Drug, chemical	Poisoning, Accidental (unintentional)	Poisoning, Intentional self-harm	Poisoning, Assault	Poisoning, Undetermined	Adverse effect	Underdosing
1-propanol	T51.3X1	T51.3X2	T51.3X3	T51.3X4	----	----
2-propanol	T51.2X1	T51.2X2	T51.2X3	T51.2X4	----	----
2, 4-D (dichlorophenoxyacetic acid)	T60.3X1	T60.3X2	T60.3X3	T60.3X4	----	----
2, 4-toluene dilsocyanate	T65.0X1	T65.0X2	T65.0X3	T65.0X4	----	----
2, 4, 5-T (trichlorophenoxyacetic acid)	T60.1X1	T60.1X2	T60.1X3	T60.1X4	----	----
14-hydroxydihydromorphinone	T40.2X1	T40.2X2	T40.2X3	T40.2X4	T40.2X5	T40.2X6
A						
ABOB	T37.5X1	T37.5X2	T37.5X3	T37.5X4	T37.5X5	T37.5X6
Abrine	T62.2X1	T62.2X2	T62.2X3	T62.2X4	----	----
Abrus (seed)	T62.2X1	T62.2X2	T62.2X3	T62.2X4	----	----
Absinthe	T51.0X1	T51.0X2	T51.0X3	T51.0X4	----	----
beverage	T51.0X1	T51.0X2	T51.0X3	T51.0X4	----	----
Acaricide	T60.8X1	T60.8X2	T60.8X3	T60.8X4	----	----

The codes in categories T36-T65 are combination codes that include the substance that was taken as well as the intent. No additional external cause codes are required for poisonings, toxic effects, adverse effects and underdosing codes. Do not code directly from the Table of Drugs and Chemicals. All codes must be verified in the Tabular List.

All codes that apply to the encounter are coded. If the same code is reported for more than one substance, the code is only reported once. If two or more drugs, medicine, or biological substances are involved, each substance is coded individually unless there is a combination code available.

The Table of Drugs and Chemicals classifies drug toxicity into four categories:

- Adverse effect - indicates the patient had an adverse effect of a drug that was correctly prescribed and properly administered.
- Poisoning - indicates improper use of a medication which includes overdose, wrong substance given or taken in error, wrong route of administration, interaction of drug(s) and alcohol, etc.
- Underdosing - refers to taking less of a medication than is prescribed by a provider or a manufacturer's instruction.

- Toxic Effects - indicates a harmful substance is ingested or comes in contact with a person.

ICD-9-CM application

The Index to External Causes of Injuries and Poisonings in Volume 2, Section 3 of the ICD-9-CM contains the codes for classifying environmental events, circumstances, and other conditions as the cause of injury or adverse effects.

The E codes in this table are defined as:

- Accidental Poisoning Codes [E850–E869]—Identify accidental ingestion of drugs for incorrect use in medical or surgical procedures, incorrect administration for ingestion of the drug, or inadvertent or accidental overdose. Codes to report poisoning by other solid and liquid substances, gases or vapors are also located in this section.
- Therapeutic Use Codes [E930–E949]—Indicate an adverse effect or reaction to a drug that was administered correctly, either therapeutically or prophylactically.
- Suicide Attempt Codes [E950–E952]—Identify the effects of the drugs or substances taken to cause self-inflicted injury or to attempt suicide.

          AAPC   www.aapc.com   *147*

- Assault Codes [E962]—Indicates drugs or substances are "purposely inflicted" by another person with the intent to cause bodily harm, injury, or death.
- Undetermined Codes [E980–E982]—Apply when the cause of poisoning or injury is unknown.

Adverse Effect

Adverse reaction occurs when a prescription medicine or drug is taken according to physician instruction, or manufacturer's instruction, and the patient develops a reaction to the medication. Adverse reactions happen in spite of proper administration.

When coding adverse reactions to a correct substance properly administered you will use two or more codes:

1. Use the first code to identify the manifestation(s).

2. The second code identifies the drug causing the reaction (use the Adverse effect column in the Table of Drugs and Chemicals). An adverse effect code should have a fifth or sixth character 5.

Example

The patient is prescribed ciprofloxacin to treat a UTI. She takes the medication as directed and becomes nauseous and can't stop vomiting. She is seen at the urgent care clinic. The correct codes and sequence are:

- R11.2 Nausea with vomiting, unspecified
- T36.8X5A Adverse effect of other systemic antibiotics, initial encounter

In the Index to Diseases and Injuries, look for Nausea/with vomiting. Next, look in the Table of Drugs and Chemicals for ciprofloxacin. The code from the Adverse effect column is reported.

Note: Codes from the Poisoning columns in the Table of Drugs and Chemicals are never used with adverse effect codes.

Poisoning

Poisoning can be accidental, intentional self-harm, assault or undetermined. Poisoning or reaction to the improper use of a medication (the wrong drug or an incorrect dosage of a correct drug is ingested) requires two or more codes. To code poisoning correctly:

1. The first code, from the Table of Drugs and Chemicals, identifies the drug. These codes have an associated intent as their fifth or sixth character to identify the

nature of poisoning (accidental, intentional self-harm, assault or undetermined).

2. The second code indicates the condition(s), manifestation(s) that resulted from the poisoning. All manifestation(s) of the poisoning are coded.

3. Additional codes are reported to identify abuse or dependence of the substance, if documented.

Example

The patient is prescribed Bactrim (sulfamethoxazole with trimethoprim) to treat a UTI. She forgets to take her morning dose and decides to take two doses in the evening. She complains of diarrhea and nausea.

The first code reported is the code from the Poisoning, Accidental (unintentional) column of the Table of Drugs and Chemicals. In the Table of Drugs and Chemicals, look for sulfamethoxazole with trimethoprim. The code from the Poisoning, Accidental (unintentional) column is T36.8X1. For the manifestations, look in the Index to Diseases and Injuries for Diarrhea (R19.7) and Nausea (R11.0).

The correct codes and sequence are:

- T36.8X1A Poisoning by other systemic antibiotics, accidental (unintentional)
- R19.7 Diarrhea, unspecified
- R11.0 Nausea

Codes in the Poisoning, Undetermined column is reported when there is documentation that indicates that the intent cannot be determined. This needs to be documented to report those codes. When there is no documentation indicating the intent of the poisoning report the codes from the Poisoning, Accidental (unintentional) column.

Underdosing

Underdosing refers to taking less of a medication than is prescribed by a provider or a manufacturer's instruction. Codes for underdosing are never used as the primary diagnosis. When the underdosing causes an exacerbation or relapse of the condition for which the drug is prescribed because of the reduction in dose, the medical condition itself should be coded. Additional codes for noncompliance or complication of care are also reported.

Example

A type 2 diabetic patient is unable to pay for his insulin and ends up in the emergency department with weakness, hallucinations, and an altered mental state due to hyperglycemia.

E11.65 Type 2 diabetes mellitus with hyperglycemia

T38.3X6A Underdosing of insulin and oral hypoglycemic [antidiabetic] drugs, initial encounter

Z91.120 Patient's intentional underdosing of medication regimen due to financial hardship

The condition that is exacerbated is reported first. Look in the Index to Diseases and Injuries for Diabetes, diabetic (mellitus) (sugar)/type 2/with/hyperglycemia E11.65. Next, look in the Table of Drugs and Chemicals for insulin and use the code from the Underdosing Column T38.3X6. From the Tabular List, A is used to indicate this is an initial encounter. Then, look for Noncompliance/with/medication regimen NEC/underdosing/intentional NEC/due to financial hardship of patient Z91.120. Verify all codes in the Tabular List.

Adult and Child Abuse, Neglect and Other Maltreatment

Adult and child abuse, neglect and other maltreatment can be alleged, suspected, or confirmed. The codes in this category are classified into suspected and confirmed:

T74.- Adult and child abuse, neglect and other maltreatment, confirmed

T76.- Adult and child abuse, neglect and other maltreatment, suspected

When a case of abuse or neglect is suspected, but is ruled out during the encounter, report the appropriate ruled code instead of a code from category T76:

Z04.71 Encounter for examination and observation following alleged physical adult abuse

 Suspected adult physical abuse, ruled out

Z04.72 Encounter for examination and observation following alleged physical child abuse

 Suspected child physical abuse, ruled out

Additional codes for suspected cases ruled out include alleged rape or sexual abuse ruled out; Z04.41 - for adult and Z04.42 for child.

When abuse or neglect is confirmed, an external cause code from categories X92-Y08 are reported to identify the cause of the injuries. A perpetrator code from category Y07 is reported when documented. Codes from category T76 are not reported for these incidents.

Complications

If a complication from medical or surgical care initiates a visit to the provider's office or an admission to the hospital, a complication code is reported as the primary diagnosis. Complication codes are found in the T80-T88 series of ICD-10-CM codes. When available, the code for the specific complication is also listed. Some of the complication codes include both the nature of the complication as well as the type of procedure that cause the complication. In this case, an additional external cause code is not required.

Example

A patient is discharged from the hospital after internal fixation of an open fracture of the right humerus. Four days after surgery, the patient's surgical wound is red, swollen, and draining fluid. The patient presents to the orthopedic clinic and the provider determines the patient has a postoperative infection due to the internal fixation device and takes a culture. The culture comes back from the laboratory positive for a Streptococcus infection.

The first code reported is the complication. Look in the Index to Diseases and Injuries for Complication/fixation device, internal (orthopedic)/infection and inflammation/arm/humerus T84.61-. In the Tabular List, sixth character 0 is selected to indicate the right humerus. Seventh character A is selected for the initial encounter. The second code listed is for the infection (refer to the use additional code note below T84.6). Look in the Index to Diseases and Injuries for Infection/streptococcal NEC (A49.1.) The codes to report are:

- T84.610A Infection and inflammatory reaction due to internal fixation device of right humerus
- A49.1 Streptococcal infection, unspecified site

The complication code is sequenced first, then the specific complication(s) for the additional code(s).

Intraoperative and postprocedural complication codes are found within the body system chapters with codes specific to the organs and structures of that body system. These codes should be sequenced first, followed by a code(s) for the specific complication, if applicable. For example, G97.0 *Cerebrospinal fluid leak from spinal puncture.*

ICD-9-CM Application

In ICD-9CM, mechanical complications for internal, prosthetic device, implanted graft codes, 996.00 - 996.59, are reported if the documentation indicates any of the following types of complications: Breakdown, Displacement, Leakage, Obstruction (mechanical), Perforation, or Protrusion.

Other complication for internal prosthetic device, implant, and graft codes, 996.70-996.79, should be reported if the documentation indicates the following types of complications: Complication NOS, Occlusion NOS, Embolism, Fibrosis, Hemorrhage, Pain, Stenosis, or Thrombus.

Section Review 5.8

1. The provider performs an open reduction and internal fixation for left fibula and tibia fractures. Select the codes.

    A. S82.402A, S82.202A

    B. S82.402B, S82.202B

    C. S82.401A, S82.209A

    D. S82.402B, S82.209B

2. A patient was sent home with a PICC line for Vancomycin treatment at home. He returns to his physician with an infection due to the PICC Line. The infection is determined to be MRSA. Select the diagnosis code(s) in the correct sequence.

    A. T82.7XXA

    B. A49.02

    C. T82.7XXA, A49.02

    D. A49.02, T82.7XXA

3. A patient was prescribed an anti-depressant. She forgot she had taken her pills for the day and took another pill by accident. She is now complaining of dizziness and excessive sweating. Select the diagnosis codes in the correct sequence.

    A. R42, R61, T43.201A

    B. R61, R42, T43.202A

    C. T43.201A, F45.8, R61

    D. T43.201A, R42, R61

Chapter 20: External Causes of Morbidity (V00-Y99)

External cause codes are supplemental to the diagnosis codes in chapters 1–19 of ICD-10-CM. The external causes of morbidity provide information on how the injury happened (cause), the intent (unintentional or accidental; or intentional, such as suicide or assault), the person's status (eg, civilian, military), the associated activity, and the place where the event occurred.

Most of the main terms that are listed alphabetically in the External Cause of Injuries Index indicate the type of accident (Fall or Collision) or intentional violent assault (Stabbing or Shooting). The terms listed under the main term are the specific incident associated with that main term.

This section is divided into 12 groups with the first characters of V, W, X, and Y.

1. Pedestrian injured in transport accident (V00-V09)

2. Pedal cycle rider injured in transport accident (V10-V19)

3. Motorcycle rider injured in transport accident (V20-V29)

4. Occupant of three-wheeled motor vehicle injured in transport accident (V30-V39)

5. Car occupant injured in transport accident (V40-V49)

6. Occupant of pick-up truck or van injured in transport accident (V50-V59)

7. Occupant of heavy transport vehicle injured in transport accident (V60-V69)

8. Buss occupant injured in transport accident (V70-V79)

9. Other land transport accidents (V80-V89)

10. Water transport accidents (V90-V94)

11. Air and space transport accidents (V95-V97)

12. Other external causes of accidental injury (W00-X58)

The sections relating to land transport accidents (V01-V89) reflect the victim's mode of transport and are subdivided to identify the victim's counterpart or the type of event. A transport accident is one in which the vehicle involved must be moving or running or in use for transport purposes at the time of the accident. The first two characters of the ICD-10-CM code identify the vehicle of which the injured person is an occupant. The ICD-10-CM codebook has definitions of transport vehicles listed in the beginning of ICD-10-CM Chapter 20.

Example

A pedestrian hit by a car while walking in the parking lot at the shopping center was taken to the emergency department. The external cause codes for this case include:

V03.00XA Pedestrian on foot injured in collisions with care, pick-up truck or van in nontraffic accident.

Y93.01 Activity, walking, marching and hiking

Y92.481 Parking lot as the place of occurrence of the external cause

This is a transport accident because the car was moving (Accident/transport). The victim is a pedestrian who was walking when it collided with a car. The accident took place in a parking lot, not a public highway, making it nontraffic. Look in the Index to External Causes for Accident/transport (involving injury to)/ pedestrian/on foot/collision (with)/car/nontraffic V03.00. In the Tabular List, a dummy placeholder X is for the sixth character and the seventh character A is selected for the initial encounter. Additional external cause codes apply to this scenario to identify the activity of the patient at the time of injury, and place of occurrence. To find the activity, look in the Index to External Causes for Activity/walking Y93.01. Look in the Index to External Causes for Place of occurrence/parking garage/lot Y92.481. The external cause status is not known so it is not coded. The guidelines state to not use Y99.9 if the status is not stated.

Payers use the information provided with external cause codes to determine the payer of liability, in determining which payer is responsible for reimbursing the claim. For example, if a patient is involved in a car accident, an external cause code from subcategory V40-V49 is reported to indicate the nature of the car accident and to identify the injured person. In most cases, a claim for injuries sustained in a car accident is reimbursed by the patient's auto insurance.

External cause codes are supplemental. They are never sequenced first. Report all external cause codes needed to explain the external causes. Place of occurrence codes are reported to identify where an injury occurred such as in the patient's home or at a baseball field. External cause codes are used for the length of treatment only if required by the payer. The activity code, place of occurrence code, and activity status code are only reported on the initial treatment, not subsequent treatment.

ICD-9-CM Application

In ICD-9-CM, the external cause codes are only reported on the initial encounter along with the Place of Occurrence code, Activity code, and Status codes.

The sequencing rules for reporting two or more external cause codes are as follows:

- External cause codes for child and adult abuse take priority over all other External cause codes.
- External cause codes for terrorism events take priority over all other External cause codes except child and adult abuse.
- External cause codes for cataclysmic events take priority over all other External cause codes except child and adult abuse and terrorism.
- External cause codes for transport accidents take priority over all other External cause codes except cataclysmic events, child, and adult abuse and terrorism.
- Activity and external cause status codes are assigned following all causal (intent) External cause codes.
- The first listed External cause code should correspond to the cause of the most serious diagnosis due to an assault, accident, or self-harm, following the order of hierarchy listed above.

Example

A student was hit in the head with a baseball when he was up to bat during an afterschool baseball game at the school baseball field. The patient was brought in by his coach. The External cause codes for this case include:

- W21.03XA Struck by a baseball, initial encounter
- Y93.64 Activity, baseball
- Y92.320 Baseball field as the place of occurrence of the external cause
- Y99.8 Other External cause status

Look in the Index to External Causes for Struck (accidentally) by/ball (hit)/baseball (W21.03-). For the activity, look for Activity/baseball (Y93.64). Next report is the place of occurrence. Look in the Index to External Causes for Place of occurrence/baseball field (Y92.320). Notice in the Tabular List that sports and athletics area of schools as the place of occurrence is excluded in the subcategory for schools (Y92.2-) indicating a code from subcategory Y92.3- is reported. The last code to report is the activity status. Look in the Index to External Causes for Status of external cause/recreation or sport not for income or while a student Y99.8. Notice that if you chose student activity, you are still directed to Y99.8.

Four external cause codes are reported to indicate how the injury occurred, the activity in which the patient was involved at the time, the place of occurrence, and the activity status of the patient at the time of the injury.

Section Review 5.9

1. A male patient was a passenger in an automobile involved in a serious collision with another automobile. He sustained a closed fracture of the coronoid process of the jaw and an open left shaft fracture, Type 1, of the radius with an open Type 1 shaft fracture of the left ulna. What are the diagnosis codes?

   A. S52.302B, S52.292B, V43.62XA

   B. S52.302A, S52.202A, S02.63XA, V43.92XA

   C. S52.302B, S52.292B, S02.63XB, V43.32XA

   D. S52.302B, S52.202B, S02.63XA, V43.62XA

2. A patient was hit in the nose playing basketball on the varsity team last evening at the gym and woke up with severe epistaxis. The family physician controlled the nasal hemorrhage with cauterization and afterwards packed the nose with nasal packs. What are the correct diagnosis codes?

   A. R04.0, W21.09XA, Y92.39, Y93.79, Y99.8

   B. R04.0, W21.05XA, Y92.39, Y93.67, Y99.8

   C. I78.0, W21.05XA, Y92.39, Y93.79, Y99.8

   D. I78.0, W21.00XA, Y92.39, Y93.67, Y99.8

3. Which statement is true regarding External cause codes? Refer to ICD-10-CM Guideline I.C.20.a.6.

    A. External cause codes are never sequenced first.
    B. External cause codes are only sequenced first if a definite diagnosis is not established.
    C. External cause codes are used to indicate the reason for a screening exam.
    D. External cause codes are used to report abnormal findings.

Chapter 21: Factors Influencing Health Status and Contact with Health Services (Z00–Z99)

Not all patient encounters are for a problem or condition. Chapter 21 of ICD-10-CM includes codes reported to identify the reason why the patient is receiving services when a disease or disorder is not the reason the services are rendered. Codes in this chapter are referred to as Z codes. Z codes are reported when the patient is not sick and presents for specific care (eg, routine physical, screening mammogram) to report a specific type of care (eg, physical therapy, chemotherapy) or to identify the status of the patient that may affect the management of care (eg, family history of colon cancer). A Z code is always the first listed code to report a newborn birth status.

Z codes can be used in any healthcare setting. They can be sequenced as primary or secondary codes. There is a list of all the Z codes that can only be reported as the first listed diagnosis. The complete list can be found in Section I.C.21.c.16., Z Codes That May Only be Principal/First-Listed Diagnosis, in the Official Coding Guidelines. Z codes are divided into sixteen categories. Using the titles of the following Z categories is helpful when locating terms in the Index to Diseases and Injuries.

Contact/Exposure

A patient can be exposed to a communicable disease and not develop signs or symptoms. Although the patient is not sick or showing any signs or symptoms, she often will need to be examined, or require a screening test or prophylactic treatment. For example, if a patient is exposed to tuberculosis, a chest X-ray will be ordered. These Z codes are found under the main term Exposure in the Index to Diseases and Injuries and listed under category code Z20. Category Z77 indicates contact with suspected exposures hazardous to health.

Inoculations and Vaccinations

The code for inoculations and vaccinations is Z23. This code indicates a patient is being seen to receive a prophylactic inoculation against a disease. Procedure codes (discussed later in the curriculum) are required to identify the actual administration of the injection and the type(s) of immunizations given.

When a patient is seen for a preventive visit or other visit, and receives an inoculation as part of the visit, Z23 is listed as an additional code.

Codes in category Z28 are reported when a vaccination(s) is not carried out. The code is selected on the reason why the vaccination(s) was not carried out.

ICD-9-CM Application

In ICD-9-CM, there are specific V codes for each type of vaccination. To locate the appropriate diagnosis code for vaccinations, look up "vaccinations" in the Index to Diseases and the subterm for the type of vaccine that is administered. The inoculation and vaccination V codes are listed in categories V03–V06.

Status

Status codes indicate a patient is a carrier of a disease, has the sequelae or residual of a past disease or condition, or has another factor influencing a person's health status. Examples of codes found in this category include a patient who had a transplant, medical device, asymptomatic HIV, and use of anticoagulants. The status Z code categories are listed in ICD-10-CM Guideline I.C.21.c.3. Status codes are distinct from history codes. History codes indicate that the patient no longer has the condition.

When a patient has a complication of a disease, illness, or surgical procedure, and the complication code indicates the condition (for example subcategory T86.2 Complications of heart transplant), the status code is not reported. Indicating the patient is status heart transplant does not provide any further information than provided with T86.2.

History of

There are two types of history: Personal history and family history. Family history is important to report because some diseases have a genetic predisposition. For example, female patients with a family history of breast cancer are at a higher risk for developing breast cancer. Family history codes are found in the Index to Diseases and Injuries under History/ family (of).

Example

A patient presents complaining of a lump in her breast. She has a family history of breast cancer. The provider orders a mammogram. The correct codes to report and sequence are:

- N63 Unspecified lump in breast
- Z80.3 Family history of malignant neoplasm of breast

Look in the Index to Diseases and Injuries for Lump and you are directed to see Mass. Mass/breast directs you to N63. Next, look for History/family (of)/malignant neoplasm/breast (Z80.3).

Personal history is reported if the patient no longer has the disease. A history of an illness, even if no longer present, is important information that may alter the type of treatment ordered. Personal history codes are found in the Index to Diseases and Injuries under History/personal (of). The history Z code categories are listed in ICD-10-CM Guideline I.C.21.c.4.

Screening

There are many screening tests performed to identify problems before a patient starts to exhibit signs or symptoms. The purpose of preventive medicine is to identify potential health problems before they become severe. For example, colonoscopies are performed as a screening test for colon cancer when a patient turns 50-years-old. The proper diagnosis code is Z12.11 *Encounter for screening for malignant neoplasm of colon*. To locate screening codes, look for Screening in the Index to Diseases and Injuries and the subterm for the condition for which the screening occurs. When the purpose of the encounter is for screening and the provider finds an abnormality, first sequence the code for the screening, followed by any abnormal findings. For example, during a screening colonoscopy the provider finds and removes a polyp. The first listed code is the screening for colon cancer (Z12.11), followed by the code for the polyp (K63.5). A screening code is not necessary if the screening is inherent to a routine examination, such as a pap smear done during a routine pelvic examination. The screening Z code categories are listed in ICD-10-CM Guideline I.C.21.c.5.

Observation

Codes for observation are not used if a specific disease or injury is being observed. In that case you would report the code to identify the injury. These codes are used only when the suspected condition being observed is ruled out. For example, if a child is suspected to have ingested household cleaner, the child would be observed for reactions. If the child does not develop any symptoms, report a code Z03.6 *Encounter for observation for suspected toxic effect from ingested substance ruled out*. The two observation Z code categories are Z03 *Encounters for medical observation for suspected diseases and conditions ruled out* and Z04 *Encounter for examination and observation for other reasons*. These codes are used in rare circumstance. Codes for observation are reported as the primary code when used with the exception of codes from subcategory Z03.7 *Encounter for suspected maternal and fetal conditions ruled out* which may be first listed or as an additional code.

Aftercare

Aftercare codes are used to report the continued care the patient receives after the acute phase of treatment. Aftercare codes are reported during the healing or recovery phase. Do not report aftercare codes if active treatment is performed for the condition. Codes from other ICD-10-CM chapters may be required to report the patient's condition for the encounter. The aftercare Z codes should not be used for aftercare for injuries. For aftercare of an injury, assign the acute injury code with the appropriate seventh character. The aftercare Z code categories are listed in ICD-10-CM Guideline I.C.21.c.7.

Follow Up

Codes from this category are used to indicate the surveillance of a condition that has healed fully and no longer exists. Do not confuse follow-up care with aftercare. Aftercare codes are reported for encounters required during the healing phase of a condition. Follow up is reported when the condition has fully healed. A provider may require a patient to come to the office following treatment to make sure the patient responded. For example, a patient with chronic tonsillitis is seen to make sure the condition is fully resolved following a six month course of antibiotics. When the patient is seen, the provider documents the tonsillitis is resolved. The follow-up Z code categories are listed in ICD-10-CM Guideline I.C.21.c.8.

Donor

Category Z52 is reported for a patient who donates tissue or blood to another patient. This code is not used for organs harvested from cadavers or for self donations. For example, prior to surgery a patient may donate his or her own blood in case he or she needs a blood transfusion as a result of surgery. In this example, do not report a code from category Z52. Instead, report the code for the reason for the surgery.

Counseling

Z codes are reported when a patient or family member receives counseling following an illness or injury, or when support is required in coping with family or social problems. There are counseling codes for genetic counseling, contraception, family problems (eg, marital, substance abuse in the family, and victims of child abuse), and dietary counseling. The counseling Z code categories are listed in ICD-10-CM Guideline I.C.21.c.10.

Example

During a postpartum visit, a provider discusses the patient's options for birth control. She decides to start taking birth control pills because she plans to try for another baby next year. The provider gives her sample and writes a prescription. The correct codes and sequence are:

- Z39.2 Encounter for routine postpartum follow-up
- Z30.11 Encounter for initial prescription of contraceptive pills

Look in the Index to Disease and Injuries for Admission (for)/ examination at health care facility/postpartum checkup (Z39.2). Next, look for Contraception/initial prescription/pills (Z30.011). Verify all codes in the Tabular List.

Routine and Administrative Examinations

Z codes are reported when a patient presents for a routine exam. Examples include well child preventative visits, routine gynecological exams, and preoperative clearance. Some of the codes for routine health examinations have an option for with or without abnormal findings. The code is selected based on the information known at the time of coding. If the provider orders a test during the examination, but results are not back, and no abnormal findings are mentioned, the option for without abnormal findings is reported. An abnormal finding is a condition the provider finds during that visit when examining the patient or an abnormal result from a test at that visit. When the option for with abnormal findings is reported, additional codes are reported for the condition. The Z code categories for routine and administrative examinations are listed in ICD-10-CM Guideline I.C.21.c.13.

Section Review 5.10

1. The provider orders serum blood tests as part of a pre-employment physical exam. What is the diagnosis?

    A. Z00.00

    B. Z00.01

    C. Z02.1

    D. Z02.79

2. The patient's dense breast tissue made the screening mammogram unreadable, and she is here today for a breast ultra-sound. Her mother and sister both have history of breast cancer.

    A. N60.01, N60.02, Z80.3

    B. Z12.31, N62, Z80.3

    C. Z13.89, R92.2, Z80.3

    D. Z12.39, R92.2, Z80.3

3. When a patient presents for a screening test and the provider finds something abnormal, what diagnosis code should be sequenced first? Refer to ICD-10-CM Guideline I.C.21.c.5.

    A. The diagnosis for the abnormality that was found

    B. The Z code to identify the screening

    C. The code for abnormal results

    D. The signs and symptoms

Documentation Dissection

Case 1

Reason for Visit: Transforaminal epidural injection

Dx: <u>Multilevel lumbar degenerative disc disease</u> [1]

History: Patient returns to outpatient pain clinic following her first lumbar transforaminal epidural steroid injection. Patient reported excellent improvement in her pain starting from day two. Patient stated that about 90 percent of her pain is improved. Patient denied any complications or side-effects from first injection.

Patient decides to have second injection done today to treat her <u>chronic pain</u>. [2] Informed consent was obtained.

Description of Procedure: The patient was positioned in the prone position, Betadine® solution prep, localized the skin over the area of foraminal of L5-S1, C-arm is oblique and slightly caudad. Using fluoroscopy as guide for needle position, using patient paraesthesia to confirm needle position, a 25 gauge spinal needle was inserted. The patient experienced paraesthesia into her left lower extremities. Negative aspiration, injecting 1 ml of 0.2 percent Sensorcaine MPF® with 40 mg of Depo-Medrol®, I did not inject Isovue® due to patient's allergies to iodine. The patient tolerated the procedure well and returned to the recovery room outpatient without any difficulty.

Plan: Plan is to see the patient back for follow up in about two-three weeks.

----

[1] Documented reason for the procedure.

[2] Treatment is stated to treat the patient's chronic pain.

What are the ICD-10-CM codes reported?

Codes: G89.29, M51.36

Rationale: The purpose of the encounter is to treat the patient's chronic pain (sign/symptom) caused by lumbar degenerative joint disease. According to the Official Coding Guidelines, I.C.6.b.1.(a), a code for chronic pain is sequenced first if the reason for the encounter is to treat the chronic pain. An additional code is reported to identify the underlying cause. In this case, the first sequenced code is found in the Index to Diseases and Injuries under Pain/chronic. Refer to code G89.29 in the Tabular List to verify the code accuracy. The second listed code is found under Degeneration, degenerative/intervertebral disc NOS/lumbar region. The correct code is M51.36.

ICD-9-CM Application

What is/are the ICD-9-CM code(s) reported?

Code(s): 338.29, 722.52

Rationale: The purpose of the encounter is to treat the patient's chronic pain (sign/symptom) caused by lumbar degenerative joint disease. According to the Official Coding Guidelines, a code for chronic pain is sequenced first if the reason for the encounter is to treat the chronic pain. An additional code is reported to identify the underlying cause. In this case, the first sequenced code is found in the Index to Diseases under Pain/chronic. Refer to code 338.29 in the Tabular List to verify the code accuracy. The second listed code is found under Degenerative/intervertebral disc/lumbar. The correct code is 722.52.

Case 2

Requesting Physician: Dr. Smith

Reason for Consultation: Opinion and advice on the care of decubitus ulceration.

The history was obtained mainly from the records and the patient's son. The patient is a 65-year-old male who was admitted to the hospital for mental status changes. He had just been released from a nursing home a few days prior and was sent home with sacral decubitus ulceration.

Past Medical History: MRSA [1] and other infections, bronchitis, CVA, Alzheimer's, COPD, CHF, CAD, DVT, hypertension and arthritis. [2]

Allergies: Betadine®, heparin and PCN.

Family History: According to the son, heart problems.

Social: Patient used to smoke many years ago. Patient does not drink alcohol.

ROS: Unable to obtain due to current mental status. Son states patient is legally blind and has urinary incontinence. The son noted that the urine this morning was very dark and purulent in nature.

Exam: Temp is currently 97.2, pulse 96, BP 198/.100; temp max yesterday was 100.5. He is minimally responsive. HEENT: he would track movement in the room with his eyes, sclera was nonicteric with moist membranes. There is no cervical lymph-adenopathy, no thyromegaly. Heart is regular rate and rhythm without murmurs. Lungs have course bilateral breath sounds. Extremities are contracted and warm. The sacral decubitus buttock area shows stage 3 ulceration into the subcutaneous tissue just in some small areas in the central aspect, but overall, the ulceration measures more than 10 cm with significant amount of full thickness necrosis of the tissue. [3]

Labs were reviewed; his white count is increasing; urinalysis showed greater than 100 WBCs.

Impression and Plan: Stage 3 sacral decubitus ulcer; urinary tract infection. [4]

My recommendation would be to take the patient to the surgical suite for debridement of the ulceration; however, the patient is not hemodynamically stable enough to undergo procedure currently. I will continue to monitor the patient until he is stable for surgery.

_____

[1] The history of MRSA is significant.

[2] These conditions are documented but there is no treatment involved with any of these conditions.

[3] The provider documented the site and stage of the decubitus ulcer.

[4] The provider's final assessment of the patient's conditions that are being treated.

_____

What are the ICD-10-CM codes reported?

Codes: L89.153, N39.0, Z86.14

Rationale: The main reason for the visit is to evaluate the patient's decubitus ulcer (pressure ulcer). The decubitus ulcer is located on the sacrum. From the Index to Diseases and Injuries, look for Ulcer/decubitus and you are directed to see Ulcer, pressure, by site. Look for Ulcer/pressure/stage 3/sacral region (tailbone) and you are referred to L89.15-. In the Tabular List, L89.153 is selected for stage 3. The provider also documents a urinary tract infection (UTI). From the Alphabetic Index, look for Infection/urinary (tract). You are referred to N39.0. In the Tabular List, N39.0 has a "use additional" note indicating to identify the infectious agent. In this case, the infectious agent is unknown and, therefore, not coded.

The patient has a history of MRSA, which is significant because the patient has a decubitus ulcer and will require surgery. When a patient has a history of MRSA, he is at a higher risk of developing the infection again. To locate the code, look for History/personal (of)/Methicillin resistant Staphylococcus aureus (MRSA). You are referred to Z86.14. Verify all codes in the Tabular List.

ICD-9-CM Application

What is/are the ICD-9-CM code(s) reported?

Code(s): 707.03, 707.23, 599.0, V12.04

Rationale: The main reason for the visit is to evaluate the patient's decubitus ulcer (pressure ulcer). The decubitus ulcer is located on the sacrum. From the Index to Diseases, look up Ulcer/pressure/sacrum and you are referred to 707.03. Pressure ulcers require an additional code to report the stage of the ulcer. The provider documents the ulcer is stage 3, which is reported with 707.23. The provider also documents a urinary tract infection (UTI). From the index, look up Infection/urinary. You are referred to 599.0. The patient has a history of MRSA, which is significant because the patient has a decubitus ulcer and will require surgery. When a patient has a history of MRSA, he is at a higher risk of developing the infection again. To locate the code, look up Methicillin/resistant staphylococcus aureus (MRSA)/personal history of. You are referred to V12.04. Verify all the codes referenced in the Index to Diseases in the Tabular List.

Glossary

Abrasion—An area on the skin, or some other surface of the body, that has been damaged by scraping or rubbing.

Acute Renal Failure—A rapid loss of kidney function.

Adverse Effect—A harmful, unintended reaction to a drug administered at the correct dose.

Aftercare—Continued care of the patient following the acute phase of treatment for an illness, injury or condition.

Antepartum—Relating to the period before birth.

Arthritis—An inflammation of joint(s), and may also involve the muscles and connective tissue.

Benign Prostatic Hypertrophy—Enlargement of the prostate gland.

Bladder—Organ that collects urine excreted by the kidneys before disposal by urination.

Cellulitis—Bacterial infection of the skin and subcutaneous tissue.

Chronic Kidney Disease—A progressive loss in renal function.

Closed Fracture—A broken bone that does not pierce through the skin.

Congenital Anomalies—Birth defects or abnormalities present at birth.

Convulsions—Involuntary muscular contractions of the extremities, trunk, and head

Decubitus Ulcer—A pressure ulcer caused by lack of circulation caused by bones compressing the skin.

Dermatitis—Inflammation of the skin.

Dermis—Layer of skin beneath the epidermis that contains blood, lymph vessels, sweat glands, and nerve endings.

Dysplasia—Abnormal development of tissue or organs.

Elective Abortion—Legally induced abortion performed by a medical professional for therapeutic or elective reasons.

Epidermis—Outer layer of the skin.

Failed Abortion—An unsuccessful elective abortion; the patient is still pregnant.

First Degree Burn—A burn that affects the epidermis only.

Follow-up Care—Medical encounters to evaluate a condition that has healed and/or no longer exists.

Gestational Diabetes—A condition in which women have high blood glucose levels only during the pregnancy without a previous history of diabetes.

Late Effect—A condition that appears or remains after the acute phase of an earlier, causal condition has resolved.

Malunion—Incomplete union of a previously fractured bone.

Meninges—The membrane that covers the brain and spinal cord.

Nonunion—Failure of a broken bone to heal.

Open Fracture—A broken bone that pierces the skin.

Osteoarthritis—Gradual loss of cartilage of the joints.

Pathologic Fracture—A broken bone caused by disease.

Perinatal—Time from birth through day 28 following birth.

Poisoning—The act of administering a toxic substance; can result by the improper use of medications.

Postpartum—Time from childbirth to six weeks after childbirth.

Puerperal Sepsis—An infection in the genital tract that develops during the postpartum period.

Second Degree Burn—A partial thickness burn involving the epidermis and the dermis.

Spontaneous Abortion—Occurs without any intervention with drugs or instrumentation.

Stress Fracture—A small fracture of a bone caused by repeated physical strain.

Subcutaneous—Tissue that lies under the skin.

Third Degree Burn—A burn that destroys both the epidermis and the dermis, often also involving the subcutaneous tissue.

Ureters—Structures that carry urine from the kidneys to the urinary bladder.

Urethra—Structure that carries urine from the urinary bladder to the outside of the body.

Urinary Incontinence—Inability to control urination.

V Codes—Codes reported to support services that are rendered when a patient does not have an acute medical condition.

Introduction to CPT®

The Current Procedural Terminology (CPT®) codebook is a compilation of guidelines, codes, and descriptions to report healthcare services performed by healthcare providers in the United States. The CPT® code set (Healthcare Common Procedure Coding System or HCPCS Level I) is copyrighted and maintained by American Medical Association (AMA) and is used with other code sets established by the Department of Health & Human Services (HHS) and other federally-named entities for healthcare reporting and reimbursement.

The first CPT® code set was developed and published by the AMA in 1966, and was established as an indexing/coding system to standardize terminology among physicians and other providers. In 1983, the Health Care Financing Administration (now the Centers for Medicare & Medicaid Services (CMS) adopted CPT® and its own HCPCS Level II, mandating that these code sets be for use in all Medicare billings. These code sets largely standardized reporting of medical services, equipment, and supplies. Medicaid agencies and commercial health plans soon adopted the code sets and began to require CPT® and HCPCS Level II codes for reporting healthcare services for reimbursement.

Under the Health Insurance Portability and Accountability Act (HIPAA) of 1996, HHS was required to establish national standards for electronic transaction of healthcare information. In August 2000, the Transactions and Code Sets Final Rule (45 CFR 160.103) named CPT®, HCPCS Level II, and their respective modifiers as standard code sets for national use. The CPT® code set includes three categories of medical nomenclature and descriptors: Category I, Category II, and Category III. These three different categories are contained within the CPT® codebook.

Category I CPT® codes utilize a five-digit numeric code, eg, 12345. These codes are the most commonly used codes for medical services, procedures, and professional services by physicians and other qualified healthcare professionals. There are over 7,000 service codes plus titles and modifiers in the Category I CPT® code set. A panel established by the AMA, reviews and updates each code set annually. The updated and revised CPT® codes are provided to CMS. It is mandatory to use Category I CPT® codes for reporting and reimbursement purposes.

Category II CPT® codes are optional "performance measurement" tracking codes designed to minimize administrative burdens because they facilitate data collection about quality of care, per the AMA. Category II codes are used for the Physician Quality Reporting System (PQRS) to provide outcome measurement for certain medical conditions. PQRS is an incentive-based program developed by CMS to record evidence-based measures and is discussed later in this chapter. Category II codes are located near the back of the CPT® codebook after the Medicine section. The format for Category II codes is alphanumeric, with the letter F in the last position, eg, 0001F. Category II codes may be reported in addition to evaluation and management (E/M) services or clinical services CPT® Category I codes.

Example

A physician counsels a patient regarding prescribed statin therapy for coronary artery disease. Report code 4013F *Statin therapy prescribed or currently being taken (CAD)* in addition to the appropriate level office visit code (99201–99215).

Category III CPT® codes are temporary codes assigned by the AMA for emerging technology, services, and procedures. Category III codes are located after the Category II code section. The format for Category III codes also has an alphanumeric structure, except with a **T** in the last position, eg, 0075T. Unlike the Category II CPT® codes, Category III codes can be reported alone, without an additional Category I code.

Example

A patient has a total replacement heart system, or artificial heart implanted as a temporary measure until transplantation or to prolong life if the patient is not eligible for transplant. Report 0051T *Implantation of a total replacement heart system (artificial heart) with recipient cardiectomy.*

The AMA updates the CPT® codebook annually. The additions and revisions can include:

- Additional code additions
- Revisions to the code verbiage
- Revisions to the guidelines
- Deletions of any outdated codes

The Organization of the CPT® Codebook

To assign the codes contained within the CPT® codebook properly, you first must understand the organizational characteristics within it. The CPT® codebook is organized by:

- CPT® sections—Category I has six sections that include services and surgical procedures separated into subsections.
- Section Guidelines
- Section Table of Contents
- Notes
- Category II codes (0001F–9007F)
- Category III codes (0019T–0380T)
- Appendices A–O
- Alphabetized Index

The CPT® subsections also include:

- Indicator icons
- Boldfaced type
- Italicized type
- Cross-referenced terms
- Anatomy illustrations
- Procedural reviews that aid with medical terminology and anatomy

Introduction Guidelines in the CPT® Codebook

Guidelines in the CPT® codebook are invaluable to professional coders and define the information necessary for choosing the correct code to describe provided medical services.

Practical Coding Note

Review each and every guideline in your codebooks. Underline or highlight specific coding information within the guidelines.

Guidelines are referenced in the introduction of each section and subsection of the CPT® codebook. Guidelines in one section do not apply to another section within the CPT® codebook.

CPT® Conventions and Iconography

An established set of conventions and symbols are used throughout the CPT® codebook. They are designed to communicate information clearly and in an easily recognizable manner.

; Semicolon and Indented Procedure—The use of the semicolon was developed so that CPT® did not have to list

full descriptions for every code in the publication. A CPT® procedure or service code that contains a semicolon is divided into two parts; the description before the semicolon and the description after the semicolon.

(a) The words before the semi-colon are considered the "common procedure" in the code descriptor.

(b) The indented descriptor is dependent on the preceding "common procedure" code descriptor.

(c) It is not necessary to report the main code (eg, 00160) when reporting the indented codes (eg, 00162 or 00164).

Example

00160 Anesthesia for procedures on nose and accessory sinuses; not otherwise specified

00162   radical surgery

00164   biopsy, soft tissue

The full descriptor for CPT® code 00162 and 00164 includes the portion before the semicolon in 00160 to make the full description of the codes:

00160 Anesthesia for procedures on nose and accessory sinuses; not otherwise specified

00162 Anesthesia for procedures on nose and accessory sinuses; **radical surgery**

00164 Anesthesia for procedures on nose and accessory sinuses; biopsy, soft tissue

+ Add-on Codes (a list is located in Appendix D)—Some of the procedures listed in CPT® are carried out in addition to the primary procedure performed. Add-on codes are never reported alone. They always accompany specific primary procedure codes. These codes are located in the parenthetical instructions listed below the add-on code. All add-on codes found in the CPT® codebook are exempt from the multiple procedure concept (see the modifier 51 definition in Appendix A).

Example

+11201 each additional ten lesions, or part thereof (List separately in addition to code for primary procedure) (Use 11201 in conjunction with 11200)

● A bullet symbol located to the left of a code indicates new procedures and services added to the CPT® codebook.

Example

● **73351** Radiologic examination, femur, 1 view

▲ A triangle symbol located to the left of a code indicates that the description of the code has been revised. Details of the revision are found in Appendix B of the CPT® codebook.

Example

▲ **74240** Radiologic examination, gastrointestinal tract, upper, with or without delayed images, without KUB

This code is listed in Appendix B showing the following changes:

▲ **74240** Radiologic examination, gastrointestinal tract, upper, withour without delayed ~~films~~ <u>images</u>, without KUB

►◄ Opposing horizontal triangles indicate new and revised text other than the procedure descriptors. These symbols indicate CPT® Editorial Panel actions.

Example

50390 Aspiration and/or injection of renal cyst or pelvis by needle, percutaneous

(For radiological supervision and interpretation, see 74425, 74470, 76942, 77002, 77012, 77021)

► (For antegrade nephrostogram and/or antegrade pyelogram, see 50430, 50431) ◄

⊘ The "forbidden" symbol identifies codes that are exempt from the use of modifier 51 (See Appendix E).

Example

⊘ **20974** Electrical stimulation to aid bone healing; noninvasive (nonoperative)

⊙ A bulls-eye symbol identifies codes that include moderate sedation. When this symbol appears next to a CPT®

code, moderate sedation is not reported separately (see Appendix G).

Example

⊙ **43200** Esophagoscopy, flexible, transoral; diagnostic, including collection of specimen(s) by brushing or washing, when performed (separate procedure)

↗ The lightning bolt symbol identifies codes for vaccines pending Food and Drug Administration (FDA) approval. Some vaccine products are assigned a CPT® Category I code in anticipation of future approval from the FDA. When the vaccine has been approved by the FDA, a revision notation will be provided on the AMA CPT® "Category I Vaccine Codes" website: www.ama-assn.org/ama/pub/category/10902.html (see Appendix K for Products Pending FDA Approval).

Example

↗ **90668** Influenza virus vaccine (IIV), pandemic formulation, split virus, for intramuscular use

The pound sign symbol identifies CPT® codes that have been resequenced and are out of numerical order. A summary of resequenced CPT® codes with the pound sign symbol are listed in Appendix N.

Example

When looking for CPT® code 46947, the following stated:

46947 Code is out of numerical sequence. *See* 46700–46947.

This directs us to look at code range 46700–46947 to locate 46947. 46947 is found under CPT® code 46762.

46947 Hemorrhoidopexy (eg, for prolapsing internal hemorrhoids) by stapling

Category I CPT® Section Numbers

The Category I CPT® codebook is divided into six main section titles. Sections are organized in numeric order with the exception of the Evaluation and Management section (99201–99499), located at the beginning of the listed sections because it contains codes most commonly used.

Evaluation and Management (99201–99499)

Anesthesiology (00100–01999)

Surgery (10021–69990)

Radiology (70010–79999)

Pathology and Laboratory (80047–89398)

Medicine (90281–99607)

Section titles have subsections divided by anatomic location, procedure, condition, or descriptor subheadings. The subheadings, structured by CPT® conventions, may list alternate coding suggestions in parenthesis (parenthetical instructions) and then list the descriptors for the numerically sequenced CPT® codes with specific coding instructions.

Example

Section: **Surgery** (10021–69990)

Subsection: **Integumentary System**

Subheading: **Skin, Subcutaneous and Accessory Structures**

Category: **Debridement**

(For dermabrasions, see 15780–15783)

(For nail debridement, see 11720–11721)

(For burn(s), see 16000–16035)

(For pressure ulcers, see 15920-15999)

11000   Debridement of extensive eczematous or infected skin; up to 10% of body surface

(For abdominal wall or genitalia debridement for necrotizing soft tissue infection, see 11004-11006)

+ 11001   each additional 10% of the body surface, or part thereof (List separately in addition to code for primary procedure)

(Use 11001 in conjunction with 11000)

Section Guidelines

Follow specific guidelines presented at the beginning of each section; these identify correct coding protocols. Guidelines define which codes are used together and provide coders with information necessary to complete coding sequences.

Example

Section: **Surgery**

Subsection: **Cardiovascular System** (33010–37799)

Guideline:

Selective vascular catheterizations should be coded to include introduction and all lesser order selective catheterizations used in the approach (eg, the description for

a selective right middle cerebral artery catheterization includes the introduction and placement catheterization of the right common and internal carotid arteries).

Additional second and/or third order arterial catheterizations within the same family of arteries supplied by a single first order artery should be expressed by 36218 or 36248. Additional first order or higher catheterizations in vascular families supplied by a first order vessel different from a previously selected and coded family should be separately coded using the conventions described above.

(For monitoring, operation of pump and other non-surgical services, see 99190-99192, 99291, 99292, 99354–99360)

(For other medical or laboratory related services, see appropriate section)

(For radiological supervision and interpretation, see 75600–75978)

CPT® Code Basics

To assign appropriate CPT® codes, the professional coder reviews the physician's documentation thoroughly and selects the procedure(s) or service(s) accurately describing the care provided. The CPT® alphabetic index is referenced for a CPT® code or code range. After locating the approximate CPT® code in the alphabetic index, the numeric section is used for code specifications. The professional coder knows not to select a CPT® code using only the alphabetic index.

The CPT® Index is alphabetized with main terms organized by condition, procedure, anatomic site, synonyms, eponyms, and abbreviations. For example:

1) A condition: eg, Cerumen, Cyst, Angle Deformity

2) The name of the procedure or medical service documented: eg, Removal, Suture, Fasciotomy

3) The name of the anatomic site or organ: eg, Neck, Skin, Femur

4) Synonyms, eponyms and abbreviations: eg, Toe/Interphalangeal Joint, Watson-Jones Procedure, EEG

Information in the alphabetic index expands by subterms listed alphabetically below each main term. The subterms further clarify the main term by noting condition, procedure, or anatomic site. With each subterm is a listing of the CPT® code or code ranges located in the numeric section of the CPT® codebook.

To clarify and ensure selection of the correct CPT® code, the code or code range from the alphabetic index is located in the CPT® numeric section.

However, when CPT® code 58900 is referenced in the numeric section, additional information for correct code assignment is defined. The defining information written in the numeric section for the CPT® code 58900 is:

Example

The procedure for a biopsy of the ovary seems straightforward.

Ovary
Biopsy 49321, 58900

However, when CPT® code 58900 is referenced in the numeric section, additional information for correct code assignment is defined. The defining information written in the numeric section for the CPT® code 58900 is:

Section: **Surgery**

Subsection: **Female Genital System (56405–58999)**

Subheading: **Ovary (58800–58960)**

Category: **Excision (58900–58960)**

58900 Biopsy of ovary, unilateral or bilateral (separate procedure)

   ⊃ *CPT® Changes: An Insider's View 2000*

   ⊃ *CPT® Assistant* Nov 99:29

   (For laparoscopic biopsy of the ovary or fallopian tube, use 49321)

CPT® conventions, symbols, and references are taken under consideration to report the correct use of the code (as seen in the 58900 example). Important considerations found in the example's descriptor include:

1. Separate Procedure—When the service or procedure is designated as a "separate procedure" it is performed alone, or is considered unrelated to another procedure/service provided during the same patient encounter.

    Modifier 59 may be appended to a "separate procedure" designated CPT® code if guidelines are met within the medical documentation. Modifier 59 guidelines and its uses will be discussed later.

2. The descriptor specifies, "*unilateral or bilateral;*" modifier 50 *Bilateral procedure* is not necessary if a biopsy is taken from both ovaries.

3. ⊃ *CPT® Assistant*—This example cites two references: *CPT® Changes: An Insider's View 2000 and* the

November 1999 issue, page 29. The *CPT® Changes: An Insider's View 2000* indicates a change was made to the procedure description in the year 2000.

4. Parenthetic instructions—below code 58900, there is a parenthetic instruction that directs you to use code 49321 if the biopsy is performed by laparoscope.

    The professional coder analyzes all information from the CPT® numeric section before assigning a CPT® code. Some health plans have specific billing instructions and coverage issue clarifications posted on their websites for review prior to code assignment.CMS publishes Internet Only Manuals (IOMs) and a Medicare Coverage Center that can help professional coders with billing and coverage instructions on their website. Online documents are not updated with every new Transmittal, Program Memorandum, or *Medlearn Matters* article, so pay particular attention to when these documents were last updated. Each Medicaid agency maintains its website and program requirements.

    Internet-Only Manuals (IOMs): www.cms.gov/Regulations-and-Guidance/Guidance/Manuals/Internet-Only-Manuals-IOMs.html

    Medicare Coverage Center: www.cms.gov/Medicare/Coverage/CoverageGenInfo/index.html

National Correct Coding Initiative (NCCI)

CMS implemented the National Correct Coding Initiative (NCCI) to promote correct coding methodologies and to control improper assignment of codes that results in inappropriate reimbursement. NCCI coding policies are based on the analysis of standard medical and surgical practice; coding conventions included in CPT®; coding guidelines developed by national medical specialty societies (eg, CPT® Advisory Committee that contains representatives of major medical societies); local and national coverage determinations; and a review of current coding practices.

NCCI procedure to procedure (PTP) edits are used by professional coders to determine codes considered by CMS to be bundled codes for procedures and services deemed necessary to accomplish a major procedure. Bundled procedure codes are not reported separately: The bundled procedure is included in the major procedural code. Beware: Reporting bundled procedure codes in addition to the major procedural code is characterized as unbundling and if repeated with enough frequency could be considered an act of fraud.

The NCCI PTP includes two types of indicator edits:

1. Column 1/Column 2 edits are edits for code pairs that should not be billed together because one service inherently includes the other, unless an appropriate modifier is used and allowed.

2. Mutually exclusive edits are edits for code pairs that, for clinical reasons, are unlikely to be performed on the same patient on the same day; eg, two different types of laboratory testing that would produce the same result as one test. Effective April 2012, mutually exclusive edits are included in the Column 1/Column 2 edit file to consolidate the edits for ease of use. Coders no longer need to access two separate edit files to search for bundling conflicts.

Column1/Column 2 Edits						
Column 1	Column 2	* = In existence prior to 1996	Effective Date	Deletion Date *=no data	Modifier 0=not allowed 1=allowed 9=not applicable	PTP Edit Rationale
11042	0213T		20100701	*	0	Misuse of column two code with column one code
11042	0216T		20100701	*	0	Anesthesia service included in surgical procedure
11042	0228T		20100701	*	0	Anesthesia service included in surgical procedure
11042	0230T		20100701	*	0	Anesthesia service included in surgical procedure
11042	10030		20140101	*	1	Standards of medical/surgical practice
11042	10060		19960101	*	1	Standards of medical/surgical practice
11042	11000		19960101	*	1	Standards of medical/surgical practice
11042	11001		19960101	19960101	9	Standards of medical/surgical practice
11042	11010		19980101	*	1	Mutually exclusive procedures
11042	11011		19990401	*	1	Mutually exclusive procedures
11042	11040	*	19960101	*	1	HCPCS/CPT procedure code definition
11042	11041	*	19960101	*	1	HCPCS/CPT procedure code definition

The Correct Coding file formats continue to include a Correct Coding Modifier (CCM) indicator (carrier only) for both the Comprehensive/Component Table. This indicator determines whether a CCM causes the code pair to bypass the edit. This indicator will be either "0," "1," or "9." The definitions of each are:

0 = A CCM is not allowed and will not bypass the edits.

1 = A CCM is allowed and will bypass the edits.

9 = The use of modifiers is not specified. This indicator is used for all code pairs that have a deletion date that is the same as the effective date. This indicator was created so that no blank spaces would be in the indicator field.

Sequencing CPT® Codes

Code sequencing and reporting instructions in the CPT® numeric section is crucial in claim submission and appropriate reimbursement. Knowing and utilizing coding references also aid with reporting CPT® codes. Managing a medical practice also involves staying current with reimbursement issues.

Understanding the Resource-Based Relative Value Scale (RBRVS) will help in physician fee schedules, benchmarking, and the proper sequencing of codes. Reviewing the physician fee schedule amount against practice costs on an annual basis may help medical practices to renegotiate health plan contracts, recognize national benchmark levels of payment, and aid with sequencing codes based on the RBRVS.

Resource-Based Relative Value Scale (RBRVS)

Medicare established the RBRVS system to reimburse physicians based on the CPT® code submitted for reimbursement. Each CPT® code has a Relative Value Unit (RVU) assigned which, when multiplied by a conversion factor (CF) and a geographic region adjustment allowance, creates the reimbursement for the medical service represented by the CPT® code.

RVUs are configured utilizing three components:

1. Physician work—time, skill, training, and intensity of service provided

2. Practice expense—reflects the cost of ancillary personnel, supplies, and office overhead

3. Professional liability/malpractice insurance

How to Use the RBRVS

CMS annually publishes Physician Fee Schedule information on its website: www.cms.hhs.gov/PhysicianFeeSched/ and posts the formula for calculating physician fee schedule payment amounts. The physician fee schedule amounts vary depending on facility vs. non-facility. Facility practice RVU expenses include services performed in emergency rooms, hospital settings (inpatient and outpatient), skilled nursing facilities, nursing homes, or ambulatory surgical centers (ASCs). The non-facility RVUs include services performed in non-hospital owned physician practices or privately owned practices. The 2014 Physician Fee Schedule (PFS) is used in the following calculation example. A key factor in determining the Physician's Fee Schedule (PFS), is the Sustainable Growth Rate (SGR) formula. The SGR formula is subject to revisions based on data that is collected during the previous year or in response to trends identified during the year. If Medicare expenditures for the previous year are more than the amount forecasted, the conversion factor will be modified to decrease payments to physicians for the coming year in an effort to meet the target SGR. Should Medicare expenditures from the previous year be less than predicted, the conversion factor would be increased for the coming year. Typically, the PFS is updated annually on March 1. Ultimately, the PFS can be suspended or adjusted by Congress.

The published formula for calculating the 2015 PFS payment amount is as follows:

PE = Physician expense

MP = Malpractice

GPCI = Geographic practice cost index (this is used to realize the varying cost based on geographic location)

CF = Conversion factor (this is a fixed dollar amount used to translate the RVUs into fees)

Non-Facility Pricing Amount = [(Work RVU * Work GPCI) + (Non-Facility PE RVU * PE GPCI) + (MP RVU * MP GPCI)] * CF

Facility Pricing Amount = [(Work RVU * Work GPCI) + (Facility PE RVU * PE GPCI) + (MP RVU * MP GPCI)] * CF

The published conversion factor for 2015 (after March 31, 2015) is $35.9335.

Example

Using the following table excerpts from the CMS website, we will calculate payment results for the E/M visit, established patient office or other outpatient visit (99212) for the state of Idaho.

RVU table for E/M codes New Patient and Established Patients (99201–99215)

HCPCS CODE	SHORT DESCRIPTION	WORK RVU	FULLY IMPLEMENTED NON-FAC PE RVU	FULLY IMPLEMENTED FACILITY PE RVU	MP RVU
99201	Office/outpatient visit new	0.48	0.71	0.23	0.04
99202	Office/outpatient visit new	0.93	1.10	0.41	0.07
99203	Office/outpatient visit new	1.42	1.48	0.60	0.15
99204	Office/outpatient visit new	2.43	1.99	1.02	0.22
99205	Office/outpatient visit new	3.17	2.37	1.31	0.29
99211	Office/outpatient visit est	0.18	0.37	0.07	0.01
99212	Office/outpatient visit est	0.48	0.71	0.20	0.04
99213	Office/outpatient visit est	0.97	1.01	0.40	0.06
99214	Office/outpatient visit est	1.5	1.43	0.61	0.10
99215	Office/outpatient visit est	2.11	1.82	0.87	0.16

Source: CMS (www.cms.gov); RVU15D/PPRVU15_Oct05_V0821

2015 Geographic Practice Cost Indices by State

Locality name (State)	Work** GPCI	PE GPCI	MP GPCI
Alabama	1.000	0.886	0.611
Alaska **	1.500	1.107	0.712
Arizona	1.000	1.000	0.877
Arkansas	1.000	0.867	0.534
Delaware	1.012	1.031	1.083
Fort Lauderdale, FL	1.000	1.030	1.715
Miami, FL	1.000	1.033	2.490
Rest of Florida	1.000	0.960	1.315
Atlanta, GA	1.001	1.005	0.943
Rest of Georgia	1.000	0.899	0.904
Hawaii/Guam/American Samoa/Northern Mariana Islands	1.002	1.162	0.618
Idaho	1.000	0.898	0.508

Source: CMS PFS Relative Value Files, RVU15D, CY 2015 GPCIs

Important: Health plans other than Medicare may not use the CMS calculations to determine provider reimbursement.

Example 1:

Calculate the Non-Facility Pricing Amount, Medicare Payment for CPT® code 99212 for the state of Idaho.

Work RVUs x Work GPCI	0.48 x 1.000 = 0.48
+ Fully Implemented Non-Facility PE RVUs x PE GPCI	0.71 x 0.898 = 0.63758
+ MP RVUs x MP GPCI	0.04 x 0.508= 0.402032
= Sum of geographic adjustment	1.1379

The sum of geographic adjustment x CF = 1.1379 x $35.9335= $40.89 Non-Facility Pricing Amount (physician office, private practice)

Example 2:

Calculate the Facility Pricing Amount, Medicare Payment for the CPT® code 99212 in Idaho.

Work RVU x Work GPCI	0.48 x 1.000 = 0.48
+ Fully Implemented Facility PE RVU x PE GPCI	0.20 x 0.898 = 0.1796
+ MP RVU x MP GPCI	0.04 x 0.508 = 0.02032
= Sum of geographic adjustment	0.67992

Sum of geographic adjustment x CF = 0.67992 x $35.9335 = $24.43 Facility Pricing Amount (Medicare Part A facilities, eg, hospitals, skilled nursing facilities, nursing homes OR physician office if it is facility owned and billed for by a hospital)

Example

Using the RBRVS system and RVUs for the sequencing of CPT® codes, while maintaining correct coding guidelines, the following example is outlined:

Two polyps were identified during a colonoscopy. The physician performed a biopsy on one polyp and removed a second polyp at a different site, during the same procedure. The CPT® codes used for reporting this procedure were 45380 and 45385.

Referencing the Physician Fee Schedule Look-Up Tool on the CMS website: www.cms.gov/apps/physician-fee-schedule/search/search-criteria.aspx, we find the following information:

HCPCS	Short Description	WORK RVU	Fully Implemented Non-Fac PE RVU	Fully Implemented Facility PE RVU	MP RVU
45380	Colonoscopy and biopsy	4.43	8.09	2.31	0.66
45385	Lesion removal colonoscopy	5.30	8.79	2.69	0.79

Use the Physician Fee Schedule Look-Up Tool to check the payments for Alabama:

HCPCS	Short Description	Alabama—Non Facility Price	Alabama—Facility Price
45380	Colonoscopy and biopsy	$431.24	$247.22
45385	Lesion removal colonoscopy	$487.64	$293.43

For this example, the professional coder may use the information provided by CMS for establishing the sequence of treatment charges. The sequence of the CPT® coding for this example is 45385, 45380-59. CPT® 45385 has the highest total RVU value and therefore is sequenced first.

An additional resource available for coding reference, available through the AMA, is *Medicare RBRVS: The Physician's Guide*. The guide is a reference for physicians, professional coders, and their staff to use for detailed background information and explanations of the physician payment system. This guide may be beneficial to the professional coder because it answers questions about the RBRVS system and allows quick access to information regarding payment rules for surgical packages and CPT® code RVUs. The guide includes:

- Annual payment rules
- Feature explanations of the physician payment system
- Quick access to relative values by CPT® code
- Tables with information for calculating the Medicare payment schedule

Steps for coding Multiple Procedures

1. Select all procedure codes

2. Check the codes against NCCI (Column 1 and 2) and Mutually Exclusive table for bundling and eliminate any bundled codes. If the documentation supports the use of a modifier to report a bundled code, append the appropriate modifier to the column 2 code.

3. Check the RVUs for the remaining codes and sequence by RVU, highest to lowest.

Note: check with your individual payer to see if they follow NCCI guidelines for bundling, if not follow each individual payer's guidelines.

Section Review 6.1

1. What is the full description for CPT® code 43622?

    A. With formation of intestinal pouch, any type

    B. Gastrectomy, total; with Roux-en-Y reconstruction and formation of intestinal pouch, any type

    C. Gastrectomy, total; with esophagoenterostomy with formation of intestinal pouch, any type

    D. Gastrectomy, total; with formation of intestinal pouch, any type

2. What CPT® code listed below includes moderate sedation?

    A. 20937

    B. 20974

    C. 20979

    D. 20982

3. Select the true statement regarding modifier 51 in the CPT® codebook.

    A. Modifier 51 can be replaced by using the RT and LT modifiers.

    B. Add-on codes should always have modifier 51 appended to them.

    C. Codes exempt from modifier 51 are identified with the universal forbidden symbol.

    D. A list of modifier 51 exempt codes can be found in Appendix A of the CPT® codebook.

4. In the National Correct Coding Initiative, files contain a Correct Coding Modifier (CCM) indicator. What does the CCM indicator 0 mean?

    A. A CCM is not allowed and will not bypass the edits.

    B. A CCM is allowed and will bypass the edits.

    C. The use of modifiers is not specified.

    D. Only modifier 59 will bypass the edits.

5. According to the parenthetical instructions for CPT® code 33690, how should right and left pulmonary artery banding in a single ventricle be reported?

    A. 33690-50

    B. 33620

    C. 33690-63

    D. 33620-50

CPT® Assistant

One of the AMA resources referenced throughout the CPT® codebook is the *CPT® Assistant*. The ➲ symbol posted after many CPT® codes indicates a *CPT® Assistant* article was published regarding that particular code. The *CPT® Assistant* is a publication that offers accurate information and guidance for CPT® code use. The monthly issues offer several professional features of varying content including:

- articles answering everyday CPT® coding questions,
- CCI bundling information,
- E/M billing guidance,
- current code use and interpretation,
- case studies demonstrating practical application of codes,
- detailed case studies demonstrating practical application of codes,
- anatomical illustrations, charts and graphs for quick reference,
- information for appealing insurance denials, and
- information to validate code usage when audited.

The *CPT® Assistant* is considered an official resource and should be utilized to ensure accurate coding.

Category II Codes and a Brief Overview of the Physician Quality Reporting System

CPT® Category II Codes

CPT® Category II Codes is the code set used voluntarily by physicians to report performance measurement. Category II CPT® codes are recognized by their four numerical digits followed by the letter "F" (eg 1234F), and have no RVU value because the codes typically describe clinical components included in E/M services. Category II codes may also describe results from tests and other procedures identified as measurable data for quality patient care. For information regarding the use of Category II codes for performance measurement, exclusion modifiers, measures, and the measure's source, go to website: www.ama-assn.org.

CPT® Category II codes are updated throughout the year and are posted on the AMA website: www.ama-assn.org. Professional advisory entities collect performance-measured evidence-based data to measure the quality of patient care. CPT® Category II codes and HCPCS G codes make up the Quality Data Codes (QDCs) for the Physician Quality Reporting Initiative established by CMS.

Physician Quality Reporting

In 2006, the Tax Relief and Health Care Act authorized CMS to establish a physician quality reporting system. CMS named the program Physician Quality Reporting Initiative (PQRI). Effective 2011, the program is named Physician Quality Reporting System (PQRS). Eligible professionals who do not successfully report specified quality measures furnished to Medicare Part B beneficiaries (including Railroad Retirement Board and Medicare Secondary Payer) are penalized by a negative payment adjustment applied to the payments received. Payment adjustments are applied two years after the reporting period. A Beginner Report Toolkit explaining the program and how to get started is available on the CMS website.

When billing for medical charges and reporting QDCs for performance measures on the CMS 1500 form, only one diagnosis from the claim should be referenced in the diagnosis pointer field (field #24e), even though all diagnoses reported on the claim will be included in PQRS analysis. In addition, when reporting QDCs on medical claims, a line-item charge must be submitted. Depending on the billing system software used for claim submissions, a line item charge of $0.00 should be entered for the QDC. If the billing system software does not allow for a $0.00 line item charge, a nominal charge of $0.01 may be entered. Whether CMS is charged the $0.00 or the $0.01 for the PQRS QDC, the line item will be denied for payment. After the claim is processed and PQRS measure data is collected and recorded by CMS, a Remittance Advice (RA) will be issued to the EP. The RA will list the remark code (N365) message for the PQRS QDC line item. N365 reads: "This procedure code is not payable. It is for reporting/information purposes only" (https://www.cms.gov/Medicare/Quality-Initiatives-Patient-Assessment-Instruments/PQRS/downloads/2015_PQRS_Implementation_Guide-07-23-15.pdf?agree=yes&next=Accept).

CPT® Category III Codes

Category III CPT® codes use four numerical digits followed by the letter T, such as 1234T. The code set contains temporary codes used for data collection in the FDA approval process regarding new and emerging technology, services, and procedures. Codes are updated twice a year, January 1 and July 1, and are implemented six months afterwards. Updates are published on AMA's website: www.ama-assn.org. Category III codes describe services and/or procedures with more specificity than Category I unlisted codes. If a Category III code is available it must be reported instead of a Category I "unlisted procedure" code.

Category III codes do not indicate the service or procedure as experimental, only that it is new and/or emerging and being tracked for trending. Once FDA approval is obtained for a Category III CPT® Code, it becomes a Category I CPT® code. If the Category III code is not FDA approved within five years, the code is either renewed for another five years or removed from the CPT® codebook. Reimbursement may be available through health plans, although no RVU is assigned.

Medical practices should be aware that the AMA updates and publishes the CPT® code set each year. Medical practices should use the implementation period between publications to update CPT® changes in their coding and patient billing systems. If the practice contracts with a third-party vendor such as a billing service, the practice should verify that the vendor meets update deadlines. This is not only a regulatory compliance issue; submission of outdated codes may negatively affect reimbursement and cause claim denials.

1) CPT® Category I is published in the late summer or early fall in two available formats: electronic files and books. The updated CPT® code set is effective January 1 of the next calendar year.

2) CPT® Category II codes are released three times a year and are effective three months after the publication date.

3) CPT® Category III and vaccine product codes update twice a year and are released January 1 and July 1 with effective dates for use six months after they are published.

Appendices

Appendices A through O are located in the CPT® codebook after the Category III CPT® codes. The Appendix section references topics important for coding specificity and provides examples for the reader.

Appendix A
Modifiers—This appendix lists modifiers categorized as:

1. CPT® Level I Modifiers—lists all of the modifiers applicable to CPT® codes

2. Anesthesia Physical Status Modifiers

3. CPT® Level I Modifiers approved for Ambulatory Surgery Center (ASC) Hospital Outpatient Use

4. Level II (HCPCS/National) Modifiers

Appendix B
Summary of Additions, Deletions, and Revisions—Appendix B contains the actual changes and additions to the CPT® codes from the previous year to the current publication.

Appendix C
Clinical Examples—Limited to E/M services, the AMA has provided clinical examples for different specialties. These clinical examples do not encompass the entire scope of medical practice, and guides professional coders to follow E/M patient encounter rules for level of service.

Appendix D
Summary of CPT® Add-on Codes—Lists codes not reported as a single or stand-alone code. The codes listed are identified throughout CPT® with the + symbol throughout the numeric section of CPT®.

Appendix E
Summary of CPT® Codes Exempt from Modifier 51—This listing is a summary of CPT® codes that are exempt from the use of modifier 51. The codes are identified in the CPT® codebook with the ⊘ symbol.

Appendix F
Summary of CPT® Codes Exempt from Modifier 63—This listing is a summary of CPT® codes that are exempt from the use of modifier 63. The listed codes will also be identified by the CPT® convention of parenthetical instruction "(Do not report modifier 63 in conjunction with...)."

Appendix G
Summary of CPT® Codes That Include Moderate (Conscious) Sedation—CPT® codes identified by the ⊙ symbol, indicates the reported procedure includes conscious sedation and it is not appropriate to report sedation codes 99143-99145.

Appendix H
Alphabetic Clinical Topics Listing (AKA—Alphabetic Listing)—This has been removed from the CPT® codebook, because CPT Category II codes, clinical conditions, and measure abstracts rapidly change and expand. This listing is now solely accessed on the AMA website www.ama-assn.org/go/cpt.

Appendix I
Genetic Testing Code Modifiers—This appendix was removed with the deletion of the molecular pathology stacking codes (83890-83914). The genetic testing code modifiers were reported with the codes that were deleted. New codes for molecular pathology were created eliminating the need for the modifiers included in Appendix I.

Appendix J
Electrodiagnostic Medicine Listing of Sensory, Motor, and Mixed Nerves—This appendix provides a summary that assigns each sensory, motor, and mixed nerve with its appropriate nerve conduction study code in order to enhance accurate reporting of codes.

Appendix K

Product Pending FDA Approval—Some vaccine products listed as CPT® Category I codes are still pending approval from the FDA and can be found in this appendix. The lightning bolt symbol identifies the pending codes throughout the CPT® code set. For updated vaccine approvals by the FDA, visit the AMA CPT® Category I Vaccine Code information on website www.ama-assn.org/ama/pub/category/10902.html.

Appendix L

Vascular Families—Based on the assumption that a vascular catheterization has a starting point of the aorta, Appendix L illustrates vascular "families" that emerge from the aorta using brackets to identify the order of vessels: First, Second, Third, and Beyond Third Order of vascular branches. The largest First Order Branch emerges from the aorta. The Second Order Branch emerges from the First Order Branch, and so on to include the vessel's Third Order Branch and Beyond Third Order Branches. If the starting point of the catheterization is other than the aorta, the orders might change.

Appendix M

Renumbered CPT® Codes-Citations Crosswalk—This listing is a summary of crosswalked deleted and renumbered CPT® codes and descriptors. This is an essential tool when referencing citations regarding coding for specific procedures.

Appendix N

Summary of Resequenced CPT® Codes

This listing is a summary of CPT® codes not appearing in numeric sequence. This allows existing codes to be relocated to an appropriate location.

Appendix O

Multianalyte Assays with Algorithmic Analyses

This is a listing of administrative codes for Multianalyte Assays with Algorithmic Analyses (MAAA) procedures. These are typically unique to a single clinical laboratory or manufacturer.

Section Review 6.2

1. What association maintains and publishes CPT® coding guidelines, codes, and descriptions?

   A. AMA

   B. CPT®

   C. CMS

   D. HCPCS

2. What are the three categories of CPT® codes?

   A. CPT®, HCPCS, HCPCS Level II

   B. Category I, II, and III

   C. CPT®, Modifiers, Index

   D. All of the above

3. What are three methods used to list main terms in the CPT® codebook alphabetic index?

   A. Condition, brand names, procedure

   B. Condition, synonyms, abbreviations

   C. Anatomic site, surgical specialty, eponyms

   D. Eponyms, procedure, instruments

4. What three components are used to configure Relative Value Units?

    A. Location of practice, location of medical school, ancillary personnel

    B. Malpractice insurance claims, physician work, practice expense

    C. Malpractice insurance costs, physician work, practice expense

    D. All of the above

5. What are the Physician Fee Schedule's definitions for facility and non-facility?

    A. Facility includes privately owned physician practices and Non-facility includes hospital owned physician practices

    B. Non-Facility includes privately owned physician practices

    C. Facility includes skilled nursing facilities, nursing homes, and hospitals

    D. Both b and c

6. Which CPT® code set is used voluntarily by physicians to report quality patient performance measurements?

    A. CPT® Category I codes

    B. CPT® Category II codes

    C. CPT® Category III codes

    D. CPT® Unlisted codes

7. CPT® Category III codes are reported to indicate which type of service or procedure?

    A. New and emerging

    B. Experimental

    C. Unlisted

    D. New and extended

8. Which CPT® Appendix lists clinical examples for E/M coding?

    A. B

    B. C

    C. D

    D. G

Surgery Guidelines

Surgery is a medical branch utilizing various operative techniques by manual and instrumental means to diagnosis and/or treat injury, deformity, and disease. The condition of the patient determines which medical procedure is performed, including all variables or comorbidities. CPT® surgical codes represent a wide variety of services. When defining specific services that are included in a given CPT® surgical code, the following services are inclusive, not separately billable.

Global Package as Defined by CPT®

Payment for surgical procedures includes a standard package of preoperative, intraoperative, and postoperative services. Preoperative and postoperative periods will differ based on the classifications of the service as a major or minor surgery.

The services included in the global surgical package may be furnished in any service location, eg, a hospital, an ambulatory surgical center (ASC), or physician office. Visits to a patient in an intensive care or critical care unit are also included when made by the surgeon. Under some circumstances, critical care services (99291–99292) are not considered part of the global package and are reimbursed separately.

Global Package—Non-Medicare Health Plans

Although most health plans have adopted the CMS global package concept, some health plans write variances within their policies. The health plan has leniency to determine if a global period is applicable to surgery procedures. If the health plan determines a global package, it will establish postoperative periods of 0, 10, or 90 days to surgical CPT® codes. Although the number of postoperative period days, 0, 10, or 90 days, remain consistent with Medicare guidelines, the variances of global packages for other health plans should be noted while reviewing patient's coverage plans.

Surgery as Defined by Medicare

Medicare has classified major and minor surgeries and has determined what services are included and not included with the global package. Medicare has also determined the preoperative and postoperative days allowed for each type of surgery.

The preoperative period included in the global fee for <u>major surgery</u> is 1 day with 90 days for the postoperative period. The preoperative period for <u>minor surgery</u> is the day of the procedure with a postoperative period of either 0 or 10 days depending on the procedure. For endoscopic procedures (except procedures requiring an incision), there is no postoperative period. Global period days are available on the CMS website www.cms.gov/apps/physician-fee-schedule/overview.aspx.

Each CPT® also has a global period status indicator as per the CMS payment policies. Surgical CPT® codes (10000–69999) have a <u>global surgery status indicator</u> determining classification for a minor or major surgery as determined by RVU calculations. Per the *Federal Register*, Vol. 74, No. 132, surgical status indicators are assigned based on risk factors associated with medical specialties.

Status Indicators

000 Endoscopies or minor procedures with preoperative and postoperative relative values on the day of the procedure only are reimbursable. Evaluation and management services on the same day of the procedure are generally not payable. (eg, CPT® 43255, 53020, 67346).

010 Minor procedures with preoperative relative values on the day of the procedure and postoperative relative values during a 10 day postoperative period are reimbursable services. Evaluation and management services on the day of the procedure and during the 10 day postoperative period are not reimbursable. (eg, CPT® 17261, 40800, 64612).

090 Major procedures with one day preoperative period and 90-days postoperative period are considered to be a component of global package of the major procedure. Evaluation and management services on the day prior to the procedure, the day of the procedure, and during the 90-day postoperative period are not reimbursable. (eg, CPT® 21048, 32664, 49582).

MMM Maternity codes; the usual global period concept does not apply. (eg, CPT® 59400, 59612).

XXX The global concept does not apply to this code. (eg, Evaluation and Management services, Anesthesia, Laboratory and Radiology procedures) (eg, CPT® 10021, 36593, 38220, 44720).

YYY These are unlisted codes, and subject to individual pricing. (eg, CPT® 19499, 20999, 44979).

ZZZ These represent add-on codes. They are related to another service and are always included in the global period of the primary service. (eg, CPT® 27358, 44955, 67335).

Services Included in the Global Package

1)   Preoperative Visits—Preoperative visits after the decision is made to operate beginning with the day before the day of surgery for major procedures and the day of surgery for minor procedures

2)   Intraoperative Services—Intraoperative services considered a usual and necessary part of a surgical procedure

3)   Complications Following Surgery—All additional medical or surgical services required of the surgeon during the postoperative period of the surgery because of complications, which do not require additional trips to the operating room

4)   Postoperative Visits—Follow-up visits within the postoperative period of the surgery related to recovery from the surgery

5)   Postsurgical Pain Management—By the surgeon

6)   Miscellaneous Services—Items such as dressing changes; local incisional care; removal of operative pack, removal of cutaneous sutures and staples, lines, wires, tubes, drains, casts, and splints; insertion, irrigation and removal of urinary catheters, routine peripheral intravenous lines, nasogastric and rectal tubes; and changes and removal of tracheostomy tubes

Services Not Included in the Global Package

1)   Initial consultation or evaluation of the problem by the surgeon to determine the need for surgery.

2) Visits unrelated to the diagnosis for which the surgical procedure is performed, unless the visits occur due to complication of the surgery.

3) Treatment for the underlying condition or an added course of treatment that is not part of the normal recovery from surgery.

4) Diagnostic tests and procedures, including diagnostic radiological procedures.

5) Clearly distinct surgical procedures during the postoperative period that are not re-operations or treatment for complications (A new postoperative period begins with the subsequent procedure.) This includes procedures done in two or more parts for which the decision to stage the procedure is made prospectively or at the time of the first procedure.

6) Treatment for postoperative complications which requires a return trip to the operating room (OR). The term operating room includes a cardiac catheterization suite, a laser suite, and an endoscopy suite. It does not include a patient's room, a minor treatment room, a recovery room, or an intensive care unit (unless the patient's condition was so critical there would be insufficient time for transportation to an OR).

7) If a less extensive procedure fails, and a more extensive procedure is required, the second procedure is payable separately.

8) For certain services performed in a physician's office.

9) Immunosuppressant therapy management for organ transplants.

10) Critical care services (codes 99291 and 99292) unrelated to the surgery where a seriously injured or burned patient is critically ill and requires constant attendance of the physician.

11) For minor surgeries and endoscopies, the Medicare program will not pay separately for an E/M service on the same day as a minor surgery or endoscopy, unless a significant, separately identifiable service is also performed, for example, an initial consultation or initial new patient visit.

Modifiers Used To Report Payable Services Within the Global Package

Special Evaluation and Management (E/M) Cases			
Modifier	Description	Appropriate Examples	Examples/Rationale No Modifier
24	**Unrelated E/M by the Same Physician or Other Qualified Healthcare Professional During a Postoperative Period:** Reports an unrelated evaluation and management service by the same physician or other qualified healthcare professional during a postoperative period. Services submitted with the modifier 24 must be sufficiently documented to establish that the visit was unrelated to the surgery.	A patient was seen in the global period by his physician for a postoperative check after colon surgery. During the visit, the patient asked for medication for his sinus condition. His throat and nose were checked and a prescription was written (eg, 99212-24).	A patient is seen in the office for a post-op evaluation after removal of a facial lesion. Proper reporting would be the code 99024—Postoperative follow-up visit.
25	**Significant, Separately Identifiable Evaluation and Management Service by the Same Physician or Other Qualified Healthcare Professional on the Same Day of the Procedure or Other Service:** It may be necessary to indicate that on the day a procedure or service identified by a CPT® code was performed, the patient's condition required a significant, separately identifiable E/M service above and beyond the other service provided or beyond the usual preoperative and postoperative care associated with the procedure performed.	A patient was seen by an emergency room physician after an automobile accident and a laceration repair of the face was required. The patient was examined for possible head injury. The E/M code (with modifier) and the laceration repair codes would be billed (eg, 99283-25, 12013).	A patient was seen in a physician's office for a planned wart destruction and the physician discusses the procedure again briefly with the patient and then performed the removal. Proper coding would be 17110. The code 17110 already has a minimal E/M included in the code.

Special Evaluation and Management (E/M) Cases			
Modifier	**Description**	**Appropriate Examples**	**Examples/Rationale No Modifier**
57	**Decision for Surgery:** An evaluation and management service provided the day before or the day of surgery that resulted in the initial decision to perform the surgery might be identified by adding the modifier 57 to the appropriate level of E/M service.	A patient was seen by a surgeon in an emergency room with severe abdominal pain. The surgeon admitted the patient and performed a laparoscopic cholecystectomy the same day (eg 99221-57, 47562).	A patient was seen in the provider's office where the surgery was planned for a week in the future. Report the appropriate E/M service code. It would be inappropriate to append a 57 modifier since the surgery is outside the 24-hour period.

Global Surgery			
Modifier	**Description**	**Appropriate Examples**	**Examples/Rationale No Modifier**
58	**Staged or Related Procedure or Service by the Same Physician or Other Qualified Healthcare Professional During the Postoperative Period:** It may be necessary to indicate that the performance of a procedure or service during the postoperative period was: a) planned prospectively at the time of the original procedure (staged); b) more extensive than the original procedure; or c) for therapy following a diagnostic surgical procedure. This circumstance may be reported by adding the modifier 58 to the staged or related procedure.	Patient had a breast biopsy and five days later the same surgeon performed a modified radical mastectomy for breast cancer (19307-58). Patient had a debridement of the open wound of the leg. Two days later another debridement was performed (11043-58).	A patient returned to the surgeon's office five days after a breast biopsy for drainage of a seroma. Report 99024 (postop visit). Do not report 10160-58 or 10160-78 as a seroma can occur after a breast biopsy. The procedure was performed in the office and is bundled with the breast biopsy.
78	**Unplanned Return to the Operating/Procedure Room by the Same Physician or Other Qualified Healthcare Professional Following Initial Procedure for a Related Procedure During the Postoperative Period:** It may be necessary to indicate that another procedure was performed during the postoperative period of the initial procedure.	A patient returns to surgery for possible abdominal bleeding on the same day following a colon resection performed earlier by the same surgeon (49002-78).	Patient in the global period of a laceration repair of the thigh has developed a small hematoma. The incision is opened 1 inch and the hematoma is drained in the office (99024). 10140-78 is not reported as the procedure did not require a return to the operating room.
79	**Unrelated Procedure or Service by the Same Physician or Other Qualified Healthcare Professional During the Postoperative Period:** The physician or other qualified healthcare professional may need to indicate that the performance of a procedure or service during the postoperative period was unrelated to the original procedure. This circumstance may be reported by using the modifier 79.	A patient returned to surgery for a closed reduction of a left ankle fracture while the patient was recovering from an open reduction to a right ankle performed by the same surgeon (27808-79).	

Section Review 6.3

1. What services are included in the Surgical Global Package?

    A. Preoperative visits, Intraoperative services, Initial consultation

    B. Intraoperative services, Diagnostic tests, Experimental procedures

    C. Bilateral procedures, Documentation, Code sequencing

    D. None of the above

2. What is the postoperative period included in the surgical global package for major surgery?

    A. 0 days

    B. 60 days

    C. 90 days

    D. 120 days

3. When surgery is performed, what services are included and are not billed separately?

    A. Postoperative E/M visits

    B. Topical anesthesia

    C. Writing orders in the post-anesthesia recovery area

    D. All of the above

4. Which modifiers are appended to E/M codes to report payable services within the global package?

    A. 24, 26, 51

    B. 24, 25, 47

    C. 24, 25, 57

    D. 24, 26, 57

5. What is the CMS global period status indicator for endoscopies?

    A. 000

    B. 010

    C. 030

    D. None of the above

HCPCS Level II

HCPCS Level II codes were created by CMS to report supplies, materials, injections, and certain procedures and services not defined in the CPT® codebook. CMS updates the codes continually, and they are recognized as a national set of standard alphanumeric codes and modifiers.

Practical Coding Note

When a CPT® code and HCPCS Level II code exist for the same service, check with the payer to determine which code to report. For example, Medicare prefers the HCPCS Level II code be reported rather than the CPT® code when a code exists in both for the same service.

There are national HCPCS Level II codes representing over 4,000 separate categories of like items or services that encompass millions of products from different manufacturers. In submitting claims, suppliers are required to use one of these codes to identify the items they are billing. The descriptor assigned to a code represents the official definition of items and services that can be billed using that code. To avoid any appearance of endorsement of a particular product through HCPCS Level II, the descriptors used to identify codes do not refer to specific products. For this reason, brand or trade names are normally not used to describe the products represented by a code.

Codes begin with a single letter followed by four digits. They are grouped according to type of service or supply within a section of HCPCS Level II beginning with a specific letter.

In the HCPCS Level II codebook, information and instructions applying to a specific category are found at the beginning of each major category. Understanding these guidelines is vital to the process of assigning code(s) to accurately represent the provision of services, equipment, and supplies.

There are several types of HCPCS Level II codes depending on the purpose for the codes and who is responsible for establishing and maintaining them.

Permanent National Codes

Representatives from the Blue Cross/Blue Shield Association (BCBSA), the Health Insurance Association of America (HIAA), and CMS maintain the national permanent HCPCS Level II codes. This panel makes decisions about additions, revisions, and deletions to the permanent national alphanumeric codes used by private and public health insurers. Since HCPCS Level II is a national coding system, none of the parties, including CMS, can make unilateral decisions regarding permanent Level II national codes. Permanent national codes are updated once a year on January 1, but codes can be added or deleted throughout the year.

Miscellaneous Codes

National codes also include miscellaneous/not otherwise classified codes, which are used when no existing national code describes the item or service being billed. Claims with miscellaneous codes are manually reviewed, the item or service being billed must be clearly described, and pricing information must be provided along with documentation to explain why the beneficiary needs the item or service.

Temporary National Codes

Temporary codes allow insurers to establish codes needed before the next January 1 annual update for permanent

national codes or until consensus can be achieved on a permanent national code. These codes are updated quarterly.

Once established, temporary codes are usually implemented within 90 days, the time needed to prepare and issue implementation instructions and to enter the new code in the CMS and contractors' computer systems and initiate user education. This time is needed to allow the instructions such as bulletins and newsletters to be sent out to suppliers to provide them with information and assistance regarding the implementation of temporary CMS codes. www.cms.hhs.gov/MedHCPCSGenInfo/Downloads/LevelIICodingProcedures.pdf.

Types of temporary HCPCS Level II codes:

1. C codes identify items that may qualify for pass-through payments under the hospital outpatient prospective payment system (OPPS). These codes are used exclusively for the OPPS purposes and are only valid for Medicare on claims submitted by hospital outpatient departments.

2. G codes are used to identify professional healthcare procedures and services that would otherwise be coded in CPT® but for which there are no CPT® codes.

3. H codes are used by those state Medicaid agencies that are mandated by state law to establish separate codes for identifying mental health services such as alcohol and drug treatment services.

4. K codes were established for use by the Durable Medical Equipment Medicare Administrative Contractors (DME MAC) when the currently existing permanent national codes do not include the codes needed to implement a DME MAC medical review policy.

5. Q codes identify services that would not be given a CPT® code, such as drugs, biologicals, and other types of medical equipment or services, which are not identified by national level II codes but are needed for claims processing purposes.

6. S codes are used by the BCBSA and the HIAA to report drugs, services, and supplies for which there are no national codes but are needed by the private sector to implement policies, programs, or claims processing.

7. T codes are designated for use by Medicaid state agencies to establish codes for items with no permanent national codes (T codes are not used by Medicare but can be used by private insurers).

Code Modifiers

A HCPCS Level II code accompanied by a modifier provides additional information regarding the service or item identified by the HCPCS Level II code. For example, a UE modifier is used when the item identified by a HCPCS Level II code is used equipment, a NU modifier is used for new equipment. The HCPCS Level II modifiers are either alphanumeric or two letters.

HCPCS Level II Organization

These sections are located in HCPCS Level II:

A Codes—Transportation codes (A0021–A0999), medical and surgical supplies (A4206–A8004), and administrative, miscellaneous and investigational services, equipment, and supplies (A9150–A9999)

B Codes—Enteral and parenteral therapy (B4034–B9999)

C Codes—Temporary codes for use with Outpatient Prospective Payment System (OPPS) (pass-through) (C1713–C9899)

E Codes—Durable medical equipment (E0100–E8002)

G Codes—Procedures/professional services (temporary) (G0008–G9472)

H Codes—Temporary national codes for governmental entities other than Medicare (H0001–H2037)

J Codes—Drugs administered other than oral method (J0120–J8999) and injectable chemotherapy drugs (J9000–J9999)

K Codes—Assigned to DME MAC (K0000–K0902)

L Codes—Orthotic procedures and devices (L0112–L4999) and prosthetic procedures (L5000–L9900)

M Codes—Medical services (M0075–M0301)

P Codes—Pathology and laboratory services (P2028–P9615)

Q Codes—Procedures, services, and supplies on a temporary basis (Q0035–Q9969)

R Codes—Diagnostic radiology services (R0070–R0076)

S Codes—Temporary national codes (non-Medicare) (S0012–S9999)

T Codes—National codes established for state Medicaid agencies (T1000–T5999)

V Codes—Vision services (V2020–V2799) and hearing, which also includes speech-language pathology services (V5008–V5364)

The beginning of each section contains information and instructions for proper use of codes applying to the specific section. Greater detail will be provided for each of these categories later in this chapter. An example of the guidelines for P codes follows:

Example

Pathology and Laboratory Services (P2028–P9615)

Under certain circumstances, Medicare allows physicians and laboratories a fee for drawing or collecting test specimens. If the test specimen is collected from a homebound patient, physicians and laboratories may also bill for a travel allowance.

P codes fall under the jurisdiction of the local carrier.

Table of Drugs—The Table of Drugs (C, J, K, Q, and S codes) is designed to easily direct the coder to drug names and their corresponding codes based on an alphabetic list of drugs with cross-references to generic and commercial names. When looking in the index under the term "Drugs," the coder is directed to the Table of Drugs as well as codes or ranges of codes based on method of administration or delivery system or specific to chemotherapy. When looking for codes specific to administration, disposable delivery systems, infusion supplies, or prescription of drugs, the index directs the coder to a code, which should be verified in the alphanumeric section or main body of the publication.

Medicare

Medicare Part B will cover certain prescription drugs under specific circumstances. CMS requires local carriers and four DME MACs to establish reimbursement amounts for covered drugs. In general, the Medicare reimbursement amount for a covered drug is 85 percent of the drug's average wholesale price (AWP).

Common routes of administration are often abbreviated using the following terms:

IA   Intraarterial administration—Administration of the drug is given within an artery

IV   Intravenous administration—Administration of the drug is given into the vein

IM   Intramuscular administration—Administration of the drug via an injection into a muscle

IT   Intrathecal—Administration of the drug is given into the subdural space of the spinal cord

SC   Subcutaneous administration—Administration of the drug via an injection just under the skin

INH Administration by inhaled solution—Administration of the drug by breathing it

VAR Various routes of administration—Administration of the drug by various routes commonly administered into, joints, cavities, tissues, or topical applications

OTH Other routes of administration—Other administration methods like suppositories or catheter injections

ORAL Administered orally—Administration of the drug via taking it by mouth

Other information pertaining to HCPCS Level II codes includes national coverage policy summaries. These policies indicate circumstances in which items or services are covered. They are published in the HHS portion of the *Federal Register* under CMS regulations. These statutory provisions, regulations, and national coverage policies should be applied when filing Medicare and other claims involving government programs.

Medicare Carriers Manual (MCM) References—Includes the Coverage Issues Manual (CIM) references, the Medicare Carriers Manual references contain CMS regulations and rulings concerning coverage for procedures, services, and supplies.

Example

50.2—Determining Self-Administration of Drug or Biological

(Rev. 123, Issued: 04-30-10, Effective: 07-30-10, Implementation: 07-30-10)

The Medicare program provides limited benefits for outpatient prescription drugs. The program covers drugs that are furnished "incident to" a physician's service provided that the drugs are not usually self-administered by the patients who take them. Section 112 of the Benefits, Improvements & Protection Act of 2000 (BIPA) amended sections 1861(s)(2)(A) and 1861(s)(2)(B) of the Act to redefine this exclusion. The prior statutory language referred to those drugs "which cannot be self-administered." Implementation of the BIPA provision requires interpretation of the phrase "not usually self-administered by the patient."

A. Policy

Fiscal intermediaries, carriers and Medicare Administrative Contractors (MACs) are instructed to follow the instructions below when applying the exclusion for drugs that are usually self-administered by the patient. Each individual contractor must make its own individual determination on each drug. Contractors must continue to apply the policy that not only the drug is medically reasonable and necessary for any individual claim, but also that the route of administration is medically reasonable and necessary. That is, if a drug is available in both oral and injectable forms, the injectable form of the drug must be medically reasonable and necessary as compared to using the oral form.

For certain injectable drugs, it will be apparent due to the nature of the condition(s) for which they are administered or the usual course of treatment for those conditions, they are, or are not, usually self-administered. For example, an injectable drug used to treat migraine headaches is usually self-administered. On the other hand, an injectable drug, administered at the same time as chemotherapy, used to treat anemia secondary to chemotherapy is not usually self-administered.

See Pub. 100-02, Medicare Benefit Policy Manual, chapter 15, section 50.2. for entire policy.

Medicare Statutes—This appendix covers statutory coverage issues (eg, Section 1862 [42 U.S.C. 1395y] (a)(1)(A)-(21), Exclusions from Coverage and Medicare as Secondary Payer).

HCPCS Level II Modifiers

Two levels of HCPCS Level II modifiers correlate to two levels of HCPCS Level II codes and, in each case; the modifiers are appended to HCPCS Level II codes to add specificity to the service or procedure performed.

Level I modifiers of CPT® are two numeric digits appended to procedure and service codes to specify special circumstances. For example, a provider performs a service involving increased technical difficulty beyond those normally required (modifier 22 *Unusual Procedural Services*) or when a physician decides to reduce or eliminate a certain portion of the service or procedure usually provided (modifier 52 *Reduced Services*).

The physical status of a patient who is receiving anesthesia is reported using a two-digit alphanumeric modifier appended to the five-digit CPT® anesthesia code. The numeric portion of the modifier indicates a normal healthy patient (P1), a patient with mild systemic disease (P2), a patient with severe systemic disease (P3), a patient with severe systemic disease that is a constant threat to life (P4), a moribund patient who is not expected to survive the operation (P5), and a declared brain-dead patient whose organs are being removed for donor purposes (P6).

Level II modifiers are two alpha characters (AA–VP) or an alpha character followed by a digit. They are divided into subsections for services related to anatomy, transportation (ambulance), anesthesia, coronary arteries, ophthalmology, professional services, end-stage renal disease, and dental care.

All the alpha modifiers are listed in the HCPCS Level II code-book. Examples include:

E1—upper left, eyelid

F5—right hand, thumb

ET—emergency services

GM—multiple patients on one ambulance trip

HF—Substance abuse program

RC—right coronary artery

Q6—Service furnished by a locum tenens physician

Ambulance Origin and Destination Modifiers

When certain single character modifiers are combined, they easily specify circumstances of a service. One example is the characters of modifiers appended to ambulance service HCPCS Level II codes. The first character denotes the origin of the ambulance service, and the second character reports the destination. Single character modifiers for ambulance services include:

D—Diagnostic or therapeutic site other than "P" or "H" when these codes are used as origin codes

E—Residential, domiciliary, custodial facility (other than an 1819 facility)

G—Hospital-based ESRD facility (hospital or hospital related)

H—Hospital

I—Site of transfer (eg, airport or helicopter pad between modes of ambulance transport)

J—Freestanding ESRD facility

N—Skilled nursing facility (SNF) (1819 facility)

P—Physician's office

R—Residence

S—Scene of accident or acute event

X—(Destination code only) Intermediate stop at physician's office on the way to the hospital

Combinations of single character modifiers are appended to HCPCS Level II ambulance service codes.

Example

HH　Ambulance trip from discharge/transfer from one hospital to another hospital

RH　Ambulance trip from the patient's residence to a hospital

SH　Ambulance trip from scene of accident to a hospital

RP　Ambulance trip from the patient's residence to a physician's office

HCPCS Level II Categories—Details

Sixteen sections of HCPCS Level II codes include instructions and policies from CMS as to the appropriate use of each code and whether the local Medicare carriers or DME carrier has jurisdiction for reimbursement. It is essential to proper coding that any policy associated with a particular HCPCS Level II code be reviewed to ensure appropriate reporting of a service. Some codes have special coverage instructions, are noncovered by Medicare, are paid at the carrier's discretion, and/or have a quantity limitation.

A Codes (A0021–A9999)

The A codes consist of transportation services including ambulance (A0021–A0999), medical and surgical supplies (A4206–A7509), administrative, miscellaneous and investigational supplies, procedures, and services (A9150–A9901).

Transportation Services Including Ambulance (A0021–A0999)

Medicare pays for ambulance services for Medicare beneficiaries when other means of transportation are contraindicated. Ambulance services (air and ground) are divided into different levels of service based on the medically necessary treatment provided during transport. These services include the following levels:

For Ground:

Basic life support (BLS)

Advanced life support, Level 1 (ALS1)

Advanced life support, Level 2 (ALS2)

Specialty care transport (SCT)

Paramedic ALS intercept (PI)

For Air:

Fixed wing air ambulance (FW)

Rotary wing air ambulance (RW)

The final rule establishing the fee schedule on April 1, 2002 implemented a statutory requirement that ambulance suppliers accept Medicare assignment; codified the establishment of new HCPCS Level II codes to report for ambulance services; established increased mileage payment under the fee schedule for ambulance services furnished in rural areas based on the location of the beneficiary at the time of boarding the ambulance; revised the certification requirements for coverage of nonemergency ambulance services; and provided for a five-year transition period based on a blended rate of the fee schedule and a reasonable cost (providers) or reasonable charge (suppliers).

Ambulance codes include:

A0422 Ambulance (ALS or BLS) oxygen and oxygen supplies, life-sustaining situation.

A0433 Advanced life support, level 2 (ALS 2)

A0434 Specialty care transport (SCT)

Medical and Surgical Supplies (A4206–A8004)

A wide range of surgical and medical supplies is included in this section of HCPCS Level II codes. Administrative, miscellaneous and investigational procedures, supplies and services are also included in this section.

Example

A4253 Blood glucose test or reagent strips for home blood glucose monitor, per 50 strips

A4270 Disposable endoscope sheath, each

Administrative, Miscellaneous and Investigational (A9150–A9999)

The last section in the A category of HCPCS codes contains a variety of services that are mostly investigational products or services that are not covered by Medicare Part B.

B Codes (B4034–B9999)

This category includes Level II codes for supplies and equipment specific to enteral and parenteral therapy. Enteral means by way of the intestine or gastrointestinal tract. This is commonly used for tube feedings. Parenteral nutrition is provided intravenously.

Example

B4164 Parenteral nutrition solution: carbohydrates (dextrose), 50 percent or less (500 ml =1 unit)—homemix

B9006 Parenteral nutrition infusion pump, stationary

C Codes (C1300–C9899)

C codes were introduced to report surgical supplies and drugs specific to procedures performed under the OPPS. C codes report use of goods that Medicare will pay in addition to the Ambulatory Payment Classification (APC) for a procedure. Only facilities using APCs can use C codes.

Example

C1753 Catheter, intravascular ultrasound

C1819 Surgical tissue localization and excision device (implantable)

E Codes (E0100–E8002)

This category contains HCPCS Level II codes specific to durable medical equipment. To be classified as durable medical equipment, the item must meet the following requirements:

- Can withstand repeated use
- Primarily and customarily used to serve a medical purpose
- Not generally useful to a person in the absence of an illness or injury
- Appropriate for use within the home

For Medicare beneficiaries, all E codes are subject to the jurisdiction of the DME MAC unless otherwise specified. Many E codes are subject to special coverage instructions and/or carrier discretion for reimbursement.

Example

E0116 Crutch, underarm, other than wood, adjustable or fixed, with pad, tip, handgrip, with or without shock absorber, each

E0255 Hospital bed, variable height, hi-lo, with any type side rails, with mattress

E0691 Ultraviolet light therapy system includes bulbs/lamps, timer and eye protection; treatment area two square feet or less

G Codes (G0008–G9472)

G codes are temporary HCPCS Level II codes assigned by CMS. There are a number of exceptions to the term "temporary" as associated with the services and procedures noted in this category. G codes are reviewed by the AMA for possible inclusion in CPT®. Until these codes are replaced by CPT®

codes and appropriate descriptions, CMS uses G codes to report specific services and procedures that do not otherwise have a Level I or Level II code.

Example

G0008 Administration of influenza virus vaccine

G0202 Screening mammography, producing direct digital image, bilateral, all views

H Codes (H0001–H2037)

H codes are used by state Medicaid agencies that are mandated by state law to establish separate codes to report alcohol and drug treatment therapies.

Example

H0013 Alcohol and/or drug services; acute detoxification (residential addiction program outpatient)

H0030 Behavioral health hotline service

H0038 Self-help/peer services, per 15 minutes

J Codes (J0120–J9999)

This category contains codes and descriptions specific to drugs and biologicals (J0120–J8999) as well as injectable chemotherapy drugs (J9000–J9999). The list of drugs described in the J category can be injected by one of three means: subcutaneously, intramuscularly, or intravenously. Medications in this category can also be applied topically, inhaled, taken orally or parenterally. There is a subcategory for contraceptive devices (eg, intrauterine devices (IUD) and vaginal rings). Each drug is associated with specific dosage units as a part of the J code description. When the administered dosage exceeds the "dose unit" in the code description, the additional units must be reported on the claim form to ensure reimbursement for the entire dosage given to the patient.

Medicare reimburses for some drugs or medications for certain medical conditions only. The diagnosis as documented in the patient's medical chart and supported by laboratory and other tests must show medical necessity. Otherwise, the service is noncovered. It is important to check with the MAC for diagnoses included for a drug as supporting medical necessity according to the Medicare policy.

Practical Coding Note

Codes for drugs are reported in the outpatient setting only if the practice purchased the drug being administered. If the injection is performed in a facility, the facility would report the drugs utilizing J codes, not the physician.

Example: Mary comes into the ED after stepping on a rusty nail while working in her yard. The wound was cleaned and bandaged. A tetanus shot was given prophylactically without complication.

Injection Coding: 90471—Immunization administration (includes percutaneous, intradermal, subcutaneous, or intramuscular injections); 1 vaccine (single or combination vaccine/toxoid).

Medicare

Drugs and biologicals are usually covered by Medicare if they are:

- The type that cannot be self-administered
- Not categorized as immunizations
- Reasonable and necessary for the diagnosis or treatment of the illness or injury for which they are administered
- Not determined by the FDA to be less than effective

Additionally, they must meet all the general requirements for coverage of items as incident to a provider's services. See Pub. 100-02, Medicare Benefit Policy Manual, chapter 15, section 50.2. for entire policy. These policies are known as Local Coverage Determinations (LCD) and can be found at www.cms.gov/DeterminationProcess/04_LCDs.asp

Example

J2550 Injection, promethazine, HCl, up to 50 mg

J7680 Terbutaline sulfate, inhalation solution, compounded product, administered through DME, concentrated form, per mg

J9020 Injection, asparaginase, not otherwise specified, 10,000 units

J9120 Injection, dactinomycin, 0.5 mg

K Codes (K0000–K0902)

K codes listed in the main body of the HCPCS Level II codebook are codes assigned to DME MAC unless otherwise indicated. The DME MAC has discretion concerning whether to pay for supplies and equipment listed in this section. This discretion also includes imposing limits on the number of items that are reimbursed during a specified period of time. This section provides temporary DME codes and descriptions.

Example

K0001 Standard wheelchair

K0730 Controlled dose inhalation drug delivery system

L Codes (L0112–L9900)

Orthotic devices are listed in the L category of HCPCS Level II codes (L0112–L4631). (Prosthetics pertains to the development and maintenance of orthopedic mechanical appliances to replace missing body parts while orthotics are designed to assist damaged body areas or parts to function and/or maintain habitus stability.) The codes and their descriptions are arranged in the order of spinal specific codes from cervical to sacroiliac followed by orthosis, and halo procedure codes. Codes pertaining to scoliosis orthotic, lower extremity orthotics, shoes, and upper extremity orthotics are included. These codes are subject to the jurisdiction of the DME MAC unless otherwise indicated. Basic prosthetic services and procedures are also included (L5000–L9900).

Example

L0180 Cervical, multiple post collar, occipital/mandibular supports, adjustable

L0970 Thoracic-lumbar-sacral orthotic (TLSO), corset front

L2750 Addition to lower extremity orthosis, plating chrome or nickel, per bar

L5105 Below knee, plastic socket, joints and thigh lacer, SACH foot

L8035 Custom breast prosthesis, post mastectomy, molded to patient model

Practical Coding Note

L codes should not be used for reporting cast material supplies for routine cast application material. The codes Medicare and some private payers require are located in the Q section.

M Codes (M0064–M0301)

The local MAC has jurisdiction over the M codes, which consist of procedures and services normally not covered by Medicare.

Example

M0300 IV chelation therapy (chemical endarterectomy)

Chelation therapy is considered experimental in the United States

M0301 Fabric wrapping of abdominal aneurysm

Code with caution: This procedure has largely been replaced with more effective treatment modalities. Submit documentation.

P Codes (P2028–P9615)

This series of HCPCS Level II codes includes laboratory services and travel allowance codes specific to specimen collection from homebound or nursing homebound patients. The codes also include two catheterization codes pertaining to collection of specimen(s) from a single patient in any place of service and collection of specimens from multiple patients.

Example

P3000 Screening Papanicolaou smear, cervical or vaginal, up to three smears, by technician under physician supervision

P9010 Blood (whole), for transfusion, per unit

P9603 Travel allowance, one way in connection with medically necessary laboratory specimen collection drawn from homebound or nursing homebound patient; prorated miles actually traveled

Q Codes (Q0035–Q9969)

These codes are assigned by CMS as temporary codes for supplies, procedures, and services. They are generally temporary until the AMA assigns a Level I CPT® code for the specific procedure, service, or supply. When a CPT® code is assigned, CMS deletes the Q code from the HCPCS Level II code set. HCPCS Level II will provide a cross-reference from the deleted Q code to the permanent code. The Q codes fall under the jurisdiction of the local MAC unless otherwise specified. They are subject to special coverage instructions and, in many cases, quantity limits within specified periods of time according to Medicare policy.

Example

Q0084 Chemotherapy administration by infusion technique only, per visit

Q0113 Pinworm examinations

Q4051 Splint supplies, miscellaneous (includes thermoplastics, strapping, fasteners, padding, and other supplies)

R Codes (R0070–R0076)

R codes fall under the local MACs jurisdiction. The codes pertain to transportation of equipment from a facility to a home or nursing home in order to perform diagnostic tests.

Example

R0070 Transportation of portable X-ray equipment and personnel to home or nursing home, per trip to facility or location, one patient seen

R0075 Transportation of portable X-ray equipment and personnel to home or nursing home, per trip to facility or location, more than one patient seen

S Codes (S0012–S9999)

Temporary S codes were assigned for specific noncovered services under the national Medicare program. Commercial payers may recognize S codes for tracking and/or reimbursement purposes. They also have the potential of being used by scientific research groups for tracking purposes.

Example

S3850 Genetic testing for sickle cell anemia

S9024 Paranasal sinus ultrasound

T Codes (T1000–T5999)

National T codes were added to HCPCS Level II in 2002 for state Medicaid agency reporting.

Example

T1002 RN services, up to 15 minutes

T1012 Alcohol and/or substance abuse services, skills development

T1013 Sign language or oral interpretive services, per 15 minutes

T1014 Telehealth transmission, per minute, professional services, bill separately

V Codes (V0000–V5364)

This category of codes consists of vision services (V2020–V2799) and hearing services, which include speech-language pathology services (V5008–V5364). Services and supplies are reimbursed at the DME regional carrier's discretion and are subject to quantity limits based on the type of supply. Many vision services are subject to special coverage instructions as well as quantity limits. Hearing and hearing-related services are not covered by Medicare with the exception of specifically allowed Level I CPT® codes.

Example

V2202 Sphere, bifocal, plus or minus 7.12 to plus or minus 20.00d, per lens

V2513 Contact lens, gas permeable, extended wear, per lens

V5010 Assessment for hearing aid

V5014 Repair/modification of a hearing aid

V5362 Speech screening

HCPCS Reimbursement

HCPCS reimbursement is at the discretion of the local MAC. If a CPT® code and a HCPCS Level II code exist for the same service, make sure that each code encompasses the same procedure, and then refer to your payer policies for guidance about which code to report for each patient.

Example

99406 Smoking and tobacco use cessation counseling visit; intermediate, greater than 3 minutes up to 10 minutes

G0436 Smoking and tobacco cessation counseling visit for the asymptomatic patient; intermediate, greater than 3 minutes, up to 10 minutes

The verbiage for each of these codes is slightly different, however. Report the HCPCS G code for patients who are covered by Medicare according to Medicare guidelines.

Section Review 6.4

1. What are three types of HCPCS codes printed in the HCPCS Level II codebook?

    A. Level II Codes, Modifiers, DME Codes

    B. Level II Codes, G Codes, Miscellaneous

    C. Miscellaneous Codes, Permanent National Codes, Temporary National Codes

    D. Dental Codes, Permanent National Codes, Unlisted Codes

2. How often can HCPCS Level II temporary codes be updated?

    A. Once annually

    B. Biannually

    C. Quarterly

    D. None of the above

3. Which set of HCPCS Level II codes are required for use under the Medicare Outpatient Prospective Payment System?

    A. A codes

    B. C codes

    C. G codes

    D. T codes

4. Which set of HCPCS Level II codes are temporary HCPCS Level II codes assigned by CMS and reviewed by AMA for inclusion in the CPT°?

    A. A codes

    B. C codes

    C. G codes

    D. T codes

5. Which set of HCPCS Level II codes would be utilized to report injected drugs?

    A. A codes

    B. C codes

    C. H codes

    D. J codes

                    AAPC   www.aapc.com   187

Modifiers

Modifiers are appended to CPT® and HCPCS Level II codes to report specific circumstances or alterations to a procedure, service, or medical equipment without changing the definition of the code. Correct reporting of medical services for reimbursement is the responsibility of physicians and medical suppliers. Modifiers correlate with their areas of healthcare:

- CPT® (HCPCS Level I) codes
- Anesthesia Physical Status
- Hospital Outpatient Ambulatory Surgery Center
- HCPCS Level II codes

Both CPT® and HCPCS Level II codebooks list modifiers and their descriptions. Appendix A lists CPT® modifiers and includes modifiers used by anesthesia and ASC hospital outpatient facilities. HCPCS Level II modifiers are usually

located in an appendix of the HCPCS Level II codebook. When appending modifiers to CPT® or HCPCS Level II codes, it is very important to use the appropriate modifier as well as use it according to the established guideline(s).

When reporting codes with more than one modifier, enter the functional modifier(s) immediately after the code; functional modifiers can also be referred to as pricing modifier. This means that payers consider it when determining reimbursement. Next, report informational modifiers; these modifiers clarify certain aspects of the procedure or service provided for the payer (eg, procedures performed on the left or right side of the patient's body).

It is important to remember that not all CPT® modifiers apply to each section of CPT®. Coders should contact their carriers to obtain a list of modifiers because each payer has different reporting requirements.

CPT® Code Modifiers

CPT® modifiers are two-digit, numeric codes.

22	**Increased Procedural Services:** When the service(s) provided is greater than that usually required for the listed procedure, it may be identified by adding modifier 22 to the usual procedure code number. Documentation must support the substantial additional work and the reason for the additional work. *(Append modifier 22 to a procedure code when the physician describes "above and beyond" circumstances within his operative report and there is no other procedure code to describe the extensive services.)* *(Appropriate example: A surgeon spends an extra 1-1/2 hours removing adhesions that are extremely vascular and increased the technical difficulty during a laparoscopic cholecystectomy with cholangiograms: CPT® 47563⊠22)* *Keywords: extended time, took longer than normal, extenuated circumstances, etc.* *(Inappropriate example: A surgeon performed the lysis of adhesions in the process of a partial colectomy. Rational: Just because your surgeon performs, adhesiolysis does not mean that it would qualify for a modifier 22.)*
23	**Unusual Anesthesia:** When a procedure usually requires either no anesthesia or local anesthesia, and due to unusual circumstances the procedure must be performed under general anesthesia. Anesthesiologists or CRNAs only use modifier 23 with anesthesia codes 00100-01999. *(Appropriate example: A patient requires general anesthesia for an ERCP: CPT® 00740⊠23.)* *Keywords: unable to tolerate without general anesthesia, etc.* *(Inappropriate use: general anesthesia is performed on a patient for the convenience of the surgeon. Unless the patient has a medical reason for the anesthesia, it would be inappropriate to use it and also to report it to the patient's insurance carrier.)*

24	**Unrelated E/M by the Same Physician or Other Qualified Healthcare Professional During a Postoperative Period:** The physician or other qualified healthcare professional may need to indicate that an evaluation and management service was performed during a postoperative period for a reason(s) unrelated to the original procedure. This circumstance may be reported by adding the modifier 24 to the appropriate level of E/M service. *(Appropriate example: Append modifier 24 to an E/M code if a physician treats a patient for migraines during a postoperative period and they are unrelated to the surgical procedure.)* *Keywords: unrelated, outside of, not related to, etc.*
25	**Significant, Separately Identifiable Evaluation and Management Service by the Same Physician or Other Qualified Healthcare Professional on the Same Day of the Procedure or Other Service:** It may be necessary to indicate that on the day a procedure or service identified by a CPT® code was performed, the patient's condition required a significant, separately identifiable E/M service above and beyond the other service provided or beyond the usual preoperative and postoperative care associated with the procedure performed. *(Example: Append modifier 25 to an E/M code when a male patient is treated by the physician for hypertension and then asks the physician to biopsy a soft tissue lump located on his back: CPT® 99204⊠25, 21920)* *Keywords: unrelated, outside of, not related to, etc.*
26	**Professional Component:** Certain procedures are a combination of a physician or other qualified healthcare professional component and a technical component. When the physician or other qualified healthcare professional component is reported separately, the service may be identified by adding modifier 26 to the usual procedure number. *(Appropriate example: Append modifier 26 to a procedure code (77001–77003) if a physician provides the professional component of fluoroscopy use during a surgical procedure, when the facility owns the equipment and employs the staff operating the equipment.)* *Keywords: independent radiologist, performed in a hospital, etc.* *(Inappropriate example: Appending modifier 26 to services that do not have a professional or technical component.)*
32	**Mandated Services:** Services related to *mandated* consultation and/or related services. *(Append modifier -32 to an E/M code if an insurance company requests a patient to receive a second opinion, before additional services/procedures are authorized.)* *Keywords: second opinion, required by insurance, etc.*
47	**Anesthesia by Surgeon:** Regional or general anesthesia provided by the surgeon may be reported by adding modifier 47 to the basic service. *Keywords: surgeon administered anesthesia, anesthesiologist not available, etc.*
50	**Bilateral Procedure:** Bilateral procedures that are performed at the same operative session. *(Appropriate example: Append modifier 50 to the procedure code when a patient undergoes surgery for a bilateral laparoscopic inguinal hernia repair: CPT® 49650⊠50)* *Keywords: bilateral, both sides, left and right, etc.* *(Inappropriate example: It is inappropriate to report this modifier in addition to the Right (RT) and/or Left (LT) modifier; this is because the 50 modifier already indicates this information.)*

          AAPC   www.aapc.com   *189*

51	**Multiple Procedures:** When multiple procedures, other than E/M services, Physical Medicine and Rehabilitation services or provision of supplies are performed at the same session by the same provider. *Keywords: a different procedure, separate from, etc.*
52	**Reduced Services:** Under certain circumstances, a service or procedure is partially reduced or eliminated at the physician's or other qualified healthcare professionals' discretion. Under these circumstances, the service provided can be identified by its usual procedure code and the addition of modifier 52. *Keywords: partially, to be reduced, part of procedure not completed.*
53	**Discontinued Procedure:** Under certain circumstances, the physician or other qualified healthcare professional may elect to terminate a surgical or diagnostic procedure. Due to extenuating circumstances, or those that threaten the well-being of the patient, it may be necessary to indicate that a surgical or diagnostic procedure was started but discontinued. *Keywords: procedure stopped before completion, no need to complete procedure, etc.*
54	**Surgical Care Only:** When one physician or other qualified healthcare professional performs a surgical procedure and another provides preoperative and/or postoperative management, surgical services may be identified by adding modifier 54 to the surgical procedure code. *Keywords: only performed the surgical procedure, no post-op management, etc.*
55	**Postoperative Management Only:** When one physician or other qualified healthcare professional performs the postoperative management and another performed the surgical procedure, the postoperative component may be identified by adding the modifier 55 to the surgical procedure code. *Keywords: post-op follow-up only, postoperative care turned over to, transfer of care, etc.*
56	**Preoperative Management Only:** When one physician or other qualified healthcare professional performs the preoperative care and evaluation and another physician performs the surgical procedure, the preoperative component may be identified by adding modifier 56 to the surgical procedure code. *Keywords: pre-op evaluation only, covering for surgeon, etc.*
57	**Decision for Surgery:** An evaluation and management service provided the day before or the day of surgery that resulted in the initial decision to perform the surgery might be identified by adding modifier 57 to the appropriate level of E/M service. *(Example: Append modifier 57 to an E/M code if a physician exams a patient in the ER and makes the decision to admit the patient and perform an appendectomy the same day: CPT® 99221⬚57, 44950)* *Keywords: decision to perform surgery, will need to go to OR, etc.*
58	**Staged or Related Procedure or Service by the Same Physician or Other Qualified Healthcare Professional During the Postoperative Period:** It may be necessary to indicate that the performance of a procedure or service during the postoperative period was: a) planned prospectively at the time of the original procedure (staged); b) more extensive than the original procedure; or c) for therapy following a diagnostic surgical procedure. This circumstance may be reported by adding the modifier 58 to the staged or related procedure. *Keywords: return to OR, will proceed with additional services in next procedure, etc.*

59	**Distinct Procedural Service:** Under certain circumstances, it may be necessary to indicate that a procedure or service was distinct or independent from other non-E/M services performed on the same day. Modifier 59 is used to identify services not normally reported together, but is appropriate under the reported circumstances. CMS NCCI documentation has specific examples for the correct use of modifier 59.
	
	 CMS provides a subset of modifier 59:
	
	     XE—Separate Encounter, a service that is distinct because it occurred during a separate encounter;
	
	     XS—Separate Structure, a service that is distinct because it was performed on a separate organ/structure;
	
	     XP—Separate Practitioner, a service that is distinct because it was performed by a different practitioner; and
	
	     XU—Unusual Non-Overlapping Service, the use of a service that is distinct because it does not overlap usual components of the main service.
	
	 The subset of modifiers are more selective versions of modifier 59 so it would be incorrect to include both modifiers on the same line.
	
	 Keywords: separate procedure, needed additional services, etc.

62	**Two Surgeons:** When two surgeons work together as primary surgeons performing distinct part(s) of a procedure. Each surgeon provides an operative report, which describes his or her portion of the surgery. *Keywords: co-surgeon, shared procedure with, etc.*
63	**Procedure Performed on Infants less than 4 kg:** Procedures performed on neonates and infants, up to a present body weight of 4 kg, may involve significantly increased complexity and physician or other qualified healthcare professional work commonly associated with these patients. *Keywords: weight, incubator, neonate, newborn, etc.*
66	**Surgical Team:** Under some circumstances, highly complex procedures are carried out under the "surgical team" concept. Such circumstances may be identified by each participating physician or other qualified healthcare professional with the addition of modifier 66 to the basic procedure number used for reporting services. *Keywords: surgical team working together, presence of other surgeons, etc.*
76	**Repeat Procedure or Service by Same Physician or Other Qualified Healthcare Professional:** The physician or other qualified healthcare professional may need to indicate that a procedure or service was repeated. This may be reported by adding the modifier 76 to the repeated service. *keywords: repeated, again, previous, etc.*
77	**Repeat Procedure by Another Physician or Other Qualified Healthcare Professional:** The physician or other qualified healthcare professional may need to indicate that a procedure or service performed by another physician or other qualified healthcare professional had to be repeated. Modifier 77 is then added to the repeated procedure/service. *Keywords: repeated by another physician, etc.*
78	**Unplanned Return to the Operating/Procedure Room by the Same Physician or Other Qualified Healthcare Professional Following Initial Procedure for a Related Procedure During the Postoperative Period:** It may be necessary to indicate that another procedure was performed during the postoperative period of the initial procedure. Modifier 78 is used for a return to the operating room for a complication during the global period of another procedure. *Keywords: complications, had to return to OR, etc.*

79	**Unrelated Procedure or Service by the Same Physician or Other Qualified Healthcare Professional During the Postoperative Period:** The physician or other qualified healthcare professional may need to indicate that the performance of a procedure or service during the postoperative period was unrelated to the original procedure. This circumstance may be reported by using modifier 79. *Keywords: not related to previous care, etc.*
80	**Assistant Surgeon:** Surgical surgeon assistant services may be identified by adding modifier 80 to the usual procedure code(s). *Keywords: assisted, surgeon called in to help, etc.*
81	**Minimum Assistant Surgeon:** Minimum assistant surgeon services are identified by adding the modifier 81 to the procedure code. Another surgeon is called in to assist for a limited period of time. *Keywords: assisted partially, helped with part of procedure., etc.*
82	**Assistant Surgeon (when qualified resident surgeon not available):** The unavailability of a qualified resident surgeon is a prerequisite for use of modifier 82 appended to the usual procedure code(s). *Keywords: surgical resident not available, etc.*
90	**Reference (Outside) Laboratory:** When laboratory procedures are performed by a party other than the treating or reporting physician or other qualified healthcare professional, the procedure may be identified by adding modifier 90 to the procedure code. *Keyword: independent lab, separate from physician, etc.*
91	**Repeat Clinical Diagnostic Laboratory Test:** When it may be necessary to repeat the same laboratory test on the same day to obtain subsequent test result(s). *Keywords: sequenced lab tests, repeat lab after 4 hours, etc.*
92	**Alternative Laboratory Platform Testing:** Reporting modifier 92 is appropriate when laboratory testing is being performed using a kit or transportable instrument that wholly or in part consists of a single use, disposable analytical chamber. *Keywords: portable, kit, disposable, etc.*
99	**Multiple Modifiers:** Under certain circumstances, two or more modifiers may be necessary to delineate completely a service. Modifier 99 should be added to the basic procedure. Other applicable modifiers may be listed as part of the service description.

HCPCS Level II Modifiers

There are numerous HCPCS Level II modifiers; many more than CPT® modifiers. HCPCS Level II modifiers are two-character codes that may be two alphabetic characters (AA) or one alphabetic and one numeric character (U4).

HCPCS Level II modifiers are required to add specificity to CPT® procedure codes performed on eyelids, fingers, toes, and coronary arteries.

Listed are a few of the HCPCS Level II modifiers with coding examples:

BO	**Orally Administered Nutrition, Not by Feeding Tube** *(Example: Append modifier BO to enteral nutrients (B4149-B4162) when administered orally [by mouth].)*
E2	**Lower Left Eyelid** *(Example: Append E2 to CPT® code 67700 when a blepharotomy, drainage of abscess, of the left lower eyelid is performed.)*

F1	**Left Hand, Second Digit**
	(Example: Append F1 to CPT® code 26340 when manipulation, finger joint, under anesthesia, each joint is performed on the second digit of the left hand.)
GA	**Waiver of Liability Statement Issued as Required by Payer Policy, Individual Case**
	(Example: Append GA to CPT® code when the diagnosis code does not meet medical necessity according to the Local Coverage Determination (LCD) of the MAC.)
GU	**Waiver of Liability Statement Issued as Required by Payer Policy, Routine Notice**
	Note: Medicare has not yet defined the use of this modifier
LT	Left Side
	(Example: Append LT to CPT® code 24000 when an arthrotomy, elbow, including exploration, drainage, or removal of foreign body is performed on the left elbow.)
NU	New Equipment
	(Example: Append NU to HCPCS code E0143 when a new walker, folding, wheeled, adjustable or fixed height is sold to a patient.)
Q6	**Service Furnished by a Locum Tenens Physician**
	(Example: Append Q6 to CPT® code 99213 when a level III established patient office visit is provided by a locum tenens while the regular physician is absent on maternity leave.)
TC	**Technical Component**
	(Example: Append TC to CPT® code 92081 when a visual field examination, unilateral or bilateral, is performed by a technician in a hospital and the report is performed by an independent physician. The physician would report 92081 with modifier 26.)

HCPCS modifiers assist the payers in identifying circumstances for payment. For example, when a substitute physician takes over the professional practice of a physician who is absent for reasons such as illness, pregnancy, vacation, or continuing medical education, the service is reported under the regular physician with a modifier Q6 appended to the services. These substitute physicians are known as locum tenens. The Q6 modifier indicates to the payer that the service was provided by the locum tenens.

Section Review 6.5

1. Which CPT® modifier would you append to a surgical code for a bilateral procedure?

    A. 22

    B. 50

    C. 51

    D. 59

2. What types of modifiers are listed in the CPT® codebook's Appendix A?

    A. CPT®, Anesthesia Physical Status Modifiers, Surgical

    B. CPT®, ASC, HCPCS, Anesthesia Physical Status Modifiers

    C. HCPCS, CPT®, Surgical

    D. CPT®, HCPCS, Category I

3. Which HCPCS Level II modifier would you append to a HCPCS Level II code for a new wheelchair purchase?

    A. GM

    B. HC

    C. NR

    D. NU

4. What modifier do you append to a CPT® code if a commercial insurance company requires the patient to acquire a medical consultation from a second physician?

    A. 22

    B. 25

    C. 32

    D. 59

5. When are HCPCS Level II modifiers appended to CPT® procedure codes?

    A. Never, HCPCS Level II Modifiers are only appended to HCPCS codes

    B. When specificity is required for eyelids, fingers, toes and coronary arteries

    C. When CPT® and HCPCS are coded together

    D. Always

Documentation Dissection

Case 1:

Preoperative Diagnosis: Bilateral upper eyelid dermatochalasis

Postoperative Diagnosis: Bilateral upper eyelid dermatochalasis [1]

Procedure: Bilateral upper lid blepharoplasty

This 55-year-old male demonstrates redundant eyelid skin in excess causing lateral vision deficits and requests surgical correction.

The procedure with risks was discussed thoroughly with the patient and questions were answered. The patient wished to proceed with surgery and the operative consent form was signed for bilateral upper lid blepharoplasty.

The patient was brought into the operating room and placed in the supine position on the operating table. An intravenous line was established preoperatively and was used for sedation. IV sedation [2] was administered preoperatively by anesthesia.

The bilateral upper eyelids were injected with approximately 2 ml of 1% Lidocaine. The face and orbital areas were prepped with hibiclens and the face was draped in the usual sterile manner. The excess and redundant skin of the upper lids was carefully measured and incisions were marked for fusiform excision with a sterile marking pen. Excessive skin of the right upper eyelid was excised with Westcott scissors. [3] Hemostasis was obtained with a bipolar cautery. Removal of excessive skin was performed on the left upper eyelid in the same fashion. [4] The lateral aspects of the upper eyelid incisions were closed with running sutures using 6-0 Prolene. Steri-Strips and skin adhesive were applied to both eyelids and were dressed with ophthalmic antibiotic ointment.

The patient tolerated the procedure well and was transferred to the recovery room in satisfactory condition. Procedure results were discussed with the patient's wife.

The patient was released to return home in satisfactory condition. Estimated blood loss was none.

_____

[1] Postoperative Diagnosis is used for coding.

[2] IV Sedation used for anesthesia.

[3] Removal of excess skin on right eyelid.

[4] Removal of skin on left eyelid.

_____

How do you utilize the alphabetic index to locate CPT® codes?

Steps to locate the procedure code: Blepharoplasty, code range 15820-15823, select appropriate code from code range, or look up Eyelid/Blepharoplasty or Skin/Revision/Blepharoplasty.

Rationale: When looking up a procedure in the CPT® Index always look for the name of the procedure first. If that term is not in the Index, then look up the body part on which the procedure was performed. If you still cannot locate the code for the procedure break the verbiage down further. In this case we used the term skin to locate the code range.

What are the CPT® and ICD-10-CM codes reported?

CPT® Codes: 15823-50 or 15823-E1, 15823-E3

ICD-10-CM Codes: H02.834, H02.831

Rationale: CPT® Codes: 15823-50 or 15823-E1, 15823-E3

Notable Coding Information: CPT® 15823 *Blepharoplasty, upper eyelid with excessive skin weighting down the eyelid* describes the procedure. Append modifier 50 to indicate the procedure was performed bilaterally. Some payers may prefer the anatomic HCPCS Level II modifiers which are reported as 15823-E1, 15823-E3. Submit the modifier based on payer preference.

ICD-10-CM Codes: Look in the Index to Diseases and Injuries for Dermatochalasis, eyelid/left/upper H02.834 and Dermatochalasis, eyelid/right/upper H02.831. There is not an option for bilateral so each eyelid is reported separately. Verification in the Tabular List confirms code selection.

ICD-9-CM Application

What is/are the ICD-9-CM code(s) reported?

Code(s): 374.87

Rationale: The postoperative diagnosis is dermatochalasis of the eyelid. Look in the ICD-9-CM Index to Diseases for Dermatochalasia, dermatochalasis. You are directed to 374.87. Verification of the code in the Tabular List confirms code selection. Only report the diagnosis code once, even though it is for both eyelids (Guideline I.B.14).

Case 2:

Preoperative Diagnosis: Right temporal metastatic tumor

Postoperative Diagnosis: <u>Right temporal metastatic tumor; metastatic lung adenocarcinoma</u> [1]

Procedure:
1. **Right temporal craniotomy**
2. **Excision of the metastatic tumor**
3. **Insertion of ICP monitor.**

Assistant: Dr. Joe M.D. (modifier 80)

Anesthesia: <u>General endotracheal</u> [2]

This 64-year-old gentleman presented with agitation and significant mental changes. Diagnostics located a right medial temporal lobe lesion and a small lesion in the right parietal lobe. Indications, surgical procedure, possible risks, and complications were discussed in detail with the patient's wife and family. It was decided to perform surgery. The surgical consent was signed by patient's wife for a **Right temporal craniotomy with excision of metastatic tumor with insertion of ICP Monitor.**

The patient was brought into the operating room and placed in the supine position on the operating table. After general endotracheal anesthesia was induced, the head was secured in the Mayfield brace with pins. The right temporal region was shaved, prepped, and draped in usual sterile manner. The <u>incision was performed to the right anterior and temporal region.</u> [3] Self-retaining retractors were placed after the incision and when the temporal muscle was incised. <u>A burr hole was then made and the bone was dissected resulting in a 4 cm circumferential opening.</u> [4] Dissection was continued through to the temporal lobe where a single encapsulated lesion present. The tumor was removed intact with minimal brain dissection. The tumor was approximately 1 x 1.4 cm. Hemostasis was obtained with a bipolar cautery. The wound was irrigated with Bacitracin 1000 mg solution. Retractors were removed and Gelfoam was placed in the cavity. The dura was closed with 4-0 Nurolon with running and interrupted sutures. An ICP monitor was placed. The <u>bone flap was returned and secured with dural closure clips.</u> [5] The wound was closed with 2-0 Vicryl. The skin was closed with 3-0 Nylon. Sterile dressing was applied using Xeroform gauze, 4x4's, ABD, and gauze applied around the scalp.

Sponge and needle counts were completed and correct x2 postoperatively. The patient tolerated the procedure well and was transferred to the recovery room in stable condition. Estimated blood loss during procedure was minimal.

<u>Dr. Joe was present for the entire case and assisted with the approach, definitive surgery, wound closure, and dressing application.</u> [6]

---

[1] Postoperative Diagnosis is used for coding.

[2] General Anesthesia.

[3] Approach.

[4] Burr hole used to access the brain.

[5] Bone flap used.

[6] Assistant Surgeon.

How do you utilize the alphabetic index to locate CPT® codes?

1st Procedure Steps: Craniotomy/with Bone Flap (refer to #5 highlighted information in the body of the note detail). The code can also be found under Brain/Tumor/Excision/Supratentorial or Excision/Tumor/Brain

Rationale: When you go to the code 61510, it states trephination in the code description. Trephination means cutting a circular shaped portion out of a part, in this case the skull. Do not let terms confuse you during code verification. You will have to look up some words in a medical dictionary until you become familiar with the codes and the terminology.

2nd Procedure Steps: Brain/Catheter/Insertion 61210 or Insertion/Brain/Catheter or look for Catheterization/Brain 61210. Check the code descriptor.

Rationale: You may have had difficulty understanding the procedures. Professional coders must utilize various methods such as the Internet, dictionary, or anatomy book to research the procedures, products, and diseases to be able to locate and assign a code to the documentation. With almost all procedures, there are several different ways to use the Index to find the correct code. For this procedure the 3rd option was the most direct and the code was quickly located with fewer steps.

What are the CPT® and ICD-10-CM codes reported for Dr. Joe?

CPT® Code: 61510-80

ICD-10-CM Codes: C79.31, C78.00, C80.1

Rationale: CPT® Code: Notable coding information: A craniectomy procedure was performed and documented in the operative report, above. Per the CPT® codebook, CPT® code 61510 describes the procedure as Craniectomy, trephination, bone flap craniotomy; for excision of brain tumor, supratentorial, except meningioma. With this procedure, the CMS website verifies CPT® code 61510 as a qualifying code for use of a surgical assistant or a co-surgeon. As the operative report indicates, a surgical assistant was present throughout the surgery. The modifier for an assistant surgeon is 80 and it is appended to the CPT® code 61510.

The above operative report also stated an intracranial pressure monitoring catheter (ICP monitor) was placed. Code 61210 *Burr holes; for implanting ventricular catheter, reservoir, EEG electrodes(s), pressure recording device, or other cerebral monitoring device (separate procedure)* is not reported as it is bundled or included in the craniectomy. Note that the description of 61210 includes "separate procedure." The ICP monitor was inserted at the time of the craniectomy, through the same incision as the removal of the brain tumor; therefore, the procedure is included in 61510.

ICD-10-CM Codes: A metastatic tumor is a secondary malignancy. Look in the Index to Diseases and Injuries for Tumor/metastatic/to specified site—*See* Neoplasm, secondary, by site. Look in the Table of Neoplasms for Neoplasm, neoplastic/temporal/lobe or pole (the lobe is specified in the detail of the report) and use the code from the secondary column—C79.31. The patient also has metastatic lung adenocarcinoma. Look in the Index to Diseases and Injuries for Adenocarcinoma and you are directed to *see also* Neoplasm, malignant, by site. Look in the Table of Neoplasms for Neoplasm, neoplastic/lung. Use the code from the Malignant Secondary column (it is stated as metastatic)—C78.0-. The dash indicates another character is required. In the Tabular List, a fifth character of zero is chosen because the laterality of the lung affected is not specified. C78.00 is the correct code. The origin, or primary site, of cancer is unknown which is reported with C80.1. In the Table of Neoplasms, look for Neoplasm, neoplastic/Malignant Primary column C80.1.

ICD-9-CM Application

What is/are the ICD-9-CM code(s) reported?

Code(s): 198.3, 197.0, 199.1

Rationale: The diagnoses are listed as right temporal metastatic tumor; metastatic lung adenocarcinoma. Look in the ICD-9-CM Index to Diseases for Tumor/metastatic/from specified site—*See* Neoplasm, by site, malignant. Next look in the Neoplasm Table for brain/temporal lobe. The secondary (metastatic) column directs you to 198.3. The patient also has metastatic lung adenocarcinoma. Look in the Alphabetic Index for Adenocarcinoma *See also* Neoplasm, by site, malignant. In the Neoplasm Table, look for Neoplasm/lung/Secondary 197.0. The origin, or primary site, of cancer is unknown so ICD-9-CM code 199.1 is reported. This is found at the very beginning of the Neoplasm Table.

Glossary

Add-on Code—CPT® code used to report a supplemental or additional procedure appended to a primary procedure (stand-alone) code. Add-on codes are recognized by the CPT® symbol + used throughout the CPT® codebook.

The Centers for Medicare & Medicaid Services (CMS)—Agency within the United States Department of Health and Human Services that administers the Medicare program and works in partnership with state governments to administer Medicaid and State Children's Health Insurance Programs.

Current Procedural Terminology (CPT®)—A code set copyrighted and maintained by the American Medical Association (AMA).

Diagnosis Pointer Field—A field on the medical claim form (CMS 1500) that relates the line item to the diagnosis on the base claim.

Global Package—The period (0–90 days as determined by the health plan) and services provided for a surgery inclusive of preoperative visits, intraoperative services, post-surgical complications, postoperative visits, post-surgical pain management by the surgeon, and several miscellaneous services as defined by the health plan, regardless of setting, eg, in a hospital, an ambulatory surgical center (AMC), or physician office.

Global Surgery Status Indicator—An assigned indicator, which determines classification for a minor or major surgery, based on RVU calculations.

Healthcare Common Procedure Coding System (HCPCS) Level II—HCPCS Level II is the national procedure code set for healthcare practitioners, providers, and medical equipment suppliers when filing insurance claims for medical devices, medications, transportation services, and other items and services.

Locum Tenens—Substitute physician who takes over the professional practice of a physician who is absent for reasons such as illness, pregnancy, vacation, or continuing medical education. When a locum tenens fills in, the regular physician submits the claim with modifier Q6 appended to the services.

Major Surgery—Surgeries classified as major have a global surgical period that includes the day before the surgery, the day of surgery, and any related follow-up visits with/by the physician 90 days after the procedure.

Minor Surgery—Surgeries classified as minor have a global surgical period that includes the preoperative service the day of surgery, surgery, and any related follow-up visits with/by the physician 0–10 days after the surgery.

National Correct Coding Initiative (NCCI)—Used by professional coder to determine codes considered by CMS to be bundled codes for procedures and services deemed necessary to accomplish a major procedure. This is to promote correct coding methodologies and to control improper assignment of codes that results in inappropriate reimbursement.

Resource-Based Relative Value Scale (RBRVS)—Physician payment schedule established by Medicare.

Relative Value Units (RVU)—CMS reimburses physicians for Medicare services using a national payment schedule based upon the resources used in furnishing physician services. RVUs are configured using work based on specialties, practice expense, and physician liability insurance.

Integumentary System

Introduction

The integumentary system is made up of structures covering the human body: skin, hair, nails, sebaceous glands, and sweat glands. The breasts and subcutaneous tissue are also included in the integumentary system.

Objectives

- Understand key components of the skin, hair, nails, and breasts
- Define key terms
- Understand the most common pathologies affecting the skin, hair, nails, and breasts
- Understand procedures and surgeries as they relate to the skin, hair, nails, and breasts
- Recognize common eponyms and acronyms for this section
- Identify when other sections of CPT® or ICD-10-CM should be accessed
- Know when HCPCS Level II codes or modifiers are appropriate

Structures of the Skin

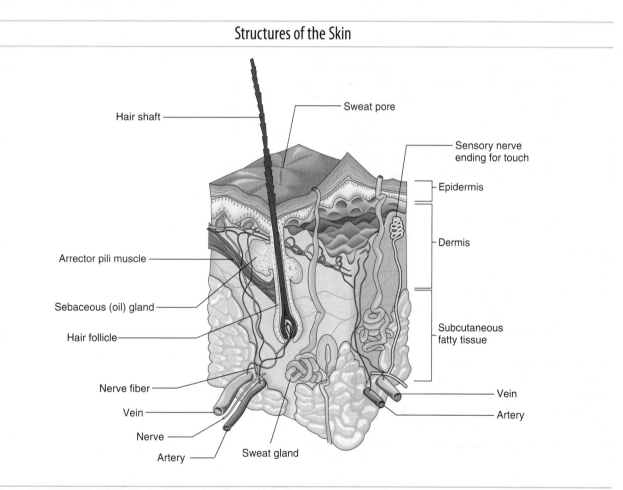

Source: EHRLICH/SCHROEDER. Medical Terminology for Health Professions, 6E. © 2009 Delmar Learning, a part of Cengage Learning, Inc. Reproduced by permission. www.cengage.com/permissions

Anatomy and Medical Terminology

The skin is the largest organ system in the body. The skin itself is made up of two primary layers. The epidermis is the outermost portion of skin. It is comprised of many layers but does not contain blood vessels. It contains pigment melanin giving skin color and allowing the skin to tan. The epidermis contains different types of cells; the most common are squamous cells (which are flat, scaly cells on the surface of the skin), basal cells (which are round cells), and melanocytes (which give the skin color).

The dermis is under the epidermis and performs most of the skin's functions. The dermis consists of blood vessels, connective tissue, nerves, lymph vessels, glands, receptors, and hair shafts. The dermis is made up of two layers; the upper portion is referred to as the papillary layer and the lower portion is the reticular layer. The dermis contains several important glands, such as the sebaceous glands secreting oil to keep the skin and hair soft and moist.

Subcutaneous tissue is located under the dermis and is primarily fat cells that give the skin a smooth appearance and acts as a cushion. The subcutaneous tissue is not a layer of the skin, but is just below the skin. It is very important to understand the layers of the skin to better comprehend skin closures discussed later in this chapter.

The protein keratin stiffens epidermal tissue to form finger nails. Nails grow from a thin area called the nail matrix, at an average rate of about 1 mm per week.

ICD-10-CM Coding

The diagnostic codes for the skin are found primarily in three chapters in ICD-10-CM:

- Chapter 2: Neoplasms
- Chapter 12: Diseases of the Skin and Subcutaneous Tissue
- Chapter 19: Injury, Poisoning, and Certain Other Consequences of External Causes

In addition to codes found in these chapters, we also will discuss codes for disorders of the breast (categories N60-N65). Diagnoses for the breast are typically found in ICD-10-CM chapter 14: Diseases of the Genitourinary System. We will cover them in this section because procedures performed on the breast are found in the Integumentary System in the CPT® codebook.

ICD-9-CM Application

In ICD-9-CM, diagnostic codes for the skin are found primarily in the following three Chapters:

Chapter 2: Neoplasms

Chapter 12: Diseases of the Skin and Subcutaneous Tissue

Chapter 17: Injury and Poisoning

Neoplasms

It is important that the coding guidelines are read and understood when it comes to applying neoplasm codes to a patient record. First one must understand how to use the Table of Neoplasms.

Practical Coding Note

The ICD-10-CM Table of Neoplasms is found after the ICD-10-CM Index to Diseases and Injuries.

Neoplasm Index	Malignant Primary	Malignant Secondary	Ca in situ	Benign	Uncertain Behavior	Unspecified Behavior
skin NOS	C44.90	C79.2	D04.9	D23.9	D48.5	D49.2
ear (external)	C44.20-	C79.2	D04.2-	D23.2-	D48.5	D49.2
basal cell carcinoma	C44.21-	___	___	___	___	___
specified type NEC	C44.29-	___	___	___	___	___
squamous cell carcinoma	C44.22-	___	___	___	___	___
elbow (*see also* Neoplasm, skin, limb, upper)	C44.60-	C79.2	D04.6-	D23.6-	D48.5	D49.2
eyebrow (*see also* Neoplasm, skin, face)	C44.309	C79.2	D04.39	D23.39	D48.5	D49.2
eyelid	C44.10-	C79.2	D04.1-	D23.1-	D48.5	D49.2
basal cell carcinoma	C44.11-	___	___	___	___	___
specified type NEC	C44.19-	___	___	___	___	___
squamous cell carcinoma	C44.12-	___	___	___	___	___

The Table of Neoplasms is broken down into six columns. The first three columns indicate malignancies, which are classified as Primary, Secondary, and Ca in Situ. After the malignancies are columns for Benign, Uncertain Behavior, and Unspecified Behavior.

- Primary Malignancy is the first location of the cancer (carcinoma) (eg, Skin; eyebrow C44.309).

- Secondary Malignancy is where the cancer spreads or metastasizes to. Use the secondary location as the first-listed code when it is the cancer receiving treatment (eg, Skin; eyebrow C79.2).

- Ca in Situ (pronounced, carcinoma in situ) occurs when the cancer is encapsulated and has not spread (eg, Skin; eyebrow D04.39).

- Benign is used when the pathology report indicates there is no cancer or pre-cancerous cells associated with the lesion (eg, Skin; eyebrow D23.39).

- Uncertain Behavior is a specific pathologic diagnosis. This is a lesion whose behavior cannot be predicted. It's currently benign, but there is a chance that it could undergo malignant transformation over time. There must be a pathology report indicating Uncertain Behavior (eg, Skin; eyebrow D48.5).

- Unspecified Behavior is used when there is no pathology report indicating what the lesion is (eg, Skin; eyebrow D49.2).

As an example, find the appropriate diagnosis code for squamous cell carcinoma of the right arm. Using the Index to Diseases and Injuries, look for Carcinoma/skin appendage directing us to — *see* Neoplasm, skin, malignant. In the Table of Neoplasms look for the term arm. The entry for arm indicates NEC indicating not elsewhere classified. Because we are dealing with the skin of the arm, however, we should look for Neoplasm/skin/arm. This directs to (*see also* Neoplasm, skin, limb, upper). Under these subterms look up squamous cell carcinoma C44.62-. Turn to C44.62 in the Tabular List to select the correct sixth character. In this case, it is the right arm C44.622.

Next let's look for Compound Nevus of the left leg. A compound nevus is one that is located within the epidermis and dermis. Using the Index to Diseases and Injuries, look for Nevus/dermal/with epidermal nevus *see* Neoplasm/skin/benign. Turn to the Table of Neoplasms and look for Neoplasm/skin/leg/Benign (column) D23.7-. Verify your code selection in the Tabular List. The benign neoplasm of the skin of the left leg is D23.72.

Finally, locate the correct diagnosis code for melanoma of the skin of the upper lip. Your first thought might be to go directly to the Table of Neoplasms. Always check the Index to Diseases and Injuries first. Find Melanoma in the Index to Diseases and Injuries, and then find skin/lip (lower) (upper) C43.0. Verify in the Tabular List.

Practical Coding Note

If a histologic term is documented, that term should be referenced before going directly to the Table of Neoplasms to determine which column of the Table of Neoplasms is appropriate. In some circumstances the histologic term will provide a category that does not requires the Table of Neoplasms (eg, lump, fibroid, adenoma, or nodule).

ICD-9-CM Application

The Neoplasm Table in ICD-9-CM is broken down into the same six columns.

Diseases of the Skin and Subcutaneous Tissue

Common skin infection and disorder diagnosis codes are found in Chapter 12 of ICD-10-CM — Diseases of the Skin and Subcutaneous Tissue, which includes codes for:

- Skin infections (bacterial and fungal)
- Inflammatory conditions of the skin including dermatitis, erythema, rosacea, and psoriasis
- Other disorders of the skin including corns and calluses, keloid scars, keratosis, diseases of the hair (eg, alopecia), diseases of sweat glands (eg, hidradenitis), diseases of the sebaceous glands (eg, acne), and ulcers

Infections of the Skin and Subcutaneous Tissue

Skin infections can be bacterial or fungal. Common bacterial skin infections include impetigo, cutaneous abscesses, carbuncles and furuncles, cellulitis, lymphangitis and lymphadenitis, and folliculitis. Common fungal skin infections include athlete's foot, jock itch, ringworm, and yeast infections.

Impetigo is caused from bacteria entering the skin, typically through cuts or insect bites, and is highly contagious. Infections commonly occur in children and infants.

Cutaneous abscesses, carbuncles and furuncles (boils) (category L02) typically are caused by a staphylococcal infection. A cutaneous abscess is a localized collection of pus in the skin. Carbuncles and furuncles are follicle-based cutaneous abscesses. Several furuncles together make up a carbuncle and often involve a group of hair follicles. The carbuncle appears as a swollen lump filled with pus and commonly is painful. Although contagious, carbuncles typically heal without treatment within a couple of weeks. They can be located anywhere on the body, but typically are found on the back and neck.

There are codes to identify whether the abscess is a cutaneous abscess, furuncle or carbuncle and to identify the site.

Category L03 is cellulitis and acute lymphangitis. Cellulitis is a bacterial infection in the deeper subcutaneous layer of the skin. The skin appears swollen, red, and warm to the touch. Lymphangitis is an infection of the lymph vessels which can result from an acute streptococcal infection of the skin caused by staphylococcal infection. Lymphangitis can be a sign that a skin infection is getting worse. Code selection is based on location, then differentiated by whether it is cellulitis or acute lymphangitis Lymphadenitis is an infection of the lymph nodes and is coded from category L04.

A pilonidal cyst is a cyst, fistula, or sinus under the skin located at the bottom of the tailbone, near the natal cleft of the buttocks. The cyst can contain hair, skin debris, and other abnormal tissue. If it becomes infected, it is considered an abscess. Coding for a pilonidal cyst or sinus is coded in category L05.

ICD-9-CM Application

In the Index to Diseases, "Carbuncle" is found in both the ICD-9-CM and ICD-10-CM Index to Diseases. The detail and terminology may differ in ICD-9-CM. For example, the detail of the location of a carbuncle on the arm is less extensive in ICD-9-CM:

ICD-9-CM:

Look in the Index to Diseases for Carbuncle/arm (any part, above wrist) 680.3

680.3 Carbuncle and furuncle, upper arm and forearm

ICD-10-CM:

Look in the Index to Diseases and Injuries for Carbuncle/upper limb L02.43- (the dash indicates another character is required). The 6th character further specifies the location of the carbuncle. Furthermore, there are separate codes for a furuncle versus a carbuncle.

L02.431 Carbuncle of the right axilla

L02.432 Carbuncle of the left axilla

L02.433 Carbuncle of the right upper limb

L02.434 Carbuncle of the left upper limb

Notice, in ICD-9-CM, the term "arm" is used to locate the code and in ICD-10-CM, the term "upper limb" is used.

Inflammatory Conditions of the Skin

Inflammatory conditions of the skin include dermatitis, erythema, rosacea, and psoriasis. There are many causes and many manifestations.

Dermatitis is inflammation of the skin. There are different types of dermatitis such as seborrheic, atopic, and contact dermatitis. Seborrheic dermatitis appears as scaly, itchy, red skin, and typically is found on the scalp. In adults, it often appears as dandruff, and in infants it is referred to as cradle cap. Atopic dermatitis is also referred to as eczema. It is an itchy rash that comes and goes, and can be chronic. Diaper rash is a form of atopic dermatitis. Contact dermatitis is inflammation caused by an external irritant. The irritant can be any type of chemical, food, or plant. The code selection for contact dermatitis depends on the irritant causing the reaction. When the irritant is a drug or other irritant, the appropriate external cause code is coded in addition to allergic or irritant contact dermatitis due to an adverse effect of a drug or irritant. Remember, if the rash is only identified as a rash, with no other description or qualification, it is coded as R21 *Rash and other nonspecific skin eruption*.

Psoriasis appears as patches of red skin covered in silvery scales. It is often very itchy and can be painful. Psoriasis is coded based on the type of psoriasis and is found in category L40.

Erythema is redness of the skin due to capillary dilation. There are multiple types of erythema. Rosacea is one of the most well-known erythemas. Rosacea typically occurs in adults appearing as red pustules on the face. Additional types of erythema include erythema multiforme and erythema nodosum. ICD-10-CM code selection is based on the type of erythema. When erythema multiforme is coded, code the associated manifestation, an additional adverse effect code if drug induced, and an additional code from L49.- to identify the percent of skin exfoliation.

Other Diseases of Skin and Subcutaneous Tissue

Other disorders of the skin include urticaria, keratosis, disorders of skin appendages (L60-L75), corns and callosites (L84), pressure ulcers (L89), and keloid scars (L91.0).

Urticaria can also be described as hives and shows on skin as raised, red, itchy wheals. Urticaria can be caused by an allergy to food or medications, external factors such as heat or friction, or can be idiopathic. The ICD-10-CM code is selected based on the cause of the urticaria.

Keratosis is an overgrowth of the horny layer of skin. Actinic keratosis (AK) is also known as solar keratosis and is caused by exposure to sun. It appears as a scaly, crusty lesion on the skin, sometimes resembling a wart. Actinic keratosis is known

as precancerous, it can be the first step leading to squamous cell carcinoma and is reported with code L57.0 along with an additional code to identify the source of ultraviolet radiation. Seborrheic keratosis is a benign growth typically not forming into cancer and is coded with a code from category L82. Warts are also a growth on the skin; however, warts are typically caused by human papilloma virus (HPV) and are often benign growths. Warts caused by HPV are reported with B07.9. Other types of warts are reported from other categories within ICD-10-CM (A18, L82, etc.).

The ICD-10-CM categories for skin appendages (L60-L75) include diagnosis for nail conditions, hair conditions, and other subcutaneous skin conditions.

One of the main diagnoses seen in diseases of the nail is an ingrown toenail (L60.0). An ingrown toenail is caused when the skin on the side of the nail is pressured against the nail itself, typically by tight fitting shoes. This pressure causes the skin to become irritated, red, and painful.

Alopecia (L63) is loss of hair, also referred to as balding. Alopecia areata is an autoimmune disease, where the immune system mistakenly attacks hair follicles causing hair loss. Telogen effluvium is alopecia caused by a metabolic or hormonal stress or by medications. Code selection is based on the type of alopecia.

Corns and callosites (calluses) (L84) are the body's way of adding protection to the skin. They typically are a result of constant friction to an area of the skin.

An ulcer is a lesion on the skin caused by superficial loss of tissue. In ICD-10-CM, skin ulcers are selected based on the type (eg, diabetic, amebic), the site and if a pressure ulcer, the stage. A pressure ulcer is also known as a bedsore or decubitus ulcer and occurs when there is loss of tissue due to pressure on the skin. They commonly are located over bony prominences, such as the hip. When a pressure ulcer code is used from category L89, the codes identify both the site and the stage of the ulcer. There are four stages of pressure ulcers:

- **Stage I**—Persistent focal erythema
- **Stage II**—Partial thickness skin loss involving epidermis, dermis, or both
- **Stage III**—Full thickness skin loss extending through subcutaneous tissue
- **Stage IV**—Necrosis of soft tissue extending to muscle and bone

In ICD-10-CM, each site has a code choice for unstageable pressure ulcers. Unstageable is not the same as unspecified. Unstageable means the base of the ulcer is covered in eschar or slough and the depth of the ulcer cannot be determined. Unspecified means the physician has not specified is the stage of the ulcer. Be sure to review ICD-10-CM chapter guidelines regarding pressure ulcers (I.C.12.a.).

ICD-9-CM Application

The ICD-9-CM and ICD-10-CM *Official Guidelines for Coding and Reporting* both contain guidelines for coding of pressure ulcers. In ICD-9-CM, two codes are required to identify the site of the pressure ulcer and the stage of the pressure ulcer. In ICD-10-CM, only one code is required to report both the location and the stage. In addition, ICD-9-CM has guidelines for reporting of bilateral pressure ulcers. In ICD-10-CM, the right and left hips have separate codes.

ICD-9-CM:

707.04 Pressure ulcer, hip

707.21 Pressure ulcer stage I

ICD-10-CM:

L89.201 Pressure ulcer of unspecified hip, stage I

L89.211 Pressure ulcer of right hip, stage I

L89.221 Pressure ulcer of left hip, stage I

Occasionally, after surgery requiring a cut to the skin or after an injury to the skin, a keloid scar will form. Keloid scar is excess growth of connective tissue during the healing process. Keloid scars can be removed or may get smaller over time. ICD-10-CM code L91.0 is used to report a keloid scar.

Injury and Poisoning

ICD-10-CM Chapter 19: Injury, Poisoning, and Certain Other Consequences of External Causes contains codes for superficial injuries (eg, abrasions, blisters, contusions) and open wounds (eg, laceration, bite, puncture) and is organized by location.

Superficial injuries occur to the outer layers of the skin. This includes abrasions, friction burns, blisters, insect bites, and splinters. Contusions are bruises or hematomas. Superficial injuries and hematomas are not coded when they are part of a more serious injury to the same site. Open wounds include lacerations, puncture wounds, and open bites. Code selection is based on the type of superficial injury or open wound and the location.

Most categories in ICD-10-CM Injury and Poisoning have a 7th character requirement for each applicable code. In most cases, there are three main 7th character values (with the exception of fractures) in this section: A, initial encounter, D, subsequent encounter and S, sequela. To assign a code for

laceration of the leg, documentation must provide enough information for proper 7th character selection.

ICD-9-CM Application

ICD-9-CM is not as detailed for code selection of open wounds. In ICD-9-CM, the code for lower leg laceration is located by finding Wound, open/leg/lower in the Index to Diseases.

ICD-9-CM: 891.0

In ICD-10-CM, the code for leg laceration is located under Laceration/leg (lower) in the Index to Diseases and Injuries which directs you to S81.819-. In the Tabular List, subcategory S81.8 lists various types of open wounds: unspecified laceration with or without foreign body, puncture wound with or without foreign body and open bite. Codes are further classified based on laterality (left, right, unspecified). In order to properly assign this code, documentation must include laterality and encounter information. The code in ICD-10-CM to report a subsequent encounter for a right leg laceration without foreign body is:

ICD-10-CM code: S81.811D

Burns and corrosions of the skin are assigned based on whether the injury is a burn or corrosion. A burn is a thermal burn that come from a heat source (except sunburns), such as a fire or hot appliance. Corrosion is a burn due to chemicals.

Current burns and corrosions (T20-T25) are classified by location, depth, extent and by agent (X code):

- Location—Codes in the burn section are categorized according to the location of the burn. According to the ICD-10-CM guidelines, a separate code is reported for each burn site.

- Depth of the burn—There are three degrees of burns:

  – First degree—involves the epidermis, and can be superficial (such as sunburn).

  – Second degree—involves the epidermis, dermis and subcutaneous tissue and is partial thickness.

  – Third degree—involves the epidermis, dermis, subcutaneous tissue, muscle, and sometimes bone.

When there are multiple degrees of burns in the same location (same three character category), code the highest degree burn for the location. When coding multiple degrees of burns in different locations, sequence the code for the burn of highest degree first.

- Total body surface area (TBSA)—the total body surface area affected by the burn. According to the Official ICD-10-CM Guidelines, a code from category T31 should be used to record burn mortality, such as in burn units, or when there is mention of a third degree burn involving 20 percent or more of the body surface (Guideline I.C.19.d.6.). The Rule of Nines assists you in coding the total body surface area of burns. In this illustration you can see how the body is broken down into percentages. Remember to take note of the age of your patient as this can change the TBSA.

- External cause codes report how the burn occurred and where (eg, while cooking in the kitchen).

Degree of Burns

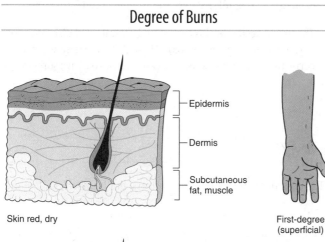

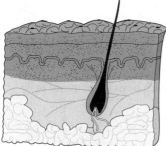

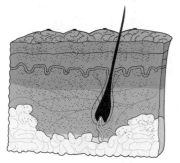

Skin red, dry	First-degree (superficial)
Blistered, skin moist, pink or red	Second-degree (partial thickness)
Charring, skin black, brown, red	Third-degree (full thickness)

Epidermis

Dermis

Subcutaneous fat, muscle

Source: EHRLICH/SCHROEDER. Medical Terminology for Health Professions, 6E.
© 2009 Delmar Learning, a part of Cengage Learning, Inc.
Reproduced by permission. www.cengage.com/permissions

ICD-9-CM Application

ICD-9-CM does not make a distinction between burns and corrosions.

Extent of total body surface area (TBSA) involved is reported with ICD-9-CM code category 948.

Example

ICD-9-CM/ICD-10-CM Comparison:

Second degree burn of the left forearm from hot soup. TBSA < 10%. Initial encounter.

ICD-9-CM:

943.21 Blisters, epidermal loss [second degree], forearm

948.00 Burn [any degree] involving less than 10 percent of body surface, third-degree burn less than 10 percent or unspecified

E924.0 Accident caused by hot liquids and vapors, including steam

Look in the Index to Diseases for Burn/forearm(s)/second degree 943.21. For the percent of third degree burn, look for Burn/extent (percent of body surface)/less than 10 percent 948.0x. Turn to the Tabular List to select a fifth digit of 0 for less than 10 percent or unspecified third degree burns. Look in the Index to External Causes for Accident (to)/caused by, due to/hot/liquid E924.0. Because we do not know the location or the activity, the E-codes for this injury cannot be reported. Verify in the Tabular List.

ICD-10-CM:

T22.212A Burn of second degree of left forearm, initial encounter

T31.0 Burns involving less than 10% of body surface

X10.1XXA* Contact with hot food, initial encounter

Look in the Index to Diseases and Injuries for Burn/forearm/left/second degree T22.212-. In the Tabular List, there is an indication a 7th character extension is required. "A" is selected for the initial encounter. There is also a note under subcategory T22.2 indicating to use an additional external cause code to identify the source, place, and intent of the burn. Then, look in the Index to Diseases and Injuries for Burn/Extent/less than 10 percent T31.0. To report the external cause, look in the Index to External Causes of Injuries for Contact (accidental)/with/hot/food X10.1-. In the Tabular List X10.1 indicates a 7th character extension is required. The 7th character extension A is selected for the initial encounter X10.1XXA.

---

*Note: If a code that requires a 7th character does not have 6 characters, a placeholder "X" must be used to fill in the empty characters.

Disorders of the Breast

There is only a small selection of categories of breast disorders in the ICD-10-CM codebook: benign mammary dysplasias (N60), inflammatory disorders of breast (N61), hypertrophy of breast (N62), unspecified lump in breast (N63), and other disorders of the breasts (N64), and deformity and disproportion of reconstructed breasts (N65).

Dysplasia is abnormal tissue. The most common mammary dysplasia is fibrocystic disease or mammary cysts. Fibrocystic changes in breasts are common and are often a diagnosis associated with an E/M code or breast exam.

Category N64 *Other disorders of breast*, is where you will find common signs and symptoms of the breasts, such as pain in the breast (N64.4 Mastodynia), and nipple discharge (N64.52). Also in this section is the code for galactocele (N64.89). A galactocele is a milk-fed cyst and is often cured by aspiration.

The final category in this section is deformity and disproportion of reconstructed breasts (N65). These codes are used when a correction to a breast is required after reconstructive surgery.

Section Review 7.1

1. A 25-year-old man complains he has premature hair loss. The provider suspects it is due to stress, but is uncertain. List the ICD-10-CM code(s) for the hair loss.

   A. L64.8

   B. L65.0

   C. L64.8, F43.8

   D. F43.8

2. A provider performs a punch biopsy of two pre-cancerous lesions on the patient's back, which he has determined to be actinic keratosis (AK). List the ICD-10-CM code for the AK.

   A. D49.2

   B. C44.519

   C. D23.5

   D. L57.0

3. A patient arrives at the hospital from a nursing home with a stage 3 bed sore on the left hip. List the ICD-10-CM code for the bedsore.

   A. L89.209

   B. L89.223

   C. L97.823

   D. L89.323

4. When coding burns, which is correct?

   A. Sequence first the code reflecting the largest area in Rule of Nines with this degree of burn.

   B. Sequence first the circumstance of the burn occurrence.

   C. Sequence first the code reflecting the highest degree of burn.

   D. Sequence first the code identifying burns to the head and neck.

5. A man arrives at the ED with a superficial injury to the scalp (length 1 cm) and a deep laceration to the right hand (length 5 cm). List the ICD-10-CM codes.

    A. S61.411A, S00.00XA

    B. S61.412A, S01.01XA

    C. S61.432A, S00.01XA

    D. S10.412A, S01.01XA

CPT® Coding

CPT® codes found in the Integumentary System include procedures performed on the skin and nails, as well as those performed on the breasts. Just prior to the Integumentary System, there are a couple of CPT® codes for fine needle aspiration, which we will discuss first.

General

Fine needle aspiration (FNA) is used to sample fluid or tissue from a cyst or mass. For a fine needle aspiration, a fine-gauge needle and syringe are used to sample fluid from a cyst. When the mass or cyst is difficult to find by palpation, ultrasound or fluoroscopic guidance (referred to as imaging guidance) is used. The code is selected based on whether imaging guidance is used.

Aspiration is used to evacuate fluid collection while catheters may be used for complete or continuous drainage of fluid collection. When a catheter is used for drainage of an abscess, hematoma, seroma, lymphocele, or cyst in the soft tissue, and image guidance is used, it is reported with 10030.

Incision and Drainage (10040–10180)

The skin can manifest infections in different ways. Some manifestations include acne, abscess, cysts, hematoma, or bulla. Upon examination the provider may decide to use a scalpel or needle to open the cyst to drain any fluid. When presented with a hematoma, the provider may insert a needle into the hematoma to withdraw fluid and provide relief for the patient. The same concept applies to an abscess.

An incision and drainage (I&D) may be performed for an abscess, cyst, or hematoma by opening the abscess or cyst with a surgical instrument and allowing the contents to drain. The surgical opening is often left open to allow for continued drainage. A drain or gauze strip may be inserted to permit continued drainage. A complicated incision and drainage involves multiple incisions, drain placements, extensive packing, and subsequent wound closure may be required at a later date.

When the patient presents with a pilonidal cyst, which is a sac under the skin at the base of the spine, the physician makes an incision to allow drainage and remove the epithelial lining by curettage. To allow for the use of CPT® 10081 the procedure must be documented as complicated. The wound usually is infected and requires tissue removal, drain placement, more extensive packing, and may require require secondary closure with Z-plasty/Z procedure.

There will be times when the patient presents with a foreign body embedded beneath the epidermis. When this happens the physician makes a simple incision directly above it and uses forceps or other instruments to enter the incision and remove the foreign body. Primary closure is common and included with this procedure. If the foreign body is embedded deeply in the subcutaneous tissue—and requires dissection of underlying tissues—it supports use of CPT® 10121.

A hematoma is a collection of bloody fluid and/or blood clots. The incision and drainage of a hematoma is performed using a hemostat to remove the blood clots. Gauze packing may be used to allow further drainage if fluid continues to enter the site. In most cases the physician places a pressure dressing over the site. The incision may be closed or left open to close by secondary intent.

CPT® 10160 describes the puncture aspiration of an abscess, hematoma, bulla, or cyst, whereas the other codes we have discussed were for incision and drainage. For a puncture aspiration, the physician uses a large needle attached to a syringe and guides it into the site and aspirates the fluid. If necessary a pressure dressing is applied.

When a patient presents with a post-operative wound infection, the physician may choose to perform an incision and drainage of the wound. The infected wound is reopened by removal of any suture material, and the wound is drained. With the use of scissors any necrotic or dead tissues are removed from the site, and it is irrigated with saline and either re-sutured or packed with gauze to allow additional drainage. In some cases, the wound is left open and may require sutures at a later date.

Debridement (11000–11047)

Debridement is the process of removing dead tissue or eschar, dirt, foreign material, or debris from infected skin, a burn, or a wound to promote healing and prevent or control infection. Several methods may be used for debridement. Contaminated, infected, and dead skin tissues may be cut away from their attachments with scissors or a scalpel. Alternatively, the affected area may be debrided by flooding it with copious amounts of a physiologic saline solution to wash away debris and other contaminants. This saline irrigation should not be confused with surgical debridement of a wound, burn, or other defect, nor is it billed separately. There are three distinct sets of debridement codes in the CPT® codebook.

Debridement codes in the Integumentary System section are used more often for friction burns, frost bite, abrasions, pressure ulcers and more, but not used for second and third degree burns of the skin. To promote healing the physician will debride the infected or necrotic tissue until healthy tissue is visible. Pay close attention to the body area that is being treated and how much tissue, muscle, or bone is being debrided from that body area.

For necrotizing soft tissue infection (NSTI) the physician removes the necrotic eschar tissue to allow for proper healing of the site. In many cases the tissue removed is sent for evaluation to determine the type of infection so proper oral or intravenous medications can be administered. In reviewing the CPT® codes 11000–11008, the reporting of these codes are based on key components such as percentage of body surface area and location of the wound. In some cases prosthetic material or mesh of the abdominal wall becomes infected and also needs to be removed. The removal of mesh is reported with add-on code 11008. 11008 is not reported alone since it's an add-on code.

CPT® codes 11010–11012 describe removal of nonviable skin and foreign material associated with an open fracture and/or open dislocation. In some cases, these codes may be used to report significant debridement of a closed fracture when a closed fracture results from blunt trauma resulting in extensive skin and soft tissue damage directly over the fracture site (*AMA Principles of CPT® Coding, 2005*). According to CPT® guidelines:

"Decontamination and/or debridement: Debridement is considered a separate procedure only when gross contamination requires prolonged cleansing, when appreciable amounts of devitalized or contaminated tissue are removed, or when debridement is carried out separately without immediate primary closure."

Practical Coding Note

The amount of debridement performed beyond the first 10 percent of body surface area can be reported separately. Additional units may be reported using an add-on code for each unit of an additional 10 percent of body surface or any fraction thereof. Underline or highlight "part thereof" as a reminder.

Debridement is not included in the global surgical package of treating the fracture/dislocation since debridement and treatment of the fracture/dislocation are two separate and distinct procedures.

Practical Coding Note

When reporting 11010–11047, documentation needs to indicate if foreign material is removed, or if partial thickness or full thickness of the skin is debrided. Partial thickness refers to the epidermis and a portion of the dermis, whereas full thickness refers to not only the epidermis but all of the dermis.

Debridement codes (11042–11047) can be used to report debridement for conditions not mentioned in the first two sets (11000–11008, 11010–11012). Examples of conditions for which these procedures may be performed include gangrene, avascular necrosis, and stasis ulcers. These codes are not used for active wound management denoted by CPT® codes 97597–97610. CPT® codes 11042–11047 are selected based on the deepest depth of the tissue debrided and the surface area of the wound. If multiple wounds of the same depth are debrided, add the surface areas of wounds to select the code(s). If the wounds are different depths, code each wound separately. The attachment of modifier 59 for multiple sites may be necessary to distinguish separately identifiable procedures performed during the same session or on the same day.

Medicine Codes for Debridement

Codes 97597–97602 describe active wound care management services to remove devitalized and/or necrotic tissue and to promote healing. Codes 97597 and 97598 report selective debridement based on total surface area of wound size. CPT® 97602 is a stand-alone code to report nonselective debridement of devitalized skin without the use of anesthesia. These codes are not reported in addition to 11042–11047.

Wound Healing

The following list of terms describes conditions the healthcare provider may note in the documentation. They apply to wound care (*Home Healthcare Nurse,* Volume 21, Number 8, August 2003, page 512).

Avascular—A lack in blood supply, devitalized, necrotic, and nonviable. Specific types include slough and eschar.

Clean Wound—Wound is free of devitalized tissue, purulent drainage, foreign material, or debris.

Closed Wound Edges—Edges of top layers of epidermis have rolled down to cover lower edge of epidermis, so epithelial cells cannot migrate from wound edges; also described as epibole. Presents clinically as sealed edge of mature epithelium; may be hard/thickened; may be discolored (eg, yellowish, gray, white).

Dehisced/Dehiscence—To split apart or open along natural or sutured lines.

Epidermis—Outermost layer of skin.

Epithelization—Regeneration of epidermis across a wound surface.

Eschar—Black or brown necrotic, devitalized tissue; tissue can be loose or firmly adherent, hard, soft, or soggy.

Full-thickness—Tissue damage involving total loss of epidermis and dermis and extending into the subcutaneous tissue and possibly into muscle or bone.

Granulation Tissue—The pink/red, moist tissue comprised of new blood vessels, connective tissue, fibroblasts, and inflammatory cells, fill an open wound when it starts to heal; it typically appears deep pink or red with an irregular, berry-like surface.

Healing Ridge—Palpatory finding is indicative of new collagen synthesis. Palpation (feeling or touching) reveals induration (hardening) beneath the skin extending to about one centimeter on each side of the wound. Becomes evident between five and nine days after wounding; typically persists until about 15 days after the wound occurs. This is an expected positive sign.

Infection—The presence of bacteria or other microorganisms is in sufficient quantity to damage tissue or impair healing. Wounds can be classified as infected when the wound tissue contains 105 or more microorganisms per gram of tissue. Typical signs and symptoms of infection include purulent exudates, odor, erythema, warmth, tenderness, edema, pain, fever, and elevated white cell count; however, clinical signs of infection may not be present especially in the immunocompromised patient or the patient with poor perfusion.

Nongranulating—Absence of granulation tissue, wound surface appears smooth as opposed to granular. For example, when a wound is clean but nongranulating, this indicates the wound surface appears smooth and red as opposed to berry-like.

Partial-thickness—Damage does not penetrate below the dermis and may be limited to the epidermal layers only.

Sinus Tract—Course of tissue destruction. It occurs in any direction from the surface or edge of the wound; and, it results in dead space with potential for abscess formation. It's also called tunneling. (It can be distinguished from undermining by the sinus tract involving a small portion of the wound edge whereas undermining involves a significant portion of wound edge.)

Slough—Soft, moist avascular (devitalized) tissue may be white, yellow, tan, or green; may be loose or firmly adherent.

Undermining—Area of tissue destruction extends under the intact skin along the periphery of a wound; commonly seen in shear injuries.

Paring or Cutting (11055–11057)

Codes in this category are used for the removal of hyperkeratotic lesions, such as corns and calluses. The physician uses a sharp instrument either to pare or cut the corn or callus from the patient's body. Local anesthetic may be used. Code selection is based on how many lesions are removed.

Biopsy CPT® Code Range (11100–11101)

Biopsy within the Integumentary System is specifically referring to biopsies of the skin. A biopsy is sampling of a suspicious lesion. This can be performed in several manners, but is most often accomplished by a punch biopsy. When the provider takes a punch biopsy of a lesion, a tool is used to obtain a circular sample of the lesion. Typical sizes are 3 mm, 4 mm, or 5 mm. Sutures often are needed to close the defect.

A shave biopsy occurs when the provider uses a sharp instrument, such as a scalpel, and excises the suspicious lesion as close to the base of the lesion as possible. When the provider chooses to do a shave biopsy, the wound is usually covered by a bandage and usually does not require suturing.

Skin biopsies are reported by the number of lesions biopsied. Obtaining tissue for biopsy during an excision, destruction, or shave removal of lesions is not reported separately. Biopsy for pathological examination must be unrelated to other procedures provided at the same time.

Removal of Skin Tags (11200–11201)

Skin tags are defined as an outgrowth of both the epidermis and dermal fibrovascular tissue. The most common area for skin tags is the neck, back, and folds of skin (such as the underarm). Often, the removal of skin tags is considered cosmetic. It is important to check carrier guidelines to determine if this is a covered service.

CPT® states skin tag removal often is performed by scissoring or any sharp method (using surgical scissors or a surgical blade to cut), ligature strangulation (tying suture material around the skin tag to stop the blood flow), electrosurgical destruction, or combination of treatment modalities, including chemical destruction or electrocauterization of wound, with or without local anesthesia. CPT® code selection is determined based on how many skin tags are removed.

Lesions

A lesion is defined as an abnormal change in the tissues in an area of the body, such as a sore, rash, wound, injury, or growth, usually localized (confined to that area). Many codes are predicated on the number of lesions involved. In this case, some key terminology should be determined. Phrases such as "each," "each additional," "second and third lesion," "more than five specimens," as well as "single vs. multiple" are key factors to consider when selecting codes where the number of lesions is a determining factor. The bulk of the excision subsection is divided between benign and malignant neoplastic lesions. The determination is left to physician discretion but the pathology report provides a definitive diagnosis and is often essential in supporting billed services. When the pathology report comes back with a diagnosis of "uncertain morphology," the AMA CPT® Assistant (May 1996, page 11) encourages providers to choose the procedure code best reflecting the manner in which the lesion removal was performed. If the provider feels that the lesion is unlikely to be malignant, the margins taken will be minimal, but if the lesion appears moderately to highly suspicious for malignancy, a moderate to wide margin will be included with the excision.

Shaving of Epidermal or Dermal Lesions (11300–11313)

Shave removal of a lesion often is confused with the biopsy of a lesion. A shave removal is removal of the lesion without taking a full thickness excision, and usually does not require suture closure. Reporting of shave removals is not only by body area but also by size. Physicians determine the medical necessity of a shave removal of a lesion versus the excision removal of the lesion.

Removal of Lesions by Excision (11400–11646)

Excision is defined as full thickness removal of a lesion of the skin. The codes are selected first based on whether the lesion is benign or malignant. Pathology will determine which code set (benign or malignant) is used for the proper coding.

Benign lesions (11400–11471) describe lesions not spreading to adjacent sites or reproducing at the expense of surrounding tissues. Benign tumors usually cause problems secondary

to the pressure exerted on surrounding structures. Benign tumors or nonmalignant neoplasms are often regular in shape and covered by a fibrous capsule. Types of benign lesions include cicatricial, fibrous, inflammatory, congenital, and cystic lesions.

At the end of the category for benign lesion removal is a series of codes for reporting the excision of skin and subcutaneous tissue for hidradenitis (11450–11471). Hidradenitis is a condition causing inflammation of the sweat glands and is characteristic of perfuse sweating. These codes are categorized based on the location of the hidradenitis and the type of repair.

A malignant lesion is a cancerous growth invading adjacent normal tissue and may metastasize or spread to distant parts of the body. Malignant lesions include basal cell carcinoma, squamous cell carcinoma, and melanoma lesions. There are various methods used to remove malignant skin lesions. The choice of methods depends on the type of lesion, size, its location, and the physician's preference. There are codes for each variety of lesion removal whether it be excisional or via destruction. The physician may combine several methods to completely remove a lesion. The following examples describe the different methods available:

Electrodesiccation—This process destroys tissue using a small instrument with a cautery needle connected to a monopolar electric source. Electricity is the source of heat as it passes through cautery blade or needle. As the needle touches tissue, the tissue is burned away (destruction).

Electrofulguration—This process destroys tissue using high frequency electric current. An insulated electrode with a metal point is held above the surface of the lesion while electrical sparks are generated in sufficient quantity to destroy the tissue. After a layer of cells is destroyed, it is scraped away with a curette (small, sharp, ring-shaped instrument). This process is repeated until the lesion is removed. This method results in a wide border of normal tissue being removed along with the malignant lesion (destruction).

Elliptical Excision—The physician usually marks the skin externally before the first incision is made. The length of the ellipse is usually two to three times the required width. The incision is through the dermis with some subcutaneous fatty tissue visible when the tissue is excised.

Removal of malignant lesions by means other than excision are coded with a procedure listed in the 17260–17286, 17999 series of CPT® codes.

Measurement of Lesions

One of the key criteria when determining a CPT® code for excising a lesion is determining and documenting the diameter of a lesion. Knowing how to measure, what to measure, and what code to select based on those criteria ensures compliance with guidelines. CPT® recognizes the metric system in code narratives for lesion measurement.

To report excisions (codes 11400–11446 and 11600–11646), the size of the lesion diameter is used in code selection. In documentation, the physician should report the following:

- Lesions should be measured with a centimeter ruler (don't estimate or guess the size of a lesion)
- Measure lesions before infiltration with an anesthetic
- Size includes the narrowest margin required for complete excision (widest lesion diameter plus the narrowest margin x 2 equals total lesion diameter)
- When frozen section pathology shows margins of excision were not adequate, an additional excision may be necessary

It is important for the coder to note the following points for coding measurement purposes:

1. Lesions are measured by their widest diameter, while repairs are measured by the length, width, and depth of the wound.

2. Measurement guidelines include the narrowest margin required in the total diameter of the lesion being excised. According to instructions, if complete tumor removal requires an additional excision at the same operative session per frozen section pathology findings, report one code based on the final widest excised diameter. Report a code from the range 11600–11646 for a re-excision at a subsequent operative session; append modifier 58 if the re-excision is performed during the postoperative period of the primary excision procedure.

3. Know how to convert millimeter measurements to centimeters if the physician states in millimeters. CPT® codes are described in centimeters (see conversion table chart). To convert mm to cm, move the decimal one character to the left or divide by 10. For example, 10 mm equals 1.0 cm.

4. To code for destruction of malignant lesions (codes 17260–17286), the diameter of the lesion is measured.

5. For certain repairs (CPT® codes 12001–12018; 12031–12057; 13100–13153), the length of the wound is measured in centimeters.

6. For other repairs (eg, full-thickness grafts) (CPT® codes 14000–14302 and 15100–15261) the size of the graft is measured in square centimeters based on the size of the recipient site.

7. Use CPT® code 15002 and 15005 to denote excisional preparation or creation of recipient site of essentially intact skin in addition to attachment code (15050–15278). When CPT® codes 15002–15005 are coded, do not code an excision of a lesion.

Practical Coding Note

Highlight the "cm" and "sq cm" in the code descriptions to remind you when to use cm and when to use sq cm. Sq cm is calculated by multiplying the length x width.

The specimen size at time of excision is important to document, considering the pathology report is going to report the size of a lesion after it has been placed in formaldehyde, which causes the tissues of the specimen to shrink some. Specimens/lesions can also become fragmented in the process of the excision, which would not report the true size of the lesion excised. If the lesion size is not reported on the operative report, the coder should ask the provider or will have to defer to the pathology report as a last resort. If the size is not available, then report the smallest lesion size for the excision code.

Conversion Table:

Millimeter/Inches	Centimeters/Square Centimeters
1 mm	0.1 cm
10 mm	1 cm
0.3937 in	1 cm
1 in	2.54 cm
0.16 sq in	1 sq cm
1 sq in	6.452 sq cm

After the lesion is excised, it is sent to pathology for analysis. Frozen section pathology refers to the process of taking a thin slice of the tissue and freezing it with use of a cryostat (a device used to keep specimens at freezing temperatures). The frozen section is then able to be rapidly evaluated by the pathologist to determine the diagnosis.

Skin cancer is the most common type of cancer and occurs more often in people with light-colored skin who have had a high exposure to sunlight. There are two common types of skin cancer: basal cell carcinoma and squamous cell carcinoma. The next most-common skin cancer is melanoma, and the least common is Merkel cell cancer.

Basal cells are found in the epidermis. When basal cells become cancerous, it is considered basal cell carcinoma. Basal cell carcinoma is the most common type of skin cancer and when found early is highly curable.

Squamous cell carcinoma arises in the squamous cells (the flat, scaly cells on the surface) and also has a high cure rate when detected early.

Melanoma is a malignancy of the skin considered a more serious skin cancer than basal cell and squamous cell carcinoma. Melanoma is measured in thickness known as Breslow's depth, and is determined by the pathologist during examination. This measurement is related to the five-year survival rate after surgical intervention. Clark level of invasion, commonly known as Clark's Level, is a method devised by pathologist Wallace Clark and measures depth of penetration of the melanoma into the skin according to anatomic layer. This determination also is made by the pathologist.

There are five Clark levels of invasion:

- **Level I:** Melanomas confined to the outermost layer of the skin, the epidermis. This is also called "melanoma *in-situ*."
- **Level II:** Penetration by melanomas into the second layer of the skin, the dermis.
- **Level III-IV:** Melanomas that invade deeper through the dermis, but are still contained completely within the skin.
- **Level V:** Penetration of melanoma into the fat of the skin beneath the dermis, penetration into the sub cutis.

Pathology of the excised lesion is necessary to choose the appropriate CPT® code. All excised lesions include simple repair, but in the case where removal of the lesion calls for an intermediate or complex closure, the closure is reported in addition to the excision of lesion code.

Lesion excisions are first divided by pathology, whether it is benign (non-cancerous) or malignant. Pathology reports for malignant lesions will likely state basal cell carcinoma, squamous cell carcinoma, carcinoma in-situ, melanoma, and melanoma *in-situ*. For benign lesions, pathology reports likely state compound nevus, benign nevus, melanocytic nevus, epidermal nevus, congenital nevus, nevus sebaceous, and dysplastic nevus. Within both the benign and malignant sections, codes are listed by body location and size excised.

Nails (11719–11765)

Nails are plates of tightly packed, hard, keratinized epidermal cells. The nail consists of:

- **Nail root:** the portion of the nail under the skin
- **Nail body:** the visible pink portion of the nail—the white crescent at the base of the nail is the lunula; the hyponychium secures the nail to the finger; the cuticle or eponychium is a narrow band around the proximal edge of the nail

- **Free edge:** the white end extending past the finger

There are several procedures performed on the nails, such as trimming of healthy nails for the diabetic patient. These services are often performed by a podiatrist or family practice physician. Report 11719 for trimming of the nondystrophic nail(s); any number. A nondystrophic nail is essentially a normal nail unaffected by abnormal development or changes in structure or appearance due to disease, injury, or aging. For Medicare, trimming of dystrophic nails is reported with HCPCS Level II code G0127.

With diabetic patients it may be necessary to have nails trimmed by a podiatrist due to the underlying issues such as increased risk of fungal nail infections and poor healing process associated with diabetes.

Code 11720 reports debridement of one nail to five nails. Nail debridement may be indicated for hypertrophic dystrophic nails, mycotic (fungal) infections, or for patients with peripheral vascular disease. Nail debridement typically is performed mechanically by using instruments such as a nail splitter, nail elevator (small, narrow spoon-shaped instrument), and/or electrical burr or sander. Code 11721 is used for six or more nails.

Avulsion (tearing away) of a nail plate is described with 11730 for partial or complete; simple; single. This procedure involves the physician removing part of or the entire fingernail or toenail. After local anesthetic is administered the physician separates the nail plate from the nail bed to remove the nail. If the physician is removing more than one nail from the finger or toes, +11732 is used for each additional nail. Remember that CPT® 11732 is an add-on code reported with units of occurrence.

When a patient presents with a hematoma (collection of blood) of the fingernail or toenail the physician removes the collection of blood by using an electrocautery unit to pierce the nail plate and drains the fluid. CPT® 11740 is reported. When more than one nail is involved, report each additional procedure with modifier 59 and the appropriate F1–FA modifier to indicate which fingernail (or T1–TA for toenails).

The excision of a nail and nail matrix (11750) is performed for severely deformed or ingrown nails. This procedure may be performed using surgical, laser, electrocautery, or chemical techniques, following administration of a local anesthetic. Code 11752 describes partial or complete removal of the nail and nail matrix, and excision of the end of the distal phalanx of the digit, usually a toe. Local anesthesia is administered.

CPT® 11755 describes biopsy of the nail unit. In the documentation it's important to identify the nail plate, bed, matrix, proximal, lateral or distal grooves, proximal or lateral fold, or the epithelium. The most common approach to a nail biopsy is a double punch, utilizing a punch tool similar to the tool used for a punch biopsy of the skin. A larger punch tool is used first, such as a 6 mm tool. To obtain the actual biopsy the physician will use a smaller punch tool, such as a 4 mm. The physician will determine if sutures are needed to close the biopsy site, or whether to let it heal by secondary intent.

Practical Coding Note

When a biopsy of the nail bed is performed after avulsion of the nail plate, it is inclusive of the avulsion procedure and is not coded separately. If a soft tissue laceration of the skin surrounding the nail has occurred, the laceration is reported separately with the simple, intermediate or complex repair codes.

Reconstruction of the nail bed (11762) differs in each case, depending on the nature and extent of the defect.

CPT® 11765 is coded when a wedge excision of the skin of the nail fold is performed to treat an ingrown toenail. This procedure is performed when there is a chronic infection resulting in diseased tissue along the nail fold. The physician makes an incision along the nail fold and a wedge-shaped excision is performed to remove the diseased tissue. In most cases the wound is left open to heal by secondary intention.

Pilonidal Cysts (11770–11772)

A pilonidal cyst is a sac under the skin at the base of the spine and can become infected. When this happens, the physician will use a scalpel to excise all of the adjacent tissue. The code selection is based on whether the excision of the cyst is simple, extensive, or complicated. A simple excision (11770) is closed in only one layer. If several layers of closure are required and the documentation indicates extensive or complicated; code selection is directed to 11771 or 11772.

Introduction (11900–11983)

In some cases, a patient presents with lesions not requiring excision, but yet need treatment. In these situations the physician will choose to inject the lesion (such as a wart, erythemas, hordeolums, or keloid scars). The physician typically injects a steroid material into these lesions. Pay close attention to number of injections, because there are only two correct codes to use; 11900 is up to and including seven lesions, while 11901 describes more than seven lesions being injected.

Tattooing typically is performed for patients who have undergone breast reconstruction. Watch your total area, as this procedure is measured in square centimeters.

Injection of filling material such as collagen is used in many facets of reconstructive and cosmetic surgery. The physician injects filling material subcutaneously to treat acne scars, facial wrinkles, and abnormality of the breast due to reconstruction. The injection includes treatment of scarring conditions. Read the procedural note to be able to report correctly how many ccs were injected. For instance, 11950 describes 1 cc or less, whereas 11954 describes over 10 ccs.

Tissue expanders are used in a number of ways. The most common are for burn victims and breast cancer patients. In the case of the burn victim, the physician places a tissue expander under the skin and the patient returns to the office for expansion, which is done with injection of saline or air into the expander. The tissue expander allows the skin to be stretched so it can be harvested for transfer to a burn site or open wound site. For the breast cancer survivor the tissue expander is placed during a more involved breast reconstruction surgery to be discussed later in this chapter. Insertion of the tissue expander for other than breast reconstruction is reported with 11960. When the tissue expander is removed and replaced with a permanent prosthesis for breast reconstruction, report 11970.

The insertion and removal of implantable contraceptive devices are coded from this section. In looking at CPT® codes 11981–11983, it is important to pay close attention to how and what is being placed (eg, implantable capsule, subcutaneous hormone pellet or non-biodegradable drug delivery implant).

Section Review 7.2

1. A patient presents to the dermatologist with a suspicious lesion on her left arm and on her right arm. After examination the physician feels these lesions present as highly suspicious and obtains consent to perform punch biopsies on both sites. After prepping the area, the physician injects the sites with Lidocaine 1 percent and .05 percent Epinephrine. A 3 mm punch biopsy of the lesion of the left arm and a 4 mm punch biopsy of the lesion of the right arm is taken. The sites are closed with a simple one layer closure and the patient is to return in 10 days for suture removal and to discuss the pathology results. The patient tolerated the procedure well.

   Select the CPT® code(s) for this procedure.

   A. 10060

   B. 11100, 11101

   C. 11400, 11400-59

   D. 11600, 11600-59

2. Patient presents with a cyst on the arm. Upon examination the physician decides to incise and drain the cyst. The site is prepped and the physician takes a scalpel and cuts into the cyst. Purulent fluid is extracted from the cyst and a sample of the fluid is sent to the laboratory for evaluation. The wound is irrigated with normal saline and covered with a bandage. The patient is to return in a week to ten days to re-examine the wound.

   Select the CPT® code for this procedure.

   A. 10060

   B. 11400

   C. 11100

   D. 10061

3. A patient presents to the primary care physician with multiple skin tags. After a complete examination of the skin the provider discusses with the patient the removal of 18 skin tags located on the patient's neck and shoulder area. Patient consent is obtained and the provider removes all 18 skin tags by scissoring technique.

   Select the CPT® code(s) for this procedure.

   A. 11201

   B. 11200, 11201-51

   C. 17000

   D. 11200, 11201

4. A patient presents for tattooing of the nipple and areola of both breasts after undergoing breast reconstruction. The total area for the right breast is 11.5 cm2 and for the left breast of 10.5 cm2.

   Select the CPT® code(s) for this procedure.

   A. 11921, 11922

   B. 11921-50

   C. 19350

   D. 19120-50

5. A patient presents to the dermatologist with a suspicious lesion of the left cheek. Upon examination the physician discusses with the patient the best course of treatment is to remove the lesion by shave technique. Consent is obtained and the physician preps the area and using an 11-blade scalpel, makes a transverse incision and slices the lesion at the base. The wound is cleaned and a bandage is placed. The physician indicates the size of the lesion is 1.4 cm. The lesion is sent to pathology for evaluation and the patient is to return in 10 days to discuss the findings.

Select the CPT® code for this procedure.

A. 11312

B. 11100

C. 11642

D. 11442

Repair/Closure (12001–13160)

Surgical repair refers to procedures reestablishing function or appearance of damaged tissue through artificial means. These procedures often involve suturing tissues back together after they have been separated or damaged by injury or trauma. A wound is any physical injury involving a break in the skin, usually caused by an act or accident (eg, chest or puncture wound, gunshot wound). Wound repairs are divided into three categories: simple, intermediate, and complex. The physician determines whether a repair is simple, intermediate, or complex.

Simple repair codes (12001–12021) are used on superficial wounds that primarily involve the epidermis, dermis, or subcutaneous tissues without involvement of deeper structures. The repair requires simple "one layer closure/suturing" and "includes local anesthesia and chemical or electrocauterization of wounds not closed." When adhesive strips are used as the only material for wound closure, an E/M service should be reported. The key components must be documented (*AMA CPT® Assistant* Vol. 10, Issue 4, April 2000, p 8.).

Intermediate repair codes (12031–12057) include repair of epidermis, dermis, or subcutaneous tissues requiring layered closure of one or more of the subcutaneous tissues and nonmuscle fascia. Also included in this definition is when a single layer closure of heavily contaminated wounds requiring extensive cleaning or removal of particulate matter.

Complex repair codes (13100–13160) include repairing of wounds requiring more than layered closure (eg, scar revision); debridement (eg, traumatic lacerations or avulsions); extensive undermining, stents or retention sutures, or cosmetic closures. "Necessary preparation includes creation of a defect for repairs (eg, excision of a scar requiring a complex repair or the debridement of complicated lacerations or avulsions)." ("A Table of Reporting Complex Repair Involving Multiple Anatomic Sites" is available in the *AMA CPT® Assistant,* Feb 2000, p 10).

The following information is important to consider when choosing repair codes:

It is permissible to use the repair codes to report wounds repaired with staples, tissue adhesives, and their use in combination with adhesive strips. If adhesive strips (example, steri-strips) are used alone to close a wound, the wound care must be billed with an E/M code rather than a code from the 10000 range. When a tissue adhesive (example, Dermabond®) is used alone report HCPCS Level II code G0168 *Wound closure utilizing tissue adhesive(s) only* may be required by some payers.

Repaired wounds must be measured and reported in centimeters to allow for correct CPT® code selection. When reporting repair services, first group the wounds by the type of repair (simple, intermediate, or complex) and then group them by anatomical area. For example, it is not appropriate to add the lengths of intermediate wounds of the face with intermediate wounds of the back.

When multiple wounds require the same type of repair and are located/listed in the same anatomical region/code, add the lengths of each wound and report them as a single item (the sum of all the lengths).

Practical Coding Note

Place a plus sign (+) next to the heading of repairs as a reminder to add repairs of the same category together.

When more than one classification of wound is repaired, list the more complicated repair first, followed by the less complicated repair, and add CPT® modifier 59 to each procedure after the first.

For excision of benign and malignant lesions requiring more than simple closure, report 11400–11446 or 11600–11646 in addition to the appropriate closure code.

For reconstructive closure, see 14000–14302, 15002–15278, or 15570–15770.

If repairs involve nerves, blood vessels, or tendons, the appropriate code would be selected from the correct system (nervous, cardiovascular, or musculoskeletal, respectively). A simple exploration of the nerves, blood vessels, or exposed tendons is considered part of the repair.

Adjacent Tissue Transfer or Rearrangement (14000–14350)

Primary and secondary defects of the integument too large to close by simply bringing the wound edges together are sometimes repaired using adjacent tissue transfer or rearrangement. Primary wound healing refers to healing of a clean incision via collagen synthesis. Wounds, which are easily repaired by bringing the wound edges together with minimal tissue loss, are said to heal by primary intention. Sometimes it is best for function and appearance to close this wound at the initial encounter with an adjacent tissue transfer or rearrangement.

When a primary defect is too large to bring together the wound edges, it can be left to heal from the bottom up via a process of laying down granulation tissue, which may or may not require closure or reconstruction at a later date. This process is referred to as wound healing by secondary intention. This can take a much longer time to go through the process of epithelialization, scar formation, and contraction of wound edges.

Sometimes wounds cannot heal properly or cosmetically due to problems with collagen synthesis (eg, Ehlers-Danlos syndrome). Formation of keloid scar tissue is a direct result of overproduction of collagen. Unsightly or troublesome scars can occur for a multitude of reasons. In certain circumstances, it is appropriate to excise a scar (this creates a secondary defect) and the resultant defect requires a complex closure using tissue transfer and rearrangement.

Adjacent tissue transfer actually involves a primary and secondary defect, both of which are repaired in the adjacent tissue transfer procedure. The primary defect is the original defect to be closed. The secondary defect is the defect created by the movement of tissue necessary to close the primary defect. Since both types of defects affect the amount of effort necessary to perform the procedure, the guidelines now specify the need to include both the primary and secondary defects as part of the measurement for this type of repair. In addition, the defect and the attendant physician's work involved for the procedure varies more with the type of flap utilized than with

the size of the lesion removed. For instance, in some cases, the primary defect may approximate the size of the secondary defect. However, in many instances, the secondary defect area must be considerably larger than the primary defect area, depending on factors such as location, skin mobility, and elasticity, or adjacent structures such as lip or eyelid. Skin grafting is necessary to close secondary defects and is considered an additional procedure. Refer to the illustrations in *CPT® Professional Edition* for an Advancement Flap and a Rotation Flap.

There are many types of adjacent tissue transfers and rearrangements such as V-Y advancement, Z, W, Limberg, or nasolabial transpositions and rotation flaps. Tissue transfer or rearrangement is best described as filling large defects by moving a flat piece of healthy tissue (preserving a connection on at least one side of its place of origin) into the defect. When applied in repairing lacerations, the procedure listed must be developed by the surgeon to accomplish the repair. They do not apply when closure or rearrangement results in the configuration.

When selecting the appropriate tissue transfer code, choose the code according to the size of the defect or wound to be covered. For example, when a lesion is removed and an adjacent tissue transfer covers the remaining open wound/defect, code according to the size of the defect (in square centimeters), not by the size of the lesion. The excision of the lesion is included in the procedure.

When two different lesions are removed from two different locations, and an adjacent tissue repair closes one wound while sutures close the other wounds, both services may be reported because two different lesions are excised. However, when reporting these services, the wound closed with sutures is reported with CPT® modifier 59 to indicate it is a different procedure and is not included in the adjacent tissue transfer.

Practical Coding Note

The adjacent tissue transfer and rearrangement codes are reported in square centimeters for CPT® codes 14000–14350. Free flap codes 15100–15121 and skin substitute grafts 15273–15274 and 15277–15278 are listed in increments of 100 sq cm. Coders should read the codes carefully for appropriate assignment. If the length and width of the site to be grafted are provided, the square centimeters are calculated by multiplying the length times the width.

Types of Skin Flaps

Advancement Flap—Undermining or freeing up tissue (from underlying fibrous attachments) surrounding a defect creates an advancement flap. This tissue is now free to move forward into the defect and be sutured to the other wound edge. This type of tissue transfer does not include any side or rotational movement of the tissues freed for advancement.

Allograft—The skin graft is transplanted from one person to another, who are not genetically identical; also called an allogenic skin graft.

Autograft—Skin graft is harvested from another healthy part of the patient's own body.

Composite Graft—This term refers to skin grafts including more than one type of tissue. The multiple tissues are aligned and used to plug a defect. This type of graft is usually done for both structural and cosmetic reasons (*AMA CPT® Assistant*, September 1997, page 3).

Derma-Fascia-Fat Grafts—This service is performed to smooth out blemishes created secondary to surgically created defects or atrophy. CPT® code 15770 refers to a composite graft of all three layers mentioned (*AMA CPT® Assistant*, Sept 1997, p 3).

Double Pedicle Flap—An incision is made in the skin along the length of the defect to be closed and the tissue between the incision and the edge of the defect is freed, leaving the ends of the flap attached. The flap is moved into place over the defect and the edges are sutured. The double pedicle flap allows the blood supply to the tissue flap to be maintained from both ends of the flap (*AMA CPT® Assistant*, July 1999, p 4).

Free Fascia Graft—This type of graft requires the elevation and transfer of fascia with microvascular anastomosis. If it is subsequently covered with a skin graft, the skin graft is reported separately (*AMA CPT® Assistant*, April 1997, p 6).

Full-thickness Graft—Graft is composed of epidermis and layers of the dermis. The graft is cut with a scalpel, placed over the defect, and sutured into place.

Heterograft—This type of graft is synonymous with a xenograft, which is a graft material transferred between species (eg, a skin graft section made of pigskin that functions as a biological dressing).

Homograft—The graft material originates from two individuals of the same species who are not genetically identical (eg, skin harvested from a cadaver and used as temporary cover). These grafts are commonly used only about 10 days, though they may last four to five weeks. They are usually used to cover large burns and stimulate the growth of new skin beneath them.

Rotation Flap—A skin incision is made to create a curvilinear flap contiguous with the defect. Once the flap is dissected free, it is pivoted into place over the defect and sutured into

place. The defect created in making the flap is sutured shut or repaired with an additional graft as necessary.

Split-thickness Graft—The graft is composed of epidermis and a small portion of the dermis.

Skin Replacement Surgery and Skin Substitutes (15002–15278)

When patients suffer disfiguring injuries, burns, or surgically created defects, skin grafting may be employed for either therapeutic or cosmetic results. Free skin graft codes are selected on the basis of type of graft as well as area, size, and location of the recipient area. The codes include simple debridement or recent avulsions.

CPT® code 15002 and 15004 includes the excision and initial preparation of wounds. CPT® codes 15100–15261 include autogenous and autogenous tissue-cultured skin grafts. Placement of the graft includes harvesting of the keratinocytes. The selected CPT® code for the procedure is determined according to the recipient site of the graft.

For three series of CPT® codes in this section (eg, 15002–15005, 15040, 15100–15101 and 15120–15121), CPT® states the determination of how much body surface area is involved is based on 100 sq cm units for adults and one percentage of body area for infants and children under 10 years of age. CPT® code 15050 is measured in cm. Codes 15002–15005 are selected based on the location and size of the resultant defect.

Application of a skin substitute and skin replacement is reported using CPT® codes 15100–15278. When the procedure is staged, append modifier 58 to the procedure.

For multiple wounds, add the surface area of all wounds from all anatomic sites that are grouped together into the same code descriptor (eg, trunk and legs). Do not add wounds from different grouping of anatomic site (eg, arms and hands).

Codes 15271, 15272, 15275, and 15276 are reported for total wounds surface area less than 100 square centimeters. Codes 15273, 15274, 15277, and 15278 are reported for total wound surface area greater than or equal to 100 square centimeters. The total surface area of all of the wounds from all anatomic sites grouped together into the same code descriptor should be added together to obtain the total surface area when selecting the code.

In the grafting procedure, the recipient site is prepared by surgical scrub and debrided for best approximation of wound margins. With a split or full-thickness graft, the skin is removed from the donor sited by a dermatome. The graft sometimes runs through a machine turning it into a mesh by cutting multiple diamond shaped holes in the graft. Once the graft is cut to size, it is placed on the recipient site. The graft is anchored with either a pressure dressing or sutures and covered with nonadherent gauze or covered with a gauze dressing.

Repair of donor site requiring skin graft or adjacent tissue repair may be coded as a separate procedure. Debridement can be coded as a separate procedure only when gross contamination requires extensive cleansing, when large amounts of devitalized or contaminated tissue are removed, or when debridement is carried out separately without having closure of the wound immediately.

Practical Coding Note

Procedures involving wrist are reported with the codes that include the arm in the code descriptor. Procedures involving the ankle are reported with codes that include leg in the code descriptor.

Flaps (Skin and/or Deep Tissues) (15570–15738)

Flaps, skin, and/or deep tissue describe a section of skin that is transferred to the recipient site while still remaining attached to a blood supply source. Most of the procedures in this section describe pedicle flaps. The term pedicle means stalk or stem, especially one acting as a support. A pedicle flap of skin is raised from its bed and placed in the recipient location while the other end of the pedicle flap remains attached at the donor site for blood supply and nourishment.

Although this process sounds similar to an adjacent tissue replacement, there are important differences to keep in mind when distinguishing between the two services:

1. The pedicle (base) of the pedicle flap is eventually cut or severed from its original blood supply after the skin transfer has been completed. In an adjacent tissue transfer, the base remains intact permanently.

2. Pedicle flaps are formed on an area distant from the defect where it is being transferred. In an adjacent tissue transfer, transfer is made from a local flap.

3. Pedicle flaps are often completed in multiple stages but can be formed and transferred in one stage. Adjacent tissue transfers are completed in a single stage.

CPT® codes 15570–15576 refer to the body location in which the formation of the pedicle is created with or without transfer. CPT® codes 15600–15630 describe the delay of flap or resectioning. These codes are usually reported for a second stage on a tubed or direct pedicle flap when performed. Use modifier 58 when these codes are performed within the global

period. CPT® code 15650 describes the transfer of the pedicle, any location. This is when a prior pedicle flap has been in the recipient area long enough to get good blood supply and the flap is removed completely from the donor attachment to a new location. The same flap may be moved in the same way to another part of the body at another time. This procedure is also known as "walking the flap." The code is reported for each transfer with modifier 58.

Muscle flaps are coded with CPT® codes 15732–15738. These codes are listed based on the donor site of the flap. Each of these codes refers to a more general anatomic area than may be listed in an operative note. If the muscle flap had been created from the gracilis, the CPT® code 15738 would be used (Plastic Surgery News, April 1994, Raymond Janevicius, MD).

Other Flaps and Grafts (15740–15777)

According to a January 1997 Coding Corner article "Free Flap Codes Dominate New 1997 Additions," each free flap code includes the following services:

- Elevation of the flap
- Isolation of the vessels
- Transfer of the flap to the recipient site
- Microvascular anastomosis of one artery
- Microvascular anastomosis of one vein or two veins
- Inset of flap into recipient site
- Primary closure of the donor site

Microvascular transfer, a free tissue transfer, or a free flap tissue are terms used to describe the process of transferring tissue from one area of the body to another using microsurgical techniques. The word "free" indicates the tissue is actually separated from its blood supply and transferred to a recipient site where it is reanastomosed to the recipient blood vessels. All of the free tissue transfer codes include transferring a portion of the fascia, which contains the vascular supply to the skin.

Code 15756 describes a free muscle or myocutaneous flap with or without skin with microvascular anastomosis. Microvascular anastomosis is a process in which a physician, under microscopic visualization, sutures together the donor and recipient vessels with microvascular instruments. This procedure usually requires a team of two physicians, one to prepare the recipient site and the other to harvest the flap. Each surgeon functions as a primary surgeon and reports the procedure performed. If microdissection of arteries, veins, and/or nerves are performed, this may be reported separately.

A variation of the free muscle flap—an innervated free muscle flap—is muscle that is transferred to another area of the body where arteries and veins are anastomosed, in addition to the motor nerve anastomosed to a recipient motor nerve. This is done to allow the transferred muscle to replace a muscle that no longer functions, such as a finger flexor or elbow flexor.

Free fasciocutaneous flaps (15757) are used in soft tissue defects around the knee (eg, Saphenous flap). Free skin flaps are also used for reconstruction of facial burns and elsewhere. A free skin flap with microvascular anastomosis can often be used in situations similar to those where the free muscle flap is used. Muscle flaps are preferred in situations where good blood supply is required (eg, an open tibial fracture).

Code 15758 describes a flap involving only the elevation and transfer of the fascia. Fascial flaps are used in areas where the bulk of the muscle or skin is not desirable and requires some soft tissue coverage. The fascial flaps are usually covered with a skin graft, which is coded separately.

Practical Coding Note

When the CPT® code description includes microvascular anastomosis, do not report use of the operating microscope (69990). Use of the operating microscope is included in the procedure. Highlight "microvascular anastomosis" in the code description to remind you not to report 69990.

CPT® codes 15775 and 15776 describe the process of excising circular portions of the scalp or other hair containing tissues and placing them in the hairline in areas lacking hair. CPT® codes 15775 and 15776 are mutually exclusive (*AMA CPT® Assistant*, September 1997, page 3). 15777 is an add-on code used when biological implant is used for soft tissue reinforcement.

Other Procedures (15780–15879)

CPT® codes 15780-15783 deals with dermabrasion treatment. Dermabrasion is when the upper top layers of the skin are scraped away using a mechanical tool or instrument, such as sandpaper or a power rotary abrasive drum. The reason for this procedure is to smooth the skin and remove scarring caused by acne, fine wrinkles, general keratosis or tattoos. These codes are chosen by the location and if it is superficial.

CPT® codes 15788-15793 are reported for chemical peels which is also another type of dermabrasion treatment. This is when the physician uses chemical agents, such as phenol or alpha-hydroxy acid, to remove abnormal pigmentation, sun damage, superficial scarring, or fine winkles. These codes are chosen by the location and the depth of the skin. For example, code 15788 is for the chemical peel on the face on the epidermal layer. If the peel goes deeper to the dermal layer you will report code 15789.

A blepharoplasty is performed to remove excess eyelid skin and in many cases, extensive herniated fat pad from both the upper and the lower eyelids. Often the excessive skin blocks the patient's visual field. Once removed, the patient will notice improvement in their ability to see. This type of surgery can be done under local anesthesia in a doctor's office. The codes are selected based on the location (upper or lower lid) and whether the fat pad is herniated. The code range for blepharoplasty is 15820–15823.

The proper HCPCS modifiers are appended to report the eyelid the surgery is performed on.

- E1 Upper left, eyelid
- E2 Lower left, eyelid
- E3 Upper right, eyelid
- E4 Lower right eyelid

If the procedure is performed bilaterally, modifier 50 can be appended in lieu of the HCPCS anatomical modifiers.

A rhytid is a wrinkle. Rhytidectomy is the removal of these wrinkles by performing a facelift. The codes for this procedure are reported based on the anatomical site of the procedure. CPT® codes 15824-15829 are reported by the anatomical area involved.

With the increase of gastric bypass surgery, there has been an increase of men and women requesting large amounts of excess skin be removed due to the large amount of weight loss. The procedures are reported with code range 15830-15839 and are selected based on anatomical site.

CPT® codes 15840-15845 are reported when a graft is harvested from some location on the body (eg, fascia lata of the leg) and is placed to the face over the paralyzed area. Codes 15840 and 15841 is for the type of graft used, 15842 is for using a free muscle flap by microsurgical technique, and 15845 is when a muscle regional muscle transfer is performed.

Lipectomy is also known as liposuction or surgical assisted lipectomy. There are techniques now where ultrasound is used to break down the fat within the tissue and make it easier to be sucked out by the cannula. There is also a tumescent type of liposuction done where the doctor injects fluids into the tissues and then the liposuction cannula sucks it out along with the fat. The codes are selected based on anatomic site. When performed on the head and neck, report 15876. When performed on the trunk, report 15877. When performed on the upper extremities report 15878. When performed on the lower extremities report 15879. The perfect candidate for liposuction is someone who is close to their ideal body weight and whose skin is in good condition. If a patient is considering liposuction, it is recommended they follow a good diet and exercise and then have liposuction on the areas in which they cannot lose the weight.

Pressure Ulcer (Decubitus Ulcers) (15920–15999)

Pressure ulcer, decubitus ulcer, and bedsores are synonyms referring to ulcerations of the skin and the underlying tissues. They are usually confined to one area and are commonly found over the bony projections such as the sacrum, coccyx, ischium, knee, and heel just to name a few areas. Pressure sores are caused by a decrease in blood supply from pressure to the skin and result in inflammation and swelling in the area which, in turn, results in necrosis (death of cells), ulceration, and possible infection. Pressure sores may be superficial, that is, confined to the skin, or they may go deep extending below the skin into layers of tissue under it. Pressure sores are commonly found in patients confined to their beds.

When using a code with the descriptor "in preparation for muscle or myocutaneous flap," such as CPT® code 15936, use the appropriate code for reporting the muscle flap or myocutaneous flap procedure in addition to the pressure sore procedure (Flaps [Skin and/or Deep Tissues]). When coding for pressure sore procedures including an adjacent tissue transfer, flap closure, or skin flap closure, choose the appropriate code under the Pressure Ulcer section of the CPT®.

Burns, Local Treatment (16000–16036)

The origin of a burn may be thermal, or caused by heat or cold, produced by chemicals, radiation, or friction. Depth and percentage of the total body surface area (TBSA) determine the severity of a burn. There are several methods used to determine the depth of the burn or injury.

Skin Depth Method—Indicative of its name. Partial-thickness burn damages the epidermis and/or part of the dermis. A full-thickness burn damages the epidermis, dermis, and extends into the subcutaneous tissue.

Rule of Nines—The most commonly used, and evaluates the percentage of body surface burned by allocating a percentage to each of the following body surfaces; head, each upper extremity, and the front and back halves of each lower extremity.

Degree of Burn

First degree burn involves damage to the outermost layer of skin (epidermis). First degree burns are characterized by tenderness. A person may require hospitalization for dehydration requiring reporting the appropriate level of E/M service.

Second degree burn involves damage to the epidermis and dermis; blisters or vesicles are usually present. Second degree burns can cause severe pain due to nerve damage.

Third degree burn involves damage not only to the epidermis and dermis, but extends into the subcutaneous tissues; tissue may be charred.

Practical Coding Note

ICD-10-CM makes a distinction between burns and corrosions. Burns are caused by a heat source such as fire or hot appliance, radiation, radiation or electricity. Corrosions are due to chemicals.

When the services involve dressings/debridement and are provided under anesthesia, use codes 16020–16030. Any local infiltration, metacarpal/digital block, or topical anesthesia, when used, is not reported separately.

Wound Preparation

Codes 15002–15005 include the excisional preparation of open wounds, burn eschar or scar, including tangential excisions and reflect a stand-alone procedure used when a skin graft is not recommended (eg, partial-thickness burns) or when grafting is delayed due to a subsequent session. To quantify the variance in the amount of work involved in the soft tissue treatment, CPT® codes 15002 and 15004 are based on surface area and includes the excisional preparation of the first 100 sq cm in the treatment of adults; in infants and children, 1 percent. Codes 15003 and 15005 were established to recognize the additional work of each additional 100 sq cm or each 1 percent in infants and children.

CPT® codes 16000–16030 report local treatment of the burn surface only. Local treatment refers to symptomatic relief for the patient (*CPT® Assistant,* Aug 1997, p 6).

These codes describe the application and dressing changes for burn wounds and any associated debridement or curettement. They do not include E/M services involving history, exam, and medical decision making for concurrent systemic problems of the patient.

When reporting a skin grafting procedure following debridement, choose the appropriate code for debridement (16000–16030) followed by the appropriate CPT® code from 15100–15650 to report the skin graft.

Practical Coding Note

Burn Repair by Autologous Cultured Human Epithelium— Unburned epidermal cells cultured into sheets are attached to petrolatum gauze squares (used as a soothing application to burns and abrasions of the skin) and sutured into place over the wound. The petrolatum gauze is removed in seven to 10 days.

Section Review 7.3

1. A patient presents to her doctor with three medium sized suspicious lesions on her leg. The physician uses a saw type instrument and slices horizontally to remove the lesions. The lesions are sent for pathology.

    What CPT® code(s) should be reported for this example?

    A. 11000, 11101 x 2

    B. 11300, 11300-51 x 2

    C. 11302 x 3

    D. 11303

2. A patient presents to the emergency department with multiple lacerations. After inspection and cleaning of the multiple wounds the physician proceeds to close the wounds. The documentation indicates the following:

    2.7 cm complex closure to the right upper abdominal area, a 1.4 cm complex repair to the right buttock, a 7.4 cm intermediate repair to the right arm, a 3.8 cm intermediate repair to the left cheek, a 8.1 cm intermediate repair to the scalp, and a 2.3 cm simple repair the right lower lip.

    What are the correct CPT® codes to report for this example?

    A. 13101, 13100-59, 12051-59, 12011-59

    B. 13100, 12035-59, 12052-59, 12012-59

    C. 13101, 12034-59, 13100-59, 12052-59

    D. 13101, 12035-59, 12052-59, 12011-59

3. **Operative Report:**

    Indications for Surgery: The patient has a suspicious 1.5 cm lesion of the left upper medial thigh. Clinical diagnosis of this lesion is unknown, but due to the appearance, malignancy is a realistic concern. The area is marked for elliptical excision with gross normal margins of 3 mm in relaxed skin tension lines of the respective area and the best guess at the resulting scars was drawn. The patient observed these marks in a mirror to understand the surgery and agreed on the location and we proceeded.

    Procedure: The areas were infiltrated with local anesthetic. The area was prepped and draped in sterile fashion. The suspicious left upper most medial thigh lesion was excised as drawn, into the subcutaneous fat. This was sent for permanent pathology. The wound was closed in layers using 3.0 monocryl and 5.0 chromic. The repair measured 5.0 cm. Meticulous homeostasis was achieved using light pressure. The patient tolerated the procedure well.

    What CPT® code(s) should be reported for this example?

    A. 11100

    B. 11311

    C. 12032, 11403-51

    D. 12031, 11600-51

4. **Operative Report:**

    Indications for Surgery: The patient has a dysplastic nevus on the right upper abdomen. The area is marked for elliptical excision with gross normal margins of 4 to 6 mm in relaxed skin tension lines of the respective area and the best guess at the resulting scars is drawn. The patient observed these marks in a mirror to understand the surgery and agrees on the location and we proceeded.

    Procedure: The area was infiltrated with local anesthetic. The area is prepped and draped in sterile fashion. The dysplastic nevus right upper abdomen lesion measuring 2.2 cm with margins is excised as drawn, into the subcutaneous fat. Suture is used to mark the specimen at its medial tip, and labeled 12 o'clock. This is sent for permanent pathology. Meticulous homeostasis is achieved using light pressure. The patient tolerated the procedure well.

    What is the correct CPT® code to report for this example?

    A. 11603

    B. 11403

    C. 11401

    D. 11601

5. **Operative Report:**

    Indications for Surgery: The patient is a 72-year-old male with a biopsy-proven squamous cell carcinoma of his left forearm. With his permission, I marked my planned excision and my best guess at the resultant scar, which included a rhomboid flap repair. The patient observed these markings in a mirror, so he could understand the surgery, and agree on the location; I proceeded.

    Description of Procedure: The patient was given 1 g of IV Ancef. The area was infiltrated with local anesthetic. The forearm was prepped and draped in a sterile fashion. I excised this lesion measuring 1.2 cm diameter as drawn into the subcutaneous fat. A suture was used to mark this specimen at its proximal tip and this was labeled at 12 o'clock. Negative margins were then given. Meticulous hemostasis was achieved using a Bovie cautery. I incised my planned rhomboid flap measuring 2 cm x 2 cm. I elevated the flap with a full-thickness of skin and subcutaneous fat. The total defect size was 5.44 sq cm. The flap was rotated into the defect and the donor site was closed and the flap was inset in layers using 4-0 Monocryl and 5-0 Prolene. Loupe magnification was used throughout the procedure and the patient tolerated the procedure well.

    What CPT® code(s) should be reported for this example?

    A. 14040

    B. 14020, 11602-51

    C. 14020

    D. 14021

Destruction (17000–17999)

CPT® codes 17000–17286 are used when reporting destruction of a lesion. According to AMA's CPT®, "Lesions include condylomata, papillomata, molluscum contagiosum, herpetic lesions, warts (eg, common, plantar, flat) milia or other benign, premalignant, or malignant lesions." Destruction means the ablation of benign, premalignant, or malignant tissues by any method, with or without curettage, including local anesthesia,

and not usually requiring closure. There are several methods of destruction: electrosurgery, cryosurgery, laser, chemical treatment, and surgical curettage.

Electrosurgery

When tissue requires destruction rather than removal, the physician may choose electrosurgery. This method does not require sutures and eliminates concern over bleeding. Healing time is prolonged (often up to three weeks) and scarring may be more pronounced with this method.

Electrosurgery may or may not be performed in conjunction with curettage. A dermal curette is used due to the semisharp cutting edge found on this tool. This edge allows easy removal of soft, cancerous tissue while not easily slicing through normal, benign collagen. Developing expertise with the curette enables the surgeon to easily determine the margins and the depth of the lesions.

Curettage without electrosurgery results in less scarring but may not fully destroy the lesion, making recurrence more likely than in those cases when the two methods are combined.

Cryosurgery

Cryosurgery is the application of freezing temperatures to produce cell death and/or tissue destruction. This method requires no injected anesthesia and no bleeding occurs. This method has a more penetrating effect and is used for malignant lesions.

Cryosurgery commonly takes these forms: liquid nitrogen administered directly to the lesion, liquid nitrogen spray, or a metal probe infused with liquid nitrogen, which lowers the probe's temperature to the nitrogen preparation. This third method, though requiring expensive equipment, provides the highest degree of control over the size and depth of the tissue to be treated.

Laser Surgery

Laser is an acronym for light amplification by stimulated emission of radiation. Laser energy is available in several types and is hailed for its precision with a lesion's margins and depth as well as its elimination of bleeding.

Argon lasers are commonly used with vascular lesions but are more likely to produce scarring than with a pulsed dye laser. Local or general anesthesia is usually used with this treatment mode. This laser may produce a burn-like wound requiring dressing changes from one week to several weeks following treatment.

Carbon dioxide lasers destroy anything within the path of the focused beam and are useful in treatment of many benign and malignant lesion types. Local anesthesia is usually used. Postoperatively, patients may require sutures or staples for skin closure.

Yellow light or pulsed-dye lasers produce a snapping sensation but usually require no anesthesia or wound care.

If lesions are destroyed from multiple body sites, more than one code is required for accurate reporting and billing.

Destruction may be accomplished by one of many methodologies including scalpel, cryotherapy, laser, and cautery. The code is selected according to procedure, not by method.

When reporting codes 17000–17003, it is not necessary to add CPT® modifier 51 (multiple procedures) to 17003 for destruction of additional lesions since it is an add-on code. In the CPT® text code 17004 is also exempt from the use of modifier 51 and is not reported with codes 17000–17003.

Example

The following example shows how to report destruction of three premalignant lesions.

17000   Destruction (eg, laser surgery, electrosurgery, cryosurgery, chemosurgery, surgical curettement), premalignant lesion (eg, actinic keratoses); first lesion

1 Unit

17003 x 2   second through 14 lesions, each

2 Units

When reporting destruction of 15 or more premalignant lesions, use code 17004 only. As an example, destruction of 16 lesions is coded as 17004.

Mohs Micrographic Surgery (17311–17315)

Mohs micrographic surgery is a unique procedure performed by a surgeon acting in two very distinct roles; first as a surgeon and second as a pathologist. The surgeon removes the tumor tissue, and maps and divides the tumor specimen into pieces. These pieces are examined under a microscope to check for positive margins; if positive margins are present, the surgeon returns for another portion of the tumor and begins again. It is very important to understand this process as CPT® codes directly apply to each step. Each time the surgeon removes a portion of the tumor, it is referred to as a stage; each stage is mapped and divided into tissue blocks.

Mohs micrographic surgery is often used for recurrent tumors and/or tumors in difficult-to-reach areas, such as the nose or eyelids. This surgical technique may leave a skin defect in which case flaps or grafts are used to correct or lessen the resulting defect. If a repair is performed using a flap or graft, the procedure may be reported separately.

Practical Coding Note

When coding for Mohs micrographic surgery technique, it is important for the coder to understand the difference between the terms "stage(s)" and "tissue block(s)." The term stage(s) refers to the removal of a layer(s) of tissue. Each removed stage is divided into tissue blocks. Each stage may be divided into one or more tissue blocks, as is common in a later or final stage, the layer may only be one tissue block.

CPT® breaks Mohs down by each stage and up to five tissue blocks. Add-on codes are available for additional stages and additional tissue blocks beyond the initial five blocks.

Example

If a total of eight excised specimens from the neck are prepared and examined during the first Mohs stage, it is appropriate to report code 17311 one time and code 17315 three times.

In addition, if a total of six excised specimens are prepared and examined during the second Mohs stage, then it would be appropriate to report code 17312 one time and code 17315 one time.

Codes 17312, 17314 and 17315 are add-on codes and need to be used in conjunction with the appropriate parent code 17311 or 17313.

Breast (19000–19499)

The female breast lies between the second and sixth ribs, between the sternal edge and the midaxillary line. About two-thirds of the breast is superficial to the pectoralis major muscle and about one-third of the breast is superficial to the serratus anterior muscle. The surface of the areola located on the nipple has small rounded elevations that mark the location of the sebaceous glands. The breast tissue has three components.

Glandular Tissue—Produces milk and is organized into 15 to 20 lobes surrounding the nipple.

Fibrous Tissue—Supports the glandular tissue.

Fat—Surrounds the breast.

The male breast consists chiefly of a small nipple and the areola. These structures overlay a thin disc of underdeveloped breast tissue.

There are many procedures done on the breasts, from a puncture of a cyst to full reconstruction. Each procedure has distinct aspects.

When a patient presents with what appears to be a breast cyst, the physician does a puncture aspiration. Pay attention to the note and remember to code for imaging guidance when applicable.

A mastotomy (19020) is done when the abscess is deep in breast tissue, forcing the physician to create an incision into the breast over the tissue or abscess. The physician will take a culture of the area and irrigate with saline solution. If the tissue is normal, the physician closes the site with sutures. If an abscess is found, the physician commonly packs the wound with gauze to assist in draining the abscess.

For breast biopsies (19081–19101) there are different approaches and imaging methods the surgeon may choose: Percutaneous (using a needle) with or without imaging guidance, or open incisional biopsy (19101) are the two types of breast biopsies performed to evaluate masses found in the breast. Percutaneous biopsies utilize a breast localization device, (clip or metallic pellet) and may be performed using stereotactic (19081), ultrasound (19083), or magnetic resonance guidance (19085).

Depending on what is found during a biopsy, the patient may undergo open breast procedures to remove the mass or, in the case of breast cancer, the patient may undergo a mastectomy. It is imperative to understand the different type of mastectomy procedures.

A lumpectomy is surgical removal of a lesion or abnormal tissue with the purpose of removing the mass in total from the breast, sparing as much breast tissue as possible. When only a cyst, fibroadenoma, or other benign or malignant tumor is removed, report code 19120. This is found by looking in the CPT® Index for Breast/Excision/Lesion.

The breast localization device placement codes 19281–+19288 vary based on the type of guidance (for example, mammogram, stereotactic, ultrasound, and magnetic resonance) the provider uses. Breast localization device are small devices (for example, clip, wire/needle) used to mark the location of a breast abnormality to make it easier for the provider to find the target area during biopsy. The goal of the procedure is to locate and identify the site of the lesion prior to breast biopsy. These codes are only for the placement of the breast localization device. When an image-guided breast biopsy is performed with placement of a breast localization device you report codes 19081–19086.

In the CPT® Index, Lumpectomy refers to codes 19301–19302. The excision of a breast lesion identified by the preoperative placement of a radiological marker is reported as CPT® code 19125, and 19126 is for each additional, lesion identified separately by radiological marker.

A mastectomy is the surgical removal of one or both breasts. The term "double mastectomy" is used when both breasts are removed during one surgical setting. There are several types of mastectomy:

Complete—The breast tissue as well as the skin, nipple, and areola are removed. Use CPT® code 19303.

Gynecomastia—The term describes the abnormal enlargement of one breast or both breasts in men. Excess fat and breast tissue are removed from the breast area, generally by dissecting the tissue away from the pectoralis fascia. The skin, nipple, and areola remain intact. Use CPT® code 19300.

Modified Radical—This procedure describes removal of breast tissue and includes skin, nipple, areola, and axillary lymph nodes, with or without the pectoralis minor muscle. The procedure differs from the radical mastectomy, because the pectoralis major muscle is not removed. Use CPT® code 19307.

Partial—A portion of the breast tissue, which involves more than removal of a lesion or tumor, is described by this term. Some normal tissue in addition to the abnormal growth or lesion may be included. In some cases, as much as a quadrant or segment of breast tissue may be removed. Codes 19296–19298 are reported separately for the placement of radiotherapy afterloading balloon/brachytherapy catheters.

Radical—Breast tissue associated with skin, nipple, areola, axillary lymph nodes, pectoralis major, and minor muscles are removed. Use CPT® code 19305.

Simple—See the definition for "complete."

Urban—This type is similar to radical mastectomy but includes the internal mammary lymph nodes. Use CPT® code 19306.

Keep the following guidelines in mind when coding for a breast biopsy and mastectomy performed on the same day and during the same operative session:

1. If the malignancy was diagnosed previously by a biopsy and the surgeon takes breast tissue after the mastectomy to biopsy skin margins for signs of malignancy, the biopsy is not coded separately when a mastectomy also is performed.

2. If a breast biopsy was taken and a mastectomy was performed, the biopsy is "subsumed" as part of the larger operation and is not reported separately (AMA's Principles of *CPT® Coding*, 2001, p 131).

3. Codes 19081–19272 require a modifier 50, if bilateral.

4. The use of an operating microscope (69990) is inclusive to codes 19364 and 19368, and should not be reported separately.

5. CPT® code 19302 includes sentinel node removal.

Codes 19281 through 19288 describe preoperative placement of the breast localization devices. Devices such as clip, metallic pellet, wire/needle, radioactive seeds are differentiated by the type of guidance being used (mammographic, stereotactic, ultrasound or magnetic resonance). Add-on codes should be assigned for each additional lesion that is identified. After the patient has undergone mastectomy, the next step to consider is reconstruction. Under the heading of repair and/or reconstruction in CPT®, find breast reconstruction procedures, along with other breast surgeries.

A mastopexy is performed cosmetically or as a medically-necessary surgery to lift the breast. A reduction mammoplasty is done for patients having an abundance of breast tissue, and due to the enlargement of the breasts, have back, neck, and shoulder pain in addition to shoulder grooving. During this surgery, the surgeon removes excess tissue from each breast reducing the size of the patient's breast by several cup sizes. The decision on how much breast tissue is removed typically is based on the patient height, weight, and body frame. Another breast surgery is breast augmentation, which is done in breast reconstruction or cosmetically for patients unhappy with their current breast size.

There are times when a patient presents after undergoing a breast augmentation or implant placement in reconstruction where the implant has ruptured. In these cases, the implant and possibly the implant material must be removed. Not all cases allow for the implant to be replaced.

Reconstruction options for the mastectomy patient can start immediately or be delayed. CPT® 19340 describes immediate insertion of breast prosthesis following mastopexy, mastectomy or in reconstruction. This means the implant is placed at the same surgical session as the mastectomy. CPT® 19342 describes delayed insertion of breast prosthesis following mastopexy, mastectomy or in reconstruction. This means the implant is placed some time after the mastectomy surgery has had time to heal or after the patient has completed chemotherapy and/or radiation therapy.

In looking at possible options for breast reconstruction, four are considered the "most popular." We already discussed the immediate or delayed insertion of the breast prosthesis, which is one of the options. Another option is the immediate or delayed insertion of a tissue expander (CPT® 19357), which allows the skin to be stretched to allow for the placement of the breast prosthesis. These procedures typically are done in two stages: Placement of the tissue expander is first, followed by removal of the tissue expander with placement of the permanent prosthesis.

Another option might be CPT® 19361, which is breast reconstruction with latissimus dorsi flap, without prosthetic implant. In this surgery, the surgeon cuts away part of the latissimus muscle from the back and tunnels it through the body under the arm and brings it out through the old mastectomy scar, allowing a fresh muscle, good blood supply, and a "strong" anchor for a prosthetic implant to be placed if needed.

Another common breast reconstruction is the transverse rectus abdominis myocutaneous (TRAM) flap. This surgery is similar to the latissimus dorsi flap in that it takes a muscle and

moves it from one location to the chest wall for breast reconstruction. With the TRAM reconstruction, the patient is not only having breast reconstruction but is receiving a tummy tuck at the same time.

Other procedures on the breast are capsulotomy and capsulectomy. Capsulotomy is incision over the previous scar and creation of a larger pocket by cutting the scar tissue surrounding the implant. The capsulectomy is when the surgeon actually removes the scar tissue around the implant.

Section Review 7.4

1. Patient presents to the dermatologist for the removal of warts on his hands. Upon evaluation it is noted the patient has nine warts on his right hand and 10 on his left hand, all of which he has indicated he would like removed today. After discussion with the patient regarding the destruction method and aftercare the patient agreed to proceed. Using cryosurgery the physician applied two squirts of liquid nitrogen on each of the warts on his right and left hand. Aftercare instructions were given to the patient's wife. The patient tolerated the procedure well.

   What CPT® code(s) should be reported for this example?

   A. 17110, 17111

   B. 17111

   C. 17004

   D. 17111 x 19

2. Patient returns to the dermatologist after biopsies were done on several lesions. In discussing the pathology results with the patient, the physician indicated she had a superficial basal cell carcinoma (BCC) on her right cheek and left hand. The physician discussed the different treatment options with the patient and she decided to try cryosurgery to destroy the skin cancers. Informed consent was obtained. The physician noted the measurements of the BCC of the face to be 0.7 cm and the BCC on the left hand to be 1.2 cm prior to destruction.

   What are the correct CPT® codes to report for this example?

   A. 17311, 17312

   B. 17000, 17003

   C. 17270, 17280-51

   D. 17272, 17281-51

3. A patient has a squamous cell carcinoma on the tip of the nose. After prepping the patient and site, the physician removes the tumor (first stage) and divides it into seven blocks for examination. Seeing positive margins, he removes a second stage, which he divides into five blocks. The physician again identifies positive margins. He performs a third stage and divides the specimen into three blocks proving to be clear of the skin cancer.

   What are the correct CPT® codes to report for this example?

   A. 17311, 17312, 17312, 17315, 17315

   B. 17311, 17312, 17312

   C. 11640 x 3

   D. 11440 x 3

4. A patient presents for reduction of her left breast due to atrophy of the breast. After being prepped and draped, the surgeon makes a circular incision above the nipple to indicate where the nipple is to be relocated. Another incision is made around the nipple, and then two more incisions are made from the circular cut above the nipple to fold beneath the breast, which creates a keyhole shaped skin and breast incision. Skin wedges and tissue are removed until the surgeon is satisfied with the size. Electrocautery was performed on bleeding vessels and the nipple was elevated to its new position and the nipple pedicle was sutured with layered closure. The last incision was repaired with a layered closure as well.

    What is the correct CPT® code to report for this example?

    A. 19324-LT

    B. 19318-LT

    C. 19350-LT

    D. 19316-LT

5. A 32-year-old female is having excision of a mass in her left breast. The physician makes a curved incision along the inferior and medial aspect of the left areola. A breast nodule, measuring approximately 1 cm in diameter, was identified. It appeared to be benign. It was firm, gray, and discrete. It was completely excised. There was no gross evidence of malignancy. The bleeding was controlled with electrocautery. The skin edges were approximated with a continuous subcuticular 4-0 Vicryl suture. Indermil tissue adhesive was applied to the skin as well as a dry gauze dressing.

    What is the correct CPT® code to report for this example?

    A. 19120-LT

    B. 19125-LT

    C. 19301-LT

    D. 19370-LT

Medicine Section

Photodynamic Therapy (96567–96571)

Photodynamic therapy describes the ablation of tumorous tissue by activation of photoactive drugs. It involves use of external light application to destroy premalignant and/or malignant lesions of the skin and adjacent mucosa by activating photosensitive drugs. It is reported according to each phototherapy exposure.

Codes 96570 and 96571 are reported in addition to endoscopy or bronchoscopy procedures of the lung and esophagus. These codes are selected based on the time. Modifier 52 may be necessary if the time reported is less than 23 minutes.

Special Dermatological Procedures (96900–96999)

These CPT® codes describe special dermatology procedures frequently rendered on a consultative basis.

Actinotherapy involves exposing the patient's skin to ultraviolet light to treat skin disease, such as acne. Various light

sources and lamps are used to produce ultraviolet light. The length of exposure to ultraviolet radiation is calculated following a skin test for erythema (sunburn). The patient's eyes are protected during treatment by special dark glasses.

Photochemotherapy combines light (photo) and chemicals to deliver an effective treatment. Goeckerman treatment involves the topical application of tar (which makes lesions more sensitive to ultraviolet B light) or petrolatum and increasingly strong doses of ultraviolet B light. This form of therapy is used to treat psoriasis, eczema, or mycosis. Psoralens and ultraviolet A light help prevent the accelerated growth of immature skin cells characterizing psoriasis.

Code 96913 describes an aggressive form of photochemotherapy used to treat severe psoriasis. This photochemotherapy consists of Goeckerman and/or psoralens ultraviolet A treatment (PUVA) and the patient must be under the direct supervision of a provider for at least four to eight hours. This procedure is usually done in an inpatient setting and includes the reporting of application of medication and dressings.

Laser treatment for inflammatory skin disease (psoriasis) involves the use of a beam of laser light concentrated on active psoriatic skin plaques. Dosage depends on the results of an initial skin test. Codes are selected based on the size of the area treated in square centimeters.

HCPCS Level II Codes

Common HCPCS Level II codes used for the Integumentary System include:

G0127 Trimming of dystrophic nails, any number

G0168 Wound closure utilizing tissue adhesive(s) only

G0295 Electromagnetic therapy, to one or more areas, for wound care other than described in G0329 or for other uses

G0329 Electromagnetic therapy, to one or more areas for chronic Stage III and Stage IV pressure ulcers, arterial ulcers, diabetic ulcers and venous stasis ulcers not demonstrating measurable signs of healing after 30 days of conventional care as part of a therapy plan of care

There are additional codes in the A section of the HCPCS Level II codebook for dressing supplies.

Modifiers

Modifier 25—Significant, Separately Identifiable Evaluation and Management Service by the Same Physician on the Same Day of the Procedure or Other Service

Minor procedures to remove skin lesions are often performed in a provider's office. When a separately identifiable evaluation and management service is performed in addition to the minor procedure, modifier 25 should be appended to the E/M code.

Modifier 50—Bilateral Procedure

A bilateral procedure modifier may be reported for bilateral debridement when reporting codes 11010–11012. To qualify as a bilateral procedure, the same procedure must be done on both sides of the body. On occasion, this situation may arise with bilateral, heavily contaminated same site fractures.

Modifier 52—Reduced Services

Modifier 52 may be reported with CPT® code +96570 if the service time was less than 23 minutes for the photodynamic therapy.

Modifier 58—Staged or Related Procedure

When repeat debridement is warranted and/or fracture care is performed on a date other than the date of the wound debridement, add CPT® modifier 58 to the appropriate treatment codes to indicate it was a staged or related procedure.

Modifier 59—Distinct procedural service

Modifier 59 may be used when the evacuation of a subungual hematoma is reported on more than one nail during the same session.

In the treatment of burns, if the physician is required to perform dressings/debridement at different sessions or patient encounters on the same date, then modifier 59 may be used to accurately identify this circumstance. Services in this category provided on different dates are separately reported (*AMA CPT® Assistant*, Jan 1999, p. 4).

Documentation Dissection

Case 1—Excision

Preoperative Diagnosis: Suspicious lesion nose and left cheek

Postoperative Diagnosis: BCC nose, Compound nevus left cheek [1]

Procedure Performed: Excision, BCC nose with excised diameter of 1.4 cm with a 2.7 cm intermediate repair [2]

Excision compound nevus left cheek with excised diameter of 2.7 cm and an intermediate repair measuring 3.2 cm. [2]

Patient presents to the surgeon with suspicious lesions of the nose and cheek. With the patient's permission the surgeon marks the areas for excision. The patient observed the markings in the mirror and agreed on the location and surgery proceeded.

Patient was given 1 g of IV Ancef. The area of the nose and cheek were infiltrated with local anesthetic. The face and nose were prepped and draped in a sterile fashion. The surgeon excised the lesion on the nose as drawn into the subcutaneous fat. A suture was used to mark the specimen at its lateral tip and this was labeled at 12 o'clock. The wound was closed first in the deep subcutaneous tissue with 4-0 Monocryl, then in the dermis with 5-0 Monocryl and then the epidermis with 6-0 Prolene. [3] Attention was then turned to the left cheek. The surgeon excised the lesion on the cheek as drawn into the subcutaneous fat. A suture was used to mark the specimen at its lateral tip and this was labeled at 12 o'clock. The wound was closed in layers using 4-0 Monocryl and 6-0 Prolene. [4] Loupe magnification was used throughout the procedure and the patient tolerated the procedure well.

----

[1] Diagnosis is BCC (Basal Cell Carcinoma) on the nose which is malignant and Compound Nevus which is benign.

[2] Procedure for both lesions.

[3] Layered closure is reported as an intermediate closure.

[4] Supporting intermediate repair.

What are the CPT® and ICD-10-CM codes reported?

CPT® Codes: 12053, 11642-51, 11443-51

ICD-10-CM Codes: C44.311, D22.39

Both repairs are in the same anatomic category (nose and cheek) and both intermediate repairs with layered closure; therefore, the repairs are added together. 2.7 nose + 3.2 cheek equals 5.9 cm. Intermediate repair of the face, 5.9 cm is reported with 12053.

For the nose, the excision was 1.4 cm. This is a malignant lesion. Look in the CPT® Index for Excision/Skin/Lesion, Malignant and you are directed to a range of codes. 11640–11646 is for excision on the face. An excised diameter of 1.4 cm is reported with 11642. The excision on the cheek is benign. Look in the CPT® Index for Excision/Skin/Lesion, Benign and you are directed to a range of codes. Benign excisions on the face are selected from range 11440–11446. An excised diameter of 2.7 cm is reported with 11443. NCCI has no bundling issues with the listed codes therefore the only modifier that would be required would be 51 for multiple surgeries.

BCC is Basal Cell Carcinoma. Look in the Index to Diseases and Injuries (Alphabetic Index) for Carcinoma/basal cell (pigmented). You are directed to *see also* Neoplasm, skin, malignant C44.9. This is found in the Neoplasm Table located after the Index to Diseases and Injuries. If you have difficulty locating the Neoplasm Table, check the Table of Contents in your ICD-10-CM codebook. In the Neoplasm Table, look for Neoplasm, neoplastic/skin/nose (external). This directs you to (*see also* Neoplasm, nose, skin). Look for Neoplasm, neoplastic/nose/skin/basal cell carcinoma. The code from the malignant column is C44.311. In the Tabular List C44.311 is basal cell carcinoma of skin of nose.

For the compound nevus of the left cheek, look in the Index of Diseases and Injuries for Nevus/skin/cheek (external) D22.39. In the Tabular List category D22 is for Melanocytic nevi. The Includes notes under this category indicate nevus NOS. D22.39 is for Melanocytic nevi of other parts of face.

ICD-9-CM Application

What is/are the ICD-9-CM code(s) reported?

Code(s): 173.31, 216.3

Look in the Index to Diseases for Carcinoma/basal cell (pigmented) (M8090/3) (see also Neoplasm, skin, malignant. M8090/3 is referenced in ICD-9-CM Appendix A. This is not used in coding; however, you must know the meaning of the last digit/3. It tells you that basal cell carcinoma is malignant. Look in the Neoplasm Table for Neoplasm/nose/skin/basal cell carcinoma/Malignant 173.31. Next in the Index to Diseases look for Nevus/(M8720/0 —see also Neoplasm, skin, benign. Look in the Neoplasm Table for Neoplasm/skin/cheek (external)/Benign 216.3. Verify codes in the Tabular List.

Case 2

Preoperative Diagnosis: Squamous cell carcinoma, left lower eyelid

Postoperative Diagnosis: Squamous cell carcinoma, left lower eyelid [1]

Procedure Performed: Excision of squamous cell carcinoma of the left lower eyelid measuring 1.0 cm with a 2.0 cm squared rhomboid flap repair [2]

Indications for Surgery: The patient is an 80-year-old female with biopsy-proven squamous cell carcinoma of her left lower eyelid. With her permission Dr. Violet marked this area for excision with gross normal margins of 2 mm, and drew her planned rhomboid flap for repair. The patient observed these markings in a mirror so she could understand the surgery, agreed on the location and we proceeded.

Description of Procedure: The patient was given 1 g of IV Ancef. The area was infiltrated with local anesthetic. The face was prepped and draped in a sterile fashion. Dr. Violet then excised the lesion as drawn into the subcutaneous fat. Suture was used to mark the specimen at its medial tip and this was labeled 12 o'clock. Meticulous hemostasis had been achieved using Bovie cautery. Dr. Violet put a stitch initially in this wound to see if she could close it primarily; however, it was pulling down on the patient's lower eyelid or creating ectropion, and because of that she felt she needed to proceed with the planned rhomboid flap reconstruction. She incised the rhomboid flap as she had drawn it, elevating the flap with the full thickness of skin and subcutaneous fat and rotated into the defect. [3] The donor site was closed and the flap was inset in layers using 4-0 Monocryl, 5-0 Monocryl and 6-0 Prolene. Loupe magnification was used throughout the procedure, and the patient tolerated the procedure well.

_____

[1] Post operative diagnosis with location.
   Squamous cell carcinoma is a malignant lesion.

[2] Procedure performed.

[3] Supporting documentation for rotation/rhomboid flap.

_____

What are the CPT® and ICD-10-CM codes reported?

CPT® Code: 14060

ICD-10-CM Code: C44.129

CPT® code 14060 is used to describe the 2.0 cm squared flap repair, even though the procedure indicates the removal of the lesion, excision is included in the flap reconstruction. In the CPT® Index look for Skin Graft and Flap/Tissue Transfer directs you to codes range 14000-14350.

Look in the Index to Diseases and Injuries for Carcinoma (malignant) (*see also* Neoplasm, malignant, by site. Look for the Neoplasm Table at the end of the ICD-10-CM Index to Diseases and Injuries. Look for Neoplasm, neoplastic/eyelid (lower) (skin)(upper)/squamous cell carcinoma. The code from the malignant column is C44.12-. The dash indicates an additional character is required. In the Tabular List locate C44.12. The sixth character identifies the laterality. In this case, the neoplasm is on the left lower eyelid making C44.129 the correct code. C44.129 is for squamous cell carcinoma of skin of left eyelid, including canthus.

ICD-9-CM Application

What is/are the ICD-9-CM code(s) reported?

Code(s): 173.12

ICD-9-CM Code: 173.12

Look in the Index to Diseases for Carcinoma/squamous (cell) (M8070/03). The M code is not used in coding. This is a morphology code found in Appendix A of ICD-9-CM. You must know the meaning of the last digit for these codes. The /3 indicates a malignant neoplasm. Look in the Neoplasm Table for Neoplasm/skin/eyelid/squamous cell carcinoma/Malignant/Primary 173.12. Verify in the Tabular List. The code for squamous cell carcinoma of eyelid, including canthus is 173.12.

Case 3

Preoperative Diagnosis: Squamous Cell Carcinoma, left ear

Postoperative Diagnosis: Squamous Cell Carcinoma, left ear [1]

Procedure Performed: Excision, squamous cell carcinoma, left ear with excised diameter of 2.7 cm and a 5.0 cm squared full-thickness skin graft repair. [2]

Indications for Surgery: The patient is a 39-year-old male with biopsy proven squamous cell carcinoma of his left ear. With the patient's permission I marked the area for excision and my best guess at the resultant scar. Because of the size and location of this lesion I discussed with the patient the need for a full thickness skin graft for the repair. The patient observed the markings in a mirror so he could understand and I proceeded.

Description of Procedure: The patient was given 1 gm IV Ancef. The area of the ear was infiltrated with local anesthetic. The face and neck were prepped and draped in sterile fashion. I then excised the lesion as drawn into the subcutaneous fat. [3] A suture was used to mark the specimen at its lateral tip and this was labeled at 12 o'clock. Meticulous hemostasis was achieved using the Bovie cautery. I then harvested a full-thickness skin graft from the patient's left perauricular area as I had drawn. [4] This was defatted using scissors. It was then inset into the ear using 5-0 plain suture. Vents were made in the skin graft with a #11 blade to allow for the egress of fluid and then a Xeroform bolster was applied and affixed to the skin using 5-0 nylon suture. The skin graft donor site was closed in layers using 5-0 Monocryl and 6-0 Prolene. Loupe magnification was used throughout the procedure and the patient tolerated the procedure well.

---

[1] Post operative diagnosis with location.

[2] Procedure performed.

[3] Documentation supporting lesion removal.

[4] Documentation supporting full thickness skin graft.

What are the CPT® and ICD-10-CM codes reported?

CPT® Codes: 15260, 11643-51

ICD-10-CM Code: C44.229

CPT® code 15260 would be first applied for the skin graft under 20 square centimeters and also CPT® 11643 is appended for removal of the skin cancer of the ear. Modifier 51 is appended to 11643 to show multiple procedures. In the CPT® Index look for Skin Graft and Flap/Free Skin Graft/Full Thickness and you are directed to code range 15200–15261. Range of codes is chosen by the anatomical area and size. In the CPT® index look for Excision/Skin/Lesion, Malignant gives you a range of codes. Codes set 11640-11644 is for the ear.

Look in the Index to Diseases and Injuries for Carcinoma (malignant) (*see also* Neoplasm, malignant, by site. Look for the Neoplasm Table at the end of the the ICD-10-CM Index to Diseases and Injuries. In the Neoplasm Table, look for Neoplasm, neoplastic/ear (external)/skin/squamous cell carcinoma. The code from the malignant column is C44.22-. The dash indicates an additional character is required. In the Tabular List of Diseases and Injuries, locate C44.22. The sixth character identifies the laterality. In this case, the neoplasm is on the left ear making C44.229 the correct code. C44.229 is for squamous cell carcinoma of skin of left ear and external auricular canal.

ICD-9-CM Application

What is/are the ICD-9-CM code(s) reported?

Code(s): 173.22

Look in the Index to Diseases for Carcinoma/squamous (cell) (M8070/03). The M code is not used in coding. This is a morphology code found in Appendix A of ICD-9-CM. You must know the meaning of the last digit for these codes. The /3 indicates a malignant neoplasm. Look in the Neoplasm Table for Neoplasm/skin/ear (external)/squamous cell carcinoma/Malignant/Primary 173.22. Verify in the Tabular List. Squamous cell carcinoma of skin of ear and external auditory canal is coded with 173.22.

Case 4

Preoperatiave Diagnosis: Macromastia, Back Pain, Neck Pain, Shoulder Pain

Postoperative Diagnosis: Macromastia, Back Pain, Neck Pain, Shoulder Pain [1]

Procedure Performed:
Right breast reduction of 320 grams [2]
Left breast reduction of 340 grams [2]

Indications for Surgery: The patient is a 47-year-old female with macromastia and associated back pain, neck pain and shoulder pain. She desires a breast reduction. In the pre-operative holding area I marked her for inferior central pedicle technique. I then performed a manual breast exam, which showed no mass in either breast or axillae.

Description of Procedure: The patient was taken to the operative suite. Bilateral knee-hi TED hose were worn, as well as pneumatic compression stockings throughout the procedure. A lower body bear hugger was placed. General anesthesia was induced. One gram of IV Ancef was given. Both arms were secured to padded arm boards using Kerlix rolls. The neck, chest, axillae, and upper abdomen were prepped and draped in sterile fashion. I then began by circumscribing around each areola using a 42 mm areolar marker. The inferior central pedicle on either side was then deepithelialized. I began on the right side, medial, lateral and superior skin flaps were raised in thickness of about 2 cm. Meticulous hemostasis was achieved using the Bovie cautery. The tissue between the elevated flaps and the inferior central pedicle was then excised. This wound was then temporarily closed using the skin stapler. [3]

Attention was then directed to the left breast, again medial, lateral and superior skin flaps were raised in thickness of about 2 cm. The tissue between the elevated flaps and the inferior central pedicle was then excised. Meticulous hemostasis had been achieved using the Bovie cautery. This wound was also temporarily closed using the skin stapler. [4] The patient was then sat up. I felt that I had achieved a very symmetrical result. The new position of the nipple areolar complex was then marked using a 38 mm areolar marker and methylene blue. I was satisfied with the position of the nipple areolar complexes, the patient was placed supine. The new position for the nipple areolar complexes were then de-epithelialized bilaterally. Incision was made in the dermis and on each side. The nipple areolar complexes were matured and inset in layers. Using 3-0 Monocryl, both interrupted and running suture and 5-0 Prolene, the vertical and transverse incisions were closed in similar fashion. The wounds were dressed with Xeroform and gauze. The patient tolerated the procedure well. She was taken to the recovery room in good condition.

----

[1] Post operative diagnosis.

[2] Procedure performed with grams removed.

[3] Description of procedure for right breast.

[4] Description of procedure for left breast.

What are the CPT® and ICD-10-CM codes reported?

CPT® Code: 19318-50

ICD-10-CM Code: N62

The correct CPT® code for this procedure is 19318-50. Code 19318 describes mammoplasty reduction; modifier 50 is necessary due to the surgery being bilateral. In the CPT® Index look for Mammaplasty/Reduction directs you to code 19318.

Macromastia is female breast hypertrophy and can cause neck pain, back pain and shoulder pain. The diagnosis is macromastia; therefore, the symptoms of pain are not coded separately. Look in the ICD-10-CM Index to Diseases and Injuries for Macromastia. You are directed to *see* Hypertrophy, breast. Look in the Index for Hypertrophy/breast N62. In the Tabular List N62 is for hypertrophy of breast.

ICD-9-CM Application

What is/are the ICD-9-CM code(s) reported?

Code(s): 611.1

Macromastia is female breast hypertrophy and can cause neck pain, back pain and shoulder pain. Since the diagnosis is macromastia, the symptoms of pain are not coded separately. Look in the Index to Diseases for Macromastia 611.1 Verify in the Tabular List.

Glossary

Actinic Keratosis—A premalignant warty lesion occurring on sun-exposed skin of the face or hands in aged light-skinned people.

Alopecia—Loss of hair.

Basal Cell Carcinoma—A slow growing malignant neoplasm.

Benign Lesion—A tumor not forming metastases, and not invading and destroying adjacent normal tissue.

Biopsy—Removal of tissue from a patient for macroscopic diagnostic examination.

Congenital Nevus—A melanocytic nevus visible at birth, often larger than an acquired nevus.

Contact Dermatitis—Acute or chronic dermatitis caused by initial irritant effect of a substance coming in contact with the skin.

Debridement—Removal of foreign materials, necrotic matter, and devitalized tissue from a wound or burn.

Decubitus Ulcer—Focal ischemic necrosis of skin and underlying tissues at sites of constant pressure or recurring friction.

Dermabrasion—Procedure used to remove acne scars or pits, performed with sandpaper or other abrasive materials.

Dermatofibroma—A slowly-growing, benign skin nodule consisting of poorly demarcated cellular fibrous tissue.

Dermatologist—A physician specializing in diagnosing and treating cutaneous and related systemic diseases.

Dermatome—An instrument for cutting thin slices of skin for grafting or excising small lesions.

Dermis—Directly below the epidermis, the dermis is the second layer of the skin.

Dysplastic Nevus—Cutaneous pigmented lesions with notched, irregular borders, considered pre-malignant.

Epidermis—Outer layer of the skin.

Eschar—A thick, crusty covering or slough developing after thermal or chemical burn or cauterization of the skin.

Gynecomastia—Excessive development of the male mammary glands.

Impetigo—A contagious superficial pyoderma, caused by Staph or group A Strep.

Intradermal Nevus—A nevus in which nests of melanocytes are found in the dermis, but not at the epidermal-dermal junction.

Keloid—A nodular, firm, often linear mass of hyperplastic, thick scar tissue.

Lumpectomy—Surgical removal of a tumor or other lump from the breast along with some surrounding tissue, conserving normal breast appearance.

Mammaplasty—Plastic surgery for altering the breast(s) size by enlarging or reducing the breasts.

Mastectomy—Surgical removal of one or both breasts to treat or prevent breast cancer.

Mastopexy—Plastic surgical fixation in doing a breast(s) lift or reshape the breast(s) to improve the look of sagging breast(s).

Mycoses—Any disease caused by a fungus.

Necrosis—Pathologic death of one or more cells, or of a portion of tissue or organ, resulting from irreversible damage.

Nevus—A circumscribed malformation of the skin, especially one that is colored by hyperpigmentation.

Pilonidal Cyst—Hair-containing cyst or sinus in the tissues of the sacrococcygeal area.

Pruritis—Relating to itching.

Psoriasis—A common inherited condition characterized by the eruption of reddish, silvery-scaled maculopapules.

Sebaceous Cyst—A common cyst of the skin and subcutis containing sebum and keratin.

Seborrhea—Overactivity of the sebaceous gland, resulting in an excessive amount of sebum.

Introduction

In this chapter we will look at how muscles and bones work together to form the framework for the body, and the many procedures used to keep this system in shape.

Objectives

- Understand the components of the musculoskeletal system
- Define key terms
- Understand the most common pathologies affecting these organs
- Understand orthopedic surgeries and how they relate to pathological conditions
- Recognize common eponyms and acronyms
- Identify when other sections of CPT® or ICD-10-CM should be accessed
- Know when HCPCS Level II codes or modifiers are appropriate

Anatomy and Medical Terminology

The musculoskeletal system contains 206 bones and more than 600 muscles, as well as ligaments, tendons, and cartilage.

The skeleton is divided into two parts: The axial skeleton and the appendicular skeleton. The axial skeleton consists of the bones of the skull, the chest, and the spine. The appendicular skeleton includes the remaining bones of the upper and lower limbs, shoulders, and pelvis.

The primary functions of the musculoskeletal system are to provide protection for the internal organs and to assist with movement. The skeleton is the basic framework for the entire body, and the bones store calcium and produce blood cells. The muscles assist with heat production, locomotion, and posture. Ligaments attach bones to other bones, and tendons attach muscles to bones. Cartilage acts as a cushion between bones in a joint.

Proficiency in coding for the musculoskeletal system requires a good working knowledge of human anatomy including location, function, and movement of all structures involved. An understanding of surgical terms used to describe procedures performed will provide additional confidence when choosing appropriate codes. There are many eponyms and acronyms

used in orthopedic surgery; a good medical dictionary is essential. Many fracture types are named after a person (eponym), and procedures are often described using acronyms (for example, ORIF is the acronym for open reduction internal fixation).

There are three basic muscle types: striated (skeletal) muscle, smooth (visceral) muscle, and cardiac muscle. The musculoskeletal system includes mostly striated muscle, which helps control body movement. Cardiac muscle is found in the heart and great vessels such as the aorta. Smooth muscle is involuntary muscle found in the internal organs, such as in the bowels and blood vessels.

Muscles can be named based on their size (gluteus maximus), shape (the deltoid is shaped like a delta or triangle), location (the sternocleidomastoid is attached to the sternum, clavicle, and mastoid process), action (flexor carpi ulnaris), number of attachments (the triceps brachii has a three-headed origin), or the direction of its fibers (the fibers of the transverse abdominus run horizontally).

When muscles are named for their action, words like flexor and extensor are often included in the name. Names of muscle action include:

Flexor—Causes flexion or bending of a limb or body part.

Extensor—Causes straightening of a limb or body part.

Adductor—Moves a part of the body towards the midline of the body.

Abductor—Moves a part of the body away from the midline of the body.

Pronator—Turns a part downward or backward by rotating.

Supinator—Turns a part upward or forward by rotating.

There are many different types of bones, and each has a specific function. Long bones such as the femur, tibia, and fibula in the legs and the humerus, radius, and ulna in the arms have large surface areas for muscle attachment. Short bones can be found in the wrists and ankles. Flat bones are found covering soft body parts; these are the shoulder blades, pelvic bones, and ribs. Sesamoid bones are shaped like sesame seeds, and are found near a joint, (for example, the patella or kneecap). Irregular bones are other various shapes (for instance, the vertebrae or facial bones such as the zygoma).

Types of Bones

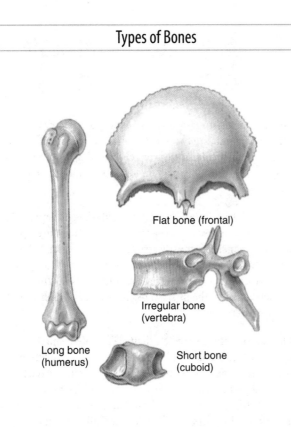

Flat bone (frontal)

Irregular bone (vertebra)

Long bone (humerus)

Short bone (cuboid)

Source: Rizzo, Fundamentals of Anatomy and Physiology, 3e, ISBN #978-1-4354-3871-2

Axilla (Axillary Mass)

A term often used to refer to the armpit area is the axilla. The axilla is the space below the glenohumeral joint which is bound by the pectoralis major anteriorly, the latissimus dorsi posteriorly, the serratus anterior medially, and the humerus laterally. There are numerous lymph nodes in this area as well as muscles and other tissue. The posterior axillary fold refers to topographical anatomy, and is composed of skin and muscular tissue of the latissimus dorsi and teres major. This is located on the back side of the armpit. The back side would be considered the back/flank. There are also times when the axilla may refer to the upper arm. When the term "axilla" is used, you will need to read further in the documentation to clarify the location or query the provider.

Fractures and Dislocations

Common injuries of the musculoskeletal system include fractures and dislocations. Understanding the terminology associated with fractures and dislocations—as well as their care, is essential to accurate coding.

There are many fracture eponyms. These often are named after the physician who first documented or described the fracture or the treatment. Common eponyms include:

Colles' Fracture—A fracture of the wrist at the distal radius. Sometimes the ulnar styloid also is involved.

Smith's Fracture—Similar to a Colles' fracture, except the bones are displaced toward the palm.

Jones Fracture—A stress fracture of the fifth metatarsal of the foot.

Salter-Harris Fracture—An epiphyseal plate fracture; a common injury seen in children.

Dupuytren's Fracture—Fracture of the distal fibula with rupture of the distal tibiofibular ligaments and lateral displacement of the talus.

Monteggia's Fracture—Fracture of the proximal third of the ulna with associated dislocation of the radial head.

Section Review 8.1

1. A Colles' fracture is a fracture of what part of the body?

    A. Elbow

    B. Wrist

    C. Knee

    D. Ankle

2. In the CPT® codebook, 25000 and 25001 are for incisions in the tendon sheath on the wrist. 25000 is for the extensor tendon and 25001 is for the flexor tendon sheath. What is the difference between extension and flexion?

    A. Extension causes bending of the wrist; flexion causes straightening of the wrist.

    B. Extension causes straightening of the wrist; flexion causes bending of the wrist.

    C. Extension causes the wrist to move forward by rotating; flexion causes the wrist to move backward by rotating.

    D. Extension causes the wrist to move backward by rotating; flexion causes the wrist to move forward by rotating.

3. In the CPT® codebook, 28400 and 28405 are used when coding a calcaneal fracture. What is the difference between these two codes?

    A. One includes internal fixation and one does not

    B. One is for a foot fracture and one is for an ankle fracture

    C. One includes manipulation and one does not

    D. One requires surgery and one does not

4. This type of connective tissue attaches a muscle to a bone:

    A. Ligament

    B. Vein

    C. Vertebra

    D. Tendon

5. The muscles that help control movement of the body, maintain posture, and help produce heat are of what type?

    A. Striated or skeletal

    B. Smooth or visceral

    C. Cardiac

    D. Involuntary

ICD-10-CM Coding

In ICD-10-CM, Chapter 13 is the Diseases of the Musculoskeletal System and Connective Tissue and Chapter 18 is Symptoms, Signs and Abnormal Clinical and Laboratory Findings. Chapter 19 is Injury, Poisoning and Certain Other Consequences of External Causes. Traumatic fracture diagnosis codes will be found in this chapter. Most of the codes within chapter 13 have site and laterality designations.

Example:

Idiopathic gout, elbow

    M10.021 Idiopathic gout, **right** elbow

    M10.022 Idiopathic gout, **left** elbow

    M10.029 Idiopathic gout, **unspecified** elbow

The site may be the bone, joint or muscle involved. When more than one bone, muscle or joint is involved there is a "multiple sites" code available such as M12.59 which is used for traumatic arthropathy, multiple sites. When a multiple sites code is not available, multiple codes should be used to indicate the different sites.

ICD-9-CM Application

Many ICD-9-CM codes used for the musculoskeletal system are found in Chapter 13 Diseases of the Musculoskeletal System and Connective Tissue. Relevant codes also may be found in other chapters, including Chapter 16: Signs, Symptoms and Ill-Defined Conditions, and Chapter 17: Injury and Poisoning.

Example

Category 715 Osteoarthrosis and allied disorders. The note below this category indicates that localized in the subcategories below, includes bilateral involvement of the same site.

Primary localized arthritis of both knees is reported with 715.16.

Many codes in this section require a fifth digit; these fifth digits are consistent throughout much of ICD-9-CM chapter 13. These are:

0—Site unspecified

1—Shoulder region (Acromioclavicular joint(s), Clavicle, Glenohumeral joint(s), Scapula, Sternoclavicular Joint(s))

2—Upper arm (Elbow Joint, Humerus)

3—Forearm (Radius, Ulna, Wrist joint)

4—Hand (Carpus, Metacarpus, Phalanges (Fingers))

5—Pelvic region and thigh (Buttock, Femur, Hip (joint))

6—Lower leg (Fibula, Knee joint, Patella, Tibia)

7—Ankle and foot (Ankle joint, Digits [toes], Metatarsus, Phalanges, foot, Tarsus, Other joints in foot)

8—Other specified sites (Head, Neck, Ribs, Skull, Trunk, Vertebral Column)

Because the full codes are site specific, the fifth digit classification no longer applies in ICD-10-CM.

Example

Effusion of right ankle joint.

ICD-10-CM

Look in the Index to Diseases and Injuries for Effusion/joint/ankle. In the Tabular List, code M25.47- Effusion, ankle and foot requires the application of a sixth character to specify the location (foot or ankle) and laterality.

M25.471 Effusion, right ankle

ICD-9-CM

Look in the Index to Diseases for Effusion/joint/ankle. In the Tabular List, code 719.0 requires the application of a fifth digit to specify the location of the effusion. There is no specification of laterality in ICD-9-CM.

719.07 Effusion of joint, ankle and foot

Codes for the musculoskeletal system can be considered acute or chronic. Most of the acute conditions are coded from chapter 19: Injury and Poisoning and Certain Other Consequences of External Causes (S00–T88) of ICD-10-CM. Most chronic or recurrent conditions are coded from chapter 13: Diseases of the Musculoskeletal System and Connective Tissue (M00–M99).

Diseases of the Musculoskeletal System and Connective Tissue (M00–M99)

Arthropathies (M00–M25)

Systemic lupus erythematosus (M32) or lupus, is an autoimmune inflammatory connective tissue disease that affects multiple body systems. Manifestations can occur in the joints, skin, cardiopulmonary system, spleen, neurologic system, renal system, hematologic system, and gastrointestinal system. It is more common in women, and the cause is unknown. In ICD-10-CM the manifestations of systemic lupus are included in the code, such as endocarditis in systemic lupus (M32.11) and lung involvement in systemic lupus (M32.13).

An arthropathy is pathology or an abnormality of a joint, and arthritic conditions are classified in this section. Many of the arthropathy codes require the use of another code first to specify an underlying disease. Rheumatoid arthritis (RA) (category M05) is a chronic systemic autoimmune disease involving the joints. Inflammation of the peripheral joints is symmetrical in RA. These codes are listed based on rheumatoid arthritis with other conditions such as splenoadenomegaly, lung disease, vasculitis and heart diseases, along with site, with or without rheumatoid factor, and laterality.

Osteoarthritis (OA) (category M15–M19) is the most common joint disorder. Symptoms include gradual onset of pain, stiffness, and occasional joint swelling. To accurately code osteoarthritis in ICD-10-CM, the documentation must include whether the arthritis is primary, secondary, or post-traumatic, the site, and laterality (right/left).

ICD-9-CM Application

Looking up Osteoarthritis in the ICD-9-CM Index to Diseases will direct you to "*see also* Osteoarthrosis." .

Example

Primary osteoarthritis of the left shoulder.

ICD-9-CM

In the ICD-9-CM Index to Diseases, Osteoarthritis refers you to Osteoarthrosis. Osteoarthrosis directs you to code 715.9 which requires a fifth-digit subclassification. There is no index entry for primary under osteoarthrosis.

715.91 Osteoarthrosis, unspecified whether generalized or localized. Fifth digit 1 lists shoulder region.

ICD-10-CM

To assign an ICD-10-CM code for primary osteoarthritis of the left shoulder, look in the Index to Diseases and Injuries for Osteoarthritis/primary/shoulder M19.01-. In the Tabular List, code M19.01- requires a sixth character to indicate the laterality.

M19.012 Primary osteoarthritis, left shoulder

Category M23 lists internal derangements of the knee. The medial collateral (MCL) and anterior cruciate (ACL) ligaments are the most commonly injured knee structures. The codes in this section are for chronic or old conditions. Acute conditions are reported from category S83 Dislocation and sprain of joints and ligaments of knee.

Major Ligaments of the Knee

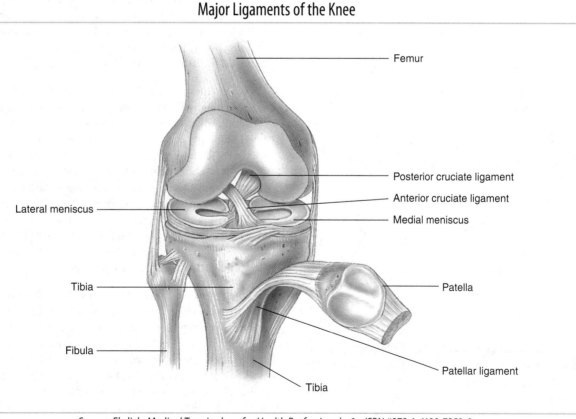

Source: Ehrlich, Medical Terminology for Health Professionals, 6e, ISBN #978-1-4180-7252-0

Another common derangement is chronic bucket handle tear of the lateral meniscus, M23.2-. A bucket handle tear occurs when an inside portion of the meniscus tears off, staying attached on both sides, and creating what looks like a bucket handle.

Dorsopathies (M40–M54)

Dorsopathies are disorders affecting the spinal column. Many of the codes listed here are sub classified according to what part of the spine is affected: cervical, thoracic, or lumbar. The fourth character classifies the type of disorder, and the fifth character the area of the spine. Diseases included in this section include kyphosis and lordosis, scoliosis, spondylosis, displacement of a vertebral disc, degenerative disc disease, and radiculopathy. Symptoms such as neck pain (M54.2 *Cervicalgia*), low back pain (M54.5 *Lumbago*), lumbago with sciatica (M54.4-), and unspecified backache (M54.9) also are found in this section.

ICD-9-CM Application

ICD-9-CM

In ICD-9-CM Index to Diseases, lumbago and lumbalgia have two code choices available:

Lumbago 724.2

    due to displacement, intervertebral disc 722.10

Lumbalgia 724.2

    due to displacement, intervertebral disc 722.10

Lumbago and lumbalgia have more expanded code options in ICD-10-CM than in ICD-9-CM.

ICD-10-CM

In ICD-10-CM Index to Diseases and Injuries, lumbago has expanded code selection:

Lumbago, lumbalgia M54.5

    with sciatica M54.4-

        due to intervertebral disc disorder M51.17

        due to displacement, intervertebral disc M51.27

    with sciatica M51.17

Spondylosis is osteoarthritis of the spine. Spondylitis is inflammation of the spine. Ankylosis is the stiffening of the joint. Ankylosing spondylitis is more common in men than in women.

Intervertebral disc disorders (M50–M51) include displaced discs, ruptured discs, Schmorl's nodes, and degenerative disc disease. The code selection is based on the disorder and the location of the disorder within the spine (cervical, thoracic, or lumbar).

Spinal stenosis (M48) is narrowing of the spinal canal. The narrowing puts pressure on the nerves, causing pain, parasthesias, weakness, or diminished reflexes. Spinal stenosis is coded based on the region of the stenosis within the spine. There is no listing in ICD-10-CM for lumbar spinal stenosis with neurogenic claudication. Neurogenic claudication is included in M48.0-. Neurogenic claudication presents as pain in the low back, buttock, thigh, and leg. It is precipitated by walking and prolonged standing. The pain is classically relieved by a change in position or flexion of the waist and not simply relieved by rest, as in vascular claudication.

The term rheumatism is a non-specific term for any painful disorder of joints, muscles, or connective tissues. These conditions are listed in ICD-10-CM under Disorders of synovium and tendon (M65–M67). Synovitis is a condition that causes joint tenderness and swelling of a joint and can be very painful. This occurs when the synovial lining of the joint becomes inflamed. When the protective lining of the tendon sheath becomes inflamed and is referred to as tenosynovitis. Category M65 contains codes for trigger finger, a condition in the tendon that causes the finger to jerk or snap straight when extending the hand. Category M67 contains codes for ganglion of the joint or tendon. A ganglion is a benign (nonmalignant) cyst that occurs above a tendon or on a joint, most commonly found on the hand or wrist.

Enthesopathies are disorders of ligaments. Capsulitis (also called synovitis) is inflammation of the tissues surrounding the joint. Adhesive capsulitis of the shoulder (M75.0-) is reduction in mobility of the shoulder, often referred to as frozen shoulder. Tendonitis is inflammation of a tendon. Tenosynovitis is inflammation of the tendon and the tendon sheath lining. Radial styloid tenosynovitis (M65.4) also is known as de Quervain's disease, and is caused by repetitive movement of the wrist. Bursitis is an inflammation of the bursa, which are small fluid-filled sacs located between movable parts of the body, especially at the joints. Synovitis, tendonitis, tenosynovitis, and bursitis all are coded by location.

Compartment syndrome is the compression of nerves and blood vessels within an enclosed space. This leads to muscle and nerve damage and problems with blood flow. Thick layers of tissue, called fascia, separate groups of muscles in the arms and legs from each other. Inside each layer of fascia is a confined space called a compartment that includes the muscle tissue, nerves, and blood vessels. If an injury occurs to this area, swelling of the tissue can cause compression and damage—and, if not treated, potential loss of the limb.

Compartment syndrome can be traumatic or non-traumatic. Non-traumatic compartment syndrome codes are located in subcategory M79.A *Nontraumatic compartment syndrome* with instructions to code first, if applicable, associated postprocedural complication. This subcategory is further divided by upper and then lower extremities, and laterality. Throughout ICD-10-CM there are a few subcategories that include an alphabetic character as the fourth character. For example, M79.A is located between subcategories M79.7 and M79.8. Traumatic compartment syndrome is found in subcategory T79.A *Traumatic compartment syndrome*. Again these codes are further divided by site and laterality. The codes in subcategory T79.A require seven characters as indicated under category T79.

Bunions are common problems disorders. Most often, acquired deformities of the toe (Hallux valgus, hallux varus, hallux rigidus, hammertoe, etc.) are found in category Other Joint Disorders (M20-M25). The Index to Diseases and Injuries for Bunions directs you to — *see* Deformity, toe, hallux valgus. Congenital deformities of the toe are rare, and are found in subcategory Q66.9.

Osteopathies and Chondropathies (M80–M94)

This section includes codes for osteomyelitis, osteoporosis, pathologic fractures (bone fractures caused by disease, not accident or injury), stress fractures, and spine deformities.

Osteomyelitis (M86) is an inflammation of the bone and/or bone marrow caused by infection. Code selection is based on whether it is acute, subacute, or chronic, and by site and laterality. There are instructions with this category to use an additional code (B95–B97) to identify infectious agent and to identify major osseous defect, if applicable (M89.7-). Further directions are given for additional codes under M89.7.

Osteochondropathies (categories M91-M94) categorizes various conditions such as osteochondrosis. This disease causes degeneration of the ossification centers found in the epiphyses of the bone and is often seen in children experiencing periods of rapid growth.

Osteoporosis (M80) is a bone disease that decreases bone density. It is coded based on the type such as age-related or other, and with or without current pathologic fracture. The loss of bone mass can cause pathologic fractures. Pathologic fractures (M84.4-) occur in weakened bone when mild or minimal force is applied. Stress fractures (M84.3-) occur from repetitive application of force. Both pathologic fractures and stress fractures require seven characters. A list of the acceptable seventh character is listed under each subcategory.

Pathologic Fracture—A fracture caused by disease, such as an infection or a tumor leading to weakness of the bone. Most

often the cause is osteoporosis. There are three subcategories for pathological fractures in ICD-10-CM:

- Pathological fracture, not elsewhere classified M84.4-
- Pathological fracture in neoplastic disease M84.5
- Pathological fracture in other disease M84.6

Subcategory M84.4 is used for chronic fracture or pathological fracture, NOS. Pathological fracture in neoplastic disease instructs to code also the underlying neoplasm. Pathological fracture in other disease instructs to code also the underlying condition. All of these codes require seven characters with the last character indicating the episode of care. Remember to use X as a placeholder if needed. Example: Pathological fracture, other site M84.48-. If this is the initial first encounter report M84.48XA.

For pathological fractures in osteoporosis use M80.-. For category M80 Osteoporosis, you are instructed to use an additional code to identify major osseous defect, if applicable (M89.7).

Traumatic fractures are coded in the chapter 19: Injury, Poisoning, and Certain Other Consequences of External Causes (S00-T88) section.

Curvature of the spine is found under deforming dorsopathies (M40–M43) which includes lordosis (curvature of the lumbar spine), kyphosis (curvature of the thoracic spine), and scoliosis. Scoliosis is curvature of the spine to the right and left. Most curves are convex to the right in the thoracic area and to the left in the lumbar area.

Injury, Poisoning and Certain Other Consequences of External Causes (S00–T88)

Sprains and Strains

A sprain (or strain) is the twisting or stretching of a joint in a way that causes pain and damage to a ligament. There is a very subtle difference between a sprain and a strain, according to the American Medical Association. A sprain involves the non-contractile tissue (the ligament) and a strain involves the contractile tissue (muscle or tendon).

Sprains and strains are coded based on their location.

Dislocations

Dislocations are injuries that occur when the joint is moved or forced out of the normal position. The joint is the place where two or more of the bones come together and allows for movement of the area. ICD-10-CM has code choices for dislocations that include the extent of the dislocation, as well as the position of the dislocation. A complete dislocation is also known as a luxation.

Dislocations of some joints have subcategories that classify the position of the dislocation: anterior, posterior, inferior, or lateral. Anterior dislocation is to the front of the normal position, posterior is behind the normal position. Interior dislocations are forced against the acromiumacromion and causes the arm to lock. Lateral dislocation occurs when the end of the bone is displaced laterally.

Nursemaid's Elbow

Nursemaid's elbow is a partial dislocation of the elbow, or proximal radial head dislocation. It is most common in small children and is caused by a sudden pull on the child's arm or hand. It is rarely seen in older children because the muscles and ligaments are stronger. Usually, it is treated easily by manipulating the elbow into a flexed position while rotating the forearm.

Nursemaid's elbow is found in the ICD-10-CM Index to Diseases and Injuries under *Nursemaid's/elbow S53.03-*. The Tabular List shows a sixth character is needed for laterality.

Practical Coding Note

Understanding terminology for dislocations will be necessary for accurate coding in ICD-10-CM.

- Subluxation is a partial or incomplete dislocation of the joint
- Dislocation Is a complete dislocation of the joint

Fractures

A fracture is the traumatic or pathologic breaking of a bone or cartilage. There are many types of fractures, and many treatments for these fractures. In ICD-10-CM, fractures usually are classified either as open or closed.

Examples of closed fractures:

- **Comminuted**—The bone is crushed or splintered into several pieces.
- **Compression Impacted**—The bone is compressed onto another bone caused by trauma or osteoporosis and common in vertebrae.
- **Depressed**—Fracture typically resulting from blunt force trauma to the skull. There is a portion of the bone that is pushed in.
- **Greenstick**—The bone is broken on one surface and bent on the other (think of the way a "green" twig will break when bent too far); this fracture occurs in children before the bones have hardened.
- **Impacted**—One part of a bone is driven forcefully into another.

- **Simple**—The bone is broken in only one place.
- **Torus or Incomplete**—One side of the bone buckles. This is mostly common in children because of their softer bones.

Examples of open fractures—The bone breaks in such a way that bone fragments stick out through the skin or a wound penetrates down to the broken bone:

- Compound
- Infected
- Missile
- Puncture
- With foreign body

Types of Fractures

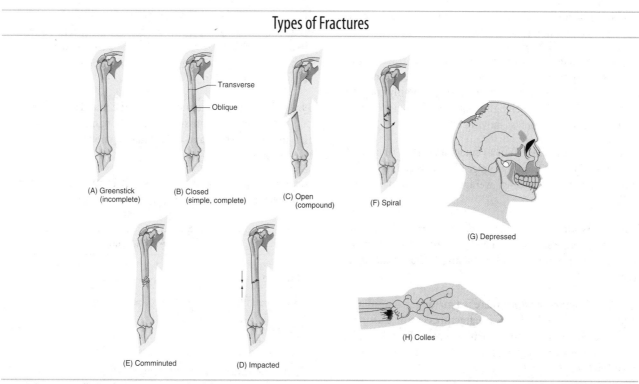

Source: Lindh, Pooler, Tamparo, and Dahl, Delmar's Comprehensive Medical Assisting (Administrative and Clinical Competencies), 4e, ISBN#978-1-4354-1914-8

ICD-10-CM lists fractures by anatomical site, type, and laterality. Further documentation in the medical record helps to choose any other specifics about the fracture (eg, pathological, what part of the bone, etc.). Many fractures are listed also by their eponyms: Hill-Sachs, Smith's fracture, etc.

Fracture types are classified differently than fracture treatments. It is important to distinguish the fracture from the treatment. The index of ICD-10-CM lists fractures by anatomical site, whether they are displaced or nondisplaced, and by other specific descriptions.

A closed fracture is one that has not broken the skin. The treatment for a closed fracture can be "closed," for example, by placing a cast, manipulating the bone without surgery, or applying traction to reduce the fracture. The treatment for a closed fracture also could be "open," in which the fracture site is opened surgically to reduce the fracture and screws or plates are applied to stabilize the fracture.

An open fracture is one where the bone is protruding through the skin. The treatment for an open fracture could be an "open" treatment, in which surgery is required to re-align the bones, or "closed," in which traction is applied to re-align the bones and the wound is sutured.

A fracture not indicated as open or closed is coded to closed. A fracture not indicated whether displaced or nondisplaced

is coded to displaced. When coding multiple injuries, code the most serious injury as determined by the provider and the focus of the treatment first. Fractures of specific sites are coded individually by site in accordance with both the provisions within categories and the level of detail furnished by medical record content.

Aftercare Z codes should not be used for aftercare for traumatic fractures. Assign the acute fracture codes with the appropriate 7th character. For example, aftercare of a torus fracture of the upper end of the right radius is S52.111D.

Gustillo Classification

Open fracture designations are based on the Gustilo open fracture classification. 7th characters are added to indicate the type of encounter. This classification is grouped into three major category types to indicate the mechanism of the injury, soft tissue damage, and the degree of skeletal involvement. One of the main categories, Type III, is further subdivided into IIIA, IIIB, and IIIC to report levels of extensive damage.

Type I Wound less than 1 cm with minimal soft tissue injury; wound bed clean, bone injury is simple with minimum comminution; with intramedullary nailing, average time to union is 21-28 weeks.

Type II Wound is greater than 1 cm with moderate soft tissue injury; wound bed is moderately contaminated; fracture contains moderate comminution; with intramedually nailing, average time to union is 26-28 weeks.

Type III Segmental fracture with displacement; fracture with diaphyseal segmental loss; fracture with associated vascular injury requiring repair; farmyard injuries or highly contaminated wounds; high velocity gunshot wound; fracture caused by crushing force from fast-moving vehicle.

Type IIIA Wound is less than 10 cm with crushed tissue and contamination; soft tissue coverage of bone is usually possibly; with intramedullary nailing, average time to union is 30-35 weeks.

Type IIIB Wound greater than 10 cm with crushed tissue and contamination; soft tissue is inadequate and requires regional or free flap; with intramedullary nailing, average time to union is 30-35 weeks.

Type IIIC Fracture in which there is a major vascular injury requiring repair for limb salvage; fractures can be classified using the MESS (Mangled Extremity Severity Score); in some cases it will be necessary to consider BKA following initial tibial fracture.

Compartment Syndrome

Compartment Syndrome usually is caused by an injury. As previously discussed, compartment syndrome is the compression of nerves and blood vessels within an enclosed space. This leads to muscle and nerve damage, and problems with blood flow.

Compartment syndrome in the ICD-10-CM Index to Diseases and Injuries directs you to codes grouped by cause (whether non-traumatic, post-surgical, or traumatic) and anatomical site. Postprocedural compartment syndrome is not listed in ICD-10-CM. You are instructed under subcategory T79.A to code first, if applicable, associated postprocedural complication.

Rotator Cuff Tear

The four muscles of the rotator cuff (supraspinatus, infraspinatus, subcapsularis, and teres minor muscles) are attached to the scapula on the back through a single tendon unit. The unit is attached on the side and front of the shoulder, on the greater tuberosity of the humerus.

The rotator cuff holds the head of the humerus into the scapula at the shoulder joint. Inflammation of the tendons of the shoulder muscles can occur in sports requiring the arm to be moved over the head repeatedly, as in tennis, baseball, and swimming. Chronic inflammation or injury can cause the tendons of the rotator cuff to tear.

If the rotator cuff is torn, surgery may be necessary. Arthroscopic surgery can remove bone spurs and inflamed tissue around the area. Small tears can be treated with arthroscopic surgery. Larger tears require open surgery to repair the torn tendon.

Physical therapy can help strengthen the muscles of the rotator cuff. If therapy is not possible because of pain, a steroid injection may reduce pain and inflammation enough to allow effective therapy.

Rotator cuff problems are indexed in ICD-10-CM by the type of problem: sprain, tear, or rupture.

ICD-9-CM Application

Example

Rotator cuff tear, right shoulder, current injury, initial encounter.

ICD-9-CM

In the ICD-9-CM Index to Diseases, look for Tear, torn (traumatic)/rotator cuff (traumatic)/current injury 840.4.

> 840. Sprains and strains of shoulder and upper arm; Rotator cuff (capsule)

ICD-10-CM

Most categories in ICD-10-CM Injury and Poisoning have a 7th character requirement for each applicable code. There are three 7th character values (with the exception of fractures):

A - Initial encounter

D - Subsequent encounter

S - Sequela

In the ICD-10-CM Index to Diseases and Injuries, look for Tear, torn (traumatic)/rotator cuff/traumatic S46.01-. In the Tabular List, a 5th character "1" is selected to indicate the right shoulder and a 7th character "A" is selected for the initial encounter.

> S46.011A Strain of muscle(s) and tendon(s) of the rotator cuff of the right shoulder, initial encounter.

External Causes of Morbidity (V00-Y99)

External cause codes capture how the injury or health condition happened (cause), the intent (unintentional, accidental, or intentional), and the place where the event occurred, the activity of the patient at the time of the event, and the person's status (eg, civilian, military).

There is no national mandatory requirement for ICD-10-CM external cause code reporting unless state-based external cause code reporting is mandated or these codes are required by a payer. Providers are encouraged to use them to provide valuable data for injury prevention strategies.

External cause codes are used with codes A00.0–T88.9, Z00–Z99. They are applicable to injuries and are used for the length of treatment. Assign the external cause code with the appropriate seventh character for each encounter. The selection is guided by the Alphabetic Index of External Causes and by Inclusion and Exclusion notes in the Tabular List. No external cause codes are needed if the cause and intent are included in a code other than chapter 20, such as T36.0X1- Poisoning by penicillins, accidental (unintentional).

ICD-9-CM Application

E codes are used for supplementary classification of external causes of injury and poisoning. Many payers require E codes to explain how the patient was injured.

An index of the E codes may be found following the Table of Drugs and Chemicals. Be as specific as possible when using E codes. Look carefully for the cause of injury and list E codes. Never select an E code as the first-listed diagnosis.

E codes are assigned for all initial treatments, not subsequent treatments according to ICD-9-CM Guideline I.C.19.a.2. This further indicates that external causes of injury codes (E-codes) may be assigned while the acute fracture codes are still applicable.

Example

Rotator cuff tear, right shoulder, current injury, initial encounter. This happened when he bumped into another player and fell while playing hockey in a public skating rink.

ICD-9-CM

In the ICD-9-CM Index to Diseases, look for Tear, torn (traumatic)/rotator cuff (traumatic)/current injury 840.4. Next look in the Index to External Causes for Bumping/in person(s)/with fall/in sports E886.0. Next in the Index to External Causes find Activity (involving)/hockey (ice) E003.1. Next in the same Index find Accident/occurring (at) (in)/skating rink E849.4. Verify in the Tabular List.

840.4 Sprains and strains of shoulder and upper arm; Rotator cuff (capsule)

E886.0 Fall on same level from collision, pushing, or shoving, by or with other person; in sports

E003.1 Activities involving ice and snow; Ice hockey

E849.4 Place of recreation

ICD-10-CM

Most categories in ICD-10-CM Injury and Poisoning have a seventh character requirement for each applicable code. There are three 7th character values (with the exception of fractures):

A - Initial encounter

D - Subsequent encounter

S - Sequela

In the ICD-10-CM Index to Diseases and Injuries, look for Tear, torn (traumatic)/rotator cuff/traumatic S46.01-. In the Tabular List, a 5th character "1" is selected to indicate the right shoulder and a 7th character "A" is selected for the initial encounter. Next in the ICD-10-CM External Causes of Injuries Index look for Pushed, pushing/by other person(s)/with fall W03. Next in the same Index find Activity/hockey (ice) Y93.22. Next in the same Index find Place/hockey rink Y92.330. Verify in the Tabular List. The notes for W03 indicate a seventh character must be used.

S46.011A Strain of muscle(s) and tendon(s) of the rotator cuff of the right shoulder, initial encounter.

W03.XXXA Other fall on same level due to collision with another person; initial encounter.

Y93.39Y93.22 Activity, ice hockey

Y92.330 Ice skating rink (indoor) (outdoor) as the place of occurrence of the external cause

Acronyms

AC	acromioclavicular
ACL	anterior cruciate ligament
AFO	ankle-foot orthosis
AKA	above-knee amputation
ANA	antinuclear antibody
BKA	below-knee amputation
C-spine	cervical spine
C1–C7	cervical vertebrae
CMC	carpometacarpal (joint)
CT	computed tomography (scan)
CTS	carpal tunnel syndrome
DC	doctor of chiropractic medicine
DDD	degenerative disc disease
DEXA/DXA	dual-energy X-ray absorptiometry

DIP	distal interphalangeal (joint)	MRI	magnetic resonance imaging
DJD	degenerative joint disease	MTP	metatarsophalangeal (joint)
DME	durable medical equipment	NSAID	nonsteroidal anti-inflammatory drug
DO	doctor of osteopathy	ORIF	open reduction internal fixation
DTRs	deep tendon reflexes	PCL	posterior cruciate ligament
EMG	electromyogram	PIP	proximal interphalangeal joint
FROM	full range of motion	PT	physical therapy
FX	fracture	RA	rheumatoid arthritis
FWB	full weight bearing	RF	rheumatoid factor
HNP	herniated nucleus pulposus	ROM	range of motion
INJ	injection	RT	right side
IM	intramuscular	SI	sacroiliac (joint)
IP	interphalangeal	SLAP	superior labral anterior posterior (superior glenoid labrum lesion or SLAP lesion of shoulder)
IT	iliotibial		
LE	lower extremity	TENS	transcutaneous electrical nerve stimulation
LP	lumbar puncture		
L-spine	lumbar spine	THR	total hip replacement
L1–L5	lumbar vertebrae	T-spine	thoracic spine
LS	lumbosacral (spine)	T1–T12	thoracic vertebrae
LT	left side	TMJ	temporomandibular joint
MCL	medial collateral ligament	UE	upper extremity
MCP	metacarpophalangeal (joint)		

Section Review 8.2

1. What is the correct 7th character, in ICD-10-CM, for a healing comminuted fracture of the right fibula, open, type 1?

   A. B

   B. D

   C. H

   D. E

2. What is the correct ICD-10-CM code for a new patient seen for a left -sided Nursemaid's elbow?

   A. S53.492A

   B. S53.032S

   C. S50.02XA

   D. S53.032A

3. How would compartment syndrome of the lower extremity caused by an auto accident be listed in the ICD-10-CM Index to Diseases and Injuries?

    A. Syndrome, compartment (traumatic), lower extremity

    B. Compartment syndrome, leg

    C. Syndrome, compartment, non-traumatic, leg

    D. Syndrome, compartment, traumatic, foot

4. How would you code a new pathological fracture of the right femur due to postmenopausal osteoporosis?

    A. M81.0

    B. M80.851A

    C. M80.051A

    D. M80.85051XA

5. What is the code for a traumatic fracture of the 5th metacarpal shaft on the right hand with delayed healing?

    A. S62.306G

    B. S62.326G

    C. S62.327D

    D. S62.316G

CPT® Coding

The musculoskeletal system comprises the longest section of CPT® and provides some of the most complex coding scenarios. The musculoskeletal system includes muscles, bones, and joints, as well as their accessory structures, the ligaments, tendons, and cartilage.

The musculoskeletal system is arranged according to body regions with three exceptions. The first exception is the General Section (20005–20999), which describes any procedure not covered by a subsection under a specific body region. The second exception is the code group for Strapping and Casting (29000– 29799), which is divided further by body region. The third exception is the heading Endoscopy and Arthroscopy (29800–29999), which is the last heading in the Musculoskeletal System chapter.

General

Fracture/Dislocation Procedures

CPT® defines "closed treatment," "open treatment," and "percutaneous skeletal fixation" clearly to clarify that treatment types are not always the same as the type of fracture.

The objective of fracture care treatment is to preserve union by restoring the broken bone(s) as fast and safely as possible. Fractures and dislocations can be treated with manipulation, which is returning the fracture to its normal anatomical position. Reduction means essentially the same thing as manipulation. According to CPT® guidelines, the term "manipulation" means "the attempted reduction or restoration of a fracture or joint dislocation to its normal anatomic alignment by the application of manually applied forces."

Some fractures are treated with fixation, either internal or external, to maintain the alignment of the bone while it heals, or to reinforce the bone permanently. Internal fixation can be done with pins, screws, plates, or wires placed directly on the bone to immobilize it. External fixation is primarily on the outside of the body, and can include a cage-like structure, as well as pins and rods.

The global concept of fracture care differs slightly from other surgical codes. The first cast application is included with fracture care. Setting and care of closed fractures and/or dislocations (without manipulation) with casts and straps are not traditional surgeries, and there is no creation of a surgical wound. Closed treatment of a fracture falls under the global procedure guidelines for CMS and commercial payers.

Closed treatment refers to a fracture/dislocation treated without making an incision into the fracture site; the site is not surgically opened and there is no direct visualization. In closed treatment, there are three different methods of fracture care:

1. **Closed Treatment Without Manipulation**—Closed treatment involves simple immobilization of the affected body part using a cast, splint, or similar device. This may be referred to as skin traction in the medical record, which refers to the longitudinal application of force to a bone using felt or strapping applied directly to the skin.

Example

CPT® 27750 Closed treatment of tibial shaft fracture (with or without fibular fracture); without manipulation

2. **Closed Treatment With Manipulation**—Bone ends do not always maintain alignment at the point of fracture. Dislocations of bone ends can be caused by muscle spasm at the site of fracture. When the affected area must be manipulated to realign the fracture or dislocation, the codes must change to include the work and risk involved. Codes indicating "with manipulation" may also specify "with or without traction."

3. **Closed Treatment With or Without the Application of Traction**—CPT® codes involving the application of traction to maintain the alignment of fractured bones or dislocations are usually worded "…with manipulation, with or without (specific type of) traction."

Example

CPT® 27752 Closed treatment of tibial shaft fracture (with or without fibular fracture); with manipulation, with or without skin or skeletal traction

Open Treatment and Reduction of a Fracture/Dislocation—Describes a situation in which a fracture is so severely displaced or out of alignment the bones cannot be manipulated through the skin. In some cases, internal repair is required because the patient's bone mass is insufficient to provide for simple healing, or the fracture occurred on a weight bearing surface, or the bone was shattered. In these cases, a deliberate surgical incision to expose the fractured bone is performed by the surgeon to visualize the fracture/dislocation and repair the defect. The ends of the broken bone(s) are brought together and held in place by some form of fixation, such as pins, wires (Kirschner wires), or rods. These types of procedures are usually performed under regional or general anesthesia.

Example

CPT® 27758 Open treatment of tibial shaft fracture (with or without fibular fracture), with plate/screws, with or without cerclage

Internal fixation is the insertion of metal rods, wires, pins, nails, or plates (or a combination of these devices) into the bone fragments, usually through an incision over the fracture site. The acronym ORIF (open reduction with internal fixation) refers to this process.

The type of fracture (eg, compound, greenstick, open, closed) in the diagnosis does not have to directly correspond to the procedure code used for the type of fracture care treatment (eg, closed, open, percutaneous) performed.

Example

A closed fracture (eg, 812.21 Closed fracture shaft of humerus) can be repaired by performing an open treatment (eg, 24515 Open treatment of humeral shaft fracture with plate/screws, with or without cerclage).

Percutaneous Skeletal Fixation—This fracture treatment is neither open nor closed. X-rays are taken by the physician to verify that the fracture can be treated by placing a fixation (eg, screw or pins) through the skin and into the bone without making an incision to expose the bone. Small stab wounds are made in the skin over the fracture and usually under X-ray imaging the insertion of screws or pins are placed through the small stab wounds. The screws or pins will hold the fracture together and then a cast, splint or brace may be applied for further stabilization.

Example

CPT® 27756 Percutaneous skeletal fixation of tibial shaft fracture (with or without fibular fracture) (eg, pins or screws)

External fixation pertains to procedures in which metal pins, screws or rods are inserted through the bone and protrude through the skin in order to attach to a metal frame or some form of stabilizing device. These devices are used for temporary or definitive treatment or for an acute or a chronic bony condition, and can be applied percutaneously or during an ORIF.

Example

CPT® 27506 Open treatment of femoral shaft fracture, with or without external fixation, with insertion of intramedullary implant, with or without cerclage and/or locking screws

Codes for application of an external fixation (20690–20692, 20696) are reported separately only when not listed as part of the basic procedure.

Coding Re-reductions of a Fracture/Dislocation

A patient who has already had a cast or strapping material applied and returns for a repeat radiograph which shows the bones are misaligned. The orthopedic surgeon may choose among several treatment options such as to realign and cast the fracture or take the patient to the operating room for ORIF. The course of treatment hinges on several factors. Sometimes a provider will try casting or other means of immobilization due to the patient's reluctance to undergo surgery. If the results of this effort are not satisfactory, the plan may be to take the patient to the operating room for an ORIF. When the second procedure is related to the first, and performed within the postoperative period, modifier 58 is applied to the second procedure.

CPT® modifier 76 *Repeat procedure by the same physician* is attached to the CPT® code when used a second time for a procedure on the same date of service or global period. Modifier 77 is used if the same procedure is repeated by another physician on the same date of service or global period. A repeat procedure may be medically necessary if the initial fracture reduction comes out of alignment or the dislocated joint slips again. Modifier 78 is used if a complication occurs from the original procedure and the patient returns to the operating room within the postoperative period.

Modifier 54 is appended to a fracture treatment code when the physician is only performing the initial fracture care treatment and the follow-up within the global period will be performed by another physician.

Accurate reporting of ICD-10-CM and CPT® codes when coding for fractures and the type of fracture care treatment depends on accurately knowing the anatomic site(s), the extent or severity of the injury, and the type of treatment(s).

Wound Exploration

Wound exploration is listed first in the CPT® chapter on the musculoskeletal system. Trauma (eg, penetrating gunshot or stab) wounds have their own category because they are defined as penetrating wounds and have to be coded a specific way.

Treatment includes the exploration and enlargement of the wound.

Excision

This section covers excision and biopsy of muscle and bone. When coding excision procedures in the musculoskeletal system, carefully read the medical report to determine the depth of the wound or tissue excised. When coding a bone or muscle biopsy, you will see some of the codes are separated into superficial or deep excisions. A muscle biopsy is considered superficial (20200) if done to a muscle close to the surface of the skin; a deep biopsy (20205) is on underlying muscle. A superficial biopsy or excision of the bone is on a bone close to the surface of the skin (eg, ilium, sternum, spinous process); a deep biopsy would include deeper bones (humerus, ischium, femur, etc.).

Introduction or Removal

Introduction and removal codes include removal of a foreign body or old hardware, aspiration of fluids, injection of medications, and application and removal of various mechanical appliances. An arthrogram is an X-ray of a joint after injecting contrast material into the joint. When coding an injection for arthrography, refer to the anatomical site.

When coding injections, watch for bundled procedures. The first set of codes listed under injection is for a therapeutic sinus tract injection (20500 and 20501). These codes are not for nasal sinuses; they refer to an abscess or cyst underneath the skin or soft tissue that has a fistula, or opening, into another area of the body, or to the outside. Antibiotics or other medicines are injected into the sinus tract or cavity to promote healing.

Removal of foreign body procedures are coded by the depth of tissue the surgeon must incise to reach the foreign body.

Surgical injections involve direct insertion of a needle into a tendon and/or joint for the aspiration of fluid and the administration of medication. A tendon sheath, ligament, trigger point, or ganglion cyst can be injected for therapeutic treatment.

A trigger point is an area of the body very tender or painful when touched or when pressure is applied. The area around it may be tender or uncomfortable, but to a lesser degree. Trigger point injections (20552–20553) are reported by the number of muscles that are given the injection, not by how many injections are given. For example, if three trigger points are given, two injections in the rhomboid minor muscle and one injection in the levator scapula muscle you report code 20552 since only two muscles received the injections. Myofascial pain is related to a muscle and its sheath of connective tissue, or fascia. Skeletal muscles are often surrounded by layers of tough connective tissue called fascia. Injury or disease in this area can result in myofascial pain.

Arthrocentesis (20600–20610) describes puncture of a joint with a large diameter needle for fluid removal and/or injection. Fluids are removed for diagnostic and therapeutic purposes. Injections reduce pain and/or inflammation to a joint, tendon, or bursa. A ganglion cyst is a type of tumor usually located in a joint capsule or tendon sheath. Codes 20604 and 20606 are with ultrasound guidance, the other codes in this range are without ultrasound guidance. Code 20612 is for the aspiration of the cyst and/or injection of an anti-inflammatory substance which often relieves the symptoms without surgery.

Injection of a substance does not include the drug itself; the drug supply may be billed separately.

External fixation codes are used when coding the stabilization of a fracture or protecting the skull, as in the application of a halo (20661–20664). Skeletal traction is used to exert force against the pull of muscles in the injured area to realign fractured bones, reduce dislocations, or treat other conditions by attaching weights to a pin or wire. Uniplane fixation (20690) is defined as pins, wires, rods or screws applied in one plane or direction, and multiplane fixation is when the "hardware" is placed in two or more planes or directions. A plane of the body is a point of reference for making an imaginary or real cut through the body or a part.

Example

> The median sagittal plane divides the body into right and left halves, from the midpoint at the top of the head through the pubic bone area. The coronal (frontal) plane divides the body into front and back halves, from the midpoint of the head through the leg down to the feet.

CPT® codes 20670 and 20680 *Removal of implant* are reported more than once if the hardware (pins, screws, nails, rods) needs to be taken out from more than one fracture site involved. Modifier 59 is required. If multiple hardware items are being removed or if more than one incision is made to remove the hardware from one fracture, the code is only reported once.

CPT® 20692 refers to the application of a multiplane external fixation device. The Ilizarov device is named for the Russian physician who described multiple fixations and its use for the treatment of highly complex closed fractures. This compression distraction device also can be used for bone lengthening in certain conditions. The multi-plane external fixation device consists of rings attached by longitudinal rods, making complete circles around the affected limb. Pins are inserted at intervals through the skin on one side, passing through the bone and out the other side.

Replantation

Replantation codes are used when the surgeon is replanting a digit or a limb after a complete amputation. If the digit or limb is amputated partially, the coder uses specific codes for repair of bones, ligaments, tendons, nerves, or blood vessels.

Replantation involves cleansing of the amputation site (traumatic); debridement of devitalized tissue; shortening of bone (if necessary); internal fixation or arthrodesis; repair of tendons; arteries; veins and nerves; skin closure including tendon, skin flaps, and grafts.

CPT® codes 20802– 20838 identify the replantation of a specific body part, for example, replantation of the hand due to a complete amputation. These codes include the necessary attachments of all underlying structures associated with a complete amputation. An incomplete amputation and subsequent reattachment should be reported according to the bone, ligament, tendon, nerve, and/or blood vessel repair, with modifier 52 appended to each of the codes.

Practical Coding Note

Highlight or underline the anatomical site (for example, arm, digit, thumb, etc.) in the code descriptions.

Grafts (or Implants)

Graft (or implant) codes are used for autogenous (from the patient) bone, cartilage, tendon or fascia lata grafts, or other tissue via separate incisions. Some musculoskeletal surgeries require bone grafts, which are coded separately unless the code description states "includes obtaining graft." The add-on codes 20930 and 20937 refer to morselized bone (bone in particle form) used for spine procedures, either from the patient (autograft) or a donor (allograft).

According to the American Academy of Orthopaedic Surgeons (AAOS), the definitions of the types of grafts referred to in CPT® code 20938 include monocortical, which is not mentioned in the code's description, and are the following:

Monocortical—A graft of cortical bone removed from the outer cortex of the ilium (Ilium—part of pelvic or hip bone).

Bicortical—A graft of cortical bone removed as one piece from the inner and outer portions of the ilium (eg, having two layers of external bone surface).

Tricortical—A graft of cortical bone from the ilium that includes the anterior-superior iliac spine and both the inner and outer iliac cortex as a single piece (eg, having three layers of external surface).

A bone graft is surgery to place new bone into spaces between or around fractures or defects in bone. New bone to be grafted around fractures or defects can be taken from the patient's own healthy bone (autograft) or from frozen, donated bone (allograft).

Bone grafts typically are harvested from the patient's iliac crest (top of the hip bone), ribs, or fibula in the lower leg. Autologous bone is harvested from the patient's pelvic bone (iliac crest) and provides calcium scaffolding for growth of new bone. Autologous bone also contains bone-growing cells (osteoblasts) and bone-growing proteins (bone morphogenic proteins).

Allograft bone provides calcium scaffolding and does not contain bone-growing cells or bone-growing proteins. Whether using autologous or allograft bone, the procedure involves shaping and inserting the bone graft through an incision directly over the area to be repaired, and keeping it in place with pins, plates, or screws. A splint or cast usually is used to prevent injury or movement while healing.

Codes for obtaining autogenous bone grafts, cartilage, tendon, fascia lata grafts, or other tissues through separate incisions are reported separately unless the code descriptor references the harvesting of the graft or implant (eg, includes obtaining graft). In cases where the descriptor does not indicate "includes obtaining graft," it would be appropriate to report the harvesting code if the graft was obtained through a separate incision.

Example

28446 Open osteochondral autograft, talus (includes obtaining graft[s])

The term "with grafting" refers to the placement of the graft. For example, code 22319 states "with grafting." If a graft is obtained from a separate incision site the graft codes 20900 or 20902 may be reported with 22319, because code 22319 indicates that a graft was used. In cases when the graft was obtained from another incision site it is appropriate to report graft code 20900 or 20902. A code that states "with graft" (or "with autograft", "with bone graft", "with or without bone graft"), in the code description indicates that the procedure was performed with a graft, but does not report how the graft was obtained.

Other Musculoskeletal Procedures

Interstitial fluid pressure monitoring (20950) is a method of detecting muscle compartment syndrome (eg, failure of the muscle or a portion of a muscle to function properly) or muscle ischemia (eg, loss of blood to the muscle). An interstitial pressure-monitoring device is inserted into the muscle compartment by using a needle, wick catheter, or other means. When the pressure monitored by the device rises, muscle compartment syndrome may be developing. When enough data is retrieved, the needle or catheter is removed.

Microsurgery (20955–20973) includes not only the anastomosis (connecting) of vessels less than two millimeters in diameter, but also the anastomosis of individual nerve fibers. Procedures involving a microvascular component include the free transfer from fibula, rib, or other bone, as well as free osteocutaneous flaps and the transfer of the great toe with the web space.

Vascularized bone grafts (20955–20962) are used when large defects exist, usually in long bones, where standard iliac bone grafts or other types of nonvascularized bone grafts are not likely to heal. Patients with congenital abnormalities that require excision of large segments of bone (eg, congenital pseudoarthrosis of the tibia) are candidates for vascularized bone grafts. The iliac crest and metatarsals are donor sites for harvesting of bone.

Free osteocutaneous (bone and skin) flaps with microvascular anastomosis are used in reconstructive surgery. Use of the operating microscope (69990) is inherent in these procedures and is not reported separately. Osteocutaneous microvascular free flaps (20969–20973) are used in not only a large bony defect, but also in an adjacent or overlying soft tissue defect to be repaired. A combined free bone and skin flap provides the reconstructive surgeon with an excellent tool to repair such defects. These flaps are useful in treating high energy extremity wounds involving loss of bone and soft tissue.

Percutaneous radiofrequency ablation (RFA) of 1 or more bone tumors (20982) can be an alternative to, or a supplement for, radiation therapy of metastatic lesions to bone from a variety of primary tumors. This technology may be applied to surgical treatment of the benign (but frequently painful) bone tumors. When performed by cryoablation report code 20983.

Head

The next few sections of CPT® are listed anatomically. Each section is divided into sub-sections depending on the procedures performed.

The first of these anatomical sections is the head. Codes for most procedures performed on the bones of the head are found here. These include the skull, facial bones, and temporomandibular joint. Codes for surgeries on the brain are found in the nervous system section.

The temporomandibular joint (TMJ) is the "hinge" of the jaw between the mandible and the temporal bone. CPT® lists many procedures for repair, reconstruction, and manipulation of this joint. The articular disc, made of cartilage and positioned between the temporal bone and the mandible, allows this joint to be extremely flexible, but can be the source of many disorders. The most common problem is displacement of the articular disc, and can require manipulation or reconstruction to restore functionality and reduce pain. Arthrotomy of the TMJ is coded with 21010; codes 21050– 21070 and 21240–21243 are other reconstructive surgical procedures. Treatment of TMJ dislocation is coded with 21480, 21485 or 21490, depending whether the surgery is open or closed.

The vertical part of the lower jaw extends from the temporomandibular joint to the angle where it curves into the mandibular body. It is called the mandibular rami. Surgery on the rami is performed for reconstruction after a fracture, or to move the lower part of the jaw forward or back to correct an orthognathic defect. Bone grafting or internal fixation including screws and plates may be used for these procedures. CPT® codes for reconstruction of the mandibular rami are 21193–21196. If a bone graft is used, it is included with 21194.

CPT® codes 21141–21160 describe reconstruction of the midface, LeFort I, LeFort II, or LeFort III procedures. These codes should not be confused with the fracture care codes for the LeFort fractures listed as CPT® codes 21421–21436. Renee LeFort, a French surgeon, was the first to describe the three lines of weakness or typical fracture lines in the upper jaw and skull.

There are several types of LeFort fractures and reconstructions classified in CPT®. A LeFort I fracture also is referred to as Guérin's fracture or horizontal fracture of the midface. This fracture typically occurs above the apices of the teeth on the maxilla. The lower portion of the face becomes disengaged from the rest of the face in this type of surgery/fracture. A LeFort II fracture results when the fracture line traverses the midface and meets at the apex of the nose. This fracture also is referred to as a pyramidal fracture due to its shape. A transverse facial fracture or craniofacial disjunction fracture is synonymous with a LeFort III fracture. When this fracture occurs, the facial bones become separated from the cranial bones. The fracture runs from ear to ear through the bony orbit of the eye.

Repair and/or reconstruction of these fractures are quite complex. This can require multiple incisions, bone grafts, and the introduction of internal hardware to hold the defects in place. Arch bars, screws, and plates are often a part of the LeFort I reconstruction. Dentition of the upper jaw usually is splinted and intermaxillary fixation may be warranted. In the reconstruction for long face syndrome (CPT® code 21141, LeFort I), the overgrown portions of the maxilla are measured preoperatively via radiograph and slated for removal via osteotomy. When more than one segment of maxilla is removed, CPT® code 21142 or 21143 is reported. This type of reconstructive surgery requires the surgeon to "down fracture the maxilla" to create a LeFort fracture with a pair of

Rowe forceps. Fracture and removal of the extra bony growth for CPT® procedures 21141–21143 creates the equivalent of a LeFort I defect, and the defect is repaired.

CPT® 21195 is inherently bilateral per CPT® (*AMA CPT® Assistant*, April 1996, p 11). If the procedure is performed on one side only, report 21195 and add modifier 52 *Reduced services*. If internal rigid fixation is used, CPT® 21196 is reported.

Practical Coding Note

Highlight or underline the references to LeFort I, LeFort II, and LeFort III for easy reference.

Write "bilateral" next to CPT® code 21195 and highlight the reference to *AMA CPT® Assistant* below the code to remind you to use a modifier 52 if performed unilaterally.

Neck (Soft Tissues) and Thorax

In the musculoskeletal section of the CPT® codebook there are specific codes that are reported for removal of a tumor or lipoma from certain anatomical sites. For example, codes 21555-21554, are reported for excision of a tumor in the neck or anterior thorax. These codes are categorized by the size of the tumor and the depth of the tumor (subcutaneous, subfascial, or submuscular).Subcutaneous soft connective tissue tumors are usually benign and are removed with minimal surrounding tissue. Radical resection of soft connective tissue tumors involve the removal of the tumor (usually a malignant tumor) and removal of excessive amounts of normal tissue from many layers including margins. Removal of tumors of a cutaneous origin are reported using codes from the integumentary system.

Code 21685 reports the enlarging of the retrolingual/hypopharyngeal airway to help correct sleep-disordered breathing (obstructive sleep apnea syndrome). Commonly described as hyoid myotomy and suspension, this procedure also is known as a modified hyoid myotomy and suspension with hyoid repositioning. This procedure affects function of the pharynx and larynx. The procedure opens the orohypopharyngeal airway, and is performed on the laryngeal skeleton.

Spine (Vertebral Column)

Some of the procedures on the musculoskeletal system also involve surgery on the nerves and nervous system. The most common of these are surgeries on the spine or vertebral column. The spine is divided into three main sections: the cervical spine, the thoracic spine, and the lumbar spine. When coding spinal surgeries, it is critical to determine first the area of the spine where the surgery is being performed. These surgeries are very complicated, and include instrumentation and bone grafts, in addition to arthrodesis. Instrumentation is reported separately in addition to arthrodesis.

Practical Coding Note

Highlight each section of the spine in different colors. For example, use pink for cervical, blue for thoracic, and green for lumbar. This will provide easy reference for the section of spine that is being coded.

According to CPT® guidelines and the AAOS, "A vertebral segment describes the basic constituent part into which the spine may be divided. It represents a single complete vertebral bone with its associated articular processes and laminae."

Example

If the surgeon documents posterior instrumentation, segmental, was applied for levels T4–T8, the appropriate code would be 22842 *Posterior segmental instrumentation (eg, pedicle fixation, dual rods with multiple hooks and sublaminar wires); 3 to 6 vertebral segments*. In this case, five vertebral segments (T4–T8) are included in the description.

If the surgeon states anterior instrumentation was placed from T2–T10, the appropriate code would be 22847 *Anterior instrumentation; 8 or more vertebral segments* because T2–T10 includes nine vertebral segments. Note that codes 22842 and 22847 are "add-on" codes and must be reported with one of the other codes that are listed below the code description.

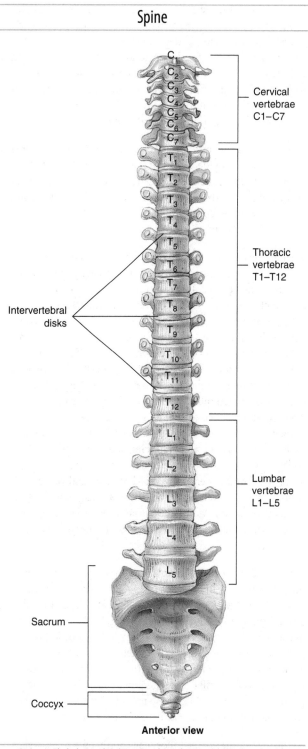

Spine

Source: Ehrlich, Medical Terminology for Health Professionals, 6e, ISBN #978-1-4180-7252-0

A vertebral interspace is the non-bony compartment between two adjacent vertebral bodies that contains the intervertebral disc and includes the nucleus pulposus, annulus fibrosus, and two cartilaginous endplates.

Access to spinal surgery sites can be accomplished through a variety of approaches. The two most common approaches are posterior and anterior. Patients are placed face down on the operating room table for the posterior approach. An incision is made directly into the area of the posterior spine. Anterior approach is accomplished by placing the patient in the supine position on the operating room table. The site for an incision depends on the area of the spine affected.

In many cases a second surgeon—such as a thoracic or general surgeon—will provide exposure (surgical dissection) to the anterior operative site. Two surgeons (often of separate specialties) working together to accomplish a single surgery is considered a co-surgery. Both surgeons are required to bill the same CPT® code with a modifier 62.

Vertebroplasty is performed on a compression fracture of the vertebra by percutaneously creating a cavity in the bone and injecting bone cement mixture to provide stability to the vertebra preventing further vertebral collapse. Codes 22510-22512 report percutaneous vertebroplasty and a code is selected based on the area of the spine involved - cervicothoracic or lumbosacral vertebra. Codes 22513-22515 are for vertebral augmentation, also known as kyphoplasty. Kyphoplasty is also performed to stabilize a spinal compression fracture. A cavity is created into the spine by a balloon or mechanical device that is inflated to expand the bone to restore the height of the vertebra. A bone cement mixture is injected to fill the cavity to stabilize the area, reducing pain, and to prevent collapse again. The code is selected based on spinal area - thoracic or lumbar vertebra. Vertebroplasty and vertebral augmentation includes bone biopsy, imaging guidance, and moderate sedation. Modifier 50 is not reported on these codes because the code description indicates unilateral or bilateral injection.

Arthrodesis is surgical immobilization of a joint, which is intended to result in bone fusion. Arthrodesis can be accomplished through use of a cortical bone graft packed in and around the spine. This procedure promotes the production of new bone cells (osteocytes) secondary to the addition of the graft material. This provides a framework for these cells to grow in and lay down new bone. This type of bone grafting procedure is what CPT® considers arthrodesis for coding purposes. Instrumentation also provides immobility to the spine via addition of screws, hooks, rods, and wires.

Arthrodesis is performed most commonly on ankles, wrists, and spinal vertebrae, but it can be performed on other joints such as thumbs, toes, and fingers.

There are a variety of techniques for approaching arthrodesis. The approach on the operative report must match the approach for the arthrodesis CPT® code selected. Lateral extracavitary approach requires resection of the ribs, and dissecting

spinal/paraspinal tissues to access the vertebral bodies/discs. The surgeon removes and fuses the vertebral body to correct compression of the spinal cord, cauda equina, and/or nerve roots due to vertebral body damage caused by tumor, fracture, or osteomyelitis.

CPT® code 22830 is used when the surgeon explores a previous spinal fusion. Although not listed as a separate procedure by CPT®, most carriers or third party payers consider exploration to be included if new work is done in the same operative site and session. In a September 1997 *CPT® Assistant* article, the AMA cites it is appropriate to bill both procedures; however, this has not done much to help reimbursement. The AMA has stated this code includes "decortication of bone and adjustment of existing plates, clamps, screws, and/or wires, but does not include their removal." This code is not to be used for bone harvesting and insertion, decompression of disc or nerve root, or insertion of new or additional spinal instrumentation. Exploration of a spinal fusion is not considered an integral part of arthrodesis. CPT® modifier 51 is appended to the additional procedure to indicate appropriate multiple procedure reduction.

Spinal instrumentation is used to treat abnormal curvature of the spine (eg, scoliosis or kyphosis) and to stabilize the spine after spinal surgery, treatment of a fracture, and/or dislocation. This set of CPT® codes is divided based on segmental or nonsegmental technique and anterior vs. posterior surgical approach.

When coding spinal instrumentation, it is important to understand the difference between segmental and non-segmental instrumentation. Segmental instrumentation is defined as fixation at each end of the construct (rod), with at least one additional interposed bony attachment. Non-segmental instrumentation is defined as fixation at each end of the construct (rod) only, and may span several vertebral segments without attachment to the intervening segments.

The spinal instrumentation codes are add-on codes; they are to be coded in addition to the primary surgery (eg, arthrodesis 22800–22812).

Add-on insertion codes 22840–22848 are not to be reported with reinsertion code 22849 and/or removal code 22850. Add-on insertion codes (22840–22848) are reported when new hardware is put in for the first time or when new hardware is put in which exceeds the previously placed hardware and includes removal of the old hardware. Reinsertion (22849) is reported when the hardware is going back in the same spinal levels as the previous placed hardware and includes the removal of the old hardware. Removal codes (22850, 22852 and 22855) are reported when only the hardware is taken out.

Abdomen

The procedure code in this subsection reports the excision of a subfascial abdominal wall tumor. There is also a code for other procedures to the abdomen; coders should always check Category III codes prior to assigning an unlisted procedure code because new technology codes supersede use of an unlisted code. Documentation should accompany the claim when reporting either an unspecified or Category III code.

Shoulder

The scapula is a flat, triangular-shaped bone on the dorsal side, or back, of the thorax. The acromion is an extension of this bone joining with the clavicle at the shoulder to form the acromioclavicular joint. Procedures in the shoulder section can be performed on the scapula, acromion, or clavicle. In the CPT® Index, look under "Shoulder." You will be directed to "see Clavicle; Scapula."

Hand and Fingers

There are four muscle groups found in the hand; each is housed in a separate compartment. An injury to the hand can cause compartment syndrome, compression, and loss of function of one muscle group or more muscle groups in the hand.

No Man's Land

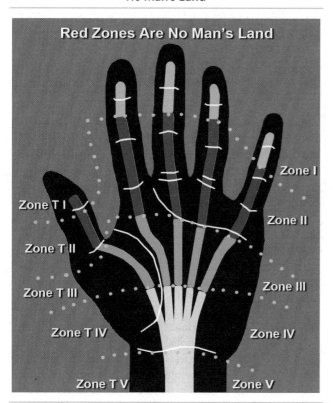

Source: AAPC

No Man's Land pertains to the area between the distal crease of the palm and the proximal end of the middle phalanx, and is also known as Zone 2. Stiffness following injury is a common problem in this area.

Tendon repairs to the hands and/or fingers are performed to provide treatment for injuries or to correct deformities of the hand. Tendons of the hands are numerous and extremely complex. Tendons are separated into two types: flexor tendons and extensor tendons. Strong fibrous digital sheaths extend from the top of the metacarpals to the bottom of the distal phalanges and cover flexor tendons.

Extensor tendon structure is most complex at the level of the proximal interphalangeal joint (PIP). These tendons often are ruptured more easily after repair due to greater strength in opposition supplied by the flexor tendons. Restrictive deformities can result from extensor tendon injuries such as Boutonnière deformity and mallet finger.

In some cases, part of a tendon has been lost due to an injury, and the ends of the tendon cannot be brought together for repair. Tendon grafts can be inserted to correct the defect. A graft is tissue bridging the defect or injured area. Grafts may be obtained from other sites in the hand or from the inner ankle.

Coders must differentiate among CPT® codes mentioning work on a single tendon versus work on multiple tendons through the same incision (eg, codes 27685 and 27686). Code 27685 is used to report a single tendon lengthened or shortened in the leg or ankle. Code 27686 is used to report each tendon of a group of multiple tendons lengthened or shortened in the leg or ankle during the same operative session.

When three tendons are lengthened, for example, 27686 is reported separately three times or by entering a "3" in the "units" field on the CMS-1500 claim form.

Muscle Group	Compartment	Function
Thenar	Thenar compartment	Opposition of the thumb
Adductor pollicis	Adductor compartment	Allows for increased pressure to thumb opposition
Hypothenar muscles	Hypothenar compartment	Produces the hypothenar eminence and provides movement to the fifth digit
Short muscles	Central compartment	Abduction and adduction of the digits

Many procedures are bundled into the repair codes and should not be identified separately. The following procedures or portions of the tendon repair are included in the tendon repair:

- Extension to expose the entire tendon
- Repair and closure of the tendon sheath
- Application of immobilization or other devices for postoperative therapy

The following procedures are not considered an integral part of tendon repair and may be reported in addition to tendon repair:

- Harvesting and insertion of tendon grafts from a distant site using CPT® code 20924
- Repair of nerves and/or arteries
- Fracture fixation

Toe-to-Hand Transfer

Toe-to-hand transfer offers the patient the possibility of recovering not only mechanical function, but also sensory function.

The toe-to-hand transfer with microvascular anastomosis, great toe "wrap-around," is significantly different from the standard great toe-to-hand transfer (great toe with web space—20973). In the wrap-around procedure, a segment of the iliac crest is harvested and fashioned to replace the amputated proximal and distal phalanges of the thumb. The microvascular aspect of the procedure includes transfer of the skin, nerves, vasculature, and nail organ from the great toe and literally wrapping this tissue around the iliac bone graft that has been fixed onto the residual first metacarpal. This procedure creates a new thumb. It looks more like a thumb than a great toe transfer to the hand. With this procedure, the harvesting of the iliac bone graft, as well as its fixation and the microvascular aspects of the procedure, are included. A skin graft harvested for closure of the great toe is reported separately.

In cases of severe injuries where no fingers are left, occasionally a double toe transfer is carried out. In this situation, two toes are transferred together. For example, the second and third toes from the foot are harvested as one tissue block. Multiple tendon repairs, multiple nerve repairs, vascular repairs, and multiple osteosyntheses are included in the transfer. In this microvascular procedure, a toe (often the proximal interphalangeal joint of the toe or the metatarsophalangeal joint of the toe) is harvested with an overlying island of skin. This is used for reconstruction of severe joint injuries, particularly in children, because the growth plate of the toe can be transferred with the joint to allow continued growth of the injured digit.

Pelvis and Hip Joint

The hip joint may be replaced with a variety of materials, including metal, polyethylene, and ceramic. A joint prosthesis is identified as a total hip arthroplasty if both the articular surfaces of the acetabulum and femur are replaced. If the femoral head is replaced and the acetabulum is not altered, the prosthesis may be considered a hemiarthroplasty. Imaging of a hip arthroplasty and its complications relies on information obtained from routine radiography and, to a lesser extent, arthrography, nuclear medicine, and sonography.

Femur (Thigh Region) and Knee Joint

There are three compartments in the knee: medial, lateral, and patellofemoral. The medial compartment is on the inner knee; the lateral compartment is on the outer side; and the patellofemoral compartment is behind the patella or kneecap. When coding surgeries on the knee joint, each compartment is considered a separate area of the knee and is coded appropriately.

"Articular" means a moveable joint. When a code refers to a procedure that is performed "extra-articular," the procedure is performed on the outer portion of the joint. "Intra-articular" is a procedure performed inside the joint itself.

Example

- 27427 Ligamentous reconstruction (augmentation), knee; extra-articular
- 27428 intra-articular (open)
- 27429 intra-articular (open) and extra-articular

Mosaicplasty is a procedure where cylindrical osteochondral (bone and cartilage) grafts are removed from a donor site and transplanted to holes prepared at the recipient site. The most commonly used donor sites are the patellofemoral area, the medial rim of the femoral trochlea, the lateral rim of the femoral trochlea, and the periphery of the intercondylar notch. Cylindrical holes are prepared at the site of the cartilage defect and filled with the cylindrical grafts harvested, to restore the original curvature of the articular surface. A mosaicplasty is coded 27416 if done via an open incision; if done via arthroscopy, use 29866 or 29867. All mosaicplasty codes include harvesting of bone and cartilage.

The head of the femur fits into the acetabulum of the innominate bone and allows rotational flexibility in the hip joint. The greater trochanter and the lesser trochanter are sites for muscle attachment. The patella fits into the groove at the distal anterior surface of the bone. The rounded condyles on the distal posterior surface of the femur articulate with the tibia.

The three types of femoral shaft fractures are as follows:

- Type I—Spiral or transverse (most common)
- Type II—Comminuted
- Type III—Open

Diaphyseal fractures result from significant force transmitted by a direct blow or from indirect force transmitted at the knee. Pathologic fractures may be the result of bone weakness from osteoporosis or lytic lesions.

Foot and Toes

Foot deformities are often a source of confusion for coders. Bunions are caused by swelling and inflammation on the first digit at the joint where the distal metatarsal joins the proximal phalanx. Hallux valgus refers to the altered angle of the great toe leaning in toward the other toes, and at times over- or under-lapping with them. The terms hallux valgus and bunions are often interchangeable because the medial bunion is almost always associated with a hallux valgus. A hammertoe deformity refers to a flexion deformity of the proximal interphalangeal (PIP) joint that is fixed, creating a claw-like appearance. The code for hammertoe correction is 28285.

Hallux rigidus is a result of arthritic changes of the first metatarsophalangeal joint, and can cause pain and swelling on the top of the foot. A cheilectomy (28289) is surgery to correct this condition. It is removal of a large portion of the dorsal metatarsal head and associated bone spurs.

Bunionectomy Codes and their Eponyms

Codes for correction of hallux valgus are 28290–28299. There are a multitude of methods for correcting this problem.

Silver Procedure (28290)—Removal of the medial eminence of the distal metatarsal bone.

Keller, McBride, or Mayo Type Procedure (28292)—Removal of the medial eminence of the distal metatarsal bone and a resection of the base of the proximal phalanx.

Keller-Mayo with Implant (28293)—Removal of the medial eminence of the distal metatarsal bone and a resection of the base of the proximal phalanx, with insertion of a double stem implant in the proximal phalanx.

Joplin Procedure (28294)—Rearrangement of the tendons of the toe to correct a bunion deformity, followed by removal of the medial eminence of the distal metatarsal bone.

Mitchell, Chevron, Austin, or Concentric Procedure (28296)—A double osteotomy in the first distal metatarsal.

Lapidus Procedure (28297)—Fusion of the metatarsal bone to the cuneiform bone to affect a distal repair of the bunion and correction of the hallux valgus.

Aiken Procedure (28298)—Removal of a wedge of the bottom of the proximal phalanx and, usually, the medial eminence of the distal metatarsal bone. The toe is immobilized with the percutaneous placement of a Kirchner wire.

According to the *AMA's Principles of CPT® Coding*, the following procedures are included (when performed on the metatarsophalangeal joint during bunion surgery): capsulotomy, synovectomy, synovial biopsy, arthrotomy, neuroplasty, tenotomy, tendon release, tenolysis, excision of osteophytes, excision of medial eminence, articular shaving, removal of bursal tissue, placement of internal fixation, and scar revision.

Other Procedures

Code 28890 has been added to identify high energy extracorporeal shock wave (ESW) treatment of the plantar fascia. ESW procedures provided in other areas are cross-referenced in parenthetical instructions guiding the user to Category III codes. The *AMA's CPT® Changes 2006: An Insider's View* states, "The language included in the code descriptor helps to differentiate this procedure, indicating that (1) it is an ESW treatment that is high energy (usually involving pain), (2) it requires performance by a physician, and (3) it necessitates use of a nonlocal anesthetic. The descriptor also includes ultrasound guidance and is specific to treatment for plantar fasciitis."

Application of Casts and Strapping

Casts are applied to immobilize a body part for treatment of a fracture or for postoperative management after an orthopedic surgical procedure.

Casts may be made from plaster, fiberglass, or synthetic material. Application and removal of the first cast or strapping device is part of the global surgical care for musculoskeletal procedures. This coding guideline holds true regardless of whether the cast is applied to treat a fracture or to immobilize an extremity after a surgical procedure.

According to both the AMA and the AAOS *Guidelines for Fractures and Dislocations*, the type of fracture does not dictate the type of treatment. CPT® describes a variety of methods for treating fractures and or dislocations: closed reduction, open reduction, open reduction with internal fixation, and percutaneous skeletal fixation. The services include the application and removal of the first casts or traction device only. Subsequent replacement of casts and/or traction devices may require reporting an additional CPT® code. See cast and strapping procedures (29000–29799).

When the cast or strapping is a replacement for the first cast within or after the follow-up period, the code for the cast application is reported. E/M services rendered with the reapplication of a cast or strapping are not reported separately. If a significant and separately identifiable service is rendered in addition to the casting, report the E/M service with a CPT® modifier 25. Remember: When reporting reapplication of a cast or strapping, removal of the old cast or strap is included.

When it comes time to remove a cast and a physician other than the physician who applied the cast removes it, removal may be reported with cast removal CPT® codes 29700–29710.

When a cast or strapping is applied for the first time at the initial visit and no surgical treatment is performed for the fracture/dislocation, the appropriate casting/strapping code should be reported along with the supplies used for casting/strapping. Supplies should be coded using HCPCS Level II codes. An appropriate E/M code should be reported for the office visit.

When a physician applies a temporary cast, splint, or strapping and another physician provides the definitive/restorative treatment of a fracture, each physician may bill for the services provided. It is not considered preoperative care and modifier 56 is not appropriate.

Example

> A patient visits the ED for a broken arm. The ED physician applies a temporary cast until the patient can see the orthopedic surgeon the next morning. The orthopedic provider manipulates the fracture and applies a cast. In this case, the ED provider would bill an E/M code for the encounter and for the temporary casting. The orthopedic provider would bill for the fracture treatment involving manipulation.

Code 29580 *Unna boot* is a compression wrap in which a dressing is made up of zinc oxide paste which also can include glycerin and calamine lotion to apply to the affected area on the lower leg or foot. Then supporting bandages are wrapped around the lower leg until the desired support is attained. This procedure is usually performed to treat or prevent disorders such as wounds that have drainage, ulcers, or postoperative edema that may result from an amputation. Do not report Unna boot with multi-layer codes 29581 and 29582.

Code 29581–29584 is reported for compression therapy for management of venous ulcers or chronic venous insufficiency. The multi-layer compression bandaging system can consist of elastic bandages only or the bandages can be paired with a knitted tubular compression garment.

Endoscopy/Arthroscopy

Surgical arthroscopic procedures always include a diagnostic arthroscopy of the same joint. If there is not a CPT® code for the therapeutic arthroscopy performed, it is not permissible to code the open procedure for the arthroscopy (*AMA CPT® Assistant*, July 1998, p. 8).

When a diagnostic scope is followed by an open procedure, such as arthrotomy, it is appropriate to code both procedures and append modifiers 59 and 51 (distinct procedural service and multiple procedures, respectively) to the diagnostic scope code. If therapeutic arthroscopic surgery is scheduled and upon arthroscopic visualization the joint is not appropriate for further surgery, only the diagnostic arthroscopic procedure should be reported.

Disarticulation is the separation of two bones at the joint, either traumatically or by surgical amputation. A surgical amputation may be done for gangrene, or for complications of diabetes and circulatory disorders. CPT® includes codes for disarticulation of the ankle (27889), hip (27295), knee (27598), and wrist (25920). Shoulder disarticulation is coded with 23920 or 23921, depending on if it is the initial surgery, or a secondary closure or scar revision.

Report only a single arthroscopic procedure for each compartment in the knee. For example, if the surgeon performs meniscectomy and debridement in the medial compartment, you can only bill a single procedure (normally the meniscectomy, which has the higher value).

Example

> 29881 Arthroscopy, knee, surgical; with meniscectomy (medial or lateral, including any meniscal shaving), including debridement/shaving of articular cartilage (chondroplasty), same or separate compartment(s), when performed

CPT® does not differentiate compartments in the shoulder clearly; they are vaguely defined, usually as anterior or posterior. The AAOS recognizes three "areas" or "regions" of the shoulder: the glenohumeral joint, the acromioclavicular joint, and the subacromial bursal space. These areas are clearly separate; procedures done in one area should not influence coding in a different area.

Non-union or malunion of a fracture occurs when a fracture does not heal properly. Surgery to correct this problem is coded differently than a normal fracture repair. When repairing a malunion of the femur, there are different codes for repairing the defect with a graft or without a graft.

The term "radical," when referring to surgery of the musculoskeletal system is used to describe removal of an extensive area of tissue surrounding an area of infection or malignancy. For example, 21620 is an *ostectomy of sternum, partial*, which would be for removal of a portion of the sternum; 21630 is for a *radical resection of sternum*, which would include most or all of the sternum and some of the surrounding tissue.

Section Review 8.3

1. The physician performs arthroscopic meniscus repair with partial medial and lateral repairs. What code would you use?

    A. 29883

    B. 29880

    C. 29882

    D. 27332

2. How would you code an arthroscopic abrasion chondroplasty of the medial femoral condyle?

    A. 29884

    B. 29862

    C. 29879

    D. 29860

3. The patient came to the office for a therapeutic injection, left shoulder subacromial space. How would you code the procedure?

    A. 20612

    B. 20610

    C. 20552

    D. 20550

4. Joe was in a motorcycle accident and fractured his right femur. The surgeon placed an intramedullary locking implant (nail) through a buttock incision. How would you code the procedure?

    A. 27503-RT

    B. 27508-RT

    C. 27510-RT

    D. 27506-RT

5. Jeff is a 13-year-old boy who fractured his left radius and ulna while snowboarding. Three weeks after the physician placed a long arm cast on Jeff, he was skateboarding and crushed the cast (without further injury to the arm). The physician replaces the cast with a short-arm fiberglass cast. How would you code the services provided after the skateboard accident?

    A. No code

    B. 29065-58

    C. 29075-58

    D. 29125-58

6. Mary has been having pain in her temporomandibular joint. Her doctor decides to manipulate the joint under general anesthesia, and schedules her for this procedure the next day. How would this procedure be coded?

    A. 21073

    B. 21480

    C. 21485

    D. 21060

7. The patient has developed plantar fasciitis, a painful condition in his heel and the sole of his foot. He has tried using shoe inserts and over-the-counter pain relievers, but is still having pain. His physician plans an injection of the tendon sheath on the bottom of his foot. How would this injection be coded?

    A. 28070

    B. 20550

    C. 28001

    D. 20553

8. Julia tripped and fell down three stairs in her apartment. X-rays show a fracture of the metatarsal bone of her left great toe, and the physician treats this fracture with a special orthotic boot. How would you code the physician's services?

    A. 27752-TA

    B. 27786-TA

    C. 28470-TA

    D. 27750-TA

9. Mrs. Williams has had a bunion on her right foot for many years and is scheduled for surgery to correct this condition. The doctor plans to do a double osteotomy of the metatarsal bone. How will he code this surgery?

    A. 28296-RT, 28296-RT

    B. 28299-RT

    C. 28293-RT

    D. 28290-RT

10. Mrs. Smith underwent an arthrodesis of her spine for spinal deformity, posterior approach, segments L3–L5. How is this arthrodesis coded?

    A. 22810

    B. 22818

    C. 22802

    D. 22800

HCPCS Level II

HCPCS Level II L codes are for orthotic and prosthetic procedures and supplies, and most of them are used with the musculoskeletal system procedures and services.

Many HCPCS Level II E codes are used with musculoskeletal and orthopedic services, such as canes, crutches, walkers, traction devices, wheelchairs, and other orthopedic devices. Some physicians provide basic orthopedic supplies, but most are supplied by a durable medical equipment (DME) provider fulfilling the physician's order.

Modifiers

Modifiers often are used in orthopedic surgery to indicate on which side of the body the surgery was performed, which finger or toe was repaired, or to indicate identical procedures were performed on both sides of the body. These modifiers are critical to report that a procedure was done twice or to a certain part of the body. Without this key information, a payer may deny the claim inappropriately considering it as either a duplicate or bundled procedure.

The most common modifiers used in orthopedic surgery are:

50 *Bilateral procedure*—When using this modifier, check with the payer to determine if the codes reported are to be separated with modifiers LT *Left Side* and RT *Right Side* for each side, or if they prefer a single code with modifier 50.

54 *Surgical care only*

57 *Decision for surgery*

58 S*taged or related procedure or service by the same physician or other qualified healthcare professional during the post-operative period*—Append this modifier when an additional procedure(s) was planned or related to the initial procedure. This does not require the procedure to be performed in the operating/procedure room. It would indicate the second surgery is not to be considered bundled into the routine post-operative services. This often happens in the case of staged reconstructive surgeries, when a second or third surgery must be performed (eg, cleft lip and palate surgery or removal of hardware after stabilization of a fracture).

59 *Distinct procedural service*—This modifier indicates a service should not be considered bundled when it normally might be bundled (eg, service performed on a repair of a laceration in the foot and a treatment of a fracture of the distal radius).

62 *Two surgeons*—When two surgeons work together to perform distinct portions of the same service (using the same CPT® code), append this modifier.

66 *Surgical team*—A surgical team is composed of three or more surgeons or other qualified health professional required for complex procedures (for example, some spine surgeries or complicated repairs).

78 *Unplanned return to the operating/procedure room by the same physician or other qualified healthcare professional following initial procedure for a related procedure during the postoperative period*—Use if the patient is returned to the operating room for an additional procedure in the post-operative period that was not planned, or for complications.

80 *Assistant surgeon*—Used for a surgical assistant who is a physician assistant (also consider Modifier AS).

LT *Left side of the body*

RT *Right side of the body*

FA *Left hand, thumb*

F1 *Left hand, second digit*

F2 *Left hand, third digit*

F3 *Left hand, fourth digit*

F4 *Left hand, fifth digit*

F5 *Right hand, thumb*

F6 *Right hand second digit*

F7 *Right hand, third digit*

F8 *Right hand, fourth digit*

F9 *Right hand, fifth digit*

TA *Left foot, great toe*

T1 *Left foot, second digit*

T2 *Left foot, third digit*

T3 *Left foot, fourth digit*

T4 *Left foot, fifth digit*

T5 *Right foot, great toe*

T6 *Right foot, second digit*

T7 *Right foot, third digit*

T8 *Right foot, fourth digit*

T9 *Right foot, fifth digit*

Documentation Dissection

Case 1

Preoperative Diagnosis: Adolescent idiopathic scoliosis

Postoperative Diagnosis: Adolescent idiopathic scoliosis

Operation:

1. Posterior spinal fusion, T5 to L2 (10 levels)
2. Posterior segmental spinal instrumentation, Expedium, T5 to L2
3. Posterolateral Smith-Peterson osteotomy, L1, T8, T9, T10, T11, T12.
4. Autograft for spine fusion
5. Allograft for spine fusion

Anesthesia: General.

History: The patient is a 13-year-old female who presented with a large right thoracic curve. She apparently had been diagnosed several years previously and had spotty follow-up. Over the course of the past year, she had developed a markedly progressive and more prominent curve. On examination, she had a large right thoracic curve with associated rib hump and significant shoulder height asymmetry. Neurovascular status was intact and preoperative MRI scan was normal. Radiographs showed right main thoracic curve that measured in excess of 60 degrees. She was brought to the operating room today for posterior instrumentation and fusion.

Procedure: After obtaining adequate general anesthesia, the patient was positioned prone on the Jackson table. Transcranial motor and somatosensory evoked potential monitoring was established and good baseline signals obtained. An Amicar drip was started. Controlled hypotensive anesthesia was induced.

After the back was prepped and draped sterilely, an incision was made from the upper thoracic to the upper lumbar region. [1] A localizing radiograph was obtained and the spine exposed subperiosteally from T5 to L2. Pedicle screws were placed in standard fashion. An opening to the pedicle was made with a high-speed bur. A pilot hole was created with a gearshift pusher. The pilot hole was probed, tapped, and reprobed to verify integrity, and then screws were placed. Screws were placed according to preoperatively determined plan, as follows: All levels on the left side (from T5 to L2), and on the right T5, T6, T7, T8, T9, T10, T12, L1, and L2. [2] Length and direction of the screws were checked with the surgeon-directed C-arm fluoroscope [3] and several minor adjustments to length were made.

Posterolateral osteotomies [4] were then performed to help mobilize the spine. These were done in sequential fashion starting at L1 and extending in a cephalad direction up to T8. [5] The osteotomies were done by excising the facet joints with Leksell rongeur and/or osteotomes, and performing a limited laminectomy and excision of the spinous processes using a Leksell rongeur. This technique was repeated in the fashion described at each level so as to help mobilize the spine to enable a better correction.

Next, 5.5 mm stainless steel rods were trimmed to appropriate length and contoured. The left-sided rod was seated first. The rod was slightly underbent relative to the on table deformity of the spine and loaded into the screws. Setscrews were placed, provisionally tightened. The rod was rotated. [6] *In situ* benders were used to gain additional correction. The convex rod was then placed. With both rods in place, the vertebral bodies were then de-rotated using paired or single screws at each level. [7] Final correction was then achieved by distracting across the concavity of the curve and compressing across convexity. Cross-connectors were then applied at the upper end of the construct between T5 and T6 and at the lower end of the construct between L1 and L2. [8] Setscrews were all tightened using the torque limiting wrench. The wound was irrigated with 1.5 liters of saline. Autogenous bone, which had been harvested and preserved in the course of performing the osteotomies and preparing the pedicle screw sites, was then packed posterolaterally as graft (approximately 20 to 25 mL total). [9] This was augmented with another 20 mL of DBX bone chips. [10] A subfascial drain was placed. One gram of Vancomycin® powder was distributed in the depths and around the margins of the wound, and then the incision closed in layers using absorbable suture with a running subcuticular stitch to the skin. Steri-Strips and sterile dressings were applied.

The patient was awakened and taken to recovery in satisfactory condition.

_____

[1] Posterior approach.

[2] Spinal fusion using pedicle screws, 10 levels.

[3] Intraoperative fluoroscopy was used.

[4] Osteotomies performed.

[5] 6 vertebral segments, 1 Lumbar and 5 Thoracic.

[6] Spinal instrumentation used.

[7] Multiple attachment points indicate segmental instrumentation.

[8] Spinal instrumentation went from T5–L2.

[9] Autograft.

[10] Allograft

_____

What are the CPT® and ICD-10-CM codes reported?

CPT® Codes: 22802, 22214-51, 22843, 22216 x 5, 20936, 20930

ICD-10-CM Code: M41.125

Rationale: CPT® Codes: Arthrodesis is a surgical procedure joining two vertebrae together. In this case, pedicle screws are used to fixate T5 through L2 together for a spinal deformity (scoliosis) (T5, T6, T7, T8, T9, T10, T11, T12, L1, and L2 = 10 levels). In the CPT® Index to Diseases, look for Arthrodesis/Vertebra/Spinal Deformity. A posterior (through the back) approach was taken, you are directed to codes 22800– 22804. Code selection is based on the number of vertebral segments. Ten levels are coded with 22802 (7 to 12 segments). Fluoroscopy is bundled with the arthrodesis and is not coded. Fluoro is included when used as guidance for ortho surgery.

Posterolateral osteotomies were performed starting at L1 and extending in a cephalad (toward the head) direction up to T8. In the CPT® Index, look for Osteotomy/Spine/Posterior/Posterolateral, and you are directed to code range 22210–22214. Osteotomies of the spine are coded based on location. One lumbar (L1) and five thoracic (T8, T9, T10, T11, T12) vertebrae are involved. Code 22214 is reported for the one lumbar segment, and 22216 x 5 reports the remaining five segments.

Spinal instrumentation also was applied. Look in the CPT® Index to Diseases for Spinal Instrumentation/Posterior Segmental (we know it is segmental because it was fixated in multiple levels), and you are directed to 22842–22844. The code is selected based on the number of levels. In this case, the spinal instrumentation was fixated from T5–L2 (T5, T6, T7, T8, T9, T10, T11, T12, L1, and L2 = 10 levels). Ten levels are coded with add-on code 22843.

Autogenous bone was used for a graft (autograft), and then supplemented with bone chips (allograft). In the CPT® Index to Diseases, look for Spine/Allograft. The selection is between morselized and structural. Bone chips were used, indicating it was morselized, which directs you to 20930. Under spine, autograft, you have an option for local. The autogenous bone was stated as being taken from the spine osteotomies, considered local, which directs you to 20936. Verification of both 20930 and 20936 determine these are the correct codes.

The listing of the codes is based on RVUs. Modifier 51 is used on code 22214 to indicate multiple procedures. Modifier 51 is not used on the remaining codes because they are add-on codes and are modifier 51 exempt.

ICD-10-CM Code: Look in the ICD-10-CM Index to Diseases and Injuries for Scoliosis/idiopathic/adolescent/thoracolumbar region. Verify code M41.125 in the Tabular List. Adolescent idiopathic scoliosis is present in 2 to 4 percent of children between 10 and 16 years of age. Juvenile idiopathic scoliosis is a type of scoliosis that is first diagnosed between the ages of 4 and 10.

ICD-9-CM Application

What is/are the ICD-9-CM code(s) reported?

Code(s): 737.30

Rationale: The diagnosis is listed as adolescent idiopathic scoliosis. Look in the ICD-9-CM Index to Diseases for Scoliosis/idiopathic, and you are directed to 737.30. The Tabular List verifies 737.30 is for scoliosis, idiopathic.

Case #2

Preoperative Diagnosis: Hammertoe, digit. 2 and 3 right. [1]

Post-Operative Diagnosis: Same as preoperative diagnosis.

Procedure: Flexor Tenotomy of the 2nd and 3rd Toe, Right Foot [2]

Anesthesia: Local

Hemostasis: Accomplished with digital tomicot

Estimated Blood Loss: Minimal

Injectables: Agent used for local anesthesia was 3.0 cc Lidocaine 2% with epi. Each toe.

Pathology: No specimen

Dressings: Applied Bacitracin® ointment. Site was dressed with Adaptic, dry sterile dressing, Kling and 3x3 gauze.

For informed consent, the more common risks, benefits, and alternatives to the procedure were thoroughly discussed with the patient. An appropriate consent form was signed, indicating he understands the procedure and its possible complications.

Operative Note: This 85-year-old male was brought to the operating room and placed on the surgical table in a supine position. Following anesthesia and hemostasis, surgical site was prepped and draped in the normal sterile fashion. Attention was then directed to the plantar aspect of the 2nd toe, right foot [3] where, utilizing a # 61 blade, a stab incision was made, taking care to identify and retract all vital structures. Utilizing a curved hemostat, the flexor tendon was grasped and withdrawn from the incision. A Z-plasty incision was made on the flexor tendon and it was lengthened. [4] Superficial closure [5] was accomplished using Steri-Strips. Approximately 1/4 cc. of Hexadrol Phosphate was instilled into each of the surgical sites. The exact same procedure was performed on the third toe right foot. [6] Site was dressed with Adaptic, dry sterile dressing, Kling and 3x3 gauze. Excellent capillary refill to all the digits was observed without excessive bleeding noted.

Condition: Patient tolerated procedure and anesthesia well. Vital signs stable. Vascular status intact to all digits. Patient recovered in the operating room, post operative instructions were given to patient which includes keeping the dressing dry and intact until I see them next week.

Scheduling: Return to the clinic in 1 week(s).

---

[1] Pre-operative and postoperative diagnosis is hammertoe, digit 2 and 3 right.

[2] Procedure performed.

[3] Operation on the 2nd toe of the right foot.

[4] Z-plasty incision made on the flexor tendon to lengthen it.

[5] Repair is superficial.

[6] The same procedure was repeated on the third toe of the right foot.

What are the CPT® and ICD-10-CM codes reported?

CPT® Codes: 28232-T6, 28232-51-T7

ICD-10-CM Code: M20.41

Rationale: CPT® Codes: An incision was made into the tendon of the toe (tenotomy) to lengthen the tendon and release hammertoe. To find the correct code, look in the CPT® Index to Diseases for Tenotomy/Toe, or Toe/Tenotomy, and you are directed to codes 28010–28011, 28232–28234, and 28240. Codes 28010–28011 are for a percutaneous procedure. Codes 28232–28234 are for an open tenotomy, and code 28240 is for tenotomy on the abductor hallicis muscle. This procedure was an open tenotomy on a tendon; the selection is narrowed down to 28232–28234. Code 28232 is for a flexor tendon, while 28234 is for an extensor tendon. The procedure was on a flexor tendon, making 28232 the correct code. The procedure was performed twice, once on the 2nd toe of the right foot, and again on the 3rd toe of the right foot. Modifiers T6 and T7 are used to indicate on which toes the procedure was performed. Modifier 51 is reported on the second code to indicate multiple procedures.

Look in the ICD-10-CM Index to Diseases and Injuries for Deformity/toe/hammer toe M20.4-. Look for code M20.4- in the Tabular List. The Tabular List specifies that a 5th character is required to report laterality (right or left foot). The documentation states the deformity is on the right foot which is reported with M20.41.

ICD-9-CM Application

What is/are the ICD-9-CM code(s) reported?

Code(s): 735.4

ICD-9-CM Code: The diagnosis is hammertoe of the 2nd and 3rd digit of the right foot. Look in the ICD-9-CM Index to Diseases for Hammer toe. We do not know if this is acquired or congenital, so the default is acquired. You are directed to 735.4. Code 735.4 is for Other hammertoe (acquired). Because it is the same diagnosis for both the 2nd and 3rd digits, it is only reported once.

Glossary

Allograft—Transplanting tissue obtained from a donor of the same species.

Ankylosis—Stiffening of the joint.

Ankylosing Spondylitis—A disease causing the bones of the spine to grow together.

Anterior Cruciate Ligament (ACL)—A ligament located in the center of the knee controlling rotation and forward movement of the tibia (shin bone).

Arthritis—Inflammation of a joint; usually accompanied by pain, swelling, and sometimes changes in structure.

Arthrogram—X–ray to view bone structures, follows an injection of contrast fluid into a joint area.

Arthroscopy—Minimally-invasive, diagnostic and therapeutic endoscopic procedure used for conditions of a joint.

Arthropathy—Pathology or abnormality of a joint and arthritic conditions

Autograft—Transplanting tissue into a new position in or on the body of the same individual.

Bursa—Fluid-filled sac located between a bone and a tendon or muscle.

Bursitis—Swelling and irritation of the bursa.

Bunion—Inflammation and deformity in the joint of the big toe.

Capsulitis—Inflammation of the tissues; also called synovitis.

Carpal Tunnel Syndrome—Median nerve is compressed as it passes through the carpal tunnel (a confined space) in the wrist.

Cartilage—Smooth material covering bone ends of a joint to cushion bones; allows the joint to move easily.

Cubital Tunnel—A tunnel of muscle, ligament, and bone on the inside of the elbow.

Dislocation—Occurs when extreme force is put on a ligament, causing the two bone ends to separate.

Dorsopathies—Disorders affecting the spinal column.

Electromyogram (EMG)—A test to evaluate nerve and muscle function.

Enthesopathy—Disease occurring at the site of attachment of ligament or muscle tendons to bones or joint capsules.

Femur—Thighbone.

Fibromyalgia (Fibrositis)—Chronic, widespread pain in muscles and soft tissues surrounding the joints throughout the body.

Fracture—A break in a bone.

Gout—Result of a defect in body chemistry (such as uric acid in the joint fluid); this painful condition most often attacks small joints.

Hammertoe—Bent deformity in the middle toe joint.

Heel Spur—Bone growth on the heel bone.

Humerus—Bone of the upper arm.

Inflammation—Normal reaction to injury or disease, results in swelling, pain, and stiffness.

Joint—Place where the ends of two or more bones meet.

Juvenile Rheumatoid Arthritis (JRA)—Form of arthritis in children ages 16 or younger causing inflammation and stiffness of joints.

Lateral Collateral Ligament (LCL)—Ligament giving stability to the outer knee.

Lateral Epicondylitis (Tennis Elbow)—Caused by damage to tendons bending the wrist backward away from the palm.

Ligaments—White, shiny, flexible band of fibrous tissue binding joints together and connecting bones and cartilage.

Medial Collateral Ligament (MCL)—Ligament giving stability to the inner knee.

Medial Epicondylitis—Condition in the elbow caused by damage to the tendons bending the wrist toward the palm.

Meniscus—Crescent-shaped disc of connective tissue between the bones of the knees acting as a shock absorber to cushion the lower part of the leg.

Morton's Neuroma—Pinched nerve usually causing pain between the third and fourth toes.

Musculoskeletal System—Complex system involving the body's muscles and skeleton, including the joints, ligaments, tendons, and nerves.

Myelogram—Injection of a dye or contrast material into the spinal canal; a specific X-ray study also allowing careful evaluation of the spinal canal and nerve roots.

Nursmaid's elbow—Partial dislocation of the elbow or proximal radial head common in small children.

Open Reduction Internal Fixation (ORIF)—The insertion of metal rods, wires, pins, nails, or plates are placed to surgically repair fractured bones, usually through an incision over the facture site.

Osteoarthritis—Wear and tear causing inflammation of the joint, resulting in swelling, pain, and stiffness.

Osteomyletis—An inflammation of the bone and/or bone marrow caused by infection.

Osteoporosis—Porous bone developing when bone no longer is replaced as quickly as it is removed.

Pathologic Fracture—Bone fracture caused by a disease, not accident or injury.

Patella—Kneecap.

Plantar Fascia—Long band of connecting tissue running from the heel to the ball of the foot.

Posterior Cruciate Ligament (PCL)—Ligament located in the back of the knee controlling backward movement of the tibia (shin bone).

Prosthesis—Artificial body part replacement.

Radius—Shorter of the two bones of the forearm.

Rheumatoid Arthritis—Inflammatory disease involving the lining of the joint (synovium).

Scleroderma—Disease of the body's connective tissue causing thickening and hardening of the skin.

Scoliosis—Lateral, or sideways, curvature and rotation of vertebrae.

Soft Tissues—Ligaments, tendons, and muscles of the musculoskeletal system.

Spondylosis—Osteoarthritis of the spine.

Spondylitis—Inflammation of the spine.

Spinal Stenosis—Narrowing of the spinal canal.

Sprain—Partial or complete tear of a ligament.

Strain—Partial or complete tear of a muscle or tendon.

Stress Fracture—Bone injury caused by overuse.

Synovial Fluid—Clear fluid released by the synovial membrane, acts as a lubricant for joints and tendons.

Tendon—Tough cords of tissue that connect muscles to bones.

Tendonitis—Inflammation in a tendon or the tendon covering.

Tibia—Shin bone or larger bone of the lower leg.

Trigger Finger—Irritation of the digital sheath that surrounds the flexor tendons of the finger.

Ulnar Bone—Longer of the two bones in the forearm.

Respiratory, Hemic, and Lymphatic Systems; Mediastinum, and Diaphragm

Introduction

This chapter will discuss CPT®, ICD-10-CM, and HCPCS Level II coding for the respiratory, hemic and lymphatic systems, and the mediastinum and diaphragm. Codes found in the respiratory portion of CPT® codes (30000–32999) describe procedures of the nose, accessory sinuses, larynx (voice box), trachea, bronchi, and the lungs and pleura. The mediastinum is the central cavity of the chest. CPT® 39000–39499 describe procedures of the cavity itself, not of the organs (such as the heart) contained within it. The thoracic diaphragm (CPT® 39501–39599) divides the thoracic cavity from the abdomen, and enables respiration and speech. The hemic and lymphatic systems (CPT® 38100–38999) include the spleen and bone marrow, and the lymph nodes and lymphatic channels.

ICD-10-CM codes for these systems are found throughout the ICD-10-CM codebook, and include Z codes (for screening services) and neoplasm coding found in the Neoplasm Table in the Index to Diseases.

Objectives

- Understand basic anatomy and functions of the respiratory system, hemic and lymphatic systems, and the mediastinum and diaphragm
- Define key terms relevant to these systems
- Provide practical advice to overcome the most common CPT® coding dilemmas involving these systems
- Discuss application of the most-frequently used CPT® modifiers
- Review diagnoses common to the respiratory system, the hemic and lymphatic systems, and the mediastinum and diaphragm
- Introduce HCPCS Level II codes and coding guidelines as they apply to these systems
- Supply hands-on examples and review material to improve your mastery of the above concepts

Anatomy and Medical Terminology

The Respiratory System

Respiration (breathing) is critical to all cellular activity. The pathway of the human respiratory system begins with oxygenated air entering the nostrils. Within the nose, fine hairs trap larger inhaled particles and form the body's first defense against harmful environmental pathogens, such as germs, fungi, and spores. Cilia are microscopic filaments bathed in nasal mucus covering the surface of the tissue in the nose. A sticky layer of mucus and the cilia draws particles to the back of the throat and into the esophagus for swallowing. The cilia and mucus simultaneously add heat and humidity to the air. The resulting filtered and conditioned air travels through the larynx into the trachea.

The larynx, also called the voice box, is a funnel-shaped organ in the back of the throat connecting the inferior portion of the pharynx with the trachea. The larynx is formed by nine cartilages connected by muscles and ligaments. The hyoid bone, a horseshoe-shaped bone in the anterior midline of the neck, is not part of the trachea and does not articulate with any other bone. It provides attachment to the muscles of the floor of the mouth and tongue above, larynx below, and epiglottis and pharynx behind. The primary functions of the larynx are to protect the trachea when swallowing, and to produce sound. The larynx is covered by the epiglottis during swallowing. The epiglottis is a lid or flap covering the larynx to protect the trachea from inhaled food or liquid. The larynx also contains vocal cords separated by a triangular opening, called the glottis, through which air flows. The glottis narrows, controlling the flow of air, which causes the vocal cords to vibrate and create sound.

The trachea, or windpipe, is a cartilage-supported tube that connects the nose and mouth to the lungs. If the epiglottis fails to cover the larynx, and food or liquid enter the trachea, the body's natural defense is to cough. Sensory receptors in the larynx detect foreign substances and the brain triggers the cough reflex to prevent choking. For boys only, the trachea takes on a unique shape during puberty. The largest cartilage of the larynx (voice box), the thyroid cartilage, grows larger and sticks out at the bottom of the throat. This is referred to as the "Adam's Apple." Everyone's larynx grows during puberty; however, the thyroid cartilage in boys tends to grow more than in girls. Although rare, some girls may have an Adam's apple. The growth of the thyroid cartilage is what causes the change in a boy's voice during puberty.

Respiratory System

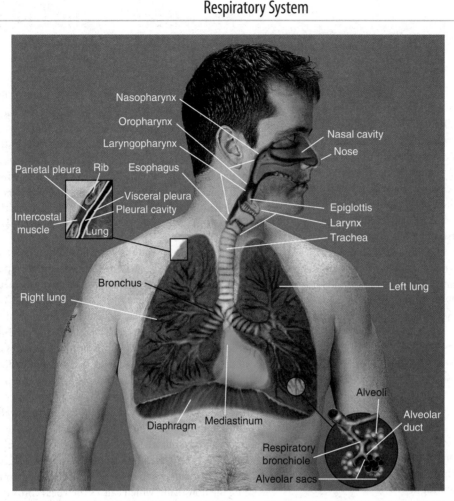

Source: EHRLICH/SCHROEDER. Medical Terminology for Health Professions, 6E. © 2009 Delmar Learning, a part of Cengage Learning, Inc. Reproduced by permission. www.cengage.com/permissions

The trachea branches into the right and left bronchi. The ridge separating the opening of the right and left bronchi is called the carina. The carina is a downward and backward projection of the last tracheal cartilage. The mucous membrane of the carina is the most sensitive area of the trachea and larynx for triggering a cough reflex. The right and left bronchi are the connection between the trachea and the lungs. The right bronchus is shorter and wider than the left bronchus. The right bronchus branches into three bronchi providing airways to the three lobes of the right lung. The left bronchus branches into two bronchi to the two lobes of the left lung. The lobar bronchi branch into tertiary or segmental bronchi, and then into smaller bronchioles. The bronchial system often is called the bronchial tree.

Bronchioles eventually branch into alveolar ducts and sacs. The alveoli, or air sacs, are primary units for the exchange of oxygen and carbon dioxide in the lungs. The exchange

occurs by diffusion across the alveoli and walls of the capillary network that surround the alveoli.

The lungs are located in the thoracic cavity on either side of the heart. The right lung is divided into three lobes and the left lung is divided into two lobes. The lobes are divided by fissures. The individual lobes are divided further into segments and then lobules. The left lung is longer and narrower than the right lung due to the heart being located in the left portion of the thoracic cavity. The right lung is shorter because the diaphragm is higher on the right to accommodate the liver that lies below it. Lung function is measured as vital capacity (VC). VC is the maximum volume of air a person can exhale after maximum inhalation. The measure is used in diagnostic pulmonary testing.

The lungs are protected by the pleura, a serous membrane that folds back onto itself to form a two-layered structure. The space between the two pleural layers is known as the pleural cavity. This cavity contains pleural fluid that prevents friction between the two membranes and allows them to slide past one another during breathing, as the lungs expand and contract. The outer layer of the pleural (parietal pleura) attaches the lung to the chest wall. The inner pleura (visceral pleura) cover the lungs. No connection exists between the right and left pleural cavities; disease or trauma to one lung may not affect the other lung.

Key Roots, Suffixes, and Prefixes for the Respiratory System

bi—two

centesis—puncture of a cavity or organ to remove fluid

ectomy—surgical removal

ostomy—a new permanent opening

otomy—cut into

oplasty—surgical repair

pnea—breathing

peri—surrounding

oscopy—to view

phonia—voice

rhino/naso—nose

broncho/bronchi—bronchus

pharyngo—pharynx

trachea—trachea

pleura—pleura

pulmono/pulmo—lung

phreno—diaphragm

pneumo/pneumato—air, gas; can also pertain to lung, respiration

spiro—breathing

Mediastinum and Diaphragm

The mediastinum is the portion of the thoracic cavity between the lungs that contains the heart, aorta, esophagus, trachea, and thymus gland, as well as blood vessels and nerves. Discussion in this chapter does not include the individual structures within the mediastinum (such as the heart, etc.), but entails only the space itself.

The diaphragm is the primary muscle used in respiration, and divides the thoracic (chest) cavity from the abdominal

cavity. Inhalation occurs when the diaphragm contracts or moves down: The air pressure in the thoracic cavity is reduced, allowing air to flow into the lungs. During exhalation, the diaphragm is relaxed and pushes air out of the chest.

Contraction of the external and internal intercostal muscles of the rib cage elevate the ribs and push the sternum forward to increase the diameter of the thoracic cavity. These muscles are necessary for respiration. During increased respiration due to disease or exercise, the muscles can become fatigued and sore.

Other muscles, not used during normal respiration, include the parasternal, scalene, sternocleidomastoid, trapezius, and pectoral muscles. These accessory muscles are engaged typically only when a respiratory disorder—such as Chronic Obstructive Pulmonary Disease (COPD) or asthma—is present.

The Hemic and Lymphatic Systems

The hemic system pertains to the production of blood, including components essential in providing defense against foreign organisms or substances. The primary structures of the hemic system are the spleen and bone marrow.

The spleen is located in the left upper quadrant of the abdomen, and serves several functions:

- Creates and stores new red blood cells
- Phagocytizes (leukocytes eat/destroy) bacteria and worn-out platelets and red blood cells
- Holds a reserve of blood in case of hemorrhagic shock
- Recycles iron
- Synthesizes antibodies
- Holds in reserve monocytes and other bodies crucial to immune and restorative function

The spleen is a component of the lymphatic system. Splenoportography is a method of using X-ray imaging to view the portal system via the spleen.

Bone marrow is the flexible tissue found in the center of many bones, primarily in the cancellous tissue of the ribs, vertebrae, sternum, and bones of the pelvis. It produces the majority of red blood cells (for oxygen distribution), most white blood cells (for immune function), and platelets (for blood clotting, among other functions).

Bone marrow also contains so-called "stem cells" that can develop into several cell types. Hematopoietic progenitor cells are stem cells (hematocytoblasts) in the bone marrow that give rise to all other blood cells. These cells are used for bone marrow transplants. Hematopoiesis begins with stems cells in the red bone marrow. Some stem cells will differentiate into mature red blood cells and platelets. Others will develop into various white cells (or WBCs) such as basophils, lymphocytes, neutrophils, eosinophils, and monocytes.

Stem cells can be harvested from the blood system by apheresis, whereby blood is filtered to remove the stem cells. The blood, with the stem cells removed, is returned to the patient. The stem cells can be preserved by cryopreservation (a process using ultra-low-temperature) until they are needed.

Lymph nodes are located throughout the body and are an important part of the lymphatic system. Lymph nodes are considered glands, and aggregations of lymph nodes are located in the neck, under the arms, and in the groin. Lymph nodes filter the lymph fluid to remove harmful bacteria, viruses, and other unknown foreign material. Lymph capillaries pick up interstitial fluid, which is carried in the lymphatic vessels and drains into two main channels: the thoracic duct or the right lymphatic duct. These ducts empty respectively into the left and right subclavian veins. The intestines contain specialized lymphatic vessels named lacteals that absorb fats and transfer the fat via the thoracic duct to the blood.

The lymphatic system includes four organs: the spleen (discussed above), tonsils, thymus gland, and Peyer's patches.

Tonsils are immune tissue located on the back of the throat, one per side. They are an initial "line of defense" against inhaled or ingested pathogens, and as such are a common site of infection (especially in children).

The thymus gland is located in the mediastinum. It reaches its maximum size during puberty, and then decreases in size as it is replaced by fat and connective tissue. It is responsible for the production of T cells, which are crucial to function of the adaptive immune system. The thymus also plays a role in auto-immunity (preventing the body from attacking its own tissue).

Peyer's patches are found in the wall of the small intestine. Bacteria always are present in large numbers in the intestine, and the macrophages in Peyer's patches prevent the bacteria from infecting and penetrating the walls of the intestine.

Section Review 9.1

1. Where does the exchange of oxygen and carbon dioxide take place within the lungs?

   A. Bronchioles

   B. Larynx

   C. Alveoli

   D. Windpipe

2. What protects the trachea from food or liquids entering?

   A. Larynx

   B. Glottis

   C. Voice box

   D. Epiglottis

3. How many lobes are in both lungs combined?

   A. 6

   B. 3

   C. 2

   D. 5

4. What is the major muscle used during respiration?

   A. Intercostal muscles of the ribs

   B. Diaphragm

   C. Abdominal muscles

   D. Chest wall or pectoral muscles

5. What is also referred to as the "Windpipe?"

    A. Bronchus

    B. Larynx

    C. Trachea

    D. Glottis

6. Which of the following is not one of the four organs of the lymph system?

    A. Spleen

    B. Thymus gland

    C. Tonsils

    D. Bone Marrow

7. What is the term for removal of part of the lymph system?

    A. Lymphoma

    B. Lymphadenectomy

    C. Lymphadenitis

    D. Lymphedema

8. Where is the mediastinum located?

    A. Left upper abdominal quadrant

    B. Muscle that separates the abdominal and thoracic cavities

    C. In between the two lungs

    D. Below the diaphragm

9. What portion of the thoracic cavity lies between the lungs and contains the heart?

    A. Mediastinum

    B. Diaphragm

    C. Lymphatic channels

    D. Bone marrow

10. What is another name for the larynx?

    A. Windpipe

    B. Trachea

    C. Voice box

    D. Epiglottis

ICD-10-CM

The Respiratory System

ICD-10-CM contains a dedicated chapter for the respiratory system. Relevant codes may be found throughout the ICD-10-CM codebook. As always, begin your search for a diagnosis code from the Index to Diseases and Injuries, and verify code selection using the Tabular List.

Subsections of the ICD-10-CM respiratory chapter (J00-J99) are:

Acute Upper Respiratory Infections (ARIs)

Pneumonia and Influenza

Other Acute Lower Respiratory Infections

Other Diseases of Upper Respiratory Tract

Chronic Lower Respiratory Disease

Lung Diseases Due to External Agents

Other Diseases Principally Affecting the Interstitium

Suppurative and Necrotic Conditions of the Lower Respiratory Tract

Intraoperative and Postprocedural Complications and Disorders of Respiratory System

Acute Respiratory Infections (J00-J06)

"Acute" means a sudden and short-term infection. Depending on the severity of the infection, breathing can become difficult and oxygen levels in the blood can drop lower than normal. According to the World Health Organization (WHO), acute respiratory infections (ARIs) continue to be the leading cause of acute illness worldwide. Infection may be caused by a virus or bacteria. Viral infections usually are self-limiting. Bacterial ARIs typically are treated with antibiotics (whereas viral infections are not). ICD-10-CM codes for ARI are separated by the anatomy of the respiratory system: nose, pharynx, larynx, bronchus, and bronchioles.

Laryngitis, typically referred to as losing one's voice, is caused by irritation and inflammation of the vocal cords. Codes for acute laryngitis describe with (J05.0) or without (J04.0) mention of obstruction. Category code J05 has an instructional note to use an additional code to identify the infectious agent (B95-B97).

Croup (J05.0, J20.9, J38.5) is a common, high-pitched, barking cough found in infants and children with nasal-type symptoms. It can cause difficulty breathing due to swelling around the vocal cords. Croup usually is treated easily at home using a vaporizer to provide cool moist air for the child to breathe. In severe cases, the entire windpipe can swell shut. Croup usually

is caused by parainfluenza viruses; however, respiratory syncytial virus (RSV), measles, adenovirus, and influenza all can cause croup.

A milder form of croup, stridulous croup, also known as laryngismus stridulous or false croup, is a sudden onset of spasmodic laryngeal closure with crowing inspiration. There is no cough, no fever, and the respiration is normal between paroxysms. Respiratory syncytial virus, or RSV (B97.4) is the leading cause of respiratory infections in children. Acute bronchitis (Category J20) and acute bronchiolitis (Category J21) commonly are diagnosed when a patient presents with symptoms of a severe and/or productive cough.

Other Disease of the Upper Respiratory System (J30-J39)

Most codes in this section pertain to chronic conditions. A condition is considered chronic if it has developed slowly over time, is persistent, and lasts over 3 weeks in duration. These conditions usually are more difficult to treat and tend to go in and out of a controlled state. Codes in this section include J34.2 for an acquired (usually by trauma) deviated septum of the nose. The septum is the bone and cartilage that separates the right and left nostrils. Note, the code for a congenitally deviated septum is Q67.4. Nasal polyps (J33.0 - J33.9) are sac-like growths inside the nose, often associated with chronic sinusitis (J32.0 - J32.9, codes are dependent on which sinus is infected and inflamed).

Pansinusitis is used when all sinuses are affected on one or both sides of the nose. When reporting sinusitis in two or more sinuses and documentation does not indicate pansinusitis report a code from subcategory J01.8- or code J32.8. Pansinusitis codes are selected on its condition being acute, chronic, or acute recurrent.

ICD-9-CM Application

Pansinusitis in ICD-9-CM does not have a specific code to report its condition and is reported with a code titled "other."

In the Index to Diseases look for Pansinusitis and Pansinusitis/acute

473.8 Other chronic sinusitis

Pansinusitis (chronic)

461.8 Other acute sinusitis

Acute pansinusitis

Pneumonia and Influenza (J09-J18)

Pneumonia, like acute respiratory infection (ARI), can be caused by a virus, fungi, or bacteria. ARI can lead to pneumonia if not treated. Many of the codes for pneumonia in ICD-10-CM are combination codes that include the causative agent, and a secondary code is not required. J15.5, Pneumonia due to Escherichia coli is a good example of this concept.

Influenza (the flu) is a viral infection that affects primarily the nose, throat, bronchi, and occasionally the lungs. Influenza can be very serious, especially in the very young and elderly. The H1N1 pandemic in 2009 was a new flu virus that circulated quickly causing many deaths. Fighting a new strain of flu, like H1N1, is difficult when there is virtually no existing immunity. Mitigating the effects of new strains of flu is a public health priority. ICD-10-CM utilizes combination codes that are based on the strain of influenza and any related manifestations, such as respiratory, gastrointestinal, and others. Avian (J09.X-), H1N1 (J10.-), novel influenza A (J09.X-) or unspecified with pneumonia or other respiratory manifestations (J10-J12).

Code only confirmed cases of avian flu, or novel influenza, or other identified influenza (see ICD-10-CM Official Coding Guidelines, 1.C.10.c).

Example

Cytomegaloviral pneumonitis.

In the Index to Diseases and Injuries, look for Pneumonia/cytomegaloviral and you are directed to B25.0.

B25.0 Cytomegaloviral pneumonitis

ICD-9-CM Application

ICD-9-CM contains an instructional note to code first underlying disease as seen for codes listed in category 484. This instructional note does not apply in ICD-10-CM with the use of combination codes and only one code is reported.

In the Index to Diseases, look for Pneumonia/cytomegalic inclusion and you are directed to 078.5 [484.1].

078.5 Cytomegaloviral disease

Use additional code to identify manifestation, as:
cytomegalic inclusion virus:
hepatitis (573.1)
pneumonia (484.1)

484.1 Pneumonia in cytomegalic inclusion diseases
Code first underlying disease (078.5)

Chronic Obstructive Pulmonary Disease (J44.0 - J44.9)

Chronic Obstructive Pulmonary Disease (COPD) is a progressive disease that worsens over time. COPD causes coughing, wheezing, shortness of breath, and difficulty breathing. The number one cause of COPD is smoking. COPD is considered an umbrella term for multiple chronic lung diseases. Category J44 in ICD-10-CM includes these condition:

- Asthma with chronic obstructive pulmonary disease
- Chronic asthmatic (obstructive) bronchitis
- Chronic bronchitis with airway obstruction
- Chronic emphysematous bronchitis
- Chronic obstructive asthma
- Chronic obstructive bronchitis
- Chronic obstructive tracheobronchitis

ICD-10-CM Coding Guidelines (1.C.10.a.1), state the codes in categories J44 (COPD) and J45 (Asthma) distinguish between uncomplicated case and those with exacerbation.

Acute exacerbation of asthma and COPD is an increase in the severity of symptoms, such as wheezing and shortness of breath. Status asthmaticus means the patient fails to respond to therapy during an asthmatic episode; this is a life-threatening complication.

Asthma codes are based on the severity of the asthma as well as if the case is uncomplicated, or complicated by exacerbation or status asthmaticus. Excludes2 notes for Asthma (J45) allows using an additional code for COPD, unspecified (J44.9).

For COPD with asthma, the Tabular List has instructional notes to code also the type of asthma, if applicable (J45.-) and use additional code to identify any exposure to tobacco or environmental smoke. COPD with an acute lower respiratory infection (J44.0) states to use an additional code to identify the infection.

Example

COPD with acute moderate persistent asthma exacerbation due to exposure of second hand cigarette smoke.

In the Index to Diseases and Injuries, look for Asthma, asthmatic/with/chronic obstructive pulmonary disease/with/exacerbation (acute) J44.1. In the Tabular List, category J44 has two instructional notes; code also type of asthma, if applicable and use additional code to identify tobacco use, tobacco dependence, or exposure to environmental tobacco smoke. To find the code for asthma, look in the Index to Diseases and Injuries for Asthma/persistent/moderate/with/exacerbation (acute) J45.41. The external cause code is located in the External Cause of Injuries Index by looking for Exposure/smoke/tobacco, second hand Z77.22.

J44.1 Chronic obstructive pulmonary disease with (acute) exacerbation

J45.41 Moderate persistent asthma with (acute) exacerbation

Z77.22 Contact with and (suspected) exposure to environmental tobacco smoke (acute) (chronic)

ICD-9-CM Application

ICD-9-CM

In the Index to Diseases, look for Asthma, asthmatic/with/chronic obstructive pulmonary disease 493.2x; 493.22. For the external cause, look in the Index to External Causes for Exposure/smoke from, due to/tobacco, second-hand E869.4.

493.22 Chronic obstructive asthma with (acute) exacerbation

E869.4 Second-hand tobacco smoke

Note: There is not an instructional note to code the external cause.

Bronchitis (chronic J42, acute J20) is commonly associated with COPD. If the provider documents both COPD and acute bronchitis, report J44.0, COPD with acute lower respiratory infection with a secondary code to identify acute bronchitis (J20). For acute bronchitis with COPD that is causing an acute exacerbation, an Excludes2 note at J44.1 states that J44.0 may also be assigned at the same time. If documentation states the patient has COPD with acute exacerbation, but doesn't mention acute bronchitis, report J44.1 *COPD with acute exacerbation is used.*

If the provider diagnoses COPD without associated manifestations or conditions (chronic bronchitis or emphysema) report COPD alone using J44.9, Chronic obstructive pulmonary disease, unspecified. When the patient does not have an exacerbation or a lower respiratory tract infection, J44.9 is the only available code choice.

In emphysema (J43.0 - J43.9) the walls between the air sacs are damaged, causing them to lose their shape and elasticity. Most people who have COPD have both emphysema and chronic obstructive bronchitis.

Example

COPD with acute bronchitis.

Look in the Index to Diseases and Injuries for Bronchitis/acute or subacute/with/chronic obstructive pulmonary disease or

Diseased, Disease/pulmonary/chronic obstructive/with acute bronchitis J44.0.

J44.0 Chronic obstructive pulmonary disease with acute lower respiratory infection

There is an instructional note under this code to use additional code to identify infection.

In this case the secondary code would be from category J20 for acute bronchitis. These are combination codes that include the infectious organism. When the organism is not stated or is not known, J20.9 Acute bronchitis, unspecified is used.

ICD-9-CM Application

ICD-9-CM

Look in the Index to Diseases for Bronchitis/with obstruction airway, chronic/with/acute bronchitis or Disease, diseased/pulmonary/diffuse obstructive (chronic)/with/acute bronchitis 491.22.

491.22 Chronic airway obstruction with acute bronchitis

Lung Diseases Due to External Agents (J60-J70)

Pneumoconiosis (pl. pneumoconioses) is a restrictive lung disease caused by inhalation of dust. Typically, it is referred to as an occupational lung disease because it affects primarily those working in mining, steel production, and occupations that deal with shipping stone. Dust causes scarring of the lungs that cannot be reversed. Other ICD-10-CM codes in this section include exposure to chemical fumes, vapors, solids, and liquids.

Example

ICD-10-CM has code selections for pneumoconiosis due to other silica or silicates and pneumonia due to inhalation of other dust.

J62 Pneumoconiosis due to dust containing silica

J62.0 Pneumoconiosis due to talc dust

J62.8 Pneumoconiosis due to other dust containing silica

J63 Pneumoconiosis due to other inorganic dusts

J63.0 Aluminosis (of lung)

J63.1 Bauxite fibrosis (of lung)

J63.2 Beryliosis

J63.3 Graphite fibrosis (of lung)

J63.4 Sideroisis

J63.5 Stannosis

J63.6 Pneumoconiosis due to other specified inorganic dusts

ICD-9-CM Application

ICD-9-CM only two codes are reported for pneumoconiosis due to other silica or silicates and pneumonia due to inhalation of other dust.

502 Pneumoconiosis due to other silica or silicates

503 Pneumoconiosis due to other inorganic dust

Suppurative and Necrotic conditions of the Lower Respiratory Tract (J85-J86)

Pyothorax (J86.0, J86.1) is collection of pus between the lung and the lining of the lung (pleural space), often caused by a lung infection that spreads outside the lung to the pleural space. Pleurisy is inflammation of the pleura, caused by a lung infection (typically pneumonia or tuberculosis). Category J86 has an instructional note to use an additional code (B95-B97) to identify the infectious agent, if known.

Other Diseases of the Pleura (J90-J94)

Pneumothorax (J93.0 - J93.9) is the collapse of the lung. A spontaneous pneumothorax (J93.0) has no traumatic cause. This is common in thin men who are heavy smokers. A pneumothorax also can occur postoperatively (J95.811); this may be referred to as iatrogenic pneumothorax. Iatrogenic denotes a response to medical treatment or surgical treatment. Traumatic pneumothoraces are found in the injury section and coded with S27.0-.

Pneumothorax

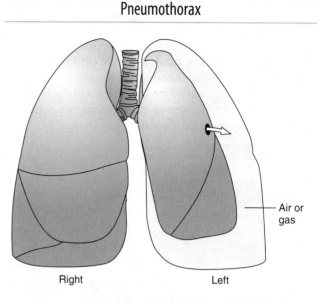

Source: EHRLICH/SCHROEDER. Medical Terminology for Health Professions, 6E. © 2009 Delmar Learning, a part of Cengage Learning, Inc. Reproduced by permission. www.cengage.com/permissions

Interstitial lung disease (ILD), also known as diffuse parenchymal lung disease (DPLD), refers to a group of lung diseases affecting the interstitium (the tissue and space around the air sacs of the lungs). ILD (Category J84) often is the result of pulmonary fibrosis from exposure to contaminants like asbestos, and is a chronic debilitating condition.

Pulmonary edema codes are located in this section of ICD-10-CM codes. In the Alphabetic Index Edema/pulmonary, instructs you to see Edema, lung. Many codes are available, ranging from J81.0 *Acute edema of lung,* J81.1, Chronic pulmonary edema, to to J68.1 Pulmonary edema due to chemicals, gases, fumes, and vapors.

Cystic fibrosis is a genetic disease that causes sticky mucus to build up in the pulmonary system and digestive tract. Coded from the Endocrine, Nutritional, and Metabolic Diseases section of ICD-10-CM, use E84.0 Cystic fibrosis with pulmonary manifestations. Identify any infectious organism present and report them with the appropriate code.

Symptoms, Z codes

When a definitive diagnosis cannot be coded, it is appropriate to code signs and symptoms. This excludes signs and symptoms that are an integral part of the disease process. Signs and symptoms not typically associated with a disease process may be reported separately (see Coding Guidelines, I.B.4-6). Chapter 18 of ICD-10-CM, Symptoms, Signs, and Abnormal Clinical and Laboratory Findings, not elsewhere classified (R00-R99) contains many, but not all, codes for symptoms. For example, respiratory system symptom codes R06.0-R06.9

describe symptoms such as shortness of breath, wheezing, and cough that cannot be coded more specifically from the respiratory ICD-10-CM section.

Z codes report personal or family history of conditions of respiratory disease. These codes are supplementary codes and are not used as the primary code. Screenings and status codes (eg, Z13.83 Encounter for screening for respiratory disorder NEC) are found among the Z codes.

Mediastinum and Diaphragm

Herniation of the diaphragm can occur due to weakening (K44.9). Report ICD-10-CM code Q79.0, if herniation is due to a congenital or gross defect of the diaphragm. *Diaphragmatic hernia with obstruction* is K44.0.

With bilateral diaphragmatic paralysis (J98.6), respiratory accessory muscles assume some or all of the work of breathing by contracting more intensely. An increased effort in the struggle to breathe may fatigue the accessory muscles and lead to ventilation failure. If the paralysis is due to severance of the phrenic nerve during a procedure, in ICD-10-CM the codes are specific to what procedure was being performed at the time of the puncture.

Look in the Alphabetic Index for Complication/intraoperative (intraprocedural)/puncture or laceration (accidental)/respiratory system has two codes - during a procedure on the respiratory system organ or structure (J95.71) or during other procedure (J95.72).

Thymic hyperplasia (E32.0) is abnormal growth of the thymus gland. Thymoma is a benign (D15.0) or malignant (C37) tumor in the thymus.

Hemic and Lymphatic Systems

ICD-10-CM codes for the Hemic and Lymphatic system appear throughout the codebook. The following are among the most significant and common diagnoses.

Lymphoma (C81-C86) is a cancer of the lymphatic system and typically presents itself with a lump along the lymphatic channels or in a lymph node. It may spread to the bone marrow. Treatment includes radiation, chemotherapy, bone marrow transplant, or a combination of all three.

Example

ICD-10-CM has two sets of codes for Anaplastic large cell lymphoma further defining the lymphoma by ALK-positive or ALK-negative. ICD-10-CM codes are combination codes that identify the type of lymphoma and the location of the affected lymph nodes.

C84.60–C84.69 Anaplastic large cell lymphoma, ALK-positive

C84.70–C84.79 Anaplastic large cell lymphoma, ALK-negative

ICD-10-CM has expanded code options for other types of lymphomas not listed in ICD-9-CM

C84.90–C84.99 Mature T/NK cell lymphomas, unspecified

C85.20–C85.29 Mediastinal (thymic) large B-cell lymphoma

C84.A0-C84.A9 Cutaneous T-cell lymphoma, unspecified

Lymphadenitis (I88.0 - I88.9) is an inflammation of a lymph node, often associated with some type of bacterial disease.

Lymphedema (acquired I89.0, post mastectomy lymphedema I97.2, or congenital Q82.0) is lymphatic system obstruction, which leads to localized fluid retention and tissue swelling. Untreated lymphedema may cause severe deformity.

Disorders involving the immune mechanism are coded to category D80-D89. Lymphoproliferative disorders pertain to several disorders marked by increased lymphocyte production. Typically, these disorders occur in patients with suppressed immune systems; examples include autoimmune lymphoproliferative syndrome (ALPS), D89.82 and Wiskott-Aldrich syndrome, D82.0.

Splenic rupture has several codes, depending on the cause. For rupture during birth use code P15.1 for newborns; for a traumatic injury, contusion, laceration, or rupture use a code from category S36.-. For all other causes, assign D73.0 -D73.89. Example, hypersplenism (D73.1) describes an enlarged, overactive spleen. This can cause a decrease in blood cells circulating throughout the body

Example

Laceration of the spleen

Laceration of spleen is reported by the severity of the condition indicating superficial, moderate, or major from Chapter 19, Injury, Poisoning, and Certain Other Consequences of External Causes.

> S36.030- Superficial (capsular) laceration of spleen
>
> S36.031- Moderate laceration of spleen
>
> S36.032- Major laceration of spleen

Multiple moderate lacerations of the spleen is coded S36.032-. A seventh character (A, D, or S) is required for these codes. The Tabular List further defines superficial, moderate, or major laceration of the spleen under the codes.

If the laceration is a complication of a surgical procedure these codes would not be used for the traumatic event. In the Alphabetic Index, look for of Complication/intraoperative (intraprocedural)/puncture or laceration (accidental)/ spleen leads you to D78.11 during a procedure on the spleen, or D78.12 during a procedure on other organ.

ICD-9-CM Application

ICD-9-CM codes for if the spleen is traumatically injured, contused, lacerated or ruptured are reported with two subcategory codes, 865.0x and 865.1x indicating if there is or is not an open wound into the cavity. A fifth digit is required to complete the code.

> 865.01 Injury to spleen without mention of open wound into cavity, hematoma without rupture of capsule
>
> 865.04 Injury to spleen without mention of open wound into cavity, massive parenchymal disruption
>
> 865.13 Injury to spleen with open wound into cavity, laceration extending into parenchyma

---

Leukemia is the most familiar disease of the blood and bone marrow; leukemia is a broad term encompassing a number of disorders. It is a form of cancer characterized by an abnormal increase of (usually white) blood cells. Codes for leukemia are listed in code range C90-C95. In ICD-10-CM the remission status is identified in the code.

- Not having achieved remission
- In remission
- In relapse

Not having achieved remission is also used for failed remission or not otherwise specified. Remission is defined as a decrease in or the absence of symptoms of cancer. A relapse is a deterioration after a period of improvement.

Section Review 9.2

1. What is the ICD-10-CM code for a patient with COPD presenting with an acute bronchitis?

    A. J44.0

    B. J21.8

    C. J44.9

    D. J44.0, J20.9

2. What is the ICD-10-CM code for a patient who presents with enlargement of his tonsils and adenoids for the fourth time in a year?

    A. J35.03

    B. J35.9

    C. J35.3

    D. J03.90

3. What is/are the ICD-10-CM code(s) for a patient with whooping cough who presents with pneumonia?

    A. J12.9

    B. A37.01

    C. A37.91

    D. J18.9, A37.91

4. What is the ICD-10-CM code for a child who presents with acute exacerbation of hay fever asthma?

    A. J45.22

    B. J45.901

    C. J45.32

    D. J45.902

5. A 20-year-old male presents in the Emergency Department with chest pain and shortness of breath. Chest X-ray reveals a tension pneumothorax. No trauma occurred: Patient smokes two packs of cigarettes per day. What ICD-10-CM code(s) is/are reported?

    A. S27.0XXA

    B. S27.0XXA, Z77.22

    C. J93.0

    D. J93.0, F17.210

6. What is the ICD-10-CM code for primary malignant thymoma?

    A. C37

    B. C73

    C. D15.0

    D. D09.8

7. What is the ICD-10-CM code for acquired lymphedema?

   A. I88.1

   B. I89.0

   C. Q82.0

   D. I88.8

8. A 4-month-old infant presents to the physician with cold-like symptoms, coughing, and wheezing. The infant is diagnosed with bronchiolitis due to RSV. What is/are the ICD-10-CM code(s) for this service?

   A. J21.0

   B. J21.8

   C. J21.0, B97.4

   D. R05, B97.4

9. A patient presents to the physician with persistent stuffiness and facial pain. The physician reports a diagnosis of nasal polyps. What ICD-10-CM code is reported?

   A. J33.0

   B. J33.8

   C. J33.1

   D. J33.9

10. A patient with right arm and shoulder pain, and a droopy eyelid is referred to a pulmonologist after finding an abnormality on chest X-ray in the right upper lobe. The pulmonologist has a CT scan performed and determines the patient has a Pancoast tumor. What ICD-10-CM code is used to report this?

    A. C34.10

    B. C34.12

    C. C34.11

    D. C34.91

CPT® Coding

Respiratory System

The Respiratory System chapter (30000–32999) of CPT® is arranged anatomically, beginning with the nose, followed by accessory sinuses, larynx, trachea and bronchi, and ending with the lungs and pleura. The anatomical section is subdivided further with codes for incision, excision, introduction, removal, repair, destruction, endoscopy, and other procedures.

Nose

"Rhino" is a prefix that pertains to the nose. Incision into the nose is rhinotomy. Incision codes for the nose are to drain and incise an abscess in the nasal cavity (30000), or on the nasal septum (30020).

Excisional codes for the nose include biopsy, removal of lesions, cysts, polyps, or the entire or part of the nose (rhinectomy). Follow CPT® parenthetical instructions to help you differentiate among the codes. For example, a parenthetical reference instructs that a simple excision of nasal polyp (30110) would normally be completed in an office setting, whereas extensive excision of a nasal polyp (30115) normally would require the facilities available in a hospital setting. Codes differ for excision of an intranasal lesion (30117–30118) and dermoid cyst (30124–30125).

Turbinates are bony structures in the nose that control and maintain airflow. Turbinates also allow for more surface area in a small space, which function to warm or cool incoming air. There are three turbinates on each side of the nose: superior, middle, and inferior. These turbinates may become swollen and require surgery to restore airflow. Methods to reduce the turbinates includes excision (30130–30140) or ablation (found in the "destruction" subsection, 30801–30802). Sometimes, the superior or middle turbinates are excised or ablated. In these instances, code 30999 is the appropriate code based on CPT® parenthetical instructions.

If a rhinectomy—total (30160) or partial (30150) removal of the nose—is performed, closure or reconstruction can be coded from the skin/repair section of CPT®.

Codes 30300–30320 report the removal of a foreign body from the nasal cavity. Typically done in an office setting, 30300 is the removal of a foreign body from a single nostril (a common procedure for young children). A more invasive procedure includes 30310, requiring general anesthesia, or 30320, removal of the foreign body requires incision into the nostril.

Rhinoplasty repairs tend to be performed for cosmetic reasons; however, rhinoplasties may be medically necessary if a patient has difficulty breathing through the nose. A septoplasty procedure is performed for a deviated septum that is congenital or from a traumatic event. Vestibular stenosis is narrowing of the nasal inlet resulting in airway obstruction. Causes include nasal trauma, infection, and previous surgery. Vestibular stenosis repairs are reported with 30465; note this code is bilateral, and applies to procedures performed on both sides of the nose. Choanal atresia is a congenital disorder where the back of the nasal passage (choana) is blocked by abnormal tissue. Intra-nasal (30540) or transpalatine (30545) approach may be used to perform repairs of this condition. Intranasal synechiae are lesions, often the result of trauma or prior surgery. These lesions may be lysed (destroyed), as reported with 30560.

Epistaxes (nosebleeds, singular is Epistaxis) are common, but sometimes require intervention to control. Control of nosebleeds codes are located in the "Other Procedures" section in the nose subsection. It is important to remember nosebleeds are typically unilateral; the coder should append the RT or LT modifier when supporting documentation is present. Nosebleeds can be bilateral, so be sure to add the 50 modifier if the CPT® code is a unilateral procedure code. Fracture of inferior turbinates is a therapeutic procedure to reduce the turbinates and improve airflow through the nose. This is reported as 30930. Do not report this code in addition to excision (30130) or resection (30140) of inferior turbinates. For fracture of the superior or middle turbinates, CPT® directs you to report unlisted procedure code 30999.

Accessory Sinuses

There are four pairs of sinuses (paranasal sinuses) in the respiratory system. All are located in and around the nasal-oral cavities. The frontal sinuses are located above the eyes on the interior or medial aspect. The ethmoid sinuses are located directly below the frontal sinuses, between the eyes and the nose. The sphenoid sinuses are located behind the ethmoid sinuses (behind the nose, and the eyes), and the maxillary sinuses are located in the cheekbones, under the eyes. All four sinuses outline the nose from the forehead to the cheeks. The sinuses are referred to as antrums. Procedures on the accessory sinuses often use the prefix "antr," such as an antrotomy (incision into the sinus).

Incisional procedures, referred to as sinusotomy procedures, can be obliterative or non-obliterative. Coders must choose the correct sinus and approach. Approach can be from the front or transorbital (through the eye). Sinusotomy may be necessary to open or drain a blocked sinus. Obliterative procedures are the last line of treatment options for chronic conditions of the sinuses not successfully treated by less invasive measures. When obliteration is part of the procedure performed, the entire mucosa of the sinus is removed and the sinus is then back filled with "fat" typically taken from the patient's own belly or thigh; non-obliterative procedures preserve the cavity.

Endoscopic procedures can be performed on the sinuses. An endoscope is introduced through the nostril to inspect the sinuses. Documentation of "flexible scope," "endoscope," or similar terms identify these procedures. Codes 31231–31235 describe diagnostic endoscopies; these "refer to employing a nasal/sinus endoscope to inspect the interior of the nasal cavity and the middle and superior meatus, the turbinates, and the spheno-ethmoid recess. Any time a diagnostic evaluation is performed all the areas are inspected and a separate code is not reported for each area," according to CPT® instruction. Diagnostic endoscopies are always included in surgical endoscopy. If a diagnostic scope is performed and the decision is made to perform a surgical scope, only the surgical scope is coded.

Codes 31237–31294 describe surgical endoscopies to treat an already-diagnosed condition. CPT® provides extensive parenthetical instruction in this section. Read and apply these guidelines carefully. The endoscope may be used for biopsy (31237), or for more extensive procedures ranging from control of hemorrhage (31238) to ethmoidectomy (removal of ethmoid tissue) (31254–31255), and more. Highlights in this section include:

- Dacryocystorhinostomy (31239) restores the flow of tears into the nose from the lacrimal sac when the nasolacrimal duct does not function.

- Concha bullosa is enlargement of the nasal turbinate; it may be resected (31240) to improve airflow.

- Maxillary antrostomy (31256) involves making an opening in the maxillary sinus to improve drainage.

- Sphenoidotomy (31288) is the creation of an opening into the anterior (front) wall of the sphenoid sinus.

- Decompression (31292–31294, depending on the structure(s) treated) relieves pressure on an optic nerve or other structures of the eye, to treat various optic neuropathies.

Larynx (Voice Box)

Excision of the larynx, parts of the larynx, or nearby anatomic structures are coded 31300–31420. Tissue may be removed, for instance, to excise malignant neoplasm. Laryngotomy (31300) is an incision into the larynx (in this case to remove a tumor). Laryngectomy is excision of the larynx, and may be total (31360–31365), subtotal (31367–31368), or partial (31370–31382). Laryngectomy can often be a difficult decision. It can be performed due to cancer or after a traumatic accident. There are options to replace the voice box with various devices, or the patient can learn esophageal speech. Watch for related procedures, such as neck dissection, during code selection. Radical neck dissection is the removal of the larynx, and lymph nodes; it may include surrounding tissue. This is to ensure all cancerous tissue is removed. For partial laryngectomy, the surgical approach (eg, laterovertical vs. anterovertical) affects code selection.

Pharyngolaryngectomy is removal of the pharynx and larynx. For procedures with reconstruction report 31395; without reconstruction, report 31390. Arytenoidectomy (31400 open, 31560 endoscopic) is excision of laryngeal cartilage where the vocal cords attach. Epiglottidectomy is excision of the epiglottis (flap of cartilage located in the throat behind the tongue and in front of the larynx).

Code 31500 describes an emergency endotracheal intubation. This procedure is reported when the patient cannot breathe on his own and the provider inserts a tube in the patient's mouth advancing it to the trachea to maintain an open airway during an emergency situation. Modifier 51 is not appended to this code.

A tracheotomy is an incision through the neck into the trachea to allow someone to breathe. An emergency tracheotomy may be performed for maxillofacial injuries, acute inflammation of the head or neck, or severe facial burns. Tracheostomies also may be performed when there is need for long-term mechanical ventilation, such as for a comatose patient.

Tracheotomy tube placement involves a fistula tract from the skin of the anterior neck to the trachea. If the tracheotomy tube must be changed before the tract is fully established (usually after about seven days), report 31502. Any tube changes after the tract is established cannot be billed and become a component of the appropriate E/M service billed for the visit.

A planned tracheostomy (31600) is a "separate procedure" that usually should not be billed if performed at the same time as a more extensive, related procedure. Planned tracheostomies on children under age two are reported using 31601. Emergency codes 31603 and 31605, which differ according to the area of access, are rarely performed because of the risk involved with these types of procedures.

There are two types of laryngoscopy (31505–31579)—direct and indirect—distinguishing between the two is imperative for correct coding of these procedures.

Indirect laryngoscopy is simpler than direct laryngoscopy. Indirect laryngoscopy involves the use of mirrors and lights to view the larynx. The provider views, biopsies or removes a lesion by visualizing the larynx through the reflection on a mirror.

- 31505 Laryngoscopy, indirect; diagnostic (separate procedure)
- 31510 with biopsy
- 31511 with removal of foreign body
- 31512 with removal of lesion
- 31513 with vocal cord injection

Direct laryngoscopy is an examination of the back of the throat and vocal cords using a laryngoscope. The provider can see the vocal cords directly. Direct laryngoscopy usually takes place in the operating room under general anesthesia or conscious sedation. This laryngoscopy category contains over a dozen codes and involves the most complex procedures. Common direct laryngoscopies are:

- 31535 Laryngoscopy, direct, operative, with biopsy;
- 31536 with operating microscope or telescope
- 31541 Laryngoscopy, direct, operative, with excision of tumor and/or stripping of vocal cords or epiglottis; with operating microscope or telescope

Many of the endoscopy codes include the use of a microscope or telescope (for example 31531 *Direct laryngoscopy for removal of a foreign body with operating microscope or telescope* or 31536, above). When a CPT® code does not include an operating microscope, but an operating microscope was used, 69990 should be coded in addition to the procedure code, but only once per operative session.

Endoscopic stroboscopy (31579) allows an examiner to gather information on the vibratory nature of the vocal cords. Using the stroboscopy, the examiner may determine the depth of cancer invasion, the presence of scar tissue or stiffness in a vocal cord, or the relative tone of the vocal cords.

A laryngeal web is a congenital malformation of the larynx, report codes located within the repair section of the CPT®

codebook. Repairs are performed via a horizontal neck incision. The surgeon exposes the laryngeal web between the vocal cords, excises the web, and inserts a laryngeal keel (spacer) between the vocal cords. At a later operative session, the surgeon removes the keel. In 31582, the stenosis (web) involves the arytenoid cartilages. The surgeon excises the affected area and places a graft (included) to allow for support for the larynx.

A cricoid split is a break in the circular cartilage of the larynx. This may be restored via laryngoplasty (31587). The split is reduced and affixed with wire; a stent also may be placed to maintain cricotracheal continuity.

Trachea and Bronchi

The trachea is also referred to as the windpipe. We have already discussed several codes relating to the trachea in this section, including several tracheostomy procedures (31600–31610). Tracheostoma revision may be simple (31613, without flap rotation to close the wound) or complex (31614, with flap rotation). Insertion of a laryngeal speech prosthesis (such as a voice button) is reported using 31611.

The primary codes in the Trachea/Bronchi section are the endoscopic codes. Surgical bronchoscopy always includes diagnostic bronchoscopy when performed by the same surgeon. Code the appropriate endoscopy of each anatomical site examined. If multiple bronchoscopies are performed, modifier 51 is used (individual payers may not require the use of modifier 51: check with your payers for details). For example, bronchoscopy with brushings and alveolar lavage is reported 31623 (report the code with the highest relative value unit, or RVU, first), followed by 31624 (append modifier 51 for those payers who require it).

Additional highlights in this section include:

- Codes 31622–31654 include fluoroscopic guidance, when performed. Do not report fluoroscopic guidance separately with these procedures.
- Bronchial alveolar lavage (31624) allows sampling of lung tissue by irrigating with saline followed by suctioning of the irrigation fluid.
- For a fiducial marker delivered via the airway using bronchoscope, report 31626. This code may be appropriate when physicians place fiducial markers used as guidance during thoracoscopic procedures or for lung wedge biopsies. Supply of the device (marker) may be reported separately using the appropriate HCPCS Level II code. If the procedure is performed in a hospital, the hospital bills for the supply, and it is not reported by the physician.
- Code 31627 describes computer-assisted, image-guided navigation during bronchoscopy. It includes 3D reconstruction (do not report with 76376, 76377). This

add-on code is used only with 31615, 31622–31631, 31635, 31636, and 31638–31643.
- CPT® provides extensive parenthetical notes throughout this section. Read and apply these guidelines carefully for best code selection. Many codes in this section are add-on codes (indicated with a "+"); others include moderate sedation, when provided, as indicated by the "bulls eye" symbol.

Endobronchial ultrasound (EBUS) allows physicians to perform a technique known as transendoscopic needle aspiration, to obtain tissue or fluid samples from the lungs and surrounding lymph nodes, without conventional surgery. The samples are for diagnosing and staging lung cancer, detecting infections, and identifying inflammatory diseases that affect the lungs. This is a less invasive procedure than a mediastinoscopy, described later in this chapter. EBUS can be performed during a bronchoscopy. Code selection is based on the number of samples or if it is performed for intervention of peripheral lesion(s).

Bronchial thermoplasty is a minimally invasive procedure used on patients that have severe asthma. A bronchoscope is inserted through the mouth or nose to the bronchus, then a catheter is inserted through the scope and thermal energy is used to reduce the amount of smooth muscles to clear the airways. Codes 31660 and 31661 are reported based on the number of lobes treated with thermoplasty.

A brush biopsy of bronchial tissue obtained by catheterization is reported with code 31717. Code 31720 is reported when a catheter is inserted in the nose through the trachea and into to the bronchus and fluid or foreign substances, such as secretions, is suctioned. Code 31725 is when the aspiration is performed by a flexible fiberscope and a tracheobronchial approach is used at the bedside.

Excision and repair codes primarily describe reconstructive procedures such as tracheoplasty (31750–31760, according to the precise location) and bronchoplasty (31770–31775, by method of repair). Also included in this section are suture of a tracheal wound (31800–31805, by location) and closure of tracheostomy or fistula, with (31825) or without (31820) plastic repair.

Lungs and Pleura

Understanding suffixes is required to master this section of codes. As a point of review, let's re-visit the suffixes that pertain to these codes:

-ostomy: new, permanent opening

-otomy: cutting into

-ectomy: surgical removal

-centesis: puncture a cavity to remove fluid

Incision for lung and pleural procedures typically involves a posterolateral incision between ribs 5–7, with the patient positioned in the right or left lateral decubitus position. Such open thoracotomy procedures fall into one of two categories, diagnostic (32096–32098) and surgical thoracotomies for definitive diagnoses (32100–32160). A diagnostic thoracotomy is for biopsy of the lung or pleura. A thoracotomy for definitive diagnoses describes more extensive procedures, such as hemorrhage control (32110) or removal of foreign body (32150).

A thoracotomy is an inherent part of other open lung procedures, so these codes are not all-inclusive. In other words, if a thoracotomy is part of the approach to perform a more extensive surgery, the thoracotomy is included and not separately coded. The CPT® codebook directs you to use open codes 32440–32540, for more extensive procedures. For example, when reporting removal of lung (32440), you do not code thoracotomy separately.

"Open" decortication (32220, 32225) is performed to remove fibrous or scarred pleura adhered to the lungs. These diseased pleura restrict lung expansion, and are found most commonly in patients with tuberculosis (ICD-9-CM 010–018) and mesothelioma (ICD-9-CM 163). Decortication increases comfort for the patient, but it does not treat the underlying condition.

Excision and Removal codes describe open procedures to remove portions of the lung and pleura. These may include biopsy by needle (32400 pleura, 32405 lung or mediastinum) or through open excision (32098 pleura). A pleurectomy is excision of the pleura (32310); note, this is a "separate procedure" and is only reported separately when it is the only procedure performed, or is unrelated to any major procedures performed on the same day. A pneumonectomy (32440) is the removal of the entire lung. Partial removal of a lobe, two lobes, segment, wedge, or other resections, requires 32480–32507.

Introduction and removal codes include chest tube insertion, 32551. Code 32551 is bundled into all thoracotomy and chest endoscopic procedures. Chest tubes are required to re-expand the lungs following these procedures; do not code them separately. The code includes connection to a drainage system when performed.

Thoracentesis involves inserting a needle or catheter into the pleural space and aspirating fluid. This is reported with code (32554) without imaging guidance and (32555) with imaging guidance. When an indwelling catheter is used for draining fluid from the chest cavity report codes 32556 and 32557 with or without imaging guidance. Codes 32560, 32561, and 32562 are used when instilling (gradually introducing) various agents. Code 32560 describes pleurodesis (talc) for recurring pneumothorax (collapsed lung). The instilled agent causes adhesion of the surface of the lung to the inside surface of the chest cavity. Codes 32561 (initial day) and 32562 (each subse-

quent day) describes fibrinolysis used to break up effusions (excess fluid that accumulates in the fluid-filled space that surrounds the lungs) and facilitate adequate drainage. Report a single unit of 32561 on the initial day and one unit of 32562 for each subsequent treatment day—even if the physician instills a fibrinolytic agent multiple times during the day.

Thoracoscopy is endoscopy of the thorax. Video-Assisted Thoracoscopic Surgery, or VATS, is a minimally invasive procedure for lung disorders. VATS allows a surgeon to accomplish the same goal as an open procedure with reduced pain, morbidity, shorter hospital stays and less recovery time. VATS is performed using a small video camera introduced into the patient's chest cavity via a scope. With the video camera, the surgeon is able to view the anatomy, along with other surgical instruments introduced into the chest via small incisions or "ports." The surgeon may insert up to four ports depending on the instruments needed to complete the procedure.

CPT® guidelines specify that surgical VATS (32650–32674) always include same-session diagnostic VATS (32601–32609). If the results of a VATS biopsy prompt the surgeon to perform a surgical VATS to excise malignant tissue, only the surgical VATS is reported. In contrast, if the results of a diagnostic VATS prompts an open procedure to excise tissue, the diagnostic VATS may be billed, and the appropriate open surgical code may be reported with modifier 58 *Staged procedure*; some payers may require a modifier 59 in this situation; check with your payers for appropriate modifier usage.

Additional highlights in this section include:

- Diagnostic thoracoscopy of the lungs, pericardial sac, mediastinal or pleural space, without biopsy (for visualization only) is reported with 32601; this is a separate procedure and should be reported if it is the only procedure performed, or is unrelated to more-extensive procedures performed at the same session. In the latter case, report 32601 with modifier 59, in addition to the unrelated, more-extensive procedure.

- Biopsy procedures (32607, 32608, and 32609) are specific to the type of tissue removed (eg, infiltrates, nodule(s) or mass(es), or pleura).

- Surgical codes describe a wide range of services, from endoscopic pulmonary decortication (32651–32652), the open procedure (32200–32225, was discussed above) to lung wedge resection (32666-32668) to total (32663) or segmental lobectomy (32669) and more. Additional codes describe control of traumatic hemorrhage (32654) total pericardiectomy (excision of pericardial sac, usually to remove malignancy) or excision of a pericardial (32661) or mediastinal (32662) cyst, tumor, or mass.

Lung Transplant codes 32850–32856 include three separate areas of work involved in the transplant:

1. Donor pneumonectomy

2. Backbench work to prepare the donor lung

3. Recipient lung transplant

Separate providers in different facilities typically code these procedures. CPT® provides explanatory guidelines preceding the code listings.

Thoracoplasty is a treatment for chronic empyema, or pus that collects in the chest cavity. After extensive unroofing of the empyema space by resecting overlying ribs and partial removal of the lining of the chest cavity, the area is packed with gauze. This staged procedure takes place over many days. All stages are included in code 32905 (surgical collapse therapy). Because the code descriptor identifies this as a staged procedure, do not add modifier 58.

Pneumonolysis (32940) separates the chest wall from the lungs to permit collapse.

Respiratory/Medicine Codes

A ventilator is a machine used to assist with ventilation of a patient who is unable to breathe sufficiently due to illness and/or following major surgery. Management of ventilator settings is usually performed by a pulmonologist or intensivist, use codes 94002–94005.

Other procedures in the pulmonary section include pulmonary function tests (PFTs). PFTs are a series of different breathing tests led by a trained pulmonary function technologist, usually done at a hospital or clinic. There are national standards and guidelines to ensure that everyone performs and interprets pulmonary function tests in the same way.

Practical Coding Note

Codes 94060 and 94070 do not include the administration of bronchodilator in spirometry; the supply of bronchodilator and antigens should be reported with 99070 or the appropriate HCPCS Level II supply code. Highlight the parenthetical instructions below both of these codes to remind you to bill for the supplies.

Spirometry makes pulmonary measurements with a spirometer. This measures inhaled and exhaled gases and assists providers in the treatment of asthma. Forced vital capacity (FVC) measures the amount of air exhaled from full inspiration to full expiration. All of the codes in this section can be used alone or with each other, depending on what the provider is trying to diagnose. They are diagnostic and measure the improvement or progression of certain respiratory disease.

Codes 94011–94013 are for infant pulmonary function testing (PFT). The tests are performed only for children up to age 2. Before this age, the patient cannot cooperate with standard spirometry. Note that 94011–94013 codes include moderate sedation.

Practical Coding Note

All pulmonary codes, with the exception of CPT® codes 94760–94762 (which are technical only) have a professional and a technical component. The appropriate modifier (26 or TC) must be added, when appropriate, to designate the service performed was for the professional or technical component only. Make a note in your CPT® codebook so you remember to add the appropriate modifier.

High Altitude Simulation Test (HAST) (94452, 94453) is a test pulmonologists use to determine the patient's liter flow of oxygen or if the patient may require supplemental oxygen.

Pressurized or nonpressurized inhalation treatment used for airway obstruction is reported with CPT® code 94640. Pentamidine administration via aerosol inhalation is coded 94642 and is most frequently used for pneumocystis carinii pneumonia treatment or prophylaxis.

Often, an apnea monitor is used on premature infants and infants with chronic lung disease and neonates and infants who have a high risk of developing apnea. This type of monitoring is performed at home and involves training parents on how to respond to the monitor's alarms and appropriately intervene. Code 94774 includes the hook up, monitoring, interpretation, and report. Whereas codes 94775–94777 report each component of the 94774 descriptor and separate the procedure by the specific components such as the monitoring, downloading information, provider interpretation, and report. These codes are reported once per 30-day period.

Mediastinum and Diaphragm

The mediastinum extends from the sternum in front to the vertebral column behind, and contains all the thoracic viscera except the lungs. The mediastinum has two parts: an upper portion, above the upper level of the pericardium, named the superior mediastinum; and a lower portion, below the upper level of the pericardium. This lower portion is subdivided into the anterior mediastinum, middle mediastinum, and posterior mediastinum.

Mediastinum

Mediastinum codes include a mediastinotomy (cutting into the mediastinum) via a cervical (neck) approach (39000) or a thoracic approach (39010). Mediastinotomy can occur for a wide variety of reasons, including exploration, drainage, foreign body removal, or biopsy.

An anterior mediastinoscopy describes a procedure in which the physician inserts a tube through an incision next to the breastbone to view the organs in the mediastinum. Anterior mediastinotomy gives direct access to the aortopulmonary window lymph nodes—common site of metastases from left upper lobe cancers—that are inaccessible to mediastinoscopy.

Resection codes are used to report removal of a cyst (39200) or to remove a tumor (39220). An endoscopic approach is coded with 39401, includes biopsy(ies) when performed; or with 39402 when biopsy(ies) of the lymph node are performed.

Mediastinoscopy is an endoscopic evaluation of the mediastinum and used primarily to stage lung cancer especially when enlarged lymph nodes are seen on chest X-ray or CT scan, to diagnose mediastinal masses or to sample lymph nodes in patients who might have lymphoma or granulomatous diseases. Mediastinoscopy is performed using a general anesthetic in an operating room. A mediastinoscope is passed through a suprasternal notch incision, allowing access to the superior posterior mediastinum.

Diaphragm

The diaphragm is the thin muscle below the lungs and heart that separates the chest from the abdomen; it is the principal muscle of breathing.

Hernia repair codes for the repair of a diaphragmatic hernia include procedures performed on a newborn (39503), an acute traumatic (injury) in the diaphragm for other than a newborn (39540), or chronic hernia resulting from an injury for other than a newborn (39541). Additional approaches for hernia repair are coded from other sections. For transthoracic (through the thoracic cavity) see 43334 and 43335 and for thoracoabdominal (through the thorax and abdomen) see 43336 and 43337.

A diaphragmatic hernia is a protrusion of abdominal contents into the thorax through a defect in the diaphragm. Surgery is required to place the bowel in the abdomen and to close the diaphragmatic defect.

Imbrication (overlapping the edges) of the diaphragm for an eventration (a protrusion through the abdominal wall) is a surgical procedure to treat diaphragmatic disorder such as paralysis from traumatic injury. The abrupt increase in intraabdominal pressure during blunt trauma (eg, car accidents, falls, or crush injuries) produces diaphragmatic injury.

The fluoroscopic demonstration of absent or decreased diaphragmatic motion is suggestive of diaphragmatic injury. Barium follow-through confirms the diagnosis by showing herniated viscera above the diaphragm, and constriction where they pass through the diaphragmatic tear.

Hemic and Lymphatic Systems

This short section of CPT® contains approximately 60 codes, including incisions, excisions, and laparoscopic procedures, among others.

Spleen

The spleen is located in the upper left portion of the abdominal cavity beneath the diaphragm and behind the stomach. The spleen is enclosed in a capsule of connective tissue, which extends inward from the surface and partially divides the organ into chambers or lobules. Within the lobules are two types of tissue: red pulp and white pulp.

Spleen

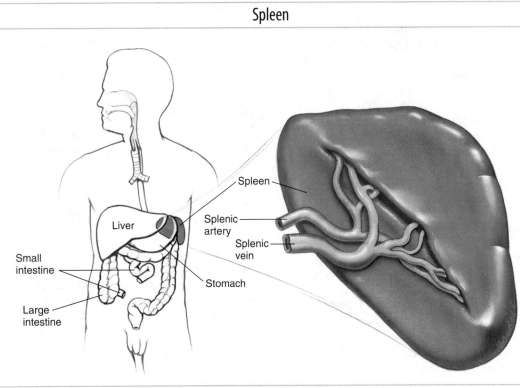

Source: Ehrlich, Medical Terminology for Health Professionals, 6e,
ISBN #978-1-4180-7252-0

Red Pulp—Contains many blood cells (mostly erythrocytes or red blood cells [RBCs]) and serves as a blood reservoir. This tissue also supplies the body with phagocytes. The term phagocyte is derived from the Greek words phagein (to eat) and kytos (cell). These cells have the ability to ingest and destroy bacteria, protozoa, cell debris, and dust particles.

White Pulp—Distributed throughout the spleen and is composed of lymphatic nodules called splenic nodules. This tissue generates protective humoral antibodies.

Excision of the spleen is a splenectomy, which may be total (38100), partial (38101—this is a designated "separate procedure"), or total at the time of another procedure (+38102). This last code refers to en bloc removal, meaning the spleen was removed as a whole or in-total; 38102 is an add-on code, which is reported in addition to the code for the "other procedure." Repair of the spleen (splenorrhaphy) is reported with 38115. A ruptured spleen may occur due to trauma; without emergency treatment, a ruptured spleen can cause life-threatening bleeding.

Surgical laparoscopic procedures on the spleen are reported with 38120 or 38129. If an X-ray of the spleen and portal system is needed, a splenoportography (38200) is performed. The radiological supervision and interpretation is also reported (75810).

General

Additional codes describe bone marrow or stem cell procedures.

Codes within the CPT® subsection describing bone marrow or stem cell procedures include the harvesting, transplantation, selection, cryopreservation, and storage of hematopoietic progenitor cells and the purging of malignant cells and T cells from these cells. Hematopoietic therapies include the repairing of progenitor cell therapy that refers to the infusion of blood-forming stem cells into the patient for the treatment of leukemia, certain other kinds of cancers, and some noncancerous blood disorders. The blood forming stem cells are derived from bone marrow, peripheral blood, or umbilical cord blood.

Codes 38204 and 38205 support the work of donor search (38204) and actual harvesting of the hematopoietic progenitor cells for transplant (38205, 38206). Transplant preparation codes include CPT® codes 38207–38215.

Practical Coding Note

Codes 38207–38215 are used to describe the various steps in the respective procedures and each code may be reported only once per day.

Bone marrow aspiration or biopsy only, code with 38220 or 38221.

Bone marrow or blood derived peripheral stem cells for transplant can be obtained by three different sources:

- Allogenic (genetically different but obtained from the same species): 38240
- Autologous (obtained from the patient): 38241
- Allogenic lymphocyte infusions: 38242
- Hematopoietic progenitor cell (HPC); HPC boost: 38243

Allogenic bone marrow transplantation describes the harvesting and preparation of a healthy donor's bone marrow for intravenous infusion to restore normal marrow function in a recipient with an inherited or acquired marrow deficiency or defect.

Autologous bone marrow transplantation is a technique for restoring bone marrow stem cells using the patient's own previously stored marrow. In aggressive cancer management, healthy bone marrow is harvested and placed in reserve while aggressive chemotherapy is employed to kill the cancerous cells. When chemotherapy is completed, the patient's healthy bone marrow is restored.

The infusion of donor (allogenic) lymphocyte cells is a procedure found to be effective in treating chronic myelogenous leukemia (CML), in relapse, after allogenic stem cell transplantation.

Lymph Nodes and Lymphatic Channels

Lymph nodes are small, bean-shaped structures grouped together along lymph pathways. These nodes or glands filter harmful products from lymph fluid and produce and store lymphocytes, which help fight infectious bacteria and viruses. Lymph nodes also contain other phagocytic cells, which engulf and destroy cellular debris, worn out cells, and other foreign material.

The movement of lymph fluid may be obstructed by tumors or during surgical procedures, if portions of the lymphatic system are removed. An example is when axillary lymph nodes are excised during a mastectomy, or for certain parasitic infections (eg, filariasis).

Lymphadenitis (inflammation of the lymph nodes) can be caused by a pathogen (eg, bacterial, viral, protozoa, rickettsia, or fungal). The lymph node involvement may be generalized with systemic infections or confined to regional lymph nodes.

Lymph nodes may need to be incised to drain an abscess. This can be done by a simple approach (38300), or an extensive procedure (38305). It often is difficult for coders to deter-

mine the difference between simple and extensive; query the provider if you are unsure.

Because lymph vessels carry material away from tissue, they sometimes carry cancer cells from original sites of origin, causing a metastasis of the cancer. Surgery for the removal of cancerous tissue varies in the amount of tissue and the structures affected or excised.

When the code indicates that a radical procedure is performed and includes lymph node dissection, then it is inappropriate to code a CPT® code from this section in addition to the primary surgical service. When a surgeon operates and establishes margins in the excised tissue but finds on the pathology report that the margins are inadequate (eg, all of the cancerous tissue is not removed), code for the removal of remaining lymph nodes.

The extent of the biopsy or excision, along with the location, determines the code (CPT® code range 38700–38780). Lymph nodes that lie under a layer of muscle and/or bone are considered deep. Limited lymphadenectomy for staging of a cancer is done to determine if a primary neoplasm has spread. There are different levels of cancer (grades or stages). Staging helps the provider diagnose the correct stage to determine the most effective treatment plan. Common staging is termed TNM (tumors, nodes, and metastasis).

Laparoscopic procedures of lymph nodes are for biopsies (38570), pelvic lymphadenectomy (38571), or pelvic lymphadenectomy and periaortic lymph node sampling (38572). Radical lymphadenectomy is the radical resection of lymph nodes to remove all of the nodes, surrounding tissue and structures. A radical surgery is considered extreme and is the opposite of a conservative surgery. This typically is performed for a high grade-cancer that has spread to surrounding tissues and structures.

Lymphangiography (38790) is an imaging technique in which a radiopaque contrast medium is injected, and an X-ray is taken to visualize the lymph vessels. The same procedure may be used with a radioactive tracer to identify sentinel nodes (38792). A sentinel node is the first lymph node (or group of nodes) reached by metastasizing cancer cells from a primary tumor.

Section Review 9.3

1. Patient is a mouth-breather. He is diagnosed with inflamed inferior turbinates and a superficial ablation is performed.

    A. 30802

    B. 30140

    C. 30801

    D. 30802-52

2. Which code(s) describe(s) bilateral endoscopic nasal procedure to diagnose breathing problems?

    A. 31231-50

    B. 31230-RT, 31230-LT

    C. 31233

    D. 31231

3. An indirect endoscopic procedure of the larynx means the larynx is viewed:

    A. Directly with a scope

    B. With mirrors

    C. Through an open incision

    D. Through an open mouth

4. Can bronchoscopy codes be coded together by a physician, and if yes, how? Are multiple procedures reported with modifier 51?

    A. No.

    B. Yes: Report multiple procedures with a modifier 51 (if required by the payer).

    C. Yes: Report distinct procedures with a modifier 59.

    D. Yes: Report multiple bronchoscopy codes together because no modifier is required.

5. A thoracotomy procedure was performed for repair of hemorrhage and lung tear. What CPT® code is reported?

    A. 32100

    B. 32110

    C. 32120

    D. 32151

6. Which CPT® code describes a pneumonectomy?

    A. 32442

    B. 32440

    C. 32440-50

    D. 32445

7. Can diagnostic VATS be billed with a surgical VATS under certain circumstances?

    A. No: A diagnostic VATS is always included in the surgical VATS.

    B. No: A surgical VATS is always included in the diagnostic VATS.

    C. Yes: Anytime a diagnostic VATS and surgical VATS are performed together.

    D. Yes: When a diagnostic biopsy is performed and submitted for pathologic evaluation, resulting in a surgical VATS.

8. Which CPT® code(s) describes VATS therapeutic wedge resection of the left upper lobe followed by left upper lobectomy?

    A. 32480

    B. 32505, 32480

    C. 32663, 32666

    D. 32663

9. A patient has a mass in her left axilla that is suspected to be a recurrence of lymphoma. She has a left axillary node excisional biopsy. The lymph node biopsied is under the pectoralis minor. What CPT® code is reported?

    A. 38500

    B. 38562

    C. 38745

    D. 38525

10. A patient with adenocarcinoma of the larynx has developed cervical adenopathy and is undergoing an excisional biopsy of the right cervical node. An incision is made above the clavicle and dissection taken down into the muscle. Blunt dissection was used to work the way down to the node, which was firm and white. The entire node was taken and the wound was closed. What CPT® code is reported?

    A. 38500

    B. 38510

    C. 38520

    D. 38542

HCPCS Level II

The Medicare pulmonary rehab codes are found in HCPCS Level II (commercial payers allow different codes to be used, eg, G0424, S9473; check your contracts). These codes are not found in the ICD-9-CM or CPT® codebooks; they are found in the HCPCS codebook.

G0237 Therapeutic procedures to increase strength or endurance of respiratory muscles, face-to-face, one-on-one, each 15 minutes (includes monitoring)

G0238 Therapeutic procedures to improve respiratory function, other than described by G0237, one-on-one, face to face, per 15 minutes (includes monitoring)

G0239 Therapeutic procedures to improve respiratory function or increase strength or endurance of respiratory muscles, two or more individuals (includes monitoring)

If supplies are used during the pulmonary rehabilitation, they are reported separately. For example, A4614 for a peak flow meter, or A7003 for a disposable nebulizer circuit (includes monitoring).

Modifiers

Modifiers from throughout the CPT® codebook may be used when coding for respiratory, hemic/lymphatic systems, or mediastinum/diaphragm procedures and services. Several specific instances of modifier use have been illustrated throughout this chapter. Rules for applying modifiers are consistent throughout all portions of the CPT® codebook. Below is a cursory review of the most-commonly used modifiers.

Modifier 22

Append modifier 22 *Increased procedural services* when the service(s) is "greater than that usually required for the listed procedure," according to CPT® Appendix A ("Modifiers"). Truly "unusual" circumstances will occur in only a minority of cases.

Modifier 25

Apply modifier 25 *Significant, separately identifiable evaluation and management service by the same physician or Other Qualified Healthcare Professional on the same day of the procedure or other service* when an E/M service occurs at the same time as another minor procedure or service. Documentation must substantiate that the E/M to which modifier 25 is appended, is both significant and separately identifiable. Any E/M service separately reported must be "above and beyond" the minimal evaluation and management normally included in a procedure or other service.

Modifier 50

Append modifier 50 *Bilateral procedure* when the provider performs a procedure bilaterally (on both sides of the body), and no available CPT® code otherwise describes the procedure as bilateral. Not every code is eligible to receive modifier 50 because not all procedures may be performed bilaterally. For Medicare payers, guidance on when to append modifier 50 can be found in the CMS National Physician Fee Schedule Relative Value File.

Modifier 51

Modifier 51 *Multiple procedures* indicates that more than one (non-E/M) procedure was provided during the same session. Many payers now use software that automatically detects second and subsequent procedures, thereby making modifier 51 unnecessary for that payer. Check with your individual payer for its guidelines, and request the payer's instructions in writing.

Modifier 57

Modifier 57 *Decision for surgery* applies to an E/M service occurring on the day of, or day before, a major surgical procedure (a procedure with a 90-day global period), and that results in the decision to perform the surgery.

Modifier 58

Append modifier 58 to a procedure or service during the post-operative period if the procedure or service was:

- Planned prospectively at the time of the original procedure

- More extensive than the original procedure
- For therapy following a diagnostic surgical procedure

Do not use modifier 58 if the patient needs a follow-up procedure because of surgical complications or unexpected postoperative findings arising from the initial surgery. For complications requiring a return to the operating room instead, append modifier 78, *unplanned return to the operating/procedure room by the same physician or other qualified healthcare professional following initial procedure for a related procedure during the postoperative period*.

Modifier 59

Use modifier 59 *Distinct procedural service* to identify procedures that are distinctly separate from any other procedure provided on the same date. According to CPT® instruction, you may append modifier 59 when the provider:

- treats a patient during a different session
- treats a different site or organ system
- makes a separate incision/excision
- tends to a different lesion
- treats a separate injury

Do not append modifier 59 to E/M codes, and do not use modifier 59 if another, more specific modifier is available.

Modifier 79

Modifier 79 *Unrelated procedure or service by the same physician or Other Qualified Healthcare Professional during the postoperative period* may be appended when an unrelated surgery by the same physician occurs during the global period of a previous surgery.

Modifier LT and Modifier RT

Modifiers LT *Left side* and RT *Right side* differentiate procedures performed on paired structures (such as eyes, lungs, arms, breasts, knees, etc.). They might also apply when a provider performs unilaterally a procedure that CPT® defines as bilateral (such cases would be rare). Finally, modifiers LT and RT may be used to provide location-specific information for those services defined either as unilateral or bilateral.

Documentation Dissection

Case 1

Preoperative Diagnosis:

Hypoxia.

Shortness of Breath

Postoperative Diagnosis:

Small Cell Carcinoma Right Lower Lobe [1]

Procedure: Surgical VATS, anatomic resection of the right lower lobe

Description of Procedure: After getting the appropriate consent for the operation and administering general anesthesia and intubation, the patient was placed in a full left lateral decubitus position with the table flexed at 30 degrees at the level between the nipples and the umbilicus to have better exposure of the right intercostal spaces. A 10-mm zero-degree thoracoscope was inserted in the right pleural cavity through a port site placed in the sixth intercostal space on the midaxillary line. Two additional port sites were placed in the fifth intercostal space on the posterior and anterior midaxillary line, respectively. The port sites were chosen with a possible thoracotomy in mind. The VATS exploration immediately revealed a mass in the base of the right lung. We wedge biopsied the mass and sent it to pathology for frozen section. [2] Results from pathology revealed small cell carcinoma so we proceeded with an anatomic resection of the mass. [3] We were able to thorascopically remove the mass via anatomic resection of the right lower lobe [4] without having to open the thoracic cavity. Green load endoscopic stapling was used to retract the right lower wedge, which was bagged and sent to pathology. Inspection of the lung revealed normal pulmonary parencheyma. After closing the port sites and inserting a chest tube, the patient was extubated and was transferred to the surgical intensive care unit for observation.

---

[1] Malignancy found in right lower lobe of lung.

[2] Diagnostic VATS biopsy performed and sent to pathology.

[3] Results came back from pathology and a decision is made in the same-surgical session to perform a surgical VATS.

[4] Lobectomy performed.

What CPT® and ICD-10-CM codes are reported for this procedure?

CPT® Code: 32663-RT

Rationale: A diagnostic biopsy VATS (32607) was first performed and sent to pathology. The results came back positive for small cell carcinoma. The results of the VATS biopsy prompted the surgeon to perform a surgical VATS with removal of the right lower lobe of the right lung. CPT® guidelines specify that surgical VATS (32650–32674) always includes same-session diagnostic VATS (32601–32609). Code 32663 is the only code reported for this case. The code is indexed under Thoracoscopy/Surgical/with Lobectomy. Modifier RT is appended to indicate the right side or right lung.

Diagnosis code is based on findings of the pathology report, small cell carcinoma of the right lower lobe.

ICD-10-CM Code: C34.31

Rationale: Look in the ICD-10-CM Index to Diseases and Injuries, look for Carcinoma referring you to *see also* Neoplasm, by site, malignant. Go to the Table of Neoplasms look for Neoplasm, neoplastic/lung/lower lobe/Malignant Primary column referring you to C34.3-. Subcategory code in the Tabular List indicates a fifth character is needed to complete the code. The concept of laterality is introduced in ICD-10-CM with code choices of left or right. This is documented as right. Fifth character 1 indicates the right lung.

ICD-9-CM Application

What is/are the ICD-9-CM code(s) reported?

Code(s): 162.5

Rationale: Look in the ICD-9-CM Neoplasm Table looking for Neoplasm, neoplastic/lung/lower lobe and use the code from the Malignant Primary column referring you to code 162.5. Verification in the Tabular List code 162.5 is reported to the highest specificity. There is not a code to report the laterality in ICD-9-CM.

Case 2

Preoperative Diagnosis:

Left upper lobe mass

PET positive lesion

Intractable back pain

Postoperative Diagnosis:

Lung cancer left upper lobe

Procedure: Mediastinotomy, bronchoscopy

Finding: Frozen section revealed a positive malignancy and compression of the left upper lobe bronchus [1] found by bronchoscopy.

Procedure: Patient was brought to the OR and placed in supine position. IV sedation and general anesthesia were administered per Anesthesia Department. A single lumen endotracheal tube was placed per Anesthesia, and the neck was prepped in standard fashion using ChloraPrep sterile towels, sheets and drapes. A standard linear incision was made over the trachea and was used to dissect down to through the pretracheal fascia without difficulty. [2] After extensive dissection and ligation of a few dense adhesions, we were able to identify two large lymph nodes in level 4 in the paratracheal region. Both were biopsied [3] extensively. The initial lymph node was found to be a reactionary lymph node; however, the second demonstrated a malignant process on frozen section. With the diagnosis in hand, we opted to terminate the mediastinotomy at that time. Hemostasis was obtained. The wound was closed and the layer of skin was closed with subcuticular.

Bronchoscopy demonstrated copious amounts of clear white secretions. [4] No evidence of purulent drainage was noted. The right bronchus was cannulated first and found to be free of any endobronchial lesions or unexpected pathology. However, the left main stem bronchus led us to a bronchiole that appeared to be compressed likely due to the malignancy in the left upper lobe lesion. The bronchus leading to left lower lobe and lingula appeared to be free of this compression. Again, copious amounts of clear secretions were noted and were removed with suction. [5] At that point, in time, the bronchoscopy was terminated. The ET tube was removed without difficulty. The patient tolerated the procedure well and was taken to the recovery room.

---

[1] Malignant based on pathology.

[2] A cervical approach (neck) was used as the report states a linear incision was made over the trachea portion of the neck.

[3] Two lymph nodes were biopsied.

[4] Diagnostic bronchoscopy with secretions removed with suction

[5] Secretions removed with suction.

What CPT® and ICD-10-CM codes are reported?

CPT® Codes: 39000, 31622-51

Rationale:

- Code 39000 is used for the cervical approach (neck) as the report states a linear incision was made over the trachea portion of the neck. Code 39010 would be used if a thoracic (chest) incision was made.

- Separate procedure was performed via a bronchoscope introduced via the oral cavity down the trachea and into the bronchus. Secretions were removed by suction. This is a diagnostic bronchoscopy and should be coded with 31622. A lavage (31624) was not performed, as there is no mention of saline irrigation and suctioning of the fluid, only suction of the secretions. Modifier 59 is not necessary because the procedures are separate from one another (they were performed by different approaches and in different areas).

ICD-10-CM: C34.12

Rationale: Diagnosis coding is based on the frozen section results, positive malignancy of the upper left lobe. Look in the ICD-10-CM Table of Neoplasms for Neoplasm, neoplastic/bronchus/upper lobe of lung /Malignant Primary column (C34.1-). In the Tabular List, the fifth character 2 indicates the left bronchus.

ICD-9-CM Application

What is/are the ICD-9-CM code(s) reported?

Code(s): 162.3

Rationale: Diagnosis coding is based on the frozen section results, positive malignancy of the upper lobe. In the Index to Diseases go to the Neoplasm Table look for Neoplasm, neoplastic/lung/upper lobe/primary. Verification in the Tabular List code 162.3 is reported to the highest specificity. There is not a code to report the laterality in ICD-9-CM.

Case 3

Preoperative Diagnosis/Indication: Traumatic pneumothorax/hemothorax [1]/pleural effusion

Postoperative Diagnosis: Decompressed pneumothorax/drained hemothorax/drained pleural effusion

Procedure: Chest thoracostomy with indwelling tube

Procedure: After consent was obtained, the patient was then placed supine with the ipsilateral arm above his head. After donning cap, mask, sterile gown, and gloves, the patient's left chest wall from mid-clavicular line to posterior axillary line and from axilla to costophrenic line was scrubbed thoroughly with chlorhexidine solution and allowed to dry. Sterile drapes were applied covering the patient's upper torso including face. Landmarks were identified between the 4th and 5th intercostal space. 10 cc's of 2% Lidocaine with epinephrine were widely infiltrated subcutaneously for local analgesia. Using a 10-blade scalpel, the skin and subcutaneous tissues were incised parallel to the rib margins to a length of approx 3 cm. Hemostats were then used to dissect bluntly to the intercostal musculature. The parietal pleura was then punctured with large Kelly clamps and the jaws were opened widely to allow an immediate escape of air. An 18 French chest tube with trocar was introduced into the pleural space to a level of 2 cm at the skin. The trocar was removed as the tube was advanced into position. The skin was approximated first, via 2-0 silk sutures in a horizontal mattress above and below the chest tube, then, the suture ends were tied around the indwelling tube. [2] The tube was then placed to suction. Sterile petrolatum gauze was placed at the skin junction and covered with sterile 4x4's. The site was then taped with pressure tape and secured. The Pleuravac [3] was checked and no air leak indicated. The patient tolerated the procedure well. There were no complications. Follow-up CXR has been ordered for placement.

---

[1] Traumatic pneumothorax with hemothorax are coded together.

[2] Chest tube was placed and left in for suction.

[3] Pleurovac is used for water seal suction.

What CPT® and ICD-10-CM codes are reported?

CPT® Code: 32551

Rationale: Look in the CPT® Index for Thorax/Tube Thoracostomy or for Thoracostomy/Tube. 32551 is a tube thoracostomy, which includes water seal connection to a drainage system.

ICD-10-CM Codes: S27.2XXA, J90

Rationale: The patient has a combination of traumatic pneumothorax and hemothorax. Look in the ICD-10-CM Index to Diseases and Injuries for Pneumothorax/traumatic/with hemothorax S27.2-. In the Tabular List S27.2- requires a 7th character extender. Remember, the 7th character extender must remain in the 7th position. Because S27.2 is only four characters, dummy placeholders must be used to keep the 7th character extender in the 7th position. The 7th character A for initial encounter is assigned. According to ICD-10-CM Guideline Section I.C.19.a., the initial encounter extender should be appended when the patient is receiving active treatment. An example of active treatment includes surgical treatment.

The patient also has traumatic pleural effusion. Look in the ICD-10-CM Index to Diseases and Injuries for Effusion/pleura, pleurisy, pleuritic, pleuropericardial referring you to J90. There is not an option for traumatic. J90 is confirmed in the Tabular List.

ICD-9-CM Application

What is/are the ICD-9-CM code(s) reported?

Code(s): 860.4, 862.29

Rationale: The patient has a combination of a traumatic pneumothorax and hemothorax. Look in the ICD-9-CM Index to Diseases for Pneumothorax/traumatic/with/hemothorax 860.4. The patient also has traumatic pleural effusion. Look in the ICD-9-CM Index to Diseases for Effusion/pleura, pleurisy, pleuritic, pleuropericardial/traumatic 862.29. Confirmation of these codes in the Tabular List indicates both codes are reported to the highest specificity.

Glossary

Allogenic: Genetically different but obtained from the same species.

Alveoli (air sacs): The primary units for the exchange of oxygen and carbon dioxide in the lungs.

Apheresis: Filtering of blood to remove stem cells or other cellular elements.

Autologous: Obtained from the patient.

Bone Marrow: The flexible tissue found in the center of many bones, primarily in the cancellous tissue of the ribs, vertebrae, sternum, and bones of the pelvis.

Bronchi: Bottom portion of the trachea that splits into airways to the right and left lung; the right is shorter and wider than the left.

Carina: The ridge that separates the opening of the right and left bronchi; a downward and backward projection of the last tracheal cartilage.

Chronic Obstructive Pulmonary Disease (COPD): A progressive disease that gets worse over time. COPD causes coughing, wheezing, shortness of breath, and difficulty breathing. The number one cause of COPD is smoking.

Cilia: Microscopic filaments bathed in nasal mucus that cover the surface of the tissue in the nose.

Concha Bullosa: Enlargement of the nasal turbinate.

Croup: A common, high-pitched, barking cough found in infants and children with nasal-type symptoms.

Diaphragm: Muscle separating the abdominal cavity from the thoracic cavity; primary muscle in respiration, contracting and relaxing thus inflating and deflating the lungs.

Dacryocystorhinostomy: Surgical procedure that restores the flow of tears into the nose from the lacrimal sac when the nasolacrimal duct does not function.

Decortication: Separating the pleura adhering to lungs to assist with expansion of the lungs.

Direct Laryngoscopy: Use of an endoscope to look directly at the larynx.

Empyema: Collection of pus between the lung and the lining of the lung (pleural space).

En Bloc: In total or in full; as a single piece.

Epiglottis: A lid or flap that covers the larynx to protect the trachea from inhaled food or liquid.

Glottis: The larynx contains vocal cords separated by a triangular opening, called the glottis, through which air flows. The glottis narrows, controlling the flow of air, which causes the vocal cords to vibrate and create sound.

Hemic: Pertaining to blood. SYN—hematic.

Hyoid Bone: A horseshoe-shaped bone in the anterior midline of the neck. It is not part of the trachea and does not articulate with any other bone. It provides attachment to the muscles of the floor of the mouth and the tongue above, the larynx below, and the epiglottis and pharynx behind.

Indirect Laryngoscopy: Use of mirrors with a rigid laryngoscope to view the larynx.

Instill: To introduce gradually.

Larynx (voice box): Connects the nasopharynx to the trachea, covered by the epiglottis during swallowing to prevent aspiration.

Lungs: The right lung has three lobes and the left lung has two lobes.

Mediastinum: That portion of the thoracic cavity between the lungs that contains the heart, aorta, esophagus, trachea, and thymus gland, as well as blood vessels and nerves.

Pleura: A serous membrane that folds back onto itself to form a two-layered structure.

Pleural Cavity: The space between the two pleural layers.

Pneumonectomy: Removal of an entire lung (all lobes).

Pneumonolysis: A procedure that separates the chest wall from the lungs to permit collapse.

Pneumothorax: Collapse of the lung.

Pulmonary Function Tests: Tests to diagnosis breathing problems.

Trachea (windpipe): Cartilaginous structure that carries air from the nasopharynx to the lungs via the bronchi.

Turbinates: Superior, middle, and inferior bony structures found in each right and left nasal cavity to assist with air movement.

Septum: Bony structure that separates the left nasal cavity from the right nasal cavity.

Splenoportography: A method of using X-ray imaging to view the portal system via the spleen.

Video-Assisted Thoracoscopic Surgery (VATS): Use of endoscope and video to perform diagnostic and surgical procedures on the thoracic cavity.

Vital Capacity (VC): The maximum volume of air that a person can exhale after maximum inhalation. The measure is used in diagnostic pulmonary testing.

Introduction

This chapter reviews the cardiovascular system. Codes relevant to this system are found in several sections of the CPT® codebook (specifically surgery, radiology, and medicine), and throughout ICD-10-CM (primarily chapter 9) and HCPCS Level II codebooks.

Objectives

- Master anatomical concepts necessary to understand the cardiovascular system
- Define key terms and recognize common eponyms and acronyms
- Explain the most common pathologies affecting this system
- Understand cardiovascular procedures and surgeries, and where in CPT® to locate relevant codes
- Introduce ICD-10-CM and HCPCS Level II codes and coding guidelines as they apply to this system
- Supply examples and review material to improve your application of the above concepts

Anatomy and Medical Terminology

The term cardiovascular means pertaining to the heart and blood vessels. The cardiovascular system is comprised of the heart, arteries, and veins.

The Heart

The heart often is known as the hardest working muscle in the human body. It sits between the lungs and behind the sternum (breastbone) in the mediastinum. The heart is a fist-sized, cone-shaped muscle (the myocardium) beating nearly 115,200 times per day, at an average rate of 80 times a minute. The heart is divided into right and left sides by a muscular wall, the septum. A two-layered, protective membrane, the pericardium (literally "around the heart"), surrounds the heart and roots of the great vessels (aorta, pulmonary trunk, pulmonary veins, and superior and inferior vena cava).

The pericardium consists of two layers, one sac inside another, the parietal pericardium and the visceral pericardium. The parietal pericardium lies posterior and adjacent to the thoracic vertebrae and superior to the diaphragm. It provides an efficient barrier to infection from surrounding structures. The visceral pericardium (or epicardium) adheres to the heart and the first several centimeters of the great vessels.

Pericardial fluid lubricates the heart's surface pericardium and facilitates movement during the heart's pumping action. The fluid, usually 10 to 30 ml in volume, can increase to 300 ml without impeding the heart's pumping action. With certain cardiac conditions, up to one liter of fluid can be retained within the pericardial space.

There are three layers of heart muscle:

1. The epicardium (or visceral pericardium) covers the heart's surface and extends to the great vessels.

2. The myocardium is the contracting muscle of the heart and consists of striated muscle fibers interlaced into bundles.

3. The innermost endocardium is composed of a thin layer of endothelium and a thin layer of connective tissue.

Layers of the Heart

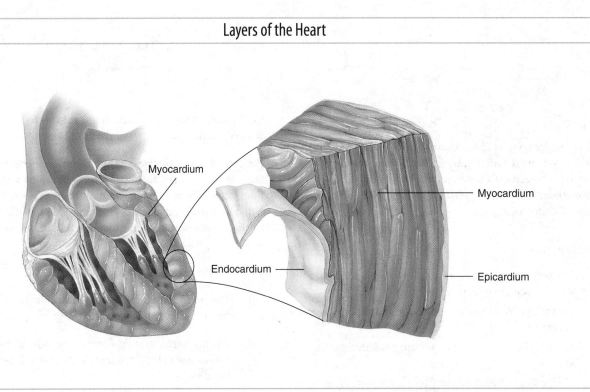

Source: Ehrlich, Medical Terminology for Health Professionals, 6e, ISBN #978-1-4180-7252-0

These layers line the inner chambers of the heart as well as the valves, chordae tendineae, and papillary muscles.

Chambers

The heart contains four chambers. The upper chambers are the atria (singular = atrium), which are "holding tanks," and receive blood as it comes into the heart. The lower chambers are ventricles, and pump blood out of the heart. The left ventricle is the most muscular chamber of the heart, because it is responsible for distributing oxygen-rich blood throughout the body (see "Oxygenation Process," below). The left atrium and ventricle are separated from the right atrium and ventricle by a septum. A large vein, the coronary sinus, drains blood from the walls of the heart and empties into the right atrium.

Valves

To ensure blood moves through the heart in one direction only, the ventricles have inlet and outlet valves. Heart valves are made of flaps (cusps/leaflets) opening and closing like one-way swinging doors. Atrioventricular (AV) valves are the tricuspid on the right, and the mitral (or bicuspid) on the left. They open from the atria to the ventricles. Both valves contain leaflets or cusps pushing upward during systole but prevent sinking or eversion into the atria. The tricuspid valve has three leaflets or cusps. The mitral valve has only two leaflets and is named mitral because its shape resembles a bishop's hat or miter.

The semilunar valves are the pulmonary (pulmonic) on the right, and the aortic on the left. The pulmonary valve is between the right ventricle and the pulmonary artery. The aortic valve leads from the left ventricle into the aorta. Intraventricular pressure during contraction of the heart muscle forces valves to open and the loss of pressure at the termination of systole allows them to close during diastole.

The tricuspid and mitral valves are inlet valves, but the pulmonary and aortic valves are outlet valves. The inlet valves are supported by the chordae tendineae (string-like tendons linking the papillary muscles of the inferior wall of the ventricles to the tricuspid valve in the right ventricle and the mitral valve in the left ventricle). When the atria contract, the valves open, and blood flows into the ventricles during diastole (ventricles relaxed, lower pressure). When the ventricles contract, the valves close preventing backflow of blood from the ventricles into the atria. The contraction of the papillary muscles prevents inversion or prolapse of these valves during ventricular contraction (systole), forcing blood out of the ventricles. The chordae tendineae are sometimes referred to as "heart strings." The "lub-dub" sounds of the heart beating are actually the sounds of the valves closing. The "lub" is the tricuspid and mitral valves closing, and the "dub" is the aortic and pulmonary valves closing.

Oxygenation Process

Oxygen deficient blood enters the right atrium through the superior or inferior vena cava. The tricuspid valve opens and the blood flows into the right ventricle. The blood is pushed up from the right ventricle through the pulmonary valve into the pulmonary artery. From there, the blood moves to the lungs, releasing carbon dioxide and picking up oxygen. Oxygen-rich blood returns to the heart through the pulmonary veins and enters the left atrium. The mitral valve opens, and blood flows into the left ventricle. The blood pushes up through the aortic valve, into the aorta, and out to the body.

Oxygen Flow of Blood

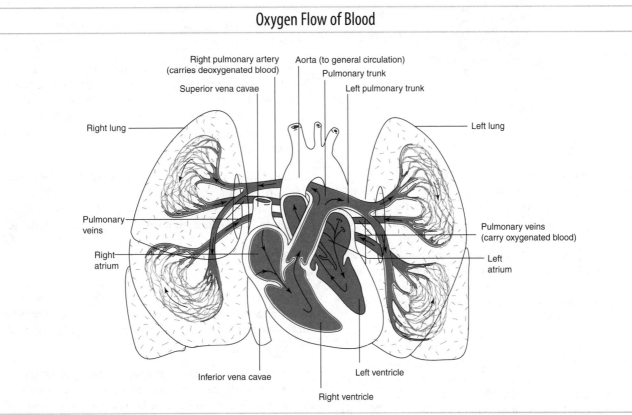

Source: Lindh, Pooler, Tamparo, and Dahl, Delmar's Comprehensive Medical Assisting (Administrative and Clinical Competencies), 4e, ISBN#978-1-4354-1914-8

Conduction System

The heart is able to move blood throughout the body as a result of its conduction system. The system contains pacemaker cells, nodes, bundle of His (AV bundle), and Purkinje fibers. Pacemaker cells have the ability to generate an electrical impulse, to pass the impulse to other cells, and to shorten the fibers in the heart when receiving the impulse.

The sinoatrial (SA) node is located in the right atrium by the superior vena cava. It is the normal pacemaker of the heart and generates an impulse between 60–100 times per minute.

The atrioventricular (AV) node is located lower in the septal wall of the right atrium. It slows the impulse conduction down between the atria and the ventricles to allow time for the atria to fill with blood before the ventricles contract. The impulse travels to the bundle of His, muscle fibers branching off to the right and left. The impulse arrives at the Purkinje fibers at the end of the bundle branches. These fibers lie across the surface of the ventricles and give the signal for the myocardium of the ventricles to contract.

Electrical Impulse

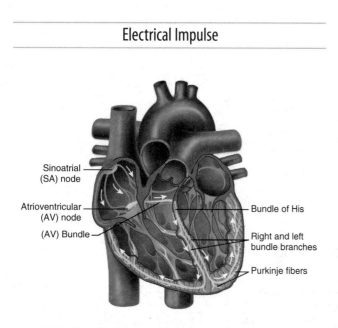

Sinoatrial
(SA) node

Atrioventricular
(AV) node

(AV) Bundle

Bundle of His

Right and left
bundle branches

Purkinje fibers

*Source: Ehrlich, Medical Terminology for Health Professionals, 6e,
ISBN #978-1-4180-7252-0*

Coronary Arteries

The heart is composed primarily of cardiac muscle tissue (myocardium) repeatedly contracting and relaxing. It therefore must have a constant supply of oxygen and nutrients as well as removal of carbon dioxide and waste products. The coronary arteries are the network of blood vessels carrying oxygen and nutrient-rich blood to the cardiac muscle tissue. The blood leaving the left ventricle exits through the aorta, the body's main artery. Two coronary arteries, referred to as the "left" and "right" coronary arteries, emerge from the beginning of the aorta, near the top of the heart.

The initial segment of the left coronary artery is the left main coronary artery. This blood vessel is about the diameter of a soda straw and is less than an inch long. It branches into two slightly smaller arteries: the left anterior descending (LAD) coronary artery and the left circumflex coronary (LCX) artery. The left anterior descending coronary artery is embedded in the surface of the front side of the heart. The left circumflex coronary artery circles around the left side of the heart and is embedded in the surface of the back of the heart. The right coronary artery travels in the right atrioventricular groove, between the right atrium and the right ventricle as it wraps around the inferior portion of the heart. The right coronary artery gives rise to the acute marginal branch that travels along the anterior portion of the right ventricle. The arteries continue to branch into progressively smaller vessels. The larger vessels travel along the surface of the heart; the smaller branches penetrate heart muscle. The smallest branches are capillaries in which red blood cells provide oxygen and nutrients to cardiac muscle tissue and bond with carbon dioxide and other meta-

bolic waste products, taking them away from the heart muscle through the coronary veins and sinus for disposal through the lungs, kidneys, and liver.

Blood Vessels

There are three varieties of blood vessels: arteries, veins, and capillaries. During blood circulation, arteries carry blood away from the heart (remember: "A" = artery = away). The capillaries connect the arteries to veins. Veins carry blood back to the heart.

To withstand the pumping pressure of the heart, an artery has three layers: a tough outer layer of tissue, a muscular middle, and an inner layer of epithelial cells. The muscle in the middle of the artery is strong and elastic. The inner layer is very smooth so blood can flow easily.

Veins are similar to arteries, but because they transport blood at a lower pressure, they are not as strong. Like arteries, veins have three layers: An outer layer of tissue, muscle in the middle, and a smooth inner layer of epithelial cells. But, vascular layers of veins are thinner and contain less tissue than arterial layers.

Unlike arteries and veins, capillaries are very thin and fragile. Capillaries are a single epithelial cell thick—so thin blood cells can pass through them only in single file. The exchange of oxygen and carbon dioxide takes place through the thin capillary wall.

Circulation

There are five systems relating to circulation in the human body: Systemic, Coronary, Pulmonary, Portal, and Lymphatic. In this chapter, we will discuss systems in the body circulating blood.

On average, the human body has approximately five liters of blood continually moving through it by way of the circulatory system. The pumping of the heart forces blood on its journey. There are three methods of circulation carrying blood throughout the body: systemic, pulmonary, and coronary.

Systemic circulation supplies nourishment to tissue located throughout the body, with the exception of the heart and lungs. Pulmonary circulation is movement of blood from the heart, to the lungs, and back to the heart again. Pulmonary circulation accomplishes the exchange of oxygen and carbon dioxide. Coronary circulation refers to movement of blood via coronary arteries and veins to and from tissues of the heart.

Key Roots, Suffixes, and Prefixes for the Cardiovascular System

Combining forms

aneurysm/o	aneurysm
angi/o; vas/o; vascul/o	vessel
aort/o	aorta
arter/o; arteri/o	artery
arteriol/o	arteriole
ather/o	yellowish, fatty plaque
atri/o	atrium
cancer/o; carcin/o	cancer
cardi/o	heart
coron/o	heart
ech/o; son/o	sound
electr/o	electrical
endocardi/o	endocardium
mediastin/o	mediastinum
my/o	muscle
myocardi/o	myocardium
ox/i	oxygen
pericardi/o	pericardium
phleb/o; ven/o	vein
pulmon/o	lung
rhythm/o	rhythm
scler/o	hard
sept/o	septum
sin/o	sinus
steth/o; thorac/o	chest
valv/o; valvul/o	valve
ventricul/o	ventricle
venul/o	venule

Prefixes

bi-	two
brady-	slow
de-	down; from
epi-	upon; above
peri-	around
poly-	many
tachy-	fast
tri-	three

Suffixes

-ary	pertaining to
-edema	swelling
-graph	instrument used to record
-graphy	process of recording
-gram	recording, writing
-ium	membrane
-megaly	enlarged
-ole	small
-oma	tumor
-pathy	disease, abnormality
-phobia	fear (abnormal)
-sclerosis	hardening, hardness
-stenosis	narrowing; stricture
-stomy	artificial opening
-tome	cutting instrument

Section Review 10.1

1. The _____ is a fist-sized, cone-shaped muscle sitting between the lungs and behind the sternum.

   A. Aortic valve

   B. Heart

   C. Capillary bed

   D. Coronary artery

2. What type of circulation refers to the movement of blood through tissues of the heart?

    A. Pulmonary

    B. Systemic

    C. Arterial

    D. Coronary

3. What term refers to a rapid heartbeat?

    A. Tachycardia

    B. Cardiomegaly

    C. Bradycardia

    D. Tachypnea

4. Which valves are the semilunar valves?

    A. Tricuspid and Aortic

    B. Pulmonary and Mitral

    C. Tricuspid and Mitral

    D. Pulmonary and Aortic

5. Where can codes relating to the Cardiovascular system be found in CPT®?

    A. 30000s

    B. 70000s

    C. 90000s

    D. All of the above

ICD-10-CM

Most diagnostic codes for the cardiovascular system are found in ICD-10-CM chapter 9, Diseases of the Circulatory System (I00-I99). Common cardiovascular conditions fall into these categories:

- Rheumatic Heart Disease
- Hypertensive Disease
- Ischemic Heart Disease
- Pulmonary Heart Disease and Diseases of Pulmonary Circulation
- Other Forms of Heart Disease
- Cerebrovascular Disease
- Diseases of Veins, Lymphatic Vessels and Lymph Nodes
- Other Disorders of Circulatory System

Acute Rheumatic Fever

Rheumatic fever (I00-I02) is a complication of strep throat with Group A streptococci that is left untreated. This is a rare, but serious life-threatening condition. The main symptoms are fever, muscle aches, swollen and painful joints. Some patients have a red rash that accompanies the acute symptoms. These symptoms typically appear 2-4 weeks after the strep infection. This can cause rheumatic heart disease that weakens the heart and can, in rare, circumstances, cause heart failure.

Chronic rheumatic fever is also called chronic rheumatic heart disease (I05-I09) and includes complications such as rheumatic mitral valve diseases (I05), rheumatic aortic valve disorders (I06), rheumatic tricuspid valve disorders (I07) multiple valve diseases (I08) and other rheumatic heart diseases (I09).

Example

Look in the Index to Diseases and Injures for Fever/rheumatic (active)(acute)(chronic)(subacute) leads to I00 Rheumatic fever without heart involvement. Under category code I01 there are many codes listed to identify heart involvement. Pericarditis (I01.0) is a sudden, severe inflammation of the heart lining due to rheumatic fever. Endocarditis (I01.1) is sudden, severe Inflammation of the heart cavities due to rheumatic fever, and myocarditis (I01.2) is sudden, severe inflammation of the heart muscle due to rheumatic fever.

Acute rheumatic fever with pericarditis

I01.0 Acute rheumatic pericarditis

> Rheumatic pericarditis (acute)

ICD-9-CM Application

In ICD-9-CM Index to Diseases the look for Fever/ rheumatic/with heart involvement/pericarditis directs you to:

391.0 Acute rheumatic pericarditis

> Fever (active) (acute) with pericarditis

> Pericarditis (acute)

Hypertension

Hypertension (HTN), or high blood pressure, is a chronic medical condition in which the blood pressure in the arteries is elevated. It is classified as either primary (essential) or secondary. About 90–95 percent of cases are termed primary hypertension, which refers to high blood pressure for which no medical cause can be found. The remaining 5–10 percent of cases (secondary hypertension) is caused by other conditions affecting the kidneys, arteries, heart, or endocrine system.

Combination codes are used to report hypertension with other diseases. Hypertension is assigned code I10 and is used whether the hypertension is controlled or uncontrolled and whether benign, essential, malignant, or unspecified. The combination codes are used when hypertension is accompanied by other conditions, such as heart disease and chronic kidney disease.

Example

Malignant hypertension.

Look in the Index to Diseases and Injuries for Hypertension, hypertensive I10.

> I10 Essential (primary) hypertension

In the Tabular list, I10 includes Hypertension that is arterial, benign, essential, malignant, primary, or systemic. The ICD-10-CM Official Guidelines for Coding and Reporting, Section I.C.9.a., gives extensive direction on code assignment when accompanied by heart disease and chronic kidney disease.

In the Tabular List, above code I10 an instructional note states to use an additional code to identify tobacco use, exposure to smoke or tobacco, or nicotine dependence, if applicable.

ICD-9-CM Application

ICD-9-CM differentiates between benign, malignant, and other hypertension. There is a Hypertension Table to assist the coder in finding the correct hypertension code.

ICD-9-CM Example

Look in the Index to Diseases for the Hypertension. This is where the Hypertension Table is located.

Hypertension, hypertensive/Malignant (column) 401.0.

> 401.0 Malignant hypertension

Hypertension with Heart Disease

Heart conditions are assigned to category I11 if a causal relationship with hypertension is stated or implied. Look for words such as "hypertensive," or phrases, such as "due to hypertension," to support the codes in this category. I11.0 *Hypertensive heart disease with heart failure* has a note to use an additional code to identify the type of heart failure (category I50-) if present. I11.9 is used for hypertensive heart disease without heart failure.

The same heart condition with hypertension, but without the causal relationship documented, must be coded separately (the heart condition and hypertension are separate and unrelated). Sequence them in order of importance for the patient admission or encounter, according to documentation.

Example

Cardiomyopathy with congestive heart failure due to malignant hypertension.

ICD-10-CM

In the Index to Diseases and Injuries look for Hypertension, hypertensive/heart/with/heart failure I11.0. An instructional note in the Tabular List states to Use an additional code to identify the heart failure. The codes reported are:

I11.0 Hypertensive heart disease with heart failure

I50.9 Heart failure, unspecified

ICD-9-CM Application

In the Hypertension Table look for Hypertension, hypertensive/heart (disease)/with heart failure/Malignant (column) 402.01. An instructional note In the Tabular List states to Use additional code to specify type of heart failure (428.0-428.43), if known. The codes reported are:

402.01 Hypertensive heart disease, Malignant with heart failure

428.0 Congestive heart failure, unspecified

Hypertensive Chronic Kidney Disease

Unlike hypertension with heart disease, there is a presumed cause-and-effect relationship between hypertension and chronic kidney disease (CKD). When conditions classifiable in N18 *Chronic kidney disease* are present with hypertension, assign codes from category I12 *Hypertensive chronic kidney disease*. I12.0 is used for hypertensive CKD Stage 5 or ESRD. Code I12.9 is used with hypertensive CKD Stage 1-4. Assign the appropriate code from N18 as a secondary code to identify the stage of CKD.

Example

Malignant hypertension with stage II chronic kidney disease:

Look in the Index to Diseases and Injuries for Hypertension, hypertensive/kidney/with stage 1 through stage 4 chronic kidney disease I12.9. In the Tabular List there is an instructional note to Use additional code to identify the stage of chronic kidney disease.

I12.9 Hypertensive chronic kidney disease with stage 1 through stage 4 chronic kidney disease, or unspecified chronic kidney disease.

N18.2 Chronic kidney disease, stage 2 (mild)

ICD-9-CM Application

Look in the Index to Diseases for the Hypertension Table, Hypertension, hypertensive/with chronic kidney disease/stage I through stage IV, or unspecified/Malignant (column) refers you to code 403.00. In the Tabular List there is an instructional note to Use additional code to identify the stage of the chronic kidney disease.

403.00 Malignant hypertension with chronic kidney disease stage II

585.2 Chronic kidney disease, Stage II (mild)

Hypertensive Heart and Chronic Kidney Disease

When a patient has both hypertensive heart disease and CKD, assign a code from category I13 *Hypertensive heart and chronic kidney disease*. A relationship is assumed between the hypertension and the CKD, whether stated or not. An additional code or codes should be assigned from category I50 to indicate the type of heart failure. An additional code from category N18 is necessary to identify the stage of kidney disease.

Hypertensive heart and chronic kidney disease ICD-10-CM code descriptions I13.0-I13.2 include "with or without" heart failure and the stage of chronic kidney disease. The specific type of heart failure and stage of CKD are also reported as additional codes.

Example

Benign hypertensive heart disease with systolic heart failure and stage III chronic kidney disease

In the Index to Diseases and Injuries look for Hypertension, hypertensive/cardiorenal (disease)/with heart failure/with stage 1 through stage 4 chronic kidney disease I13.0.

I13.0 Hypertensive heart and chronic kidney disease with heart failure and stage 1 through stage 4 chronic kidney disease, or unspecified chronic kidney disease

I50.20 Unspecified systolic (congestive) heart failure

N18.3 Chronic kidney disease, stage 3 (moderate)

Hypertensive Cerebrovascular Disease

When patients have hypertensive cerebrovascular disease (I60-I69), code the cerebrovascular condition first, followed by the appropriate hypertension code.

Hypertensive Retinopathy

Two codes are necessary to identify this condition. First, assign a code from the subcategory H35.03- *Hypertensive retinopathy* used with the appropriate code from categories I10-I15 to indicate the type of hypertension.

Example

Hypertensive retinopathy for ICD-10-CM needs a sixth character that specifies the laterality of the retinopathy. Look in the Index to Diseases and Injuries for Retinopathy/hypertensive H35.03-.

> H35.031 Hypertensive retinopathy, right eye
>
> H35.032 Hypertensive retinopathy, left eye
>
> H35.033 Hypertensive retinopathy, bilateral
>
> H35.039 Hypertensive retinopathy, unspecified eye

There is also an instructional note in the Tabular List under subcategory code H35.0, Code also any associated hypertension.

Secondary Hypertension

To code for secondary hypertension, two codes are assigned. Assign a code to show the underlying cause or condition and a second code from category I15 to indicate the type of hypertension. Sequencing is determined by the reason for the admission or encounter.

Example

A patient is being seen for benign hypertension which is due to primary aldosteronism.

Transient Hypertension and Elevated Blood Pressure

Assign R03.0 *Elevated blood-pressure reading, without diagnosis of hypertension*, is reported when the provider has not made a formal diagnosis of hypertension. Do not report this code when the patient has an established diagnosis of hypertension. Code R03.0 can also apply to patients experiencing what is sometimes referred to as "white coat syndrome" or "white coat hypertension." For transient hypertension complicating pregnancy, assign a code from category O13 *Gestational [pregnancy-induced] hypertension without significant proteinuria*.

Hypertension, Controlled or Uncontrolled

Controlled hypertension refers to an existing state of hypertension under control by therapy. Uncontrolled hypertension may refer to untreated hypertension or hypertension not responding to current therapy. Either of these are reported with code I10 *Essential (primary) hypertension* which is used for benign, essential, malignant, and unspecified and controlled or uncontrolled.

Myocardial Infarction (MI)

An MI, or heart attack, is a sudden decrease in coronary artery blood flow resulting in death of the heart muscle. When an MI is suspected, the provider often orders lab tests to determine the levels of creatinine phosphokinase (CPK) and troponin in the patient's blood. Elevated levels of CPK and troponin can

---

indicate damage to the heart muscle. If you have a diagnosis of elevated CPK or elevated troponin, the elevated lab result is coded from Abnormal findings (R70-R79) in ICD-10-CM. Once a myocardial infarction (MI) has been diagnosed, it is classified based on the affected heart tissue and the time frame in which it occurs.

ICD-9-CM Application

ICD-10-CM Official Guidelines for Coding and Reporting, Section I.C.9.e.4 states that a code form category I22 subsequent STEMI and NSTEMI myocardial infarction, is to be used when a patient who has suffered an AMI has a new AMI within the 4 week time frame of the initial AMI. This time period is a significant change from ICD-9-CM that indicates less than 8 weeks old.

Acute MI (AMI)

For an acute MI, select from category I21 according to site. Subcategories I20.0-I21.2 and I21.3 identify a ST elevation myocardial infarction (STEMI) in a STEMI, the coronary artery is completely blocked and virtually all the heart muscle being supplied by the affected artery starts to die. Code I21.4 is used for NSTEMI (non-ST elevation myocardial infarction), nontransmural MIs, or acute subendocardial MIs. In an NSTEMI, the plaque or blockage only partially occludes the coronary artery and only a portion of the heart muscle being supplied by the affected artery dies.

There is an instructional note under categories I21 and I22 in the Tabular List to Use additional code, if documented, to identify use or exposure or dependence to tobacco, or status post administration of tPA (rtPA).

Practical Coding Note

Category I22 Is always reported with a code from Category I21. The sequencing of the codes will depend on the circumstances of the encounter. .

Example

Initial episode of acute myocardial infarction

In the Index to Diseases and Injuries look for Infarct, infarction/myocardium, myocardial I21.3.

> I21.3 ST elevation (STEMI) myocardial infarction of unspecified site

ICD-10-CM reports which coronary artery is involved in a ST elevation STEMI and non-ST elevation (NSTEMI) myocardial infarction (example, anterior or inferior wall).

I21.01 ST elevation (STEMI) myocardial infarction involving left main coronary artery

I21.02 ST elevation (STEMI) myocardial infarction involving left anterior descending coronary artery

I21.09 ST elevation (STEMI) myocardial infarction involving other coronary artery of anterior wall

---

ICD-9-CM Application

ICD-9-CM has fifth digits (0, 1, and 2) to report the episode of care for when the infarction occurred. ICD-10-CM identifies initial and subsequent with separate categories of codes (I21 and I22).

In the Index to Diseases look for Infarct, infarction/myocardium, myocardial 410.9x.

> 410.91 Acute myocardial infarction NOS, initial episode

Old MI

There is only one code for an old MI, I25.2. With an old MI, the patient is asymptomatic and does not require any further treatment. If a patient presents with symptoms less than four weeks post-MI, it is considered acute. If the patient requires continued care or is symptomatic after 4 weeks, the appropriate aftercare code is used and not a code from category I21.

Practical Coding Note

I21.3 *ST elevation (STEMI) myocardial Infarction of unspecified site* is used for a default for acute myocardial infarction. It is also assigned when documentation states STEMI (only) or transmural MI.

Arteriosclerosis

Arteriosclerosis is hardening of the arteries. If it is arteriosclerosis of the coronary arteries, assign a code from category I25 *Chronic ischemic heart disease*. Code selection indicates whether the atherosclerosis is of native artery, bypassed artery, or transplanted heart. Angina pectoris is characterized by chest pain and is common in patients with arteriosclerosis. When both conditions are documented, a causal relationship is assumed between arteriosclerosis and angina pectoris unless it is specifically stated the angina is due to another cause. Combination codes are used to report arteriosclerosis with angina pectoris (I25.11-, I25.7-). Because the angina is included in the code it is not necessary to report it separately.

Apply I25.10 when documentation shows that the patient has had a coronary artery bypass graft (CABG) and the physician

---

did not specify where the coronary artery disease (CAD) is being treated and whether it is in a native vessel or in one of the replaced vessels.

If documentation specifies CAD of a native coronary artery, and the patient is not a heart transplant patient, select a code from subcategory I25.11- *Atherosclerotic heart disease of native coronary artery with angina pectoris.* The 6th character of the code will identify the presence of angina or spasm.

Whether the patient has had a previous CABG is important for several reasons:

- ICD-10-CM coding may be different if the patient has atherosclerosis of native coronary arteries (I25.1) versus previous bypass grafts (I25.7-).
- The patient has CAD and documentation specifies no history of a prior coronary artery bypass graft (CABG).
- The patient had a prior percutaneous transluminal coronary angioplasty (PTCA) of a native artery and the patient is admitted with reocclusion of this lesion.

Use I25.82 *Chronic total occlusion of coronary artery* when the patient has 100 percent coronary artery occlusion for several months. Use I70.92 *Chronic total occlusion of artery of the extremities* when a patient has 100 percent occlusion of an artery supplying the arms or legs. Instructional note states to code first atherosclerosis of arteries of the extremities (I70.2-, I70.3-, I70.4-, I70.5-, I70.6-, I70.7-).

Apply I24.0 if documentation shows debris causes an acute blockage of a coronary artery (occlusion, embolism, thromboembolism) not resulting in a myocardial infarction. If your documentation shows lipid rich plaque built up over time in the coronary artery (atherosclerosis), choose code I25.83. If your documentation shows calcified coronary lesion choose code I25.84. Both I25.83 and I24.84 state to code first coronary atherosclerosis (I25.1-, I25.7-, I25.81-).

Codes for arteriosclerosis of the non-coronary arteries are found mostly in category I70-. The fourth character for this category generally identifies the type of artery (native, bypass). The fifth and sixth character in Category I70 identifies either the location, laterality, or complication depending on the category.

Practical Coding Note

In ICD-10-CM, Atherosclerosis/coronary/artery directs you to I25.10 *Atherosclerotic heart disease of native coronary artery without angina pectoris.* In addition, the coding for ICD-10-CM requires the documentation to state when there is presence of angina pectoris. If angina pectoris is present, see if the documentation mentions spasm.

ICD-9-CM Application

In ICD-9-CM, Atherosclerosis/coronary (artery) directs the coder to 414.00 *Coronary Atherosclerosis of unspecified type of vessel, native or graft.* The coder is dependent on reading the Coding Clinic to know to report code 414.01 for the default code if a history of a bypass was not documented.

Endocarditis

Endocarditis is inflammation or infection of the inner lining of the heart (endocardium). Left untreated, it can damage or destroy heart valves. Bacterial infection is the most common source of endocarditis, but it may be caused by fungi. In some cases, no cause can be identified. Most codes for endocarditis can be found in code range I33-I39. Rheumatic endocarditis is an exception: Acute rheumatic endocarditis is coded as I01.1 and chronic rheumatic endocarditis as I09.1.

Sometimes multiple codes are necessary to report acute endocarditis when the infectious organism is known or when the underlying disease is known. The order will depend on the type of endocarditis. For example, acute streptococcal endocarditis is codes I33.0, B95.-.

Heart Failure

Heart failure (also, congestive heart failure or CHF) occurs when the heart cannot pump enough blood to supply the body's other organs. Multiple codes may be necessary to describe the condition. At other times, combination codes may be used. For example, hypertensive heart failure (explained above) requires at least two codes. In contrast, acute systolic and diastolic heart failure are reported with combination code I50.41.

Example

Category I50 *Heart failure* has a code first note in ICD-10-CM. The note indicates to code first heart failure following surgery (I97.13-) and then a code from category I50 as the additional code.

To code heart failure following cardiac surgery in ICD-10-CM, two codes are reported:

I97.130 Postprocedural heart failure following cardiac surgery

I50.9 Heart failure, unspecified

Note: Heart failure can be further specified as acute, chronic, acute on chronic, systolic, diastolic, or combined when documented.

ICD-9-CM Application

To code heart failure following cardiac surgery only one code is reported:

429.4 Functional disturbances following cardiac surgery

This code is excluded from category 428 *Heart failure* in ICD-9-CM.

Example

ICD-10-CM indexes PVD due to diabetes with one code. For proper code selection the provider must document if the patient has gangrene or not. Look in the Index to Diseases and Injuries for Diabetes, diabetic/type 2/peripheral angiopathy

E11.51 Type 2 diabetes mellitus with diabetic peripheral angiopathy without gangrene

---

Pericarditis

Pericarditis is inflammation of the sac surrounding the heart (pericardium), caused by infection. Chest pain is significant on inspiration, and onset often is sudden and can be worse when lying down. Most codes for pericarditis are found in code range I30-I32. Multiple codes may be necessary to describe the patient's condition if underlying disease is documented.

Peripheral Arterial Disease (PAD)

PAD is similar to coronary artery disease, except it affects the arteries outside the heart and brain. It is the most common type of peripheral vascular disease (PVD). If the only diagnosis given is PAD or PVD, report unspecified code I73.9. If the PVD is due to diabetes, a combination code must be used to show the condition: E08-E13 with fifth and sixth character of .51 or .52 depending on the presence of gangrene.

Valve Disorders

There are various heart valve disorders. Most prominent are stenosis, regurgitation, and prolapse. Valve stenosis is a condition of the heart in which one or more of the heart valve openings is narrow (or stenotic) and restricts the flow of blood through the heart. Valve regurgitation occurs when the valve does not close properly and blood backflows, or leaks back, into the heart chamber. Valve prolapse occurs when valve leaflets prolapse, or fall backward, into the heart chamber. ICD-10-CM code selection is driven by which valve(s) are affected and whether the condition is congenital or acquired. For congenital heart valve stenosis, see categories Q22 and Q23. For non-congenital disorders, you must know if the condition is rheumatic, acute, or involves multiple valves.

Section Review 10.2

1. A patient presents to his physician's office for a follow-up visit and review of test results. He complained of shortness of breath and chest pain during exercise and the physician ordered an echocardiogram. The physician documents aortic valve stenosis. What ICD-10-CM code is reported?

    A. I08.0

    B. Q23.0

    C. I35.0

    D. I06.0

2. A patient presents to the ED and is subsequently admitted on the same day diagnosed with an acute anteroapical wall infarction. What ICD-10-CM code is reported?

    A. I21.19

    B. I21.09

    C. I22.9

    D. I21.4

3. Patient is diagnosed as having renal failure with hypertension. He is end stage receiving dialysis. What ICD-10-CM codes are reported?

    A. I10, N18.6, Z99.2

    B. I12.9, N18.6, Z99.2

    C. I12.0, N18.6, Z99.2

    D. I13.0, N18.6, Z99.2

4. A patient is diagnosed with acute on chronic diastolic congestive heart failure (CHF). What ICD-10-CM code(s) is/are reported?

    A. I50.33

    B. I50.31, I50.32

    C. I50.43

    D. I50.32

5. Patient presents to her physician's office after a syncopal episode. An ECG is performed in the office and the patient is diagnosed with a Mobitz type I AV block. What ICD-10-CM code is reported?

    A. I44.0

    B. R55

    C. I44.1

    D. I44.2

CPT®

Codes throughout the CPT® codebook report procedures and diagnostic tests of the heart. For example, a coronary artery bypass graft (CABG) is coded from the 30000 section of CPT®, ECGs are coded from the 90000 section, and the radiologic portion of an interventional procedure is coded from the 70000 section.

Surgery, Cardiovascular System (33010–37799)

Heart and Pericardium

A pericardiocentesis (33010, 33011) involves drawing off collected fluid (via a specialized needle) built up inside the double-layered pericardial sac. Too much fluid can impede the

contraction and effectiveness of the heart, this is called cardiac tamponade.

A tube pericardiostomy (33015) refers to an artificial opening made to insert a tube for drainage purposes, for specimen collection, or culture.

A pericardiotomy (33020) refers to an incision made for a clot/foreign body removal. This procedure requires subxiphoid, sternal splitting, or a left anterior thoracostomy incision for pericardial biopsy, irrigation, drainage, or collection of cultures. They are not identified separately. For thoracoscopic removal of an intrapericardial blood clot or foreign body, report code 32658.

Practical Coding Note

Make a note in the Pericardium section to see 32658 for thoraco-scopic removal of intrapericardial blood clot or foreign body.

A pericardiectomy (33030, 33031) describes the removal of the fibrous sac (pericardium) surrounding the heart. This procedure is performed due to adhesive pericarditis, constrictive pericarditis, or other diseases affecting the pericardium. The use of cardiopulmonary bypass significantly increases the risk to the patient. The surgeon will usually induce hypothermia, cardiac standstill, and the off-loading of circulation to an artificial pump/oxygenator requiring employment of a technician specially trained to run it. Blood is oxygenated and CO_2 gas is released in the pump/oxygenator. Once this process is complete, blood is returned to the aorta by the pump, which helps to mimic the beating of the heart by pumping the blood back to the body. Code selection is based on whether cardiopulmonary bypass is used.

Practical Coding Note

Many cardiothoracic CPT® codes require use of cardiopulmonary bypass, while others may be performed with or without the use of bypass. The coder must pay close attention to the operative notes and choose codes based on whether documentation supports the use of bypass. Highlight or underline "cardiopulmonary bypass" when used in the code description.

Cardiac tumors may be inside or outside the heart and require different levels of service. After the heart is opened (33120), the tumor is resected with a margin of normal heart tissue. Any problems created by this resection (damage to heart valves, holes in the walls, injury to coronary arteries) are repaired and are not coded separately. Cardiopulmonary bypass is only required if a significant portion of the heart or a major vessel is removed with the tumor, or for resection of margins of normal tissue around the tumor. The heart is not opened for an excision of an external cardiac tumor (33130).

Transmyocardial revascularization (TMR) (33140, 33141) is a surgical procedure to treat severe angina. The surgeon makes a thoracotomy incision (transthoracic) to expose the surface of the heart and locate a viable ischemic area. The laser is inserted and fired between heartbeats to make channels through the left ventricle enhancing flow of oxygen carrying blood back to the severely damaged muscle.

Blood filling the ventricle protects the surrounding heart tissue from injury by the laser. The procedure also stimulates growth of new blood vessels within the heart muscle.

Pacemaker or Implantable Defibrillator

A pacemaker or implantable defibrillator system is made up of a pulse generator (battery and electronics) and one or more electrodes (leads). To code these procedures, you need to know:

- the type of system
- whether the placement is temporary or permanent
- whether the device is single, dual, or multiple leads
- placement of electrodes
  - transvenous
  - endoscopic
  - epicardial
  - coronary sinus
- what is being done to the system?
  - removal
  - replacement
  - insertion
- which component(s) (pulse generator, leads) are being removed, replaced, or inserted?
  - all at once
  - individually

When reading descriptors for pacer/defibrillator codes, the first word generally defines the procedure performed; for instance, 33202 is an insertion code, and 33218 is a repair code. Next, you need to know the type of system. A pacemaker uses low-energy electronic pulses to overcome conduction disorders of the heart. An implantable defibrillator delivers electrical shocks and sometimes paces the heart. CPT® separates some of the codes by the type of system. For example, relocating a skin pocket for a pacemaker is 33222; relocating a skin pocket for an implantable defibrillator is 33223. Relocation of a pacemaker skin pocket could be performed for erosion or threatened erosion of a pulse generator pocket. The preexisting pocket is opened, the generator removed, the pocket is debrided, cultures taken, and then the pocket is extended to a deeper position. After flushing with antibiotic solution, the generator is replaced and the pocket is closed with multiple layers of 2.0 Dexon and the skin closed with 4.0 Ethicon.

Practical Coding Note

Codes in this section identify procedures for pacemakers and and implantable defibrillators.

Underline the words identifying the procedure, such as "insertion," "revision," "repair," and "removal." Highlight "pacemaker" in one color and "defibrillator" in another color for easy identification.

For pacemakers, you need to know if it is a temporary or permanent pacemaker. Temporary pacemakers are used to treat a number of temporary heartbeat problems, such as a slow heartbeat caused by a heart attack, heart surgery, or an overdose of medicine. They also are used during emergencies until a permanent pacemaker can be implanted or until the temporary condition abates. Temporary pacemaker placement codes are 33210–33211.

Permanent pacemakers are used to control long-term heart rhythm problems. A permanent pacemaker continuously stimulates cardiac contractions at a certain rate by electrical impulses. Placement of a permanent pacemaker can help to keep the heart rate and blood pressure at safe levels. Permanent pacemakers are comprised of two components: a pulse generator (battery) and an electrode(s). This device operates by sensing the patient's heart beat (the electrode) and eliciting a small electrical impulse (the pulse generator) similar to the SA node to initiate a heart beat in the event the patient's native heart rate drops below a preset rate.

The pulse generator is usually placed into a surgically created subcutaneous pocket on the chest just under the clavicle. The electrode is threaded into the right heart via the large subclavian vein and manipulated into the myocardium (transvenous).

For pacemakers, there also are different codes for a single or dual chamber system. CPT® codes 33206 and 33207 are for single chamber pacemaker system placements. CPT® code 33208 is for a dual chamber pacemaker system placement. These codes are for entire systems. If only the generator is placed, look to 33212, 33213 and 33221. Do not report 33212, 33213, 33221 in conjunction with 33233 for removal and replacement of the pacemaker pulse generator. Use 33227–33229, as appropriate, when pulse generator replacement is indicated.

Electrodes (also referred to as leads) can be placed transvenously into the right side of the heart or into the coronary sinus (for left ventricular pacing), or they can be placed on the heart (epicardial) by open (thoracotomy) or endoscopic technique. When epicardial lead placement is performed with insertion of a generator, report 33202, 33203 in conjunction with 33212, 33213, and 33221.

Example

Insertion of a pacemaker pulse generator, with existing dual leads, is coded:

33213 Insertion of pacemaker pulse generator only; with existing dual leads

Placement of a permanent pacemaker can be achieved with a single lead/electrode placed in either the right atrium or the right ventricle.

Placement of a single pacemaker lead is referred to as a single chamber pacemaker. When a pacemaker wire is situated in the right ventricle and right atrium, the pacing system is referred to as a dual chamber pacemaker. Biventricular pacing (33224–33226) is established when a third lead is threaded into the coronary sinus and over the heart to provide stimulation to the left ventricle. The lead provides for synchronous contraction of both ventricles when there is damage to the left bundle branch or Purkinje fibers on the left side of the heart.

There are two general types of implantable defibrillators. Transvenous implantable pacing cardioverter-defibrillator (ICD) use a combination of antitachycardia pacing, low energy cardioversion or defibrillating shocks to treat ventricular tachycardia or ventricular fibrillation. The subcutaneous implantable defibrillator (S-ICD) uses a single subcutaneous electrode to treat ventricular tachyarrhythmias. Subcutaneous implantable defibrillators do not provide antitachycardia pacing or chronic pacing. Some patients suffer life-threatening arrhythmias, such as ventricular tachycardia, and require a small shock of electricity to reset the pacing of the heart. With these devices, the patient is provided with additional cardiac support by adding the pacing component. Review the CPT® codebook for the codes for implantable debrillator insertion (33240, 33230, and 33231), removal of only the implantable defibrillator pulse generator (33241), and removal with replacement of the pulse generator (33262–33264). Do not report 33262–33264 in conjunction with 33241.There are codes to describe the services for subcutaneous implantable defibrillators. The insertion or replacement of the system is reported with 33270. The removal of a lead is reported with 33272. Removal and replacement of the complete system requires codes 33272, 33241, and 33270.

You may need more than one code to describe the full procedure. If a new system is put in after removal of an old system, for instance, you code removal of the pieces and insertion of the new system.

Example

Patient presents for replacement of his permanent dual chamber pacemaker with another transvenous dual permanent chamber pacemaker.

Codes for this case are as follows:

33235 Removal of transvenous pacemaker electrode(s); dual lead system

33208-51 Insertion of new or replacement of permanent pacemaker with transvenous electrode(s); atrial and ventricular

33233-51 Removal of permanent pacemaker pulse generator only

Valve Procedures

Valves of the heart direct blood flow from the right to the left. The valves open and close passively; these movements depend on pressure gradients in the cardiac chambers.

Some of the conditions caused by valves not working properly include:

Mitral Regurgitation—The backwash of blood into the left atrium. Thickening, scarring, rigidity, and calcification of the valve leaflets allow the backwash effect to occur. Blood cannot move efficiently through the heart to the rest of the body leading to possible fatigue or shortness of breath, depending on the severity.

Aortic Stenosis—The narrowing of the aortic valve due to disease or the degeneration inherent in the natural aging process. Narrowing causes left ventricular hypertrophy as a result of the increased pressure necessary to pump the blood through the stenotic valve.

Aortic Regurgitation—The aortic valve between the aorta and the left ventricle does not close properly, and blood leaks backward through the valve. This causes an overload of the left ventricle which can cause an eventual decrease in the muscular elasticity necessary for effective pumping.

When coding for cardiac valve surgery, the following information should be considered:

1.   Which valve was diseased or replaced?

2.   What was the type of replacement valve used?

Valve procedures include repair and replacement. Codes are assigned by valve (aortic, mitral, tricuspid, or pulmonary) and procedure. Valvuloplasty (repair) may be accomplished by sutures, patches, or rings. It involves work on the whole valve, including the leaflets of the valve and the ring or the annulus. Annuloplasty involves work solely on the ring (annulus).

Replacement of the valve can be performed using either a mechanical or biological prosthesis. If more than one valve is operated on, report separate codes for each procedure.

Codes listed in CPT® for mitral, tricuspid, and pulmonary valve surgery do not always include cardiopulmonary bypass. Most open aortic valve surgery is performed while the patient is on cardiopulmonary bypass, because the heart cannot pump blood during surgery.

Codes 33361–33369 report transcatheter aortic valve replacement with a prosthetic valve through various approaches (percutaneous femoral artery, open femoral artery, open axillary artery, etc.), and there are also separate codes for various transcatheter approaches with the use of cardiopulmonary bypass. These procedures require two surgeons, report with modifier 62. Review the guidelines in the CPT® codebook for 33361–33369. Diagnostic coronary angiograms may be reported separately when certain criteria is met. The requirements are included in the CPT® coding guidelines.

The replacement of the aortic valve (33405) with a prosthetic valve (other than a homograft or stentless valve) is a procedure where the diseased leaflets are excised and replaced with an artificial valve by sewing it to the annulus (ring of tissue where the valve leaflets normally attach to the aorta). This procedure is performed with cardiopulmonary bypass. If an allograft valve (freehand) is used during aortic valve replacement, the leaflets of a homograft valve must be sized and trimmed, as necessary, to prevent occlusion of the aortic sinuses.

A valvuloplasty for the mitral valve may be used when the efficiency of the mitral valve has been compromised due to an enlargement or dilation of the annulus or ring. This repair may be accomplished with or without a prosthetic ring.

CPT® code 33476 describes correction of stenosis in the infundibulum of the heart. The infundibulum, also known as the outflow tract, extends to the pulmonary artery. If the outflow tract is stenosed, the outflow is obstructed. The blood backs up and pools in the right ventricle. By resecting obstructive muscle bands, the outflow impediment can be corrected. A commissurotomy is surgical opening or division of a fibrous band or ring. When the valve must also be opened and the outflow tract is augmented (gusset), report code 33478.

Coronary Artery Anomalies

The coronary arteries begin at the aortic sinuses, located just above the aortic valve in the ascending aorta. The three major coronary arteries are the right coronary artery (RC, arises from the right aortic sinus), and the left coronary artery (arises from the left aortic sinus) which gives rise to the left anterior descending (LD, or LAD) artery and the smaller left circumflex artery (LC, or LCX).

The RC travels down the atrioventricular groove towards the base of the heart, and one of the branches is the posterior descending artery (PDA), which supplies the interior wall, ventricular septum and the posteromedial papillary muscle. The RC also supplies the SA nodal artery in some patients, and the LC artery supplies the SA nodal artery in others.

The LAD artery, branches off the left coronary artery and supplies blood to the front of the heart. The LCX branches off the left coronary artery and encircles the heart muscle. This artery supplies blood to the back of the heart.

A fistula describes an abnormal passageway from a hollow organ to the surface or from one organ to another. An arteriovenous fistula describes the communication between a vein and an artery (allowing oxygenated and deoxygenated blood to mingle). The fistula may eventually develop an AV aneurysm or bulging pouch. (The site of the fistula can be previously determined by cardiac catheterization). The venous end of the fistula can be ligated with sutures. If the fistula is to a cardiac chamber, the chamber is opened, and the chamber end of the fistula is closed with a stitch.

In a Takeuchi procedure (33505), holes are made in the aorta and pulmonary artery at the level of the anomalous coronary artery and where the vessels touch each other. The holes are sewn together to create a direct aortopulmonary opening. A flap of pulmonary artery wall is created with the anomalous coronary artery, creating a tunnel. Blood is diverted from the aorta into this tunnel.

Coronary Artery Bypass Grafts (CABG)

Coronary artery bypass graft (CABG) is a surgical procedure performed to go around (or bypass) blockages in the coronary arteries to improve blood flow to heart muscle. Arterial or venous grafts are harvested from the patient's body to be used as conduits (grafts) to the coronary arteries.

To code a CABG procedure, a coder must know:

- How many grafts were performed?
- How many were arterial? Which artery(ies)?
- How many were venous? Which vein(s)?
- How were the grafts harvested? Open or endoscopic?
- Did the patient have a previous CABG?

CPT® divides codes by venous, arterial, and combination arterial-venous. If only venous grafting is performed, 33510–33516 *Venous grafting only for CABG* is applicable. If arterial grafting is performed, 33533–33536 *Arterial grafting for CABG* is applicable. If both arterial and venous grafting are performed, two codes are reported from code ranges 33517–33523 *Venous grafting for combination CABG* (these are add-on codes) and 33533–33536 *Arterial grafting for CABG*. The codes indicate the number of the specific type of graft. For example, CPT® code 33512 describes a three venous graft only CABG, and CPT® code 33534 describes a two arterial graft CABG.

You must know which arteries and veins were procured for the grafts; some procurements are reported separately and some are bundled. According to CPT®, procurement of most arteries and the saphenous vein is bundled into the code set. Harvesting may be reported separately for the following:

- upper extremity artery (eg, radial): 35600

- upper extremity vein: 35500
- femoropopliteal vein: 35572

How the vein is harvested also is important. Endoscopic harvesting of veins for coronary artery bypass grafting is reported separately with add-on code 33508.

Whether the patient has had a previous CABG is important for several reasons:

- ICD-10-CM coding may be different if the patient has atherosclerosis of native coronary arteries (I25.1-) versus previous bypass grafts (I25.7-).
- Add-on code 33530 should be coded for additional reimbursement for reoperation CABG or valve procedures performed more than one month after the original procedure.

Septal Defect

A septal defect refers to a condition in which the septum, dividing the right and left sides of the heart, does not close completely. Code 33641 describes the repair of an atrial septal defect, secundum (a hole between the right and left atria). The most common type of atrial septal defect is an ostium secundum (second opening). This opening is normal for a developing fetus in utero but closes at birth.

Tetralogy of Fallot describes a congenital heart condition characterized by four anomalies:

- Stenosis of the infundibulum (cone-shaped outflow passage of the right ventricle)
- Ventricular septal defect (VSD)
- Abnormally positioned aorta; receives mixed arterial and venous blood
- Hypertrophy (increased size) of the right ventricle

Shunting Procedures

The subclavian-to-pulmonary shunt procedure (also known as the Blalock-Taussig procedure) is a palliative (temporary) procedure performed in children who are not getting enough blood to the lungs to be oxygenated (blue babies). These procedures are performed in situations where the heart defect results in too little blood flow to the lungs, resulting in low oxygen levels in the blood, or cyanosis. Shunts may be performed either from the front of the chest (sternotomy) or the side (thoracotomy), depending on the child's specific anatomy. The shunt is typically a short segment of an artificial blood vessel connecting a branch off of the aorta to one of the pulmonary arteries to allow more blood flow to the lungs. Because these shunts are synthetic, they will not grow; the child outgrows the shunt, resulting in gradually falling oxygen levels.

The typical diagnosis associated with this procedure used to be tetralogy of Fallot, although now most patients with tetralogy of Fallot undergo complete correction early in infancy. Currently, the shunt procedure is used in more complex defects, such as tricuspid atresia.

Transposition of the Great Vessels

This condition describes a total reversal of the origin of the aorta and the pulmonary artery. In this condition, the aorta leads from the right ventricle and the pulmonary artery from the left ventricle. A shunt between the arterial and venous blood flow must be placed for the patient to survive. (The ductus arteriosus is a small artery in the fetus allowing pulmonary artery blood to flow into the aorta).

Truncus Arteriosus

Truncus arteriosus is the common arterial trunk opening out of both ventricles in the heart while the fetus is in stages of early development in utero. In later embryonic development, this opening divides into the aorta and pulmonary artery when a spiral septum grows to separate and divide the two great vessels.

If nature does not make the division or closure, surgery is performed to eliminate development of left ventricular failure and increased pulmonary pressure. If the pulmonary pressure exceeds the systemic pressure, the patient is considered inoperable.

Frequently, patients with a persistent truncus arteriosus (one failing to divide normally) also have a second abnormality, such as a hole in the septum between the two ventricles, referred to as ventricular septal defect (VSD).

Arteries and Veins

The primary procedures performed on blood vessels include establishing both inflow and outflow of blood through the vessels; any lesser procedures required to establish inflow/outflow are included in the major procedure.

Aneurysm

A local abnormal dilation of an artery due to a congenital defect or weakness of the vessel wall is known as an aneurysm. Atherosclerosis is a common cause of aortic aneurysms, but those in the periphery are usually caused by damage due to trauma or bacterial or fungal infection. The dangers of aneurysms include rupture, emboli to a peripheral artery, pressure on surrounding tissues, and the obstruction of blood flow to organs fed by arterial branches.

Endovascular Repair of Abdominal Aortic Aneurysm

An endovascular abdominal aneurysm repair involves open femoral or iliac artery exposure and then access with a device manipulated and positioned and deployed, leaving the endograft to repair the aneurysm.

Endovascular Repair of Iliac Aneurysm

Endovascular repair of an iliac aneurysm (34900) involves access through the femoral artery to place a graft in the iliac artery to cover the aneurysm and eliminate the risk of rupture. A self-expanding stent with hooks substitutes for suture material. One incision or two incisions over each femoral artery in the groin for deployment of the endograft into the iliac artery completes the reconstruction. Other interventional procedures performed during the time of the repair are reported separately.

Direct Repair of Aneurysm or Excision (Partial or Total) and Graft Insertion for Aneurysm, Pseudoaneurysm, Ruptured Aneurysm, and Associated Occlusive Disease

Aneurysms involve ballooning or "out pouching" of a vessel wall. The ballooned portion of the vessel wall in a true aneurysm is made up of one or more layers of the actual vessel wall. In a false aneurysm, a hematoma is present. The hematoma can be surrounded by a capsule of periarterial fibrous tissue and adventitia. When the false aneurysm communicates with the arterial lumen, it pulsates. These aneurysms tend to occur around the site of a graft anastomosis or where a catheter has been inserted.

Codes 35001–35152 include necessary preparation of the artery for anastomosis as well as endarterectomy. Endarterectomy is an integral part of these procedures and is not reported as a separate item on the claim. Endarterectomy is excision of diseased layers of an artery.

When reporting partial or total excision of an occluded artery and replacement of the excised artery with a graft, see codes under subsection Repair Blood Vessel Other Than for Fistula, With or Without Patch Angioplasty (specifically codes 35201–35286). Excision of a diseased artery and replacement with the graft are bundled in the single code.

Practical Coding Note

Aneurysm Coding Guidelines

The following information is considered when coding aneurysm repair:

- Identify the site and type of aneurysm being treated
- Identify the type of graft material in use

- Determine whether a surgical excision or revision was performed
- Determine whether there were any vascular, medical, surgical, or mechanical complications resulting in other surgical procedures or treatments
- Grafts include preparation of the artery for anastomosis and endarterectomy when necessary
- If the repair is performed with a bypass graft, refer to codes 35501–35152
- The aneurysm is not necessarily excised in a direct repair procedure. In some cases, vascular clamps are placed above and below the aneurysm to occlude blood flow into and away from the weakened area. The aneurysm is cleaned out and the graft is sewn into the vessel. Part of the wall of the aneurysm may be excised, and the aneurysm shell is wrapped around the graft.

Deep Vein Thrombosis

Venous obstruction may be permanent or temporary. Obstruction of a portion of the trunk or main branches causes vessels distal to the obstruction to dilate and can result in permanent damage to valves and vessel walls due to pressure, hypoxemia, stretch, and malnutrition. Edema may result from damage to peripheral vessels. Injury to veins can cause clots to form in response to inflammation or trauma to the endothelium. Stasis of the venous blood contributes to the formation of a blood clot or thrombus. As the thrombus grows along the axis of blood flow, part of it may break off and become an embolism. It can lodge in upstream vessels. Most often emboli lodge in the pulmonary capillaries, called a pulmonary embolus.

When thrombosis occludes a vessel, collateral vessels may compensate. If collateral circulation is inadequate, edema can result. Treatment includes anticoagulant therapy or surgical removal if the thrombus is large. Inflammation of a vein, usually in the leg, due to presence of a thrombus is thrombophlebitis. Such inflammation can occur due to chemical damage, bacterial infection, or from an unknown origin. Thrombophlebitis in deep veins or deep vein thrombosis (DVT) of the legs causes calf pain and tenderness.

Thromboendarterectomies are used when calcified plaque or persistent clot formations do not respond to balloon angioplasty procedures. This procedure differs from a thrombectomy, because along with the thrombus being removed, the inner lining of the artery (intima and some media) is removed. Thromboendarterectomies may or may not include a patch graft. Codes are reported based on the arteries requiring surgery (eg, femoral, popliteal, iliac, etc).

Practical Coding Note

Code 35301 is reported with add on code 35390 when a second thromboendarterectomy operation is performed more than one month after the original operation involving the carotid artery. If a prior surgery is performed, documentation of timing will be essential.

Angioplasty

Angioplasty opens narrow or blocked vessels. When performed percutaneously, it is a PTA (percutaneous transluminal angioplasty). Do not confuse the codes in this section with the codes for PTCA, which is performed on the coronary arteries. The codes for PTCA are in the Medicine section of CPT®, and will be discussed below. Balloon angioplasty involves inserting a balloon catheter into a narrow or occluded blood vessel to dilate the vessel by inflating the balloon.

Practical Coding Note

Make a note next to the codes in this section to see codes 92920–92944 for PTCA (Coronary).

Codes for angioplasty are chosen by vessel and method. For example, an open aortic angioplasty is 35452, but a percutaneous aortic angioplasty is 35472. Note that there are separate codes for percutaneous transluminal angioplasty of the lower extremities in the category Endovascular Revascularization (Open or Percutaneous, Transcatheter).

Practical Coding Note

When billing, report the supervision and interpretation code(s) from the Radiology section in addition to a code from the range 35450–35476, when the physician performs the open transluminal or percutaneous transluminal angioplasty as well as supervises and interprets the radiologic procedure. Also remember to code the appropriate nonselective or selective catheterization codes.

For radiological supervision of transluminal angioplasty, select the appropriate CPT® code from 75962–75968 and 75978.

Bypass Graft

These grafts are performed on the non-coronary vessels, as determined by the type of graft and the vessels bypassed. There are three sections: vein, *in-situ* vein, and other than vein. You must know the anastomosis sites (where the graft is connected on the ends). For example, if a synthetic bypass graft is placed from the femoral artery to the popliteal artery, report 35656.

The "*in-situ*" graft is a method used for revascularization of lower and upper extremities to avoid amputation. For codes 35583–35587, the saphenous vein is isolated and remains in place. The proximal and distal ends are mobilized. Side branches and all tributaries are tied off along the vein graft section and valves are destroyed or incised. The upper and lower ends of the saphenous vein are anastomosed to the artery (for example, femoral artery and popliteal artery) creating a new circulatory pathway. A bypass vein graft (35500–35572) involves bypassing an arterial blockage with a section of vein reversed so the vein valves are in the direction of arterial flow.

Practical Coding Note

An "*in-situ*" graft occurs when the vein is left in its native place, while the arterial flow is bypassed from artery to vein to artery to circumvent a blockage and create a new circulatory pathway.

Next to the *In-Situ* Vein codes, write "artery-vein-artery."

The valves inside the vein are stripped to allow arterial blood flow toward the foot. Codes 35600–35671 are reported for bypass performed with use of synthetic vein (prosthetic) material for grafting.

Add-on code 35681 is reported when the graft is composed of autogenous vein and prosthetic graft. Add-on codes 35682–35683 report harvest and anastomosis of two or more vein segments from distant sites from a limb other than the vessel undergoing bypass.

Any venipuncture, arterial punctures, and closures of surgical wounds are considered inherent to these procedures. Any additional procedures performed to improve blood flow (toward or away from the graft site), as well as intraoperative angiograms, are considered inherent. Procurement of the saphenous vein is included in the description of 35501–35587. To report harvesting of femoropopliteal vein segment, use add-on code 35572 or composite (prosthetic and vein) or multiple vein segments from distant sites, use add-on codes 35681–35683.

Practical Coding Note

Some bypass graft coding tips are:

1. Any additional procedures performed to improve blood flow toward or away from the graft site, as well as intraoperative angiograms, are considered inherent in these codes and should not be separated out for billing.

2. If a vein and synthetic graft are used in combination (a composite graft), 35681 is reported. This code does not require modifier 51.

3. Venipunctures, arterial punctures, and closures of any surgical wounds are considered inherent and are not coded separately.

4. When reporting a bypass graft, report the type of graft, or device used.

5. Note the point-to-point insertion/anastomosis of the graft.

6. The harvesting of a saphenous vein graft is included in the description of the work for codes 35501–35587 and should not be reported separately.

Arterial Transposition

Arterial transposition codes are used to describe the transposition or anastomosis of a diseased artery to a healthy artery.

The reimplantation of a visceral artery to an infrarenal aortic prosthesis is an add-on code for the added work of reimplanting arteries, such as the renal or mesenteric artery to an aortic graft after resection of an aneurysm. Report 35697 for each visceral artery reimplanted.

Excision, Exploration, Repair, Revision

Bypass surgery does not cure atherosclerotic vascular disease. Symptoms are relieved, and almost without fail, the patient's quality of life dramatically improves; however, the condition producing plaque is ongoing and insidious in nature. If a patient has advanced disease, the vessel may again occlude within a three- to five-year-period after the initial surgical procedure.

Vascular Injection Procedures 36000–36481 are discussed in the Interventional Radiology section.

Central Venous Access Procedures

Central venous access devices (CVAD) (36555–36598) are catheters placed in large veins for patients who require frequent access to the bloodstream. According to CPT® guidelines, the tip of the catheter must terminate in the subclavian, brachiocephalic, or iliac veins, the inferior or superior vena cava, or right atrium to qualify as a CVAD.

There are five code categories: insertions, repairs, partial replacements, complete replacements, and removals. Devices may be inserted centrally or peripherally. Central insertion is into the jugular, subclavian, or femoral veins; or the inferior vena cava. Peripheral insertion is into the basilic, cephalic, or other peripheral veins. Devices may be tunneled or non-tunneled, and may be accessed via an exposed catheter or a subcutaneous port or pump.

If the centrally inserted central venous catheters are tunneled, they are also known as partially implanted vascular access devices. This latter group includes the Hickman® catheter, which is inserted and secured into a large vein in the chest for long-term use to administer drugs or nutrients. A tunnel is made under the skin to another site where the catheter exits. The catheter is placed in the vein leading to the heart and the end of the catheter is pulled through the tunnel. Medication, blood products, nutritional support, and new bone marrow can be delivered through the part of the catheter extending outside the body, and blood can be drawn from the body through the catheter.

If an existing CVAD is removed and a new one placed via a separate venous access site, report both the removal of the old device and insertion of the new device. Any imaging procedures used to gain access to the venous entry site, or to manipulate the catheter into the final central position, are reported using 76937 and 77001, as appropriate.

Intraosseous

Intraosseous infusion (36680) is accomplished by insertion of a special needle through the skin, muscle tissue, and into the bone marrow cavity of either the tibia or fibula. This method is required when infants have inaccessible vessels and fluids need to be infused directly into the bone marrow blood vessels.

Portal Decompression Procedures

Patients with cirrhosis and other diseases of the liver can develop portal hypertension due to an occlusion of the portal vein. The portal vein is a short but very wide vein formed by many of the veins draining the digestive system. In cases where it is occluded, it becomes necessary to create a surgical diversion between the portal vein and either the inferior vena cava or one of its tributaries. This subsection describes decompression of the portal vein by forming venous anastomoses with the listed combinations.

Transvenous intrahepatic portosystemic shunt (TIPS), is a procedure used to reduce portal pressure. TIPS involves threading a catheter into the portal vein and inserting a self-expanding stent to bridge the portal and hepatic veins to divert blood from the portal vein to the hepatic vein. It is performed when pressure in the portal vein is so high it causes internal bleeding from blood vessels in the esophagus.

Transcatheter Procedures

This subsection of vascular codes describes procedures to resolve a vascular condition across the vessel. The vessel is accessed (often percutaneously, depending on location) and a drug infusion or biopsy or removal of a foreign body is performed inside the vessel.

If an angioplasty is performed for the purpose of placing the stent, the angioplasty is included in the stent placement and not coded separately. If the provider has tried to resolve the intravascular lesion with angioplasty but places a stent as the last resort, only the stent placement may be coded.

Endovascular Revascularization (37220–37235) is discussed in the Interventional Radiology section below.

Ligation and Other Procedures

The walls of large arteries have three layers: a tough elastic outer coat, a layer of muscular tissue, and a smooth, thin inner coat. Veins return blood to the heart through a series of one-way valves keeping blood flowing from the superficial veins to deep veins in the muscles.

If vein walls are weak and damaged, or if valves are stretched or injured, unusually high pressure can build, resulting in swelling and potential blood clot formation.

Over time, the conditions contribute to a variety of venous diseases, including varicose veins, which are dilated, twisting, or bulging, and superficial veins often asymptomatic or causing aches and cramping.

Asymptomatic varicose veins require no therapy unless for cosmetic appearance. Tests to determine the extent of disease include duplex scan to determine the presence or absence of blood flow and the direction of flow or a venogram, which involves the injection of contrast dye directly into veins to visualize flow.

The saphenous vein, which runs from the ankle to the groin, can be stripped out through one or more incisions (37700–37735). The procedure is performed on an outpatient basis.

The stab avulsion (ambulatory stab phlebectomy) removes the varicose veins through incisions 2 to 3 mm in length using a small, hooked instrument. This procedure may be done as an outpatient surgical procedure with the use of anesthesia, and may be performed in conjunction with ligation and stripping.

Section Review 10.3

1. Patient undergoes a 3 venous, 2 arterial CABG using the saphenous vein, femoropopliteal vein, and the radial artery, harvested by the surgeon performing the grafts. The venous grafts were procured using endoscopic harvesting techniques. What CPT® codes are reported?

    A. 33534, 33512, 35572

    B. 33534, 33519, 35572, 35600, 33508

    C. 33514, 35572, 35600

    D. 33533, 33521, 35572, 35600, 33508

2. Patient presents for removal and replacement of her permanent dual chamber transvenous pacemaker system (generator and leads). What CPT® codes are reported?

    A. 33213, 33234-51, 33233-51

    B. 33206, 33207-51, 33233-51, 33235-51

    C. 33235, 33208-51, 33233-51

    D. 33240, 33235-51, 33233-51

3. Patient had mitral valve prolapse, and a mitral valve ring was inserted with cardiopulmonary bypass. What CPT® code is reported?

    A. 33426

    B. 33464

    C. 33425

    D. 33430

Interventional Procedures

Interventional Cardiology/Radiology (IVR) is a branch of medicine diagnosing and treating diseases using minimally invasive techniques under imaging guidance (fluoroscopy, ultrasound, etc.). A catheter threaded through vessels, rather than an open technique, is used to perform the procedure(s). To report such procedures in full, you may need to report multiple codes from different sections of CPT® (eg, Surgery, Radiology, and Medicine). We will discuss each of these separately, and use a two-part example to illustrate proper coding principles.

IVR Terms

Angiography—Radiographic visualization of blood vessels following introduction of contrast material.

Antegrade—Moving or extending anteriorly, moving with the flow.

Bifurcation—Division into two branches.

Contralateral—Situated on, pertaining to, or affecting the opposite side, as opposed to ipsilateral.

Digital Subtraction Angiography—Arteriography using electronic circuitry to subtract the background of bone and soft tissue to provide a useful image of arteries injected with contrast medium.

First Order Vessel—Primary branch off the main trunk of a vascular system.

Ipsilateral—Situated on, pertaining to, or affecting the same side, as opposed to contralateral.

Main Trunk of the Arterial System—Aorta.

Main Trunk of the Venous System—Vena cava.

Non-Selective Catheterization—Catheter placed in the main trunk, contrast may be injected, images may be taken, but the catheter is not moved into any other branches.

Retrograde—Moving backward or against the usual direction of flow.

Roadmapping—Overlaying of two images. A stored image is superimposed upon a current fluoroscopic image, or a current image can be copied for storage and later used in roadmapping (angiograms to see landmarks—not diagnostic).

Second Order Vessel—Secondary branch and comes off the first order vessel.

Selective Catheterization—A catheter is placed in the branches further off the main trunk (first, second, third, or higher order).

Third Order and Higher Vessel(s)—Tertiary branch and further, comes off the second order vessel.

Trifurcation—Division into three branches or parts.

Vascular Family—Network of vessels arising from the aorta's main branch or network of vessels arising from one primary branch off the access site.

Vascular Injection Procedures (36000–36598)

CPT® guidelines listed under the Vascular Injection Procedure section address proper application of these codes. Guidelines address services included with IVR procedures; all "necessary local anesthesia, introduction of contrast media with or without automatic power injection, and/or necessary pre- and post-injection care specifically related to the injection procedure" is included. Catheters, drugs, and contrast material are not included. Additional guidelines for interventional procedures state:

- Selective catheterizations should be coded to the highest level accessed within a vascular family.

- The highest level accessed when coded includes all of the lesser order selective catheterizations used in the approach (if a second order vessel is catheterized, the first order vessel and non-selective catheterization is bundled).

- Additional second and/or third order arterial catheterization within a vascular family of arteries or veins supplied by a single first order should be expressed by using 36012 or add-on codes 36218, or 36248, as appropriate.

- Additional first order or higher catheterizations in vascular families supplied by a first order vessel different from a previously selected and coded family should be separately coded using the above guidelines (you may code separately for catheterizations within each new vascular family).

To code an interventional radiology procedure, you must consider:

- The number of catheter access sites (each access site is coded as a separate procedure).

- The number of catheter end points. This will tell you how many vascular families and how many vessel orders were accessed.

- The number of vessels visualized. This will tell you how many radiology supervision and interpretation codes you need (the radiology codes will be discussed separately after the surgical codes).

Vascular Family Order

Think of the vessel order like turns off the highway. The main trunk (non-selective) is the main highway. If you take an off ramp to get gas it is one turn off the main highway (first order vessel). If you go further down the road after getting gas, for instance to get a bite to eat, it is two turns off the main highway (second order vessel). You get back on the main highway and realize you need to stop again. When you get off the main highway the next time, is a new ramp off the main highway (first order of new vascular family). Always "drive back" to the main trunk when coding vascular families and vascular order.

A single primary branch with all of its secondary and tertiary branches is defined as a vascular family. A vascular family is a group of vessels fed by a primary branch of the aorta or a primary branch of the vessel. Appendix L of the CPT® codebook contains the vascular families and their orders. It may be helpful when trying to determine order and families for coding. Please note the Appendix makes the assumption the starting point is catheterization from the aorta. If the starting point is different, the orders may be different.

Example 1

Part 1 (Surgical):

In the hospital, from a right femoral artery puncture, a catheter was placed in the aorta (nonselective 36200), and then the catheter was manipulated into the left common iliac (first order 36245), then into the external iliac and the common femoral artery (second order 36246), and then into the superficial femoral artery (third order 36247). Only the final catheter position is reported (36247). Angiography of the left lower extremity is performed. Check Appendix L for the vascular family order starting from the aorta.

Selective vs. Nonselective Catheterization

Nonselective catheterization is placement of a catheter into the desired blood vessel. No manipulation is needed and the catheter is not advanced into other branches of the vascular family or is only negotiated into a vessel such as the thoracic or abdominal aorta.

Selective catheterization means the needle or catheter must be manipulated into other branches of the vascular family. This is usually performed under fluoroscopic guidance and involves more work and risk.

Vascular Systems

Five vascular systems are considered when performing interventional procedures. These are the systemic (arterial and venous), pulmonary, coronary, portal system, and lymphatic system. Each of these systems may be accessed when providing diagnostic and/or therapeutic services and are coded separately.

Injection procedures from different systems are coded separately. Cardiac catheterization, their related injection procedures and radiological supervision and interpretation services are coded from the Medicine section of CPT® with codes 93451–93581.

Arterial System Coding

The surgical component is coded separately from the radiologic component; however, there may not be a one-to-one correspondence between the two services. To code complex procedures, first describe the exact procedural service provided without regard to the type and number of images provided. Once described, report the exact imaging service. Determine the beginning point (the puncture site) and the end point (the injection site/highest order catheter position). How many branches of each vascular family did the catheter traverse? Each branch represents a different order of selection and is coded accordingly.

Code only the highest order catheter selection within each family. Selective catheterization includes the introduction and all lesser order selective catheterization used in the approach.

Example 2

Part 1 (Surgical):

Consider a femoral puncture for selective catheterization for visualization of the right brachial artery. Look in Appendix L and you will see that the right brachial artery is a third order vessel (36217). The innominate (first order 36215) and subclavian (second order 36216) are bundled, because the catheter had to pass through these arteries to get to the brachial artery. The surgical portion is 36217.

Depending on the arterial system, additional second and/or third order arterial catheterization(s) within the same arterial family are coded by listing add-on codes 36218 or 36248.

Each vascular family is coded separately. Because the right and left vessels belong to two different vascular families, cases of

bilateral catheterization are coded separately. Additional first order or higher catheterization in vascular families, supplied by a first order vessel different from a previously selected family, are coded separately using the conventions described.

Coding is modified in cases of anomalous anatomy. If two punctures are required, each vascular access is coded independently.

Example 3

Part 1 (Surgical):

From a right femoral access the catheter is advanced into the aorta just above the renal arteries and an aortogram is performed. Next the catheter is manipulated into the superior mesenteric artery (visceral artery), and then into the inferior mesenteric artery and angiography is performed in both vessels. Look in Appendix L and you will see that the superior and inferior mesenteric arteries are first order vessels (separate vascular families). The selective catheterization is below the diaphragm; therefore, 36245 is reported twice. Modifier 59 is appended to the second code to show a separate first order family (36245, 36245-59). Report 36245, 36245-59.

There are exceptions when coding for selective catheter placement and angiography. There are codes which include the selective catheterization for the injection of contrast, and the radiological supervision and interpretation for the aortic arch, carotid, intracranial, vertebral, and renal angiography.

Example 4

Angiography of the aortic arch followed by selective catheterization with angiography of the right and left common carotids, right and left internal carotids, and the right and left vertebral arteries, with visualization and report of the internal cerebral arteries is reported as follows:

36224-50 Selective catheter placement, internal carotid artery, unilateral, with angiography of the ipsilateral intracranial carotid circulation and all associated radiological supervision and interpretation, includes angiography of the extracranial carotid and cervicocerebral arch, when performed.

36226-50 Selective catheter placement, vertebral artery, unilateral, with angiography of the ipsilateral vertebral circulation and all associated radiological supervision and interpretation, includes angiography of the cervicocerebral arch, when performed.

Modifier 50 is appended because the procedures are performed bilaterally. Some payers may prefer modifiers LT and RT instead of modifier 50. Verify payer policy. For the CPC® exam, report modifier 50 for bilateral procedures. According to the CPT® coding guidelines, the procedure codes include radiological supervision and interpretation. Codes from the Radiology section are not reported in this case.

Venous System Coding

Rules are similar to arterial selective catheterization with one exception—there are no codes for each additional second, third, or higher order catheterization. Instead, CPT® dictates use of code 36012 (second order, or more selective). Codes must be reused to describe the total number of separate catheterizations performed during a given procedure.

Pulmonary System Coding

There are only two vascular families in this system. Each family is fed by either the right or left pulmonary artery. Highest order catheterization includes the work of lesser order catheterization. Subsequent catheterization is listed by reusing the codes.

Example

If two segmental injections are performed in the right lung after placement of the catheter into the right pulmonary artery, code 36015 is listed twice. Modifier 59 is added to one of the codes to show each procedure was separate (eg, 36015, 36015–59). Code 75741-26 is reported for the radiological supervision and interpretation. Modifier 26 denotes the professional service. Report 36015, 36015-59, 75741-26.

To code venipuncture procedures, whether in the office, emergency department, or hospital setting, several issues may arise. Consider the following:

1. What is the site of the puncture?

2. Is the procedure a direct puncture or a cut-down procedure?

3. Did a physician perform the procedure?

Sclerotherapy is a procedure obliterating veins through a reaction caused by a chemical solution injected directly into the vein. Sclerotherapy can be used after surgical removal of large varicose veins to obliterate small residual spider veins.

Portal System Coding

Code 36481 describes percutaneous nonselective portal vein catheterization (for radiological supervision and interpretation, see 75885 or 75887). The code is listed in addition to selective catheterization of the portal system as described by codes

36011 and 36012. Percutaneous catheterization of the portal vein is more labor intensive than establishing normal venous access, venous selective codes do not contain the work value of code 36481.

Endovascular Revascularization (Open or Percutaneous, Transcatheter)

Endovascular revascularization procedures (37220–37235) include in ascending order, transluminal angioplasty, placement of stent, atherectomy and placement of stent with atherectomy. These procedures are applied in three arterial areas: iliac (excluding atherectomy), femoral/popliteal, and tibial/peroneal.

These procedures include the work of accessing and selectively catheterizing the vessel, traversing the lesion, radiological supervision, and interpretation directly related to the intervention(s) performed, embolic protection, if used, closure of the arteriotomy, imaging for the procedure, and imaging performed to document completion of the intervention. Diagnostic angiography is reported separately with modifier 59, when performed prior to the intervention(s).

Iliac vascular territory is divided into the common iliac, internal iliac, and external iliac. Only one primary code is used for the initial iliac artery treated in each leg (37220 or 37221). Add-on codes (37222, 37223) must be used for interventions performed in either of the two other vessels in the iliac area. For example, placement of a stent in the common iliac and angioplasty of the external iliac are reported with 37221 and 37222. Stent intervention supersedes angioplasty; the primary procedure is the stent (37221), and the add-on procedure is the angioplasty (37222).

Atherectomy in the iliac area is reported separately because atherectomy in the supra-inguinal vessels (iliacs, visceral, aorta, renal, and brachiocephalic) utilize Category III CPT® codes 0234T–0238T. These category III codes do not include accessing and selectively catheterizing the vessel or closure of the arteriotomy; they are coded separately.

For the femoral/popliteal territory, all interventions performed in the common femoral, profunda femoral, superficial femoral, and popliteal arteries are described by a single code. The hierarchy listed above still applies.

The tibial/peroneal territory includes the anterior tibial, posterior tibial, and peroneal arteries. The dorsalis pedis artery is considered continuation of the anterior tibial artery, and the medial malleolar artery is considered continuation of the posterior tibial artery.

These procedures are inclusive of all of the services provided for the vessel; only one code from this subsection is reported for each lower extremity vessel treated, unless it is bilateral.

When bilateral procedures are performed, the code will be repeated with a modifier 59 appended to the second code.

When reporting endovascular interventions, report the most comprehensive treatment given within a vessel. The hierarchy of intensity will differ from numeric order. Follow the extensive guidelines in CPT® when coding endovascular revascularization for the lower extremities.

Practical Coding Note

The intensity of these services from the most intensive to the least intensive is as follows:

- Stent and atherectomy
- Atherectomy
- Stent
- PTA

Intravascular stent placement codes for vessels other than lower extremity artery(s) for occlusive disease, cervical carotid, intracoronary, extracranial vertebral, intrathoracic carotid, intracranial, or coronary report codes 37236-37239. These codes also bundle in radiological supervision and interpretation, and (if performed) same-vessel angioplasty. Code 37236 reports the placement of the stent in the initial artery and add-on code 37237 is for each additional artery where the physician places a stent. Code 37238 reports the placement of a stent in the initial vein and add-on code 37239 is for each additional vein where the physician places a stent. One code is reported when one or more stents are placed in a single vessel. Also, report one code if one intervention can treat a single lesion that extends from one vessel to another. Pay close attention to the parenthetical instructions in this section of codes.

Vascular Procedures Radiology (75600–75989)

If the physician provides both portions of an interventional service, report Radiology codes—in addition to surgery codes. Remember modifier 26 *Professional Component* may be required when reporting radiology procedures performed in a facility/hospital setting, or when using equipment not belonging to the provider.

The following radiology guidelines apply to interventional procedures:

- Diagnostic angiography radiologic supervision and interpretation (S&I) codes should *not* be used with interventional procedures for:
  - contrast injections, angiography, roadmapping, and/or fluoroscopic guidance for the intervention
  - vessel measurement
  - post-angioplasty/stent angiography

Such work is captured in the interventional S & I codes.

- Diagnostic angiography performed at the time of an interventional procedure is separately reportable if:
  - no prior catheter-based angiographic study is available and a full diagnostic study is performed, and the decision to intervene is based on the diagnostic study, OR
  - a prior study is available, but as documented in the medical record:
    a. the patient's condition with respect to the clinical indication has changed since the prior study, OR
    b. there is inadequate visualization of the anatomy and/or pathology, OR
    c. there is a clinical change during the procedure requiring new evaluation outside the target area of intervention.

- Diagnostic angiography performed at a separate setting from an interventional procedure is separately reportable.
- Diagnostic angiography performed at the time of an interventional procedure is NOT separately reportable if it is specifically included in the interventional code descriptor.

In the Radiology section of CPT®, when a code descriptor states *selective*, the catheter must be placed in the vessel to report the code. If the code does not state selective, the vessel must be visualized with interpretation and report documented to report the code.

Some codes are unilateral and some codes are bilateral; pay careful attention to code descriptors and CPT® parenthetical notes. Unlike the surgical codes, you may report a non-selective S&I if it is documented.

Example 1

Part 2 (Radiology):

In the hospital, from a right femoral artery puncture, a catheter was placed in aorta, and then it was manipulated into the left superficial femoral artery and angiography of the left lower extremity was performed. For the angiography report 75710-26 *Angiography, extremity, unilateral, radiological supervision and interpretation*. Modifier 26 is appended to denote the professional service. This code is found in the CPT® Index under Angiography/Leg Artery.

By combining parts 1 (surgical) and 2 (radiologic) of this example, complete coding for this case is: 36247, 75710-26.

Example 2

Part 2 (Radiology):

Consider a femoral puncture for selective catheterization for visualization of the right brachial artery (36217). For the angiography report 75710-26 *Angiography, extremity, unilateral, radiological supervision and interpretation.* Modifier 26 is appended to denote the professional service. This code is found in the CPT® Index under Angiography/Arm Artery.

By combining parts 1 (surgical) and 2 (radiologic) of this example, complete coding for this case is: 36217, 75710-26.

Example 3

Part 2 (Radiology):

In the hospital, from a right femoral artery puncture, a catheter was placed in the aorta just above the renal arteries and an aortogram is performed. Next the catheter is manipulated into the superior mesenteric artery (visceral artery), and then into the inferior mesenteric artery and angiography is performed in both vessels. Look in the CPT® Index for Angiogram/Abdominal and you will see a range of codes. The correct code is 75726 *Angiography, visceral, selective or supraselective (with or without flush aortogram), radiological supervision and interpretation*, which is reported twice. The aortogram is included in 75726. Modifier 26 is appended to indicate the professional service. Modifier 59 is needed on the second code to show that this was performed in another family.

By combining parts 1 (surgical) and 2 (radiologic) of this example, complete coding for this case is: 36245, 36245-59, 75726-26, 75726-26-59.

Section Review 10.4

1. Catheter advanced from the left femoral artery into the aorta, manipulated into both the left and right renal arteries for imaging. What CPT® code(s) is/are reported?

    A. 36245, 36245-59

    B. 36252

    C. 36245, 36245-59, 36252

    D. 36251

2. During an inpatient stay, a patient is taken to the cath lab. A catheter is placed in the aortic arch, right and left vertebral arteries, and right and left common carotids. Imaging with interpretation and report is performed in each location. What CPT® codes are reported?

    A. 36247, 36246-59, 36245-59, 36222-50-51, 36226-50-51

    B. 36217, 36216-59, 36215-59, 36218, 36222-50-51, 36226-50-51

    C. 36226-50, 36222-50-51

    D. 36224-50, 36228-50-51

3. A 5 French pigtail catheter was placed in the abdominal aorta and a run-off was performed following injection of 80 cc of contrast. Oblique DSA images of the iliac circulation were performed following 2 injections, each 15 cc. The catheter was not moved to another position within the aorta for the additional injections. What CPT® codes are reported?

    A. 36200, 75630-26

    B. 36215, 36215-59, 75630-26

    C. 36215, 36215-59, 36200, 75630-26

    D. 36200, 75716-26

4.   A catheter was advanced into the left and right renal artery, and the superior mesenteric artery (SMA), and imaging was performed in all vessels. What CPT® codes are reported?

   A.   36245-RT, 36245-LT, 36245-59, 36252-59, 75726-26

   B.   36245-RT, 36245-LT-59, 36245-59, 75726-26

   C.   36252, 36245-59, 75726-26

   D.   36245, 36248 x 2, 75726-26

5.   A catheter is placed at the level of the renal arteries for the abdominal aortography and then moved to the level of the bifurcation of the aorta for pelvic angiography demonstrating stenosis in the left external iliac. The right external iliac, femoral, and popliteal arteries are normal. What CPT® codes are reported?

   A.   36245, 36245-59, 75630-26

   B.   36245, 36245-59, 75716-26, 75625-26

   C.   36245, 36200, 75716-26

   D.   36200, 75716-26, 75625-26

Radiology

Radiology codes were discussed for interventional coding, above. We will now look at some other tests falling under the Radiology section for Cardiology.

Heart (75557–75574)

This section contains codes for cardiac magnetic resonance imaging (MRI) and computed tomography (CT). Cardiac MRI differs from traditional MRI in its ability to provide a physiologic evaluation of cardiac function. Only one procedure from code range 75557–75563 may be reported per session. Only one add-on code for flow velocity (75565) may be reported per session. Cardiac MRI can be performed at rest and/or during pharmacologic stress. Stress test codes (93015–93018) also may be reported, if appropriate.

Cardiac computed tomography (CT) and coronary computed tomographic angiography (CTA) are described by 75571–75574. Contrast enhanced cardiac CT and coronary CTA include any quantitative assessment when performed as part of the same encounter. Only one CT heart service may be reported per encounter.

Cardiovascular System (78414–78499)

This section has codes for SPECT, planar, PET, and blood pool imaging studies.

Cardiac SPECT (single photon emission computed tomography) scans—also known as myocardial perfusion imaging—are non-invasive tests used to assess the heart's structure and function. SPECT scans use small amounts of radioactive substances injected into a vein and a special camera to produce images of the heart. Using these pictures, a computer measures blood flow through the heart and detects areas of abnormal heart muscle. Myocardial perfusion imaging studies are reported with 78451–78454.

Cardiac blood pool imaging is performed when a radioactive solution is introduced into the bloodstream and monitored as it travels through the heart; these procedures are coded from 78472–78483 and 78494–78496.

Myocardial perfusion and cardiac blood pool imaging studies can be performed at rest and/or during stress. When performed during exercise and/or pharmacologic stress, the appropriate stress testing codes (93015–93018) should be reported.

Positron Emission Tomography (PET) is a type of nuclear imaging to evaluate heart function after administration of a natural biochemical substance, such as glucose or fatty acids. PET scans can be used to look for coronary artery disease by examining how blood flows through the heart; it can evaluate damage to heart tissue after a heart attack. PET is reported using 78459 and 78491–78492.

Medicine, Cardiovascular (92920–93799)

Therapeutic Services and Procedures (92920–92979)

Cardiopulmonary resuscitation (CPR) is described using 92950. This code has no timeframe associated with it, and is not bundled into the critical care E/M codes.

Cardioversion is use of defibrillator paddles to restore normal rhythm of the heart by electrical shock. Code 92960 is for external placement of the paddles; 92961 is for internal placement. These codes are meant for elective (planned) cardioversion. A parenthetical note in CPT® with 92961 instructs, "do not report 92961 in conjunction with 93282–93284, 93287, 93289, 93295, 93296, 93618–93624, 93631, 93640–93642, 93650, 93653–93657, 93662."

Thrombolysis of a coronary artery (destruction of a blood clot) is coded by method of administration: 92975 is for intracoronary infusion and 92977 is for IV infusion.

Add-on codes 92978 and 92979 describe intravascular ultrasound (IVUS) when performed during a diagnostic or therapeutic intervention. During IVUS, a catheter with a transducer at its tip is inserted and threaded through a selected coronary artery(s) or coronary bypass graft(s). These procedures are coded per vessel, and include all transducer manipulations and repositioning within the specific vessel being examined, both before and after therapeutic intervention.

Percutaneous transluminal coronary angioplasty, or PTCA (92920–92921), is a non-surgical procedure relieving narrowing and obstruction of coronary arteries. This allows more blood and oxygen to be delivered to the heart muscle. PTCA is accomplished with a small balloon catheter inserted into an artery in the groin or arm, and advanced to the narrowing in the coronary artery. The balloon is then inflated to enlarge the narrowing in the artery. Code 92921 is an add-on code for additional coronary angioplasty in each additional branch of a major coronary artery.

Percutaneous transluminal coronary atherectomy (92924–92925) is a technique in which a cutting device (a blade or rotating blade) removes plaque buildup from the artery wall. The procedure includes angioplasty when performed.

Percutaneous intracoronary stent placement (92928–92929) is a procedure in which a perforated stainless steel tube (or stent) is mounted on a balloon catheter in a "crimped" or collapsed state and inserted into a coronary artery. When the balloon is inflated, the stent expands or opens up and pushes itself against the inner wall of the coronary artery. This holds the artery open when the balloon is deflated and removed. The stent placement code includes angioplasty when performed.

PTCA atherectomy with intracoronary stent placement, and angioplasty when performed, is reported with 92933–92934.

There are PTCA codes for revascularization of:

- Coronary artery bypass graft such as the internal mammary, free arterial or free venous grafts with any combination of intracoronary stent, atherectomy and angioplasty (92937, 92938).

- Acute total/subtotal occlusion during acute myocardial infarction of a coronary artery, or coronary artery bypass graft, with any combination of intracoronary stent, atherectomy, and angioplasty, including aspiration of thrombectomy when performed, single vessel (92941)

- Chronic total occlusion of a coronary artery, coronary branch, or coronary artery bypass graft, with any combination of intracoronary stent, atherectomy and angioplasty (92943–92944)

The base code that includes the most intensive service for the target vessel is reported. Percutaneous coronary intervention (PCI) performed during the same session in additional recognized branches of the target vessel is reported with add-on codes.

The codes for PTCA, intracoronary stent placement, percutaneous transluminal coronary atherectomy, percutaneous transluminal pulmonary artery balloon angioplasty, and IVUS are coded per vessel. It is important to look for the specific artery when utilizing these codes because there are specific bundling issues.

It is important to understand how these codes work together: One vessel may have a stent placed, while another vessel may have a PTCA performed. Special modifiers are used with these codes, to show which coronary artery is being accessed. Modifier LC stands for left circumflex coronary artery, modifier LD stands for left anterior descending coronary artery, modifier LM stands for left main, modifier RC stands for right coronary artery, and modifier RI stands for ramus intermedius.

Practical Coding Note

Pay attention to parenthetical notes. Following code 92961, there is a parenthetical note that includes the codes that should not be reported in addition to this code. If you report the codes listed in the parenthetical, you will be unbundling services.

Example

A patient was admitted to the ED with angina and shortness of breath, and was diagnosed with an acute myocardial infarction of the left descending coronary artery. He was urgently taken to the cardiac catheterization lab, and the coronary thrombus was aspirated. A stent was placed (92941-LD). Note the cardiac catheterization is included in code 92941.

Example

A patient is admitted to the cardiac catheterization lab with a chronic total occlusion of a venous bypass graft to the left anterior descending. Atherectomy is performed and a stent is placed in the bypass graft (92943-LD). Angioplasty is also performed in the left circumflex (92920-LC).

Cardiography (93000–93042)

The electrocardiogram (ECG or EKG) is a diagnostic tool used to measure and record electrical activity of the heart, interpretation of which allows for diagnosis of a wide range of heart conditions. EKG codes 93000–93010 are differentiated by which part of the procedure the physician is reporting. Code 93000 is for the complete global procedure—both the professional (interpretation and report) and technical (machine ownership, etc.) components. Because the codes are separated in this manner, modifiers 26 and TC are not necessary when reporting these services. If the physician owns the ECG machine and performs the official interpretation and report, 93000 is reported. If the physician performs the official interpretation and report only, use 93010. If the physician's ECG machine is used, but someone else performs the interpretation and report, 93005 is reported by the physician owning the ECG machine.

Cardiovascular stress tests are defined in a similar manner. Code 93015 is for the global procedure, cardiovascular stress test using maximal or submaximal treadmill or bicycle exercise, continuous electrocardiographic monitoring, and/ or pharmacological stress test with physician supervision, with interpretation and report. Due to the nature of the exam, physician monitoring during the test is required. If a physician monitors the test only, 93016 is reported. If a physician interprets the study and writes the official report, 93018 is reported. If a physician performs both services, both 93016 and 93018 are reported.

The Holter monitor (93224–93227) is a device invented by Dr. Norman Holter to record the heart rhythm continuously for up to 48 hours. Coding is similar to ECGs and stress tests; you may report the complete service, or portions thereof, as appropriate.

Practical Coding Note

In CPT®, highlight the parenthetical instruction directing use of modifier 52 if the recording is for less than 12 hours.

Implantable and Wearable Cardiac Device Evaluations (93279–93299)

There are a lot of guidelines for this section of CPT®, primarily to define the various devices. Read through them to become more familiar with terminology for the code set. Cardiac device evaluation services are diagnostic medical procedures using in-person and remote technology to assess device therapy and cardiovascular physiologic data. Important coding concepts for this section include:

- Codes 93279–93292 are reported per procedure.
- Codes 93293 –93296 are reported no more than once every 90 days, and cannot be reported if the monitoring period is less than 30 days.
- Codes 93297–93298 are reported no more than once every 30 days, and cannot be reported if the monitoring period is less than 10 days.
- A physician or qualified healthcare professional may not report an in-person and remote interrogation of the same device during the same period. Report only remote services when an in-person interrogation device evaluation is performed during a period of remote interrogation device evaluation.
- Programming device evaluation and in-person interrogation device evaluations may not be reported on the same date by the same physician.
- CPT® 93296 or 93299 is for reporting by a service center during a period in which a physician performs an in-person interrogation device evaluation. They are technical component only codes.
- Do not report 93268–93272 when performing 93279–93289, 93291–93296, or 93298–93299.
- Do not report 93040–93042 when performing 93279–93289, 93291–93296, or 93298–93299.

Echocardiography (93303–93352)

Echocardiography records graphically the position and motion of the heart walls or the internal structures of the heart and neighboring tissue using echoes obtained from ultrasonic waves directed through the chest wall. There are transesophageal echoes (TEE, 93312–93317) and transthoracic echoes (TTE, 93303–93308). Within each group, codes are separated by whether a congenital cardiac anomaly exists; there are codes for complete and follow-up (or limited) studies.

According to CPT®, a complete TTE without spectral or color flow Doppler (93307) is a comprehensive procedure including 2-dimensional, and when performed, selected M-mode examination of the left and right atria, left and right ventricles, the aortic, mitral, and tricuspid valves, the pericardium, and adjacent portions of the aorta. Despite significant effort, identification and measurement of some structures may not always be possible. In such instances, the reason an element could not be visualized must be documented.

A complete TTE with spectral and color flow Doppler (93306) is a comprehensive procedure including spectral Doppler and color flow Doppler in addition to the 2-dimensional and selected M-mode examinations, when performed. Complete, bundled TTE (93306) includes the TTE, spectral Doppler, and color flow Doppler (93307 + 93320 or 93321 + 93325). Watch for parenthetical notes following codes to ensure proper code selection.

There is also a grouping of codes (93350–93351) for TTE with cardiovascular stress testing. In addition to code 93350, stress test codes 93016–93018 also are reported.

Add-on code 93352 is for contrast agent used during stress echo. Usually there is a pre and post injection of the contrast, but the code may only be reported once per stress echocardiography.

Cardiac Catheterization (93451–93581)

Cardiac catheterization is the most commonly performed minimally invasive diagnostic test enabling evaluation of the heart's chambers, valves, and coronary arteries. This test provides information related to overall function of the heart and may reveal a stenotic lesion (hardening or narrowing) of coronary artery(ies) or cardiac valve.

Cardiac catheterization may be performed on the right heart, left heart, or as a combined (right heart and left heart) procedure. Left heart catheterization requires arterial access; right heart catheterization requires venous access. The following procedures are considered inclusive components of cardiac catheterization and not separately billed: local anesthesia or sedation, introduction of catheters, positioning and/or repositioning of catheters, recording of pressures, obtaining blood samples for blood gas measurement or dilution curves and cardiac output measurements, final evaluation and report of procedure.

Codes for catheter placement (93451–93533) are considered global codes. This means they are considered to have both a technical and professional component. The technical component (modifier TC) is for the provision of technical personnel, equipment, supplies, and costs associated with the performance of the test or procedure. The professional component (modifier 26) is for the physician's work providing the service, such as interpreting a test or performing a procedure, and writing a formal report. When performed in a facility setting where the provider does not own the equipment, modifier 26 must be added to these codes. Codes are further differentiated by catheter placement in patients with congenital cardiac anomalies (93530–93533), which are abnormalities present in the heart from birth. ICD-10-CM codes used will demon-

strate cardiac anomaly catheter placement codes are reported appropriately.

Most procedures for non-congenital conditions are reported with one code, but catheterizations for congenital heart conditions may be reported with multiple codes. Cardiac catheterization for congenital conditions (93530–93533) does not include injection codes and radiological supervision and interpretation (see 93563–93568). For studies of non-congenital conditions, the catheterization codes include:

- Intraprocedural injection(s) for angiography
- Imaging supervision, interpretation and report

Note: additional injection procedures (93565–93568) may be used with non-congenital cardiac catheterization codes. These injection add-on codes are professional services; therefore, modifier 26 is not required.

Intracardiac Electrophysiological Procedures/Studies (93600–93662)

Electrophysiological studies (EPS) involve invasive testing of the electrical conduction system of the heart (the system generating the heart beat). Tilt table studies are used to evaluate cardiovascular function by using a tilt table with continuous ECG and intermittent blood pressure monitoring. There are definitions listed in CPT® guidelines to ensure proper understanding of the codes. Comprehensive studies are reported with 93619–93622. If less than a comprehensive study is performed, portions performed are coded separately. Many codes in this section are add-on codes, and/or are modifier 51 exempt. All codes in this section contain both a professional and technical component, and you need to apply modifiers 26/TC if the global service is not provided.

Intracardiac catheter ablation procedures use radiofrequency energy to destroy cardiac tissue selectively. Code 93650 is for ablation of AV node function/AV conduction to create complete heart block. Code 93653 is for treatment of supraventricular tachycardia (SVT) by ablation of fast or slow atrioventricular pathway, accessory atrioventricular connection, cavo-tricuspid isthmus or other single atrial focus or source of atrial reentry. Code 93654 is for intracardiac ablation for treatment of ventricular tachycardia (V-tach) or ventricular ectopy including intracardiac electrophysiologic 3D mapping, when performed, and left ventricular pacing and recording when performed. Both codes include comprehensive electrophysiological evaluation including insertion and repositioning of multiple electrode catheters with induction or attempted induction of an arrhythmia with right atrial pacing and recording, right ventricular pacing and recording, and bundle of His recording.

Section Review 10.5

1. Left and right heart catheterization, selective coronary angiogram, left ventriculogram, ascending aortogram to access the aortic root, descending aortogram, right iliac angiogram, Perclose closure. Access is from the right femoral artery and right femoral vein. What CPT® codes are reported for the physician's services in a facility?

    A. 93454-26, 93565, 75625-26

    B. 93458-26, 93567, 75600-26, 75625-26, 75710-RT

    C. 93460-26, 93567

    D. 93460, 93567, 75600-26, 75625-26, 75710-RT

2. Angioplasty of the diagonal branch with intravascular ultrasound (IVUS). What CPT® code(s) is/are reported?

    A. 92920-LD, 92978-26

    B. 92920-LC, 92978-26

    C. 92920-26, 92979-26

    D. 92920-LC

3. A patient presents for a cardiac stress test at the hospital. The same physician supervises the test, interprets the study, and documents the official report. What CPT® code(s) is/are reported?

    A. 93015

    B. 93015-26

    C. 93016, 93017, 93018

    D. 93016, 93018

4. The EP specialist documents that a comprehensive electrophysiologic evaluation was performed in the hospital, including induction of arrhythmia, right atrial pacing, and bundle of His recording. The specialist documented the study and wrote a report. What CPT® code(s) is/are reported?

    A. 93619

    B. 93620-26

    C. 93618-26, 93610-26, 93600-26

    D. 93620-26, 93621

5. A complete TTE (transthoracic echocardiography) was performed with spectral Doppler and color flow. Report the global service. What CPT® code(s) is/are reported?

    A. 93307, 93320, 93325

    B. 93306

    C. 93312, 93320, 93325

    D. 93312

Modifiers

The cardiology section uses the same modifiers as other sections, with the exception of the LC, LD, LM, RC, and RI modifiers already discussed. What follows is a quick review of recommended use for many of the most often-accessed modifiers in cardiology.

Modifier 22

Consider appending modifier 22 *Increased procedural services*, when the service(s) is "greater than usually required for the listed procedure," according to CPT® Appendix A ("Modifiers").

CPT® codes describe a range of services: Although one procedure may go smoothly, the next procedure of the same type may take longer or be more difficult. The "easy" and "hard" procedures are expected to average over time. In some cases, however, surgery may require significant additional time or effort falling outside the range of services described by a particular CPT® code. When you encounter such circumstances, and no available code better describes the work involved, modifier 22 may be appropriate.

Truly "unusual" circumstances will occur in only a small minority of cases. Situations calling for modifier 22 may include:

- Excessive blood loss for the particular procedure.
- Presence of an excessively large surgical specimen (especially in abdominal surgery).
- Trauma extensive enough to complicate the particular procedure and not billed as additional procedure codes.
- Other pathologies, tumors, malformation (genetic, traumatic, surgical) directly interfering with the procedure but are not billed separately.
- Services rendered are significantly more complex than described for the CPT® code in question.

Provider documentation must demonstrate the special circumstances, such as extra time or highly complex trauma, warranting modifier 22.

Modifier 26 and Modifier TC

When a physician conducts diagnostic tests or other services using equipment he or she doesn't own, modifier 26 *Professional component* may be used to indicate the physician provided only the professional component (the administration or interpretation) of the service. The facility providing the equipment may receive reimbursement for the service's technical component (the cost of equipment, supplies, technician salaries, etc.) by reporting the appropriate CPT® code with modifier TC *Technical component* appended.

Apply modifiers 26 and TC only to those codes having both a professional and a technical component. Such codes are found primarily in the Radiology and Medicine portions of CPT®. The professional portion of the service includes the physician interpretation and report. The technical component pays for operation and maintenance of equipment, necessary supplies, etc. The CMS National Physician Fee Schedule Relative Value File separately lists a code value with modifier 26, with modifier TC, and with no modifier appended.

If the physician provides both components of the service (for instance, by providing the service in his or her office), he or she may report the appropriate CPT® code without either modifier 26 or modifier TC.

Modifier 51

Modifier 51 *Multiple procedures*, indicates more than one (non-E/M) procedure was provided during the same session. Many payers use software automatically detecting second and subsequent procedures, making modifier 51 unnecessary. Check with individual payers for guidelines, and request the payer's instructions in writing.

Modifier 58

Append modifier 58 to a procedure or service during the post-operative period if the procedure or service was:

- Planned prospectively at the time of the original procedure
- More extensive than the original procedure
- For therapy following a diagnostic surgical procedure

The subsequent procedure or service either is related to the underlying problem/diagnosis prompting the initial surgery, or anticipated at the time the surgeon performs the initial surgery, according to CPT® instruction. A "more extensive" procedure need not be more complex or time-intensive than the original procedure; it need only "go beyond" the work performed during the initial procedure.

Do not use modifier 58 if the patient needs a follow-up procedure because of surgical complications or unexpected postoperative findings arising from the initial surgery. For complications requiring a return to the operating room, append modifier 78 *Unplanned return to the operating/procedure room by the same physician or other qualified healthcare professional following initial procedure for a related procedure during the postoperative period*.

Modifier 59

Use modifier 59 *Distinct procedural service* to identify procedures not normally reported together, but are appropriate under the circumstances. According to CPT® instruction, you may append modifier 59 when the provider:

- sees a patient during a different session
- treats a different site or organ system
- makes a separate incision/excision
- tends to a different lesion
- treats a separate injury

Do not append modifier 59 to E/M codes, and do not use modifier 59 if another, more specific modifier is available.

Modifiers 76 and 77

Modifiers 76 and 77 describe repeat procedures, and often are used with serial ECGs and chest X-rays when performed on the same date.

Modifier 78

Apply modifier 78 *Return to the operating room by the same physician for a related procedure during the postoperative period* when all of the following conditions are met:

- The physician must undertake the subsequent surgery because of conditions (complications) arising from an initial surgery;
- The subsequent surgery occurs during the global period of the initial surgery; and
- The subsequent surgery requires a return to the operating room.

Modifier 79

Modifier 79 *Unrelated procedure or service by the same physician during the postoperative period* may be appended when an unrelated surgery by the same physician occurs during the global period of a previous surgery.

HCPCS Level II

HCPCS Level II codes applicable to cardiology may include drug codes, such as J1245 for Persantine, which may be needed for testing. When reporting drug codes, pay careful attention to dosage to be sure you are reporting the proper number of units.

Additional HCPCS Level II codes relevant to this section include:

G0278 Iliac and/or femoral artery angiography, non-selective, bilateral or ipsilateral to catheter insertion, performed at the same time as cardiac catheterization and/or coronary angiography, includes positioning or placement of the catheter in the distal aorta or ipsilat-

eral femoral or iliac artery, injection of dye, production of permanent images, and radiologic supervision and interpretation (List separately in addition to primary procedure)

G0389 Ultrasound B-scan and/or real time with image documentation; for abdominal aortic aneurysm (AAA) screening

G0422 Intensive cardiac rehabilitation; with or without continuous ECG monitoring with exercise, per session

G0423 Intensive cardiac rehabilitation; with or without continuous ECG monitoring; without exercise, per session

M0300 IV chelation therapy (chemical endarterectomy)

There may be other codes applicable to the specialties of Cardiology, Cardiothoracic Surgery, Cardiovascular Surgery, and Interventional Cardiology/Radiology. Requirements for using these codes should be checked with CMS and/or the individual payer.

Documentation Dissection

Case 1—CABG

Diagnosis: Multivessel coronary artery disease with angina.

Operative Procedure: Coronary artery bypass graft x 4 (CABG)

1. Left internal mammary to the left anterior descending.

2. Sequential vein graft from the aorta to the second and third marginal branches.

3. Saphenous vein to the acute marginal branch of the right coronary.

Procedure: The patient was supine with standard padding and positioning. Anesthesia was obtained and monitoring lines were established. Cardiac sterile prep and drape were performed. The sternum was opened through a vertical midline incision. The left ankle was opened with a small incision, and the saphenous vein harvested through a series of small incisions using endoscopic technique. [1]

The sternum was divided with a reciprocating saw and the sternum was opened. The pericardium was incised, and the coronary anatomy was inspected. Measurements were taken of the proposed targets. The left chest wall was elevated and the mammary artery taken down with cautery. A Blake drain was placed in the left pleural space. The sternal retractor was placed. The pericardium was distended and the patient was fully heparinized. The aorta was cannulated near the innominate vessel. Retrograde and antegrade cardioplegic cannulas were established along with a double-stage venous uptake cannula. The mammary artery was dilated and flow was excellent. The LIMA (left internal mammary artery) was brought in the left lobe of the thymus and through an incision in the pericardium.

The conduits were excellent. The ACT was over 400; cardiopulmonary bypass was begun. Core temperature was dropped to 28 degrees. The aorta was cross clamped and 500 cc of antegrade followed by 300 cc of retrograde cardioplegia were administered. The root was vented and maintenance cardioplegia was given retrograde every 15–20 minutes with doses of 300 to 350 cc of cold potassium crystalloid.

The large acute marginal branch was grafted first. It was isolated with tape and opened with a #15 blade and fine scissors. It easily took a 1 mm probe. A segment of vein was grafted to the acute marginal branch and confirmed with probes. The graft was brought up to the right lateral ascending aorta where a linear incision was made and the top end created to the vein with continuous 6-0 Prolene. [2]

The heart was flipped up to expose the inferior wall. There was significant palpable disease in the proximal PDA. A segment of saphenous vein was beveled and sewn in a parallel end-to-side manner. [3] Then the mid OM-2 was opened, a diamond-shaped anastomosis created to the venotomy and the final suture line confirmed with probes. The length was very adequate, and a tension-free anastomosis to the aorta was created in the manner described above. [4]

Rewarming was begun. The distal LAD was opened and grafted to the tip of the left mammary and also confirmed probe patent. There was excellent flow of blood from the LIMA. The heart pinked up and began to beat spontaneously and measured 56 cc of flow in the trunk of the LIMA graft. [5]

The root was vented while Valsalva maneuvers were repeated, and the left ventricle compressed. After this was done many times and the cross clamp released, the vein grafts filled well and stripped well. There was no proximal or distal bleeding. The patient came back with a nodal rhythm, was paced through temporary V-wires, and finally came back in sinus rhythm. The patient came off bypass without pressors. Flows in the grafts were good.

The cannulation sites were all closed and protamine was given to reverse heparin. Hemostasis was satisfactory. Two RV pacing electrodes were left. The linea alba was approximated with interrupted Polydek. Two mediastinal chest tubes and a right pleural Blake drain were left. The aortic cannulation site was closed with a pursestring and oversewn sutures. The mediastinum was irrigated with antibiotic solution.

The vein tunnel was irrigated with antibiotic solution, the entrance incisions closed with two layers of Vicryl, and the leg was wrapped with an elastic wrap. The sternum was approximated with #6 wire, the midline fascia with interrupted Polydek, and a multilayer Dexon closure on the remaining subcutaneous tissue and skin.

The patient tolerated the procedure well and there were no complications. The patient will be sent to the ICU in satisfactory condition.

---

[1] Endoscopic technique used for saphenous vein harvesting—33508.

[2] 1st venous conduit placed.

[3] 2nd venous conduit placed.

[4] 3rd venous conduit placed.

[5] 1st arterial conduit placed.

What are the CPT® and ICD-10-CM codes reported?

Correct CPT® Codes: 33533, 33519, 33508

ICD-10-CM Codes: I25.119

Rationale: CPT® Codes: The physician performed a CABG with one arterial graft to the left anterior descending and three venous grafts. One of the venous grafts was a sequential graft, meaning one vein graft was anastomosed to the second and the third marginals of the right circumflex artery before anastomosis to the aorta. This counts as two venous grafts. See the illustration in CPT® Professional and the note under 33517-33530 "To determine the number of bypass grafts in a coronary artery bypass (CABG), count the number of anastomoses (contact point(s) where the bypass artery or vein is sutured to the diseased coronary artery(s)." The other venous graft was to the acute marginal of the right coronary artery. In the CPT® Index, see Coronary Artery Bypass Graft (CABG)/Arterial Bypass, and you are directed to range 33533–33536. Code selection is based on the number of arterial grafts used, in this case one, the left internal mammary artery (LIMA). The arterial graft is reported with 33533. The guidelines above code 33533 indicate to look at codes 33517–33523 for combined arterial-venous grafts. Again, based on the number of grafts, 3 venous grafts are reported with add-on code 33519. The harvest of the saphenous vein was performed endoscopically, reported with add-on code 33508. This is found in the CPT® Index under Vein/Endoscopic Harvest/for Bypass Graft 33508.

ICD-10-CM Code: ICD-10-CM utilizes combination codes. Chapter Specific Coding Guidelines (I.C.9.b) when one of these combination codes is used, it is not necessary to use an additional code for angina. In the ICD-10-CM Index to Diseases and Injuries, look for Disease/artery/coronary/with angina pectoris, you are directed to see Arteriosclerosis, coronary (artery). Look in the index for Arteriosclerosis/coronary (artery)/native vessel/with/angina pectoris I25.119. Verify in the Tabular List.

ICD-9-CM Application

What is/are the ICD-9-CM code(s) reported?

Code(s): 414.01, 413.9

Rationale: In the ICD-9-CM Index to Diseases, look for Disease/artery/coronary, you are directed to see Arteriosclerosis, coronary. Under Arteriosclerosis/coronary/native artery, you are directed to 414.01. Because there is no mention of prior bypass, native artery is coded. The second diagnosis is stated as angina which directs you to 413.9 in the ICD-9-CM Index to Diseases. Verification in the Tabular List confirms code selection.

Case 2—Valve Replacement

Diagnosis: Aortic valve stenosis

Operation: Aortic valve replacement using a #23 St. Jude mechanical valve

Findings: The left ventricle is certainly hypertrophied· The aortic valve leaflet is calcified and has very severe restrictive leaflet motion. It is a tricuspid type of valve.

Procedure: The patient was brought to the operating room and placed in supine position. After the patient was prepared, <u>median sternotomy incision was carried out</u>. [1]

She was cannulated after the aorta and atrium were exposed and received full heparinization. She went on cardiopulmonary bypass and the aortic cross-clamp was applied. Cardioplegia was delivered through the coronary sinuses in a retrograde manner. The patient was cooled to 32 degrees. Iced slush was applied to the heart. <u>The aortic valve was then exposed through the aortic root by transverse incision. The valve leaflets were removed and the #23 St. Jude mechanical valve was secured into position by circumferential pledgeted sutures</u>. [2] At this point, aortotomy was closed. The patient came off cardiopulmonary bypass after aortic cross-clamp was released. Protamine was given without adverse effect. Sternal closure was then done using wires. The subcutaneous layers were closed using Vicryl suture. The skin was approximated using staples.

----

[1] This shows an open procedure is being performed.

[2] Valve being placed.

What are the CPT® and ICD-10-CM codes reported?

CPT® Code: 33405

ICD-10-CM Code: I35.0

Rationale: CPT® Code: In the CPT® Index, see Replacement/Aortic Valve, and you are directed to 33361–33365, 33367-33369, 33405–33413. Check the codes. Code 33405 describes this procedure.

ICD-10-CM Code: In the Index to Diseases and Injuries, look for Stenosis/aortic (valve), and you are directed to I35.0. Verification of the code in the Tabular List confirms code selection.

ICD-9-CM Application

What is/are ICD-9-CM code(s) reported?

Code(s): 424.1

Rationale: In the Index to Diseases, see Stenosis/aortic (valve), and you are directed to 424.1. Verification of the code in the Tabular List confirms code selection.

Case 3—Intracoronary Stent

Diagnosis: Coronary atherosclerosis:

After local anesthesia in the femoral area, appropriate catheters were placed. After systemic heparinization with ACT greater than 300, the guiding catheter was advanced into the ostium of the <u>RCA</u>. [1] Utilizing fluoroscopic guidance and after confirming the lesion, the stent system was advanced and positioned. <u>The stent was inflated using the stent balloon. After confirming the stent displacement, the balloon was deflated and withdrawn</u>. [2] Attention was then turned toward the <u>LAD</u> [3] system. The distal lesion was then dilated with a balloon. <u>The stent was then placed in a standard manner</u>. The proximal lesion was dilated with a balloon and another stent was placed in the artery in a similar manner. [4] At the completion of the procedure, the patient was transferred to the floor in stable condition without complaints of chest pain.

Results—

Pre-stent distal LAD—95%

Post-stent—No residual

Pre-stent proximal LAD—90%

Post-stent—No residual

Pre-stent RCA—95%

Post-stent—No residual

_____

[1] RCA = right coronary artery.

[2] First stent deployed.

[3] LAD = left anterior descending.

[4] Second and third stent deployed in a different coronary artery.

_____

What are the CPT® and ICD-10-CM codes reported?

CPT® Codes: 92928-RC, 92928-LD

ICD-10-CM Code: I25.10

Rationale: CPT® Codes: Three coronary stents were placed through catheters (transcatheter). In the CPT® Index, look up Coronary Artery/Insertion/Stent, you are directed to 92928–92929. The codes are selected based on one procedure per vessel (RC, LD or LC). Even though a balloon was used (angioplasty), it was to dilate the vessel and to deploy the stent and is included in 92928. One stent was placed in the right coronary artery (92928-RC). Two stents were placed in the LAD. Only one procedure can be reported per coronary vessel; therefore, code 92928-LD is reported only once. PCI performed in a main coronary artery is assigned a base code as indicated in the subsection guidelines for Coronary Therapeutic Services and Procedures in CPT®. The coronary modifiers are necessary to indicate one intervention per coronary artery.

ICD-10-CM Code: In the Index to Diseases and Injuries, look for Arterosclerosis, arteriosclerotic/coronary (artery) referring you to I25.10. Verification of this code in the Tabular List confirms code selection. The native artery is assumed unless there is a statement regarding a prior bypass graft.

ICD-9-CM Application

What is/are the ICD-9-CM code(s) reported?

Code(s): 414.01

Rationale: In the Index to Diseases, look for Arteriosclerosis/coronary/native artery, and you are directed to 414.01. Verification of this code in the Tabular List confirms code selection. The native artery is assumed unless there is a statement regarding a prior bypass graft.

Case 4—Interventional Radiology

Procedure: Thoracic aortogram; bilateral carotid angiography

Details of Procedure: The patient was brought to the angiographic suite in the 12-hour post absorptive state. Consent was obtained from the patient and his family and they understood the risks and benefits of cerebral angiography, including a 1 percent risk of stroke. The patient was assessed for conscious sedation, placed on the angiographic table in the usual fashion for cerebral angiography. He was prepared and draped using sterile technique. Using 2 percent Lidocaine and the Seldinger technique, a 5 French sheath was placed in the right common femoral artery.

A 5 French marker pigtail catheter was positioned just above the aortic valve and digital subtraction angiography was obtained. [1] Then, that catheter was removed and a 5 French angled Terumo catheter with a 0.03 angled Terumo wire was used to negotiate the brachiocephalic and internal carotid artery. The catheter was threaded into the proximal portion of right internal carotid artery and [2] AP and lateral projections of the cervical portion of the carotid, the carotid bifurcation and the intracranial vessels were obtained using digital subtraction angiography. The catheter was then redirected into the left common carotid, [3] where similar angiography was repeated.

Findings: There is a normal aortic arch. [4] There are no proximal lesions in the left carotid, the subclavian, or the brachiocephalic.

The right common and internal carotid arteries are widely patent. There is minimal stenosis in the right internal carotid artery (less than 20 Percent). The petrous portion of the internal carotid is normal. The middle cerebral artery is widely patent and provides crossover to the left cerebral hemisphere, filling the entire middle cerebral artery. The anterior communicating artery is normal, and it crosses over to the left cerebral anterior communicating artery.

Left common carotid artery has a 50 percent stenosis just before the carotid bifurcation. [5] The left internal carotid artery is totally occluded in its proximal portion and has an irregular angiographic appearance. [6] Left external carotid artery is patent and there is minimal extracranial to intracranial to the middle cerebral artery flow on injection of the left common carotid artery. [7]

Plan: Medical therapy.

----

[1] Aortic arch angiography is performed.

[2] Catheter placed into right internal carotid.

[3] Catheter placed into the left common carotid.

[4] Non-selective RS&I of the aortic arch.

[5] Left and right common carotids RS&I.

[6] Left and right internal carotids RS&I.

[7] Although external carotid mentioned, catheter not selectively placed into vessel so cannot code.

What are the CPT® and ICD-10-CM codes reported?

CPT® Codes: 36224, 36223-59

ICD-10-CM Code: I65.22

Rationale: CPT® Codes: Selective catheterization of the right internal carotid arteries was performed after arch aorto-gram and angiography was performed. Code 36224 includes selective catheterization, the S&I, and angiography of the right internal carotid, intracranial carotid circulation, extracranial carotid, and cervicocerebral arch. Next the selective catheterization of the left common carotid and a report indicating blockage of the left internal carotid, flow through the left external carotid, and minimal extracranial flow to the left cerebral anterior communicating artery (36223). Modifier 59 indicates another vascular family. The codes are 36224, 36223-59. Some payers may require RT and LT. In the Index, look up Catheterization/Carotid Artery directing you to 36100, 36221–36224, 36227–36228.

ICD-10-CM Code: Findings indicate stenosis in the left common carotid bifurcation with total occlusion of the internal carotid artery. Look in the Index to Diseases and Injuries look for Occlusion, occluded/artery/carotid directing you to I65.2-. In the Tabular List, a fifth character is needed to complete the code. Code I65.22 *Occlusion and stenosis of left carotid artery* is correct. The internal carotid artery is not listed, but under category I65 you see Includes obstruction (complete) (partial) of precerebral artery.

ICD-9-CM Application

What is/are the ICD-9-CM code(s) reported?

Code(s): 433.10

Rationale: Findings indicate stenosis in the left common carotid bifurcation with total occlusion of the internal carotid artery. Look in the Index to Diseases for Occlusion/artery/carotid directing you to 433.1. In the Tabular List, a fifth digit of 0 is used to indicate there is no mention of cerebral infarction.

Glossary

Anastomosis—Joining of two or more blood vessels.

Angiography—Radiographic visualization of blood vessels following introduction of contrast material.

Angioplasty—Procedure to open narrow or blocked vessels.

Annuloplasty—Surgical reconstruction of the ring (annulus) of a heart valve.

Antegrade—Moving or extending anteriorly, moving with the usual direction of flow.

Arrhythmia—Irregularity of heart rate or rhythm; loss of rhythm.

Arteriosclerosis—Hardening of the arteries.

Atherectomy—Procedure to remove plaque from arteries.

Atherosclerosis—Build up of plaque on artery walls.

Atria—Upper chambers of the heart; right atrium, left atrium.

Atrioventricular (AV)—Relating to both the atria and the ventricles of the heart.

Bifurcation—Division into two branches.

Bundle of His (AV bundle)—Muscle fibers in the heart's conduction system branching off to the right and left sides of the heart.

Capillaries—Smallest branches of arteries and veins.

Cardioversion—Use of defibrillator paddles to restore normal rhythm of the heart by electrical shock.

Chordae Tendineae—String-like tendons linking papillary muscles to the tricuspid valve in the right ventricle and the mitral valve in the left ventricle.

Conduction System—Generates and distributes electrical impulses over the heart and along the septum to stimulate contraction, allowing blood to move throughout the body.

Contralateral—Situated on, pertaining to, or affecting the opposite side, as opposed to ipsilateral.

Coronary Circulation—Movement of blood through coronary vessels supplying tissues of the heart.

Endocarditis—Inflammation or infection of the inner lining of the heart (endocardium).

Epicardial—Relating to the outermost (on top) layer of the heart wall.

Implantable Defibrillator—Implantable device delivering an electrical shock to restore a normal heart rhythm.

Infarction—Death of tissue.

Intracoronary—Within the heart.

Ipsilateral—Situated on, pertaining to, or affecting the same side, as opposed to contralateral.

Myocardial—Relating to the myocardium (second layer of the wall of the heart).

Nonselective Catheterization—Catheter placed in the main trunk, contrast may be injected, images may be taken, the catheter is not moved into any other branches.

Non-Tunneled Catheter—A catheter inserted through the skin directly into a great vessel.

Occlusion—Closure; the act of closing.

Papillary Muscles—Muscles attached to the lower portion of the interior wall of the ventricles and connected to the chordae tendineae.

Prolapse—Sinking of an organ or other part.

Pulmonary Circulation—Movement of blood from the heart, to the lungs, and back to the heart again.

Purkinje Fibers—Conduction myofibers branching off of the right and left bundle branches into cells of the myocardium.

Regurgitation—Flowing backwards.

Retrograde—Moving backward or against the usual direction of flow.

Revascularization—Reestablishment of blood supply to a part.

Selective Catheterization—Catheter placed in branches further off the main trunk (first, second, third or higher order).

Sinoatrial—Refers to the sinus of the venae cavae of the mature heart, and the right atrium.

Stenosis—Narrowing, stricture.

Subendocardial—Under or below the endocardium.

Syncope—Loss of consciousness and postural tone.

Systemic Circulation—Supplies nourishment to tissue located throughout the body, with the exception of the heart and lungs.

Thrombolysis—Destruction of a blood clot.

Transluminal—Through or across the lumen (tube) of an artery or vein.

Transvenous—Through or across a vein.

Trifurcation—Division into three branches or parts.

Tunneled Catheter—Catheter tunneled through the skin and subcutaneous tissue to a central vessel. The entrance point of the catheter is distant from the entrance to the vascular system.

Valvular Prolapse—Valve leaflets fall backward into the heart chamber.

Valvuloplasty—Surgical reconstruction of a valve.

Ventricle—Lower chamber of the heart; right ventricle, left ventricle.

Introduction

The digestive system consists of the alimentary or digestive tract and its accessory organs. The digestive tract is a long, hollow, muscular tube beginning at the lips and ending at the anus. It includes the mouth, pharynx, esophagus, stomach, small intestines, and large intestines. Accessory organs include the salivary glands, liver, pancreas, and gallbladder.

The major function of the digestive system is to digest or break down foods that are taken into the body. The digestive process mechanically and chemically breaks down food so it can be absorbed into the body to nourish cells and provide energy.

The long, hollow organs of the digestive tract have smooth muscle fibers running in circular and longitudinal directions. These circular fibers contract and enable the food to move from one organ to the next. This action is named peristalsis.

Objectives

- Define and understand key terms associated with the digestive tract and procedures performed in this section
- Understand anatomy associated with procedures performed in this section
- Explain the organization and content of the CPT® Surgery/Digestive System subsections
- Learn to assign appropriate CPT® surgery codes from the digestive subsection

Anatomy and Medical Terminology

Lips/Mouth

The lips form the entrance to the oral cavity and digestive tract. The oral cavity includes the mouth and its associated structures; soft and hard palates, teeth, gums, tongue, and salivary glands. The mouth performs three main functions: digestion, breathing, and speech. The digestive process begins when food enters the mouth. The teeth and tongue break the food into small particles by mastication, or chewing. The salivary glands secrete saliva and enzymes that aid in digestion. The tongue functions to mix saliva with food and to keep the food pressed between the teeth for chewing before it pushes the food backward for swallowing.

There are three categories of teeth:

Incisors—*The teeth in the front of the mouth. They are shaped like chisels and are useful in biting off large pieces of food. Each person has eight incisors (four on the top, four on the bottom).*

Cuspids—*The pointy teeth immediately behind the incisors. Also called the canines, these teeth are used for grasping or tearing food. Each person has four cuspids (two on the top and two on the bottom).*

Molars—*The flattened teeth used for grinding food. They are the furthest back in the mouth, and their number can vary among people.*

Digestive System

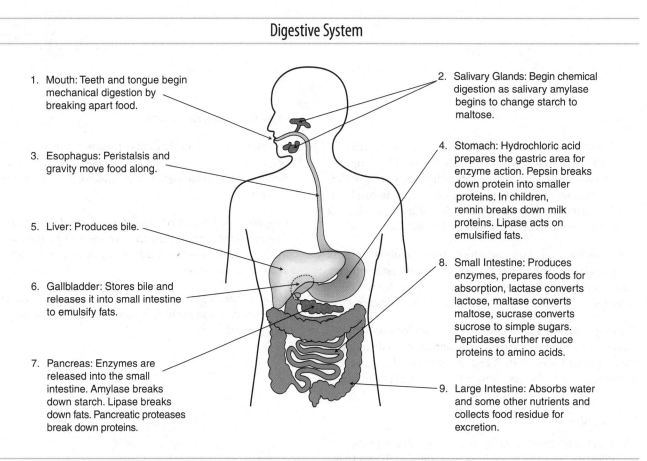

1. Mouth: Teeth and tongue begin mechanical digestion by breaking apart food.

2. Salivary Glands: Begin chemical digestion as salivary amylase begins to change starch to maltose.

3. Esophagus: Peristalsis and gravity move food along.

4. Stomach: Hydrochloric acid prepares the gastric area for enzyme action. Pepsin breaks down protein into smaller proteins. In children, rennin breaks down milk proteins. Lipase acts on emulsified fats.

5. Liver: Produces bile.

6. Gallbladder: Stores bile and releases it into small intestine to emulsify fats.

8. Small Intestine: Produces enzymes, prepares foods for absorption, lactase converts lactose, maltase converts maltose, sucrase converts sucrose to simple sugars. Peptidases further reduce proteins to amino acids.

7. Pancreas: Enzymes are released into the small intestine. Amylase breaks down starch. Lipase breaks down fats. Pancreatic proteases break down proteins.

9. Large Intestine: Absorbs water and some other nutrients and collects food residue for excretion.

Source: Lindh, Pooler, Tamparo, and Dahl, Delmar's Comprehensive Medical Assisting (Administrative and Clinical Competencies), 4e, ISBN#978-1-4354-1914-8

Pharynx

The pharynx serves as a passageway for both the respiratory and digestive systems. It is a five-inch tube located immediately behind the mouth. It serves as an airway and a passageway for food. It aids in the closure of the nasopharynx and larynx when swallowing, keeping the food out of the respiratory tract and in the digestive tract.

Esophagus

The esophagus is a long, straight tube about 10 inches long that arises from the pharynx, passes through the diaphragm, and continues into the stomach. The diaphragm is a muscular and membranous partition that separates the chest cavity from the abdominal cavity. The muscular walls of the esophagus move food into the stomach by peristalsis.

Stomach

The stomach is a large chamber that receives liquids, solids, and semisolid food from the esophagus. The stomach has four parts: cardia, fundus, body, and antrum (also known as the pylorus). It digests the food received from the esophagus and passes the partially digested food, known as chyme, into the duodenum (upper part of the small intestine).

Small Intestine

The small intestine is a coiled, muscular tube that occupies the central and lower abdomen. The small intestine is divided into the duodenum, jejunum, and ileum. The duodenum is the first portion of the small intestine and is connected to the stomach. It is about 10 inches long. Small ducts from the pancreas, liver, and gallbladder open into the duodenum via the hepatopancreatic ampulla (ampulla of Vater). The jejunum, the middle third of the small intestine, is about 7 ½ feet in length. Vigorous, peristaltic waves move the fluid contents to the ileum. The ileum, which is approximately 12 feet in length, is the last and longest section of the small intestine. Most of the absorption of food takes place in the ileum. The ileum connects to the large intestine.

Large Intestine

The large intestine is about five feet long and averages 2.5 inches in diameter. It receives the digestive products from the small intestine. It is divided into the cecum, appendix, ascending colon, transverse colon, descending colon, sigmoid colon, rectum, and anus. Unabsorbed food material is stored in the large intestine. Water is reabsorbed as the food material travels through the large intestine and eventually is eliminated from the body.

Pancreas

The pancreas is a soft, oblong gland about six inches long and one inch thick beneath the great curvature of the stomach. It consists of five parts: the head, neck, body, tail, and uncinate process. The pancreas empties digestive fluid (mixture of enzymes) into the duodenum and insulin into the bloodstream. Insulin is a hormone produced in the pancreas by the islands of Langerhans. This hormone is essential for the use of sugar by the body tissue. Lack of insulin that is not produced by the body is usually the key cause for Type I diabetes mellitus and many studies indicate that obesity is the key cause for Type II diabetes mellitus.

Liver

The liver is the second largest single organ in the body (after the skin). It weighs about 4 pounds. The liver lies in the upper abdomen, on the right side under the diaphragm and above the duodenum. *The human liver has four lobes: right lobe and left lobe, which may be seen in an anterior view, plus the quadrate lobe and caudate lobe.* Liver functions are so numerous and important that we cannot survive without the liver. Proteins, when digested, become amino acids, and ammonia is a byproduct that is toxic to cells. The liver converts ammonia into urea, which is then excreted by the kidney or sweat glands. The liver also converts excess glucose into glycogen or fat. Bile salts are produced by the liver and when bile is secreted into the duodenum, fat is emulsified and absorbed by the intestine. The liver is also the only organ in the human body that can regenerate itself—which is why an adult can donate a portion of a liver to a child, and that transplanted portion will regrow, usually within six weeks of the procedure.

Gallbladder/Biliary System

The gallbladder is a sac-like structure attached to the inferior surface of the liver, and serves as a reservoir for bile. Bile is produced by the liver and aids in the digestive process. It periodically empties into the duodenum by way of the cystic ducts.

Medical Terminology

Abdomin/o	abdomen, abdominal
An/o	anus
Appendic/o	appendix
-ase	enzyme
Bil/i	bile
Bucc/o	cheek
Cec/o	cecum
Celi/o	abdomen
-cele	hernia
Cheil/o	lip
-chezia	defecation
Chol/e, chol/o	bile, gallbladder
Choledoch/o	common bile duct
Cholecyst/o	gallbladder
Cirrh/o	orange/yellow
Col/o	large intestine, colon
Dent/i, dent/o, dont/o	teeth
Dia	through, throughout, completely
Duoden/o	duodenum
-ectasia, -ectasis	dilation, expansion
-emesis	vomiting
End/o, ent/o	within, inner, containing
Enter/o	small intestine
Esophag/o	esophagus
Gastr/o	stomach
Gingiv/o	gingivae, gums of the mouth
Gloss/o	tongue
Hepat/o	liver
Herni/o	rupture, protrusion of part of a structure through the tissues containing it
Ile/o	ileum
Jejun/o	jejunum
Labi/o	lips
Lapar/o	abdomen
Lingu/o	tongue
Lith/o	stone
-lysis	release

Or/o	mouth	-rrhea	flowing, flux
-ostomy, -stomy	artificial or surgical opening	-scope, -scopy	action involving the use of an instrument for viewing
-otomy	incision into		
Pancreat/o	pancreas	Sial/o	saliva
-pepsia	digestion	Sialaden/o	salivary gland
Peritone/o	peritoneum	Sigmoid/o	sigmoid colon
-phagia	eating, devouring	Splen/o	spleen
-plasty	technique involving molding or surgically forming	Stomat/o	mouth
		Uvul/o	uvula, grape
Proct/o	anus, rectum	Viscer/o	the viscera, internal organs
Rect/o	rectum		

Section Review 11.1

1. The suffix meaning artificial or surgical opening:

    A. -ectasis

    B. -stomy

    C. -cele

    D. -lysis

2. The prefix meaning lip:

    A. an/o

    B. cec/o

    C. cheil/o

    D. col/o

3. What is the function of the gallbladder?

    A. It plays a role in maintaining glucose levels in the blood.

    B. It conveys and stores bile.

    C. It breaks down and stores waste products.

    D. It produces acidic juices for digestion.

4. Name the three sections of the small intestine.

    A. Sigmoid, rectum, ilium

    B. Jejunum, duodenum, ilium

    C. Cecum, jejunum, ileum

    D. Duodenum, jejunum, ileum

5. What is the name of the large intestine that runs horizontally across the abdomen?

    A. Sigmoid colon

    B. Transverse colon

    C. Descending colon

    D. Ascending colon

6. What organ in the human body has the capability to regenerate?

    A. Pancreas

    B. Kidney

    C. Liver

    D. Intestine

7. What are the two processes of digestion?

    A. Mechanical and chemical

    B. Chewing and absorption

    C. Ingestion and defecation

    D. Secretion and propulsion

8. What are the three categories of teeth?

    A. Enamel, Root, Crown

    B. Incisors, Cuspids, Molars

    C. Baby teeth, Adolescent teeth, Wisdom teeth

    D. There are not three categories of teeth

9. Approximately how long is the large intestine in normal anatomy?

    A. 6 ft. long

    B. 9 ft. long

    C. 3 ft. long

    D. 5 ft. long

10. How many lobes are in the liver?

    A. 4 lobes

    B. 3 lobes

    C. 2 lobes

    D. 5 lobes

ICD-10-CM

The diagnosis codes for the diseases of the digestive system are found in multiple sections of ICD-10-CM. There are no chapter-specific coding guidelines for diseases of the digestive system in the ICD-10-CM Official Guidelines, but there are chapter-specific guidelines for infectious diseases in chapter 1 and neoplastic diseases in chapter 2 of the Official Guidelines, Section I.C.

These diagnosis codes are found in chapter 11 Diseases of the Digestive System (K00-K95), chapter 1 Infectious and Parasitic Diseases (A00-B99), chapter 2 Neoplasms (C00-D49), chapter 17 Congenital Malformations, Deformations, and Chromosomal Abnormalities (Q00-Q99), and chapter 18 Symptoms, Signs, and Abnormal Clinical and Laboratory Findings, Not Elsewhere Classified (R00-R99). Additional codes may also be found in the Factors Influencing Health Status and Contact with Health Services (Z00-Z99).

Esophageal and Swallowing Disorders

Barrett's Esophagus—an abnormal growth of stomach or intestinal cells at the distal end of the esophagus. These tissue changes may be the forerunner of cancer of the lower esophagus. This condition may develop because of chronic gastroesophageal reflux disease, which exposes the esophagus to stomach acids.

Esophagitis—an inflammation of the lining of the esophagus. If left untreated, this condition can become very uncomfortable, causing problems with swallowing, ulcers, and scarring of the esophagus. Esophagitis can be caused by an infection or irritation in the esophagus. Infections like candida (candidiasis, monilia, yeast, thrush) and herpes can cause esophagitis. Medications such as aspirin or other non-steroidal anti-inflammatory drugs (NSAIDS) also may cause esophagitis. Continued exposure to gastric acids caused by reflux will erode the esophagus. All of these conditions can also cause the esophagus to dilate or constrict, causing esophageal stricture.

Esophageal Varices—extremely dilated submucosal veins in the lower end of the esophagus. They are most often caused by portal hypertension and cirrhosis of the liver. Esophageal varices have a strong tendency to develop bleeding.

Mallory-Weiss Tear—occurs in the mucous membrane of the esophagus, where it connects to the stomach. Tears usually are caused by forceful or long-term vomiting, or by epileptic convulsions. The tear may be followed by vomiting bright red blood or by passing blood in the stool.

Hiatal Hernia—an anatomical abnormality in which part of the stomach protrudes or herniates through the opening of the diaphragm and up into the chest.

Swallowing Disorders or Dysphagia—any condition that causes impairment of the movement of solids or fluids from the mouth, down the throat, and into the stomach. They can have a severe effect on caloric intake and nutritional status. Swallowing disorders may affect the ability to swallow liquids, solids, or both. They also make an individual susceptible to pneumonia, when substances being swallowed are inhaled into the lungs.

Gastritis and Peptic Ulcer Disease

Gastritis (K29) is an acute or chronic inflammation of the stomach. A common cause of gastritis is a bacterium named helicobacter pylori, or H. pylori. These bacteria lives in the lining of the stomach. This infection can lead to ulcers and even cancer. Long-term use of NSAIDS also causes gastritis and ulcers. Long-term alcohol use is another common cause of gastritis.

Peptic Ulcer Disease (K25) is a sore or opening in the inner lining of the stomach or duodenum. Ulcers develop when the intestine or stomach's protective layer is broken down. When this happens, digestive juices can damage the intestine or stomach tissue. These digestive juices can also damage the esophagus. The two most common causes of peptic ulcers are H. pylori infections and the prolonged use of NSAIDS.

In ICD-10-CM Gastritis (K29) is identified by specific four character codes to indicate without bleeding or with bleeding. Peptic ulcers may also be referred to as gastric or stomach ulcers. There is also a Use additional code instruction note to indicate alcohol abuse and dependence (F10.-).

Example

K29.00 Acute gastritis without bleeding

K29.01 Acute gastritis with bleeding

ICD-9-CM Application

In ICD-9-CM Gastritis is identified with 535.5 and has a 5th digit sub classification to indicate without mention of hemorrhage or with hemorrhage.

Example:
535.00 Acute gastritis without mention of hemorrhage
535.01 Acute gastritis with hemorrhage

Peptic Ulcers

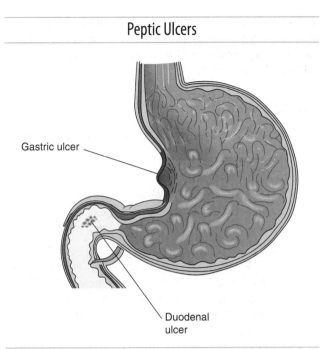

Gastric ulcer

Duodenal ulcer

Source: Lindh, Pooler, Tamparo, and Dahl, Delmar's Comprehensive Medical Assisting (Administrative and Clinical Competencies), 4e, ISBN#978-1-4354-1914-8

Hernias

Hernias occur when the contents of a body cavity bulge out of the area where they are normally contained. These hernias can be congenital (present at birth), acquired, or recurrent. The code block for hernias is K40-K46 specific to the type of hernia as well as whether an obstruction or gangrene is present. Inguinal hernias (K40) occur in the groin area and can be either direct or indirect. Direct hernias usually occur in middle-aged or elderly because of the weakening of the abdominal wall. Indirect hernias are can occur at any age. An umbilical hernias (K42) is common and caused by an opening in the abdominal wall. Ventral hernias (K43) occur at the site of a previous abdominal surgery and also called incisional hernia. A diaphragmatic hernia occurs when there is an abnormal opening in the diaphragm. Diaphragmatic hernias can be acquired (K43) or congenital (Q79.0).

Gastrointestinal Bleeding

Gastrointestinal bleeding describes every form of hemorrhage in the gastrointestinal tract, from the pharynx to the rectum. GI bleeding can range from microscopic bleeding, only detectable by a lab test, to massive bleeding where pure blood is passed (resulting in hypovolemia, shock, and even death). GI bleeding has many causes: esophageal varices, Mallory-Weiss tears, peptic ulcer disease, diverticular disease, hemorrhoids, and fissures, to name a few.

Gastroenteritis

Gastroenteritis (K52) is an infection or irritation of the digestive tract, particularly the stomach and intestines. Major symptoms include nausea and vomiting, diarrhea, and abdominal cramps. These symptoms are sometimes accompanied by fever and overall weakness. It can be caused by either a virus or bacteria. Gastroenteritis typically lasts about three days. Adults usually recover without problem, but children, the elderly, and anyone with an underlying disease are more vulnerable to complications such as dehydration.

Inflammatory Bowel Disease (IBD)

Inflammatory Bowel Disease (IBD) is a group of inflammatory conditions of the colon and small intestine. The major types of IBD are Crohn's disease and ulcerative colitis.

Ulcerative colitis is a chronic inflammatory disorder limited to the colon. It causes inflammation and sores in the lining of the rectum and colon. Ulcers form where inflammation has killed the cells that usually line the colon, then bleed and produce pus. Inflammation in the colon also causes the colon to empty frequently, leading to diarrhea.

Crohn's disease (regional enteritis) is a chronic, inflammatory process of the bowel that often leads to fibrosis and obstructive symptoms, which can affect any part of the gastrointestinal (GI) tract from the mouth to the anus. Most Crohn's disease involves the small bowel, particularly the terminal ileum. The characteristic presentation of Crohn's disease is abdominal pain and diarrhea, which may be complicated by intestinal fistulization, obstruction, hemorrhage, abscess or a combination of complications. Unpredictable flares and remissions characterize the long-term course of this illness.

In ICD-10-CM, Crohn's disease is found under enteritis and colitis in Category K50. These are combination codes that include the anatomic site as well as the complication(s) associated with Crohn's disease.

Example

K50.012 Crohn's disease of small intestine with intestinal obstruction

ICD-9-CM Application

In ICD-9-CM Crohn's Disease is reported with category 555. The forth digit identifies anatomic site.

Example: 555.0 Regional enteritis of small intestine.

Practical Coding Note

Anatomy and terminology of the large and small intestine will be vital to assigning the correct code for Crohn's disease. Be sure to read the inclusion terms provided under some categories as these provide guidance as to conditions associated with the code.

Diverticular Disease

Diverticulosis is the condition of having pockets or projections (diverticula) extending from the walls of the colon. The pockets of colonic mucosa and submucosa develop through weaknesses of the muscle layers in the colon wall when the colon contracts and exerts pressure on the walls. Diverticulosis occurs most frequently in the sigmoid colon. It can cause changes in bowel function, such as discomfort, diarrhea, or constipation. In its advanced stages, the lower colon may become very fixed, distorted, and even narrowed. When this occurs, there may be thin or pellet-shaped stools, constipation, and an occasional rush of diarrhea.

Diverticulosis

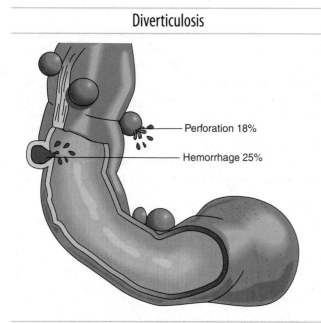

Source: Lindh, Pooler, Tamparo, and Dahl, Delmar's Comprehensive Medical Assisting (Administrative and Clinical Competencies), 4e, ISBN#978-1-4354-1914-8

Bacteria in the colon can cause infection of the diverticular pockets, referred to as diverticulitis. It can be mild with only slight discomfort in the left lower abdomen. Alternatively, it can be extreme with severe tenderness and fever, requiring treatment with antibiotics and dietary restrictions. Diverticulitis can cause bleeding and perforation.

In ICD-10-CM the codes for diverticular disease are located in category K57 and contain combination codes to include

the condition and any complication. The fourth character of the code identify location of the disease and if a perforation or abscess is present. The fifth character identifies with or without bleeding.

Example:

K57.01 Diverticulitis of small intestine with perforation and abscess with bleeding

K57.50 Diverticulosis of both small and large intestine without perforation or abscess without bleeding.

Practical Coding Note

In Category K65 for Peritonitis the Excludes1 note shows that codes for diverticulitis and diverticulosis with abscess and peritonitis are in category K57 are not coded together. Codes in K57 are combination codes.

ICD-9-CM Application

In ICD-9-CM codes are listed by location of small intestine and colon with subcategories for diverticulitis or diverticulosis (562). Instructional note indicates to Use an additional code for any associated peritonitis (567.0-567.9).

55-year-old male has a GI endoscopic exam that shows he has diverticulitis of the lower portion of the small intestine with some bleeding. Exam also showed he has peritonitis. The codes to report are:

562.03 Diverticulitis of small intestine with hemorrhage

567.9 Unspecified peritonitis

Irritable Bowel Syndrome (IBS)

Irritable Bowel Syndrome (IBS) (K58) is known by a variety of other terms: spastic colon, spastic colitis, and nervous or functional bowel. Most often, it affects the large intestine, but other parts of the intestinal tract can be affected. When IBS occurs, the colon does not contract normally, but in a disorganized, violent manner. The contractions may be exaggerated and sustained, lasting for prolonged periods. One area of the colon may contract with no regard to another. At other times, there may be little bowel activity. These abnormal contractions result in changing bowel patterns with constipation and pain being most common. ICD-10-CM codes for IBS include with or without diarrhea. If the patient has diarrhea it is not separately reported.

Foreign Bodies

Foreign bodies in the gastrointestinal tract are usually swallowed, either purposely or accidentally. They can cause perforation or obstruction. Foreign bodies in the esophagus should be removed or manipulated endoscopically into the stomach.

ICD-10-CM codes for a foreign body entering through the gastrointestinal tract are found in category T18 and listed by the location of the foreign body.

Anorectal Disorders

Rectal prolapse can be partial or complete. Partial rectal prolapse occurs when the mucous membrane lining the anal canal protrudes through the anus. Complete rectal prolapse occurs when the full thickness of the bowel protrudes through the anus.

An abscess is a localized pocket of pus caused by infection. An abscess can occur in the perirectal and perianal areas.

Hemorrhoids are dilated or enlarged varicose veins, which occur in and around the anus and rectum. They may be external (distal end of the anal canal) or internal (in the rectum) and slip to the outside of the anus (prolapsed). Hemorrhoids can be complicated by the following conditions: thrombosis, strangulation, prolapse, and ulceration.

Anal fissures are tears in the mucosa and skin of the anal canal due to passing a large stool, straining during childbirth, and laceration from passing a foreign body.

Anal fistulas are tiny channels or tracts that develop because of an infection, inflammation, or abscess. The channel has one opening in the anal canal and runs to the perianal skin, rectum, bladder, or vagina.

Pancreatitis

Pancreatitis (K85) is an inflammation of the pancreas. It can be acute or chronic. Binge alcohol drinking is a common cause of acute pancreatitis. Gallbladder disease also may cause this condition. Certain drugs, such as diuretics, can produce the disorder, as can extremely high blood fat levels (triglycerides). In pancreatitis, the digestive enzymes of the pancreas break out into the tissues of the organ rather than staying within the tubes (ducts) causing severe damage to the pancreas.

Benign and Malignant Neoplasms of the Gastrointestinal Tract

Benign and malignant neoplasms can occur throughout the entire digestive tract, from the lips to the anus. Coding for neoplasms usually requires specific physician documentation regarding the behavior of the neoplasm and the exact location of the neoplasm within the gastrointestinal tract. To code for neoplasms accurately, one should start with the Index to Diseases and Injures. For example, the Index to Diseases and Injuries will confirm that an adenocarcinoma is malignant. Then, go to the Table of Neoplasms. The Table of Neoplasms has six columns for the behavior of neoplasms and anatomical listings for the location of the neoplasm. Be sure to confirm the code found in the Index to Diseases and Injuries or the Table of Neoplasms in the Tabular Listing.

Polyps occur frequently in the digestive tract. Polyps are defined as an abnormal growth of tissue projecting from a mucous membrane. They are attached by a narrow stalk. Polyps often are benign, but they can become malignant over time if not removed. Coding for polyps can be accomplished by using the Index to Diseases and Injuries confirming the code choice in the Tabular List.

Any personal history or family history of any type of neoplasm are always significant clinically and should be coded in addition to the reason for treatment. Personal histories of malignant neoplasms in the gastrointestinal tract are coded using codes from category Z85. Family histories of malignant neoplasms in the gastrointestinal tract are coded using Z80.0.

When an examination is performed for screening for a malignant neoplasm in the gastrointestinal tract, there are several Z codes from which to choose.

Subcategory Z12.1 identifies screening for malignant neoplasms of the intestinal tract. The fifth character identifies the location in the intestinal tract:

Z12.10 Encounter for screening for malignant neoplasm of intestinal tract, unspecified

Z12.11 Encounter for screening for malignant neoplasm of colon

Z12.12 Encounter for screening for malignant neoplasm of rectum

Z12.13 Encounter for screening for malignant neoplasm of small intestine

Subcategory Z12.8 Encounter for screening for malignant neoplasm of other sites uses fifth character 1 to identify screening for malignant neoplasm of oral cavity, Z12.81.

Congenital Disorders

Several congenital disorders can have an effect on the gastrointestinal tract. Several of the disorders are immediately apparent at birth, but others are not known until a problem arises later in life. Some conditions never really cause problems and are found incidentally during another procedure. Regardless of the age of the patient, the ICD-10-CM codes for a congenital disorder are found in Chapter 17 Congenital Malformations, Deformations, and Chromosomal Abnormalities (Q00–Q99).

Cleft lip and palate are congenital conditions that result due to abnormal facial development during gestation. A cleft is a fissure, opening, or gap, resulting in a deformity. The deformity can affect the lip, soft palate, hard palate, and even the nasal cavities.

Meckel's diverticulum is a congenital diverticulum. It is a remnant of the connection from the yolk sac to the small intestine present during embryonic development. Sometimes the diverticular pocket contains gastric tissue, and sometimes it contains pancreatic tissue. This type of diverticulum normally will remain asymptomatic. The condition is managed by surgical resection.

Congenital megacolon is a congenital, abnormal dilation of the colon. It is often accompanied by a paralysis of the peristaltic movements of the bowel.

Redundant colon is a congenital variation on the normal anatomy of the colon. It simply means that the colon is longer than normal. It typically is not found until an X-ray or colonoscopy is performed. It usually does not cause any serious health concerns.

Imperforate anus or anal atresia is a birth defect where the rectum is malformed. In some instances, the anus is very narrow or missing altogether. In other instances, the defect is higher up in the rectum. These defects need to be corrected surgically very soon after birth. Sometimes, a colostomy is needed.

Section Review 11.2

1. A 42-year-old patient visits his doctor for chest pain and a dry cough lasting for two months. After evaluating the patient, the physician states the patient has GERD. What is/are the correct diagnosis code(s)?

   A. K21.0

   B. K21.9

   C. K63.9, R05

   D. R07.9. R05

2. A 28-year-old female has constant abdominal pain and diarrhea. The provider runs blood tests and takes a stool sample. A colonoscopy with biopsy is performed to rule out ulcerative colitis. The provider determines the patient has IBS. What is/are the correct diagnosis code(s)?

   A. K22.0

   B. K58.0, R10.9, R19.7

   C. K51.90, K58.0

   D. K58.0

3. A patient with a large prolapsed hemorrhoid arrives at the Emergency Department. After multiple attempts, the provider is unable to reduce it. The physician applies granulated sugar to the hemorrhoid and is able to reduce the hemorrhoid. What is the correct diagnosis code?

   A. K64.4

   B. K64.0

   C. K64.8

   D. K64.5

4.   A patient is seen in the outpatient GI lab of the hospital for rectal bleeding. A colonoscopy revealed three polyps in the transverse colon. The polyps were removed by snare technique. What is the correct diagnosis code for this procedure?

   A. K63.5

   B. D12.3

   C. K92.1

   D. K62.5

5.   The patient is a 65-year-old female with Type II diabetes. She is being seen today by her primary care physician for extreme abdominal bloating and discomfort after eating. The patient also complains of constant heartburn. This has occurred frequently and is not relieved by anything the patient has tried. The patient recorded her blood sugar this morning as 178. Her A1C taken in the office was 8.2. The physician diagnoses gastroparesis due to the patient's diabetes. Code the ICD-10-CM diagnosis code(s).

   A. E10.43

   B. K31.84

   C. E11.43

   D. E11.43, K31.84

CPT® Digestive System (40490–49999)

The digestive system subsection includes diagnostic and definitive treatment procedures of the digestive system (eg, GI endoscopy, laparoscopy, and analytic procedures). This subsection is similar to other surgery sections in that it is arranged by anatomic region and then by procedure.

The digestive tract includes the work of different organs (called accessory organs) to complete digestion; therefore, the Digestive System subsection includes procedures on the pancreas, liver, and gallbladder.

Lips 40490–40799 Biopsy, Vermilionectomy and Cheiloplasty

The CPT® codes 40490–40799 from the digestive system subsection start with the lips. The lips are composed of skin, muscle, and mucosa, which are divided into three main regions: the cutaneous, vermilion, and mucosal. The cutaneous portion of the upper lip extends from the bottom of the nose to the nasolabial folds laterally to the vermilion border or "lipstick area" of the lips. The lower cutaneous lip extends from the vermilion border to the extension of the nasolabial folds laterally to the mental crease at the chin. The vermilion portion is the pink-to-red colored portion of the lip, which is composed of a modified mucosal membrane. The mucosal portion lies inside the mouth and abuts the teeth. It is important to note that if a procedure is performed on the skin of the lips, do not code from this section; choose a code from the integumentary system instead.

Biopsy of the lip, code 40490, is performed on any portion of the lip, starting at the vermilion border and continuing inside the mouth to the mucosal area. A biopsy would be performed when there is a concern for malignancy by visual of scaling, fissuring, plaques, or other lesions.

Vermilionectomy, code 40500, is the shaving or excision of the vermilion border of the lip. This code also includes the repair of the excisional area by mucosal advancement. If more tissue is excised or removed from the lip area, choose from the code range 40510–40530. Wedge resections or full thickness excisional codes are chosen not only for the tissue excised but also on the reconstruction that is performed to correct the defect. These reconstructions are built into the nature of the code, and should not be reported with any other repair codes. It is important when reporting procedure codes 40510-40527 not to choose codes from both this section and the integumentary system.

Cheiloplasty is plastic surgery of the lips. The proper reporting of the codes 40650–40761 is based on the documented indication of the vertical height associated with the repair (eg, up to half-vertical height or over one-half vertical height). These procedures can be performed to repair congenital conditions, such as a cleft lip or an injury or disease such as a malignancy causing a cosmetic deficit. It can also be performed for strictly cosmetic reasons.

Mouth 40800–42699

The space between the cheek, lips, and teeth is referred to as the vestibule of the mouth, or buccal cavity.

Procedures performed on this area of the mouth, which include mucosa and submucosal tissues, 40800–40899, are incisions, excisions, destructions, and repairs. A vestibulo-plasty is a repair procedure performed in the vestibule of the mouth.

The floor of the mouth includes the tongue, sublingual space under the tongue, submandibular space under the mandible, and masticator space. The masticator space is the space between the floor of the mouth and the hyoid bone. A frenum is defined as a fold or flap of skin or mucous membrane that supports or restricts the movement of a part or organ, such as the small band of tissue that connects the underside of the tongue to the floor of the mouth. There are also two frenums in the mouth attaching the upper and lower lip to the gums. If an incision is made in these structures, it is named a frenotomy.

Glossectomy (41120–41155) is the surgical removal of all or part of the tongue. The code is chosen based on the extent of the tissue that is removed. Malignancy of the tongue is the most common reason for a glossectomy.

A palatopharyngoplasty or uvulopalatopharyngoplasty (code 42145) reports the removal of elongated excessive tissues of the uvula, soft palate, and pharynx. Incisions are made in the soft palate mucosa. Excessive submucosal tissue is removed and the uvula is partially excised. The remaining mucosa is loosened and the soft palate is reapproximated, increasing the diam-eter of the oropharynx. This surgery is typically performed on patients with oropharyngeal obstruction, contributing to obstructive sleep apnea. The patient benefits with increased oxygen intake at night after removal of excessive tissue. Laser treatment may require multiple visits to complete the process. Subsequent visits for laser treatment would be included in the primary code and not coded separately. When this procedure is performed with another procedure identified separately, the primary procedure is listed first followed by the subsequent procedures appended with the CPT® modifier 51. If significant additional time and effort are documented, append modifier 22 and submit a cover letter and operative report to prove medical necessity.

Practical Coding Note

For removal of torus mandibularis or maxillary torus palatinus in addition to a palatopharyngoplasty, see CPT® codes 21031 or 21032, respectively.

Palatoplasty is a surgical procedure to reconstruct the palate or roof of the mouth. It is performed when a baby is born with a congenital cleft palate. The cleft size and location determine the type and extent of the procedure that is performed. If a bone graft is utilized at the time of the palatoplasty, the graft should be reported in addition to the palatoplasty.

There are three salivary glands, the parotid, submandibular, and sublingual. The procedures performed on the salivary glands and the salivary ducts are assigned codes 42300–42699. These procedures are used to treat abscesses, cysts, and stones located in the salivary glands and ducts. Most tumors in the salivary glands are benign. The most frequently seen malig-nant tumors are adenocarcinomas.

Excision of a parotid gland (42410–42426) or tumor is deter-mined by the amount of tissue excised, the lobe that is affected and if nerve dissection was performed.

Sialodochoplasty, CPT® codes 42500–42505, is performed by inserting a hollow plastic silicone tube into the duct. The duct is allowed to heal and may be sutured around the tube. Repair of the duct is complex and may be delayed. The tube is later removed and the opening is restored.

Pharynx, Adenoids and Tonsils 42700–42999

Codes 42820–42836 describe tonsillectomy and adenoidectomy procedures. These procedure codes are distinguished by the age of the patient (under age 12 and over). Adenoidectomies and tonsillectomies are normally performed bilaterally and are only reported once without the addition of modifier 50.

Codes 42830–42836 describe adenoidectomy procedures and are determined not only by the age of the patient but also by whether the procedure is "primary" or "secondary."

- A primary procedure is the initial procedure performed to remove tissue
- A secondary procedure may be necessary if the adenoid tissue grows back

The excision of tonsil tags is reported using code 42860. Tonsil tags are the portions of the tonsil not excised during the primary resection or that have developed polyps. The provider uses a mouth gag to visualize the tonsillar pillars, and cauter-izes or snares the affected tissue. Closure is normally not required.

If radical resection of the tonsils is necessary, CPT® codes 42842–42845 are used. The surgeon removes the tonsils, tonsillar pillars, or the retromolar trigone along with any infected area of the maxilla or mandible involved in the tumor. Normally, a tracheostomy is performed and the involved tissue is resected. In addition to the above areas, radical resection may include a hemiglossectomy or total glossectomy as well as a full neck dissection.

In code 42842, the wound site is extremely extensive and it is packed open and grafted at a later session. In 42844, the wound is less extensive and may be closed with local flap (eg, tongue, buccal). In 42845, a flap is rotated up from the chest. If the wound includes the resection of the mandible or maxilla, a fibular bone graft or metal plate may be used to reconstruct the jaw.

The removal of a small portion of the pharyngeal wall or pyriform sinus is commonly called a limited pharyngectomy (42890). Occasionally, the removed area includes part of the thyroid (hyoid bone) and wall of the pyriform fossa. The procedure includes an anterior transhyoid pharyngotomy, lateral pharyngotomy, and median labiomandibular glossectomy. Reconstructive surgery is required for closure.

If an advancement of the lateral or posterior pharyngeal wall is necessary, report CPT® code 42892. If a myocutaneous flap, normally achieved using the pectoralis major muscle and its overlying skin, is rotated and inserted through a previously created tunnel between the clavicle and overlying skin and sutured into place to reconstruct the pharynx, report CPT® code 42894.

Esophagus 43020–43135

Esophagectomy codes, 43100–43135 are used to report the removal of all or part of the esophagus. The code choice is based on whether the esophagectomy is partial, near total, or total; whether the approach is cervical or thoracic; and if any reconstruction is performed. Esophagectomies are usually performed for malignancies of the esophagus. A colon interposition is performed by using a piece of the colon to rebuild the esophagus at the time of the esophagectomy.

Diverticula in the esophagus are sac-like pouches in one or more layers of the esophagus. As food is ingested, it becomes trapped in the diverticulum where it may become inflamed or regurgitated. When symptoms become severe, surgery is performed to correct the problem.

Diverticulectomy of the hypopharynx or esophagus, with or without myotomy; cervical approach or thoracic approach is reported using codes 43130–43135, respectively. Whether using the cervical approach or the thoracic approach, the diverticulum is excised and the esophageal mucosa is re-anastomosed.

Endoscopy 43180–43273

Endoscopic procedures are used to visualize the digestive organs, via the use of either a flexible fiber-optic tube or ridged instruments. Endoscopic instruments allow physicians to diagnose and treat various conditions, such as ulcers, inflam-

mation, tumors, infections, or bleeding. It is important to choose and report the appropriate code for each anatomic site examined. If the provider converts an endoscopic procedure to an open procedure, report only the open procedure. According to National Correct Coding Initiative (NCCI) policy, which is followed by most payers, do not report the attempted endoscopic procedure. For the CPC® exam, the NCCI policy is followed for endoscopic procedures converted to open procedures. Report only the open procedure.

Code 43180 is reported when a rigid endoscope is inserted in the mouth to the esophagus removing the diverticulum of the hypopharynx or cervical esophagus. A small incision is made to the cricopharyngeus muscle to show the diverticulum. The telescope or operating microscope is used for this procedure and a parenthetical note indicates add-on code 69990 is not reported separately. Code 43191 - 43196 describe rigid esophagoscopy procedures and codes 43200–43232 describe flexible esophagoscopy procedures that are the direct visualization of the esophagus that do not extend into the stomach. The scopes can be inserted via into the mouth (transoral) or into the nose (transnasal). It is important to note that codes 43191 *Esophagoscopy, rigid, transoral,* 43197 *Esophagoscopy, flexible, transnasal,* and 43200 *Esophagoscopy, flexible, transoral* are the parent codes. This means that the other codes in this series are indented in the CPT®; everything prior to the semicolon is inherent to the remaining codes in the series.

Practical Coding Note

Place a line down the left side of codes 43192-43196, 43198 and 43201–43232 with a highlighter to remind you they are indented codes.

Band ligation of esophageal varices (43205) describes the application of a tight band around an esophageal varix (a tortuous, dilated vein; a varicose vein in the esophagus) that cuts off circulation and effectively eliminates the varix.

Hot biopsy (43216) is used to remove small tumors, polyps, or other lesions.

Hot Biopsy Forceps—Uses monopolar current, requiring a grounding pad placed somewhere on the patient. The use of "hot" forceps enables the provider to simultaneously excise a lesion and control bleeding and, if needed, preserve the specimen for histological examination.

Electrocautery snare (43217) can also be used to remove small tumors, polyps, or other lesions. A snare is a wire loop used to encircle tissue for removal rather than grasp tissue, as done with forceps. Usually monopolar current is used with snares, although bipolar snares are available.

Practical Coding Note

CPT® code 43229 is used when techniques other than hot biopsy, bipolar cautery, or electrocautery snares (eg, laser) are used for lesion treatment. Make a note of this next to codes 43216 & 43217.

If more than one tumor is removed by multiple techniques, which have distinct CPT® codes, each type of removal should be separately reported.

Example

Biopsy of one tumor, excision of a different tumor by hot biopsy and removal of a polyp by snare technique would require three separate codes:

43202 Esophagoscopy, flexible, transoral; with biopsy, single or multiple

43216 Esophagoscopy, flexible, transoral; with removal of tumor(s), polyp(s), or other lesion(s) by hot biopsy forceps.

43217 Esophagoscopy, flexible, transoral; with removal of tumor(s), polyp(s), or other lesion(s) by snare technique

A modifier 59 would need to be appended to show they were different sites.

With balloon dilation (43220) (less than 30 mm diameter), the endoscope is passed through the esophagus, and while viewing the stricture, a tube with an inflatable balloon at its tip is passed through the endoscope and positioned at the narrowed section of the esophagus. The balloon is then briefly inflated to dilate the narrowed area. The balloon is then deflated and removed. Do not use this code if the procedure is performed without direct visualization. Instead, use an appropriate code from the series 43450–43453 under the Manipulation subheading (in these procedures, the provider dilates by palpation [feel], rather than visualization through a scope).

Esophagogastroduodenoscopy (EGD) procedures include the visualization of the esophagus, stomach, and proximal duodenum or jejunum. The code range for these procedures is 43235–43259. If during the exam the physician does not report the examination of the proximal duodenum or jejunum, per CPT® instructions you may report the examination using this code range and append a 52 modifier to report that the full examination was not completed.

EGD Procedure

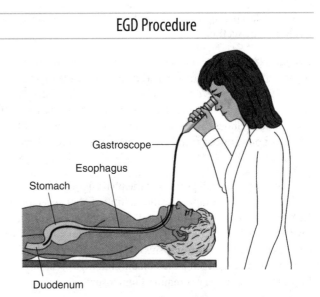

Gastroscope
Esophagus
Stomach
Duodenum

Source: LINDH/TAMPARO/POOLER/DAHL. Delmar's Comprehensive Medical Assisting, 4E. © 2010 Delmar Learning, a part of Cengage Learning, Inc. Reproduced by permission. www.cengage.com/ permissions

CPT® codes 43196, 43226 and 43248 describe dilation of the esophagus by insertion of a guidewire followed by dilation over the guidewire. The procedure involves inserting the scope, placing a guidewire, removing the scope, dilating the esophagus guided by the wire with a series of dilators and, when the dilation is complete, removing the guidewire. Code 43226 is reported when only a flexible, transoral esophagoscopy is performed (not beyond the pyloric valve). Code 43196 is reported when a rigid, transoral esophagoscopy is performed and code 43248 should be reported for guidewire dilation of the esophagus in conjunction with a full EGD.

Percutaneous placement of a gastrostomy tube or percutaneous endoscopic gastrostomy (PEG), via an EGD is described by code 43246. When the provider changes a gastrostomy tube without an EGD, use code 43760. There is no code for PEG tube removal. According to the AMA, PEG tube removal is included in the evaluation and management service.

When PEG tube placement requires the skills of two providers, both providers should report code 43246 with modifier 62 (cosurgery). A "gastrostomy button" serves as an alternative to a gastrostomy tube; it is used for patients with an existing stoma (opening). It is reported the same as any other gastrostomy tube based on method of placement.

CPT® codes 43227 or 43255 may be reported for endoscopic control of bleeding when the bleeding is not a complication of the endoscopy. If the bleeding is a result of the endoscopic procedure, it is considered an inherent part of the primary procedure and not coded separately at the same operative session. If the patient is returned to the endoscopy suite later in the day or on another day with a bleeding complication, the procedure performed to resolve the complication might be reported separately. Fundoplasty involves mobilization of the fundus of the stomach, which is then wrapped around the lower esophageal sphincter to correct esophageal reflux or a hiatal hernia.

Hiatal hernia may be a congenital abnormality or secondary to trauma. In paraesophageal hiatus hernia, a portion of the stomach is adjacent to the esophagus; the hernia is reduced surgically because of the risk of strangulation. The repair of paraesophageal hiatal hernia (43332–43337) is coded based on the approach and if mesh or other prosthesis was implanted.

Endoscopic retrograde cholangiopancreatography (ERCP) uses a combination of endoscopy and fluoroscopy to diagnose and treat certain problems of the biliary or pancreatic ductal systems. ERCP is used primarily to diagnose and treat conditions of the bile ducts, including gallstones, inflammatory strictures (scars), leaks (from trauma and surgery), and malignancies. ERCP is primarily used for therapeutic reasons; however, it can be applied for diagnostic purposes. There has been development of other safer and relatively non-invasive investigations, such as magnetic resonance cholangiopancreatography (MRCP) and endoscopic ultrasound. The ERCP code range is 43260–43273.

Coding Tip

Modifier 52 - When a patient is scheduled for an endoscopic procedure (upper or lower) and the procedure is partially reduced or eliminated because the physician elected to based on the findings during the procedure. It is appropriate to report the planned procedure with the addition of modifier 52, signifying that the service is reduced. This reduces the service without disturbing the identification of the basic service.

Stomach 43500–43999

Procedures performed on the stomach are reported with the code range 43500–43999. The Stomach subsection includes procedures such as gastrectomy, endoscopy, and laparoscopic procedures, as well as gastric bypass procedures, to name a few.

A gastrectomy is the removal of all or part of the stomach; this procedure typically is used to treat ulcers, malignancy, noncancerous polyps, or perforations of the stomach wall. Codes 43620–43635 describe various gastrectomies. The difference between these codes is not only the amount of stomach removed, but also the type of reconstruction selected. If the lower end of the stomach is diseased, the surgeon places clamps on either end of the area, and that portion is excised. The upper part of the

stomach is attached to the small intestine. If the upper end of the stomach is diseased, the end of the esophagus and the upper part of the stomach are clamped. The diseased part is removed, and the lower part of the stomach is attached to the esophagus.

After gastrectomy, the surgeon may reconstruct the altered portions of the digestive tract so that it may continue to function. Several different surgical techniques can be used to attach the remaining portion of the stomach to the small intestine. These techniques range from a simple anastomosis to the jejunum (43632) or the duodenum (43631) to the more complex reconstructions that would include a Roux-en-Y. A Roux-en-Y looks like the letter "Y." Typically, the two upper limbs of the Y represent a proximal segment of small bowel and the distal small bowel it joins with (which is often a blind end), and the lower part of the Y the distal small bowel (beyond the anastomosis). Roux-en-Y reconstruction is used in several different types of reconstructions throughout the CPT® codebook. Code 43634, *Gastrectomy, partial, distal; with formation of intestinal pouch*, describes another type of reconstruction where the distal end of the jejunum is folded in upon itself to form a pouch, then the bottom of the pouch is connected to the remaining portion of the small intestine. If the surgeon performs these procedures laparoscopically, report an unlisted code 43659 *Unlisted laparoscopy procedure, stomach* because there are no laparoscopic codes to describe these approaches.

Bariatric and gastric bypass procedures are reported when a patient is seeking treatment for morbid obesity. There are several different types of procedures (Roux-en-Y, banding, etc.) and approaches, open vs. laparoscopic, to complete this treatment. Likewise, there are several code ranges from which to choose as well. A laparoscopy is a minimally invasive technique where the surgeon inflates the abdomen and inserts trocars (scopes) to perform the procedure. Laparoscopic gastric restrictive procedures are reported with code ranges 43644–43645 and 43770–43775. Open gastric bypass surgeries are reported with code range 43842–43848.

Practical Coding Note

Subsequent band adjustments are included in typical postoperative care and the adjustments are not reported separately. Band adjustment refers to changing the gastric band component diameter by injection or aspiration of fluid through the subcutaneous port component.

The Endoscopic procedures of the stomach are located in the endoscopy subsection, and are reported with the codes 43235–43259.

Nasogastric/orogastric intubation that requires the skill of a surgeon and fluoroscopic guidance is reported 43752. This code is not reported when nursing staff places the tube.

Gastric intubation code 43753 is reported when the physician pumps the stomach due to an overdose or poisoning, or a gastrointestinal hemorrhage. The physician will pass a tube through the mouth or nose into the stomach and a lavage (pumping saline or warm water) is performed suctioning out the stomach contents.

Gastric intubation codes 43754 and 43755 are reported when the contents of the stomach are aspirated for diagnostic purposes, such as for acid analysis in code 43754. Code 43755 is reported when many specimens are obtained for acid analysis. Administration of gastric secretion stimulating drugs is included with these codes.

Many abdominal procedures require the patient to have a nasogastric or orogastric tube to help decompress the stomach. When the viscera are handled during intraabdominal surgery, peristalsis of the bowel ceases for 24 to 72 hours. If the stomach fills, the suture line could become compromised secondary to distention or vomiting. An NG (nasogastric) tube is inserted to help keep the stomach empty. This tube also serves to prevent vomiting. The insertion of a nasogastric or orogastric tube requiring the skill of a physician and fluoroscopic guidance is reported as CPT® code 43752. Placement of the NG (nasogastric) tube is always bundled with abdominal surgery.

Nasogastric and Gastrostomy Tubes

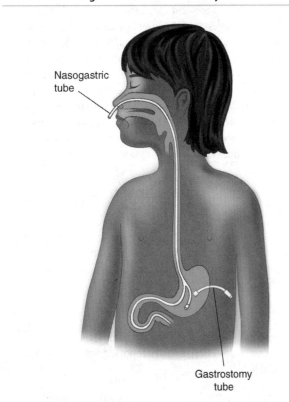

Nasogastric tube

Gastrostomy tube

Intestines 44005–44799

Intestinal procedures begin with code 44005 and end with 44799; these codes represent the different procedures performed on the intestines, except the rectum, which is covered with the code range 45000–45999. The code description sounds similar from one code to the next; carefully review the note and the code description to assure correct coding.

CPT® code 44005 describes enterolysis (freeing of intestinal adhesion). This procedure is listed as a separate procedure. When it is performed alone and is not related to another, more extensive procedure performed at the same time, it may be reported. However, when it is an integral part of another, more extensive procedure, it is not normally reportable and is incidental. Exploration, biopsy, or removal of a foreign body from the small intestine may be performed using a duodenotomy (44010), enterotomy (44020), or colotomy (44025).

Codes 44120–44128 are used for reporting an enterectomy, which is the resection of one or more segments of the small bowel and normally with an anastomosis between the remaining bowel ends. The correct code is determined by the amount removed and the type of repair performed. Code 44121 is an add-on code and is to be used in conjunction with code 44120. It reports "each additional resection and anastomosis." CPT® modifier 51 is not applicable.

CPT® codes 44126–44128 report enterectomy for congenital atresia, single resection, and anastomosis of proximal segment of intestine. CPT® code 44126 denotes "without tapering" and 44127 reports, "with tapering." Tapering means a gradual narrowing of a hollow organ such as the intestine. Code 44128 is used for "each additional resection and anastomosis." This code is used when appropriate with 44126 or 44127. Code 44130 is used to report an enteroenterostomy. An enteroenterostomy is a separate procedure that is a surgical anastomosis of two parts of the intestine with creation of an opening between them.

Codes 44132 and 44133 include cold preservation of the donor enterectomy eliminating the steps of preparing and maintaining the allograft. Code 44132 is used to report a cadaver donor enterectomy and 44133 is used to report a partial enterectomy from a living donor.

A colectomy (44140–44160) is the removal of part or the entire colon (large intestine). Removal of the entire colon is unusual. More common is the removal of part of the intestine, which is a partial colectomy. These are four common types of partial colectomies:

1. Right colectomy is the removal of all or part of the right colon, performed to treat lesions of the cecum, ascending colon, and hepatic flexure.

2. Left colectomy is removal of all or part of the left colon, performed to treat conditions affecting the splenic flexure, sigmoid, or descending colon.

3. Anterior resection is removal of all or part of the rectosigmoid colon, or the lower part of the descending sigmoid and rectosigmoid colon.

4. Abdominal perineal resection is removal of the lower rectosigmoid colon, rectum, and anus.

The code descriptors available in CPT® to report partial colectomies do not indicate the exact portion of the colon removed but do reflect the difficulty of the procedure according to the additional procedures (cecostomy, colostomy, ileostomy, and resection) performed in conjunction with the removal. The level of the anastomosis or -ostomy can also determine code choices. The same principle is true when reporting total colectomies. Selection of the correct code is based on the related procedures performed with the colectomy.

Practical Coding Note

Documentation in the operative report of a puncture made into the abdomen and the end of the bowel that was brought out indicates the creation of a stoma (colostomy).

Laparoscopic procedures are divided into subsections incision, enterostomy—external fistulization, and repair. There is an open procedure referenced in the parenthetical note under code 44188 to refer the coder to 44320.

Enterostomy—External
Fistulization of Intestines (44186–44188)

Code 44186 reports surgical laparoscopy to advance a feeding tube through the stomach and duodenum into the jejunum to allow gastrojejunostomy enteral therapy; while code 44187 represents a jejunostomy or ileostomy that is performed for reasons other than placing a feeding tube. A cecostomy (44188) is the surgical construction of an opening into the cecum with a tube through the abdominal wall (tube cecostomy) or by skin level approach, in which the cecum is sewn to the surrounding peritoneum. Its primary purpose is decompression of colonic obstruction.

Excision (44202–44213)

Code 44202 describes a surgical enterectomy, performed laparoscopically, and includes a resection of the small intestine with a single resection and anastomosis. CPT® code 44203 is an add-on code that reports each additional small intestine resection and anastomosis.

Codes 44204 and 44205 report laparoscopic partial colectomies with anastomosis, and removal of the terminal ileum with ileocolostomy. Colectomy, or removal of part of the colon, is one of the most common laparoscope procedures; it involves locating the affected area with help of the laparoscope, sealing and cutting the vessels surrounding the diseased portion of the colon. The diseased segment is extracted through a trocar, or in some cases, through an enlarged abdominal incision. The healthy parts of the colon are secured together. Surgical tape or stitches close the incisions following surgery.

Surgical laparoscopy or colectomy codes (44206–44212) describe laparoscopic colectomy, which is a treatment for colon conditions including diverticulitis, Crohn's disease (occurring in the small intestine as well as the colon), chronic ulcerative colitis, constipation, and sigmoid volvulus.

Code 44213 reports laparoscopic colon resection for middle to low rectal cancer, followed by an end-to-end colorectal anastomosis between the splenic flexure and the rectum, requiring mobilization of the entire splenic flexure.

Repair (44227)

The single repair code reports the laparoscopic closure of an enterostomy with resection and anastomosis.

Endoscopic procedures are split into two subsections in the intestine section. The first section is for endoscopic procedures of the small intestines (44360–44379), beyond the second portion of the duodenum, and stomal endoscopy (44380–44384), where the scope is inserted via an existing ileostomy. Colonoscopies performed via the stoma can be found in this section, as well, with codes 44388–44408.

Enterostomy procedures are the creation of external stomas, or openings in the body for the discharge of body waste. The coding for ostomies is determined by the portion of the digestive tract that is brought to the surface of the abdomen and if the procedure is not already included in the verbiage of a more extensive procedure. Ostomies can be of the small or large intestines, and may be permanent or temporary.

Code 44701 describes operating table colonic lavage. This technique has been used in patients with inadequate bowel preparation at the time of elective or semi-elective surgery. The lavage is performed after the resection and anastomosis of the colon are completed.

Meckel's Diverticulum and Mesentery (44800–44899)

Diverticulosis refers to the presence of non-inflamed outpouching of the intestine. Diverticulitis is inflammation of the diverticulum. A diverticulum is a blinding outpouch or herniation of the intestinal mucosa through the muscular coat of the large intestine, usually the sigmoid colon.

Meckel's diverticulum is an outpouching of the bowel, a vestige of embryonic development found on the ileum within 10 cm of the cecum. The pouch may be lined with gastric mucosa or it may contain pancreatic tissue. The gastric mucosal lining sometimes ulcerates, bleeds, or perforates. It may become inflamed and mimic appendicitis. In addition, a Meckel's diverticulum is sometimes attached to the umbilicus by a fibrous band, which may focus around the twisted bowel, causing obstruction.

CPT® code 44800 is used to report excision of Meckel's diverticulum or the omphalomesenteric duct. The defect in the ileum is closed with sutures or staples or the segment of ileum may be excised and reapproximated.

Appendix

Appendectomies can be performed via an open (44950–44960) or laparoscopic (44970) approach. It is important to note this procedure is considered incidental to other intra-abdominal procedures, unless the procedure is performed for an indicated purpose (44955) such as, rupture, fecalith, and intussusceptions (to name a few).

Colon and Rectum 45000–45999

The code range 45000–45999 describes procedures on or through the rectum. Endoscopic procedures in this section include colonoscopy, sigmoidoscopy, and proctosigmoidoscopy. Proctosigmoidoscopy procedures (45300–45327) involve the visual examination of the rectum and sigmoid colon using a rigid, stiff hollow tube. Sigmoidoscopy procedures (45330–45350) involve the visual examination of the entire rectum and sigmoid colon, and may include a portion of the descending colon using a flexible instrument. Proper code selection for a proctosigmoidoscopy versus a sigmoidoscopy will depend on the instrument used. Colonoscopy procedures (45378–45398) are the visual examination of the entire colon, from the rectum to cecum, and might include the terminal ileum. According to CPT® for a diagnostic or screening colonoscopy that does not reach the splenic flexure you report flexible sigmoidoscopy code 45330. For a diagnostic or screening colonoscopy that passes the splenic flexure but does not go all the way to the cecum you report code 45378 with modifier 53. When the diagnostic or screening colonoscopy goes all the way to the cecum you report code 45378 with no modifier. For therapeutic or surgical colonoscopy that does not reach the splenic

flexure you report flexible sigmoidoscopy codes 45331-45347. For therapeutic or surgical colonoscopy that passes the splenic flexure but does not go all the way to cecum you report codes 45379-45398 with modifier 52. For therapeutic or surgical colonoscopy that goes all the way to the cecum report codes 45379-45398 with no modifier. Refer to the CPT® subsection guidelines for Endoscopy and read all parenthetical notes in this series of codes.

To determine the appropriate code you must understand the different techniques to remove lesions, polyps, or tumors through the endoscope. The techniques include bipolar cautery, which is the use of an electric current that flows from one tip of the forcep to the other. Another technique used is hot biopsy forceps, which utilizes tweezers-like forceps connected to a monopolar electrocautery unit and a grounding pad, for the removal of the specimen(s). The opposite of the hot biopsy forceps is the cold biopsy forceps, which does not employ electrocoagulation to remove the specimen. The provider simply grasps the polyp and pulls it from the colon wall. An electrocautery snare is a wire loop that is used to encircle the specimen to remove it. The final technique is the use of a laser that uses a waveguide to direct the laser through the endoscope to the operative field.

NOTE—When multiple specimens are removed during the same endoscopic session by different techniques, report a code for each procedure performed, and sequence the codes with the highest value first, and append modifier 59 to the additional codes.

Anus 46020–46999

Codes 46020–46999 report procedures performed on the anus. Hemorrhoids are one of the most common diagnoses for anal procedures. There are two types of hemorrhoids, internal and external, that are differentiated by their position with respect to the dentate line. The dentate line, or pectinate line, is a line that divides the upper two-thirds and lower one-third of the anal canal.

Internal hemorrhoids are varicosities of veins draining the territory of branches of the superior rectal arteries on the inside of the rectum. Because the interior of the rectum lacks pain receptors, most patients with internal hemorrhoids do not feel pain unless the hemorrhoids become irritated (which could cause bleeding). If left untreated, hemorrhoids can become prolapsed or strangulated.

External hemorrhoids are those that occur outside the anal verge. External hemorrhoids are varicosities of the veins draining the territory of the inferior rectal arteries, which are branches of the internal pudendal artery. They are sometimes painful, and often accompanied by swelling and irritation.

Thrombosis of an external hemorrhoid occurs when a vein ruptures and a blood clot develops.

Complications associated with hemorrhoids are defined as follows:

Prolapse—An internal hemorrhoid that descends and protrudes past the anal sphincter.

Thrombosis—A clot of blood within the hemorrhoid that causes acute pain.

Strangulation—A hemorrhoid in which the blood supply has become occluded by the constricting action of the anal sphincter.

Ulceration—A hemorrhoid in which there is inflammation or necrotic changes of the tissue.

Fistula—A tube-like tract with one opening in the anal canal and the other opening usually in the perianal skin of the rectum.

Fissure—An acute longitudinal tear, painful linear groove, or a chronic ovoid ulcer of the anal canal.

There are various treatment options for patients with hemorrhoids, which can include a hemorrhoidectomy by banding or ligation via a rubber band (46221), to complete hemorrhoid excisions with treatment for anal fissures or fistulas (46257–46258 and 46261–46262).When multiple methods are used to remove multiple hemorrhoids, use a separate code for each specimen removed.

Code 46505 is used to report chemodenervation of internal anal sphincter. This identifies the injection of botulinum toxin into the sphincter muscle to allow for healing of a fissure that develops at that orifice site.

CPT® code 46706 describes fibrin glue repair of an anal fistula. Fibrin glue is a topical biological adhesive that can be used to coagulate blood at a wound site, which serves to diminish the risk of postoperative bleeding. It has been found that the use of fibrin tissue glue for low output enterocutaneous (abnormal connection between intestine and skin) speeds healing and reduces the patient's hospital stay. If the initial application does not close the fistula, it can be used again.

Liver 47000–47399, Biliary Tract 47400–47999, and Pancreas 48000–48999

Liver

The liver is the largest gland of the body, weighing 1200–1600 grams. It is wedge-shaped and covered by a network of connective tissue (Glisson's capsule).

The procedures performed on the liver are reported with the code range 47000–47399. Liver injuries can result from trauma such as stabbing, gunshot wounds, and blunt traumas, which can cause hemorrhaging of the liver. To report these types of repairs, choose the codes from the range 47350–47362, depending on the extent of the wound and hemorrhaging involved.

CPT® code 47010 describes a hepatotomy for open drainage of an abscess or cyst. This procedure may be performed in one or two stages and should not be reported twice. For percutaneous drainage of a liver abscess, report code 49405. This procedure may be performed in stages as well and should not be reported twice. It includes initial insertion and final removal of the catheter under radiologic guidance.

Probably the most common procedures performed on the liver would be a hepatectomy of a portion of the liver. Although the liver is the only organ in the human body to regenerate itself, a person cannot live without a sufficient amount of liver left in the body prior to the regeneration. The codes for the partial removal are arranged by the portion of the liver removed. A partial lobectomy (47120) would be used to remove a single tumor from a lobe of the liver. The liver is made up of four lobes, the left, right, caudate, and quadrate lobes. It is also separated into eight segments, the caudate (1), lateral (2, 3), medial (4a, 4b) and right (5, 6, 7, 8). It is important to know this prior to code selection because 47120 should be reported for each tumor, if removed from different lobes of the liver.

Liver Transplantation

Five codes—47143, 47144, 47145, 47146 and 47147—are used to report cadaver to recipient allotransplantation. Three codes—47143, 47144 and 47145—describe backbench preparation of the cadaver donor whole liver graft, and codes 47146 and 47147 describe backbench preparation of a cadaver or living donor liver graft prior to allotransplantation. Codes 47133 and 47140 include cold preservation, but the codes do not include preparation and maintenance of the allograft.

Liver allotransplantation requires three components of physician work: cadaver or living donor hepatectomy (harvesting of graft and cold preservation), backbench preparation, and recipient allotransplantation (which includes recipient care). Backbench refers to standard preparation of the organ for transplant into the recipient. The process may include reconstructive alterations to the blood vessels and tubes, depending on the recipient needs. The backbench procedure is basically the same for all organ transplants, with some modification due to tailoring requirements of the specific organ allograft.

Backbench preparation of the whole liver graft (47143) includes a cholecystectomy, dissection, and removal of surrounding soft tissues to prepare the vena cava, portal vein, hepatic artery, and common bile duct for implantation. Code 47144 includes the whole liver graft preparation and the tri-segment split into two partial grafts; code 47145 reports the preparation of the whole liver graft plus the lobe split into two partial grafts. The back-bench procedures performed immediately prior to transplant may be reported with 47146 when it includes a venous anastomosis. Code 47147 is reported when the procedure involves arterial anastomosis.

Normally, a transplant involves a surgical team with the use of CPT® modifier 66 appended to the procedure code(s). Modifier 66 is used to identify highly complex procedures requiring the concomitant services of several physicians, often of different specialties, with highly skilled and trained personnel using complex equipment.

The liver is the only human organ that can self-regenerate. If a part of the liver is removed, the remaining parts can grow back to its original size. With living donor liver transplantation, the healthy donor's liver regenerates to full size within a few weeks of operation, and there is no long-term impairment of liver function. The transplanted liver portion also regenerates, increasing in size to an appropriate match for the recipient. Adult-to-adult living donor liver transplantation using the right portion of the liver evolved from successful experiences with transplantation of children and cadaver donor split-liver transplantation. The latter procedure involves splitting a whole cadaver liver into two parts, allowing transplantation of two recipients.

Repair

Liver injuries often occur from a penetrating injury (eg, knife or gun shot) or blunt trauma (eg, from a steering wheel or a fall) and either may lead to a laceration or hemorrhage. Intervention for liver injuries consists of hemorrhage control, debridement, or drainage. It may be necessary to remove the liver lobes, but more often, the major goal is to control the hemorrhage. CPT® code 47361 describes repairs for complex liver injuries that require greater service than those described by codes 47360. Code 47362 describes re-exploration of the wound for removal of packing. This procedure is carried out one to three days after the original procedure. Attach modifier 58 to code 47362.

Biliary Tract

Biliary tract procedures are reported with 47400–47999; the biliary tract includes the liver, gallbladder, and pancreas. The biliary tract functions to create, transport, store, and release bile into the duodenum to aid in the digestive process. The most common procedure performed on the biliary tract is a cholecystectomy, which can be performed laparoscopically (47562–47564) or open (47600–47620). Additional procedures can be performed during a cholecystectomy, such as a

cholangiography (47605 open and 47563 laparoscopy) or an exploration of the common bile duct (47610 open and 47564 laparoscopy). These additional procedures are performed if the surgeon has a question about the possibility of a calculus lodged in the bile duct.

Pancreas

Pancreas procedures are coded 48000–48999. Most common are the Whipple-type procedures. A Whipple procedure, 48150, may also be called a pancreaticoduodenectomy or pancreatoduodenectomy. This procedure is a major surgical operation involving the pancreas, duodenum, and other organs. This operation normally is performed to treat malignancies in the head of the pancreas, or malignant tumors involving the common bile duct or duodenum near the pancreas. Coding depends on how much of the duodenum is removed (total to near total) and if a pancreatojejunostomy is performed. In the absence of the anastomosis to the jejunum (pancreatojejunostomy), report code 48154. Choice of codes also depends on the extent of excision of additional structures.

Internal anastomosis of a pancreatic cyst to the gastrointestinal tract may be performed and reported using code 48520. Code 48540 should be used when Roux-en-Y anastomosis to drain enzymes from the pancreatic duct is used. This procedure is characterized by the approach.

Pancreas Transplantation

Codes 48551 and 48552 include the backbench description of cadaver to recipient allotransplantation, to include preparation and reconstruction. Code 48550 reports a donor pancreatectomy, including cold preservation, with or without duodenal segment for transplantation.

Pancreatic allotransplantation requires three components of physician work: cadaver donor pancreatectomy (harvesting of graft and cold preservation), backbench preparation, and recipient allotransplantation (which includes recipient care). The process may include reconstructive alterations to the blood vessels and tubes, depending on the recipient needs. The backbench procedure is basically the same for all organ transplants, with some modification due to tailoring requirements of the specific organ allograft.

Backbench preparation of the cadaver donor pancreas graft prior to transplantation (48551) includes dissection of the allograft from surrounding tissue, splenectomy, duodenotomy, ligation of bile duct, ligation of mesenteric vessels, and Y-graft arterial anastomoses from the iliac artery to the superior mesenteric artery and to the splenic artery. Any additional work involved in the allograft prior to transplantation would be reported with code 48552.

Abdomen, Peritoneum, and Omentum 49000–49999

Procedures performed on the abdomen, peritoneum, and omentum are reported with 49000–49999, and can be performed via laparotomy or laparoscopy.

Hernia repairs, 49491–49659, are performed due to a protrusion of internal organs (eg, intestines or omentum) through a weakening in the abdominal wall. To determine which code is appropriate, coders need to know if the surgery was performed via open approach or laparoscopy, the hernia site (lumbar, inguinal, or ventral), patient's age, type of hernia (initial or recurrent), clinical presentation of the hernia (eg, reducible, incarcerated, strangulated, or recurrent), and the use of mesh.

Herniorrhaphies are repaired by the physician who reduces bulging tissue back into the abdominal cavity and sutures the abdominal wall back into place. Herniorrhaphies can include the placement of mesh (eg, Marlex or Prolene) which is placed to add reinforcement to the repair (+49568). The mesh-insertion code 49568 is an add-on code and can be used with the procedure codes for ventral and incisional hernia repairs (49560–49566).

Types of hernias include:

Inguinal Hernia—The abdominal contents protrude into the inguinal canal. This type of hernia is the most common (75 percent to 80 percent) and the method of repair is determined by the age of the patient.

"Sliding" Inguinal Hernia (49525)—The peritoneal organs (eg, ascending colon, bladder, or cecum) protrude in such a way that the wall of the internal organ forms a portion of the hernial sac.

Lumbar Hernia (49540)—These posterior abdominal wall or retroperitoneal outpouchings occur between the 12th rib and the iliac crest.

Femoral Hernia (49550–49557)—The intestine protrudes along the femoral canals. They are found more frequently in adults and may occur due to multiple pregnancies, obesity, or connective tissue degeneration, and are common to the aging process.

Incisional or Ventral Hernia (49560–49566)—Protrusion occurs at the incisional site following abdominal surgery. If mesh or prosthesis is used for the repair, code 49568 should be listed in addition to the code for the hernia repair.

Epigastric Hernia (49570–49572)—Protrusion occurs in the midline between the xiphoid process and the umbilicus.

Umbilical Hernia (49580–49587)—Protrusion occurs at the umbilicus as a result of an abnormally large or weak umbilical ring.

Spigelian Hernia (49590)—Although uncommon, this type of hernia consists of protruding properitoneal fat, a peritoneal sac, or a viscous-containing sac through the Spigelian zone. This zone is in the lower abdominal region on either the right or left side lateral to the rectus muscle.

An omphalocele is a congenital anomaly in which variable amounts of abdominal contents protrude into the base of the umbilical cord. A double membrane (amnion and peritoneum) covers the abdominal contents. This type of hernia is rare and when it does occur, it is usually associated with other anomalies.

The omphalocele is surgically converted to an incisional hernia in the first stage of omphalocele repair (CPT® code 49610). Six to 24 months later, the hernia will be reducible.

Practical Coding Note

Bilateral hernia repairs are reported with CPT® modifier 50.

By definition, an incarcerated hernia is constricted by the defect and cannot be reduced by simple manipulation. If the blood vessels leading into the sac become obstructed, necrosis of the strangulated part may occur, leading to peritonitis. A strangulated hernia is considered a medical emergency. CPT® notes, "The excision/repair of strangulated organs or structures such as testicle(s), intestine, ovaries are reported by using the appropriate code for the excision/repair (eg, 44120, 54520, and 58940), in addition to the appropriate code for the repair of the strangulated hernia."

The use of mesh or prosthesis may only be reported in addition to incisional or ventral hernia repairs (code 49568). Do not attach modifier 51 (multiple procedures) to code 49568. CPT® codes 49495–49501 may or may not include a hydrocelectomy. A hydrocele is a fluid filled sac-like cavity or duct that may occur in children with congenital hernias. Treatment of choice involves excision of the hydrocele, since simply drawing off the fluid is only a temporary remedy.

CPT® Radiology Section—Gastroenterology Codes

The radiology section contains several code ranges dedicated to digestive system procedures. Each code description includes the modality or type of service, anatomic site, and use of contrast material. Code ranges for digestive radiology include 74210–74363 for studies of the gastrointestinal tract, 76700–76776 for diagnostic ultrasound studies of the abdomen, 78201–78299 for nuclear medicine studies of the gastrointestinal tract, 74240–74249 for radiological examinations of the gastrointestinal tract to measure the patient's gastric emptying, and 74261–74283 for radiological studies of the colon.

Reporting radiological studies of the gastrointestinal tract are required for procedures such as a laparoscopic cholecystectomy with intraoperative cholangiogram and fluoroscopy. The coder reports codes 47563, Laparoscopy, surgical; cholecystectomy with cholangiography when performed by the surgeon, and 74300-26, Cholangiography and/or pancreatography; intraoperative, radiological supervision and interpretation when performed by the radiologist who reads and interprets the cholangiography. In the hospital setting, the surgeon may review the X-ray; however, the radiologist would report the reading and write the report. You would not report the fluoroscopy code (76000) because it is included in 74300; the code description for 76000 states, "separate procedure."

Diagnostic ultrasound studies of the abdomen and retroperitoneum are an imaging technique that bounces sound waves far above the level of human perception through interior body structures. The sound waves pass through different densities of tissue and reflect back to a receiving unit at varying speeds. The unit converts the waves to electrical pulses that are displayed immediately via a picture on screen. Real-time scanning displays structure images and movement with time. An example of this would be a patient undergoing an ultrasound, real time, of a transplanted kidney with duplex Doppler scan including image documentation. The appropriate code is 76776 *Ultrasound, transplanted kidney, real time, and duplex Doppler with image documentation.*

Nuclear medicine involves the use of radioactive elements such as radionuclides and radioisotopes for diagnostic imaging and radiopharmaceutical therapy to destroy diseased tissue, such as malignancies. Nuclear medicine studies also can be utilized to diagnosis other diseases or anomalies. One of these studies is the hepatobiliary system imaging, including gallbladder when present, with serial images, 78226, which is used to study biliary function in diagnosing acute cholecystitis, cholestasis, obstructions, leaks, biliary-enteric fistulas, and cysts.

Gastric emptying is a radiologic exam to aid in diagnosing neoplasms, ulcers, obstructions, and other diseases. Several of these procedures include KUB in the description of the code, which is an acronym for kidneys, ureter, and bladder.

Computed tomographic colonography (74261) also can be referred to as virtual colonoscopy. These procedures provide detailed, cross-sectional views of the colon by use of an X-ray machine linked to a computer. A variation of this technique is CT pneumocolon, which uses thicker collimation and intravenous contrast without 3-D reconstruction.

Remember that some codes include both a technical and professional component. To report only the professional component, append modifier 26. To report only the technical component, append modifier TC. To report the complete procedure (eg, both the professional and technical compo-

nents), submit without a modifier. Also, remember that all permanent images must be saved in the patient's medical record.

CPT® Medicine Section—Gastroenterology Codes

Gastroenterology describes services related to function and disorders of the gastrointestinal tract including stomach, intestines, and associated organs. The codes described in this subsection are for diagnostic and therapeutic procedures.

Esophageal Tumors and Lesions

Although a barium X-ray may demonstrate obstructive lesions of the esophagus, endoscopy with biopsy and cytology is a diagnostic approach that is commonly used. A cytology washing, (spraying the surface of the tumor with a jet of water during endoscopy gently abrades the tumor surface) can increase the yield of positive washings.

Codes 91010–91013 report an esophageal motility study. An esophageal motility study is a manometric study of the esophagus or gastroesophageal junction and is performed with or without provocation. Multilumen manometry catheter with at least three separate pressure transducers is passed into the esophagus. The equipment senses "squeeze pressure" at different sites along the esophagus.

Heartburn, with or without regurgitation of gastric contents into the mouth, is a prominent symptom of gastroesophageal reflux disease (GERD). Complications of GERD include esophagitis, esophageal stricture, esophageal ulcer, and Barrett's metaplasia. To diagnose GERD, the physician may perform an esophageal acid reflux test to determine the pH level or acidity of the esophagus.

Practical Coding Note

Codes 91010–91065 and 91122 include the professional and technical components. The codes may be modified by appending modifier 26 or TC.

Biliary drainage with cholecystokinin (CCK) utilizes a light microscope and polarized scope exam of "B" bile for cholesterol and bilirubinate crystals.

The Hollander test is administered to test the completeness of a vagotomy.

A breath hydrogen or methane test, reported with code 91065, is reported for the detection of lactase deficiency, fructose intolerance, bacterial overgrowth, or orocecal gastrointestinal transit in a noninvasive procedure that measures expiratory breath specimens collected in stages over time.

Capsule endoscopy (CPT® 91110-91112) is a procedure to produce images for the diagnosis of gastroenterology diseases, particularly in identifying diseases of the small bowel. For the procedure, the patient swallows a capsule that encases a digital camera, light-emitting diodes, batteries, and a transmitter. Images taken by the camera are transmitted to a recording device worn on a belt by the patient, who is able to perform regular daily activities during the study. The images are downloaded from the belt for review.

The technology helps to evaluate obscure gastrointestinal bleeding (eg, recurrent or persistent iron deficiency anemia, fecal occult blood test (FOBT) positivity, or visible bleeding) after a negative initial or primary endoscopy (colonoscopy or upper endoscopy).

Code 91120 identifies the measurement of rectal sensation, rectal tone, and compliance of the rectal wall and sensory properties in response to controlled balloon distention of the rectum. Guidelines instruct coders to report code 90911 for biofeedback nonrectal sensation testing and code 91122 for anorectal manometry.

HCPCS Level II—Gastroenterology Codes

The HCPCS Level II codebook contains codes for screening exams for Medicare patients. When a Medicare patient is screened for a malignant neoplasm of the gastrointestinal tract, there are several codes located in the HCPCS Level II codebook that should be used instead of codes from the CPT® codebook.

For Medicare patients codes G0104–G0106 and G0120–G0122 are used when performing a sigmoidoscopy, colonoscopy, or barium enema when screening for gastrointestinal malignancies.

Abbreviations

EGD	esophagogastroduodenoscopy
ERCP	endoscopic retrograde cholangiopancreatography
GERD	gastroesophageal reflux disease
GI	gastrointestinal
IBD	inflammatory bowel disease
IBS	irritable bowel syndrome
LLQ	left lower quadrant
LUQ	left upper quadrant
PEG	percutaneous endoscopic gastrostomy
PEH	paraesophageal hernia
RLQ	right lower quadrant
RUQ	right upper quadrant

Section Review 11.3

1. Code peritoneoscopy with laparoscopic partial colectomy and anastomosis.

    A. 44140

    B. 44204

    C. 49320, 44140

    D. 49320, 44204

2. Code intraoral incision and drainage of hematoma of tongue, submandibular space.

    A. 41008

    B. 41009

    C. 41015

    D. 41017

3. Code proximal subtotal pancreatectomy, with total duodenectomy, partial gastrectomy, choledochoenterostomy, and gastrojejunostomy, with pancreatojejunostomy.

    A. 48150

    B. 48152

    C. 48153

    D. 48154

4. A 43-year-old male has a chronic posterior anal fissure. The posterior anal fissure was excised down to the internal sphincter muscle. Which CPT® code should be used?

    A. 46200

    B. 46261

    C. 46270

    D. 46275

5. A 55-year-old patient underwent a repair of an initial left inguinal hernia. An incision was made at the groin and a hernia sac was readily identified and cleared from the surrounding tissue and inverted into the preperitoneal space and plugged. Mesh was tacked to the surrounding muscle layers, and then placed over the entire floor. The correct CPT® code(s) is (are):

    A. 49500-LT

    B. 49505-LT

    C. 49505-LT, 49568

    D. 49650-LT, 49568

Documentation Dissection:

Case 1: Colonoscopy Report

This is a 45-year-old male with <u>rectal pain, rectal bleeding, and some left-sided lower abdominal pain.</u> [1] The colonoscopy procedure and the risks, not limited to bleeding, perforation, infection, side effects from medication, need for surgery, etc., and were fully explained to the patient. An informed consent was taken.

Instrument Used: CF-Q160.

Sedation: Versed 5 mg IV in incremental doses and Demerol 100 mg IV in incremental doses.

Extent of Exam: Up to cecum as identified by ileocecal valve and appendiceal orifice.

Length of Scope Insertion: 110 cm.

Postop Diagnoses/Impression:

1.   Moderate-sized, internal hemorrhoids.

2.   Mild diverticulosis.

Description of Procedure: With the patient being in the left lateral position, first digital examination of the rectum was done, which was unremarkable. Then, the CF-Q160 was <u>passed through the rectum under direct visualization and advanced all the way to cecum.</u> [2] The cecum was identified by ileocecal valve and appendiceal orifice.

There were a couple of <u>tics/diverticula seen on the left side</u> . [3] A careful look was taken while withdrawing the scope. Retroflex view in the rectum showed moderate-sized <u>internal hemorrhoids</u>. [4]

Plan:

1.   Anusol-HC suppositories for hemorrhoids.

2.   High-fiber diet.

3.   If there is no family history, a follow-up colonoscopy in ten years.

----

[1] Reveals the reason for the procedure.

[2] Reveals the extent of the exam on the colon.

[3] Indicates the findings and location of the diagnosed diverticula of the exam.

[4] Internal hemorrhoid originates at the top (rectal side) of the anal canal.

What are the CPT® and ICD-10-CM codes reported?

CPT® Code: 45378

ICD-10-CM Codes: K64.8, K57.90

Rationale: CPT® Code: A diagnostic colonoscopy. In the CPT® Index, look for Endoscopy/Colon/Exploration or Colonoscopy/Proximal to Splenic Flexure and you are directed to code 45378. Verification of the code confirms code selection.

ICD-10-CM Codes: In the Index to Diseases and Injuries, look for Hemorrhoids/internal (without mention of degree) and you are directed to K64.8. Then look for Diverticulosis and you are directed to K57.90. There is no mention of exactly where the diverticulitis is located making this the correct code. Verification of the codes in the Tabular List.

What is/are the ICD-9-CM code(s) reported?

Codes: 455.0, 562.10

Rationale: In the Index to Diseases, look for Hemorrhoids/internal and you are directed to 455.0. Then look for Diverticulosis and you are directed to 562.10. Verification of the codes in the Tabular List confirms code selection.

Case 2: Procedure: Esophagogastroduodenoscopy with placement of feeding tube

Indications: Feeding difficulties. Patient intubated and sedated due to respiratory distress and pneumonia. Placement of NG tube revealed coffee ground emesis. [1]

Endoscopic Procedure Performed: Esophagogastroduodenoscopy performed with regular gastroscope to the second part of duodenum (depth of insertion 100 cm). [2] Diet: NPO >6 hours. Prep: None. Patient was in the supine position. Percutaneous endoscopic gastrostomy [3] placement using a 20 Fr. Ponsky Gauderer pull.

Therapeutic Outcomes: Successful placement of feeding device

Specimens: No specimens obtained

Procedure Medications: 75 mg Meperidine administered by IV; 3 mg Midazolam administered by IV

Recommendations: Can use tube in 4 hrs if bowel sounds are present

Diagnoses:

1. Non-erosive duodenitis of duodenal bulb

2. Normal examination of whole stomach

---

[1] When emesis is referred to as coffee ground it is due to a particular appearance of vomit. This is a classic sign of upper gastrointestinal bleeding.

[2] Shows the extent of the exam.

[3] Also known as a PEG tube, is a tube placed in the patient's stomach for feeding.

What are the CPT® and ICD-10-CM codes reported?

CPT® Code: 43246

ICD-10-CM Codes: R63.3, K29.80

Rationale: CPT® Code: The patient had an EGD with placement of a feeding tube. Look in the CPT® Index for Endoscopy/Gastrointestinal/Upper/Tube placement and you are directed to 43246. Verification of the code confirms code selection.

ICD-10-CM Codes: To support the medical necessity of the feeding tube, look for Difficult, difficulty/feeding and you are directed to R63.3. The provider also diagnosis duodenitis. In the Index to Diseases and Injuries, look for Duodenitis. There is no mention of bleeding so you are directed to K29.80. Verification of both codes in the Tabular List confirms selection.

ICD-9-CM Application

What is/are the ICD-9-CM code(s) reported?

Codes: 783.3, 535.60

Rationale: To support the medical necessity of the feeding tube, look in the Index to Diseases for Difficulty/feeding and you are directed to 783.3. The provider also diagnoses duodenitis. In the Index to Diseases, look for Duodenitis and you are directed to 535.60. Verification of both codes in the Tabular List confirms code selection.

Glossary

Anastomosis—Surgical connection of two tubular structures.

Anoscopy—Procedure that uses a scope to examine the anus.

Bariatric Surgery—Gastric restrictive procedures that are used to treat morbid obesity and are accomplished by placing a restrictive device around the stomach to decrease it functional size.

Barium Enema—Radiographic contrast medium enhanced examination of the colon.

Biliary—Gallbladder, bile, or bile duct.

Bypass—To go around.

Calculus—Concretion of mineral salts, also called a stone.

Cholangiography—Radiographic recording of the bile ducts.

Cholangiopancreatography—Radiographic recording of the biliary system and pancreas.

Cholecystectomy—Surgical removal of the gallbladder.

Cholecystoenterostomy—Creation of a connection between the gallbladder and intestine.

Cholecystography—Radiographic recording of the gallbladder.

Colonoscopy—Endoscopic examination of the entire colon that may include part of the terminal ileum.

Colostomy—Artificial opening between the colon and the abdominal wall.

Congenital—Existing from birth.

Conscious (Moderate) Sedation—A decreased level of consciousness in which the patient is not completely asleep.

Crohn's Disease—Regional enteritis.

Diaphragm—Muscular wall that separates the thoracic and abdominal cavities.

Diaphragmatic Hernia—Hernia of the diaphragm.

Dilatation—Expansion.

Diverticulum—Protrusion of the intestinal wall.

Duodenography—Radiographic recording of the duodenum, or the first part of the small intestine.

Dysphagia—Difficulty swallowing.

Endoscopy—Inspection of body organs or cavities through an existing opening or through a small incision.

Enterolysis—Releasing of adhesions of intestine.

Epiglottidectomy—Excision of the covering of the larynx.

Eventration of Intestines—Protrusion of the intestines through the abdominal wall.

Evisceration—Pulling the viscera outside of the body through an incision.

Exenteration—Major operation during which an organ and its adjacent structures are removed.

Exstrophy—Condition in which an organ is turned inside out.

Exteriorization—To expose an internal structure outside the body for observation, surgery, or experimentation, such creating a passage from the bladder to the abdominal wall.

Fistula—Abnormal opening from one area to another area or outside of the body.

Fluoroscopy—Procedure for viewing the interior of the body using X-rays and projecting the image onto a television screen.

Fulguration—Use of electric current to destroy tissue.

Fundoplasty—Repair of the bottom of an organ or muscle.

Gastrointestinal—Pertaining to the stomach and the intestine.

Gastroplasty—Operation of the stomach for repair or reconfiguration.

Gastrostomy—Artificial opening between the stomach and the abdominal wall.

Hepatography—Radiographic recording of the liver.

Hernia—Organ or tissue protruding through the wall or cavity that usually contains it.

Hypogastric—Lowest middle abdominal area.

Ileostomy—Artificial opening between the ileum and the abdominal wall.

Incarcerated—A constricted, irreducible hernia that may cause obstruction of the organ contained within the hernia.

Intussusception—Slipping of one part of intestine into another part.

Jejunostomy—Artificial opening between the jejunum and the abdominal wall.

Laparoscopy—Exploration of the abdomen and pelvic cavities using a scope placed through a small incision in the abdominal wall.

Lavage—Washing out of an organ.

Marsupialization—Surgical procedure that creates an exterior pouch from an internal abscess.

Omentum—Peritoneal connection between the stomach and other internal organs.

Peritoneal—Within the lining of the abdominal cavity.

Peritoneoscopy—Visualization of the abdominal cavity using a scope placed through a small incision in the abdominal wall.

Polyp—Tumor on a pedicle that bleeds easily and may become malignant.

Proctosigmoidoscopy—Endoscopic examination of the sigmoid colon and rectum.

Reanastomosis—Reconnection of a previous connection between two places organs or spaces.

Rectocele—Herniation of the rectal wall through the posterior wall of the vagina.

Reducible—Able to be corrected or put back into a normal position.

Sialolithotomy—Surgical removal of a stone located in the salivary gland or duct.

Varices—Varicose veins.

Volvulus—Twisted section of intestine.

Urinary System and Male Genital System

Introduction

In this chapter, we will explore the anatomy and function of the kidneys, ureters, bladder, and urethra. We also will cover diseases and procedures for the male genital system. Because urine must pass through the prostate when leaving the male body, there are significant diseases affecting the male reproductive system. We will discuss a few of these, as well.

Objectives

The objectives for this chapter include:

- Describe the anatomy of the urinary system
- Describe the anatomy and functions of the male reproductive system (the female reproductive system is covered elsewhere)
- Understand the structures and processes forming and eliminating urine
- Understand and learn where to locate diseases specific to the urinary system within ICD-10-CM
- Learn the components of the CPT® codebook specific to the genitourinary system and male genital system
- Determine when and how to apply modifiers
- Discover which HCPCS Level II codes are significant to the genitourinary system

Anatomy and Medical Terminology

The Urinary System

The urinary system removes waste called urea from your blood. Urea is produced when foods are broken down in the body. Urea is carried in the bloodstream to the kidneys. The urinary system works with the lungs, skin, and intestines to keep chemicals and water in your body balanced.

The urinary system of the human body consists of two kidneys, two ureters, one bladder, and one urethra. In ICD-10-CM and CPT® coding, terms such as renal and nephro usually are interchangeable. The definition of renal is pertinent to the kidney, the meaning of nephro is kidney.

Within the renal sinus of the kidney is the renal pelvis. The renal pelvis (pyelo-) is the expanded proximal end of the ureter (where the ureter attaches to the kidney). It receives urine through the major calyces. The primary function of the renal

pelvis is to act as a funnel for urine flowing to the ureter. Urine passes through the ureters and flows into the bladder, where it is stored.

At the time of urination, the bladder muscles will tighten and squeeze urine from the bladder into the urethra. The urethra is the outlet for urine to exit the body. The proximal opening of the urethra is called the bladder neck: In men, it is adjacent to the prostate gland. If the bladder neck does not open appropriately or completely during voiding, the bladder neck may become obstructed. This can be caused in men by an enlarged prostate. In women, vaginal or pelvic prolapse is the most common cause of bladder neck obstruction.

The kidneys are bean-shaped organs approximately the size of your fist. They are located near the middle of the back, just below the rib cage to the left and right of the spine. Kidneys remove urea from the blood through tiny filtering units called nephrons. Each nephron consists of a ball formed of small capillaries, called a glomerulus, and a small tube called a renal tubule. Urea, together with water and other waste substances, form urine as they pass through the nephrons down the renal tubules of the kidney.

The ureters are muscular tubes carrying urine from the kidneys to the bladder. Ureters originate in the renal pelvis and end in the bladder. They are approximately 25–30 cm (10-12 inches) long and 3-4 mm in diameter. The muscles in the ureter walls constantly tighten and relax (peristalsis) to force urine downward away from the kidneys. If urine is allowed to stand still, or back up, a kidney infection (pyelonephritis) can develop.

The urinary bladder is a hollow, muscular, expandable organ collecting urine. It can be referred to as "vesical" or "cyst" in coding of procedures. The bladder sits on the pelvic floor and is held in place by ligaments attached to other organs and the pelvic bones. The bladder stores urine until nerves from the bladder send a message to the brain that the bladder is full and the urge to empty (void) intensifies. When you urinate, the brain signals the bladder muscles to tighten, squeezing urine out of the bladder. At the same time, the brain signals the sphincter muscles to relax. As these muscles relax, urine exits the bladder through the urethra.

The urethra is a tube connecting the urinary bladder to the outside of the body. In the male, the urethra is the conduit for fluid waste and semen. It is shaped like an "S" to follow the line of the penis. The portion of the urethra passing through the prostate gland is known as the prostatic urethra. The prostatic portion of the urethra passes along the neck of the urinary bladder (vesical or bladder neck) and through the prostate gland. This section of the urethra is designed to accept the drainage from the tiny ducts within the prostate and is equipped with two ejaculatory tubes. The female urethra is straight, approximately 4 cm long, and leads out of the body via the urethral orifice and has no reproductive function.

Urinary System with Renal Pelvis

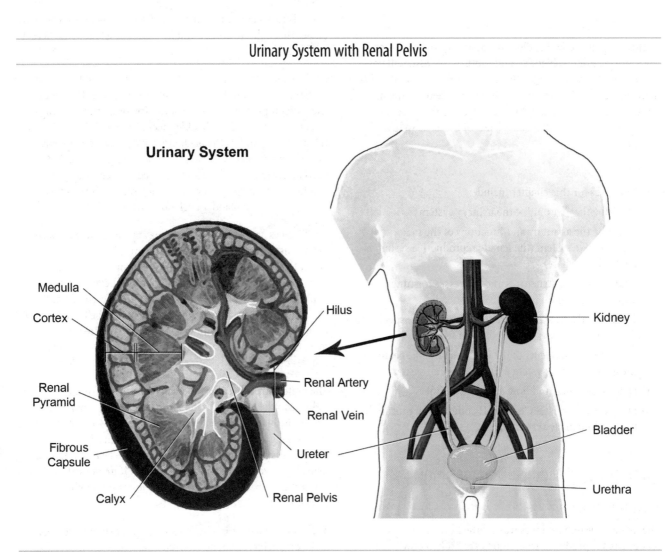

Source: AAPC

Male Reproductive System

The male reproductive system consists of the testicles (or testes), the duct system (which includes the epididymis and vas deferens), and the accessory glands (which include the seminal vesicles, prostate gland, and the bulbourethral glands [Cowper's glands]).

The testes produce and store sperm cells. They are surrounded on the front and sides by a serous membrane called the tunica vaginalis. The testicles are oval shaped and about 2 inches (5 cm) in length and 1 inch (3 cm) in diameter in the adult male.

They are considered part of the endocrine system because they secrete hormones. As a male develops, the pituitary gland—which is located near the brain—induces the testicles to produce testosterone.

The epididymis and vas deferens (deferent duct) make up the duct system. The epididymis is a coiled tube within the scrotum that connects the testicles to the vas deferens. The vas deferens is a muscular tube that transports semen from the epididymis into the pelvis, and then connects to the prostatic urethra.

The scrotum holds testicles outside the body. The testicles need to be kept cooler than body temperature to create sperm. When the body is cold, the scrotum shrinks to hold the testes closer to the body and save heat; when it is warm, the scrotum becomes larger to get rid of extra heat.

Seminal vesicles are a pair of tubular glands located behind the bladder and above the prostate gland. They are sac-like structures and measure about 5 cm (2 inches) in length. The seminal vesicles and prostate gland, also known as the accessory sex glands, provide fluids that lubricate the duct system and nourish the sperm.

Sperm develop in the testicles within a system of tiny tubes called the seminiferous tubules. Testosterone and other hormones cause the cells to transform into sperm cells. These cells then use their tails to push themselves into the epididymis, where they complete their development. Sperm then move to the vas deferens, or sperm duct.

The prostate gland surrounds the neck of the bladder and urethra in a male. It is approximately the size of a walnut. It is partly muscular and partly glandular. It is made up of three lobes: a center lobe, a right lobe, and a left lobe. The function of the prostate gland is to secrete the liquid portion of the seminal fluid. Seminal fluid carries sperm. During orgasm, the muscular glands of the prostate help to propel the prostate fluid and sperm (produced in the testicles) into the urethra. The semen leaves through the tip of the penis during ejaculation.

The penis is made up of two parts: the shaft and the glans. The shaft is the main part of the penis and the glans is the tip (sometimes called the head) of the penis. At the end of the glans is a small slit or opening called the meatus. This is where semen and urine exit the body through the urethra. The foreskin, or prepuce, is the loose skin covering the end of the penis. Excision of the prepuce is called circumcision.

Section Review 12.1

1. Where is urine formed?

    A. Kidneys

    B. Renal Pelvis

    C. Bladder

    D. Ureters

2. Urine is expelled from the body through the:

    A. Ureters

    B. Bladder

    C. Urethra

    D. Seminal vesicles

3. What are the reproductive glands located in the scrotum?

    A. Urethra

    B. Vas Deferens

    C. Seminal Vesicles

    D. Testes

4. Which organ is not considered part of the urinary system?

    A. Kidney

    B. Bladder

    C. Spleen

    D. Urethra

---

5. Which gland in the male reproductive system is partly muscular and partly glandular?

   A. Prostate

   B. Seminal Vesicle

   C. Bladder Neck

   D. Testes

Key Roots, Suffixes, and Prefixes for the Genitourinary System

By using the prefixes and suffixes, you are able to ascertain the description of most any condition. For instance, -cele: rectocele (prolapse of the rectum into the vagina), cystocele (prolapse of the bladder into the vagina), urethrocele (prolapse of the urethra into the vagina).

-cele	herniation, or prolapse
cyst/o	relating to a bladder
dys-	painful, bad, disordered, difficult
-ectomy	excision, surgical removal
ex/o	outside of, without
hydr/o	relating to fluid, water or hydrogen
-ia	state of being, condition (abnormal)
-ia/sis	condition of
-itis	inflammation
lith/o	calcification, stone
-lysis	destroy
nephr/o	relating to the kidney
-oma	tumor
orchi/o	relating to the testicles
-orrhaphy	suturing
osche/o	relating to the scrotum
-oscopy	to examine through a scope
-osis	condition, process
-ostomy	indicates a surgically created artificial opening
-otomy	incision into
-pexy	fixation or suspension
pyel/o	relating to the renal pelvis
vesic/o	relating to the urinary bladder

ICD-10-CM Coding

Abnormalities of the urinary tract are among the most common birth defects, affecting as many as one in 10 babies. Some of these abnormalities are minor problems, many causing no symptoms (such as having two ureters leading from one kidney to the bladder). Other abnormalities cause problems such as urinary tract infections, blockages, pain, kidney damage or failure, stasis (stagnation of normal flow), and formation of stones (calculi).

Some of the most common urinary tract defects include renal agenesis, hydronephrosis, polycystic kidney disease, multicystic kidneys, lower urinary tract obstruction, bladder exstrophy and epispadias, hypospadias, and ambiguous genitalia.

Common diagnoses related to draining a perirenal or renal abscess include renal and perinephric abscess, complications of transplanted kidney, and kidney replaced by transplant. A nephrectomy (removal of a kidney) may be performed on a patient with a diagnosis of a malignant neoplasm of the ureteric orifice, malignant neoplasm of the kidney, malignant neoplasm of renal pelvis, congenital obstruction of uretero-vesical junction, or complete disruption of kidney parenchyma.

Coders should have an understanding of potential documentation problems and know what to do when they encounter such problems.

Example

In ICD-10-CM Alphabetic Index the main term Urosepsis directs the coder to code to condition. The ICD-10-CM Official Guidelines for Coding and Reporting, I.C.1.d.(ii)., indicates there is no default code for the term urosepsis. If urosepsis is stated as the diagnosis, the coder must query the provider for additional information to determine the correct code.

A policy regarding the meaning of urosepsis and salient parts of that policy could be attached to the medical record to further document the patient's condition. In any case, seek clarification from the physician when urosepsis is documented. Find out if the physician means the patient has a urinary tract infection, or sepsis. Review expansive information on coding sepsis and urosepsis in the Official Guidelines for Coding and Reporting.

Diseases specific to the kidneys, ureters, bladder, and urethra are covered primarily in chapter 14 of ICD-10-CM, Diseases of the Genitourinary System (N00-N99). The diseases are listed in anatomical order beginning with the kidney, followed by the ureters, bladder, and urethra. These are followed by Diseases of the Male Genital Organs (N40-N53), which also are listed in anatomical order beginning with the prostate, followed by the testes and penis. Diagnoses for the genitourinary system also can be found in the Congenital Malformation, Deformations, and chromosomal Abnormalities chapter 17, Neoplasm chapter 2, and the chapter 18 for Symptoms, Signs, and Abnormal Clinical and Laboratory Findings, Not Elsewhere Classified.

Diseases of the Genitourinary System (N00-N99)

Inflammation and infection codes usually are located at the beginning of each anatomic section, and often are identified by the suffix -itis. Chapter 14 begins with glomerular diseases which include glomerulonephritis, nephrotic syndrome, nephritis, and nephropathy.

Nephritis is inflammation of the kidneys. It usually is caused by bacteria or their toxins. Glomerulonephritis is a form of nephritis in which lesions primarily involve the glomeruli. This condition may be acute, rapidly progressive, or chronic. Nephrotic syndrome is a condition marked by increased glomerular permeability to proteins. It usually is caused by glomerular injury. The codes for nephritis, glomerulonephritis and nephrotic syndrome (categories N00-N12) are located in an area of ICD-10-CM where combination codes are utilized and may include both conditions with the use of one code.

Pyelonephritis (category N10-N16) is an infection of the kidney. It differs from nephritis in that pyelonephritis is usually the result of a bacterial infection that has ascended from the urinary bladder. If the organism causing the infection is known, use an additional code to identify the organism. In most cases, Escherichia coli (E. coli) is the responsible microbe (B96.20-B96.29).

Example

Acute pyelonephritis due to E. Coli

N10 Acute tubulo-interstitial nephritis

B96.20 Unspecified Escherichia coli [E. coli] as the cause of diseases classified elsewhere

Note: In the ICD-10-CM Tabular List, under category N10 Infections of kidney, you will find use additional instructions:

Use additional code (B95-B97), to identify infectious agent.

Hydronephrosis (N13) is the accumulation of fluid in the renal pelvis and kidney due to a urinary obstruction. If the obstruction is not treated, the urine may cause infection. Some causes of obstruction are kidney or ureteral stones, neurogenic bladder, and hyperplasia of the prostate (BPH) or enlargement of the prostate. Neurogenic bladder is a dysfunction of the urinary bladder caused by the nerves supplying the bladder, or lesions of the central nervous system.

Renal (kidney) failure (N17-N19) is inability of the kidneys to function properly. There are many causes for renal failure. The condition may be partial, temporary, acute, chronic, or complete. In chronic kidney disease (CKD) (N18), the kidneys' ability to filter waste from the blood declines slowly. CKD has five stages, based on the patient's glomerular filtration rate (GFR). According to the National Kidney Foundation (NKF), the stages of CKD are:

Stage	GFR
Stage 1	> 90
Stage 2	60-89
Stage 3	30-59
Stage 4	15-29
Stage 5	0-14

End-stage renal disease (ESRD-N18.6) is the stage of chronic renal failure requiring renal replacement therapies. These may include dialysis (the process of removing toxic materials from the blood) or kidney transplantation. When the documentation states the patient has CKD, stage 5, and the patient requires chronic dialysis, ESRD (N18.6) is reported.

Encounters for patients presenting with hypertension and chronic kidney disease (CKD) are coded from the ICD-10-CM categories I12-I13. Although coders rarely are allowed to assume information that is not documented specifically, ICD-10-CM guidelines state whenever a patient has both chronic kidney disease and hypertension (presume cause and effect relationship), you should code primary hypertension from category I13 unless secondary hypertension (category I15) is specified in the documentation. Secondary hypertension is defined as high arterial blood pressure due to or with a variety of primary diseases, such as renal disorders, CNS disorders, endocrine, and vascular diseases.

Renovascular disease can be coded as malignant, benign, or unspecified. Renovascular disease is a progressive condition caused by narrowing or blockage of the renal arteries or veins. Generally, this term describes three disorders:

1. Renal artery occlusion: The arteries carrying blood to the kidneys are blocked. This condition can affect one or both of the arteries. Renal veins carry the filtered blood away from the kidneys to the inferior vena cava.

2. Renal vein thrombosis: A rare condition occurring when one or both of these veins develop clots.

3. Renal atheroembolism: Fatty materials build up and block the renal arterioles (the smallest arteries leading to the capillaries).

Calculi (stones) are reported by location: kidney (N20.0) or ureter (N20.1), kidney with ureter (N20.2), or lower urinary tract (N22). Although the male patient may have a diagnosis of prostatic calcification (stone within the prostate, N42.0), most calculi are located in the urinary system. If the stone is small, the patient may pass it without surgical intervention. If the stone cannot be passed, additional treatment—including surgery or procedures to break up the stone so that it can be passed—may be necessary.

Impaired renal function resulting from other conditions is coded from category N25. Some conditions causing impaired renal function include renal osteodystrophy, nephrogenic diabetes insipidus, and secondary hyperparathyroidism. The underlying disease is coded first, followed by a code to describe the renal impairment from category N25. To use these codes, the physician must document specifically the condition is caused by the impaired renal function.

Diabetes insipidus causes renal impairment through excessive urination, due either to inadequate amounts of the antidiuretic hormone in the body (central diabetes insipidus, E23.2), or by failure of the kidney to respond to the antidiuretic hormone (nephrogenic diabetes insipidus, N25.1). Nephrogenic diabetes can cause severe dehydration if undiagnosed.

Hyperparathyroidism is an excessive level of parathyroid hormone in the body. The parathyroid is responsible for maintaining serum calcium levels. When parathyroid hormone levels are elevated, increased bone reabsorption, decreased new bone formation, and decreased bone mass result (renal osteodystrophy, N25.0).

Small kidney, category N27, may be unilateral or bilateral. It can result from several conditions. Congenital dysplasia is when the kidney does not grow with the rest of the body or is small at birth. The kidney also can be damaged because of a blockage in drainage (reflux nephropathy); severe kidney infection (pyelonephritis); decreased blood supply to the kidney; or glomerulonephritis. If one kidney is small and the other one is completely normal, it is possible to lead a normal life. One small kidney may cause problems such as high blood pressure, even if the other kidney is normal. If both kidneys are small, there may be inadequate excretion.

Potential Locations of Renal Calculi

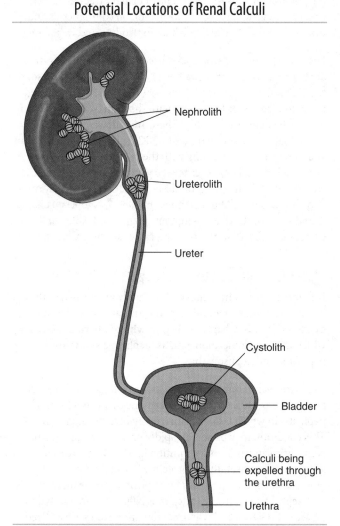

Nephrolith

Ureterolith

Ureter

Cystolith

Bladder

Calculi being expelled through the urethra

Urethra

Source: EHRLICH/SCHROEDER. Medical Terminology for Health Professions, 6E. © 2009 Delmar Learning, a part of Cengage Learning, Inc. Reproduced by permission. www.cengage.com/permissions

Kidney disorders such as nephroptosis, hypertrophy of the kidney, kidney cysts, strictures of the ureter, hydroureter, postural proteinuria, vesicoureteral reflux, vascular disorders of the kidney, ureteral fistula, and other unspecified disorders of the kidney and ureter are coded in category N28.

Subcategory code N28.1 is used for acquired cysts of the kidney. Acquired cysts rarely show symptoms but can indicate a patient has a higher risk of renal cell carcinoma. For this reason, this diagnosis may be used for a kidney ultrasound or CT to screen the patient for renal cell carcinoma. If a patient has congenital cyst of the kidney, a diagnosis code from subcategory Q61.0x *Congenital renal cyst* is reported.

Vesicoureteral reflux (VUR), N13.7-, is the backflow of urine from the bladder into the ureter. This typically is due to a congenital anomaly of the ureterovesical junction. VUR is a common cause of urinary tract infections in children. It is diagnosed in children by performing a renal ultrasound and then a voiding cystourethrography. The fifth character selection is based on whether the patient also has reflux nephropathy, and the sixth character further specifies without or without hydroureter, unilateral or bilateral.

Other Diseases of Urinary System (N30-N39)

Cystitis (N30) is inflammation of the bladder, usually because of a urinary tract infection (UTI). Many diseases and procedures pertaining to the bladder begin with the prefix cyst-, such as cystitis (inflammation of the bladder). There are many forms of cystitis; they are classified as acute, chronic, interstitial, and trigonitis. Interstitial cystitis, also known as painful bladder syndrome, is a chronic inflammation of the bladder, usually with an unknown etiology (cause). People with interstitial cystitis usually cannot hold much urine in their bladders and may experience urinary frequency. Treatment for interstitial cystitis can include medication or hydrodistention of the bladder, which alleviates many of the symptoms.

Voiding disorders (N32) are conditions affecting normal functions of urinating and can include bladder neck obstruction, bladder diverticulum, neurogenic bladder, and detrusor instability. Urinary incontinence is probably the most common voiding disorder. These disorders can be found in "signs and symptoms" subcategory code R32.

Types of incontinence are:

- Urge incontinence: Leakage of urine occurring immediately after an urgent, irrepressible need to void
- Stress incontinence: Leakage of urine due to abrupt increases in intra-abdominal pressure caused by coughing, sneezing, laughing, bending, or lifting
- Overflow incontinence: Dribbling of urine from an overly full bladder
- Functional incontinence: Urine loss due to cognitive or physical impairments such as stroke or dementia
- Mixed incontinence: Any combination of the above types of incontinence

With the exception of stress incontinence, the ICD-10-CM codes are not gender specific.

Urinary tract infection (UTI) (N39.0) is a bacterial infection affecting any part of the urinary tract. When bacteria, usually E. coli, get into the bladder or kidney and multiply in the urine, the result may be a UTI. A UTI usually presents with dysuria (painful burning on urination), frequency of urination, urgency, and cloudy urine. Although uncomfortable, a UTI is treated easily with antibiotics. The young and women are more prone to UTIs. In women this is because the urethra is shorter than in men and the infection may be related to sexual activity. In the elderly, UTI frequency is equal in men and women, with increased incidence in men due partly to enlargement

of the prostate. As the prostate enlarges, it can press on the urethra causing obstruction resulting in urination and bladder problems. When less urine is flushing the urethra, there is a higher incidence of E. Coli colonization. Although there is no single cause for UTIs, a predisposition for UTIs may run in families. Patients with diabetes and anatomical malformations of the urinary tract and paralysis may experience UTIs more frequently.

When the organism causing the UTI is known, such as E. Coli, use an additional code to report the organism. When it is not known, it is not necessary to report an additional code.

Example

UTI due to E. Coli

N39.0 Urinary tract infection, site not specified

B96.20 Unspecified Escherichia coli [E. coli] as the cause of diseases classified elsewhere

Note: In the ICD-10-CM Tabular List, under N39.0, you will find an instructional note to Use additional code (B95-B97), to identify infectious agent.

Diseases of the Male Genital Organs (N40-N53)

Prostate

One of the most common disorders of the prostate is benign hyperplasia of the prostate (BPH), coded in category N40 *Enlarged Prostate*. BPH is a benign enlargement of the prostate gland caused by excessive growth of prostatic nodules. If the prostate gland becomes enlarged, the urethra may become compressed, resulting in partial or complete obstruction and causing symptoms of urinary hesitancy, frequency, dysuria (painful urination), urinary retention, and an increased risk of urinary tract infections. These symptoms commonly are referred to as LUTS (lower urinary tract symptoms). There is no specific code for LUTS; you will need to code each symptom individually.

Prostatitis (N41) is inflammation of the prostate gland, usually because of infection. It can be either acute or chronic, and is easily treatable. A patient presenting with prostatitis may have an elevated prostate specific antigen (PSA). If this is the case, the patient will need to be monitored closely because an elevated PSA may be an indicator of prostate cancer. Elevated PSA without a diagnosis of cancer should be coded as an abnormal finding in category R97.2. Dysplasia of the prostate is abnormal shape and size of the tissues of the prostate. It can be a pre-malignant condition. If the documentation states prostatic intraepithelial neoplasia III (PIN III), ICD-10-CM code D07.5 *Carcinoma in situ of prostate* should be used. PIN I and PIN II are coded to N42.3 for dysplasia of the prostate.

Spermatic Cord, Testis, Tunica Vaginalis, Epididymis

Hydrocele (N43) is an accumulation of serous fluid in a sac-like cavity, especially the spermatic cord, testis, or tunica vaginalis. Encysted hydrocele describes a cyst above the testis. When an infection is noted in a hydrocele, an additional code is used to report the infecting organism, if known.

Orchitis (N45) is an inflammation of the testis, which can be caused by trauma, ischemia, metastasis, mumps, or secondary infection. Epididymitis is an inflammation of the epididymis, usually because of infection, or—rarely—due to trauma. When orchitis or epididymitis is present due to another disease, the underlying disease is coded first.

Penis

Phimosis is a stricture, stenosis, or narrowing of the preputial orifice preventing the foreskin from being pushed back over the glans penis. Phimosis (N47.1) and balanitis (N48.1) are the most common diagnosis codes reported when a circumcision is performed on an infant. Use code Z41.2 *Encounter for routine and ritual male circumcision*, unless there is a medical reason to perform the procedure.

Male infertility codes are listed within category N46 and include azoospermia (absence of spermatozoa in the semen), oligospermia (insufficient number of sperm in the semen), and extratesticular causes of infertility.

Penile disorders such as leukoplakia of penis (white, thickened patches on glans penis), balanoposthitis (inflammation of glans penis and prepuce), other inflammatory disorders of penis and priapism (prolonged penile erection), vascular disorders, edema, impotence, and Peyronie's disease (curvature of the erect penis) are coded in category N48.

Congenital Malformations of Genital Organs (Q50-Q56)

The most common congenital problems of the penis are hypospadias (Q54.-) and epispadias (Q64.0). These conditions are abnormal urethral meati. In hypospadias, the urethral meatus is on the underside of the penis instead of at the end. This is the more common of the two conditions. Epispadias is when the meatus is on the upper side of the penis. These conditions occur in several levels of severity and usually require surgical repair in childhood.

Neoplasms

Genitourinary cancer diagnoses are found within the Neoplasm chapter of ICD-10-CM and are specific to the anatomy of the organ. It is important for the coder to read documentation closely to identify the information needed to choose the most specific code. Use the Table of Neoplasms to select codes to describe primary and secondary (metastatic) tumors, benign tumors, and tissue of uncertain behavior. Uncertain behavior neoplasm codes should only be reported when the pathologist has documented the tissue has characteristics of several different diseases, or when it is described as hypoplasia or pre-cancerous. It should also be coded when the specific morphology indicates the neoplasm is of uncertain behavior.

Within the genitourinary and male reproductive systems, the kidney, bladder, prostate, testes, and penis are the most likely areas to develop cancer with smoking being the major risk factor for bladder and kidney cancer.

Renal cell carcinoma (RCC) is the most common type of kidney cancer. It occurs twice as frequently in men as in women. RCC includes clear cell, papillary, chromophobe, and collecting duct carcinomas, and is difficult to detect in its early stages. Classic symptoms, which usually occur in the late course of the disease, are blood in the urine (hematuria), flank pain, palpable mass, recurrent fever, rapid weight loss, abdominal or lower back pain, or fatigue.

Bladder cancer is 3–4 times more common in men than women and the fifth most common cancer in the U.S. When diagnosed in a localized stage, bladder cancer is very treatable. Smoking, as well as chronic bladder problems such as infections and kidney stones, are risk factors. Types of bladder cancer include:

- Transitional cell bladder cancer begins in the cells lining the bladder; cancers confined to the lining of the bladder are superficial bladder cancers.
- Squamous cell bladder cancer begins in squamous cells, which are thin, flat cells that may form in the bladder after long-term infection or irritation.
- Adenocarcinoma develops in the inner lining of the bladder, usually because of chronic irritation and inflammation.

Prostate cancer is the second most common cause of cancer-related death in men in the U.S. Prostate cancer can be slow growing or aggressive. Treatment options range from observation, to surgery, radiation, hormonal therapy, and chemotherapy. Symptoms include painful or burning urination, inability to urinate or difficulty in starting to urinate, blood in the urine or semen, frequent or urgent need to urinate, and lower back, pelvic, or thigh pain. Age is the most significant risk factor; screening for prostate cancer is recommended for men over the age of 50.

Testicular cancer most often occurs in young men. Types of testicular cancer include:

- Germ cell tumors, which occur in the cells that produce sperm

- Stromal tumors occur in the testicular tissue where hormones are produced

Symptoms include a small, hard, often painless lump, change in testicular consistency, feeling of heaviness in the scrotum, ache in the lower abdomen or groin, sudden collection of fluid in the scrotum, and pain or discomfort in the testicle or scrotum.

Penile cancer is rare. The most common types of penile cancer are squamous cell carcinoma, adenocarcinoma, melanoma, basal cell penile cancer, and sarcoma. Symptoms include a wart-like growth or lesion, open sore that will not heal, reddish rash, and persistent, smelly discharge under the foreskin. The most common causative factor is poor hygiene.

Injuries and Complications

Injuries to the genitourinary organs are located in the Injury, Poisoning, and Certain Other Consequences of External Causes section (S30-S39) for injuries of the kidney and pelvic organs and subcategory S39 for injuries of external genitalia. Codes for intraoperative and postprocedural complications and disorders of genitourinary system are in category N99.

The Injury, Poisoning, and Certain Other Consequences of External Causes section includes complications of genitourinary prosthetic devices, implants and grafts, which include inflammation, infection, leakage, displacement and mechanical complications of genitourinary devices (T83).

Symptoms, Signs, and Abnormal Clinical and Laboratory Findings

Symptoms and signs involving the genitourinary System (R30-R39), the digestive system and abdomen (R10-R19), and male genital organs (N40-N53) often are used when a final diagnosis is not documented.

At times, a patient will be referred to an urologist for an abnormal digital rectal exam. Although there is no specific diagnosis, R68.89 would be an appropriate diagnosis. Screening for malignant neoplasms for the prostate, bladder, or other genitourinary organs are codes from category Z12.-.

Section Review 12.2

1. Mrs. Green is a 53-year-old woman with bilateral nephrolithiasis. What is the ICD-10-CM code?

    A. N20.1
    B. N21.1
    C. N20.0
    D. E83.59, N29

2. Mr. Jones is a pleasant 85-year-old male who has gross hematuria, likely from a prostatic source. He has had a TURP in the past. What is the ICD-10-CM code for gross hematuria?

    A. N40.0
    B. R31.9
    C. R31.0
    D. R31.2

3. Jake is a 16-year-old male involved in an MVA this morning. He was the only occupant of the vehicle. No other details are available. CT examination shows the patient has a minor fractured (lacerated) right kidney. What is the ICD-10-CM code for the fractured kidney?

    A. S37.001A
    B. S37.091A
    C. S37.041A
    D. S37.011A

---

4.   The patient is a 68-year-old male with urinary retention and enlarged prostate gland. He has failed conservative treatment and presents for TURP. What is/are the ICD-10-CM code(s)?

    A. N40.1, R33.8

    B. R33.8, N40.1

    C. N40.0

    D. N41.9

5.   Mr. James is a well-known patient with a known bladder diverticulum with calculus. What is the ICD-10-CM code?

    A. K57.90

    B. N21.8

    C. N32.3

    D. N21.0

6.   Mr. Brown presents today with a sudden onset of chills and fever with dull pain in the flank over the kidneys, which are tender when palpated. He has urgency and frequency of urination. Diagnosis is acute pyelonephritis. What is the ICD-10-CM code?

    A. N12

    B. N11.0

    C. N11.8

    D. N10

7.   Mr. Black is a 53-year-old male who presents today for follow up of his stress incontinence. He has been using timed voiding and Kegel exercises but his symptoms continue. Code the diagnosis.

    A. N39.41

    B. R32

    C. N39.46

    D. N39.3

8.   A 60-year-old man with prostate cancer is status post radical prostatectomy. Prostate specific antigen (PSA) test detects high-grade disease. He is here to discuss gold fiducial marker seed placement for adjuvant radiation therapy. What is the ICD-10-CM code?

    A. Z85.46

    B. C61

    C. D40.0

    D. D49.5

9.   This is a 65-year-old woman who was found to have a right renal tumor and is status post hand-assisted laparoscopic nephrectomy. Pathology report reveals a diagnosis of renal oncocytoma. What is the ICD-10-CM code?

    A. D30.01

    B. C64.9

    C. C65.1

    D. D30.11

10. Mr. White is a 13-year-old male who presents with complaints of urinary hesitancy, frequency and dysuria. A microscopic urinalysis confirmed the presence of white blood cells (WBC) and diagnosis of UTI is confirmed. What is the ICD-10-CM code?

   A. R35.0

   B. R39.11

   C. R30.0

   D. N39.0

CPT® Coding

Urinary System (50010–53899)

The Urinary System section of CPT® includes procedures on the kidneys, ureters, bladder, and urethra. You will notice CPT® begins with the kidney and follows the anatomy of the body. Urine is created in the kidneys and flows from the kidneys to the ureters, from the ureters to the bladder where it is stored, and finally leaves the bladder via the urethra.

Practical Coding Note

CPT® Professional Edition has an illustration of the Urinary System section. Circle the enlarged, upper end of the ureter, where it connects to the kidney, and label it renal pelvis. The prefix pyel/o refers to the renal pelvis. Some procedures performed on the renal pelvis include pyelotomy and pyeloplasty, and are found in the subsection for the kidneys.

Each subsection contains incision codes, excision codes, repair codes, and—with the exception of the ureter—"other procedure" codes. There is a subsection under the urethra for codes performed via a scope. Read the description of each code carefully; some of the procedures specifically state unilateral or bilateral. If procedures do not state "bilateral," and the procedure is performed on both the right and left sides, modifier 50 or the RT and/or LT modifiers, depending upon the carrier, need to be added. Bilateral services may be billed for procedures on the kidneys and ureters only. The bladder and urethra are singular structures.

Use of an operating microscope is not included with many of these codes and should be reported separately using CPT® 69990. Reading the description of each code and the associated information noted below each code will assist you when choosing the correct and complete code(s).

A surgical endoscopy (eg, laparoscopy, cystoscopy) always includes any diagnostic endoscopy performed at the same session; diagnostic endoscopy is not reported separately.

Kidney (50010–50593)

Incision

An incision into an organ or structure can be made for diagnostic purposes (such as obtaining tissue for a biopsy), for foreign body or stone removal, to explore the organ, or to drain fluid or place a tube for fluid drainage. Access to the organ can be obtained using a knife, electrosurgical unit, or laser. Procedures ending with -otomy (eg, pylonephrotomy) typically are coded with incision codes for the specific location. Incision codes include stent and catheter insertions.

Treatment for renal abscess can be open or percutaneous. An open treatment for draining an infection (abscess) on the kidney or on the surrounding renal tissue begins with a small incision in the skin of the flank. Muscles, fat, and fibrous membranes overlying the kidney are cut and a portion of the eleventh or twelfth rib may be removed to facilitate the procedure. The abscess cavity is explored and irrigated and multiple drainage tubes (for example, dePezzer or Malecot catheter) are inserted through a separate stab incision. The drain tube ends are sutured to the skin. The fascia and muscles are sutured and the wound is packed with gauze, and the skin and subcutaneous tissue may be left open for drainage to prevent formation of a secondary body wall abscess.

Practical Coding Note

CPT® code 49020 describes open drainage of peritoneal abscess. Make a note next to CPT® code 50020 to see 49020 for peritoneal abscess.

Nephrotomy is an incision into the kidney for exploration. Pyelotomy (50120) and nephrotomy (50045) are not the same procedure, although both procedures are done on or within the kidney. Nephrotomy relates to the kidney and pyelotomy relates to the renal pelvis, which is the larger superior portion of the ureter.

Stones also can be removed from the kidney by an open incision. This is referred to as nephrolithotomy (nephr/o=kidney, lith/o=calculus, tomy=incision into) with calculus removal. The kidney usually is approached through a flank incision. The muscles below the skin are cut and the 12th rib may be removed to facilitate access. The kidney is freed from the fatty tissue surrounding it, and the renal artery is identified. The kidney is injected with a drug protecting the kidney from damage while its blood supply is cut off. A sheet of waterproof material is placed around the kidney, and a solution of iced saline is poured over it to induce hypothermia. After X-rays are taken to identify the location of calculi, an incision is made into the convex portion of the kidney tissue over the area where the calculus is located. The calculus is removed, and the interior of the kidney is examined for the presence of other calculi. The area is irrigated with sterile fluid to wash out any calculus fragments. If any of the calyces are obstructed or stenotic (abnormally narrowed), they are repaired. The incision of the kidney is closed. The kidney is returned to its bed of fatty tissue on the back of the abdominal cavity and the fascia surrounding it is closed with sutures. A drain tube is inserted into the wound and a layered closure is performed to close the wound. CPT® 50060 is reported for this procedure.

Use code 50065 when a second surgery needs to be performed to remove the calculus. Use code 50070 when the removal of a calculus is complicated by a congenital kidney abnormality such as an ectopic kidney or horseshoe kidney.

Percutaneous (through the skin) removal of stones (50080–50081) is coded by the size of the stone, and usually will require fluoroscopic guidance and an existing nephrostomy tube or tract. A small incision is made into the skin and a passageway is created either to the kidney (nephrostomy) or the kidney pelvis (pyelostomy). A guidewire and dilators may be passed through an endoscope during the procedure. The calculus may be removed using forceps, a basket, or lithotriptor (an instrument that crushes the stone). A stent (a tube that holds the ureter open for drainage) may be inserted to prevent postoperative swelling. The stent insertion is not reported separately.

In most cases, the nephrostomy tube has been placed during a previous surgical setting; if this is not the case, a nephrostomy tract must be created and reported using CPT® 50395.

Practical Coding Note

For endoscopic removal of a calculus, use CPT® codes:

Renal
50561 if through established nephrostomy or pyelostomy

or 50580 if through nephrotomy or pyelotomy

Ureteral
50961 if through established ureterostomy

or 50980 if through ureterotomy

Ureter and Pelvis
52320 for cystourethroscopy or

52352 for cystourthreroscopy with ureterscopy and/or pyeloscopy

---

Excision

Excision codes describe either total or partial removal of the organ. It is important to note that code 50200, for percutaneous renal biopsy, has a parenthetical note indicating to report code 10022 if the renal biopsy is performed by fine needle aspiration. Excision procedures are considered open procedures. If, within the procedural note, the surgeon states "-ectomy," the excision/removal codes within CPT® should be considered. This category in the kidney subheading includes renal biopsy, nephrectomy, and ablation. If the procedure is performed via laparoscope or cystoscope, refer to codes from Laparoscopy (50541–50549) or Endoscopy (50551–50580) categories. An open approach for a radical nephrectomy (50230) is removal of the kidney, upper ureter, neural and vascular structures at the apex of the renal pelvis, surrounding fat, adrenal gland, and involved renal lymph nodes.

A renal (kidney) biopsy can be performed to diagnose a kidney problem or to determine how quickly a kidney disease is progressing. Most renal biopsies are performed percutaneously with a needle or trocar. The code selection is based on the method of biopsy, needle/trocar, or open.

The majority of the codes in excision are for nephrectomies (nephr = renal, -ectomy = surgical removal). A nephrectomy can be partial or total. When a nephrectomy with total ureterectomy and bladder cuff is performed through the same incision, use CPT® code 50234. Access through the lower ureter and bladder using a separate incision is reported with CPT® code 50236 *Nephrectomy with total ureterectomy and bladder cuff; through separate incision*. If the nephrectomy is part of a renal transplant, use codes 50300–50365.

Renal Transplantation

Renal allotransplantation requires three components of physician work: cadaver or living donor, harvesting of graft, and cold preservation; backbench preparation; and recipient allotransplantation (which includes recipient care). The process may include reconstructive alterations to the blood vessels and tubes, depending on the recipient needs. The backbench procedure is basically the same for all organ transplants with some modification due to tailoring requirements of the specific organ allograft.

Backbench preparation of the cadaver donor renal allograft (50323) includes dissection and removal of perinephric fat, diaphragmatic, and retroperitoneal attachments; excision of the adrenal gland; and preparation of ureters, renal veins and renal arteries. Standard backbench preparation of a living donor renal allograft (open or laparoscopic) prior to the transplant includes dissection and removal of perinephric fat and preparation of ureters, renal veins and arteries, and ligation. Codes 50327–50329 describe backbench reconstruction of the cadaver or living donor renal allograft prior to transplant; and, code selection is based on the type of anastomosis (venous, arterial, ureteral). Each anastomosis is reported separately.

Practical Coding Note

Normally, a transplant involves a surgical team. CPT® modifier 66 is used to identify highly complex procedures requiring the concomitant services of several physicians, often of different specialties, with highly skilled and trained personnel using complex equipment. Make a note in this section to use modifier 66 if applicable.

A surgeon who removes the kidney and upper ureter from a cadaver for transplantation performs a donor nephrectomy (code 50300 for cadaver donor). The surgeon uses a midline incision in the skin from the xiphoid process to the symphysis pubis for adequate exposure. The surgeon dissects and removes the kidney, renal vessels, and ureter, usually removing sections of the inferior vena cava and aorta with the kidney. The kidney is placed in cold saline solution and flushed with cold electrolyte solution to rinse the remaining donor blood from the kidney and lower its temperature.

Code 50340 is reported when only the kidney and upper portion of the ureter is removed in a patient who is to receive a kidney transplant at a later time. Use code 50360 when the kidney and ureter are implanted in the recipient, no removal is performed. Code 50365 is reported when removal of the kidney and ureter are performed in the same surgical session as the implantation of the new kidney.

Introduction

Introduction codes describe aspiration, injection, and instillation. There are also codes for removal and replacement of internally dwelling ureteral stents, and externally accessible transnephric ureteral stents.

Renal pelvis catheter procedures differentiate between how ureteral stents are removed, or removed and replaced using different approaches. Prior to the addition of these codes, the only method of reporting ureteral stent exchange was through the existing endoscopic approach codes. Parenthetical statements beneath each code give further guidance in reporting modifier 50 for bilateral procedures or locating other codes that may be more appropriate to the procedure performed.

Ureteral stents are either indwelling or externally accessible. There are separate CPT® codes for placement of indwelling stent or externally accessible stents, and for stent removal or removal with replacement. Services are reported with different codes based on the approach (percutaneous, transnephritic, or transurethral). The codes in this series are for stent placement without cystoscopy. Most of the codes include radiological supervision and interpretation, so the imaging guidance is not reported separately.

Aspiration and/or injection of a renal cyst or pelvis (50390) following local anesthesia is performed using a needle placed percutaneously in the skin of the back. Using radiologic guidance, the provider advances the needle toward the renal pelvis or renal cyst and injects or drains fluid. See the parenthetical instruction for radiologic supervision and interpretation codes.

A physician evaluating the fluid or tissue extracted from a fine needle aspiration is reported as 88172 or 88173. When using 50390, the coder is reporting only the surgical procedure. Associated preoperative and postoperative services are not included.

Installation of a therapeutic agent into the renal pelvis and ureter generally is performed to treat tumors in the interest of preserving renal function.

CPT® code 50395 is used for the introduction of a guide into the renal pelvis and/or ureter with dilation to establish a percutaneous nephrostomy tract. The percutaneous nephrostomy usually is performed under fluoroscopic control in the radiology department. Diagnostic ultrasound also may be used with fluoroscopy. This procedure aids in outlining the interior structures of the kidney where the nephrostomy opening will be made.

After injection of a local anesthetic, a long, thin needle with a solid, slender, removable probe inside its shaft is inserted into the skin of the back and advanced inward toward the kidney. When the needle reaches the desired location within the kidney, the slender probe is removed with collection of urine for examination and with the injection of contrast material. The passageway may be enlarged, stretched, or dilated to allow insertion of a nephrostomy tube. The surgeon fixes the tube in place by suturing it to the skin or by attaching it to a special disc that has been sutured to the skin. Use CPT® code 50435 if the surgeon changes the nephrostomy catheter percutaneously.

Repair

Repair of an organ is performed to treat injury, disease, congenital abnormalities or stricture (obstruction). If the operative report contains the suffix -orrhaphy, -pexy, or -ostomy, reference the repair codes within the appropriate subheading of the organ involved. Nephrorrhaphy (nephr = kidney, orrhaphy = suture) is suturing of the kidney, which may be required after an injury or wound (for example, stab wound).

The horseshoe kidney is the most common type of renal fusion anomaly. It consists of two distinct functioning kidneys connected by fibrous tissue. The congenital anomaly is more common in males than females. Many patients with a horseshoe kidney remain asymptomatic, and the horseshoe kidney is an incidental finding during radiological examination. Symptoms, when present, usually are due to obstruction, stones, or infection. Symphysiotomy (50540) may be performed after pyeloplasty (renal reconstruction) to improve drainage.

Laparoscopy

Laparoscopic surgery is a minimally invasive surgical technique performed through small incisions as opposed to the larger incisions in open surgical procedures. Trocars, or cannulas, are placed through these incisions and used to access the structures to be treated. The abdomen usually is insufflated with carbon dioxide (CO2) gas. This lifts the abdominal wall away from the internal organs, improving visualization and access to the surgical field. Instruments are then placed through the trocars to perform the surgical procedure. Surgical explorations in the abdominal and pelvic cavities are performed using an endoscope (or scope) placed through a small incision in the abdominal wall. Code selection is based on the procedure performed through the scope.

Endoscopy

Endoscopy includes a rigid or flexible tube, a light delivery system, a lens system to transmit the image from the scope, and additional channel(s) may be used to allow entry of medical instruments. Although most endoscopic procedures are performed through a natural opening (eg, urethra or anus), some endoscopic procedures are performed through an established nephrostomy or pyelostomy (surgically created artificial opening), or through a nephrotomy or pyelotomy (small incision made in the organ). The code selection is based

on the approach and on the procedure performed through the endoscope.

Practical Coding Note

A renal endoscopy through established nephrostomy or pyelostomy, with or without irrigation, instillation, or ureteropyelography (CPT® code 50551), does not include the radiologic service. It also does not include the charge for X-rays, or other radiology technical components rendered as a necessary part of this procedure. Make a note to remind yourself to check for additional procedure codes if applicable.

CPT® 50551 usually is performed under fluoroscopic control in the radiology department. The professional services of the radiologist or other supervising provider, such as X-ray interpretations, are reported separately. An endoscopy with ureteral catheterization—with or without dilation of ureter—is accomplished when the provider passes a long thin tube over a guidewire into the kidney or down the ureter into the bladder. The catheter extends from the kidney to the bladder.

If the ureter is to be dilated, a catheter containing a deflated balloon is passed over the guidewire into the ureter. The provider positions the catheter so the deflated balloon lies inside the narrowed or constricted part of the ureter. The balloon is inflated to dilate the ureter. The balloon catheter may be deflated and removed or may be left in place, inflated for eight to 12 hours, and then removed. When the provider performs this procedure, use CPT® code 50553.

Other Procedures of Kidney

Lithotripsy refers to the crushing of calculi, while extracorporeal refers to outside of the body. In this procedure, extracorporeal shock waves are focused on stones and administered in a controlled manner to crush them. Local or general anesthesia may be used. Two different methods are available. The patient is positioned in a special chair-like device called a gantry and lowered into a tub of liquid medium (degassed, deionized water) with shock waves directed through the liquid to the kidney stones. In the second method, the one most commonly used, the patient is placed on a treatment table. The shock waves are directed through a water-cushion, or bellow that is placed against the body at the location of the kidney stone. The treatment table is equipped with video X-ray to allow visualization of the calculus. The shock waves are administered in groups of 25, 50, or 75 until the calculus is fragmented. Over several days or weeks, the tiny stone fragments pass harmlessly through the urinary system and are excreted during urination.

Percutaneous ablation of renal tumor(s) (50592) uses radiofrequencies under CT, MRI, or ultrasound guidance. An internally cooled radiofrequency needle is placed into a renal tumor through a small incision. The tumor tissue is then heated until there is sufficient and permanent cell damage and tumor necrosis.

Practical Coding Note

Percutaneous radiofrequency ablation of renal tumors (50592) is frequently performed for the treatment of renal masses as a palliative therapy for inoperable Stage IV renal cell carcinoma. The code reports a unilateral procedure, and a modifier 50 is required to report a bilateral procedure. As the bull's-eye icon indicates, moderate sedation is inherent and not reported separately.

Percutaneous cryotherapy ablation of renal tumor(s) (50593) also is performed using CT, MRI, or ultrasound guidance, but differs from the radiofrequency ablation in that a cryoprobe is placed in the tumor and cycles of freezing and thawing are used to cover the tumor tissue in an ice ball, which destroys the tumor. If this procedure is performed bilaterally, a modifier 50 should be appended.

Ureter (50600–50980)

Incision

Incision codes for the ureter include ureterotomy and ureterolithotomy procedures. During an ureterotomy for insertion of indwelling stent (50605) the provider makes an incision in the ureter and inserts a catheter (stent) into the ureter. To access the ureter, the provider makes an incision in the skin of the flank and cuts the muscles, fat, and fascia. The provider makes the next incision into the ureter. A slender catheter is inserted into the ureter, the incision is sutured, and a layered closure is performed.

When reporting incision procedures of the ureter, note that 50610–50630 are very specific regarding the ureterolithotomy (eg, 50610 upper one-third of the ureter, 50620 middle one-third of the ureter and 50630 lower one-third of the ureter). Ureteral stent insertion codes 50693-50695 are placed through the skin (percutaneously) into the ureter. These codes include a diagnostic nephrostogram, ureterogram, and image guidance not reporting them separately. When stents are inserted via cystoscopy, report 52332.

Excision

Ureterectomies typically are performed for ureteral cancers. Care should be used when reporting an ureterectomy with bladder cuff (separate procedure) (50650). Services listed as separate procedures are an integral component of another service or procedure and should not be reported in addition to the code for which it is considered an integral component.

Repair

Ureteral repair often is performed for stricture (obstruction), inflammatory disease, injury, or for repositioning or reconnection (anastomosis). It may be necessary for the surgeon to divide and reconnect the ureter to bypass a defect or obstruction. When the ureter is divided and repositioned, the description will state -ostomy as a suffix (eg, ureterostomy, ureterocalycostomy, which is ananastomosis of ureter to renal calyx). Plastic repair of the ureter is referred to as an ureteroplasty.

Surgery is performed to lyse adhesions near the ureter. These adhesions can cause obstruction of ovarian veins and pelvic pain.

Practical Coding Note

Place the universal female symbol (♀) next to CPT® code 50722.

A large portion of the codes in the repair section are for anastomosis. Anastomosis refers to the joining of two anatomical structures. These codes refer to the joining of a ureter to another body part, such as the renal pelvis (50740); renal calyx (50750); to another part of the same ureter (50760); to the other ureter (50770); or to the bladder (50782). These procedures may be necessary due to traumatic severance in an injury or the presence of diseases or tumor.

Creation of a ureteral conduit (50820) is a procedure diverting the flow of urine through an opening of the skin to a segment of small intestine. Urinary diversion is usually required for cancer or obstruction. When creation of a diversion is performed with removal of the bladder (cystectomy), see code 51596. Continent diversion codes include harvesting a piece of intestine to create the diversion and reconnection of the remaining bowel (intestinal anastomosis); intestinal anastomosis is not coded separately.

Laparoscopy

There are only a few laparoscopic codes for the ureter. Like kidneys, ureters get calculi (stones). A laparoscopic ureterolithotomy is the removal of a calculus from the ureter.

Laparoscopic ureteroneocystostomy with cystoscopy and ureteral stent placement is coded with 50947. Code 50948 is for laparoscopic ureteroneocystostomy without cystoscopy and ureteral stent placement.

An unlisted laparoscopic service performed on the ureter can be reported with CPT® code 50949. Laparoscopic procedures of the ureter are usually performed via either an abdominal or a back approach.

Endoscopy

With these procedures, the renal and ureteral structures are examined with an endoscope passed through an established opening between the skin and ureter. A guidewire is inserted, the ureterostomy tube is removed, and the endoscope is entered into the kidney or renal pelvis. This procedure usually is performed with local anesthesia. The codes are selected based on the approach (through an established ureterostomy or through an ureterotomy), and by the procedure performed through the endoscope.

Bladder (51020–52700)

The bladder is a hollow, muscular organ located in the pelvis. Its shape changes with urine filling, retention, and emptying. Three openings are found in the bladder. The ureterovesical valves mark the end of the ureters in the bladder's base. A single opening, called the bladder neck, connects the bladder to the urethra. The bladder neck is situated at the inferior aspect of the bladder. The bladder neck and base are shaped like a triangle called the trigone of the bladder. This triangular shape does not change regardless of the amount of urine contained within the bladder.

The ureterovesical junction is the anatomical area where the ureters join the bladder and has three major components:

- Lower ureter
- Trigone muscle (named for its triangular shape)
- Adjacent bladder wall

The ureterovesical junction provides a passageway for urine from the upper urinary tract to the lower urinary tract. It also prevents backflow (reflux) of the urine in the opposite direction. While the bladder is filling, the pressure within the ureterovesical junction remains low and the detrusor muscles are relaxed. Pressure exerted by waves of peristalsis in the ureters sends urine in spurts through the junction into the bladder.

Incision

The incision codes include cystotomy, cystostomy, and cystolithotomy. A cystotomy is an incision into the bladder and can be performed for ureteral catheter or stent insertion and removal or destruction of calculi (cystolithotomy).

Removal

The removal codes include aspiration by needle, trocar or intracatheter. Percutaneous bladder aspiration typically is used for sterile urine collection for bacterial study. It also can be used for temporary relief of acute urinary retention. The codes are selected based on the equipment used (needle, trocar, or intracatheter). Aspiration can be performed using imaging guidance.

The difference between using 51102 for suprapubic catheter insertion and 51040 is the technique. In 51040, the physician places the catheter through an open incision in the bladder. In 51102, a suprapubic catheter is placed in the bladder through the skin, but without an open incision into the bladder.

Excision

This range of CPT® codes includes procedures for partial removal of the bladder or complete removal. The excision is coded based on the disease being removed, diverticulum or tumor. Urinary diversion may be accomplished by uretero-sigmoidostomy or ureterocutaneous transplantations (51580–51585), ureteroileal conduit or sigmoid bladder (51590–51595), or using a segment of the small and/or large intestine to construct a neobladder (51596).

The urachus is an embryonic tube connecting the urinary bladder to the umbilicus during development of the fetus that normally closes before birth, generally in the fourth or fifth month of gestation. Sometimes the obliterative process of the urachus does not complete, causing complications later in life, including the development of urachal cyst or sinus. Urachal cysts are more common in children; infected urachal sinuses are more common in adults. Code 51500 reports the excision of the urachal cyst or sinus.

Cystectomy (bladder removal) is designated as partial or complete. During these procedures it is necessary to divert urine from the ureters to either an opening in the skin (ureterostomy), or to a sigmoid or neobladder. When the bladder is removed and the urine diverted to the skin via a stoma, the urine is collected in an appliance, or bag, attached to the outside of the patient's abdomen. An utereroileal conduit or sigmoid bladder (51590) can be catheterized from the skin, but does not require an appliance attached to the patient's skin to collect the urine. The opening in the skin can be covered by a Band-Aid®. A neobladder is constructed using a segment of the small and/or large intestine and the patient voids through his or her urethra if a neobladder is created (51596).

A bilateral pelvic lymph node dissection is included with all of the cystectomy procedures except creation of the neobladder. If bilateral pelvic lymph node dissection is performed with creation of the neobladder, it must be reported separately (38770).

Practical Coding Note

Next to the code 51596 for construction of a neobladder, make a note to code 38770 (Pelvic lymphadenectomy) if applicable. Use modifier 50 for bilateral procedures.

CPT® 51597 is a procedure where the physician removes the bladder, lower ureters, lymph nodes, urethra, prostate (if applicable), colon, and rectum due to a vesical, prostatic, or urethral malignancy. This code is used only when the need for the excision is related to a lower urinary tract or male genital malignancy, and not for gynecological or intestinal malignancy.

Introduction (51600–51720)

Injection or insertion procedures of the bladder often are performed in an office or minor procedure suite. These codes include catheter insertion (51701–51703); suprapubic catheter changes (51705–51710); and bladder irrigation and/or instillation procedures (51700).

Three codes are used to report catheter insertion. Use code 51701 for the insertion of a non-indwelling bladder catheter, which is a standard method for determining post-void residual urine volumes. Use codes 51702 and 51703 to report the insertion of a temporary indwelling catheter such as a Foley catheter, which is left in the bladder for a time. It is held in place with a balloon filled with sterile water. The urine drains into a bag, which can be emptied from an outlet device.

An indwelling catheter is used with many disorders, procedures, or problems such as; retention of urine, leading to urinary hesitancy, straining to urinate, decrease in size and force of the urinary stream, interruption of urinary stream, sensation of incomplete emptying, and obstruction of the urethra by an anatomical condition making it difficult to urinate (such as, prostate hypertrophy, prostate cancer, or narrowing of the urethra).

Urodynamics

Urodynamics (51725-51798) codes have both a professional and technical component. If billed without a modifier, the service must be performed in a physician's office by, or under the direct supervision of, a physician. The necessary equipment to perform these procedures is owned by the physician. If the equipment is owned by and the service performed in a facility location, append modifier 26.

Urodynamic studies assess the bladder, urethra and associated nerves and muscles for appropriate functioning. These studies usually are performed for incontinence, frequent urination, problems emptying the bladder, and urinary tract infections. The studies help define the cause of the urinary dysfunction so it can be treated through surgical repair, injection, or medication.

A cystometrogram (CMG) measures how much fluid the bladder can hold, how much pressure builds up inside the bladder, how full it is before the urge to urinate, and whether the bladder is emptied completely. Catheters placed in the bladder contain a pressure-measuring device called a manom-

eter. Another catheter may be placed in the rectum or vagina to record intra-abdominal pressures. As the bladder slowly fills with warm water, the manometer records the volume of water and bladder pressure. If the bladder contracts suddenly while being filled, the manometer records the leakage. When the bladder is filled, the patient is asked to void while the manometer measures the neurologic activity and pressures, as well as any residual urine.

CMG procedure codes are selected based on the type of study performed. When intra-abdominal voiding pressure studies are performed with CMG codes 51728 or 51729, it is reported in addition to the primary procedure with add-on code 51797. Uroflowmetry (51736–51741), commonly called uroflow, measures the amount of urine and the flow rate. Electromyography (EMG) studies (51784–51785) measure the electrical activity associated with the bladder during filling and emptying. In stimulus evoked response studies (51792), the head of the penis is stimulated and equipment measures the delay time for travel of stimulation through the pelvic nerves to the pudendal nerve. This procedure usually is not performed with CMGs.

Bladder scan ultrasonography (51798) is used to assess post-void urinary bladder retention. When a post void residual is the only service clinically provided, do not report a pelvic ultrasound code (CPT® 76856, complete study; or 76857, limited study) instead of, or in addition to, this service. Similarly, if a complete pelvic ultrasound code is billed appropriately, do not bill separately for a post-void residual determination because payment for this already has been included in the payment for the complete pelvic study.

Repair

Anterior vesicourethropexy or urethropexy repair (51840–51841) is used to correct incontinence, which is the involuntary leakage of urine from the bladder during coughing, sneezing, or straining. Anterior refers to the front. A vesicourethropexy refers to repair of the supporting structures of the bladder and the urethra, while urethropexy only involves the urethra. During this procedure, stretched or prolapsed organs are repaired and supported back into place. In some procedures, structures are placed in the tissue surrounding the urethra and into the vaginal wall. The sutures are pulled tight and tacked to the symphysis pubis (on the back of the pubic bone) or Cooper's ligament, and the urethra is moved forward (eg, Marshall Marchetti-Krantz or Burch procedure).

Code 51841 reports secondary repair or time or increased time or work complicating the procedure. When reporting 51841, the operative and diagnostic documentation should support the complicated procedure. Code 51845 describes an abdominovaginal vesical neck suspension (female specific code). The Stamey technique (code 51845) is performed vaginally, or through a small incision above the pubic bone. A suture is used to suspend the tissue adjacent to the urethra on each side, and cystoscopy ensures the urethra and bladder are not injured during the procedure.

Practical Coding Note

Place the universal female symbol (♀) next to CPT® code 51845.

The Raz procedure (CPT® code 51845) corrects urethral and bladder neck hypermobility when there is minimal or no herniation of the bladder into the vagina. An inverted U-shaped incision is made in the vaginal wall and bands of fibrous tissue around the bladder neck and urethra are released. A needle is passed through the incision, and the suspending sutures are pulled, lifting the front of the vagina and urethra. For an urethropexy with a hysterectomy, report 58152 or 58267.

Closure of vesicovaginal or vesicouterine fistula (51900–51925) is female specific. When a patient is diagnosed with a malignant neoplasm of the uterine adnexa or endometriosis of the uterus or urinary-genital tract fistula (female) or endometrial cystic hyperplasia, the provider often excises the fistula (this is an abnormal opening between the vagina or uterus and the bladder) and closes the defect creating a smooth surface. The codes are selected based on the approach. When a vesico-uterine fistula closure is performed with a hysterectomy, use 51925.

Practical Coding Note

Place the universal female symbol (♀) next to CPT® code range 51900–51925.

Laparoscopy

Procedures to alleviate incontinence include an open supra-pubic incision, as in the Marshall-Marchetti suspension or the Burch procedure (51840–51841). Some procedures are performed with a vaginal incision. A laparoscopic extraperitoneal approach has been used to perform a modification of an open Marshall-Marchetti procedure (51990). A laparoscope is used and the physician manipulations tools so that the pelvic organs can be observed through the laparoscope. The bladder is suspended by placing sutures in the tissues around the urethra to supporting structures. Code 51992 reports the laparoscopic sling procedure for stress incontinence.

Cystoscopic monitoring excludes passage of the needle through the bladder or the urethra and judges the proximity of the needle pass to the area needing support. In a laparoscopic

approach, the urethra can be restored to its normal position by suturing tissue next to the urethra to the pubic bone. In females, the procedure is performed to alleviate uncontrolled leakage of urine with coughing, laughing, sneezing, dancing, or running due to loss of urethral support from childbirth, or as a result of the aging process (51990).

Endoscopy—Cystoscopy, Urethroscopy, Cystourethroscopy

Codes in this section of the Bladder heading also include procedures of the ureter, pelvis, vesical (bladder) neck, and prostate. These procedures are performed using a cystoscope inserted transurethrally (through the urethra).

Cystoscopy procedures are organized according to urethra and bladder, ureter and renal pelvis, and bladder neck and prostate. Radiological services are reported separately. Read code descriptions carefully to identify the specific procedure performed and area treated. Of particular difficulty can be codes referencing the urethra or ureters because the words look quite similar, particularly in their combining forms.

Cystoscopy

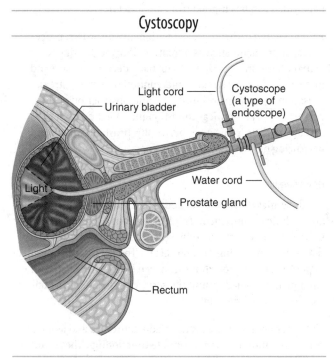

Source: Lindh, Pooler, Tamparo, and Dahl, Delmar's Comprehensive Medical Assisting (Administrative and Clinical Competencies), 4e, ISBN#978-1-4354-1914-8

A cystourethroscopy is direct visual examination of the urethra and the bladder using an endoscope (a lighted instrument called a cystourethroscope or panendoscope). Throughout this procedure, a flow of sterile distilled water or saline solution passes through the scope and into the bladder distending the tissues to facilitate visualization. The urethra and bladder are examined systematically.

During the laparoscopic procedure, when ureters are buried in scar tissue, the surgeon may place thin tubes into ureters buried in scar tissue for easier identification. When performed alone or with other unrelated services, it may be reported separately.

Cystourethroscopy, commonly referred to as a cysto, (52000) is a diagnostic cystoscopy and indicated as a separate procedure. A separate procedure indicates when it is performed with a more complex procedure, it is not reported. If performed with another separate identifiable procedure(s) and documentation supports its use, and it is not a NCCI edit where it is bundled with another procedure, append modifier 59 to code 52000. Cystourethroscopy codes including endoscopy of the ureter (ureteroscopy) are found in 52344–52355. Non-endoscopic ureteral catheterization during a cystourethroscopy is reported with 52005, which does not include visualization within the ureter, but only placement of a catheter(s) into the ureter(s) with or without irrigation, instillation of medication or ureteropyelography. The insertion of a ureteral catheter should not be confused with the insertion of an indwelling ureteral stent(s) (52332). If a catheter is inserted into the ureter, it usually is removed at the end of the case, whereas a stent remains afterward. Stents provide support for healing or to hold tissue in place. If a stent remains in the ureter for an extended time, it will need to be replaced. A stent exchange is coded 52332; this code is a unilateral procedure, when performed bilaterally append modifier 50. If a stent exchange is performed, the removal of the initial stent (52310) is not coded.

Transurethral Surgery

The urinary collecting system is examined with a cystourethroscope passed through the urethra to the bladder. Code 52204 reports biopsy tissue extracted from the bladder or urethra. This procedure normally is performed with a diagnosis such as chronic interstitial cystitis, trigonitis, hematuria and hyperplasia of prostate, or malignant neoplasm of prostate. This code is reported once regardless of the number of biopsies obtained.

A cystourethroscopy can determine whether a female or male has interstitial cystitis. Under general anesthesia or conduction (spinal or epidural) anesthesia, the bladder is filled as the surgeon inspects the inside of the bladder with a cystoscope. When the bladder is filled to capacity, the bladder volume is measured, and the cystoscope is inserted again to look for signs of interstitial cystitis: glomeruli (small bleeding points) or Huhner's ulcers.

Fulguration is destruction of tissue (usually malignant tumors) by using high-frequency electric current, most commonly with electrocautery or laser. Report code 52214 when the destruction of lesions of the trigone, bladder neck, prostatic fossa, urethra, or periurethral glands is performed through a cystourethroscope.

Code 52224 is used for treatment of bladder lesion(s) measuring less than 0.5 cm and includes a biopsy if performed. Codes 52234-52240 are used for cystourethroscopy transurethral resection of bladder tumor (TURBT) with fulguration and/or resection. These codes are based on the size of the tumor removed and only reported once, regardless of the number of tumors removed. If there are different size tumors being removed in one surgical session, only the largest tumor removed is reported. For example, a physician performs fulguration on two bladder tumors through a cystourethroscope. The first tumor measures 2.5 cm and the second tumor measures 5.5 cm. Only report code 52240 for removal of both bladder tumors.

CPT® cystourethroscopy code 52270 is female specific and code 52275 is male specific. Both codes involve a cystourethroscopy with an incision of the urethra (internal urethrotomy) and, in particular, an incision for relief of urethral stricture. CPT® 52285 is female specific and reported for the treatment of the female urethral syndrome, which has symptoms of a urinary tract infection although the urine is sterile when analyzed. An infection may be isolated to the urethra (urethritis) and treated with antibiotics.

Practical Coding Note

Place the universal female symbol (♀) next to CPT® codes 52270 and 52285.

Place the universal male symbol (♂) next to CPT® code 52275.

Transurethral surgery of the ureter and pelvis include all of the same parameters as a regular cystourethroscopy. This subset of services takes the procedure one step further by including cannulation of the ureter(s). CPT® codes 52341–52346 take care of ureteral strictures. Cystourethroscopy with ureteroscopy and/or pyeloscopy and fulguration and resection of a ureteral or renal pelvic tumor are addressed with CPT® codes 52351–52355. Code selection with the subsets depends on the procedure performed.

Vesical Neck and Prostate

Vesical neck and prostate procedures include the transurethral resection of the prostate (TURP) and laser procedures of the prostate. Code 52601 is used to report the transuretheral electrosurgical resection of prostate, including control of postoperative bleeding, complete.

If residual or regrowth from a previous TURP occurs and the prostate is resected with a transurethral approach, report code 52630. GreenLight laser of the prostate is coded 52648. Transurethral microwave therapy (TUMT) is reported 53850.

TURP

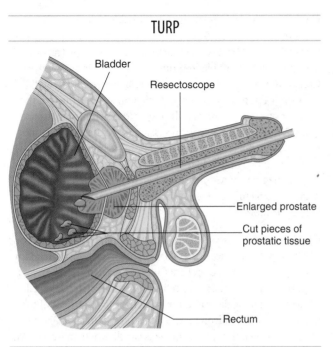

Bladder

Resectoscope

Enlarged prostate

Cut pieces of prostatic tissue

Rectum

Source: Lindh, Pooler, Tamparo, and Dahl, Delmar's Comprehensive Medical Assisting (Administrative and Clinical Competencies), 4e, ISBN#978-1-4354-1914-8

Practical Coding Note

Some of the codes in this section are male specific (52450, 52601, 52647, 52648, 52649, and 52700) and describe procedures of the prostate. Place the universal male symbol (⊗) next to these codes.

When an obstruction (tissue) in the neck (outlet) of the bladder is excised, the surgeon uses a cystourethroscope to reach the targeted region. This procedure, resection of the bladder neck (CPT® code 52500), often is part of a more complex service and not identified separately.

During laser coagulation and laser vaporization of prostate, the surgeon uses a laser to excise the prostate through an endoscope, which is inserted into the urethra. Dilation of the urethra is sometimes necessary to allow insertion of the endoscope. Code 52647 reports laser coagulation of the prostate and includes control of postoperative bleeding; vasectomy, meatotomy, cystourethroscopy, urethral calibration, and/ or dilation and internal urethrotomy, and these procedures are not reported separately if performed at the same session. During this procedure laser energy (non contact laser) is directed to an enlarged prostate with a fiber optic tube. Heat from the laser penetrates the prostate to destroy prostate cells and creates scars in the prostate. Code 52648 is used for laser vaporization of the prostate and includes transurethral resection of the prostate as part of the complete package. To accomplish this, a vasectomy, meatotomy, cystourethroscopy,

or internal urethrotomy may be necessary. For contact laser vaporization with or without transurethral resection of prostate, use 52648.

Laser procedures deliver sufficient heat to the prostate so either coagulation necrosis or frank vaporization occurs, depending on the amount of energy delivered to the tissue. Laser prostatectomy can be divided into three different procedures: visual laser ablation of the prostate (VLAP), interstitial laser coagulation (ILC), and holmium laser resection of the prostate (HoLRP).

VLAP is performed under general anesthesia, regional anesthesia, or local prostatic block. With the patient in the dorsal lithotomy position, a standard transurethral approach to the prostate is utilized with a rigid cystoscope. A deflecting bridge is used to direct the fiber to the desired area of treatment. Nd:YAG continuous wave laser can be delivered to the prostatic tissue. The amount of energy delivered to each patient is dependent on the time of exposure and power.

The majority of ILC is performed under regional or general anesthesia. Cystourethroscopy is performed to delineate any pertinent landmarks and identify the treatment target. Using the cystoscope, the diffuser-tip laser fiber is advanced into the prostate. A visible marker on the laser fiber is used to reach the desired depth within the prostate. The fiber is inserted at an angle to the urethra. Intraoperative transrectal ultrasonography can be used to confirm the placement of the fiber inside the prostate. Laser energy is applied in each location for three to four minutes. Code 52649 describes laser enucleation of the prostate with morcellation. Morcellation is when solid tissue, such as a tumor, is divided up into little pieces which can be removed.

HoLRP is performed under regional or general anesthesia. A resectoscope is inserted and a bilateral bladder neck incision is made to the depth and amount of tissue to be removed. The median lobe is undermined and detached back into the bladder.

Following laser resection (vaporization), the lobe is released, until only a bridge of tissue remains at the bladder neck. If the median lobe is very large, it is cut into smaller pieces prior to detachment. Prostate pieces are removed from the bladder at the end of the procedure.

Urethra (53000–53899)

The urethra is the canal from the bladder to the outside of the body for elimination of urine.

The male urethra is divided into three sections:

- Prostatic Urethra—The most proximal portion begins at the vesical neck at the apex of the trigone of the urinary bladder and extends through the prostate gland ending at the superior fascia of the urogenital diaphragm.

- Membranous Urethra—Begins at the superior fascia of the urogenital diaphragm, extends at the deep transverse perineal muscle ending at the inferior fascia of the urogenital diaphragm.
- Penile (Cavernous) Urethra—Begins at the inferior fascia of the urogenital diaphragm and terminates at the external urethral meatus of the glans penis.

The female urethra is a narrow membranous canal imbedded in the anterior wall of the vagina behind the symphysis pubis.

The urethra perforates the fascia of the urogenital diaphragm, and its external orifice is situated directly in front of the vaginal opening and about 2.5 cm behind the glans clitorides (or clitoris). The lining membrane is in longitudinal folds. Many small urethral glands open into the urethra. In males and females, a sphincter mechanism controls the expulsion of urine from the bladder through the meatus. Muscles inside and adjacent to the urethral wall are required to prevent leakage in times of physical stress.

Active tone and compression are necessary to maintain continence and prevent incontinence (involuntary leaking or expulsion of urine). Coaptation (closure) of the urethral lumen aids in forming a watertight seal to prevent urine leakage or dribbling. The procedural subcategories follow the normal CPT® format.

Incision

An urethrotomy (53000–53010) is an incision to resolve a narrowing (stricture) of the urethra. In males, the narrowing may be due to scar tissue resulting from infection or previous surgery, and left untreated, can affect the flow of urine.

In the drainage of deep periurethral abscesses, the surgeon drains an abscess in the urethra resulting from a urethral infection or traumatic injury. The surgeon makes an incision with blunt or sharp dissection, the incision is carried into the abscessed area to provide drainage. Drains are usually inserted and the incision is closed in layers. For a subcutaneous abscess, use 10060–10061. For an abscess or cyst in the Skene's gland, use CPT® code 53060.

Extravasation is leakage of fluid from a vessel into surrounding tissue. Codes 53080 and 53085 are used when the physician has to drain urine that has leaked into the perineum.

Excision

The excision range of CPT® codes includes codes specific to males and females. A urethrectomy is the surgical removal of all or part of the urethra. CPT® 53210 is female specific and reports total removal of the urethra. 53215 is male specific and reports the total removal of the urethra. Both codes include

the surgical formation of an opening into the urinary bladder (cystostomy).

A diverticulum is a pouch or sac occurring normally or created by herniation of the lining mucous membrane through a defect in the muscular coat of a tubular organ, according to *Dorland's Medical Dictionary*. CPT® 53230 is female specific to the excision of a urethral diverticulum; 53235 is specific to males.

The bulbourethral glands (53250), or Cowper's glands, are two pea-shaped glands in the male, located beneath the prostate gland at the beginning of the internal portion of the penis; they add fluid to semen during the process of ejaculation. The bulbourethral glands are homologous to the Bartholin's glands in the female.

Skene's glands (53270, female specific) also are known as the lesser vestibular or paraurethral glands.

Paraurethral glands are located at the opening of the vagina next to the urethra and the vestibular glands are just outside the hymen. These glands can become inflamed and cause pain with intercourse. If medical therapy fails, a microscope is used to locate them and a CO2 laser beam is targeted to vaporize the glands with minimal damage to the surrounding tissue.

Repair

The CPT® codes in the repair section are specific to urethroplasties, insertion, and/or removal/replacement of prosthetic devices such as inflatable urethral/bladder neck sphincters. The procedures also vary greatly in complexity, and several procedures are specific to either male or female.

A sling operation for male urinary incontinence involves (53440–53442) taking fibrous connective tissue or synthetic material to make a sling which is placed across the muscles surrounding the urethra and anchoring the sling with screws, staples or sutures on each side of the pelvic bone. The approach restores some of the normal anatomy, stabilizes the area to prevent movement and slightly compresses the neck of the bladder.

Three codes are female specific in this range. CPT® 53430 reports the reconstruction of the female urethra and code 53502 reports a suture procedure of a urethral wound or injury. Code 53500 reports a transvaginal urethrolysis and includes cystourethroscopy. Urethrolysis involves cutting obstructive adhesions that fix the urethra to the pubic bone. When the procedure is performed through an incision in the vagina, it is called transvaginal urethrolysis, which is the procedure commonly used for mending urethral obstruction resulting from surgical repair of stress incontinence.

Manipulation

Treatments for urethral strictures are listed as manipulation codes (53600-53665). These codes are selected based upon the type of dilation, patient's gender, and if anesthesia is used. Most of the codes within this category are gender specific. Initial or subsequent dilation is described separately.

A dilation procedure used to correct a diagnosis of chronic interstitial cystitis, trigonitis, cystitis cystica, or polyuria requires the provider to use dilators to widen the urethra. A suppository or instillation of a saline solution often is used. Code the dilation based on whether it is the initial dilation or subsequent dilations.

When general or spinal anesthesia is administered for dilation of female urethral stricture, use 53665. With codes 53660 and 53661, any associated preoperative and postoperative services are not included. CPT® 53605 reports dilation of the penile urethra. General or spinal anesthesia is used.

Other Procedures

Transurethral destruction of prostate tissue (53850-53852) is male specific. When the provider performs a transurethral destruction of prostate tissue by microwave thermotherapy, the endoscope is inserted into the penile urethra. The urethra may need to be dilated to allow for instrument passage. After the endoscope is passed, a microwave thermotherapy stylet is inserted into the urethra and the diseased prostate is treated. Use 53852 when the provider elects to perform the procedure by radiofrequency thermotherapy. This procedure often is performed on patients with a diagnosis of hyperplasia of prostate.

CPT® 53855 is for insertion of a temporary prostatic urethral stent, including urethral measurement. A temporary prostatic stent is often used for temporary relief of an obstructed urethra caused by Benign Prostatic Hyperplasia (BPH). Obstruction can also occur after surgery for BPH, prostate cancer, or after radiation therapy.

Section Review 12.3

1. A Urologist examines the urinary collecting system with a cystourethroscope and removes four bladder tumors by fulguration. Two tumors measured 1.5 cm and the other two tumors measured 2.5 cm and 3.0 cm. What code(s) should be reported?

    A. 52234 x 2, 52235 x 2
    B. 52240
    C. 52234
    D. 52235

2. The patient presents with recurrent bladder outlet obstruction secondary to prostate enlargement and requires transurethral resection of the prostate (TURP). The patient previously had a TURP 10 years ago. Code the TURP:

    A. 52601
    B. 52630
    C. 52648
    D. 52500

3. Patient presents for insertion of a draining tube due to a neurogenic bladder. The physician performs the procedure by making a small skin incision into the lower abdominal wall, then an open incision in the bladder for placement of the catheter for drainage. Code the procedure:

    A. 51102
    B. 51040
    C. 51045
    D. 51705

4. Excision of urachal cyst and an incarcerated umbilical hernia repair were performed on a six-year-old male. Code the procedure:

    A. 49580

    B. 49587

    C. 49585

    D. 51500

5. The urologist is asked by the general surgeon to place ureteral catheters for visualization of ureters during a complicated bowel surgery. Cystoscopy is performed and ureteral catheters are inserted. The general surgeon removes the catheters at the end of the case. Code the procedure.

    A. 52332

    B. 52005

    C. 52310

    D. 50605

Male Genital System (54000–55899)

The Male Genital System section of CPT® includes procedures on the penis, testis, epididymis, tunica vaginalis, scrotum, vas deferens, spermatic cord, seminal vesicles and prostate.

Penis (54000–54450)

Paraphimosis describes the foreskin of the penis trapped in a retracted position. When the foreskin is retracted, it can act as a tourniquet, leading to vascular compromise and necrosis. To relieve the condition, a dorsal slit (54000-54001) is performed. Codes are selected based on whether or not the patient is a newborn.

Services for excision or destruction of lesions on the skin generally are coded in the Integumentary system; however, in the Penis subheading of CPT®, there are codes for lesion excision and destruction under Destruction (54050–54065). These include chemical, electrodesiccation, cryosurgery, laser surgery, and surgical excision of penile lesions. The codes are differentiated by simple or extensive and by technique (simple procedure only).

Excision codes for the penis include biopsy, excision of penile plaque, removal of foreign body, amputation, and circumcision. A biopsy of the penis is helpful in diagnosing Lichen Planus, a condition causing lesions on the penis. Penile plaque (Peyronie's disease) can cause pain, abnormal curvature, erectile dysfunction, indentation, loss of girth and shortening. Peyronie's disease often resolves on its own; however, sometimes surgery is necessary. Surgical corrections include excision of the penile plaque (54110–54112). Penile cancer commonly is treated with a penectomy (amputation of the

penis). Penectomies are partial, complete, or radical. A radical penectomy includes the removal of lymph nodes in the groin. Circumcision codes, 54150–54161, are selected based on the age of the patient and the instrumentation used, such as a clamp (eg, Gomco, Plastibell). Anesthesia for a circumcision can be obtained by dorsal penile nerve block (DPNB) or subcutaneous ring block (SCRB). If anesthesia is not used when reporting code 54150, modifier 52 should be appended to the CPT® code.

Plastic operations performed on the penis for urethroplasty and for straightening (hypospadias and epispadias) are reported with codes from the repair section. The description of many of these codes begins with urethroplasty, but it is appropriate the services are reported here because they refer to the portion of the urethra passing through the penis. To assign codes for hypospadias repair use codes 54300–54352. The documentation must be clear about the extent of the work involved. Hypospadias repair typically is completed in one stage; however, in more severe cases, it will require additional stages. The stages affect the code selection. Plastic repair of epispadias is reported with 54380–54390.

Practical Coding Note

Highlight or underline the stage of each repair code.

Example

54304 Plastic operation on penis for correction of chordee or for first stage hypospadias repair with or without transplantation of prepuce and/or skin flaps.

54308 Urethroplasty for second stage hypospadias repair (including urinary diversion); less than 3 cm.

Codes 54400-54417 describe services for insertion or removal of penile prostheses. A penile prosthesis is used to treat organic erectile dysfunction (ICD-10-CM N52.9). The code for removal or repair is determined by the type of prosthesis involved. A multi-component, inflatable penile prosthesis is coded with 54405 and includes placement of the pump, cylinders, and reservoir.

For repair of a component or components of a multi-component inflatable penile prosthesis, report 54408. Any time the provider removes and replaces all the components of a multi-component inflatable penile prosthesis at the same operative session, report 54410. When the removal and replacement of all components of a multi-component, inflatable penile prosthesis is performed through an infected field, report 54411. This procedure includes the irrigation and debridement of the infected tissue. Code 54415 is reported when the removal of a non-inflatable, semi-rigid or an inflatable, self-contained penile prosthesis is performed without replacement of the prosthesis. Code 54416 reports the removal and replacement of a non-inflatable, semi-rigid or inflatable, self-contained penile prosthesis at the same operative session. Code 54417 is reported for the removal and replacement of a non-inflatable, semi-rigid or inflatable, self-contained penile prosthesis through an infected field at the same operative session. This also includes the irrigation and debridement of the infected tissue.

Foreskin manipulation (54450) is used when adhesions between the uncircumcised foreskin and the head of the penis prevent retraction of the foreskin. By stretching the foreskin back over the head of the penis, these adhesions are broken. The physician may insert a clamp between the foreskin and the head of the penis and spread the jaw of the clamp to break the adhesions.

Testis (54500–54699)

There are no incision codes for the testis. These services are described in the Epididymis subsection.

A biopsy of the testis (54500–54505) is performed to examine the testicular tissue for sperm production. This is a rare procedure to determine the cause of male infertility. Append modifier 50 to codes 54500 or 54505 when both testes are biopsied. Orchiectomy is the removal of the testis; codes are selected based on the approach and extent of the procedure (partial or radical). Orchiectomies can be performed for endocrine control of prostatic tumors and primary tumors of the testes. In a radical orchiectomy, the complete testis is removed. Undescended testes are considered pre-cancerous and often are removed as a preventive measure. When a bilateral orchiectomy is performed on a child, hormone replacement therapy will be necessary. Another surgical option for undescended testes is orchiopexy (in the Repair section). In this procedure, the testes are descended surgically and sutured

in place. A parenthetical note under code 54640 directs you to also report separately inguinal hernia repair (49495–49525) when performed. If the undescended testes are not palpable, or are in the abdomen, the orchiectomy or orchiopexy may be performed open or by abdominal laparoscopy (54690–54692).

Transplantation of testis(es) to the thigh (54680) is performed because of scrotal destruction. In this procedure, the testicle(s) is placed under the skin of the thigh to preserve function and viability. This usually is a temporary location for the testicle, where it will remain until scrotal reconstruction is complete.

Epididymis, Tunica Vaginalis, Scrotum, Vas Deferens, Spermatic Cord, and Seminal Vesicles (54700–55680)

The epididymis and vas deferens make up a system of tubes providing maturation, storage, and transportation of sperm. Epididymovasostomy, or anastomosis of epididymis to vas deferens (54900), is performed when an obstruction of the flow of spermatozoa from the epididymis to the vas deferens occurs. This procedure usually is performed because of stricture, congenital defect, or insufficient production of sperm in semen.

The tunica vaginalis is a thin pouch holding the testes within the scrotum and is made up of two layers. A hydrocele is a collection of fluid in the scrotum between layers of the tunica vaginalis. The codes in the tunica vaginalis section are for treatment of a hydrocele. Hydroceles can be communicating or non-communicating. A communicating hydrocele occurs from incomplete closure of the tunica vaginalis so a small amount of abdominal fluid may flow in and out of the thin pouch. The fluid fluctuates throughout the day and night, altering the size of the mass. A non-communicating hydrocele may be present at birth and usually resolves spontaneously within one year. A non-communicating hydrocele in an older child may indicate other problems, such as infections, torsion (twisting of the testes), or a tumor.

The scrotum is a skin-covered sac lying below the pubic bone. The lower portion of the spermatic cord, the epididymis, and the testes are contained in this sac. Each side (hemiscrotum) contains a testis, an epididymis, and a spermatic cord. The muscles in the scrotum, called the cremasteric muscles, move the testicles slightly within the scrotum depending on the surrounding temperature.

The vas deferens is a coiled tube carrying sperm out of the testes. Incision of the vas deferens (55200) usually is performed to obtain a sample of semen or to test the patency of the tubes. This is a separate procedure, and should not be reported when a more complex service is performed at the same site.

Vasectomy (removal of a small portion of the vas deferens) usually is performed for birth control, and is reported

55250. This code is reported once, whether the procedure is performed unilaterally or bilaterally. The code also includes post-operative semen examination. Vasectomy reversal procedures are reported 55400; if performed bilaterally, modifier 50 should be added.

The spermatic cord includes arteries and veins circulating blood to and from the testes and other structures in the scrotum. These structures together support the testicles in the scrotum.

The seminal vesicles are a hollow pair of muscular organs situated between the posterior bladder wall and the rectum. The seminal vesicles produce a fluid providing nutrients for the sperm and lubricates the urethra. This fluid mixes with other fluids to create semen.

Prostate (55700–55899)

A prostate biopsy (needle or punch, single or multiple, any approach) is reported with 55700, and may require imaging guidance. If imaging guidance is used, report 76942 in addition. Code 76942 has both professional and technical components; modifier 26 should be applied if the procedure is performed in a facility location. No modifier is needed if the physician provides the service in the office and owns the equipment and writes an interpretation of the service.

The codes for prostatectomy procedures, which usually are performed for cancer of the prostate are determined by the approach and whether a lymph node biopsy or dissection was performed (55801–55845). If a lymph node dissection is performed at a different surgical session than the initial removal of the prostate, report 38770 and append modifier 50 if the dissection is bilateral. Code 55801 reports a subtotal perineal prostatectomy. Subtotal means the prostatic capsule is incised removing the hypertrophied or hyperplastic adenoma of the gland. This leaves the capsule of the prostate intact and it is sutured closed. Code 55810 reports a perineal radical prostatectomy. In a radical procedure, the entire gland is removed along with the seminal vesicles and the vas deferens. Code 55812 is perineal radical prostatectomy with lymph node biopsy or biopsies. This is a limited pelvic lymphadenectomy. Only local lymph nodes are removed during this procedure. 55815 is a radical perineal prostatectomy with bilateral pelvic lymphadenectomy including the external iliac, hypogastric, and obturator nodes. This includes all lymph nodes along the back wall of the pelvic and abdominal cavities are removed. Code 55821 reports a subtotal prostatectomy using a suprapubic approach (access is incision in the lower abdomen just above the pubic area/pubic bone). The bladder is opened and the prostate exposed. The prostate is removed by blunt dissection with the surgeon's index finger. This can be performed in one or two stages. Code 55831 reports a subtotal prostatectomy

using a retropubic approach (access is retroperitoneal, without opening the bladder).

Codes 55840–55845 report radical removal of the prostate gland using a retropubic approach, with or without nerve sparing. Nerve sparing is when the bundles of nerves on either side of the prostate gland are not removed (spared). 55842 includes lymph node biopsy or biopsies. This procedure includes a limited number of lymph nodes removed. 55845 includes a bilateral pelvic lymphadenectomy including removal of the external iliac, hypogastric, and obturator nodes. Code 55866 is reported for a laparoscopic retropubic radical prostatectomy.

When the prostate is exposed for insertion of a radioactive substance, use 55860–55865. Final code selection depends on whether a lymph node biopsy or dissection also was performed.

Radiation treatment for prostate cancer may require the surgeon to place needles, catheters, or interstitial devices (such as fiducial markers) for radiation therapy (55875–55876). Ultrasonic guidance or imaging is not included and is reported separately when performed.

Section Review 12.4

1. Patient presents for treatment of multiple condyloma on the penis. The excised diameter is 0.8cm. Code the procedure.

   A. 11420

   B. 11421

   C. 11621

   D. 54060

2. Patient presents for bilateral vasectomy. After the patient is prepped and draped a unilateral vasectomy is performed. Because the vas deferens could not be located on the left side, he will be scheduled for left vasectomy under general anesthesia next week. How would the initial vasectomy be reported?

   A. 55250-53

   B. 55250-RT

   C. 55250

   D. 55250-52

3. Using the scenario above, how would you code the return to the operating room for vasectomy on the left side during the postoperative period?

   A. 55250-58

   B. 55250-78

   C. 55250-76

   D. 55250-LT

4. A right side epididymectomy and spermatocelectomy are performed on a 15-year-old male. What code is reported for this procedure?

   A. 54860

   B. 54861

   C. 54840

   D. 54830

5. A newborn has a circumcision. A dorsal penile nerve block was used for anesthesia. The provider used a Plastibell for the circumcision. What CPT® code is reported?

   A. 54150

   B. 54160

   C. 54161

   D. 54150-52

HCPCS Level II

HCPCS Level II codes used for urological procedures primarily describe supplies and drugs, including catheters, irrigation trays, and drugs to treat prostate cancer and decreased testosterone levels. Many carriers consider catheterization supplies included with the procedure. The most common HCPCS Level II codes used for urological procedures are:

Catheter supplies:

A4353 Intermittent urinary catheter, with insertion supplies

A4357 Bedside drainage bag, day or night, with or without anti-reflux device, with or without tube, each

A4358 Urinary drainage bag, leg or abdomen, vinyl, with or without tube, with straps, each

A4338 Indwelling catheter; Foley type, two-way latex with coating (Teflon, silicone, silicone elastomer, or hydrophilic, etc.), each

A4340 Indwelling catheter, specialty type, (eg, Coude, mushroom, wing, etc.), each

A4344 Indwelling catheter, Foley type, two-way, all silicone, each

A4346 Indwelling catheter; Foley type, three-way for continuous irrigation, each

Chemotherapy injection for prostate cancer:

J3315 Injection, triptorelin pamoate, 3.75 mg

J9218 Leuprolide acetate, per 1 mg

J9217 Leuprolide acetate (for depot suspension), 7.5 mg

Testosterone injection for decreased testosterone

J1071 Injection, testosterone cypionate, up to 1 mg

Modifiers

Modifiers are used to report or indicate a service or procedure has been altered by some specific circumstance but has not changed in its definition or code. The modifiers listed below are some of the common modifiers used when coding urological procedures.

Modifier 22 Increased Procedural Services

When the work required to provide a service is substantially greater than typically required, it is identified by adding modifier 22 to the usual procedure code. Documentation must support the substantial additional work and reason for the additional work; for example, the operative report states the procedure took over two hours longer than it typically would. Many carriers require documentation for claims submitted with modifier 22.

Modifier 50 Bilateral Procedure (Also, Modifiers LT/RT Left Side/Right Side)

Unless otherwise identified in the listings, bilateral procedures performed at the same operative session are identified by adding modifier 50 to the appropriate CPT® code. Depending upon the carrier, modifiers RT and LT may be used instead of modifier 50. If appending modifier 50, you will want to increase the fee for the procedure. Modifier 50 is used to report bilateral procedures on the testis or scrotum.

Modifier 51 Multiple Procedures

Modifier 51 Multiple procedures, indicates more than one (non-E/M) procedure was provided during the same session. Many payers use software automatically detecting second and subsequent procedures, making modifier 51 unnecessary. Check with individual payers for guidelines, and request the payer's instructions in writing.

Modifier 52 Reduced Services

Under certain circumstances, a service or procedure is reduced partially or eliminated at the physician's or other qualified healthcare professional's discretion. Under these circumstances, the service provided can be identified by its usual procedure number and addition of modifier 52. This allows reporting reduced services without disturbing the identification of the basic service. For instance, if the physician performs a urethroscopy but is unable to view the bladder, modifier 52 is appended to 52000.

Modifier 53 Discontinued Procedure

Due to extenuating circumstances, or those threatening the well-being of the patient, it may be necessary to indicate a surgical or diagnostic procedure was started but discontinued. This circumstance is reported by adding modifier 53. For instance, during an operative procedure the patient's blood pressure cannot be controlled, and continuation with the surgical procedure threatens the well-being of the patient. Modifier 53 is appended to the CPT® code.

Modifier 58 Staged or Related Procedure or Service by the Same Physician or Other Qualified Healthcare Professional During the Postoperative Period

It may be necessary to indicate performance of a procedure or service during the postoperative period was: (a) planned or anticipated (staged); (b) more extensive than the original procedure; or (c) for therapy following a surgical procedure. This circumstance is reported by adding modifier 58 to the staged or related procedure. For instance, the patient has a TURP and during the postoperative period returns to the clinic to confirm his bladder is emptying appropriately. Modifier 58 is added to 51798.

For treatment of a problem requiring a return to the operating/procedure room (eg, unanticipated clinical condition), see modifier 78.

Modifier 76 Repeat Procedure or Service by the Same Physician or Other Healthcare Professional

It may be necessary to indicate a procedure or service was repeated subsequent to the original procedure or service. This circumstance may be reported by adding modifier 76 to the repeated procedure/service. For instance, a patient has a cystoscopy to control bleeding from a bladder diverticulum, but continues to have bleeding after the procedure and the procedure must be repeated. Modifier 76 is added to the second cystoscopy procedure.

Modifier 58 is used if there is a planned return to the operating room during the global period. Use modifier 77 if the repeated service was performed by another provider not within the same practice group.

Modifier 78 Unplanned Return to the Operating/Procedure Room by the Same Physician or Other Healthcare Professional Following the Initial Procedure for a Related Procedure During the Postoperative Period

It may be necessary to indicate another procedure was performed during the postoperative period of the initial procedure (unplanned procedure following the initial procedure).

When this procedure is related to the first, and requires the use of an operating/procedure room, it is reported by adding modifier 78 to the related procedure. For instance, a status-post radical retropubic prostatectomy with bilateral lymph node dissection (55845) patient is found to have post-operative bleeding and is returned to the operating room. Modifier 78 is added to the procedure used to control the post-operative bleeding.

Modifier 79 Unrelated Procedure or Service by the Same Physician or Other Healthcare Professional During the Postoperative Period

The physician may need to indicate the performance of a procedure or service during the postoperative period was unrelated to the original procedure. This circumstance is reported using modifier 79. For instance, an ESWL is performed on the right kidney. During the global period of the initial surgery, the patient returns to the operating room for a second ESWL procedure, but on the left kidney. Modifier 79 is reported on the ESWL procedure performed on the left kidney.

Section Review 12.5

1. When a bilateral procedure is performed as unilateral, what modifier is reported?

   A. 50

   B. 52

   C. 53

   D. 58

2. To report a repeat procedure by the same physician, what modifier is reported?

   A. 76

   B. 78

   C. 58

   D. 79

---

3. What modifier is appended to report the technical component of a procedure?

    A. TC

    B. 26

    C. TC and 26

    D. None of the above

4. What modifier is appended to report a bilateral procedure?

    A. 51

    B. 50

    C. RT and LT

    D. B or C

5. When a procedure is terminated due to circumstances that threaten the well-being of the patient, which modifier is appended to the procedure code?

    A. 52

    B. 53

    C. 54

    D. 26

Documentation Dissection

Operative Note Coding 1

Preoperative Diagnosis: History of transitional cell carcinoma in the bladder and kidney

Postoperative Diagnosis: History of transitional cell carcinoma in the bladder and kidney [1]

Procedure: Cystoscopy [2]

Bladder biopsies [2]

Bilateral retrograde pyelogram [2]

Cytology [2]

Anesthesia: General

Estimated Blood Loss: Less than 5 cc

Complications: None

Counts: Correct

Indications: The patient is a very pleasant 71-year-old female status-post right nephroureterectomy for transitional cell carcinoma of the kidney, with later recurrence of bladder tumor. She understood the risks and benefits of today's procedure, and she elected to proceed.

Procedure Description: The patient was brought to the operating room and placed on the operating room table in the supine position. After adequate LMA anesthesia was accomplished, she was put in the dorsal lithotomy position and prepped and draped in the usual sterile fashion.

A 21-French rigid cystoscope was introduced through the urethra and a thorough cystourethroscopy [3] was performed. Bladder cytology was sent. A TigerTail® ureteral catheter was placed in the patient's right ureteral orifice, and a small amount of cytology was obtained. This was very difficult because the ureteral stump is extremely small. [4] We then performed a retrograde pyelogram [5] through that ureteral stump and saw no filling defects or abnormalities.

We then turned our attention to the left ureteral orifice and cannulated it with a TigerTail® catheter. We obtained cytologies and then performed a retrograde pyelogram that showed no filling defects or irregularities.

We then performed random bladder biopsies and fulgurated [6] the biopsy sites. There was no evidence of malignancy visible anywhere in the patient's bladder.

The bladder was emptied and lidocaine jelly instilled in the urethra. She was extubated and taken to the recovery room in good condition.

Disposition: The patient was taken to the postanesthesia care unit and then discharged home.

Bilateral Retrograde Pyelogram: A right retrograde pyelogram through ureteral stump showed no filling defects or abnormalities. A left retrograde pyelogram was performed, and showed no filling defects or irregularities.

----

[1] Postoperative diagnosis is used for coding.

[2] Multiple procedures performed.

[3] Cystourethroscopy was performed.

[4] Although this states it is "very difficult" there is no indication of the extra work or extra time required to repair it, so modifier 22 is not used.

[5] Retrograde pyelogram performed.

[6] Biopsies and fulguration.

What are the CPT® and ICD-10-CM codes reported?

CPT® Codes: 52224, 74420-26

ICD-10-CM Codes: Z85.51, Z85.528

Rationale: Documentation of a preoperative and postoperative diagnosis usually is provided by the physician. At times, the preoperative and postoperative diagnosis will be the same—document the postoperative diagnosis, if one is provided. In reviewing the operative note, you may be provided additional diagnoses not listed in the postoperative note, such as in "indications." These additional diagnoses should be documented on the claim, if the diagnosis is proven. As there are no additional diagnoses documented within the operative note, you will need to report the personal history of malignant neoplasm. Using ICD-10-CM Alphabetic Index look for History/personal (of)/malignant neoplasm (of)/bladder, Z85.51; and History/personal (of)/malignant neoplasm (of)/kidney NEC, Z85.528.

CPT® codes—Anesthesia, local or general, usually is not reported by the physician performing the procedure. This information is for documentation purposes only.

A cystoscopy, bladder biopsy, fulguration, bilateral retrograde pyelogram, and cytology were performed. In reading through the note, this is confirmed; all of the procedures listed were performed and no additional procedures were described. Using CPT®, first look up the procedures performed in the Index.

Cystoscopy (52000)

Retrograde Pyelogram tells you *See* Urography, Retrograde (74420).

Cystoscopy, with biopsy directs you to *See* Biopsy/Bladder/Cystourethroscopy 52204, 52224, or 52250.

Cytology is not a procedure, but a specimen, and is not reported.

After identifying the CPT® codes to report, read the description of the procedures. Because cystoscopy is a separate procedure, 52000 is not reported.

Retrograde pyelogram, 74420, was performed in a facility location, and modifier 26 is appended. When appending modifier 26 (supervision and interpretation) for the retrograde pyelogram, there must be documentation within the record of the findings.

Cystoscopy with fulguration and bladder biopsy (52224) describes the procedure performed. Code 52250 cystoscopy with insertion of radioactive substance, with or without biopsy, can be eliminated because no radioactive substance was inserted.

Within this note, the surgeon states the ureteral stump is very small. This makes the procedure difficult, but modifier 22 is not appended. To append modifier 22 the surgeon must state there was an excessive amount of time spent performing the procedure or describe in detail the condition making the procedure difficult. A ureteral stump is the remaining portion of the ureter left following a nephroureterectomy.

ICD-9-CM Application

What is/are the ICD-9-CM code(s) reported?

Code(s): V10.51, V10.52

Rationale: Look in the ICD-9-CM Index to Diseases for History personal (of)/malignant neoplasm (of)/bladder V10.51 and History personal (of)/malignant neoplasm (of)/kidney V10.52. Verify in the Tabular List.

Operative Note 2

Preoperative Diagnosis: Phimosis

Voiding dysfunction

Sexual dysfunction

Postoperative Diagnosis: Phimosis [1]

Voiding dysfunction [1]

Sexual dysfunction [1]

Procedure: Circumcision [2]

Anesthesia: General

Indications: The patient is a 17-year-old [3] white male with severe phimosis since birth that does not allow him to retract his foreskin. He also notes bleeding and pain with sexual contact and some irritation from urine being trapped under the foreskin. He understood the risks and benefits of circumcision, and he and his grandparents (who are his guardians) elect to proceed.

Procedure Description: The patient was brought to the operating room and placed on the operating room table in the supine position. After adequate LMA anesthesia was accomplished, he was given a dorsal penile block and a modified ring block with 0.25% Marcaine plain. [4]

Two circumferential incisions were made around the patient's penis to allow for the maximal aesthetic result. Adequate hemostasis was then achieved with the Bovie, and the skin edges were reapproximated using 4-0 chromic simple interrupted sutures with a U-stitch at the frenulum. [5]

The patient was extubated and taken to the recovery room in good condition.

Disposition: The patient was taken to the postanesthesia care unit and then discharged home

_____

[1] Postoperative diagnosis is used for coding.

[2] Procedure performed.

[3] The patient is over 28 days of age.

[4] Dorsal penile nerve block and a ring block were given for postoperative pain control.

[5] There is no mention of instrumentation.

_____

What are the CPT® and ICD-10-CM codes reported?

CPT® Code: 54161

ICD-10-CM Code: N47.1

Rationale: CPT® Code: Circumcision is another very straightforward procedure. In a surgical setting, you have only to decide the age of the patient to determine the appropriate CPT® code. In the CPT® Index look up Circumcision/Surgical Excision 54161. Because the patient is older than 28 days of age, report 54161. In CPT®, a newborn is 28 days of age or less.

This patient had a general anesthetic. The penile block for postoperative pain control is not reported because it was performed by the surgeon; therefore, included in the procedure as noted in the Surgery Guidelines in CPT®.

ICD-10-CM Code: Look in the Alphabetic Index for Phimosis N47.1. Although phimosis is not the only code listed for diagnosis, it is the only code pertinent to the procedure of circumcision. Voiding dysfunction and sexual dysfunction are both symptoms of phimosis; and therefore, not reported.

ICD-9-CM Application

What is/are the ICD-9-CM code(s) reported?

Code(s): 605

Rationale: Look in the Index to Diseases for Phimosis N47.1. The symptoms listed are symptoms of phimosis and are not reported separately.

Glossary

Ablation—Removal or destruction of a body part or tissue or its function. Ablation is performed by surgical means, hormones, drugs, radiofrequency, heat, cold, chemical application, or other methods.

Abscess—Circumscribed collection of pus resulting from bacteria, frequently associated with swelling and other signs of inflammation.

Adhesion—Abnormal fibrous connection between two structures (soft tissue or bony structures) may occur as the result of surgery, infection, or trauma.

Allograft—Graft from one individual to another of the same species.

Anastomosis—Surgically created connection between ducts, blood vessels, or bowel segments to allow flow from one to the other.

Anomaly—Irregularity in the structure or position of an organ or tissue.

Anuria—Suppression, cessation, or failure of the kidneys to secrete urine.

Aspiration—Drawing fluid out by suction.

Atony—Absence of normal muscle tone and strength.

Atresia—Congenital closure or absence of a tubular organ or an opening to the body surface.

Autograft—Tissue or organ transferred to a new position in the body of the same individual.

Azoospermia—Failure of sperm development or the absence of sperm in semen; one of the most common factors in male infertility.

Balanoposthitis—Inflammation and/or infection of the glans penis and prepuce.

Blunt Dissection—Surgical technique used to expose an underlying area by separating along natural cleavage lines of tissue, without cutting.

Brachytherapy—Form of radiation therapy in which radioactive pellets or seeds are implanted directly into the tissue being treated to deliver their dose of radiation in a more directed fashion. Brachytherapy provides radiation to the prescribed body area while minimizing exposure to normal tissue.

Calculus—Abnormal, stone-like concretion of calcium, cholesterol, mineral salts, or other substances forming in any part of the body.

Carcinoma *In Situ* (CIS)—Malignancy arising from cells of the vessel, gland, or organ of origin remaining confined to that site, has not invaded neighboring tissue.

Chordee—Ventral (downward) curvature of the penis due to a fibrous band along the corpus spongiosum seen congenitally with hypospadias, or a downward curvature seen on erection in disease conditions causing a lack of distensibility in the tissues.

Chronic Interstitial Cystitis—Persistently inflamed lesion of the bladder wall, usually accompanied by urinary frequency, pain, nocturia, and a distended bladder.

Circumcise—Circular cutting around the penis to remove the prepuce or foreskin.

Conduit—Surgically created channel for the passage of fluids.

Condyloma—Infectious, tumor-like growth caused by the human papilloma virus, with a branding connective tissue core and epithelial covering occurring on the skin and mucous membranes of the perianal region and external genitalia.

Cryotherapy—Surgical procedure using intense cold for ablation or treatment.

Cystitis—Inflammation of the urinary bladder. Symptoms include dysuria, frequency of urination, urgency, and hematuria.

Cystitis Cystica—Inflammation of the bladder characterized by the formation of multiple cysts.

Cystocele—Herniation of the bladder into the vagina.

Cystostomy—Formation of an opening through the abdominal wall into the bladder.

Cystotomy—Surgical incision into the urinary bladder or gallbladder.

Cutaneous—Relating to the skin.

Debridement—Removal of dead or contaminated tissue and foreign matter from a wound.

Dilation—Artificial increase in the diameter of an opening or lumen made by medication or by instrumentation.

Dissect—Cut apart or separate tissue for surgical purposes or for visual or microscopic study.

Diverticulum—Pouch or sac in the wall of an organ or canal.

Dysuria—Pain upon urination.

Electrocautery—Division or cutting of tissue using high-frequency electrical current to produce heat, which destroys cells or ablates tissue.

Epididymis—Coiled tube on the back of the testis, the site of sperm maturation and storage and where spermatozoa are propelled into the vas deferens toward the ejaculatory duct by contraction of smooth muscle.

Epididymo-orchitis—Inflammation of the testes and epididymis.

Epispadias—Male anomaly in which the urethral opening is abnormally located on the dorsum of the penis, appearing as a groove with no upper urethral wall covering.

Exenteration—Surgical removal of the entire contents of a body cavity, such as the pelvis or orbit.

Extrophy of Bladder—Congenital anomaly occurring when the bladder everts itself, or turns inside out, through an absent part of the lower abdominal and anterior bladder walls with incomplete closure of the pubic bone.

Fascia—Fibrous sheet or band of tissue that envelops organs, muscles, and groupings of muscles.

Fibrosis—Formation of fibrous tissue as part of the restorative process.

Fistula—Abnormal tube-like passage between two body cavities or organs or from an organ.

Fixate—Hold, secure, or fasten in position.

Flap—Mass of flesh and skin partially excised from its location but retaining its blood supply, moved to another site to repair adjacent or distant defects.

Fluoroscopy—Radiology technique allowing visual examination of part of the body or a function of an organ using a device projecting an X-ray image on a screen.

Foley Catheter—Temporary indwelling urethral catheter held in place in the bladder by an inflated balloon containing fluid or air.

Foreign Body—Any object or substance found in an organ and tissue not belonging under normal circumstances.

Free Graft—Unattached piece of skin and tissue moved to another part of the body and sutured into place to repair a defect.

Fulguration—Destruction of living tissue using sparks from a high-frequency electric current.

Hematoma—Tumor-like collection of fluid in some part of the body caused by a break in a blood vessel wall, usually as a result of trauma.

Hematospermia—Blood in the seminal fluid, often caused by inflammation of the prostate or seminal vesicles, or prostate cancer. In primary hematospermia, the presence of blood in the seminal fluid is the only symptom.

Hematuria—Blood in the urine, which may present as gross visible blood or as the presence of red blood cells visible only under a microscope.

Homograft—Graft from one individual to another of the same species.

Horseshoe Kidney—Congenital anomaly in which the kidneys are fused together at the lower end during fetal development, resulting in one large, horseshoe shaped kidney, often associated with cardiovascular, central nervous system, or genitourinary anomalies.

Hydronephrosis—Distention of the kidney caused by an accumulation of urine, because it cannot flow out due to an obstruction caused by conditions such as kidney stones or vesicoureteral reflux.

Hydroureter—Abnormal enlargement or distension of the ureter with water or urine caused by an obstruction.

Hyperplasia—Abnormal proliferation in the number of normal cells in regular tissue arrangement.

Hypertonicity—Excessive muscle tone and augmented resistance to normal muscle stretching.

Hypertrophic—Enlarged or overgrown from an increase in cell size of the affected tissue.

Hypospadias—Fairly common birth defect in males in which the meatus, or urinary opening, is abnormally positioned on the underside of the penile shaft or in the perineum requiring early surgical correction.

Incontinence—Involuntary escape of urine.

Impotence—Psychosexual or organic dysfunction in which there is partial or complete failure to attain or maintain erection until completion of the sexual act.

Laceration—Tearing injury; a torn, ragged-edged wound.

Laser Surgery—Use of concentrated, sharply defined light beams to cut, cauterize, coagulate, seal or vaporize tissue.

Lithotripsy—Destruction of calcified substances (eg, stones/calculi) in the gallbladder or urinary system by fragmenting the concretion into small particles to be washed out. This may be done by surgical or noninvasive methods, such as focused sound waves or ultrasound.

Lumen—Space within an artery, vein, intestine or tube.

Lysis—Destruction, breakdown, dissolution, or decomposition of cells or substances by a specific catalyzing agent.

Marsupialization—Creation of a pouch in surgical treatment of a cyst in which one wall is resected and the remaining cut edges are sutured to adjacent tissue creating an open pouch of the previously enclosed cyst.

Meatus—Opening or passage into the body.

Molluscum Contagiosum—Common, benign, viral skin infection, usually self-limiting, appears as a gray or flesh-colored umbilicated (dimpled or belly button shaped) lesion by itself or in groups, and later becomes white with an expulsable core containing the replication bodies. It is often transmitted sexually in adults, by autoinoculation, or close contact in children.

Nephrostomy—Placement of a stent, tube, or catheter forming a passage from the exterior of the body into the renal pelvis or calyx, often for drainage of urine or an abscess, for exploration, or calculus extraction.

Neurogenic Bladder—Dysfunctional bladder due to a central or peripheral nervous system lesion, may result in incontinence, residual urine retention, infection, stones, and renal failure.

Nocturnal Enuresis—Bed-wetting.

Oligospemia—Insufficient production of sperm in semen, a common factor in male infertility.

Orchiectomy—Surgical removal of one or both testicles via a scrotal or groin incision, indicated in cases of cancer, traumatic injury, and sex reassignment surgery.

Patency—State of a tube-like structure or conduit being open and unobstructed.

Perforation—Hole in an object, organ, or tissue, or the act of punching or boring holes through a part.

Perineal—Pertaining to the pelvic floor area between the thighs; the diamond-shaped area bordered by the pubic symphysis in front, the ischial tuberosities on the sides and the coccyx in the back.

Peritoneum—Strong, continuous membrane forming the lining of the abdominal and pelvic cavity. The parietal peritoneum, or outer layer, is attached to the abdominopelvic walls and the visceral peritoneum, or inner layer, surrounds the organs inside the abdominal cavity.

Peyronie's Disease—Development of fibrotic hardened tissue or plaque in the cavernosal sheaths in the penis. This causes pain and a severe chordee or curvature in the penis, typically during erection.

Phimosis—Condition in which the foreskin is contracted and cannot be drawn back behind the glans penis.

Priapism—Persistent, painful erection lasting more than four hours and unrelated to sexual stimulation, causing pain and tenderness.

Prepuce—Fold of penile skin covering the glans.

Prolapse—Falling, sliding, or sinking of an organ from its normal location in the body.

Prostate—Male gland surrounding the bladder neck and urethra that secretes a substance into the seminal fluid.

Puncture Aspiration—Use of a knife or needle to pierce a fluid-filled cavity and then withdraw the fluid using a syringe or suction device.

Retroperitoneal—Located behind the peritoneum, the membrane that lines the abdominopelvic walls and forms a covering for internal organs.

Scrotum—Skin pouch holding the testes and supporting reproductive structures.

Seminal Vesicles—Paired glands located at the base of the bladder in males, releases the majority of fluid into semen through ducts joining with the vas deferens forming the ejaculatory duct.

Skene's Gland—Paraurethral ducts draining a group of female urethral glands into the vestibule.

Sound—Long, slender tool with a type of curved, flat probe at the end for dilating strictures or detecting foreign bodies.

Spermatic Cord—Structure of the male reproductive organs consisting of the ductus deferens, testicular artery, nerves and veins draining the testes.

Stent—Tube to provide support in a body cavity or lumen.

Stoma—Opening created in the abdominal wall from an internal organ or structure for diversion of waste elimination, drainage, and access.

Stress Urinary Incontinence (SUI)—Involuntary escape of urine at times of minor stress against the bladder, such as coughing, sneezing, or laughing.

Stricture—Narrowing of an anatomical structure.

Subcutaneous Tissue—Sheet or wide band of adipose (fat) and areolar connective tissue in two layers attached to the dermis.

Testes—Male gonadal paired glands located in the scrotum secreting testosterone and containing the seminiferous tubules where sperm is produced.

Thermotherapy—Therapeutic elevation of body temperature between 107.6 and 113.0 degrees Fahrenheit.

Torsion of Testis—Twisting, turning or rotation of the testicle upon itself, so as to compromise or cut off the blood supply.

Transprostatic Implant—A system that permanently retracts prostate tissue away from the urethra without cutting,heating or removing prostate tissue. Used for the treatment of symptoms due to urinary outflow obstruction secondary to benign prostatic hyperplasia (BPH).

Trigone—Triangular, smooth area of mucous membrane at the base of the bladder, located between the ureteric openings posteriorly and the urethral opening anteriorly.

Tumor—Pathologic swelling or enlargement; a neoplastic growth or uncontrolled, abnormal multiplication of cells.

Tunica Vaginalis—Serous membrane partially covers the testes formed by an outpocketing of the peritoneum when the testes descend.

Urachus—Embryonic tube connecting the urinary bladder to the umbilicus during development of the fetus, normally closes before birth, generally in the fourth or fifth month of gestation.

Urethra—Small tube lined with m\ucous membrane leading from the bladder to the exterior of the body.

Ureterocele—Saccular formation of the lower part of the ureter, protruding into the bladder.

Urethral Caruncle—Small, polyp-like growth of a deep red color found in women on the mucous membrane of the urethral opening.

Urge Incontinence—Involuntary escape of urine coming from sudden, uncontrollable impulses.

Urostomy—Creation of an opening to the abdominal surface to divert urine flow.

Vascularization—Surgically induced development or growth of vessels in a tissue; the process of blood vessel generation.

Vas Deferens—Duct that arises in the tail of the epididymis, stores and carries sperm from the epididymis toward the urethra.

Vesical Fistula—Abnormal communication between the bladder and another structure.

Vesicoureteral Reflux—Urine passage from the bladder back into the ureter and kidneys, can lead to bacterial infection and an increase in hydrostatic pressure, causing kidney damage.

Introduction

In this chapter we will discuss CPT®, ICD-10-CM, and HCPCS Level II coding for the female reproductive system. This chapter includes coding for labor, delivery, abortion, and infertility. We will discuss chapters 14 and 15 of ICD-10-CM and the proper use of Z codes for services related to the female reproductive system.

Objectives

- Describe the structures associated with the female reproductive system
- Use appropriate medical terminology to identify services and select codes
- Apply the ICD-10-CM Guidelines for assigning codes and the special guidelines for coding complications of pregnancy, childbirth, and the puerperium
- Select CPT® and HCPCS Level II codes to describe the services and procedures related to the female reproductive system
- Apply CPT® and HCPCS Level II modifiers when appropriate

Anatomy

The central organ of the female reproductive system is the uterus. The uterus is comprised of two primary components, the cervix uteri and the corpus uteri. The cervix uteri, or neck of the uterus, is the lower portion of the uterus tapering to connect to the vagina. In its normal anatomic location the cervix protrudes into the upper vaginal canal. The fornix or fornices refer to the anterior and posterior recesses of the upper vagina surrounding the vaginal attachment to the cervix. The opening in the cervix communicates with the vagina and is known as the os or external os. The internal os of the cervix communicates with the corpus of the uterus. The body, or fundus, of the uterus is known as the corpus uteri. This is the part of the uterus where the fetus develops during pregnancy.

Two fallopian tubes, one on either side of the uterus, lead from bilateral ovaries into the uterus. They also are called oviducts, uterine tubes, tubes, and salpinges (singular salpinx). The distal ends of the fallopian tubes are called the infundibulum. The fimbriae, or fingers, near the ovaries, help capture the ovum (egg or oocyte) at ovulation as they make their way into the tubes, and to the uterus. The ovaries are the actual egg-producing reproductive organs. They also produce hormones related to the female reproductive cycles, and are therefore part of both the female reproductive and the endocrine systems. Together the fallopian tubes, ovaries, and ligaments are the uterine adnexa. Adnexa means appendages or adjunct parts.

The vagina is a tubular, muscular canal leading from the uterus to outside the body. The top of the vagina surrounds the cervix, as described above. The distal vagina opens to the vulva and perineum. Occasionally the vagina will contain a congenital partition, or vaginal septum. This septum may be either longitudinal, essentially creating a double vagina, or transverse. A transverse septum may block menstrual flow or, if incomplete, may be a cause of dyspareunia (pain during intercourse), or may obstruct delivery.

The vulva is the external genital organ of the female. It contains structures including the labia majora and minora, mons pubis, clitoris, and the vestibule or introitus of the vagina. The introitus is also the location of the hymen, a fold of mucous membrane surrounding or partially covering the external vaginal opening.

Several glands also are found in the vulva. Bartholin's glands (also called the greater vestibular glands) are located slightly inferior and to either side of the vaginal introitus. Skene's glands (also called the lesser vestibular glands, or paraurethral glands) are located on the anterior wall of the vagina around the lower end of the urethra.

The perineum is the area between the pubic symphysis and the coccyx, between the legs. This word can refer to only the superficial structures in this region, or it can be used to include both superficial and deep structures.

Female Reproductive System

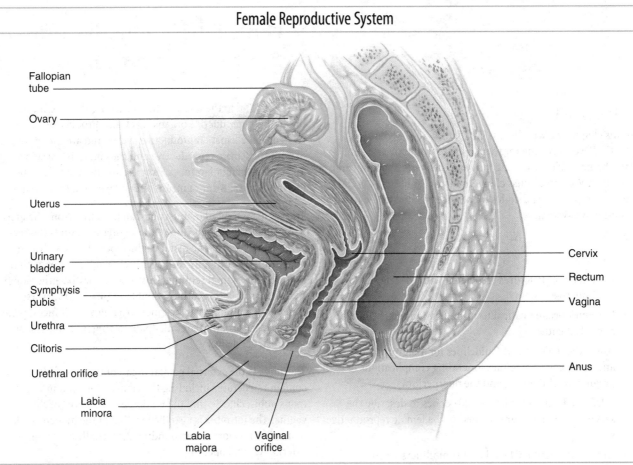

Fallopian tube
Ovary
Uterus
Urinary bladder
Symphysis pubis
Urethra
Clitoris
Urethral orifice
Labia minora
Labia majora
Vaginal orifice
Cervix
Rectum
Vagina
Anus

Source: EHRLICH/SCHROEDER. Medical Terminology for Health Professions, 6E. © 2009 Delmar Learning, a part of Cengage Learning, Inc. Reproduced by permission. www.cengage.com/permissions

Key Root Words for the Female Reproductive System

Vulv/o	vulva
Colp/o	vagina
Cervic/o	cervix
Uter/o	uterus
Hyster/o	uterus
Metri/o	uterus
Metr/o	uterus
Salping/o	fallopian tubes
Oophor/o	ovary
Gonad/o	gonad

Section Review 13.1

1. The uterine adnexa refers to which two structures of the female reproductive system?

    A. Vulva and perineum

    B. Vagina and uterus

    C. Uterus and fallopian tubes

    D. Fallopian tubes and ovaries

2. Which of the following are also known as the greater vestibular glands?

    A. Bartholin's glands

    B. Skene's glands

    C. Ovaries

    D. None of the above

3. The two structures that make up the uterus are:

    A. The uterus and uterine tubes

    B. The cervix and uterine fundus

    C. The vulva and corpus uteri

    D. The vagina and cervix

4. If you know that the suffix ~scopy means to use a scope to examine a body structure, what word means a scope procedure to examine the vagina?

    A. Hysteroscopy

    B. Laparoscopy

    C. Colposcopy

    D. Enteroscopy

5. Which of the following structures in the female reproductive system are not bilateral?

    A. Ovaries

    B. Bartholin's glands

    C. Cervix

    D. Salpinx

ICD-10-CM

In ICD-10-CM, common diagnoses for this system are found in Chapter 14: Diseases of the Genitourinary System (N00-N99) and Chapter 15: Pregnancy, Childbirth and the Puerperium (O00-O9A). Codes for neoplasms are found in Chapter 2: Neoplasms (C00-D49). Also in ICD-10-CM, Chapter 21:

Factors Influencing Health Status and Contact with Health Services are listed in Z00-Z99.

Neoplasms

Neoplasms, or tumors, are common throughout the female reproductive system and can originate in the ovaries, uterus, tubes, cervix, vagina, and vulva. These often are fast-growing malignancies that are hard to detect and may require radical procedures to treat. After a specific neoplasm has been confirmed by biopsy, look in the ICD-10-CM Alphabetic Index for the histology, such as Cancer, and you are directed to code from the Table of Neoplasms and to look for the specific structure that is the origin of the cancer.

There are many tests used to try and identify cancers of the female reproductive system. These tests may be indicative of disease, but not conclusive. An abnormal CA-125, Pap smear, or other tests should not be coded as cancer. Chapter 18, Signs, Symptoms, and Abnormal Clinical and Laboratory Findings, Not Elsewhere Classified, includes codes for abnormal findings used for reporting until a biopsy proves cancer is present. Find these codes in the Alphabetic Index under Findings, abnormal, inconclusive, without diagnosis or Abnormal. Then, look for the specific test or the type of substance tested.

There are also a number of hyperplastic conditions occurring in the female reproductive system. These are unusual growths with some characteristics of malignancies, but are not malignant. This type of tissue is referred to as pre-cancerous. Two of the most common are CIN (cervical intraepithelial neoplasia) and VIN (vulvar intraepithelial neoplasia). Both can be found under the main terms Dysplasia or Neoplasia in the ICD-10-CM Alphabetic Index. These hyperplastic conditions are staged as I, II, or III (eg, CIN II or VIN I). Stages I and II are coded as hyperplasia of the cervix or vulva, but stage III is coded as cancer (or carcinoma) *in situ* (or CIS).

Dysplasia of the cervix, vagina and vulva are found in the ICD-10-CM Index to Diseases and Injuries under Dysplasia; however, to find the codes under this main term for CIN and VIN, you are required to know if it is mild, moderate, or severe. Look in the Alphabetic Index for Dysplasia/cervix.

ICD-10-CM Index to Diseases and Injuries:

Dysplasia

  cervix (uteri) N87.9

    mild N87.0

    moderate N87.1

    severe D06.9

The same codes are also indexed under the main term Neoplasia but selected by grade. In ICD-10-CM, look in the Index to Diseases and Injuries for Neoplasia/intraepithelial/cervix:

Neoplasia

  intraepithelial (histologically confirmed)

    cervix (uteri) (CIN) (histologically confirmed) N87.9

      glandular D06.9

grade I N87.0

grade II N87.1

grade III (severe dysplasia) (see also Carcinoma, cervix uteri, in situ) D06.9

ICD-9-CM Application

ICD-9-CM Index to Diseases:

Dysplasia

  cervix (uteri) 622.10

    cervical intraepithelial neoplasia I (CIN I) 622.11

    cervical intraepithelial neoplasia II (CIN II) 622.12

    cervical intraepithelial neoplasia III (CIN III) 233.1

    CIN I 622.11

    CIN II 622.12

    CIN III 233.1

    mild 622.11

    moderate 622.12

    severe 233.1

Another common neoplasm of the female reproductive system is leiomyoma (pleural is leiomyomata), more commonly called a fibroid or myoma. These benign tumors are often found on or embedded in the musculature (myometrium) of the uterus. Fibroids can cause pelvic pain, heavy menstrual flow, frequent urination or low back pain. In the Alphabetic Index, look for Leiomyoma/uterus with code range D25.0-D25.9 by the specific type of fibroid.

- Intramural (D25.1) - These grow within the muscle of the uterine wall
- Submucous (D25.0) - These grow into the inner cavity of the uterus
- Subserosal (D25.2) - These project to the outside of the uterus
- Unspecified (D25.9) - Not specified in documentation

Female Genitourinary System

Chapter 14 of ICD-10-CM includes codes for non-neoplastic conditions of the reproductive organs for women who are not pregnant. Conditions arising during pregnancy are coded from chapter 15. Code assignment is fairly straightforward in this chapter, and care should be taken when coding for bleeding to differentiate between excessive or frequent menstruation with a regular cycle, *Menorrhagia* (N92.0), Metrorrhagia *(Bleeding unrelated to menstruation)* (N92.1), *Premenopausal menorrhagia* (N92.4) and *Postmenopausal bleeding* (N95.0).

Complications of Pregnancy, Childbirth and the Puerperium

Chapter 15 codes are used for Pregnancy, Childbirth, and the Puerperium and range from O00-O99. Chapter 15 codes have sequencing priority over codes from other chapters. Any condition a woman has during pregnancy, childbirth, or postpartum encounters that impacts the pregnancy or the pregnancy impacts the condition's treatment—whether pre-existing or new—should be coded from Chapter 15. Only if the physician states the condition is unrelated to the pregnancy, should a code from one of the other chapters be chosen with reporting Z33.1 as an additional code. Codes can be added to describe further condition(s) during pregnancy.

Example: A woman with well-controlled type II diabetes (E11.9) gets pregnant. Now her diabetes is coded from subcategory O24.11- with a code from category E11 to describe any manifestations or complications of the diabetes.

Note: Gestational diabetes is coded from subcategory O24.4- and is only reported when the patient has developed diabetes during the pregnancy until the pregnancy ends. Do not report category codes E10 and E11 with the gestational diabetes code. Code O24.01- or O24.11-is reported when the patient had pre-existing diabetes or already had diabetes before the pregnancy.

Example

A woman with well-controlled type 2 diabetes (E11.9) becomes pregnant. She is now in her 16th week of pregnancy.

O24.112 Pre-existing diabetes mellitus, type 2, in pregnancy, second trimester

E11.9 Type 2 diabetes mellitus without complications

Z3A.16 16 weeks gestation

The majority of codes in Chapter 15 have a final character to identify the trimester of the pregnancy. At the beginning of Chapter 15 trimesters are defined

- 1st Trimester - less than 14 weeks 0 days
- 2nd Trimester 14 weeks-0 days to less than 28 weeks 0 days
- 3rd Trimester - 28 weeks-0 days until delivery.

The trimester may not be part of the code if the condition being described occurs in a specific trimester or is not applicable to the condition. In ICD-10-CM some codes also have subcategories for conditions complicating childbirth and complicating the puerperium.

An instructional note at the beginning of Chapter 15 indicates to use an additional code (Z3A.-) to identify the weeks of gestation for codes O00-O9A. Look for of Pregnancy/weeks of gestation to codes in category Z3A. The weeks of the pregnancy correspond to the fourth and fifth character of the code, with the exception of less than 8 weeks (Z3A.01) and greater than 42 weeks (Z3A.49).

Example

Patient presents at 10 weeks of pregnancy with mild hyperemesis

O21.0 Mild hyperemesis gravidarum

Z3A.10 10 weeks gestation of pregnancy

In the Alphabetic Index look for Pregnancy/complicated by/hyperemesis directs you to *see also* Hyperemesis gravidarum, Look for Hyperemesis/gravidarum (mild) directs you to O21.0. The Tabular List confirms code selection that mild hyperemesis gravidarum starting before end of 20th week of gestation. Also report the weeks of gestation, Pregnancy/weeks of gestation/10 weeks with Z3A.10.

ICD-10-CM also contains a 7th character that is assigned to specific codes (Category O31, O32, O33.3 – O33.6, O35, O36, O40, O41, O60.1 – O60.2, O64, and O69) that identifies which fetus has the condition being reported. Seventh character 0 is used for a single gestation (one baby) or when it is not possible to identify which fetus is affected.

Example

A patient is pregnant and presents for ultrasound at 38 weeks with the fetus in breech position.

O32.1XX0 Maternal care for breech presentation

Z3A.38 38 weeks gestation of pregnancy

Look in the Alphabetic Index for Pregnancy/complicated by/breech position directs you to O32.1. In the Tabular List this subcategory code requires a seventh character. 0 is used for where a fetus is unspecified or single gestation. In this case only one fetus is present. Because the code is four characters in length two X placeholders are necessary to maintain the seventh character position. The complete code is O32.1XX0. Look for Pregnancy/weeks of gestation/38 weeks directs you to Z3A.38

Sites of Ectopic Pregnancy

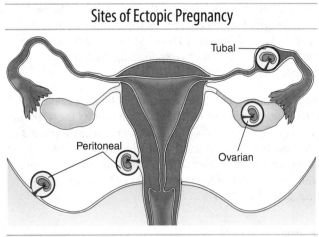

Source: Lindh, Pooler, Tamparo, and Dahl, Delmar's Comprehensive Medical Assisting (Administrative and Clinical Competencies), 4e, ISBN#978-1-4354-1914-8

Chapter 15 starts with codes related to ectopic (Category O00) and molar (O01, O02) pregnancies. An ectopic pregnancy is a pregnancy occurring outside the uterine cavity. Most often it is in the fallopian tube and is frequently called a tubal pregnancy. Molar pregnancy (blighted ovum) is an abnormal pregnancy in which a non-viable fertilized egg implants in the uterus. Hydatidiform mole is an abnormal pregnancy with cystic growth of the placenta. A molar pregnancy is a gestational trophoblastic disease (GTD). In both ectopic and molar pregnancies, surgery is often necessary. This is followed by codes for abortions (Category O03). Abortion is early fetal death. When it is spontaneous, it is referred to as a miscarriage with symptoms of bleeding, cramping, and passing of tissue. An induced abortion may be therapeutic, or elective. ICD-10-CM and CPT® recognize three types of abortions: spontaneous (also named a miscarriage), induced (caused by a deliberate procedure), or missed (when prior to 20 weeks gestation). A missed abortion occurs when the fetus dies before completion of 20 weeks of gestation but the products of conception are retained. Typically, this type of abortion is identified when the patient presents to her obstetrician with concerns of lack of fetal heartbeat, reduced fetal movement or for a regular check up or routine ultrasound and it is discovered the fetus has died. Codes in Category O04-O08 are used for complications of a termination of pregnancy, whether induced or spontaneous.

Supervision of high risk pregnancy is category O09. Look in the Alphabetic Index for Pregnancy/supervision of/ high risk will lead to specific conditions that are considered to be high-risk, although the list is not all inclusive.

This is followed by Edema, proteinuria and hypertensive disorders in pregnancy, childbirth and the puerperium (O10-O16). Codes for Other maternal disorders predominantly related to pregnancy (O20–O29) come next. Many of these codes have a fifth or sixth character (1, 2, or 3) for the trimester of the

pregnancy; 0 or 9 reports unspecified trimester depending on the situation. Trimesters are counted from the first day of the last menstrual period.

Code O80 is *only* used for a normal delivery. Normal delivery is defined as requiring minimal or no assistance, with or without episiotomy, without fetal manipulation or instrumentation or spontaneous, cephalic, vaginal, full-term, single, live-born infant. It is always used with code Z37.00 to indicate the outcome of the delivery and is only used on the maternal record not the newborn record. Use an additional code from category Z3A to indicate the weeks of gestation. Full term is defined as 37 completed weeks gestation. Code O80 is always a principal diagnosis and is not used with any other code from Chapter 15.

Z codes for pregnancy are for use when none of the complications or problems listed in the codes from Chapter 15. Code Z33.1 is used in the rare circumstances when a patient is pregnant and receives a healthcare service that is unrelated to the pregnancy. This code is never reported with the complication pregnancy codes, O00-O9A. Codes from category Z34 describe encounters to supervise or manage a normal pregnancy. These codes have a fourth character to identify the pregnancy as a first pregnancy or other (subsequent) pregnancy. The fifth character tells the trimester at the time of the prenatal visit. Supervision of high-risk pregnancy codes are located in Category O09. Other Z codes describe encounters for birth control, normal well-woman encounters, and other situations where the patient encounters healthcare but has no problems.

Acronyms

BC	Birth Control
CA	Cancer
CIN	Cervical Intraepithelial Neoplasia
CIS	Carcinoma *in Situ*
C/S	Cesarean Section or Cesarean Delivery
DNC	Dilation and Curettage (also D&C)
IND	Incision and Drainage (also I&D)
IVF	*In Vitro* Fertilization
LEEP	Loop Electrosurgical Excision Procedure
NST	Non-Stress Test
PID	Pelvic Inflammatory Disease
TAH-BSO	Total Abdominal Hysterectomy—Bilateral Salpingo-Oophorectomy
TOLAC	Trial of Labor After Cesarean
US or U/S	Ultrasound
VBAC	Vaginal Birth After Cesarean (delivery)
VIN	Vulvar Intraepithelial Neoplasia

Section Review 13.2

1. Choose the code for VIN III.

    A. N90.0

    B. N90.1

    C. D07.1

    D. D07.2

2. Which one of the following is not part of the definition of code O80?

    A. Live-born

    B. With episiotomy

    C. With forceps

    D. Spontaneous

3. A pregnant patient presents to the ED with cramping and bleeding. On examination the cervix is dilated and there are no retained products of conception. The physician documents an abortion at 10 weeks. What is the type of abortion?

    A. Missed abortion

    B. Spontaneous abortion

    C. Induced abortion

    D. None of the above

4. A woman with a long history of essential hypertension is managed throughout her pregnancy and delivers today. The hypertension has not resolved after the delivery. How should this be coded?

    A. I10

    B. O13.3

    C. O10.03

    D. O10.03, I10

5. A 68-year-old female presents with vaginal bleeding. It has been 5 years since her last period. Choose the code to describe her bleeding.

    A. N92.5

    B. N92.3

    C. N92.4

    D. N95.0

CPT® Coding

Codes for surgical treatment of the female genital system can be found in the range 56405–59899. In this section find gynecologic procedures, as well as codes for maternity care and delivery (starting with code 59000) and codes for treatment of abortion (starting with code 59812). Codes in this subsection of the Surgery chapter of CPT® are arranged from the outside of the body to the inside of the body. Coding begins with procedures on the vulva, perineum, and introitus.

Vulva, Perineum, and Introitus

The most common problems treated surgically on the vulva are infections and cancer. Infections tend to be localized abscesses and cysts, or manifestations of sexually transmitted diseases. Abscesses usually are treated with incision and drainage (I&D). A scalpel is used to open the abscess pocket, the material is expressed or drained, and the wound is treated locally with antibiotics. Occasionally, abscesses do not clear up after incision and drainage. Instead, the abscess pocket reseals itself and fills with purulent material again. When this happens, the physician may decide to perform a marsupialization. In this procedure, a scalpel is used to cut an opening in the top of the abscess pocket. The leaflets created by this procedure are pulled away from the pocket and attached to the surrounding skin with stitches or glue. This allows the abscess cavity to become a pouch (marsupialization—like a pouch on a kangaroo) so it will continue to drain and not reseal immediately. In more radical treatments, or for very large abscesses, the abscess and surrounding tissue may need to be excised.

Note: Treatment of abscesses and cysts of Skene's glands are coded in the Urinary subsection using codes 53060 or 53270.

For other types of infectious lesions, such as genital warts, or when there is widespread infection, the area may be treated with cryotherapy (freezing), laser surgery, or other methods.

Excision of the vulva typically is performed for cancer. Excisions may be simple, radical, partial, or complete in various combinations (eg, partial simple or partial radical). Simple vulvectomies include the skin and superficial subcutaneous tissues. Radical vulvectomies include removal of deep subcutaneous tissue and lymph nodes. Documentation must specify removal of deep tissue for a radical vulvectomy to be coded.

Practical Coding Note

To help distinguish between the codes for vulvectomy procedures, highlight the word partial in codes 56620 and 56630. Highlight the word complete in codes 56625, 56633, and 56640.

The vulva has two sides; a procedure described as a complete unilateral vulvectomy is a partial vulvectomy because 50 percent of the vulvar area tissue has been removed. Additionally, there is no minimum amount of tissue that must be removed for a partial vulvectomy. Very minor excisions may be coded with these codes. Helpful definitions regarding vulvectomy codes are found in the CPT® codebook in the Female Genital System under the heading, Vulva, Perineum, and Introitus.

Repair codes in the vulva section refer primarily to repairs related to congenital anomalies, except code 56810, which is used for repair of traumatic injuries. Note that any repairs related to delivery are reported with codes from the labor and delivery section.

There are also two endoscopy codes in this section. These procedures refer to inspection of the vulva and describe examination and biopsy alone.

Vagina

Codes related to incision and excision of the vagina are similar to those for the vulva, with a few exceptions. Code 57022 is the only code related to treatment of post-obstetric problems not listed in the labor and delivery section. Use code 57023 for drainage of a non-obstetric hematoma.

A frequent problem occurring as women age, and a particular problem for women who have had multiple children, is prolapse of the uterus and/or vagina. Symptoms of prolapse include discomfort and pain; protrusion of organs from the introitus; pressure; constipation if the vagina begins to fold in on the rectum (rectocele); and urinary incontinence if the vagina disrupts the anatomic position of the bladder (cystocele), urethra (urethrocele), or both (cystourethrocele). There are several possible treatment options for these conditions depending on the severity of the prolapse, age, lifestyle of the patient, and other issues.

A minimally invasive treatment option is use of a pessary. A pessary is a flexible ring shaped like a small donut; it is inserted into the vagina where it provides additional support for the uterus, bladder, and rectum. For older women who are not sexually active, colpocleisis may be performed. In this procedure the vaginal walls are sewn together, eliminating prolapse from the vagina. For younger or sexually active women, more invasive repairs may be needed.

A colpopexy can be performed via various approaches (abdominal, laparoscopic, or vaginal). In this procedure, suture material and/or mesh may be used to suspend the vagina from the boney structures in the pelvis. This may be performed with hysterectomy for severe prolapse. If the patient has a rectocele, it may be necessary to perform a posterior colporrhaphy, or posterior repair. This involves plastic repair of the vagina and the fibrous tissue separating the vagina and rectum whereby the rectovaginal fascia is plicated by folding and tacking to strengthen the area. Extra vaginal tissue is removed from the posterior wall. If the bladder and/or urethra are involved, an anterior colporrhaphy or anterior repair may be needed. This is performed in the same way on the anterior vaginal wall. If both procedures are performed, it is referred to as an anterior and posterior repair, or an A & P repair. In either case, the vaginal wall may be reinforced with mesh material. A special add-on code is available for using mesh to reinforce the walls, 57267.

If the structures supporting the urethra have been stretched, an additional procedure may be needed to create a sling to support the urethra (coded from the vagina section if performed transvaginally [57288]. Use code 51990 or 51992 if performed laparoscopically).

Other codes found in this section include 57170 for fitting of diaphragm or cervical cap for contraception, 57300–57330 for repair of fistula tract between the rectum and vagina, 57415 for removal of an impacted foreign body in the vagina when the patient is under anesthesia (other than local), and 57420–57421 for colposcopy of the entire vagina and cervix, if present.

Cervix

The section on the cervix (cervix uteri) primarily includes various biopsy procedures performed with or without colposcopy and performed transvaginally. One procedure that can be performed using either approach is conization of the cervix. In this procedure, a cone-shaped sample of tissue is removed from the cervix by either cold knife, laser method (57520 or 57455 if performed with colposcopy) or loop excision, also referred to as loop electrosurgical excision procedure, or LEEP (57522, or 57461 with colposcopy). When performing a LEEP, the physician uses a loop electrode to remove a portion of the cervix. The loop is a very hot wire; it cuts through the cervix and cauterizes the edges of the incision at the same time. The procedure is both a biopsy and a treatment for dysplasia following an abnormal Pap smear or cervical biopsy. Documentation should indicate whether a biopsy or treatment was performed, as well as the approach and method. Documentation of LEEP alone is insufficient to assign a code.

Also of note in this section is the code for cervical cerclage (57700). This is a treatment for non-pregnant women with a history of miscarriage due to an incompetent cervix and should not be used for obstetrical cerclage.

Uterus

In this section we find a number of codes related to the endometrium, including endometrial sampling (biopsy),

and dilation and curettage (D&C). The endometrium is the glandular lining of the uterus. These procedures are performed to identify any growths in the uterus and, in the case of D&C, also may provide treatment for thickened uterine lining or for retained menstrual blood and tissue. These codes should not be confused with D&C to induce or complete abortion or miscarriage, which are coded in the abortion section.

Other significant procedures in this section include hysterectomies. There are several different hysterectomy codes differing primarily in how much tissue (eg, lymph nodes, vaginal tissue, etc.) is removed at the same session and the approach: abdominal, vaginal, or endoscopic. The basic hysterectomy is 58150. This is a total abdominal hysterectomy with or without bilateral salpingo-oophorectomy, often called a TAH-BSO. This means the uterus, tubes, and ovaries are all removed. Note the service is coded the same whether neither of the tubes or ovaries or one or both tubes and one or both ovaries are removed. This procedure is performed for bleeding, benign, and malignant neoplasms, endometriosis, and prolapse.

More extensive procedures are performed for cancer, including the most extensive (58240), which is removal of essentially the entire pelvic contents. These procedures also can be performed vaginally, vaginally with laparoscopic assistance, or entirely laparoscopically. Note the differences in coding when procedures are performed vaginally. Tubes and ovaries are not automatically included. Also, the size of the uterus, by weight, affects code selection.

Other codes unique to the uterus section are hysteroscopies. In these procedures, a scope or endoscope is placed into the uterus through the cervix via the vagina. These procedures treat and diagnose conditions of the endometrium, and include procedures such as lysis of intrauterine adhesions, division of intrauterine septum, removal of leiomyomata, and occlusion of the fallopian tubes for sterilization.

Oviducts and Ovaries

Important coding in this section includes the laparoscopy subsection. These procedures include laparoscopic lysis of adhesions, partial and total removal of adnexa (which includes ovarian cystectomies), treatment of lesions on the ovaries, pelvic viscera or peritoneal surfaces (often performed to treat pelvic endometriosis), and other procedures. A common procedure performed using a laparoscope is tubal ligation. Tubal ligation is blocking of the tube or passageway from the ovaries to the uterus. This can be performed by fulguration (destruction of tissue by high-frequency electrical current), occlusion (by using a band, clip or ring), or by cutting and tying the tubes.

Tubal Ligation Methods

Banded   Cauterized   Tied and Cut

Source: AAPC

Ovary

Most of the codes in the ovary subsection are rarely performed as they describe open procedures often bundled when performed with other procedures; however, in this section are a group of radical hysterectomies for treatment of ovarian cancer. They include debulking procedures performed to reduce the size and number of tumors prior to chemotherapy and radiation therapy, as well as other radical excisions.

The last three codes in this section are for oocyte retrieval and implantation of fertilized embryos.

Maternity Care and Delivery

The codes in the Maternity Care and Delivery section are used to describe services related to antepartum, delivery, and postpartum care. All typical care—including initial and subsequent history and physical exam and routine labs throughout the normal antepartum period (usually about 13 visits), delivery and postpartum care—is part of the global OB package. Extra visits related to complicated maternity care, or any other unrelated problems treated by the physician, are billed separate. Also included is the work of the delivery, either vaginal or cesarean section, and normal postpartum care in the hospital and afterward in the clinic.

There are four codes for the global delivery package:

- 59400 is for the entire global package including vaginal delivery.
- 59510 is for the global package including cesarean delivery.
- 59610 and 59618 are for global delivery when the patient has had a previous cesarean delivery but now labors to deliver vaginally. Use 59610 if the baby is delivered vaginally, and 59618 if delivered by cesarean after trying to delivery vaginally. Do not use these codes if there is no period of labor prior to delivery.

Reporting of twin delivery can be challenging and will vary depending on the payer. A suggested plan for reporting twins is:

For the global package, both twins delivered vaginally—report code 59400 for twin A and code 59409-51 for twin B. If the patient had a previous cesarean delivery, report code 59610 and code 59612-51.

For the global package, one twin delivered vaginally and one twin delivered by cesarean delivery—report code 59510 for twin B and code 59409-51 for twin A. If the patient had a previous cesarean delivery, report code 59618 and code 59612-51. Note, in this case the 2nd twin delivered, twin B, is listed first because the delivery is by cesarean and of higher value, with the vaginal delivery of twin A listed second. Some payers may prefer modifier 59 be appended instead of modifier 51.

When both twins are delivered by cesarean delivery, report either code 59510 or 59618 for the global service. Only one code is listed because only one cesarean incision is made. In some cases a modifier 22 can be added if the cesarean delivery was significantly more difficult than usual. Documentation will need to be submitted if modifier 22 is reported.

There are additional codes to use if the global OB package must be divided because of change of insurance or change of doctor. Antepartum care, delivery, and postpartum care can be billed separately when necessary.

A number of services may be performed during the antenatal period, but are not part of the global OB package. Included in this group are amniocentesis (59000 and 59001), fetal stress and non-stress tests, and several services are listed in the Radiology chapter of CPT®.

Amniocentesis

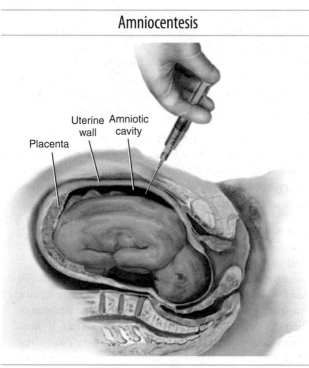

Uterine   Amniotic
wall   cavity
Placenta

Source: Lindh, Pooler, Tamparo, and Dahl, Delmar's Comprehensive Medical Assisting (Administrative and Clinical Competencies), 4e, ISBN#978-1-4354-1914-8

The most common radiologic service performed in pregnancy is the limited ultrasound (76815). This ultrasound usually is performed to confirm the size, placental placement, and anticipated delivery date. This procedure is performed so routinely, many payers include one ultrasound in the typical delivery reimbursement. Other ultrasounds in the obstetrical section require additional specific documentation, as outlined in the CPT® codebook. Non-obstetrical ultrasounds also have specified documentation requirements. All billable ultrasound services require an image of the service be captured and stored either on paper or electronically.

Abortions

Abortion codes are chosen based on the type of abortion involved: spontaneous, induced, or missed. It is important to know the definitions of each type of abortion to select the appropriate code (see the information in the ICD-10-CM section of this chapter). Also, it is important to note if a patient has a spontaneous abortion (eg, miscarriage), but does not require surgical completion, management is coded using E/M codes, including prolonged services when appropriate. A missed abortion treated non-surgically is coded with E/M codes only. Administration of pitocin to speed the process of expelling the products of conception (or POC) is not considered surgical treatment.

An incomplete abortion is an abortion where there are retained products of conception (POC). With a complete abortion, all of products of conception are expelled. It is possible for documentation to reflect a patient had a complete abortion initially and then returned with pain and bleeding at a later time and was found to have retained products of conception, thereby the abortion is incomplete.

An ectopic pregnancy occurs when a fertilized egg implants outside the uterus. It can develop in the fallopian tube, cervix, wall of the uterus (interstitial), abdomen, or ovary. This is a serious, life threatening condition to the mother. Codes 59120-59140 are reported for open surgical treatment of ectopic pregnancies and chosen according to where the pregnancy implants and is developing. This is further broken down if other anatomical areas are removed. Codes 59150 and 59151 are reported for laparoscopic treatment of ectopic pregnancies.

To select an appropriate code for termination of pregnancy, codes 59812-59857, you must know the following:

- What was the cause of or reason for termination?
- When was the pregnancy terminated?
- What services were rendered (CPT®)?
- Was patient in labor before termination?
- Was labor enhanced?
- Was labor induced?
- Were products of conception already expelled? Completely?

With this information in hand, you can determine an appropriate code, as follows:

Surgical management (eg, D&C or D&E) of incomplete abortion (defined by ACOG as the expulsion of some products of conception with the remainder evacuated surgically): Report 59812 *Treatment of incomplete abortion, any trimester, completed surgically.*

Surgical management (eg, D&C or D&E) of missed abortion (defined by ACOG as a pregnancy containing an empty gestational sac, a blighted ovum, or a fetus or fetal pole without a heartbeat):

Prior to 14 weeks 0 days gestation: report 59820 *Treatment of missed abortion, completed surgically; first trimester.*

14 weeks 0 days gestation to prior to 20 weeks 0 days gestation: report 59821 *Treatment of missed abortion, completed surgically; second trimester.*

After 20 weeks 0 days: 59821-22 (append modifier 22 to indicate the increased difficulty of the procedure after 20 weeks)

For septic abortion, report 59830.

Induced abortion via D&C or D&E (without hospital admission and labor):

Prior to 14 weeks 0 days: report 59840 *Induced abortion, by dilation and curettage.*

14 weeks 0 days to prior to 20 weeks 0 days: 59841 *Induced abortion, by dilation and evacuation.*

20 weeks 0 days or more by D&E: 59841-22.

Induced abortion via intra-amniotic injections, with hospital admission, visits and delivery:

Prior to 20 weeks 0 days gestation: 59850 I*nduced abortion, by one or more intra-amniotic injections (amniocentesis-injections), including hospital admission and visits, delivery of fetus and secundines,* 59851 *Induced abortion, by one or more intra-amniotic injections (amniocentesis-injections), including hospital admission and visits, delivery of fetus and secundines, with dilation and curettage and/or evacuation,* or 59852 *Induced abortion, by one or more intra-amniotic injections (amniocentesis-injections), including hospital admission and visits, delivery of fetus and secundines, with hysterotomy (failed intra-amniotic injection)* (May be used whether or not fetus has heartbeat prior to delivery).

After 20 weeks 0 days, report maternity care and delivery codes 59400–59515, as appropriate.

Induced abortion via vaginal suppositories/cervical dilation, with hospital admission, visits and delivery:

Prior to 20 weeks 0 days gestation: 59855 *Induced abortion, by one or more vaginal suppositories (eg, prostaglandin) with or without cervical dilation (eg, laminaria), including hospital admission and visits, delivery of fetus and secundines,* 59856 *Induced abortion, by one or more vaginal suppositories (eg, prostaglandin) with or without cervical dilation (eg, laminaria), including hospital admission and visits, delivery of fetus and secundines; with dilation and curettage and/or evacuation,* or 59857 *Induced abortion, by one or more vaginal suppositories (eg, prostaglandin) with or without cervical dilation (eg, laminaria), including hospital admission and visits, delivery of fetus and secundines; with hysterotomy (failed medical evacuation)* (May be used whether fetus does or does not have heartbeat prior to delivery).

After 20 weeks 0 days, report maternity care and delivery codes 59400–59515, as appropriate.

Related Coding

Although not properly part of the female reproductive system there are a couple of additional codes to know about not listed in the female reproductive system section. Just before the female reproductive system codes start is a small subsec-

tion called Reproductive System Procedures. The single code (55920) is for placement of needles or catheters into pelvic organs and/or genitalia for subsequent interstitial radioelement application. This code can be used for either males or females and is used when a more specific code (for example, placement of needles into the prostate, 55875, or placement of uterine tandems or vaginal ovoids, 57155) is not appropriate.

There are two codes for intersex surgery. One for male to female (55970), and one for female to male (55980). These codes include all of the work associated with genital reassignment surgery, but do not include any adjunct services (for example, construction of breasts or mastectomy).

There is also a single time-based code for medical genetics counseling. This code is used only by non-physician counselors trained in genetics. Physicians who provide genetic counseling should use E/M codes to describe the service. This code (96040) is listed once for 16–30 minutes of face-to-face counseling provided. Physicians who provide genetic counseling should use E/M codes to describe the service. It should be noted that this code is for one-on-one genetic counseling only. For education regarding genetic risks by a non-physician to a group, use codes 98961–98962 from the Medicine section. For genetic counseling and/or risk factor reduction intervention provided to patient(s) without symptoms or established disease, by a physician or other qualified healthcare professional use codes 99401–99412 from the Evaluation and Management section.

HCPCS Level II

In addition to the normal drug and supply codes used in HCPCS Level II coding, there are two particular HCPCS Level II codes of special importance in female reproductive system coding. The first is G0101 for the Medicare breast and pelvic exam. Medicare expects that at least 7 of the 11 elements described in the Female Genitourinary Exam defined by the 1997 Evaluation and Management Guidelines (discussed in Chapter 19) will be documented to bill the service. They include:

- Inspection and palpation of breasts (eg, masses or lumps, tenderness, symmetry, nipple discharge)
- Digital rectal examination including sphincter tone, presence of hemorrhoids, rectal masses
- External genitalia (eg, general appearance, hair distribution, lesions)
- Urethral meatus (eg, size, location, lesions, prolapse)
- Urethra (eg, masses, tenderness, scarring)
- Bladder (eg, fullness, masses, tenderness)
- Vagina (eg, general appearance, estrogen effect, discharge, lesions, pelvic support, cystocele, rectocele)

- Cervix (eg, general appearance, lesions, discharge)
- Uterus (eg, size, contour, position, mobility, tenderness, consistency, descent or support)
- Adnexa/parametria (eg, masses, tenderness, organomegaly, nodularity)
- Anus and perineum

Additionally, code Q0091 is used for obtaining a Pap smear. In CPT®, code 99000 is used to describe this service, but it is rarely paid as it is considered to be bundled into an E/M service performed on that date.

Modifiers

The standard CPT® E/M modifiers apply to female reproductive system coding, including modifier 25 when an E/M service is performed on the date of another separate service. Of note,

no modifiers are required on E/M services performed and billed separately during the antenatal period. Although there is a global period involved, the global concept does not attach until after the delivery is billed. Use of modifier 24 is inappropriate unless the insurer requires it (or some other modifier) to indicate the service was not part of the global care.

Modifier 51 *Multiple procedures* indicates more than one surgical procedure was provided during the same surgical session. Modifier 51 is not appended to Evaluation and Management, radiology, pathology/laboratory, or medicine codes.

Section Review 13.3

1. Physician performs an incision and drainage of an abscess located on the labia majora. What CPT® code is reported?

    A. 10060

    B. 56405

    C. 56420

    D. 53060

2. Patient comes in with uterine bleeding. Physician performs a diagnostic dilation and curettage by scraping all sides of the uterus. What CPT® code is reported?

    A. 58100

    B. 59160

    C. 57505

    D. 58120

3. A patient delivers twins at 32 weeks gestation for her first pregnancy. The first baby is delivered vaginally, but during the delivery the second baby has turned into a breech position. The physician decides to perform a cesarean delivery for the second baby. What CPT® code(s) is/are reported?

    A. 59400, 59409-51

    B. 59510-22

    C. 59510, 59409-51

    D. 59618, 59612-51

---

4. A 52-year-old female patient is scheduled for surgery for a right ovarian mass. Through an open incision, the surgeon finds a healthy left ovary. A right ovarian mass is visualized and the decision is made to remove the mass and the right ovary. What CPT® code is reported?

    A. 58940

    B. 58925

    C. 58920

    D. 58720

5. A 63-year-old female patient has severe intramural fibroids. The surgeon performs an open total abdominal hysterectomy with removal of the fallopian tubes and ovaries. What CPT® code is reported?

    A. 58200

    B. 58150

    C. 58548

    D. 58262

Documentation Dissection

Case 1

Preop Dx: Recurrent VIN III

Postop Dx: Recurrent VIN III

Procedure:
1. CO_2 laser ablation of vulvar dysplasia

2. Excision vulvar dysplasia

Indications: 36-year-old female, heavy smoker, with long history of severe dysplasia of the vulva, cervix and perianal area. Now has discomfort and pain with sitting on the left side and on exam found to have painful verrucous lesion, similar in appearance to previous dysplasia. Patient refused in-office biopsy and opted for see-and-treat management with CO2 laser and excision.

Operative Findings: [1] After application of 3% acetic acid, acetowhite area is seen almost circumferentially around the vaginal opening. Thick acetowhite at 7 o'clock around introitus and a cluster of verrucous acetowhite lesions from 3–5 o'clock. A small acetowhite lesion was seen on the vulva approximately 1 cm to the right of the posterior fourchette.

Procedure: Patient was taken to the operating room where general anesthesia was induced. She was prepared and draped in normal sterile fashion in dorsal lithotomy position in the candy cane stirrups. Wet towels were used around the vulva and anus to drape and a wet sponge was placed in the vagina. A sponge soaked in 3% acetic acid was placed over the vulva and perianal area for several minutes, and the findings were noted as above. Laser ablation [2] of the vulvar lesion at 7 o'clock was performed. The area with verrucous lesions (1 cm) was excised using a scalpel [3] and needle-tipped cautery. Hemostasis was secured with cautery. Additional laser ablation was done of small acetowhite and hyperpigmented areas around the introitus and margins of the excision. The excision defect was closed with 3-0 Polysorb with interrupted stitches. [4] Silvadene cream was liberally applied to the area. The patient tolerated the procedure well, all sponge and needle counts were correct. The patient was taken to the PACU in stable condition.

[1] Although the findings are not enough to code from, they often give important details that can help a coder follow the operative report.

[2] Multiple treatment modalities are covered with code 56501.

[3] Although multiple modalities were used, the code can only be billed once for the VIN III lesions. Also code for the excision of the verrucous lesion.

[4] Closure is bundled into this procedure.

What are the CPT® and ICD-10-CM codes reported?

CPT® Codes: 11421, 56501-51

ICD-10-CM Codes: B07.9, D07.1

Rationale: CPT® Codes: Look in the CPT® Index for Excision/Skin/Lesion, Benign for the range of codes. Code 11421 describes excision of 1 cm verrucous lesions of the genitalia. This lesion is still contained, some would call it "premalignant" but is not malignant yet, so it is an excision of a benign lesion. Next in the Index look for Destruction/Lesion/Vulva, and you are given a selection of simple (56501) or extensive (56515). The documentation does not mention extensive destruction; therefore, report 56501. Modifier 51 is needed for additional procedures performed during the same session.

ICD-10-CM Codes: In the ICD-10-CM Index to Disease and Injuries, look for Verruca B07.9. Then look for Neoplasia/intraepithelial/vulva/grade III (severe dysplasia), and you are directed to D07.1. Verification of the code in the Tabular List confirms code selection.

ICD-9-CM Application

What is/are the ICD-9-CM code(s) reported?

Code(s): 078.10, 233.32

Rationale: In the Index to Diseases look for Verruca 078.10 . Verify in the Tabular List. Then look for Dysplasia/vulva/VIN III directing you to code 233.32. Verify this code in the Tabular List. VIN III is listed as an inclusional term under 233.32

Case 2

Preoperative Diagnosis(es)

1.   Uterine prolapse.

2.   Cystocele

3.   Pelvic pain.

Postoperative Diagnosis(es)

1.   Uterine prolapse.

2.   Cystocele

3.   Vulvar lesion

Procedure Performed

Total vaginal hysterectomy.

Anterior colporrhaphy.

Vulvar biopsy.

Indications for Procedure: Patient is a 65-year-old, with uterine prolapse; specifically, cystocele, that was associated with pelvic pain. She is taken to the Operating Room for definitive management of her prolapse and pelvic pain. She has no stress urinary incontinence and is sexually active.

Findings at the Time of the Surgery: There was a Grade II to III cystocele. She also had a Grade I to II uterine prolapse. The adnexa were not enlarged. There was also moderate erythema of the labia minora and introitus, with some white epithelial changes below the clitoris that appear consistent with possible lichen sclerosis. This site was biopsied and sent to Pathology.

Description of Procedure: The patient was taken to the Operating Room, where general anesthesia was found to be adequate. The patient was prepped and draped in the usual dorsal lithotomy position in the Yellowfin leg rests. The external genitalia were examined with findings as above. An excisional biopsy [1] of the lesion was performed. After the exam under anesthesia, [2] a short weighted speculum was placed in the vagina, and a Deaver retractor was used. The cervix was easily identified and was grasped with single-toothed tenaculum. We then proceeded to inject approximately 13 cc of low-dose pitressin. Then, with the aid of the Bovie cautery, we proceeded to place an incision along the cervical uterine junction. The anterior and posterior cul-de-sac were entered without difficulty. The posterior vaginal cuff was made hemostatic with placement of a running lock suture with 0-Vicryl. A long weighted speculum was then placed through the vagina into the peritoneum. [3] The uterosacral's were then grasped, clamped, cut, and ligated with the LigaSure. We then proceeded to sequentially isolate all the ligaments and blood supply, including the uterine, cardinal ligaments, and finally the utero-ovarian ligaments, [4] with the aid of the LigaSure. The utero-ovarian ligaments were doubly clamped with Heaney clamps, along with LigaSure. An additional transfixion suture was placed at both utero-ovarian ligaments for additional hemostasis. The uterus was removed from the vagina and weighed 200 grams. [5] After completion of the hysterectomy, all pedicles were inspected and were found to be hemostatic. The vaginal cuff was closed with 0-Vicryl in a running locked fashion.

We proceeded with the anterior colporrhaphy [6] component of the surgery. Allis clamps were placed along the vaginal epithelium anteriorly [7] and the vaginal epithelium was entered with the Metzenbaum. The epithelium was then separated and dissected off the cystocele, and the endopelvic fascia was then easily identified. After completely dissecting the vaginal epithelium to the lateral aspects, we then proceeded with plication of the cystocele, which was performed with 0 Vicryl on a GU needle. Care was taken to place a Kelly plication stitch. The redundant vaginal epithelium was then cut with the Metzenbaum. The vaginal epithelium was then re-approximated with interrupted single sutures of 0-Polysorb. There was excellent hemostasis at the end of the case. Vaginal packing was placed. The patient tolerated the procedure well and was taken to the PACU in stable condition.

Addendum: Pathology report confirmed lichen sclerosus (acrodermatitis atrophicans) from the vulvar biopsy.

_____

[1] This is an excisional biopsy.

[2] This cannot be billed separately when a therapeutic procedure is performed at the same session.

[3] This is the approach.

[4] The ligaments were clamped but this is not removal of the ovaries or tubes, which is coded separately for vaginal hysterectomy.

[5] Uterus weighs less than 250 grams and is coded differently.

[6] Separate procedure on the vagina alone.

[7] Indicates anterior colporrhaphy.

_____

What are the CPT® and ICD-10-CM codes reported?

CPT® Codes: 58260, 57240-51, 56605-59

ICD-10-CM Codes: N81.2, N90.4, L90.4

Rationale: CPT® Codes: In the CPT® Index, look for Hysterectomy/Vaginal, and you are given a range of codes. 58260 is the correct code choice for a uterus weighing less than 250 grams. In this case the uterus weighed 200 grams. Second, an anterior colporrhaphy was performed. In the Index, look for Colporrhaphy/Anterior and you are directed to 57240 and

57289. 57240 is the correct code for an anterior colporrhaphy with repair of a cystocele. In addition, there was a vulvar biopsy performed which is found in the Index under Biopsy/Vulva. Since only one lesion was biopsied, 56605 is the correct code choice. Modifier 51 is appended to the second code to indicate multiple procedures. Code 56605 is a separate procedure. CPT® surgery guidelines for a separate procedure indicates when a separate procedure code is carried out independently append modifier 59. Some payers may follow CMS NCCI edits which indicate modifier 51.

ICD-10-CM: In the ICD-10-CM Index to Diseases and Injuries, look for Prolapse, prolapsed/uterovaginal/incomplete directing you to code N81.2. Looking in the Tabular List confirms this code selection. The pathology report confirms lichen sclerosus (acrodermatitis atrophican. Look for Lichen/sclerosus/vulva directs you to N90.4 and the Tabular List confirms this code with a description of Lichen sclerosus of external female genital organs. Look for Acrodermatitis/atrophicans (chronica) directing you to code L90.4. In the Tabular List there is an excludes2 note that indicates acrodermatitis chronica atrophicans can also be used if both conditions exist.

ICD-9-CM Application

What is/are the ICD-9-CM code(s) reported?

Code(s): 618.2, 701.8

Rationale: In the ICD-9-CM Index to Diseases, look for Prolapse/uterovaginal/incomplete and you are directed to 618.2. Next, look for Cystocele/female/with uterine prolapse/incomplete and you are directed to the same code, 618.2. Next, look for Lichen/sclerosus and you are directed to 701.0. However, verification of 701.0 does not include acrodermatitis atrophicans. Look for Acrodermatitis / atrophicans (chronica) directs you 701.8 which can be verified in the Tabular List.

Glossary

Amnionicity—The number of amniotic sacs in a multiple gestation pregnancy.

Bartholin's Gland—Two glands located in the vulvar area, slightly below and to either side of the vaginal introitus; also called the greater vestibular glands.

Cerclage—Placement of stitches to hold the cervix closed. May be performed during pregnancy to treat an incompetent cervix.

Chorionicity—The number of placentae in a multiple gestation pregnancy

Colpocleisis—The vaginal walls are sewn together eliminating prolapse of or through from the vagina.

Colpopexy—Procedure to return the vagina (and sometimes the uterus) to its normal anatomic position in the pelvis.

Colporrhaphy—Any procedure to repair the vagina; typically refers to plicating and tacking the weakened fibrous tissue between the bladder and vagina (cystocele) or the rectum and vagina (rectocele).

Conization of Cervix—Removal of a cone-shaped piece of mucosal tissue from the cervix, as a biopsy and/or to treat hyperplasia. If performed with a loop electrode, it may be referred to as a LEEP conization.

Corpus Uteri—The main body, or fundus, of the uterus, above the cervix.

Dilation and Curettage (D&C)—Dilation means enlarging or stretching and curettage means scraping.

Ectopic Pregnancy—Life threatening condition to the mother when a fertilized egg implants outside the uterus developing in the fallopian tube, cervix, wall of the uterus (interstitial), abdomen, or ovary.

Fulguration—The destruction of tissue, usually malignant tumors, by means of a high-frequency electric current applied with a needlelike electrode.

Gravida—The number of times a woman has been pregnant. G2 P2 indicates two pregnancies and two live births.

Hymenotomy—A fold of mucous membrane surrounds or partially covers the external vaginal opening, called the hymen. When this membrane completely covers the vaginal opening, or is too tough, surgery may be used to cut it away.

Hysterectomy—Removal of the uterus.

Induced Abortion—Intentional termination of pregnancy. SYN: medical A, therapeutic A, or elective A.

Introitus—Opening from outside of the body into the vagina. It is located in the vulva.

Lysis—Destruction; often used in relation to scar tissue or adhesions. It can be used by itself or can be used as a suffix, as in adhesiolysis, which means destruction of adhesions.

Marsupialization—Surgery used to cut an opening in the top of an abscess pocket. The leaflets created by this procedure are pulled away from the pocket and attached to the surrounding skin with stitches or glue, creating a pouch. This can be performed using a scalpel, scissors, or bovie.

Missed Abortion—The fetus dies before completion of 22 weeks of gestation but the products of conception are retained.

Para—The number of live births. G2 P2 indicates two pregnancies and two live births.

Perineum—Area between the pubic symphysis and the coccyx, between the legs. This word can refer to only the superficial structures in this region, or it can be used to include both superficial and deep structures.

Pessary—A flexible ring placed in the vagina, helps support the pelvic floor and treat prolapse and incontinence.

Post-partum—Period of time after childbirth up to six weeks following childbirth.

Puerperium—Period of time after childbirth up to six weeks (42 days) following childbirth.

Skene's Gland—Located in the vulvar area, several glands found on the anterior wall of the vagina around the lower end of the urethra. They also are called the lesser vestibular glands, or periurethral glands.

Spontaneous Abortion—Miscarriage or the natural loss of pregnancy when there is an expulsion of products of conception before completion of 22 weeks of gestation.

Urethrocele—Condition resulting from vaginal prolapse, resulting in prolapse of the urethra.

Urethrovaginal Fistula—An abnormal opening between the urethra and the vagina. Occurs with prolapse or development of an urethrocele; or because of previous surgery in the area.

Vaginal Septum—A congenital anomaly. Extra tissue divides the vagina either longitudinally or horizontally. A longitudinal vaginal septum sometimes is called a double vagina.

Vulva—The external female genitalia including the labia majora and minora, mons pubis, clitoris, vestibule (introitus) of the vagina, and the urethra.

Introduction

This chapter will discuss CPT®, ICD-10-CM, and HCPCS Level II coding for the Endocrine and Nervous systems. The majority of CPT® codes relevant to these systems are found within the 60000–64999 range, with additional codes found in the Medicine section (90000-series). Procedures may range from major or minor surgery, to diagnostic and therapeutic injection, and electro-diagnostic testing (such as electromyography or nerve conduction studies).

ICD-10-CM codes for the Endocrine system are found primarily in chapter 4, Endocrine, Nutritional and Metabolic Diseases (E00-E89). Codes specific to the Nervous system may be found in chapter 6, Diseases of the Nervous System (G00-G99). Additional relevant codes (eg, for neoplasms) are located throughout ICD-10-CM.

Objectives

- Master anatomical concepts important to understand the endocrine and nervous systems
- Review terminology relevant to these systems
- Provide practical advice to overcome the most common CPT® coding dilemmas involving these systems
- Alert you to important documentation issues and possible shortcomings, as they apply to procedures of the endocrine and nervous systems
- Discuss application of most-frequently used CPT® modifiers
- Introduce ICD-10-CM and HCPCS Level II codes and coding guidelines as they apply to these systems
- Supply hands-on examples and review material to improve your mastery of the above concepts

Anatomy

The Endocrine System

The endocrine system is comprised of glands located throughout the body producing various hormones. Endocrine glands are ductless glands that secrete hormones directly into the circulatory system. Hormones regulate many body functions, including growth and development, mood, metabolism, and tissue function.

The thyroid gland is located anteriorly in the neck, just below the thyroid cartilage, or "Adam's Apple." It controls how quickly the body uses energy, makes proteins, and determines sensitivity of the body to other hormones. The butterfly-shaped gland is composed of two wings, or lobes, connected by an isthmus over the trachea. Surgeons may remove all or a portion of the thyroid (for instance, due to neoplasm). Lobectomy describes excision of all (total) or a portion (partial) of one lobe of the thyroid. Isthmusectomy describes excision of the isthmus (the "body of the butterfly") of the thyroid.

There are four parathyroid glands. They are found on the posterior surface of the thyroid gland. These glands maintain the body's calcium level for proper functioning of the nervous and muscular systems. Parathyroidectomy describes excision of the parathyroid gland(s).

The thymus is located in the chest, behind the sternum and in front of the heart. The thymus produces T-lymphocytes, or T cells, and produces and secretes hormones to control immune function. The gland is composed of two identical lobes. The thymus is prominent during infancy and childhood and usually shrinks after puberty, by adulthood it is replaced by fat but continues to produce T cells. Thymectomy (partial or total) describes excision of the thymus. This may be achieved by a number of surgical approaches, including transcervical (via the neck), transthoracic (via the chest), or sternal split (also via the chest).

The adrenal (or suprarenal) glands sit directly atop the kidneys, one per side ("adrenal" means "near the kidneys"). Each gland is comprised of two portions, the medulla and the cortex. The cortex is divided further into three distinct zones: the zona glomerulosa, zona fasciculata, and zona reticularis. Each portion (and sub-portion) of the adrenal glands performs a distinct function. The adrenal glands are responsible primarily for releasing stress hormones, including cortisol from the cortex and adrenaline and norepinephrine from the medulla, among other hormones. Excision of the adrenal glands (partial or complete, open or laparoscopic) is an adrenalectomy.

The pancreas lies near the bottom of the stomach. It is a dual-function gland performing both endocrine and exocrine (digestive) functions. The islets of Langerhans (also called islet cells) of the pancreas produce the hormones insulin and glucagon. These hormones are important in regulating blood glucose levels (endocrine function). As a digestive organ, the pancreas secretes digestive enzymes flowing through the pancreatic duct to the small intestine (exocrine function).

CPT® subheading Parathyroid, Thymus, Adrenal Glands, Pancreas, and Carotid Body includes the Pancreas; however, there are no codes for the pancreas listed. Codes pertaining to the pancreas are listed in the Digestive System subsection.

Endocrine System

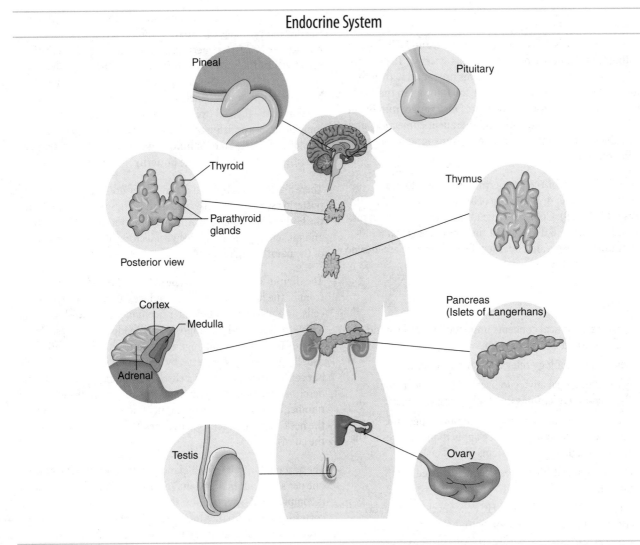

Source: RIZZO. Fundamentals of Anatomy and Physiology, 3E. © 2010 Delmar Learning, a part of Cengage Learning, Inc. Reproduced by permission. www.cengage.com/permissions

The carotid body contains some glandular tissue, but is not an endocrine structure. CPT® nevertheless locates it within the endocrine system code set (60000–60699). It is located in the neck, at the division (bifurcation) of the common carotid artery into the internal and external carotid arteries, and serves primarily as an "oxygen sensor" helping regulate breathing and blood pressure.

CPT® groups two additional glands, the pituitary gland and pineal gland, into nervous system codes (61000-64999). This is due to the glands' location within the brain.

The pituitary gland (hypophysis cerebri) is located just under the hypothalamus of the brain, which controls it. It is roughly the size of a pea, and has two lobes (anterior and posterior pituitary gland), each serves a different purpose. This "master gland" regulates a wide variety of functions including: growth, metabolism, milk production and uterine contractions in pregnant women. The anterior pituitary produces the following hormones: growth hormone (GH), thyroid stimulating hormone (TSH), adrenocorticotrophic hormone (ACTH), melanocyte-stimulating hormone (MSH), follicle-stimulating hormone (FSH), luteinizing hormone (LH) and prolactin

(PRL). The posterior pituitary produces antidiurectic hormone (ADH) or vasopressin, and oxytocin (OT).

The pineal gland (also pineal body, epiphysis cerebri, or epiphysis) is found deep within the brain, above the cerebellum and between the left and right hemispheres. It resembles a pine cone, but is approximately the size of a grain of rice. It produces the hormone melatonin, which modulates wake/sleep patterns and seasonal functions, and serotonin, which acts as a neurotransmitter and vasoconstrictor. Serotonin stimulates smooth muscle contraction and inhibits gastric secretions.

The testes and the ovaries secrete sex hormones as endocrine glands. The principal male sex hormone is testosterone, and the ovaries produce testosterone and estrogen. CPT® includes procedures for these organs in the Male Genital System (54000–55899) and the Female Genital System (56405–58999).

The Nervous System

As described in chapter 2, the nervous system is comprised of two parts:

1. The brain and spinal cord (the central nervous system, or CNS)

2. The remaining network of nerves running throughout the body (the peripheral nervous system, or PNS)

The PNS sends information to, and receives instruction from, the CNS. The CNS commands the entire body, including both conscious and subconscious movement and function.

To understand the anatomy and terminology of the nervous system, we'll reduce this complex system to several basic components. We'll begin by discussing individual nerves and how they operate. We will overview the major nerves of the PNS. Next, we'll discuss the spinal cord; the spinal cord is housed within the spinal column or vertebrae. A review of spinal skeletal anatomy will be helpful. We will also discuss the various structures of the brain.

Nerves

Individual nerves come in a variety of sizes and have specialized functions. A single nerve, or neuron, is comprised of a soma (or cell body, containing the cell nucleus), several dendrites, and an axon.

Neuron

Function	Characteristics and Location	Morphology
Neurons (nerve cells) These cells have the ability to react to stimuli. **1. Irritability—** Ability of nerve tissue to respond to environmental changes. **2. Conductivity—** Ability to carry a nerve impulse (message).	Nerve tissue is composed of _neurons_ (nerve cells). Neurons have branches through which various parts of the body are connected and their activities coordinated. They are found in the brain, spinal cord, and nerves.	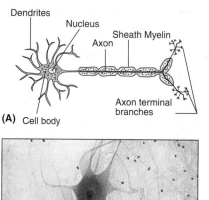

Source: RIZZO. Fundamentals of Anatomy and Physiology, 3E. © 2010 Delmar Learning, a part of Cengage Learning, Inc.
Reproduced by permission. www.cengage.com/permissions

Dendrites resemble tree branches, and increase the number of possible connections among nerve cells. Signals picked up by dendrites travel through the cell and continue along the axon, and are transmitted to the next cell. Axon terminals (synaptic bulbs) of a transmitting neuron and dendrites of a receiving neuron do not touch; they are separated by a small space, called a synapse. Across a synapse minute electrical impulses are passed from one nerve to another via chemical messengers called neurotransmitters (such as serotonin). Any disruption of normal production or function of neurotransmitters may cause problems, including mood and attention disorders.

The majority of nerves in the PNS are myelinated. Myelination means the axon is coated with a myelin sheath, a layer of fatty cells (Schwann cells) acting as insulation. At regular intervals along the axon, there are gaps in the myelin sheath (the nodes of Ranvier) allowing faster transmission of nerve impulses. If the myelin sheath were not present, nerve impulses passing along an axon could generate unwanted responses in nearby neurons. This could result in muscle contraction and jerky, irregular movements. People with myelin sheath damage (for instance, due to multiple sclerosis) often have difficulty with muscle control.

A nerve plexus is a network of intersecting nerves combining spinal nerves serving the same body area. There are several nerve plexi in the body, including:

Cervical Plexus—Serves the head, neck and shoulders

Brachial Plexus—Serves the chest, shoulders, arms and hands

Lumbar Plexus—Serves the back, abdomen, groin, thighs, knees, and calves

Sacral Plexus—Serves the pelvis, buttocks, genitals, thighs, calves, and feet

Solar or Coccygeal Plexus—Serves internal organs

Because the lumbar and sacral plexi are interconnected, they sometimes are called the lumbosacral plexus.

Major Nerves of the Peripheral Nervous System

Femoral Nerve—Sensory and motor nerve supplying the front of the thigh and part of the lower leg.

Common Fibular Nerve (common peroneal)—Sensory and motor nerve supplying the knee and superior tibiofibular joints and tibialis anterior muscle. It divides into superficial and deep fibular (peroneal) nerves; a branch of the sciatic nerve supplying movement and sensation to the lower leg, foot, and toes.

Intercostal Nerves—The upper thoracic nerves innervate primarily the chest and upper abdomen; the only nerves not originating from a plexus.

Median Nerve—Innervates most flexor muscles of the forearm and provides sensation for the thumb, index, middle fingers, and a portion of the ring finger. It is the only nerve passing through the carpal tunnel.

Musculocutaneous Nerve—Sensory and motor nerve of the coracobrachialis, biceps brachii, and the greater part of the brachialis (the bicep and side of forearm). It arises from the brachial plexus.

Radial Nerve—Innervates the triceps brachii muscle of the arm and all 12 muscles in the posterior osteofascial compartment of the forearm.

Saphenous Nerve—Sensory nerve of the knee joint, subsartorial, and patellar plexuses, and the skin on medial side of the leg and foot.

Sciatic Nerve—The largest nerve of the body, derived from spinal nerves L4 through S3, runs through the buttock and down the lower limb. It supplies the skin of the leg and the muscles of the back of the thigh. It divides just above the knee into the tibial and common fibular (common peroneal) nerves.

Subcostal Nerves—Sensory and motor nerves of the skin of lower abdomen and lateral side of gluteal region, and parts of abdominal transverse, oblique, and rectus muscles.

Tibial Nerve—Sensory and motor nerve, supplies the muscles and skin of the knee, calf, and sole of the foot, and the toes; a branch of the sciatic nerve.

Ulnar Nerve—Provides sensation for the little finger and a portion of the ring finger, and innervates some muscles of the hand and forearm.

The Spinal Cord (and Spine)

The spinal cord is a bundle of nerves that extends from the base of the brain downward, to the space (conus medullaris) between the first and second lumbar vertebrae. The spinal cord lies within the vertebral column, which protects it. Below the conus medullaris, the spinal nerves continue as the cauda equine.

Spinal Cord & Nerves

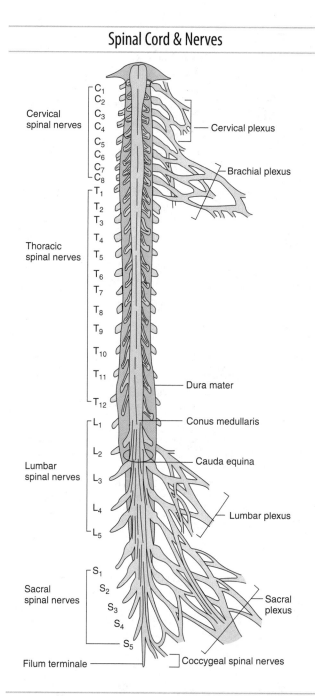

Source: Rizzo, Fundamentals of Anatomy and Physiology, 3e, ISBN #978-1-4354-3871-2

The spinal cord has three main functions:

1. To serve as a conduit for motor information traveling down the spinal cord (to the muscles)

2. To serve as a conduit for sensory information traveling up the spinal cord (to the brain)

3. To serve as a center for coordinating a number of reflexes

The spinal cord nerve segments are grouped by region, as follows:

- Eight cervical segments form 8 pairs of cervical nerves.
- Twelve thoracic segments form 12 pairs of thoracic nerves.
- Five lumbar segments form five pairs of lumbar nerves.
- Five sacral segments form five pairs of sacral nerves (some anatomy texts consider this to be a single segment).
- Three coccygeal segments join, forming one pair of coccygeal nerves.

The spinal nerves for each segment exit at the level of the corresponding vertebra. As is true of spinal surgeries in the musculoskeletal region of CPT® (22010–22899), to assign CPT codes 62263–63746 correctly, you will need to identify the region of the spine (cervical, thoracic, lumbar, sacral) where the procedure is performed.

Procedures of the spine and spinal column (CPT® 62263–63746) also may differentiate among vertebral segments and vertebral interspaces.

- A vertebral segment describes the basic constituent part into which the spine may be divided. It represents a single complete vertebral bone with its associated articular processes and laminae.
- A vertebral interspace is the non-bony compartment between two adjacent vertebral bodies containing the intervertebral disc. It includes the nucleus pulposus, annulus fibrosus, and two cartilagenous endplates.

For example, CPT® 63075 describes discectomy (removal of an intervertebral disc), and is reported for a single cervical interspace. In contrast, CPT® 63081 describes vertebral corpectomy (removal of a portion of the vertebral body), and is reported for a single cervical vertebral segment.

The anatomy and terminology of individual vertebral segments is especially relevant to procedures found in the Nervous System/Spinal portion of CPT®.

Individual Vertebral Segment

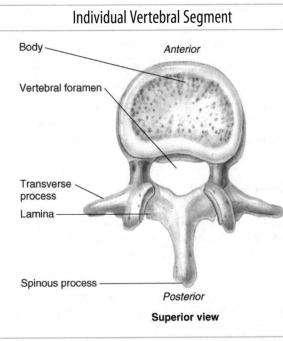

Body — Anterior

Vertebral foramen

Transverse process

Lamina

Spinous process — Posterior

Superior view

Source: EHRLICH/SCHROEDER. Medical Terminology for Health Professions, 6E. © 2009 Delmar Learning, a part of Cengage Learning, Inc. Reproduced by permission. www.cengage.com/permissions

The main portion of the vertebra is the body (corpus). The vertebral foramen is the opening through which the spinal cord passes. The posterior projection of the vertebra is the spinous process. The projections on either side of the vertebra are the transverse processes. Between the spinous process and each transverse process lie the laminae. Many procedures will involve laminectomy (complete excision of laminae, in addition to the entire posterior portion of the vertebra [spinous process]) or laminotomy (partial excision of one or more lamina), for instance for nerve decompression.

Facet joints—also called paravertebral facet joint and/or zygapophyseal or Z joints— are located on the posterior spine on each side of the vertebrae where it overlaps the neighboring vertebrae. The facet joints provide stability and give the spine the ability to bend and twist. They are made up of two surfaces of the adjacent vertebrae that are separated by a thin layer of cartilage. Often, these joints are the site of diagnostic or therapeutic (pain relief) injection, which is discussed further in the CPT® portion of this chapter.

The Brain

The brain is divided into distinct regions, as follows:

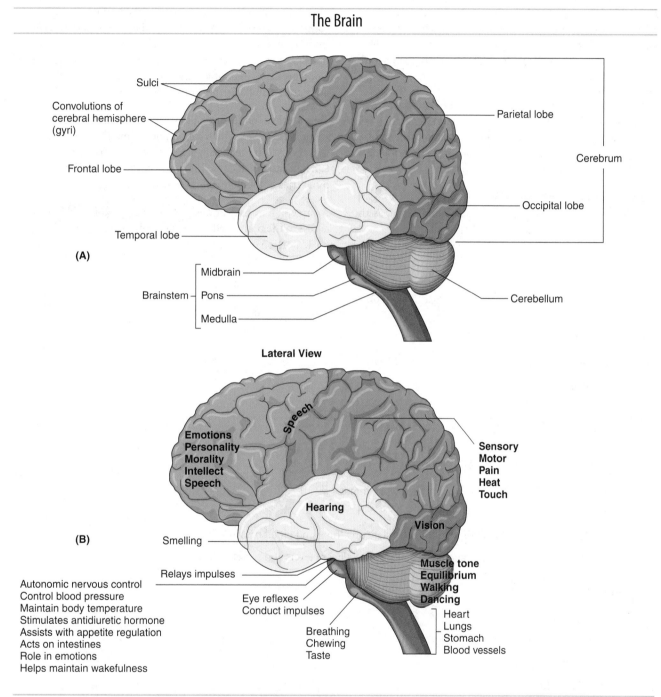

The Brain

(A) Lateral View

Sulci · Convolutions of cerebral hemisphere (gyri) · Frontal lobe · Temporal lobe · Parietal lobe · Cerebrum · Occipital lobe · Cerebellum · Brainstem — Midbrain, Pons, Medulla

(B)
Emotions / Personality / Morality / Intellect / Speech
Speech
Sensory / Motor / Pain / Heat / Touch
Hearing
Vision
Smelling
Muscle tone / Equilibrium / Walking / Dancing
Relays impulses
Eye reflexes / Conduct impulses
Heart / Lungs / Stomach / Blood vessels
Breathing / Chewing / Taste

Autonomic nervous control
Control blood pressure
Maintain body temperature
Stimulates antidiuretic hormone
Assists with appetite regulation
Acts on intestines
Role in emotions
Helps maintain wakefulness

Source: RIZZO. Fundamentals of Anatomy and Physiology, 3E. © 2010 Delmar Learning, a part of Cengage Learning, Inc. Reproduced by permission. www.cengage.com/permissions

The cerebrum contains the frontal, temporal, parietal, and occipital lobes.

The frontal lobe is the front part of the brain, and is involved in planning, organizing, problem solving, selective attention, personality, and a variety of "higher cognitive functions," including behavior and emotions. The frontal lobe is part of the cerebrum.

There are two temporal lobes, one on either side of the brain. The right lobe involves visual memory, the left lobe mainly involves verbal memory. The temporal lobes help sort new information, and are believed to be responsible for short-term memory. The temporal lobes also evaluate hearing input and smell.

The parietal lobes lie behind the frontal lobes and above the temporal lobes, at the top of the brain. They contain the primary sensory cortex controlling sensation. The right lobe processes visuo-spatial information, while the left lobe processes spoken and/or written information.

The occipital lobe is in the back of the brain and processes visual information, including visual recognition of shapes and colors.

The cerebellum is located at the "bottom" of the brain, below the occipital lobe, and helps to coordinate movement (for instance, balance and muscle coordination).

The brainstem is the low extension of the brain where it connects to the spinal cord. Most of the cranial nerves come from the brainstem. This region controls neurological functions necessary for survival (breathing, digestion, heart rate, blood pressure) and for arousal (being awake and alert). The pons and medulla are portions of the brainstem.

The ventricles of the brain are structures containing cerebrospinal fluid (CSF), which bathes and cushions the brain and spinal cord. The ventricles are continuous with the central canal of the spinal cord. The brain and spinal cord are covered by a series of tough membranes called meninges.

A surgeon may use various methods and/or approaches to gain access to the brain, and these will be discussed further in the CPT® portion of this chapter.

Section Review 14.1

1. The endocrine system is comprised of:

    A. Nerves

    B. Glands

    C. Skeletal Parts

    D. Tissue

2. The pancreas gland has what two functions?

    A. Maintaining calcium levels and to secrete hormones

    B. Produces melatonin and adrenaline

    C. Controls immune function and helps regulate breathing and blood pressure

    D. Produces insulin and glucagon to regulate blood glucose levels and secretes digestive enzymes

3. Adrenal means:

    A. Near the kidneys

    B. Back of the thyroid

    C. Near the stomach

    D. Within the brain

4. What does it mean when a patient is going to have a thymectomy performed by the surgical approach of a sternal split?

    A. Excision of thymus by cutting into the neck

    B. Excision of the thyroid by cutting into the chest

    C. Excision of the thymus by cutting into the chest

    D. Excision of the isthmus by cutting into the neck

5. Which endocrine gland does not have lobes?

    A. Thyroid

    B. Pineal

    C. Pituitary

    D. Thymus

6. The nervous system is composed of what two parts?

    A. Central and Peripheral Nervous systems

    B. Sensory and Reflex systems

    C. Brain and Skeletal muscles

    D. Nerves and Neurons

7. Which nerve is the largest nerve of the body?

    A. Femoral

    B. Intercostal

    C. Radial

    D. Sciatic

8. What is not a region of the spinal cord nerve segments?

    A. Lumbar

    B. Cervical

    C. Vertebra

    D. Coccygeal

9. What is a vertebral segment?

    A. A single complete vertebral bone with its associated articular process and laminae

    B. Non-bony compartment between two adjacent vertebral bodies

    C. The lamina between the spinous and transverse process

    D. Overlaps the vertebrae to give the spine the ability to bend and twist

10. What part of the brain is affected when one has a stroke and is unable to speak or write?

    A. Frontal lobe

    B. Cerebellum

    C. Temporal lobe

    D. Parietal lobe

ICD-10-CM

The Endocrine System

ICD-10-CM codes related to the endocrine system are concentrated in the Endocrine, Nutritional and Metabolic Diseases,(E00-E89) chapter. Disorders of the individual glands are ordered by location (eg, disorders of the thyroid gland (E00-E07), disorders of parathyroid (E20-E21), diseases of thymus gland (E32), etc.).

Use the Alphabetic Index to Diseases and Injuries to find the disorder/disease, and confirm code selection by referring to the Tabular List. Be sure to heed all Includes, Excludes1 and Excludes2 information.

Select Endocrine Diagnoses Definitions

Acromegaly—Characterized by enlarged skeletal parts, especially the nose, ears, jaws, fingers, and toes; caused by hypersecretion of growth hormone (GH) from the pituitary gland.

Cushing's Syndrome—An excess of cortisol, caused either by an overactive adrenal gland or glucocorticoid medications; may result in excess fatty tissue of the face, neck, and body, curvature of spine, weakness, and other symptoms.

Goiter—An enlarged thyroid gland, caused by overproduction of thyroid hormone (TSH) or a neoplasm. A diet deficient in iodine can result in a goiter; however, this is rarely the cause.

Hyperparathyroidism—Overactive parathyroid; may result in bone deterioration, reduced renal function, kidney stones, and other difficulties.

Hyperaldosteronism—Oversecretion of aldosterone by the adrenal glands; results in fluid retention and hypertension.

Hypoparathyroidism—Underactive parathyroid; may result in muscle cramps, and cataracts, among other difficulties.

Hypothyroidism—Underactive thyroid; too little thyroid hormone produced (the opposite of hyperthyroidism); may result in children with intellectual disability and small stature. In adults, this condition results in lower metabolism, fatigue, and fluid in the tissues—myxedema.

Panhypopituitarism—Damage to or absence of pituitary gland, which may result in impaired sexual function, weight loss, fatigue, depression, and other symptoms.

Prolactinoma—A benign tumor of the pituitary gland, production of a hormone called prolactin. In women, high blood levels of prolactin can result in infertility and changes in menstruation. In men, the most common symptom of prolactinoma is impotence.

Thyroiditis—Inflammation of the thyroid gland.

Thyrotoxicosis—Refers to the hypermetabolic clinical syndrome resulting from serum elevations in thyroid hormone levels. An overproduction of thyroid hormones, caused by hyperthyroidism, or an overactive thyroid gland is a type of thyrotoxicosis; however, hyperthyroidism and thyrotoxicosis are not synonymous.

ICD-10-CM instructions in the Tabular List of chapter 4 specify: "All neoplasms, whether functionally active or not, are classified in chapter 2." Codes in the Endocrine, Nutritional and Metabolic Diseases, such as E05.8 *Other thyrotoxicosis* and *E07.0 Hypersecretion of calcitonin*, "may be used to identify such functional activity associated with any neoplasm, or by ectopic endocrine tissue." That is, the neoplasm should be reported first, and any functional activity caused by the neoplasm should be reported as a secondary code.

Adrenal Deficiency

Addison's disease occurs when the adrenal glands do not produce enough of the hormone cortisol and in some cases, the hormone aldosterone. The diseases related to the deficiency are due to autoimmune disorders, in which the immune system makes antibodies attacking the body's own tissues or organs, slowly destroying them. Chronic, worsening fatigue and muscle weakness, loss of appetite, and weight loss are characteristic of the disease. The ACTH stimulation test (CPT® codes 80400–80406 and 82024) is the most specific test for diagnosing Addison's disease. Treatment of Addison's disease involves replacing, or substituting, the hormones. ICD-10-CM lists two different codes for Addison's disease (E27.-), with or without crisis.

ICD-9-CM Application

ICD-9-CM has Addison's disease with or without crisis reported with the same code.

255.41 Glucocorticoid disorder

> Addisonian crisis
>
> Addison's disease NOS

Parathyroid Disorder

Primary hyperparathyroidism is a disorder of the parathyroid glands. Most people with this disorder have one or more enlarged, overactive parathyroid glands secreting too much parathyroid hormone (PTH or parathormone). In secondary hyperparathyroidism, a problem such as kidney failure makes the body resistant to the action of parathyroid hormone. In hyperparathyroidism, the hormonal balance is disrupted and blood calcium rises, resulting in hypercalcemia. In 85 percent of people with this disorder, a benign tumor (adenoma) has formed in one of the parathyroid glands, causing it to become overactive. In other cases, excess hormone is due to enlarged parathyroid glands, a condition called hyperplasia. Hyperparathyroidism is diagnosed using tests showing blood levels of calcium as well as parathyroid hormone are too high (code 83970). Surgery to remove the enlarged parathyroid gland (codes 60500–60505) cures about 95 percent of cases.

Diabetes

The ICD-10-CM Official Guidelines for Coding and Reporting provide extensive notes and instruction for coding diabetes and its manifestations. You should review these guidelines in full. The following summary identifies key points.

Diabetes mellitus refers to a group of diseases affecting how the body uses glucose (blood sugar). Patients with diabetes often suffer from one or multiple, often serious, complications (damage to the nerves, kidneys, eyes, cardiovascular system, etc.).

When beta cells in the pancreas do not produce enough insulin, glucose builds up in the blood, causing hyperglycemia (the opposite—low glucose levels—is called hypoglycemia). Along with the pancreas, the liver helps to manage blood-sugar levels by storing excess glucose in a form called glycogen. When glucose levels are low, alpha cells in the pancreas secrete the hormone glucagon, which stimulates the liver to convert glycogen back into glucose (glycogenolysis) releasing it into the blood for use by the body.

The diabetes mellitus codes are combination codes that include the type of diabetes, the body system affected and the complications affecting that body system. The diabetic codes are categorized by the type of diabetes into five categories (E08-E13) including due to an underlying condition (E08), drug or chemical induced (E09), Type 1 (E10), Type 2 (E11), and other specified (E13). Assign as many codes from category E08-E13 as needed to identify all of the associated conditions the patient has.

- Type 1: The patient's pancreatic beta cells no longer produce insulin. People with type 1 diabetes must take insulin. Type 1 diabetes is also referred to as juvenile type diabetes.

- Type 2: The patient's beta cells do not produce sufficient insulin or the beta cells have developed insulin resistance. Unlike people with type 1, people with type 2 may or may not have to take insulin.

For example; the documentation states chronic kidney disease secondary to diabetes. The proper code assignment would be E11.22 *Type 2 diabetes mellitus with diabetic chronic kidney disease*, followed by N18.9 *Chronic kidney disease, unspecified*.

If the documentation doesn't specify the type, a code from category E11 Type 2 diabetes mellitus is assigned.

Example:

Diabetes with diabetic gangrene:

Look in the Alphabetic Index to Diseases for Diabetes, diabetic/ with/gangrene E11.52.

E11.52 Type 2 diabetes mellitus with diabetic peripheral angiopathy with gangrene

---

ICD-9-CM Application

ICD-9-CM reports two codes if a patient has diabetes with a manifestation. Assign the diabetic code first followed by the associated condition. Diabetic codes, with the exception of secondary diabetes, fall into category 250. The fourth digit indicates whether there are any complications or manifestations. The fifth digit (0, 1, 2, or 3) indicates the type of diabetes (Type 1 or 2) and if it is controlled or uncontrolled. Type 1 diabetes and uncontrolled must be documented by the physician to report that fifth digit.

Example

Diabetes with diabetic gangrene:

Look in the ICD-9-CM Alphabetic Index for Diabetes, diabetic/ with/gangrene 250.7 [785.4]

250.70 Diabetes with peripheral circulatory disorder

785.4   Gangrene

In the Alphabetic Index code 785.4 for gangrene is in slanted brackets which indicates that code is reported as an additional code with the diabetes code as the primary code. In the Tabular List for subcategory code 250.7x there is an instructional note to Use additional code to identify manifestation and gangrene is listed as an additional code.

Secondary diabetes (category E08-E09) identifies complications/manifestations associated with secondary diabetes mellitus. Secondary diabetes is caused by another condition or event, such as cystic fibrosis, neoplasm of pancreas, poisoning, etc.

Example

Patient being seen today for treatment of secondary diabetes due to Cushing's syndrome.

The ICD-10-CM Official Guidelines instructs when reporting secondary diabetes due to an underlying condition, code first the underlying condition then the diabetes code.

In the Tabular List under category code E08 Diabetes mellitus due to underlying condition, there is an instructional note:

Code first the underlying condition, such as:

    congenital rubella (P35.0)

    Cushing's syndrome (E24.-)

    cystic fibrosis (E84.-)

    malignant neoplasm (C00-C96)

    malnutrition (E40-E46)

    pancreatitis and other diseases of the pancreas (K85-K86.-)

Look in the Alphabetic Index for Diabetes, diabetic/due to underlying condition E08.9. According to the code first note under E08, Cushing's syndrome (E24.-) is reported first. In the Tabular List, a fourth character of 9 is selected for unspecified.

    E24.9 Cushing's syndrome, unspecified

    E08.9 Diabetes mellitus due to underlying condition without complications

Category code E09 drug or chemical that induced diabetes has an instructional note to code first the drug or chemical (T36-T65).

ICD-9-CM Application

Secondary diabetes in ICD-9-CM is reported from category 249. Two codes are reported if a patient has secondary diabetes with a manifestation. The fourth digit indicates whether there are any complications or manifestations. The fifth digit (0 or 1) indicates if it is controlled or uncontrolled. Uncontrolled must be documented by the physician to report that fifth digit.

ICD-9-CM Official Guidelines instruct to code secondary diabetes first if the patient is being treated for the secondary diabetes. If the encounter is for the treatment for the condition causing the diabetes (eg, cystic fibrosis), then that is coded first.

Example

Patient being seen today for treatment of secondary diabetes due to Cushing's syndrome.

    249.00   Secondary diabetes mellitus without mention of complication

    255.0   Cushing's syndrome

Look in the ICD-9-CM Alphabetic Index for Diabetes, diabetic/ secondary 249.0. In the Tabular List, a fifth digit 0 is selected to indicate the diabetes is not stated as uncontrolled, or unspecified. Next, look for Syndrome/Cushing's 255.0.

The Nervous System

ICD-10-CM codes specific to the nervous system are listed primarily in chapter 6, Diseases of the Nervous System (G00-G99). Use the Alphabetic Index (ICD-10-CM) to find the disorder/disease, and confirm code selection by referring to the Tabular List. Be sure to heed all Includes, Excludes1 and Excludes2 information, as well as required additional characters for specificity.

Meningitis

Meningitis is inflammation of the lining of the brain and/or the spinal cord, which also causes changes in the cerebrospinal fluid (CSF) surrounding the brain and spinal cord. Meningitis may be caused by a number of agents, including bacteria, virus, and others. When coding for meningitis, you must know the agent responsible (for example, pneumococcal, streptococcal, gram-negative anaerobes, arbovirus, etc.). In some cases (eg, G02 *Meningitis in other infectious and parasitic diseases classified elsewhere*), you must code the underlying disease first (B57.41 *Meningitis in Chagas' disease*). B57 includes American trypanosomiasis with involvement of organ other than heart as noted under B57. For unspecified meningitis, report G03.9.

Example

Streptococcal A meningitis.

Look in the ICD-10-CM Alphabetic Index for Meningitis/streptococcal (acute) G00.2. In the Tabular List, G00.2 has a note to use an additional code to further identify the organism. The organism is Streptococcus A. In the Alphabetic Index, look for Streptococcus, streptococcal/group/A, as cause of disease classified elsewhere B95.0.

    G00.2 Streptococcal meningitis

    B95.0 Streptococcus, group A, as the cause of diseases classified elsewhere

---

Encephalitis, Myelitis, and Encephalomyelitis

Encephalitis is swelling/inflammation of the brain. Myelitis is swelling/inflammation of the spinal cord. Encephalomyelitis is combined brain/spinal cord inflammation. Because the brain and spinal cord are constrained within the skull and spinal column, respectively, swelling can cause severe dysfunction or even death.

When coding for these disorders, check ICD-10-CM notation as to whether you should first code the underlying disease, and whether additional external cause codes are necessary.

Organic Sleep Disorders

Organic sleep disorders, including organic insomnia (inability to sleep), hypersomnia (excessive sleep), sleep apnea (pauses in breathing during sleep), parasomnia (night terrors, sleep-walking, and related abnormal movement during sleep), and others, may be found in category G47. See subcategory F51.- for sleep disorders not documented as organic.

Other Degenerative Diseases of the Nervous System

Codes G30-G32 describe degenerative diseases of the nervous system. Diagnoses in this range include Alzheimer's disease (G30) and dementia with Parkinsonism or frontotemporal dementia (G31)—among others.

Example

Late onset of Alzheimer's with dementia without behavioral disturbance.

Look in the ICD-10-CM Alphabetic Index for Disease/Alzheimer's/late onset G30.1 [F02.80].

G30.1 Alzheimer's disease with late onset

F02.80 Dementia in other diseases classified elsewhere, without behavioral disturbance

Code selection is straightforward, but be sure to abide by the ICD-10-CM instructions regarding use of additional codes to identify associated conditions, or to report underlying diseases (which may cause a degenerative disease of the CNS) as primary. Watch also, Excludes notes. For instance, senile degeneration of brain (G31.1) specifically excludes senility not otherwise specified (R41.81).

Select Diagnoses Definitions

Amyotrophic Lateral Sclerosis (ALS, or Lou Gehrig's Disease)—A type of motor neuron disease affecting nerve cells in the brain and spinal cord controlling voluntary muscle movement.

Ataxia—Lack of muscle movement coordination.

Cerebral Lipidoses—Genetic disorder causing lipid accumulation the brain.

Cerebral Palsy—A group of disorders involving brain and nervous system functions such as movement, learning, hearing, vision, and thought; there are several types of cerebral palsy, including spastic, dyskinetic, ataxic, hypotonic, and mixed.

Dyskinesia—Uncontrolled muscle movement.

Hydrocephalus—Abnormal accumulation of cerebrospinal fluid in the ventricles or cavities of the brain.

Myelopathy—Dysfunction of the spinal cord.

Myoclonus—Spontaneous, uncontrolled twitching of a muscle or group of muscles.

Neuropathy—Dysfunction of the nerves (eg, peripheral neuropathy is dysfunction of the nerves of the peripheral nervous system).

Paraplegia—Impairment in motor or sensory function of the lower extremities.

Reye's Syndrome—Affects all organs of the body but is most harmful to the brain and the liver and it is defined as a two phase illness because it generally occurs in conjunction with a previous viral infection such as the flu or chicken pox.

Syringomyelia—Disorder in which a cyst (syrinx) forms within the spinal cord; the cyst expands over time damaging the cord.

Pain (Not Elsewhere Classified)

The ICD-10-CM Official Guidelines for Coding and Reporting provide extensive notes and instruction for coding pain (category G89). You should review these guidelines in full. The following summary identifies key points.

When seeking a pain diagnosis, identify as precisely as possible the pain's location and/or source. If pain is the primary symptom and you know the location, the Alphabetic Index will generally provide all the information you need.

You only report pain diagnosis codes from the G89 category as the primary diagnosis when:

- The acute or chronic pain and neoplasm pain provide more detail when used in conjunction with codes from other categories: or
- The reason for the service is for pain control or pain management.

You do not report codes from the G89 category as the first-listed diagnosis if you know the underlying (definitive) diagnosis and the reason for the service is to manage/treat the underlying condition. You may report the acute/chronic pain code (G89) as a secondary diagnosis if the diagnosis provides additional, relevant information not adequately explained by the primary diagnosis code.

If the patient has a documented, more-comprehensive diagnosis causing the documented acute/chronic pain, but the documentation indicates the primary reason for the visit/service is management/control of the pain, you should report a diagnosis code from the G89 category as the primary or first-listed ICD-10-CM code.

The official ICD-10-CM Guidelines I.C.6.b.1 specify you should not report a diagnosis from the G89 series "if the pain is not specified as acute or chronic, post-thoracotomy pain, postprocedural, or neoplasm related pain."

As a rule, acute pain is sudden and sharp. It can range from mild to severe and may last a few minutes or a few weeks or months. Acute pain typically does not last longer than six months and usually disappears when the physician identifies and treats the underlying cause or condition for the pain.

Chronic pain may last for months or years, and may persist even after the underlying injury has healed or the underlying condition has been treated. There is no specific timeframe identifying when you can define the pain as chronic. Base code assignment on provider documentation.

Chronic pain syndrome is not the same as chronic pain. You should report chronic pain syndrome (G89.2) only when the provider has documented that exact condition.

Demyelinating Diseases of the Central Nervous System are found among codes G35–G37. Examples include multiple sclerosis (an autoimmune disease of the brain and spinal cord), some types of myelitis. Code selection is straightforward, but be sure to abide by ICD-10-CM instruction regarding the use of additional codes to identify associated conditions and/or cause. Watch also, Excludes and Includes notes.

Select Diagnoses Definitions

Anoxic Brain Damage—Brain injury due to lack of oxygen; report an E code in addition to identifying cause (birth trauma is excluded from 348.1 *Anoxic brain damage*).

Cataplexy—Sudden onset of muscle weakness with loss of tone and strength; triggered by intense emotion.

Diplegic—Paralysis of like parts on either side of the body.

Dural Tear—The dura is the outermost of the three layers comprising the meninges, which surround the brain and spinal cord. A tear in the dura may result in loss of cerebrospinal fluid (CSF). Code 349.31 is specific to an inadvertent tear during a procedure; assign 998.2 for an accidental puncture or tear by a catheter or instrument during a procedure.

Grand Mal Status—Sudden loss of consciousness followed by generalized convulsions in epilepsy; see also Petit Mal Status.

Encephalopathy—Disorder or disease of the brain; does not refer to a single disease, but rather to a syndrome caused by any number of diseases. Reported to 348.3x when not elsewhere classified.

Epilepsy—A brain disorder characterized by electrical-like disturbances. May be convulsive or nonconvulsive, generalized or localized; symptoms may include occasional impairment and loss of consciousness, abnormal movement, and sensory disturbance.

Hemiplegic—Paralysis affecting one side of the body.

Monoplegic—Paralysis in one limb (arm or leg)

Multiple Sclerosis—The body directs antibodies and white blood cells against proteins in the myelin sheath surrounding nerves in the brain and spinal cord, causing inflammation and injury to the sheath and ultimately to the nerves. The damage slows or blocks muscle coordination, visual sensation, and other nerve signals.

Narcolepsy—Brief, recurrent, uncontrollable episodes of sound sleep, often during the day.

Petit Mal Status—Minor, involuntary muscle movement or brief (usually less than 15 seconds) disturbance in brain function (staring spell) due to abnormal electrical activity in the brain. Person is usually wide awake and thinking clearly immediately after the seizure.

Quadraplegic—Paralysis in all four limbs (arms and legs).

Migraine

Within this set of codes, category G43 describes migraine, defined as "benign vascular headache of extreme pain" and commonly associated with "irritability, nausea, vomiting and often photophobia; premonitory visual hallucination of a crescent in the visual field (scotoma)." Per ICD-10-CM instruction, migraine does not include headache not otherwise specified (R51) or various syndromes as described by G44.

Migraines may occur with or without aura. Aura is a group of symptoms that occur prior to the onset of a migraine, and usually includes visual disturbances, such as loss of part of the visual field, flashing lights, lines across the visual field, etc.

For each code in the G43 set, you must specify they type of migraine, with or without aura, intractable or not intractable, with or without status migrainosus.

Status migrainosus is an unrelenting, debilitating headache of severe intensity lasting more than 72 hours with less than an hour of pain-free period.

An intractable migraine is sustained and continual and does not respond to normal treatment.

Migraines may occur with or without cerebral infarction. Migraines related to menstruation is reported to G43.83-.

Example

Abdominal migraine that has lasted for more than 72 hours that is not responding to medication.

In the Alphabetic Index look for Migraine/abdominal, there are four options that further define abdominal migraine: with and without refractory migraine, intractable or not intractable. The code for intractable abdominal migraine is:

G43.D1 Abdominal migraine, intractable

ICD-9-CM Application

ICD-9-CM requires a fifth digit (0, 1, 2, or 3) to indicate if the migraine is intractable and with status migrainosus.

Example

Abdominal migraine that has lasted for more than 72 hours that is not responding to medication.

Look in the ICD-9-CM Alphabetic Index for Migraine/abdominal (syndrome) 346.2x. In the Tabular List, a fifth digit of 3 is selected to indicate the migraine is intractable and with status migrainosus.

362.43 Variants of migraine, not elsewhere classified, with intractable migraine, so stated, with status migrainosus.

Nerve, Nerve Root and Plexus Disorders

Nerve, nerve root and plexus disorders are found in code sets G50-G59. Examples include trigeminal nerve disorders (pain resulting in disorder of Cranial Nerve V, the nerve connecting part of the face to the brain), lesions of the nerve roots and plexus, nerve inflammation (neuritis—the most prominent of these is carpel tunnel syndrome, G56), and hereditary and idiopathic peripheral nerve disease (neuropathy).

Code selection is straightforward, but be sure to abide by the ICD-10CM instructions regarding the use of additional codes to identify associated conditions and/or cause. Watch also, Excludes and Includes notes.

Select Diagnoses Definitions

Bell's Palsy—A temporary form of facial paralysis, occurs with damage to Cranial Nerve VII, the nerve controlling movement of the muscles in the face.

Carpel Tunnel Syndrome—Compression of the median nerve (median nerve entrapment); may result in pain, tingling, numbness, and a burning sensation in the hand.

Causalgia—Intense burning pain and sensitivity to vibration or touch.

Demyelination—Damage to the myelin sheath of neurons, occurs in Multiple Sclerosis (MS).

Geniculate Ganglionitis—Involves severe pain deep in the ear, may be caused by compression of the somatic sensory branch of Cranial Nerve VII. This may also develop following herpes zoster, oticus.

Mononeuritis—Inflammation of a single nerve.

Muscular Dystrophy (MD)—A group of disorders involving muscle weakness and loss of muscle tissue; progresses over time.

Myoneural Disorders—Disorders affecting both muscles and nerves (eg, Myasthenia gravis).

Myotonia—Slow relaxation of the muscles after voluntary contraction or electrical stimulation; individuals with myotonia (a symptom of certain neuromuscular disorders) may have trouble releasing their grip on objects, or may have difficulty rising from a sitting position.

Neuralgic Amyotrophy (Parsonage-Aldren-Turner Syndrome, Brachial Neuritis, Brachial Plexitis)—Pain and muscle weakness affecting the upper extremity, often in response to stressors such as surgery, infection, minor trauma, etc.

Polyneuritis—Inflammation of several peripheral nerves simultaneously.

Trigeminal Neuralgia—Inflammation of the trigeminal nerve. Cranial Nerve V (CN V) delivers feeling to the face.

Neoplasms

Neoplasms may occur throughout the endocrine and nervous systems. Selecting a neoplasm diagnosis code is the same as for any other system.

Go to ICD-10-CM Alphabetic Index to look for the main term describing the neoplasm type. Don't go directly to the Table of Neoplasms. Although the Alphabetic Index often directs you to the Neoplasm Table, checking the Alphabetic Index first is an important step. You won't find all the codes you need in the Table of Neoplasms. ICD-10-CM lists certain conditions only in the Alphabetic Index; in other cases, using the Alphabetic Index saves time and reduces confusion. If the Alphabetic Index doesn't provide the information you need, consult the Table of Neoplasms.

Section Review 14.2

1. Select the code for a patient diagnosed with thyrotoxicosis crisis with an overactive nodular goiter.

   A. E05.00

   B. E05.10

   C. E05.21

   D. E05.20

2. A 42-year-old male with thyroid cancer is being admitted to the hospital for hypersecretion of calcitonin (functional activity) caused by the cancer. Choose the ICD-10-CM code(s) to report.

   A. E07.0, C73

   B. C73, E07.0

   C. E07.0, Z85.850

   D. E07.0

3. A 65-year-old female with type 1 diabetes may need amputation of her lower left leg due to having diabetic gangrene. Select the ICD-10-CM code(s) to report.

   A. E10.52

   B. I96, E10.52

   C. I96, E10.9

   D. E11.52, I96

4. A 70-year-old patient has toxic myelitis due to inhaling vapors of carbon tetrachloride when using a fire extinguisher to put out a fire. The appropriate codes to report are:

   A. G92, T59.4X1A

   B. G92, T58.2X1A

   C. T53.0X1A, G92

   D. G92, T53.0X1A

5. A 27-year-old had a MVA accident a couple days ago and is coming in to see his primary care physician for acute pain in his neck down his spine since having the accident. Select the ICD-10-CM code(s) on how this visit should be reported.

   A. R52

   B. G89.11, M54.2

   C. M54.2, Z04.3

   D. F45.41

CPT® Coding

CPT® codes relevant to the endocrine and nervous systems will come primarily from the 60000 series, with some additional services in the 90000 series.

The Endocrine System

This portion of CPT®, like most others, is arranged anatomically, from the head downward, and classifies procedures into basic types such as incision, excision, removal, etc.

The Thyroid Gland

Procedures include incision and drainage, biopsy, and excision or aspiration of thyroid cyst.

Report 60000 for incision and drainage of an infected thyroglossal duct cyst. This cyst is formed from a duct that has not closed or has not disappeared by the time the thyroid gland has moved into its permanent position in the neck during embryonic development. When these cysts become infected, they must be drained (60000).

The majority of codes describe excision procedures, including total or partial removal of the thyroid and may include related procedures such as neck dissection. Lobectomy describes removal of a single lobe of the thyroid, while isthmusectomy (for example, 60210–60225) describes excision of the isthmus of the thyroid, the connective passage between the two lateral lobes of the thyroid gland. The codes state which sides are being addressed and whether the isthmus is transected or resected. In general, the parathyroid glands located on the posterior (back) of the thyroid gland are preserved during excision of the thyroid.

Practical Coding Note

Code 60254 includes a radical neck dissection, and a tracheostomy is always an inherent part of a radical neck dissection. The tracheostomy is performed to preserve the airway, which can be compromised due to postoperative swelling. Make a note next to 60254 to remind you the tracheostomy is included and not coded separately.

A thyroid goiter is a dramatic enlargement of the thyroid gland. Goiters are often removed because of cosmetic reasons or, more commonly, because they compress other vital structures of the neck. If a massive goiter is compressing the trachea and esophagus, a subtotal or total thyroidectomy may be performed to remove the mass.

Ultrasound can be performed in diagnosing thyroid nodules and masses suspicious for malignancy.

If a dominant solitary nodule is present, the physician may remove the lobe (lobectomy). If a hot nodule is producing too much hormone resulting in hyperthyroidism, the physician may remove the lobe harboring the affected nodule. A total or near total thyroidectomy is generally prescribed for thyroid carcinoma. Some patients with papillary carcinomas of small size may require a lobectomy with removal of the isthmus. A lymph node dissection within the anterior and lateral neck is indicated in patients with papillary or follicular thyroid cancer if the lymph nodes can be palpated. Patients with medullary carcinoma of the thyroid require total thyroidectomy and aggressive lymph node dissection.

Parathyroid, Thymus, Adrenal Glands, Pancreas, and Carotid Body

Multiple endocrine neoplasias Type 1 (MEN1), or Wermer's syndrome, is an inherited disorder causing groups of endocrine glands, such as the parathyroid, the pancreas, and the pituitary, to become overactive simultaneously. The usual treatment is an operation to remove the three largest parathyroid glands and all but a small part of the fourth (60500–60505).

Exploration of the parathyroid glands traditionally warrants a cervical approach (60500). In some instances where parathyroid adenomas cannot be located in the cervical region, further exploration via a transthoracic approach (60505) is needed. A portion of the parathyroid can be transplanted onto the sternocleidomastoid muscle after total thyroidectomy (+60512). This procedure preserves the function of the parathyroid, and transplantation to nonhomologous tissue permits easy resection in the event the transplant requires revision or resection at a later date.

Practical Coding Note

Next to code 60500, write "typically cervical approach." Highlight or underline "transthoracic approach" in the description of code 60505.

Resection of the thymus (thymectomy) can be done via a variety of approaches. Remember, whenever the thoracic cavity is opened, the negative pressure allowing for expansion of the lungs is disrupted. It is considered routine to place a chest tube for all intrathoracic surgeries to permit expansion of the lungs. This procedure, chest tube placement, is not a separately billed service.

Most pheochromocytomas are benign tumors of the chromaffin cells of the adrenal medulla. These tumors are usually confined to the adrenal glands but can occur near the bladder or the heart. This type of tumor manufactures extra catecholamines, including hormones like epinephrine and norepinephrine. Patients experience hypertension, headaches, profuse sweating, and anxiety from the overproduction of these hormones. Treatment for this condition is surgical excision. When there is a tumor in or adjacent to the adrenal gland, the correct CPT® code is 60540 or 60545. When the tumor is located elsewhere in the abdomen, CPT® directs the coder to 49203–49205 depending on the size or number of tumors involved.

Surgical access for the excision of a carotid body tumor is usually through an incision in the neck. In many cases, the tumor can be removed allowing for the carotid artery to remain intact (60600). In some cases, the tumor is imbedded too deep to dissect it free and a portion of the carotid artery must be removed (60605).

Unlisted Procedure

Unlisted procedures of the endocrine system are reported using 60699. Report an unlisted procedure code only when no CPT® code or category III code properly describes the procedure the provider performs. Do not select a code "close enough" in lieu of an unlisted procedure code.

When filing a claim using an unlisted procedure code, submit a cover letter of explanation and the full documentation of services.

Endocrinology

Endocrinology services in the medicine portion of CPT® are limited to 95250–95251 for continuous monitoring of glucose (CGM) over a 72-hour period. CGM is indicated for patients with type 1, type 2, or gestational diabetes who require better regulation of blood glucose levels. Monitoring may be performed with an invasive device or a noninvasive device. The invasive device monitors glucose levels by a sensor inserted in the subcutaneous tissue of the lower abdomen. The noninvasive device is worn like a wristwatch and measures glucose with an electric current and biometric sensor. After 72 hours, data are downloaded to a computer.

The Nervous System

CPT® divides the nervous system into three primary categories:

1. Skull, Meninges, and Brain (61000–62258)

2. Spine and Spinal Cord (62263–63746)

3. Extracranial Nerves, Peripheral Nerves, and Autonomic Nervous System (64400–64999)

Many codes within this section of CPT® may be performed with radiologic imaging, and often radiological supervision and interpretation may be reported separately. Pay attention

to CPT® parenthetical notes following code descriptors, as well as instructions in section headings. The guidance that follows is not all-inclusive, but will highlight areas of primary significance.

Skull, Meninges, and Brain

The skull or cranium is the bony protection surrounding the brain and is made up of 22 bones. Fourteen of these bones form the face and jaw and are referred to as the facial bones. The other eight bones, known as the cranial bones, protect the brain.

There are six cranial fontanels in the infant skull. A fontanel is a space covered by tough membranes between the bones of an infant's cranium, which has yet to close. They are named for their locations. The two well-known fontanels are the posterior (between the occipital and the two parietal bones) and the anterior (located between the frontal and two parietal bones). The two lesser known paired fontanels are the posterolateral (eg, mastoid) situated between the temporal bone and the mastoid process, and the anterolateral (eg, sphenoid) located between the temporal, parietal, and frontal bones.

Twist Drill, Burr Holes or Trephine, Craniectomy, or Craniotomy

Various methods may be used to pierce the skull and/or access the brain. Cisternal or lateral cervical punctures are similar in performance to a lumbar puncture for gaining access to the cerebellomedullary cistern (the largest of the subarachnoid cisterns between the cerebellum and the medulla oblongata). Cisternal puncture is described as the passage of a hollow needle through the posterior atlantooccipital membrane into the cerebellomedullary cistern, also known as the cisterna magna.

Practical Coding Note

When an injection of contrast material is performed for Myelography or CT scan to provide lumbar imagery, use CPT® code 62284.

Additional methods include twist drill holes for puncture (eg, 61105–61108) and burr holes (eg, 61120–61210), which are dime-sized openings in the skull (also called keyhole craniotomy). A trephine is a surgical instrument with a cylindrical blade used to create an opening in the skull. The reason for access, and location (for instance, for aspiration of hematoma or cyst, intracerebral) determine code selection.

A hematoma is a localized collection of blood, which has usually clotted. Hematomas are found in organs, spaces, or tissue, and are the result of a break in the wall of blood vessels. A subdural hematoma (61108) refers to a leakage of blood between the dura and arachnoidal membranes. This injury creates a space, which does not normally exist, and usually results from trauma. Because the cranium is a closed or finite space, hematomas must be drained. To allow them to expand unchecked can result in displacing brain tissue (under pressure) resulting in anoxia/death to those tissues and eventual death to the individual. Code 61156 refers to the removal by aspiration of a hematoma or cyst intracerebral or inside the cerebrum. Evacuation of a chronic intracranial subdural hematoma through burr holes can be done with sedation and local anesthetic at the skin incision site. The procedures take about one hour.

Craniectomy or craniotomy (61304–61576) is more extensive than twist drill holes or burr holes; the opening is larger. Technically, craniotomy is any bony opening cut into the skull. A section of skull, called a bone flap, is removed to access the brain underneath. Typically, the bone flap is replaced; if the bone flap is not replaced, the procedure is called a craniectomy.

When coding this range, the coder must know the reason for the surgery (abscess, tumor, etc.) as well as the surgical approach (eg, subtemporal, suboccipital, or transcranial). Infratentorial refers to beneath the tentorium cerebelli and supratentorial refers to the structures above the tentorium cerebelli (the tent of dura mater that separates the cerebellum from the occipital and temporal lobes). Extradural refers to outside of the dura mater.

There are a variety of causes affecting the skull and its contents, which may require a craniotomy or craniectomy:

- Tumors of the supporting cells of the brain called gliomas
- Cancers that have metastasized to the brain
- Abscess
- Meninges can give rise to mostly benign tumors called meningiomas growing quite large and compressing the brain causing damage
- Obstruction to the flow of cerebrospinal fluid produces hydrocephalus, and on occasion requires craniotomy
- The vessels at the base of the brain may give rise to aneurysms with possible rupture and can cause bleeding around the brain (subarachnoid hemorrhage)

Craniotomy is labeled by the part of the skull opened. A frontal craniotomy indicates the opening is in the frontal bone; a parietal craniotomy involves opening the parietal bone. If parts of two adjacent bones are opened, both bones are mentioned (eg, frontotemporal craniotomy). Surgery on the back of the brain beneath the tentorium is usually carried out by removal of the lower part of the occipital bone. This is called a suboccipital craniectomy. The craniectomy may be midline or to one side or the other. When bone removal is more to the side, just behind the mastoid bone, it may be called a retromastoid craniectomy.

Incision in the scalp is designed to expose the skull over the lesion to be removed. The bone flap may be removed through a series of small holes (burr holes) made in the skull. The skull is cut between each adjacent burr hole in a progressive manner until the bone flap is separated from the surrounding skull. After the bone flap is removed, underlying dura is cut to expose the lesion. If the lesion is a meningioma and is attached to the dura, the surgeon may cut the dura around the tumor to leave a margin of normal dura. When there is a loss of dura, various substitutes can be used such as bovine pericardium (covering of the heart), banked human dura, GORE-TEX® plastic, or an absorbable collagen matrix. When the surgery is for a malignant brain tumor, the surgeon may wish to line the cavity left by removal of the tumor with an absorbable wafer impregnated with an anticancer drug. This has been shown to extend life by two to four months.

Following removal of the lesion, all bleeding is secured, the dura is sutured closed and the bone flap restored to the skull with wire sutures or titanium miniplates and screws. Burr holes in cosmetically exposed areas are covered with small titanium plates. If the bone cannot be replaced (infected or invaded by tumor) a prosthesis can be used. These are usually made of titanium mesh or plastic. The scalp is then sutured closed. When there is a fracture or other injury to the skull that is causing compression of the brain tissue, the surgeon will perform surgery to release or decompress the pressure. This procedure is done by elevating, and in some instances removing, the bone or bony fragments. CPT® codes 61330–61340, 61343, 61345, 61450, and 61458 describe decompression services via a variety of approaches and for a variety of reasons. The transcranial approach to access the bony structures of the orbit involves going through the frontal bone above the eyebrow and lifting back (retracting) the forebrain.

Decompression of the posterior fossa entails alleviating the buildup of extra CSF via an incision below the occipital area. Decompression in this area is tricky due to the close proximity of the cranial nerves, the cerebellomedullary cistern (the largest cerebellar cistern, which is located between the cerebellum and the medulla oblongata), and the structures of the posterior brain. Occasionally, an abnormality is situated in the low brainstem or cerebellum and may extend to the upper spinal cord. In these instances a cervical laminectomy may also accompany the suboccipital craniectomy.

Code 61450 includes the language "decompression of sensory root of gasserian ganglion." A ganglion is a knot-like mass or group of nerve cells located outside the central nervous system. The gasserian ganglion is synonymous with the trigeminal ganglion and is a large, flat ganglion of the fifth cranial nerve, the trigeminal nerve.

A tractotomy is the surgical interruption of a nerve track in the spinal cord or brain stem. CPT® code 61480 reports tractotomy of the mesencephalic region of the brain. The mesencephalon is the middle part of the brain stem formed during embryogenesis. The predominant nerve cell groups present in the adult mesencephalon include the motor neurons of the oculomotor and trochlear nerves. Severing of the spinothalamic tracts is done for intractable pain, and severing of the cerebral peduncles is done for dyskinesias such as Parkinson's disease. A peduncle is best described as a stalk-like or stem-like structure that connects the parts of the brain. The peduncles are usually made completely of either white or gray matter. The cerebral peduncle is made of gray matter. The gray matter is a major component of the CNS consisting of neuronal cell bodies. The white matter of the CNS consists mostly of myelinated axons.

Osteomyelitis, as mentioned in code 61501, is an inflammation of the bone caused by a pyogenic (pus-producing) organism. The infected part of the cranial bone is removed. CPT® codes 61512 and 61519 mention excision of a meningioma. A meningioma is a hard, slow-growing, usually vascular tumor that occurs mainly along the meningeal vessels and superior longitudinal sinus. This type of tumor invades the dura and skull and leads to erosion and thinning of the skull.

Some particularly aggressive types of tumors occurring in the brain may benefit from the use of chemotherapy applied directly into the cavity from which tumor tissue has been removed. Such intracavitary chemotherapy treats the edge of the tumor resection cavity with a chemotherapy agent at many times the concentration possible by administering the agent either orally or by injection. It is most often done with a chemotherapy agent impregnated into biodegradable wafers. Following resection, several of the biodegradable wafers may be inserted into the cavity formed when tumor tissue is removed prior to closing the incision. As the wafers dissolve over the following two weeks or more, chemotherapy is gradually released into the surrounding tissue.

CPT® code +61517 is an "add-on" code that reports the implantation of the intracavitary chemotherapy agent and can only be used with codes 61510 or 61518 as described in the parenthetical note. Electrocorticography (codes 61536–61539) may be used during craniotomy procedures to accurately identify a particular area of the brain. This procedure involves applying electrodes directly to the cortex of the brain. Codes 61537 and 61540, report procedures performed without the application of electrodes.

Code 61541 refers to cutting across the corpus callosum, the largest of the tracts connecting the left and right hemispheres of the brain (also called commissures). It makes communications between centers in the paired hemispheres possible. The choroid plexus (61544) is located in the lateral ventricles of the brain and is a general term for a network of lymphatic vessels, nerves, or veins. The choroid plexus produces cerebral spinal fluid and also acts as a filtering system. It removes metabolic waste, foreign substances, and excess neurotransmitters from the CSF. Craniopharyngioma (61545) is a tumor in a portion of the pituitary gland.

Pituitary tumors can cause a patient to develop visual field defects, absent menstrual cycles, infertility, decreased libido, impotence, decreased body hair, and decreased production of other stimulating hormones. Most of these tumors occur in the anterior lobe and are benign, small, and encapsulated. Often, these can be successfully removed by a surgery called a transsphenoidal hypophysectomy. The operation is performed through the nose to avoid entering the cranium. Codes 61546 and 61548 involve excision of the hypophysis or pituitary gland and are selected by the surgical approach.

Craniosynostosis (61550–61559) refers to the premature closure of the sutures of the skull. These codes are determined by anatomical position of the anomaly and whether the procedure involved a craniotomy or craniectomy.

When a part of the brain can be identified as the source of seizures, surgical removal of that source will often eliminate the seizures. Several different types of surgery can be offered. The temporal lobe is the most common part of the brain involved in seizures and these patients undergo temporal lobectomy. Extratemporal lobectomy, hemispherotomy, and corpus callosotomy are also used in patients with seizure sources in different parts of the brain. In patients who are not candidates for brain surgery, the vagus nerve stimulator can be used to reduce seizure frequency.

CPT® code 61566 refers to the surgical removal of the amygdala and hippocampus (brain structures located in the medial temporal lobe) for control of epilepsy. The procedure is achieved through a small cortical incision to resect the amygdala and hippocampus. Direct recordings of brain activity from the surface of the cortex can be preformed during the surgery (61567).

Skull Base Surgery

CPT® provides extensive notes for skull base surgery codes 61580–61619. Usually the skills of several surgeons of different surgical specialties work together or in tandem. Each surgeon reports only the code for the procedure performed. These procedures are performed to treat lesions involving the skull base, and consist usually of three distinct parts:

1.   An approach procedure to gain access to the lesion

2.   A definitive procedure to biopsy, excise, or otherwise treat the lesion

3.   A repair/reconstructive procedure of the defect left following the definitive procedure

To find the appropriate skull-base surgery approach code, look to the surgeon's documentation to determine the fossa targeted and whether the incision was through the dura. Confer with the surgeon to verify the exact structures he moved or removed to select the code best describing the procedure. Documentation in the medical record may not always match CPT® code descriptor language.

The definitive portion of the procedure is determined according to the area of the skull base (anterior, middle, or posterior cranial fossa) from which the surgeon performs the procedure. When coding for skull-base surgeries, the approach and definitive procedure codes should match. An anterior approach (such as 61586) should accompany a code describing, for instance, removal of a lesion in the same portion of the skull (the anterior cranial fossa). Other factors, such as whether the dura is entered, also determine code selection.

Often (but not always), the surgeon must perform a secondary repair following skull-base surgery. Report the repair/reconstruction codes (61618–61619) separately, "if extensive dural grafting, cranioplasty, local or regional myocutaneous pedicle flaps or extensive skin grafts are required," according to CPT® guidelines. Such secondary repairs will occur during a later operative session, which may require application of modifier 58 (the repair was planned) or modifier 78 (the repair was unplanned), as appropriate to the situation.

Endovascular Therapy

Endovascular treatment of arterial disease involves the use of balloons or stents to treat a diseased artery. Endovascular procedures are less invasive than open vascular procedures, and are done under local anesthesia and sedation rather than full anesthesia. Endovascular techniques may be used to treat vascular issues within the head, neck, or spine (for instance, vascular malformation of the central nervous system).

Procedures described by 61623–61642 generally include selective catheterization of the target vessel only, and radiological supervision and interpretation often are reported separately. Look to parenthetical references in CPT® for instruction.

Surgery for Aneurysm, AV Malformation, or Vascular Disease

CPT® divides codes 61680–61711 into four categories. Each of these procedures includes craniotomy, when appropriate.

1. Codes 61680–61692 specify surgery of intracranial arteriovenous malformation. Arteries and veins are fused abnormally in a tumor-like mass, bypassing the capillaries that normally nourish the surrounding tissue. The malformation may be supratentorial (above the tentorium cerebelli, or in the cerebrum), infratentorial (in the lower part of the brain or cerebellum), or dural (within the dura). These procedures may be coded as simple or complex, as determined by accessibility and difficulty of repair.

2. Codes 61697–61703 describe repair of intracranial (within the skull) aneurysms. An aneurysm is a bulge or abnormal dilation caused when the walls of a blood vessel weaken. These repairs are classified as either simple or complex. According to CPT®, a repair is complex if the aneurysm(s) is larger than 15 mm, involves calcification of the aneurysm neck (the constricted portion at the "base" of the aneurysm), incorporates normal vessels into the aneurysm neck, or requires temporary vessel occlusion, trapping, or cardiopulmonary bypass to complete the repair.

   The carotid circulation supplies blood to the anterior (front) and middle portions of the brain (via the internal carotid artery), while the vertebrobasilar circulation supplies the cerebellum and brain stem via vessels coming up the vertebral arteries. Code 61703 *Surgery of intracranial aneurysm, cervical approach by application of occluding clamp to cervical carotid artery (Selverstone-Crutchfield type)* describes a unique procedure involving approach through the neck to occlude the carotid artery. After occlusion, the surgeon performs a craniotomy and occludes the aneurysm with a clip. Once bleeding is controlled, the carotid clamp is removed, the dura is closed, and the bone flap is repositioned and secured. The scalp and neck incisions are closed.

3. Codes 61705–61710 describe other techniques and approaches for repairing intracranial abnormalities:

   - A combined approach through the neck and skull; the surgeon interrupts blood flow to the abnormality in both directions (61705)
   - Intracranial electrothrombosis (cautery) to obliterate the lesion (61708)
   - Intra-arterial embolization, injection procedure, or balloon catheter (61710)

4. Code 61711 *Anastomosis, arterial, extracranial-intracranial (eg, middle cerebral/cortical) arteries* describes the joining of arteries to bypass an aneurysm or other defect.

Cranial Stereotaxis and Stereotactic Radiosurgery

Stereotactic techniques are a minimally-invasive form of surgical intervention using three-dimensional coordinates to locate small targets inside the body, and to perform on the target some action such as ablation (removal), biopsy, lesion injection, stimulation, implantation, or radiosurgery (SRS). This technique may use an external frame attached to the head, or imaging markers attached to the scalp (frameless or image-guided surgery), to orient the surgeon in his approach.

CPT® provides extensive explanation and instruction preceding stereotactic radiosurgery codes 61796–61800. Familiarize yourself with these guidelines prior to attempting code selection.

When treating cranial lesion by stereotactic radiosurgery (61796–61799), the number and type of lesions treated differentiate the codes. Complex lesions include those that are adjacent to the optic nerve/optic chasm/optic tract (5 mm or less), or within the brain stem. Certain types of lesions automatically are considered complex—including schwannomas, arteriovenous malformations, pituitary tumors, glomus tumors, pineal region tumors, and cavernous sinus/parasellar/petroclival tumors. Simple cranial lesions are less than 3.5 cm in maximum dimension and do not otherwise meet the definition of a complex lesion.

Codes 61797 and 61799 are "each additional codes" and may be reported after the initial procedure.

For a frame-based stereotactic system, report 61800 *Application of stereotactic headframe for stereotactic radiosurgery (List separately in addition to code for primary procedure)*

Cranial Neurostimulators

Placement of intracranial neurostimulators is reported using 61850-61888. A neurostimulator pulse generator system is a surgically implanted, pacemaker-like device delivering preprogrammed intermittent electrical pulses to a particular nerve(s) or brain structure(s). These systems treat conditions not responding satisfactorily to medication alone, including intractable pain in the trunk and/or limbs, peripheral neuropathy (G60-G65), Parkinson's disease (G20), epileptic seizure (G40), and others.

These procedures include access by burr hole, craniectomy, craniotomy, etc., and apply for any type of intracranial neurostimulator (simple or complex).

Deep brain stimulation (DBS) refers to high frequency electrical stimulation of anatomic regions deep within the brain utilizing neurosurgically implanted electrodes. These DBS electrodes are stereotactically placed within targeted nuclei on one (unilateral) or both (bilateral) sides of the brain. Three targets for DBS are the thalamic ventralis intermedius nucleus (VIM), subthalamic nucleus (STN), and globus pallidus interna (GPi). The work of stereotactic localization of deep cerebral nuclear structures and the basic operative work of opening the skull, inserting the electrode array into the initial target and the final closure of the wound is reported using CPT® codes 61863–61867.

Follow CPT® instructions preceding the codes, as well as parenthetical notes, for proper code selection.

Repair

Codes 62000– +62148 describe repairs to the skull (for instance, due to fracture or encephalocele).

Depressed skull fractures often require emergency management of lacerated vessels. If the patient has CSF leakage from the nose or ear, antibiotic prophylaxis is often used. Patients are monitored closely and protected against heat loss (hypothermia), hyperthermia, hyponatremia, fluid imbalance, and airway obstructions. After severe head injuries, amnesia for periods immediately before and after loss of consciousness can occur. Duration of posttraumatic amnesia often provides a good estimate of the extent of brain damage in closed head injuries. When a neurosurgeon treats a patient for a depressed skull fracture to restore anatomical position, the skull is exposed where the depression is found. When the surgeon drills a burr hole(s) and pulls upon the skull to elevate the bone, the coder will use CPT® code 62000 for the service. When multiple fracture lines are found and stabilized, use code 62005. If the skull fracture has damaged the dura and brain, use code 62010. When repairing the dura and CSF leakage, use code 62100.

Encephalocele, a serious neurologic abnormality, often develops in the first two months of gestation. Encephalocele is a protrusion of nervous tissue and meninges through a skull defect and is associated with an incomplete closure of the cranial vault (cranium bifidum). Hydrocephalus is often associated with encephalocele and requires definition by CT or ultrasound. A surgeon can correct an encephalocele defect in the skull vault with cranioplasty (62120) or with a craniotomy (62121).

Follow CPT® parenthetical notes, when applicable, for proper code selection.

Neuroendoscopy

CPT® contains a specific code set, 62160–62165, to describe procedures performed by neuroendoscopy. The endoscope is less invasive than a comparable "open" (incisional) procedure. The code descriptors are straightforward. Follow CPT® parenthetical notes, when applicable, for proper code selection.

Do not report an endoscopy code in addition to the code describing the identical open procedure. If the surgeon must "convert" an endoscopic procedure to an open procedure because of complications, report only the successful open procedure.

CSF Shunt

The standard surgical treatment for hydrocephalus (an accumulation of cerebrospinal fluid, or CSF) includes placement of an extracranial shunt, or tube, to divert excess CSF from the ventricles of the brain to another body area (most often the abdominal cavity). Coding for these procedures depends on the location of both the proximal portion of the shunt and the drain site.

Intracranial shunts are created by means of ventriculocisternostomy, or ventriculocisternal shunting (62180).

Code 62180 describes the Torkildsen type operation. This technique involves performance of a ventriculocisternostomy to form communication between the lateral ventricles and the cisterna magna. This procedure drains excess CSF into the subarachnoid space, especially the cistern magna where fluids will be absorbed. Burr hole(s) are drilled into the skull and a shunt is inserted toward the lateral ventricle (with or without the aid of an endoscope) until the CSF (cerebrospinal fluid) flows through the shunt. The distal end of the shunt is directed toward the cisterna magna. The two ends are connected and tested. The dura is sutured and the scalp is reapproximated and closed in sutured layers.

Endoscopic third ventriculostomy (62201) uses a laser under neuroendoscopic guidance to create a duct from the third lateral ventricle to the cisterna magna without need for a shunt.

Extracranial shunts may require periodic revisions, including irrigation and complete or partial replacement (eg, 62194, 62225, 62230, 62256, and 62258).

The reprogrammable shunt allows noninvasive pressure adjustments to correct over—or underdrainage of CSF; reprogramming is reported 62252.

Spine and Spinal Cord

Injection, Drainage, or Aspiration

CPT® supplies extensive notes prior to these codes (62263–62319), as well as numerous parenthetical instructions. Read and understand these guidelines prior to selecting a code. Highlights in this section include:

- During epidural lysis of spinal adhesions (Racz catheter procedure or epidural adhesiolysis), 62263–62264, the surgeon inserts a needle near the patient's tailbone and threads a catheter through the needle to inject medication into adhesions. The needle may be removed after the procedure, but the catheter may remain in place for several days to continue treating the lesions.

- Percutaneous aspiration (code 62268) is a procedure where the surgeon removes contents of a cyst or syrinx (a fistula or diseased area) with a needle. Using a C-arm X-ray machine to verify placement of the needle, the surgeon aspirates the cyst or syrinx of its contents and removes the needle. This procedure is often used to treat intraspinal abscess, syringomyelia, and other disorders of the meninges.

- Diagnostic spinal puncture ("spinal tap") is reported 62270; therapeutic procedure for drainage of CSF is reported 62272.

- A patient diagnosed with spasmodic torticollis, multiple sclerosis, lumbosacral plexus lesions, or causalgia of the lower limb may receive an injection of neurolytic substance (eg, alcohol, phenol, iced saline solution) to destroy nerve tissues or adhesions. When a surgeon provides this service to the subarachnoid area, use CPT® code 62280. For neurolytic injection/infusion to the epidural space, choose between 62281 and 62282.

- When myelography is performed on the cervical, thoracic, or lumbosacral regions utilizing a lumbar injection, codes 62302-62305 are reported based on the region under investigation. When two or more regions are being evaluated, code 62305 is reported. Radiological supervision and interpretation are included in these codes.

- For non-neurolytic substances (anesthetic, antispasmodic, opioid, steroid, etc.) administered through a single injection or via a continuous infusion or intermittent bolus by indwelling catheter into the epidural or subarachnoid space, choose 62318–62319 depending on the location. These codes include use of contrast material for localization or epidurography.

- For transforaminal epidural injection of a non-neurolytic substance, select from 64479–64484.

- For a continuous epidural injection, catheter placement involves using a special needle called a Touhy needle, which is inserted between the vertebrae into the epidural space. The epidural space is between the endosteum of the spinal column and the dural membrane, and the needle does not puncture the dura. A small catheter is threaded through the needle into the epidural space and the needle is withdrawn. The catheter is taped in place to prevent movement and the anesthetic agent is injected or infused through the catheter. CPT® codes 62318 and 62319 represent catheter placement and injection or infusion by catheter.

- For injection of an anesthetic agent for autonomic nerves, see nerve-specific codes 64505–64530.

- For paravertebral facet (zygapophyseal) joint injections report 64490-64495. Imaging guidance and localization are required for these procedures. If imaging is not used, report 20552–20553. If ultrasound guidance is used, report 0213T–0218T.

Catheter, Reservoir/Pump Implantation

Procedures for so-called "pain pumps" (for instance, for pain management or spasticity treatment) are reported with 62350–62370.

An intrathecal catheter placement involves penetration of the dural membrane and diffuses medication into the spinal fluid, whereas the epidural catheter placement does not penetrate the dura. When an intrathecal or epidural catheter is connected to an implantable reservoir, an implantable infusion pump (IIP), or an external pump required for treatment of intractable spasticity or pain associated with cancer or other conditions, one of two CPT® codes (62350, 62351) is reported.

Programmable implantable infusion pump (PIIP) and IIPs are important drug delivery systems used for treatment of a wide range of clinical conditions, such as cancer therapy and chronic pain therapy. The objectives of implantable drug delivery systems include provision of long-term access to various compartments of the nervous systems (epidural, subarachnoid, hepatic artery) to enable site specific drug therapy; reduction in infections at the injection site associated with external access devices; and provision of drug delivery through a device or system promoting patient mobility and independence.

Functional requirements of infusion pumps include reliability, precision, and safety, simplicity in handling and maintenance, light weight, and biological, and chemical compatibility with the drug to be infused into the implantable pumps, easy access, and long acting power source. All benefits of these pumps necessarily require that the delivery system use a drug that is effective for the clinical condition in question. IIPs have been developed primarily to promote patient independence from the hospital setting during long term infusion therapy, particularly for pain control and chemotherapy administration. The components include the infusion pump and reservoir, bacteriostatic filters, fluid administration sets, and delivery catheters. When providers provide trial dosing to assess patient appropriateness for therapy, dose changes, reprogramming, and refilling of the pump, several services, and procedures are reportable.

Available codes distinguish between programmable and non-programmable pumps. CPT® parenthetical instructions provide guidance on coding for associated procedures, such as refilling and maintenance of implantable infusion pump.

Laminotomy, Laminectomy

Laminectomy (excision of lamina and spinous process) and laminotomy (partial excision of lamina) are performed primarily for nerve decompression. Read code descriptors carefully to determine if related procedures, such as facectec-

tomy, foraminotomy, excision of herniated intervertebral discs, etc., are included.

These procedures are grouped according to spinal region (cervical, thoracic, and lumbar). Note that some procedures are reported per segment (eg, 63015–63017), while others are reported per interspace (eg, 63020–63044). The interspace is the space between two vertebral bodies. It is a non-bony compartment. Generally, a single code is reported for the first segment/interspace, with add-on codes used to report additional segments/interspaces. As an example, 63020 describes laminotomy of a single cervical interspace. For each additional cervical interspace treated, one unit of add-on code 63035 would be reported.

Cauda equina codes 63015 and 63045 refer to the long spinal nerves emerging from the lower end of the spinal cord. These long nerves resemble a horse's tail, or a cauda equina. The term, spondylolisthesis (code 63012) refers to the forward displacement of a vertebra over a lower segment, usually in the lumbar region. Decompression of nerves, or the removal of pressure from nerves, is included with all of these codes. Facectectomy refers to the surgical removal of the articular facets of a vertebra. Foraminotomy is the surgical removal of bone from around the edges of the intervertebral foramina. The foramen is the opening formed by the anterior segment (the body), and the posterior part, the vertebral arch of the vertebra which surrounds the spinal cord. A herniated intervertebral disc is a disc that has ruptured and spread out of its capsule.

Codes 63040–63044 specifically describe re-exploration, or a repeat procedure.

Follow CPT® parenthetical instruction regarding proper reporting of bilateral procedures and allowable code combinations. Anatomically these procedures are considered unilateral, because either the right or the left lamina can be excised to expose disc material. A modifier 50 should be appended when both sides are worked on.

Excision by laminectomy of lesion other than a herniated disc is reported using 63250–63290, as appropriate to the type of lesion and its location. Add-on code +63295 describes reconstruction of dorsal spinal elements following an intraspinal procedure. CPT® provides parenthetical notes outlining correct use of this code.

Extradural Exploration/Decompression

Exploration and Decompression codes 63055– +63103 are grouped according to approach (transpedicular/costovertebral approach for posterolateral extradural exploration, anterior/anterolateral, or lateral extracavitary approach). The approach determines whether the procedure will include removal of bone (for instance, vertebral corpectomy).

Example

The provider makes an incision along the rib corresponding to the second thoracic vertebra above the involved intervertebral disc. The rib is removed for access and eventually used for graft material. The disc is removed and the end plates stripped of their cartilage. The physician makes a slot in one vertebral body and a hole in the other to accept the graft, which is made of several sections of rib. The physician ties the grafts together with heavy suture material. A closure is performed with layered sutures and a chest drain may be inserted. Use CPT® code 63077 when reporting this procedure. Code 63078 is reported for each additional thoracic interspace.

A discectomy may be performed when a patient is diagnosed with displacement of a thoracic intervertebral disc without myelopathy, degeneration of thoracic or thoracolumbar intervertebral disc, spinal stenosis of the thoracic region or pain in the thoracic spine.

Osteophytectomy is removal of an osteophyte, which is a bony outgrowth. They sometimes develop on the upper and lower edges of the vertebral bodies and can exert pressure on the spinal cord.

A vertebral corpectomy is a vertebral body resection or the removal of the body of a vertebra and includes the discectomy above and/or below the vertebral segment. Vertebral corpectomy is removal of the body of a vertebral segment. When a lumbar vertebral corpectomy is performed via an anterior approach (abdominal incision), a second surgeon of a different specialty may be called to provide surgical exposure. This constitutes co-surgery. Both surgeons would bill the same corpectomy code with a modifier 62.

Read code descriptors carefully to determine if related procedures, such as osteophytectomy, etc., are included.

The section of codes for Lateral Extracavitary Approach for Extradural Exploration/Decompression (63101–63103) reports the lateral extracavitary approach that neurosurgeons may perform for a variety of diagnoses, including:

- Correct fixed short segment thoracic kyphosis
- Treatment of herniated thoracic disc
- Decompression of the spinal cord and osseous fusion of the spine following traumatic thoracolumbar fracture
- Prevent collapse of the involved vertebral segment

CPT® provides instructional guidance for this section (for instance, regarding the proper use of modifier 62 with discectomy procedures), as well as numerous parenthetical notes. Read and understand these guidelines prior to selecting a code.

Incision

Cervical spondylosis usually results from a degenerative change in the intervertebral disc and annulus with formation of bony osteophytes narrowing the cervical canal or neural foramina. It is often diagnosed by an MRI. A decompressive laminectomy is indicated, if the patient has myelopathy and cord compression confirmed by imaging studies. If surgery is indicated, anatomic pathology and symptoms determine whether an anterior or posterior approach is used.

A laminectomy with cordotomy (63194–63199) may be performed in one stage with resection of one or both spinothalamic tracts or in two stages. Cordotomy refers to a section of the nerve fibers that pass up the spinal cord in special tracts. The spinothalmic tracts transmit the sensation of pain to consciousness.

Excision by Laminectomy of Lesion Other than Herniated Disc

These codes are used to describe excisions of lesions (eg, arteriovenous malformations, intraspinal (other than neoplasm), and biopsy/excision of intraspinal lesions). Codes are selected based on their location along the spine and if the lesion is extradural or intradural.

Excision of Intraspinal Lesion, Anterior or Anterolateral Approach

These codes describe either intradural or extradural excision of intraspinal lesions with variable anterior surgical approaches.

These codes (63300–63308) are selected according to spinal region (cervical, thoracic), whether intra- or extradural, and (in some cases) by specific approach. CPT® provides instructional guidance regarding the proper use of modifier 62 for this section.

Spinal Stereotaxis and Stereotactic Radiosurgery

Codes 63600– 63621 describe procedures similar to cranial stereotactic codes 61720–61800. Stereotaxis may include lesion creation (63600), stimulation not followed by other surgery (63610), and biopsy, aspiration, or excision of lesion (63615).

CPT® provides extensive explanation and instruction preceding stereotactic radiosurgery codes 63620– 63621. Familiarize yourself with these guidelines prior to attempting code selection. Unlike the cranial stereotactic codes, the spinal codes do not differentiate lesions as "simple" or "complex."

Neurostimulators (Spinal)

Spinal neurostimulators are placed to treat chronic back pain by delivering low voltage electrical stimulation to the dorsal columns of the spinal cord to block the sensation of pain. The systems consist of electrodes implanted along the spine, which are connected to a programmable pulse generator or receiver.

The electrodes may be either a catheter electrode array, or arranged on a "paddle."

Implantation of electrode arrays is reported 63650–63655, according to method. Two codes (63661, 63662) describe removal of spinal neurostimulator electrodes, according to type (electrode array or plate/paddles). Two additional codes describe revision (63663, 63664)—which includes replacement when performed—of spinal neurostimulator, according to type (electrode array or plate/paddles). All of the above services include fluoroscopy if performed.

Implantation or replacement of pulse generator or receiver is reported 63685; revision or removal of the same is reported 63688. Programming may be reported separately.

Repair

Spina bifida is one of the most serious neural tube defects. Manifestation of neurologic symptoms is directly related to severity, varying from the occult type with no findings to a complete open spine (rachischisis) with severe neurologic disability and death. In spina bifida cystica, the protruding sac can contain spinal meninges (meningocele [for repair procedures, see codes 63700–63702] or myelomeningocele [for repair procedures, see CPT® codes 63704–63706]). It is most commonly found in the lower thoracic, lumbar, or sacral region and usually extends for three to six vertebral segments.

If the defect is leaking CSF, antibiotics and urgent neurosurgical evaluation and repair (63707–63709) can reduce the risk of meningeal or ventricular infection. A graft using dural tissue is reported with code 63710.

Shunt, Spinal CSF

These codes are similar to shunt CPT® codes 62190–62192, except they originate from the lumbar spine rather than the brain and do not end in the atrial or jugular blood vessels. Hydrocephalus is a condition marked by an excessive accumulation of fluid resulting in dilation of the cerebral ventricles and raised intracranial pressure. When a patient is diagnosed with hydrocephalus (eg, communicating, congenital, or obstructive) the surgeon may recommend a shunt procedure, which allows excess cerebral spinal fluid to be drained. The shunt is inserted through the dura into the subarachnoid space, is passed around the flank to the peritoneal, pleural, or other space for drainage.

Extracranial Nerves, Peripheral Nerves, and Autonomic Nervous System

The peripheral nervous system is comprised of the cranial nerves (12 pairs), the spinal nerves (31 pairs), and the autonomic ganglia and any plexuses through which they run. The spinal nerves come from the spinal cord through the vertebral foramina. The cranial nerves emerge from the cranium or skull.

There are two major divisions between the nerve fibers that comprise the peripheral nervous system. They are somatic and autonomic. The somatic nerves primarily innervate the skeletal muscles and the sensory organs. The term autonomic nervous system refers to nerves working automatically. The nerves of the autonomic nervous system innervate and regulate gland cells, smooth muscles (eg, stomach, bladder, blood vessels, and the heart muscle). There are two distinct branches of the autonomic nervous system: sympathetic and parasympathetic. These two divisions act in an opposing manner to counteract each other and keep homeostasis (equilibrium) in the body.

The following list contrasts the features of the two branches:

Feature	Sympathetic	Parasympathetic
Location of controlling nodes	Thoracic and lumbar areas of spinal cord	Cranial and sacral areas of the spinal cord
Location of the ganglia	Near the spinal cord	Near the target organs
Neurotransmitter used to convey impulses	Norepinephrine	Acetylcholine
Physiologic purpose/function	Speeds up bodily functions in preparation for emergency response	Slows down bodily functions to normal after sympathetic response to give the body a rest

This code section (64400–64495) applies to extracranial nerves only; for intracranial surgery on cranial nerves, see 61450, 61460, or 61790.

Diagnostic or Therapeutic Nerve Block

Nerve blocks are reported according to the nerve/plexus targeted. CPT® provides extensive parenthetical notes in this section to guide code selection, and indicates when associated procedures (such as image guidance) may be reported separately.

Transversus abdominis plane (TAP) blocks (64486-64489) are reported based on whether the procedure was performed unilaterally or bilaterally and method of administration, either through injections or continuous infusions. Imaging guidance is included if performed.

The term "facet joint injection" may describe either a nerve block (64490–+64495) or more-extensive nerve destruction

(64633–64636) When reporting nerve blocks, focus on the "joint"—the area between adjacent nerves—that the provider targets; one nerve block "level" will involve two nerves.

Example

The physician provides diagnostic nerve blocks for C2, C3, and C4, she is addressing three nerves but only two levels (the joint at C2/C3 and the joint at C3/C4).

Be sure to apply 64490–64495 per level, rather than per injection (the physician may provide more than one injection per level).

Codes 64490–64495 describe unilateral procedures. If the provider addresses both the left and right side at the same level, CPT® guidelines allow modifier 50 to report a bilateral procedure. Because these codes include image guidance, radiology codes for a CT or fluoroscopy are not reported separately.

Somatic Nerves

Somatic nerves are the voluntary motor and sensory nerves supplying skeletal muscle and somatic tissues. Sympathetic nerves are part of the involuntary, autonomic nervous system.

When coding nerve blocks, consider the following factors:

1. What type of substance was injected? If it is classified as anesthetic, a code from the range 64400–64484 for somatic nerves or 64505–64530 for autonomic nerves would be appropriate. Examples of some anesthetic agents include Novocaine, Xylocaine, and Marcaine. If the agent is classified as a neurolytic substance, codes 64600–64681 would be appropriate.

2. Differentiate between somatic and sympathetic nerves. CPT® identifies these nerves by name.

3. Differentiate between a single level or multiple level before assigning a code for somatic nerve injection. Regional blocks (eg, 64421) are achieved by injecting the anesthetic along the course of the nerve or into the epidural or subarachnoid space.

4. Consider duration of infusion. Use codes for continuous infusion by catheter and daily management for anesthetic agent administration.

Practical Coding Note

Go through the CPT® codes and highlight or underline when the code specifies "single" or "continuous."

The trigeminal nerve (64400) is the fifth and largest cranial nerve and is actually a pair of nerves that exit the brain on the right and left sides. The facial nerve (64402) is the seventh cranial nerve and has six branches. It may be blocked during intraocular surgery to relax the eyelids. The greater occipital nerve (64405) provides feeling to the area at the back of the skull (middle portion of the occipital area) and is a branch of the second cervical spinal nerve. A block at this site is used to diagnose and relieve headache from tension or spasm of the cervical muscles, or to provide anesthesia to the scalp during operative procedures and treat pain from cranial lesions.

The vagus nerve (64408) is the tenth cranial nerve. It is the longest cranial nerve and extends from the head and neck to the chest and abdominal area. A block to this nerve anesthetizes the breathing passages from the epiglottis to the smallest airways in the lung and may be used prior to general anesthesia.

The phrenic nerve (64410) is a branch of the cervical plexus and is made up of fibers from the third, fourth, and fifth cervical spinal nerves. The phrenic nerve may be blocked to treat intractable hiccoughs (hiccups) and relieves pain from lesions of the pericardial region.

The spinal accessory nerve is the eleventh cranial nerve and consists of the cranial accessory nerve plus five or six cervical spinal nerve roots. A block of this nerve provides motor paralysis during surgery and relieves spasms of the sternocleidomastoid and upper trapezius muscles. This is reported using code 64999.

The cervical plexus (64413) is made up of nerves from the C1, C2, C3, and C4 spinal nerves. A block to this nerve is also known as a paravertebral cervical block. These blocks are easy to perform and provide anesthesia during certain lymph node dissections, plastic repairs, and carotid endarterectomy procedures.

The brachial plexus (64415) supplies the muscles and skin of the chest, shoulders, and arms. The brachial plexus block is often referred to as an interscalene block. The axillary nerve (64417) is a branch of the brachial plexus. The suprascapular nerve (64418) also comes from the brachial plexus and supplies the shoulder joint and deep shoulder structures.

The intercostal nerves (64420, 64421) branch off the first through eleventh thoracic spinal nerves. They extend along each rib. An intercostal nerve block may be performed on one or more intercostal nerves. Usually multiple nerves are blocked, since three nerves need to be blocked to provide complete anesthesia to any one site. They may provide pain relief for rib fractures, surgical incisions, pleurisy, chest tube placement, and herpes zoster.

The ilioinguinal and iliohypogastric nerves (64425) branch off the twelfth thoracic and first lumbar spinal nerves. A block of these nerves provides relief from pain due to inguinal hernia repair and pediatric orchiopexy (fixation of an undescended testis in the scrotum). The pudendal nerve (64430) originates from the sacral plexus and divides into five branches supplying the genital, perineum, the coccyx and pubic bone, and pelvic region.

The paracervical nerve (64435) is actually a group of nerves. It supplies the uterus, vagina, bladder, and rectum of the female, and is also known as the uterovaginal plexus or uterine nerve. A block to the paracervical nerve provides relief to the pudendal nerve.

The sciatic nerve (64445) is the largest nerve of the body and extends from the sacral plexus through the pelvis, buttocks, and into the thigh. A sciatic nerve block provides relief for chronic pain and may be combined with other blocks to provide anesthesia during surgery to structures below the knee. NOTE that 64446 refers to a continuous sciatic nerve block, which includes postoperative pain management. When a nerve or digital block is given for pain management code 64450 is used. It is mainly used to turn off a pain signal from a specific part of the body.

A paravertebral facet joint injection (64490–64495) may involve injection of a steroid and an anesthetic agent into the facet joint of a vertebra or around the facet joint nerve to relieve chronic low back pain. The paravertebral somatic nerves (64490–64495) are distinguished from the paravertebral sympathetic nerves (64520). These nerves curve around each vertebra. Blocks to these nerves and other regional blocks may be used to diagnose and treat certain pain disorders.

Autonomic Nerves (Sympathetic)

Injection procedures involving sympathetic nerves (belonging to the involuntary nervous system) are listed in CPT® codes 64505–64530. Nerve blocks to these nerves produce vasodilation, increased blood flow, and a consequent rise in skin temperature.

A stellate ganglion nerve block (64510) is used to treat reflex sympathetic dystrophy and herpes zoster. A lumbar or thoracic sympathetic nerve block (64520) is indicated for patients suffering vasospasm in the legs or sympathetic dystrophy. A celiac plexus block (64530) provides relief of abdominal pain in acute or chronic pancreatitis; pancreatic, liver, and bladder cancer; or sympathetic bowel imbalance. Identify whether the blocked nerves belong to the somatic or sympathetic nervous system.

Neurostimulators (Peripheral Nerve)

Electrical stimulators may be applied either to the surface of the skin or percutaneously. They may also be implanted after an incision has been made. Placement and revision/replacement of peripheral nerve neurostimulators (simple or complex) is reported using 64550–64595, depending on the nerve targeted and type of neurostimulator. The code descriptors are straightforward. Follow CPT® instruction preceding the codes, as well as parenthetical notes, for proper code selection.

Destruction by Neurolytic Agent

Neurolytic agents are any agent destroying nerve tissue. The purpose is to provide ongoing relief of pain due to disease or other abnormality of the nerve root. These procedures are also referred to as rhizotomy. This type of treatment may provide relief for weeks, up to one year. Neurolytic agents for nerve destruction may include chemical, thermal, electrical, or radiofrequency methods. Codes in this range (64600–64681) are specific as to the nerves/plexus, muscles, or glands targeted. CPT® instructions preceding these codes, as well as all parenthetical references, provide necessary guidance to report these procedures with accuracy.

Chemodenervation refers to the process of interrupting the complex chemical reactions at the junction of the nerve endplate and the muscular surface it is designed to innervate. This procedure is usually done with C. botulinum toxin. A toxin is a poisonous chemical substance and is a by-product of growth and/or metabolism of certain microorganisms. There are seven serologically distinct toxins produced by the bacterium botulinum behaving as neurotoxins in the human body. A neurotoxin interrupts the flow of neurotransmitters (in the case of botulinum it interrupts the flow of acetylcholine) where the nerve meets the muscle it is set to innervate. This action is particularly useful in treating patients with spasmodic problems such as dystonia and cerebral palsy.

Although CPT® procedure codes 64612–64617 are listed with the "destruction" services, these services do not include the destruction to muscles in the extremities. CPT® code 64616 accounts for denervation to unilateral neck muscles. To report chemodenervation of one side of the larynx, assign code 64617. When performed bilaterally, append modifier 50. These codes are not for use with cosmetic procedures such as minimizing facial wrinkles or in the treatment of excessive sweating using botulinum toxin. This involves the injection into muscles (not nerves) of the neck and larynx.

When muscles of the extremities or trunk are injected, codes 64642–64647 are reported. Codes are assigned based on how many muscles are injected and where the muscles are located. Report codes 64642 for extremities when 1–4 muscles are injected, and 64643 for each additional extremity receiving 1–4 injections. When an extremity receives 5 or more injections, report code 64644. For each additional extremity receiving 5 or more injections, assign add-on code 64645. When chemodenervation is administered to trunk muscles, report 64646 or 64647 depending on how many muscles are injected.

In trigeminal nerve disorders (trigeminal neuralgia), bouts of excruciating, lancinating pain lasting up to two minutes accompanied with sensory divisions (most often maxillary) are common. Chewing or brushing teeth often activates this type of pain. In resistant cases where a craniectomy is performed, the intracranial arterial and sometimes venous loops are found to compress the trigeminal nerve root where it enters the brain stem.

Electrolytic, chemical, or balloon compressive lesions of the gasserian ganglion can be made via a percutaneous stereotaxically positioned needle to destroy the nerve tissue (64600). Destruction of blepharospasm or hemifacial spasm (64612) refers to the entire destruction procedure and is reported once, although more than one injection may be required for the procedure.

Neuroplasty

These codes describe the freeing of intact nerves from scar tissue and include external neurolysis and/or transposition (in this context, changing the position or placement of the nerve). The codes are applied according to the nerve targeted.

The repair of a compressed nerve in a finger, hand, or foot (64702–64704) is accomplished by decompressing the nerve from the surrounding tissue. When the surgeon performs neuroplasty by making a horizontal incision in the wrist at the metacarpal joints to locate the nerves and frees the ulnar nerve, use CPT® code 64719.

Transposition means the nerve has been moved from one place to another. Neurolysis is the liberation of a nerve from adhesions or the relief of tension of a nerve due to stretching. To restore feeling in the hand, soft tissues are resected and the nerve is freed from the underlying bed. This procedure is also known as carpal tunnel release (64721) and is commonly performed.

Transection and Avulsion

Transection (to divide by transverse incision) and avulsion (tearing away) of nerves codes are selected according to the nerve targeted.

When a surgeon transects over the supraorbital nerve (64732) (the ophthalmic branch of the trigeminal nerve is sensory in nature), the patient's pain to the head and neck area is eliminated.

CPT® parenthetical notes provide guidance for proper reporting of bilateral procedures.

Excision

Excision of nerves is coded according to the nerve targeted. Biopsy of somatic nerve is reported 64795.

Neurorrhaphy

Neurorrhaphy is the surgical suturing of a divided nerve. Codes in the range 64831–+64876 describe suturing only; the appropriate code is selected according to the nerve(s) targeted.

Codes 64885–64911 describe neurorrhaphy with nerve graft, vein graft, or conduit. Most codes are selected according to location (head or neck, hand or foot, etc.) and nerve length (more or less than 4 cm). Add-on codes 64901 and 64902 describe each additional nerve graft, single and multiple strands, respectively. If the surgeon repairs two or more nerves using grafts, report 64901–64902, as appropriate.

Unlisted Procedures

Unlisted procedures of the nervous system are to be reported using 64999. Call on an unlisted procedure code only when no CPT® code or Category III code properly describes the procedure the provider performed. Do not select a code that is "close enough" in lieu of an unlisted procedure code.

When filing a claim using an unlisted procedure code, submit a cover letter of explanation and the full documentation of services.

Operating Microscope

Report +69990 *Microsurgical techniques, requiring use of operating microscope (List separately in addition to code for primary procedure)* only for procedures requiring microsurgery or microdissection, and only when the primary surgery does not include micro-dissection as an integral part of the operation. Do not claim 69990 if the surgeon uses the microscope only for magnification or corrective vision. Do not claim 69990 for magnifying loupes.

Because 69990 is an add-on code, you can report it only with another, primary procedure.

CPT® provides instructions for when you may report 69990 in addition to other procedures, but be aware that not all payers will abide by AMA rules. The National Correct Coding Initiative bundles 69990 extensively, when CPT® otherwise allows separate coding.

Neurology and Neuromuscular Procedures

Neurology and neuromuscular procedures include a wide range of services, and may be found in the Medicine chapter (90000-series) of CPT®.

Sleep Studies

CPT® provides extensive direction for proper reporting of these services, including the proper use of modifier 26 to report professional services.

Polysomnography includes sleep staging with varying "parameters of sleep" studied. CPT® defines sleep staging to include a 1-4 lead electroencephalogram (EEG), an electro-oculogram (EOG), and a submental electromyogram (EMG). Additional parameters of sleep that may be recorded include:

- ECG
- airflow
- ventilation and respiratory effort
- gas exchange by oximetry, transcutaneous monitoring, or end tidal gas analysis
- extremity muscle activity, motor activity-movement
- extended EEG monitoring
- penile tumescence
- gastroesophageal reflux
- continuous blood pressure monitoring
- snoring
- body positions

These studies (and other sleep studies described in CPT®) require continuous monitoring and recording. If fewer than six hours of recording takes place, modifier 52 should be appended to identify a reduced service with codes 95800, 95801 and 95806, 95807, 95810, 95811. If less than seven hours of recording for 95782, 95783, append modifier 52.

CPT® 95808 and 95810 identify diagnostic polysomnograms, depending on the parameters of sleep recorded. Code 95811 requires sleep staging with four or more additional parameters of sleep and further includes initiation of treatment. The patient must be six years of age or older to report codes 95810 and 95811.

A multiple sleep latency test (95805) is a daytime sleep study measuring how sleepy the patient is and how long it takes the patient to fall asleep.

Actigraphy testing (95803) is done to study a patient's circadian rhythms and sleep schedule.

Electroencephalography (EEG)/Special EEG

Routine EEG codes 95816–95822 include 20–40 minutes of recording. Extended EEG codes 95812–95813 include reporting times longer than 40 minutes. Hyperventilation and photic stimulation are not a mandatory part of routine EEG.

Code 95819 is appropriate if an awake/asleep study was intended even if the patient did not sleep. Report 95819 (rather than 95816) if an awake only study is planned but the patient falls asleep.

Patients may undergo special EEG monitoring (95950/95951) to determine the reasons for seizures and to localize the portion of the brain affected. EEG monitoring as described by 95953 more precisely localizes certain types of seizures; when employed, it often follows monitoring as described by 95950 or 95951.

The descriptors for 95950-95953 specify "each 24 hours;" if 12 hours or less of monitoring are provided, report the appropriate CPT® code with modifier 52 appended.

Most EEGs run on digital machines, but using a digital recorder alone does not support digital analysis 95957. Rather, digital analysis as described by 95957 requires analysis using quantitative analytical techniques such as data selection, quantitative software processing, and dipole source analysis. This kind of analysis entails additional work to process the data, as well as extra time to review the data.

Muscle and Range of Motion Testing

Manual muscle testing codes (95831–95834) are specific to the area tested (extremity (excluding hand) or trunk, hand, total body with/without hands). All codes include physician report.

Range of motion measurement codes are reported per extremity or trunk section (95851), or for the hand (95852).

Tensilon test for myasthenia gravis (a neuromuscular disorder characterized by weakness of voluntary muscles) is reported 95857. In myasthenia gravis, the muscles improve immediately following administration of Tensilon (edrophonium chloride).

Electromyography

EMG is used to evaluate the cause of weakness, paralysis, involuntary muscle twitching, or other symptoms.

To reporting EMG limb testing (95860–95864, depending on the number of limbs studied), the provider must evaluate extremity muscles innervated by at least three nerves (for example, radial, ulnar, median, tibial, peroneal or femoral— but not sub branches) or four spinal levels, with a minimum of five muscles studies per limb.

"Related paraspinal areas" include all paraspinals except for T1 or T12. If the provider studies the paraspinals from T2–T11, report 95869; report only one unit of 95869, regardless of the number of levels studied or if bilateral.

When four or fewer muscles are tested report limited EMG 95870 or 95885.

Guidance for Chemodenervation

For EMG when administering chemodenervation, report the guidance separately using 95873 or 95874. Codes 95873 and 95874 are the only acceptable needle guidance codes with chemodenervation procedures. Use 95873 or 95874 only with injection codes 64612–64616, 64642–64647. Do not report 95873 or 95874 in addition to other needle EMG diagnostic study codes, such as needle electromyography codes 95860–95870.

Nerve Conduction Tests

CPT® provides extensive instruction in the heading preceding nerve conduction studies (NCS) 95905–95913, as well as several parenthetical notes to guide code application.

The codes for NCS are reported by the number of studies performed. Refer to CPT® Appendix J for a list of separately billable sensory, motor, and mixed nerves.

Code 95905 describes specifically studies conducted using preconfigured electrode arrays, such as the NeuroMetrix NC-stat System.

Intraoperative Neurophysiology

Continuous intraoperative neurophysiology testing and monitoring (IOM) is reported using add-on codes 95940 and 95941.

Report add-on code 95940 when the IOM is continuous in the operating room and when there is only one patient that is personally monitored in 15 minute increments. Add-on code 95941 is reported when the IOM is not performed in the operating room or when there is more than one patient being monitored in an operating room per hour. Prior to IOM, the monitoring physician may first conduct one or more studies to establish a patient's "baseline" responses. Report these baseline studies separately. CPT® provides a list of approved baseline studies/primary procedures for use with IOM, which includes EMG, nerve conduction studies, evoked potentials and others. You may report multiple baseline studies, when necessary.

When determining IOM time, do not count "standby time" in the operating room or the time spent conducting any baseline studies. Only a dedicated physician, with the sole task of monitoring the patient during the surgery, should separately claim IOM services.

CPT® provides extensive instructions for reporting these services correctly.

Evoked Potentials and Reflex Tests

Codes for evoked potential (EP) studies include two auditory studies (92585, 92586), four sensory studies (95925–95927, 95938), and one visual study (95930). EP studies measure the brain's electrical activity in response to stimulation of specific nerve pathways.

A comprehensive auditory evoked response (AER) exam (92585) measures middle latency and late cortical responses, and evaluates brainstem response. A limited audiometry examination (92586) describes limited auditory brainstem response (ABR) testing.

Regardless of the number of skin sites (dermatomes) tested, you may report only a single unit of 95925–95927.

Report 95928 (upper limbs), 95929 (lower limbs), or 95939 when both upper and lower limbs are studied, as appropriate, for central motor (rather than sensory) EP study.

Analysis and Programming of Neurostimulators

A neurostimulator pulse generator system is a surgically implanted, pacemaker-like device delivering preprogrammed intermittent electrical pulses to a particular nerve(s) or brain structure(s). Codes 95970-95982 are specific to location: spinal cord or peripheral nerve (95970–95972), cranial nerve (95974–95975), deep brain (95978–95979) and gastric (95980–95982).

Neurostimulators may be either simple or complex. A simple neurostimulator is capable of affecting three or fewer of the following, while a complex neurostimulator is capable of affecting more than three:

- Rate
- Pulse amplitude
- Pulse duration
- Pulse frequency
- Eight or more electrode contacts
- Cycling
- Stimulation train duration
- Train spacing
- Number of programs
- Number of channels
- Alternating electrode polarities
- Dose time (stimulation parameters changing in the time periods of minutes including dose lockout times)
- More than one clinical feature (eg, rigidity, dyskinesia, tremor)

Coding for complex neurostimulator programming is always time-based.

Unlisted Neurological or Neuromuscular Diagnostic Procedure

Unlisted neurological or neuromuscular diagnostic procedures are to be reported using 95999. Call on an unlisted procedure code only when no CPT® code or Category III code properly describes the procedure the provider performs. Do not select a code "close enough" in lieu of an unlisted procedure code.

Category III

Category III codes are temporary codes for emerging technologies, services, and procedures. These alphanumeric codes are important tracking mechanisms and also may become future Category I codes. You should report a Category III code accurately describing the service when there is no option under the Category I codes. If a Category III code is available, this code must be reported instead of a Category I unlisted code.

A number of Category III codes describe endocrine or nervous system procedures (for instance, 0201T *Percutaneous sacral augmentation [sacroplasty], bilateral injections, including the use of a balloon or mechanical device, when used, 2 or more needles, includes imaging guidance and bone biopsy, when performed*).

Section Review 14.3

---

1. Patient is a 59-year-old female with failed back syndrome. She has undergone a recent test dose of intrathecal narcotics with good pain response. She has been brought to the operating room at this time for preparation and insertion of Medtronic programmable pain pump and intrathecal catheter. Select the procedure codes for this surgery.

    A. 62360, 62350-51

    B. 62362, 62318-51

    C. 62361, 62318-51

    D. 62362, 62350-51

2. College student comes into the ER with symptoms of headache and a high fever for the past two days. A lumbar puncture is performed and spinal fluid is sent to the lab to check for meningitis. Choose the correct procedure code.

    A. 62282

    B. 62272

    C. 62270

    D. 62267

3. A 35-year-old male has a left chronic subdural hematoma. He will be undergoing left burr hole evacuation of subdural hematoma. The correct procedure code for this surgery is:

    A. 61108

    B. 61154

    C. 61156

    D. 61105

4. A patient has severe spinal stenosis located between L3–L5 inferior to disc space. A laminectomy is performed on L4 along with a decompression of L3–L4 and L4–L5. Choose the appropriate code for this procedure.

    A. 63005

    B. 63012

    C. 63020

    D. 63047

5. A 50-year-old with left internal carotid artery stenosis is having a left carotid thromboendarterectomy with electroenceph-
    alogram monitoring. The patient had electroencephalogram (EEG) leads placed on his head prior to surgery. Throughout
    the whole time of the dissection, EEG patterns were symmetrical. Select the CPT® code for this EEG Monitoring.

    A. 95954-26

    B. 95957-26

    C. 95955-26

    D. 95958-26

HCPCS Level II

You will find codes throughout the HCPCS Level II codebook
for endocrine and nervous system coding. Primarily, you
will report drug supplies (often using J codes, for example
J0585 *Injection, onabotulinumtoxinA, 1 unit for Botox®*),
some supply codes (such as L8680 *Implantable neurostimulator electrode (with any number of contact points), each*, and
temporary national codes (S codes) for emerging procedures
or technology (for instance, S2348 *Decompression procedure,
percutaneous, of nucleus pulposus of intervertebral disc, using
radiofrequency energy, single or multiple levels, lumbar*).

Check the index or Table of Drugs for easy code location and
assignment.

Modifiers

When reporting endocrine and nervous system-related
services and procedures, you will access the full gamut of
CPT® modifiers, as well as several Level II modifiers. We will
review recommended use for many of the most often-accessed
modifiers.

Modifier 22

Consider appending modifier 22 *Increased procedural services*
when the service(s) is "greater than that usually required
for the listed procedure," according to CPT® Appendix A
(Modifiers).

CPT® codes describe a "range" of services: Although one
procedure may go smoothly, the next procedure of the same
type may take longer or be more difficult. The "easy" and
"hard" procedures are expected to average over time. In some
cases, however, the surgery may require significant additional
time or effort that falls outside the range of services described
by a particular CPT® code. When you encounter such circumstances, and no available code better describes the work
involved, modifier 22 may be appropriate.

Truly "unusual" circumstances will occur in only a small
minority of cases. Types of situations that may require the use
of modifier 22 include:

- Excessive blood loss for the particular procedure.
- Presence of excessively large surgical specimen (especially
  in abdominal surgery).
- Trauma extensive enough to complicate the particular
  procedure yet not significant enough to bill as additional
  procedure codes.
- Other pathologies, tumors, malformation (genetic,
  traumatic, surgical) directly interfering with the
  procedure but are not billed separately.
- Services rendered that are significantly more complex
  than what the appropriate CPT® code describes.

Provider documentation must demonstrate the special circumstances, such as extra time or highly complex trauma, that
warrant modifier 22.

Modifier 24

Apply modifier 24 *Unrelated evaluation and management
service by the same physician or other qualified healthcare
professional during a postoperative period* to describe an unrelated E/M service during the global period of another procedure. Modifier 24 designates the provider is evaluating the
patient for a new problem, and the evaluation is not included
in a previous procedure's global surgical package.

When you report modifier 24, the E/M service must meet three
criteria:

- The E/M service occurs during the postoperative period of
  another procedure.
- The current E/M service is unrelated to the previous
  procedure (you should be able to connect the E/M service
  to a separate, distinct diagnosis).
- The same provider (or one with the same tax ID) who
  performed the previous procedure provides the E/M.

Modifier 25

To apply modifier 25 *Significant, separately identifiable evaluation and management service by the same physician or other qualified healthcare professional on the same day of the procedure or other service* appropriately, for an E/M service at the same time as another minor procedure or service, documentation must substantiate that the E/M is both significant and separately identifiable. Any E/M service separately reported must be "above and beyond" the minimal evaluation and management normally included in a procedure or other service.

When deciding if an E/M service is separate and significantly identifiable, consider whether you can find in the documentation a clear history, exam, and medical decision-making apart from any other minor procedures the provider performs on the same day. If you can easily identify these E/M components, and they are separately identifiable, report the E/M with modifier 25.

For all services, you must assign a diagnosis that explains the reason the physician performed the service. The diagnosis assigned to the E/M service may or may not be the same as the diagnosis assigned to the other procedure/service provided during the same visit.

Modifier 26 and Modifier TC

When a provider conducts diagnostic tests or other services using equipment he or she doesn't own, modifier 26 *Professional component* may be used to indicate that the physician or other qualified healthcare professional provided only the professional component (the administration or interpretation) of the service. The facility providing the equipment may receive reimbursement for the service's technical component (the cost of equipment, supplies, technician salaries, etc.) by reporting the appropriate CPT® code with modifier TC *Technical component* appended. Modifier TC is not reported by outpatient hospital facilities to Medicare.

Apply modifiers 26 and TC only to those codes having both a professional and a technical component. The professional portion of the service includes the physician interpretation and report, and the technical component pays for operation and maintenance of equipment, necessary supplies, etc. The CMS National Physician Fee Schedule Relative Value File (PFSRV) separately lists a code values with modifier 26, with modifier TC, and with no modifier appended.

If the physician provides both components of the service (for instance, by providing the service in his or her own office), he or she may report the appropriate CPT® code without either modifier 26 or modifier TC.

Modifier 50

Append modifier 50 *Bilateral procedure* when the provider performs a procedure bilaterally (on both sides of the body), and no available CPT® code otherwise describes the procedure as bilateral. For example, if a neurosurgeon performs a bilateral lumbar laminotomy, appropriate coding would be 63030 *Laminotomy (hemilaminectomy), with decompression of nerve root[s], including partial facetectomy, foraminotomy and/or excision of herniated intervertebral disc; one interspace, lumbar (including open or endoscopically assisted approach)* with modifier 50 appended.

Not every code is eligible to report modifier 50 because not all procedures may be performed bilaterally. For Medicare payers, guidance on when to append modifier 50 can be found in the CMS PFSRV (Centers for Medicare & Medicaid Services Physician Fee Schedule Relative Value www.cms.gov).

Modifier 51

Modifier 51 *Multiple procedures* indicates more than one (non-E/M) procedure was provided during the same session. Many payers now use software that automatically detects second and subsequent procedures, making modifier 51 unnecessary. Check with your individual payer for its guidelines, and request the payer's instructions in writing.

Modifier 52

Apply modifier 52 *Reduced services* when the physician or other healthcare professional plans or expects a reduction in the service, or the provider electively cancels the procedure prior to completion. The reduction of services must have occurred by choice (either the surgeon's or the patient's), rather than necessity. For instance, the physician may determine the patient requires a service, but at a lesser level than the complete code description indicates, or the patient may elect to cancel the procedure prior to completion.

Modifier 53

Modifier 53 *Discontinued services* describes an unexpected problem beyond the physician's, or healthcare professional's, or patient's control that necessitates terminating the procedure.

CPT® Appendix A instructs, "Under certain circumstances, the physician or other qualified professional may elect to terminate a surgical or diagnostic procedure.

"Due to extenuating circumstances or those that threaten the well being of the patient, it may be necessary to indicate that a surgical or diagnostic procedure was started but discontinued. This circumstance may be reported by adding the modifier 53 to the code reported by the physician for the discontinued procedure."

Modifiers 54, 55, and 56

All procedures with a global surgical package have three parts: pre-operative services (for example, pre-operative exam), the surgery itself, and postoperative care (follow-up visits, minor complications). In some circumstances, a physician or other qualified healthcare professional (or physician group billing under the same provider number) will furnish only part of the total surgical service as described by the global surgical package. When this occurs, modifiers 54 *Surgical care only*, 55 *Postoperative management only*, and 56 *Preoperative management* only may be appropriate.

For example, most patients seen in the ED require follow up by another provider. In such cases, the ED provider should report any applicable procedures using modifier 54, and the provider providing follow up would report the same codes with modifier 55.

Modifier 57

Modifier 57 *Decision for surgery* applies to an E/M service occurring on the day of, or day before, a major surgical procedure (a procedure with a 90-day global period), and resulting in the decision to perform the surgery.

To append modifier 57, the E/M service must meet four conditions:

1. The E/M service must occur on the same day of or the day before the surgical procedure.

2. The E/M service must directly lead to the surgeon's decision to perform surgery.

3. The surgical procedure following the E/M must have a 90-day global period. For a separate and significantly identifiable E/M service on the same day as a minor procedure, append modifier 25.

4. The same provider (or one with the same tax ID) provides the E/M service and the surgical procedure.

Modifier 58

Append modifier 58 to a procedure or service during the post-operative period if the procedure or service was:

- Planned prospectively at the time of the original procedure
- More extensive than the original procedure
- For therapy following a diagnostic surgical procedure

The subsequent procedure or service either is related to the underlying problem/diagnosis prompting the initial surgery, or anticipated at the time the surgeon performs the initial surgery, according to CPT® instruction. A "more extensive"

procedure need not be more complex or time-intensive than the original procedure; it need only "go beyond" the work performed during the initial procedure.

Do not use modifier 58 if the patient needs a follow-up procedure because of surgical complications or unexpected postoperative findings that arise from the initial surgery. For complications that require a return to the operating room instead append modifier 78 *Unplanned return to the operating/procedure room by the same physician or other qualified healthcare professional following initial procedure for a related procedure during the postoperative period.*

Modifier 59

Use modifier 59 *Distinct procedural service* to identify procedures that are distinctly separate from any other procedure provided on the same date. According to CPT® instruction, you may append modifier 59 when the provider:

- Treats a patient during a different surgical session
- Treats a different site or organ system
- Makes a separate incision/excision
- Tends to a different lesion
- Treats a separate injury

Do not append modifier 59 to E/M codes, and do not use modifier 59 if another, more specific modifier is available.

Modifier 62

Append modifier 62 *Two surgeons* when two surgeons work together to complete a procedure described by a single CPT® code. To qualify as co-surgeons, the operating surgeons must share responsibility for the surgical procedure, with each serving as a primary surgeon during some portion of the procedure. Because co-surgeons each perform a distinct part of the procedure, they cannot share the same documentation. Each provider should document his own operative notes.

Not all CPT® codes may receive modifier 62. For Medicare payers, guidance on when modifier 62 may apply can be found in the CMS PFSRV.

Modifier 78

Apply modifier 78 *Unplanned return to the operating/procedure room by the same physician or other qualified healthcare professional following initial procedure for a related procedure during the postoperative period* when all of the following conditions are met:

- The physician or other healthcare professional must undertake the subsequent surgery because of conditions (complications) arising from an initial surgery;

- The subsequent surgery occurs during the global period of the initial surgery; and
- The subsequent surgery requires a return to the operating room.

Modifier 79

Modifier 79 *Unrelated procedure or service by the same physician or other healthcare professional during the postoperative period* may be appended when an unrelated surgery by the same physician occurs during the global period of a previous surgery.

Modifier LT and Modifier RT

Modifiers LT *Left side* and RT *Right side* differentiate procedures performed on paired structures (such as eyes, lungs, arms, breasts, knees, etc.). They might also apply when a provider performs unilaterally a procedure that CPT® defines as bilateral (such cases would be rare). Finally, modifiers LT and RT may be used to provide location-specific information for those services defined either as unilateral or bilateral.

Section Review 14.4

---

1. Select the HCPCS Level II code to report a patient having a spinal needle inserted into the nucleus pulposus of the L3/L4 intervertebral disc until the desired decompression is accomplished using radio frequency energy.

   A. S2350

   B. S2348

   C. S9090

   D. S2351

2. A 45-year-old female has carpal tunnel syndrome. She is in surgery to have a neuroplasty performed on her left wrist. During the surgery the patient's blood pressure starts dropping and the surgeon decides to stop the operation. How should the procedure code be reported?

   A. 64721-52

   B. 64721-53

   C. 64721-54

   D. No procedure is billed

3. A young child has been hit by a car. The neurosurgeon was called to the ER in which he examined the patient and finds the young child has a subdural hematoma. The surgeon makes the decision that the child needs to be taken to OR to drain the hematoma. Select the modifier appended to the Evaluation and Management service.

   A. 22

   B. 25

   C. 57

   D. 54

4. A 6-week-old baby had a cerebrospinal fluid shunt placed two days ago. The shunt is having a complication in which it is not draining the excess CSF. The baby is going back to the operating room for shunt removal and shunt replacement by the same surgeon who placed the original one. Choose the procedure code reported.

   A. 62258-79

   B. 62256-58

   C. 62258-78

   D. 62230-76

5. A patient is coming to the physician's office for a follow up for a repaired damaged nerve to her finger. During the visit she tells the doctor she fell and hit her little toe this morning and now it is red and swollen and wants to make sure it is not broken. The physician examines the toe and reassures her that it is not fractured. The doctor also examines the finger, which is healing well with no infection. Select the E/M service for this visit.

    A. 99212-24

    B. 99212-55

    C. 99212-79

    D. No service is billed since patient is in the post-operative period

Documentation Dissection

Case 1

Preoperative Diagnosis:
Primary hyperparathyroidism.

Postoperative Diagnosis:
Primary hyperparathyroidism.

Procedure Performed:
1. Exploration of parathyroid adenoma.

2. Intraoperative recurrent laryngeal nerve monitoring.

3. Intraoperative PTH assay.

Anesthesia: General anesthesia.

Estimated Blood Loss: Minimal.

Gross Findings:
A 37-year-old female has been found to have primary hyperparathyroidism. Her preoperative localizing studies were all negative including repeat sestamibi scans and ultrasounds. After informed consent, this morning she received an isotope injection and we scanned her neck. No adenoma could be localized on the scan this morning. She was taken to the Operating Room where exploration using the Gamma probe demonstrated a right lower parathyroid adenoma. It measured approximately 250 mg. Her preoperative PTH level was 96. Five minutes after excision, it dropped to 24, ten minutes post excision her PTH level was 15. The patient tolerated the procedure well.

Procedure in Detail:
This morning the patient was taken to the Nuclear Department, received an isotope injection and had her neck scanned. She was brought to the holding area then to the Operating Room where she was given general endotracheal anesthesia, a roll was placed behind the shoulders, the neck was extended, the head was padded. The neck and chest were prepped and draped in the usual sterile fashion. We used the Gamma probe to listen over the neck area and could not identify any particular area that seemed to be hot. Reviewing her old sestamibi scans, there was some vague hint of increased activity in the right lower position. We anesthetized the skin and subcutaneous tissue and made an incision starting below the sternal notch extending to the 4th intercostal spaces. The manubrium was completely divided and the sternotomy is carried to the level of the fourth interspace with a sternal retractor in place to separate the sternum. [1] Identified on the lateral aspect of the lower pole of the thyroid was a 2 cm. tan-reddish nodule. It was clearly an enlarged parathyroid. As we manipulated this, a manipulation blood draw was taken by Anesthesia. We then freed up the pedicle, divided the vessels between clips and sent the lesion for frozen section. [2] The medastinum was then looked at with no abnormal tissue, growths, or signs of infection and small, smooth, normal appearing lymph nodes. [3] Anesthesia drew blood samples at five and 10 minutes respectively. Frozen section revealed this to be a hypercellular parathyroid

gland. At this point after securing meticulous hemostasis a chest tube was placed from the right anterior chest wall and extending to the contralateral apex via the mediastinum for drainage. The sternum was approximated with interrupted wires removing the sternal retractor. She was extubated. The cervical fascia was closed with 3-0 Monocryl, platysma was closed with 4-0 Vicryl, and skin was closed with 4-0 Monocryl in subcuticular fashion. Sterile dressings were applied. All sponge, needle and instrument counts were correct. The patient tolerated the procedure well, was transferred to the Recovery Room in stable condition.

---

[1] Surgical approach of sternal split.

[2] Tissue was excised for pathological examination.

[3] Mediastinal Exploration

What are the CPT® and ICD-10-CM codes reported?

CPT® Code: 60505

ICD-10-CM Code: E21.0

Rationale: A patient with hyperparathyroidism is having her parathyroid glands explored by having tissue excised for pathological examination. The physician exposed the thyroid by splitting open the sternum (sternal split). A mediastinal exploration was performed with results of no abnormalities. This procedure is indexed in the CPT® codebook under Parathyroid Gland/Exploration 60500–60505. Intraoperative nerve monitoring is not reported when performed by the surgeon. The patient has primary hyperparathyroidism. In the ICD-10-CM Index to Diseases and Injuries, look for Hyperparathyroidism/primary E21.0.

ICD-9-CM Application

What is/are the ICD-9-CM code(s) reported?

ICD-9-CM Code(s): 252.01

Rationale: The patient has primary hyperparathyroidism. In the ICD-9-CM Alphabetic Index, look for Hyperparathyroidism/primary 252.01.

Case 2

Preoperative Diagnosis: Shunt infection

Postoperative Diagnosis: Same

Operation: Replacement of externalized shunt with medium pressure ventriculoperitoneal shunt

Anesthesia: General

Estimated Blood Loss: <10 cc's

Complications: None

Specimen: CSF

Indications: Admitted for shunt tap documenting shunt infection resulting in externalized shunt. Culture of the exit site reveals a staphylococcus aureus [1] infection. Additional problems with chronic headaches and fibrous dysplasia,

Procedure:
After obtaining adequate general anesthesia, the patient was prepped and draped in the standard fashion. The right parietal scalp incision was reopened and the shunt catheter identified. The shunts reservoir was delivered from the wound and the distal catheter freed from it. The abdominal incision was reopened and the rectus sheath identified. A shunt passer was then passed from the abdominal wound to the head wound. The passer was then used to bring the wound distal catheter [2] from the head wound to the abdominal. The old ventricular catheter was then removed after freeing it from tethering material by twisting the catheter. A large piece of choroid plexus was entwined in the inlets of the catheter. [3] A new ventricular-catheter was then inserted into the tract of the old catheter and fed into a distance equal to that of the old catheter (5 cm). [4] Good flow was seen. It was attached to the shunt reservoir that was then seated after attaching a 0-25 shunt assistant valve to it. A small amount of CSF was then withdrawn from the distal end. An abdominal trocar was then used to pierce the rectus sheath and muscle and the abdominal cavity entered. The distal catheter was then fed into the peritoneal cavity.

The subcutaneous tissues were closed in a multi-layer fashion and the skin with staples. The monitor line was sewn to the scalp. The patient tolerated the procedure well, had an estimated blood loss of <10 ccs and was taken to the PICU in stable condition, Sponge, needle and cottonoid counts were correct.

_____

[1] The diagnoses for the infection of shunt and type of infection.

[2] Distal catheter was revised by having it from the head fed to the peritoneal cavity.

[3] This indicates a mechanical complication of the catheter.

[4] The removal and replacement of the ventricular catheter.

_____

What are the CPT® and ICD-10-CM codes reported?

CPT® Codes: 62230, 62225-51

ICD-10-CM Codes: T85.79XA, B95.62, T85.09XA

Rationale: The first procedure reported is the distal catheter being freed and repositioned by being attached from the head wound to the peritoneal cavity. The second procedure code is replacement of the ventricular catheter. Both of these codes are in indexed in the CPT® under Replacement/Cerebrospinal Fluid Shunt.

Look in the ICD-10-CM Index to Diseases and Injuries for Complication(s)/ventricular (communicating) shunt (device)/infection and inflammation T85.79x. In the Tabular List, the seventh character A is selected to indicate initial encounter (ICD-10-CM Guidelines indicate initial encounter is active treatment. Surgery is given as an example of active treatment). Because this is a 5 character code, the dummy placeholder X is used to place the seventh character (A) in the seventh position. Under subcategory T85.7, there is a note to use an additional code to identify the infection. Look in the ICD-10-CM Index to Diseases and Injuries for Infection, infected, infective/staphylococcal, unspecified site/as the cause of disease classified elsewhere/aureus/methicillin resistant (MRSA) B95.62. There is also a blockage of the ventricular catheter. Look in the ICD-10-CM for Complication/ventricular (communicating) shunt (device)/mechanical/obstruction T85.09x. A seventh character is required. Use a dummy place holder to keep the seventh character in the seventh position. Seventh character A is selected for the surgical encounter (initial encounter).

ICD-9-CM Application

What is/are the ICD-9-CM code(s) reported?

ICD-9-CM Codes: 996.63, 041.11, 996.2

Rationale: The first diagnosis is indexed in the ICD-9-CM under Complications/infection/due to/ventricular shunt guiding you to code 996.63. There is a note under subcategory code 996.6 that states: Use additional code to identify specified infection. The second diagnosis is indexed under Infection/staphylococcal/aureus guiding you to code 041.11. Also listed is the complication blockage of the ventricular catheter noted in "A large piece of choroid plexus was entwined in the inlets of the catheter" which is reported with code 996.2 found in the index under Complication/mechanical/device NEC/nervous system and verified in the Tabular List.

Glossary

Additional terms are defined throughout the chapter.

Actigraphy Testing—Measures the movement of a limb; the term actigraphy refers to methods utilizing miniaturized sensors translating physical motion into a numeric presentation.

Anastomosis—A surgical connection between two (usually hollow) structures.

Chemodenervation—An interruption of messages sent between nerves and muscles by administration of a chemical substance.

Chemonucleolysis—Injection of an enzyme to dissolve the gelatinous cushioning material in an intervertebral dis.

Cranioplasty—Surgical repair of a defect or deformity of a skull.

Decompression—When referring to nerves of the spine: Freeing of a pinched nerve, for instance from between adjacent vertebrae.

Encephalocele (Cephalocele, Meningoencephalocele)—Rare disorder in which the bones of the skull do not close completely, creating a gap through which cerebral spinal fluid, brain tissue and the meninges can protrude into a sac-like formation.

Fossa—Any one of three hollows (anterior, middle, and posterior) in the base of the cranium for the lobes of the brain.

F-Wave—A voltage change observed after electrical stimulation is applied to the skin surface above the distal region of a nerve; often used to measure nerve conduction velocity.

H-Reflex—(Hoffman reflex) A reflectory reaction of muscles after electrical stimulation of sensory fibers in their innervating nerves (for example, those located behind the knee).

Ligation—To tie off.

Meninges—Collective name for the membranes enveloping the central nervous system. The meninges consist of three layers: the dura mater, the arachnoid mater, and the pia mater. Its primary function (along with cerebrospinal fluid) is to protect the brain and spinal cord.

Meningocele—Protrusion through a bone defect in the vertebral column, of the meninges covering the spinal cord.

Myelomeningocele—A birth defect in which the backbone and spinal canal do not close before birth; a type of spina bifida (a developmental birth defect caused by the incomplete closure of the embryonic neural tube). The spinal cord and the meninges protrude.

Neurolytic Agent—Agent used to destroy nerves; for instance alcohol, phenol, etc.

Osteomyelitis—An acute or chronic bone infection.

Spinal tap—Spinal puncture (CPT® 62270–62272); a procedure to withdraw cerebrospinal fluid.

Stereotactic Head Frame—A guiding device, positions the head for precise treatment during stereotactic radiosurgery.

Tentorium Cerebelli (Cerebellar Tentorium)—An extension of the dura mater, separates the cerebrum from the cerebellum.

Transection—To divide by cutting transversely; a cross section along a long axis.

Trephination (Trepanning, Trephining, Burr Hole)—Drilling a hole in the skull to expose the dura matter.

Vasospasm—A condition in which blood vessels spasm, leading to vasoconstriction and possible stroke or other injury; may arise in the context of subarachnoid hemorrhage.

Zygapophyseal Joint (Z Joint, Paravertebral Facet Joint, Facet Joint)—Located on the posterior spine on each side of the vertebrae where it overlaps the neighboring vertebrae; the facet joints provide stability and give the spine the ability to bend and twist. They are made up of two surfaces of the adjacent vertebrae that are separated by a thin layer of cartilage.

www.aapc.com 461

Eye and Ocular Adnexa, Auditory Systems

Introduction

The eye and ear are both part of the nervous system, but both CPT® and ICD-10-CM treat them separately from the rest of the nervous system codes. That's because the eye and the auditory systems are very specialized anatomically, and as sense organs vital to our overall well-being, warrant separate consideration.

To understand coding of disorders or procedures for the eye or the ear, it helps to have an understanding of the interdependencies of the components of sight and sound. We will take a good look at how these structures work together to serve our senses, and then how surgeries can support sight and hearing.

Objectives

- Understand the components of the eye and ear
- Define key terms
- Understand the most common pathologies affecting these sense organs
- Understand eye surgeries and ear surgeries and how they relate to pathologies
- Recognize common eponyms and acronyms for these specialties
- Identify when other sections of CPT® or ICD-10-CM should be accessed
- Know when HCPCS Level II codes or modifiers are appropriate

Anatomy and Medical Terminology

The eye and ear are both complex organs that have unique structures and nomenclature. The most important concept to understand regarding the eye is refraction. The ear has two key functions that must be understood: conduction and balance.

The Eye

Vision is all about light. Light enters the eye; sensors there read the image and transmit information to the brain. On its way to those sensors, the light travels through several transparent layers of the eye, and these layers are responsible for refraction of the light. In refraction, the eye bends and focuses light rays into a sharp image. If the light is refracted imperfectly, vision blurs. People who wear glasses or contacts are adding a corrective layer of refraction to their eyes to improve their sight.

Surgery can be performed to correct the error in refraction, as well.

The eyeball is just that; a ball. It is composed of a tough membrane called sclera. The sclera is the outer coat of the globe and is continuous with the dura via the dural sheath of the optic nerve at the back of the eye. The sclera at the front of the eye is known as the white of the eye, and is covered with a thin protective layer of conjunctiva. The sclera is tough so that the contents of the eye are protected, and also so that the shape of the eye remains consistent.

The middle layer of the eye is the choroid layer, a dark, unreflective layer, which contains a rich supply of blood. The inner layer is the retina, with light and color receptors, which send light data to the brain via the optic nerve.

The shape of the eyeball affects refraction. If the eyeball is too oblong, the patient will be nearsighted (myopia), and refraction will cause blurring of far away objects. In farsightedness (hyperopia), the eyeball is foreshortened, and close-up vision is impaired.

The Eye

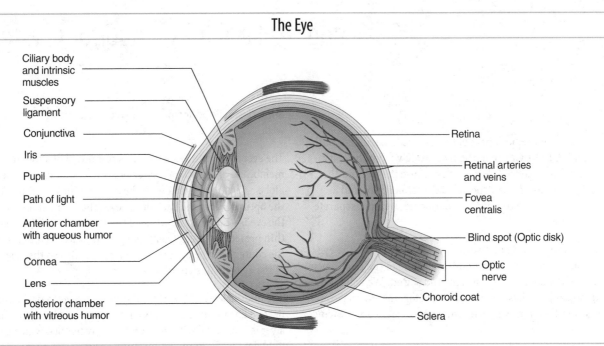

Ciliary body and intrinsic muscles
Suspensory ligament
Conjunctiva
Iris
Pupil
Path of light
Anterior chamber with aqueous humor
Cornea
Lens
Posterior chamber with vitreous humor

Retina
Retinal arteries and veins
Fovea centralis
Blind spot (Optic disk)
Optic nerve
Choroid coat
Sclera

Source: RIZZO. Fundamentals of Anatomy and Physiology, 3E. © 2010 Delmar Learning, a part of Cengage Learning, Inc. Reproduced by permission. www.cengage.com/permissions

Fluids within the eyeball help maintain its consistent shape. Any reduction in fluid within the eye will affect the shape of the eye, just like letting air out of a beach ball, and will affect refraction. Severe dehydration and numerous medical conditions can affect the shape of the eye, and cause blurry vision.

Each eye has six muscles that work in tandem to control movement of the eyeball up and down and from side to side as we focus on an object. If we follow the path of light in the eye, it first enters through the cornea, which is the bay window of the eye. The cornea has five layers, and they act to refract the light entering the eye. The layers from the surface of the cornea inward are: the epithelium layer, Bowman's layer (a tough basement membrane), stroma (collagen fibers supporting keratocytes), Descemet's layer (an inner basement membrane), and endothelium layer (crucial layer that keeps the cornea from getting too wet). The layers are important, because sometimes corneal defects will be managed by removing one or two layers (lamellar keratoplasty), rather than full-thickness cornea (penetrating keratoplasty). This is done to preserve the fluid balance of the eye and prevent leaks through full-thickness incisions. The cornea meets the sclera in a ring called the limbus, also known as the sclerocorneal junction. Often, physicians will reference the limbus when describing the site of incision in eye surgery. Behind the cornea is the anterior segment of the eye, which is filled with a clear, salty fluid called aqueous humor. The anterior seqment is divided into the anterior chamber (back of cornea to the iris) and posterior chamber (back of iris to the lens) and it is filled with aqueous humor.

The aqueous humor functions as another source for refraction, and also provides stability to the corneal walls.

Light from the aqueous humor next enters the crystalline lens, a convex disc suspended on threads just behind the iris. We know the iris as our source of eye color, but this colorful tissue is actually a muscle that expands and contracts to regulate the amount of light entering the posterior chamber of the eye through the pupil. If the light is too bright, the iris expands so that the size of the pupil shrinks. If there is too little light, the iris contracts to enlarge the pupil and allow more light into the eye. The threads (ciliary zonules) holding the lens and the ciliary body to which they are connected automatically tug at the lens to change its shape to help focus on items near or far. This refraction function gets slower and less effective with age, which explains why so many older adults find themselves getting prescriptions for reading glasses (presbyopia).

After the light has been bent by the crystalline lens, it enters the vitreous humor, a gel-like mass that fills the large posterior segment of the eye. The vitreous humor presses against the inner layer of the eye, maintaining the eyeball's shape and keeping the blood-rich choroid layer in contact with the retina. The light is placed upon the retina's rods and cones (photoreceptors) like a projected image at a movie theater, and these images are transmitted via the optic nerve to the brain. Rods located around the edges of the retina utilize low lighting and distinguish differences in shapes and distances while cones utilize bright light conditions and distinguish color. The macula is an oval-shaped highly pigmented yellow spot near the center of the retina. Near its center is the fovea centralis which contains the highest concentration of cone cells.

To trace again the refraction path: Light travels from cornea to aqueous humor to lens to vitreous humor to retina. The stability of the eyeball and the refractive elements must all be perfect for vision to be 20-20. There is plenty to go wrong, and that's why the eyeball is nestled in a bony socket lined in protective fat. A direct blow to the eye often will damage soft tissue around the bony orbit, but not harm the eye itself. Further protecting the eye are eyelashes and eyebrows, which protect from foreign bodies as well as excess light, and the eyelids that keep eyes from drying out. The lacrimal system produces tears in glands behind the eyebrows. These tears flow through ducts into the eyes where they drain out the lacrimal puncta, or flow into the nose (which explains why we blow our noses when we cry).

The visual field can be affected by many things: Blood, foreign bodies, or other tissue can obstruct the pathway to the retina. Examples include excessive skin on the eyelids, shielding a portion of the eye from light, a cloudy condition (eg, cataract) in any of the refractive properties of the eye, or damage to the retina. Sometimes a change in the visual field is the chief complaint when a patient schedules an appointment with the ophthalmologist.

The Ear

In the context of the ear, conduction refers to the transfer of sound waves. Sound waves take two paths in humans. The waves can be captured by the pinna, or outer ear, and travel by air along the external auditory meatus to the tympanic membrane. True to its name, the tympanic membrane vibrates to telegraph its message to the middle ear, where the malleus picks up the vibration, and transfers it to the incus and stapes. These three tiny bones, the ossicles, carry the message to the oval window. As the stapes footplate moves the oval window, and creates waves in the perilymph of the scala vesibuli of the cochlea, the round window membrane moves, which causes movement of the endolymph inside the cochlear duct. This causes the basilar membrane to vibrate, which in turn causes the organ of Corti (inner hair cells) to send electrical impulses along the auditory nerve to the brain. Secondary to this air conduction is bone conduction. The mastoid bones contain tiny air cells that also form a conductive path for sound. The mastoid cells transmit sound effectively, although not as efficiently as sound traveling from the pinna through the auditory canal. Loss of the mastoid function damages hearing, but more importantly, mastoid cell sensitivity can be augmented in patients who have experienced a hearing loss along the more traditional air conduction pathway. In either case, when the sound waves reach the auditory nerve, they are transmitted to the brain.

The ear is also a center for balance. Information within the vestibule and the three semicircular canals is sent to the brain, signaling the body to compensate by adjusting posture or movement as appropriate for the orientation of the body. The inner ear is responsible for balance in addition to conduction of sound. Vertigo or extreme dizziness, is often a symptom of inner ear disorders, such as Mèniére's disease.

The entry to the ear is well protected by the meaty exterior, and the ear canal is lined with hairs and lubricated with cerumen to filter out foreign bodies. To equalize the pressure between the middle ear and outer world, the Eustachian tubes link the middle ear to the nasopharynx. Without this opening, the pressure of air in the middle ear would not change when the pressure outside does and this would inhibit vibrations and hamper our ability to hear. It is the change in air pressure that causes our ears to pop on airplanes or when changing altitudes. Without the Eustachian tubes, we would not be able to do this.

Key Roots, Suffixes, and Prefixes for Eye and Ear

acous/o	hearing
blephar/o	eyelid
canth/o	corner of eyelid
cochle/o	cochlear
conjunctiv/o	conjunctival
dacry/o	relating to lacrimal system, tear
dipl/o	two
goni/o	angle
irid/o	iris
kerat/o	corneal
myring/o	tympanic membrane
-opia	vision
ot/o	ear
phak/o	lens
phot/o	light
-ptosis	droop
retin/o	retinal
rhin/o	nose
scler/o	ocular sclera
staped/o	stapes
tars/o	margin of eyelid

Key Roots, Suffixes, and Prefixes for Eye and Ear (cont.)

trabecul/o	relating to meshwork for drainage of aqueous humor
uve/o	uveal
vitre/o	vitreous

Section Review 15.1

1. Using your CPT® codebook and looking up Strabismus in the Index, strabismus surgery would be performed to correct which of the following eye disorders?

   A. Removing a cloudy lens

   B. Balancing the strength of extraocular muscles

   C. Draining an orbital abscess

   D. Reconstructing a damaged eyelid

2. Which of the following organs has NO refractive properties?

   A. Cornea

   B. Lens

   C. Vitreous

   D. Iris

3. Code 69210 in your CPT® codebook describes removal of impacted earwax from the external auditory canal. What type of conduction is interrupted by impacted earwax?

   A. Bone conduction

   B. Air conduction

   C. Bone and air conduction

   D. Neither bone nor air conduction

4. The incus bone is between the malleus and the stapes. In which part of the ear does the incus reside?

   A. The external ear

   B. The middle ear

   C. The inner ear

   D. The Eustachian tube

5. Which of the following statements is true regarding the vitreous humor?

   A. It presses against the cornea so that the cornea keeps its shape.

   B. It signals the iris when to contract or expand.

   C. It produces tears that flow in the eyes and in the nose.

   D. It holds the retina firmly against the blood-rich choroid

6. What is a blepharoplasty?

    A. Excision of tumor of the tear duct.

    B. Corrective surgery for refraction error.

    C. Surgical repair of the eyelid.

    D. Suture repair of the sclera.

7. Keratoconus is a defect of which component of the eye?

    A. Cornea

    B. Lens

    C. Choroid

    D. Macula

8. What occurs in myringotomy?

    A. The external auditory canal is reconstructed.

    B. Myringa is removed from the inner ear.

    C. The tympanic membrane is excised.

    D. The tympanic membrane is incised.

9. The patient has a disorder of the ear and it is causing her to have extreme vertigo. Which part of the ear is diseased?

    A. The inner ear

    B. The middle ear

    C. The external ear

    D. None of the above

10. Based on what you have learned so far, which of the following statements is true?

    A. All organs of the eye and all organs of the ear occur bilaterally.

    B. Most procedures for the eye or for the ear are performed by specialists.

    C. The eye and ear are the two most important sense organs in the body.

    D. All of the above.

ICD-10-CM

The ICD-10-CM Chapter 7 contains codes for the Eye and Adnexa (H00-H59) and provide Coding Guidelines for Glaucoma. Chapter 8 contains codes for the Ear and Mastoid Process (H60-H95). There are no coding guidelines in ICD-10-CM specific to the Ear and Mastoid process. An understanding of common disorders of these organs can help you in selecting the correct codes. Although the majority of codes for the eye are found in Disorders of the Eye and Adnexa (H00-H59) and ear are found in Diseases of the Ear and Mastoid Process (H60-H95), there are a significant number of diagnosis codes for these organs found in other chapters of ICD-10-CM. It is imperative that the reader begin the search for a code in the Index to Diseases and Injuries to ensure the proper code is selected.

The Eye

Most disorders of the eye fall into these general categories:

- Infection and inflammation
- Neoplastic disease
- Injury

- Glaucoma
- Cataracts
- Retinopathy
- Retinal detachment
- Strabismus

Codes within Disorders of the Eye and Adnexa are organized according to anatomic site, beginning with eyelid and lacrimal system (H00-H05), followed by Disorders of the conjunctiva (H10-H11), Disorders of sclera, cornea, iris, and ciliary body (H15-H22), Disorders of lens (H25-H28) including cataracts, Disorders of choroid and retina (H30-H36), Glaucoma (H40-H42), Disorders of vitreous and globe (H43-H44), Disorders of optic nerve and visual pathways (H46-H47), Disorders of ocular muscles, binocular movement, accommodation and refraction (H49-H52), Visual disturbances and blindness (H53-H54), Other disorders or eye and adnexa (H55-H57), Intraoperative and postprocedural complications and disorders of eye and adnexa (H59).

Infections and inflammation are listed in all categories based on the exact location of the infection or inflammation. Some eye infections are found in the Infectious and Parasitic Diseases chapter, such as herpes zoster (B02.30) or herpes simplex (B00.50), trachoma (A71.-). Remember to report secondarily the infectious agent, if known, for example, B95.62 for MRSA.

ICD-10-CM codes require a fifth or sixth character to identify which eye is affected by the condition being reported. This is the concept of laterality - right, left, bilateral, unspecified.

Neoplastic Disease—Codes for neoplasms of the eye are straightforward. Remember to begin in the Index to Diseases and Injuries and then go to the Table of Neoplasms as directed. Do not look for Eye in the Table of Neoplasms. Instead, look for the specific accessory organ or structure of the eye. Category C69 contains the codes malignancy for these sites. The fourth character of the code identifies the location of the neoplasm. The fifth character identifies the laterality (right, left, unspecified).

Sometimes, ophthalmologists will note the patient has a dark spot on the retina. The retina is delicate and blood-rich, making it difficult to biopsy. Instead of a biopsy, the physician will monitor the spot, sometimes called a retinal freckle, for change. Report D49.81 for this condition.

Keep in mind, a melanoma of the eye may not be reported from the Table of Neoplasms.

Example

Melanoma (malignant) C43.9

    benign—*see* Nevus

    in situ D03.9

        abdominal wall D03.59

        ala nasi D03.39

        ankle D03.7-

    malignant, of soft parts except skin—*see* Neoplasm, connective tissue, malignant

In the Table of Neoplasms look for Neoplasm, neoplastic/connective tissue NEC/Malignant Primary, and eye is not listed. There is an instructional note under connective tissue NEC that indicates that for sites that do not appear in this list, code to neoplasm of that site. Look for Neoplasm, neoplastic/eye NEC/Malignant Primary C69.9-. In the Tabular List the code to report is C69.90.

ICD-9-CM Application

In ICD-9-CM melanoma of the eye is given a code in the Alphabetic Index.

ICD-9-CM

Melanoma

    eye 190.9

    benign (M8720/0)—*see* Neoplasm, skin, benign

    in situ—*see* Melanoma, by site

Cataracts—Not only do the refractive elements of the eye need to be accurate in their ability to focus, they also need to be free of defects that could obscure vision. Cataracts describe flaws or clouds that develop in the crystalline lens, and are reported with codes from categories H25-H28 depending on the type of cataract. These categories will have separate codes for right, left and bilateral. Congenital cataracts are found in category Q12. Cataracts occur naturally with age, but can occur secondary to trauma, foreign bodies, disease, or drugs. If a cataract impedes vision sufficiently, surgery can be performed to remove the crystalline lens, and an artificial intraocular lens (IOL) can be placed.

The lens has many layers, and specific codes can be selected to identify cataracts by their layer. The outer layer is harder, like an M&M candy's outer shell. Often, when a cataract is removed from the eye, the physician opts to retain the posterior outermost shell so that there remains an organic separation between the posterior and anterior segments. Later, this remaining shell may develop opacities as well, and this is called an after-cataract or secondary cataract. Removal of an after-cataract is a fairly simple surgery. After-cataract is coded with H26.40.

Retinopathy—Retinopathy describes changes that occur in the blood vessels within the retina. These aneurysms, hemorrhages, and proliferation of small vessels damage the retina and put the patient's vision at risk. Retinopathy is most commonly seen as a complication of diabetes, but can be caused by prematurity in newborns, by systemic hypertension, or other pathologies.

The effect of diabetes on the eye is called diabetic retinopathy. In the earliest phase of the disease, called background or nonproliferative diabetic retinopathy, the arteries in the retina become weakened and leak, forming small, dot-like hemorrhages. These leaking vessels often lead to swelling or edema in the retina and decreased vision. The phases of nonproliferative retinopathy are mild, moderate, and severe.

Example:

Uncontrolled DM Type II with proliferative retinopathy

ICD-10-CM indexes the majority of diabetic codes with manifestations using only one code for both. These are considered combination codes that include the condition with the manifestation or complication.

Look in the Alphabetic Index for Diabetes, diabetic/Type 2/with/retinopathy/proliferative E11.359.

E11.359 Type 2 diabetes mellitus with proliferative diabetic retinopathy without macular edema.

ICD-9-CM Application

In ICD-9-CM two codes are reported for a patient that has diabetes with a manifestation.

Look in the Index to Diseases for Diabetes, diabetic/with/retinopathy/proliferative 250.5x *[362.02]*.

250.52 Diabetes with ophthalmic manifestations, Type II uncontrolled

362.02 Proliferative diabetic retinopathy

A fifth digit is required to indicate the type of diabetes and if the diabetes is controlled or uncontrolled. The patient being a Type 2 diabetic and it is uncontrolled, the fifth digit 2 is reported. In the Index to Diseases code 362.02 for the proliferative retinopathy is in slanted brackets indicating this code is reported as the additional code. In the Tabular List under subcategory code 250.5 has an instruction note to Use additional code to identify manifestation. Retinopathy is listed to use as an additional code.

Circulation problems cause areas of the retina to become oxygen deprived or ischemic. New, fragile vessels develop as the circulatory system attempts to maintain adequate oxygen levels within the retina. These vessels hemorrhage easily and blood may leak into the retina and vitreous causing spots or floaters along with decreased vision.

In the advanced phase of the disease, continued abnormal vessel growth, and scar tissue may cause serious problems such as retinal detachment or glaucoma.

Vessels in retinopathy can be cauterized by lasers and patients with retinopathy must be monitored regularly so that any new disease is treated before permanent damage to vision occurs.

Retinal Detachment—Injury or anatomic defect can cause the retina to be freed from the blood-rich choroid at the back of the eye. When the retinal layer floats away, it loses its supply of nutrients. Nutrients must return or vision is lost. Corrective action might include the injection of fluid, air, or external eye pressure to push the retina back into place, or bursts of laser to burn the retina to the choroid. Scleral buckling techniques are used in a large number of patients. Vitrectomy occasionally is performed to gain access to the retina. At the end of surgery, gas or silicone oil is injection into the eye to replace the vitreous gel to restore normal pressure.

Glaucoma—Fluid levels in the eye are important to its health, but too much pressure from fluid can lead to a hypertensive condition in the eye called glaucoma. When ocular pressure rises, pathological changes occur that can damage or destroy vision. The fluid in the front of the eye flows through an anatomical pathway. If this pathway is blocked, pressure against blood vessels can cut off blood to the eye, and blindness can follow quickly. Typically, the progression of disease is more insidious. In either case, the physician can perform surgery to revise the flow of aqueous in the eye and reduce the pressure. Glaucoma codes are covered in H40 except for congenital glaucoma, which is found in subcategory Q15.0.

ICD-10-CM codes for Glaucoma include the type and stage of the glaucoma. Laterality is also included in the choice of codes. A seventh character is added to identify the stage of the glaucoma. Unspecified equates to not documented, while indeterminate stage equates to the physician being unable to determine the stage.

- 0 stage unspecified
- 1 mild stage
- 2 moderate stage
- 3 severe stage
- 4 indeterminate stage

Coding Guidelines state when a patient has bilateral glaucoma that is documented as the same type and stage, a code is assigned for bilateral glaucoma with the appropriate seventh character for the stage. When the patient has bilateral glaucoma with different type or different stage, a code is assigned for each eye instead of a bilateral code. Specific guidelines exist for subcategories H40.10-, H40.11-, H40.20- (I.C.7.a.) with attention to how the codes are indexed in the Alphabetic Index.

Glaucoma is classified according to the type of angle closure. The angle referenced is along the exterior ring of the iris, where it joins the trabecular meshwork at the base of the cornea. This meshwork collects aqueous that has flowed through the anterior chamber so that it can be recirculated in the eye. If the angle is closed, the flow of aqueous is reduced or shut off, creating a surplus of aqueous and raising the pressure within the eye. Closed-angle glaucoma is also known as narrow-angle glaucoma. Increased pressure causes the iris to bulge forward narrowing or blocking the drainage angle formed by the cornea and iris. Acute closed-angle glaucoma occurs quickly, for example, within minutes or hours following an injury to the eye. Chronic closed-angle glaucoma can be due to a defect caused by illness or age. Open-angle also known as wide-angle glaucoma (chronic glaucoma), is the most common type of glaucoma, and it is the leading cause of blindness in adults in the United States. It can only be detected by regular eye exams. Gradually the pressure increases in the eye due to clogging of the drainage system or overproduction of aqueous fluid.

Strabismus (H49-H50) —Coordinated eye movement is essential to depth perception, single vision, and other aspects of sight. When the eyes do not move in synchrony, it is often because of misalignment of mismatched strength in the eye muscles. The eye muscles come in three pairs: Superior and inferior rectus, on top and bottom; lateral and medial rectus on each side; and superior and inferior oblique, across the top and bottom of the eyeball. Variations in strabismus are called tropias. In esotropia, the eye deviates inward; in exotropia, outward. In hypertropia, the eye deviates upward; and in hypotropia, downward. Usually, these disorders are corrected in childhood, but sometimes, illness or injury can cause strabismus in adults. Balance is restored to the eyes by lengthening or shortening of muscle.

Injury—Most eye injury codes are found in the Injury and Poisoning chapter of ICD-10-CM. For example: Acute chemical conjunctivitis look in the Alphabetic Index for Conjunctivitis/chemical acute H10.21- . In the Tabular List H10.21 has a note to code first from T51-T65. Superficial injury to the eye and adnexa are reported with codes from category S05, with subcategories for the type of injury and with or without the presence of a foreign body. Burns to the eye and adnexa are handled with category T26 with the distinction made between burns and corrosions. Corrosions are the result of chemicals while burns are the result of a heat source, such as fire, steam, electricity, or radiation.

Practical Coding Note

ICD-10-CM lists many of the codes for eye disorders or injuries based on which eye was affected (left, right, bilateral, or unspecified). Note that documentation for eye care may utilize different abbreviations for right and left. Right is typically documented as OD and left with OS, OU for both eyes.

ICD-9CM Application

ICD-9-CM codes for eye disorders or injuries are reported with one code that does not specify which eye is affected.

ICD-9-CM

372.06 Acute chemical conjunctivitis

930.9 Foreign body on external eye, unspecified site

Codes in subcategories T85.2- and T85.3- are used for complications of intraocular lens, or other ocular prosthetic devices, implants or grafts. Codes from these categories are used if there is a mechanical complication due to corneal graft (T85.31-) or for a displacement of an artificial intraocular lens (T85.32-). Complications of a corneal transplant use codes from subcategory T86.84-.

Intraoperative and postprocedural complications codes are in category H59. Codes from this category are used if cataract fragments remain in the eye following cataract surgery (H59.02-) or if an accidental puncture to the eye occurs during the surgical procedure (H59.2-)

Codes for eyelids not only identify the laterality but in some categories identify whether the condition affects the upper eyelid or the lower lid.

Example

H02.84- Edema of eyelid

H02.841 Edema of right upper eyelid

H02.842 Edema of right lower eyelid

H02.843 Edema of right eye, unspecified eyelid

H02.844 Edema of left upper eyelid

H02.845 Edema of left lower lid

H02.846 Edema of left eye, unspecified eyelid

H02.849 Edema of unspecified eye, unspecified eyelid

Tropias

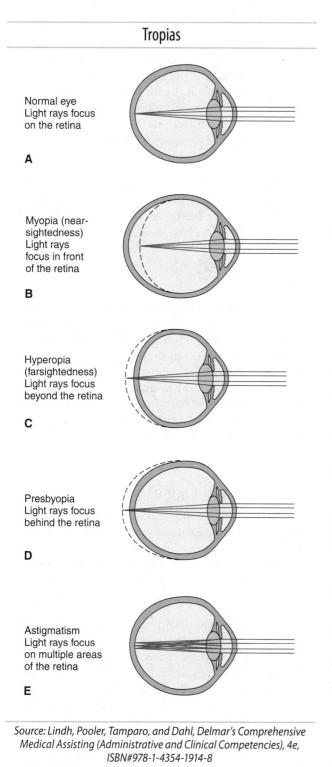

Normal eye
Light rays focus
on the retina

A

Myopia (near-sightedness)
Light rays
focus in front
of the retina

B

Hyperopia
(farsightedness)
Light rays focus
beyond the retina

C

Presbyopia
Light rays focus
behind the retina

D

Astigmatism
Light rays focus
on multiple areas
of the retina

E

Source: Lindh, Pooler, Tamparo, and Dahl, Delmar's Comprehensive Medical Assisting (Administrative and Clinical Competencies), 4e, ISBN#978-1-4354-1914-8

The Ear

Most disorders of the ear fall into the following categories:

- Infection and inflammation
- Neoplastic disease
- Injury

- Vertigo
- Hearing loss
- Congenital disorders

Infection and Inflammation—When the patient has an infection or inflammation, first determine the location. The codes within Diseases of the Ear and Mastoid Process (H60-H95) are organized according to anatomic site, beginning with external ear, moving to middle and inner ear, hearing loss, and ending with codes describing intraoperative and postprocedural complications and disorders. Some ear infections are found in the Infectious and Parasitic Diseases chapter; for example, epidemic vertigo (A88.1) and herpes infections such as B02.21 *Postherpetic geniculate ganglionitis* or B00.1 *Herpes simplex otitis externa*. Remember, to report the infectious agent as an additional diagnosis, if known; for example, B96.3 *Hemophilus influenzae [H. Influenzae]* as the cause of disease classified elsewhere or B95.5 *Unspecified stretococcus* as the cause of diseases classified elsewhere.

By far the most common codes used in this chapter are the codes for otitis media (OM), or middle ear infection. In otitis media, the infection occurs between the eardrum and the oval window. Some infections are difficult to destroy, and become chronic. Other infections are sudden onset, which is acute. Codes for OM are selected based upon whether the infection is acute or chronic, and whether there is pus or viscous fluid, or mucous. OM typically follows an upper respiratory infection with the infective agent traveling along the Eustachian tube into the middle ear.

The ICD-10-CM codes listed for otitis media are reported by laterality (right, left, or bilateral).

Example

Suppurative otitis media in the right ear.

ICD-10-CM

Look in the ICD-10-CM Index to Diseases and Injuries for Otitis/media/suppurative H66.4-. In the Tabular List, a fifth character is required to identify the laterality.

H66.40 Suppurative otitis media, unspecified, unspecified ear

H66.41 Suppurative otitis media, unspecified, right ear

H66.42 Suppurative otitis media, unspecified, left ear

H66.43 Suppurative otitis media, unspecified, bilateral

ICD-9-CM Application

Otitis media codes in ICD-9-CM are selected based upon whether the infection is acute, chronic, or unspecified and whether it is suppurative (purulent) or nonsuppurative (mucoid, with effusion, serous). The codes do not indicate laterality.

ICD-9-CM

Look in the ICD-9-CM Index to Diseases for Otitis/media/suppurative 382.4.

382.4 Unspecified suppurative otitis media

Neoplastic Disease—Acoustic neuroma, also called a vestibular schwannoma, is likely most common neoplasm related to the ear. It is a slow growing tumor of the 8th cranial nerve (vestibulocochlear) that connects the inner ear to the brain. Although benign, it causes problems for the patient because it interferes with balance and hearing, and usually must be excised. Acoustic neuroma is reported with D33.3 *Benign neoplasm of cranial nerves*. The Table of Neoplasms has a fairly complete listing of subcategory sites under Ear, but always begin in the Alphabetic Index to ensure your code is listed in the Table of Neoplasms.

Injury—Most ear injury codes are found in the Injury and Poisoning chapter of ICD-10-CM. Open wound codes are selected based upon the site damaged. Superficial injuries are not specified to a high level of detail because the superficial ear doesn't include any of the components vital to hearing. You should find selection of ear injury codes straightforward. Seventh character extensions will be required for injuries to identify the episode of care. Refer to ICD-10-CM Guideline I.C.19.a for the definitions of the seventh characters.

Vertigo—Vertigo is an illusion of movement. The person with vertigo feels that he is moving or the surroundings are moving when they are not. Vertigo is usually classified as being peripheral or central in origin. Peripheral vertigo is caused by disease in the inner ear, such as neuroma, trauma, inflammation, or infection. Central vertigo is generally milder, and arises from brain pathology; for example, in a patient with multiple sclerosis. There are numerous tests to determine the origin of the vertigo. Vertigo can be a symptom (R42) or, if the cause is known, reported with a code from category H81. Mèniére's disease is the most common form of peripheral vertigo, and the cause is unknown, although the cause of the symptoms is thought to be increased pressure in the endolymph of the cochlea. Vertigo is accompanied by hearing loss and tinnitus, or ringing in the ears. Vertigo can cause nystagmus or reflexive jerky eye movements as a response to the messages of the inner ear.

Hearing Loss—The ICD-10-CM differentiates conductive hearing loss from sensorineural hearing loss (H90-H94). Conductive hearing loss has its origin in the continuity of the transmission of sound from the external ear across the tympanic membrane through each of the ossicles and across the oval window to the round window and into the cochlea. Any disruption within that conductive chain can cause hearing loss, and the site of the disruption is reported in addition to its laterality.

Sensorineural hearing loss occurs along the nerve conduction beginning in the cochlear nerve and traveling to the brain. Sensory hearing loss is defined as a defect in the cochlea, and neural hearing loss identifies a problem between nerve hair cells and nerve fibers in the brain. Sometimes, there are mixed reasons for the hearing loss, and the classification has codes for that, as well.

Congenital Disorders—Many chromosomal syndromes have anomalies of the ear as a component. Typically, the individual anomaly being treated is reported in addition to the code for the syndrome itself; for example, many children born with Down's syndrome (Q90.-) also have some form of hearing loss. Other syndromes occur with microtia or less visible defects to the ear. A combination of codes from Diseases of the Ear and Mastoid Process (H60-H95) and the congenital section for the ear (Q16-Q18) may be necessary to capture the clinical picture completely.

Symptoms and Z Codes

When the coding for the diagnosis isn't self-evident, there may be a reason: The patient may have scheduled an appointment because of symptoms that turned out to be benign, or the patient may be in the office for a follow-up or a screening test. When this happens, ICD-10-CM has Z codes and symptom codes to report.

The signs and symptoms chapter has generic codes for vertigo when a link to vestibular disease hasn't been established (R42) and codes for abnormal test results when the diagnosis is still unknown (R94-). Do not neglect Z codes as you consider the eye and ear. Codes specific to the eye and ear include codes for family histories for blindness, deafness, and other anomalies, and personal histories of cornea, globe, and lens replacements. There are codes identifying the reason for the encounter as fitting and adjustment of glasses, contacts or hearing aids, issuance of prescriptions, or aftercare following plastic reconstruction. Other codes report eye vision and hearing screening exams. Read the guidelines and notes carefully and refer to the Tabular List as well for sequencing advice.

Example

Screening exam for cataracts.

Look in the ICD-10-CM Index to Diseases and Injuries for Screening/cataract Z13.5.

> Z13.5 Encounter for screening for eye and ear disorder

ICD-9-CM Application

Z codes in ICD-10-CM are reported with V codes in ICD-9-CM.

ICD-9-CM

Look in the ICD-9-CM Index to Diseases for Screening/condition/eye NEC V80.2.

> V80.2 Special screening for neurological, eye, and ear diseases; other eye condition

---

Acronyms

AACG	acute angle closure glaucoma
AC	anterior chamber
AD	right ear
AMD	age related macular degeneration
AO	left ear
AU	both ears
BOM	bilateral otitis media
BSOM	bilateral serous otitis media
CACG	chronic angle closure glaucoma
CE	cataract extraction
DA	dark adaptation
ERG	electroretinogram
ETD	Eustachian tube dysfunction
FA	fluorescein angiography
FB	foreign body
FTG	fulltime glasses
GDD	glaucoma drainage device
GP	gas permeable
IOL	intraocular lens
IOP	intraocular pressure
LL	lower lid
LOM	left otitis media
LSOM	left serous otitis media
NLD	nasal lacrimal duct
NLDO	nasal lacrimal duct obstruction
NPDR	non-proliferative diabetic retinopathy
OAG	open angle glaucoma
OD	right eye
OS	left eye
OU	both eyes or each eye
PCIOL	posterior chamber IOL
PMMA	polymethylmethacrylate
PSC	posterior subcapsular cataract
RD	retinal detachment
RK	radial keratotomy
ROP	retinopathy of prematurity
T&A	tonsils and adenoids
TM	trabecular meshwork
TM	tympanic membrane
VALE	visual acuity, left eye
VARE	visual acuity, right eye
VF	visual field
WNL	within normal limits

AAPC

www.aapc.com   473

Section Review 15.2

1. The patient is a 40-year-old male with Type I diabetes in good control. He is seen today for a follow up of his mild nonproliferative diabetic retinopathy. Code the diagnoses.

    A. E10.329, H35.02

    B. E10.329

    C. H35.029

    D. E11.329

2. Mrs. Johns brought in her nine-month-old baby today, complaining that he has been fussy and inconsolable. Indeed, James cried during the entire visit. Mrs. Johns believes her child has another case of otitis media, as this is the exact behavior exhibited last time. However, the exam reveals no infection, no fever. Code the diagnosis.

    A. Z01.10

    B. Z00.129

    C. H66.90

    D. R68.12

3. The pathology report comes back and the tumor is a malignant acoustic schwannoma. What is the correct diagnosis code?

    A. D49.89

    B. D33.3

    C. C72.50

    D. C71.0

4. The patient is seen in the emergency department. While dressing for work, she caught her earring in her shirt, and the force of her arm's motion ripped the earring free, tearing her earlobe. She is here to have the left earlobe repaired and to receive a tetanus shot. What diagnosis codes are assign?

    A. S01.311A, Z23

    B. S01.332A, Z23

    C. S01.342A, Z23

    D. S01.312A, Z23

5. The child is exhibiting leucocoria in the left eye, and I ordered an MRI of the skull to rule out retinoblastoma.

    A. H44.532

    B. C69.22

    C. H17.12

    D. H44.50

6. I prescribed topical antibiotics today for Jack Jones, who presented with pink eye in both eyes. Apparently, his four children are all being treated for the same condition by their pediatrician.

    A. H10.021

    B. H10.023

    C. H10.029

    D. H10.519

7. Mable reports her hearing is not what it used to be. Indeed, I have been forced to repeat everything loudly today, and within very close range. I am setting her up for hearing testing with Acme Audiology.

     A. H90.8

     B. R94.120

     C. H91.09

     D. H91.90

8. The patient underwent an enucleation for retinal cancer and today presents with right orbital cellulitis, a foreign body response to the temporary implant placed following the surgery. The implant was removed, and the patient admitted for observation and IV antibiotics.

     A. T85.79XA, H05.011, Z85.840

     B. T86.698A, H05.11, Z80.8

     C. H05.011, Z80.8

     D. T85.79XA, H05.011, Z85.840

9. The patient reports she turned her head quickly while pruning a dogwood tree in her yard, and a branch entered her right ear. She states that when she performs a Valsalva maneuver, she can hear air course through her ear. Upon examination, a small perforation of the right eardrum is noted, which I suspect will heal independent of treatment. We will reevaluate her ear in two weeks. There is no FB present.

     A. H72.00, W60.XXXA, Y92.017, Y93.H2

     B. S00.401A, H72.00

     C. S09.21XA, W60.XXXA, Y92.017, Y93.H2

     D. S09.21XA , W45.8XXA, Y92.017, Y92.157

10. The patient has been compliant with his Xalatan eye drops and his IOP is now WNL at 20 mm Hg. The glaucoma seems to be in good control. He will continue the current regime and return for a follow-up exam in six months.

     A. H40.9

     B. H40.10X0

     C. Z86.69

     D. H40.20X1

CPT®

Codes throughout the CPT® codebook may be used to report procedures on the eye and ear. Flaps and repairs from the Integumentary chapter can be performed on the skin of the eye and ear. The codes specific to Eye and Ocular Adnexa (65091–68899) and Auditory System (69000–69979), with a few exceptions, are almost exclusively reported by specialists. That's because, as we have seen, the eye and ear are very complex organs and surgeries affecting these sensory systems are delicate and require great skill.

The Eye

Eyeball (65091-65290)

CPT® codes within the Eye and Ocular Adnexa chapter begin with a sequence of codes for the most extreme procedures performed on the eye: its removal. An eye typically is removed for one of three reasons: the eye has a malignancy, and its removal is to safeguard the patient's health; the eye is blind and very painful, and its removal is to relieve the patient's symptoms; or the eye is blind and disfiguring, and the patient will receive a cosmetic implant in its place.

There are three types of removals. In evisceration, the contents of the eyeball are scooped out but the sclera shell remains connected to the eye muscles so that a prosthesis fitted into the globe will have natural movement. In enucleation, the connections (muscles, vessels, and optic nerve) are severed and the entire eyeball is removed en masse. In exenteration, surrounding skin, fat, muscle, and bone is removed. Exenteration is the most extreme type of surgery, and is reserved for patients who have serious malignancies.

In any removal, a temporary implant may be placed to protect the void that may later hold a permanent implant. This temporary implant is included in the procedure and not reported separately. The implant codes reference permanent implants that have aesthetic properties.

Anterior Segment (65400–66999)

Procedures that cut into the globe or the anterior segment of the eye disturb its fluid balance and invite the possibility of infection. A laser will be used to surgically cauterize, cut, destroy, or repair the eye, instead of a knife. The laser light can enter through the cornea directly to any site in the globe without incision or causing harm in its travels. The targeted light is focused on the defect. The lasers are very specific in what they can do.

When you are reviewing the codes in the CPT® Eye and Ocular Adnexa sections, assume that any procedure with a laser approach is going to be preferred to an open approach.

Cornea

The excision of a lesion of the cornea is a surgical procedure (eg, karetectomy, lamellar, partial. Lamellar refers to partial thickness of the cornea). An excision is the removal of an entire defect while a biopsy is removal of tissue for a diagnostic examination.

Practical Coding Note

Codes 65400 and 65410 should not be reported together on the same date of service. The biopsy is considered inclusive of the excision.

A pterygium is a benign growth of the conjunctiva that is attached to the sclera and extends from the inner canthus to the border of the cornea with an apex that points to the pupil. A pterygium may require surgical excision or transposition away from the field of vision when it is blocking the field of vision. A circumcorneal incision may be accomplished with the use of a conjunctival flap to repair a pterygium site following excision or transposition.

CPT® codes found under the subheading for removal or destruction include a diagnostic scraping of the cornea to obtain a smear and/or culture. The tissue removed during scraping (65430) may be cultured to determine a diagnosis. Removing the epithelial layer by scraping or cutting will stimulate the growth of the cornea's outermost layer to treat cases of corneal erosion or degeneration.

Code 65435 should be used to report removal of corneal epithelium with or without chemocauterization by abrasion or curettage. When a rust ring is removed from the cornea, chemical cauterization may be applied. An alternative to the chemocauterization procedure is the use of an acid to destroy the corneal epithelium. Code 65436 reports the application of a chelating agent such as EDTA.

Multiple punctures (65600) of the anterior cornea to treat corneal erosion are done in an attempt to stimulate growth of the cornea's outermost layer. A fine needle is used to "tattoo" the epithelium surface by creating hundreds of tiny pricks.

Keratoplasty is the plastic repair of the cornea. This procedure is also known as a corneal transplant. It includes the use of fresh or preserved grafts and preparation of donor material for cornea transplant. Keratoplasty procedures are normally performed using an operating microscope. A patient diagnosed with peripheral opacity of the cornea, anterior, stromal, or posterior pigmentation of the cornea; or keratoconus, to name a few diagnoses, might undergo a keratoplasty lamellar transplant.

A lamellar corneal transplant refers to the thin, outermost layers (not usually deeper than the stroma) of the cornea. A trephine is used to punch a measured circular hole in the cornea of the donor eye, and the corneal tissue is prepared and set aside. This process is repeated in the cornea of the patient and the defective tissue is removed. The identically sized donor material is sutured into position. Code 65710 reports a lamellar keratoplasty.

A penetrating corneal transplant refers to a full-thickness corneal transplant (65730–65755). The procedure is similar to the lamellar transplant except the donor material is full-thickness. In aphakic patients, vitreous, and/or aqueous may be withdrawn from the eye prior to corneal removal. An aphakic patient is a patient who has had cataract surgery and does not have an artificial or natural lens.

A key consideration when determining a code for keratoplasties is determining the lens status of the patient. Aphakia is the absence of the lens of the eye. Code 65750 reports a keratoplasty for an aphakic patient.

Code 65755 reports a keratoplasty; penetrating for the pseudophakic patient. A pseudophakic patient is one who does not have a natural lens but an artificial intraocular lens (IOL).

Practical Coding Note

CPT® codes 65710–65757 are not used to report refractive kera-toplasty procedures for the fitting of contact lens for treatment of disease. Code 92072 is reported for this purpose. Make a note next to these procedures as a reminder.

Keratomileusis (65760) is a procedure to alter visual acuity. In this procedure, a partial-thickness central portion of the cornea is frozen, reshaped on an electronic lathe, repositioned, and sutured back into place. This procedure to correct high degrees of myopia has largely been replaced by photorefrac-tive keratectomy (PRK) and LASIK, a noninvasive surgery in which an Excimer laser is used to reshape the cornea of the eye. In PRK the cornea's entire epithelial layer is removed to expose the area, whereas in LASIK surgery a thin, hinged flap is created on the cornea to access the treatment area to reshape the stromal layer of the cornea to correct the refractive error. PRK and LASIK procedures are reported with code 66999. A letter and operative report should accompany the claim.

In a keratophakia procedure (65765), a trephine is used to punch a measured circular hole in the cornea of the donor eye. An incision is made at the juncture of the cornea and the sclera. The patient's cornea is then separated into two layers. The donor cornea is inserted between these layers. This change in corneal curvature corrects a preexisting refractive error. Refractive corrections are generally cosmetic and may not be reimbursable.

In an epikeratoplasty procedure (65767), the trephine punches measured circular holes in the cornea of the donor's eye. A lens, made up of the stroma and the Bowman's membrane layers of the cornea, is shaped on a lathe. This lens is sutured into position on the surface of the patient's cornea correcting a preexisting refractive error.

A new anterior chamber is created with a plastic optical implant replacing a severely damaged cornea in a keratopros-thesis procedure (65770).

In a radial keratotomy (65771) procedure, the patient's cornea is measured and multiple, nonpenetrating cuts are made in a bicycle spoke pattern on the cornea to reduce myopia. A variety of peripheral cornea tangential cuts may be made for astigmatic correction. This procedure is often performed with circumferential subconjunctival or retrobulbar block anesthesia.

Practical Coding Note

Make a note next to code 65771 to remind you that photorefrac-tive keratectomy and LASIK are reported with the unlisted code 66999.

If previous surgery results in astigmatism, corrective surgery is performed. In this corneal relaxing procedure (65772), an X cut is made on the cornea to repair the error. Slices along the edge of the cornea are removed. In corneal wedge resec-tion (65775), a wedge is cut from the cornea. The wedging procedure is the most preferred technique used by surgeons to correct surgically induced astigmatism.

Corneal incisions or wedges for correction of surgically induced astigmatism require diagnostic codes of H52.2- *Astigmatism*, T85.3- *Mechanical complication of other ocular prosthetic devices, implants and grafts*, Z94.7 *Corneal transplant status*, Z98.4- *Cataract extraction status*, and Z98.83 *Filtering bleb after glaucoma surgery status*. The surgically induced astigmatism must be two diopters or more of change documented pre- and postoperatively and not resolved by spectacles.

The corneal epithelium is a five-to-seven cell-layer-thick covering of the anterior surface of the cornea, which protects the interior cornea from foreign objects and helps produce tears with secretions on the front surface of the superficial epithelial cells.

Ordinarily, superficial cells are shed from the epithelial surface and replaced by those from below and basal epithelial cells replace the deeper corneal epithelial cells. A constant supply of corneal epithelial cells is required and an interruption (eg, due to chronic conditions such as radiation keratitis, drug toxicity, and ocular cicatricial pemphigoid) can cause serious ocular problems. Chronic inflammation may occur character-ized by corneal scarring and opacification, corneal thinning, and possible corneal perforation, all of which may lead to loss of visual acuity. Insufficient corneal epithelial stem cells in the limbal region can be caused by burn injuries or Stevens-Johnson syndrome, an acute inflammatory disorder of the skin and mucous membranes.

Treatment of chronic epithelial defect includes limiting or removing its causes. Effective therapy includes frequent topical lubrication, punctal occlusion, and therapeutic contact lenses. More invasive surgical therapies include temporary or permanent tarsorrhaphy (sutures are used to close the palpe-bral fissure at least partially) (67875) and the use of human amniotic membrane for transplantation (65780) may be an alternative or adjunctive therapy.

Other alternative procedures include limbal cell allografts from a cadaver or living donor (65781). Corneal tissue relies on stem cells located in the limbal epithelium, the zone where corneal and conjunctival epithelia meet, to regenerate. If the graft is taken from a living donor, a conjunctival limbal graft is placed with the limbal edge of the graft at the recipient limbus. Harvesting of an allograft is reported with code 68371. A limbal conjunctival autograft (65782) includes obtaining the graft from the healthy eye.

65785 is for implantation of intrastromal corneal ring segments. This procedure is performed for the treatment of keratoconus. Keratoconus is a corneal disorder that is a progressive corneal thinning that causes irregular astigmatism and decreased visual acuity. The segments are implanted in the deep corneal stroma to modify the corneal curvature.

Anterior Chamber

A paracentesis procedure (65800–65815) is performed for the removal of aqueous humor from the anterior chamber for diagnostic analysis or to quickly reduce eye pressure temporarily as a therapeutic procedure. Code 65810 describes paracentesis of the anterior chamber with removal of vitreous and/or discission (cutting into or incision) of the anterior hyaloid membrane. This is usually performed with a YAG (yttrium-aluminum-garnet) laser. The anterior hyaloid membrane is a layer of collagen separating the vitreous from the lens. The posterior hyaloid membrane separates the back of the vitreous from the retina.

Surgeries on the iris and trabecular meshwork, including goniotomy, are usually a therapeutic treatment for glaucoma to improve the flow of aqueous in the eye. This disease is characterized by increased intraocular pressure. If left untreated, this disease will damage the optic nerve and retina, causing blindness.

A goniotomy (65820) is a surgical procedure for children in which a lens (goniolens, gonioscopy lens) is used to see the anterior chamber and an opening is made in the anterior trabecular meshwork. A trabeculotomy (65850) is a procedure to create an opening in the meshwork for the drainage of aqueous humor. A trabeculotomy is performed on children only to treat congenital glaucoma.

Trabeculoplasty is the repair of the trabecular meshwork by laser surgery in one or more sessions. Code 65855 reports a trabeculoplasty by laser surgery of glaucoma. In all other references to eye surgery by laser, one or more sessions include all additional treatments to the same eye in a defined period of time. Code 65860 for severing adhesions of anterior segment, laser technique reports the severing of goniosynechiae (adhesions of the iris to the posterior surface of the cornea) before they cause a more serious problem. Codes 65865 to 65875 report incisional technique for severing adhesions in the anterior segment of the eye including anterior and posterior chamber synechiae. An instructional note at 65865 states to use code 65855 for trabeculoplasty performed by laser surgery.

Anterior Sclera

Anterior sclera includes excision, aqueous shunt, and repair or revision codes.

Iris, Ciliary Body

An iridotomy (66500) is an incision into the iris. A patient diagnosed with adhesions or disruptions of the pupillary membranes (eg, iris bombe), occlusion or seclusion of the pupillary membrane may require an iridotomy procedure (incision into the iris). With an iris bombe condition, the iris bulges forward into the anterior chamber due to pressure built up from an accumulation of aqueous fluid between the iris and the lens in the posterior chamber. The surgeon makes an incision in the corneal-scleral junction (limbus), and then slices through the iris in a side-to-side technique (66505). This procedure increases the flow of the fluids that was initially slowed due to pupillary blockage. No tissue is removed in this procedure.

An iridectomy is the removal of part of the iris. To remove a lesion from the iris, a surgeon may choose to perform an iridectomy with a corneoscleral section or corneal section (66600). Using deep laser burns, an incision is made through a conjunctival flap. An argon laser is used to excise the affected iris along with other involved structures.

A cyclectomy (66605) consists of removing part of the ciliary muscle along with the lesion. The ciliary muscle is a ring of striated smooth muscle of the ciliary body that is attached to the lens. This muscle controls accommodation by changing the shape of the lens and regulates the flow of aqueous humor into Schlemms' canal.

A patient with degeneration of the iris and ciliary body (iris atrophy, iridoschisis, translucency of the iris, miotic cysts of the pupillary margin, or changes in the chamber angle) may require a surgical procedure to repair or suture the iris and/or ciliary body (66680, 66682). The surgeon places an ocular speculum in the patient's eye and makes an incision in the limbus to approach and repair a tear of the iris. These types of tears are often the result of bleeding from the torn tissues due to trauma. Any bleeding is controlled by cautery and the iridodialysis (coredialysis, or localized separation/tearing of the iris from the ciliary body) is sutured with fine surgical thread. The surgically created iridectomy site remains open.

In cases where high intraocular pressure cannot be otherwise controlled, portions of the ciliary body are destroyed to reduce the production of aqueous humor. Codes 66700–66740 report the use of a heat probe, laser, or freezing probe.

Cyclodialysis (66740) involves an incision and insertion of a spatula that separates the ciliary body from the sclera spur to lower intraocular pressure either by decreasing aqueous humor formation or by increasing uveovascular scleral outflow of aqueous.

In an iridotomy/iridectomy procedure, part of the iris is removed or an incision is made into the iris to permit aqueous flow from the posterior chamber to the anterior chamber, reducing intraocular pressure. A slit-lamp microscope and laser are used together to facilitate this procedure.

Lens and Intraocular Lens Procedures

When an extracapsular extraction is performed, the posterior part of the lens capsule remains intact. At times, this structure may become opaque or membranes may grow secondary to the original procedure (secondary membranous cataract). Opaque membranes are excised with a needle knife. When coding incision of secondary cataract, it is important to differentiate between the techniques of stab incision or laser surgery.

Example

Procedure 66820, for example, describes a cut into the limbus to access and remove a secondary cataract. Today, this procedure is performed by laser: An upside down "U" is cut through the secondary cataract, which then falls out of the visual field like an opened curtain. This type of laser incision is reported with 66821.

Some surgeries require incisions. Removal of a lens with a cataract requires an incision allowing the lens to be extracted and an intraocular lens (IOL) to be inserted into the eye. Currently, cataract surgery is performed microscopically, and tiny incisions in the limbus fulfill the code requirement. The defective lens is broken down into smaller segments and systematically vacuumed from the eye. The artificial lens is folded in on itself and inserted through the incision. When in place, the artificial lens opens and is secured. Recovery is a fraction of what once was required for cataract surgery.

During laser surgery, the pupil is typically dilated allowing the physician to have a broader view and greater ability to reach more tissue in the eye. A speculum is placed in the eye to hold it open, and anesthetic is applied to the cornea. For some surgeries, injections are sometimes required to numb the eye. A retrobulbar or Tenon's capsule injection are two common approaches for delivery of anesthetic. These nerve blocks are bundled into the procedures and not reported separately when performed by the surgeon.

The majority of procedures performed on the anterior segment of the eye are considered microsurgeries as they are performed using an operating microscope (69990). The scope is not reported separately for procedures 65091-68850. All procedures that include use of an operating microscope are listed in the section note above code 69990.

Posterior Segment (67005–67299)

Vitreous

A vitreous hemorrhage is an extravasation of blood into the vitreous. It often produces a black reflection on ophthalmoscopy. A vitreous hemorrhage may occur in such conditions as retinal vein occlusion, diabetic retinopathy, posterior vitreous detachment, retinal neovascularization, retinal tears, or ocular trauma. Localized bleeding from retinal vessels can usually be controlled by photocoagulation.

Vitreous hemorrhages, along with diagnoses such as degeneration, crystalline deposits, prolapse, or other disorders of the vitreous, are health issues that warrant the surgeon to recommend a procedure to remove the vitreous. A vitrectomy is the surgical removal of part or all of the vitreous (a clear jelly-like substance that fills the posterior [rear] cavity of the eyeball). An open sky technique, as described in code 67005, refers to an incision made at the corneal edge or limbus. A needle is passed to the back of the anterior segment where displaced vitreous humor is removed by aspiration. If the vitrectomy is performed with a mechanical tool instead of a syringe, code 67010 should be reported.

Some of the codes in the Vitreous category of CPT® refer to a pars plana approach.

The pars plana refers to the flattened posterior portion of the ciliary body located 4 mm behind the corneoscleral junction. Sometimes during cataract extraction surgery, the vitreous moves forward into the wound and this material must be removed. This removal procedure (67015) could be coded in addition to the cataract surgery, depending on payer reimbursement policies.

Code 67025 reports the injection of a vitreous substitute and refers to the injection of Healon or silicone and not air or balanced salt solutions.

During a vitrectomy procedure, part or all of the vitreous may be removed. Special instruments, such as a rotoextractor or vitreous infusion suction cutter (VISC), are used. A VISC is capable of aspirating, cutting, and removing vitreous and, at the same time, introducing irrigating fluid into the posterior cavity. A panretinal procedure means that all four quadrants of the retina are treated. Code 67040 reports a vitrectomy with endolaser panretinal photocoagulation.

Retina or Choroid

Retinal detachment is a separation of the retina from underlying retinal pigment epithelium. A retinal detachment is painless. Early symptoms may include vitreous floaters, flashes of light, or blurred vision. Direct ophthalmoscopy can indicate retinal irregularities and a bullous retinal elevation with darkened blood vessels.

Retinal detachments may be caused by injury, previous surgery, inflammation, and vitreous hemorrhage. This condition occurs when the inner layer of retinal tissue falls away from the underlying support tissue into the vitreous. Because the tissue is detached from its choroid blood supply, vision is lost in that part of the retina.

Cryotherapy refers to the use of subfreezing temperatures to destroy tissue, while diathermy uses high frequency electric currents for the same purpose. Photocoagulation uses a laser to coagulate and destroy the tissue.

Codes 67101–67108 require a diagnosis of retinal detachment. It is quite common to confuse the use of posterior segment codes with or without retinal detachment. The operative report must be reviewed carefully to determine the appropriate CPT® code to report from this code group. If several methods are combined, such as diathermy, cryotherapy, and photocoagulation, report the code describing the principal modality. Also note that several of these codes do not allow for separate reporting of implants or drainage of fluid.

Retinal breaks and lattice degeneration detachments may require a procedure to secure the retina by cryotherapy (freezing) or by diathermy (heat). Prophylactic treatments for retinal detachment are coded according to the method used. CPT® notes that the procedure may require one or more sessions. CPT® modifier 58 (staged procedure) should not be attached to these codes because the definitions of these codes denote repetitive services and staging is inclusive.

The choroid is a vascular tunic that is between the sclera and retina. A patient diagnosed with localized lesions of the choroid, caused by age-related macular degeneration, may undergo a procedure requiring ocular photodynamic therapy (OPT) utilizing a photosensitive drug or a laser treatment that treats choroidal neovascularization.

The laser procedure (67220) describes destruction of a localized lesion of choroid, one or more sessions, by photocoagulation using laser. Ocular photodynamic therapy (67221) utilizes low energy targeted laser light to activate a photoactive drug administered intravenously to remove abnormal tissue.

Ocular Adnexa (67311—67999)

There are many procedures performed on the ocular adnexa, and these do not require entry into the globe or anterior segment.

Extraocular Muscles

The muscles controlling vertical eye movement are the superior rectus, inferior rectus, superior oblique, and inferior oblique. Muscles controlling horizontal movement include the medial rectus and lateral rectus. Strabismus is an imbalance in the muscles of the eyeball that control the movement of the eyeball.

Six Muscles Controlling Eye Movement

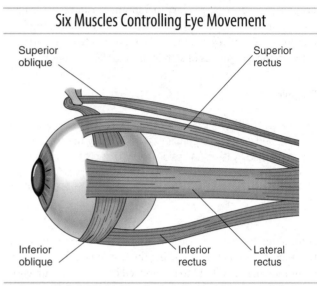

Source: Ehrlich, Medical Terminology for Health Professionals, 6e, ISBN #978-1-4180-7252-0

Recession is a weakening procedure whereby an extraocular muscle (EOM) is severed from the eye, allowed to retract, and then sutured to the sclera at a selected distance from the original place of attachment. A resection procedure involves detaching the extraocular muscle from the eye, removing part of the muscle tissue, and then resuturing it to the eye, usually at the original site.

Codes 67311–67318 are the primary strabismus codes that identify resection or recession procedures used to strengthen or weaken each eye muscle or a combination of eye muscles. An exotropia is when an eye turns outward. A patient diagnosed with exotropia may require this procedure to be performed on the horizontal muscles.

In some cases, the procedure is not completed until the patient is awakened and lengthy sutures extruding from the back of the eye adjusted to ensure perfect binocular vision. These adjustable sutures are reported with add-on code 67335.

Orbit

Orbitotomies without bone flaps, and using a frontal or transconjunctival approach for exploration/drainage to remove lesions, foreign bodies, or bone removal for decompression, are reported using codes 67400–67414. Incisions are made in either the upper or lower eyelid for these procedures.

Orbitotomies with bone flaps or windows for exploration with or without biopsy, for removal of lesions, foreign bodies with drainage, or for bone removal for decompression, are reported using codes 67420–67450. These procedures include a C-shaped incision down to the periosteum overlying the lateral orbital rim.

Code 67445 is a surgical procedure during which part of the orbital side bone is removed to allow lateral movement rather than pushing the eye forward. A lateral approach (eg, Kroenlein), is used. This procedure is sometimes necessary in the treatment of Grave's disease. Grave's disease is a thyroid disease that can cause exophthalmos, which is the protrusion of one or both of the eyeballs.

Injection procedures include codes 67500–67515. Retrobulbar injections are used to introduce medication or alcohol to the muscle cone behind the eye. Therapeutic agents are introduced by injection along the surface of the globe beneath the conjunctiva and between the sclera and Tenon's capsule. Tenon's capsule is a thin membrane which envelopes the eyeball from the optic nerve to the limbus, separating it from the orbital fat and forming a socket in which it moves.

Eyelids

A surgeon may perform a blepharotomy (67700) to drain an eyelid abscess when a patient is diagnosed with a hordeolum or other deep inflammation, abscess, or cysts. The patient is usually placed under a local anesthesia, a small incision is made in the eyelid and the abscess is drained and irrigated. If the abscess or hordeolum is extensive, the provider may place a small drain in the wound.

When a patient is diagnosed with an orbital hemorrhage or blepharophimosis (decrease in the size of the fissure between the eyelids without fusion of the eyelid), the provider often performs a canthotomy. A canthotomy (67715) involves creating an opening into the skin at the canthus to repair its shape.

A chalazion is a small, localized swelling, or mass located at the margin of an eyelid. It is often caused by inflammation and/or blockage of a meibomian gland (tarsal gland), one of the sebaceous glands between the dense white fibrous tissue supporting the eyelid (aka tarsi) and the eyelid's conjunctiva. Excision of the chalazion should be reported with a code from 67800–67805 depending on the number of chalazia excised and whether both eyelids are affected.

When a patient is seen for ingrown eyelashes (trichiasis) irritating the eye, such as senile entropion, cicatricial entropion, hypertrichosis of the eyelid (abnormal growth of eyelashes), or other disorders of the eyelid, operative intervention may be required. Trichiasis often irritates the cornea or conjunctiva, resulting in scarring or thickening of the cornea if left untreated. The ophthalmologist may perform a procedure

to correct the condition. In the procedure, the surgeon uses a biomicroscope, an instrument consisting of a microscope combined with a rectangular light source, to pluck out the offending eyelashes with forceps.

Tarsorrhaphy involves suturing the edges of the eyelids to close the palpebral fissure, which is the linear opening between the eyelids. This temporary closure provides relief for the patient with an eroded or painful cornea. Code 67875 is reported when the provider uses Frost sutures for temporary closure of the eyelids.

Code 67880 is reported when construction of the intermarginal adhesions, median tarsorrhaphy or canthorrhaphy (repair of the canthus—the angle of the slit between the eyelids at either end) is performed. Permanent intermarginal adhesions are created by excising tissue from the margins of the eyelids along the mucocutaneous junction. Sutures are passed through the eyelid margin and skin of the upper and lower lids. For each eye, the process may be repeated a number of times.

Brow ptosis is the drooping of the eyebrows. This occurs in old age or secondary to paralysis or weakness of the frontalis muscle such as in Bell's palsy or myasthenia gravis. Dissection is carried down to the brow area as the surgeon pulls superiorly to properly position the brow area above the supraorbital rim. Code 67900 reports the repair of a brow ptosis by supraciliary, midforehead, or coronal approach.

Blepharoptosis is drooping of an upper eyelid and may require surgical intervention by various techniques. Code 67901 reports the repair of blepharoptosis using the frontalis muscle technique with suture or other material (eg, banked fascia).

Practical Coding Note

Code 67902 is distinguished from code 67901 by the fact that the "sling" material is fascia lata, which is a thin fibrous tissue transplanted from the thigh. In the description of 67901, highlight "with suture or other material" and in the description of 67902, highlight "with autologous fascial sling" to distinguish between the two codes.

The implanting of an upper eyelid load to correct lagophthalmos is reported using code 67912. Lagophthalmos is the inability to fully close the upper eyelid, which can result in damage to the cornea from a drying out of its surface due to lack of moisture. The condition may be present at birth but more commonly it is associated with paralyzing conditions such as Bell's palsy or stroke. Head trauma and tumors also may cause lagophthalmos. The surgical insertion of a predetermined gold weight into the upper eyelid enables the lid to close more easily.

Ectropion is the turning outward of the margin of the lower eyelid and procedures to repair the condition are described in codes 67914–67917. Sutures may be used to shorten the posterior tissues of the eyelid. For code 67915, thermocauterization is used to shrink the posterior tissues of the eyelid margin to treat the everted lid. A tarsal wedge of tissue can be excised to eliminate the ectropion with sutures placed to repair the incision. In another of these procedures, a canthotomy incision is made and the tarsal plate is advanced and secured with sutures to correct the condition. Code 67916 is used to correct ectropion with excision of a tarsal wedge.

Entropion is an inversion of the margin of the eyelid. Repair of this condition involves the use of sutures, thermocauterization and an excised tarsal wedge with a variation of suture repair. Codes 67921–67924 are used to report the various types of entropion repairs.

CPT® codes 67930–67935 are used to report the suture of recent partial-thickness and full-thickness eyelid wounds. These wounds are irrigated and sutured in layers.

Codes 67961–67966 are used to report full-thickness excision and repair of the eyelid. In these surgical procedures, a piece of eyelid is excised and surrounding tissue is rearranged to compensate for the defect. If more than one-fourth of the lid margin is removed, code 67966 is reported. These codes include preparation for skin graft or pedicle flap with adjacent tissue transfer or rearrangement.

Conjunctiva (68020—68899)

The categories under the Conjunctiva subheading of CPT® identify the following types of surgical procedures:

- Incision and Drainage
- Excision and/or Destruction
- Injection
- Conjunctivoplasty
- Other Procedures
- Lacrimal System

A conjunctival cyst is an abnormal, thin-walled sac of fluid in the conjunctiva. A sebaceous cyst occurs in the sebaceous gland located in the skin of the eyelid. When a conjunctival cyst or a sebaceous cyst undergoes a procedure in which a vertical or horizontal incision is made in the posterior surface of the eyelid to drain fluid or matter, report 68020.

Trachoma (68040) is a chronic and contagious inflammation of the conjunctiva with hypertrophy. This condition is most contagious in its early stages and is transmitted by eye secretions, hand-to-eye contact, or by sharing contaminated articles (eg, towels, handkerchiefs, and eye make-up). After the incubation period, which is about seven days, conjunc-

tival hyperemia, eyelid edema, photophobia, and lacrimation appear, usually bilaterally. Unless treatment is given, a cicatrix (scar) follows. Secondary bacterial infection is also common. The treatment involves the use of trachoma biomicroscopic guidance to evert the eyelid margin and express the conjunctival follicles.

An excision of a conjunctival lesion including adjacent sclera may be performed on a patient who is diagnosed with a malignant or benign neoplasm of the conjunctiva. Other diagnoses may include carcinoma in situ of the eye, granuloma, or hyperemia of the conjunctiva. Local anesthesia is provided and a lid speculum is inserted, and the lesion is then excised with a curette. Use code 68130 for this procedure.

A provider may inject a corticosteroid or antibiotic medication into the subconjunctival space to treat a patient for diagnoses such as keratoconjunctivitis, chronic conjunctivitis, or scleritis. Code 68200 reports a subconjunctival injection.

Conjunctivoplasty is an important part of reconstruction because the conjunctiva is vascularized and provides moisture to the inner aspect of the eyelids and to the anterior sclera. The conjunctiva ends at the limbus; there is no conjunctival covering over the cornea. However, in prosthetics following evisceration, the conjunctiva may traverse an artificial cornea. When the conjunctiva is damaged, buccal mucosa may be harvested and used as a graft (68325). Remember, the conjunctiva forms a cul de sac 360 degrees around the eye. Any foreign body that enters the orbit of the eye must pierce the conjunctiva to get there. The extraocular muscles are rooted into the globe posterior to the cul de sac. CPT® procedural codes for removal of excess skin from the eyelid are found in the integumentary chapter. Blepharoplasty codes in the Eye and Adnexa chapter involve the more complex structures within the eye.

During a conjunctival flap procedure (68360, 68362), the conjunctiva is elevated from the Tenon's capsule and a small tongue of free conjunctiva is advanced via a flap where it is secured with sutures.

The lacrimal system serves to keep the conjunctiva and cornea moist through the production, distribution, and elimination of tears. An incision of the lacrimal gland (68400) or in the lacrimal sac (68420) is made to drain abscesses.

The lacrimal puncta are small openings in the inner canthus of the eyelids that channel tears produced by the lacrimal gland. A snip incision of the lacrimal punctum is commonly performed for stenosis of the lacrimal punctum, epiphora (overproduction of tears), or tear film insufficiency. A snip incision (68440) to the punctum is made and the punctum enlargement is verified with a dilating probe.

For total or partial lacrimal gland removal (68500–68505) an incision can be made either beneath the superior orbital rim or in the lid crease of the upper lid. The lacrimal duct is isolated and dissected from its position in the lacrimal fossa.

Practical Coding Note

CPT® code 68500 is not used if the removal is due to tumor. Highlight "except for tumor" in the code description as a reminder.

For a biopsy procedure of the lacrimal gland (68510), a portion of the gland is excised for analysis.

The lacrimal sac is an enlarged portion of the lacrimal duct that eliminates tears. Excision of the lacrimal sac (68520) requires an incision midway between the nose bridge and medial canthal tendon. The sac is separated and removed. For biopsy (68525), a section of the lacrimal sac is removed.

For removal of a foreign body or stone in the lacrimal passages, code 68530 is reported. The surgical access to the site is the same as that for sac removal.

For excision of a lacrimal gland tumor, access to the site is also the same as that for gland removal. The tumor is removed with a rim of normal lacrimal gland tissue. If the tumor has invaded the lacrimal fossa, part of the affected bone is removed. Code 68540 reports an excision of a lacrimal gland tumor by frontal approach and code 68550 reports an excision of a lacrimal gland by osteotomy. An osteotomy is an incision into the bone.

Lacrimal canaliculi are the two passages that connect the puncta to the lacrimal sac. An injury to the eye may sever this passage. A probe may be used to locate the distal and proximal ends of the canaliculi, and the ends are reattached. The wound is closed with sutures. Code 68700 reports a plastic repair of the canaliculi. Code 68720 reports a dacryocystorhinostomy, which creates a fistula or connection between the lacrimal sac and the nasal mucosa.

For a conjunctivorhinostomy procedure (68745–68750), the sac is connected to the nasal mucosa by a series of interrupted sutures. A glass tube or a stent may be inserted (68750) to create a connection between the lacrimal system and the nasal mucosa.

Code 68760 describes the surgical closure of a section of the canalicular and lacrimal system that includes the lacrimal punctum. A heat source is used to seal the punctum. Code 68761 reports a punctum closure using either a permanent silicone plug or a temporary collagen plug.

Medicine Codes— Ophthalmological Services

Services described by ophthalmology medicine codes include general services (medical examination and evaluation), special services, ophthalmoscopy, electroretinography, contact lens services, prescription, and fitting of ocular prosthesis, spectacle services, and the supply of materials.

General Ophthalmological Services (92002–92014)

These CPT® codes are specific to the typical services rendered during an ophthalmological visit.

The CPT® codes used for the reporting of general ophthalmological services are based on new and established patient criteria and level of service provided. For supply of spectacles, use the appropriate supply codes in the HCPCS Level II code set.

To determine what level of service to code, the provider and coder must be familiar with the terms "intermediate" and "comprehensive" as they apply to ophthalmological services.

Intermediate ophthalmological services include an evaluation of a new or existing condition complicated by a new diagnostic or management problem (not necessarily related to the primary diagnosis), including a history, general medical observation, external ocular and adnexal examination, and other diagnostic procedures as indicated.

According to CPT®, this service "may include the use of mydriasis for ophthalmoscopy." Mydriasis is the increase in pupil size that normally occurs in the dark or artificially using drugs. A mydriatic agent to dilate the pupils facilitates visualization of the ocular media and fundus.

Comprehensive ophthalmological services include an evaluation of the complete visual system. This service may require more than one visit. The service includes a history; general medical observation; external examination (examination of the eye and adnexa [following the eyelids, lashes, eyebrows, alignment of the eye, and motility of the eye, conjunctiva, cornea, and iris]); ophthalmoscopic examination of the ocular media, the retina, and optic nerve, gross visual fields; and a basic sensorimotor examination. Refer to the CPT® Ophthalmology subsection guidelines for definitions and examples for intermediate and comprehensive ophthalmological services.

Intermediate	Comprehensive
History	History
General medical observation	General medical observation

Intermediate	Comprehensive
External ocular and adnexal exam	External and ophthalmoscopic exam
Other diagnostic procedures as indicated	Gross visual fields
May include mydriasis	Basic sensorimotor exam
	Often includes biomicroscopy, exam with cycloplegia or mydriasis and tonometry.
	Always includes initiation of diagnostic and treatment programs

Special Ophthalmological Services (92015–92140)

A special evaluation of part of the visual system is made that goes beyond the services included under general services. These special ophthalmological services may be reported in addition to a general ophthalmological services or E/M services.

Interpretation and report by the physician is an integral part of special ophthalmological services where indicated. Technical procedures are often part of the service, but should not be mistaken to constitute the service itself.

CPT® code 92015 *Determination of refractive state* includes prescription of lenses. Reimbursement for 92015 is controversial because many payers bundle this service into the intermediate or comprehensive eye exam.

Fluorescein angioscopy and quantitative visual field examination can be reported separately, when performed.

Practical Coding Note

When only one eye is assessed, use modifier 52 to report reduced services. The modifier 50 should not be used with CPT® codes 92002–92065 and 92081–92100. Both of these levels of services constitute integrated services in which medical decision making cannot be separated from the examining techniques.

Itemization of service components, such as a slit lamp examination, keratometry or retinoscopy, is not applicable.

A gonioscope is used to examine the trabecular meshwork, located at the "angle" of the eye where the iris and cornea meet. A special contact lens (a goniolens) is placed on the cornea to eliminate the curvature of the cornea, allowing light to be reflected into the angle of the anterior chamber. This procedure is considered noninvasive and helps to locate foreign bodies in

the anterior chamber, to evaluate tumors, cysts, and trauma or to view anatomic structures behind the iris.

Codes 92081–92083 report visual field examination, unilateral or bilateral. Measurements are taken of space visible to an eye fixated straight ahead. Level of service is dependent upon degree of field measured, point of field, and thresholds. The CPT® guidelines note that basic confrontational fields are a part of all eye exams.

CPT® code 92100 reports serial tonometry. Serial tonometry is a measurement of the outflow of aqueous from the eye and it determines if the fluids in the eye are at proper levels and circulating properly. When this service is performed, a serial tonometry monitors the pressure over a long period to look for a time of day rhythm (a number of measurements separated by many hours).

Ophthalmoscopy (92225–92260)

Ophthalmoscopy, direct or indirect, is an examination used primarily to examine the fundus or posterior portion of the interior of the eye. The anterior portion of the eye, composed of the cornea, iris, and lens is also examined in the course of focusing on the interior of the eye. Indirect ophthalmoscopy is most commonly used by retinal surgeons for preoperative diagnostic evaluation and during surgery for repair of retinal detachment.

Fluorescein angiography involves laser scanning for reconstructing images for display on a cathode ray tube. This procedure helps to evaluate the surface of the eye for disease or injury. Fluorescein dye is a dye that emits light when a specific light is used to enhance the imaging during fluorescein angiography. A number of abnormalities may be identified in this process such as microscopic aneurysms, arteriovenous shunts, and neovascularization.

Use CPT® code 92235 to report fluorescein angiography that includes multiframe imaging, interpretation, and report. Multiframe imaging involves multiple, rapid photographs that are taken approximately one second apart. The procedure includes interpretation and report. When both eyes are tested, report the bilateral modifier 50 or RT/LT.

Indocyanine green angiography (92240) is a diagnostic study in which retinal and choroidal inclusions are displayed and photographed utilizing computer technology. It can be used in conjunction with a fluorescein angiography study if the fluorescein does not provide enough diagnostic information. Both studies may be performed on the same eye, on the same day, and are reimbursed separately.

A written report or medical documentation should accompany insurance claims when CPT® codes 92235 and 92240 are performed on the same date of service.

Ophthalmodynamometry (92260) is a procedure used to obtain an approximate measurement of the pressure in the central retinal arteries. It measures indirectly the flow of blood in the carotid artery on each side of the body. This procedure is often performed on patients who are blacking out in one eye or experiencing periodic attacks of weakness, etc. If this procedure is performed on only one eye, the reduced service modifier 52 should be reported, because CPT® indicates the code represents a bilateral procedure.

Contact Lens Services (92310–92326)

Prescription of contact lens is not a part of general ophthalmological services. The fitting of lens includes patient instruction, training, and incidental revision, as necessary.

CPT® codes 92310–92317 report the prescription and medical supervision for the fitting of corneal contact lenses. CPT® codes 92310 and 92314 describe services to both eyes except for aphakia. Modifier 52 should be reported if the prescription and fitting of a contact lens is for only one eye.

CPT® states that the supply of contact lenses may be reported as part of the service of fitting or it may be reported with appropriate supply codes.

Spectacle Services (Including Prosthesis for Aphakia) (92340–92371)

Fitting of spectacles may be reported separately using CPT® codes 92340–92371. This service includes measurement of anatomical facial characteristics, writing of laboratory specifications, and final adjustment of the spectacles to the visual axes and anatomical tomography. The prescription of spectacles, when required, is an integral part of the general services.

The Ear

Understanding anatomy of the ear is essential to procedural coding for the ear because procedures for the ear are organized anatomically: external, middle, and inner ear.

External Ear (69000–69399)

Many of the external ear procedures are simple procedures that can be performed by any practitioner; for example, 69200 *Removal foreign body from external auditory canal; without general anesthesia.* As you can imagine, this is a popular code among pediatricians. Repair codes in the External Ear subheading are often performed by plastic surgeons, and relate to plastic defects that may be congenital or due to injury.

Incision

Perichondritis is an infection of the perichondrium of the pinna. Perichondritis may be initiated by trauma, insect bites, incisions or superficial infections of the pinna, in which pus accumulates between the cartilage and the perichondrium. The blood supply to the cartilage is provided by the perichondrium. If the perichondrium is separated from both sides of the cartilage, the resulting avascular necrosis leads to a deformed pinna. Septic necrosis also plays a role. Perichondritis tends to be indolent, long lasting, and destructive. Gram-negative bacteria usually causes perichondritis.

The provider may perform an incision and drainage by means of suction to the external ear to approximate the blood supply to the cartilage. Code 69000 reports simple drainage of the external ear for abscess or hematoma.

Code 69005 reports a more complex external ear drainage procedure for an abscess or hematoma. The complicated procedure requires additional time to clean the abscess cavity and usually includes insertion of a small drain tube or packing of the abscess with the application of antibiotic eardrops.

Excision

Basal cell and squamous cell carcinomas frequently develop on the pinna after regular exposure to the sun. Early lesions can be successfully treated with cautery and curettage or radiation therapy. More advanced lesions affecting the cartilage require surgical excision of V-shaped wedges or of larger portions of the pinna.

If an entire lesion is removed from the external ear with a simple repair, code 69110 is reported. Code 69120 reports a complete amputation of the external ear.

Excision exostosis(es), external auditory canal refers to the removal of a benign bony growth from the ear canal. To remove an exostosis, the surgeon makes an incision through the skin above the exostosis to expose the bone beneath it. The bony growth is chipped away with a chisel or drill. Code 69140 reports the excision of an exostosis or exostoses of the external auditory canal.

Removal

Removal of a foreign body (example, bead) from the inside of the ear canal is reported with code 69200 without general anesthesia or 69205 with general anesthesia. Modifier 50 (or LT and RT, depending on the payer) is appended to these codes if both ears are involved.

Cerumen refers to ear wax. When impacted cerumen is removed by irrigation or lavage 69209 is used. When impacted cerumen is removed from the ear by instrumentation, such as a cerumen spoon, vacuum evacuation or forceps, report code 69210. Use modifier 50 (or LT and RT, depending on the payer) if procedure is performed bilaterally. When cerumen is not stated to be impacted, you are instructed to report an Evaluation and Management code.

CPT® code 69220 describes routine cleaning performed every three to six months to remove skin debris and drainage from the mastoid cavity after a radical or modified radical mastoidectomy. Code 69222 is reported when the cleaning is more extensive, such as when an infection is present, or anesthesia is required. Simple procedures are generally performed in the office, while complex procedures are generally performed in the operating room.

Repair

Otoplasty (69300) is a surgical procedure (cosmetic) performed to correct protruding ear(s). When a surgeon performs an otoplasty, an incision is made on the posterior auricle. A new antihelical fold is created. The cartilage and ear size may also be reduced. This code includes moderate sedation.

A common diagnosis in a medical record may include macrotia, bat ear, Stahl's ear, or other types of congenital anomalies of the ear.

Code 69320 is used when the surgeon performs a single-stage reconstruction of the external auditory (canal) for congenital atresia. Reconstruction of the external auditory canal corrects congenital malformations when no middle ear reconstruction is necessary. If this procedure is performed bilaterally, append modifier 50. Some payers require two line items showing the CPT® code with the modifier appended to the second line item, while others require the procedural code with modifier 50 as a single line item.

Ear

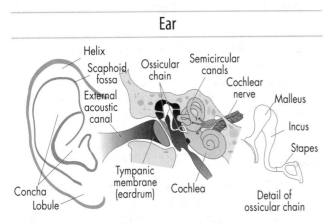

The tympanic membrane is a thin, sensitive tissue and is the gateway to the middle ear; the membrane vibrates in response to sound waves and the movement is transmitted via the ossicular chain to the internal ear. Many surgeries to the middle ear involve repair to the tympanic membrane and reconstruction to the various components of the ossicular chain.

Source: Copyright OptumInsight. All rights reserved

Middle Ear (69420–69799)

The middle ear includes the tympanic membrane (eardrum), the auditory ossicles, and four openings. The auditory ossicles consist of three small bones commonly known as the hammer, anvil, and stirrup. These three bones are medically known as the malleus, incus, and stapes, respectively. These middle ear bones are linked, to allow the transmission of sound waves. The middle ear cavity is air-filled and has four openings. The footplate (forming the base of the stapes) sits over the oval window that covers the vestibule of the inner ear. The round window opens into the cochlea of the inner ear. The Eustachian tube has an opening that leads to the upper part of the throat behind the nose. The aditus is an inlet that leads to the mastoid cavity, or sinus, behind the middle ear.

The Eustachian tube opens on the front wall of the middle ear and extends to the pharynx. The Eustachian tubes are 3 to 4 cm long and are lined with a mucous membrane. These tubes permit equalization of air pressure between the internal ear and the outside of the body. Occlusion of the Eustachian tube leads to the development of otitis media. Most procedures on the Eustachian tubes are performed in the physician's office.

Incision

A myringotomy is the surgical incision of the tympanic membrane to relieve pressure and release pus from an infection. In this procedure, fluid is gently suctioned out of the middle ear. This surgical procedure is also known as tympanostomy.

When a surgeon performs Eustachian tube inflation, a catheter is inserted via nasal cavity with the aid of a nasopharyngoscope. Air is forced into the catheter to inflate the Eustachian tube and the catheter is removed. This procedure is performed when a patient is diagnosed with chronic serous otitis media, a permanent perforation of the tympanic membrane with or without permanent changes in the middle ear, and to relieve the pain.

Tympanostomy

Tympanic refers to procedures of the middle ear. The tympanic cavity is the main cavity of the ear between the eardrum and the inner ear. The tympanum, or myringa, is the membrane in the ear that vibrates to sound.

A tympanostomy involves the surgical insertion of ventilation tubes, also called pressure equalization (PE) or tympanostomy tubes, into the eardrum, where they remain to allow for continual drainage of fluid and normalization of pressure in the ear space.

Bilateral tympanostomies (myringotomies) with the insertion of ventilation tubes is one of the most common surgical procedures performed in the United States today for children with recurrent otitis media. Code 69436 reports a tympanostomy requiring insertion of a ventilating tube. To report a bilateral tympanostomy with ventilation tube insertion, use modifier 50.

Mastoidectomy

The mastoid bone is a bone located behind the ear (felt as a hard bump behind the ear). The air cells inside are connected to the middle ear through an air-filled cavity called the mastoid antrum.

Mastoidectomy is a surgical procedure designed to remove infection or growths in the mastoid bone. Access to the middle ear, antrum, and mastoid for chronic ear disease and cholesteatoma is performed by drilling away bone to visualize these areas, rid the disease, and reconstruct the conductive hearing mechanism.

A cholesteatoma is a sac that expands by collection of cells and debris. Depending on the amount of infection or cholesteatoma present, various degrees of mastoidectomies can be performed. In a simple mastoidectomy (69501), the surgeon opens the bone and removes any infection. A tube may be placed in the eardrum to drain any pus or secretions present in the middle ear. Antibiotics are then given intravenously (through a vein) or by mouth.

A modified radical mastoidectomy (69505) involves a post-aural or endaural incision and a posterior tympanomeatal flap is reflected forward in order to drill out the mastoid cortex. Granulations and cholesteatoma are removed. The posterior bony canal wall is removed to the level of the facial nerve and ossicles are removed if involved in the cholesteatoma. The posterior skin flap and eardrum are repositioned and a meatoplasty is performed. Both a modified radical and a radical mastoidectomy usually result in less than normal hearing.

A radical mastoidectomy (69511) removes the most bone and is indicated for extensive spread of cholesteatoma. The posterior and superior bony canal walls are taken down. The Eustachian tube orifice mucosa, middle ear mucosa, granulations, and cholesteatoma are removed. The eardrum and middle ear structures may be completely removed. Usually the stapes (the stirrup-shaped bone) is spared, if possible, to help preserve some hearing.

Repair

A tympanoplasty (codes 69631–69646) is a surgical procedure that involves repairing or reconstructing the eardrum. In a tympanoplasty without mastoidectomy procedure, code 69631, the middle ear is explored. If adhesions or squamous debris is located, the surgeon removes them and palpates the ossicles. Tympanoplasty may involve one or more of the following procedures:

1. A canaloplasty is the repair of the external ear canal usually due to trauma, especially basilar skull fracture trauma.

2. An atticotomy is the cutting of an opening in the wall of the "attic," which is the cavity of the middle ear that lies above the tympanic cavity and contains the upper portion of the malleus and most of the incus.

3. Ossicular chain reconstruction involves the repair of the three small bones in the ear called ossicles. The three small bones are the malleus, incus, and stapes. These bones may be replaced with prosthetic bones. This procedure is usually performed for chronic ear infection, trauma, or perforation of the eardrum.

Inner Ear (69801–69949)

The inner ear consists of a bony labyrinth within the temporal bone lying on either side of the head. This complex structure has three parts: the semicircular canals, the vestibule, and the cochlea. The three semicircular canals maintain equilibrium and merge into the vestibule, which contains fluid. The oval window, in the middle ear, covers the vestibule, which contains perilymph fluid.

Incision and/or Destruction

A patient diagnosed with active Ménière's disease (eg, cochleovestibular or vestibular) may undergo a procedure called a labyrinthotomy. Code 69801 is reported for labyrinthotomy with perfusion of vestibuloactive drug(s) via transcanal approach. A small catheter or needle is inserted into the middle ear for the administration of drugs such as aminoglycosides, corticosteroids, antibiotics or local anesthetics.

Vertigo may be caused by acute labyrinthitis (a viral inflammation of the inner ear), benign positional vertigo (a condition due to abnormally floating crystals in the inner ear that stimulate the nerve endings of the inner ear), delayed symptom of head injury, or result of cervical spine problems. Procedures to decrease the severity of symptoms include endolymphatic sac decompression (69805), which involves making an incision behind the involved ear and exposing the mastoid bone. The mastoid cavity is drilled out until the endolymphatic sac is exposed and opened. The posterior ear canal wall remains intact. If a shunt is inserted into the sac to allow for future drainage, report 69806.

Code 69820 is used for fenestration of the semicircular canal. A partial mastoidectomy is performed. The mastoid antrum and horizontal semicircular canal are identified. The posterior ear canal wall is removed. The incus and head of the malleus are removed. A small opening is created in the horizontal canal. The eardrum and canal skin are repositioned and the mastoid is packed, and the incision repaired.

Labyrinthectomy

In individuals with complete or near complete hearing loss in one ear due to Ménière's, a surgical procedure termed a labyrinthectomy (69905–69910) may be performed. An incision is made in the posterior canal skin and the skin flap and posterior eardrum are reflected forward. Under microscopic visualization, the incus and stapes are removed. A right angle hook is fed through the oval window to remove the contents of the vestibule. The surgeon may drill a connection between the oval and round window. The middle ear is packed and the eardrum and canal skin are repositioned, and the ear canal is packed. This procedure may be performed with a mastoidectomy 69910.

A vestibular nerve section is performed when a patient is diagnosed with acute mastoiditis accompanied with other complications or vestibular neuronitis (a benign disorder characterized by sudden onset of severe vertigo that can last seven to 10 days). In a vestibular nerve section, using a translabyrinth approach, the surgeon drills out the mastoid cavity, removes the semicircular canals, and then removes the bone over the internal auditory canal. The dura is opened and the vestibular nerve is cut. The dura is closed and the mastoid cavity is packed. Code 69915 reports a vestibular nerve section by translabyrinth approach. For a transcranial approach use 69950.

A cochlear implant is an electronic device that is implanted under the skin and is used to treat sensory deafness. Electrodes in the middle ear assist in the creation of sound sensation for a patient who has this device implanted. The first cochlear implant procedure was performed in 1978 in Australia. Code 69930 reports cochlear device implantation, with or without a mastoidectomy.

Temporal Bone, Middle Fossa Approach

This subheading describes the middle fossa approach to the temporal bone and includes primary procedures and an unlisted code for other procedures. The temporal bones form the sides and part of the base of the skull. They are among the hardest of all bones, and enclose the organs of the hearing and balance systems. The middle fossa approach provides surgical access to lesions of the geniculate ganglion and the labyrinthine portion of the facial nerve as well as to the internal acoustic canal, and helps preserve cochlear function.

Bell's palsy is a unilateral facial paralysis resulting from dysfunction of the facial nerve (cranial nerve VII). If no specific cause such as brain tumor or stroke is identified, the condition is known as Bell's palsy. A patient diagnosed with Bell's palsy shows symptoms of weakness to an entire half of the face. The extent of nerve damage determines patient

outcome. A total nerve decompression and repair are common surgical procedures to repair facial nerve damage. Several approaches are used via temporal bone, mastoid approach, or through the external auditory canal. If the nerve has been transected because of trauma, it can be repaired with sutures.

Code 69955 reports a total facial nerve decompression and/or repair. This code includes a graft. Code 69970 is reported when the surgeon, through a middle cranial fossa approach, removes a temporal bone tumor.

The Medicine Section—Special Otorhinolaryngologic Services (92502–92700)

CPT® codes described in the Special Otorhinolaryngologic subsection of CPT® describe diagnostic and treatment services not included in an evaluation and management service (99201–99214, 99241–99245).

Aural rehabilitation is auditory training or therapy provided by the physician or the clinically trained staff member. It includes speech, language, and/or hearing loss, and physical and mental development. Once an assessment is made, the physician provides the patient with a plan that may involve speech therapy and/or hearing aids, etc.

Code 92512 reports nasal function studies (eg, rhinomanometry). This study is used to evaluate the normal and abnormal function of the nose. The rhinomanometer measures the flow and pressure of air through the nose to assess the degree of obstruction, if any. This test can be performed by anterior or posterior measurements.

Vestibular Function Tests (92531–92548)

Vestibular function tests evaluate conditions such as vertigo (92531–92534). Vertigo is an abnormal sensation of rotary movement associated with difficulty in balance, gait, and navigation of the environment. Lesions (disturbances in the inner ear), in the 8th cranial nerve or vestibular nuclei and their pathways in the brainstem and cerebellum can cause vertigo. Often the physician will perform clinical evaluations of the vestibular apparatus. Evaluation by the physician includes tests such as rapidly alternating movement (eg, finger-to-finger, heel-to-shin test, gait testing).

Other vestibular function tests begin by artificial stimulation of the vestibular apparatus to produce nystagmus. Nystagmus is the involuntary rhythmic oscillation of the eyeball and could be a clinical manifestation of diseases such as multiple sclerosis or an Arnold-Chiari malformation (downward displacement of the cerebellar tonsils through the foramen magnum, the opening at the base of the skull). Nystagmus is the most useful response that can be monitored by clinician observation or more reliably, by electronystagmography. CPT® codes for the evaluation of nystagmus include code 92531 for spontaneous nystagmus including gaze, and code 92532 for positional nystagmus. When these procedures are performed with recording codes 92541 and 92542 are reported.

Optokinetic nystagmus (92534) is described as a slow pursuit of moving stripes that are interrupted involuntarily by fast saccades in the opposite direction. Caloric vestibular tests are performed to validate a diagnosis of asymmetric function in the peripheral vestibular system. 92537, Caloric vestibular test with recording when performed bilaterally, one cool and one warm in each ear for a total of four irrigations. 92538, Caloric vestibular test with recording when performed monothermal is used for one irrigation in each ear (total of two irrigations).

Audiologic Function Tests (92550–92597)

This subheading of CPT® relates to services performed by a physician or audiology technician to diagnose the cause of hearing loss. The audiometric testing listed implies the use of calibrated electronic equipment. When using these codes, the physician and coder are indicating that the services were performed on both ears, unless the use of a modifier 52 indicates otherwise.

When a physician or audiology technician is performing a screening test for pure tones, air only, the patient responds to different pitches and intensities of tones. It is a limited test. If the patient fails to respond appropriately, additional testing is recommended.

Speech audiometry (92555, 92556) is a valuable clinical measurement of hearing. This type of audiometry tests the ability of the patient to discriminate various speech sounds.

A visual reinforcement audiometry (VRA) test (92579) is usually performed on infants and/or difficult to test children and adults. This type of testing addresses the type and severity of hearing loss. The service includes a history and otologic exam (conducted in a sound booth). Lighted toys are used for children as reinforcement for response to auditory stimuli.

Codes for testing evoked otoacoustic emissions—92587 and 92588—report a non-invasive audiologic function test used to identify hearing defects in newborns and young children. The physician places a probe tip in the ear canal. This probe emits a clicking sound that passes through the tympanic membrane, middle ear, and then to the inner ear where the sound is identified by cochlear hair cells. The computer records the echo transmitted from the hair cells.

Evaluative and \Therapeutic Services (92601–92633)

Codes 92601–92604 report the diagnostic analysis of cochlear implants for patients in two age ranges (under seven years of

age in codes 92601 and 92602; and age seven years and up in codes 92603 and 92604).

Codes 92610 and 92611 report evaluation of oral and pharyngeal swallowing function and motion fluoroscopic evaluation of swallowing function by cine or video recording, respectively. Code 92597 reports an evaluation for the use and/or fitting of a voice prosthetic device to supplement oral speech.

Speech generating devices (SGD) are speech aids that provide functional speaking abilities to individuals with severe speech impairment. Digitized speech, sometimes referred to as devices with whole message speech output, utilize words or phrases that have been recorded by an individual other than the SGD user for playback upon command of the SGD user. Synthesized speech translates a user's input into device generated speech using algorithms representing linguistic rules. Users of synthesized speech SGDs are not limited to prerecorded messages and they can independently create messages as their communication needs dictate.

A flexible fiberoptic endoscope is used in codes 92612–92617 to evaluate swallowing by cine or video recording and to report laryngeal sensory testing by cine or video recording. The codes include technical and professional components. Flexible endoscopic evaluation of swallowing with sensory testing provides an assessment of hypopharyngeal sensitivity, which gives clinicians information regarding a patient's ability to protect the airway during the ingestion of food and provides evidence regarding the patient's control of secretions. A patient's laryngopharyngeal sensory capacity can be tested using endoscopically administered air pulse stimuli to the mucosa of the larynx innervated by the superior laryngeal nerve.

Two codes describe central auditory function testing services using both speech and nonspeech stimuli to allow reporting multiple individual tests performed during a clinical visit. Code 92620 reports the initial 60 minutes of tests performed and code 92621 reports each additional 15-minute increment. The time may be spent in evaluation with a single test performed repeatedly or for a battery of multiple tests performed during a single encounter. These codes are not to be reported in conjunction with 92521, 92522, 92523, or 92524. To report evaluation of speech fluency, speech sound production and evaluation of language comprehension and expression assign 92521, 92522, 92523 or 92524 as appropriate. Code 92507 and its companion code 92508 report the treatment of speech, language, voice, communication and/or auditory processing disorders; code 92507 reports individual treatment and code 92508 reports group treatment. Code 92625 reports tinnitus assessment to include pitch, loudness matching, and masking.

Section Review 15.3

1. The patient is complaining of severe corneal pain and believes a wood chip entered his eye. He was working in his wood-working shop without goggles this morning. After placing two drops of proparacaine 0.5% in the right eye, I administered fluorescein and examined the cornea under ultraviolet light using a slit lamp. Seidel sign negative for penetrating injury. A small piece of wood was identified under a flap of lamellar cornea, and I was able to dislodge the wood and flush it from the eye. A single suture was placed to secure the flap.

    What CPT® code is reported for this procedure?

    A. 65270

    B. 65275

    C. 65280

    D. 65285

2. The 55-year-old patient presents with 1 cm lesion in his right ear canal posterior to the tragus. The lesion is red and raised, typical of basal cell carcinoma. After administration of lidocaine, I performed a shave biopsy. Electrocautery was required to control bleeding. The tissue sample was sent to pathology. What CPT® code is reported for this procedure?

    A. 69100

    B. 69105

    C. 11301

    D. 11100

3. Today we excised bilateral recurrent pterygium under topical anesthetic. The conjunctival incisions were repaired simply. What CPT® code is reported for this procedure?

    A. 65420-50

    B. 65426-50

    C. 68110-50

    D. 68115-50

4. The patient underwent a plastic repair of the external auditory canal for stenosis, a late effect of a burn. After excising the subepithelial stenotic tissue and a wedge of skin from the floor of the external auditory canal, a rubber tube was placed inside the external canal. The patient will return in two weeks to monitor his progress. What CPT® code is reported for this procedure?

    A. 69433

    B. 69799

    C. 69310

    D. 69140

5. The patient has hypertropia in her right eye with prior operations and today we are performing a recession of the superior oblique muscle to balance this muscle and eliminate strabismus. Adjustable sutures are applied. She is pseudophakic. What CPT® codes are reported for this procedure?

    A. 67318, 67335-51

    B. 67314, 67335, 67331

    C. 67318, 67331, 67335

    D. 67314, 67335, 67320

6. The patient with severe mixed hearing loss from chronic otitis media undergoes a round window implant with floating mass transducer. What CPT® code is reported for this procedure?

    A. 69799

    B. 69667

    C. 69714

    D. 69710

7. The patient has an oversized and embedded dacryolith in the lacrimal sac, and a dacryocystectomy is performed. What CPT® code(s) is/are reported for this procedure?

    A. 68500

    B. 68420

    C. 68520

    D. 68520, 68420-51

8. The patient underwent mastoidotomy for ossicular chain reconstruction with tympanic membrane repair, atticotomy, and partial ossicular replacement prosthesis. What CPT® code is reported for this procedure?

    A. 69632

    B. 69635

    C. 69636

    D. 69637

9. What code is used to report surgery to remove an aqueous shunt from the patient's eye?

    A. 65265

    B. 65920

    C. 67120

    D. 67121

10. The ophthalmologist performs a review of history, external exam, ophthalmoscopy, biomicroscopy and tonometry on an established patient with a new cataract. What CPT® code is reported for this procedure?

    A. 99212

    B. 92002

    C. 92012

    D. 99202

HCPCS Level II

HCPCS Level II codes report the supply of injectable or implantable drugs used in the treatment of ear and eye disorders, as well as supply of prostheses, visual aids, contact lenses, glasses, and hearing aids. Glaucoma screening codes for ophthalmologists or optometrists participating in the Physician Quality Reporting System (PQRS) are found in the temporary G codes (G0117 and G0118). Many of the pros-thetics and DME reported through HCPCS Level II are no longer distributed by physicians. Instead, they write prescriptions for these items. The most important codes to consider as you study the HCPCS Level II codes for ophthalmic and ENT procedures are the supply of drugs for injections. The Table of Drugs and Biologicals in your HCPCS Level II codebook will list these alphabetically, so they are easy to locate. Always confirm your code choice in the Tabular Section of your HCPCS Level II codebook.

Modifiers

Eye and Ear specialists use many of the same modifiers as other physicians. There are some modifiers, however, that take on significant importance for them. Because the eyes and ears are bilateral organs, identifying a procedure as bilateral (50) or identifying laterality (RT and LT) becomes very important to payment processes. Insurance typically won't cover the removal of a cataract more than once per eye; if the payer does not know which eye was treated, it will not know which one is left to treat.

Another issue for payers is whether the patient has his own lens (phakic), an artificial lens (pseudophakic) or no lens (aphakic). Aphakic patients may be eligible for benefits not available to others.

50	Bilateral procedure
E1	Upper left eyelid
E2	Lower left eyelid
E3	Upper right eyelid
E4	Lower right eyelid
LS	FDA—monitored IOL implant
LT	Left
PL	Progressive addition lenses
RT	Right

Documentation Dissection

Case 1

Preoperative Diagnosis: Left lower eyelid basal cell carcinoma

Postoperative Diagnosis: Same

Operation: Excision of left lower eyelid basal cell carcinoma with flaps and full thickness skin graft and tarsorrhaphy.

Indication for Surgery: The patient is a very pleasant female who complains of a one year history of a left lower eyelid lesion and this was recently biopsied and found to be basal cell carcinoma. She was advised that she would benefit from a complete excision of the left lower eyelid lesion. She is aware of the risks of residual tumor, infection, bleeding, scarring and possible need for further surgery. All questions have been answered prior to the day of surgery. She consents to the surgery.

Operative Procedure:
The patient was placed on the operating room table in the supine position and an intravenous line was established by hospital staff prior to sedation and analgesia. Throughout the entire case the patient received monitored anesthesia care. The patient's entire face was prepped and draped in the usual sterile fashion with a Betadine solution and topical tetracaine and corneal protective shields were placed over both corneas. A surgical marking pen was used to mark the tumor. 3 mm markings were obtained around the tumor. [1] The tumor was noted to encompass approximately 1/3 of the left lower eyelid. [2] A wedge resection was performed and this was marked and 2 % Xylocaine with 1:100,000 epinephrine, 0.5 % Marcaine with 1:100,000 epinephrine was infiltrated around the lesion. This was excised with a #15 blade. This was sent for intraoperative fresh frozen sections. Intraoperative fresh frozen sections revealed persistent basal cell carcinoma at the medial margin. Another 2 mm of margin [3] was discarded and a revised left lower eyelid medial margin was sent for permanent sections. The area could not be closed primarily thus a tarsoconjunctival advancement flap was advanced from the left upper eyelid to fill the defect. [4] This was sutured in place with multiple 5-0 Vicryl sutures. The anterior lamella defect of skin was closed by harvesting a full-thickness skin graft from the left upper eyelid and placing it in the left lower eyelid defect. [5] This was sutured in place with multiple interrupted 5-0 chromic gut sutures. The eyelids were sutured shut both on the medial aspect of the Hughes flap as well as the lateral aspect of the Hughes flap with a 4-0 silk suture. [6] A pressure dressing and TobraDex ointment were applied. The patient tolerated the procedure well and was transported back to the recovery area in excellent condition.

----

[1] 3 mm margin is excised in addition to the lesion.

[2] The size of the lesion is 1/3 of the left lower eyelid.

[3] An additional 2 mm is excised.

|4| A flap is used to close the defect.

|5| A FTSK from the upper eyelid is used to repair the defect of the lower eyelid.

|6| A tarsorrhaphy is performed.

_____

What are the CPT® and ICD-9-CM codes reported?

CPT® Codes: 15260, 67966-51-E2, 67971-51-E2, 67875-51-E2

ICD-10-CM Code: C44.119

Rationale: In this case an excision of a basal cell carcinoma is performed. More than 1/3 of the lower eyelid is excised. A full thickness graft, as well as a flap (adjacent tissue transfer), is required for the closures. From the CPT® Index, look up Excision/Lesion/Eyelid. Refer to the codes referenced in the Index. Under code 67840 there is a parenthetical note that states, "For excision and repair of eyelid by reconstructive surgery, *See* 67961, 67966."

Code 67961 is an excision and repair of the eyelid including preparation for skin graft or flap with adjacent tissue transfer or rearrangement involving up to one-fourth of the lid margin. In this case the excision is larger. Code 67966 reports the excision and reconstruction with a flap or an excision over one-fourth of the lid margin, which is one of the correct codes for this case.

From the CPT® Index, look up Reconstruction/Eyelid/Tarsoconjunctival Flap Transfer 67971. Also performed is a full-thickness skin graft from the left upper eyelid which was placed on the left lower eyelid defect. Skin grafts are always reported according to the recipient site. Look in the CPT® Index for Skin Graft and Flap/Free Skin Graft/Full Thickness 15200–15261. The size is not reported, so 15260 is assigned. A tarsorrhaphy (eyelids sewn shut) is performed. Look in the CPT® Index for Tarsorrhaphy 67875. Review the code descriptions for accuracy.

When multiple procedures are performed, they are sequenced in order from the most labor intensive (highest RVUs) to the lowest. In this case, the proper sequence is 15260, 67966, 67971, and 67875. The procedures are performed on the left lower eyelid which is reported with modifier E2. When multiple procedures are performed, modifier 51 is appended to the procedure codes (except for add-on codes and modifier 51 exempt codes) that are listed after the first-listed CPT® code.

To determine diagnosis code, look in the ICD-10-CM Index to Diseases and Injuries for Carcinoma/basal cell. You are directed to see Neoplasm, skin, malignant. Look in the Neoplasm Table for Neoplasm, neoplastic/skin/eyelid/basal cell carcinoma and use the code from the Malignant column, C44.11x. Sixth character 9 specifies the left eyelid.

ICD-9-CM Application

What is/are the ICD-9-CM code(s) reported?

Code(s): 173.11

Rationale: Look in the ICD-9-CM Index to Diseases for Carcinoma/basal cell. There is guidance to *see also* Neoplasm, skin, malignant. Look for Neoplasm, neoplastic/skin NOS/eyelid/basal cell carcinoma/Malignant/ Primary. You are referred to 173.11. Refer to the Tabular List to verify the code accuracy.

    AAPC   www.aapc.com   *493*

Case 2

Preoperative Procedure: Chronic otitis media with effusion

Postoperative Procedure: Chronic otitis media with effusion

Indications: The 23-month-old child status post tubes one year ago. The tubes have extruded and his problem has returned. Therefore, the above procedure was planned. Prior to the procedure, all of the risks vs. benefits were discussed at length with the patient's mother. An informed consent was obtained.

Findings: Dull membranes bilaterally with serous fluid.

Procedure in Detail: After appropriate written consent was obtained from the patient's parents he was taken to the operating room, placed supine on the operating stretcher. General anesthesia [1] was given by mask. Once an adequate depth of anesthesia had been achieved, the right ear was examined with an operating microscope. [2] The tympanic membrane was noted to be retracted and dull. A tube was noted in the external auditory canal which was removed with an alligator forceps. [3] A small radial incision was made on the tympanic membrane [4] and the serous fluid was suctioned from the middle ear. A Paparella style tube was placed. [5] Saline drips were applied.

Attention was then turned to the left ear. [6] Again, the tympanic membrane was noted to be retracted and dull. A small radial incision was made. [7] A small amount of serous fluid was suctioned from the middle ear and a Paparella style tube was placed. [8] Saline drops were applied. The patient was then awakened and taken to the recovery area in stable condition. Estimated blood loss was less than 5cc. He tolerated the procedure well without complications.

----

[1] General anesthesia is used.

[2] The right ear is examined using the operating microscope.

[3] The previously placed tube in the external auditory canal is removed.

[4] An incision is made into the tympanic membrane.

[5] The ventilating tube is placed in the incision made in the right ear.

[6] The procedure is now performed on the left ear.

[7] An incision is made into the left tympanic membrane.

[8] A ventilating tube is inserted in the incision that was made in the left ear.

What are the CPT® and ICD-10-CM codes reported?

CPT® Code: 69436-50

ICD-9-CM Code: H65.23

Rationale: In this case, a tympanostomy is performed using ventilating tubes. The patient had this procedure performed previously. The previously placed tube has fallen into the external auditory canal. A ventilating tube (Paparella style) is inserted in both the left and right ears using the same surgical technique.

Look in the CPT® Index for Tympanostomy/General Anesthesia 69436. General anesthesia is used, which makes 69436 the correct code. The procedure is performed on both the left and right ear, which requires appending modifier 50.

To locate the code for the removal of the ventilating tube in the right ear, turn to Removal/Tube/Ear, Middle in the CPT® Index. You are referred to 69424. The code description matches the procedure performed but there is a parenthetical note following this code that states, "Do not report 69424 in conjunction with 69205, 69210, 69420, 69421, 69433–69676, 69710–69745, 69801-69930." Code 69436 is in the range of codes. For this scenario, only code for the tympanostomy with insertion of the ventilating tubes. The removal is included and not reported separately.

Next we need to determine the ICD-10-CM code.

The operative note indicated there is serous fluid bilaterally (both ears) and both tympanic membranes are dull, but intact, so there is no rupture of the tympanic membrane. Look in the ICD-10-CM Index to Diseases and Injuries for Otitis/media (hemorrhagic) (staphylococcal) (streptococcal)/chronic/with effusion (nonpurulent). You are directed to *see* Otitis, media, nonsuppurative. Look for Otitis/media/nonsuppurative/chronic /serous which directs you to H65.2-. Sixth character 3 specifies the condition is bilateral. The finding indicate that serous fluid was found.

ICD-9-CM Application

What is/are the ICD-9-CM code(s) reported?

Code(s): 381.3

Rationale: The indication for the surgery is chronic otitis media with effusion. This means the patient has fluid in the middle ear that cannot drain. In ICD-9-CM the diagnosis is supported by the information in the description of the procedure. The note states "serous fluid was suctioned" in each ear. To locate the diagnosis code, look in the ICD-9-CM Index to Diseases for Otitis/media/chronic/with effusion. You are referred to 381.3. Verify the code description is the Tabular List.

Glossary

Acoustic Neuroma—Also called a vestibular schwannoma; a benign tumor arising from nerve cells of the auditory nerve.

After-Cataract—When a cataract is removed from the eye, the physician opts to retain the posterior outermost shell so there remains an organic separation between the posterior and anterior chambers. Later, this remaining shell may develop opacities as well, and this is called after-cataract or secondary cataract.

Anterior Segment—The cornea up to the vitreous body which includes the aqueous humor, iris, and lens.

Aqueous Humor—A clear, salty fluid filling the area behind the cornea and up to the lens. Aqueous humor fills the anterior chamber (between back of cornea and the iris) and posterior chamber (peripheral part of the iris to the lens) of the eye.

Blepharoplasty—Surgical repair of the eyelid.

Cataract—Flaws or clouding that develop in the crystalline lens.

Cerumen—Ear wax.

Cholesteatoma—A benign growth of skin in the middle ear, usually caused by chronic otitis media.

Choroid—The middle vascular layer between the retina and the sclera in the posterior segment of the eye. The choroid nourishes the retina.

Ciliary Body—A thickened layer of the vascular tunic which contains the muscle that controls the shape of the lens.

Cochlea—An inner ear structure that looks like a snail shell. It is divided into two canals and the organ of Corti.

Conduction—Receptions or conveyance of sound, heat, or electricity. Sound waves are conducted to the inner ear through bones in the skull.

Conjunctiva—A thin protective layer lining the eyelid and covering the sclera.

Cornea—The bay window of the eye. The cornea has five layers, and they act to refract the light entering the eye.

Crystalline Lens—A convex disc suspended on threads just behind the iris.

Dacryolith—Calculus in the lacrimal sac or duct.

Endolymph—Fluid within the semicircular canals and the tubes of the cochlea of the inner ear.

Enucleation—Removal of a structure such as the eyeball.

Esotropia—A condition where the eye deviates inward.

Eustachian Tube—A tube in the ear linking the middle ear to the nasopharynx. This tube equalizes pressure between the middle ear and the outer world.

Evisceration—A procedure where the contents of the eyeball are scooped out but the sclera shell remains connected to the eye muscles so that a prosthesis fitted into the globe will have natural movement.

Exenteration—Removal of a complete structure and the surrounding skin, fat, muscle, and bone.

External Auditory Meatus—Pathway from the pinna (outer ear) to the tympanic membrane.

Exotropia—A condition where the eye deviates outward.

Glaucoma—A hypertensive condition of the eye caused by too much pressure from fluid.

Goniotomy—A procedure where an opening is made in the trabecular meshwork of the front part of the eye. The provider uses a goniolens during the procedure.

Hypertropia—A condition where the eye deviates upward.

Incus—A tiny bone (ossicle) in the middle ear.

Iris—A muscular ring around the pupil regulating the amount of light that enters the pupil. Also known as our source of eye color.

Limbus—The border where the cornea meets the sclera. Also known as the sclerocorneal junction.

Malleus—A tiny bone (ossicle) in the middle ear that picks up vibration from the tympanic membrane.

Mastoid—A bone in the skull just behind the ear containing tiny air cells that also form a conductive path for sound.

Mastoiditis—Inflammation or infection of the mastoid bone.

Mèniére's Disease—The most common form of peripheral vertigo, accompanied by hearing loss and tinnitus. The cause is unknown, although the symptoms may be caused by an increase in fluid pressure in the inner ear.

Microtia—A congenital deformity of the ear whereby the pinna (external ear) is underdeveloped.

Nystagmus—Reflexive jerky eye movements as a response to the messages of the inner ear.

Optic Nerve—The nerve that transmits images from the eye to the brain. Damage to the optic nerve can result is loss of or impaired vision.

Ossicles—Three tiny bones in the middle ear; malleus, incus, and stapes.

Otitis Media—Middle ear infection.

Oval Window—A membrane covered window from the inner ear to the middle ear.

Perilymph—Surrounds the semicircular canals, utricle, and saccule of the vestibular system, and it surrounds the ducts in the cochlea. Inner channels are filled with endolymph.

Puncta—Tiny openings of the tear ducts.

Pupil—The opening of the center of the eye where light enters.

Refraction—Bending and focusing of light rays into a sharp image.

Retina—Layer of tissue in the back of the eye that is light sensitive.

Retinal Detachment—The retina is freed from the blood-rich choroid at the back of the eye. When the retinal layer floats away, it loses its supply of nutrients. Nutrients must return or vision is lost.

Retrobulbar—Space behind the eye.

Round Window—A membrane-covered window that separates the middle ear from the inner ear, allowing vibrations to pass through to the cochlea.

Sclera—The white outer skin of the eye, and is covered with a thin protective layer of conjunctiva.

Sclerocorneal Junction—The ring where the cornea meets the sclera. Also known as the limbus.

Secondary Cataract—*See* after-cataract.

Semicircular Canals—Three tiny tubes in the inner ear filled with fluid (endolymph) to assist in balance.

Stapes—Tiny stirrup-shaped bone (ossicle) in the middle ear.

Strabismus—A condition where the eyes are not properly aligned with each other.

Tenon's Capsule—Connective tissue surrounding the posterior eyeball.

Trachoma—Bacterial infection of the eyes.

Tympanic Membrane—Thin, delicate tissue separating the outer ear from the middle ear. The tympanic membrane is part of the inner ear.

Uvea—The area beneath the sclera where the iris, choroid, and ciliary body meet.

Vestibular Schwannoma—A benign tumor arising from nerve cells of the auditory nerve (8th cranial nerve), also known as an acoustic neuroma.

Vestibule—Inner part of the ear connecting the semicircular canals and the cochlea. The vestibule contains the sense organs responsible for balance.

Vertigo—A whirling or spinning perception of motion resulting in the loss of balance.

Visual Field—The total area that can be seen by peripheral vision.

Vitreous Humor—A gel-like mass that fills the large posterior segment of the eye.

Introduction

This chapter includes information necessary to understand correct anesthesia coding. Anesthesia codes take up only a few pages in CPT®, but coding guidelines for anesthesia services are unique. Note also, anesthesia providers are not limited strictly to reporting anesthesia codes 00100–01999. The objectives for this chapter are:

- Understand anesthesia coding guidelines
- Define key terms related to anesthesia
- Understand how anatomy applies to anesthesia coding
- Recognize acronyms for anesthesia coding
- Identify when other services may be billed in conjunction with anesthesia
- Distinguish between anesthesia services and moderate sedation
- Know which HCPCS Level II modifiers are appropriate

Anatomy and Medical Terminology

This section concentrates on terminology related to anesthesia and the difficult areas of anesthesia code selection. After learning basic concepts for assigning an anesthesia code anatomically and by description, we will add more difficult concepts in the CPT® section.

Anesthesia codes are grouped anatomically, beginning with the head. Because anesthesia codes are reported as related to the surgical service provided, coders must be knowledgeable in anatomical terminology from many different specialties.

Selecting an anesthesia code follows the same basic steps as assigning procedure codes for other specialties. Coders either will use the Index under Anesthesia, in the back of the CPT® codebook to locate the correct anatomic area, or turn to the blue edged "Anesthesia 00100" pages with an index page at the beginning of the section and look under the appropriate anatomic heading.

Example

To look up the code for a thyroid biopsy, you can look in the Index or in the tabular section of the CPT® codebook.

1. In the Index

- Anesthesia

    Biopsy

        Ear   00120

        Liver   00702

        Salivary Glands 00100

The code we are looking for is not found under Anesthesia/Biopsy. If the anesthesia code is not found under the procedure, next you look for the anatomic structure.

- Anesthesia

    Thyroid   00320–00322

Refer to the code range in the tabular section to determine which code is correct.

2. In the tabular section

After reviewing 00320–00322, we find we need to determine how the biopsy is obtained. If a needle biopsy is performed, report 00322. If another method was used, report 00320.

The following sections show the breakdown of anatomic anesthesia code assignments:

Head
00100 through 00222

Neck
00300 through 00352

Thorax (Chest Wall and Shoulder Girdle)
00400 through 00474

Intrathoracic
00500 through 00580

Spine and Spinal Cord
00600 through 00670

Upper Abdomen
00700 through 00797

Lower Abdomen
00800 through 00882

Perineum
00902 through 00952

Pelvis (Except Hip)
01112 through 01190

Upper Leg (Except Knee)
01200 through 01274

Knee and Popliteal Area
01320 through 01444

Lower Leg (Below Knee, Includes Ankle and Foot)
01462 through 01522

Shoulder and Axilla
01610 through 01682

Upper Arm and Elbow
01710 through 01782

Forearm, Wrist, and Hand
01810 through 01860

Radiological Procedures
01916 through 01936

Burn Excisions or Debridement
01951 through 01953

Obstetric
01958 through 01969

Other Procedures
01990 through 01999

As with any other specialty, care must be taken to review the exact wording of each code—including any pertinent comments and exclusions, for example, "Pelvis (Except Hip)." Some exclusions must be taken literally; for instance, the hip codes are found under the "Upper Leg" section. Other exclusions may be taken more liberally. As an example, 00103 describes reconstructive procedures of the eyelid and gives examples (eg, blepharoplasty, ptosis surgery) of reconstructive surgery; however, this code may be assigned even if the procedure is not specified in the code descriptor.

Pay close attention to anesthesia codes not reported together or comments sending coders to another section. Parenthetic instructions give you guidance for these circumstances.

Example

Parenthetical instruction for codes not reported together:

00834 *Anesthesia for hernia repairs in the lower abdomen not otherwise specified, younger than 1 year of age* includes the descriptor "younger than 1 year of age." It is not appropriate to report code +99100 *Anesthesia for patient of extreme age, younger than 1 year and older than 70 (List separately in addition to code for primary anesthesia procedure)*, which is an age related code, in addition to 00834.

Parenthetical instruction referring to another section:

00796 *Anesthesia for intraperitoneal procedures in upper abdomen including laparoscopy; liver transplant (recipient)*. The parenthetical instruction states "(For harvesting of liver, use 01990)." Although the liver is located in the upper abdomen, the harvesting of liver is reported with code 01990, which is listed under "Other procedures" as *Physiological support for harvesting of organ(s) from a brain-dead patient*.

Parenthetical reminders and/or comments are located under each related code.

Practical Coding Note

Highlight or underline all references to age within the description of the anesthesia code:

00834 Anesthesia for hernia repairs in the lower abdomen not otherwise specified, younger than 1 year of age.

Anesthesia for the integumentary (skin) system is generalized under either 00300 or 00400, depending on the anatomic location. Code 00300 includes muscles and nerves of the head and neck. However, other nerve and muscle codes may be found anatomically, as with the knee (01320 *Anesthesia for all procedures on nerves, muscles, tendons, fascia, and bursae of knee and/or popliteal area*) or wrist (01810 *Anesthesia for all procedures on nerves, muscles, tendons, fascia, and bursae of forearm, wrist, and hand*).

Many of the anesthesia codes indicate, "not otherwise specified." This allows the code to be reported for the anatomic area, unless a more specific code exists. For example, code 00920 describes anesthesia for procedures on male genitalia (including open urethral procedures); not otherwise specified. Although a bilateral vasectomy involves the male genitalia, a code exists to report it separately as 00921—this code takes precedence as it is a specified anesthesia code.

Until the new anesthesia coder becomes familiar with anatomical codes, it is best to use the index found in the back of the book, and look for the term Anesthesia, to begin learning. Keep in mind codes are not always found under the surgical description and the coder may need to default backward to find the most accurate description.

Example

The code ranges for anesthesia for a simple mastectomy are not listed under mastectomy, but rather under breast. The codes range from 00402–00406; the coder should not assign a code until he or she has reviewed the suggested code range in the blue tab section. When reviewing the suggested codes listed under the Thorax (which includes the chest wall and shoulder girdle), 00402, 00404, and 00406 describe reconstructive procedures or radical/modified radical procedures—they do not accurately describe a simple mastectomy. The coder defaults to 00400 *Anesthesia for procedures on the integumentary system on the extremities, anterior trunk and perineum; not otherwise specified* to assign the anesthesia code for a simple mastectomy.

Practical Coding Note

Add "Mastectomy" in the index as a subentry under Anesthesia. Make a note to "see Anesthesia, Breast."

> Anesthesia
>
> > Mastectomy…*see* Anesthesia, Breast.

Anesthesia "crosswalk" books are available to assist coders by "crosswalking" the known surgical code to an appropriate anesthesia code. All anesthesia codes are assigned a base unit value (BUV), which is discussed later in the chapter. When more than one code is suggested by the crosswalk, the coder must determine the code based on the code description most accurately describing the service performed. It is also important to remember, publications may contain unintentional cross-walking errors. Always read the full description of the code you are referred to by the index or a crosswalk to make sure it accurately reports the anesthesia service provided and documented.

Although the large majority of anesthesia codes may be assigned to specific coding areas, there is a default code—found under the "Other Procedures" section—to report unlisted anesthesia services (01999 *Unlisted anesthesia procedure(s)*).

Types of Anesthesia

There are three different types of anesthesia: General, Regional, and Monitored Anesthesia Care (MAC):

General Anesthesia—A drug-induced loss of consciousness

Regional Anesthesia—A loss of sensation in a region of the body, such as:

- **Spinal Anesthesia**—An anesthetic agent is injected in the subarachnoid space into the cerebral spinal fluid (CSF) in the patient's spinal canal for surgeries performed below the upper abdomen.
- **Epidural Anesthesia**—An anesthetic agent is injected in the epidural space. A small catheter may be placed for a continuous epidural. An epidural can also remain in place after surgery to assist with postoperative pain.

- **Nerve Block**—An anesthetic agent is injected directly into the area around a nerve to block sensation for the region the surgery is being performed. Commonly used for procedures on the arms or legs.

Monitored Anesthesia Care (MAC)—Anesthesia service where the patient is under light sedation or no sedation while undergoing surgery with local anesthesia provided by the surgeon. The patient can respond to purposeful stimulation and can maintain his airway. The service is monitored by an anesthesia provider who is prepared at all times to convert MAC to general anesthesia if necessary.

Anesthesia Providers

The anesthesiologist is a physician licensed to practice medicine and has completed an accredited anesthesiology program. These physicians may personally perform, medically direct, or medically supervise members of an anesthesia care team.

A certified registered nurse anesthetist (CRNA) is a registered nurse who has completed an accredited nurse anesthesia-training program. The CRNA may be either medically directed by an anesthesiologist or non-medically directed.

An anesthesiologist assistant (AA) is a health professional who has completed an accredited Anesthesia Assistant training program. The AA may only be medically directed by an anesthesiologist.

An anesthesia resident is a physician who has completed his medical degree and is in a residency program specifically for anesthesiology training.

A student registered nurse anesthetist (SRNA) is a registered nurse who is training in an accredited nurse anesthesia program.

Anesthesia Coding Terminology

One-Lung Ventilation (OLV) is a term used in anesthesia related to thoracic surgery. OLV occurs when one lung is ventilated and the other lung is collapsed temporarily to improve surgical access to the lung. Several anesthesia codes separately identify utilization of one-lung ventilation.

Pump Oxygenator describes when a cardiopulmonary bypass (CPB) machine is used to function as the heart and lungs during heart or great vessel surgery. CPB maintains the circulation of blood and the oxygen content of the body. When a CPB machine is used, the anesthesia record should describe when the patient went on and off pump. When a pump oxygenator is not used, the surgeon is operating on a "beating" heart.

Practical Coding Note

Highlight the statement "with pump oxygenator" in anesthesia codes indicating the inclusion of pump oxygenator and "utilizing one lung ventilation" in anesthesia codes indicating the inclusion of OLV.

Examples:

00561 Anesthesia for procedures on heart, pericardial sac, and great vessels of chest; with pump oxygenator, younger than 1 year of age.

00529 Anesthesia for closed chest procedures; mediastinoscopy and diagnostic thoracoscopy utilizing one lung ventilation.

Intraperitoneal describes organs within the peritoneal cavity. These procedures may be performed in both the upper and lower abdomen. Correct anesthesia code assignment requires anatomical knowledge of the related organs. Intraperitoneal organs in the upper abdomen include the stomach, liver, gallbladder, spleen, jejunum, ascending, and transverse colon. Intraperitoneal organs in the lower abdomen include the appendix, cecum, ileum, and sigmoid colon.

Extraperitoneal or **Retroperitoneal** describes the anatomical space in the abdominal cavity behind or outside the peritoneum. Extraperitoneal organs in the lower abdomen include the ureters and urinary bladder. The kidneys, adrenal glands, and lower esophagus are extraperitoneal organs of the upper abdomen. Also located in the retroperitoneum are the aorta and inferior vena cava.

It is important for coders to understand it doesn't matter where trocars are placed for laparoscopic procedures; code assignment is dependent on the actual procedure being performed. For example, the operative report may indicate a trocar was placed in the upper abdomen. Remember that this statement is describing the approach for the procedure, not that an upper abdominal procedure was performed.

Radical surgery is usually extensive, complex, and intended to correct a severe health threat such as a rapidly growing cancer. For example, a radical hysterectomy involves the removal of the uterus, cervix, upper part of the vagina, and the tissues supporting the uterus and lymph nodes.

Diagnostic or **Surgical Arthroscopic** procedures may be performed on the temporomandibular joint, shoulder, elbow, wrist, hip, knee, and ankle. Coders should assign only a diagnostic code when no surgical procedure is performed. For example, if a knee arthroscopy is listed as "diagnostic" and a meniscectomy is performed, a surgical arthroscopic meniscectomy code is assigned.

Postoperative pain management is usually the responsibility of the surgeon, and payment is bundled into the surgeon's global fee. However, postoperative pain management may be requested by the surgeon and billed separately by anesthesia as long as the anesthesia for the surgical procedure is not dependent on the efficacy of the regional anesthetic technique. For example, if an epidural is the mode of anesthesia for the surgical procedure, the epidural cannot be reported for postoperative pain management.

Postoperative pain management coding depends on what is injected, the site of the injection and placement of either a single injection block or a continuous block by catheter. Pay close attention to whether it is a single injection or continuous infusion. The CPT® code reported is appended with modifier 59 *Distinct procedural services* to signify the service is separate and distinct from the anesthesia care provided for the surgery.

Codes obtained from the surgery and radiology section are flat-fee, and no time is reported separately. Only anesthesia codes are reported with time units; this will be described later in this chapter.

When ultrasound or fluoroscopic guidance is utilized for pain management procedures and appropriately documented, codes are reported separately with modifier 26 *Professional component* unless the code selected includes imaging guidance (fluoroscopy or CT).

Nerve block codes, for example 64415 (brachial plexus block), may be used as an adjunct to general anesthesia if placement is for postoperative pain management. Nerve block codes should not be reported separately if the block is the mode of anesthesia for a procedure being performed. For example, if a carpal tunnel procedure is performed with an axillary block, a code from the anesthesia section (01810 + related anesthesia time) is reported. No separate code is reported for the axillary block.

Practical Coding Note

Make a notation in the section for nerve blocks indicating the codes are not reported separately if the block is the mode of anesthesia for a procedure being performed.

Continuous catheter codes, for example 64448 *Injection, anesthetic agent; femoral nerve, continuous infusion by catheter (including catheter placement)*, are reported for continuous administration of anesthesia for postoperative pain management. If the infusion catheter is placed for operative anesthesia, the appropriate anesthesia code plus time is reported. If the continuous infusion catheter is placed for postoperative pain management, the daily postoperative management of the catheter is included in 64448. The note below 64448 states "Do not use 64448 in conjunction with 01996."

Code 01996 *Daily hospital management of epidural or subarachnoid continuous drug administration* is assigned for daily hospital management of epidural or subarachnoid continuous drug administration. Continuous infusion by catheter such as femoral (64448) or sciatic nerve (64446) is not an epidural catheter; 01996 is never reported with these codes. Anesthesiologists may report an appropriate E/M service to re-evaluate postoperative pain if documentation supports the level of service reported and billed.

Practical Coding Note

CPT® codes 64446–64449 each have a parenthetical statement stating not to report the code in conjunction with 01996. Turn to CPT® code 01996 and make a note indicating not to report in conjunction with CPT® codes 64446–64449.

Spinal anatomy is important to understand. The spinal column has seven cervical vertebrae, 12 thoracic vertebrae, five lumbar vertebrae and the sacrum. Cervical vertebrae (C1–C7) are immediately inferior to the skull. Thoracic vertebrae (T1–T12) are in the middle region, between the cervical and lumbar, with the ribs being supported from T1 through T10. Lumbar vertebrae (L1–L5) are located in the lower back. The lumbar region is where back pain most frequently occurs because this is where most of the body weight is carried. Sacral vertebrae (S1–S5) are fused together to form the sacrum. The sacrum fits between the hip bones connecting the spine to the pelvis. The top part connects with L5 and the bottom part connects with the coccyx.

Epidural is reported when the anesthetist or anesthesiologist injects anesthesia into the epidural space of the spine, including the cervical, thoracic, or lumbar area. Subarachnoid or spinal anesthesia is reported when anesthesia, opioids, or steroids are injected into the subarachnoid or cerebrospinal fluid (CSF) space. As with the nerve blocks, epidural/subarachnoid injection may be either a single injection or a continuous catheter. For example, a continuous infusion in the thoracic area is reported as 62318 *Injection(s), including indwelling catheter placement, continuous infusion or intermittent bolus, of diagnostic or therapeutic substance(s) (including anesthetic, antispasmodic, opioid, steroid, other solution), not including neurolytic substances, includes contrast for localization when performed, epidural or subarachnoid; cervical or thoracic.* When these techniques are used for postoperative pain management, the same rules apply.

When an epidural or subarachnoid catheter is placed for a laboring patient, the injection codes typically are not reported. CPT® codes to describe labor epidural/subarachnoid services are listed under the Obstetric section of the anesthesia codes.

Practical Coding Note

Make a note in your CPT® codebook, next to codes 62318-62319, to refer you to the OB Section of Anesthesia (01958–01969) to report catheter placement for a patient in labor.

Daily hospital management of continuous epidural or subarachnoid drug administration (01996) cannot be reported on the day of the epidural or subarachnoid catheter placement. It may be reported starting with the first postoperative day.

Section Review 16.1

1. Using your CPT® Index, look up Anesthesia for a diagnostic thoracoscopy. Which of the following is the correct anesthesia code?

    A. 00528

    B. 00529

    C. 00540

    D. 00541

---

2. Using your CPT® Index, look up Anesthesia for a modified radical mastectomy with internal mammary node dissection. Which of the following is the correct anesthesia code?

   A. 00400

   B. 00402

   C. 00404

   D. 00406

3. Using the main section of Anesthesia (blue tab) in your CPT®, look up Anesthesia for laparoscopic cholecystectomy. Which of the following is the correct anesthesia code?

   A. 00700

   B. 00790

   C. 00840

   D. 00860

4. Using your CPT® Index, look up Anesthesia for a diagnostic shoulder arthroscopy. Which of the following is the correct anesthesia code?

   A. 01622

   B. 01630

   C. 01634

   D. 01638

5. Report the appropriate anesthesia code(s) for a patient who had general anesthesia for a total shoulder replacement. At the surgeon's request, the anesthesiologist placed a brachial plexus continuous catheter for postoperative pain management. The day after surgery, the patient was seen by the anesthesiologist for follow-up care. What are the correct codes for this encounter?

   A. 01630, 64416 -59, 01996

   B. 01638, 64415-59

   C. 01638, 64415-59, 01996

   D. 01638, 64416-59

6. Report the appropriate anesthesia code(s) for an obstetric patient who had an epidural catheter placed for a normal delivery. The catheter was dislodged and was replaced before the patient delivered a healthy baby girl.

   A. 62319

   B. 01967

   C. 01967 x 2

   D. 01961

ICD-10-CM Coding

One of the first steps in selecting a diagnosis code is to determine the reason for the patient encounter. The majority of anesthesia services are provided to patients during surgery. An anesthesia provider usually reports fewer diagnosis codes than either the hospital or surgeon. Although the anesthesia provider completes a pre-anesthesia assessment to gather important information, including a medical history of the patient, the diagnoses listed on the pre-anesthesia assessment are not routinely reported. Supporting diagnosis codes may be reported if they are relevant to either substantiate medical necessity or support physical status modifiers, which will be discussed in the next section.

It is important for anesthesia coders to pay attention to "history of" codes. It is not appropriate coding to report a patient presenting for hernia repair surgery with a history of transient ischemic attack (TIA) as current symptoms. History codes are located within the Z codes, and rules regarding their use are listed in the ICD-10-CM Official Coding Guidelines under I.C.21.c.4. Coders have an important responsibility to code with a high level of accuracy because incorrectly reported diagnosis codes may result in claim rejection.

Example

History of polyps in the colon.

ICD-10-CM

In the ICD-10-CM Index to Diseases and Injuries look for History/ personal (of)/benign neoplasm/colonic polyps Z86.010.

Z86.010 Personal history of colonic polyps

ICD-9-CM Application

In ICD-9-CM the history codes are reported with V codes.

In the ICD-9-CM Index to Diseases look for History (personal) of/ digestive system disease/polyps, colonic V12.72.

V12.72 Diseases of the digestive system, Colonic polyps

For operative notes the postoperative diagnosis is coded because the preoperative diagnosis may change intra-operatively. For example, if a patient is admitted with pain in the right lower quadrant and subsequently has an appendectomy, the postoperative diagnosis may be acute appendicitis.

With the exception of the anesthesia-related information discussed, diagnosis codes for anesthesia are assigned in the same manner as any other diagnosis. These steps will help coders focus on quick and correct diagnosis code selection.

- Identify reason for anesthesia service
- Review for other pertinent information and supporting diagnosis codes
- Check Alphabetic Index and then check the code in the Tabular List
- Locate main entry term
- Pay attention to notes listed in main terms
- Understand coding conventions (See ICD-10-CM Official and Additional Conventions)
- Look for additional instructions in the tabular (numeric) section
- Make sure code is to highest level of specificity
- Assign pertinent related ICD-10-CM code(s)

Pain diagnosis codes are separately identified in the G89 section of the ICD-10-CM. Routine and expected postoperative pain should not be coded. When the provider is treating postoperative pain, a code from category G89 is selected based on whether the pain is documented as acute or chronic. When the pain is not stated as acute or chronic, the default is to code it as acute. When the underlying condition causing the pain is treated, the condition should be listed first and if appropriate a second code from G89 can be used. See guidelines I.C.6.b.

Example

A patient has surgery to treat a herniated disc causing chronic back pain. The coder selects a code for a herniated disc. A diagnosis for pain is not reported because the pain is a symptom of the herniated disc. However, if the anesthesia provider is asked to place an epidural for acute postoperative back pain in addition to the anesthesia for the surgery, the coder reports the diagnosis code for a herniated disc (M51.9) and acute postoperative pain (G89.18).

Section Review 16.2

1. Using your ICD-10-CM Index to Diseases and Injuries, look up the diagnosis code for a patient with a postoperative diagnosis of pancreatic mass. Which of the following is the correct diagnosis code?

    A. K86.8

    B. D01.7

    C. C25.9

    D. D37.8

2. Using your ICD-10-CM Index to Diseases and Injuries, look up the diagnosis code for a patient with a preoperative diagnosis of abdominal pain, right lower quadrant and a postoperative diagnosis of uterine fibroids. Which of the following is the correct diagnosis code?

    A. R10.9

    B. R10.31

    C. D26.9

    D. D25.9

3. A patient was scheduled for monitored anesthesia care (MAC) to remove an eyelid cyst. Normally the surgeon would provide moderate sedation for the removal; however, this patient has a history of failed moderate sedation. Select the correct diagnosis code(s).

    A. H02.829

    B. H02.829, T88.52XA

    C. H02.829, Z92.83

    D. Z92.83

4. A 74-year-old patient was scheduled for a total knee replacement due to degenerative joint disease (DJD) of his knee. The patient had surgery in 2012 for gastroesophageal reflux disease (GERD). Which of the following is/are the correct diagnosis code(s)?

    A. K21.9

    B. M25.462

    C. M17.9

    D. M17.9, K21.9

5. Which of the following is the correct diagnosis code to report a linear tibial closed fracture, proximal end, of the left leg, initial encounter?

    A. S82.191A

    B. S02.191B

    C. S82.102A

    D. S82.102B

CPT® Coding

CPT® Anesthesia Guidelines are found under the blue tab just before the Anesthesia section codes. Often these are the guidelines used by insurance companies to process claims for anesthesia services.

Services included with the base unit value of anesthesia codes reported are all usual preoperative and postoperative visits, anesthesia care during the procedure, administration of fluids and/or blood products during the surgery, and non-invasive monitoring (ECG, temperature, blood pressure, pulse oximetry, capnography and mass spectrometry). Unusual forms of monitoring—for example, arterial lines, central venous (CV) catheters and pulmonary artery catheters (eg, Swan Ganz)—are not included in the base unit value of the anesthesia code.

Base unit values are not separately listed in the CPT®. The American Society of Anesthesiologists (ASA) determines the base unit values for anesthesia codes. The ASA publishes a Relative Value Guide® including the base unit values assigned to each anesthesia code. This guide is not required for this course nor the CPC® certification exam.

Base unit values are determined by the difficulty of the procedure performed. For example, a temporal artery biopsy or ligation carries a lower base unit value than a procedure on major vessels of the neck. Specialty books specific to anesthesia coding contain base unit values for each anesthesia code. Medicare also publishes a list of base unit values available on its website under the Anesthesiologists Center.

Determining the base value is the first step in calculating anesthesia charges and payment expected. Time reporting is the second step.

Anesthesia time begins when the anesthesiologist begins to prepare the patient for anesthesia in either the operating room or an equivalent area. Pre-anesthesia assessment time is not part of reportable anesthesia time because it is considered in the base value assigned. Anesthesia time ends when the anesthesiologist is no longer in personal attendance. Ending time is generally reported when the patient is safely placed under postoperative supervision, usually in the Post Anesthesia Care Unit (PACU) or equivalent area.

Time does not need to be continuous. For example, an axillary block may be performed in a holding room, prior to surgery. If the axillary block is the mode of anesthesia, then the time for placement of that block is counted. The anesthesiologist may then leave, and when the patient is brought to the operating room, and the anesthesiologist again counts anesthesia time. The time for the block is then added to the total anesthesia time for the case. For example, If the axillary block time was 15 minutes, and the total anesthesia care for the surgery is one hour, then the total anesthesia time is 15 minutes (block

time) + 60 minutes (surgery anesthesia time) = 75 minutes total anesthesia time. Only the anesthesia code for the case is reported.

Practical Coding Note

In the Anesthesia Guidelines in the CPT® codebook, highlight the definition of anesthesia starting time in one color, and the definition for the anesthesia ending time in another color.

Time reporting on claims may vary, and there is no national guidance. Time units are added to the base unit value as is customary in the local area.

Medicare requires exact time reporting, without rounding to the nearest five minutes. For example, if anesthesia time starts at 11:02 and the patient is turned over to PACU at 11:59, the reported anesthesia time is 57 minutes. Medicare divides the 57 minutes by 15 minute increments for total value of 3.8 units. If the procedure has a base value of 6 units, adding 3.8 units for a total of 9.8 units, which is then multiplied by the Anesthesia Conversion Factor for the geographic location where the services are provided. Using the 2012 Anesthesia Conversion Factor assigned to Salt Lake City, Utah of $21.44, the total Medicare payment is $210.11 (9.8 x $21.44 = $210.11)

Other insurance companies may process the anesthesia time reported in increments varying from exact time (like Medicare), to 10, 12, or 15 minutes, or some other time increment.

For example, let's use a 10 minute time increment to convert to the time unit value. If the procedure has a base value of 4 units, and the same 57 minutes from the example above is divided by 10 minute increments, the time value is 5.7, which is generally rounded up to 6, depending on the insurance. By adding 6 time units to the base unit value of 4 there is a total of 10 units, which is then multiplied by the applicable Anesthesia Conversion Factor.

Example

00322 Anesthesia for all procedures on esophagus, thyroid, larynx, trachea and lymphatic system of neck; needle biopsy of thyroid

Anesthesia time: 120 minutes

Conversion factor: $21.44

Medicare:

Base Value	3
Time (120 min/15)	8
Total units	11 x $21.44 = $235.84

Commercial Insurance (using 10 min increments in this example):

Base Value	3
Time (120 min/10)	12
Total units	15 x $21.44 = $321.60

We will tackle adding additional units in the Physical Status and Qualifying Circumstances section.

Multiple (surgical) procedures may be performed on one patient during anesthesia administration. When this occurs, surgery representing the most complex procedure is reported because this service carries a higher base unit value. Anesthesia time is reported as usual, from the time the anesthesiologist begins to prepare the patient until the patient is safely placed under postoperative supervision. Because only one of the procedures is reported, the modifier 51 *Multiple procedures* is not applicable to the anesthesia section. Only one anesthesia code is reported during anesthesia administration except in the case where there is an anesthesia add-on code (explained below). Total time for both procedures is reported as anesthesia time.

Example

A patient has two surgical procedures at one time:

00830 Anesthesia for hernia repairs in the lower abdomen not otherwise specified

00832 Anesthesia for hernia repairs in lower abdomen; ventral and incisional hernias

Inguinal hernia repair (00830) has 4 base units and the ventral hernia repair (00832) has 6 base units. Only the ventral herniorrhaphy (00832) is reported because it is more complex and has a higher base value than the inguinal hernia surgery.

It is important to remember: although both diagnosis codes may be reported, the diagnosis code related to the ventral hernia is reported in the primary position. Reporting the inguinal hernia diagnosis as secondary may help explain why the reported anesthesia time is longer than normally expected for the procedure reported.

An exception to this multiple procedure rule is applied when the patient has additional add-on procedures applicable to the anesthesia service. The anesthesia section of the CPT® has add-on codes listed under Burn Excision or Debridement and Obstetric codes. These add-on procedures may not be reported alone—they must be reported with the applicable primary anesthesia code referenced in parenthesis. Turn to code 01951

listed under Burn Excisions or Debridement to visualize the following example.

Example

Add-on code +01953 Anesthesia for second- and third-degree burn excision or debridement with or without skin grafting, any site, for total body surface area (TBSA) treated during anesthesia and surgery; each additional 9% total body surface area or part thereof (List separately in addition to code for primary procedure) is reported if the total body surface area (TBSA) treated during surgery exceeds 9%. This add-on code is reported in addition to 01952 Anesthesia for second- and third-degree burn excision or debridement with or without skin grafting, any site, for total body surface area (TBSA) treated during anesthesia and surgery; between 4% and 9% of total body surface area for each additional 9 percent or part thereof of the TBSA treated. A TBSA of 40 percent is reported as follows:

01952 + TM First 4 to 9 percent of TBSA

+01953 x 4 Represents the remaining 31 percent of TBSA in increments of 9 percent (the remaining 4 percent is considered a "part thereof")

Note: The first anesthesia code, 01952 is reported with time units. The add-on code 01953 is reported in units only.

Physical Status Modifiers

Physical Status Modifiers are anesthesia modifiers describing the physical status of the patient. These modifiers are not recognized by Medicare for additional payment, and no base values are listed in the CPT®. However, because insurance companies are familiar with the Anesthesia Coding Guidelines in the CPT®, non-Medicare payers typically pay additional base units. The carrier usually will not require a specific diagnosis code to substantiate the physical status modifier billed, as long as the preoperative assessment documentation supports the modifier billed (unless medical necessity is an issue).

The following modifiers are assigned to patients based on their individual physical status:

P1—A normal healthy patient—No extra value added

P2—A patient with mild systemic disease—No extra value added

P3—A patient with severe systemic disease—1 extra unit

P4—A patient with severe systemic disease that is a constant threat to life—2 extra units

P5—A moribund patient who is not expected to survive without the operation—3 extra units

P6—A declared brain-dead patient whose organs are being removed for donor purposes—No extra value added

To report a physical status modifier, the anesthesia code selected is appended with the appropriate P modifier. For example, a Non-Medicare patient who has a severe systemic disease that is a constant threat to life and is undergoing a direct coronary artery bypass graft (CABG) with a pump oxygenator is reported as 00567-P4.

To re-review our earlier discussion of calculating base plus time, we will now add 2 physical status units to our calculation. The Medicare assigned base unit value for anesthesia for a CABG is 18 units. Let's assume the anesthesia time reported calculates to 20 time units. Our new calculation is 18 base, plus twenty (20) time (18+20 = 38 units). The additional units for the physical status modifier are not factored in the Medicare calculation. Using the 2012 Anesthesia Conversion Factor assigned to Salt Lake City, Utah of $21.44, the total Medicare payment is $814.72 (38 x $21.44 = $814.72). For non-Medicare payers, the calculation is is eighteen (18) base plus twenty (20) time units plus two (2) physical status modifier (18+20+2=40). Using the same conversion factor, the total non-Medicare payment is $857.60 (40 x 21.44=$857.60).

Qualifying Circumstances

Qualifying Circumstances (QC) are anesthesia add-on codes assigned to report anesthesia services performed under difficult circumstances affecting significantly the character of an anesthesia service. Each of the procedure codes will identify a different circumstance, and more than one may be listed when applicable, unless the reported code already contains the risk factor. When this occurs, the code has a parenthetical reference underneath specifying the qualifying circumstance code is not reported with the referenced code.

Qualifying circumstances are add-on codes and may not be reported without an associated anesthesia procedure code. These add-on codes are not recognized by Medicare for additional payment, and no base values are listed in CPT®.

The ASA assigned base unit values for the qualifying circumstances. The following codes are assigned to each patient based on the documented qualifying circumstance:

+99100—Anesthesia for patient of extreme age, younger than one (1) year and older than seventy (70)—1 extra unit

+99116—Anesthesia complicated by utilization of total body hypothermia—5 extra units

+99135—Anesthesia complicated by utilization of controlled hypotension—5 extra units

+99140—Anesthesia complicated by emergency conditions (specify)—2 extra units

Documentation must support the qualifying circumstance code(s) reported. Emergency conditions do not apply to after normal-hour care or routine obstetric labor. An emergency is defined as existing when a delay in the treatment of the patient would lead to a significant increase in the threat to the patient's life or body parts.

As with the physical status modifiers, qualifying circumstance codes add to the value of an anesthesia service. We've reviewed calculating base plus time plus physical status modifiers, so we will now add 2 emergency circumstance units to our calculation.

As we discussed in our earlier example, the Medicare assigned base unit value for anesthesia for a CABG is eighteen (18) units and we used an anesthesia time calculation of 20 time units. Our new calculation is 18 base plus 20 time units (18+20 = 38 units). Using the 2012 Anesthesia Conversion Factor assigned to Salt Lake City, Utah of $21.44, the total Medicare payment is $814.72 (38 x $21.44 = $814.72). Additional units for physical status modifiers and qualifying circumstances are not recognized by Medicare. Some non-Medicare payers will allow the additional units to be factored in the calculation to determine the anesthesia fee. When an anesthesiologist medically directs CRNAs, (covered under HCPCS Level II below) the qualifying circumstance code is usually assigned to the anesthesiologist.

For non-Medicare payers, the calculation is 18 base units plus 20 time units plus 2 physical status modifier plus 2 for the qualifying circumstances (18+20+2+2=42 units). Using the same conversion factor, the total non-Medicare payment is $900.48 (42 x 21.44).

Coders should now understand the calculation for anesthesia services is BASE + TIME + PHYSICAL STATUS MODIFERS + QUALIFYING CIRCUMSTANCES multiplied by the CONVERSION FACTOR for non-Medicare payers. For Medicare, the calculation for anesthesia services is BASE + TIME multiplied by the Medicare conversion factor for the region.

Calculate anesthesia units:

- + Base units
- + Time units
- + Additional Units
  - » Status modifier
  - » Qualifying Circumstances
- = Total units

Practical Coding Note

Place the calculation of time in the Anesthesia Guidelines in your CPT® codebook.

Additional Billable Items by Anesthesiologist

When we first discussed base values, we learned the services included and mentioned unusual forms of monitoring are not included. Patients who undergo anesthesia for surgery often require a higher level of cardiovascular monitoring than can be obtained using standard, non-invasive monitoring techniques.

When the anesthesia provider places an invasive monitoring device, an additional code is reported. Monitoring is included in the base value, so if another provider—such as the surgeon or a perfusionist—places the line or catheter, no additional information is reported by the anesthesia provider on the claim form. Anesthesia providers may only report service(s) they perform.

Time is not reported separately for flat fee procedures. Unlike anesthesia codes which require anesthesia time be documented and reported, flat fee procedure codes found in the surgery section of the CPT® do not require time to be documented for reporting or payment. If a flat fee service is provided it is not included in the anesthesia time. For example, if an epidural is placed for pain management prior to the induction of anesthesia, and an arterial line is also placed, the time for these services is not counted in the total anesthesia time.

When a CV catheter is inserted and used to thread a pulmonary artery catheter (PAC), only the PAC code 93503 *Insertion and placement of flow directed catheter (eg, Swan-Ganz) for monitoring purposes* is reported. If a central venous catheter and Swan-Ganz catheter are separately placed, each procedure is reported. The central venous line will require modifier 59 to show it was completely separate and necessary.

Payments for these services are based on the physician fee schedule, as are other surgical services. Monitoring is NOT reported separately.

The most common codes reported in addition to the anesthesia service are:

31500—*Intubation, endotracheal, emergency procedure*: Emergency intubation may be reported separately when an anesthesia provider is requested to intubate a patient who is NOT undergoing anesthesia. Normal intubation for patients undergoing anesthesia is included in the base value of the anesthesia code.

36620—*Arterial Catheterization or cannulation for sampling, monitoring or transfusion; percutaneous* (placed in a radial artery through needle puncture of the skin)

36555 or 36556—*Insertion of non-tunneled centrally inserted central venous catheter*: Because these codes are age-related, the appropriate code assignment is based on whether the patient is under 5 years of age or over.

93503—*Insertion and placement of flow directed catheter for monitoring purposes (eg, Swan-Ganz) for monitoring purposes*

Practical Coding Note

Make a note in your CPT® book of the following procedures outside of the anesthesia code range which are commonly billed by anesthesiologists:

Intubation (31500)
— when not undergoing anesthesia

CVP—central venous catheter (36555, 36556)
— monitoring
— quick administration

Arterial line insertion (36620, 36625)
— based on technique used

Swan-Ganz (93503)
— included if done through CVP
— separate vessels code for both

For example, anesthesia coders will look for documentation to support placement of a pulmonary artery catheter by the anesthesia provider. It may be identified as either a pulmonary artery catheter (PAC) or Swan-Ganz (SG), and should have procedural notes documented in either the comments section of the anesthesia record, in progress notes, or on a separate procedure form.

Example

CVP was placed in the right internal jugular and a Swan-Ganz catheter was inserted in the left internal jugular by Dr. Smith.

This documentation shows two placements:

1. CVP in the right internal jugular; and
2. Swan-Ganz in the left internal jugular.

A physician who is also performing the service for which conscious sedation is being provided may report moderate sedation codes. Anesthesia providers do not typically provide anesthesia and surgery at the same time. Moderate sedation also can be provided by a physician other than the surgeon; and, an anesthesiologist may provide moderate sedation in these circumstances.

Moderate sedation is provided without anesthesia equipment and backup for general anesthesia. In addition, moderate sedation codes do not include minimal sedation, deep sedation, or monitored anesthesia care. Coders are directed to the anesthesia section of the CPT® to report services. Only anesthesia providers report anesthesia codes.

Monitored Anesthesia Care (MAC) is distinctly different from moderate sedation. MAC may involve the administration of sedatives, analgesics, hypnotics, anesthetic agents, or other medications as necessary for patient safety based on each patient's health status. The patient does not lose consciousness, is arousable, and is able to maintain an open airway. The patient's anesthesia plan is determined on a case-by-case basis. When using MAC, the anesthesia provider must be qualified and prepared at all times to convert to general anesthesia, if necessary. If the patient loses consciousness and the ability to respond purposely, the anesthesia care is a general anesthetic. MAC services are paid in the same way as general or regional anesthesia services—although many insurance companies request special modifiers to identify the service as monitored anesthesia care. We will discuss MAC and these modifiers more completely in the HCPCS Level II section.

Modifiers

Modifiers related to anesthesia may be found in Appendix A of CPT®. HCPCS Level II related-anesthesia modifiers will be covered in the HCPCS Level II section. After defining the modifiers briefly, we will discuss their application to anesthesia services. Full descriptions are listed in Appendix A.

Modifier 23 *Unusual anesthesia*—This modifier may be reported to describe a procedure usually not requiring anesthesia (either none or local) but, due to unusual circumstances, is performed under general anesthesia. For example, a pediatric patient may require general anesthesia for

the surgeon to perform a procedure not requiring anesthesia under usual circumstances.

Modifier 47 *Anesthesia by surgeon*—This modifier is reported by the surgeon when he also provides regional or general anesthesia for the surgical service, and does not apply to local anesthesia. This modifier is not to be reported with anesthesia procedure codes. Anesthesia providers do not report this modifier.

Modifier 53 *Discontinued procedure*—This modifier may be reported to describe a procedure started and, due to extenuating circumstances, was discontinued. Although this modifier is not strictly anesthesia related, carrier policy often identifies this as the modifier to report when anesthesia services are discontinued.

Modifier 59 *Distinct procedural service*—This modifier is used to indicate a procedure or service is distinct or independent from other Non-Evaluation and Management procedures. Documentation must support a different session, procedure, surgery, site, organ system, incision/excision, or injury. This modifier is often appended to post-operative pain management services to indicate it is separate from the anesthesia administered during the surgery.

Modifier 73 *Discontinued out-patient hospital/ambulatory surgery center (ASC) procedure prior to the administration of anesthesia*—This modifier is listed as approved for ASC and hospital outpatient use. Although this modifier is not strictly anesthesia related carrier policy often identifies this as the modifier to report when anesthesia services are discontinued prior to administration of anesthesia. Note: Physician reporting of discontinued procedures is referred to Modifier 53.

Modifier 74 *Discontinued out-patient hospital/ambulatory surgery center (ASC) procedure after administration of anesthesia*—This modifier is listed as approved for ASC and hospital outpatient use. Although this modifier is not strictly anesthesia related, carrier policy often identifies this as the modifier to report when anesthesia services are discontinued after administration of anesthesia. Note: Physician reporting of discontinued procedures is referred to Modifier 53.

Section Review 16.3

1. Which of the following is not included in the base unit value of anesthesia services?

    A. Pre-anesthesia visit

    B. Post-anesthesia visit

    C. Arterial line placement

    D. Routine Monitoring

---

2. Which of the following best describes the start of anesthesia time?

    A. During the pre-anesthesia visit.

    B. When the anesthesiologist begins to prepare the patient.

    C. When the surgeon begins to treat the patient.

    D. When the OR nurse calls start of room time.

3. When more than one surgery is performed during a single anesthetic administration, which of the following is true regarding the anesthesia code reported?

    A. The anesthesia code representing the most complex procedure is reported.

    B. An anesthesia code is reported for each separate surgery performed.

    C. The anesthesia code representing the longest surgery is reported.

    D. None of the above

4. Which of the following physical status modifiers best describes a normal, healthy patient who is undergoing anesthesia?

    A. P6

    B. P4

    C. P3

    D. P1

5. A 67-year-old patient is undergoing anesthesia for a re-operation after a coronary bypass two months ago. Which of the following qualifying circumstances may be reported separately?

    A. +99100

    B. +99116

    C. +99135

    D. None of the above

6. Which of the following codes is used to report placement of a flow directed Swan-Ganz catheter?

    A. 36160

    B. 93503

    C. 36013

    D. 36556

7. An anesthesiologist was called to the emergency room to intubate a patient who was having respiratory difficulty. Which procedure code is reported?

    A. 31502

    B. 43753

    C. 36620

    D. 31500

8. A 42-year-old patient is going for immediate surgery due to a ruptured appendix. An anesthesiologist was not available to administer general anesthesia. The surgeon administers the regional anesthesia with an epidural spinal block and performs the surgery. Which modifier is reported by the surgeon for administering anesthesia?

    A. 22

    B. 23

    C. 47

    D. 59

Direction, Supervision, and Monitoring

Medical direction occurs when an anesthesiologist is involved in two, three, or four anesthesia procedures at the same time; or a single anesthesia procedure with a qualified anesthesia resident, CRNA, or anesthesiologist assistant. According to the Center for Medicare & Medicaid Services (CMS), when an anesthesiologist is medically directing, he must provide the following seven services:

1. Perform a pre-anesthetic examination and evaluation.

2. Prescribe the anesthesia plan.

3. Personally participate in the most demanding procedures of the anesthesia plan including, if applicable, induction and emergence.

4. Ensure that any procedures in the anesthesia plan that he or she does not perform are performed by a qualified anesthetist.

5. Monitor the course of anesthesia administration at frequent intervals.

6. Remain physically present and available for immediate diagnosis and treatment of emergencies.

7. Provide the indicated post anesthesia care.

If one or more of the above services are not performed by the anesthesiologist, the service is not considered medical direction.

While medically directing, anesthesiologists should not be providing services to other patients. However, they are allowed to provide any of the following services to other patients without affecting their ability to provide medical direction:

- Addressing an emergency of short duration in the immediate area.

- Administering an epidural or caudal anesthetic to ease labor pain.

- Monitoring an obstetrical patient periodically rather than continuously.

- Receiving patients entering the operating suite for the next surgery.

- Checking on or discharging patients from the post anesthesia care unit.

- Coordinating scheduling matters.

Medical supervision occurs when an anesthesiologist is involved in five or more anesthesia procedures during the same time (concurrent); or when the anesthesiologist does not perform the required services listed under medical direction above.

Non-medically directed CRNAs are working without medical direction.

Monitored Anesthesia Care (MAC) is the intraoperative monitoring by an anesthesiologist or qualified individual under the direction of an anesthesiologist of a patient's vital physiological signs, in anticipation of:

- The need for administration of general anesthesia.

- The development of an adverse physiological patient reaction to the surgical procedure.

Monitored anesthesia care includes the performance of the following by the anesthesiologist, CRNA, or qualified individual under the direction of an anesthesiologist:

- Pre-anesthetic examination and evaluation

- Prescription of the anesthesia care required

- Completion of an anesthesia record

- Administration of any necessary oral or parenteral medication

- Provision of indicated postoperative anesthesia care

The anesthesiologist, CRNA, or a qualified individual under the medical direction of an anesthesiologist, must be continuously present to monitor the patient and provide anesthesia care.

Medical Direction Modifiers from HCPCS Level II (discussed below) allow reporting of the appropriate medical direction/supervision/non-medically directed status.

HCPCS Level II Modifiers

The HCPCS Level II codes are part of a set of national standard codes recognized under the Health Insurance Portability and Accountability Act of 1996 (HIPAA). Level I codes are the descriptive codes we've discussed under the CPT® section, which primarily list medical services and procedures performed by physicians and other healthcare providers. Level II codes, described as alphanumeric codes, are used to report products, supplies and other services (such as durable medical equipment). In addition, the HCPCS Level II codebook contains standardized code modifiers, which expand greatly on the anatomical Level II modifiers listed in Appendix A of the CPT®.

In this section, we discuss anesthesia-related modifiers and the associated terms. We will also use anesthesia terms discussed in previous sections, such as CRNA. Anesthesiologist Assistant will be spelled out because the abbreviation (AA) must not be confused with the HCPCS Level II modifier containing the same letters.

HCPCS modifiers are applied to report the circumstances surrounding the various methods of anesthesia delivery. These modifiers report if the anesthesiologist personally performed the anesthesia, provided medical supervision of the anesthesia, or provided medical direction of the anesthesia. These modifiers are reported only with anesthesia CPT® codes:

- AA—Anesthesia services performed personally by anesthesiologist
- AD—Medical supervision by a physician: more than four concurrent anesthesia procedures

Note: "Concurrency" refers to all current ongoing anesthesia cases during the same time under the direction or supervision of an anesthesiologist.

- QK—Medical direction of 2, 3, or 4 concurrent anesthesia procedures involving qualified individuals
- QY—Medical direction of one certified registered nurse anesthetist (CRNA) by an anesthesiologist
- GC—This service has been performed in part by a resident under the direction of a teaching physician

The following medical supervision/direction modifiers are reported with CRNA or anesthesiologist assistant services:

- QX—CRNA service: with medical direction by a physician
- QZ—CRNA service: without medical direction by a physician

Note: State scope of practice may prohibit an Anesthesiologist Assistant from reporting claims with a non-medical direction modifier. If a provider moves from QK—Medical direction of 2, 3, or 4 concurrent anesthesia procedures involving qualified individuals to AD—Medical supervision by a physician: more than four concurrent anesthesia procedures, the CRNA still reports QX as the CRNA would not necessarily know the number of cases the anesthesiologist is overseeing.

Medical Direction modifiers are associated with specific providers and are reported in the first position after the anesthesia CPT® code because payment often is related to the modifier reported.

Additional anesthesia-related modifiers usually are reported in the second position after any related medical direction modifiers, as they are considered informational or statistical. Modifiers affecting payment always should be reported in the position before information/statistical modifiers.

Physical status modifiers, which have already been discussed, are also listed in HCPCS Level II. Physical status modifiers also are reported in the second or third position, as applicable. For example, 00910-AA-P3 (to report a personally performing physician service with a physical status 3 patient) and 00142 QK-QS-P3 and 00142 QX-QS-P3 (to report the medically directing physician and CRNA service with a physical status 3 patient under monitored anesthesia care).

When reporting MAC services, CMS and other insurance carriers may require the use one of the following HCPCS Level II modifiers:

- QS—Monitored anesthesia care service
- G8—Monitored anesthesia care for deep complex, complicated, or markedly invasive surgical procedure
- G9—Monitored anesthesia care for patient who has a history of severe cardiopulmonary disease

When reporting a G8 or G9 modifier, it is not necessary to report a QS modifier separately because the description of these modifiers includes Monitored Anesthesia Care.

Note: Anesthesia modifiers are reported only with anesthesia codes; they are not listed with other CPT® code categories.

Anesthesia-Related Teaching Rules

Effective January 1, 2010, CMS updated their teaching rules to align payment with that of other teaching specialties. For a number of years, teaching anesthesiologists were paid less to teach anesthesia residents than their constituents.

To interpret Medicare's teaching rules for anesthesia correctly, the following italicized teaching information is taken directly from chapter 12, Section 50 on the Medicare On-Line Manual at www.cms.gov/manuals/downloads/clm104c12.pdf. The chapter should be reviewed in its entirety before billing anesthesia services to Medicare.

Payment at Personally Performed Rate

The Part B Contractor must determine the fee schedule payment, recognizing the base unit for the anesthesia code and one time unit per 15 minutes of anesthesia time if:

- The physician personally performed the entire anesthesia service alone;

- The physician is involved with one anesthesia case with a resident, the physician is a teaching physician as defined in §100, and the service is furnished on or after January 1, 1996;

- The physician is involved in the training of physician residents in a single anesthesia case, two concurrent anesthesia cases involving residents or a single anesthesia case involving a resident that is concurrent to another case paid under the medical direction rules. The physician meets the teaching physician criteria in §100.1.4 and the service is furnished on or after January 1, 2010;

- The physician is continuously involved in a single case involving a student nurse anesthetist;

- The physician is continuously involved in one anesthesia case involving a CRNA (or AA) and the service was furnished prior to January 1, 1998. If the physician is involved with a single case with a CRNA (or AA) and the service was furnished on or after January 1, 1998, carriers may pay the physician service and the CRNA (or AA) service in accordance with the medical direction payment policy; or

- The physician and the CRNA (or AA) are involved in one anesthesia case and the services of each are found to be medically necessary. Documentation must be submitted by both the CRNA and the physician to support payment of the full fee for each of the two providers. The physician reports the "AA" modifier and the CRNA reports the "QZ" modifier for a nonmedically directed case.

Payment at the Medically Directed Rate

For services furnished on or after January 1, 1994, the physician can medically direct two, three, or four concurrent procedures involving qualified individuals, all of whom could be CRNAs, AAs, interns, residents, or combinations of these individuals. The medical direction rules apply to cases involving student nurse anesthetists if the physician directs two concurrent cases, each of which involves a student nurse anesthetist, or the physician directs one case involving a student nurse anesthetist and another involving a CRNA, AA, intern, or resident.

For services furnished on or after January 1, 2010, the medical direction rules do not apply to a single resident case that is concurrent to another anesthesia case paid under the medical direction rules or to two concurrent anesthesia cases involving residents.

The GC modifier is reported by the teaching physician to indicate he rendered the service in compliance with the teaching physician requirements in §100.1.2. One of the payment modifiers must be used in conjunction with the GC modifier.

Anesthesia   Chapter 16

Section Review 16.4

1. A 78-year-old patient is undergoing lens surgery for cataracts. An anesthesiologist is performing monitored anesthesia care (MAC) personally. Which modifier(s) is/are appropriately reported for the anesthesiologist's service?

    A. 00142-QK

    B. 00142-QS

    C. 00142-AA-QS

    D. 00142-AA

2. A 22-year-old patient delivered a healthy baby boy by cesarean delivery under general anesthesia. The anesthesiologist performed all required steps for medical direction and was medically directing two other cases concurrently. Which modifier(s) is/are reported for the anesthesiologist and CRNA services?

    A. 01961-AA

    B. 01961-QK and 01961-QX

    C. 01961-QK and 01961-QZ

    D. 01961-QY and 01961-QX

3. An anesthesiologist is medically supervising five cases at the same time. Which modifier(s) appropriately report the anesthesiologist and CRNA services?

    A. AA and QZ

    B. QK and QZ

    C. AD alone

    D. AD and QX

4. A CRNA is performing a case personally without medical direction from an anesthesiologist. Which modifier is appropriately reported for the CRNA services?

    A. QX

    B. QZ

    C. QK

    D. QS

5. A 69-year-old Medicare patient with a history of severe cardiopulmonary disease is undergoing surgery under monitored anesthesia care (MAC). Which modifier(s) is/are appropriate?

    A. QS

    B. G8

    C. G9

    D. G9 and QS

514   2016 Medical Coding Training: CPC®   CPT® copyright 2015 American Medical Association. All rights reserved.

Documentation Dissection

Review the following operative notes and apply the knowledge you've learned in this section to find the correct diagnosis and or procedure codes, as applicable.

Case 1

A 44-year-old healthy patient is undergoing anesthesia for knee surgery. Review the following operative report and assign the correct information, as indicated at the end of the report.

Operative Report

Postoperative Diagnosis: Left knee osteoarthrosis [1]

Operation: Total Knee Arthroplasty [2]

Anesthesia: General. [3]

Anesthesia Provided By: Dr. Who, Anesthesiologist [4]

Anesthesia Start: 8:21 [5]

Surgery Start: 8:30

Surgery End: 10:49

Anesthesia End: 11:00 [6]

Procedure: In the preoperative holding area the site and side and the procedure were confirmed with the patient. Risks, benefits, and alternatives were discussed.

The patient was taken to the operating room, and after adequate general anesthesia the left leg was carefully placed in the left leg holder. The leg was prepped and draped in the usual sterile fashion. A mid-line incision was made over the knee joint. Sequential examination of the knee joint was performed and localized primary arthritis [7] was noted throughout the left knee.

Unilateral flaps were developed and a median retinacular parapatellar incision was made. The extensor mechanism was partially divided and the patella was everted. Some of the femoral bone spurs were resected using an osteotome and a rongeur. Ascending drill hole was made in the distal femur and the distal femoral cut, anterior and posterior and chamfer cuts were accomplished for a 67.5 femoral component.

At this point, the ACL was resected. Some of the fat pad and synovium were resected, as well as both medial and lateral menisci. A posterior cruciate retractor was utilized, the tibia brought forward and a centering drill hole made in the tibia. The intramedullary guide was used for cutting the tibia. It was set at 8 mm. A trial reduction was done with a 71 tibial base plate. This was pinned and drilled and then trial reduction done with a 10-mm insert. This gave good stability and a full range of motion.

The patella was measured with the calibers and 9 mm of bone was resected with an oscillating saw. Further trial reduction was done and two liters of pulse lavage were used to clean the bony surfaces. A packet of cement was hand mixed, pressurized with a spatula into the proximal tibia. Multiple drill holes were made on the medial side of the tibia where the bone was somewhat sclerotic. The tibia baseplate was secured and the patella was inserted, held with a clamp. The extraneous cement was removed. At this point, the tibial baseplate was locked into place and the femoral component seated solidly. The knee was extended, held in this position for another 5–6 minutes until the cement was cured. Further extraneous cement was removed. The pneumatic tourniquet was released hemostasis was obtained with electrocoagulation. Retinaculum, quadriceps and extensor were repaired with multiple figure-of-eight #1 Vicryl sutures, the subcutaneous tissue with 2-0 and the skin with skin staples. [8]

A sterile dressing was applied. The patient was aroused from anesthesia and taken to the recovery room in stable condition having tolerated the procedure well.

---

[1] Anesthesia diagnosis code should be the same as the surgeon's postoperative diagnosis.

[2] Anesthesia procedure code will be obtained from the "00" code section under Knee and Popliteal Area.

[3] Pay attention to the type of anesthesia. MAC may require a modifier.

[4] In order to assign the correct medical direction modifier, coder must determine who provided the service.

[5] Exact starting anesthesia time is necessary to report total time spent with the patient.

[6] Exact ending anesthesia time is necessary to report total time spent with the patient.

[7] This additional information will help direct coder to correct diagnosis code assignment.

[8] Unless specific coding information is necessary, anesthesia coding may not always require thoroughly reading through the operative report.

What are the CPT® and ICD-10-CM codes reported?

    CPT® code and Modifiers: 01402-AA-P1

    ICD-10-CM Code: M17.12

    Time: 2 hours 39 minutes (or 159 minutes)

    Rationale: Total knee arthroplasty is reported with anesthesia code 01402 *Anesthesia for open or surgical arthroscopic procedures on knee joint; total knee arthroplasty*. General anesthesia was provided by a personally performing anesthesiologist, which is identified with an "AA" modifier. The patient was healthy, which is reported with P1. In the Index, look up Anesthesia/knee for the code range.

    The anesthesia diagnosis code should be the same as the surgeon's postoperative diagnosis. More specific diagnosis information was provided in the operative report indicating the arthritis is localized, primary. Look in the ICD-10-CM Index to Diseases and Injuries for Osteoarthrosis and you are directed to *see also* Osteoarthritis. Look for Osteoarthritis/primary/knee M17.1-. A fifth character of 2 is used to specify the left knee.

    Anesthesia start time was 8:21 and end time was 11:00, for a total of two hours and 39 minutes. Exact start and stop times are necessary to determine the precise time. Surgery times are not considered when reporting anesthesia time.

ICD-9-CM Application

What is/are the ICD-9-CM code(s) reported?

    Code(s): 715.16

    Rationale: A more specific diagnosis information is provided in the operative note that the arthritis is localized, primary. In the Index to Diseases, look for Osteoarthrosis/localized/primary directing you to 715.1 and a fifth digit is necessary. As indicated at the beginning of Chapter 13, the knee is considered part of the lower leg, so the fifth digit is 6. The correct diagnosis is 715.16 *Osteoarthrosis, localized primary, lower leg*.

Case 2

A 71-year-old patient is undergoing monitored anesthesia care for eye surgery. Dr. Smith is medically directing this case, and two other concurrent cases, with CRNAs. [1] Review the following operative report and assign the correct information, as indicated at the end of the report.

Postoperative Diagnosis: Diabetic Cataract, O.S. [2]

Operation: Extracapsular cataract removal with insertion of intraocular lens, left eye. [3]

Anesthesia: Monitored anesthesia care. [4]

Anesthesia Provided by: Jane Doe, CRNA with medical direction by John Smith, anesthesiologist [5]

Anesthesia Start: 7:01 [6]

Surgery Start: 7:16

Surgery End: 7:47

Anesthesia End: 7:52 [7]

Indications for Procedure: Patient is a 71-year-old white female with Type II controlled diabetes. She is complaining of decreased vision in her left eye. On examination, she was noted to have significant cataract formation of the left eye, an ophthalmic manifestation of her diabetes. [8] After discussing these findings with the patient, including the risks, benefits, and options available to her, she wished to proceed with the above-named procedure.

Operative Procedure: The patient was taken to the operative area, prepped, and draped in the usual sterile fashion. Two drops of povidone iodine and a thorough lavage of the conjunctival sac with a complete washing of Betadine was performed. Anesthesia was obtained by utilizing a mixture of 2% Xylocaine jelly along with intravenous sedation. After adequate anesthesia was obtained, a lid speculum was placed between the two eyelids of the left eye and the eye was approached from the temporal position.

A Super Blade was used to perform a paracentesis at the four o'clock position and a 2.85 mm keratome blade was used to perform a clear corneal temporally located incision. Healon 5 was instilled into the capsular bag and balanced salt solution was used to perform a soft shell. The cystitome capsulorrhexis forceps were used to perform a round 4.5-mm anterior capsulotomy and a balanced salt solution was used to hydro-dissect between the capsule and cortex. At this point, a 30-degree Kelman high-efficiency phacoemulsification tip was introduced into the eye and phacoemulsification was carried out in a divide-and-conquer technique over 4.5 seconds with an average power of 5.9%. Irrigation and aspiration was utilized to remove the remaining cortical material and all cortical material, including nuclear segments, were removed. Healon 5 was instilled into the anterior chamber and at this point, no vitreous had presented to the wound. An Alcon Model MA60 AC lens with a diopter power of 19.5 and a length of 13 mm was inserted into the capsular bag after the corneal incision was enlarged to 3.4 mm. The optic was placed inside the capsular bag with the haptics resting in the ciliary sulcus. The Healon 5 was removed using the bimanual irrigation and aspiration hand piece and Miochol was instilled into the anterior chamber to replace the aqueous, offering good pupillary constriction.

The left eye was treated with Ocuflox drops, povidone-iodine solution and a pressure patch. The patient tolerated the procedure well and was returned to the recovery room in stable condition.

---

[1] To assign a correct medical direction modifier, the coder must know how many concurrent cases are being medically directed by one anesthesiologist.

[2] Anesthesia diagnosis code should be the same as the surgeon's postoperative diagnosis.

[3] Anesthesia procedure code will be obtained from the "00" code section under Head section.

[4] Pay attention to the type of anesthesia. MAC requires a modifier identifying the type of anesthesia provided.

[5] In order to assign the correct medical direction modifier, coder must determine who provided the service.

[6] Exact starting anesthesia time is necessary to report total time spent with the patient.

[7] Exact ending anesthesia time is necessary to report total time spent with the patient.

[8] Pay attention to diabetes related conditions, which require following specific coding guidelines.

What are the CPT® and ICD-10-CM codes reported?

CRNA:

CPT® Codes: 00142-QX-QS-P2

Anesthesiologist:

CPT® Codes: 00142-QK-QS-P2, 99100

ICD-10-CM Codes: E11.36

Time: 51 minutes

Rationale: Start with Head area of anesthesia codes. Lens surgery is reported with anesthesia code 00142 *Anesthesia for procedures on eye; lens surgery*. In the Index, look up Anesthesia/Eye/Lens directing you to 00142. The "QX" medical direction modifier for a medically-directed CRNA is reported in the first position because it affects payment (payment modifiers are primary). The statistical modifier for Monitored Anesthesia Care (QS) is reported as the second modifier. P2 is used to report a healthy patient with diabetes type II (controlled).

For the anesthesiologist, the "QK" medical direction modifier, for a physician who is medically directing two or more CRNAs, is reported in the first position because it affects payment (payment modifiers are primary). The statistical modifier for Monitored Anesthesia Care (QS) is reported as the second modifier. P2 is used to report a healthy patient with diabetes type II (controlled).

The patient has a diabetic cataract on her left eye. Look in the ICD-10-CM Index to Diseases and Injuries for Diabetes, diabetic/type 2/with/cataract/leads to a combination code E11.36. Verification in the Tabular List confirms there is no further specification for code E11.36. Long term use of insulin is not used as no mention is made in the medical record.

Anesthesia start time was 7:01 and end time was 7:52, for a total of 51 minutes. Surgery times are not considered when reporting anesthesia time.

ICD-9-CM Application

What is/are the ICD-9-CM code(s) reported?

Code(s): 250.50, 366.41

Rationale: 250.50 and 366.41 *Cataract, diabetic*. Coding instructions indicate to "code first diabetes." In the Index to Diseases look for Diabetes, diabetic/with/cataract directing you to 250.5. A fifth digit is required, because diabetes is identified in the Indications for Procedure as Type II, controlled the fifth digit 0 is reported, 250.50. There is an instruction note in the Tabular List to Use additional code to identify manifestations. Code 366.41 is for cataract.

Case 3

A 19-year-old patient is undergoing anesthesia for a suspected miscarriage. <u>General anesthesia is provided by a non-medically directed CRNA.</u> [1] Review the following operative report and assign the correct information, as indicated at the end of the report.

<u>Preoperative Diagnosis:</u> [2] Vaginal bleeding, suspected pregnancy

Postop Diagnosis: <u>Spontaneous abortion.</u> [3]

Operation Performed: <u>Dilatation and curettage.</u> [4]

Anesthesia: <u>General anesthesia</u> [5]

Anesthesia Provided by: <u>Mary Smith, CRNA</u> [6]

Anesthesia Start: <u>4:01</u> [7]

SURGERY START: 4:11

Surgery End: 4:38

Anesthesia End: <u>4:51</u> [8]

Indications for Procedure: <u>Patient is a 19-year-old female who has not received obstetric care. She was admitted through the emergency room with vaginal bleeding and believes she is approximately six weeks pregnant.</u> [9]

Operative Procedure: Satisfactory level of general anesthesia with endotracheal intubation was obtained. Patient was in the supine position with legs placed in the lithotomy position, prepped, and draped in the usual sterile fashion. Her urinary bladder was catheterized. <u>Examination revealed an 11-week sized uterus with partial retention of products of conception.</u> [10] The cervix was grasped with a single-toothed tenaculum and a dilator was inserted to enlarge the opening. A suction curette was passed into the uterus where a large amount of tissue and blood were removed. The endometrial lining of the uterus was scraped on all sides. The patient was awakened by Anesthesia and taken to the post-anesthesia care unit in good condition.

---

[1] To assign a correct medical direction modifier, the coder must know the medical direction status of the CRNA.

[2] Preoperative diagnosis is not reported, although it may be a clue for coding the procedure.

[3] Anesthesia diagnosis code should be the same as the surgeon's post operative diagnosis.

[4] Anesthesia procedure code will be obtained from the "00" code section under the Obstetric section.

[5] Pay attention to the type of anesthesia. MAC may require a modifier.

[6] In order to assign the correct medical direction modifier, coder must determine who provided the service.

[7] Exact starting anesthesia time is necessary to report total time spent with the patient.

[8] Exact ending anesthesia time is necessary to report total time spent with the patient.

[9] The anesthesia record should confirm an emergency status, which is qualified by "threat to life."

[10] Confirmation of trimester and gestation of less than 22 weeks with retention of products of conception.

What are the CPT® and ICD-10-CM codes reported?

CPT® Codes: 01965-QZ-P1, 99140

ICD-10-CM Code: O03.4, Z3A.11

Time: 50 minutes

Rationale: Begin with the Obstetric anesthesia codes. In the Index, look for Anesthesia/Abortion/Incomplete directing you to 01965. Coder choices are incomplete or missed abortion (01965 *Anesthesia for incomplete or missed abortion procedures*) or induced abortion (01966 *Anesthesia for induced abortion procedures*). An induced abortion is an elective procedure that generally is provided in a physician's office without an anesthesiologist. The pre-operative diagnosis is also a clue and was not an induced abortion. Anesthesia was complicated by emergency conditions and a separate qualifying circumstances code, 99140 Anesthesia complicated by emergency *conditions (specify) (List separately in addition to code for primary anesthesia procedure)*, is reported. In the Index look up Emergency Department Services/Anesthesia directing you to 99140. Note: Time, alone, is not an indication of emergency status. General anesthesia was provided by a non-medically directed CRNA, which is identified with a QZ modifier. Add P1 for physical status.

In this case, the patient has retained products of conception making this an incomplete abortion. Look in the ICD-10-CM Index to Diseases and Injuries for Abortion/incomplete (spontaneous) O03.4. Note that spontaneous is a nonessential modifier to Abortion. Chapter 15 has a note to use an additional code from category Z3A to identify the specific week of pregnancy. The provider notes an 11-week uterus. Look for Pregnancy/weeks of gestation/11 weeks Z3A.11.

Anesthesia start time was 4:01 and end time was 4:51 for a total of 50 minutes. Surgery times are not considered when reporting anesthesia time.

ICD-9-CM Application

What is/are the ICD-9-CM code(s) reported?

Code(s): 634.91

Rationale: Look in the Index to Diseases for Abortion/spontaneous 634.9x Spontaneous abortion; without mention of complication. The fifth digit is 1 to indicate incomplete. Although the pregnancy was under 22 weeks, this was not a missed abortion 632. A missed abortion is an abortion in which the fetus dies but is retained within the uterus. This was not the case, because the patient was bleeding and part of the products of conception had been expelled on admission.

Glossary

Add-on Codes—Procedures commonly carried out in addition to the primary procedure performed. Add-on codes may *not* be reported alone, and are identified with a + sign.

Anesthesiologist Assistant—A health professional who has completed an accredited Anesthesia Assistant training program.

Anesthesiologist—A physician who is licensed to practice medicine and has completed an accredited anesthesiology program.

Anesthesia Time—Begins when the anesthesiologist (or anesthesia provider) begins to prepare the patient for the induction of anesthesia and ends when the anesthesiologist (or anesthesia provider) is no longer in personal attendance.

Arterial Line—A catheter inserted into an artery. It is used most commonly to measure real-time blood pressure and to obtain samples for arterial blood gas.

Base Unit Value—Value assigned to anesthesia codes for anesthetic management of surgery and diagnostic tests. Base unit values will vary depending on the difficulty of the surgery or diagnostic tests, and the management of anesthesia.

Cardiopulmonary Bypass (CPB)—A technique used during heart surgery to take over temporarily the function of the heart and lungs.

Central Venous Catheter—A catheter placed in a large vein such as the internal jugular, subclavian, or femoral vein with the tip of the catheter close to the atrium, or in the right atrium of the heart.

Certified Registered Nurse Anesthetist (CRNA)—A registered nurse who has completed an accredited nurse anesthesia training program.

Controlled Hypotension—Technique used in general anesthesia to reduce blood pressure to control bleeding during surgery. Watch anesthesia record for notes regarding deliberate or controlled hypotension.

Conversion Factor—A unit multiplier used to convert anesthesia units into a dollar amount for anesthesia services. Conversion Factors are reviewed annually by CMS and vary geographically. Conversion Factors also may be negotiated with insurance companies.

CVP (Central Venous Pressure)—Direct measurement of the blood pressure in the right atrium and vena cava. CVP reflects the amount of blood returning to the heart and the ability of the heart to pump the blood from the right heart into the pulmonary system.

Emergency—A delay in treatment would lead to significant increase in the threat to life or body part.

Flat Fee—A flat fee is based on the physician fee schedule. Payments are made under the Relative Value Unit, rather than by Conversion Factor. Time is not a consideration for payment. Examples are arterial lines, CV line, emergency intubation, and Swan Ganz catheter insertion.

General Anesthesia—A drug-induced loss of consciousness during which patients cannot be aroused.

Hypothermic Circulatory Arrest—Implies a temperature of 20 degrees centigrade or less.

Medical Direction—Occurs when an anesthesiologist is involved in two, three, or four concurrent anesthesia procedures, or a single anesthesia procedure with a qualified anesthetist. CMS and other carriers publish criteria to be met to report medical direction.

Medical Supervision—Occurs when an anesthesiologist is involved in five or more concurrent anesthesia procedures, or fails to meet required medical direction criteria.

Monitored Anesthesia Care (MAC)—Refers to a technique for many surgical procedures that do not require deep sedation or general anesthetic. Anesthesia provider must be prepared to convert to general anesthesia, if necessary.

PAC—Pulmonary Artery Catheter (eg, Swan Ganz)—A flow directed catheter inserted into the pulmonary artery. PACs are used to measure pressures and flows within the cardiovascular system.

Physical Status modifier—Modifier used to report the physical status assigned to each patient undergoing anesthesia. Patients are ranked by their individual health status.

Pump Oxygenator—Term used when a cardiopulmonary bypass (CPB) machine is used to function as the heart and lungs during heart surgery.

Qualifying Circumstances—Circumstances significantly affecting the character of an anesthesia service. These add-on

procedures may be reported only with anesthesia codes. More than one may be reported, if applicable. Qualifying circumstances may not be reported separately when a code descriptor already indicates the circumstance.

Regional Anesthesia—Loss of sensation in a region of the body, produced by application of an anesthetic agent.

Relative Value Unit—A unit measure used to assign a value to services. It is determined by assigning weight to factors such as physician work, practice expense and malpractice expense.

Resident (anesthesia resident)—A physician who has completed his or her medical degree and entered a residency program specifically for anesthesiology training.

SRNA (Student Registered Nurse Anesthetist)—A registered nurse who is training in an accredited nurse anesthesia program.

Surgical Field Avoidance—Anesthesia provider avoids an area where the surgeon is working (usually on procedures around the head, neck or shoulder girdle).

Total Body Hypothermia—Deliberate reduction of a patient's total body temperature, which reduces the general metabolism of the tissues. Evaluate the anesthesia record for notes regarding total body hypothermia. Generally, temperature is reduced 20 percent to 30 percent below a patient's normal temperature. This may not be reported separately when code indicates it is included.

Introduction

Radiology is a branch of medicine using radiation—including ionizing radiation, radionuclides, nuclear magnetic resonance, and ultrasound—to diagnose and treat disease. Using radiography (X-rays), physicians visualize and identify internal structures, and thereby navigate within the body. X-ray technology includes a variety of advanced applications, such as computerized axial tomography (CAT or CT scan), magnetic resonance imaging (MRI), ultrasound technology, nuclear medicine, radiation oncology, and positron emission tomography (PET).

Objectives

- Understand anatomical planes, anatomical directions, and positioning in radiology
- Review key terms associated with radiology
- Understand the use and coding of contrast material
- Differentiate between the different types of imaging and films
- Gain the knowledge of when to include additional CPT® codes from other sections
- Understand the importance of parenthetic instructions
- Distinguish between the 26 and TC modifiers and when to use them.

Anatomy and Medical Terminology

To obtain effective images, the radiologist or the radiology technician will need to place the patient in the correct position and then adjust equipment to the correct angle, height, and settings to take the image. We will discuss the planes, positioning, and projection.

Planes are ways in which the body can be divided. The most common planes are the frontal (coronal) plane cutting the body into front (anterior) and back (posterior) halves; the sagittal plane cutting the body into right and left portions; and the transverse (axial) (horizontal) plane cutting the body into upper (superior) and lower (inferior) halves. The midsagittal plane divides the body into equal portions of right and left.

Example

CT Scan Report:

No visualized displaced rib fractures. There are multilevel degenerative changes of the spine. No evidence of acute fracture of the lower thoracic or lumbar spine on axial, sagittal, or coronal images. Fat filled left inguinal canal is noted.

In this CT scan report, the physician used different plane images to verify the absence of a fracture of the lower thoracic or lumbar spine.

To know what is being viewed, you will need to understand directional and positional terms. Directional terms were reviewed in the anatomy chapter. Some main positional terms include:

Anatomic Position—Erect, facing forward, arms rotated outward with the palms forward, hands open with thumbs pointed out. The feet are together or slightly apart.

Supine Position—Lying down on the back with the face up. This position is also known as dorsal recumbent (lying down).

Prone Position—Lying face down on the front of the body. This position is also known as ventral recumbent.

Lateral Position—Position in which the side of the subject is next to the film. This can be performed as erect lateral (standing side) or lateral decubitus (lying down side).

Oblique Position—Slanted position where the patient is lying at an angle neither prone nor supine. In radiology, you may see right anterior oblique (RAO), left anterior oblique (LAO), right posterior oblique (RPO), or left posterior oblique (LPO). The anterior or posterior terminology indicates the part of the body closer to the film. For example, in RAO, a person is on his right side, with the anterior part of the body closer to the film.

CPT® Example

71020 Radiologic examination, chest, 2 views, frontal and lateral

Radiological projections refer to the path in which the X-ray beam flows through the body. Radiological projections often are stated in the medical documentation, and referred to in CPT® code descriptions. Common projections include:

Anteroposterior (AP)—The X-ray beam enters the front of the body (anterior) and exits the back of the body (posterior).

Posteroanterior (PA)—The X-ray beam enters the back of the body (posterior) and exits the front of the body (anterior).

Lateral—The X-ray beam enters one side of the body and exits the other side. Lateral projections are named by the side of the body placed next to the film.

Oblique—The X-ray beam enters at an angle neither frontal (AP or PA) or lateral.

Radiographic Projection Positions

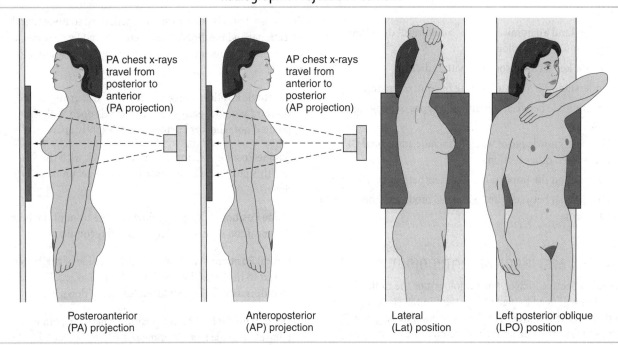

PA chest x-rays travel from posterior to anterior (PA projection)

AP chest x-rays travel from anterior to posterior (AP projection)

Posteroanterior (PA) projection

Anteroposterior (AP) projection

Lateral (Lat) position

Left posterior oblique (LPO) position

Source: EHRLICH/SCHROEDER. Medical Terminology for Health Professions, 6E. © 2009 Delmar Learning, a part of Cengage Learning, Inc. Reproduced by permission. www.cengage.com/permissions

Section Review 17.1

1. The axial plane divides the body into what sections?

    A. Left and right

    B. Posterior and anterior

    C. Front and back

    D. Superior and inferior

2. What position is the body placed in when it is in an oblique position?

   A. Lying on the back, face up

   B. Lying down, face down

   C. At an angle, neither frontal nor lateral

   D. Lying on the side

3. What X-ray projection enters the front of the body and exits through the back of the body with the patient lying down on the back?

   A. AP

   B. PA

   C. Lateral

   D. Oblique

4. Which plane divides the body into anterior and posterior sections?

   A. Sagittal

   B. Axial

   C. Transverse

   D. Coronal

5. The path of the X-ray beam is known as?

   A. Position

   B. Projection

   C. Plane

   D. Sight of vision

ICD-10-CM Coding

Radiology services are ordered for a wide variety of symptoms, illnesses, or conditions. Diagnostic coding supports medical necessity for radiological services.

Coders should keep in mind each procedure ordered and performed must be validated by medical necessity. Medical necessity is best illustrated by a solid, accurate, and specific diagnosis. Diagnoses must reflect a sign, symptom, condition, or injury. In the case of a screening film, a V code diagnosis must be used to indicate what problem is under surveillance or screening.

A radiology service can be performed as routine, screening, or for a sign or symptom. A routine screening might be performed with a preventive medicine exam, such as a routine chest X-ray. If a chest X-ray is performed as part of a preventive medicine exam, it is coded with a Z code. Look in the

ICD-10-CM Index to Diseases and Injuries for Examination/radiological. There is a subentry for with abnormal findings. These entries default to the codes for a general adult medical examination.

Z00.00 Encounter for general adult medical examination without abnormal findings

Z00.01 Encounter for general adult medical examination with abnormal findings

ICD-9-CM Application

In ICD-9-CM if a chest X-ray is performed as part of a preventive medicine exam, it is coded separately with a V code.

In the ICD-9-CM Alphabetic Index look for Examination/radiological NEC V72.5

V72.5 Radiological examination, not elsewhere classified.

Screening examinations are used when there are no signs or symptoms, but the provider is looking for a specific disease or illness. Such services might include mammography or a bone density study. When the radiological service is part of a screening for a particular disease or illness, such as mammography to screen for breast cancer, you use the screening diagnosis from the Z codes. Mammography for screening of breast cancer, is Z12.31 *Encounter for screening mammogram for malignant neoplasm of breast.*

ICD-9-CM Application

ICD-9-CM has two codes to report a routine screening mammogram:

V76.11 Screening mammogram for high-risk patient

V76.12 Other screening mammogram

Another type of screening performed is when a patient requires clearance for surgery. When an X-ray is performed as part of a pre-operative examination, a code from Z01.810-Z01.818 is used.

If the sign or symptom is the only diagnosis the coder has, the sign or symptom is used as the diagnosis for the radiological service. Similarly, when a test is ordered for a sign or symptom, and the outcome of the test is a normal result with no confirmed diagnosis, the coder reports the sign or symptom prompting the physician to order the test.

Example

A physician orders mammography for breast pain. The findings on the mammogram are normal. In this instance, the coder uses pain in breast (N64.4) for the ICD-10-CM code for the mammography.

If the radiologist has interpreted the radiology test, and the final report is available at the time of coding, the coder reports the confirmed diagnosis based on the report. This is specified in ICD-10-CM Coding Guidelines, section IV, "Diagnostic Coding and Reporting Guidelines for Outpatient Services," K, "Patients receiving diagnostic services only:"

For patients receiving diagnostic services only during an encounter/visit, sequence first the diagnosis, condition, problem, or other reason for encounter/visit shown in the medical record to be chiefly responsible for the outpatient services provided during the encounter/visit. Codes for other diagnoses (eg, chronic conditions) may be sequenced as additional diagnoses.

For encounters for routine laboratory/radiology testing in the absence of any signs, symptoms, or associated diagnosis, assign Z01.89 , encounter for other specified special examinations. If routine testing is performed during the same encounter as a test to evaluate a sign, symptom, or diagnosis, it Is appropriate to assign both the Z code and the code describing the reason for the non-routine test.

For outpatient encounters for diagnostic tests that have been interpreted by a physician, and the final report is available at the time of coding, code any confirmed or definitive diagnosis(es) documented in the interpretation. Do not code related signs and symptoms as additional diagnoses.

Sometimes, providers will order a radiological examination with a "rule out" or "questionable" diagnosis. In this instance, if the report has not been read and a final diagnosis given, the coder will need to communicate with the physician to obtain the sign or symptom for the ordered test.

Example

A patient presents to the radiology facility with forearm pain following a schoolyard fall. The ordering physician writes the order for a two-view film of the forearm (73090). The diagnosis is rule-out fractured forearm.

Because rule-out conditions are not assigned diagnosis codes, the coder must make some decisions. If the X-ray is positive for a fracture, the coder can simply add the code for a closed forearm fracture. (Note: Unless the fracture is labeled "open," the coder chooses the "closed" fracture category in ICD-10-CM.) If the X-ray is negative for a fracture, the coder must handle the problem by inquiring from the medical professional what signs or symptoms (ICD-10-CM R00-R99) the patient exhibited. At no time, however, does the coder have the authority to assume the patient was experiencing arm pain to coincide with the anatomic location of the X-ray. If no information was provided at the time of the X-ray, other than the rule-out, and the X-ray is negative, there is no medical necessity for this study.

Each payer may have varying guidelines on how the communication needs to be documented.

Example

INDICATION: Rule out cervical mass vs. left vocal cord paralysis

CT NECK WITH CONTRAST

TECHNIQUE: Axial CT cuts were obtained from the top of the orbits down to the thoracic inlet using 100 cc of Isovue 300. 1.3 mm axial CT cuts were also obtained through the larynx. Sagittal and coronal computer reconstruction images were also obtained.

Indications for nonionic contrast: None

FINDINGS: No mass lesion within the posterior nasopharynx or oropharynx. There are multifocal punctuate calcifications in the right palatine tonsil. The submandibular and parotid glands are unremarkable. There are subcentimeter anterior cervical and left submandibular lymph nodes. There are subcentimeter left internal jugular lymph nodes. The left pyriform sinus is slightly larger than the right and there is dilatation of the left laryngeal ventricle. There is probably atrophy of the left true vocal cord best seen on the 1.3 mm thick images. The left arytenoid cartilage appears to be in a deviated medial position as opposed to the right. The thyroid glands are unremarkable. The visualized upper mediastinum is unremarkable. Please refer to the CT of the chest report.

IMPRESSION

1. Left vocal cord paralysis

2. No cervical mass or adenopathy

In this case, the initial reason for the CT scan is a "rule out" diagnosis (cervical mass). The scan showed no cervical mass, but confirmed diagnosis of left vocal cord paralysis.

The *Medicare Claims Processing Manual,* chapter 23, §10.1.2 outline the guidelines for documenting orders from the treating practitioner. According to these guidelines, an order may include the following forms of communication:

- A written document signed by the treating physician/practitioner, which is hand-delivered, mailed, or faxed to the testing facility;
- A telephone call by the treating physician/practitioner or his or her office to the testing facility; or
- An electronic mail (email) by the treating physician/practitioner or his or her office to the testing facility.

Occasionally, when a radiologist reads an X-ray, she will find something on the X-ray for which she was not looking. This is considered an incidental finding and would be reported with an additional diagnosis. An incidental finding should not be used as a primary diagnosis.

Written Interpretation

Once the written interpretation is dictated and typed, there can be no alterations to the report for billing or coding purposes. Instances such as these occur frequently and should be brought to the attention of the radiologist for more accurate documentation on future interpretations, and informative orders from the referring physician.

Section Review 17.2

1. Mary visited her family physician for a lump in her breast. The physician ordered a mammogram to rule out breast cancer. The radiologist did not find any abnormal findings. What diagnosis is reported for the professional portion of the mammography?

    A. C50.911

    B. N63

    C. D24.1

    D. Z12.31

2. A young boy presents to the emergency department with pain in his lower left leg after being kicked in a soccer game. The X-ray report reveals a fractured tibia and fibula. What diagnosis code(s) is (are) reported by the radiologist for reading the X-ray (do not report the External cause code)?

    A. M79.609

    B. S72.8X2A

    C. S82.311A

    D. S82.202A, S82.402A

---

3. A patient with sinusitis and left vocal cord paralysis is sent to have a CT scan of the brain. The impression is vague, low-density white matter changes in the right frontal region. This is a nonspecific finding. The radiologist requests an MRI scan for further characterization. What diagnosis code(s) should the radiologist use for the reading of the CT?

    A. J32.9, J38.00

    B. R93.0, J32.9, J38.01

    C. R93.0

    D. J38.00

4. Mr. Davis has his yearly preventive medicine exam. The physician orders a preventive chest X-ray. What diagnosis is reported for the chest X-ray?

    A. Z01.811

    B. Z00.01

    C. Z00.00

    D. Z02.9

5. A 63-year-old female is having a hip arthroplasty due to severe rheumatoid arthritis in the hip. During her pre-operative exam, a chest X-ray is taken. What diagnosis is used for the chest X-ray?

    A. M06.9

    B. Z01.810

    C. Z01.811

    D. Z01.818

CPT®

Radiological procedures may be performed on any part of the body. They sometimes are performed as stand alone services (such as a chest X-ray or ankle X-ray), or in addition to other services (such as MRI guidance for needle placement during a biopsy). To code radiological services correctly, a coder should have a general recognition of the types of radiology equipment, determine which equipment is used for the evaluation, and understand the applicable guidelines in the Radiology section.

Radiology Guidelines

Separate Procedures

As we have discussed in prior chapters, designated "separate procedures" may be performed as an integral part to another procedure, or alone. Separate procedures should be coded only if performed alone, or performed with an unrelated service. There are very few "separate procedure" codes in the Radiology section.

Unlisted Procedures

Radiological services not covered by a specific CPT® code are coded with an unlisted code. Although most unlisted procedures end in the digits 99, in the radiology section there are some unlisted procedures ending in 96, 97, and 98 (for example, 76496 *Unlisted fluoroscopic procedure (eg, diagnostic, interventional)*).

Anytime an unlisted service code is reported, the claim should be accompanied by a special report describing the procedure and the reason the procedure was medically necessary. You also will want to explain the equipment, time, and effort involved.

Supervision and Interpretation

"S & I" codes describe the supervision and interpretation of a radiological procedure. Interventional radiologic procedures are used to diagnosis and treat conditions using invasive procedures. Common procedures containing a supervision and interpretation component include vascular procedures performed on the veins and arteries.

When a procedure requires radiological guidance, a code from the surgery or medicine section may be reported along with the supervision and interpretation code from the radiology section. When the same physician provides both the surgical procedure and the radiological guidance, the physician will report both codes. When a physician performs the surgery, and a radiologist performs the supervision and interpretation, each will report the code for his or her portion of the service. For all codes, especially S & I codes, it is imperative to read the parenthetical instructions designed to help prevent coding errors.

Remember: The radiologist billing the supervision and interpretation must be present at the time of the procedure to bill the supervision and interpretation code and provide a written report. Radiology S & I codes can be reported with modifier 26 for the professional services or the modifier TC for the technical services. Both of these modifiers are explained further in the chapter.

CPT® Example

75962 Transluminal balloon angioplasty, peripheral artery other than renal, or other visceral artery, iliac or lower extremity, radiological supervision and interpretation.

Administration of Contrast Material(s)

Contrast material is a substance or material that "lights up" the structure being studied so it can be visualized. The phrase "with contrast" represents contrast material administered in three ways:

- Intravascularly—using a vein or artery
- Intra-articularly—in a joint
- Intrathecally—within a sheath, or within the subarachnoid or cerebral spinal fluid.

According to CPT® guidelines, "Oral and/or rectal contrast administration alone does not qualify as a study "with contrast." Oral contrast is either barium or a mixture of fruit juice and an iodine-containing liquid. Or, the patient may receive a barium enema. When contrast is given orally or rectally, it is not appropriate to report a "with contrast" code.

Some studies, such as an MRI or CT scan, may be performed without contrast, followed by "with contrast." In these instances, there often is a single code to report both sets of images.

Gadolinium is a contrast used with MRIs. Iodine (or a hypoallergenic synthetic) is used for intravenous pyelograms (IVP), CT scans, arthrograms, and angiograms. The radiology technician routinely asks the patient if he or she is allergic to or has shown sensitivity to shellfish (also high in iodine concen-

tration). If the patient replies positively, a nonionic contrast substitute is infused to lessen or prevent a potential allergic reaction.

As you code for contrast imaging, you also may need to code an additional procedure. Watch for parenthetic instructions following the imaging codes to see if another procedure—such as the injection procedure for the contrast—should be reported. The contrast material is not included in the radiological procedure and can be reported separately, typically with a HCPCS Level II code to identify the substance used. The contrast material is reported by the facility, unless the procedure is performed in a physician's office, where the physician owns the equipment.

The Radiology Report

The radiologist's written report is the documentation for the professional component of the radiological procedure, and must be signed.

Types of Radiological Services

The Radiology section in the CPT® codebook is divided into the following subsections:

- Diagnostic Radiology (Diagnostic Imaging) 70010–76499)
- Diagnostic Ultrasound (76506–76999)
- Radiologic Guidance (77001–77022)
- Breast, Mammography (77051–77063)
- Bone/Joint Studies (77071–77086)
- Radiation Oncology (77261–77799)
- Nuclear Medicine (78012–79999)

Scout Films:

Films: Scout, Comparison, Diagnostic, Screening, and Spot

Scout films may be performed prior to an actual imaging study with contrast or delayed imaging. Scout films are not coded separately as they are considered part of the basic procedure. In some instances, a screening film is used to detect an undiagnosed illness or condition. Screening films may be used to prediagnose or confirm a suspected condition. Comparison films are sometimes ordered to define the presence of an injury or pathology.

Comparison films may be ordered to pinpoint an abnormality or deformity between a normal and injured body part. Unless there is diagnosed pathology or injury in both areas, only the X-rays taken of the affected area are coded. Comparison of anatomical structures may be considered part of the physician's medical decision-making process and final diagnosis.

Diagnostic films may be required to evaluate the extent of the presenting symptoms or conditions or to track the progression of the patient's condition or illness. Diabetic patients, or patients with poor wound healing potential, may have malunion or nonunion of a fractured bone. Careful X-ray monitoring is required to track the patient's progress and customize a treatment plan relative to their healing potential.

If splinting or casting is applied to a fracture, periodic films may be required to determine healing of the bone or maintenance of accurate alignment.

Spot films are submitted for a radiologist's interpretation when another physician performs the radiology supervision and interpretation procedure. Radiology supervision and interpretation codes require the radiologist to supervise performance of the procedure and provide a written interpretation of the procedure. If the radiologist was not present during the performance of the procedure, then he or she has not fulfilled the entire criteria for assigning an S & I code. To correctly code this scenario, the radiology code is appended with a reduced service modifier 52 based on the lack of direct radiologist supervision. Even with a well-defined and carefully written interpretation, payers may not consider this service as payable.

Practical Coding Note

Films that are unreadable, improperly positioned, or underdeveloped are considered "operator error" and not coded. Some technicians will make a note in the medical record for medicolegal documentation, but the coder should not penalize the patient when errors or omissions occur during the filming process.

Portable, Handheld X-ray Device

This low intensity X-ray imaging device is a lightweight portable handheld instrument using a low-level isotope as its penetrating energy source. It can picture any part of the human anatomy inserted in the space between the energy source and the viewing mechanism. The device can be useful in making an immediate diagnosis in the following settings: isolated areas, accident scenes, sports events, and emergency rooms. It is also useful in the instances where fluoroscopy would ordinarily be used: localization of foreign bodies, selected surgical procedures, and the evaluation of premature or low birth weight infants.

Diagnostic Radiology (Diagnostic Imaging)

Diagnostic radiology consists of X-rays, MRI, and CT scan studies.

A plain X-ray is like taking a picture or snapshot of the inside of the body. The X-ray machine sends photons through the body with the film on the other side to record the images using ionizing radiation. Bone blocks the protons and appears white on the X-ray film, making it easy to discover a fractured bone. Contrast material also blocks the protons and shows white on the film. Structures containing air, such as lungs, appear black on X-ray images. Muscle, fat, and fluid appear as shades of gray. Such imaging allows initial diagnosis of many abnormalities within the body.

Plain X-ray

Although more and more radiology departments are replacing actual X-ray film with digital X-ray acquisition, the ultimate purpose is the same: to focus X-ray energy on a body part creating an image of a solid or dense internal structure. In medical practice today, X-ray is used to diagnose and treat various problems. It is considered both a diagnostic and therapeutic tool.

CT scans use a series of X-rays to produce cross-sectional pictures of the body. CT scans commonly are used to diagnose tumors, identify internal injuries caused by trauma, and to diagnose vascular disease. For instance, CTA, or computerized tomographic angiography, is a CT scan of the blood vessels.

CT Scans

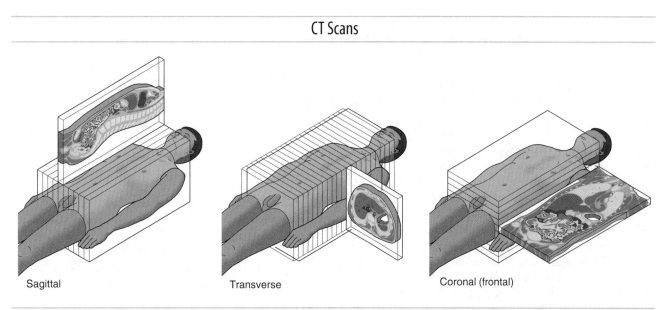

Sagittal   Transverse   Coronal (frontal)

Source: Ehrlich, Medical Terminology for Health Professionals, 6e, ISBN #978-1-4180-7252-0

CT

Multiplanar Diagnostic Imaging (MPDI) is a process translating the data produced by CT scanning by providing reconstructed oblique images contributing to diagnostic information. MPDI is also known as planar image reconstruction or reformatted imaging.

Practical Coding Note

According to CPT®, if radiographic arthrography is performed, the coder must also use the arthrography supervision and interpretation code for the appropriate joint. Fluoroscopy is considered included in these codes. On the other hand, if CT or MRI is performed with radiographic arthrography, the coder must use the appropriate joint injection code, the accurate CT or MRI code, and the correct imaging guidance code for needle placement for contrast injection. When intrathecal injection is required, code 61055 or 62284 should be added.

MRI

MRI often is used to diagnose conditions in ligament, or the brain, spinal cord, heart, and internal organs such as the lungs, liver, prostate, etc. MRI produces "slices" of images by using a magnetic field and the protons within your body. The slices can be combined to produce 3-D images that may be viewed from different angles. This precise imaging helps physicians differentiate between healthy and unhealthy tissue.

MRI can assist in the differential diagnosis of mediastinal and retroperitoneal masses, including abnormalities of the large vessels such as aneurysms and dissection of vessels. When a clinical need exists to visualize the parenchyma of solid organs to detect anatomic disruption or neoplasia, this can be accomplished in the liver, urogenital system, adrenals, and pelvic organs without the use of radiological contrast materials. When MRI is considered reasonable and necessary, the use of paramagnetic contrast materials may be covered as part of the study. MRI may also be used to detect and stage pelvic and retroperitoneal neoplasms and to evaluate disorders of cancellous bone and soft tissues, or in the detection of pericardial thickening. Primary and secondary bone neoplasm and aseptic necrosis can be detected at an early stage and monitored with MRI. Patients with metallic prostheses, especially of the hip, can be imaged to detect the early stages of infection of the bone to which the prosthesis is attached. MRI may be performed with and without contrast.

Magnetic resonance angiography (MRA) is an MRI of the blood vessels. MRA is a noninvasive diagnostic test and is an application of MRI. By analyzing the amount of energy released from tissues exposed to a strong magnetic field, MRA provides images of normal and diseased blood vessels as well as visualization and quantification of blood flow through these vessels. Phase contrast (PC) and time-of-flight (TOF) are the available MRA techniques at the time of publication. PC measures the difference between the phases of proton spins in tissue and blood and measures both the venous and arterial blood flow at any point in the cardiac cycle. TOF measures the difference between the amount of magnetization of tissue and blood and provides information on the structure of blood vessels, thus indirectly indicating blood flow. Three-dimensional (3D) images can be obtained using this method. Contrast-enhanced MRA (CE-MRA) involves blood flow imaging after the patient receives an intravenous injection of a contrast agent. Gadolinium, a nonionic element, is the foundation of all contrast agents currently in use. Gadolinium affects the way in which tissues respond to magnetization, resulting in better visualization of structures when compared to unenhanced studies. Unlike ionic (eg, iodine-based) contrast agents used in conventional contrast angiography (CA), allergic reactions to gadolinium are extremely rare. Gadolinium does not cause kidney failure occasionally seen with ionic contrast agents. Digital subtraction angiography (DSA) is a computer-augmented form of CA obtaining digital blood flow images as contrast agent courses through a blood vessel. The computer "subtracts" bone and other tissue from the image, improving visualization of blood vessels. Physicians elect to use a specific MRA or CA technique based upon clinical information from each patient.

Digital Subtraction Angiography (DSA) is a diagnostic imaging technique applying computer technology to fluoroscopy for visualizing the same vascular structures observable with conventional angiography. Because the radiographic contrast material can be injected into a vein rather than an artery, the procedure reduces the risk to patients, and can be performed on an outpatient basis.

When coding for diagnostic radiology, a coder needs to determine the anatomic location, the type of radiology used (X-ray, CT, MRI), the number of views, the type of views taken, and whether contrast material was used.

To identify the location, the coder will sometimes have to break apart a word into word parts. Consider "myelography" as an example: Myel/o is the root word meaning spinal cord, and –graphy means the act of recording data. Myelography is recording data on the spinal cord. A myelography can be performed on different sections of the spinal cord and is coded according to the section studied. For example, a myelography of the cervical region is coded with CPT® code 72240. Notice the myelography code is a supervision and interpretation code. The coder should check if additional services need to be coded from other sections of the CPT® codebook. Using our example of the cervical region, a coder must review the parenthetical instructions under CPT® code 72240 which note, "For complete cervical myelography via Injection procedure at C1–C2 see 61055, 72240."

When the anatomical location has been identified, codes for radiologic examination by X-ray often are selected based on the number of views. The number of views is not synonymous with the number of films used. A radiology technician may be required to shoot several films of the same view. The language

used in CPT® refers to the number of views, not the number of films.

CPT® Example

73560 Radiologic examination, knee; 1 or 2 views

73562   3 views

73564   complete, 4 or more views

Sometimes, the code descriptor states a minimum number of views. When this terminology is used, the code includes any number of views in excess of the number provided in the description. For example, the description for CPT® code 73610 is *Radiologic examination, ankle; complete, minimum of 3 views*. Whether three, four, or more views are taken, 73610 is appropriate.

For some radiologic examinations, the type of view taken, instead of the number of views, is the determining factor for code selection. When this is the case, if the physician only documents the number of views, there will be insufficient documentation for code selection.

CPT® Example

74000 Radiologic examination, abdomen; single anteroposterior view

74010   anteroposterior and additional oblique and cone views

74020   complete, including decubitus and/or erect views

Practical Coding Note

Radiology codes by anatomical location are grouped together based on the type of imaging used (X-Ray, MRI, CT, etc). Within your CPT® codebook, bracket the codes for each type of imaging and label the bracket as that type of imaging. After bracketing the codes, go through and underline the differences in each of the similar codes. This will aid in quick determination of the correct code during the certification exam. Upon finding the appropriate code, read the guidelines for that subsection of CPT®, along with any parenthetical notes listed below the code.

Acronyms			
		MRA	Magnetic resonance angiography
		MRI	Magnetic resonance imaging
AP	Anteroposterior	PA	Posteroanterior
CT	Computed tomography	RL	Right lateral
CTA	Computed tomography angiography	S & I	Supervision and interpretation
KUB	Kidneys, ureter, bladder	TMJ	Temporomandibular joint
LL	Left lateral		

Section Review 17.3

1. A contrast radiograph of the salivary glands and ducts is performed, resulting in a diagnosis of salivary fistula. What are the CPT® and ICD-10-CM codes for the supervision and interpretation of this procedure?

   A. 70380-26, K11.5

   B. 70380-26, K11.3

   C. 70390-26, K11.5

   D. 70390-26, K11.4

2. CT images of the abdomen and pelvis were obtained without IV contrast, as a follow up to a splenic injury. What is/are the CPT® code(s) for the CT scan?

   A. 74010

   B. 72170

   C. 74176

   D. 74170, 72194

3. A parent brings a child to the Emergency Department after realizing the child swallowed a metal jack. A radiological exam from the nose to the rectum is performed. What is/are the CPT® code(s) for this service?

   A. 70160-26, 70370-26, 71010-26, 74245-26

   B. 76010-26

   C. 70160-26, 70360-26, 71015-26, 74245-26

   D. 70160-26, 70370-26, 74245-26

4. A patient presents to her physician 48 hours after an assault with right eye pain, nasal airway obstruction, and deformity. The physician orders an X-ray of the facial bones with a Waters view, Caldwell view, and a lateral view. What is the CPT® code for the X-ray?

   A. 70486

   B. 70220

   C. 70150

   D. 70140

5. A patient presents to the physician with stiffness and numbness in the neck, shoulders, and arms. The physician orders an MRI of the cervical spine, with and without contrast, to rule out cervical spinal stenosis. What is/are the CPT® code(s) for the MRI?

    A. 72020

    B. 72127

    C. 72141, 72142

    D. 72156

Diagnostic Ultrasound

Diagnostic ultrasound uses sound waves to visualize internal structures such as muscles, tendons, and organs. The images then can be used to measure the size—and observe the movement and functioning—of structures such as the heart or blood vessels. During pregnancy, ultrasound is used to view the fetus. Ultrasound also is used for guidance in various procedures.

There are different types of ultrasound scans. Some types include A-mode (A-scan), B-mode (B-scan), M-mode, and Real-time scan. A-mode (amplitude mode) is a one-dimensional scan typically only seen in ophthalmic ultrasounds. M-mode (motion mode) is a one-dimensional scan showing the movement of a moving structure (such as the heart). B-mode (brightness mode) is a two-dimensional scan. Real-time scans are B-scans in motion.

3-D scans also are now available; 4-D scans are 3-D ultrasounds in motion.

4D Ultrasound

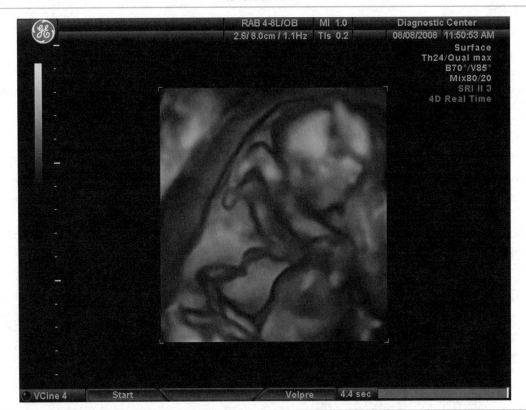

Twins at 17 weeks gestation. Courtesy: AAPC

A coder will need to understand the different types of scans to select the correct code.

A Doppler study is a type of ultrasound penetrating solids or liquids. This type of study is useful in imaging the flow of blood. The Doppler can create images either in shades of gray or, when processed by a computer, color images. The use of Doppler imaging is separately reportable, except when used alone for anatomic structure identification with real-time ultrasound. To report a Doppler study there must be a permanent record of the images and a written report.

An example of where you need to know the different scans for code selection is in ophthalmic ultrasounds in the Head and Neck anatomical subsection. For ophthalmic ultrasounds, there is a biometric A-scan, biomicroscopy, quantitative A-Scan, Biomicroscopy, Quantative A-Scan, and corneal pachymetry. For an A-scan, you look straight ahead. For a B-scan, you look in many different directions. A biomicroscopy is a slit lamp exam, which is a low-power microscope combined with a high-intensity light source focused to shine in a thin beam. This test may detect cataracts, macular degeneration, retinal detachment, and other eye diseases. A corneal pachymetry is a test to determine corneal thickness. Topical anesthesia is required for corneal pachymetry because the probe must touch the corneal surface. Corneal pachymetry is one of the biometric studies not requiring permanently recorded images.

Some anatomic regions have "complete" and "limited" ultrasound codes. Elements comprising a "complete" exam are listed in the code description in parentheses. For example, the guidelines in the abdomen and retroperitoneum subsection give the definitions of a complete ultrasound exam for the abdomen and the retroperitoneum. The abdomen real-time scan includes the liver, gallbladder, common bile duct, pancreas, spleen, kidneys, and the upper abdominal aorta and inferior vena cava. If the intent of the procedure is to visualize all of these, but one is obstructed from view, the physician must document why he or she was not able to visualize the organ or structure. If less than a complete exam is completed, the coder reports the "limited" ultrasound code.

Pelvic ultrasounds are divided further between obstetric (76801–76828) and non-obstetric (76830–76857). An obstetric ultrasound is either a pregnant uterus ultrasound or a fetal ultrasound. The components of each pregnant uterus ultrasound are listed within the guidelines of the obstetrical pelvis subsection. The fetal ultrasounds differ according to what is evaluated. Fetal ultrasounds include a biophysical profile (BPP) examining the health of the fetus, including information on the amniotic fluid, fetal breathing, fetal tone, and gross body movements. This profile can be performed with or without non-stress testing.

Non-obstetric ultrasounds include a transvaginal ultrasound, a sonohysterography, and non-obstetric pelvic ultrasounds. A transvaginal (meaning "through the vagina") ultrasound is used to look at the female reproductive organs—the uterus, ovaries, cervix, and vagina—to search for ovarian cysts, tumors, infection, etc. Transvaginal ultrasound is also used in obstetrics early in pregnancy and to evaluate the cervix.

Sonohysterography is an ultrasound of the uterus. Saline infusion sonohysterography occurs when sterile saline is introduced into the uterus through the cervix. The procedure is used to evaluate symptoms such as abnormal uterine bleeding, infertility, or abnormalities of the uterine lining.

Further information about the non-obstetrical pelvic ultrasound codes can be found in the guidelines in the CPT® codebook.

Ultrasonic Guidance codes are selected based on the type of procedure performed (such as pericardiocentesis, vascular access, needle placement, etc). During an encounter, either a diagnostic ultrasound code or an ultrasound guidance code may be reported, but not both.

Radiologic Guidance

As with ultrasound guidance, services classified as radiologic guidance are used to help the provider see inside the body as he or she is performing noninvasive or percutaneous procedures. The radiologic guidance codes are organized by the type of radiological guidance used—whether it is fluoroscopic, CT, MR, or other type of guidance—and selected based on the precise procedure performed.

Fluoroscopy is a continuous X-ray displayed onto a screen for monitoring. The continuous image is used like a real-time movie to view the movement of a body part, or of an instrument or dye moving through the body. Fluoroscopic guidance codes are used for catheter insertion, needle placement, and localization of a needle or catheter.

Like fluoroscopy, CT allows the physician to view a constant image on a screen to monitor the movements made within the body. It often is used in the treatment of tumors. CT-guided stereotactic localization is used to make sure radiation beams are targeting the tumor instead of surrounding tissue or other vital organs. CT also can be used to assist monitoring parenchymal tissue ablation and the placement of radiation therapy fields. Parenchyma is the functional tissue of an organ. Parenchymal tissue ablation is destruction of the parenchymal tissue containing the cancerous cells. MR may be used for needle placement and parenchymal tissue ablation as well.

Breast, Mammography

Mammography is an X-ray of the breast using special equipment. It has been the long-standing tool for screening and diagnosing breast disease. Mammography codes are selected based on the imaging device, procedure performed, whether it is screening or diagnostic, and whether it is unilateral or bilateral.

A screening mammogram often is used to detect breast cancer. The National Cancer Institute recommends women age 40 and over have a screening mammogram every one to two years, or more frequently for those at high-risk. A screening mammogram is performed when no symptoms exist and typically takes less time than a diagnostic mammogram. Screening mammograms are always bilateral.

Diagnostic mammograms may be unilateral or bilateral, and focus on a symptom. The radiology technician may need to focus on a specific area to get a better view of a suspected problem. Diagnostic mammograms also may be combined with software using computer algorithm analysis designed to help the radiologist interpret mammograms. When this software is used, it is considered computer-aided detection (CAD) and an add-on code is reported with the mammogram.

Digital breast tomosynthesis takes mutliple images of the breast and produces a 3D image of the breast. This provides a clearer image of the breast. There are codes for unilateral or bilateral diagnostic digital breast tomosynthesis and an add-on code for screening tomosynthesis during a screening mammogram.

A ductogram, or galactogram (galact is a root word meaning milk), is imaging of the ducts in the breast. It typically is used to find the reason for nipple discharge. Additional studies found in this section include MRI of the breast.

Example

Mammography with CAD

Reason for Exam: Lump in breast, history of breast cancer at age 73.

Ordered: MAMMOGRAPHY, DIGITAL, BILATERAL

Report: Bilateral CC, MLO, and XCCL views were taken.

Impression: The breast tissue is heterogeneously dense. This may lower the sensitivity of mammography. There are no dominant masses or suspicious calcifications. There is architectural distortion and increased density in the upper outer left breast consistent with post-op and post radiation changes.

Assessment: BIRADS 2: BENIGN FINDINGS

Recommendation: Routine screening mammogram

This examination was reviewed with the aid of R2 Image Checker Computer Aided Detection, Version 9.0

CPT® Code:

77056 Mammography; bilateral (Payers requiring the use of HCPCS would be reported with G0204)

+77051 Computer-aided detection with further review for interpretation, with or without digitization of film radiographic images; diagnostic mammography

Correct ICD-10 codes: N63 *Unspecified lump in breast*, Z85.3 *Personal history of malignant neoplasm of breast*.

In this case, indications confirm a diagnostic mammography should be reported. The mammography was performed bilaterally. Although the recommendation states "routine screening," this is a recommendation, not the type of procedure. The patient had a lump in her breast, thereby indicating the need for a diagnostic mammogram. Finally, documentation states the mammography was performed with CAD, allowing the add-on code for CAD to be reported.

Section Review 17.4

1. During a physical examination, hepatomegaly is revealed. The physician orders an ultrasound of the liver to evaluate the hepatomegaly. What CPT® code is reported?

    A. 74000

    B. 76705

    C. 74022

    D. 76700

2. A patient 20-weeks pregnant with twins goes to her OB/GYN for an ultrasound to check the position of both fetuses. What CPT® code(s) is/are used for the ultrasound?

    A. 76805, 76810

    B. 76816

    C. 76816, 76810

    D. 76815

3. A complete B-scan ultrasound without duplex Doppler of the kidney is performed in the physician's office on a patient following a kidney transplant. What is the CPT® code for the ultrasound?

    A. 76705

    B. 76775

    C. 76776

    D. 76811

4. A patient with left breast pain and a lump in the breast visits her physician. After examination, the physician orders a mammogram of the left breast. The mammography is performed using computer-aided detection software. What CPT® code(s) is/are reported for the mammography?

    A. 77055

    B. 77057-52

    C. 77055, 77051

    D. 77057-52, 77052

5. The use of ultrasound to examine and measure internal structures of the skull and to diagnose abnormalities and disease is echoencephalography. What is the code for echoencephalography and/or real time with image documentation, including A-mode encephalography as a secondary component where indicated?

    A. 76506

    B. 76510

    C. 76511

    D. 76512

Bone/Joint Studies

Bone and joint studies are performed to determine bone or joint abnormalities—whether it be the length of the bone, age of the bone, composition of the bone, or how the joint moves when stress is applied.

A bone age study typically is performed on children to estimate the maturity of a child's skeletal system, based on the appearance of the growth plate in the bone. A bone length study is used to determine discrepancies in limb length. Osseous surveys are radiological procedures used to detect fractures, tumors, or degenerative conditions of the bone.

Osseous surveys are coded based on whether the service is limited or complete, or if the survey was performed on an infant.

Dual-energy X-ray absorptiometry (DXA or DEXA), is a common test performed to determine bone density. This test helps to evaluate risk of bone fractures (which often are the result of osteoporosis). DEXA scans are coded based on the location of the body part being scanned.

Radiation Oncology

Radiation oncology is a multi-disciplinary medical specialty involving physicians, physicists and dosimetrists, nurses, biomedical scientists, computer scientists, radiotherapy technologists, nutritionists, and social workers. It is a highly specialized and complex method for delivering radiation treatment to tumors.

The radiation oncology subsection in the CPT® codebook is divided into:

- consultation; clinical management
- treatment planning
- radiation physics and dosimetry, devices, and special services
- treatment deliveries
- radiation treatment management
- hyperthermia
- clinical intracavitary hyperthermia
- clinical brachytherapy

When a patient first visits the radiation oncologist, there is a consultation to determine if radiation will benefit the patient. According to CPT®, this service is coded from the appropriate evaluation and management, medicine, or surgical codes.

After the initial consultation, the patient and provider will plan the treatment. Clinical treatment planning is how the provider determines the ports, blocks, and doses of radiation. According to your CPT® guidelines, clinical treatment planning involves interpretation of special testing, tumor localization, treatment volume determination, and treatment time/dosage determination, choice of treatment modality, determination of the number and size of treatment ports, selection of appropriate treatment devices, and other procedures.

The appropriate code (77261–77263) is based on the level of planning: simple, intermediate, or complex. Planning levels are defined by the number of treatment areas, ports, and blocks, and consider special dose time, and if rotational or special beams are required.

A port is the place where radiation enters the body and is often marked with tattooing. Blocks are special pieces of lead designed specifically for each patient to shield healthy normal tissue from receiving the radiation allowing the radiation to focus solely on the tumor.

During the treatment planning process, the provider and patient go through simulation. Simulation may be carried out on a dedicated simulator, a radiation therapy treatment unit, or diagnostic X-ray machine. The provider must be present. The therapeutic radiology simulation-aided field setting codes are used for this procedure (77280–77295). This process requires the patient to lie very still on a table while the provider determines the port entry. The simulation is selected based on the number of ports, blocks, and the use of contrast material, and 3-D simulation.

The information gained in simulation is then sent to medical radiation physicists and medical radiation dosimetrists. Dosimetry is the calculation of the dose of radiation. These highly trained physicians design and create the blocks to shield the healthy tissue. They also plan the dose delivery. The services of the physicists and dosimetrists are coded using the codes in the subsection for Medical Radiation Physics, Dosimetry, Treatment Devices and Special Planning (77295, 77300–77370).

Radiation Treatment Management

The actual delivery of radiation is reported by the facility. The oversight of the delivery is reported by the physician (77427–77499), including review of the port films, dosimetry, dose delivery, treatment parameters, and treatment set-up. This oversight is considered radiation treatment management, and is reported by the number of fractions.

Patients typically receive radiation treatment in "fractions." The treatment itself is quick and only takes a matter of minutes, but is delivered frequently, including daily or twice per day. When the delivery is twice per day, it is considered two fractions as there is a distinct break in therapy.

This phase of treatment is reported in units of five fractions or treatment sessions, regardless of the actual time-period in which the services are furnished. The services need not be furnished on consecutive days. Code 77427 is also reported for three or four fractions beyond a multiple of five at the end of a course of treatment. One or two fractions beyond a multiple of five at the end of a course of treatment are not reported separately.

Special Treatment Procedures

CPT® 77470 reports the physician's work necessary for the management of special procedures such as total body irradiation, combination with chemotherapy, or other combined modality therapy, stereotactic radiosurgery, and intraoperative radiation therapy.

Stereotactic, Radiation Treatment Delivery, Neutron Beam, and Proton Beam Treatment Delivery

The treatment delivery sections reported by the facility only include the following Radiation Oncology subsections:

- Stereotactic Radiation Treatment Delivery
- Radiation Treatment Delivery (except for the stereoscopic guidance)

- Neutron Beam Treatment Delivery
- Proton Beam Treatment Delivery

Stereotactic Radiation Treatment Delivery (77371–77373)

Stereotactic radiation treatment is also called radiation surgery, radiosurgery, stereotactic external-beam radiation, and stereotactic radiosurgery. Although it is not actual surgery, it involves precise positioning by use of special equipment to deliver large radiation doses to tumors in the brain and not to normal tissue. It is also used to treat other brain disorders and is being studied in the treatment of lung and other types of cancer.

Radiation Treatment Delivery (77401–77425)

Code 77387 reports guidance for localization, of target volume for delivery of radiation treatment delivery, includes intrafraction tracking when performed.

Neutron Beam Treatment Delivery (77422–77423)

Code 77422 describes high-energy neutron radiation treatment delivery to a single treatment area using a single port or parallel opposed ports with no blocks or simple blocking. Code 77423 describes high-energy neutron radiation treatment delivery to one or more isocenters with coplanar or noncoplanar geometry with simple or complex blocking, wedging, or compensators.

Proton Beam Treatment Delivery (77520–77525)

Proton treatment delivery uses protons (positively charged particles) to target tumors in sensitive areas. Because of the physical makeup of protons, they release most of their energy when they hit the tumor, and do not pass beyond the tumor. Proton treatment delivery is used for lung, brain, and prostate tumors and tumors in pediatric patients. Code selection is based on the number of ports and blocks used.

Practical Coding Note

Bracket the codes reported by the facility only, and label as "Facility only." These codes do not need modifier 26 or TC appended to them: 77261–77263; 77336; 77371–77373; 77401-77417; 77385–77386; 77422–77423; 77424–77425; 77520–77525.

Hyperthermia

Hyperthermia is the use of heat. Hyperthermia used with radiation therapy is under investigation. Some insurance carriers currently only allow for deep hyperthermia and some do not allow hyperthermia at all. Make sure you review your insurance carrier contracts and guidelines.

Clinical Brachytherapy

Clinical brachytherapy uses radioactive material sealed in needles, seeds, wires, or catheters. The sealed radioactive material is placed in or near a tumor. You also may hear this referred to as internal or implant radiation therapy. Interstitial brachytherapy are seeds, or other sealed radioactive material inserted into tissue at or near the tumor site. Intracavitary brachytherapy is when it is inserted into a body cavity with an applicator. Remote high dose rate (HDR) afterloading brachytherapy involves the precise insertion of catheters into the tumor. The catheter(s) is/are then connected to a remote afterloading brachytherapy unit, which delivers radiation.

Nuclear Medicine

Nuclear medicine is the use of small amounts of radioactive material to examine organ function and structure. Therapeutic nuclear medicine can be used to treat cancer and other medical conditions. The radiopharmaceuticals used in nuclear medicine are not included in the coding of the tests, and should be reported separately (typically using a HCPCS Level II code) by the facility.

The radiopharmaceuticals, or radiotracers, can be swallowed, inhaled, or injected into a vein. The radioactive material is detected by a gamma camera, a PET scan, or a probe.

PET & SPECT

PET is a noninvasive diagnostic imaging procedure assessing the level of metabolic activity and perfusion in various organ systems of the body. A positron camera (tomograph) is used to produce cross-sectional tomographic images, which are obtained from positron emitting radioactive tracer substances (radiopharmaceuticals) such as 2-[F-18] Fluoro-D-Glucose (FDG), administered intravenously to the patient.

SPECT acquires information on the concentration of radionuclides introduced into the patient's body. It is useful in the diagnosis of several clinical conditions including: stress fracture, spondylosis, infection (eg, discitis), tumor (eg, osteoid osteoma), analysis of blood flow to an organ, as in the case of myocardial viability, and to differentiate ischemic heart disease from dilated cardiomyopathy.

Single Photon Emission Computed Tomography (SPECT) studies represent an enhanced methodology over standard planar nuclear imaging. When a limited anatomic area is studied, there is no additional information procured by obtaining both planar and SPECT studies. While both represent medically acceptable imaging studies, when a SPECT study of a limited area is performed, a planar study is not to be reported separately. When vascular flow studies are obtained using planar technology in addition to SPECT studies, the appropriate CPT® code for the vascular flow study should be reported, not the flow, planar and SPECT studies. In cases where planar images must be procured because of the extent of the scanned area (eg, bone imaging), both planar and SPECT scans may be necessary and reported separately.

Absorptiometry

Single photon absorptiometry (CPT® 78350), also known as a bone density study, describes a noninvasive radiological technique that measures the absorption of a monochromatic or dichromatic photon beam by bone material. The device, which is placed directly on the patient, uses a low dose of radionuclide to measure the mass absorption efficiency of the energy released. The exam provides a quantitative measurement of the bone mineral of cortical and trabecular bone to assess treatment response at appropriate intervals.

Dual photon absorptiometry (CPT® 78351) is a noninvasive radiological technique measuring absorption of a mono- or dichromatic beam by bone material in one or more sites. This procedure is not covered under Medicare because it is still considered to be in the investigational stage.

Pulmonary Perfusion Imaging

CPT® 78597–78598 report the imaging of a patient twice: one after inhalation of a radioactive aerosol to determine pulmonary ventilation, and again after injection of a radioactive particulate to determine lung perfusion. This procedure is used in the diagnosis of pulmonary embolism, bronchopulmonary sequestration, and pulmonary trauma.

Other Procedures (78800–78999)

Nuclear medicine codes 78800, 78802, and 78804 report the studies required to complete nuclear medicine whole body or SPECT tumor imaging studies. Imaging for specific tumors detected through the infusion of labeled indium-111 antibody (78800) requires multiple day studies. Whole body imaging for pretreatment planning prior to therapy must be performed on two or more days. In codes 78802 and 78804, the imaging procedure requires whole body gamma camera images at 2 to 24 hours and again at 48 to 72 hours after injection. A third set of images may be required at 90 to 120 hours. Image interpretation requires qualitative assessment of blood clearance, normal uptake by kidneys and lungs, and uptake within tumor. Report code 78802 imaging studies for whole body performed on a single day and 78804 for whole body performed on multiple days.

Codes 78811–78816 differentiate the three different levels of work associated with PET and PET/CT imaging. Code 78811 is a limited PET study (eg, chest, head/neck); code 78812 describes a PET study of the skull base to midthigh; and code

78813 reports a PET study of the whole body. Code 78814 describes a PET procedure with concurrently acquired CT for attenuation correction and anatomical localization of a limited area. Code 78815 reports a study using PET with concurrently acquired CT for attenuation correction and anatomical localization of the skull base to mid-thigh, and code 78816 refers to a whole body study using PET with concurrently acquired CT for attenuation correction and anatomical localization.

Practical Coding Note

For code series 78814–78816, if a diagnostic CT is performed for other than attenuation correction or anatomical localization concurrently with the PET study, use modifier 59 with CT codes. There must be a separate order for the diagnostic CT and for the PET or CT performed for attenuation or anatomical localization.

Therapeutic (79005–79999)

Radiolabeled monoclonal antibodies (CPT® code 79403) can locate tumor cells and either kill them or deliver tumor-killing substances to them without harming normal cells. Monoclonal antibodies (mAb) of murine origin can target tumors and detect disease when labeled with radionuclides that emit gamma rays. Satumomab pendetide (OncoScint CR/OV) labeled with indium-111 has been approved by the FDA for the single-use detection of extrahepatic intra-abdominal metastases from colorectal or ovarian cancer. Report code 78802 or 78804 for pre-treatment imaging.

Practical Coding Note

The oral and intravenous administration codes in this section include the mode of administration. For intraarterial, intracavitary and intra-articular administration, use the appropriate injection and/or procedure codes, as well as imaging guidance and radiological supervision and interpretation codes.

Code 79005 was established to report radiopharmaceutical therapy by oral administration; code 79101 was established to report radiopharmaceutical therapy by intravenous administration. Coders should pay particular attention to the parenthetical notes referring to code 79101. Code 79445 reports radiopharmaceutical therapy by intra-arterial administration and coders are instructed to use a HCPCS Level II code to report the use of therapeutic radiopharmaceuticals. When the services are performed in a facility, the facility reports the radiopharmaceuticals.

Codes 79200, 79300, and 79440 indicate route of administration (intracavitary, interstitial and intra-articular).

Nuclear medicine codes are selected based on the test performed.

HCPCS Level II

HCPCS Level II codes exist for mammography and PET scans. For mammography, systems have been developed to produce digital images. This is sometimes used in telemammography to be able to provide mammography to underserved areas. There are HCPCS Level II codes for mammography producing a direct digital image.

Whole body PET scans may be used for staging melanoma. When a Medicare patient receives a PET scan for melanoma without the specified indications covered by Medicare, the service is coded using a HCPCS Level II code.

HCPCS Level II Example

G0219 PET imaging whole body; melanoma for non-covered indications

During MRI or CT scans, contrast material can be used. The contrast material clarifies soft tissue during the scan. When contrast material is used, a HCPCS Level II code can be coded in addition to the scan. When the services are performed in a facility, the facility reports the radiopharmaceuticals.

Modifiers

The two most common modifiers used with radiological services are:

- 26 *Professional Services*
- TC *Technical Services*

To evaluate the total cost of a radiology service, the equipment, overhead, technician cost, and the radiologist are considered. Radiology services can be performed in the hospital, provider's office, or an independent radiology center. To make sure both the facility and radiologist are paid for their services, the radiology services can be split into the professional and technical components.

The cost of the equipment, overhead of the supplies, and resources such as the room, electricity, and the salary of the radiology technician, all are included in the technical component. The technical component is reported by the facility or office who owns the equipment. Patients receiving MR, CT, PET scans, or more advanced radiological procedures typically are sent to the hospital or independent diagnostic testing facility (IDTF) for the service. When a service is performed in a hospital, the hospital has the overhead of the equipment,

supplies, and radiology technician. In this case, the hospital bills for the technical component. To report the technical component, modifier TC is appended to the CPT® code from the radiology section.

After the radiology procedure has been performed, it has to be read (interpreted) by a physician or other qualified practitioner. The provider's specialty can be radiology, but it is not required to code the services. The interpretation and report of the radiological service is considered the professional component. When a patient has a radiology service in the hospital, but a radiologist independent of the hospital reads or interprets the radiology service, the radiologist reports the professional service. To report the professional component, modifier 26 is appended to the CPT® code from the radiology section.

A facility owning the equipment and employing the radiologist would bill for both the technical and professional component. Both components together are considered "global." Sometimes, a physician's office will own the equipment and will read the X-ray and provide the report. An example of this might be an orthopedic office with X-ray equipment. When the office owns the equipment, has the overhead cost of the procedure, reads the X-ray, and provides the report, the office bills the global procedure. A global procedure is reported using the correct CPT® code without a modifier appended.

Example cost structure for Professional and Technical Components:

71020 Radiologic examination, chest, 2 views, frontal and lateral

CPT® Code	TC	26	Global
71020	$20.42	$10.55	$30.97

*Fees are based on the 2012 Medicare Physician Fee Schedule (2012B).

Additional modifiers applicable to radiological procedures include:

76 Repeat procedure or service by same physician or other qualified healthcare professional

77 Repeat procedure or service by another physician or other qualified healthcare professional

79 Unrelated procedure or service by the same physician during the postoperative period or other qualified healthcare professional

RT Right

LT Left

Section Review 17.5

1. A patient receives complex radiation oncology treatments two times a day for three days. Which radiology code(s) is/are appropriate for this series of clinical management fractions?

   A. 77427 x 3, 77431 x 3

   B. 77427

   C. 77525 x 3, 77523 x 3

   D. 77427, 77431

2. A DXA body composition study is performed on a patient. What CPT® code(s) is/are reported for the scan?

   A. 77080, 77081

   B. 77080

   C. 77086

   D. 76499

3. A male patient being treated for prostate cancer receives brachytherapy treatment. Twelve radioactive seeds were interstitially applied within the prostate. What is the CPT® code for the radiological component?

   A. 0395T

   B. 77778

   C. 77771

   D. 77789

4. Patient is in the orthopedic's office with an injured ankle. The orthopedic thinks it is only a sprained ankle, but decides to take an ankle X-ray to rule out a fracture. A two-view ankle X-ray is taken in the physician's office. The orthopedic reviews the ankle X-ray and it is negative for a fracture. The report is placed in the medical record. How is the X-ray reported by the orthopedic physician?

   A. 73600-26

   B. 73600-TC

   C. 73600-26-TC

   D. 73600

5. A patient with osteoporosis reports to her physician's office for a DXA bone density study of her spine to monitor the severity of her condition. What is the correct CPT® code for the DXA scan?

   A. 77080

   B. 77081

   C. 77086

   D. 77081-52

Documentation Dissection

Case 1

Tunneled Dialysis Catheter Placement

Clinical History: 60-year-old female patient presents with end-stage renal disease. [1] Infected right internal jugular dual-lumen dialysis catheter removed 9/02/20xx.

Technique: Informed consent was obtained. The patient was identified and placed in the supine position.

The right internal jugular vein was examined with ultrasound [2] and found to be compressible, with a partial thrombus, likely secondary to prior catheter. An image was recorded and placed in the medical record.

The right side of the neck and chest was prepped and draped in the usual sterile fashion. 1% Lidocaine with epinephrine local anesthesia was administered. Under ultrasound guidance [3] and using a micropuncture needle, the right internal jugular vein was accessed and a guidewire passed. The needle was exchanged for the micropuncture introducer/sheath.

A subcutaneous tunnel [4] was developed over the chest wall connecting to the puncture site in the neck. Under fluoroscopic observation, [5] a 23 cm tip to cuff double lumen Duro-flow catheter, after being advanced through the subcutaneous tunnel, was passed into the right internal jugular vein via a peel-away sheath. The catheter tip was placed in the right atrium. [6] Both ports had good forward flush and return. The catheter was sutured at the skin exit site and it was flushed with heparinized saline.

The incision in the neck was closed with Dermabond.

The patient tolerated the procedure well and the procedure was without complications. Dr. Wilson, the interventional radiologist performed the entire procedure and reviewed and interpreted all images obtained. [7]

Impression: Uncomplicated placement of a right internal jugular vein, 23 cm tip to cuff, double lumen tunneled catheter.

----

[1] The patient has ESRD.

[2] Ultrasound was utilized for catheter placement.

[3] Ultrasound guidance noted again.

[4] The catheter was tunneled.

[5] Flouroscopic guidance was used.

[6] The catheter was tunneled from the right internal jugular vein to the right atrium.

[7] The interventional radiologists performed the procedure and reviewed and interpreted all of the images for the ultrasound guidance and fluoroscopic guidance.

What are the CPT® and ICD-10-CM codes reported?

CPT® Codes: 36558, 76937-26, 77001-26

ICD-10-CM Codes: Z49.01, N18.6

Rationale: The documentation indicates the use of ultrasound guidance and additional use of fluoroscopic guidance.

This is found in the CPT® Index under Central Venous Catheter Placement/Insertion/Central/Tunneled without port or pump 36557–36558, 36565. Venous access is found in the CPT® Index under Ultrasound/Guidance/Vascular Access 76937. Modifier 26 is appended for the professional service.

Look in the CPT® Index for Venous Access Device/Fluoroscopic Guidance 77001. Modifier 26 is appended for the professional service.

ICD-10-CM Codes: The patient is being seen for replacement of a dialysis catheter previously removed. Look in the Index to Diseases and Injuries for Management (of)/renal dialysis catheter Z49.01 or for Preparatory care for subsequent treatment NEC/for dialysis Z49.01. Category Z49 has a note to Code also associated end stage renal disease N18.6.

ICD-9-CM Application

What is/are the ICD-9-CM code(s) reported?

Code(s): V56.1, 585.6

Rationale: The patient is having a dialysis catheter inserted for End Stage Renal Disease. Look in the Index to Diseases for Admission (encounter)/for/dialysis/catheter/removal or replacement/extracorporeal (renal) V56.1. Category V56 has a note to use an additional code to identify the associated condition. To find the code for ESRD, look for Disease/renal/end stage, and you are directed to 585.6

Case 2

CT abdomen Without Contrast Performed at Outpatient Diagnostic Center

Indication: Follow-up splenic injury [1]

Comparison: Archived images of outside CT of the abdomen and pelvis [2] from 2:40 p.m. on August 12, 20xx

Technique: MDCT images of the abdomen and pelvis were obtained without IV contrast. [3]

Findings: There is limited visualization due to lack of IV contrast. However, when compared to the prior exam, there is no significant change in the overall size of the parenchymal laceration/hematoma [4] associated with the left spleen. This suggests there has not been significant bleeding in the interim. Multiple focal areas of mildly increased attenuation within the splenic parenchyma correspond with areas of focal hematoma/contrast pooling seen on the prior study. This may be related to evolution of clot formation within the laceration. Stable amount of fluid noted adjacent to the liver. This has lower Hounsfield units than the blood that is seen around the spleen. There is some residual contrast in the renal collecting systems and bladder. The bladder appears grossly intact. Small amount of fluid in the pelvis. Right flank subcutaneous tissue edema consistent with contusion/ecchymosis. The IVC is flat, consistent with volume depletion. Scattered atherosclerotic calcifications of the aorta. No evidence of free intra-abdominal air. Moderate degenerative changes of the visualized spine. Dependent atelectasis in the bilateral lung bases. No visualized displaced rib fractures. There are multilevel degenerative changes of the spine. No evidence of acute fracture of the lower thoracic or lumbar spine on axial, sagittal, or coronal images. Fat filled left inguinal canal is noted.

Impression:

1. Grossly stable size of 2 cm parenchymal laceration of the left spleen [5] as compared to outside exam. Evaluation is limited due to lack of IV contrast. There is also blood layering around the liver. This is likely due to the splenic injury.

2. Volume depletion [6] as evidenced by small caliber of the inferior vena cava [7]

3. No definite evidence of acute fracture of the lower thoracic or lumbar spine.

---

[1] Reason for the CT.

[2] CT of the Abdomen and of the Pelvis were performed.

[3] CTs were without contrast.

[4] There is a parenchymal laceration, this is significant in the ICD-10-CM coding.

|5| Primary diagnosis.

|6| Secondary Diagnosis.

|7| Volume depletion indicated by the inferior vena cava indicates a volume depletion of plasma in the blood (hypovolemia).

_____

What are the CPT® and ICD-10-CM codes reported?

CPT® Codes: 74176-26

ICD-10-CM Codes: S36.031D, E86.1

Rationale: The exam is by CT (computed tomography), performed without contrast. The abdomen and pelvis were examined.

The report indicates that a CT of both the abdomen and of the pelvis was performed without contrast. To find in the CPT Index, look under CT Scan/without Contrast/Abdomen or Pelvis. After reviewing the codes, code 74176 for CT abdomen and pelvis, without contrast is selected. Modifier 26 is used to indicate the professional portion of the CT.

ICD-10-CM Codes: Look in the Index to Diseases and Injuries for Laceration/spleen/moderate S36.031x. In the Tabular List, there is a note under S36.031 that indicates a moderate laceration is 1–3 cm. This laceration is 2 cm making this the correct code selection. S36.031 requires a seventh character. This is a follow up study making D for subsequent encounter the correct seventh character selection. Volume depletion is also coded. Look in the Index to Diseases and Injuries for Depletion/plasma NOS E86.1

ICD-9-CM Application

What is/are the ICD-9-CM code(s) reported?

Code(s): 865.03, 276.52

Rationale: In the ICD-9-CM Index to Diseases, look for Hematoma/internal organs/spleen, you are directed to *see* Hematoma/spleen which guides you to 865.01. The case note documents laceration extending in to parenchyma. Hematoma/spleen/with laceration- *see* Laceration/spleen with parenchyma. The diagnosis is 865.03. There is a secondary diagnosis of volume depletion. In the ICD-9-CM Index to Diseases, look under Depletion/plasma and you are directed to 276.52.

Glossary

Angiography—Radiographic image of the blood vessels, using contrast material.

Aortography—Radiographic image of the aorta and branches, using contrast material.

Atherectomy—To remove plaque from an artery.

Brachytherapy—Radiation placed in or near a tumor within the body. Catheters, needles, seeds or wires may be used.

Bronchography—Radiographic image of the bronchi of the lungs, using contrast material.

Cephalogram—Radiographic image of the head.

Cholangiography—Radiographic image of the bile duct.

Cineradiography—Radiography of an organ in motion, (for example, a beating heart).

Colonography—Radiographic image of the (interior) colon.

Computed Tomography (CT)—Using specialized equipment, two-dimensional X-ray images are taken around a single axis of rotation. The images are combined to create a three dimensional image or pictures of the inside of the body. These cross-sectional images of the area being studied may be examined on a computer monitor, printed or transferred to a CD.

Corpora Cavernosography—Radiographic image of the corpora cavernosa and draining veins using contrast medium.

Cystography—Radiographic image of the bladder.

Dacryocystography—Radiographic image of the lacrimal drainage system.

Discography—Radiographic image of the disc of the spine.

Doppler—A type of ultrasound, especially useful for imaging blood flow. The Doppler can create images either in shades of gray or, when processed by a computer, in color.

Dual-Energy X-ray Absorptiometry (DEXA/DXA)—Test performed to determine bone density.

Ductogram—Imaging of the ducts in the breast.

Duodenography—Radiographic examination of the duodenum and pancreas.

Echocardiography—Imaging using sound waves to create a moving picture of the heart.

Echoencephalography—Ultrasound image of the brain.

Epidurography—Imaging of the epidural space in the spine.

Fluoroscopy—A continuous X-ray image, used to view the movement of a body part, or of an instrument or dye moving through the body.

Hyperthermia—A type of cancer treatment in which tissue is exposed to high temperatures (up to 113°F).

Hysterosalpingography—Fluoroscopic imaging (with contrast) of the uterus and fallopian tubes.

Intraluminal—Within the lumen.

Laryngography—Radiographic image of the larynx.

Lymphangiography—Diagnostic imaging to view lymphatic circulation and lymph nodes; utilizes X-ray technology and the injection of a contrast agent.

Magnetic Resonance—Magnetic fields align the protons within the body to produce image "slices," which are combined to produce 3-D images, may be viewed from different angles; performed either with or without contrast.

Myelography—Radiographic image of the spinal cord.

Nephrotomography—CT image of the kidneys.

Orthopantogram—Panoramic, radiographic image of the entire dentition, alveolar bone, and other adjacent structures on a single film; taken extra-orally.

Pachymetry—Measurement of corneal thickness.

Pancreatography—Radiographic image of the pancreatic ducts following injection of radiopaque material.

Pelvimetry—Measurement of the dimensions and capacity of the pelvis.

Positron Emission Computed Tomography (PET)—Nuclear imaging assessing the level of metabolic activity and perfusion in various organ systems of the body.

Portography—X-ray visualization of the portal circulation, using radiopaque material.

Pyelography—Radiographic imaging of the renal pelvis of a kidney following injection of a radiopaque substance through the ureter or into a vein.

Shuntogram—Placement of a radioactive isotope in the shunt reservoir in the head to measure the speed with which it moves to the abdomen. Shuntogram is the term used for angiography of an A/V fistula for renal dialysis.

Sialography—Radiographic image of the salivary ducts and glands.

Single Photon Emission Computed Tomography (SPECT)—Nuclear imaging using radioactive tracers to show how blood flows to organs and tissues.

Sonohysterography—Ultrasound imaging of the uterus.

Splenoportography—Radiography of the splenic and portal veins; includes injection of a radiopaque medium.

Teletherapy—Any treatment where the source of the therapeutic agent (for instance, radiation) is at a distance from the body.

Transcatheter—Performed via the lumen of a catheter.

Ultrasound—High frequency sound waves are used to produce two-dimensional images in examining structures inside the body or for detecting abnormalities.

Urethrocystography—Radiography of the urethra and bladder using a radiopaque substance.

Urography—Imaging of the kidneys, ureters, or bladder.

Vasography—Radiographic image of the vas deferens and ejaculatory duct following dye injection.

Velocity Flow Mapping—A non-invasive method to image blood flow through the heart by displaying flow data on the two-dimensional echocardiographic image.

Venography—A radiographic image of the veins following injection of contrast dye.

Xeroradiography—Creation of radiographs by photoelectric process, using metal plates coated with a semiconductor (for instance, selenium).

Introduction

In this chapter, we will discuss CPT®, ICD-10-CM, and HCPCS Level II codes related to pathology and laboratory services. These services apply to all parts of the body and nearly all disease processes, and are defined by the process used to perform the service, or by the substance analyzed (the analyte). CPT® codes are found primarily in the Pathology and Laboratory chapter. Most (not all) codes have both a professional and a technical component (discussed below). ICD-10-CM codes may come from nearly any chapter; we will focus on codes most specific to testing. We will cover some of the rules for assigning codes, rather than providing a comprehensive overview of codes. There is a small number of HCPCS Level II codes used for specific services; we will address these, also.

Objectives

Objectives for this chapter include:

- Define terms and concepts specific to pathology and laboratory coding
- Apply ICD-10-CM Guidelines for assigning codes for diagnostic services, and identify specific codes helpful in describing the medical necessity and outcomes of specific lab tests
- Select CPT® and HCPCS Level II codes describing the services and procedures for Pathology and Laboratory services
- Apply CPT® and HCPCS Level II modifiers, when appropriate

Terminology

Services related to Pathology and Laboratory have their own terminology built on the same root words, prefixes, and suffixes discussed in other chapters, with a few terms unique to these diagnostic services.

Pathology is the study of diseased tissue and cells (path = disease, -logy = study of). Pathology services include necropsies (autopsies), which are examinations of dead bodies to determine the cause(s) of death. Cytopathology is the study and diagnosis of diseases on a cellular level (cyto = cell). Cytogenetics goes one step further to study the genes within the cells, to determine whether diseases have inherited components, and to identify the specific genetic components of certain disease processes.

Laboratory, in this context, refers to tests performed primarily in a medical laboratory (also called a clinical laboratory). Tests of clinical specimens provide information for the diagnosis, treatment, and prevention of disease.

Molecular diagnostics is the measurement of DNA (deoxyribonucleic acid), RNA (ribonucleic acid), proteins, or metabolites to detect genotypes, mutations, or biochemical changes. Hematology is the study of the components and behavior of blood (hemat = blood). Immunology is the study of the immune system and its components and function. Microbiology (micr/o = small, bio = life) includes four subspecialties: bacteriology (study of bacteria), mycology (study of fungi), parasitology (study of parasites), and virology (study of viruses).

Many Pathology and Laboratory CPT® codes (80047–80076) describe a panel of tests. When a panel code is used, each test listed in the panel description must be performed. Do not report two or more panel codes including the same tests. For example, 80047 is not reported with 80053 because they both include a number of the same tests. Separately report tests not included in the panel.

Tests may be identified as quantitative or qualitative. Qualitative testing determines the presence or absence of a drug only. Quantitative testing identifies not only the presence of a drug, but the exact amount present (quantitative shares the same root word as quantity). For example, a patient is brought to the ED after an auto accident. If there is suspicion the individual has been drinking, a qualitative test might be performed to confirm the presence or absence of alcohol in the bloodstream. If alcohol is detected, a separate quantitative test is needed to determine the quantity of alcohol involved. Tests also may be semi-quantitative. Semi-quantitative tests describe an amount within a specified range or over a certain threshold, but do not identify a specific quantity.

Gross examination (eg, 88300) is examination of the entire specimen without sectioning of the specimen into slides for examination under a microscope. Microscopy (88302–88309) is examination of a specimen under a microscope. Most codes for microscopic examination also include gross inspection.

The word forensic refers to studies used or applied in the investigation and establishment of facts or evidence in a court of law. The Latin term *in vivo* refers to studies performed "within the living body."

The Clinical Laboratory Improvement Amendments (CLIA) passed in 1988 establishes quality standards for all laboratory testing. It ensures the accuracy, reliability and timeliness of patient test results regardless of where the test is performed. Diagnostic test systems are placed into one of three CLIA regulatory categories based on potential for risk to public health: waived tests, tests of moderate complexity, and tests of high complexity. Any lab or clinic performing any diagnostic test must have a CLIA number. This number certifies the complexity of tests to be performed in the testing location. No diagnostic tests should be performed (whether billed or not) without a CLIA certificate. All bills for tests must include the CLIA number of the testing location. Certificates for waived tests can be issued by application, without any inspection. Certificates for more complex testing require inspections, calibration of equipment, and other tests to assure the quality and accuracy of tests performed.

Key Root Words for Pathology and Laboratory Coding

Bacteri/o	bacteria
Bi/o	life
Cyt/o	cell
Gen/o	gene
Hemat/o	blood
Immun/o	immune
Micr/o	small
Myc/o	fungus
Parasit/o	parasite
Path/o	disease
Vir/o	virus

Section Review 18.1

1. The word "pathology" refers to the study of:

    A. Deterioration

    B. Direction

    C. Disease

    D. Distress

2. Which word describes the study of small life forms?

    A. Hematology

    B. Immunology

    C. *In vivo*

    D. Microbiology

3. Which term is used with the word pathologist to describe someone specializing in legal or investigational studies?

    A. *In vivo*

    B. Forensic

    C. Laboratory

    D. None of the above

4. A test determining the presence or absence of a substance is considered what type of test?

    A. Qualitative

    B. Quantitative

    C. Forensic

    D. Hematologic

5. If a patient has a test result indicating a blood alcohol level of .05, what type of test was performed to determine this information?

    A. Microbiology

    B. Qualitative

    C. Quantitative

    D. Urine dip test

ICD-10-CM

Pathology and Laboratory studies identify infectious and parasitic diseases, presence and morphology of neoplasms, quantities of various naturally occurring substances in various bodily fluids and other tissue, pregnancy status, hormonal changes, and many other factors about health and disease. As such, almost any code in any chapter of ICD-10-CM can be appropriate as an indicator for a test or a finding. In this section, we will look at the rules for assigning ICD-10-CM codes based on medical necessity and diagnostic findings. We will discuss specific codes to use when findings are inconclusive or negative/normal.

Assigning ICD-10-CM Codes for Diagnostic Services

When a provider orders a laboratory test or pathologic examination, a reason for the order must be reported. This reason is the "medical necessity" for the service. Common reasons to order a test include:

- Screening—There are no indications of disease or personal or family history indicating a disease or disorder exists, but a study is performed to check for evidence of disease.

- Signs and/or symptoms—There are indications the patient may have a disease process and further study is needed to identify the specific disease or other causes of the symptoms.

- Previous abnormal finding—The patient had a previous test indicating some abnormality, but it was not diagnostic of a specific disease. The finding must be rechecked or the patient must be followed for any changes to the finding.

- Current disease—The patient has a currently active disease to be followed for worsening symptoms or improvement.

- Personal or family history of disease—The patient or members of the patient's family had a disease and the patient needs to be checked for personal recurrence or manifestation of a hereditary disease.

It is critical to code as precisely as possible the reason the test or study is ordered. If a patient's test or study returns a more specific diagnosis than was known at the time the study was ordered, the findings of the test are coded rather than the reason the test was ordered.

Example

1. A young man is planning to get married. He and his fiancé have agreed to get HIV tests prior to their wedding. He has no symptoms or reason to think he has the disease. When the first test is ordered use Z11.4 *Encounter for screening for human immunodeficiency virus [HIV]*. If the test is negative, this is the only code used. If the test results come back indicating an abnormality, use R75 Inconclusive laboratroy evidence of HIV. If the test results come back positive for HIV exposure without clinical manifestations (no symptoms), use code Z21 *Asymptomatic human immunodeficiency virus [HIV] infection status*. This code is used until the patient develops symptoms of AIDS, when code B20 is used.

2. A middle-aged woman presents for her annual physical exam and Pap (Papanicolaou) smear. She has no symptoms of disease. When the first test is ordered, code Z12.4 *Encounter for screening for malignant neoplasm of the cervix*. If the test is negative, this is the only code used. If the test results come back indicating an abnormality, use a code from category R87 *Abnormal findings in specimens from female genital organs*. Choose the most specific information

known from the Pap smear report. If further testing is negative (or continues to be inconclusive), this is the only code used. If the test results come back positive for cancer or cervical hyperplasia or another condition, choose the appropriate code for the condition based upon the diagnosis described in the Pap smear report.

Always code to the highest degree of certainty. Never code "possible," "rule out," or "exclusion" diagnoses; instead code the sign or symptom indicating the reason the test was ordered. If a more specific diagnosis is confirmed by the test, code for the test result rather than the indications for the test. If test results are inconclusive, code for abnormal findings.

Abnormal Findings

ICD-10-CM Volume 1, chapter 18 (Symptoms, Signs, and Abnormal Clinical and Laboratory Findings, Not Elsewhere Classified R00-R99), codes R70-R79 are for Abnormal findings on examination of blood, without a diagnosis. R80-R82 Abnormal findings on examination of urine, without diagnosis, R83-R89 Abnormal findings on exam of other body fluids, substances and tissues, R90-R93, Abnormal findings on diagnostic imaging, R94 Nonspecific abnormal results of function studies, and R97 Abnormal tumor markers may be used as either the reason (medical necessity) for a follow-up study, or as the outcome of a study (either screening or ordered due to a sign or symptom without a specific diagnosis). These codes should not be used when a more specific diagnosis is known, but are useful when a test returns an abnormal result without confirmatory clinical findings. For example:

- A 50-year-old man has a screening prostate specific antigen (PSA) as part of his annual exam. The results are elevated but the patient has no clinical indications of prostate cancer. Code R97.2 (elevated PSA).
- A 68-year-old woman, status post-hysterectomy for prolapse, has a vaginal Pap smear as part of her annual breast and pelvic exam. Results show low-grade squamous intraepithelial lesion (LGSIL). Code R87.622.

To code a nonspecific abnormal finding, start with the Alphabetic Index under the main term Findings, abnormal, inconclusive, without diagnosis or under the main term Abnormal. Some codes are found under other main terms.

Example

Elevated PSA.

Look in the ICD-10-CM Index to Diseases and Injuries for Elevated, elevation/prostate specific antigen [PSA] R97.2.

R97.2 Elevated prostate specific antigen (PSA)

ICD-9-CM Application

ICD-9-CM

Coding of abnormal findings on laboratory test is coded similarly in ICD-9-CM.

Look in the ICD-9-CM Index for Elevation/prostate specific antigen (PSA) 790.93.

790.93 Elevated prostate specific antigen [PSA]

Supplementary Classification of Factors Influencing Health Status and Contact with Health Services (Z Codes)

Z codes describe the reason for a test or study or the outcome of a study when results are negative or normal.

- Exposure to communicable diseases—Use the codes in category Z20 if the individual has been exposed to a communicable disease but has no signs or symptoms of infection.
- Carrier—Use codes in category Z22 for patients who are carriers or suspected carriers of a communicable disease but have no signs or symptoms of disease themselves.
- Drug-resistant organisms—Category Z16 is for use when a patient is known to have a specific disease resistant to typical drugs used to treat it. These codes are used for additional codes to identify resistance and non-responsiveness to drugs. You are instructed to code first the infection. There are also codes that include the infection and the organism. It is important to verify In the Tabular List.
- Personal history—Categories Z85-Z87 list codes for individuals who have a personal history of various diseases requiring ongoing monitoring or therapy after the disease has been eradicated. These codes may be used only after there is no further indication of the disease, and after all active treatment directed toward the specific disease has ended.

Example

Personal history of breast cancer.

Look in the Index to Diseases and Injuries for History/personal (of)/malignant neoplasm (of)/breast Z85.3.

Z85.3 Personal history of malignant neoplasm of breast

ICD-9-CM Application

In ICD-9-CM the term "personal" is a nonessential modifier to History.

Look in the Index to Diseases for History (personal) of/malignant neoplasm (of)/breast V10.3.

V10.3 Personal history of malignant neoplasm, Breast

- Allergy to medication—Category Z88 describes patients with previous allergies to specific medications. Do not use these codes for a current allergy. These codes are for a personal history of drug allergy without a current reaction.

- Other history—There are other personal history codes and most do not apply to Laboratory and Pathology services but a few can be useful, including Category Z91.1 *Patient's noncompliance with medical treatment and regiment* that is specific to the reason for non-compliance and Z92 *Personal history of medical treatment*.

- Family history—Some tests are performed because a patient has family members with disorders. Categories Z80-Z84 describe these conditions; use only when the patient does not have a current diagnosis of the disease.

- Reproduction and development—Categories Z30-Z39 describe various encounters related to reproduction and contraception, including category Z36 *Encounter for antenatal screening of mother*. Do not use these codes when the patient has a current active illness or disorder.

- Organ or tissue replacement—Categories Z94 report times when a patient has had a transplant. These are not codes to be used in the primary position. The first code should describe any disease, symptom, or other reason for the encounter.

- Procedures for aftercare—Category Z47-Z48 includes many codes describing a follow-up visit or procedure. Some codes useful for Pathology and Lab services include

Z51.11 *Encounter for antineoplastic chemotherapy* and Z79 *Long-term (current) drug use*. The long-term drug use codes supply the medical necessity for many follow-up lab tests. These codes are not used as the primary diagnosis, but should be listed as a secondary code with the primary code listed as the condition or disease requiring drug use.

- Donor—Category Z52 is for examination of donors. Any tests or studies performed to identify an individual as a donor should be coded with one of these codes.

- Pregnancy testing—Use subcategory Z32 for pregnancy examination or test. The fifth character identifies the result of the test.

- Screening—Tests are considered screening tests when there are no specific indications of disease or disorder. There are a number of codes representing various screening tests. They generally are found in categories Z11-Z13.

Abbreviations and Acronyms

BAC	Blood alcohol content (or concentration)
Cr	Creatinine
CSF	Cerebrospinal fluid
Hct	Hematocrit
Hgb or Hb	Hemoglobin
MRSA	Methicillin-resistant Staphylococcus Aureus
PSA	Prostate specific antigen
UA	Urine analysis

Section Review 18.2

1. A patient has been exposed to rabies. He has no signs or symptoms of infection. A test is performed to check for rabies in his blood. What code is used to describe the necessity for the test?

    A. Z23

    B. B97.89

    C. Z20.3

    D. A82.9

2. A woman has identified a lump in her breast. After examination, the physician decides a biopsy is indicated. A specimen is sent for pathologic examination. The finding is carcinoma of the breast. What diagnosis is assigned for the pathologic examination?

   A. N63

   B. C80.1

   C. C50.919

   D. Z01.419

3. A patient with rheumatoid arthritis takes non-steroidal anti-inflammatories (NSAIDs) to manage pain. He also has regular blood tests to verify he has not developed any liver problems due to his use of the NSAIDS. What code(s) is (are) used to describe the need for the test when the results are normal (the patient has no symptoms of liver disease)?

   A. Z79.1

   B. M06.9, Z79.1

   C. M06.9

   D. Z79.1, M06.9

4. A patient has a history of prostate cancer with removal of the prostate and has completed radiation therapy with no recurrence for 2 years. A PSA is performed to check for any recurrence. The results show a PSA within normal limits. What is/are the diagnosis code(s) for this test?

   A. C61

   B. Z08, Z85.46

   C. Z12.5

   D. Z00.00

5. A woman comes in for her annual exam with a cervical Pap smear. The results are not normal, although they are not diagnostic of any specific disease. A second Pap smear is obtained and this test identifies only normal cells. What diagnosis code is used to identify the medical necessity for the second Pap smear?

   A. N92.6

   B. N92.3

   C. N92.4

   D. R87.619

CPT® Coding

Codes in the Pathology and Laboratory chapter of CPT® represent a wide diversity of codes and describe the work of performing a test, usually on some body fluid or tissue. All of these services are performed by a physician or by technologists under responsible supervision of a physician. Some of the tests are simple and can be performed readily in a physician's office. Some are quite complex and require special equipment and/or processes in addition to expert handling and interpretation. Some of these services produce only a test result returned to

the ordering provider. For other services, there is an expectation an expert will interpret test results further to provide more information or a final diagnosis based on a combination of clinical information and examination of the specimen. For each subsection within this chapter, there are specific rules and limitations, which will be discussed below.

Organ or Disease-Oriented Panels (80047–80081)

Codes in this section describe panels of tests often ordered together. These codes are used whenever all of the specific tests listed under the panel heading are performed, whether the panel is described with the same title or not. If one or more of the tests listed is not performed, the panel code may not be used, and the specific tests must be coded separately. If more tests than those listed in the panel are performed, the panel is coded and additional tests are listed separately. The codes for each individual test are listed beside the test under each heading.

According to AMA guidelines, "These panels were developed for coding purposes only and should not be interpreted as clinical parameters." This guideline does not limit a laboratory from creating its own panels of tests and then assigning the appropriate codes. Also, these panels do not limit the physician from ordering other tests as medically necessary.

Most of the panels are self-explanatory, but a couple of caveats should be noted. Several of the panels require all the tests in another panel be performed in addition to several other tests (eg, General Health Panel (80050) includes a Comprehensive Metabolic Panel (80053) as well as a blood count and thyroid stimulating hormone). To bill for the more extensive panel, every test listed in the less comprehensive panel must be performed in addition to any added tests listed in the more comprehensive panel.

Several panels allow either of two different tests to be performed. These two tests produce the same information, but can be performed in different ways.

Example

> Obstetric Panel (80055) includes "Blood count, complete (CBC), automated and automated differential WBC count" OR "Blood count, complete (CBC), automated and appropriate manual differential WBC count." Either of these tests fulfills the requirements to bill the panel.

Codes 80055 and 80081 are both used for obstetrical panels, with the difference being the addition of HIV testing on 80081. It would not be appropriate to order 80055 and 87389 separately.

The acute hepatitis panel is used for differential diagnosis in a patient with symptoms of liver disease or injury. When the time of exposure or the stage of the disease is not known, a patient with continued symptoms of liver disease—despite a completely negative hepatitis panel—may need a repeat panel approximately two weeks to two months later to exclude the possibility of hepatitis. Once a diagnosis is established, specific tests can be used to monitor the course of the disease.

Therapeutic Drug Assays (80150–80299)

Some drugs must be maintained at a therapeutic level to work effectively. Many of these same drugs can have negative side effects or even be toxic if levels get too high. These drugs require regular monitoring to confirm the level of drug in the patient's system. Many of these drugs are listed in the section called Therapeutic Drug Assays. Therapeutic drug assays are quantitative; and, although the tissue most often examined is blood, these codes may be used for assays on serum, plasma, or cerebrospinal fluid. The concept of peak and trough is used during therapeutic drug assays. For the physician to properly adjust medication dosages, specimens (usually blood) are collected at a given time after a dose has been administered (the peak). The exact time is dependent upon the drug, the administration interval, and the amount of time it takes the drug to be absorbed by the body. The "trough" (or low-point) specimen is collected immediately before the next dose of the drug. Repeated tests during a drug assay are legitimate and should be coded.

A number of drugs requiring monitoring for therapeutic levels are listed with specific codes in this section. Other drugs may be found in the Chemistry section as well. If there is no code for the drug being tested in either the Therapeutic Drug Assay section or the Chemistry section, use code 80299 *Quantitation of therapeutic drug, not elsewhere specified* to describe the service.

Drug Screening (80300–80377)

Drug screening is reported with codes in the 80300 to 80377 range. CPT® codes 80300-80304 report drug screening based on drug classification and the method for testing the specimen, for example, non-TLC (thin layer chromatography), TLC, immunoassay, and other non-specified presumptive procedures. Drug Class List A includes heroin, cocaine, ecstasy and LSD. Drug Class List B includes such drugs as amphetamines, ketamine, and cannabis. Codes 80320-80377 report definitive drug testing of specific types of drugs—such as alcohol, amphetamines and anabolic steroids as well as drugs or substances that are not otherwise specified. The Definitive Drug Classes Listing is used to identify drugs and metabolites included in each definitive drug class.

Evocative/Suppression Testing (80400–80439)

Evocative/Suppression Testing describes how well various endocrine glands are functioning. Each code in the Evocative/ Suppression Testing subsection includes several tests. The tests are performed after administration of an evocative or suppressive agent specific to the gland being tested. The administration of the agent is coded separately, as determined by the route of administration.

The evocative or suppressive agent is intended either to cause the gland to secrete its hormone or cause the gland to cease production of the hormone. The tests measure the initial levels and subsequent levels of the hormone. Based on the test results, physicians can determine if it is lack of the agent or failure of the gland to respond to the agent causing a glandular dysfunction.

Each of the tests listed in the panel code must be performed the number of times listed in the code. For example, code 80430 *Growth hormone suppression* panel requires glucose to be measured three times and human growth hormone to be measured four times. If extra tests are performed, they should be coded separately. If fewer than the listed number of tests are performed, the panel code cannot be used and each test must be coded separately.

When physician attendance is not required and ancillary staff administers the agent, do not report these codes separately. In the inpatient setting, these codes are only reported if the physician performs the service personally. In the office setting, the service can be reported when performed by office personnel if the physician is directly supervising the service.

While supplies necessary to perform testing are included in the testing, the HCPCS Level II J codes for the drugs can be reported separately for the diagnostic agents.

Do not report evaluation and management services separately, including prolonged services (in the case of prolonged infusions), unless a significant service can be identified separately and is provided and documented. If separate evaluation and management services are provided and reported, the injection procedure is included in this service and is not reported separately.

Consultations (80500–80502)

There are two pathology consultation codes. These codes are unlike the consultation codes in the Evaluation and Management chapter but are similar to the radiologic consultation codes. Pathology consultation codes are used when tissue samples are sent from another lab or pathologist for a second opinion on the diagnosis or other information. Code 80500 is used when only the specimen is reviewed. Code 80502 is used when clinical information is sent along with the specimen so the patient's history, treatments and other medical information can be taken into consideration as part of the specimen review.

If the pathologist performs an evaluation and management service (face-to-face contact with the patient), report the evaluation and management code, rather than the clinical pathology consultation codes. This rule holds even when the test review is performed as part of the evaluation and management service.

Documentation of clinical pathology consultations requires a written report and request from the attending physician. Reporting of a test result without medical interpretive judgment is not considered a clinical pathology consultation.

Specific criteria must be met for these codes to be used:

1. The consultation must be requested; the pathologist should not provide the service automatically.

2. The service must require the interpretive judgment of the pathologist. For example, if the clinical chemist routinely evaluates and reports abnormal results, a pathologist's consultation service has not been rendered.

3. A written report of findings must be prepared by the pathologist, forwarded to the surgeon or other provider, and be included in the patient's records.

4. The tests reviewed must be outside the clinically significant normal range, based on the patient's condition.

Urinalysis (81000–81099)

Urinalysis includes both simple and complex tests and analyses. All tests are performed on urine specimens. Some of the tests most commonly performed in physician offices can be found in this section.

Code 81000 is a simple dipstick test checking for common changes in urine indicating disease. Similar, but more involved tests are coded with 81001–81003, requiring special equipment or evaluation of the specimen under the microscope. Codes 81005–81020 are complex analyses measuring quantities of these changes, or screening for other conditions.

Urine pregnancy test by color comparison (81025) is similar to tests commercially available over the counter.

Volume measurement for timed collection (81050) measures the amount of urine produced over a period, usually 24 hours (often called a 24-hour urine).

Dipstick urinalysis and urine pregnancy tests are CLIA waived tests.

Molecular Pathology (81200–81408)

The lab tests in the molecular pathology section examine nucleic acid to determine changes in genes that may indicate a germline, (eg, an inherited constitutional chromosome abnormality), or somatic conditions (eg, neoplasm), or testing for histocompatibility antigens (eg, human leukocyte antigen (HLA)). These lab tests are a developing area of medical testing in finding clues to illnesses and their likelihood, and possible future treatments.

These codes are not reported by how the test is performed to determine the result, but reported on the analyte (gene-to-gene variant).

The code description for these lab codes are broken down this way:

Code 81220 *CTFR (cystic fibrosis transmembrane conductance regulator) (eg, cystic fibrosis) gene analysis; common variants (eg, ACMG/ACOG guidelines)*

- Gene abbreviation *(CFTR)* and gene name *(cystic fibrosis transmembrane conductance regulator)*

- Example of disease being tested (cystic fibrosis)

- "Gene analysis"

- What is being tested for (common variants)

- Example of variants being tested (ACMG/ACOG guidelines)

The molecular pathology guidelines instruct when procedures, such as microdissection (codes 88380 and 88381), are performed prior to cell lysis, those codes are reported separately.

Tier 2 codes (81400-81479) are reported when procedures are not listed in the Tier 1 pathology codes (81161, 81200–81383). The Tier 2 codes are generally performed less commonly than the Tier 1 codes. These codes are very specific and are listed by levels (Level 1–Level 9).

Modifier 26 is appended to these codes when the physician provides an interpretation and report (professional component) for these laboratory procedures.

Multianalyte Assays with Algorithmic Analyses (MAAA) (81500–81599)

MAAAs are algorithmic analysis using the results of assays (molecular pathology assays, fluorescent in situ hybridization assays and nonnucleic acid–based assays) and patient information when appropriate to report a numeric score(s) or probability of developing specific conditions.

Chemistry (82009–84999)

Tests in the chemistry section detect many substances in the body, including naturally occurring, therapeutic or non-therapeutic drugs, and other substances. All codes in this section describe quantitative analyses, unless otherwise specified. If a quantitative test for a therapeutic drug is performed and not listed here, it may be found in the Therapeutic Drug Assays subsection.

Most of the tests listed in this section are in alphabetic order. Some tests can be found at the end of the section in a more

random order. The Alphabetic Index to CPT® can be helpful in locating the correct code if you know what the test is called.

Also included in this section are the molecular diagnostic codes, also known as nucleic acid or genetic tests. These codes describe the various steps in preparing a specimen for genetic analysis.

The tests in this section may be performed on any body fluid or tissue. If the same test is performed on more than one type of specimen, you may bill each separately. Codes in this section describe tests for specific substances by any method.

Albumin Serum Testing (82040–82045)

Albumin testing is used in a variety of settings to help diagnose disease, to monitor changes in health status with treatment or with disease progression, and as a screen serving as an indicator for other kinds of testing. Low albumin levels can reflect kidney diseases, liver diseases, or prolonged malnutrition. Burn patients and patients who have protein-losing enteropathies and uropathies have low levels of protein, despite normal synthesis and require supplemental protein in many cases. Code 82045 reports albumin testing for cardiovascular events preceded by ischemia.

Fecal Occult Blood (82270–82274)

Different types of fecal hemoglobin assays exist, each directed at a different component of the hemoglobin molecule.

1. Immunoassays recognize antigenic sites on the globulin portion and are least affected by diet or proximal gut bleeding, but the antigen may be destroyed by fecal flora.

2. The heme porphyrin assay measures heme derived porphyrin and is least influenced by enterocolic metabolism or fecal storage. The capacity to detect proximal gut bleeding reduces its specificity for colorectal cancer screening but makes it more useful for evaluating overall GI bleeding in finding of iron deficiency anemia.

3. The guaiac-based test (82270–82272) is the most sensitive test for detecting lower bowel bleeding.

Code 82270 is reported once for the testing of up to three separate specimens (comprising either one test or two tests per specimen). The patient may be given three cards or a single triplet card for consecutive collection. The test is not reported until the cards have been returned and the test performed. Code 82656 reports a noninvasive stool test to determine exocrine pancreatic function.

Blood Glucose (82947, 82948, and 82962)

Blood glucose values are often necessary for the management of patients with diabetes mellitus where hyperglycemia and hypoglycemia are often present. They are also critical in the determination of control of blood glucose levels in the patient with impaired fasting glucose (FPG 110–125 mg/dL), the patient with insulin resistance syndrome and/or carbohydrate intolerance (excessive rise in glucose following ingestion of glucose or glucose sources of food), in the patient with a hypoglycemia disorder such as nesidioblastosis or insulinoma, and in patients with a catabolic or malnutrition state.

In addition to those conditions, glucose testing may be medically necessary in patients with tuberculosis, unexplained chronic or recurrent infections, alcoholism, coronary artery disease (especially women), or unexplained skin conditions (including pruritus, local skin infections, ulceration, and gangrene without an established cause). Many medical conditions may be a consequence of a sustained elevated or depressed serum glucose level. These include coma, seizures or epilepsy, confusion, abnormal hunger, abnormal weight loss or gain, and loss of sensation. Evaluation of glucose may also be indicated in patients on medications known to affect carbohydrate metabolism.

Glycated Hemoglobin and Protein (82985, 83036)

Glycated hemoglobin/protein levels are used to assess long-term (3 to 4 months) glucose control in diabetes. Alternative names for these tests include glycated or glycosylated hemoglobin or Hgb, hemoglobin glycated or glycosylated protein, and fructosamine.

Glycated hemoglobin (equivalent to hemoglobin A1, HbA1c or similar abbreviations) refers to total glycosylated hemoglobin present in erythrocytes, usually determined by affinity or ion exchange chromatographic methodology.

Helicobacter Pylori Testing (83009, 83013 and 83014)

A Helicobacter pylori bacterial infection contributes to the development of diseases, such as dyspepsia, gastritis, and ulcers in the stomach and duodenum. These bacteria have long threads that protrude and attach to the underlying stomach cells. The mucous layer protecting the stomach cells from acid also protects H. pylori, which can multiply and cause infection. Several methods are available for diagnosis. In the breath test, urea is given by mouth to indicate the presence of bacteria in the breakdown of urea into carbon dioxide. A blood test can measure protein antibodies present in the blood in defense of H. pylori. This antibody indicates whether the infection is present, or was present but no longer in the system. Codes 83013 and 83014 report H. pylori breath test analysis for urease activity and code 83009 reports a blood test analysis.

Lactoferrin Measure (83630)

A test to measure lactoferrin in the feces can determine the presence of intestinal inflammation, differentiate inflammatory from noninflammatory gastrointestinal disease, monitor patient response to therapy, and predict inflammatory bowel disease recurrence.

Lipoprotein (83695, 83700–83704, 83718)

Code 83695 reports direct quantitative measurement of lipoprotein a {Lp(a)} in serum, which is an indicator for increased risk for myocardial infarction, stroke, coronary artery disease, vein graft stenosis, and retinal arterial occlusions when present in elevated blood concentrations. The test can be run using ELISA and immunoturbidometric platforms with monoclonal antibodies against unique apo(a) epitopes used in the determination for Lp(a) being performed on a venipuncture serum sample.

Codes 83700 and 83701 describe a group analysis of lipoproteins by methodology. Code 83700 describes electrophoretic separation and quantitation and 83701 describes high-resolution fractionation and quantitation of lipoproteins including subclasses when performed. Code 83704 reports nuclear magnetic spectroscopy, which is a quantification method useful in assessing and managing cardiovascular disease among patients with elevated triglyceride levels and abnormalities associated with insulin resistance and diabetes.

Cholesterol Measures (83721)

Code 83721 (lipoprotein, direct measurement; direct measurement, LDL cholesterol) is used to report the direct measurement of the LDL cholesterol. It should not be used to report calculated LDL cholesterol. Direct measurement of LDL cholesterol in addition to total cholesterol (code 82465) or lipid panel (code 80061) may be reasonable and necessary if the triglyceride level is too high to permit calculation of the LDL cholesterol. In such situations, code 83721 is reported with modifier 59.

Prostate Specific Antigen (PSA) (84152–84154)

PSA is used in differentiating benign from malignant disease in men with lower urinary tract signs and symptoms (eg, hematuria, slow urine stream, hesitancy, urgency, frequency, nocturia, or incontinence). It is also useful in patients with palpably abnormal prostate glands on physical exam, and in patients with other laboratory or imaging studies suggestive of the possibility of a malignant prostate disorder. PSA is also a marker used to follow the progress of prostate cancer once a diagnosis has been established, such as in detecting metastatic or persistent disease in patients who may require additional treatment. PSA testing may also be useful in the differential diagnosis of men presenting with undiagnosed disseminated metastatic disease. Use ICD-10-CM code R97.2 *Elevated prostate specific antigen (PSA)* to report elevated PSA. If a more specific diagnosis has been made, use the code for that diagnosis.

Pregnancy Associated Plasma Protein-A (PAPP-A) (84163)

Code 84163 describes a screening test to identify women at increased risk of carrying a fetus with a chromosomal abnormality, such as trisomy-18 or trisomy-21. A positive result does not mean the pregnancy is affected but, rather, it indicates further testing is necessary (eg, chorionic villus sampling or amniocentesis).

Electrophoresis (84165, 84166)

Electrophoresis is a method of separating nucleic acids or proteins based on size, electric charge, and other physical properties. Code 84165 describes specific analysis of serum. For example, lipoprotein electrophoresis is a type of protein electrophoresis focused on determining the amount of lipoprotein (such as cholesterol). Code 84166 reports a protein electrophoresis for fluids other than serum, such as urine or CSF, with concentration.

Thyroid Testing (84436, 84439, 84443, 84479)

Thyroid function studies identify the presence or absence of hormonal abnormalities of the thyroid and pituitary glands. These abnormalities may be either primary or secondary and often—but not always—accompany clinically defined signs and symptoms indicative of thyroid dysfunction. Measurements of serum sensitive thyroid-stimulating hormone (TSH) levels, complemented by determination of thyroid hormone levels [free thyroxine (fT-4) or total thyroxine (T4) with triiodothyronine (T3) uptake] are used for diagnosis and follow-up of patients with thyroid disorders. Additional tests may be necessary to evaluate certain complex diagnostic problems or in hospitalized patients where many circumstances can skew tests results.

When a test for total thyroxine (total T4 or T4 radioimmunoassay) or T3 uptake is performed, calculation of the free thyroxine index (FTI) can be useful to correct for abnormal results for either total T4 or T3 uptake due to protein binding effects. Use code 728.87 to report muscle weakness as the indication for the test. Use code 194.8 *Malignant neoplasm of other endocrine glands and related structures, other* to report multiple endocrine neoplasia syndromes (MEN-1 and MEN-2).

Hematology and Coagulation (85002–85999)

Blood counts are used to evaluate and diagnose diseases relating to abnormalities of the blood or bone marrow. These include primary disorders such as anemia, leukemia, polycythemia, thrombocytosis, and thrombocytopenia. Many other conditions secondarily affect the blood or bone marrow, including reaction to inflammation and infections, coagulopathies, neoplasms, and exposure to toxic substances. Many treatments and therapies affect the blood or bone marrow, and blood counts may be used to monitor treatment progress.

The complete blood count (CBC) includes a hemogram and differential white blood count (WBC). The hemogram includes enumeration of red blood cells, white blood cells, and platelets, as well as the determination of hemoglobin, hematocrit, and indices.

Symptoms of hematological disorders are often nonspecific, and are commonly encountered in patients who may or may not prove to have a disorder of the blood or bone marrow. Many medical conditions are not primarily due to abnormalities of blood or bone marrow and may have hematological manifestations resulting from the disease or its treatment. As a result, the CBC is one of the most commonly indicated and ordered laboratory tests.

If additional but related procedures are necessary to confirm the result after a test is ordered and performed, these additional tests are considered part of the ordered test and not reported separately.

Example

1.   If a patient with leukemia has thrombocytopenia, and a manual platelet count (code 85032) is performed in addition to the performance of an automated hemogram with automated platelet count (code 85025), it is inappropriate to report codes 85032 and 85025 because the former provides a confirmatory test for the automated hemogram and platelet count (code 85025).

2.   If a patient has an abnormal test result and repeat performance of the test is done to verify the result, the test is reported as one unit of service rather than two.

Bone Marrow Aspiration

When a bone marrow aspiration is performed alone, report code 38220. Appropriate coding for the interpretation is code 85097 when the only service provided is the interpretation of the bone marrow smear. When the provider performs both procedures, report both CPT® codes. The pathological interpretations (codes 88300 to 88309) are not reported in addition to code 85097 unless separate specimens are processed.

Prothrombin Time (85610)

Basic plasma coagulation function is readily assessed with a few simple laboratory tests: the partial thromboplastin time (PTT), prothrombin time (PT), thrombin time (TT), or a quantitative fibrinogen determination. The prothrombin

 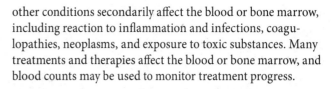

time (PT) test is one in vitro laboratory test used to assess coagulation. The PT/INR is most commonly used to measure the effect of warfarin and regulate dosing of the medication. Warfarin blocks the effect of vitamin K on hepatic production of extrinsic coagulation pathway factors. A prothrombin time is expressed in seconds and/or as an international normalized ratio (INR). The INR is the PT ratio resulting if the WHO reference thromboplastin is used in performing the test. Assign a code from subcategory code 289.8x *Other specified disease of blood and blood-forming organs* only, when a specific disease exists and is indexed to 289.8x (eg, myelofibrosis). Do not assign a code from subcategory code 289.8x to report a patient on long-term use of anticoagulant therapy (eg, to report a PT value or recheck need for medication adjustment). Assign code V58.61 to referrals for PT checks or rechecks (*AHA Coding Clinic*, March–April, pg 12, 1987, 2nd quarter, pg 8, 1989).

Immunology (86000–86849)

Immunology is the study of the immune system. Codes in this section identify and quantify antigens, antibodies, and allergens. Antigens may be viruses, bacteria, or other immune triggers our body fights off by creating antibodies. Antibodies are elements the human body creates to deal with antigens, although sometimes antibodies are created in response to inflammatory changes or other stimuli in the body. Allergens are substances causing a histamine response in the body. Identifying and quantifying these elements can tell a physician which disease a patient has, whether someone has been exposed to a disease or has an active immunity, or has other immune issues to be treated.

Most codes in this section are qualitative or semi-quantitative and describe multistep processes. Each substance should be coded as precisely as possible. If there is no code to describe the level of precision identified (eg, the specific class), the more generic code may be used multiple times to describe each separate substance tested.

Tumor Antigen Immunoassay (86300–86304)

Immunoassay determinations of serum levels of certain proteins or carbohydrates serve as tumor markers. When elevated, serum concentration of these markers may reflect tumor size and grade. A CA 125 (86304) level may be obtained as part of the initial preoperative work-up for women presenting with a suspicious pelvic mass to be used as a baseline for purposes of postoperative monitoring and treatment. CA 125 is a high molecular weight serum tumor marker elevated in 80 percent of patients who present with epithelial ovarian carcinoma. It is also elevated in carcinomas of the fallopian tube, endometrium, endocervix, and many other benign conditions. An elevated level may also be associated with the presence of a malignant mesothelioma.

Tumor antigen CA 19–9 (86301) is used in following the course of patients with established diagnosis of pancreatic and biliary ductal carcinoma. CA 15–3 (86300) is often medically necessary to aid in the management of patients with breast cancer. Serial testing is used in conjunction with other clinical methods for monitoring breast cancer. For monitoring, if medically necessary, use either CA 15–3 or CA 27.29 (86300), not both. CA 27.29 is equivalent to CA 15–3 in its usage in management of patients with breast cancer.

Hematology (86355, 86357, 86367)

These codes describe procedures used in the evaluation of hematologic conditions. Code 86355 reports B cells, total count; code 86357 reports natural killer (NK) cells; and code 86367 is used to report stem cells in the evaluation of hematologic conditions. These codes are used for quantitative analysis and do not include an interpretive report. B cells, which are produced in the bone marrow, secrete antibodies.

Each B cell can make one specific antibody. NK cells are the most aggressive cells of the immune system. They are the first line of defense against mutant and virus infected cells like severe acute respiratory syndrome (SARS) or West Nile Virus and they destroy infected and cancerous cells. NK cells make up about 5 to 16 percent of the total lymphocyte population. Stem cells are primitive cells giving rise to other types of cells. Adult and embryonic stem cell research focuses on the etiology, progression, and treatment of disease.

HIV Testing (86689, 86701–86703, 87390, 87391, 87534–87539)

Diagnosis of human immunodeficiency virus (HIV) infection is primarily made through the use of serologic assays. These assays take one of two forms: antibody detection assays and specific HIV antigen procedures. The antibody assays are usually enzyme immunoassays (EIA), which are used to confirm exposure of an individual's immune system to specific viral antigens. These assays may be formatted to detect HIV-1, HIV-2, or HIV-1 and 2 simultaneously and to detect both IgM and IgG antibodies. When the initial EIA test is repeatedly positive or indeterminate, an alternative test is used to confirm the specificity of the antibodies to individual viral components. The Western Blot test is performed after documenting that the initial EIA tests are repeatedly positive or equivocal on a single sample.

Testing for evidence of HIV infection using serologic methods may be medically appropriate in situations where there is a risk of exposure to HIV. However, in the absence of documented AIDS defining or HIV associated disease, an HIV associated sign or symptom, or documented exposure to a known HIV infected source, the testing is considered to be screening and may not be covered (eg, history of multiple blood component transfusions, exposure to blood or body fluids not resulting in consideration of therapy, history of transplant, history of illicit drug use, multiple sexual partners, same sex encounters, prostitution, or contact with prostitutes).

The CPT® Editorial Panel has issued a number of codes for infectious agent detection by direct antigen or nucleic acid probe techniques not yet developed or are only being used on an investigational basis. Laboratory providers are advised to remain current on FDA approval status for these tests.

Blood Banking and Tissue Typing (86077–86079, 86805–86849)

Codes to describe blood banking (86077–86079) and tissue typing (86805–86822) services also are found in the section on Immunology. This may be confusing to coders who might expect to find the codes, particularly in the blood banking codes, in the subsections on Hematology or Transfusion Medicine. However, these codes deal with procedures specific to immunologic reactions to foreign tissue in the human body. Blood banking services deal specifically with various transfusion reactions. Tissue typing studies consider the immunologic factors making a specimen appropriate for transplant or not a transplant candidate.

Blood banking services need not take place in a blood bank. The codes describe specific services, not specific locations. They may be coded anytime the described services are performed.

Transfusion Medicine (86850–86999)

Blood is a raw material from which a range of therapeutic products including platelet concentrates, red cell concentrates (packed red blood cells or RBCs), and fresh plasma is made. Large amounts of plasma are also needed for the production of plasma derivatives, such as albumin, coagulation factors, and immunoglobulin.

The two most common reasons for a blood transfusion are:

- Replace blood lost during an operation or after an accident
- Treat anemia (lack of red blood cells)

Small amounts of blood lost through surgery can be replaced by solutions of salt or glucose or by the use of synthetic substances such as dextrin or gelatin. Larger amounts of lost blood or rapid blood loss may require blood transfusion. Anemia has a number of causes, but in all cases, there is an insufficient supply of red cells to carry oxygen. Medicines, vitamins, and blood transfusions are treatments for anemia.

Following donation, each individual unit of blood is tested for viruses possibly transmitted by blood (eg, hepatitis B, hepatitis C, and HIV—the virus causing AIDS).

Only blood testing negative is used for transfusion. Each donation also is tested to determine the ABO and Rh D blood group. A patient's blood is tested prior to a transfusion for compatibility with the donated blood.

ABO blood group is the major human blood group system and the type depends upon the presence or absence of two genes—the A and B genes. These genes are encoded on chromosome 9 (in band 9q34.1). They determine part of the configuration of the red blood cell surface. A person can be A, B, AB, or O. If a person has two A genes, their red blood cells are type A. If a person has two B genes, their red cells are type B. If the person has one A and one B gene, their red cells are type AB. If the person has neither the A nor B gene, they are type O. The situation with antibodies in blood plasma is just the opposite. Someone with type A red cells has anti-B antibodies (antibodies directed against type B red cells) in their blood plasma. Someone with type B red cells has anti-A antibodies in plasma. Someone who is type O has both anti-A and anti-B antibodies in plasma. And someone who is type AB has neither anti-A nor anti-B antibodies in their plasma.

Antibody Screening (86850)

Antibody screening for unexpected anti-RBC antibodies is routinely done on pre-transfusion specimens from prospective recipients and prenatally on maternal specimens. Unexpected antibodies are specific for RBC blood group antigens other than A and B, such as Rh(D), Kell(K), or Duffy(Fya). Early detection is important because such antibodies can cause hemolytic disease of the newborn (HDN), serious transfusion reactions, and may complicate testing and procurement of blood.

Direct Coombs' Test (86880)

Direct antiglobulin testing detects antibodies coating the patient's RBCs *in vivo*. Washed RBCs are directly tested with antihuman globulin and observed for agglutination. A positive test, if correlated with clinical findings, suggests autoimmune hemolytic anemia, a transfusion reaction, or HDN.

Indirect Coombs' Test (86885 and 86886)

Indirect antiglobulin testing is screening for unexpected anti-RBC antibodies. Once an antibody is detected, its specificity is determined. Knowing the specificity of the antibody is helpful in assessing its clinical significance, selecting compatible blood, and managing HDN.

ABO Typing (86900)

ABO serologic typing of donor and recipient blood is done to prevent transfusion of incompatible red blood cells (RBC). As a rule, blood for transfusion should be of the same ABO type as the recipient. Individuals with type O blood do produce antigens as a result, type O people are universal donors for transfusions, but they can receive only type O blood.

Rh Typing (86901)

Rh(D) serologic typing determines whether the Rh factor Rh(D) is present (Rh-positive) or absent (Rh-negative) on the RBC. Rh-negative patients should always receive Rh-negative blood except in life-threatening emergencies when Rh-negative blood is unavailable. Rh-positive patients may receive Rh-positive or Rh-negative blood.

Compatibility Test (86920–86923)

Compatibility testing is reported with codes 86920–86923. Code 86920 provides an immediate spin crossmatch and code 86922 uses an antiglobulin technique. Code 86923 reports the cross-match service when the laboratory information system verifies ABO compatibility of the unit of blood with the intended recipient.

Microbiology (87003–87999)

The Microbiology section includes: Bacteriology (the identification and study of bacteria); Mycology (the identification and study of fungi); Parasitology (the identification and study of parasites); and Virology (the identification and study of viruses).

Identification is performed by one of two methods: presumptive or definitive. Presumptive identification is performed by identifying the characteristics of the microorganism. In other words, the tester looks at growth patterns, color, success in culturing the specimen in certain media, etc. Definitive identification requires other methods to identify the genus and species of the microorganism, and may require DNA analysis (coded separately).

Codes are specific to the source material for the study. Starting with code 87260, the source material must be primary only. In other words, the source is the individual's blood or other tissue for direct examination. Secondary sources, including materials grown on media, are not coded with these codes.

The infectious agent should be coded as specifically as possible. Testing of unidentified infectious agents or agents without a specific code may be coded by testing technique using 87300–87301.

This section also includes codes for the work of identifying drugs to which the organism may be susceptible or resistant. Although most of the codes in this section require special equipment and expertise, a few codes describe services performed routinely in a physician's office. The most common is the rapid strep test, or RADT. This is a reagent strip test for group A Streptococcus and commonly is performed to test for strep throat. This is billed with 87880 and is a CLIA waived test.

CPT® subsection guidelines for Microbiology instruct to report modifier 59 when the same lab test is performed on multiple specimens or sites. For example, a Chlamydia culture taken from the vaginal area and another culture using urine report code 87110 twice, appending modifier 59 to the second code (87110, 87110-59).

Bacterial Urine Culture (87086–87088, 87184, and 87186)

A bacterial urine culture is a laboratory procedure performed on a urine specimen to establish the probable etiology of a presumed urinary tract infection. It is common practice to do a urinalysis prior to a urine culture. A urine culture may also be used as part of the evaluation and management of another related condition. The procedure includes aerobic agar-based isolation of bacteria or other cultivable organisms present, and quantification of types present based on morphologic criteria. Isolates deemed significant may be subjected to additional identification and susceptibility procedures as requested by the ordering physician. The physician's request may be through clearly documented and communicated laboratory protocols.

Code 87086 should be used one time per encounter. Colony count restrictions ordinarily do not apply to CPT® 87088 since counts may be highly variable according to syndrome or other clinical circumstances (eg, antecedent therapy, collection time, degree of hydration). Codes 87088, 87184, and 87186 may be used multiple times in association with, or independent of, code 87086 since urinary tract infections may be polymicrobial.

Infectious Agent Detection by Nucleic Acid (DNA or RNA); HIV-1 or 2 (87536 and 87539)

HIV (human immunodeficiency virus) quantification is achieved using a number of different assays measuring the amount of circulating viral RNA. Assays vary both in methods used to detect viral RNA as well as in ability to detect viral levels at lower limits. However, all employ some type of nucleic acid amplification technique to enhance sensitivity, and results are expressed as the HIV copy number. HIV copy number is also referred to as "viral load," it is an expression of the concentration of the HIV virus in the blood. It is used as a guide to treatment decisions and to monitor response to treatment.

Quantification assays of HIV plasma RNA are used to assess relative risk for disease progression and predict time to death, as well as to assess efficacy of antiretroviral therapies. HIV quantification is often performed together with CD4+ T cell counts providing information on the extent of HIV induced immune system damage.

CPT® codes for quantification should not be used simultaneously with other nucleic acid detection codes for HIV-1 (87534, 87535) or HIV-2 (87537, 87538).

Human Papillomavirus Detection (87623–87625)

Human papillomavirus (HPV) testing is done to detect whether certain types of HPV are present. HPV can cause an abnormal Pap test result. There are many types of HPV. Some types cause common, plantar, filiform, or flat warts. Other types cause genital warts, a sexually transmitted disease affecting men and women. In women, high-risk types of HPV (such as types 16, 18, 31, and 45) cause changes in the cells of the cervix; they are seen as abnormal cells on a Pap test. Abnormal cervical cells may resolve without treatment; however, some untreated cervical cell changes can lead to cervical dysplasia and cervical cancer. HPV testing detects the genetic material of human papillomavirus. Like a Pap test, an HPV test is done on a sample of cells collected from the cervix.

Immunoassay with Optical Observation (87802–87807)

The procedures described in these codes assist physicians in making a rapid and accurate diagnosis of diseases such as influenza (87804) and respiratory syncytial virus (RSV) code (87807) through antigen detection followed by conventional viral culture and using a direct optical immunoassay. Common methods of collection for testing include nasopharyngeal swabs, bronchoalveolar lavage fluids, nasal washes, and throat swabs.

Anatomic Pathology (88000–88099)

The Anatomic Pathology subsection includes all of the postmortem pathologic examinations, or necropsies, more commonly called autopsies. Codes in this section vary based on whether the study is gross only, or gross and microscopic. There are further differentiations based on whether the central nervous system (brain and spinal cord) is included in the examination.

Additionally, 88040 is for forensic necropsy examination; 88045 is for coroner's call.

Forensic examinations are detailed exams for legal evidence. Coroner's call is for a response to a crime scene.

Cytopathology (88104–88199)

Cytopathology is a branch of pathology studying diseases on the cellular or individual cell level. The most common cytopathologic study is the Pap smear, which is an examination of cervical and/or vaginal cells.

Pap Smears (88141–88155, 88164–88167, 88174–88175)

During a Pap test, a small sample of cells from the surface of the cervix is collected and spread or smeared on a slide (Pap smear) or the cervical samples are placed into a vial of liquid preservative and sent to a lab for examination under a microscope. The cells are examined for abnormalities indicating cancer or changes leading to cancer (pre-cancerous).

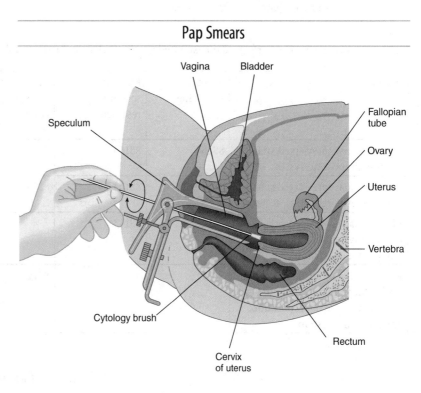

Pap Smears

Source: Lindh, Pooler, Tamparo, and Dahl, Delmar's Comprehensive Medical Assisting (Administrative and Clinical Competencies), 4e, ISBN#978-1-4354-1914-8

Cervical cancer has well-defined stages, and chances of a cure are much higher when it is detected before it has spread from the cervix to other parts of the body.

All abnormal diagnostic Pap smears requiring an interpretation by the pathologist are assigned the additional pathologist code 88141 regardless of screening (manual or computer) method or slide preparation method. Code 88141 is never reported alone but is always combined with a technical service code. Three subsets of codes report cervical and vaginal screening and physician interpretation services.

Pap smear results are reported by two methods: Bethesda and non-Bethesda. Under the Bethesda system, Pap test samples having no cell abnormalities are reported as "negative for intraepithelial lesion or malignancy." Samples with cell abnormalities are divided into the following categories:

- ASC—atypical squamous cells
- ASC-US—atypical squamous cells of undetermined significance, pronounced "ask-us" for ASC-US.
- ASC-H—atypical squamous cells cannot exclude a high-grade squamous intraepithelial lesion
- AGC—atypical glandular cells
- AIS—endocervical adenocarcinoma *in situ*, Ca *in situ or CIS* (carcinoma *in situ*)
- LSIL—low-grade squamous intraepithelial lesion
- HSIL—high-grade squamous intraepithelial lesion

Similar studies can also be performed on aspirated fluids or cells obtained by washing or brushings.

Pap Tests	Manual screening	Manual screening plus rescreening	Manual screening and computer assisted rescreening	Manual screening and computer assisted rescreening using cell selection	Automated computer screening
Conventional spray-fixed smear, Bethesda reporting system	88164	88165	88166	88167	88147
Conventional spray-fixed smear, non-Bethesda reporting system	88150	88153	88152	88154	88147
Liquid-based specimen preparation any system of reporting, by any vendor's instrument	88142	88143			88147
Pathologist diagnostic interpretation of an abnormal diagnostic smear, any type of preparation, any reporting system	88141	88141	88141	88141	88141

Flow Cytometry (88182–88189)

Flow cytometry (88182–88189), abbreviated FCM, is a technique for counting and examining microscopic particles, such as cells and chromosomes, by suspending them in a stream of fluid and passing them by an electronic detection apparatus. It allows simultaneous multiparametric analysis of the physical and/or chemical characteristics of up to thousands of particles per second. Flow cytometry is used routinely in the diagnosis of health disorders, especially blood cancers, but has many applications.

Cytogenetic Studies (88230–88299)

Cytogenetics is a branch of genetics concerned with the study of the structure and function of the cell, especially chromo-

somes. It includes routine analysis of G-Banded chromosomes, other cytogenetic banding techniques, as well as molecular cytogenetics such as fluorescent *in situ* hybridization (FISH) and comparative genomic hybridization (CGH).

Also in this section are codes for storage and thawing of materials for cytogenic analysis.

Surgical Pathology (88300–88399)

Basic surgical pathology services include accession, examination, and reporting. Documentation of all three components is required to bill the service. One code, 88300, is used when only gross examination is needed. The other codes all require both gross and microscopic examination. Successive codes represent increasing levels of physician work. The type of specimen, including how the specimen was obtained, determines the code selected. For example, a colon biopsy is assigned to Level IV (88305), a colon segmental resection for a condition other than a tumor is assigned to a Level V (88307), and a colon segmental resection for tumor is assigned to a Level VI (88309).

This section also includes codes for special treatment of specimens including special stains and decalcification of specimens.

Appendix (88302, 88304)

Two surgical pathology codes are described for the appendix: 88302 represents *Appendix, incidental*, (the appendix is being removed during the same operative session of another procedure); 88304 represents Appendix, *other than incidental* (appendectomy is the only surgery being performed).

Needle Core Biopsies (88305, 88307)

Needle core biopsies are coded 88305 or 88307, depending on the source. If there is an immediate determination of adequacy of the core biopsy using a cytologic touch preparation, report 88333 for the intraoperative consultation of the initial site and 88334 for each additional site.

Cervical Loop Electrical Excision (88305, 88307)

The ectocervical portion of a cervical loop electrosurgical excision procedure (LEEP) is coded like a cervical conization (88307). If it is submitted as separate specimens, each procedure is coded as 88305 or 88307, depending on the work involved. Small endocervical samples are comparable to an endocervical biopsy or endocervical curettage (ECC), and 88305 is the appropriate code. A larger endocervical LEEP is comparable to a cervical conization and is coded 88307.

Lymph Nodes

There are exceptions for coding separately for lymph node examinations. For example, the examination is not reported separately:

- When the CPT® designation specifically includes lymph nodes (eg, 88309, mastectomy or laryngectomy with regional lymph nodes) or
- When lymph nodes are ordinarily attached to the specimen (eg, a lymph node adjacent to the neck of the gallbladder with a cholecystectomy [88304] or colectomy for neoplasm with mesenteric lymph nodes [88309]).

There are circumstances warranting separate codes. For example, periaortic lymph nodes generally are not removed with the colon or gallbladder and, if submitted, are coded separately. When multiple regional lymph node resections are dissected, each is examined separately to establish the pres-

ence and extent of metastases and each dissection is reported separately. A radical prostate resection does not include regional lymph nodes and each regional lymph node dissection is reported separately in addition to 88309. A sentinel lymph node biopsy is not a component of a regional lymph node dissection, and the work in evaluating the sentinel lymph node is a distinct service. When a sentinel lymph node biopsy is accompanied by a lymph node dissection, both services are coded separately.

Special Stains (88312–88314)

Special stain codes are used per stain, per specimen regardless of the number of slides stained. For example, one specimen with one special stain used on multiple slides receives the appropriate special stains code only once; however, one specimen receiving three special stains is coded separately for each special stain used.

Consultations (88321, 88323)

Consultations with reports on referred slides and material requiring preparation of slides refer to a single accession from another laboratory can include multiple specimens. For example, a pathologist obtains prior mastectomy and colectomy specimens for comparison of different tumors with a fine needle aspiration (FNA) biopsy of a possible recurrence. Each is coded separately. Slides from a radical hysterectomy with multiple specimens representing different lymph node groups or peritoneal samplings are coded as a single consultation. Code 88325 reports the review of the patient's chart, laboratory results, oncologist's consultations, etc. It is not intended for use when review of the record is limited to pathology reports.

Intraoperative Cytologic Exam (88329–88334)

Intraoperative consultations (88329–88334) are services performed during operative sessions including frozen sections and touch preps (quick tissue examinations for abnormal cells requiring further excision). Code 88331 describes the exam of the initial frozen section (single specimen) and code 88332 is reported for each additional tissue block with frozen section. Two codes describe intraoperative cytologic exams (via touch or squash preparation) and consultation to provide immediate diagnosis during an intraoperative consultation without the involvement of frozen section. They are distinguished by the initial site (88333) and examination of each additional specimen (88334). Code 88334 is reported one time for each additional specimen in addition to the initial site exam (88333) and the frozen section evaluation (88331).

DNA Ploidy and S-Phase Analysis (88358)

Code 88358 is not used to report any service other than DNA ploidy and S-phase analysis. One unit of service for code 88358 includes both DNA ploidy and S-phase analysis.

Quantitative Immunohistochemistry (88361)

Quantitative immunohistochemistry by digital cellular imaging is reported as CPT® code 88361 and the code should not be used to report any service other than quantitative immunocytochemistry by digital cellular imaging. Digital cellular imaging includes computer software analysis of stained microscopic slides.

In Situ Hybridization (ISH) (88365, 88367, 88368)

ISH is used as a definitive marker for certain cancers. Codes 88367 and 88368 describe manual and computer assisted analyses for the first single probe stain. Fluorescence in situ hybridization (FISH) (code 88365) uses fluorescent dyes to identify each of the human chromosomes. This code is also reported for the first single probe stain. If additional stains are performed use the appropriate add-on code. Quantitative studies, as identified by code 88358 (morphometric analysis), performed as an adjunct to ISH procedures, are used increasingly to identify chromosomal abnormalities such as trisomy of chromosomes 18 and 21.

Practical Coding Note

Medicare does not pay for duplicate testing codes 88342 (immunohistochemistry or immunocytochemistry, per specimen) and codes 88184–88189 (flow cytometry) should not be reported for the same or similar specimens. The diagnosis should be established using one of these methods. The provider may report both CPT® codes if both methods are required because the initial method is nondiagnostic or does not explain the light microscopic findings. The provider can report both methods utilizing modifier 59 and document the need for both methods in the medical record.

If the abnormal cells in two or more specimens are morphologically similar and testing on one specimen by one method (88342 or 88184–88189) establishes the diagnosis, the other method should not be reported on the same or similar specimen. Similar specimens include, but are not limited to:

- Blood and bone marrow
- Bone marrow aspiration and bone marrow biopsy
- Two separate lymph nodes
- Lymph node and other tissue with lymphoid infiltrate

In Vivo Laboratory Procedures (88720–88749)

CPT® code 88740 is performed to determine whether a patient has carbon monoxide poisoning. Code 88741 is used to determine if a patient suffers from methemoglobinemia. Methemoglobinemia is a blood disorder in which an abnormal amount of methemoglobin builds up in the blood.

Other Procedures (89049–89240)

This group of CPT® codes is a catchall for all other laboratory and pathology procedures not easily classified with other service codes. Some of the service codes describe collection of various body fluids routinely performed by lab personnel (eg, gastric intubation, nasal smears, sputum collection, and sweat collection).

Cell Count (89050)

Miscellaneous body fluids (eg, cerebral spinal fluid, joint fluid) are listed when cells are counted in fluids other than blood. Patients presenting with suspected meningitis, for example, have CSF withdrawn and several tests run. One of these tests is microscopic examination. The presence of any cells—red blood cells, white blood cells, or microbes—is considered significant.

Sputum Induction (89220)

Sputum induction is a noninvasive procedure using an ultrasonic nebulizer to induce a sputum specimen for microbiological staining for diagnosis of a variety of organisms, including Mycobacterium tuberculosis and Pneumocystis carinii pneumonia (PCP). Sputum induction is an alternative to bronchoalveolar lavage to obtain a rapid diagnosis. Documentation in the medical record should include the following:

- Date and time of procedure
- Length of procedure
- Mode of therapy
- Medication administered (if applicable)
- Patient tolerance
- Pre- and postheart rates
- Pre- and postbreath sounds
- Cough effort

Sweat Test (89230)

CPT® code 89230 reports the collection of sweat stimulated with an inducer by pilocarpine iontophoresis. An elevated level of chloride in sweat is the most commonly used test for a laboratory diagnosis of cystic fibrosis.

Reproductive Medicine Procedures (89250–89398)

The subsection Reproductive Medicine Procedures is used to report the changing technology and medical practice in the field of reproductive medicine. According to a patient fact sheet of the American Society for Reproductive Medicine, infertility may be due to problems in either the male or the female partner. Male problems may be contributory in 30 percent to 40 percent of infertile couples. The initial screening evaluation of the male partner includes a history and two semen analyses. Commonly called a "sperm count," the number of live and motile sperm in a sample are estimated. Semen cultures check for bacteria causing genital infection. Biochemical analysis of semen measures various chemicals in semen such as fructose.

Other tests include:

1. Antisperm antibodies (89325) tests for antibodies binding to sperm and may reduce fertility.

2. Sperm penetration assay (Hamster egg penetration test, 89329) measures sperm-egg membrane fusion, using hamster eggs and the male's sperm to test the capability of the sperm to penetrate the egg during in vitro fertilization (IVF).

Code 89250 reports the culture of immature oocytes, but excludes the term "fertilization," which may or may not be performed.

Code 89272 reports separate techniques for additional culture from an eight-cell embryo (4–7 days) to blastocyst. Insemination is reported separately with CPT® codes 89280 and 89281. Code 89281 reports the additional work of microfertilization of greater than 10 oocytes in culture techniques involving tissue culture of human oocytes/embryos in the presence of oviductal, uterine, granulosa, or other substrate cells. Microscopic and cytochemical examination of the substrate cells may be used to determine their viability or functionality.

Code 89268 reports the insemination of oocytes to achieve fertilization, which involves introduction of human spermatozoa isolated from seminal plasma into a culture dish containing oocytes. Semen analysis and sperm preparation must be performed prior to this procedure to assess sperm parameters necessary for fertilization. This procedure also includes microscopic examination of spermatozoa and oocytes to determine viability or functionality. Culture of human oocytes/embryos involves the identification, isolation, and incubation of these cells in culture medium and the maintenance of oocytes/embryo viability and functionality. Laboratory services provided are reported separately from physician services.

Code 89272 reports the extended culture of human oocytes/embryos and includes the identification, isolation, and incubation of these cells in culture medium and includes maintenance of culture viability and functionality. This does not include the work of 89250.

CPT® Category III codes are used to report cryopreservation of ovarian tissue (0058T) and immature oocyte(s) (0357T). Category III codes are found in the CPT® codebook right before the appendices.

HCPCS Level II

HCPCS Level II codes beginning with P are specific for pathology services. (P2028–P9615). They are of limited use as most pathology and laboratory services are coded from CPT®.

- Chemistry and Toxicology Tests (P2028–P2038)
- Pathology Screening Tests (P3000–P3001)
- Microbiology Tests (P7001)
- Miscellaneous Pathology and Lab Tests (P9010–P9615)

Modifiers

CPT® modifier 26 indicates only the professional component of the service was performed, and HCPCS Level II modifier TC indicates only the technical component of the service was performed. Virtually all of the codes in the Pathology and Laboratory Chapter have both a professional and a technical component. If both the professional and technical components are performed by the same provider, this is referred to as the global service and no modifiers are used.

The technical component of any test includes the work of preparing and running the test, as well as the equipment and supplies involved. It also includes the time and skill of the individual who performed the test. When a test is performed in a hospital or other facility setting, the reimbursement for the technical component of the service belongs to the facility. If a physician's office performed only the testing but sent the results for interpretation, the test code is billed with modifier TC.

The professional component is the interpretation of the results with a written report of the interpretation. Quite a few services in the Pathology and Laboratory Chapter do not have a professional component because the ordering physician receives the results and makes his own interpretation, combined with his or her clinical findings. To bill the professional component of a service, a physician must write an interpretive report based on the test results. When this is done, the code is billed with modifier 26.

If the service is performed in a physician's office and a report is written with the interpretation of the results, the code is billed without a modifier. Although other CPT® modifiers (notably 59, 76, and 77) are used in the appropriate circumstances as described in other chapters, three other modifiers apply specifically to the Pathology and Laboratory codes.

Modifier 90 is used when an office or facility bills for a test performed at an outside reference laboratory. This can be done only when the reference lab has billed the facility for testing and the facility or physician office bills the insurer for the test. There are many payer-specific rules about billing for a reference lab; coders need to know the rules for each specific payer.

Modifier 91 is used to indicate a repeat diagnostic test was needed. It is similar to modifiers 76 and 77, but does not specify a provider. This is appropriate for tests not having a separate professional component. This modifier is used when medical necessity dictates another test is needed. If a test is repeated because of an error, or because the specimen was insufficient, this is not a separately billable service.

Modifier 92 describes testing using special single-use transportable equipment or kit. This equipment often is used when tests are performed in other patient locations, but the use of the modifier is not limited to other locations. It may be reported any time the equipment is used. Modifier 92 is added to the code describing the basic test performed.

Modifier QW is used when the service provided is a CLIA waived test. Although this is required for Medicare claims, other payers may require it because it indicates the service provider has a CLIA waived certificate.

Clinical Laboratory Improvement Amendments (CLIA)

Congress passed the Clinical Laboratory Improvement Amendments (CLIA) in 1988. CLIA requires all laboratories examining materials derived from the human body for diagnosis, prevention, or treatment purposes to be certified by the Secretary of Health and Human Services. The Centers for Medicare & Medicaid Services (CMS) administers the CLIA laboratory certification program for the Secretary in conjunc-

tion with the Centers for Disease Control and Prevention (CDC) and the Food and Drug Administration (FDA), one of its most important programs (a description of the program is available online from CMS at www.cms.gov/clia/).

All laboratory testing sites (eg, physician's offices, hospitals, independent laboratories, ambulatory surgical centers, community clinics, ESRD facilities, health fairs, health maintenance organizations [HMO], home health agencies [HHA], rural health clinics [RHC], pharmacies, industry, mobility units, student health centers, blood banks, and tissue repositories) must be registered with CLIA. These sites must have either a registration certificate or a CLIA certificate of waiver to legally perform lab tests in the United States. Claims will be denied for labs not meeting these stipulations and when denied, the provider may not bill the patient for services provided. Violation of CLIA regulations is punishable by fines and imprisonment.

Tests typically performed in the provider's office are less complex and are classified as waived. The provider must have a certificate of waiver to perform these tests in office. Modifier QW usually needs to be appended to the HCPCS Level I or Level II code for Medicare claims given the designation CLIA waived. Modifier QW can be found in the HCPCS Level II codebook. A comprehensive list of these tests can be found at www.cms.gov/CLIA/downloads/waivetbl.pdf (CLIA waived tests are produced by a variety of pharmaceutical manufacturers).

Section Review 18.3

1. A patient with deep vein thrombosis requires heparin to maintain therapeutic anticoagulation levels. He has regular PTTs drawn to monitor his level of anticoagulation. What code describes this testing?

    A. 85730

    B. 85520

    C. 80299

    D. None of these

2. What is the code and any required modifier(s) for dipstick urinalysis, non-automated, without microscopy performed in a physician office for a Medicare patient?

    A. 81025-26-QW

    B. 81002-26-QW

    C. 81002-QW

    D. 81002

---

3. A patient presents with right upper quadrant pain, nausea, and other symptoms of liver disease as well as complaints of decreased urination. Her physician orders an albumin; bilirubin, both total and direct; alkaline phosphatase; total protein; alanine amino transferase; aspartate amino transferase, and creatinine. How should this be coded?

    A. 82040, 82247, 82248, 84075, 84155, 84460, 84450, 82565

    B. 80076, 82565

    C. 80076

    D. 80076-22

4. A 27-year-old male dies of a gunshot wound. An autopsy is performed to gain evidence for the police investigation and any subsequent trial. What code describes this service?

    A. 88005

    B. 88025

    C. 88040

    D. 88045

5. A patient with AIDS presents for follow-up care. The total T-cell count is ordered to evaluate progression of the disease. Choose the code(s) for this study.

    A. 86703

    B. 86360

    C. 86361, 86359

    D. 86359

Document Dissection

Case 1

Ordering Physician: William Jones, MD [1]

Clinical Indications: [2] HCV. Liver function tests: Bili 0.6, alk phos 89, AST 40, ALT 59.

Gross Description: [3] A) Received in formalin labeled "Smith, liver" are four needle core biopsy fragments ranging in size from 0.5 up to 1.4 cm in maximum length. The specimens are entirely submitted in cassette A.

Microscopic Description: [4] The architecture is intact without nodularity, with approximately 16 portal tracts available for evaluation with no architectural distortion. There is minimal portal lymphocytic infiltrate, and mild focal portal fibrous expansion, confirmed by trichrome stain, [5] with no pericellular fibrosis. There is minimal focal lobular inflammatory activity. There is no steatosis. There are no iron deposits or hepatocyte intractyoplasmic globules identified by iron and PAS-D stains, [6] respectively.

Final Diagnosis: [7]

A) Native liver, core needle biopsy: [8]

1. Chronic hepatitis with minimal focal portal and lobular activity and mild focal portal fibrous expansion, confirmed by trichrome stain, consistent with hepatitis C induced disease, Grade 1, Stage 1 [9]

2. No steatosis

3. No iron deposition detected by iron stain

4. No hepatocyte cytoplasmic inclusions detected by PAS-D stain

---

_____

[1] The name of the ordering physician must always be recorded as part of the documentation.

[2] Although not strictly required, including any clinical indications when available is very helpful, especially when results are negative as this is the medical necessity for the service.

[3] Surgical Pathology services always require a gross description. This area also contains critical information regarding the number of specimens received.

[4] Except for code 88300, surgical pathology codes require a microscopic examination.

[5] Notes must specify any special preparations used along with the findings associated with that preparation. First stain performed.

[6] Another two stains performed.

[7] The final diagnostic statement is key to coding surgical pathology services. This is the physician's interpretation.

[8] Knowing the procedure used to obtain the specimen is also key as this will be part of determining the right level of service.

[9] The final diagnosis is both the physician work component and the diagnosis to be used to select an ICD-10-CM code. Note as well that the results of each separate stain and treatment are listed with their findings, even when the findings are negative.

_____

What are the CPT® and ICD-10-CM codes reported?

CPT® Codes: 88307, 88312, 88313x2

ICD-10-CM Code: B18.2

Rationale: CPT® Codes: Surgical pathology of one cassette of specimens of the liver from a core needle biopsy is coded using 88307. Look in the CPT® Index for Pathology and Laboratory/Surgical Pathology/Gross and Micro Exam/Level V. You may not know what Level it is (II–VI), if you look at codes 88302–88309, find Liver, biopsy—needle/wedge, 88307. The PAS-D stain is reported with 88312. The trichome and iron stain are reported with 88313 each so, x2. For both of these, in the CPT® Index look for Pathology and Laboratory/Smear and Stain-See Smear and Stain. Smear and Stain/Blood Smears/ Surgical Pathology which directs you to 88312–88313, 88319.

ICD-10-CM Code: The diagnosis is chronic hepatitis type C. Look in the ICD-10-CM Index to Diseases and Injuries for Hepatitis/C (viral)/chronic B18.2. Verification in the Tabular Index confirms code selection.

ICD-9-CM Application

What is/are the ICD-9-CM code(s) reported?

Code(s): 070.54

Rationale: The diagnosis is chronic hepatitis type C. Look in the ICD-9-CM Alphabetic Index for Hepatitis/Type C/chronic and you are directed to 070.54. Verification in the Tabular List confirms code selection

---

Case 2

Ordering Physician: Annette Brown, MD [1]

Cytology Report: [2] Screening cervical Pap smear, Bethesda system

Collected: 1/30/20xx [3] **Received:** 2/3/20xx

Patient History:

LMP: 1/24/xx

Additional Information: Kidney transplant [4]

Specimen Source:

A) Endo/ecto cervical

Cytologic Impression, Manual Screening with Physician Supervision: [5]

Negative for intraepithelial lesions or malignancy [6]

Sampling Adequacy: Endocervical cells present.

Comments: Menstrual sample.

----

[1] As with surgical pathology, the ordering physician must always be documented as part of the report.

[2] Although not always recorded as part of the report it is helpful to know what type of study was requested. This heading also tells us that the specimen was a Pap smear and that it was cervical rather than vaginal.

[3] The date collected is the date of service.

[4] Clinical data will be helpful in coding ICD-10-CM for negative results.

[5] Choosing a code includes know how the screening was performed. That information is included here.

[6] This is the physician's interpretation. It is the Bethesda reporting system.

What are the CPT® and ICD-10-CM codes reported?

CPT® Code: 88164

ICD-10-CM Codes: Z12.4, Z94.0

CPT® Code: The procedure is a manual screening of a cervical Pap smear. Look in the CPT® Index for Pap Smears/Bethesda System and you are directed to 88164-88167. Code 88164 is correct because the manual screening of the cervical smear was done under physician supervision.

ICD-10-CM Codes: Screening Pap smears are performed to diagnose cervical cancer and precancer or dysplasia. Look in the ICD-10-CM Index to Diseases and Injuries for Screening/neoplasm (malignant) (of)/cervix Z12.4. The patient has had a kidney transplant. Look in the Index to Diseases and Injuries for Transplant(ed) (status)/kidney Z94.0. Verify code selection in the Tabular List.

ICD-9-CM Application

What is/are the ICD-9-CM code(s) reported?

Code(s): V76.2, V42.0

Rationale: Screening Pap smears are performed to diagnose cervical cancer and precancer or dysplasia. To find the diagnosis, look in the Index to Diseases for Screening/malignant neoplasm/cervix and you are directed to V76.2. The patient has had a kidney transplant. Look in the Index to Diseases for Transplant(ed)/kidney and you are directed to V42.0. Verification of the codes in the Tabular List confirms code selections.

Glossary

Autopsy—Examination of a dead body to determine the cause(s) of death (syn. necropsy).

Bacteriology—Branch of science concerned with the study of bacteria.

Cytopathology—The study of the cellular changes in disease.

Cytogenetics—A branch of genetics concerned with the study of the structure and function of the cell, especially the chromosomes.

Clinical Laboratory—Place where tests are performed on clinical specimens to get information about the health of a patient as pertaining to the diagnosis, treatment, and prevention of disease.

Clinical Laboratory Improvement Amendments (CLIA)—Quality standards for all laboratory testing to ensure the accuracy, reliability, and timeliness of patient test results.

CLIA waived tests—Simple tests that may be performed in non-laboratory settings, such as a physician office.

Definitive Identification—Identification of the genus and species of the microorganism.

Forensic—Pertaining to or applicable to personal injury, murder, and other legal proceedings.

Gross—Examination of the entire specimen without sectioning of the specimen into thin slides to be examined without the use of a microscope.

Hematology—The medical specialty pertaining to the anatomy, physiology, pathology, symptomatology and therapeutics related to blood and blood forming tissues.

Immunology—The study of the immune system, its components and function.

In Vivo—Studies performed within the living body.

Microbiology—The study of microorganisms, including fungi, protozoa, bacteria and viruses.

Microscopy (Microscopic)—Examination under a microscope of minute objects.

Molecular Diagnostics—The measurement of DNA, RNA, proteins or metabolites to detect genotypes, mutations or biochemical changes.

Mycology—The study of fungi, their identification, classification, edibility, cultivation, and biology, including pathogenicity.

Necropsy—Examination of a dead body and organs to determine the cause(s) of death (syn. autopsy).

Panel—A group of tests performed together and listed in the code description.

Pathology—The medical science and specialty practice concerned with study of diseased tissue and cells.

Presumptive Identification—Identification of a microorganism based on the growth patterns, color, success in culturing the specimen in certain media, etc.

Parasitology—The branch of biology and of medicine concerned with the study of parasites.

Qualitative—A test determining the presence or absence of a drug.

Quantitative—A test identifying not only the presence of a drug, but the exact amount present.

Semi-quantitative—Test identifying the amount of an analyte within a specified range but does not identify a specific quantity.

Virology—The study of viruses and of viral disease.

Introduction

Evaluation and management (E/M) services are placed prominently at the forefront of the CPT® codebook, signaling the importance of these codes. For many providers, E/M services represent the bulk of codes reported. For each E/M service, code selection is based on location, physician work, and the extent of medical decision making demonstrated during the visit. E/M codes are reported by physicians and physician extenders of all medical specialties.

Objectives

- Define E/M
- Differentiate between a new patient and an established patient
- Identify service location(s) and type(s)
- Understand the requirements for the different levels of service
- Learn how properly to "level" an E/M service
- Abstract a provider's note to arrive at the levels of service

Anatomy and Medical Terminology

E/M is not specific to one medical specialty, nor is it specific to one body system or anatomical area. To code E/M services appropriately, you will need to understand terms and anatomy related to the entire body.

During each visit, a physician uses a variety of methods to evaluate a patient. The physician observes the patient during the encounter and documents mannerisms and behavior. The skin and symmetry of the body are inspected.

After inspection and observation (visual evaluation), a physician may explore a body system further using palpation, auscultation, and percussion. Palpation refers to examination of the body by touch. Body parts are palpated to look for organ size or condition (eg, abdominal masses), or for tenderness (eg, there is no tenderness to palpation). Auscultation is listening to body sounds. A stethoscope may be used to listen to the heart and lungs for sounds. Percussion is creating sounds from tapping on body areas to examine body organs and body cavities. The vibrations of the sounds help identify abnormalities. Lungs sound hollow when percussed.

As we discuss the physical exam component of an E/M code later in this chapter, we will introduce terminology used for each body area examined.

Medical Abbreviation

BP	Blood pressure
CC	Chief complaint
HEENT	Head, eyes, ears, nose, throat
h/o	History of
HPI	History of present illness
Hx	History
NAD	No apparent distress
NKDA	No known drug allergies
PE	Physical examination
PERLA	Pupils equal and reactive to light and accommodation. (In other words, normal)
PMH	Past medical history
pt	Patient
R/O	Rule out
ROS	Review of systems
WNL	Within normal limits

ICD-10-CM Coding

E/M services are used to "evaluate and manage" all symptoms, illnesses, and diseases. Diagnosis coding for E/M services is not limited to one set of diagnosis codes, or to one section of the ICD-10-CM codebook.

The primary diagnosis for any E/M service should be the reason the visit was initiated. This can be a symptom such as a cough or a disease such as diabetes. A visit also may be for preventive care, which requires a Z code to describe the reason for the service.

Preventive Care E/M codes will be accompanied by ICD-10-CM codes from Chapter 21: *Factors Influencing Health Status and Contact with Health Services (Z00–Z99)*. Z codes are for use in any healthcare setting and may be used as either a first-listed or secondary code, depending on the circumstances of the encounter.

In the ICD-10-CM Index to Diseases and Injuries, look for Examination/medical (adult)(for)(of)/general (adult) Z00.00 and with abnormal findings Z00.01.

Z00.00 Encounter for general adult medical examination without abnormal findings

Z00.01 Encounter for general adult medical examination without abnormal findings

ICD-9-CM Application

A preventive care visit in ICD-9-CM is a V code.

In the ICD-9-CM Index to Diseases, look for Examination (general) (routine)(of)(for)/medical (for)(of)/general/routine V70.0.

V70.0 Routine general medical examination at a healthcare facility

A diagnosis can be considered acute, chronic, or an acute phase of a chronic condition. When the condition is an acute phase of a chronic condition and there is a code to describe each of the phases, list the acute code first and the chronic code second. Be aware of combination codes, such as acute and chronic cholecystitis (K81.2), where a single code is reported for both conditions.

Practical Coding Note

If the same condition is described as both acute (subacute) and chronic, and separate subentries exist in the Alphabetic Index at the same indentation level, code both and sequence the acute (or subacute) code first.

Symptoms typically are coded from chapter 18—Symptoms, Signs, and Abnormal Clinical and Laboratory Findings, Not Elsewhere Classifed (R00-R99) of the ICD-10-CM codebook. Symptoms should be used as a diagnosis only if no definitive diagnosis is provided. For example, if the patient comes in with cough, congestion, and a headache, but the provider determines the patient has an upper respiratory infection, only the upper respiratory infection is used as a diagnosis. Conversely, if a patient is seen for chest pain but the provider has not yet provided a definitive diagnosis, "chest pain" is used for the diagnosis.

Signs and symptoms routinely associated with a disease process are not to be coded separately from the definitive diagnosis. Signs and symptoms not associated with a disease process routinely should be coded separately. The coder must understand the pathophysiology of diseases to determine if a sign or symptom is part of the disease process, or if it should be reported separately. For example, a patient has a fever and cough and the provider diagnoses the patient with pneumonia. Fever and cough are part of the disease process for pneumonia; they are not coded separately. If the same patient also complains of elbow pain, the elbow pain is reported separately because it is not part of the disease process for pneumonia.

When a patient with multiple conditions is seen, *only* those conditions affecting care, or requiring provider care or management, are coded.

The guidelines to report signs and symptoms when there is not a definitive diagnosis for ICD-10-CM is I.C.18.a. ICD-10-CM contains a number of combination codes that identify both the definitive diagnosis along with the usual symptoms of that diagnosis. When reporting these combination codes, an additional code to report symptoms is not required (I.18.d.).

Example

I20.1 Angina pectoris with documented spasm

In this example, the spasm is a symptom included in the code for the angina pectoris. The documented spasm is not reported with a separate code.

CPT® Coding

E/M codes (99201–99499) describe a provider's service to a patient including evaluating the patient's condition(s) and determining the management of care required to treat the patient. Services based solely on time, such as physician standby services, also may be defined as E/M services (These will be discussed in detail later in the chapter).

There are seven components making up an E/M service: History, Exam, Medical Decision Making (MDM), Counseling, Coordination of Care, Nature of Presenting Problem, and Time. Three of these components—History, Exam, and MDM—are considered key components to determining the overall level of an E/M Service.

To support coding of an E/M service, the provider must document the three key components in his or her medical documentation of the patient encounter. Each key component may be documented at several levels, as specified by E/M code descriptors. As an example, the history component may be documented as problem focused, expanded problem focused, detailed, or comprehensive.

Using his or her best clinical judgment, experience, and training, the provider determines the extent of the history, exam, and medical decision making required, based on Medical Necessity (what is necessary to treat the patient for a given condition/complaint). For instance, the physician could spend one hour documenting an exhaustive medical history for a patient with a splinter in her finger, but this would not be necessary or appropriate to the circumstances. Likewise, if a new patient presents with a wide variety of health problems, including hypertension, diabetes, and symptoms of stroke such as slurred speech, a quick five-minute history would not suffice. Medical necessity is supported by ICD-10-CM code assignment.

Serious problems may arise when the provider documents a history and/or exam at a level not supported by medical necessity. The Medicare *Claims Processing Manual* (30.6.1.A) states, "It would not be medically necessary or appropriate to bill a higher level of evaluation and management service when a lower level of service is warranted. *The volume of documentation should not be the primary influence upon which a specific level of service is billed*" [emphasis added].

In the majority of cases, an overall E/M service level is determined by "adding together" the key components the provider has documented. When applicable, CPT® code descriptors will indicate the key component requirements for reporting a specific code. For example, the code descriptor for a level I new patient outpatient visit, 99201, specifies to report the service, the required key components are a problem focused history, a problem focused examination, and straightforward medical decision making (We will discuss these terms in greater detail, below).

In some cases, to report a given level of service, you must meet all three key components (as in the example of 99201 just provided). In other cases, the code descriptor may allow you to report a given level of service by meeting two of the three key components at the specified level. For example, the code descriptor for a level II established patient outpatient visit specifies that to report the service, at least two of three key components—a problem focused history, a problem focused examination, and straightforward MDM—must be documented.

Practical Coding Note

In the description of the majority of evaluation and management codes, the number of key components is specified. For example:

99201—Office or other outpatient visit for the evaluation and management of a new patient, which requires these 3 key components:

99213—Office or other outpatient visit for the evaluation and management of an established patient, which requires at least 2 of these 3 key components:

Highlight or underline the components required for each code.

The Evaluation and Management Services Guidelines in your CPT® codebook outline six steps to determining the level of an evaluation and management service:

1. Select the category or subcategory of service and review the guidelines;
2. Review the level of E/M service descriptors and examples;
3. Determine the level of history;
4. Determine the level of exam;
5. Determine the level of medical decision making; and
6. Select the appropriate level of E/M service.

Categories and Subcategories

E/M codes are divided into categories representing the type of service, such as office visits, emergency department visits, nursing facility care, etc. Some categories are divided further (subcategories) to indicate specific details reflecting the status of the patients as new or established, and/or inpatient or outpatient. Subcategories are divided into levels, which are assigned a five digit code (eg, 99201). Individual code descriptors provide specific details such as place and or type of service; content of the service provided; nature of the presenting problem; and the time generally required to provide the service. The example below represents the basic format of an E/M service category.

Example

Office or Other Outpatient Services *(category)*

New Patient *(subcategory)*

99201 Office or other outpatient visit for the evaluation and management of a new patient, which requires these 3 key components:

- A problem focused history
- A problem focused examination
- Straightforward medical decision making

Counseling and/or coordination of care with other physicians, other qualified healthcare professionals, or agencies are provided consistent with the nature of the problem(s) and the patient's and/or family's needs.

Usually, the presenting problem(s) are self limited or minor. Typically, 10 minutes are spent face-to-face with the patient and/or family. [1]

New vs. Established Patients

Many (not all) E/M service categories differentiate between "new" and "established" patients. The "Decision Tree for New vs. Established Patients" included in the CPT® Evaluation and Management Services guideline provides a quick method to determine if a given patient is new or established, as defined by the AMA (CMS follows CPT® definitions of new and established patients). A patient is new if he or she has not received any *face-to-face* professional services from the physician or qualified health professional, or a physician/qualified health professional of the exact same specialty and subspecialty within the group practice, within the last three years (36 months). This is often referred to as the "three year rule."

If a patient is seen by another member of the group within the past three years, but the physician/qualified health professional is of a different specialty or subspecialty, the patient may still be new. For example, a patient sees an orthopaedist in a group practice to be evaluated for possible hip replacement. The same patient has seen an internist in the same group practice several times over the past three years. The patient is "new" to the orthopedist but "established" for the internist.

Where the patient is seen is not a factor in determining new vs. established. For example, Mrs. Jones' general practitioner, Dr. Smith, joins a new group practice across town. As long as Dr. Smith has seen Ms. Jones within the past three years, she is an established patient at the new location. Likewise, if a physician has provided services face-to-face with a patient in the hospital, and sees the same patient in his or her office within three years, the patient is established.

---

[1] AMA—CPT® 2014 Professional Edition

E/M Service Categories

Office or Other Outpatient Services

Office or Other Outpatient Services is divided into subcategories of new and established patients, as described above. This category represents visits performed in the physician's office, outpatient hospital, or other ambulatory facility such as an urgent care center or nursing home. For new patient services, all three key components must be documented to the extent stated in the code descriptor (as outlined earlier). For established patient services, two of three key components are required.

Note: A Level I *New* Patient Visit (99201) does not correspond equally to the work performed in a Level I *Established* Patient Visit (99211).

Hospital Observation Services

When a patient has a condition needing to be monitored to determine a course of action, he may be admitted to "observation status." For example, if a patient presents to the Emergency Department (ED) with a concussion, the provider can admit the patient to observation status. After a period of monitoring, the patient may be discharged, or—if the condition worsens—may be admitted to the hospital as an inpatient for additional treatment.

The patient is not required to be in a specific area of the hospital to be deemed in "observation status." There is no distinction between a new or established patient for observations services. When the patient is seen at another site of service (eg, ED), and observation status is initiated at the site of service, all E/M services provided by the admitting physician are considered to be part of the initial observation care and not reported separately.

Hospital Observation includes three types of service: Observation Care Discharge Services, Observation Care, and Subsequent Observation Care. The initial observation care should be reported only by the physician admitting the patient to observation status. Initial Observation Care codes require three of three key components be met to report the chosen level of service.

Subsequent Observation Care is used when the patient is seen on a day other than the date of admission or discharge.

Observation Care Discharge Services are used to report the final exam and discharge of the patient. Typically, a patient is admitted to observation care for less than 24 hours; however, a patient can remain in observation care for up to three days. The Initial Observation Care and the Observation Care Discharge should be reported separately only if they occur on separate dates of service.

Example

A patient arrives at the hospital and is admitted to observation status at 9:30 p.m., Oct 1. The patient is discharged from observation status and sent home at 8:30 a.m., Oct 2. In this case, a code from Initial Observation Care would be reported for Oct 1, and the Observation Care Discharge Services would be reported for Oct. 2.

If the patient is admitted to observation status, and discharged on the same date of service, a code from the Observation or Inpatient Care Services (Including Admission and Discharge Services), range 99234–99236, is reported.

When a patient is admitted to the hospital during an observation stay, the observation services should not be reported separately. The observation services provided on the same date as a hospital admission should be included as part of the admission. An observation discharge should not be reported on the same date as the hospital admission.

Hospital Inpatient Services

Hospital Inpatient Services are subcategorized into Initial Hospital Care, Subsequent Hospital Care, Observation or Inpatient Care Services (Including Admission and Discharge Services), and Hospital Discharge Services. These services do not distinguish between new and established patients. Initial Hospital Care requires three of three key components be met to report the chosen level of service.

Initial Hospital Care should be reported only by the admitting physician, according to CPT® Guidelines. CMS, by contrast, allows the use of the initial hospital care codes in place of inpatient consultation codes (we will discuss this in detail when reviewing consultation services below).

Any services performed on the same date, when related to the admission, should be included in the initial hospital care code and not reported separately. This includes office visits, observation visits, and nursing facility visits if provided by the same provider on the same date of service.

Subsequent Hospital Care is used to report the subsequent visits to the patient while the patient is in the hospital. These codes include the provider reviewing the medical record, diagnostic test results, and changes in the patient's status since the last physician assessment. Subsequent Hospital Care codes require two of the three key components be met.

Observation or Inpatient Care Services (Including Admission and Discharge Services) codes should be used to report an admit and discharge on the same date of service. These codes require that all three key components be met.

Hospital Discharge Services report the total time spent by the physician on the date of discharge. Discharge services include the final examination, discussion of the stay, continuing care instructions, discharge paperwork, prescriptions, and referral forms. This service is reported by the amount of time spent by the physician on the date of discharge, even if the time is not continuous. Discharge services are time-based; the time must be documented in the patient's record to qualify for a discharge time of over 30 minutes. Visits to the patient on the date of discharge by physicians who are not the attending physician should be reported using Subsequent Hospital Care codes (99231–99233).

Consultations

Consultation codes are divided into two subcategories based on the location of the consult: Office or Other Outpatient Consultations, and Inpatient Consultations. All consultation services must meet all three key components.

According to CPT®, a consultation has the following components:

- A physician (or other appropriate source) requests another physician (or appropriate source) to evaluate a patient's specific problem or condition and render an opinion. The request can be written or verbal; if verbal, the request must be documented in the patient's medical record.
- The consultant either will recommend care for the patient's condition, or will determine whether to accept care of the patient.
- The consultant must submit a written report back to the requesting physician (or other appropriate source).

For office or outpatient consultations if another physician/ qualified healthcare provider requests an opinion or advice on the same condition, or a new condition, for the same patient, the consulting provider can again report a consultation code. Inpatient consultation codes can only be reported once per admission by the same doctor or doctors in the exact same practice seeing the same patient.

Consultations requested by a patient or family member should be reported using the appropriate codes from categories other than consultation; Office or Other Outpatient Visits, Home Service, or Domiciliary or Rest Home. When a consultation is mandated by a third party payer, or by government, legislative, or regulatory requirement, append modifier 32 *Mandated services* to the consultation code.

Referrals and Transfer of Care

A consultation differs from a referral. A referral occurs when a patient is sent to another physician for care of a specific problem or condition. The requesting physician is not expecting to receive recommendations back from the referring physician, and does not expect to continue treating the patient for the condition.

Example

Consultation: A patient's family physician requests the patient to see a cardiologist to evaluate a heart murmur found during examination and give recommendations for the patient's care.

Referral: A patient's family physician refers the patient to see a cardiologist to treat a heart murmur found during examination.

CPT® defines a transfer of care as, "the process whereby a physician who is providing management for some or all of a patient's problems relinquishes this responsibility to another physician who explicitly agrees to accept this responsibility and who, from the initial encounter, in not providing consultative services."

When transfer of care has been established, the provider accepting care bills subsequent visits with the appropriate established patient visit codes based on the location; Office or Other Outpatient Established Patient Visit (99211–99213), Domiciliary or Rest Home (99334–99337), Home Visit (99347–99350), Subsequent Hospital Care Services (99231–99233), or Subsequent Nursing Facility (99307–99310).

Reporting Consultations for Medicare

Medicare does not pay for consultation codes (except telehealth consultations), and requires that consultation services be billed with the most appropriate (non-consultation) E/M code for the service.

- Outpatient consultations should be reported by selecting the appropriate level code from the Office or Other Outpatient Services (99201–99215).

- Inpatient consultations should be reported using the Initial Hospital Care code (99221–99223) for the initial evaluation and a Subsequent Hospital Care code (99231–99233) for subsequent visits. The physician who admitted the patient as a hospital inpatient (whether that physician is the "consultant" or another physician), should append modifier AI *Principal physician of record* to indicate that he or she is the admitting physician, and to distinguish the physician from others who may provide inpatient services.

Other, non-Medicare payers may allow you to continue to report Consultation codes. Check with individual payers for guidelines.

Emergency Department Services

An Emergency Department (ED) is a section of a hospital organized and designated to treat unscheduled patient visits for immediate medical attention. Emergency departments must be open 24 hours a day, seven days a week. A patient may receive critical care treatment in an emergency department. In this event, critical care codes (discussed below), rather than ED services, will be reported.

Reporting of ED services does not distinguish between new and established patients. Code selection is the same whether the patient has seen the provider before or not. ED visits require all three key components be met.

Another service found in this category is the physician direction of emergency medical services (EMS) emergency care, advanced life support (99288). This code reports the services of a physician, located in a facility's emergency department or critical care department, who is in two-way communication with emergency services personnel. The physician directs the personnel in performing life-saving procedures.

Critical Care Services

Critical care service codes report the direct delivery of medical care to a critically injured or critically ill patient. According to CPT®, "a critical illness or injury acutely impairs one or more vital organ systems, such that there is a high probability of imminent or life threatening deterioration in the patient's condition."

Critical care is a condition, not a location. A patient does not have to be in an intensive care unit (ICU) or other designated area to meet the requirements of critical care. Nor do all patients in an ICU or other designated unit qualify automatically for critical care. Any patient meeting the definition of critically ill or critically injured may qualify for critical care services.

Critical care bundles a number of services, such as cardiac output measurements (93561, 93562), that typically may be required for critically ill or critically injured patients. A complete list of services bundled with critical care may be found in the critical care portion of the CPT® codebook. Any procedures performed by the physician that are not included in the procedures bundled in critical care can be separately reported (example, 31500 *Intubation, endotracheal, emergency procedure*). The physician needs to document that the separate reportable procedures are not included in the critical care time. If this is not documented, then time needs to be deducted from the critical care time to report those services.

Practical Coding Note

To identify services included in critical care codes easily, bracket or highlight the paragraph listing the included services in your CPT® codebook. In addition, locate each code included in the critical care codes, and write "included in critical care" next to it.

Critical Care services are reported based on the time the physician spent dedicated, and directly available, to the patient. The physician cannot work on any other patient during this time; however, the time is not required to be continuous, and the physician is not required to be in the same room as the patient. The physician can report only time spent on the same unit or floor as the patient.

All time spent on the management of the patient's condition on the same floor or unit as the patient is totaled throughout the day and reported with 99291 and 99292. When the time is less than 30 minutes, critical care codes are not reported. Code 99291 is used to report when the total time is between 30 and 74 minutes. Each additional 30 minutes, or part thereof, is reported with a unit of 99292.

Example

A physician provides 125 minutes of critical care to a patient. These services would be reported as 99291, 99292 x 2:

99291 for the first 74 minutes;

99292 for the next 30 minutes (minutes 75–104); and

99292 for the remaining 21 minutes.

Practical Coding Note

Use the Critical Care Time Table in the CPT® codebook to calculate Critical Care Time.

For younger patients, specific code ranges may apply when reporting critical care:

- Neonates (28 days of age or younger)—Inpatient critical care services are reported with neonatal critical care codes 99468 and 99469.
- Infants 29 days through 24 months of age—Inpatient critical care services are reported with pediatric critical care codes 99471–99472.
- Critically ill infant or young child, 2 through 5 years of age—Inpatient critical care services are reported with pediatric critical care codes 99475–99476.

- Neonates and infants up through 71 months (5 years, 11 months) of age—Outpatient critical care services are reported with critical care codes 99291 and 99292. If the patient is later admitted to critical care report all services with the appropriate neonatal or pediatric critical care codes 99468–99476.
- Critical care services to pediatric patients six years of age or older are reported with the critical care codes 99291 and 99292.

Practical Coding Note

Find the above guidelines in the critical care section and highlight them for easy reference.

Nursing Facility Services

Nursing facility services are subcategorized into Initial Nursing Facility Visit, Subsequent Nursing Facility Visits, Nursing Facility Discharge, and Other Nursing Facility Services. E/M services provided to patients in a nursing facility or a psychiatric residential treatment service are reported with these codes.

Initial nursing facility care codes require all three key components be met. Subsequent nursing facility care codes require two of the three key components be met.

For Medicare, the initial visit may be reported by more than one physician, but the physician of record for an admission to the nursing home should append a modifier AI to indicate primary physician of record.

Nursing facility discharge codes report the services provided by a physician to discharge the patient. The codes are reported by time, which includes all time spent on the patient for the date of discharge.

The final code in this section is for an Annual Nursing Facility Assessment by the provider. Government regulations required Nursing Facilities to perform Minimum Data Set/Resident Assessment Instrument (MDS/RAI) annually. When a physician completes this information and performs the comprehensive nursing facility service, report code 99318.

Domiciliary, Rest Home, or Custodial Care Services

This category includes E/M services provided to patients residing in Domiciliary, Rest Home, or in Custodial Care. Domiciliary care refers to care provided in a supervised home setting. Assisted living facilities are considered domiciliary care.

Domiciliary, Rest Home, or Home Care Plan Oversight (CPO)

Care plan oversight indicates oversight of the services provided to patients in certain locations. Oversight of patients in a domiciliary, a rest home, or in the patient's own home is reported with codes from this category, based on the physician time.

Home Services

E/M services provided to a patient in a private residence are reported from this category. The codes distinguish between new and established patients.

Prolonged Services

Codes in this category are subcategorized based on whether the physician has direct (face-to-face) contact with the patient, and are reported based on location and time.

Prolonged services with direct patient contact are add-on codes reported in addition to one of the designated E/M codes listed in the parenthetical instructions after each code.

Prolonged services without direct patient contact are used to report services for time spent managing the patient's care without direct face-to-face patient contact. Prolonged services without direct patient contact may be reported on a different date than the E/M services to which it is related.

A third subcategory is available for clinical staff that provide direct (face-to-face) contact with the patient in the office or other out-patient setting, based on time, and require direct supervision from a physician or qualified health care provider.

Prolonged services are reported in addition to a primary E/M service. Prolonged service codes should be reported only in addition to other E/M codes which have time stated in the description. As an example, the descriptor for level V established patient outpatient service 99215 specifies, "Typically, 40 minutes are spent face-to-face with the patient and/or family." By contrast, Emergency Department services 99281–99285 do not include a stated time component; prolonged services may not be reported in addition to Emergency Department services. Below each prolonged service add-on code is parenthetical instructions indicating with which E/M codes the add-on code can be reported.

Prolonged services may not be reported for services of fewer than 30 minutes.

Occasionally, a request is made for a physician to be available to perform a possible procedure. For example, when there is a delivery involving risk to a neonate, the OB/Gyn delivering the neonate may request a pediatrician to "stand by" in case a surgical procedure is needed on the neonate. Standby services must be at least 30 minutes to be reported, and cannot be reported if the physician standing by performs a procedure

with a global package. Code 99360 reports Physician Standby Services.

Case Management Services

The Case Management Services Category includes Anticoagulant Management and Medical Team Conference.

Warfarin is an anticoagulant (blood thinner) used to prevent blood clots. Common brand names for warfarin include Coumadin® and Jantoven®. The use of Coumadin® can also be referred to as "Coumadin therapy." Due to the critical nature of thinning blood or reducing its clotting factor, patients on warfarin require constant oversight, along with International Normalized Ration (INR) testing. The medication is adjusted, as needed, to provide the best level of anticoagulation in the blood. The patient is reminded of the specific dietary needs, and observed for possible bruising. Anticoagulation management codes are used to report this oversight, which includes ordering, review, and interpretation of the INR testing, communication with the patient, and dosage adjustments, as necessary. The initial management must include at least 60 days of therapy and include a minimum of eight reported INR measurements. Each subsequent 90 days of therapy, including at least three INR measurements, may be reported using 99364.

Medical Team Conference codes report meeting or conference time (face-to-face) of at least three qualified healthcare professionals, with or without the presence of the patient or patient's family member. The healthcare professionals should be of different specialties, and all should be involved directly in the patient's care. The code is selected based on whether the patient or patient's family is present. If the patient or patient's family is not present, the code is selected based on the type of provider: physician or nonphysician qualified healthcare professional.

Care Plan Oversight Services

When the care of a patient involves complex and multidisciplinary care modalities, physician supervision is required to monitor the patient's progress and adjust the care plan as necessary. These services are reported with the codes from the Care Plan Oversight Services Category. The codes are selected based on the location of the patient, and the amount of time spent within a 30-day period to oversee the patient's care.

Preventive Medicine Services

Preventive Medicine, Individual Services, also referred to as "well visits," describe E/M services provided to a patient without a sign, symptom, condition, or illness. The comprehensive exam as described here is an age-appropriate examination of the patient, and not the same as the comprehensive exam referred to in other E/M code categories. The preventive medicine codes are determined based on the age of the patient, and whether the patient is new or established.

During preventive medicine exams, a provider may discover an abnormality or address a condition already in existence. If the abnormality or condition requires the provider to perform a significant amount of work, above what normally would be performed for a preventive service, the additional work can be reported with a separate E/M service code. The additional E/M code would be reported with modifier 25 appended. When determining whether a problem required a significant amount of work, it would be appropriate to see if you could separate the documentation into two distinct separate notes, one to support each service.

The reporting and payment of preventive services and additional E/M codes will depend largely on payer policy. While Medicare pays for certain preventive medicine visits, many commercial policies do not include preventive visits as a benefit.

Other Preventive Medicine Services include Counseling Risk Factor Reduction and Behavior Change Intervention services.

Preventive Medicine Counseling is a service provided to patients to prevent risky behavior from developing or to prevent injury from happening. The counseling occurs to address issues such as drug abuse, family problems, diet and exercise, etc. These services may not be reported in addition to preventive medicine visits (99381–99397). Code selection is based on the face-to-face time spent with the patient and according to whether the counseling is provided to an individual or in a group setting.

Behavior Change Interventions, Individual services are provided to patients who have already exhibited the risky behavior. Smoking cessation (quitting smoking) counseling, and alcohol and substance abuse counseling, are found in the behavior change intervention codes. The codes are selected based on the substance and the amount of time spent with the patient.

Non Face-to-Face Physician Services

Non Face-to-Face Physician services are becoming increasingly popular with the advancement of technology. Services include Telephone Services and Online Medical Evaluations. Not all telephone encounters or online correspondence may be reported using these codes. Telephone services resulting in a visit to the physician within the next 24 hours, or next available urgent appointment, would be considered part of the service and would not be reported separately. To bill for a telephone service not resulting in a visit, the call must be initiated by an established patient, or established patient's guardian. If the physician calls the patient within seven days of an E/M for something related to that E/M visit, the call would not be reported separately.

Online Medical Evaluations have similar guidelines. Online evaluations must be permanently stored. Online communications with the patient involving E/M services provided by the physician within seven days prior to the communication would not be reported separately.

Codes are also available to report interprofessional consultative discussion and review provided via telephone/internet assessment by a consulting physician. Code selection is based on the amount of time for medical consultative discussion and review.

Special Evaluation and Management Services

Obtaining Basic Life or Disability Insurance requires a medical evaluation and completion of forms by the physician on the patient's behalf. In this category, codes exist to report these services. The code is selected based on the type of benefit being sought (basic life or disability, work related or medical disability).

Newborn Care Services

After the delivery of a newborn, the newborn is evaluated by a pediatrician or other qualified practitioner. Codes in this category are reported based on the location of the delivery and episode of care (initial or subsequent).

Additional critical services may be provided to the newborn immediately after delivery. These services include attendance at the delivery and stabilization of the newborn (99464) and the resuscitation, provision of positive pressure ventilation, and/or chest compressions (99465). Resuscitation does not include intubation (31500).

Inpatient Neonatal Intensive Care
Services and Pediatric Neonatal Critical Care Services

This category of E/M codes includes codes for Pediatric Critical Care Transport; Neonatal Critical Care, Pediatric Critical Care; and Initial and Continuing Intensive Care Services.

Sometimes, a critically ill pediatric patient needs to be transported from one facility to another for care. When a physician or other qualified provider is in attendance for direct care to the patient during transport, the service can be reported using 99466 and 99467. The codes are reported based on time, beginning when the physician assumes primary responsibility of the patient and ending when the receiving facility has assumed responsibility for the patient. Only direct, face-to-face time during the transport may be reported.

Inpatient Neonatal and Pediatric Critical Care visits are reported using 99468–99476. The code is selected based on the age of the patient, and whether a visit is initial or subsequent.

Practical Coding Note

Underline or highlight the portion of the code descriptions defining the age of the patient.

Example

99468 Initial inpatient neonatal critical care, per day, for the evaluation and management of a critically ill neonate, <u>28 days of age or younger</u>.

This category of codes is only intended for use for <u>inpatient</u> neonatal and pediatric critically ill patients (patients 5 years of age and under). Outpatient critical care services provided to patients 5 years of age and under should be reported with critical care codes 99291 and 99292. Critical care services provided to patients over 5 years of age are reported with 99291 and 99292, whether they are inpatient or outpatient services.

Practical Coding Note

Make a note is this subsection, "Do not use for outpatient services."

Critical care includes many related services, such as X-rays, gastric intubation, and more. CPT® lists all included services in the Critical Care services guidelines preceding adult critical care codes 99291–99292. Pediatric critical care codes 99471–99476 include all the same services as adult critical care, plus additional services (such as ventilator management and lumbar puncture) as listed in the Inpatient Neonatal and Pediatric Critical Care services guidelines. Always check your CPT® codebook prior to coding for additional services with critical care to be sure those additional services are separately reportable.

If a neonate is intubated or resuscitated in the delivery room by the provider admitting the neonate to critical care, the intubation and/or resuscitation are reported separately. Modifier 59 is required to show the services were provided prior to admission to neonatal critical care.

Practical Coding Note

To identify easily services included in critical care codes, bracket or highlight the paragraph listing the included services in your CPT® codebook.

For easy reference, make a note in this subcategory directing you to instructions for 99291 and 99292 that lists services included with critical care.

Codes 99477–99480 describe initial (99477) and subsequent (99478–99480) *intensive* care for a child. Intensive care is not the same as critical care. CPT® clarifies children requiring intensive care are not critically ill, but require "intensive observation, frequent interventions, and other intensive care services."

The initial care code applies only to neonates, age 28 days or less. CPT® provides parenthetical notes to direct coding for services provided to children who do not meet the requirements of 99477. Subsequent care is reported per day, and depends on the infant's body weight: 1500 grams or less (99478), 1500–2500 grams (99479), or 2501–5000 grams (99480).

There are additional codes (99485-99486) to report the supervision of transport of a critically ill or critically injured pediatric patient. This includes two-way communication with the transport team before transport, at the referring facility and during the transport. These codes are selected based on time.

Care Management Services

Patients with one or more chronic illnesses may require coordination of chronic care. The patient's condition must be expected to last at least 12 months or until the death of the patient to report codes 99487–99490. When chronic care services are performed by clinical staff directed by a physician or other qualified healthcare professional, code 99490 is reported. Services less than 20 minutes per month are not reported. When the care is more complex, requiring establishment or substantial revisions of a comprehensive care plan requiring medical decision making of moderate or high complexity, and requires clinical staff care management services for at least 60 minutes, codes 99487-99489 are reported. The provider overseeing the care plan and coordination reports the code based on time and whether the patient is seen within the reporting period or not. The time reported is based on the provider's time, other qualified healthcare professionals and clinical staff. The codes are reported based on the total time within in a calendar month. Patients who receive this type of service live at home or in a domiciliary, rest home, or assisted living facility.

According to CPT® coding guidelines, "Care management services include care plan oversight services (99339, 99340, 99374–99380), prolonged services without direct patient contact (99358, 99359), anticoagulant management (99363, 99364), medical team conferences (99366, 99367, 99368), education and training (98960, 98961, 98962, 99071, 99078), telephone services (99366, 99367, 99368, 99441, 99442, 99443), on-line medical evaluation (98969, 99444), preparation of special reports (99080), analysis of data (99090, 99091), transitional care management services (99495, 99496), medication therapy management services (99605, 99606, 99607) and, if performed, these services may not be reported separately during the month for which 99487, 99489, 99490 are reported."

Practical Coding Note

Use the table provided in the CPT® coding guidelines to determine the correct code(s) based on time.

Transitional Care Management Services

A patient discharged from an inpatient setting (acute hospital, rehabilitation hospital, long-term acute care hospital), partial hospital, observation status in a hospital, or skilled nursing facility/nursing facility to the patient's community setting (home, domiciliary, rest home, or assisted living) may require transitional care in order to prevent repeat admissions. The codes in this subsection can only be reported once in a 30 day period. The codes (99495–99496) are selected based on the level of medical decision making (moderate or high) and when the first face-to-face encounter occurs after discharge (within 14 calendar days after discharge or seven calendar days after discharge).

Other Evaluation and Management Services

The only code in this section is unlisted E/M service code 99499. This code is reported only if no other available E/M code describes the service provided. When reporting an unlisted service or procedure code, documentation must substantiate the nature of the service. Whenever possible, avoid reporting an unlisted code.

Section Review 19.1

1. Mr. Andrews, a 34-year-old male, visits Dr. Parker's office at the request of Dr. Smith for a neurological consultation. He presents with complaints of weakness, numbness, and pain in his left hand and arm. Dr. Parker examines the patient and sends his recommendations and a written report back to Dr. Smith for the care of the patient. Which category or subcategory of evaluation and management codes would you select from for the visit to Dr. Parker?

    A. Office visit, new patient

    B. Office visit, established patient

    C. Outpatient consultation

    D. Case management services

2. A mother takes her 2-year-old back to Dr. Denton for an annual well child exam. The patient has a comprehensive check-up and vaccinations are brought up to date. Which category or subcategory of evaluation and management codes would you select from for the well child exam?

    A. Office visit, established patient

    B. Preventive medicine, established patient

    C. Subsequent hospital care

    D. Preventive medicine, individual counseling

3. John, a 16-year-old male, is admitted by the emergency department physician for observation after an ATV accident. The patient was discharged from observation by another provider the next day. What category or subcategory of evaluation and management codes would you select from for the emergency department physician?

    A. Office visit, new patient

    B. Emergency department services

    C. Initial hospital care

    D. Initial observation care

4. Dr. Hedrick, a neurosurgeon, was asked to assist in a surgery to remove cancer from the spinal cord. He was a co-surgeon working with an orthopedic surgeon. Dr. Hedrick followed up with the patient during his rounds at the hospital the next day. What category or subcategory of evaluation and management services would Dr. Hedrick's follow-up visit be reported from?

    A. Outpatient visit, established patient

    B. Inpatient consultation

    C. Nonbillable

    D. Subsequent hospital care

5. During a soccer game, Ashley, a 26-year-old female, heard a popping sound in her knee. Her knee has been unstable since the incident and she decided to consult an orthopedist. She visits Dr. Howard, an orthopedist she has not seen before, to evaluate her knee pain. Dr. Howard's diagnosis is a torn ACL. What category or subcategory of evaluation and management code would you select for the visit to Dr. Howard?

    A. Office visit, new patient

    B. Office visit, established patient

    C. Outpatient consultation

    D. Preventive visit, new patient

Determine the Level of Services

As previously described, within each E/M category or subcategory, code descriptors define the specific details of the service to include: place and or type of service; content of the service provided; nature of the presenting problem; and the time generally required to provide the service.

Most E/M services are provided at varying levels of intensity. The extent of the patient's illness or injury will determine the amount of physician work and skill required to evaluate and treat the patient. This physician effort (when documented appropriately and supported by medical necessity) drives the E/M service level.

Levels of E/M codes in each category are often referred to as level I, level II, level III, etc., depending on the last number of the code referred to in the category.

Example

New Patient Office or Other Outpatient Visits:

99201 Office visit, new patient: *level I*

99202 Office visit, new patient: *level II*

99203 Office visit, new patient: *level III*

Each level of service has a unique description and requirement for its category or subcategory.

Example

Codes 99203 (Office or other outpatient visit, level III, new patient) and 99213 (Office or other outpatient visit, level III, established patient) have different requirements for the level of history, exam and medical decision making:

E/M Code	99203	99213
Key Components Required	3 of 3	2 of 3
Level of History	Detailed	Expanded Problem Focused
Level of Exam	Detailed	Expanded Problem Focused
Level of Medical Decision Making	Low Complexity	Low Complexity

Each of the key components identified above (history, exam, MDM) is broken down into further divisions:

History	Exam	Medical Decision Making
Chief Complaint History of Present Illness (HPI) Review of Systems (ROS) Past, Family, Social History (PFSH)	Constitutional Eyes Ears, Nose, Throat, Mouth Cardiovascular Respiratory Gastrointestinal Genitourinary Musculoskeletal Skin Neurological Psychiatric Hematologic/ lymphatic/ immunologic	Number of diagnosis and management options Amount and complexity of data to be reviewed Level of risk

The level of each key component is used to determine the overall level of the evaluation and management service.

The levels of history, exam, and medical decision making are defined in your Evaluation and Management Guidelines of your CPT® codebook. They are further defined, with specific detail, in the 1995 and 1997 Evaluation and Management Guidelines.

Practical Coding Note

Use the 1995 and 1997 Evaluation and Management Guidelines to build grids in your CPT® codebook to help you determine the levels of history, exam, and medical decision making.

1995 E/M Documentation Guidelines and 1997 E/M Documentation Guidelines

The 1995 Documentation Guidelines for Evaluation and Management Services and the 1997 Documentation Guidelines for Evaluation and Management Services were developed to assist providers in determining the level of service provided to a patient. Both sets of guidelines can be found on the CMS website (www.cms.gov/Outreach-and-Education/Medicare-Learning-Network-MLN/MLNEdWebGuide/EMDOC.html).

Either the 1995 or the 1997 set of guidelines can be used for any particular E/M service. The main difference between the 1995 and 1997 Documentation Guidelines for Evaluation and Management services is the leveling of the exam component. The set of guidelines most beneficial to the provider (eg, results in a higher level of code) should be used. There are instances when the insurance carrier or company policy will dictate which guideline is used or if either set of guidelines can be used. When determining the level of a visit, it is important to know company policy, as well as payer policy to determine the correct level of codes.

Chief Complaint

Both the 1995 and 1997 Documentation Guidelines require a chief complaint. A chief complaint is a medically necessary reason for the patient to meet with the physician. The chief complaint is part of the history component. If there is not a chief complaint, the service is preventive and is reported using a dedicated preventive service code.

The chief complaint is often stated in the patient's words, for example, "My throat is sore," or "I am having pain in my back."

Occasionally, documentation states the reason for a visit is "follow up." A simple statement of "follow up" is not sufficient for a chief complaint. It is necessary for a provider to document the condition being followed up on. A more concise statement would be, "follow up of ankle pain," or "follow up of diabetes."

Determining the Level of History

The history is used for the provider to troubleshoot the chief complaint based on an interview with the patient. History is divided into the following components:

- History of Present Illness (HPI)
- Review of Systems (ROS)
- Past, Family, and Social History (PFSH)

Some categories of service only require an interval history, such as subsequent hospital care, follow-up inpatient consultations and subsequent nursing facility care. An interval history is the history during the time period since the physician last performed an assessment of the patient. As such, the PFSH is not required for an interval history.

History of Present Illness (HPI)

Based on the chief complaint, a provider will ask questions to get a complete description and chronologic account of the problem to be treated. The description of HPI is listed in the Evaluation and Management Guidelines of the CPT® codebook. The 1995 and 1997 Documentation Guidelines for

Evaluation and Management Services recognizes eight HPI components:

1. Location: The anatomical place, position, or site of the chief complaint (eg, back pain, sore elbow, cut on leg, etc.)

2. Quality: A problem's characteristics, such as how it looks or feels (eg, yellow discharge, popping knee, throbbing pain, etc.)

3. Severity: A degree or measurement of how bad it is (eg, improved, unbearable pain, blood sugar 205, etc.)

4. Duration: How long the complaint has been occurring, or when it first occurred (eg, since childhood, first noticed a month ago, on and off for several weeks, etc.)

5. Timing: A measurement of when, or at what frequency, he or she notices a problem (eg, intermittent, constant, only in the evening, etc.)

6. Context: What the patient was doing, environmental factors, and/or circumstances surrounding the complaint (eg, while standing, during exercise, after a fall, etc.)

7. Modifying factors: Anything that makes the problem better or worse (eg, improves with aspirin, worse when sitting, better when lying down, etc.)

8. Associated signs and symptoms: Additional complaints that may be related.

Practical Coding Note

In the CPT™ codebook, add duration to the list of components listed in definition of History of Present Illness in the E/M guidelines.

The history of present illness can be considered brief or extended. A brief history of present illness will document one to three elements of the history of present illness. An extended history of present illness will document four or more elements.

Example

History of Present Illness:

Brief:
This 2-year-old patient presents with a barking (quality) cough occurring at night (timing).

Two HPI elements (quality and timing) results in a brief HPI.

Extended:
This 2-year-old patient presents with a barking (quality) cough which began two nights ago (duration). The coughing occurs mainly at night (timing). The mother has noted a slight (severity) fever (associated sign or symptom).

Five HPI elements (quality, duration, timing, severity, and associated sign or symptom) results in an extended HPI.

The 1997 E/M Documentation Guidelines also allow credit in the HPI for patients who are seen for chronic conditions, such as if the patient is being seen to follow up with his COPD, DM, and hypertension when the status of those conditions is the reason for the visit. For services provided on or after September 10, 2013, CMS also allows statements of this type to be credited under the 1995 E/M Documentation Guidelines.

It is not sufficient, however, simply to document the chronic problem: The status of at least three chronic (or inactive) conditions must be documented to meet the requirements of an extended HPI. This option is available only for an extended HPI. If the status of fewer than three chronic (or inactive) conditions is documented without documentation of any of the eight HPI elements, the Documentation Guidelines for a brief or extended HPI have not been satisfied.

Example

He is a Type II diabetic under good control and is very diligent with managing his sugars. He has a history of high blood pressure, which is benign and under good control with a Beta blocker. He is also having pain in his knees from his osteoarthritis. The pain lessens with Motrin but has been getting worse in the past several months.

Review of Systems (ROS)

The Review of Systems (ROS) consists of questions to inventory the body systems to assist in identifying signs or symptoms the patient has experienced or is currently experiencing. The questioning of multiple body systems assist the provider in finding subtle changes in the patient and further focus on problems.

Note: The ROS is not a hands-on patient exam. Do not confuse the findings of a review of systems with those for a hands-on exam.

Both 1995 and 1997 E/M Documentation Guidelines define the ROS as an account of body systems obtained through questioning to identify patient signs and/or symptoms. The ROS might include verbal questioning by the provider or by a separate patient intake or questionnaire form. The ROS may include the systems directly related to the problems identified in the HPI and/or additional body systems.

The 14 systems recognized for the ROS include:

1. <u>Constitutional symptoms</u>—General symptoms such as fever, weight loss, fatigue, energy level, etc.

2. <u>Eyes</u>—Questions surrounding the patient's vision. For example, does the patient wear glasses, or have blurry vision.

3. <u>Ears, nose, mouth, throat (ENMT)</u>—A provider may ask about hearing loss, nose bleeds, runny nose, dizziness, dental disease, throat pain, etc.

4. <u>Cardiovascular (CV)</u>—Symptoms in the cardiovascular system can include asking about chest pain, high blood pressure, palpitations, tachypnea, varicose veins, etc. This component will focus on the heart, veins, and arteries.

5. <u>Respiratory</u>—Shortness of breath, chest pain, asthma, and cough are some of the symptoms sought in the respiratory review of systems.

6. <u>Gastrointestinal (GI)</u>—Nausea, diarrhea, trouble swallowing, jaundice, heartburn, indigestion are some of the symptoms associated with the gastrointestinal system.

7. <u>Genitourinary (GU)</u>—The urological system reviews incontinence, pain or burning during urination, and difficulty with flow. The reproductive systems might cover dysmenorrhea, menorrhagia, menopause, contraception, pain during intercourse for the female. The male review might include hernias, testicular pain, or impotence.

8. <u>Musculoskeletal (MS)</u>—The muscles and joints work together for body movement. A review of the musculoskeletal system will include questions about joint pain, stiffness, arthritis, limitation in movement, etc.

9. <u>Integumentary</u>—This system covers both the skin and the breasts. Symptoms sought can include rashes, dryness, nipple discharge, tenderness, or may include information about self-breast exams.

10. <u>Neurological</u>—Focusing on the central and peripheral nervous system, questions about symptoms such as paralysis, weakness, clumsiness, or loss of balance may be asked.

11. <u>Psychiatric</u>—Questions about insomnia, mood, nervousness, or depression may be asked during a psychiatric review.

12. <u>Endocrine</u>—The endocrine system is comprised of glands and the secretion of hormones, keeping our bodies in balance. A provider will ask about effects of a gland not functioning properly, such as thyroid trouble, heat or cold intolerance, excessive sweating, thirst, or urination.

13. <u>Hematologic/lymphatic</u>—The provider asks about symptoms such as bruising, anemia, frequent infections, fatigue, and swollen lymph nodes.

14. <u>Allergic/immunologic</u>—This system reviews the body's ability to fight infection or the response to environmental factors. Symptoms reviewed might include allergies to food, environmental allergens, urticaria, hives, etc.

Some symptoms can fall into one or more body systems of the review. For example, when a provider is asking if there is any chest pain, he or she could be asking for an indication of cardiac problems, respiratory illnesses, psychiatric illnesses, musculoskeletal problems, or gastrointestinal distress. When using chest pain as an element of review of systems, it can only be used for one review of systems. If counted as cardiac, it cannot be used as respiratory. Each statement in a medical record can be used only once.

There are three types of review of systems:

1. Problem pertinent—A problem pertinent review of systems addresses only the body system directly related to the problem.

2. Extended—The system directly affected and related systems are reviewed. For an extended review of systems, the provider will inquire about two to nine systems.

3. Complete—A complete review of systems is when a provider reviews 10 or more body systems. A complete review of systems can be documented by either individually documenting 10 or more systems, or by documenting the positive or pertinent negatives responses individually and adding a notation that all other systems were reviewed and are negative.

Example

Problem pertinent (1 ROS):
CC: Finger pain
ROS: Positive for pain in right index finger. Denies loss of movement or sensation.

Extended (2–9 ROS):
CC: Headache
ROS:

Constitutional: Negative for chills, fatigue, and fever.
E/N/T: Negative for diminished hearing, nasal congestion, hoarseness, and sore throat.
Cardiovascular: Negative for chest pain, dizziness, and pedal edema.
Respiratory: Negative for chronic cough, dyspnea, and frequent wheezing.
Gastrointestinal: Negative for abdominal pain, constipation, diarrhea, heartburn, hematemesis, melena, nausea, and vomiting.
Neurological: See HPI

Complete (10+ ROS):
CC: Radiating numbness in back
ROS:
Const: Denies chills, fatigue, fever and weight change.
Eyes: Denies visual disturbance.
CV: Denies chest pain and palpitations.
Resp: Denies cough, dyspnea and wheezing.
GI: Denies constipation, diarrhea, dyspepsia, dysphagia, hematochezia, melena, nausea, and vomiting.
GU: Urinary: denies dysuria, frequency, hematuria, incontinence, nocturia, and urgency.
Musculo: Denies arthralgias and myalgia.
Skin: Denies rashes.
Neuro: Denies symptoms other than stated above.
Psych: Denies psychiatric symptoms.

Medical necessity determines the extent of the ROS. For instance, it might be considered necessary to obtain a complete ROS when a new patient presents, but medically unnecessary to repeat that complete review on every follow-up visit.

For most payers, if there is separate documentation of at least one pertinent positive or negative ROS element, and the provider states the remaining systems are reviewed and negative, credit should be given for a complete ROS. For example, the ROS for a new patient visiting a cardiologist may read, "Denies additional cardiac complaints; the remaining systems were reviewed and otherwise negative."

Past, Family, and Social History (PFSH)
PFSH describes occurrences with illness, surgeries, and treatments the patient and the patient's family have incurred, as well as social factors influencing the patient's health.

The past history focuses on the patient's prior medical treatments and can include:

- Prior major illnesses and injuries
- Prior operations
- Prior hospitalizations
- Current medications
- Allergies

- Age appropriate immunization status
- Age appropriate feeding/dietary status

Family history describes occurrences in the patient's family and typically includes a list of diseases or hereditary conditions that may place the patient at risk (for example, a family history of hypertension, diabetes, or cancer). This section also may include the age of death or living status of immediate family.

Social history identifies current and past patient activities, such as:

- Social status or living arrangements (if child, social status of parents)
- Employment status
- Occupational history
- Drug, tobacco, alcohol use (if child, exposure to second-hand smoke)
- Education level
- Sexual history
- Any social event/occurrence impacting patient's condition

There are two types of PFSH: Pertinent and complete. Pertinent PFSH is a review of history areas directly related to the chief complaint. Only one history component must be documented for a pertinent PFSH. A complete PFSH will depend on the category of evaluation and management service.

For the following categories, a complete PFSH requires two of the three history areas to be documented (Past, Family, or Social):

- Office or other outpatient services, established patient
- Emergency Department
- Domiciliary care, established patient
- Home care, established patient

For other categories, at least one item from each history area (Past, Family, and Social) must be documented. These categories include:

- Office or other outpatient services, new patient
- Hospital observation services
- Hospital inpatient services, initial care
- Consultations
- Comprehensive Nursing Facility assessments
- Domiciliary care, new patient
- Home care, new patient

Example

Pertinent PFSH:

CC: Breast pain

The patient has a positive family history of breast cancer (mom, aunt).

Complete PFSH:

She has no history of any prior stroke or Bell's palsy. She has had no facial droop previously. She has history of anemia, gastro-esophageal reflux disease, depression, and osteoporosis. She has no history of diagnosed hypertension, diabetes, cancer, asthma, bleeding problems, thyroid disease, TIA, heart disease, or arrhythmia.

Her only prior surgery was a lumbar procedure, perhaps 20 years ago.

She does not smoke cigarettes or drink alcohol. She does have children and grandchildren locally.

She has some family history of hypertension, she believes. There is no family history definitive of stroke.

Totaling the Level of History

According to the documentation guidelines, the Chief Complaint, Review of Systems, and Past, Family, and Social History may be listed as separate elements of history, or they may be included in the description of the history of present illness. It is pertinent for a coder to be able to determine the levels of history regardless how they are documented.

When the level of each element of history has been determined, the levels are combined to determine the overall level of history. There are four levels of history defined in your Evaluation and Management Guidelines:

- Problem Focused
- Expanded Problem Focused
- Detailed
- Comprehensive

To determine the level accurately, it is best to use a grid method:

History of Present Illness (HPI)	Review of Systems (ROS)	Past, Family, Social History (PFSH)	Level of History
Brief	N/A	N/A	Problem Focused
Brief	Problem Pertinent	N/A	Expanded Problem Focused
Extended	Extended	Pertinent	Detailed
Extended	Complete	Complete	Comprehensive

Practical Coding Note

Place a grid for the levels of history in your CPT® codebook for easy reference.

All three history elements must support the work level to meet the overall history level requirement. The lowest element within the history component always will determine the overall history level. For example, if the HPI and ROS both support a detailed history level, but the PFSH supports only an expanded problem focused history level, the history level will stay at the expanded problem focused level.

History of Present Illness (HPI)	Review of Systems (ROS)	Past, Family, Social History (PFSH)	Level of History
Brief	N/A	N/A	Problem Focused
Brief	Problem Pertinent	N/A	Expanded Problem Focused
Extended	Extended	Pertinent	Detailed
Extended	Complete	Complete	Comprehensive

The level of history required for each level of service is stated in the description of the CPT® code.

Example

99201 Office or other outpatient visit for the evaluation and management of a new patient, which requires these 3 key components:

- A problem focused history
- A problem focused examination
- Straightforward medical decision making

Counseling and/or coordination of care with other physicians, other qualified healthcare professionals, or agencies are provided consistent with the nature of the problem(s) and the patient's and/or family's needs.

Usually, the presenting problem(s) are self limited or minor. Physicians typically spend 10 minutes face-to-face with the patient and/or family.

Documentation Dissection: History

CC: sneezing, watery eyes [1]

History: 4-year-old female presents today sneezing, watery eyes and nasal [2] congestion. [3]

Symptoms started two days ago [4] after spending all day working with her mom in the garden. [5]

Patient's eyes are not watering as much since she started taking a prescription decongestant [6] issued at previous visit, [7] but only has two dosages left.

ROS: Eyes—Watery [8]
ENT—Nasal congestion, sneezing [9]
Cardio—Denies chest pain [10]
Respiratory—Denies shortness of breath, wheezing [11]

Personal History: Multiple sinus infections over last two years [12]

Social History: Attends private preschool [13]

Table A: History

History				
HPI Location Severity Timing Modifying Factors | Quality Duration Context Assoc Signs & Symptoms	Brief (1-3)	Brief (1-3)	Extended (4 or more)	Extended (4 or more)
ROS Const GI Integ Hem/lymph Eyes GU Neuro All/Immuno Card/Vasc Musculo Psych All other negative Resp ENT, mouth Endo	None	Pertinent to problem (1 system)	Extended (2-9 systems)	Complete
PFSH Past history (current meds, past illnesses, operations, injuries, treatments) Family history (a review of medical events in the patient's family) Social history (an age appropriate review of past and current activities)	None	None	Pertinent (1 history area)	Complete (2 (est) or 3 (new) history areas)
	Problem Focused	Expanded Problem Focused	Detailed	Comprehensive

Looking at the grid, you must meet or exceed all levels of history. Because we do not have a complete ROS, we do not have a comprehensive level of history. The highest level of history for which we have met all three levels of history components is a detailed history.

----

[1] Chief complaint.

[2] Location: eyes and nasal.

[3] Associated Signs & Symptoms: Congestion.

[4] Duration: 2 days ago.

[5] Context: working in garden.

[6] Modifying factors: Decongestant.

[7] Patient status is established.

[8] ROS: Eyes.

[9] ROS: Nose.

[10] ROS: Cardiovascular.

[11] ROS: Respiratory.

[12] Personal History.

[13] Social History.

Key Points to Consider When Selecting a History Level

- If documentation establishes the provider cannot obtain a history from the patient or other source (for example, if the patient is unconscious), the provider is not penalized, nor are the overall medical necessity level and provider work discounted automatically.
- Additional history supplied by a family member or a caregiver and documented by the provider can be credited toward the overall E/M service's MDM component.
- A ROS and/or PFSH taken from a previous encounter may be updated without complete re-documentation for most payers. The provider should indicate the new history status and indicate where the original documentation is stored.

There is a fine line between the signs and symptoms the patient shares in the HPI, and those obtained via the ROS. Individual payers have the power to interpret the documentation guidelines in their own way, and many prohibit using one documented statement to count for two separate history elements. For example, if the documentation reads, "The patient states that her hip has been painful," credit would not be given to both the HPI location and to the musculoskeletal ROS (this is "double-dipping"). If, on the other hand, the documentation reads, "The patient states that her hip has been painful. She denies any other musculoskeletal complaint," there is a distinct component of both the HPI (painful hip) and a separate musculoskeletal ROS (no other musculoskeletal complaint). There are times when two separate audits of the same service may produce different results, and neither party can be proven technically or medically wrong. A reviewer may argue an HPI element is a "quality" versus an "associated sign and symptom or other element," or that "no known drug allergies" documentation constitutes an ROS element rather than a past history element. Correct interpretation requires consistency, verifiable references, a logical argument, and—ultimately—medical necessity.

Section Review 19.2

1. Patient presents to the clinic today for a follow-up of his hospitalization for pneumonia. He was placed back on Singulair® and has been improving with his breathing since then. He has no complaints today. What is the level of history?

    A. Problem focused

    B. Expanded problem focused

    C. Detailed

    D. Comprehensive

2.   The patient presents to the clinic today for an asthma exacerbation. She has been having a cough and difficulty breathing that has been getting worse for the last two to three days. She currently uses inhalers, but could not find any of her inhalers for this past week. She denies any fever or chills. Has a productive cough today.

What is the level of history?

   A.   Problem focused

   B.   Expanded problem focused

   C.   Detailed

   D.   Comprehensive

3.   History of Present Illness

This is a 73-year-old man who is a veterinarian. He is seen here for the first time today. He has a history of squamous cell carcinoma on the left arm and a basal cell carcinoma on the right forehead near the temple both in January 2007. He says he has had a lesion on his forehead for approximately one year. He is concerned about what it is. He thinks it may be another skin cancer. He is also concerned about a lesion just lateral to his right eye; he is concerned this may be a skin cancer, too. It has been present for quite a while as well. He would also like a full skin check today. He uses a hat for sun protection. He has lived in California and has had significant sun exposure in the past.

Review of Systems: Otherwise well, no other skin complaints.

Past Medical History

Coronary artery disease status post bypass surgery, history of squamous and basal cell carcinomas as noted above, hay fever, and hyperlipidemia. He has had lipomas removed.

Medications: Tylenol, tramadol, thyroxin, fish oil, flax seed oil, simvastatin, Zyrtec®, 5 percent saline in eyes.

Allergies: No known drug allergies.

Family History: No family history of skin cancer or other skin problems.

Social History: Patient is a veterinarian. He recently moved to the Rochester area from Pennsylvania. He is married.

What is the level of history?

   A.   Problem focused

   B.   Expanded problem focused

   C.   Detailed

   D.   Comprehensive

4.   Established patient

Chief Complaint: Fever.

Present Illness: The patient is a 2-year 3-month-old female with less than one day of a high fever with decreased appetite. There has been no vomiting or diarrhea. Parents are unaware of any cough. Tylenol has been given which reduced the fever.

Past Medical History: Otherwise negative.

Current Medications: Tylenol® 160 mg q.4 h. per infant Tylenol® drops.

Allergies: NONE.

Immunizations: Up-to-date.

Review of Systems: As per HPI. Rest of review of systems reviewed and negative.

Personal, Family, Social History: The patient is not exposed to secondhand cigarette smoke.

What is the level of history?

    A. Problem focused

    B. Expanded problem focused

    C. Detailed

    D. Comprehensive

5.   Emergency Department

The patient is a 47-year-old white male who presented to the emergency room after the four-wheeler he was operating struck a ditch and rapidly came to a halt. This threw him against the windshield where he struck the mid part of his face and lower lip. This resulted in lip and chin lacerations. He was brought to the emergency room where he was evaluated by Dr. Jones and a CT scan suggested a hyper dense abnormality within the brain. A bleed could not be ruled out. This being the case, admission was recommended.

His past history includes previous tonsillectomy, previous hospital admission for a syncopal episode associated with pain in the groin area, and hypercholesterolemia. He has no known allergies. His current medications are Zocor® and Accutane®. He is a nonsmoker, moderate drinker of alcohol.

The review of systems is negative for nausea, vomiting, blurred vision, or headache.

What is the level of history?

    A. Problem focused

    B. Expanded problem focused

    C. Detailed

    D. Comprehensive

Determining the Level of Exam

An E/M service's exam component is, as the name implies, the physician's physical examination of the patient. The 1995 and 1997 Documentation Guidelines for Evaluation and Management Services define differently the specific elements determining the exam level. The primary weakness of the 1995 guidelines is the inability to acknowledge the more specific work and documentation provided by a specialist. The primary weakness of the 1997 guidelines is that it requires too many specific documentation elements. Consider your specialty's nature, and the typical documentation the physician generates, to determine which guidelines set to use.

Both 1995 and 1997 guidelines recognize the same body areas, including:

- Head, including the face
- Neck
- Chest, including the breast and axillae
- Abdomen
- Genitalia, groin, and buttocks
- Back, including spine
- Each extremity

Both guidelines recognize the same organ systems, including:

- Constitutional
- Eyes
- Ears nose, mouth, and throat
- Cardiovascular
- Respiratory
- Gastrointestinal

- Genitourinary
- Musculoskeletal
- Skin
- Neurologic
- Psychiatric
- Hematologic, lymphatic, and immunologic

Both 1995 and 1997 guidelines require the provider to elaborate on abnormal findings and describe unexpected findings. Both guidelines also allow a brief note of "negative" or "normal" to document normal findings or unaffected areas or systems. Most carriers require you to work with either the body areas or organ systems, not both.

Each body area or organ system is inspected for specific findings. Here is a brief explanation of the examination components and some commonly used verbiage in medical record documentation. This list is not all inclusive, but will give you a good understanding of what you might see in a medical record.

Constitutional—Overall appearance of the patient, including development and attention to grooming. Vital signs, such as blood pressure, pulse rate and regularity, respiration, temperature, height, weight, etc., are included in constitutional. Sample documentation: NAD (no apparent distress).

Head, including the face—The head is checked for swelling and lumps. The face is checked for abnormalities such as coloring of the skin, asymmetry of the face, etc. Sample documentation: Head is NCAT (normocephalic and atraumatic).

Skin—Skin is checked for lesions, rashes, temperature, and moisture. Hair and nails are checked for abnormalities. Sample documentation: There is no significant rash or ulceration. Color good. Skin warm and moist. Hair with average texture.

Eyes—Inspection of the conjunctivae and lids. An ophthalmoscope may be used to examine the optic discs and posterior segments of the eye. Sclera are checked for jaundice. Sample documentation: PERRLA (Pupils Equal Round Reactive to Light and Accommodation). Sclera white, conjunctivae pink.

Ears, nose, mouth, and throat (ENMT)—The nose and ears are checked for external appearance, scars, lesions, or masses. The nasal mucosa septum and turbinates are checked for swelling and redness. The mouth and pharynx are checked for abnormality. Sample documentation: TMs (tympanic membranes) gray with normal light reflex, EAC (external auditory canal) clear. Nasal mucosa pink, septum midline, no sinus tenderness. Oral mucosa pink, dentition good, pharynx without exudate.

Neck—Neck is checked for lumps and swelling. Sample documentation: Neck is supple (bends easily), no thyromegaly (enlarged thyroid). No JVD (jugular venous distention).

Chest/respiratory—Observation of rate, rhythm, depth and effort of breathing, observing the chest for asymmetry and tenderness. Listening (auscultation) to breath sounds. Sample documentation: Equal chest wall excursion. There are no intercostal retractions or the use of accessory muscles with respirations. Breath sounds are clear and symmetrical. There are no wheezes, rales, or rhonchi.

Breast and axilla—The breasts are checked for asymmetry, tenderness, lumps, and/or discharge. The axillae are palpated for masses. Sample documentation: Breasts symmetrical without masses. Nipples without discharge. No LAD.

Cardiovascular—Palpation of heart, auscultation of the heart with notation of abnormal sounds and murmurs, examination of carotid arteries, abdominal aorta, femoral arteries, pedal pulses, and extremities for edema and/or varicosities. Sample documentation: The chest wall is normal in appearance. The heart has RRR (regular rate and rhythm) with no murmur.

Pulse Sites in the Body

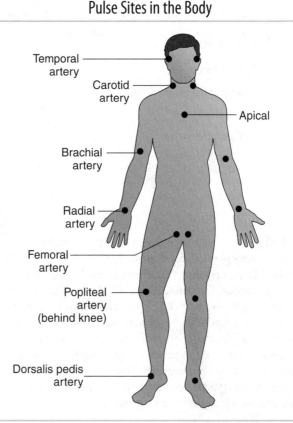

Source: Lindh, Pooler, Tamparo, and Dahl, Delmar's Comprehensive Medical Assisting (Administrative and Clinical Competencies), 4e, ISBN#978-1-4354-1914-8

Abdomen/GI—The abdomen is checked for tenderness and masses. Palpation is used to check size of liver, spleen, and kidneys. Auscultation is used to listen to bowel sounds, bruits, or rubs. Sample documentation: Abdomen is soft and nontender. There is no tenderness to palpation, rebound, or guarding. Positive bowel sounds. No masses or hepatosplenomegaly. No CVA (costovertebral angle) tenderness, also sometimes listed as no CVAT.

Genitalia, groin, and buttocks/Genitourinary (GU)—The male genitalia is checked for abnormalities, lesions, tenderness, lumps, etc. The prostate is checked for swelling or tenderness. The female genitalia is checked for abnormalities, lesions, tenderness, discharge, etc. The anus is checked for lesions or tenderness. Sample documentation, female: External genitalia: no rash, or swelling. Vagina: Blood: minimal and brown. Blood Clots: None Cervix: Speculum exam: No active bleeding Digital exam: Closed Cervical motion tenderness: Absent, stenotic. Uterus: Normal. Adnexa: Normal. Sample documentation, Male: No penile discharge or lesions, no scrotal swelling, no inguinal or femoral hernia. Prostate smooth and nontender.

Musculoskeletal/back, including spine/Each extremity—Extremities are checked for range of motion, strength and tone. The spine is checked for deformities or abnormalities in curvature. Sample documentation: Strength and tone are grossly normal to the upper and lower extremities. Good ROM (range of motion) in all joints. No evidence of swelling or deformity.

Neurologic—Sensation, Cranial Nerves, Deep Tendon Reflexes (DTRs) with notation of pathological reflexes are checked. Sample documentation: No focal neurologic deficit, weakness, paresthesias, or incoordination.

Psychiatric—The patient's mental status, level of consciousness, mood and affect are checked along with remote and recent memory. Sample documentation: Alert and orient x 3. Thought processes are coherent, insight is good.

Hematologic/lymphatic/immunologic—Lymphatic is counted when there is palpation of the lymph nodes in the neck, axillae, groin and/or other area. Sample documentation: No LAD (lymphodenopathy).

Review of System (ROS) Elements vs. Physical Exam Elements

When reading a chart note, it can be difficult to distinguish between elements belonging to the review of systems (ROS) and those elements relevant to the exam. The ROS and the exam elements are not interchangeable, and for most payers you may not count a single element toward both the ROS and the exam.

The ROS is a series of written or verbal "questions and answers" relevant to signs or symptoms the patient is experiencing at the time of service. Often, the ROS is gathered by having the patient complete a history or intake form given to the patient at the front desk check-in. The form is a list of questions generally asking the patient to check off and/or briefly explain signs and symptoms the patient currently has or has had in the past.

ROS Questionnaire Example:

Have you now or have you ever had any of the conditions listed below? If yes, please describe.

Respiratory:

- Severe shortness of breath or wheezing
- Had a cough for more than one month
- Chest pain when you cough hard or take a deep breath
- Cough up blood
- Difficulty breathing
- Shortness of breath when exercising

The ROS also may occur verbally with the provider or other staff. For instance, an assistant may ask the patient, "Do you have any problems breathing? Do you have shortness of breath when exercising, walking, or climbing the stairs?" The patient's response might be documented in a note by the provider as briefly as: "Patient states his chest hurts when he coughs but not when he takes a deep breath. No SOB. No complaints of pain in joints. No problems sleeping."

In contrast to ROS elements, the exam elements are actual visual or hands-on findings. For example, the provider uses an otoscope to inspect the middle ear visually, an ophthalmoscope to check the eyes and their reaction to light, and a stethoscope to listen to lung, heart, and bowel sounds. The provider will document what she sees with statements such as:

- Eyes: Pupils are equal and reactive to light
- Chest: bilateral rales and rhonchi
- GI: Bowel sounds are normal
- Extremities: no cyanosis or edema

When reading the notes, ask yourself if the notation is something the patient answered, or if it is something the provider observed. An answered question belongs to the ROS; whereas something seen, heard, or measured by a provider is an exam element.

The 1995 and 1997 guidelines define the four levels of exam (problem focused, expanded problem focused, detailed, and comprehensive) differently. The 1995 guidelines define the levels of exam as follows:

- Problem Focused—a limited examination of the affected body area or organ system (that is, a limited exam on only one affected body area or organ system)

- Expanded Problem Focused—a limited examination of the affected body area or organ system and other symptomatic or related organ system(s) (that is, a limited exam of at least two body areas or organ systems)

- Detailed—an extended examination of the affected body area(s) and other symptomatic or related organ system(s) (that is, an extended examination of at least two body areas or organ systems)

- Comprehensive—a general multi-system examination or complete single-organ system examination (The medical record for a general multi-system examination should include findings about eight or more of the 12 organ systems)

The 1997 guidelines define levels of exam based on bulleted elements within the body areas and organ systems. This may vary based on what type (specialty) exam is being performed.

"Gray Areas" in the 1995 Documentation Guidelines

The 1995 guidelines, although generally clear, contain two gray areas complicating your ability to determine the exam level:

- An expanded problem focused exam and a detailed exam both require examination of at least two body areas and/or organ systems; the expanded problem focus level requires that these exams are "limited," whereas the detailed level requires that these exams are "extended." The terms limited and extended are not defined specifically.

- The definition of a comprehensive single system exam is defined only as "complete." The term complete is not defined specifically.

The 1997 guidelines eliminate this subjectivity by exactly specifying—using bulleted items—the exam requirement for a particular body area or organ system. These requirements provide objective criteria against which to measure physician documentation. A detailed list of bulleted exam requirements may be found on pages 11–43 of the 1997 Documentation Guidelines for Evaluation and Management Services as available at www.cms.gov/Outreach-and-Education/Medicare-Learning-Network-MLN/MLNEdWebGuide/Downloads/97Docguidelines.pdf.

When using 1997 guidelines, the physician may select from the general multi-system exam or any of the single organ system exams. The coder must review each documented element to determine which single-organ system exam is the most appropriate E/M service level selection. For instance, a problem focused, general multi-system examination requires the documentation of at least one bullet. For an expanded problem focused exam, at least six bullets must be documented. For a detailed examination, there should be documentation to support two bullets in at least six organ systems or body areas, or 12 bullets in two or more organ systems or body areas.

Physicians should focus on the medical necessity of an exam, and should never document "just one more bullet" to achieve a higher service level.

"The type (general multi-system or single organ system) and content of examination are selected by the examining physician and are based upon clinical judgment, the patient's history, and the nature of the presenting problem(s)," according to the 1997 guidelines. For instance, it might be considered necessary to perform a comprehensive exam when a new patient presents, but medically unnecessary to repeat a complete review on every follow-up.

Documentation Dissection: Exam

Physical Examination:

Constitutional: [1] Vital Signs: Resp: 26. Temp: 98.7. Weight: 47 lbs.

HEENT: PERRLA. [2] Ears negative. [3] Nares wet with clear rhinorrhea. [4] Throat red and swollen, postnasal drip present.

Cardiovascular: RRR [5]

Skin: Reveals no rash, petechia or purpura. [6]

Table B: Exam

Examination				
Body Areas: Head, Including face Neck Abdomen Genitalia, groin, buttocks Chest, inc. Breast and Axilla Each extremity Back, including spine	1 body area or organ system	2–7 systems— limited exam	2–7 systems— detailed exam	8 or more systems
Organ Systems: Constitutional Respiratory Musculoskeletal Psychiatric Cardiovascular GI Skin Hem/Lymph/Imm ENMT, GU Neurological Eyes				
	Problem Focused	Expanded Problem Focused	Detailed	Comprehensive

There are five organ systems examined with limited documentation in our example, which is considered Expanded Problem Focused Exam.

----

[1] Constitutional.

[2] Eyes.

[3] Ears.

[4] Nose.

[5] Cardiovascular.

[6] Skin.

Section Review 19.3

1. **Physical Exam:**

   General: His physical exam shows an intubated male. He is at times somewhat combative. There is a brace on the right shoulder.

   Skin: His skin is warm and dry. No rashes, ulcers, or lesions.

   Lungs: The lungs are diminished breath sounds, though no crackles are noted.

   Cardiac: Cardiac exam is tachycardic, no distinct murmurs appreciated. Extremities show no significant edema.

   Abdomen: Abdominal exam is soft. No masses or tenderness. No hepatosplenomegaly

   Extremities: No clubbing or cyanosis. Bilateral lower: No misalignment or tenderness.

   Based on the 1995 Documentation Guidelines, what is the level of exam?

   A. Problem focused

   B. Expanded problem focused

   C. Detailed

   D. Comprehensive

2. **Physical Exam:**

   General Appearance: Healthy appearing individual in no distress

   Abdomen: Soft, non-tender, without masses. No CVA tenderness

   Female Exam:

   Vulva/Labia Majora: No erythema, ulcerations, swelling, or lesions seen.

   Bartholin Glands: No cysts, abscesses, induration, discharge, masses, or inflammation noted.

   Skene's: No cysts, abscesses, induration, discharge, masses, or inflammation noted.

   Clitoris/Labia Minora: Clitoris normal. No atrophy, adhesions, erythema, or vesicles noted. Labia unremarkable.

   Urethral Meatus: Meatus appears normal in size and location. No masses, lesions, or prolapse.

   Urethra: No masses, tenderness or scarring.

   Bladder: Without fullness, masses or tenderness.

   Vagina: Mucosa clear without lesions, Pelvic support normal. No discharge.

   Cervix: The cervix is clear, firm, and closed. No visible lesions. No abnormal discharge.

   Uterus: Uterus non-tender and of normal size, shape, and consistency. Position and mobility are normal.

   Adnexa/Parametria: No masses or tenderness noted.

Based on the 1995 Documentation Guidelines, what is the level of exam?

    A. Problem focused

    B. Expanded problem focused

    C. Detailed

    D. Comprehensive

3. **Physical Exam:**

    General/Constitutional: No apparent distress. Well nourished and well developed.

    Ears: TM's gray. Landmarks normal. Positive light reflex.

    Nose/Throat: Nose and throat clear; palate intact; no lesions.

    Lymphatic: No palpable cervical, supraclavicular, or axillary adenopathy.

    Respiratory: Normal to inspection. Lungs clear to auscultation.

    Cardiovascular: RRR without murmurs.

    Abdomen: Non-distended, non-tender. Soft, no organomegaly, no masses.

    Integumentary: No unusual rashes or lesions.

    Musculoskeletal: Good strength; no deformities. Full ROM all extremities.

    Extremities: Extremities appear normal.

    What is the level of exam?

    A. Problem focused

    B. Expanded problem focused

    C. Detailed

    D. Comprehensive

4. **Physical Exam:**

    General: Alert, smiling child.

    HEENT: There is clear rhinorrhea. Pharynx is without inflammation.

    Neck: Supple.

    Chest: Lungs are clear without wheeze or rhonchi.

    Abdomen: Soft, nontender.

    What is the level of exam?

    A. Problem focused

    B. Expanded problem focused

    C. Detailed

    D. Comprehensive

5.   **Physical Exam:**

Constitutional: Vital Signs: Pulse: 161. Resp: 30. Temp: 102.4. Oxygen saturation 90 percent

General Appearance: The patient reveals profound intellectual disability. Tracheostomy is in place.

Eyes: Conjunctivae are slightly anemic.

ENT: Oral mucosa is dry.

Neck: The neck is supple and the trachea is midline. Range of motion is normal. There are no masses, crepitus or tenderness of the neck. The thyroid gland has no appreciable goiter.

Respiratory: The lungs reveal transmitted upper airway signs and bilateral rales, wheezes, and rhonchi.

Cardiovascular: The chest wall is normal in appearance. Regular rate and rhythm. No murmurs, rubs, or gallops are noted. There is no significant edema to the lower extremities.

Gastrointestinal: The abdomen is soft and nondistended. There is no tenderness, rebound, or guarding noted. There are no masses. No organomegaly is appreciated.

Skin: The skin is pale and slightly diaphoretic.

Neurologic: Cranial nerves appear intact. The patient moves all four extremities symmetrically. No lateralizing signs are noted. Gross sensation is intact to all extremities.

Lymphatic: There are no palpable pathologic lymph nodes in the neck or axilla.

Musculoskeletal: Gait and station are normal. Strength and tone to the upper and lower extremities are normal for age with no evidence of atrophy. There is no cyanosis, clubbing, or edema to the digits.

What is the level of exam?

A.   Problem focused

B.   Expanded problem focused

C.   Detailed

D.   Comprehensive

Determining the Medical Decision Making (MDM)

MDM is perhaps the most important of the three primary components of E/M code selection. It is also the most subjective. Whether you use the 1995 or 1997 E/M Documentation Guidelines, the nature of the presenting problem and medical necessity of the encounter are the best MDM indicators. You will choose an overall MDM level based on three factors:

- The number of diagnoses or management options;
- The amount and/or complexity of data to be reviewed; and
- The risk of complications and morbidity or mortality.

Diagnoses or Management Options

The number of diagnoses or management options is based on the relative difficulty level in making a diagnosis, and the status of the problem. Although audit tools vary, the number of diagnosis and management options typically is determined using a points system. Under this system, points are assigned according to how sick a patient is, and the amount of physician work involved.

- Minor problems, such as those resolving regardless if the patient had sought medical attention, are worth one point. A patient may have four minor, documented problems. For coding purposes, a maximum of two such problems can be counted.

- Established, stable, or improved conditions are worth one point each.
- Established, worsening conditions are worth two points each.
- A new problem (new to the provider) without any additional workup is worth three points. You may only count such a problem once per encounter, even if there are multiple occurrences in the encounter (a workup is defined as anything the physician does after making the diagnosis the patient left with. For example, if the physician suspects a particular diagnosis and sends the patient on for a diagnostic test to confirm a suspicion, the diagnostic test counts as workup).
- A new problem with additional workup is counted as four points

Table C: Medical Decision Making or Management Options

Number of diagnosis or treatment options			
Problem	Number	Points	Total (Number x Points)
Self limited or minor (max 2 points)	Max = 2 points	1	
Established problem to provider (stable or improved)		1	
Established problem to provider (worsening)		2	
New problem to provider with no additional work up planned	Max = 3 points	3	
New problem to provider with additional work up planned.		4	
	Total		

Data Amount and Complexity

The amount and complexity of data for review is measured by the need to order and review tests, and the need to gather information and data. Planning, scheduling, and performing clinical labs and tests from the medicine and radiology portions of CPT® are indications of complexity, as is the need to request old records, or to obtain additional history from someone other than the patient (such as a family member, caregiver, teacher, etc.). Documented discussions with the performing physician about unusual or unexpected patient results also may result in credit. If a physician makes an independent visualization and interpretation, for example, with an

MRI or a Gram stain—and he or she is not billing separately for the service—it would be credited in this component of code selection.

A points system is very effective for measuring the amount and complexity of data for review:

- Clinical lab(s) ordered or reviewed are worth one point.
- Any test(s) reviewed/ordered from the medicine section of the CPT® codebook are worth one point.
- Any procedures reviewed/ordered from the radiology section of the CPT® are worth one point. Regardless of the number of radiological procedures reviewed/ordered, only one point may be assigned (eg, five radiology reports reviewed count as one point only).
- Discussing patient's results with the performing or consulting physician is worth one point—if it is captured in the documentation.
- Decisions to obtain old records or additional history from someone other than the patient are worth one point.
- Review and summary of data from old records or additional history gathered from someone other than the patient is worth two points.
- Independent or second interpretation of an image tracing or specimen is worth two points. Note this means not just the review of the report, but of the actual film image or tracing.

Table D: Data Amount and Complexity

Reviewed/Ordered Data	Points
Review and/or order lab test(s)	1
Review and/or order test(s) in the radiology section of CPT®	1
Review and/or order test(s) in the medicine section of CPT®	1
Discussion of test results with performing physician	1
Decision to obtain old records and/or obtain history from someone other than the patient	1
Review and summarization of old records and/or obtaining history from someone other than the patient and/or discussion of case with another healthcare provider.	2
Independent visualization of image, specimen or tracing (NOT simply a review of report, do not use if billing for the interpretation)	2

The Table of Risk

Risk is measured based on the physician's determination of the patient's probability of becoming ill or diseased, having complications, or dying between this encounter and the next planned encounter. Risk indications include the nature of the presenting problem, the urgency of the visit, co-morbid conditions, and the need for diagnostic tests or surgery.

Documentation Guidelines determine the risk level using the Table of Risk (Table E). The Table of Risk is divided into three columns; each column correlates with an overall risk level. The three columns list presenting problems, diagnostic procedures ordered, and management options selected. Only one item within the table of risk needs to be identified to meet a level of risk. It is important to keep in mind medical necessity also plays a very important role in the level of risk. Identifying one bullet within a level of risk is sufficient for determining the level of risk.

Table E: Table of Risk

Level of Risk	Presenting Problem(s)	Diagnostic Procedure(s) Ordered	Management Options Selected
Minimal	One self-limited or minor problem, eg, cold, insect bite, tinea corporis	Laboratory tests requiring: • venipuncture • Chest X-rays • EKG/EEG • Urinalysis • Ultrasound, eg, echocardiography • KOH prep	• Rest • Gargles • Elastic bandages • Superficial dressings
Low	• Two or more self-limited or minor problems • One stable chronic illness, eg, well controlled hypertension, non-insulin dependent diabetes, cataract, BPH • Acute uncomplicated illness or injury, eg, cystitis, allergic rhinitis, simple sprain	• Physiologic tests not under stress, eg, pulmonary function tests • Non-cardiovascular imaging studies with contrast, eg, barium enema • Superficial needle biopsies • Clinical laboratory tests requiring arterial puncture • Skin biopsies	• Over-the-counter drugs • Minor surgery with no identified risk factors • Physical therapy • Occupational therapy • IV fluids without additives
Moderate	• One or more chronic illnesses with mild exacerbation, progression, or side effects of treatment • Two or more stable chronic illnesses • Undiagnosed new problem with uncertain prognosis, eg, lump in breast • Acute illness with systemic symptoms, eg, pyelonephritis, pneumonitis, colitis • Acute complicated injury, eg, head injury with brief loss of consciousness	• Physiologic tests under stress, eg, cardiac stress test, fetal contraction stress test • Diagnostic endoscopies with no identified risk factors Deep needle or incisional biopsy • Cardiovascular imaging studies with contrast and no identified risk factors, eg, arteriogram, cardiac catheterization • Obtain fluid from body cavity, eg lumbar puncture, thoracentesis, culdocentesis	• Minor surgery with identified risk factors • Elective major surgery (open, percutaneous or endoscopic) with no identified risk factors • Prescription drug management • Therapeutic nuclear medicine • IV fluids with additives • Closed treatment of fracture or dislocation without manipulation

| High | • One or more chronic illnesses with severe exacerbation, progression, or side effects of treatment
• Acute or chronic illnesses or injuries that pose a threat to life or bodily function, eg, multiple trauma, acute MI, pulmonary embolus, severe respiratory distress, progressive severe rheumatoid arthritis, psychiatric illness with potential threat to self or others, peritonitis, acute renal failure
• An abrupt change in neurologic status, eg, seizure, TIA, weakness, sensory loss | • Cardiovascular imaging studies with contrast with identified risk factors
• Cardiac electrophysiological tests
• Diagnostic Endoscopies with identified risk factors
• Discography | • Elective major surgery (open, percutaneous or endoscopic) with identified risk factors
• Emergency major surgery (open, percutaneous or endoscopic)
• Parenteral controlled substances
• Drug therapy requiring intensive monitoring for toxicity
• Decision not to resuscitate or to de-escalate care because of poor prognosis |

Source: CMS: Evaluation & Management Services Guide

Totaling the MDM Component

To select an overall MDM level, at least two of three elements (number of diagnoses or management options; amount and/or complexity of data to be reviewed; risk of complications and/or morbidity or mortality) for that level must be met.

Table F: Medical Decision Making (MDM)

Final Result of Tables C, D, E = Level of Medical Decision Making (MDM)					
Table C	Number of diagnosis/ treatment options	1	2	3	4
Table D	Amount of data reviewed/ordered	1	2	3	4
Table E	Level of risk	Minimal	Low	Moderate	High
MDM Level		Straightforward	Low	Moderate	High

Documentation Dissection: Medical Decision Making

From History: "Patient's eyes are not watering as much since she stated taking a prescription decongestant issued at previous visit, but only has two dosages left." [1]

Assessment and Plan—

1. allergic rhinitis [2] —OTC eye drops.

   Allergy skin testing ordered [3]

Return to office in 10 days if symptoms have not improved.

Number of Diagnosis or Treatment Options

Number of diagnosis or treatment options			
Problem	Number	Points	Total (Number x Points)
Self limited or minor (max 2 points)	Max = 2 points	1	
Established problem to provider (stable or improved)	1	1	1
Established problem to provider (worsening)		2	
New problem to provider with no additional work up planned	Max = 3 points	3	
New problem to provider with additional work up planned.		4	
	Total		1

Complexity and Amount of Data Reviewed

Reviewed/Ordered Data	Points
Review and/or order lab tests	1
Review and/or order tests in the radiology section of CPT®	1
Review and/or order tests in the medicine section of CPT®	1
Discussion of test results with performing physician	1
Decision to obtain old records and/or obtain history from someone other than the patient	1
Review and summarization of old records and/or obtaining history from someone other than the patient and/or discussion of case with another healthcare provider.	2
Independent visualization of image, specimen or tracing (NOT simply a review of report, do not use if billing for the interpretation)	2

Medical Decision Making

Final Result of Tables C, D, E = Level of Medical Decision Making (MDM)					
Table C	Number of diagnosis/treatment options	1	2	3	4
Table D	Amount of data reviewed/ordered	1	2	3	4
Table E	Level of risk	Minimal	Low	Moderate	High
MDM Level		Straightforward	Low	Moderate	High

[1] Indicates an established problem that is improving.

[2] Table of Risk indicates:
   Acute uncomplicated illness or injury, (eg, cystitis, allergic rhinitis, simple sprain) is a Low level of risk.

[3] Test from the Medicine Section ordered.

Section Review 19.4

1. Office Visit:

    Here for six mo. check up

    HPI: Follow-up evaluation of DM and hypertension. She is under a lot of stress. No other new problems or complaints.

    A/P DM: essential hypertension

    Plan is to continue the same. Return to office in six months for follow up.

    What is the level of Medical Decision Making?

    A. Straightforward

    B. Low

    C. Moderate

    D. High

2. ER Visit:

    Data: BUN 74, creatinine 8.8, K 4.9, HGB 10.8, Troponin 0.01. I reviewed the EKG which shows some LVH but no ST changes. I also reviewed the CXR, which showed moderate pulmonary vascular congestion, but no infiltrate.

    Impression: New problem of pulmonary edema due to hypervolemia. No evidence of acute MI or unstable angina. The patient also has ESRD, which is stable, and poorly controlled HTN, which is most likely due to hypervolemia.

    Plan: I spoke with the dialysis unit. We can get him in for an early treatment this afternoon as opposed to having to wait for his usual shift tomorrow. For that reason, it is okay to discharge him from the ER to go directly to the unit.

    What is the level of Medical Decision Making?

    A. Straightforward

    B. Low

    C. Moderate

    D. High

3. IMPRESSION: Right recurrent gynecomastia.

    PLAN: The patient had a right breast ultrasound on November 17, and it showed a hypoechoic area measuring 1.7 x 0.7 x 1.2 cm in the 11 o'clock position of the right breast. There was no Doppler flow, and the transmission suggested that this was a cystic lesion. Follow-up in a month was suggested at that time. Because of this ultrasound and because this is symptomatic, I have recommended a simple mastectomy under general anesthesia. The patient is in agreement. I filled out the prison forms requesting permission, and I described the operation to the patient.

    What is the level of Medical Decision Making?

    A. Straightforward

    B. Low

    C. Moderate

    D. High

4. Subsequent Hospital Visit

    Labs: BUN 56, creatinine 2.1, K 5.2, HGB 12.

    Impression:

    1. Severe exacerbation of CHF
    2. Poorly controlled HTN
    3. Worsening ARF due to cardio-renal syndrome

    Plan:

    1. Increase BUMEX to 2 mg IV Q6.
    2. Give 500 mg IV DIURIL times one.
    3. Re-check usual labs in a.m.

    Total time: 20 minutes.

    What is the level of Medical Decision Making?

    A. Straightforward
    B. Low
    C. Moderate
    D. High

5. Established patient

    Chief Complaint: Gallstones and reflux.

    History of Present Illness: This is a 61-year-old woman who comes back to see me today with a two-year history of severe 'gallbladder' attacks. Also of note, she has had ongoing reflux problems for many years. Within the last few months, her reflux has worsened.

    Assessment/Plan: This is a 61-year-old woman with likely symptomatic cholelithiasis and reflux. Her number one concern right now is the 'gallbladder attacks.' This sounds like symptomatic cholelithiasis. As a result, we recommended for her to have laparoscopic cholecystectomy with intraoperative cholangiogram. The risks and benefits were explained to the patient who understood and agrees for us to proceed.

    With regards to her reflux, it is partially controlled by her medication. She also is overweight and might have symptom improvement after weight loss. She is also very hesitant to proceed with the Nissan fundoplication because her husband had the surgery done before and had some problems with vomiting afterwards. She does have objective evidence of reflux as well and is a good candidate for surgery. However, we will let her decide whether she wants to proceed with surgery or not.

    What is the level of Medical Decision Making?

    A. Straightforward
    B. Low
    C. Moderate
    D. High

Totaling the Level of Visit

When the level of each key component (History, Exam, and Medical Decision Making) has been determined, the overall level of the visit can be calculated. To determine the level of visit based on the key components, you will need to read the requirements for the category or subcategory for the level of codes. For example, established patient office visits require two of the three key components be met to substantiate the codes.

Documentation Dissection: Level of Visit

Utilizing a grid method will help us determine the level of visit for the office visit we have broken down through this chapter.

CC: sneezing, watery eyes [1]

History: 4-year-old female presents today sneezing, watery eyes, and nasal congestion. [1]

Symptoms started two days ago after spending all day working with her mom in the garden. [1]

Patient's eyes are not watering as much since she started taking a prescription decongestant issued at previous visit, but only has two doses left. [1]

ROS: Eyes—watery [1]

      ENT—Nasal congestion, sneezing. [1]

      Cardio—Denies chest pain. [1]

      Respiratory—Denies shortness of breath, wheezing. [1]

Personal History: Multiple sinus infections over last two years [1]

Social History: Attends private preschool [1]

Physical Examination: [2]
Constitutional: Vital Signs: Resp: 26. Temp: 98.7. Weight: 47 lbs. [2]

HEENT: PERRLA Ears negative. Nares wet with clear rhinorrhea. Throat red and swollen, postnasal drip present. [2]

Respiratory: RRR [2]

Skin: Reveals no rash, petechia or purpura. [2]

Assessment and Plan— [3]
    1.   allergic rhinitis—OTC eye drops. [3]

Allergy skin testing ordered [3]

Return to office in 10 days if symptoms have not improved. [3]

Two of three key components are needed to make established patient level visit.

Established patient office visit table				
HISTORY (Table A)	Problem focused	Expanded problem focused	Detailed	Comprehensive
EXAM (Table B)	Problem focused	Expanded problem focused	Detailed	Comprehensive
MDM (Table F)	Straightforward	Low	Moderate	High
LEVEL OF VISIT	99212	99213	99214	99215

In this example, the level of visit is 99213.

_____

[1] History (Table A) Detailed.

[2] Exam (Table B) Expanded Problem Focused.

[3] Medical Decision Making (Table F) Straightforward.

Section review 19.5

1. An established patient is seen in clinic for allergic rhinitis. A problem focused history, expanded problem focused exam, and a low level of medical decision making were performed. What E/M code would be reported for the visit?

    A. 99212

    B. 99213

    C. 99214

    D. 99215

2. A patient is admitted to the hospital for a lung transplant. The admitting physician performs a comprehensive history, a comprehensive exam, and a high level of medical decision making. What CPT® code should be reported?

    A. 99221

    B. 99222

    C. 99223

    D. 99234

3. A new patient is seen in the pediatric office for ear pain. The patient has had pain for four days and it keeps her awake at night. She has had a slight fever (99). She has not been swimming or actively in water for the past couple of months. She denies any cough, nasal congestion, or stuffiness, or loss of weight. The provider does a limited exam on the ears, nose, throat, and neck. The patient is determined to have otitis media. Amoxicillin is prescribed.

   What E/M code would be reported for the visit?

   A. 99201

   B. 99202

   C. 99203

   D. 99204

4. Mrs. Standerfer's family physician visits her in the nursing home after a spell of dizziness and confusion reported by the staff at the nursing home. She sat down after lunch and stated she was dizzy. She slept for two hours after the spell. She states she is doing much better now. She has a known history of electrolyte imbalance and is on fluid restriction at the nursing home. She has not experienced any chest pain, Dyspnea, unexplained weight changes, or intolerance to heat or cold. No complaints of head or neck pain. During the exam, the physician takes her BP both supine and standing, and notes her pulse and fever. A detailed exam of the eyes, ears, nose, and throat is performed along with a detailed neurological exam. The physician orders blood work to determine if her electrolytes are out of balance again.

   What E/M code would be reported for this visit?

   A. 99307

   B. 99308

   C. 99309

   D. 99310

5. A 45-year-old patient is seeing the neurologist, Dr. Williams, at the request of his family physician to evaluate complaints of weakness, numbness, and pain in his left hand and arm. The pain started last year after rocks fell on him while mining. He still has significant, sharp, burning wrist pain and reports the problems are continuing to get worse. He is limited in his job as a machinist for a mining company due to the pain and numbness. He has no swelling in his hand, no neck pain, or radiating pain.

   His past medical history is negative for significant diseases. He has had carpal tunnel surgery. He has a family history of hypertension, heart disease, and stroke. He is married with children and smokes one pack of cigarettes/day.

   A detailed exam is performed of the mental status, cranial nerves, motor nerves, DTRs, sensory nerves, and head and neck.

   After performing an EMG and Nerve Conduction Study, Dr. Williams determined the patient has left ulnar neuropathy at the cubital tunnel region, as well as an ongoing carpal tunnel syndrome. Repeat carpal tunnel surgery is recommended, along with a possible cubital tunnel surgical procedure. If the patient does not have surgery, he risks permanent nerve damage. A report is sent back to the physician requesting the consult.

   What E/M consultation code would be reported for this visit?

   A. 99242

   B. 99243

   C. 99244

   D. 99245

Contributory Factors to E/M Service Leveling

Contributory factors for selecting an E/M service include counseling, coordination of care, and nature of the presenting problem. The first two factors are important in E/M, but are not required for each visit. Nature of the presenting problem is considered as the disease, illness, condition, injury, symptom, signs, finding, complaint, or other with or without a diagnosis.

Counseling

Counseling may be included during the visit of a patient and reflect conversations with the patient and/or family regarding risk reduction, treatment options, benefits and risks associated with differing treatment options and other education given to the patient and/or family. This often occurs when a patient has a complicated illness or injury with different treatment options to consider. It is also common when a patient is newly diagnosed with an acute or chronic illness posing a threat to life.

Example

I had an extremely extensive 60+ minute examination, and series of discussions, with the patient and her family members. Over half of the time was spent on counseling the patient and family members.

At great length, with the patient and her daughter, and later with her son-in-law who arrived secondarily, and later again with her husband, who arrived at the end of my visit, I discussed how with diabetic injury, especially with neuropathy, she would be at risk, over time, of valvular dysfunction in the leg veins. I discussed the anatomy and physiology of orthostatic hypotension, and how this can be very pronounced, especially in long-term diabetics, and this would be made even worse with respect to her gait and balance, with her underlying peripheral neuropathy. Superimposing orthostatic hypotension on top of the neuropathy could certainly make her at risk for falling to greater degree.

Nature of Presenting Problems

The Nature of a Presenting Problem is the reason for the visit: the sign, symptom, illness, or disease being treated. Nature of a presenting problem includes five types:

- Minimal: A problem that may not require the presence of the physician; however, services provided are under the physician's supervision. Problems presenting are usually for services not billed for as an office visit. Examples include removal of sutures, supervised drug screen, or a patient needs a release for school or work.
- Self-limited or minor: Does not permanently alter health status and with management and compliance has an outcome of "good." Self-limited or minor problems are those that usually will heal on their own, without

physician intervention. Some examples include poison ivy or poison oak exposure, a sore throat, or a patient with resolved tonsillitis after a completed course of antibiotic treatment.

- Low severity: Risk of morbidity/mortality without treatment is low and full recovery with no functional impairment is expected. Problems of low severity can include management of a hypertensive patient on medication, established patient for follow up of osteoporosis, and a patient with a painful bunion.
- Moderate severity: Risk of morbidity/mortality without treatment is moderate, uncertain prognosis or increased probability of prolonged functional impairment. Examples of moderate problems include a diabetic with complications, a status-post MI patient who is not doing well on his medication, or possibly a patient with new onset of right lower quadrant abdominal pain.
- High Severity: Risk of morbidity/mortality without treatment is highly probable; uncertain prognosis or high probability of severe prolonged functional impairment. High severity problems might include a status post transplant patient developing new symptoms or a cancer patient with signs of paralysis.

Practical Coding Note

Appendix C: Clinical Examples in your CPT® codebook can be used as a good indication when determining the nature of the presenting problem. Keep in mind the level of visit is still dependent on the key components documented in the medical record.

Time

Time may be considered the controlling factor to qualify for a particular E/M service level, "When counseling and/or coordination of care dominates (more than 50 percent) the physician/patient and/or family encounter…," according to CPT® guidelines. The E/M category selected must include a time reference. As an example, the descriptor for level V established patient outpatient service 99215 specifies, "Physicians typically spend 40 minutes at the bedside and on the patient's hospital floor or unit." By contrast, Emergency Department services 99281–99285 do not include a stated time component; these services may not be reported with time as the deciding component.

Time may include face-to-face time in the office or other outpatient setting, or floor/unit time in the hospital or nursing facility, and includes time spent with parties who have assumed responsibility for the care of the patient or decision making whether or not they are family members.

Time the physician spends taking the patient's history or performing an examination does not count as counseling time. The physician must look at the entire patient encounter and decide if he or she spent the majority of time in counseling and/or coordinating care or if the key components of history, exam, and MDM should be the deciding factor when choosing an E/M level.

Counseling and coordinating care could include discussion with the patient (or his or her family) about one or more of the following, according to CPT® guidelines:

- diagnostic results
- impressions and/or recommended diagnostic studies
- prognosis
- risks and benefits of treatment options
- instructions for treatment and/or follow-up
- importance of compliance with chosen treatment options
- risk-factor reduction
- patient/family education

The provider's documentation should support the content and extent of the patient counseling. For example, Amy Jo is diagnosed with a hairline fracture of the wrist. Amy Jo is very concerned about how this will impact her career as a gymnast. Dr. Jones spent 20 minutes of a 30-minute visit counseling Amy Jo on the care to be followed to prevent further damage of the weak wrist, including no lifting of heavy objects, and no gymnastic activities involving direct pressure on the wrist (such as hand springs, head stands, etc.). In this case, the level of the visit will be based on the time.

The most important part of coding by time is complete and adequate documentation of the visit — including documentation of the total visit time and the total time the physician spends counseling.

HCPCS Level II Codes

HCPCS Level II codes for E/M services are sometimes reported for Medicare patients. Medicare has specific guidelines for many of their HCPCS Level II Codes. Some of the codes you might see reported for evaluation and management services include:

- Home health and hospice services (G0179–G0182)
- Telehealth consultation codes (G0406–G0408, G0425–G0427)
- Diabetic evaluation for loss of protective sensation (LOPS) (G0245–G0246)
- Initial preventive physical examination (IPPE) for Medicare beneficiaries (G0402)

The IPPE for Medicare beneficiaries must be provided during the first 12 months of the patient's Medicare enrollment. The IPPE has specific guidelines to bill the service. The guidelines can be found in the Medicare *Internet Only Manuals* (*IOMs*).

Other services you may often see reported with or instead of evaluation and management services include:

- Breast and pelvic exams for cervical or vaginal cancer screening (G0101)
- Digital rectal exam for prostate cancer screening (G0102)
- Wound closure utilizing tissue adhesive(s) only (G0168)

The breast and pelvic exam, and the digital rectal exams, often are performed with a preventive medicine exam. Medicare provides specific coding guidelines for the diagnosis used for these services.

Code G0168 describes wound closure utilizing tissue adhesive(s) only. This differs from CPT® instructions, which state, "Wound closure utilizing adhesive strips as the sole repair material should be coded using the appropriate E/M code." Steri-Strips are an example of adhesive strips which are a fabric-based tape or a type of adhesive flexible material used to close a small laceration without stitches. Tissue adhesive is when a substance, such as an agent or material, is used to cause adherence of tissue to tissue in sealing two cut surfaces together (eg, Dermabond).

Practical Coding Note

Next to the paragraph under Repair in the Integumentary system, make a note to use G0168 for repair using tissue adhesive only, for those payers that recognize HCPCS Level II codes.

Modifiers

The most common modifiers used with evaluation and management services include:

Modifier 24 *Unrelated evaluation and management service by the same physician or other qualified healthcare professional during a postoperative period.*

Modifier 25 *Significant, separately identifiable evaluation and management service by the same physician or other qualified healthcare professional on the same day of the procedure or other service.*

Modifier 32 *Mandated Services.*

Modifier 57 *Decision for surgery.*

Modifier 24 is to be used when patient is seen by the same physician, another physician, or other qualified healthcare professional of the same specialty who belongs to the same group practice during a postoperative period for an unrelated evaluation and management service. This occurs when a patient develops a symptom unrelated to the surgery. Some payers will allow modifier 24 on an E/M service when it is for a complication related to the surgery; check your payer guidelines.

Example

January 22—Mr. Porter is seen by Dr. Parker in the ED for an injury to his PIP joint in his right pointer finger requiring amputation of the finger.

March 24—Mr. Porter sees Dr. Parker in his office for an infection in his leg.

In this case, the initial procedure (the finger amputation) has a 90 day global period. The patient is seen in the office during the global period for a completely unrelated condition. Modifier 24 would be appended to the evaluation and management visit for March 24.

Modifier 25 is used commonly to indicate a significant and separately identifiable service was provided on the same day as an E/M service. Medicare states the procedure/service and the office visit do not require different diagnosis codes. The best way to determine if the documentation supports an evaluation and management service with a modifier 25 in addition to a procedure/service is to separate the note into separate notes.

Example

Pt comes in for FU of her HTN, hyperlipidemia, depression, and has some musculoskeletal pain she is concerned about. She would like a skin lesion removed. She also requests a tetanus shot. She has some left shoulder pain that started about two weeks ago. It is not related to any increased activity, however. She points between her scapula and her spine when she brings her elbows back. No weakness in the upper extremities or numbness. No cough, no chest pain, no SOB.

Review of Systems: Essentially negative other than she has a lesion on her belly she would like looked at and removed, if possible.

Physical Examination: Weight 241 #. BP 134/82. Pulse 68. Respiratory rate 16. Temperature 97. Eyes: anicteric. Ears: clear. Throat: normal. Neck: no JVD, no bruits. Abdomen reveals a flesh-colored lesion along the bra line, which is slightly irritated and erythematous. Extremities: no cyanosis, clubbing, or edema. Shoulder reveals good ROM, some tenderness and spasm along the medial scapula on the left compared to the right. Distal neuro and vascular supply is grossly intact.

Assessment: HTN, hypercholesterolemia, musculoskeletal strain and depression.

Plan: We will increase her Zoloft® to 100 mg per pt request and have her stay on this for at least one year and wean off in the spring of next year. Today her lipids revealed LDL of 131, total cholesterol 220. We will continue with the Zocor® given her two risk factors and her age. For HTN, continue Uniretic®. Her abdomen was prepped and draped, and 1 cc of 1% Lidocaine was administered subcutaneously. A sharp excision was performed on the lesion, which measured approximately 5 cm, Hemostasis was achieved without any suture. Pt tolerated procedure well. Specimen was not sent because it is flesh-colored. Pt will FU as needed. Instructions were given for wound care.

Evaluation and Management Documentation:

Pt comes in for FU of her HTN, hyperlipidemia, depression, and has some musculoskeletal pain she is concerned about.

She also requests a tetanus shot. She has some left shoulder pain that started about two weeks ago. It is not related to any increased activity, however. She points between her scapula and her spine when she brings her elbows back. No weakness in the upper extremities or numbness. No cough, no chest pain, no SOB.

Review of Systems: Essentially negative.

Physical Examination: Weight 241 #. BP 134/82. Pulse 68. Respiratory rate 16. Temperature 97. Eyes: anicteric. Ears: clear. Throat: normal. Neck: no JVD, no bruits. Extremities: no cyanosis, clubbing or edema. Shoulder reveals good ROM, some tenderness and spasm along the medial scapula on the left compared to the right. Distal neuro and vascular supply is grossly intact.

Assessment: HTN, hypercholesterolemia, musculoskeletal strain and depression.

PLAN: We will increase her Zoloft® to 100 mg per pt request and have her stay on this for at least one year and wean off in the spring of next year. Today her lipids revealed LDL of 131, total cholesterol 220. We will continue with the Zocor® given her two risk factors and her age. For HTN, continue Uniretic®.

Procedure Documentation:

She has a lesion on her belly she would like looked at and removed, if possible.

Physical Examination: Abdomen reveals a flesh-colored lesion along the bra line, which is slightly irritated and erythematous.

Plan: Her abdomen was prepped and draped, and 1 cc of 1% Lidocaine was administered subcutaneously. A sharp excision was performed on the lesion, which measured approximately 5 cm, Hemostasis was achieved without any suture. Pt tolerated procedure well. Specimen was not sent because it is flesh-colored. Pt will FU as needed. Instructions were given for wound care.

Modifier 32 is used to show a service was mandated by a third party payer (eg, Workers' Compensation) or government, or that the service is a legislative or regulatory requirement.

Modifier 57 is used when the decision for surgery is made during an E/M service on the day of, or the day before a surgery. Payers will have different guidelines for the use of modifier 57; check your payer policies.

For Medicare, modifier 57 should only be used for major surgeries. If the decision to perform a minor surgery (global days 0-10) is made during a visit, modifier 25 would be appended to the appropriate E/M service code. For the decision to perform a major surgery (90 day global) on the day of or day before the surgery, modifier 57 would be appended to the appropriate E/M code. To know which procedures are major surgery and which are minor, you will need to refer to the global days in the Medicare Physician Fee Schedule.

Documentation Dissection

Case 1: Established Patient Office Visit

Chief Complaint: Right shoulder pain [1]

This is a 47-year-old, otherwise healthy, right-hand-dominant male tool maker with a 6-8 week history [2] of gradual insidious onset [3] of right shoulder pain. [4] He has noted popping along the medial aspect of the scapula, [5] but this is not particularly associated with the pain. The pain seems to be localized more laterally. He has been taking Naprosyn® [6] for some low back discomfort, which helps his shoulder as well.

ROS: No HEENT, respiratory, cardiovascular, gastrointestinal, genitourinary, or nerve complaints. MS is positive for joint pain, muscle tenderness, and weakness. [7]

Past History: Medications: Naprosyn®, Allergic to Penicillin. Prior surgery on lower back (1994). [8]

Family History: None [8]

Social History: positive for tobacco and alcohol use. [8]

Physical Examination:

Right shoulder is non-swollen. No deformity. No muscular atrophy. He does have crepitus that localizes to his scapulothoracic articulation medially and posteriorly, but there is no tenderness or apparent pain. He has full active range of motion. No instability. Negative impingement. He does have some pain primarily with resisted supraspinatus function, but no distinct weakness. [9]

X-Ray: X-rays, three views of the right shoulder viewed in office, [10] show normal anatomic relationships. No soft tissue calcifications. Acromial humeral interval maintained. The X-ray will be officially read by the radiologist.

Assessment and Plan:

Right rotator cuff tendonitis. [11] After discussion of treatment options, he wished to proceed with shoulder injection done with 2 cc of Xylocaine® under a sterile technique from a posterior approach. [12] He is started on a rotator cuff exercise program. Return in 3-4 weeks for follow-up.

---

[1] Chief complaint.

[2] Duration.

[3] Timing.

[4] Location.

[5] Associated Sign & Symptom.

[3] Modifying factor.

[7] Review of Systems:
Eyes
ENMT
Respiratory
Cardiovascular
Gastrointestinal
Genitourinary
Neurological
Musculoskeletal

[8] Complete PFSH.

[9] Musculoskeletal system examined.

[10] X-rays independently reviewed by physician. Will be reported by the radiologist.

[11] Definitive diagnosis.

[12] Major joint injection; shoulder.

What are the CPT® and ICD-10-CM codes reported?

CPT® Codes: 99213-25, 20610

ICD-10-CM Code: M75.81

Rationale: CPT® Codes: Established patient requires two of the three key components to meet the criteria for a visit.

History—HPI (extended), ROS (extended), PFSH (Complete) = Detailed

Exam—Problem focused

MDM—New problem, Independent review of X-ray, Risk—Low (acute uncomplicated injury and minor surgery with no identified risk factors) = Low

A detailed history, problem focused exam, and low medical decision making supports a level III office visit (99213).

After evaluation, the provider discussed treatment options with the patient and performed a joint injection. In the CPT® Index, look for Injection/Joint and you are directed to 20600, 20604–20606, 20610, 20611. The shoulder is considered a major joint; therefore, 20610 is the correct code. Modifier 25 is appended to the E/M code to indicate that a significant separate identifiable E/M services was performed with a same day procedure.

Look in the ICD-10-CM Index to Diseases and Injuries for Tendinitis, tendonitis. The provider states there are no calcifications showing on the X-ray and does not mention adhesive or that the condition is a result of overuse. There is a note to *see also* Enthesopathy. Enthesopathy/shoulder region directs you to *see* Lesion, shoulder. Lesion/shoulder (region)/specified NEC M75.8-. Specified NEC is used because we know the condition is tendonitis. In the Tabular List, M75.8- requires another character to specify laterality. Fifth character 1 indicates the right shoulder is affected.

ICD-9-CM Application

What is/are ICD-9-CM code(s) reported?

Code(s): 726.10

Rationale: Look in the ICD-9-CM Index to Diseases for Tendonitis. There is no subentry for shoulder. There is an entry for adhesive, shoulder. Adhesive tendonitis is when there is a loss of motion, referred to as a frozen shoulder. The entry of Tendonitis states to *see also* Tenosynovitis. Look for Tenosynovitis/shoulder you are directed to 726.10. Code 726.10 is for *Disorders of bursae and tendons in the shoulder region, unspecified.*

Case 2: Emergency Department Visit

Chief complaint: Dizziness, nausea, vomiting.

History of Present Illness

A 43-year-old very pleasant gentleman with history of hypertension who presents to the emergency room with chief complaint of abrupt onset [1] of nausea, vomiting, and dizziness. [2] The patient said that while he was sitting [3] he felt like the room was spinning, he felt very unstable, [4] associated with severe nausea. Denies any abdominal pain, [5] fever, chills, [6] headache, [7] or shortness of breath. [8] Symptoms are exacerbated by certain movements. [9] Denies any sick contacts. This is the first time this has ever happened. The patient arrived via EMS. After receiving 12.5 mg of Phenergan® [10] intravenously, he feels better at this time.

The patient said that he has some mild nausea. [11] He has had one episode of nonbloody, nonbilious emesis in the emergency room.

Past Medical History: Hypertension. [12]

Past Surgical History: Negative. [12]

Social History: Occasional use, nonsmoker, no drug use. [13]

Family History: Negative for hypertension [14]

Review of Systems

All pertinent positives and negatives as above, all 10 systems [15] reviewed and the remaining are negative.

Physical Examination

Temperature 97, heart rate 66, blood pressure 169/92, respiratory rate 20, O2 sat 97% on room air. General examination: The patient in no acute distress. [16] HEENT: Normocephalic, atraumatic. [17] Pupils are 4 and reactive. [18] There is a slight horizontal nystagmus with left lateral gaze. [19] Mucous membranes are moist. [20] Neck is supple. There is no Kernig's, no Brudzinskj's. Hallpike maneuver was negative. The patient was symptomatic with both directions. [21] Lungs are clear auscultation bilaterally. Chest symmetric. [22] Cardiovascular: S1, S2, regular rate and rhythm. [23] Abdomen is soft, nontender, [24] no CVA tenderness. [25] Neurologically, the patient is alert and oriented x3. Cranial nerves II-XII are grossly intact. Strength is 5/5. Reflexes are symmetric. Cerebellum is intact with good finger-to-nose. Sensation is grossly intact. [26] Lymph: No appreciable cervical, axilla, inguinal lymphadenopathy. [27]

Diagnostics

CBC: White blood cell count of 14, hemoglobin 15, hematocrit 45, platelets are 179. Chem-7 identifies glucose of 202, BUN of 13, creatinine 0.8. [28]

ED Course

The patient underwent an MRI of the brain, [29] which was interpreted as negative per the attending radiologist. He was treated with intravenous Zofran® [30] and oral Antivert®, [31] feels better at this time.

Plan: The patient will be discharged at this time. Advised to follow up with his primary care physician. Return if increased symptoms.

Diagnosis: Vertigo. [32]

Disposition: Discharged stable condition.

---

[1] Timing.

[2] Associated signs and symptoms.

[3] Context.

[4] Quality.

[5] GI ROS.

[6] Constitutional ROS.

[7] Neuro ROS:

[8] Respiratory ROS.

[9] Modifying factors.

[10] Modifying factors.

[11] Severity.

[12] Past Medical History.

[13] Social History.

[14] Family History.

[15] Complete ROS.

[16] Constitutional.

[17] Head.

[18] Eyes.

[19] Neurological.

[20] Mouth.

[21] Neurological.

[22] Respiratory.

[23] Cardiovascular.

[24] Abdominal.

[25] Genitourinary.

[26] Neurological.

[27] Lymphatic.

[28] Labs reviewed.

[29] MRI ordered.

[30] IV Zofran.

[31] Oral meds.

[32] Definitive diagnosis.

What are the CPT® and ICD-10-CM codes reported?

CPT® Code: 99284

ICD-10-CM Code: R42

Rationale: CPT® Code: Emergency department visits require all three key components be met.

History—HPI (Extended), ROS (Complete), PFSH (Complete) = Comprehensive

Exam—Comprehensive exam (eight systems—Constitutional, eyes, ENMT (mouth), Cardiovascular, Respiratory, Genitourinary, Neurologic, Lymphatic)

MDM—New problem, no additional work up, Lab and Radiology reviewed, Risk moderate (IV fluids with Zofran®, oral meds) = Moderate MDM

Comprehensive history, comprehensive exam, medical decision making moderate supports a 99284 for the emergency department.

ICD-10-CM Code: Look in the ICD-10-CM Index to Diseases and Injuries for vertigo. There are many different subentries for the type of vertigo; however, the type of vertigo is not specified. R42 is the default code for vertigo. Verification in the Tabular List confirms R42 is to be used for vertigo, NOS.

ICD-9-CM Application

What is/are ICD-9-CM codes reported?

Code(s): 780.4

Rationale: Definitive diagnosis is Vertigo. Look for Vertigo in the ICD-9-CM Index to Diseases. There are many different subentries (types) of vertigo. There is no more description on the vertigo, so we are directed to 780.4. Code 780.4 is for dizziness and giddiness with Vertigo, NOS listed as an inclusion term.

Glossary

Auscultation—Listening to body organs.

Chief Complaint—The reason the patient presents for an encounter.

Counseling—A discussion with a patient and/or family concerning diagnosis, prognosis, risk factors, etc.

Critical Care—Care provided for a critical illness or injury which acutely impairs one or more vital organ systems, and is an imminent or life-threatening condition.

Established Patient—A patient who has seen a provider of the exact same specialty and subspecialty in the same group within the past three years.

Family History—A review of the health status of immediate family, including cause and age of death, if appropriate. Also includes a review of hereditary diseases existing in the family.

History of Present Illness—A chronological description of the onset and progression of the illness for which treatment is being sought.

New Patient—A patient who has not been seen by a provider of the exact same specialty and subspecialty in the same group for the past three years.

Medical Necessity—Reasonable and necessary services to effect cure or a change in the condition for which the patient is being seen.

Observation Status—The patient's condition requires monitoring but the decision to admit to inpatient status has not been made.

Palpation—Touching the body during a physical examination in which an object is felt to determine size, shape, firmness, or location.

Percussion—Creating sounds from the body by tapping.

Review of Systems—A series of questions regarding signs and symptoms that are associated with the patient's chief complaint.

Introduction

The objective for this chapter is to introduce you to a diverse group of noninvasive or minimally invasive services. You will learn steps to correct coding concepts, proper application of modifiers, diagnosis coding tips and some applicable HCPCS Level II references. This chapter covers multiple specialties. Included in this category are:

Immunizations

Vaccines, Toxoids

Psychiatry

Biofeedback

Dialysis

Gastroenterology

Ophthalmology

Otorhinolaryngology

Cardiovascular

Noninvasive Diagnostic Vascular Studies

Pulmonary

Allergy & Clinical Immunology

Endocrinology

Neurology/Neuromuscular Procedures

Medical Genetics & Genetic Counseling Services

Central Nervous System Assessments/Tests

Health & Behavior Assessment/Intervention

Hydration, Therapeutic, Prophylactic, Infusions & Injections

Photodynamic Therapy

Special Dermatological Procedures

Physical Medicine & Rehabilitation

Nutritional Therapy

Acupuncture

Osteopathic & Chiropractic Manipulative Treatment

Education & Training for Patient Self-Management

Non-Face-To-Face Nonphysician Services

Qualifying Circumstances for Anesthesia

Moderate Sedation

Home Health Procedures/Services

Medication Therapy Management Services

Anti-Infective Immunizations

Codes 90281–90399 describe anti-infective immunizations derived from human blood or products created in a laboratory through modification of genetic human and/or animal protein. Each code is specific to the type of anti-infective administered, with 90399 reserved for an immune globulin not described in a code.

Do not report modifier 51 if these services are performed with another procedure.

When microorganisms enter the body through a barrier breach (example: cut on skin), the inflammatory response directs immune system components to the infected site. Common pathogens responsible for infection are fungi, gram-positive, and gram-negative organisms. The body's immune system produces antibodies (or immunity) when foreign substances (antigens) are introduced. Immune globulins are concentrations of antibodies collected from pooled blood given to immediately protect against infectious agents or given to individuals with weakened immune systems such as chemotherapy patients.

The administration of these products is reported in addition to the product. Codes 96365–96368, 96372, 96374, 96375 are reported for the administration of immune globulin. It is important to select the correct administration code to describe the appropriate delivery technique. When the delivery is by infusion, (96365–96371), adhere to the times as stated in the code descriptor. For example, the base code may describe up to one hour, with the add-on code reported for each additional hour. A minimum time of 31 minutes is required when reporting the add-on code for an additional hour.

Practical Coding Note

The coder must refer to the nurse's notes for delivery technique and start and stop infusion times of each drug/substance administered to correctly report the service. These codes also may describe addition of sequential substances as an add-on to the base code. Generally included in the service are local anesthesia, IV start, vascular access, flush at conclusion of an infusion, standard tubing, syringes, and supplies. When fluids are used for delivery of the substance/drug, fluid administration is incidental to the administration and is not separately reported. Codes 96365–96371 are not to be reported for chemotherapy administration.

Physician work for these services usually includes development of the treatment plan and direct supervision of staff. If a significant, separately identifiable Evaluation and Management (E/M) service is performed at the same encounter, the appropriate E/M code is reported with modifier 25.

Practical Coding Note

If the substance is ordered due to exposure to infection, report a Z code as the diagnosis. Example: Z20.820 Contact with and (suspected) exposure to varicella (90396).

In ICD-10-CM the type of drug used for the vaccine or immunization is identified in the CPT® or HCPCS code. Only one diagnosis code exists in ICD-10-CM (Z23).

Example

Patient was given the measles-mumps-rubella vaccination (MMR).

In the Index to Diseases and Injuries look for Vaccination (prophylactic)/encounter for Z23.

Z23 Encounter for immunization

ICD-10-CM also provides codes for when the immunization is not carried out or for under immunization status. These codes are found in category Z28.

Z28.04 Immunization not carried out because of patient allergy to vaccine or component

Z28.3 Under immunization status

ICD-9-CM Application

ICD-9-CM has a specific code for each type of vaccination given to the patient for the different types of vaccinations that are administered to a patient.

In the Index to Diseases look for Vaccination/prophylactic (against)/mumps/with measles and rubella (MMR) V06.4.

V06.4 Need for prophylactic vaccination and inoculation against combination of diseases, Measles-mumps-rubella [MMR]

Vaccines and Toxoids

Codes 90476–90748 describe vaccines and toxoids reported for the product only. Each code is specific to the type of vaccine/toxoid administered. A vaccine is made from a weakened live or killed form of a microbe. A toxoid is a bacterial poison or exotoxin weakened and no longer has toxic properties; however, it still can stimulate the production of antibodies.

Some codes are specific to certain age categories. It is important for the coder to select the correct code applicable to the age described in the code.

The coder also must code the administration of the vaccine/toxoid. The administration codes are 90460–90474. Codes are selected by the age of the patient and method of delivery.

Report codes 90460–90461 only if the provider counsels the patient/family face-to-face during administration of the vaccine/toxoid to a child through 18 years of age. The provider must counsel the patient/family about benefits and risks of the proposed injection of vaccine/toxoid when reporting codes containing counseling in the code descriptor. For a vaccine with multiple components (combination vaccine) you report 90460 for the first component and each additional component is reported with 90461. For example, MMR is a combination vaccine made up of three vaccine components: mumps, measles, and rubella. Report the administration codes with counseling with:

90460 Mumps

90461x2 Measles and Rubella

Example

The administration of two vaccines for a 4-year-old with counseling, (DTaP and Varicella) is reported as follows:

- 90700 DTaP Vaccine, IM
- 90716 Varicella virus vaccine
- 90460 x 2 Administration code for the first vaccine component (Diptheria) in the DTaP vaccine and for the Varicella
- 90461 x 2 Administration code for the two remaining vaccine components (Tetanus toxoid and acellular pertussis) in the DTap vaccine.

Code 90460 is reported for vaccines that are not combination vaccines (eg, 90716) and is also reported for the first vaccine component in combination vaccines. The add-on code 90461 is only reported for additional component(s) in combination vaccine(s).

Report codes 90471–90474 if no counseling is provided for a child less than 18 years of age and for the administration of vaccine(s)/toxoid(s) to patients over 18 years of age. These administration codes are not reported by each vaccine component in a combination vaccine, but reported by how each vaccination is given (IM, orally, subcutaneously etc.). For example a MMR vaccine given intramuscularly without counseling is reported with one administration code, 90471.

Example

The administration of several vaccines in tandem, (DTaP polio measles, mumps, and rubella (MMR), and Varicella vaccine) would be reported as follows:

- 90700 DTaP Vaccine, IM
- 90471 Administration of DTaP, IM
- 90713 Poliovirus Vaccine, SQ or IM
- 90707 MMR Vaccine, SQ
- 90716 Varicella Virus Vaccine (VAR), SQ
- 90472 x 3 Administration of Poliovirus, MMR, and Varicella Virus Vaccine

Do not report modifier 51 with these services.

If a significant, separately identifiable E/M service is provided at the same encounter, the appropriate E/M service may also be reported with modifier 25.

Subcutaneous injections (Sub-Q) are delivered into the subcutaneous layer of skin, just below the epidermis and dermis. Typical injection sites are the outer area of the upper arm, upper buttocks just behind the hipbone, front outer area of the thigh, midway between the upper thigh and knee or just above or below the waist. Injections generally are not administered within a 2-inch circle of the navel because large nerves are present close to the skin.

Intramuscular injections (IM) are administered directly into a muscle.

Immunizations are given to prevent a disease/illness. They induce the immune system to produce immunity against specific microorganisms/viruses. When a foreign object or antigen is introduced into a healthy body, an immune response follows during which the healthy body forms antigen specific antibodies. Some immunizations are described as active, which

means the patient is acquiring antigens through the introduction of a weakened live or dead pathogen and produces antibodies in response (eg, CPT® codes 90476–90749).

Tips for Coding Vaccines/Toxoids

Keep in mind the following coding tips:

1. All vaccines and immunizations are reported with ICD-10-CM code Z23.

2. These services are separate from chemotherapy and allergy injections.

4. Medicare allows payment for administration of flu shots, pneumococcal vaccine, and hepatitis B vaccine using HCPCS Level II codes G0008, G0009, and G0010, respectively.

5. When an immunization is the only service provided, a minimal service may be listed in addition to the vaccine/toxoid product(s), if the payer does not recognize the administration CPT® codes.

6. Codes 90460–90474 must be reported in addition to the vaccine and toxoid codes (90476–90749).

7. An office visit (any level) may not be coded separately when the primary reason for the visit is to receive the injection. In the case of hepatitis B, Medicare carriers do make exceptions to this statement, if the patient has been exposed to hepatitis B. There is very often additional work required to trace the initial source of exposure. The Z code Z20.5, indicating exposure, would help to show medical necessity for an E/M service. Some carriers may reimburse for the E/M service, the G code, and the CPT® code for the product. Others will reimburse for the E/M code and the injectable product only. Check with the payer in your region if this situation arises.

8. All CPT® codes for vaccines/toxoids are modifier 51 exempt.

Section Review 20.1

1. A child was bitten by a dog that tested positive for rabies and is seen for an injection of rabies immune globulin.

    A. 90396, 96365

    B. 90375, 96372

    C. 90384, 96369

    D. 90389, 90471

2. An elderly diabetic patient visited a neighborhood clinic to receive influenza and pneumonia intramuscular immunizations.

    A. 90658, 90732, 90471, 90472

    B. 90662, 90732, 90472

    C. 90736, 90657, 90471, 90472

    D. 90660, 90732, 90471

3. A 35-year-old patient plans to travel to a country with a high incidence of yellow fever. The patient receives the yellow fever immunization.

    A. 90717, 90471

    B. 90749, 90472

    C. 90717, 90460

    D. 90749, 90471

Psychiatry

Codes 90785–90899 are reported for psychiatric services. Psychiatric services may be performed in both outpatient and inpatient settings. For example, a patient being treated for medical conditions may exhibit behavior concerns detrimental to the progress of the medical condition(s). The attending physician may request consultation from a psychiatrist in an attempt to modify behavior. The encounter may be diagnostic, therapeutic, or a combination. The hospital patient may receive only E/M services, or the physician may render both E/M and other services such as electroconvulsive therapy.

Psychiatric services may include psychotherapy, behavior modification, and addictive disease therapy. Insight-oriented, behavior-modifying, and/or supportive therapy refers to the development of insight or affective understanding, use of behavior modification techniques, discussion of reality, and supportive interaction to initiate therapeutic change. Some examples are group interactive sessions, setting rules and limitations, goal setting and clear steps to accomplishment. Practitioners include physicians who specialize in psychiatry, clinical psychologists, and clinical social workers. Encounters may be individual, group sessions, or family psychotherapy.

Psychiatrists may reference Axis I–V in their documentation. This criterion is based on the *Diagnostic and Statistical Manual of Mental Disorders* (DSM) classification system. It is the primary system used to diagnose and classify mental disorders. Each disorder and applicable diagnosis code includes a set of diagnostic criteria, descriptive details, associated features, familial patterns, age, culture, and gender specific features. The Axis System allows for much greater diagnostic detail. Often, situations may be exacerbated to a degree an additional diagnosis is applicable. Example: Major mental illness is captured in Axis I. The condition may be exacerbated by external influence and will add a condition reportable in Axis IV.

Axis I—All psychiatric diagnoses are listed on Axis I except intellectual disability and personality disorders

Axis II—Developmental diagnoses and disorders first diagnosed in infancy or childhood

   Includes intellectual disability and personality disorders.

Axis III—Physical diseases

Axis IV—Psychological stress factors affecting the patient

Axis V—Global functioning of the patient

Evaluates the patient's ability to cope with his or her present situation.

Interactive complexity is an add-on code reported for patients with communication factors that complicate the delivery of psychiatric services. This code cannot be reported with E/M codes. The only appropriate base codes are listed in a parenthetical note following code 90785.

Psychiatrists often report CPT® codes 90785–90792 instead of E/M codes. Psychiatric diagnostic interviews are performed to determine if there is a treatable diagnosis. The correct code is chosen based on whether other medical services are performed.

Psychotherapy is treatment for mental illness and behavioral disturbances in which the physician or therapist establishes a professional contract with the patient. These services can be provided in both the inpatient and outpatient setting.

Whether medical E/M services were provided also affect code selection. Remember, there are specific psychotherapy codes including E/M; codes from the E/M section can be reported in addition to psychotherapy services. The add-on codes including medical E/M services are noted in the description by stating "when performed with an evaluation and management service."

Codes for psychotherapy are determined based on time. There are add-on codes for psychotherapy used when a significant and separately identifiable E/M service is performed on the same date. The time performing the E/M service can not be counted in the time used to determine the psychotherapy code.

Example

99204 New Patient office or other outpatient visit

+90833   when performed with an evaluation and management service (List separately in addition to the code for primary procedure)

In this example, CPT® add-on code 90833 is reported as an additional code if medical E/M services were performed in addition to psychotherapy services described in CPT® subsection guidelines for Psychotherapy.

Codes for psychotherapy for patients in crisis are reported when patients have a life threatening condition or a very complex medical condition. The codes are selected based on time. The services performed include psychotherapy, mobilization of resources to defuse the crisis and restore safety, and implementation of psychotherapeutic interventions to minimize the potential for psychological trauma.

According to CPT® subsection guidelines for Psychotherapy you do not report psychotherapy codes if the face-to-face time is documented less than 16 minutes. When 16 minutes or more is documented for psychotherapy, choose the code closet to the actual time.

16–37 minutes—90832 and 90833

38–52 minutes—90834 and 90836

53–more minutes—90837–90838

Terms common in psychiatric documentation include:

- Bipolar disorder—Periods of uncontrollable mood swings between mania and depression
- Cognitive—Thoughts or thinking
- Compulsion—Repetitive ritualistic behavior
- Coping mechanism—Personal adjustment to stress without losing sight of a goal
- Delusions—False beliefs
- Depressive neurosis—State of sadness or anxiety and loss of interest in normal activities
- Disorientation—Confusion about time, place, or person
- Egocentrism—Inability to see any viewpoint other than one's own
- Fragmentation—Feeling of falling apart or fear of impending loss
- Generalized anxiety disorder—Constantly feeling tense and apprehensive; inability to relax
- Grandiosity—Elevated feeling of self-worth
- Hallucinations—Sensory impairment; seeing and hearing things not present
- Hypochondriasis—Misinterpretation of normal experiences to be a disease
- Inappropriate effect—Expression not fitting the situation
- Loosening of associations—Thought or speech disturbances; fragmentation
- Mood and affect—Mood is an emotion, such as depression and anger. Affect is the behavior indicating the expression of the mood
- Obsessive-compulsive disorder—Repetitive, ritualistic behavior
- Panic attacks—Intense anxiety; feeling of loss of control
- Paranoia—Suspiciousness; feelings of persecution
- Post-traumatic stress disorder—Emotional disturbance resulting from a previous traumatic event
- Psychosomatic—Illness triggered by mind and thought rather than from a virus, injury, or bacteria
- Psychosis—Loss of boundary; gross impairment of reality

- Schizophrenia—Delusional; flawed perception of the world
- Short-term memory—Ability to recall information for a very short time span

Practical Coding Note

Diagnosis Coding: If a definitive condition has been documented, it is reported as the diagnosis. If the patient is being observed for behavior patterns pending diagnosis, it may be appropriate to report a Z code for observation of certain conditions.

Example

Chronic paranoid schizophrenia with acute exacerbation.

ICD-10-CM does not specify in the code description for a schizophrenic disorder if it is chronic, with exacerbation or in remission. In the Alphabetic Index look for Schizophrenia/paranoid and directs you to F20.0

F20.0 Paranoid schizophrenia

ICD-9-CM Application

ICD-9-CM does specify in the code description for a schizophrenic disorder if it is chronic, with exacerbation to in remission. In the ICD-9-CM Alphabetic Index look for Paranoid/schizophrenia (acute) 295.3. In the Tabular List fifth digit 4 is selected to indicate chronic with acute exacerbation.

295.34 Paranoid type, chronic with acute exacerbation

Example

ICD-10-CM has specific codes for certain types of phobias.

Arachnophobia (fear of spiders).

F40.210 Arachnophobia

Look in the Index to Diseases and Injuries for Phobia, phobic/animal/spiders F40.210.

ICD-9-CM

ICD-9-CM has very few phobic disorders in subcategory 300.2. There is no code for arachnophobia and is reported as a specified code.

Look in the Index to Diseases for Phobia, phobic (reaction)/specified NEC 300.29.

300.29 Other isolated or specific phobias

The final heading in the Psychiatry subsection includes CPT® codes for pharmacologic management, narcosynthesis, electroconvulsive therapy (ECT), and psychophysiological therapy incorporating biofeedback training and hypnotherapy.

Psychiatric somatotherapy (90863–90870) is the biological treatment of a mental disorder. Modalities include pharmacological management, narcosynthesis, and the use of electroconvulsive therapy (ECT).

Pharmacologic management is reported with an add-on code (90863). This service is reported in addition to psychotherapy (90832, 90834, 90837). The time spent performing pharmacologic management cannot be used to determine the time reported for the psychotherapy code according to CPT®. Pharmacologic management can also be performed during an E/M service by providers allowed to report E/M services. Do not report 90863 with E/M codes. The work spent providing the pharmacologic management will be captured in the selection of the E/M code. Narcosynthesis (90865) is therapy rendered when the patient is under the influence of a drug such as a sedative or narcotic.

Biofeedback is a training technique allowing the patient an element of voluntary control over autonomic body functions. Biofeedback techniques may be incorporated as part of a service including psychotherapy. Codes 90875 and 90876 report any modality of individual psychophysiological therapy incorporating biofeedback training. These codes identify a face-to-face service and include psychotherapy.

Time is a factor when reporting a CPT® code for individual psychophysiological therapy. If the time used to perform the service is increased or decreased, a modifier is used to indicate the time difference. CPT® modifier 52 is used if the session is less than 20 minutes.

Biofeedback in conjunction with psychotherapy assists in modifying the patient's physiological behavior through relaxation techniques. Codes 90901 and 90911 are not reported separately for individual psychophysiological therapy.

Hypnotherapy (90880) is a modality to evaluate or alter patient behavior while the patient is in a state of lowered critical judgment.

Section Review 20.2

1. A patient was referred to a psychiatrist for management after displaying erratic and unusual behavior at work. The patient disclosed a difficult family situation and the psychiatrist arranged a family therapy session to include the patient. What is the correct code for the family psychotherapy session?

    A. 90849

    B. 90833

    C. 90847

    D. 90853

2. A patient receiving psychotherapy is ready to begin mainstream efforts into the community. The psychiatrist discusses the patient's mental health history with a social agency who assists in locating employment and living arrangements.

    A. 90887

    B. 90882

    C. 90889

    D. 90875

3. A patient experienced a stressful personal event and met with her psychiatrist in his office for 45 minutes for the purpose of evaluating her potential to return to work.

    A. 90839

    B. 90845

    C. 90792

    D. 90834

Biofeedback

Biofeedback is a medical modality designed to control autonomic body responses by auditory and/or visual stimuli to the senses. Electrical devices help the patient acquire the ability to control heart rate, blood pressure, skin temperature, salivation, peripheral vasomotor activity, or gross muscle tone. These responses are managed by control techniques to duplicate the desired response of the biofeedback modality.

Physicians, psychiatrists, therapists, and technicians provide biofeedback in physical therapy, pain management, and psychiatric services

Code 90901 reports biofeedback training used to improve and regulate vital signs (eg, heart rate, blood pressure, muscle tension of the autonomic or involuntary nervous system). Time is not considered a factor when using this code since training is administered over several sessions.

Code 90911 is specific to reporting of biofeedback training for perineal muscles, anorectal, or urethral sphincter. The description of this code includes EMG and/or manometry, for example, rectal manometry, which is the measurement of pressure differences.

Biofeedback training codes 90901 and 90911 should not be confused with needle electromyography testing or H&F reflex studies. These tests may be coded separately when provided concurrently with biofeedback.

In some instances, biofeedback techniques may be incorporated as part of a service also using psychotherapy. These services are identified in codes 90875 and 90876 as individual psychophysiological therapy incorporating biofeedback. In these instances, the descriptor language identifies each type of service rendered, as well as any time frames.

Section Review 20.3

1. A patient with long-time stress urinary incontinence underwent biofeedback training for improvement of urine leakage.

 A. 90911

 B. 90901

 C. 53899

 D. 91120

Dialysis and End Stage Renal Disease Services

Dialysis is a procedure removing toxins from blood in patients with chronic renal failure or acute renal failure. Dialysis typically is required three times weekly. End-stage renal disease requires dialysis until a suitable organ donor is identified. There are a number of potential complications to dialysis, including infection of the access site, sepsis, hypotension (low blood pressure), anemia, and air embolism. Vital signs are documented every 30 minutes and blood samples are checked for clotting time.

Peritoneal Dialysis

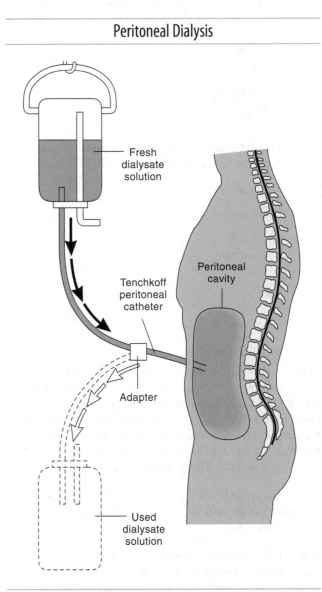

Source: EHRLICH/SCHROEDER. Medical Terminology for Health Professions, 6E. © 2009 Delmar Learning, a part of Cengage Learning, Inc. Reproduced by permission. www.cengage.com/permissions

Codes 90935–90940 are reported for hemodialysis. Hemodialysis is removal of toxins from the blood directly: 90935 is reported for one evaluation by a physician or other qualified healthcare professional; 90937 is reported for repeat evaluations, with or without substantial revision of the prescribed treatment.

Report 90940 for evaluation of the blood flow through the graft or AV fistula during hemodialysis. An AV fistula for hemodialysis is created by connecting an artery directly to a vein to allow more blood to flow into the vein; as a result, the vein becomes larger and stronger. If vessels are small or will not properly form a fistula, an artery and vein can be connected with a synthetic tube or graft implanted under the skin.

Codes 90945–90947 are reported for dialysis other than hemodialysis, such as peritoneal or hemofiltration.

In peritoneal dialysis a sterile solution (dialysate) is run through a tube into the peritoneal cavity and the solution is left a time to absorb waste products, and is drained from the abdominal cavity. Hemofiltration is similar to hemodialysis; however, a different principle is utilized. Blood is pumped through a hemofilter but no dialysate is used. Salts and water lost through this process are replaced with substitution fluid infused into the patient during treatment.

Codes 90951–90962 are reported once per month for end-stage renal disease services. Codes are selected based upon the age of the patient and on the number of face-to-face physician or other qualified healthcare professional visits. The scope of the physician work will include establishment of the treatment cycle, outpatient E/M of the visits, management of the patient during the dialysis, and telephone calls for a full month of treatment.

If a complete assessment has been provided, but the patient had less than one month of the services, you may report codes 90951–90962 according to the number of visits performed.

Significant, separately identifiable E/M services provided at the encounter unrelated to dialysis and not performed during the dialysis encounter may be reported separately, using modifier 25.

Codes 90967–90970 are reported based on the age of patient and each day end-stage renal disease services are provided less than a full month. These codes are reported for certain circumstances, some examples include transient patients, patients admitted to the hospital, treatments terminated due to recovery or death of the patient, or patients who have received a renal transplant. For example, home dialysis patients who are admitted as inpatients will have a break in their home dialysis. In this case, report codes 90967–90970 for each day outside of the inpatient hospitalization. Report as appropriate, codes 90935–90937, 90945, 90947, for dialysis during the inpatient stay.

Example

5-year-old patient received ESRD related services at home for 10 days and had to be admitted to the hospital for inpatient management on the 11th day.

90968 x10 End-stage renal disease (ESRD) related services for home dialysis less than a full month of service, per day for patients 2-11 years of age.

Because the ESRD services in the home setting was not performed for the full month, code 90968 needs to be reported in 10 units to indicate the services performed per day.

Codes 90989–90993 are reported for patient and helper dialysis training. If a complete training course has been accomplished, report 90989. If the training course has not been completed, report 90993 per training session.

Patients who are candidates for home dialysis receive instruction from a home training nurse. The nurse will assess the room where dialysis supplies will be maintained and the area for water treatment. The quality of the water supply will be tested. Minor plumbing and wiring changes may be required in some cases. Some dialysis organizations may require training for the patient and their helper be completed in the center. Others may arrange training at home by a home care nurse. The patient receives written instructions, a list of medication to be filled, and emergency contact information. During the first week of training, the nurse sets up the machine and inserts the needles into the vascular access. As the patient and helper become familiar with the procedure, they will gradually assume the steps under the direction of the nurse. Typical training time is several weeks.

Practical Coding Note

Procedure coding: For declotting of an A/V fistula report 36831, 36833, 36860, 36861 or 36870 (percutaneous thrombectomy and intra-graft thrombolysis). Report code 36861 when an external cannula is declotted and the clot (thrombus) is removed with a balloon catheter. Report 36833 if a revision is made to the graft after removing the clot.

Diagnosis Coding: Patients who require dialysis often have other chronic disease processes related to the dialysis. Specifically, when the patient has hypertension, renal failure, and heart failure, the coder reports a combination code in lieu of reporting each condition separately. Report from code range category I11 for hypertensive heart disease, category I12 for hypertensive chronic kidney disease, and category I13 for hypertensive heart and chronic kidney disease.

HCPCS Level II Coding: Dialysis patients often experience fatigue and anemia. Aranesp (darbepoetin alfa) is a drug often administered to dialysis patients to encourage production of red blood cells. Report this drug with J0882 for dialysis patients. The coder must review the record to report the correct number of units delivered to the patient.

Dialysis Coding Guidelines

1. A dialysis procedure, other than hemodialysis, such as peritoneal or hemofiltration dialysis, with a single physician evaluation is reported with code 90945. The medical record should clearly indicate the technique that was used.

2. A dialysis procedure, other than hemodialysis, such as peritoneal or hemofiltration dialysis requiring repeated evaluations, with or without substantial revision of dialysis prescription, is reported with code 90947.

3. When the physician or healthcare provider trains a patient (including the assistant or patient caregiver) to help with dialysis, code 90989 is reported. This code is reported contingent upon completing the entire training course.

4. Code 90993 is reported per training session if the patient, including the assistant, as applicable, did not complete the training course.

Section Review 20.4

1. An inpatient with ESRD was placed on a regular schedule of hemodialysis treatments. The patient received dialysis at the hospital and was re-evaluated once by the physician for possible revision of the prescribed treatments. On re-evaluation, the physician determined no change in regimen was needed. Code for the dialysis and physician re-evaluation.

    A. 90937

    B. 90940

    C. 90945

    D. 90947

2. An 18-year-old ESRD patient is receiving dialysis services and has had two face-to-face visits with her physician within 25 days. On the 26th day, she was admitted to the hospital for inpatient management without a complete assessment. She remained in the hospital until the end of the month. Code for the physician services for the 25 days.

    A. 90969

    B. 90960

    C. 90969 x 25

    D. 90957

3. A patient with renal failure needs to begin dialysis treatments. He and his daughter both underwent complete training for managing dialysis at home.

    A. 90993

    B. 90966

    C. 90989

    D. 90997

Gastroenterology

These services are covered in the Digestive System in chapter 11. These codes describe minimally invasive and noninvasive services in the gastrointestinal tract, and generally are used for analyzing suspected conditions.

Ophthalmological Services

These services are covered in the Eye and Ocular Adnexa, Auditory Systems in chapter 15. These codes describe evaluation of the visual system such as glaucoma, cataract, and retinal disease. The codes are applicable to new or established patients and include special ophthalmological services such as fluorescein angiography, prescription, and fitting of lenses, assessment of eye muscles, and spectacle services including prosthesis service for aphakia (lens has been surgically removed and has not been replaced).

Special Otorhinolaryngologic Services

Special Otorhinolaryngologic services include evaluation of speech production and ability to express thought and identify acoustic characteristics of speech communication sounds. More information about these services is covered in chapter 15-Eye and Ocular Adnexa, Auditory Systems.

Cardiovascular Services

Cardiovascular Services in the Medicine Section include heart catheterization, stent placement, thrombectomy (removal of clot material), atherectomy (removal of plaque), and balloon angioplasty (catheter with a balloon to push back plaque) of the coronary arteries, electrocardiograms, echocardiograms (ultrasonic signals) and electrophysiological evaluations. More information about these services is covered in chapter 10-Cardiovascular System.

Noninvasive Vascular Diagnostic Studies

Noninvasive Vascular Diagnostic Studies are reported for investigation of blood flow in the head, extremities, viscera, and penis. Types of studies include duplex scans and transcranial Doppler studies.

Duplex scans are ultrasonic scanning procedures confirming patterns and direction of blood flow. The scan produces real time, two-dimensional images of arteries and veins. A different type of equipment is used to perform physiological studies, which evaluate pressure recordings.

Cerebrovascular arterial studies evaluate right and left anterior and posterior circulation territories (including both the vertebral and basilar arteries) using ultrasound technology. If two or fewer territories are evaluated, report the code for a limited study.

Practical Coding Note

Conditions indicating a reason for these studies include occlusion and stenosis of an artery, with or without infarction, arterial syndromes, transient ischemic attack, atherosclerosis, aneurysms, embolisms, thrombosis, and arterial injuries.

Section Review 20.5

1. A patient with obvious swelling in her left foot visited her physician. There was no known injury. The physician evaluated for possible blood clot before considering treatment. The physician ordered a stat duplex scan of the arteries of left leg and foot. The scan indicated no evidence of a clot.

   A. 93970

   B. 93930

   C. 93965

   D. 93926

2. A dialysis patient underwent a duplex scan of his hemodialysis access site to determine the pattern and blood flow in the arteries and veins.

   A. 93978

   B. 93965

   C. 93971

   D. 93990

3. A patient with chronic gastrointestinal disturbances underwent complete ultrasonic scanning of the intestinal vascular structure to determine if blood flow was adequate.

   A. 93982

   B. 93975

   C. 93931

   D. 93981

Pulmonary Studies

These services are covered in the Respiratory, Hemic, Lymphatic, Mediastinum, and Diaphragm Systems in chapter 9. These services include ventilator management, measurement of lung capacity, aerosol breathing treatments, and pulmonary stress testing.

Allergy and Immunology

Services in the Allergy and Clinical Immunology subsection of CPT® describe allergy testing by sensitivity tests and allergen immunotherapy services. Other related services, such as medical conferences covering use of mechanical and electronic devices (precipitators, air conditioners, air filters, humidifiers, or dehumidifiers) and climatotherapy, physical therapy, and occupational and recreational therapy, is referenced from the Evaluation and Management section of CPT®.

Allergy symptoms are produced when the patient's immune system overreacts to the introduction of foreign substances (allergens) and produces inordinate amounts of IgE (immunoglobulin E). Allergic responses may be immediate or delayed.

Immunotherapy is based on the premise that low doses of the offending allergen will bind with IgG (immunoglobulin G) and produce blocking IgG antibodies. This prevents the production of excess amounts of IgE.

A patient with suspected allergies is tested to determine which allergens are causing sensitivity. An extract is made containing the specific antigens causing a positive reaction and applied to a scratch, small puncture, or is induced intracutaneously. The site is observed for redness, swelling, and/or itching.

Codes 95004–95079 are reported for testing of persons who exhibit hypersensitivity to certain materials. Symptoms may include allergic asthma, atopic dermatitis, rhinitis, allergic conjunctivitis, and urticaria. Onset of symptoms may be seasonal.

Allergy Skin Test

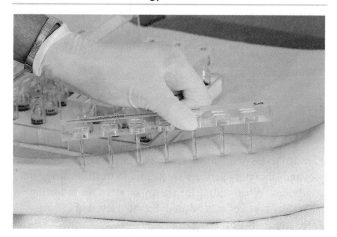

Source: LINDH/TAMPARO/POOLER/DAHL.
Delmar's Comprehensive Medical Assisting, 4E.
© 2010 Delmar Learning, a part of Cengage Learning, Inc.
Reproduced by permission. www.cengage.com/permissions

Skin tests are easy methods to detect reaction to certain substances, and may be performed by pricks or by intradermal injections. Solutions for testing may be created from ingested or inhaled materials. The test is considered positive if a reaction occurs within 15 minutes and a wheal of more than 5 mm larger than the substance appears on the skin. Select the code describing the type of test method. Codes 95004–95079 include test interpretation and report by the physician. Both interpretation and report are included in the reimbursement. If the provider does not issue a report, append modifier 52 for reduced services.

Code 95004 reports tests done with allergenic extracts, producing an immediate reaction. These types of allergy extracts include dust, plant pollen, dog dander, and molds.

Codes 95017–95018 reports sequential and incremental allergy tests. Code selection is based on whether the test is performed using venoms or drugs and biologicals. Drugs refer to pharmaceuticals used to treat diseases. For example, some patients are allergic to penicillin but must be treated with this particular drug. Immunotherapy may be used to help them tolerate necessary drug therapy.

Biologicals are drugs made from living organisms and include vaccines, serums, antitoxins, and antivenins. Examples of biologicals are diphtheria antitoxin, influenza virus vaccine, tetanus toxoid, and hepatitis B immunoglobulin. Patients suspected of being allergic to biologicals made with egg protein may be treated prior to immunization. Stinging insects inject venom into their victims when they sting. Examples of venom extract used in allergy testing include venom from wasps, yellow jackets, and hornets.

Code 95028 describes intracutaneous (intradermal) tests administered using allergenic extracts. Allergenic extracts are classified as bacterial, fungal, and viral. Bacterial extracts include tuberculin, staphage lysate, and streptokinase. Fungal extracts include blastomycin, coccidioidin, histoplasmin, candida, and trichophytin. CPT® codes for these tests include the reading of delayed reactions, usually 24–72 hours later. It is inappropriate to code an established E/M service with code 95028 unless the E/M service is performed for reasons unrelated to the allergy tests.

Code 95052 reports photo patch tests performed to identify antigens causing contact dermatitis. Photo patch tests identify antigens applied to the skin or taken internally causing a photoallergic reaction.

Patients with albinism lack normal pigment in the skin and are very light sensitive. Drugs such as tetracycline actually change light and patients taking tetracycline or a drug that produces a similar reaction to light may develop redness, swelling, or even blistering when exposed to the light. In photo testing, a patient is exposed to full spectrum ultraviolet or visible light for specified periods. Sites are checked immediately and again 24 hours later. Code 95056 describes photo tests used to diagnose patients sensitive to sunlight or artificial light.

Code 95060 reports an ophthalmic mucous membrane test. A small amount of antigen, in liquid or powder form, is applied to the lower eyelid of one eye and the eye is observed for an allergic reaction. The other eye serves as a control.

Code 95065 reports a direct nasal mucous membrane test. A nasal mucous membrane test is performed to diagnose allergic rhinitis. The allergen is applied to tiny paper discs placed directly on the mucous membranes in the nose.

Codes 95070 and 95071 describe a challenge or provocation testing of the bronchi by inhalation of different substances. These tests enable the physician to observe a patient's breathing in response to different antigens. Inhalation of antigens may be used to test for allergies to occupational gases, fumes, or dust. It is necessary to specify the antigen tested. Pulmonary function tests are integral to these procedures but may be listed separately.

Codes 95115–95199 describe the professional services of allergen immunotherapy. Codes should be selected based upon number of injections or number of stinging insect venoms.

CPT® codes 95145–95170 allow the supply of antigen to be reported as a "multiple dose vial" or a "treatment board." Treatment boards are defined by CPT® as small amounts of antigens drawn from a number of separate bottles containing different antigens. The mixture is injected into the patient. Approximately 40–50 percent of allergists use this method rather than multiple dose vials.

Code 95165 reports supervision and provision of single or multiple antigens in multidose vials or a treatment board for immunotherapy. The number of doses should be specified.

Code 95170 reports whole body extract of biting insect or arthropods. With this code, the number of doses should be specified.

If a patient is allergic to a drug, vaccine, or other substance needed to combat a life-threatening illness, a rapid desensitization procedure may prove to be a life-saving measure. The patient is given small doses of a desensitizing agent (such as insulin, penicillin, or horse serum) gradually increased over a relatively short period of time.

The desensitization time period may range from four to 24 hours while the patient is carefully monitored for a serious reaction. If a serious reaction does occur, epinephrine is immediately administered and then treatment is slowly resumed. Insulin is used to treat diabetes, and penicillin is an antibiotic used to treat many bacterial infections. Patients may also be allergic to horse serum, which is used to prepare various vaccines, or snake antivenin. The number of hours spent providing this service should be reported in column G of the CMS-1500 form.

Code 95180 should be reported for rapid desensitization, which involves injecting an extract of the allergen in gradually increasing doses. This treatment must be done under well-controlled conditions and may be used when the allergens are difficult to avoid or control.

ICD-9-CM Application

In ICD-9-CM the adverse effect codes do not indicate if this is the patient's initial encounter, subsequent encounter, or sequalae.

Example

Patient is in the ED due to anaphylactic shock from eating peanuts.

ICD-10-CM

In the Index to Diseases and Injuries, look for Anaphylactic/shock or reaction - *see* Shock, anaphylactic.

Shock/anaphylactic/due to food/peanuts T78.01-. In the Tabular List, a seventh character is required. Because this is an ED visit, the seventh character A would be appended to indicate the initial encounter. The ICD-10-CM code is five characters which requires a dummy placeholder (X) to keep the seventh character in the seventh position.

T78.01XA Anaphylactic reaction due to peanuts, initial encounter

ICD-9-CM

In the Index to Diseases, look for Anaphylactic reaction or shock/food/peanuts 995.61.

995.61 Anaphylactic reaction due to peanuts

Related Laboratory Services

Elevated levels of IgE are noted in patients suffering from allergies and laboratory services are helpful in treating allergenic conditions. When coding for allergy services, the following laboratory services may be used. Elevated levels of IgE are noted in patients suffering from allergies.

Code 86003 reports allergen-specific IgE; quantitative or semi-quantitative, each allergen. Code 86005 reports an allergen-specific IgE; qualitative, multiallergen screen; by dipstick, paddle, or disk. Use code 82785 to report gamma globulin; IgE; quantitative.

Practical Coding Note

CMS does not allow Medicare payment for the complete service, CPT® codes 95120–95134. Providers should code for the injection, and the provision of the extract should be reported to Medicare separately using other codes as described.

CPT® codes 95115 or 95117 should be used for the injection component.

One of the preparation codes, 95145, 95146, 95147, 95148, 95149, 95165, or 95170, should be used to report the supply component.

CPT® code 95144 should not be used when describing a complete service. Medicare will only allow payment for this code if the provider preparing the single dose vial is a different provider than the one providing the injection service. Medicare calculates payment by multiplying the per dose allowance by the number of doses for which you code. When submitting a claim to Medicare, specify the number of doses in the unit's field of the CMS-1500 form.

Example

If the allergist prepared a multidose vial of antigens (eg, eight doses) and only injects one dose, code the eight doses of antigen and one injection service. When the remaining doses are injected, only the injection services should be coded.

Section Review 20.6

1. A patient with chronic skin rashes on the hands visits an allergist for evaluation and receives 12 percutaneous scratch tests with various household products.

   A. 95004 x 12

   B. 95004

   C. 95144

   D. 95044 x 12

2. A patient suffers from nasal congestion, rhinitis, and facial swelling after being stung by honeybees and undergoes allergen immunotherapy. The physician provides a single injection of bee venom.

   A. 95120

   B. 95144

   C. 95130

   D. 95145

3. A patient exhibits severe allergic reaction to peanuts. An allergist prepares and provides four vials of single dose antigens for the patient to inject if he accidently ingests peanut products.

   A. 95145 x 4

   B. 95144 x 4

   C. 95120 x 4

   D. 95170 x 4

Endocrinology

These services are covered in the Endocrine and Nervous System in chapter 14. Services include continuous monitoring of glucose over a 72-hour period.

Neurology and Neuromuscular Procedures

These services are covered in the Endocrine and Nervous System in chapter 14. Services include sleep studies, electroencephalography (brain function), electromyography (interpretation of electrical signals from muscles), nervous system testing, analysis and programming of neurostimulators, and motion analysis. Refer to Appendix J in the CPT® codebook for information about sensory, motor, and mixed nerves.

Medical Genetics and Genetic Counseling Services

Code 96040 describes services provided by a qualified genetic counselor to determine the genetic risk of hereditary diseases. It is a time-based code to be reported for each 30 minutes face-to-face time with the patient and/or family. The provider must document the time spent in the encounter to report the correct number of units. The counselor typically will obtain an extensive family history, and the service will include review of medical data. The counselor may engage in extensive research of certain syndromes and other diseases to determine the potential risk.

Parents who have an impaired child often desire to determine the possible risks of other offspring and may arrange genetic counseling. Laboratory studies may be performed such as analysis of chromosomes, metabolic, muscular, and blood factor disorders. Patients may also request genetic testing to investigate their risk for certain neoplastic diseases.

Practical Coding Note

Coders who work in molecular laboratories involved in genetic testing should refer to the Genetic Testing modifiers located in Appendix I of the CPT® codebook.

Section Review 20.7

1. A nurse practitioner who is a trained genetic counselor met with a couple and their child who has Duchenne's muscular dystrophy. The couple is considering another child but wants to know the potential risk of the disorder in other children. The session lasted 1.5 hours.

    A. 96040

    B. 96040 x 4

    C. 96040 x 2

    D. 96040 x 3

Central Nervous System Assessments/Tests

Psychological services (96101–96127) include psychological testing for neuro-cognitive and mental status. Health and Behavior Assessment interventions (96150–96155) focus on cognitive, social, and behavior factors, with a goal of prevention or improvement of the patient's physical health problems. Coding for these services is determined by the time documented by the provider and if the session is performed for an individual, in a group, or in the presence of family.

Referrals for psychological testing may be generated through physicians, school counselors, and social service programs.

Practical Coding Note

Some codes in the psychology section are time-based codes. The practitioner should document the time to allow for correct reporting of the service. Payers may require modifier AH be appended to the claim to indicate a Clinical Psychologist, or modifier AJ to indicate a Clinical Social Worker as the provider of service.

Section Review 20.8

1. A patient needs a renal transplant. The patient has been on dialysis and is awaiting a suitable donor. A clinical psychologist meets with the patient to assess the patient's ability to comply with the requirements and drug regimen if a donor match is found. The session lasts 2 hours.

    A. 96152 x 2

    B. 96150 x 8

    C. 96154 x 8

    D. 96155 x 5

2. A 4-year-old has not reached the expected developmental milestones for her age group. She was referred by her pediatrician for extensive developmental testing. The psychologist initiated multiple function studies, using standardized instruments and reported the results to her pediatrician.

    A. 96118

    B. 96125

    C. 96111

    D. 96120

3. A child displayed emotional outbursts, inability to interact appropriately with peers and his teacher, and was not effective in grasping lessons deemed suitable for his age. The school counselor requested psychological testing to determine if the child had been placed in classes appropriate to his abilities. Testing was administered by a clinical psychologist who spent 10 hours face-to-face with the patient, and 3 hours preparing the report of the results.

    A. 96103

    B. 96102

    C. 96110

    D. 96101 x 13

Hydration, Therapeutic, Prophylactic, Diagnostic Injections/Infusions and Chemotherapy, Highly Complex Drugs or Highly Complex Biologic Agent Administration

Hydration

Codes 96360–96361 are reported for hydration administration. These are time-based codes. The infusion consists of pre-packaged fluid and electrolytes. These codes are not to be used for infusion of other substances. The scope of the physician work involves development of the treatment and supervision of the staff.

Hydration codes should not be reported separately if the fluid is used solely to facilitate administration of other drugs, such as chemotherapy. The coder should review the record to determine if the fluids were delivered to a dehydrated patient who needed hydration therapy.

The start and stop times for the infusion, as well as the agent, will be recorded in the nurse's notes for guidance in selecting the appropriate code(s). If the administration occurs in the facility, the physician should not report these codes. The solution should be reported in addition to the administration charge using a HCPCS Level II code.

Non-Chemotherapy Complex Drugs and Substances

Codes 96365–96371 are reported for the injection and infusion of complex non-chemotherapy drugs and substances. These codes are very specific as to time, technique, substances added during the infusion time, and additional set-up and establishment of a new infusion. They should not be reported by a physician when performed in a facility setting.

If a different type of administration is used, report it as subsequent, even if it is the first service from the infusion group.

Example: Initial infusion of 1 hour, different drug administered by IV push; report the IV push as a subsequent service. When several techniques or drugs are given, always determine the primary service. Chemotherapy is primary to nonchemotherapy infusion, which is primary to hydration.

Do not report the add-on code for additional hour of time unless at least 31 additional minutes are utilized.

If multiple drugs are infusing at the same time through the same IV line, they are considered concurrent. Concurrent infusions may be reported only once per patient encounter unless protocol dictates that two separate IV lines must be used. If infusion of a different drug through the same access site begins after the completion of the initial infusion, a sequential infusion is reported. Clinical justification for subsequent rather than concurrent should be clearly stated in the documentation.

Chemotherapy

Codes 96401–96425 are reported for chemotherapy administration by infusion, IV push, or injection. The codes are specific as to time, technique, and additional substances added during the administration. These substances are prepared specifically for the patient and require advanced staff training to manage the administration. Significant patient risk is a consideration for this service. The substance is reported in addition to the administration using the appropriate HCPCS Level II code(s). Injectable chemotherapy drugs are located in the J9xxx range.

Codes 96440–96549 are reported for services other than standard infusion/injection techniques.

When a thoracentesis is performed and the chemotherapy is delivered into the pleural cavity, code 96440 is reported. Thoracentesis is included in this code.

Report code 96446 when peritoneocentesis is performed and the chemotherapy is delivered into the peritoneal cavity. Peritoneocentesis is included in this code.

Report code 96450 when chemotherapy is delivered into the central nervous system, for example, by intrathecal technique. This code includes spinal puncture.

If a ventricular reservoir has been implanted for chemotherapy administration into the subarachnoid or intraventricular areas, report code 96542.

Code 96549 is reported for an unlisted chemotherapy procedure.

For refilling or maintenance of the implanted reservoir, report code 96522. Vascular access devices frequently become clogged when in place over a period of time. For irrigation of an access device that has been implanted for the purpose of drug delivery, report code 96523 if no other services are performed on that day. If a significant, separately identifiable E/M service is performed on the same day, it may be reported separately by using the appropriate E/M code and appending modifier 25.

Practical Coding Note

If the infusion time is 15 minutes or less, IV push should be reported as the technique. These infusion services include use of local anesthesia, start of the IV, access to indwelling IV, access to port or catheter, end of procedure flush and standard tubing, supplies, and syringes.

When multiple substances are delivered, only one initial administration code is reported unless a separate IV site is required. For example, an ICU patient requires two lines. A central line is placed for a Dopamine drip for hypotension and another line is required for antibiotics. Do not report the add-on code for an additional hour of time unless at least 31 additional minutes are utilized. If multiple drugs are mixed in the same bag, report one administration code unless the time extends to at least 1 hour, 31 minutes. The drugs are separately reportable.

When multiple types of infusions are reported, an established hierarchy should be utilized. For physician reporting, report the initial service as the primary reason for the encounter. For facility reporting, chemotherapy is reported primary to therapeutic, prophylactic, and diagnostic delivery, which is primary to hydration. Infusions are primary to IV push, which is primary to injections.

Patients receiving chemotherapy will have a malignancy. Utilize the Neoplasm Table in ICD-10-CM for the correct site for reporting neoplasms. The primary site will be the origin of the cancer. Cancers metastasized to secondary sites are reported with the secondary category. There may be more than one secondary site. If the physician clinically is unable to determine the origin of the cancer, report C80.1 as the primary site (although this code should rarely be used). Blood cancers, such as leukemia and lymphoma, will be located in the index instead of the Neoplasm Table.

Section Review 20.9

1. A patient presented with vomiting and diarrhea for the past three days. The physician determined the patient is dehydrated and ordered infusion of hydration fluids to run for two hours.

   A. 96360, 96361

   B. 96361 x 2

   C. 96360, 96361 x 2

   D. 96360 x 2

2. A patient has an implanted intravenous pump for the purpose of prescribed drug delivery at preset intervals. The patient is seen by the physician who provides maintenance and refills the pump with the medication.

   A. 96523

   B. 96522

   C. 96521

   D. 95990

3. A cancer patient will receive chemotherapy by intrathecal delivery. A spinal puncture will be necessary to accommodate the catheter.

    A. 96523

    B. 96413

    C. 96420

    D. 96450

Photodynamic Therapy

This service is covered in the Integumentary System in chapter 7. These services include application of light to destroy abnormal tissue.

Special Dermatological Procedures

These procedures are covered in the Integumentary System in chapter 7. These services include treatment of dermatitis and laser ablation of psoriasis.

Physical Medicine and Rehabilitation

Codes 97001–97546 are reported for this service. The services are intended to improve functional loss, and commonly are prescribed for patients who have been affected by stroke, amputation, major cardiac events, and hip fractures. The functionality of younger patients may be fully restored. In older patients, therapy may be prescribed with a goal of being able to perform activities of daily living. Response to therapy is often achieved more quickly with younger patients.

The provider will develop an initial treatment plan outlining the problem(s), goals, modalities to be used, and projected time to reach the goal. The patient is referred to a therapy center for implementation of the therapy. The procedures are performed by qualified physical, occupational, and speech therapists. The referring provider should review the progress each 30 days. If satisfactory progress is not noted, the provider likely either will modify or discontinue the therapy. Although a provider may be on site at the therapy center to provide supervision and oversight, the referring provider will be responsible for monitoring the patient's progress and prescribing changes to the treatment plan. Physical therapists may be independent practitioners and bill for services under their own provider number or may work incident to a physician. Medicare rules for billing and payment of therapy services may be different from CPT® information. Refer to the CMS website under therapy services for CMS guidelines: www.cms.hhs.gov.

Evaluation and Re-evaluation

Codes 97001–97006 are reported by the therapist for the initial evaluation and re-evaluation of a patient for physical therapy, occupational therapy, or athletic training.

Documentation requirements include:

- Physician's referral and treatment recommendations
- Plan of treatment including measurable objective information
- Medicare requires the attending physician to see the patient at least once every 30 days
- Noting any changes in a patient's clinical status since the last visit
- Modalities and procedures performed (including time) and who performed them (direct supervision vs. nondirect supervision)
- Patient improvement and/or tolerance to treatment
- Patient education
- Expected outcome of treatment
- Estimated future treatment

Modalities

Supervised—Codes 97010–97028 are modalities not requiring one-on-one contact by the therapist. These modalities include hot or cold packs, traction, vasopneumatic devices, paraffin bath, whirlpool, diathermy, infrared, ultraviolet, and some types of electric stimulation. More than one modality may be utilized during the therapy session. Modifier 51 should not be appended for codes 97001–97755. Vasopneumatic devices apply pressure to reduce swelling. Diathermy is deep dry heat with high frequency current to reduce pain and increase movement.

Constant Attendance—Codes 97032–97039 are modalities requiring one-on-one (constant attendance) patient contact by the therapist. These modalities include contrast baths, Hubbard tank, ultrasound, manual electric stimulation, and iontophoresis (introduction of ions into the tissue by electricity). These codes are reported for each 15-minute increment and require provider documentation of time for correct reporting of units. A Hubbard tank is a large sized tank that is used for underwater exercises. The patient will be fully immersed in the tank. The purpose of a contrast bath is to stimulate blood circulation by alternately spraying the feet and legs with warm and cold water for about one minute each.

Therapeutic Procedures—Codes 97110–97546 are reported for therapeutic procedures performed to improve function and require one-on-one interaction by the provider. These services involve balance, coordination, exercise, aquatic therapy, improvement of cognitive functions, manual manipulation, and sensory processing. Code 97542 is reported for fitting and training of wheelchair use. Codes 97545 and 97546 are reported for work conditioning. Many of these codes are reported per 15-minute increments and require provider documentation of time for correct reporting of units. Code 97150 is reported for group therapy of two or more patients.

Active Wound Care Management—Codes 97597–97610 are reported for wound care management. Necrotic tissue must be removed to encourage healing of a wound. The provider must document the technique used to remove the tissue and the surface area of the wound. Services are reported for each session and require one-on-one interaction by the provider. Removal by debridement is reported with codes 97597–97602. Tissue removal by vacuum (negative pressure therapy) is reported with 97605–97608. Non-physicians usually perform these procedures. Surgical debridement services are reported with 11040–11047. Do not report 97597–97602 with 11040–11047.

Tests and Measurements—Codes 97750–97755 are reported for measurements and tests. Code 97750 is for the reporting of performance measurement. When assistive technology is used to improve patient functionality, 97755 is reported. Examples of assistive technology include modification of keyboards, screen magnifiers, and Braille technology.

Orthotic Management and Prosthetic Management—Codes 97760–97762 are reported for management of prosthetics and orthotics. 97761 is reported for patient training in the use of an extremity prosthesis.

Practical Coding Note

Orthotic and prosthetic products are custom-made for the patient and reported separately using HCPCS Level II codes L0112–L9900. Modifiers used in therapy are: GN *Speech/language therapy*, GO *Occupational therapy*, and GP *Physical therapy*. Medicare rules governing coverage and payment of therapy services may be different from CPT®. Refer to the Medicare section under Billing for Therapy at www.cms.hhs.gov.

Section Review 20.10

1. A patient sustained a severe ankle sprain playing basketball. The ankle was still stiff without complete range of motion. The physician referred the patient for physical therapy. Prior to treatment, the therapist evaluated the patient and determined a treatment plan. The patient had a one-hour therapy on the same day.

   A. 97001-GP, 97110-GP x 4

   B. 97002-GP, 97112-GP x 4

   C. 97110-GP x 4

   D. 97530-GP

2. A patient underwent a knee arthroplasty (joint replacement) and requires physical therapy to learn to walk with the artificial joint. The therapist evaluates the patient, and initiates therapeutic exercises and gait training. The exercises are for 45 minutes and the gait training is 15 minutes at this session.

   A. 97001-GP, 97110-GP, 97116-GP

   B. 97002-GP, 97116-GP

   C. 97001-GP, 97110-GP X 3, 97116-GP

   D. 97001-GP, 97116-GP

3.   A patient has a collapsed arch on her left foot. The physician prescribed a custom orthotic insert to be worn inside the patient's shoe to support the collapsed arch. The patient visits the physician to receive the orthotic and is instructed how to position it inside the shoe for maximum results. The patient walks around the treatment room and hallway to determine if there is a comfortable fit. The session lasted 15 minutes.

   A. 97760

   B. 97761

   C. 97762

   D. 97116

Medical Nutritional Therapy

Codes 97802–97804 are reported for special dietary assessments for patients requiring special dietary management. Examples may include patients with diabetes, renal failure, and vitamin or electrolyte deficiencies. Codes 97802 and 97803 are reported for face-to-face interaction with the patient and are reported in 15-minute increments. Code 97804 is reported for a group session with two or more participants and is reported in 30-minute increments. The provider reports the time of the encounter to allow for correct coding of the service.

Practical Coding Note

Enteral and parenteral therapy products are reported separately with HCPCS Level II codes B4034–B9999.

Section Review 20.11

1.   An anorexic patient is experiencing signs of severe dietary deficiency and electrolyte imbalance. She will need medical nutrition therapy to treat these symptoms. The provider spent 30 minutes with the patient to discuss the seriousness of her eating disorder and the necessity of nutrition therapy. This is the initial assessment.

   A. 97804

   B. 97802

   C. 97802 x 2

   D. 97803 x 2

Acupuncture

Codes 97810–97814 are reported for acupuncture services. These services involve placement of needles, with or without electric stimulation. Typically, the procedure is performed for patients experiencing pain. Needles are inserted at specific body sites, which may be far from the pain site. A needle will be manipulated intermittently and rapidly. An electrical current also may be applied. The provider is face-to-face with the patient.

Services are reported in 15-minute increments. Code 97810 is reported for use of one or more needles without electrical stimulation. Code 97811 is an add-on code for each additional 15-minute increment with re-insertion of needle(s). Code 97813 is reported when electric stimulation is used; 97814 is an add-on code and is reported with electric stimulation, each additional 15-minute increment, and with re-insertion of needle(s). The provider must document the time of the encounter to correctly code the service.

Practical Coding Note

If a separate E/M service is provided at the same encounter, and is significantly outside the normal pre and post procedure work, it may be additionally reported using modifier 25. Do not include the time of the acupuncture service in the E/M service.

Section Review 20.12

1. A patient with a long history of migraine headaches decides to try acupuncture in an attempt to reduce the headache pain. The provider used acupuncture with electrical stimulation during a 15-minute face-to-face encounter with the patient.

   A. 97810

   B. 97810, 97811

   C. 97813

   D. 97814

Osteopathic Manipulative Treatment

This service involves the provider (Osteopathic Physician, DO) using hands to move muscles and joints and includes stretching, gentle pressure, and resistance. The purpose is to improve pain, promote healing, and increase mobility.

Codes 98925–98929 are reported for application of manual manipulation to improve somatic and related disorders. The codes are reported by the number of body regions manipulated, and may be performed by several different methods. Typically, the body regions are head, cervical, thoracic, lumbar, sacral, pelvic regions, all extremities, rib cage, abdominal, and viscera regions.

Practical Coding Note

If a separate E/M service is provided at the same encounter, and is significantly outside the normal pre-and post-procedure work, it is additionally reported using modifier 25. Services may be related to the symptoms for which the osteopathic manipulative treatment (OMT) was provided. Diagnosis codes may be related to nerve disorders, arthropathy, osteoarthrosis, inflammation, intervertebral disc disorders, injuries to nerves, and other musculoskeletal disorders.

Section Review 20.13

1. A patient with polyneuropathy in the feet underwent osteopathic manipulation to improve tingling and numbness sensations. The provider manipulated both feet during the session.

   A. 98926

   B. 98925

   C. 98925, 98926

   D. 98929

Chiropractic Manipulative Treatment

Codes 98940–98943 are reported for chiropractic services (CMT). Services typically are performed in the spinal region, but may include the extremities and abdominal region. Codes are reported per number of regions manipulated, with 98940–98942 reported specifically for spinal manipulation. Code 98943 is reported for extraspinal manipulation.

There are five spinal regions and five extraspinal regions that may be referred to in the provider notes. The spinal regions are cervical, thoracic, lumbar, sacral, and pelvic. The extraspinal regions are head, all extremities, rib cage, and abdomen.

Practical Coding Note

Diagnosis codes are related to neuropathy, spinal lesions, osteoarthrosis, spondylosis, inflammation, intervertebral disc disorders, spinal stenosis, scoliosis, injuries and muscle spasms. If the diagnosis describes an acute condition, include modifier AT *Acute treatment* on the service line. Medicare rules governing chiropractic services may be found at www.cms.hhs.gov.

Section Review 20.14

1. A patient presented with a complaint of continuing left shoulder pain after falling from her patio onto a wooden step. No fracture was identified at the time of the fall. After assessing the patient, the chiropractor manipulated the shoulder region.

    A. 98943

    B. 98940

    C. 98943, 98940

    D. 98942

2. A patient continued to have low back pain after lifting a heavy bin while cleaning the basement. The chiropractor manipulated both the lumbar and sacral areas.

    A. 98941

    B. 98943

    C. 98940

    D. 98942

3. A patient received manipulations in the cervical, thoracic, and lumbar spine by a chiropractor.

    A. 98941

    B. 98940

    C. 98943

    D. 98940 x 2

Education and Training
for Patient Self-Management

Codes 98960–98962 are reported for patient self-management training and education when prescribed by a physician. The service will be provided by a nonphysician practitioner who is qualified to instruct a standardized program for treatment of confirmed illness or disease, or to delay comorbidity. The purpose of the service is to teach the patient how to self-manage his or her health problems, such as diabetes.

Training and education will be applicable to the condition(s) identified by the appropriate diagnosis code(s). Codes will be selected based on the number of patients. Caregivers may be included in the sessions. The codes are reportable in 30-minute increments and require the provider to document the time of the encounter.

Section Review 20.15

1. A registered dietician provided diabetes management education to seven patients for 90 minutes.

   A. 99078

   B. 98961

   C. 98960 x 3

   D. 98962 x 3

2. A diabetic patient who has not been successful with managing his diet meets personally with a registered dietician for one hour to develop a diet plan.

   A. 98961

   B. 98960 x 2

   C. 98961 x 2

   D. 98962

Non Face-to-Face Nonphysician Services

Telephone Services

Qualified nonphysician practitioners providing telephone services to an established patient, parent, or guardian report codes 98966–98968. If the telephone discussion results in a determination to see the patient within 24 hours or at the next available urgent appointment, the code is not reported. In lieu of reporting the code, the telephone service is considered a part of the pre-work for the upcoming encounter. The codes may be billed if the call does not result in an urgent appointment and does not relate to an assessment and/or management service within the past seven days.

Codes are selected by the time of the call, which must be documented by the provider. Code 98966 is billed for a discussion of 5–10 minutes. Code 98967 is billed for a discussion of 11–20 minutes. Code 98968 is billed for a discussion of 21–30 minutes.

Practical Coding Note

Coverage and reimbursement for codes 98966–98968 are payer specific. Discuss with your payer the circumstances of coverage. Codes 99441–99443 should be reported if a physician provides the telephone service. Refer to E/M Services in chapter 19 for additional information.

Online Medical Evaluation

Code 98969 is reported for online medical evaluation using Internet or other electronic communication modes to answer an established patient's online inquiry. Service may include parent or guardian inquiry. The service is reported by a qualified nonphysician practitioner once per seven-day period, per provider, for the same episode of care. The response must be timely and the ability to store the communication is required. If services are provided within seven days or within the post-operative period of a previously completed procedure, the service is considered to be covered by the previous encounter. It is expected that the communication will include a total of telephone calls, laboratory orders, and prescription management that relate to the online patient encounter.

Practical Coding Note

Coverage and reimbursement for code 98969 is payer specific. Discuss with your payer the circumstances of coverage. Code 99444 is reported if a physician provides the online service.

Section Review 20.16

1. A patient called her physician to discuss the refill of a current prescription. She spoke with the registered nurse who discussed the patient's current status and advised that the prescription would be called into her pharmacy. The call lasted 12 minutes.

   A. 98966

   B. 98968

   C. 99442

   D. 98967

2. A patient in a rural setting with limited travel resources visited his physician for a physical examination. Lab work was done. The physician advised the patient that if the results were negative, he did not need to return to the office. The nurse emailed the patient that the results were negative, and the patient did not need to return for six months unless new symptoms appeared. One month later, the patient emailed the office with a request to change his current medication to a less-expensive generic version. The nurse answered the email advising one of his medications could be changed to a generic version, and refills would be called to the pharmacy as needed. She also responded to several questions the patient had about his general health conditions. She spent 25 minutes entering this information.

   A. 98966

   B. 99444

   C. 98968

   D. 98969

Special Services, Procedures and Reports

Codes 99000–99091 are miscellaneous codes involving special services, procedures and reports. They are reported by physicians or other qualified healthcare professional to identify a supplemental component of a primary service.

Physicians often contract with an independent laboratory to test specimens and provide reports. Code 99000 is reported for transfer of a laboratory specimen from a physician office to a laboratory. Code 99001 is reported for transfer of a specimen from the patient in a site other than a physician office.

When a physician order involves a service related to custom-made devices, such as prosthetics and orthotics and the device is manufactured at an outside vendor, report code 99002. These items will need to be fitted and adjusted by the physician or other qualified care professional and will require delivery to the physician office.

Report code 99024 for a related post-operative visit during the global period of a procedure to indicate the E/M service provided. This code is not separately payable, but considered a component of the procedure. Refer to the Surgery Guidelines section for a description of the "surgical package."

Report codes 99026 and 99027 for mandated hospital on-call personnel. These codes typically are not reimbursed by the payer, but are required by certain hospital personnel (for example, special procedures radiology technicians, surgery, anesthesia, and post-anesthesia recovery staff). The codes are reported per hour for on-call status.

Practical Coding Note

Do not report codes 99026 and 99027 for physician stand-by services. Refer to the E/M Services in chapter 19 for information about physician stand-by.

Codes 99050–99060 are reported for patient encounters outside the normal posted business hours or special circumstances at the request of the patient. These codes are reported in addition to the basic service. Report code 99050 for services provided in the office that are outside the normal posted hours or when the office is normally closed, for example, holidays and weekends.

If the practice maintains evening, weekend, or holiday hours, report code 99051 for patients seen during these times. Report code 99053 for services provided at a 24-hour location between 10 pm and 8 am.

If a service is normally provided in the office, but is provided outside the office at the request of the patient, report code 99056.

Report code 99058 for in the office emergency services that are a disruption to the office schedule.

Report code 99060 for out of the office emergency services that are a disruption to the office schedule.

Practical Coding Note

Coverage and reimbursement for codes 99050–99060 are payer specific. Discuss the circumstances of coverage with your payer.

Code 99070 is reported for supplies provided by the physician and other qualified healthcare professional not usually included in an office visit. Items may include sterile trays, drugs, vaccines, and immune globulins. They may be reported separately if not considered integral to a procedure. Reimbursement may be on an acquisition cost basis.

Practical Coding Note

Eyeglasses are not included in 99070. Refer to the HCPCS Level II codes for specific eyeglasses codes. Some payers (Medicare and possibly others) will require individual listing of the items/drugs using HCPCS Level II codes instead of 99070. Query your payer for billing instructions.

Code 99071 is reported for physician or other qualified healthcare professional cost of educational materials that are dispensed to the patient for specific educational information.

Code 99075 is reported for time the physician spends providing medical testimony.

Code 99078 is reported for group educational sessions when conducted by a physician or other qualified healthcare professional trained by education, licensure/regulation when relevant.

Code 99080 is reported for completion of forms and reports exceeding usual and standard information.

Code 99082 is reported for unusual travel by a physician, for example, accompanying a patient.

Code 99090 is reported for analyzing stored data in a computerized mode.

Code 99091 is reported for interpretation of data stored in a digital mode and transmitted to the physician or qualified healthcare professional trained by education, licensure/regulation when relevant. Transmission may be by the patient or caregiver. The provider must spend at least 30 minutes to report this code. Refer to Evaluation & Management in chapter 19 for additional information about these services.

Practical Coding Note

Coverage and reimbursement for codes 99071–99091 are payer specific. Discuss with your payer the circumstances of coverage.

Section Review 20.17

1. A physician provided medical testimony in a suspicious death case.

   A. 99090

   B. 99080

   C. 99056

   D. 99075

2. A hospital must provide an on call radiology technician trained in MRI services for emergent cases presenting to the emergency department from 6 pm until 7 am. The technician is required to return to the hospital within 40 minutes of notification.

   A. 99060

   B. 99027 x 13

   C. 99026 x 13

   D. 99058

3. An independent laboratory charges a fee to transport medical specimens from physicians' offices to the laboratory for testing.

    A. 99000
    B. 99056
    C. 99050
    D. 99002

4. A physician agreed to meet a patient at the office on Sunday afternoon to assess a repeat problem. Special equipment in the physician office is needed to evaluate the condition. Normal office hours are Monday–Friday.

    A. 99058
    B. 99056
    C. 99060
    D. 99050

Qualifying Circumstances for Anesthesia

These services are covered in Anesthesia Services in chapter 16. These codes describe certain circumstances increasing the risk of anesthesia services, such as extreme age, emergent life-threatening situations, and reduction of body temperature (hypothermia) or blood pressure (controlled hypotension). They are add-on codes and may only be reported with the primary anesthesia code.

Moderate (Conscious) Sedation

These services are covered in Anesthesia Services in chapter 16. These services describe a drug-induced depression of consciousness. Face-to-face attendance is required and the patient must be able to respond to commands.

Other Services and Procedures

Codes 99170–99199 are reported for certain specified miscellaneous services. Code 99170 is reported for an anogenital magnified examination of a child that includes image recording when performed. This procedure is performed when there is suspicion of trauma. The examination is initiated in cases of suspected penetrating sexual abuse. Anogenital trauma typically heals very quickly and may not be determined easily.

Practical Coding Note

Diagnosis codes may be related to injuries in the rectal and/or genital area and suspected adult or child abuse. If an examination is performed with no confirmation of diagnosis, report Z04.41 Encounter for examination and observation following alleged adult rape (suspected adult rape, ruled out; adult sexual abuse, ruled out) or Z04.42 Encounter for examination and observation following alleged child rape (suspected child rape, ruled out, suspected child sexual abuse, ruled out).

Code 99172 is reported for determination of visual acuity, ocular alignment, color vision, and visual field. The service must use graduated visual acuity stimuli allowing a quantitative estimate of visual acuity (sharpness of vision). Code 99173 is reported for a screening test of visual acuity.

Practical Coding Note

Do not report codes 99172 and 99173 if a general ophthalmological service or an E/M of the eye is performed. If an additional E/M service is performed unrelated to these tests, it may be reported separately using modifier 25. Diagnosis codes supporting these services include neoplasms, migraine headaches, detached retina, diabetic retinopathy, macular degeneration, retinal hemorrhage, glaucoma, color deficiency, night blindness, and other specified ocular disorders.

Code 99174 is reported for bilateral instrument based ocular screening. Ocular photoscreening is a diagnostic tool for testing preverbal children and children with developmental disorders for amblyogenic factors, such as strabismus, media opacities, and severe refractive disorders. The test only requires that the patient focus on a target in a darkened room long enough for a specialized camera or video system to capture images of the papillary reflexes and red reflexes. The code includes remote analysis and a report.

Practical Coding Note

Do not report 99174 with 92002–92014, 99172, and 99173. Diagnosis codes supporting this service will be in the H52-H53 range.

Code 99175 is reported for administration of ipecac or similar material for initiation of emesis. The provider will observe the patient until the stomach has emptied. The purpose of the service is to eliminate stomach contents when the patient has ingested a poisonous or toxic substance.

Practical Coding Note

Refer to the Table of Drugs and Chemicals in the ICD-10-CM codebook for diagnosis code information.

Code 99183 is reported for hyperbaric oxygen therapy when supervised and attended by a physician or other qualified healthcare professional. Procedures such a wound debridement and/or E/M services may be reported separately when provided during a hyperbaric oxygen therapy session in a dedicated treatment facility.

Practical Coding Note

Hyperbaric oxygen therapy may be utilized for infections, embolism, thrombosis, osteomyelitis, necrotizing fasciitis, vascular and crushing injuries, toxic effect of gasses, effect of high altitude, and complications of reattached limbs.

Code 99190–99192 is reported for the operation of a pump with oxygenator or heat exchanger, and includes assembly and operation of the unit. Codes are selected based on time.

Practical Coding Note

Appropriate diagnosis codes are related to cardiac failure in category I50. They also may be reported for cardiogenic shock.

Section Review 20.18

1. A patient ingested a toxic substance and was administered ipecac in the Emergency Department to empty the stomach.

   A. 99195

   B. 43755

   C. 99199

   D. 99175

2. A physician performed a magnified anogenital examination on a young child to determine if assault had occurred.

   A. 99175

   B. 99170

   C. 99174

   D. 99195

Home Health Procedures and Services

Codes 99500–99602 are reported by nonphysician practitioners who provide services in a home setting. Home setting is defined as the environment in which the patient resides and may include assisted living facilities, group homes, and custodial care facilities. Each code is specific to the service rendered.

If a significant, separately identifiable E/M service is provided over and above the service described in the code, the E/M may be separately reported using modifier 25 if the provider is authorized to report E/M codes.

Code 99500 is reported for home visit for prenatal services or pregnant, patient with pregnancy complications. The assessments are to determine the health of the mother and fetus. Applicable diagnosis codes are selected from ICD-10-CM chapter 15—Complications of Pregnancy, Childbirth, and the Puerperium.

Practical Coding Note

Diagnosis codes can be in category O10 if a condition has been confirmed.

Code 99501 is reported for home visit for postnatal follow-up care. During the follow-up visit, the mother is carefully assessed to make certain she is healthy and able to take care of her baby. She is given information about breast feeding, reproductive health and contraception, as well as evaluated for indications of post partum depression and timely identification of other potential problems.

Practical Coding Note

Diagnosis codes are reported from Z39 range.

Code 99502 is reported for home care assessment of a newborn. Services include assessment of maternal/family risk factors, home and social environment, perinatal history, infant nutrition, basic care/caregiver skills, parenting skills, newborn assessment, resources, and referrals.

Practical Coding Note

A diagnosis code Z00.110 or Z00.111 is reported for this service.

Code 99503 is reported for home care management of respiratory conditions, including evaluation of apnea, oxygen management, and changes in medication such as bronchodilators. The service includes inspecting and cleaning equipment, evaluation of the home environment, and educating patients about managing their diseases, medication, and equipment.

Practical Coding Note

Review diagnosis codes related to respiratory neoplasms, cystic fibrosis, obstructive bronchitis, asthma, pneumonia, and other pulmonary conditions.

Code 99504 is reported for home care management of a ventilator. The service includes regular assessments of equipment, checking the patient's breathing, and adjusting the setting on

the ventilator (oxygen, carbon dioxide, and pH level) per physician orders.

Practical Coding Note

Diagnosis codes are reported in the J80, J81.0, J82, J84, J96, or P19, P22, P91 for newborns .

Code 99505 is reported for home care of ostomies and stomas. The service includes evaluation of the site, troubleshooting for skin or stoma problems, any required refitting or resizing due to body or lifestyle changes, and responding to patient's questions.

Practical Coding Note

Diagnosis code should be reported in category Z43 , along with the condition that required the ostomy/stoma.

Code 99506 is reported for home visit for intramuscular injections. Diagnosis codes are determined by the condition as stated by the physician plan of care. Medications may be reported with appropriate HCPCS Level II code, in addition to the injection administration code.

Code 99507 is reported for home care visit for catheter maintenance. The service will vary depending on the type, location, and reason for the catheter. The nurse will inspect the catheter for indications of malfunction and the site for indications of infection. If the patient has a suprapubic catheter, the site must be cleaned daily with soap and water and covered with dry gauze. The nurse may provide patient training for self-catheterization.

Practical Coding Note

Diagnosis code is Z46.82, plus the condition that required the catheter.

Code 99509 is reported for a home visit for assistance with activities of daily living. The patient must be unable to perform two or more activities of daily living such as eating, toileting, transferring, bathing, dressing, and continence. The healthcare provider visits the home to conduct a comprehensive assessment of the patient's needs. A care plan is developed with the client's physician and other community programs.

Practical Coding Note

Diagnosis codes are reported describing the impairment preventing independent daily activities. Do not report this code for speech therapy (92507–92508), nutrition assessment (97802–97804), or self-management training (97535).

Code 99510 is reported for a home visit for counseling sessions including marriage counseling. Participants may be an individual or family.

Practical Coding Note

Diagnosis codes to report are located by looking in the Alphabetic Index for Counseling, including any specific problems addressed in the physician order for services.

Code 99511 is reported for a home visit for the management of fecal impaction and/or administration of enema. Fecal impaction results from a mass of hardened stool that may need to be removed manually. The home care provider will use fingers to break up the mass into small pieces to prevent injury to the patient. When an enema is required, the home care provider typically will use a disposable enema unit. After lubrication, the liquid is gently squeezed into the patient's anal canal.

Practical Coding Note

Refer to diagnosis codes K56.49, and category K59

Code 99512 is reported for home visits for hemodialysis. A home health nurse commonly visits the patient three times a week to provide hemodialysis. Each treatment lasts from two to four hours.

Practical Coding Note

The diagnosis codes may include I12 and I13 code ranges and N18.0-N18.9. Do not report this code for peritoneal dialysis (90945–90947).

Home Infusion Procedures

Codes 99601 and 99602 are reported for home visits for infusion of specialty drug administration and are reported per visit. The home health provider brings the supplies and medication required, administers, and oversees the infusion. Report 99601 for a session up to two hours. Report 99602 for each additional hour of infusion.

Practical Coding Note

These codes may be reported for peritoneal dialysis and other therapeutic and prophylactic agents. Medications given are reported separately.

Section Review 20.19

1. A post-surgical patient is discharged from the hospital to home. The patient still has a urinary catheter needing attention for the next several days. The physician arranged the home care through a home care agency.

    A. 99505

    B. 99509

    C. 99512

    D. 99507

2. A patient was discharged recently from the hospital following a colon resection with colostomy. A nurse made a home visit to assist with the patient's colostomy.

    A. 99505

    B. 99509

    C. 99511

    D. 99512

3. A nurse visited a patient in the home to manage infusion of a thrombolytic agent for two hours.

    A. 99512

    B. 99605

    C. 99601, 99602

    D. 99601

Medication Therapy Management Services

Codes 99605–99607 are reported by a pharmacist for the purpose of patient assessment, intervention, or management of medication interaction/complications. Required documentation includes patient history, current medications, and recommendations in a face-to-face encounter. Do not report these codes for discussion of products relative to routine dispensing.

Code selection is determined on whether the patient is new or established, and the time reported for the management service.

Practical Coding Note

Report diagnosis code in the Z71 and Z76 range.

Section Review 20.20

1. A patient on multiple prescriptions had concerns about possible drug interactions with a new prescription. She requested consultation from the local pharmacist before leaving the pharmacy. The pharmacist met with her for 23 minutes to discuss possible interactions with her current medications and assured her that it was not likely the new medication would cause significant side effects.

    A. 99605

    B. 99606

    C. 99605, 99607

    D. 99606, 99607

Documentation Dissection

Case 1

Physical Therapy

Patient Name: Jill Smith	Date of Service: 10/10/201x
Medical Record#: 12345	Date of Birth: 01/01/1957
Provider: Alexis Timmins, MD	Treating Clinician: Robert Thomas, PT
Certification from: 09/01/201x	Certification to: 10/30/201x

Patient has a history of breast cancer, left breast; post mastectomy, [1] has lymph node swelling [2] in the left axillary region. She requires manual manipulation drainage of the affected area, and has presented to the outpatient physical medicine department. Today's treatment stimulated the lymph nodes to lessen the backlog of fluid. The patient states she is feeling very relaxed, and the pain from the swelling is reduced.

Diagnosis: Swollen lymph nodes
              Status-Post Mastectomy

Treatment: Manual manipulation drainage—15 minutes

Patient: Jill Smith   Diagnosis: Lymph Node Swelling   Ref. Physician: Will Jones, MD

Visit	Date	97160 group	Date	97160 group	Date	97160 group
Therapeutic Exercise (list each below)	10/10/201x					
Therapeutic Activities (list each)						
	ROM WS GR MPR PPT-___min		ROM WS GR MPR PPT-___min		ROM WS GR MPR PPT-___min	
97110 TE Treatment Time	____ min		____ min		____ min	
97530 TA Treatment Time	____ min		____ min		____ min	
Manual Therapy	97140		97140		97140	
Manual lymphatic drainage [3]	15 min [4]		____ min		____ min	
	____ min		____ min		____ min	
Modalities (list each below)						
Cold Packs	____ min		____ min		____ min	
Hot Packs	____ min		____ min		____ min	

Visit	Date	97160 group	Date	97160 group	Date	97160 group
	____ min		____ min		____ min	
	____ min		____ min		____ min	
Total Time (Code Treatment Time)	15 min					
Time In						
Time Out						
PT Initials	RT					

---

[1] The patient has an acquired absence of the breast.

[2] The reason for PT is lymph node swelling.

[3] Manual lymphatic therapy is considered Manual Therapy.

[4] The service was performed for 15 minutes.

What are the CPT® and ICD-10-CM codes reported?

CPT® Code: 97140

ICD-10-CM Code(s): R59.0, Z90.12, Z85.3

Rationale: CPT® Code: The note states the patient was sent to the outpatient physical medicine department. Go to the index of your CPT® codebook under Physical Medicine/Therapy/Occupational Therapy. Manual Therapy is referenced by code 97140. Review the description of code 97140. The descriptor indicates manual therapy techniques, one or more regions, and does include lymphatic drainage. This is the correct code for the service.

Review the therapy notes to determine the time. Report the number of units per 15-minute increments of time as stated in the notes. 97140 x 1.

ICD-10-CM Codes: Look in the ICD-10-CM Index to Diseases and Injuries for Enlargement, enlarged/lymph gland or node R59.9. The documentation states the lymph node swelling is localized to the left axillary region. The subentry for localized directs you to code R59.0. The patient is post-mastectomy. Look in the Index to Diseases and Injuries for Absence/breast(s) (and nipple(s)) (acquired) Z90.1-. A fifth character is required to identify laterality; Z90.12 indicates the left breast. The patient also has a history of breast cancer. Look in the Index to Diseases and Injuries for History/personal (of)/malignant neoplasm (of)/breast Z85.3. Verify codes in the Tabular List.

ICD-9-CM Application

What is/are ICD-9-CM code(s) reported?

Code(s): 785.6, V45.71, V10.3

Rationale: The patient is having manual therapy to drain the swollen lymph nodes. To find the diagnosis for swollen lymph nodes, look in the ICD-9-CM Alphabetic Index for Swelling/lymph nodes. This directs you to 785.6 *Enlargement of lymph nodes*. For the status post mastectomy, you will need to look for Absence/breast(s) (acquired), directs you to V45.71. The patient also has a history of breast cancer. Look for History (personal) of/malignant neoplasm (of)/breast V10.3.

Case 2

A <u>diabetic</u> [1] patient had an <u>ulcer</u> [2] on the <u>right foot</u>. [3] Although it was not infected, it was deep and needed <u>debridement</u>. [4] The wound measured <u>15 square centimeters</u>. [5] No infection was present. <u>Using local anesthetic,</u> [6] the <u>devitalized tissue was removed with surgical scissors</u>. [7] A special gel and dressing was applied. The patient was instructed to change the dressing daily, apply the special gel to the wound and wear a plastic shield on the foot when showering. Patient was instructed to return in one week.

_____

[1] The patient is diabetic.

[2] The ulcer would be considered a wound.

[3] The ulcer was on the right foot.

[4] The patient's ulcer was debrided.

[5] The wound was 15 square centimeters

[6] Local anesthesia was used.

[7] The wound was debrided with surgical scissors.

_____

What are the CPT® and ICD-10-CM codes reported?

CPT® Code: 97597

ICD-10-CM Code(s): E11.621, L97.519

Rationale: CPT® Code: Go to the index of your CPT® codebook and see Wound/Debridement/Selective. Select Wound Debridement. This was a Selective debridement because the physician used sharp scissors to selectively choose the tissue to be removed. Index references codes 97597–97598. Review the descriptor of these codes. Code 97597 describes tissue removal by scissors, selective debridement, without anesthesia, up to 20 centimeters. This is the correct code for the service.

Rationale: Look in the ICD-10-CM Index to Diseases and Injuries for Diabetes, diabetic/with/foot ulcer E11.621. In the Tabular List, there is a note to use an additional code to identify the site of the ulcer (L97.4-, L97.5-). Look in the Index to Diseases and Injuries for Ulcer/lower limb/foot specified NEC/right L97.519. We do not know the severity of the ulcer. Verify in the Tabular Index.

ICD-9-CM Application

What is/are ICD-9-CM code(s) reported?

Codes: 250.80, 707.15

Rationale: In the ICD-9-CM Index, look for Diabetes, diabetic/ulcer/lower extremity/foot. You are guided to 250.8x [*707.15*]. Turn to 250.8x In the Tabular List. You will select 0 for the fifth digit because the type of diabetes is not specified and there is documentation that the diabetes is uncontrolled.

Under 250.8x, there is a note to Use additional code to identify manifestation, as: any associated ulceration (707.10–707.9), diabetic bone changes (731.8). The second code listed in the index in slanted brackets indicates to use 707.15 for the ulcer on the foot as the additional code.

Glossary

Allergy—Hypersensitivity.

Artery—Vessel carrying blood from the heart to the tissues.

Autonomic—Involuntary.

Biofeedback—Development of a person's ability to control his or her autonomic nervous system.

Bipolar disorder—Disorder in which mood swings from euphoric to depression.

Catheterization—To insert a catheter into a body structure.

Chemotherapy—Killing of cancer cells by administering anti-neoplastic agents.

Chiropractic—Treatment predominately by manipulation of spinal and musculoskeletal structures.

Cognitive—Thoughts or thinking process.

Comorbidity—Presence of two or more illnesses at the same time. There may be an association between the illnesses.

Compulsion—Repetitive behavior with ritualistic characteristics.

Debridement—Removal of damaged tissue to promote healing.

Decompensation—Deterioration; exacerbation of an illness or condition.

Desensitize—Lessen sensitivity by administering the specific antigen in low doses.

Dialysis—Removal of toxins from the blood by diffusing over a membrane or filter in patients with renal failure.

Disorientation—Confusion.

Doppler Study—Use an ultrasonic probe to determine blood flow.

Enteral Nutrition—Nutrients for patients with impaired ability to chew/swallow or ingest food, typically delivered by gastric or nasogastric tube.

Extracranial—Outside the skull.

Extraspinal—Outside the spine.

Gait Training—Method of restoration of balance, extremity swings, stance.

Gastroenterology—Study of the stomach, intestine, esophagus, liver, gallbladder & pancreas.

Genetics—Study of hereditary factors.

Grandiosity—Unrealistic concept of self importance.

Hallucination—False sense of perception.

Home care—Prescribed medical care provided in a patient's home.

Hydration—To replenish fluids.

Immune globulin—Antibodies derived from blood plasma providing short term, protection against certain infections.

Infusion—A therapeutic agent introduced into the body by a vein.

Injection—A fluid introduced into tissue, cavity or vessel, usually by needle.

Loosening of Association—Frequent change of subject, often with minimal relationship.

Manipulation—Thrusting movement to achieve realignment of joints or spine.

Modality—A therapeutic agent.

Neuropsychology—Study and treatment of psychiatric and neurological disorders.

On call—Medical personnel with special training and skills available to provide services when summoned.

Orientation—Awareness.

Orthotic—A custom made mechanical appliance used in orthopedics.

Panic Attack—Intense anxiety; often feels like a loss of control.

Parenteral Nutrition—Nutrients delivered intravenously to patients who are postoperative, in shock, or otherwise unresponsive.

Prosthetic—An artificial body part.

Psychology—Study of behavior, thoughts, feelings.

Psychotherapy—Method of treating mental disorders. Treatment may involve education, pharmacology, suggestion, and psychoanalysis.

Range of Motion—Natural movement.

Reflux—To flow backward.

Rehabilitation—Effort to restore to optimal function.

           AAPC   www.aapc.com   651

Short Term Memory—Ability to recall information for a very brief period.

Therapeutic—To promote healing.

Toxoids—Substance no longer toxic, but capable of forming antibodies.

Vaccine—Preparation (bacteria or virus) of nonpathogenic material but can induce immunity to prevent disease.

Vein—Vessel that carries blood to the heart.

Venom—A poison transmitted by bites or stings.

Prepare Now for Change

The practice and business of medicine are driven by change, from blockbuster drugs and breakthrough treatments, to revised code sets and new regulatory requirements. An effective professional coder must remain educated and responsive. Significant developments that coders should embrace, now, include:

- Physician quality reporting and value based payment models
- Risk adjustment
- Bundled payments
- Physicians' evolving role
- More care moving outside the Physician Office
- Leveraging technology to improve efficiency and effectiveness
- Electronic health record (EHR) Meaningful Use
- Fraud and abuse prevention
- The importance of a compliance plans for every Medicare and Medicaid provider

This chapter will discuss these and other healthcare trends, in greater detail.

Physician Reporting

The Centers for Medicare & Medicaid Services (CMS) wants to transition the current "fee for service" reimbursement model (which rewards volume of care) to a "pay for performance" model (which rewards high-quality, high-value care). To do so, CMS must gather data on what works to keep patients healthy, entice providers to adopt more efficient processes, and identify those providers who treat patients according to high-quality, high-value protocols. This has been the impetus behind the Physician Quality Reporting System (PQRS) and the Value-Based Payment Modifier (VM), which require and incentivize physician quality reporting.

PQRS

The 2006 Tax Relief and Healthcare Act (TRHCA) (P.L. 109–432) required a physician quality reporting system, including an incentive payment for eligible professionals (EPs) who satisfactorily reported data on quality measures for covered professional services furnished to Medicare beneficiaries during the second half of 2007. CMS named this program the Physician Quality Reporting Initiative (PQRI). In 2011, it was expanded to the Physician Quality Reporting System (PQRS).

Beginning in 2015, physicians not participating in the PRQS program are penalized 1.5 percent of Medicare reimbursement, and 2 percent in subsequent years. Those who reported satisfactorily for the 2015 program year will avoid the 2017 PQRS negative payment adjustment. Participation in PQRS also is mandatory to avoid further payment penalties under the value-based payment modifier (discussed below).

PQRS offers options for individual eligible professionals (EPs) and group reporting. EPs include doctors of optometry and chiropractic, among others, and mid-level providers such as physician assistants, clinical psychologists, physical and occupational therapists, and more. Individual EPs do not need to sign up or pre-register to participate in the PQRS.

PQRS program requirements and measure specifications differ from year to year. EPs are responsible for ensuring they are using the PQRS documents for the correct program year. More information on PQRS can be found on the CMS website: https://www.cms.gov/Medicare/Quality-Initiatives-Patient-Assessment-Instruments/PQRS/How_To_Get_Started.html.

Value Based Payment Modifier

The Affordable Care Act (ACA) requires the Centers for Medicare & Medicaid Services (CMS) to enact a Value-Based Payment Modifier (VM), beginning in 2015. The "Value Modifier" is not a modifier in the sense most familiar to coders (e.g., modifier 25, modifier 59, etc.). Rather, the VM creates a payment differential among EPs receiving reimbursement under the Medicare physician fee schedule (MPFS), according to whether, and how effectively, those providers demonstrate quality of care relative to cost.

CMS has employed a mixture of rewards and penalties to encourage provider participation in its initiatives. With the value-based payment modifier, CMS is upping the ante "by providing upward payment adjustments under the PFS [physician fee schedule] to high performing physicians (and groups of physicians) and downward adjustments for low performing physicians (and groups of physicians)."

The VM will be phased in over several years:

- In 2015, physicians in groups of 100 or more EPs who submit claims to Medicare under a single Taxpayer

Identification Number (TIN) were subject to the VM, based on their performance in calendar year 2013. Group size is determined by Medicare Provider Enrollment, Chain, and Ownership System (PECOS) data.

- In 2016, physicians in groups of 10 or more EPs who submit claims to Medicare under a single TIN will be subject to the VM, based on their performance in calendar year 2014. Per CMS, "If a group practice does not report quality measures via 2014 PQRS GPRO [group practice reporting option], CMS will calculate a group quality score if at least 50 percent of the EPs in the group report measures individually and meet the criteria to avoid the 2016 PQRS payment adjustment."

- In 2017, CMS will apply the VM to all remaining EPs, including "physicians and nonphysician eligible professionals in groups with two or more eligible professionals and to solo practitioners," based on their performance in 2015.

VM payment adjustments (upward, downward, or neutral) are based on several factors, including "quality tiering" analyses to determine if a group's or individual EP's performance is statistically better, the same, or worse than the national mean. Initially, quality tiering is voluntary for large physician groups (100 or more EPs), but within a few years it will be mandatory for all providers.

CMS's approach to implementing the VM is based on participation in PQRS. As such, EPs who do not to participate in PQRS may face a double payment penalty: First, from PQRS, and again from the VM. Conversely, EPs who meet PQRS program requirements will receive VM bonus payments, based on a percentage of allowable MPFS charges within a reporting period. This payment differential is in addition to the penalties and incentives already built into PQRS. Reporting to PQRS in 2015 was the last opportunity for EPs in solo practice, or those who practice in small groups, to avoid payment penalties in 2017.

Risk Adjustment

Medicare Risk Adjustment varies reimbursement for Medicare Advantage or managed care enrollees' health expenditures according to the severity of the individual patient's illness. Payments are higher for less-healthy members (i.e., those who are more expensive to treat) and lower for healthier members. Providers are reimbursed based on the difference between the calculated payment and the actual cost of patient care; therefore, they are incentivized to find to document and code all of a patient's diseases, and to manage resources carefully.

The Balanced Budget Act of 1997 mandated Risk Adjustment Methodology to improve payment accuracy and to strengthen the Medicare Program. The methodology was fully imple-

mented for Medicare Advantage in 2007. Currently, payments are adjusted based on a calculation of chronic medical conditions, plus five demographic factors:

1. Age
2. Sex
3. Medicaid status
4. Disabled status, and
5. Original reason for entitlement

Historically, physicians and medical groups focused on CPT® coding because procedural codes drove reimbursement. By contrast, a pure risk-adjusted model relies solely on diagnosis coding. Diagnosis codes are categorized into disease groups to include conditions that are clinically related, with similar cost implications. Payments are based on the most severe manifestation of disease, when less severe manifestations also are present. Financial losses due to incomplete documentation or diagnosis coding can mount quickly. Providers, facilities, and other health professionals must diagnose patients and document conditions thoroughly, while accepting a greater responsibility for the cost of care.

Risk adjustment is now used across all facets of healthcare. For example, Medicaid and commercial plans are using risk adjustment models to assist in predicting patients' future needs, and to plan for potential complications. The ACA calls for all commercial plans to institute a risk adjustment model, if they are not already using one.

Bundled Payments

Coders often speak of "bundled" procedures, or those that are included (and therefore are not separately reported and reimbursed) in another, more extensive service. For example, CPT® guidelines state that a surgical endoscope always includes a diagnostic endoscope of the same type. If a diagnostic scope precedes a surgical scope, only the surgical scope is coded and paid.

Bundled payments employ the same concept, allotting a single payment to cover the entire cost of a particular service or diagnosis, rather than paying separately for individual line items. Bundled payments are common in facility settings, including outpatient settings such as ambulatory surgical centers. As payers seek to curb healthcare costs and move toward alternative payment models, bundled payments are likely to become more prevalent. As coders, we must be sure that all separately reportable services are coded, without unbundling.

Physicians' Evolving Role

A key component of government healthcare reform has been to shift care away from acute, episodic care toward primary care and prevention. For example, the ACA improves coverage of prevention benefits and promotes primary care services by:

Eliminating cost-sharing for Medicare covered preventive services

Waiving the deductible for colorectal cancer screening

Covering personalized prevention plan services, including comprehensive health risk assessments on an annual basis

Providing a 10 percent bonus payment from 2011 to 2016 to primary care providers and general surgeons practicing in designated health professional shortage areas

Increasing mental health services payments by 5 percent for 2010

The ACA also includes provisions that are dependent on outcomes and quality of services being provided. For example:

As of 2012, Medicare no longer pays for certain preventable hospital readmissions.

Beginning in 2015, Medicare payments to certain hospitals decreased by 1 percent for hospital-acquired conditions such as infections.

The ACA establishes a hospital value-based purchasing program in Medicare to pay hospitals based on performance on quality measures. Higher scoring hospitals receive higher payments; lower scoring hospitals receive lower payments.

Expanding the roles and scope of services for non-physician providers is one way healthcare is responding both to the shortage of primary care physicians and to cost containment. Non-physician providers, such as nurse practitioners (NPs) and physician assistants (PAs), will likely come to play a more central role in providing care for routine and common illnesses or procedures, shifting the role of the physician to focus on more complex problems.

Pharmacists will also begin to play a greater role in providing comprehensive patient care. In particular, with health and wellness becoming a more focal point of healthcare, pharmacists' scope of practice may expand as more of a health coach to patients with chronic conditions such as diabetes and hypertension. In this capacity they will augment physician and nursing care by helping identify patient challenges to managing their condition and counseling them, as well as reinforcing and supporting all aspects of physicians' prescribed treatment plans.

With the push to better coordinate care among healthcare providers, patient centered medical homes are being established as a new model of care. A medical home is not a building, a house, or other facility. It is a concept that healthcare delivery, especially for those with chronic conditions, is coordinated by a team of professionals such as doctors, nurses, pharmacists, physical therapists, nurse educators, etc. that communicate and coordinate care—most likely through a secure computer platform.

In this new era, physicians will need to re-evaluate not only the purpose of medical services, but their role in the continuum of care. Physicians also must learn to leverage the clinical skills and scope of practice of nurses, NPs, PAs, and pharmacists. Coders will need to report a growing number of preventive services and services for a larger range of providers. Because reporting requirements for non-physician providers often differ from those of providers, coders must be aware of the differences and how they affect claims reporting.

Patient Care Moves Beyond the Physician Office

Cost pressures, advances in technology, and the increasing demand are redefining how patients access care. As a result, alternative solutions are beginning to make their way into the healthcare system.

Retail Clinics

Retail health clinics have been expanding across the country in an attempt to bring access closer to consumers and at lower costs. Clinics typically are staffed by a nurse practitioner or a physician assistant, and provide services for minor conditions such as colds, earaches, and sore throat. Clinics also have begun the move to full primary care, and are expanding into chronic-disease management. In addition to the convenience of these clinics, they are also less expensive (typically costing consumers half as much as a doctor appointment for similar conditions). [1]

Internet-based Visits

Advances in Internet and web-based technology are creating new opportunities for alternative ways of interacting with healthcare providers. A 2009 survey found that more than 50 percent of consumers would be willing to use the telephone, email, or online consultation in lieu of going to a doctor's office for a visit. Several large health systems such as Kaiser and insurers such as Aetna and Cigna are adopting these innovations and beginning to reimburse for online visits. As the proof of concept is tested, this trend is expected to grow.

[1] Convenient Care Association, "Reducing Costs for Consumers and Third-party Payers," www.ccaclinics.org

Electronic Patient Engagement

Technological advances are also redefining the way in which healthcare providers are communicating with patients. As a society we see heavy use of texting, email, Internet, and social media as a way to effectively communicate. Secure messaging between patient and provider is now used to communicate information such as test results, appointment reminders, immunization records, and other important health information. In addition, EHR portals are being made available for patients to login to see their personal health information. CMS encourages secure patient access and messaging as one of the Stage 2 Meaningful Use core objectives.

Remote Patient Monitoring

Mobile technology is getting smaller, more sophisticated, and cheaper. As a result, it is being integrated into healthcare as a way to monitor patients, improve outcomes, and reduce the need for face-to-face office visits. One example is the use of biometric monitoring. These devices make it possible to gather continuous health data (such as blood pressure, weight, and heart rate) unobtrusively. With predictive health analytics, major risks or abnormalities can be detected, triggering the need for an office visit or even more preemptive action by a provider to avoid complications such as strokes and heart attacks. Biometrics also opens the door for improved wellness programs and disease management. Information from remote monitoring is being actively used to populate personal health records, allowing health coaches or physicians to monitor patients and deliver targeted health information based on changes to a patient's health risk.

Coders may be reporting a wider variety of place of service (POS) codes in future years, and may be reporting more services for mid-level providers such as PAs and nurses for whom reporting requirements and scope-of-practice privileges may vary. As well, coders will have to master documentation and reporting requirements for non face-to-face services and the use of remote technologies.

Technology Advancements for Business Processes

Technology continues to advance in astonishing ways. Who would have thought 10 years ago that our personal mobile devices would have the abilities they do for voice recognition, for video conferencing, for managing documents, and much more? Clinicians and other medical professionals must adopt technology to advance efficiency and effectiveness. For example:

- Greater integration between diagnostic devices and electronic health records continue to evolve, providing fast access to information
- Coders and billers are becoming more efficient with online coding tools where access to code descriptions, lay terms, CCI edits, and LCDs are instantaneous

- Real time claim scrubber technology is being developed to ensure accuracy before a claim is submitted
- Prior authorizations and benefit verification with payers is becoming automated
- The ability to communicate with providers and other clinical staff throughout the office is more efficient, resulting in faster and more accurate transfer of information
- Online tools are being marketed to help manage the complexity of compliance plans in a medical office

Technology and Medical Coding

ICD-10-CM, CPT®, and HCPCS Level II codebooks are the basic, hands-on tools used by a medical coder to locate and assign diagnosis and procedure codes. Understanding coding conventions and guidelines and applying the proper methods to locate codes using codebooks are the most fundamental skills a coder can develop. These skills are invaluable when sitting for coding certification exams.

Technology can be used to increase efficiency and allow rapid access to vast amounts of information and data. The process of medical coding is no exception. The skilled medical coder must be able to understand the basic functionality of medical coding software and its place in the real world of medical coding.

Gaining experience in the use of medical coding software is valuable when entering the workforce. The ability to utilize medical coding technology may be key to landing your first coding job as many employers look for this skill when considering an applicant's qualifications.

There are a number of medical coding software tools available for use in the medical coding industry. Medical coding software may be used as a stand-alone tool or integrated into practice management, billing, and electronic health record systems. As an example, code look-up tool AAPC Coder enables coders to quick look up of CPT®, HCPCS Level II, ICD-9-CM, and ICD-10-CM medical codes. Users access CCI edits, LCD policies and approved diagnosis codes for applicable NCD policies that help ensure proper payment. Like most look up tools, AAPC Coder includes an ICD-9 to ICD-10 cross reference tool.

The Electronic Health Record

A critical barrier to healthcare efficiency is that data is fragmented between providers, payers, and consumers. To improve efficiency, the dissemination and coordination of information (data sharing) must improve first.

Several key pieces of legislation within the ARRA were aimed at transforming healthcare's use of technology. These include government grants and funding for the development of Health Information Exchanges (HIEs), which allow participants to share and access patient information through a central repository or network. Many HIEs already exist to varying degrees. An interface between the clinic and the hospital, between a clinic and an outside lab, or even a clinic and a pharmacist exchange patient information seamlessly. There, however, is an interest in moving to much broader exchanges involving central repositories where information is shared between hospitals, outpatient clinics, health plans, pharmacies, long term care, clinical educators, ERs, state and federal healthcare, and more.

The ARRA also includes a national broadband plan with the goal of expanding and improving broadband access across the country. A major objective of the plan would be to leverage improved broadband to further promote and facilitate the adoption of health information technology solutions.

Perhaps most significantly, the Health Information Technology for Economic and Clinical Health (HITECH) Act, a provision of the ARRA, allocates $36 billion in incentive payments for providers that become "meaningful users" of electronic health records (EHRs). The resulting EHR Incentive Programs provide incentive payments to eligible professionals, eligible hospitals, and critical access hospitals (CAHs) as they adopt, implement, upgrade, or demonstrate meaningful use of certified EHR technology.

On July 13, 2010 CMS issued a final rule that defined Stage 1 Meaningful Use criteria. On August 23, 2012, CMS issued a final rule that defined Stage 2 criteria. Meaningful Use will be assessed on a year-by-year basis as CMS establishes more comprehensive Stage 3 Meaningful Use criteria for future years. Meaningful Use criteria differ for EPs and for facilities.

The implications of EHR adoption are many. All staff—not just physicians—will need to become more computer savvy. All aspects of the medical office or facility, including clinical operations, IT security, reporting, coding, compliance, and patient interaction, will be affected. Coders will have an important role to play, ensuring that compliance and coding rules are observed when EHR templates are built. For example, EHRs may allow physicians to pull forward documentation from prior visits, but if the documentation is not current or medically-relevant to the present visit, E/M levels may be assigned inappropriately.

For more information on EHR meaningful use requirements, visit the CMS website: https://www.cms.gov/Regulations-and-Guidance/Legislation/EHRIncentivePrograms/Getting_Started.html.

Focus on Fraud and Abuse

To control costs, health reform is expanding existing programs and undertaking new efforts to reduce waste, fraud, and abuse. Increased funding is being allocated to the Department of Health & Human Services (HHS) and the Office of Inspector General, the FBI, Medicare and Medicaid integrity Programs, and the Department of Justice. The ACA's fraud and abuse provisions:

- Mandate provider screening and enhance oversight for new providers and suppliers, including initial claims of DME suppliers;

- Require providers to supply, upon request, documentation of DME and home health referrals;

- Require Medicare and Medicaid program providers and suppliers to establish compliance and ethics programs containing core elements established by HHS;

- Instruct CMS to develop an integrated data repository to capture and share data across federal and state programs, including reporting adverse actions taken against providers.

- Allow sharing of IRS data to identify fraudulent providers or providers with tax debts;

- Enforce the Anti-Kickback statute by making violations of the statute also a violation of the False Claims Act;

- Mandate that overpayments be returned within 60 days;

- Increase and create new penalties for false statements made in relation to false claims investigations; and

- Require disclosure during enrollment/re-enrollment of any affiliations (prior or current) with individuals/suppliers that have uncollected debt, payments suspended, are excluded, or have billing privileges revoked (This may result in denial of enrollment/re-enrollment).

These provisions, along with the creation or extension of several audit programs—such as the recovery audit contractors (RACs) and Zone Program Integrity Contractor (ZPICs)—raise the stakes for compliance, complete documentation, and proper coding.

Mandatory Compliance Programs

The Patient Protection and Affordable Care Act (ACA), section 6401, requires the Secretary of Health and Human Services (HHS), in consultation with the HHS inspector general, to establish core healthcare compliance elements. When these core elements are implemented (currently, no date has been set), the law further requires medical providers to "establish a compliance program that contains the core elements" as a condition of enrollment in Medicare, Medicaid, and Children Health Insurance Program (CHIP).

In other words, under the ACA, a compliance program will become mandatory to participate with CMS. If physician groups establish better compliance programs, focusing on promoting quality and integrity in everyday processes, the hope is there will be less fraud and abuse in the revenue cycle process, resulting in fewer correction activities and less waste in our system. Already, many providers that participate with Medicare Part C programs must attest annually to the various Medicare Advantage Plans that they have policies, procedures, and employee training in the area of compliance.

Further, on April 20, 2015 the Office of Inspector General (OIG) and HHS, in collaboration with the American Health Lawyers Association, the Association of Healthcare Internal Auditors, and the Health Care Compliance Association, announced a program of educational outreach to healthcare organizations regarding compliance plan oversight.

Taken together, the ACA requirement and OIG/HHS initiative suggest that now is ideal time to begin building a compliance program in your office or facility. The "OIG Compliance Program for Individual and Small Group Physician Practices," published in the Oct. 5, 2000 *Federal Register*, continues to be an excellent guide. The seven, basic Elements of Healthcare Compliance defined in the OIG Compliance Program include:

1. Conducting internal monitoring and auditing

2. Implementing compliance and practice standards

3. Designating a compliance officer or contact

4. Conducting appropriate training and education

5. Responding appropriately to detected offenses and developing corrective action

6. Developing open lines of communication

7. Enforcing disciplinary standards through well-publicized guidelines

Opportunities for Professional Coders

In a changing healthcare environment, the skills of the professional coder are even more vital. To maintain their place in the changing landscape of revenue management coders must remain abreast of the changes to come and remain current about how those changes affect providers. The industry and our patients rely on professional coders as the hub for successful implementation. And, while medical coding relies on universal skills, coders are finding themselves working in a number of expanding and new roles in healthcare reimbursement. AAPC surveys indicate more coders are evolving into auditors, compliance officers, practice managers, risk manage-

ment professionals, educators, and consultants. This opportunity is driven by three forces:

- **Increased government involvement**—State and federal regulations and mandates provide more opportunity for coders to evolve into auditors, compliance officers, risk managers, and practice managers.

- **More covered individuals**—A larger patient pool needs both more useful codes and a larger number of codes reported. The increased number of professional coders needed have the opportunity to simplify and implement processes that provide better and less expensive care. Expertise in EHRs means that coders will be problem solvers.

- **Heightened cost pressure**—Increased focus on cost containment means more visibility on revenue cycle management, Coders will continue to progress as responsibility for accuracy, expedience, and follow up grows. Providers will continue to turn to coders for interpretation and implementation as pressures mount.

It is impossible to predict how the changes discussed in this chapter will be successful without the skills and judgment professional coders can provide. Increased governmental scrutiny, patient growth, and a careful eye on cost will only continue as will the need for professional medical coders anxious to learn and develop their skills.

AMA www.ama-assn.org/ama/pub/physician-resources/solutions-managing-your-practice/coding-billing-insurance/medicare/the-resource-based-relative-value-scale/overview-of-rbrvs.shtml

Anatomy and physiology online at www.prostate.com.ph/anatomy.html

Bureau of Labor and Statistics www.bls.gov/oco/ocos103.htm

Cell Based Wellness Systems at www.carbonbased.com/.

Choi, James, MD, Ikeguchi, Edward F., MD, Te, Alexis E, MD, Kaplan, Steven A, MD: "Laser Prostatectomy," Reviews in Urology, Summer 1999

CMS EHR Incentive Programs—Stage 2, www.cms.gov/Regulations-and-Guidance/Legislation/EHRIncentivePrograms/Stage_2.html

CMS Internet Only Manual www.cms.hhs.gov/Manuals/IOM/list.asp

Coders Desk Reference 2010, published by Ingenix

Cohen, B, *Medical Terminology, An Illustrated Guide*, Lippincott Williams & Wilkins, Baltimore, 2008.

Combined text for HIPAA www.hhs.gov/ocr/privacy/hipaa/administrative/privacyrule/adminsimpregtext.pdf

CPT® 2013

D. Riza, MD and A. S. Deshmukh, MD: "A Laparoscopic assisted Extraperitoneal Bladder Neck Suspension: An Initial Experience." Journal of Laparoendoscopic Surgery, Volume 4, Number 5, 1994

Davis, F.A. Company, Philadelphia; 2001, *Tabers Cyclopedic Medical Dictionary*, 19th edition

Dorland's Medical Dictionary, 28th edition; Saunders

FDA—Fluoroscopy: www.fda.gov/Radiation-EmittingProducts/RadiationEmittingProductsandProcedures/MedicalImaging/MedicalX-Rays/ucm115354.htm

Healthy Hearing [Health_Hearing_Newsletter@newsletter.healthyhearing.com].

Heuther, S and McCance, K, Pathophysiology, C.V. Mosby, St. Louis, 1990, page 755.

HIPAA www.hhs.gov/ocr/privacy/

HIPAA minimum necessary www.hhs.gov/ocr/privacy/hipaa/understanding/coveredentities/minimumnecessary.html

Incontinence and Surgical Techniques, Health communities.com at www.urologychannel.com/incontinence/stress/treatment_surg.html

Magnetic Resonance Imaging, information for patients (National Society for Magnetic Resonance in Medicine): www.ismrm.org/public/

Marieb, E and Hoehn, K, *Human Anatomy & Physiology*, 7th edition, Pearson Benjamin Cummings, San Francisco, 2007.

Medline Plus, X-Ray: www.nlm.nih.gov/medlineplus/ency/article/003337.htm

National Cancer Institute: www.cancer.gov/cancertopics/factsheet/Detection/mammograms

 AAPC www.aapc.com 659

OIG Compliance Plans: www.oig.hhs.gov/authorities/docs/physician.pdf

Physician Fee Schedule: www.cms.hhs.gov/PhysicianFeeSched/01_Overview.asp#TopOfPage

Puget Sound Blood Center at www.psbc.org

RSNA, RadiologyInfo, CT-Body: www.radiologyinfo.org/en/info.cfm?pg=bodyct

Thibodeau and Patton, C.B. Mosby, St Louis, eleventh edition, 2000, *Structures and Function of the Body*

What You Need to Know About Dermatology at dermatology.about.com/library/blnailanatomy.htm.

A

Abdominal
  aorta, 319, 535, 592
  cavities(y), 28, 269, 285, 340, 359, 378, 391, 443, 500, 625
  laparoscopy, 390
  masses, 571

Ablation, 222, 227, 251, 280, 327, 378, 380, 381, 386, 441, 535, 635

ABN, 8-10, 17

Abnormal
  Pap, 411, 561
  pregnancy, 408
  result, 155, 550

Abortion, 135, 136, 159, 403, 408, 410, 411, 413, 414, 420

Abrasion, 158, 476

Abscess, 202, 207, 209, 224, 249, 279, 287, 345-347, 357, 370, 377, 387, 399, 410, 439, 443, 481, 485

Abuse, 11, 12, 96, 97, 107, 136, 148, 149, 152, 155, 182, 344, 579, 643, 653, 657, 658

Accessory
  glands, 368
  ligaments, 32
  muscles, 269, 276, 592
  organs, 339, 349
  sinus(es), 84, 162, 267, 279, 280
  structures, 46, 164, 247

Accountability Act, 11, 12, 17, 161, 512

Acne, 202, 207, 213, 219, 227

Acoustic neuroma, 472, 495, 496

Actinic keratosis, 203, 233

Actinotherapy, 227

Acupuncture, 617, 637

Acute
  appendicitis, 66, 141, 503
  bronchiolitis, 272
  bronchitis, 113, 272, 274
  cholecystitis, 360
  condition(s), 238, 239, 638
  exacerbation, 113, 120, 273, 274, 622
  gastritis, 344
  inflammation, 281
  labyrinthitis, 487
  laryngitis, 272
  mastoiditis, 488
  myocardial infarction (MI), 110, 111, 306, 325
  pain, 357, 434
  pyelonephritis, 371
  sinusitis, 59, 272

Add-on procedure, 321

Adenocarcinoma, 347, 374, 375, 562

Adenoidectomy procedures, 350

Adenoids, 37, 350, 473

Adenoma, 58, 202, 391, 430

Adenovirus, 272

Adherence, 14, 17, 609

Adhesiolysis, 188, 420, 443

Adhesive
  capsulitis, 240
  pericarditis, 310

Adipose tissue, 29

Administration code, 540, 617-619, 634, 645

Administrative simplification, 11-13

Adnexa, 77, 104, 384, 403, 411, 415, 463-496, 593, 627

Adrenal
  gland, 21, 48, 378, 379, 430, 438
  medulla, 437

Adrenalectomy, 421

Advancement flap, 216

Adverse
  effect, 86, 91, 135, 147, 148, 158, 203
  reaction, 148

Aftercare code, 125, 306

Afterloading brachytherapy, 539

AIDS, 77-79, 82, 120, 558, 559

Aiken procedure, 257

Airway obstruction, 273, 274, 280, 284

Alcohol abuse, 58, 97, 344

Alcoholism, 145, 556

Allergen immunotherapy, 628, 629

Allergen(s), 558, 585, 628-630

Allergic
  asthma, 628
  immunologic, 585
  reaction, 121, 529, 629
  rhinitis, 629

family, 320

graft, 313

punctures, 316

system, 318, 320

Arteriogram, 600

Arteriosclerosis, 35, 306, 307, 336

Arteriosclerotic, 112

Arteriotomy, 35, 321

Arteriovenous

fistula, 313

malformations, 442, 445

Arthralgia, 32

Arthritis, 32, 68, 97, 124, 126, 158, 238, 246, 265, 266

Arthrocentesis, 250

Arthrodesis, 32, 250, 253, 254

Arthrogram, 249, 265

Arthropathy

joint disease, 32

pathology, 265

Arthroscopic

procedure, 258

surgery, 244, 258

Arthrotomy, 193, 252, 257, 258

Artificial

cornea, 482

heart, 161

lens, 479

opening, 116, 301, 309, 370, 380

valve, 312

Arytenoidectomy, 281

Ascending aorta, 312

Aseptic necrosis, 531

Aspiration, 114, 206, 207, 224, 249, 250, 282, 287, 325, 353, 378, 379, 382, 399, 401, 437-439, 443, 445, 479, 557, 563, 564

Assault, 147, 148, 151, 152

Assays, 173, 553, 555, 558, 560

Assistant surgeon, 4, 192, 261

Asthma exacerbation, 273

Astigmatic correction, 477

Astigmatism, 46, 471, 477, 478

Asymptomatic HIV, 134, 153

Atherectomy, 321, 322, 325, 326, 336, 545, 627

Atherosclerosis, 35, 109, 120, 306, 307, 313, 314, 336, 627

Atresia, 280, 314, 348, 354, 399, 486

Atrial fibrillation, 111

Atrioventricular, 34, 111, 298-300, 312, 327, 336

Atrophy, 37, 217, 478Atticotomy, 487

Audiometric, 489

Auditing, 2, 13, 658

Auditory

apparatus, 47

canal, 465, 485, 486, 488, 592

impulses, 47

nerve, 465, 495, 496

ossicles, 486

stimuli, 489

system, 475

training, 488

Augmentation, 225, 254

Aura, 101, 434

Auscultation, 4, 571, 592, 593, 616

Autogenous

bone, 251, 262

vein, 316

Autograft, 217, 250, 251, 265, 399, 477

Autoimmune disease, 93, 124, 203, 238, 434

Autoimmunity, 270

Autoinoculation, 401

Autologous

bone, 251, 287

graft, 109

Autonomic nerves, 443, 447, 448

Autopsy, 570

Avascular necrosis, 208, 485

Avian flu, 114, 273

Avulsion procedure, 213

Avulsions, 215, 217

Axial skeleton, 32, 235

Axilla, 236, 592

Axillary

block, 500, 505

mass, 236

nerve, 447

Axis system, 620

B

Bacillary angiomatosis, 78

Back/flank, 236

Backache, 240

Backbench preparation, 357, 358, 379

Bacterial

infection, 103, 121, 202, 307, 315, 371, 373, 482, 556

pneumonia, 114

Cisternal puncture, 438

Classification system, 1, 620

Cleft
lip, 139, 261, 348, 349
palate, 139, 350

CLIA, 548, 554, 560, 566, 570

Climatotherapy, 628

CMS
contractor, 5
global, 175
policy, 9
regulations, 3, 181
rules, 8

CNS disorders, 371

Coagulopathies, 557

Colectomy, 41, 354, 355, 563

Collapse therapy, 284

Colon
biopsy, 563
cancer, 153, 154
conditions, 355
resection, 177, 355
surgery, 176

Colonography, 360, 545

Colonoscopy, 41, 154, 348, 356, 360, 361, 365

Colostomy, 348, 355, 365

Colotomy, 354

Colpocleisis, 410, 419

Colpopexy, 410, 419

Colporrhaphy, 43, 410, 411

Combination code, 67, 75

Co-morbid, 145, 600

Comparison films, 529

Compartment syndrome, 240, 241, 244, 251, 255

Compliance plan, 13, 14, 658

Complication, 67, 69, 71, 81, 86, 87, 91, 93, 95, 97, 102, 104, 106, 111, 114, 116, 124, 125, 130, 132, 133, 135, 136, 143, 148-149, 153, 176, 184, 191, 241, 244, 249, 273, 276, 302, 307, 345, 346, 352, 353, 408, 469, 470, 477, 610

Composite graft, 217, 316

Compression therapy, 258

Computer-aided detection, 536

Concurrent
cases, 513
infusions, 633

Concussion, 574

Conduction system, 34, 299, 327, 336

Condyloma, 399

Condylomata, 222

Congenital
abnormality, 353
anomaly, 139, 359, 372, 380
defect, 44, 314, 390
disorder, 280, 348

Conjunctival flap, 476, 478, 482

Conjunctivitis, 103, 104, 120, 470, 482, 628

Conjunctivoplasty, 482

Conjunctivorhinostomy, 483

Connective tissues, 124, 240

Conscious sedation, 172, 281, 508, 643

Constipation, 346, 355, 410

Consultation services, 575, 576

Contact
dermatitis, 121, 203, 233, 629
lenses, 477, 485, 491

Contraception, 155, 411, 551, 645

Contraceptive devices, 184, 213

Contralateral, 318, 336

Contrast
imaging, 529
injection, 531
material, 249, 319, 359, 380, 438, 443, 523, 529, 530, 532, 538, 541

Contusion, 55, 143, 277

Conversion factor, 167, 505, 507, 521

Convulsions, 101, 158, 344, 434

Coombs Test, 559

COPD, 38, 75, 113-115, 269, 273, 274, 295, 584

Cordotomy, 445

Corneal
defects, 464
graft, 470
pachymetry, 535
removal, 476
scarring, 477

Coronary
arteries, 109, 120, 181, 192, 300, 306, 307, 310, 312, 313, 315, 325, 327, 627
circulation, 300, 336

Corpus callosotomy, 440

Cosmetic, 209, 213, 215, 280, 317, 349, 437, 448, 475, 477, 486

Co-surgeon, 4, 191

Co-surgery, 254, 445

Emesis, 341, 644

EMG, 246, 266, 383, 450, 451, 623

Emphysema, 38, 113, 274

Empyema, 284, 295

En bloc, 286, 295

Encephalocele, 442, 460

Encephalomyelitis, 79, 432

Endarterectomy, 314, 315, 447

Endobronchial
    lesions, 39
        ultrasound, 282

Endocarditis, 238, 307, 336

Endocardium, 34, 297, 298, 301, 307, 336, 337

Endocervical, 562, 563, 569

Endocrine, 21, 25, 42, 48, 49, 55, 64, 77, 92, 93, 95, 109, 275, 303, 368, 371, 390, 403, 421-461, 553, 557, 585, 631

Endocrine
    gland, 48
        system, 21, 48, 49, 92, 303, 368, 421, 422, 430, 437, 438, 585

Endograft, 314

Endometrial sampling, 411

Endometriosis, 44, 127, 129, 384, 411

Endometrium, 129, 411, 558

Endoscopic, 175, 280-283, 285, 310, 311, 313, 351-353, 355, 356, 361, 378-380, 411, 442, 443, 489

Endotracheal intubation, 281

Endovascular
    interventions, 322
        procedures, 441

revascularization, 315, 317, 321, 322

Enteral nutrition, 651

Enterectomy, 354, 355

Enteroenterostomy, 354

Enterolysis, 354, 365

Enterostomy, 355

Enterotomy, 354

Enthesopathy, 266

Entropion, 46, 481, 482

Enucleation, 386, 476, 495

Eosinophils, 50, 51, 270

Epididymis, 21, 43, 127, 368, 369, 374, 389, 390, 400

Epididymitis, 374

Epididymovasostomy, 390

Epidurography, 443, 546

Epiglottidectomy, 281, 365

Epikeratoplasty procedure, 477

Epilepsy, 100, 120, 434, 440, 556

Episiotomy, 408

Epispadias, 44, 370, 374, 389, 400

Epistaxis, 280

Epstein-Barr virus, 51

Erythema
    multiforme, 203
    nodosum, 203

Erythemas, 203, 213

Erythrocyte, 50, 91

Erythrocyte disorders, 50

Eschar, 122, 203, 208, 209, 220, 234

Escherichia coli, 273, 371, 373

Esophageal
    stricture, 344, 360
    tumors, 360
    ulcer, 360
    varices, 344, 345, 351

Esophagectomy, 351

Esophagitis, 116, 344, 360

Esophagogastroduodenoscopy, 352, 361

Esophagoscopy, 163, 351, 352

Esotropia, 104, 470, 495

ESRD, 3, 127, 130, 182, 304, 371, 566

Ethmoidectomy, 280

Eustachian tube(s), 22, 106, 465, 471, 473, 486, 487, 495

Evocative/suppression testing, 553

Exacerbation, 92, 113, 120, 148, 273, 274

Exam
    element, 593
    level, 568, 591, 594

Exenteration, 365, 400, 476, 495

Exocrine glands, 48

Exophthalmos, 481

Exostosis, 485

Exotropia, 104, 470, 480, 496

Exploration/drainage, 193, 285, 480

Exstrophy, 365, 370

External cause, 68, 105, 145, 147, 149, 151, 152, 203, 205, 244, 245, 433

Extracapsular extraction, 479

Extracorporeal shock, 257, 380

disease, 108, 109, 112, 134, 136, 302-304, 306, 307, 539, 626

failure, 108, 109, 112, 114, 120, 134, 302-305, 307, 308, 626

function, 324

murmur, 576

muscle, 23, 32, 109-111, 120, 297, 298, 300, 303, 305, 306, 310, 313, 324, 325, 446

valve, 59, 308, 336

Heartburn, 115, 360, 585, 586

Helicobacter pylori, 78, 344, 556

Hematemesis, 41, 586

Hematochezia, 586

Hematocrit, 51, 551, 557

Hematologic, 25, 50, 51, 238, 558, 585, 592, 593

Hematoma, 111, 207, 212, 314, 400, 410, 438, 439, 485

Hematopoietic therapies, 286

Hematuria, 43, 67, 374, 385, 400, 556

Hemiarthroplasty, 256

Hemifacial spasm, 449

Hemiglossectomy, 351

Hemilaminectomy, 454

Hemiparesis, 45, 101, 110

Hemiplegia, 68, 100, 101, 110

Hemispherotomy, 440

Hemofiltration, 625, 626

Hemoglobin, 50, 51, 90, 551, 555-557

Hemogram, 557

Hemophilia, 50

Hemorrhage, 104, 280, 283, 345-346, 354, 358, 439, 461, 469, 479-481, 643

Hemorrhoid, 357

Hemorrhoidectomy, 357

Hemostasis, 51

Hemothorax, 38

Hepatic
artery, 357, 444
flexure, 41, 354
vein, 317

Hepatitis B, 58, 559, 619, 629

Hepatitis C, 58, 559, 567, 568

Hepatosplenomegaly, 593

Hepatotomy, 357

Hereditary conditions, 586

Hernia, 41, 116, 120, 276, 285, 341, 344, 345, 353, 359, 361, 365, 366, 390, 448, 503, 593

Herniated disc, 444, 445, 503

Herniorrhaphies, 359

Herniotomy, 41

Herpes infections, 471

Hiatal hernia, 344, 353

Hidradenitis, 202, 210

HIPAA, 11-13, 17, 161, 512

History elements, 587

HITECH, 13, 17, 657

HIV
disease, 77, 79, 80, 134
exposure, 549
infection, 78, 79, 134, 558
status, 79

virus, 79, 560

Hives, 203, 585

Hoarseness, 586

Holter monitor, 326

Homograft, 217, 312, 400

Horseshoe kidney, 378, 380, 400

Hospice services, 609

Hospital
admission, 413, 414, 575
inpatient, 73, 575, 576, 586
observation, 574, 581, 586

Human papillomavirus, 561

Hydration administration, 633

Hydrocele, 359, 374, 390

Hydrocelectomy, 359

Hydrocephalus, 433, 439, 442, 443, 446

Hydronephrosis, 43, 370, 371, 400

Hydrophilic, 393

Hymenotomy, 419

Hyoid myotomy, 252

Hypercalcemia, 51, 430

Hypercholesterolemia, 611

Hyperglycemia, 51, 149, 431, 556

Hyperkalemia, 49

Hyperlipemia, 51

Hyperlipidemia, 611

Hyperparathyroidism, 372, 430, 431

Hyperplasia, 128, 276, 371, 373, 384, 385, 388, 400, 406, 431

Hyperplastic conditions, 406

N

Nail
biopsy, 212
debridement, 164, 212

Narcolepsy, 434

Nasal
congestion, 586, 605
polyp(s), 272, 279

Nasogastric tube, 354, 651

NCCI, 165, 169, 191, 198, 351, 385, 419

NCD, 5, 18, 656

NDC, 12

Nearsighted, 463

NEC classification, 57

Neck pain, 240

Necropsy, 561, 570

Necrosis, 122, 128, 144, 203, 208, 220,
234, 359, 381, 386, 389, 485, 531

Necrotizing fasciitis, 644

Needle
aspiration, 207, 282, 378, 379, 563
biopsy, 497, 505, 567, 568
placement, 528, 531, 535
trocar, 378, 382

Neoplasia, 130, 373, 406, 408, 531, 557

Neoplasm type, 435

Neoplastic disease, 37, 87, 91, 120, 241,
467, 468, 471, 472

Neovascularization, 479, 480, 484

Nephrectomy, 43, 370, 378, 379

Nephritis, 21, 43, 371

Nephrogenic diabetes, 372

Nephrolithiasis, 128

Nephrolithotomy, 377

Nephropathy, 21, 43, 78, 371-373

Nephroptosis, 372

Nephrorrhaphy, 380

Nephrosclerosis, 43

Nephrostomy, 378-380, 401

Nephrotomy, 377, 378, 380

Nerve
block, 389, 446-448, 499, 500
conduction, 172, 421, 451, 472
decompression, 426, 444, 488
disorders, 435, 449, 638
graft, 449

Nervous systems, 421, 435, 437, 444

Nervousness, 92, 585

Nesidioblastosis, 556

Neuralgia, 45, 435, 449

Neuralgic amyotrophy, 435

Neuritis, 45, 435

Neuroendoscopy, 442

Neurogenic
bladder, 371, 373, 401
claudication, 240

Neurohypophysis, 21, 49

Neurologic system, 238

Neurological disorders, 651

Neurolysis, 45, 449

Neuroma, 266, 472, 495, 496

Neuromuscular
disorder, 450

procedures, 450, 617, 631

Neuropathy, 22, 78, 93, 120, 433, 435,
442, 608, 638

Neuroplasty, 257, 449

Neurorrhaphy, 45, 449

Neurostimulator, 101, 102, 442, 446, 448,
451-453

Neutron beam, 538, 539

Nevus, 201, 212, 234, 468

Night
blindness, 643
terrors, 433

Nocturia, 399, 556, 586

Nocturnal Enuresis, 401

Nondystrophic nail, 212

Nonessential modifiers, 57, 60, 75

Nonselective catheterization, 319, 337

NSTEMI, 111, 120, 306

Nuclear
medicine, 256, 359, 360, 523, 529,
539-541, 600

Numbness, 22, 435, 586, 611

Nursing facility, 182, 573, 575-577, 581,
583, 586, 608

Nystagmus, 472, 488, 489, 496

O

Obesity, 69, 93, 95, 97, 341, 353, 359, 365

Obliteration, 280

Obliterative procedures, 280

Observation Care, 574, 575

Obstetric
panel, 553

Routine
  care, 133, 142
  exam, 155
  radiography, 256
  ultrasound, 408

Roux-en-Y
  anastomosis, 358
  reconstruction, 353

Rule-out conditions, 526

Ruptured
  aneurysm, 314
  discs, 240
  spleen, 286

RVU, 167-169, 171, 172, 175, 198, 282

RVU
  calculations, 175, 198
  expenses, 167
  table, 168

S

S codes, 71, 81, 179, 180, 186, 451, 453, 639

S&I codes, 322, 528, 529

SA node, 111, 299, 300, 311

Sacroplasty, 452

Sarcoma, 78, 79, 375

SARS, 558

Scar revision, 215, 257, 258

Schizophrenia, 622

Schwannomas, 442

Sciatica, 240

Scleritis, 482

Sclerosis, 43, 60, 301, 424, 433-435, 443, 472, 488

Sclerotherapy, 321

Scoliosis, 33, 185, 240, 241, 254, 266, 638

Scope instrument, 23

Scotoma, 434

Scout films, 529

Screening
  codes, 154, 491
  film, 525, 529
  mammogram, 153, 526, 536
  Pap, 569
  services, 267
  test, 153, 154, 472, 489, 557, 643

Scrotal
  destruction, 390
  reconstruction, 390

Sebaceous cyst, 234, 482

Seborrheic
  dermatitis, 103, 203
  keratosis, 203

Security rule, 12

Segmental
  instrumentation, 253, 254
  lobectomy, 283

Seizure disorder, 100, 101

Selective
  catheterization, 315, 319-321, 323, 337, 441
  debridement, 208

Semen analysis, 565

Semi-quantitative, 547, 558, 570

Senile entropion, 481

Sensory
  deafness, 488
  disturbance, 434

divisions, 449

information, 425

nerves, 447

neurons, 47

organs, 46, 446

processing, 636

properties, 361

receptor, 46

systems, 475

testing, 489

Sepsis, 59, 76, 78, 80-82, 120, 135, 159, 371, 624

Septic shock, 78, 80-82, 135

Septicemia, 51, 59, 76

Septoplasty, 280

Sequelae, 68, 110, 125, 136, 153

Seroma, 177, 207

Sexual dysfunction, 98

Shave
  biopsy, 209
  removal, 209, 210

Short-term memory, 428, 622

Shoulder
  disarticulation, 258
  pain, 67, 225, 611

Shunt
  procedure, 313, 314, 446
  reservoir, 546

Shuntogram, 546

Sialodochoplasty, 350

Sigmoidoscopy, 356, 361

Simulation, 284, 538

Sinus, 115, 202, 209, 249, 272, 280, 298, 300, 301, 310-312, 351, 367, 382, 440, 442, 486, 592

Twist Drill, 438, 439

Tympanoplasty, 487

Tympanostomy, 106, 486, 487

U

Ulcer, 29, 69, 122, 203, 204, 220, 344, 345, 357, 360

Ulcerative colitis, 345, 355

Ultrasonic guidance, 391, 535

Ultrasonography, 383, 386

Umbilical hernia, 116, 120, 359

Uniplane fixation, 250

Unlisted codes, 171, 175

Unna boot, 258

Unusual circumstances, 188, 290, 329, 453, 509

Urachal cysts, 382

Uremia, 43, 108

Ureteral
    catheter, 382, 385
    stones, 371

Ureterectomy, 378, 381

Ureterocalycostomy, 381

Ureterocutaneous transplantations, 382

Ureterolithotomy, 381

Ureteroplasty, 43, 381

Ureteropyelography, 380, 385

Ureteroscopy, 385

Ureterostomy, 378, 381, 382

Urethral
    infection, 387
    malignancy, 383

strictures, 388

Urethrectomy, 387

Urethritis, 385

Urethrocele, 370, 410, 420

Urethrodynia, 43

Urethrolysis, 387

Urethropexy, 383, 384

Urethroplasty, 389

Urethroscopy, 384, 393

URI, 67, 115

Urinalysis, 43, 128, 130, 554, 560, 600

Urinary
    catheter, 393
    frequency, 373, 399
    hesitancy, 373, 383
    incontinence, 127, 128, 130, 159, 373, 387, 402, 410
    obstruction, 128, 371
    retention, 129, 373, 382

Urine culture, 560

Urodynamics, 383

Uroflowmetry, 383

Uropathies, 555

Urosepsis, 80, 120, 370, 371

Urticaria, 203, 585, 628

Uterine
    adnexa, 384, 403
    cavity, 408
    contractions, 49, 422
    lining, 411, 535
    prolapse, 128

Uvulopalatopharyngoplasty, 350

V

Vaccinations, 153, 618

Vaccine/toxoid, 184, 618, 619

Vaginal
    attachment, 403
    delivery, 412
    hysterectomy, 23
    incision, 384
    prolapse, 420

Valve
    prolapse, 308
    regurgitation, 308
    stenosis, 140, 308

Valvular dysfunction, 608

Valvuloplasty, 312, 337

Varicose vein, 351

Varicosities, 356, 592

Vascular
    access, 317, 320, 535, 618, 625, 634
    catheterization, 173
    condition, 317
    disease, 212, 308, 316, 441, 530
    disorders, 111, 372, 374
    family, 319, 320
    order, 319
    system, 318, 337
    tumor, 440

Vasectomy, 44, 386, 390, 391, 498

Vasodilation, 448

Vasopneumatic devices, 635

VATS, 283, 295

Venipuncture, 316, 321, 556, 600

Venogram, 317

Venous
anastomosis, 358
grafts, 313, 325
thrombosis, 111

Ventilating tube, 487

Ventilation, 276, 281, 284, 450, 486, 487, 499, 500, 540, 579

Ventilator management, 580, 628

Ventral
hernia, 120, 359, 506
herniorrhaphy, 506

Ventricular
contraction, 298
failure, 314
fibrillation, 311
infection, 446
pacing, 311, 327
reservoir, 634
septum, 312
tachycardia, 311, 327

Ventriculocisternostomy, 443

Vermilionectomy, 349

Vertebral
arteries, 320, 441
column, 238, 252, 284, 424
corpectomy, 425, 444, 445
foramen, 426
foramina, 446
interspace, 253, 425
segment, 253, 425, 426, 445

Vertigo, 47, 106, 465, 471, 472, 487, 488, 496

Vesicourethropexy, 383

Vesicouterine fistula, 384

Vestibular
neuronitis, 488
schwannoma, 472, 495, 496

stenosis, 280

Vestibuloplasty, 350

Viral
disease, 570
infection, 51, 114, 273, 433

Vision
loss, 103
services, 47, 180, 186

Visual disturbance, 101, 586

Vitrectomy procedure, 479

Vitreous
floaters, 479
hemorrhage, 479, 480

VLAP, 386

Voiding
cystourethrography, 373
disorder(s), 373

Vulvovaginitis, 78

V-Y advancement, 216

W

Wart, 176, 203, 213

WBC, 91, 553, 557

Wedge resection, 283, 477

Whipple-type procedures, 358

Wound
care, 208, 215, 223, 611, 636
closure, 207, 215, 609

X

Xenograft, 217

X-ray
beam, 523, 524
equipment, 186, 541

film, 530
image, 400, 546
imaging, 248, 269, 295, 530
interpretations, 380
machine, 360, 443, 530, 538

Xenograft, 217

Y

Yeast infections, 202

Z

Zona
fasciculata, 421
glomerulosa, 421

Zygoma, 31, 235